দ্বিভাষার্থকাভিধান,

OR

A DICTIONARY

OF THE

BENGALI LANGUAGE

দ্বিভাষার্থকাভিধান,

OR

A DICTIONARY

OF THE

BENGALI LANGUAGE

WITH

Bengali Synonyms

AND

AN ENGLISH INTERPRETATION,

COMPILED FROM NATIVE AND OTHER AUTHORITIES.

BY

THE REV. WILLIAM MORTON

GYAN

Published by

Gyan Publishing House
5, Ansari Road
Daryaganj, New Delhi-110002
Phone: 011-47034999, 9811692060
E-mail: books@gyanbooks.com

Distribution Network
gyanbooks.com
India, USA, Canada, UK, Australia

ISBN: 978-81-212-5975-0 (PB)
First Published, 1828

2nd Impression 2024

Printed at: Gyan Press, Delhi.

দ্বিভাষার্থকাভিধান, OR A DICTIONARY OF THE BENGALI LANGUAGE
Author: WILLIAM MORTON

দ্বিভাষার্থকাভিধান,

OR

A DICTIONARY

OF THE

BENGALI LANGUAGE

WITH

Bengali Synonyms

AND

AN ENGLISH INTERPRETATION,

COMPILED FROM NATIVE AND OTHER AUTHORITIES.

BY

THE REV. WILLIAM MORTON,

MISSIONARY FROM THE INCORPORATED SOCIETY FOR THE PROPAGATION OF THE GOSPEL IN FOREIGN PARTS.

অহস্কৃতাব্যকারশ্চকুশাগ্রীয়ধিয়াবৃতৌ।
নৈবশব্দাম্বুধেঃপারংকিমন্যেজড়বুদ্ধয়ঃ॥

Bishop's College:

PRINTED BY H. TOWNSEND.

1828.

TO

THE MOST REVEREND THE PRESIDENT,

THE RIGHT REVEREND AND OTHER MEMBERS

OF THE INCORPORATED SOCIETY

FOR THE PROPAGATION OF THE GOSPEL

IN FOREIGN PARTS,

THIS WORK,

COMPILED BY THE FIRST MISSIONARY

OF THEIR APPOINTMENT TO INDIA

AND THE FIRST FRUITS OF HIS AUXILIARY LITERARY LABOURS

IN THAT EXTENSIVE FIELD,

IS MOST HUMBLY AND RESPECTFULLY DEDICATED

BY

THEIR OBLIGED AND GRATEFUL SERVANT,

WILLIAM MORTON.

PREFACE.

THE Dictionary of the Bengáli language now offered to the public, is the result of several years' assiduous application more particularly directed to this special object. Early on his arrival in this country, the Compiler became sensible of the want of such a compendium, a mean between the meagreness of a mere vocabulary and the diffuseness of the more elaborate species of Dictionaries. At the period when this work was undertaken, there were extant only the vocabulary of Mr. Foster and the large quartos of Dr. Carey.

The former, considered as the first effort in Bengáli Lexicography of any European, must be considered to bear high and ample testimony to the skill and judgment of the author, as well as to his extensive acquaintance with the language. Deficient, it certainly is; but the Compiler's unassuming profession, *Vox et praterea nihil*, precludes any charge on that ground. Still it contains a mass of most valuable materials for succeeding lexicographers, though in a state, it must be confessed, somewhat chaotic and difficult of application by a tyro in the language; and the student, as he advances, must often be struck with the Compiler's accurate acquaintance with the idiomatical and colloquial applications of terms, considered as mere vocables, little connected with their general notions. Those who have made most proficiency in this tongue are duly sensible of the real excellence of the work, and it must be evident, to one competent to pass a judgment, that Mr. Foster could have been no sciolist in the general principles of language. Had his arrangement been better, his Vocabulary would only have needed due enlargement to answer all the purpose of a standard Dictionary. The work it must be owned, however, is extremely defective, is disfigured and deteriorated by a large admixture of Hindustáni, &c. and is become, moreover, both scarce and dear. Yet it would be an extreme injustice, quite unworthy of an aspirant to literary excellence, to withhold a tribute due to the labours of one to whom the Compiler of the present work acknowledges himself under the greatest obligations.

The ponderous quartos of Dr. Carey include a compilation of a widely different character, in bulk, assuredly, exceeding the product of all others together in this field; and if estimated by that measure, they must be allowed, without dispute, to take the first place in the list of works of their class. From these also the Compiler has drawn freely, as from a storehouse of vocables, for the accumulation of which Dr. Carey has laid him and all other learners of Bengáli under great and lasting obligation. A student of the provincial language would greatly err, however, in the expectation of finding in these large volumes the actual existing vocabulary of the population, free from a strange and heterogeneous edmixture of foreign terms, Persian, Arabic, &c. with every imaginable corruption of the colloquial medium on the one hand, as well as of high unnaturalized Sanscrit words on the other. The approved standard among respectably educated natives is equally removed from both extremes, from the barbarism and vulgarity of the one, from the pedantry and unintelligibility of the other. In no accredited Dictionary of any literary language are the gross vulgarisms of the boor and the low artizan admitted to hold a place, which decency and good taste refuse them.

With regard to the higher style, indeed, the derivatives of the learned language of India differ materially from many Western tongues; inasmuch as the former are absolutely dependant, for scientifical, theological, and general literary terms and phraseology, on the polished language of the Brahmins; the Bengáli perhaps more so than any of its cognate dialects: and, in general, a polished and learned style must necessarily be formed on the model of the Sanscrit, as well as furnished from its vocabulary. A due discrimination is, however, indispensable in detailing the meanings of pure Sanscrit terms, many of whose native applications are quite unknown to the derivative dialect. Dr. Carey's great work is as much depreciated in value as it is augmented in bulk, by a mass of matter utterly irrelevant to the study of the provincial tongue; in nearly every instance, the Sanscrit Dictionary of Dr. Wilson being transcribed verbatim into its pages, to the utter confusion of the student, who is thus set afloat on an unknown ocean of words without pilot or compass. That in the course of time, as the Bengáli becomes cultivated, refined and polished, large accessions will accrue from the higher source, may not be doubted; nor should many words or senses, at present little in use or only employed in some few of the higher compositions, be rejected, if elegant in themselves or necessary to a just expression of current ideas. Many such will be found in the present compilation.

Exotic terms, whether of Arabic, Persic or European origin, are not of the language whose vocabulary it is intended to give, and are therefore designedly excluded, as actual corruptions of a dialect sufficiently rich to be independent of foreign accessions, which it is incapable of enuntiating justly or euphonically, to the manifest injury of its harmony and uniformity, while it may draw naturally and to any extent desirable from the Sanscrit.

The Sanscrit is distinguished, even beyond the polished language of the ancient Greeks, by the extent of its capabilities in the composition of terms, and the facility with which the most complex notions are united in their expression. The Bengáli bears this mark of its affiliation in an eminent degree. The rules for the most current compositions are so easy and regular and they apply so universally, that to collect those even in daily use in the alphabetical order of a Dictionary, would be a task as useless as laborious, and swell the bulk of a volume without corresponding advantage; rather, to the manifest inconvenience of the student, who instead of a portable octavo would be compelled, as at present, to wade in search of a common simple term, through an endless list of formatives and compounds; of which from 50 to 250 and upwards may be numbered in every part of the volumes of Dr. Carey. Nay, in two places, under তৎ *that* and এতৎ *this*, the body of the vocables of the language is duplicated and triplicated, occupying together no fewer than 390 pages of the whole work! It cannot but excite astonishment, considering the really extensive acquirements and acknowledged talents of the respectable author, that his labour should have been so fruitlessly expended both to himself and to those whom it was intended to benefit. On the other hand, the more philosophical compounds, such as are formed by aggregation or coalescence of terms, are actually limited only by the vocabulary of these latter, and are producible *ad libitum*: the attempt to include such is therefore out of the question. The more usual only are comprized in the present work.

The Sanscrit Dictionary of Dr. Wilson is beyond all praise from the Compiler of this volume, as the production of a Scholar who thought for himself, and who, even in availing himself of the labours of his predecessors, has, by an exercise of judgement and discrimination and by personal toil, rendered that his own which has received its modification and arrangement from his mind. Of this invaluable work large use has been made, to the manifest enrichment of the present publication.

The Amara Cosha and other works altogether native have been carefully consulted, and in some of the latter pages, a few hints have been taken from the small vocabulary recently published by Tárachand Datt. The Abridgement of Carey's Dictionary being merely a reduction of the bulk of that work, retaining all its peculiarities though meagre in its explanatory portion, has been of no additional service.

The Shabda Calpa Druma, now in course of publication by Baboo Rádhá Cánta Deb, whose talents and useful labours reflect the greatest credit on himself and his fellow countrymen of this province, and promise to be of eminent service to the students of Hindoo literature, has been consulted as far as published. The Compiler having been, with equal kindness and liberality, favoured by that gentleman with a copy of the extant portion of his elaborate work, takes this opportunity of offering his grateful acknowledgements to him for the aid thence derived.

In the native part of the work, the Amara Cosha, an edition of the same with Bhásha interpretation, and the school vocabulary of Rámchandra Sharma, have been of considerable use; though by far more than three fourths of even that part of the work are entirely original, the result of personal reading and selection, with such aid as could be derived from native assistants. From these latter, it would not easily be credited by the mere European student, how little effective co-operation is obtained where thought and research are required; as a single term cannot safely be admitted uncorroborated by citation or other sufficient authority; and even in the more mechanical species of assistance, the most rigid inspection must be incessantly exercised. It is with true regret that the Compiler is compelled by strict verity to exclude from any participation in the merits of the present publication, whatever they may be, those by whom he has been assisted, the extent of whose services has been limited entirely to the labour of reference or the detection of literal errors and idiomatical inaccuracies. He hails, however, with delight, the augmenting disposition to cultivate every department of literature, in which several well known native scholars have been eminently forward, and begs to throw the present mite of contribution into the general treasury from which the great cause of knowledge, which is the cause of Man in all the varieties of his race and conditions of his being, is to be advanced.

After the foregoing observations, a simple inspection will sufficiently explain the plan of the present work, which is to embody with explanatory English the synonyms of the Bengáli language, to answer the donble purpose of furnishing—to the European, the means as well of fixing the peculiar application of the terms explained, hy corresponding native words, as of varying bis phraseology; and to the native student, together with an explanation of bis national tongue in its own words, a similar in the Englisb language; so that whether he design to study the latter or to confine bimself to the former, he may in either case be furnished witb the requisite assistance. Nothing of this kind has yet appeared, which alone might serve to justify the present attempt to supply the deficiency.

It will be found to contain the great hody of the language with its most important derivatives and compounds, and even those of regular formation, wherever any peculiarity of notion or application exists. Tbose not so circumstanced, as also a large proportion of negatives, &c. formed by the prefixes অ, ন, &c. bave been omitted in coincidence with the Compiler's object, which was to comprize all that was indispensable to the study of the language within the compass of a moderate Octavo, by its size and price accommodated to general use. A few of the earlier sheets are less furnisbed with synonyms than the rest of tbe work; but througbout, the explanatory portion, it is believed, is not chargeable with many serious deficiencies, being fuller than in any work preceding it, not excepting the quartos of Dr. Carey, some of whose omissions, by no means few nor nnimportant, have also been supplied. The synonyms follow in the order of the English explanatory terms. The notation of parts of speecb bas been omitted as inapplicable to the native grammar, (to the rules of which alone the language can he advantageously snbjected,) a semicolon only being used wberever, according to Englisb notions, a word assumes the form of a different part of speech, the same word in Bengáli answering, in numerous instances, the purposes of several. The nnmber of words originally promised has been exceeded by nearly 3,000; and a considerably greater expenditure of time and labour and consequent augmentation of charge than were contemplated, have been unavoidable, from the necessity, in part, of more extensive reading and the consultation of numerous authorities, in part, from successive removals and domestic calamities.

That he mnst have fallen into errors, and that deficiencies will be found to attacb to his work as to every thing buman, the Compiler is perfectly assured; bis bope is they will neither bave been greater nor more nnmerous than, considering the nature of the compilation, tbe little aid to be derived from native assistants, the peculiarities of the idiomatical applications of terms in a language not bis own, and tbe difficulty of decision in numberless instances—was to be expected. He can safely aver, however, that the whole is the result of actual personal labour, having no wbere excused bimself from the dnty of verifying, as far as possible, sucb interpretations as he has taken from others, and that his most strenuous endeavours have not been wanting to render the work, as far as his abilities, attainments and resources admitted, worthy of tbe encouragement of a discerning Public; and it will be found, he ventures to think, from the peculiarity of its plan, peculiarly calculated to aid the now accelerating progress of general edncation in this country.

The labour of such a compilation, especially tbat of fixing npon the just synonymons expressions, can only be appreciated by sucb as have been similarly engaged, who well know the reason Scaliger had for bis strong language on the subject—

> "Si qnem manet sententia jndicis olim,
> Damnatum ærumnis suppliciisqne caput;
> Lexica contexat, nam cetera, quid moror? omnes
> Pœnarum facies hic labor unns habet."

Such as it is, it is now submitted to the Public and subjected to the animadversion of Scholars, in the words of a still more classical authority—

> "Si quid novisti rectius istis,
> Candidns imperti: si non, bis utere mecum."

It remains to state, that this work was undertaken with the sanction and encouragement of that polisbed scholar and empbatically excellent man, the late lamented Bishop Heber, wbose splendid talents and brilliant accomplishments were, alas! so early shrouded from our admiration by the curtain of Fate. It bas been patronized hy the Venerable Society in whose service the Compiler has the happiness to labour, and is printed at their sole charge, a manifest and striking proof of tbeir zeal, not more in the cause of a pure and primitive Christianity, than for the advancement of general literature.

DICTIONARY, &c.

অ.

অ, যে শব্দের পূর্ব্বে থাকে, তাহার অন্যথা হয়, a prefix negative or privative.

অই, পূর্ব্বস্মৃত; সম্মুখস্থিত, yon, yonder, there.

অংশ, ভাগ, a share, part, division.

অংশগত, ভাগযুক্ত, included in a share or part.

অংশাংশ, ভিন্নাংশ, distinct shares, an allotment.

অংশাংশি, পরস্পর ভাগ করা, division into shares.

অংশী, ভাগের অধিকারী, sharing, participating; a partner.

অংশু, কিরণ, a ray. [quillity.

অকম্প, শান্ত, অনুদ্বিগ্ন, quiet, unagitated; quietness, tran-

অকরুণ, নির্দয় unmerciful, unfeeling. [*of reproach*).

অকর্ণবেধ, যাহার কর্ণ ছিদ্রিত নয়, having the ears unbored (*term*

অকর্ম্ম, কুক্রিয়া; নিষ্ফল, useless, fit for nothing; a bad action.

অকল্পন, প্রকৃত, যথার্থ, inartificial, genuine, true.

অকস্মাৎ, হঠাৎ, by chance, suddenly, unawares.

অকাল, অসময়; অন্নাভাব, premature, out of season; a famine.

অকিঞ্চন, দরিদ্র, destitute, poor, quite needy.

অকুলন, অনুপস্থিত, wanting, unprovided, not at hand.

অকূপার, সমুদ্র, the ocean.

অকৃপ, কৃপাহীন, unmerciful, inexorable.

অক্ত, অভিষিক্ত, smeared, plastered, anointed. [ment.

অক্রম, ক্রমরাহিত্য, irregularity, confusion, want of arrange-

অক্রিয়া, আলস্য, inaction, inoperativeness, irreligion.

অক্ষ, পাষ্টি, a die, spot on a die, a wheel, a lawsuit, a bead.
অক্ষতা, কুমারী, a virgin.
অক্ষর, বর্ণ; অনাশ্য, a letter, type, beatitude; imperishable.
অক্ষাংশ, ভূগোলীয় পরিমাণ বিশেষ, a degree of latitude or longitude.
অক্ষি, চক্ষুঃ, an eye.
অখর্ট, অকস্মাদ্বাসনা, childish whim, fancy, caprice.
অখিল, সমুদায়, whole, all, entire.
অগ, দৃঢ়, অটল, immovable; a mountain, tree.
অগত, বর্ত্তমান, not gone, present.
অগত্যা, অনুপায়ে, unavoidably, without resource.
অগদ, ঔষধ, medicine, medicament.
অগম, অসম্ভ্রান্ত, not honorable, disregarded.
অগাধ, অতলস্পর্শ, unfathomable, very deep.
অগার, গৃহ, a house.
অগুণ, অকর্ম্মণ্য; মন্দ, useless, worthless, evil; bad effect.
অগ্নি, অনল, fire, the god of fire, digestive power, bile.
অগ্ন্যবতার, অতিকোপান্বিত, fire incarnate, *i. e.* distorted with passion, furious.
অগ্র, আদ্যভাগ; অন্তভাগ, the front, peak, point, pinnacle; preliminary.
অগ্রণী, যে অগ্রে লইয়া যায়, leading, conducting; a leader.
অগ্রপশ্চাৎ, পূর্ব্বাপর, backwards and forwards, sooner or later.
অগ্রিম, প্রধান, উত্তম, first, chief, eldest, best.
অঘ, পাপ, sin, guilt.
অঘন, মেঘরহিত, clear, cloudless, thin, not crowded.
অঙ্ক, চিহ্ন, a mark, badge, cypher, the flank, heart, numerical figure.
অঙ্কগ, অবগণ্ড, a child in arms. [tortion.
অঙ্কবৃদ্ধি, অধিকাঙ্ক, addition, raising a number or price; ex-
অঙ্কুর, বৃক্ষ ধান্যাদির কল, a sprout, germ, seed, bud, plant.
অঙ্কুশ, হস্তিশাসন দণ্ড, an elephant goad.
অঙ্গ, অবয়ব, the body, a limb, member, part.
অঙ্গগ্রহ, আকর্ষণী, a spasm, cramp, pain, ache.
অঙ্গজ, পুত্র, born of one's body; a son.
অঙ্গনা, সুরূপা স্ত্রী, a well-shaped woman.

অঙ্গপ্রত্যঙ্গ. সকল অবয়ব. in all parts, cap-a-pie.
অঙ্গবশ, স্বায়ত্ত হস্তপাদাদি, the use of the limbs.
অঙ্গরাগ, অঙ্গ সৌন্দর্য্যকারক বর্ণ, a cosmetic, color for painting
the body. [dance, coition.
অঙ্গসঙ্গ, অঙ্গের পরস্পর সংযোগ, contact, obsequious atten-
অঙ্গাঙ্গী, গাণতা, connection, partnership, chicane, collusion.
অঙ্গার, দগ্ধকাষ্ঠ, coal, charcoal, cinder.
অঙ্গী, অবয়ব বিশিষ্ট, embodied; *adv. in comp.* acquiescingly.
অঙ্গীকার, স্বীকার, acquiescence, consent, promise.
অঙ্গুরী, আঙ্গটী, toe or finger-ring.
অঙ্গুলী, হস্তপাদের শেষ অবয়ব, a toe or finger.
অঙ্গুষ্ঠ, বৃদ্ধাঙ্গুলী, the thumb,
অঙ্ঘ্রি, চরণ, the foot, the leg.
অঙ্ঘ্রিপ, বৃক্ষ, a tree. [incident.
অচরিত্র, অস্থির, চঞ্চল, unsteady, changeable, destitute of
অচল, অনড় immoveable, resolute, decrepit; a mountain.
অচির, অস্থির, শীঘ্র, transitory, evanescent, not durable.
অচিরক্রিয়, সতর্ক, prompt in action, active.
অচিরাৎ, অবিলম্বে, promptly, forthwith.
অচিরাভী, ক্ষণিক, অল্পকালিক, temporary, transient.
অচ্ছ, নির্ম্মল, transparent, good. well. [vernment.
অচ্ছত্র, অরাজক, without a king, destitute of a regular go-
অচ্যুত, অনশ্বর, undecaying, imperishable; *ep. of Vishnu.*
অজ, জন্মরহিত, ছাগল, unproduced; a god, spirit or the
male principle of creation; a he-goat.
অজয়, অপরাজয়নীয়, invincible.
অজস্র, নিরন্তর, incessant.
অজা, ছাগী, প্রকৃতি, plastic nature, matter or the female
principle of creation, a she-goat.
অজিন, চর্ম্ম, leather.
অজ্বর, সুস্থ, tranquil, without distress or disease.
অঞ্চল, বস্ত্রের শেষ ভাগ, a border, quarter of a town or country.
অঞ্জন, কজ্জল, black pigment, antimony. [handful.
অঞ্জলি, যুক্ত করদ্বয়, the hands joined palm upwards, a
অটন, চলন, the act of moving, walking.
অটবী, বন, a fôrest, thicket.

অটল, দৃঢ, permanent, immovable, incontrovertible.
অটুট, অখণ্ড, not defective, uninjured, unbroken, entire.
অট্ট, রাজবাটী, a palace, upper-roomed house, *in comp.* exceeding great.
অট্টালক, } ইষ্টকাদি নির্ম্মিত উচ্চ গৃহ, a palace, edifice of brick or
অট্টালিকা, } stone, a house.
অঠেল, স্থিরতর, not displaceable, unanswerable.
অণিমা, অলৌকিক শক্তি, super-human power.
অণু, সূক্ষ্ম বস্তু, an atom, a particle.
অণ্ড, ডিম্ব, an egg, spawn, roe, testicle.
অণ্ডকটাহ, বিশ্ব, the universe.
অণ্ডদ্রব, অসাহস, a sinking at danger, want of fortitude
অতঃপর, ইহার পর, afterwards.
অতএব, এই হেতু, therefore, wherefore.
অতন্দ্রা, অবিলম্বক, unprocrastinating, punctual.
অতসী, শোণ, flax.
অতি, শব্দের পূর্ব্বে থাকিলে অর্থের বৃদ্ধি করেন, *pref.* excessive, very.
অতিকায়, প্রকাণ্ডশরীর, gigantic.
অতিক্রম, লঙ্ঘন, a transgression, surpassing limits.
অতিক্রান্ত, অন্যথাকৃত, transgressed, exceeded, surpassed.
অতিথি, পরগৃহাগত ব্যক্তি, a guest, stranger.
অতিপন্থাঃ, রাজপথ, a high road, a good road.
অতিপর, অতিশত্রু, a decided enemy, not an acquaintance.
অতিপাত, রীতি বিধি বিরুদ্ধ আচার, neglect of what is customary or enjoined.
অতিপার্শ্ব, সন্নিকট, close to the side, alongside, near.
অতিপ্রসঙ্গ, বিস্তার, পুনরুক্তি, unnecessary diffuseness on or intrusion of a topic.
অতিমাত্র, অত্যন্ত, excessive, much; exceedingly, &c.
অতিরথী, অতিযোদ্ধা, opposing many chariot-warriors.
অতিরিক্ত, অত্যন্ত, superabounding, excessive.
অতিরেক, আধিক্য, surplus.
অতিশয়, অত্যন্ত, exceeding, great, very, excessively.
অতিশয়, অধিক, exceeded, excessive.
অতিসার, উদরাময়, a diarrhoea, dysentery.
অতিসারী, অতিসারগ্রস্ত, moving excessively; much affected [with diarrhœa.

অতীত, গত, অতিক্রান্ত, past, gone, elapsed.
অতীন্দ্রিয়, ইন্দ্রিয়ের অগোচর, imperceptible to the senses.
অতীব, অপরিমিত রূপে, excessively.
অতীয়ত্তা, বৃহত্ত্ব, immensity.
অতুন্দ, ক্ষীণ, lank, thin.
অতুর, পীড়িত, দুঃখিত, weak, infirm.
অতুল, অনুপম, unequalled, peerless; unrivalled.
অতেমন, অসমান, dissimilar, unlike.
অত্যন্ত, অতিশয়, very, excessive, immoderate, abundant, great, much.
অত্যন্তবাসী, যোগী, a devotee living in the greatest abstrac- [tion.
অত্যয়, ত্যাগকরা, অধিক, departure, excess, a surpassing.
অত্যয়িত, অতিক্রান্ত, exceeded, outraged, overstepped.
অত্যর্থ, অতিশয়, excessive, exceeding; exceedingly, &c.
অত্যাচার, দৌরাত্ম্য, violence, outrage, oppression, inconsistence.
অত্যুক্তি, অসম্ভাবিত কথন, hyperbole; diffuseness.
অত্যুত্তর, সিদ্ধান্ত, compleat refutation, the extreme north, the most distant time; last, hindermost.
অত্র, এস্থানে, here, in this place.
অত্রত্য, এস্থানের, belonging to this place.
অত্রাযোগ, অযোগ্যতা, failure of sufficiency on emergency.
অত্বক্, ছালহীন, destitute of skin, rind or bark.
অত্বর, অশীঘ্র, not hasty, cool, deliberate.
অথ, অথচ, অনন্তর, moreover, and, also.
অথবা, কিম্বা, otherwise, or.
অথর্ব্ব, অতিবৃদ্ধ, old, superannuated.
অথো, অধিকন্তু, furthermore, moreover, and, hence.
অদত্তা, অবিবাহিতা, not given in marriage, a spinster.
অদন, ভোজন, food, a meal, act of eating.
অদয়, কৃপাহীন, pitiless, unfeeling, uncompassionate.
অদর্শন, অন্তর্দ্ধান, disappearance, being out of sight.
অদৃষ্ট, অদেখা, unseen, unperceived; fate, luck, unseen danger.
অদেবক, অপূজাজীবী, not living on the service of a god.
অদ্ভুত, অলৌকিক, supernatural, marvellous, amazing.

অঘস্মর, অবক্ষুধিত, ravenous, gluttonous.
অদ্য, এই দিনে, to-day.
অদ্যকার, অদ্যতন, এইদিনের, belonging to to-day, to day's.
অদ্রি, পর্ব্বত, a mountain.
অদ্বয়, এক কেবল, single.
অধঃ, নীচে, beneath, below.
অধম, নিকৃষ্ট, vile, base, mean, abominable, wicked.
অধমর্ণ, ঋণী, a debtor.
অধমাধম, অতি নিকৃষ্ট, excessively vile or base.
অধর, নীচের ওষ্ঠ, the lower lip.
অধস্তন, নীচস্থ, lying beneath, situated under.
অধস্তাৎ. নীচ হইতে, beneath, from below.
অধি, প্রাধান্য বোধক হম, *pref.* over, superior; possession, right, property, &c.
অধিক, অতিরিক্ত, more, more than.
অধিকন্তু, বিশেষতঃ, especially, principally; further, also.
অধিকরণ, আধার, a possession; the seventh case.
অধিকাধিক, নিয়মিতের অধিক, more and more.
অধিকার, স্বামিত্ব; রাজ্য; government, estate, reign, right, privilege, inheritance, class of persons.
অধিকারী, স্বামী; কর্ত্তা; possessing right, &c.; a proprietor; capable of, having in one's power.
অধিক্ষিপ্ত, প্রতিক্ষিপ্ত. turned away, sent, despatched.
অধিগত, অবগত; প্রাপ্ত, known, found, acquired, obtained.
অধিগম লাভ; প্রাপ্তি, the obtaining of a thing, acquisition of knowledge, a finding. [god.
অধিদেবতা, ইষ্টদেবতা; অধিষ্ঠাতা, a presiding deity, guardian
অধিদৈব, ক্ষুদ্র দেবগণ, a division of creation including the inferior deities, demigods, &c.
অধিদৈবত, দেব বিদ্যা, theology; a presiding deity. [owner.
অধিপ, অধিপতি, অধিরাজ, প্রভু, a king, sovereign, lord, master,
অধিপ্রজ. জগৎ, the world as continued by procreation.
অধিবাস, শুভ কর্ম্মের পূর্ব্ব কর্ত্তব্য ক্রিয়া, a preliminary ceremony on festive occasions.
অধিবিদ্য, শাস্ত্রবিদ্যা; পাণ্ডিত্য, learning, philosophy.
অধিভূত, প্রকৃতি, nature, the material parts of creation.

অধিমাত্র, ওঁকারের বিদ্যা প্রাপ্তি, a knowledge of the mysteries of the sacred syllable ওঁ.

অধিমাস, মল মাস, an intercalary month.

অধিরাজ, ভূপতি, বড় রাজা, a sovereign, emperor.

অধিলোক, প্রকৃতি, the material world.

অধিষ্ঠাতা, প্রতিপালক, কর্ত্তা, a regent, governor, president, ruler.

অধিষ্ঠাত্রী, অধিদেবতা, presiding, ruling, governing.

অধিষ্ঠান, অবস্থিতি, a habitation, possession, practice, line or principle of conduct.

অধীত, শিক্ষিত, read, studied, instructed.

অধীন, বশতাপন্ন, subject to, beneath, dependant, subservient.

অধীশ্বর, অধিরাজ, a sovereign, lord.

অধুনা, এইক্ষণে, now, lately.

অধোগত, অবগত, descended, gone down.

অধোভব, অধম, নীচস্থ, inferior, placed or situated below.

অধ্যক্ষ, কর্ম্মকর্ত্তা, a chief, superintendant, guardian, governor.

অধ্যক্ষর, ওঁকার, the mysterious syllable ওঁ.

অধ্যধীন, অত্যধীন; দাস, wholly subject; a slave.

অধ্যবসায়, যত্ন করা, perseverance, devotedness to.

অধ্যয়, পাঠ, a lecture, lesson, section.

অধ্যয়ন, পঠন; পাঠ, repetition of a lesson; a reading, lecture.

অধ্যস্ত, পরিবর্ত্তী, substituted, placed instead of.

অধ্যাত্ম, আত্মসম্বন্ধীয়, spiritual, belonging to spirit, inherent; speech, enunciation.

অধ্যাপক, উপদেষ্টা, a teacher, instructor; teaching.

অধ্যায়, পাঠ, a lecture, section, chapter.

অধ্যারূঢ, চড়িত, mounted upon.

অধ্যারোপ, বিরুদ্ধারোপ, an imputing or attributing of what does not belong to a person or thing; the assigning of a fictitious character.

অধ্যারোহণ, চড়ন, a mounting upon, climbing up.

অধ্যাস, ভ্রমকরা, the substituting or mistaking one for another.

অধ্যাসিত, নিবাসী পরিপূর্ণ দেশ, inhabited, settled with inhabitants.

অধ্যাসীন, আসনস্থ, seated, sitting in state.

অধ্যাহরণ, ঊহা, the supplying of an ellipsis, investigation.

অধ্যাহার, উহ্যবাক্য, an ellipsis.
অধ্যুষিত, অধ্যাসিত, inhabited.
অধ্যূঢ়া, প্রথম বিবাহিতা স্ত্রী, the first married of several wives.
অধ্যেতা, অভ্যাসী; ছাত্র, a student, one who reads.
অধ্যেষণা, প্রার্থনা, earnest request, solicitation, prayer.
অধ্ব, পথ, a road, way, path.
অধ্বনীন, অধ্বন্য,-পথিক, a traveller, messenger.
অধ্বর, বলি; যজ্ঞ, a sacrifice.
অনক্ষর, অপণ্ডিত, অজ্ঞ, unlettered, ignorant.
অনঘাত, তাল, the beating of time in music.
অনডুহী, অনড্বাহী,—গরু, a cow.
অনড্বান, বৃষ, a bull.
অনণু, মটর প্রভৃতি, coarse grain, as pease, tares, &c.
অনন্ত, অশেষ; নিত্য, endless, eternal, boundless, numberless.
অনন্তভাব, নিত্যতা, endlessness, eternity.
অনন্তর, অব্যবহিত; পর, afterwards; succeeding, incessant, only, unequalled.
অনন্য, ভিন্ন নাই, identical, the same, not different.
অনন্যপূর্ব্বক, অনুপম, unprecedented. not experienced by others, not preceded.
অনপর, নিজ, ব্রহ্ম, own; an appellation of Brahma.
অনবরত, যাহার বিরাম নাই, incessant, perpetual, constant.
অনবসাদ, দৃঢ়তা; স্থৈর্য্য, continuance or stability of a state, a not running to ruin.
অনবস্থা, দরিদ্রতা, want, need, adversity: infinite (in logic.)
অনর্থ, নিষ্ফল, useless, answering no purpose.
অনল, অগ্নি, fire, a species of reed.
অনস, গাড়ী, a cart, carriage. [to a close, not finished.
অনস্ত, অনস্তমিত,-অনস্তাগত, not set (as a star), not brought
অনহিত, হিংসক, injurious, disadvantageous.
অনাগত, ভবিষ্যৎ, not come, not arrived, future.
অনাগাঃ, নিষ্পাপী, sinless, free from transgression.
অনাচার, অশুচিকর্ম্ম, improper conduct, impurity.
অনাজ, শস্য; তরকারী, corn, edible vegetables.
অনাড়, গুপ্ত; দুর্জ্ঞেয়, secret, not easily discovered.
অনাড়িপনা, জড়তা, inactivity, dulness, stupidity.

অনাড়ী, জড়; অচেতন, inactive, dull, stupid, motionless.
অনাথ, অস্বামিক, forlorn, orphan, without a protector.
অনাদি, জন্মরহিত, without beginning, eternal.
অনামা, অনামিকা,—চতুর্থাঙ্গুলী, the fourth finger.
অনালোক, অপ্রিয়দর্শন, disagreeable to the sight, unwelcome.
অনায়ক, স্বামিহীন, without an owner or leader, unappropriated, unclaimed.
অনায়াস, অল্পশ্রম, ease, facility; easy.
অনারত, নিত্য, অনিবারিত, incessant, perpetual.
অনাশ, নাশঅভাব, অহিংসক, non-destruction; harmless.
অনিয়ত, নিত্য, অনিয়মিত, incessant, perpetual, constant, undetermined, unregulated, not resolved.
অনিল, বায়ু, the wind.
অনিসর্গ, অস্বাভাবিক, unnatural, excited, depressed; an unnatural state of mind.
অনীক, অনীকিনী,—সৈন্য, an army, forces.
অনীদৃশ, অতুল্য, not thus, unlike, dissimilar.
অনীশ, অনধিকারী, without right or authority, subject, dependant.
অনীশ্বর, যিনি ঈশ্বর নয়, that which is not God.
অনীশ্বরবাদ, নাস্তিকতা, atheism, denial of God.
অনীহ, অলস্য, inactive, indolent.
অনু, পশ্চাৎ, *pref*. following, agreeing, according to.
অনুকম্পা, দয়া, কৃপা, pity, compassion, tenderness.
অনুকরণ, অনুবৃত্তি, imitation; imitative.
অনুকর্ষণ, আকর্ষণ, a drawing, attraction, repetition.
অনুকল্প, প্রধান কল্পের ন্যূন, an alternative, consequential step or measure, secondary injunction.
অনুকার, অনুরূপ করা, an imitation.
অনুকূল, সহকারী, coinciding, friendly, cooperating, assisting.
অনুক্রম, শ্রেণী, a series, succession, method, order.
অনুক্রমণিকা, সূচীপত্র, an index, table of contents.
অনুক্রোশ, কৃপা, pity, compassion, tenderness.
অনুক্ষণ, সর্বসময়, at every instant, perpetually, continually.
অনুগত, আশ্রিত, gone after, dependent on, attached to.
অনুগম, পশ্চাদ্গমন, a following, a consequence.
অনুগ্রহ, প্রসন্নতা, grace, favour, kindness.
অনুচর, সহচর, an attendant, follower.

অনুজ, কনিষ্ঠ ভ্রাতা, younger, junior.
অনুজীবী, অন্যাবলম্বী, living upon, supported by, dependent on.
অনুজ্ঞা, অনুমতি, a command, injunction.
অনুতপ্ত, অনুশোচী, penitent, repentant, filled with regret.
অনুতাপ, শোক; পশ্চাত্তাপ, repentance, regret, remorse.
অনুদর, ক্ষীণ, lank, thin.
অনুদিন, প্রতিদিন, daily, as constant as the day.
অনুদৈর্ঘ্য, অনুলম্ব, longitudinal.
অনুদ্বাহ, অবিবাহ, celibacy. [flexion, consideration.
অনুধাবন, পশ্চাদ্গমন; মনোযোগ, a pursuit, running after, re-
অনুনয়, স্তুতি, humility, submission, intreaty.
অনুপাত, সমভাব, proportion, arithmetical proportion.
অনুপাতক, ক্ষুদ্র পাপ, a small crime, venial fault.
অনুপান, ঔষধের সহকারী, a vehicle for medicine.
অনুপার্শ্ব, পার্শ্ব সম্বন্ধীয়, lateral.
অনুপ্রবেশ, পশ্চাদ্গমন, a following another into a place.
অনুপ্রয়াস, অনুপ্রাস,-নিষ্ফল পরিশ্রম, tardy exertion, labour after a thing is done. [verse.
অনুপ্রস্থ, প্রস্থ সম্বন্ধীয়, latitudinal, following the width, trans-
অনুবৎসর, প্রতি বৎসর, yearly, annual. [quence of something.
অনুবদ্ধ, সম্বন্ধীয়, related to, bound or connected in conse-
অনুবন্ধ, পাপ; মূল, an offence, guilt; a root, affix.
অনুবর্ত্তন, অনুসার, a following, a being consequent, attendance, complaisance. [the Veda.
অনুবাক, বেদাংশ, শ্রুতি, an explanatory text or sentence from
অনুবাদ, পুনঃকথন, a response, abusive reply, quotation.
অনুবৃত্তি, পশ্চাদ্গমন, a consequence, a following.
অনুবোধ, স্মৃতি, অনুসূচনা, a recollection, reviving of ideas, after-thought.
অনুভব, মানসজ্ঞান, apprehension, comprehension, guess, inference, supposition, hypothesis, experience.
অনুভাব, দৃঢ় অনুমান; নিশ্চয়, firm opinion, certainty, indication, hint. [cated, &c.
অনুভূত, মানস দ্বারা জ্ঞাত, experienced, felt, guessed, indi-
অনুমত, স্বীকৃত, allowed, permitted.

অনুমতি, সম্মতি, আজ্ঞা, a permission, command, advice.
অনুমন্তা, অনুমতিকারক, one who orders or permits.
অনুমরণ, পশ্চাৎমরণ, a widow's burning on a separate pile from her deceased husband.
অনুমান, যুক্তির দ্বারা নির্ণয়, an inference, guess, hypothesis.
অনুমাপন, অনুমান করাণ, a leading to an inference, a causing to infer.
অনুমৃতা অনুগামিনী, a woman who burns on a separate pile.
অনুমোদন, পরসন্তোষে সন্তোষ পাওন, to receive pleasure from sympathy.
অনুযায়ী, পশ্চাদ্গামী, following, arising as a consequence.
অনুযোগ, অপমান, a reproof, reprehension.
অনুরক্ত, অনুগত, attached; fond, enamoured.
অনুরঞ্জন, অনুরাগ-আসক্তি, attachment, delight in, fondness.
অনুরুদ্ধ, স্বীকৃত, complied with, acquiesced in, conceded to.
অনুরূপ, সদৃশ, corresponding, resembling, like.
অনুরোধ, অপেক্ষা, প্রণয়, expectation, waiting for, partiality acquiescence, complaisance.
অনুলেপ, অঙ্গলেপ, a perfumed unguent; an anointment of the body.
অনুলোম, যথাক্রম, favorable. helping, going with the grain.
অনুশয়, পশ্চাত্তাপ; প্রতিদ্বেষ, repentance, revenge, ancient enmity, an object of pursuit.
অনুশাসন, বশীভূত করণ, the giving rules for acquiring a science; to discipline.
অনুশিষ্ট, উপদেশপাত্র, docile, teachable, subject to rules.
অনুশীলন, আলোচনা, attention, study, devotedness to.
অনুশোক, পশ্চাত্তাপ, repentance, regret, remorse.
অনুশ্রব, শ্রুতিধর, learned by dictation, or hearing repeated.
অনুষঙ্গ, সম্বন্ধ, প্রণয়, agreement of a word with succeeding words, attachment, love.
অনুষেক, পুনর্জলসেক, a wetting or watering again.
অনুষ্ঠান, আরম্ভ; উত্থাপন, a doing or practising, practice, commencement, application, diligence, topic, subject.
অনুসন্ধান, অন্বেষণ, aim, search, research, scrutiny, enquiry.

অনুসরণ, পশ্চাদ্গমন, following after.
অনুসার, পূর্বানুরূপ similarity, a consequence, accordance.
অনুসূচন, দর্শান, the occasioning of reflection on a subject, indication.
অনুসূচনা, বিবেচনা, reflexion, indication.
অনুন, মোটা, coarse, gross, thick, entire, close.
অনুপ, জলযুক্ত, জলময়, wet, watery, overflowed.
অনেক, বহু, many, much.
অনেকপ, হস্তী, an elephant.
অনেকশ, প্রশস্তরূপে, by large numbers or quantities.
অনোখা, অনুপম, unprecedented, unparallelled.
অন্ত, } শেষ ভাগ; সীমা, near; an end, death, *pref.* inward,
অন্তঃ, } within, inwardly, inner.
অন্তঃকরণ, মন, বুদ্ধি, চিত্ত, the heart, will.
অন্তঃপুর, পুরীর মধ্য, inner or women's apartments, seraglio.
অন্তঃপ্রজ্ঞ, চিত্তজ্ঞ, acquainted with the heart, knowing the thoughts.
অন্তঃসত্ত্বা, গর্ভিণী, pregnant.
অন্তঃসলিল, অন্তর্জল, subterraneous water; a secret, concealed [idea.
অন্তক, নাশকারী, mortal, deadly, ending; death.
অন্তর, মধ্য; পৃথক; দূর, within, between, on the margin, opportunely; interval, distance, midst, outside, opportunity, the supreme soul; difference, remainder, sake, behalf; own, similar; *ad.* without, except, and, moreover.
অন্তরঙ্গ, আত্মীয়; সহকারী, a relative, near friend, intimate.
অন্তরতা, দূরতা; মধ্যতা, inclusiveness, exclusiveness, distance, inwardness, outwardness.
অন্তরা, মধ্য; নিকট, between, near, except; a line in poetry.
অন্তরাত্মা, জীবাত্মা, the inward spirit, the soul.
অন্তরাপত্যা, গর্ভিণী, pregnant.
অন্তরায়, ব্যাঘাত, an impediment, obstacle.
অন্তরাল, মধ্যস্থল, a space between two objects.
অন্তরিক্ষ, অন্তরীক্ষ,-আকাশ, the sky, atmosphere.
অন্তরীপ, শুষ্ক, dried up, left dry: a head-land.
অন্তরীয়, মধ্যের, an inner garment; inner.

অন্তরেণ, ভিতরে; ভিন্ন, within, between, except.
অন্তর্গত, মনোবর্ত্তি. included. forgotten.
অন্তর্জনন, মনোমধ্যজন্মান, a producing in, or working on the mind.
অন্তর্জল, ভূমধ্যজল, water absorbed by the earth or passing off subterraneously; half-immersed.
অন্তর্দ্ধা, অন্তর্দ্ধান, অদর্শন, a disappearing, vanishing.
অন্তর্দ্ধি, অদৃশ্যত্ব. invisibility, a concealed state.
অন্তর্ধ্যান, মনশ্চিন্তা, inward meditation; contemplation.
অন্তর্ভবন, অন্তরভাব, মনোভবন, an existing inwardly, or within.
অন্তর্যজন, অন্তর্যাগ,—মানস পূজা, ধ্যান, inward or mental worship.
অন্তর্যমন, ব্যাপ্তি, a pervading.
অন্তর্হিত, লুক্কায়িত, vanished, disappeared.
অন্তিক, সমীপ, near, contiguous, proximate.
অন্তিম, চরম, very near, last, ulterior.
অন্তেবাসী, ছাত্র, a disciple; an outcast.
অন্ত্য, শেষস্থ, last, ultimate.
অন্ত্যেষ্টি, শব দাহনাদি, a last or funeral sacrifice.
অন্ত্র, আঁত, the entrails, bowels, viscera.
অন্দু, স্ত্রীপাদালঙ্কার, an ornament for a woman's foot, a chain.
অন্ধ, নেত্রহীন, blind; overgrown with weeds or bushes.
অন্ধকার, তমোভাব, darkness.
অন্ধলা, অন্ধ, blind.
অন্ধস্, খাদ্য, food.
অন্ধিসন্ধি, ছিদ্র, a chink, crevice, flaw, flaw in one's conduct.
অন্ন, পক্ব তণ্ডুলাদি, boiled rice, food in general.
অন্নদাস, অন্নার্থ দাস, an eye-servant, regarding only his food.
অন্নব্রহ্ম, অন্ন স্বরূপ ব্রহ্ম, Bramha as identified with food.
অন্নযোগ, অন্নপ্রস্তুত করণ, the providing of food, abundance.
অন্নরস, অন্নের সারভাগ, chyle.
অন্নাদ ভোক্তা, an eater.
অন্নান্নাদাত্মা, খাদ্যভোক্তাস্বরূপ, Brahma as identified with the food and the eater.
অন্নাহারী, ভোক্তা, eating food; an eater.
অন্য, ভিন্ন, another, other, different.
অন্যগামী, ব্যভিচারী, going to others, adulterous.
অন্যৎ, পৃথক, ভিন্ন, another, other.

অন্যতম, অনেকের মধ্যে এক, one of several, the best of all.

অন্যতর, দুয়ের মধ্যে এক, one of two, rather, either, other, different.

অন্যথা, ভিন্ন প্রকার, বিরুদ্ধ, the contrary, reverse, a different idea, different conduct; contrary, different; contrarywise, differently.

অন্যপূর্ব্বা, পরপূর্ব্বা previously betrothed to another man.

অন্যভৃৎ, কাক, a crow.

অন্যমনস্ক, অন্যচিত্ত, thinking on something else, absent, absorbed in other thoughts, averse.

অন্যাৎ, অন্য প্রকার, otherwise, yet, in another respect.

অন্যাদৃক, অন্যাদৃশ, ভিন্নরূপে, otherwise, in another manner.

অন্যান্য, ভিন্নভিন্নলোক, others.

অন্যেদ্যুঃ, ভিন্নকালে, on another day, at another time.

অন্যোন্য, পরস্পর, mutual, reciprocal.

অন্বক্ষ, পশ্চাদ্গামী, following.

অন্বয়, বংশ, কুল, race, lineage, regimen in grammar, a consequence or conclusion in logic.

অন্বয়ী, সম্পর্কী, agreeing with, following upon.

অন্বহ, প্রত্যহ, daily.

অন্বাচয়, যোগকরণ, the connecting of succeeding objects in writing or discourse.

অন্বাধি, পুনর্ব্বার আধি করণ, a deposit made with one for ultimate deposit with another.

অন্বায়তম, অনুপ্রস্থ, latitudinal, following the width.

অন্বারব্ধ, দক্ষিণের সহিত সংযুক্ত বামহস্ত, brought in contact with the right, (spoken of the left hand, in contracts.)

অন্বাহার্য্য, মাসিক, monthly obsequies to ancestors.

অন্বাহিত, পুনর্ব্বার আধিকৃত, deposited for ultimate delivery to another.

অন্বিত, যুক্ত, connected, agreeing with, inherent, fraught with, possessed of.

অন্বেষণ, অনুসন্ধান, search, research, enquiry.

অপ্, জল, water.

অপ, অন্যথা কিম্বা মন্দ বোধক শব্দ, *pref.* away from, ill, evil.

অপকরণ, অনিষ্ট করণ, to do wrong, hinder, obstruct.
অপকর্ম, কুশীলতা, evil tendency, wrong bias, pre-observance.
অপকর্ষণ, অন্যায় রূপেতে কর্ষণ, an unfair seizing, a biassing, a drawing from what is right.
অপকলঙ্ক, অভিদুর্নাম, indelible stain, blot, disgrace.
অপকার, অনিষ্ট, ক্ষতি, hindrance, detriment, injury.
অপকীর্ত্তি, দুর্যশ, ill-fame, infamy.
অপক্রম, পলায়ন, a withdrawing, flight, retreat.
অপক্বরস, অন্নরস, chyle.
অপক্বাশী, অপক্ব ভোজী, feeding on raw food or unripe fruits.
অপগম, প্রস্থান, departure, deviation.
অপঘন, অবয়ব, a member, limb.
অপঘাত, বধ, murder, tragical or sudden death.
অপচয়, ক্ষতি, loss, detriment, dispersion, waste.
অপচার, অপাক, indigestion.
অপচ্ছায়া, ভূত, প্রেত, an apparition, phantom, unhealthy or injurious shadow.
অপত্য, পুত্র, কন্যা, a child.
অপত্রপা, লাজুকতা, bashfulness.
অপত্রপিষ্ণু, লজ্জাশীল, bashful. [ploy; a reptile.
অপদ, পাদ রহিত; কর্ম্মচ্যুত, without feet, out of office or em-
অপদান, সমাপ্তি, a finished work, approved occupation.
অপদার্থ, অযোগ্য; শূন্যতা, nothing, vanity; unfit, incompetent.
অপদেবতা, মনঃকল্পিত প্রেত পিশাচাদি, apparition, ghost.
অপদেশ, ছল, pretext, pretence. [cursing.
অপধ্বংসক, খণ্ডক; ঘৃণাকারী, breaking to pieces, abhorring,
অপনয়ন, মরণ, a taking from; act of dying. [ground.
অপনুত্তি, অপনোদন,-আছড়াওন, a dashing or beating on the
অপবর্গ মুক্তি, detachment from matter, beatitude.
অপবর্ত্ত্য, সংক্ষেপ করা, an abridging.
অপবাদ, নিন্দা; অখ্যাতি, accusation, libel.
অপবাহ, অল্প করণ, a deduction.
অপবিদ্ধ, চূর্ণিত, pulverized, broken small.
অপব্যয়, বৃথাব্যয়, prodigality, profuse expenditure.
অপভাষা, অসাধুবাক্য, low, vulgar, contemptible, or obscene language.

অপভ্রংশ, কুৎসিত বাক্য, চ্যুতি, common vulgar talk, low term; fall, want of success, failure.
অপমান, তিরস্কার, dishonour, insult, disgrace, affront.
অপমৃত্যু, রোগ ব্যতিরেকে মৃত্যু, inauspicious or untimely death.
অপর, অন্য, other, another.
অপরলোক, অন্যলোক; পরলোক, other people, another world.
অপররাত্র, রাত্রির শেষ ভাগ, the end of the night.
অপরম্পার, নিয়ত, continual.
অপরাধ, পাপ, দণ্ডযোগ্য কর্ম্ম, a fault, guilt, sin.
অপরাদ্ধ, অপরাধী, পাপী, guilty, faulty, criminal.
অপরাহ্ন, বৈকাল, afternoon.
অপরাহ্নতন, বৈকালিক, belonging to the afternoon.
অপরিণাম, অবস্থার অনন্যথা, original or unchanged state; unchangeable.
অপরুদ্ধ, ক্ষুব্ধ, affected, pained, distressed.
অপরূপ, আশ্চর্য্য, preternatural, ugly, distorted, queer.
অপরেদ্যুঃ, পরদিবস, the morrow, day following.
অপর্ণ, পত্রহীন, অপূর্ণিত সংখ্যা, leafless, an incomplete number.
অপলপন, পরিবাদ, a slandering, belieing, talking scandal, [denying.
অপসব্য, বামহস্ত, the left hand or side.
অপসরণ, প্রস্থান, পলায়ন, a withdrawing, retreating.
অপস্মার, মৃগীরোগ, epilepsy.
অপহনন, হত্যা, a killing, murdering.
অপহরণ, চৌর্য্য, plundering, purloining, unfair taking.
অপহা, হন্তা, a murderer.
অপহার, চৌর্য্য, pillage, plunder, depredation, robbery.
অপহ্নব, চৌর্য্য, অপলাপ, denial, concealment.
অপাংনিধি, সমুদ্র, the sea.
অপাঙ্গ, চক্ষুর প্রান্ত ভাগ, the outer corner of the eye, small circle on the forehead: lame, ugly, deformed.
অপাঙ্গদর্শন, ঈষদ্দর্শন, glance, imperfect view.
অপাঠ, মিথ্যা পাঠ, false reading, interpolation, unauthentic [writing.
অপাদান, গ্রহণ, করণ, a taking from, origin.
অপান, গুহ্য দেশ, the anus, a not drinking, air inhaled.
অপাবৃত্ত, অনিরুদ্ধ, unrestrained.

অপায়, বিনাশ, hindrance, obstruction, death.
অপি, ও, also, and, likewise, moreover; *pref.* over.
অপিচ, অপিতু,—আর, moreover, also, and.
অপিধান, পরিচ্ছদ, a covering.
অপিনদ্ধ, অস্ত্রবিশিষ্ট, covered with armour, accoutred.
অপূপ, পিষ্টক, bread, a cake. [eminent; fate, destiny.
অপূর্ব. অদৃষ্ট, উত্তম, unprecedented, uncommon, excellent,
অপূর্বাহ্ন, বৈকাল, afternoon; without a forenoon.
অপেক্ষ, অনুরোধী, আশান্বিত, expectant, expecting, requisite.
অপেক্ষা, অনুরোধ, আশা, expectation, hope, dependance,
need, remains of food &c.; than, rather.
অপেক্ষণ, দর্শনাপেক্ষা, an expecting or waiting for. [sion.
অপোহ, নির্ণয়, নিষ্পত্তি, an ascertaining by investigation, deci-
অম্পতি, সমুদ্র, জলস্বামী, the sea, the lord of waters.
অপ্সরা, স্বর্গবেশ্যা, female demigods, dancers and courte-
zans of heaven. [now.
অব, মন্দ ও নীচার্থক শব্দ, *pref.* away, down, ill, bad; *adv.*
অবকথন, উপাসনা, স্তব, a flattering, fulsome flattery, low talk.
অবকর, আবর্জ্জনা, sweepings, refuse, dust, a dunghill.
অবকর্ত্তন, চরকা, a spinning wheel.
অবকলন, অগণন, a making false or useless calculations.
অবকাশ, অবসর, leisure, opportunity. [temned.
অবকুঞ্চিত, বক্রীকৃত, হেয়, dishevelled, unreasonable, con-
অবকুট্টন, খিট্‌খিট্, an improper complaining, querulousness.
অবকুণ্ঠন, অসাহস, ভীরুতা, a shrinking from fear, distress,
agitation.
অবকুহুন, কুকোঁথানি, a hideous and disagreeable groaning.
অবকূজন, কুরব, a disagreeable noise, croaking, howling,
groaning.
অবকৃষ্ট, বহিষ্কৃত, মন্দ, removed, expelled, rejected.
অবক্রন্দন, উচ্চৈঃস্বরযুক্ত ক্রন্দন, a loud and clamorous weeping.
অবক্রয়, নিন্দ্যক্রয়, an unfair purchase.
অবক্রীড়ন, কুৎসিত খেলা, rough play, unfair play.
অবক্রুদ্ধ, অতিরাগযুক্ত, unnecessarily or unseasonably enraged.
অবক্রুষ্ট, কুরবোক্ত, expressed by yells or howling, howled over.
অবক্বণ, কুধ্বনি, discord in music, sound of a lute.

অবক্ষুধা, পেটুকতা, a ravenous appetite. [sarcasm.
অবক্ষেপ, কুক্ষেপ, ব্যঙ্গ, a careless or unskilful throw, irony,
অবখণ্ডন, খনন, to dig, break unskilfully, mangle.
অবখাত, খামা, a dangerous pit.
অবখেল, কুৎসিত খেলা, foul play.
অবগণিত, অমানিত, despised, disregarded, miscalculated.
অবগণ্ড, শিশু, an infant.
অবগম, জ্ঞান, knowledge, acquaintance with.
অবগাঢ়, ডুবিত, স্নাত, bathed, immersed.
অবগাহন, স্নান, ডুব, a bathing, immersion, ablution.
অবগুণ্ঠন, অবগুণ্ঠিকা,—ঘোমটা, a veil.
অবগোচর, অর্দ্ধদর্শিত, dimly or imperfectly perceived.
অবগোরণ, উত্থান, a lifting the hand or weapon to strike.
অবগ্রন্থন, কুরচনা, bad or irregular workmanship, an entangling, irregular writing.
অবগ্রহ, অবগ্রাহ, অনাবৃষ্টি, drought; an elephant's forehead.
অবঘাত, অপঘাত, বধ, a mortal blow, murder.
অবঘূর্ণ, ঘূর্ণজল, a whirlpool, a careless or unskilful whirling.
অবঘ্রাণ, নিন্দিত গন্ধ, a disagreeable smell.
অবচূর্ণ, অসূক্ষ্ম চূর্ণ, coarse powder. [unlawful endeavour.
অবচেষ্টা, আনাড়িপনা, awkward or uncouth action, awkward or
অবচ্ছেদ, সীমা, পর্য্যন্ত, a limit, boundary.
অবচ্ছেদাবচ্ছেদ, সমস্ত, সাকল্য, the whole of any thing.
অবজীর্ণ, অতিবৃদ্ধ, decrepid, withered with age.
অবজ্ঞা, অনাদর, হিংসা, disregard, contempt, despite.
অবট, গর্ত্ত, ছিদ্র, a hole, cavern, cavity.
অবতংস, চূড়া, মণি, a crest, ear-ring, gem, gold, ray, rein.
অবতমস, ঘোরতা, gloom, imperfect darkness.
অবতান, চাঁদনি, an awning.
অবতার, দেবতাদের মনুষ্যাদি রূপে প্রকাশ, a descent, incarnation.
অবতারণিকা, তোলা; নৌকা, a quotation, a boat.
অবতীর্ণ, উপস্থিত, descended, incarnate.
অবত্ত, নিবেদিত, offered, immolated.
অবথর, বলহীন, decrepid.
অবদান, উৎসর্গ, বলি, oblation, immolation.
অবদীর্ণ, চিরাণ, ফাটিত, torn, rent, cleft, cracked.

অবদূন, অনুতাপিত, regretted, repented of.
অবদ্যোত, ঈষদুজ্জ্বল, a glimmering, faint light.
অবদ্রুত, গোলমালে পলায়িত, fled in disorder, imperfectly melted or dissolved.
অবধান, মনোযোগ, attention, care, regard.
অবধারণ, নিশ্চয়, স্থির করণ, a settling, determining on, emphasis.
অবধি, পর্য্যন্ত, extremity, limit, border; to, from.
অবধীরিত, অবজ্ঞাত, undervalued, despised, contemned.
অবধূত, তপস্যান্বিত, devoted to God, but regardless of ceremonies.
অবধূত, পরিষ্কৃত, shaken out, brushed.
অবনর্দ্দন, কুৎসিত শব্দ, a harsh discordant sound.
অবনায়, নামান, দ্বেষ, a causing to descend, throwing down, dislike, hatred.
অবনাহ, কুরূপে অস্ত্রাদি সাজন, a girding on of armour unskilfully.
অবনি, পৃথিবী, the earth, the world.
অবপক্ষ, অকর্ম্মণ্য পক্ষপাতী, a useless partizan, useless wing.
অবপাল, পালরহিত, without a keeper or protector, neglected.
অববাদ, নিন্দা, accusation, reproach, command, friendship, kindness.
অববৃত, আচ্ছাদিত, covered, protected.
অববেষ্টন, ঘেরণ, to encircle, surround, swathe.
অববোধ, অশুদ্ধ জ্ঞান, imperfect idea, false judgment, prejudice.
অবভান, অবভাস,—মায়া, deceptive or false appearance.
অবভৃথ, প্রায়শ্চিত্তের পরস্নান, ablution after a sacrifice.
অবম, কর্ম্মাযোগ্য দিবস, a solar day; vile, bad, inferior.
অবমতি, অবজ্ঞা; স্বামী, contempt; a master, lord.
অবমান, অখ্যাতি, dishonour, disgrace.
অবমূর্দ্ধশয়, অধঃশিরাশায়ী, hanging or falling with the head downwards.
অবমৃষ্ট, ভ্রষ্ট, deflowered, forced, defiled.
অবয়ব, অঙ্গ, a limb, member, part, feature.
অবয়বী, অঙ্গবিশিষ্ট, made up of parts or members.
অবর, কনিষ্ঠ, younger, posterior, inferior, least.
অবরত, ক্ষান্ত, desisted, ceased.
অবরতঃ, অবরস্তাৎ,—পশ্চাৎ, afterwards, beneath, subsequently.
অবরস, অস্বাদু, বিরস, unpleasant taste; ill-tasted, tasteless.

অবরোধ, বদ্ধকরা, a blockade, shutting up, siege, prevention, coverlid, queen's apartments.
অবরোহ, নামন, অধোগমন, a descent, an alighting.
অবলজ্জা, নিন্দিত লজ্জা, false modesty, improper shame.
অবলম্ব, আশ্রয়, a prop, support, fulcrum, perpendicular.
অবলম্বন, আশ্রয়, ঠেস্, a prop, support; -দে- to apply a prop; ক- to take as a support, maintain, depend on.
অবলা, বলহীনা; নারী, weak; a woman. [to brand.
অবলাঞ্ছন, অকীর্ত্তি জনক চিহ্ন রাখন, to fix a mark of disgrace,
অবলিপ্ত, অভ্যঙ্গিত, smeared over, anointed, proud, conceited.
অবলেহ, চাটন, the lapping of a liquid; a lozenge.
অবলোকন, দর্শন, to look at, survey.
অবশেষ, শেষাংশ, residue, remnant, surplus, last remains.
অবশ্য, সর্ব্বথাকর্ত্তব্য, certain, necessary; certainly, necessarily.
অবশ্যত্তব, সর্ব্বথাকর্ত্তব্যতা, necessity, importance, urgency.
অবশ্যায়, নীহার, শীতল, frost, cold, pride.
অবষ্টব্ধ, বেষ্টিত, surrounded, near, supported, protected.
অবষ্টম্ভ, আরম্ভ, সূচনা, beginning, intimation, excellence, symmetry, a pillar.
অবস্, অবস্তাৎ—পর, পশ্চাৎ, inferiorly, after, beneath, behind.
অবসথ, অবস্থান, house, residence, town. [poor.
অবসন্ন, শ্রান্ত, wearied, exhausted, relaxed, decayed, ended,
অবসর, অবকাশ, leisure, opportunity.
অবসাদ, শ্রান্তি, গ্লানি, weariness, lassitude, flaccidity.
অবসান, অবসায়,-শেষ, exit, extinction, end, decline, decision, decay.
অবসারণ, বহিষ্করণ, to dislodge, cause to remove, disband.
অবসেয়, নাশ্য, destructible, mortal, ruinable.
অবস্কন্দ, কটক, a camp.
অবস্কন্দন, খণ্ডন, পরিহরণ, to refute, repel.
অবস্কর, ওঁচলা, sweepings, refuse, ordure.
অবস্থা, দশা; দুর্দশা, condition, situation, state, trouble.
অবস্থান, স্থিতি, a lodging, residing, settling, residence.
অবস্থাপন, স্থিতি করান, to settle, fix, establish.
অবস্থিতি, অবস্থান, residence, dwelling, settlement.

অবস্বন, কুশব্দ, harsh sound, noise, howl, yell.
অবহনন, মর্দ্দন, to pound or thresh, unhusk.
অবহা, স্থির, not passing away or flowing on, permanent.
অবহার, গ্রহন,মোচন, a removing or taking away, forgiveness.
অবহিত্থা. কাপট্য, dissimulation, concealed conduct.
অবহেল, অবহেলা,—অনাদর, disregard of authority, contempt, disrespcct.
অবাক্, বাক্যরহিত, speechless, mute; beneath, below.
অবাক্‌শিরাঃ, অবমূর্দ্ধশয়, hanging with the head downwards.
অবাগ্র, নিম্নাগ্র, নত, bowed, hanging down, nodding.
অবাচী, দক্ষিণ, south, the south.
অবাদ, অবিতণ্ডা, a saying of no authority, non-contradiction.
অবান্তর, অন্তরস্থ, অন্য, included, intervolved.
অবাপ্ত, পুনঃপ্রাপ্ত, re-obtained, recovered, transplanted.
অবার, ওপার, the hither side of a river.
অবি, মেষ, a sheep, mountain, the sun, preservation.
অবিকট, মেষপাল, a flock of sheep.
অবিধ, অভেদ, similar, common, undistinguished.
অবিধা, অবিশেষ, want of method or distinction.
অবী, রজস্বলা, a woman in her courses.
অবীরা, পতিপুত্ররহিতা, a woman without husband or son.
অবেক্ষণ, দর্শন, a surveying, inspection.
অবেক্ষা, ধ্যান, মনোযোগ, attention, fixedness of mind, inspection.
অব্জ, চন্দ্র, পদ্ম, the moon, a conch, a lotus.
অব্জিনী, পদ্মিনী, a bed of lotuses.
অব্জিনীপতি, সূর্য্য, the sun.
অব্দ, বৎসর, মেঘ, a year, æra; a cloud.
অব্ধি, সমুদ্র, the sea, a receptacle of water.
অভ্র, মেঘ, a cloud.
অব্রুবন, অব্রুবান,—অবগণ্ড, not speaking; an infant.
অভরণ, অলঙ্কার, a jewel, ornament.
অভাব, অবিদ্যমানতা, non-existence, deficiency, failure.
অভিক, অভিলাষী, desirous, lustful.
অভিখ্যা, সংজ্ঞা, পদবী, appellation, name, beauty.
অভিগমন, নিকট গমন, motion towards, a going to.
অভিঘাত, নাশ, বধ, destruction, murder.

অভিচার, নাশক মন্ত্রাদি, an incantation to injure or destroy.

অভিজন, পরিজন, a family, head of a family, birth-place, family residence.

অভিজাত, সদ্বংশজ, nobly-born, fit, learned.

অভিজ্ঞ, পণ্ডিত, wise, learned, acquainted with.

অভিজ্ঞান, অসন্দেহ, চিহ্ন, conviction, certainty, token, sign, signal, flag.

অভিতঃ, চতুর্দিক, round about, in front, swiftly, wholly.

অভিধা, অভিধান,—সংজ্ঞা, কোষ, word, name, appellation, vocabulary, explanation.

অভিধেয়, শব্দের প্রতিপাদ্য, নাম, the thing to be explained or spoken, a name; explicable, fit to be spoken.

অভিধ্যা, পরদ্রব্যাভিলাষ, a coveting what is another's.

অভিনব, নূতন, new, recent.

অভিনয়, কাপ, a representation, theatrical entertainment.

অভিনিবেশ, মনোযোগ, engagedness of mind, devotedness to, zeal.

অভিনিপাতিত, ব্যাপ্ত, shed abroad upon (as the solar rays).

অভিনিষ্পত্তি, সমাপ্তি, conclusion, termination, decision.

অভিনেতা, সংকারক, an actor in a drama.

অভিনেয়, অভিনয়যোগ্য, proper to be represented; a character or part in a drama.

অভিপন্ন, বশীভূত, subdued, fugitive, refugee, guilty, involved in calamity.

অভিপ্রায়, তাৎপর্য্য, a design, object, scope, moral.

অভিপ্রেত, সম্মত, intended, designed, aimed at.

অভিবাদ, পাদস্পর্শপূর্ব্বক প্রণাম, salutation, prostration, reverence.

অভিবিনীত, অতিধার্ম্মিক, punctual in sacred and moral actions.

অভিব্যক্তি, প্রকাশ, revelation, declaration, expression, a making evident.

অভিব্যাপ্তি, নিকটাগমন, a flowing spreading towards, contact.

অভিভব, পরাজয়, a subduing, humbling, defeat, conquest.

অভিমত, সম্মত, মনোনীত, approved, chosen.

অভিমন্ত্রণ, সংস্কার, a consecration, benediction by religious formula.

অভিমর্ষণ, ওষ্ঠচাটন, মলন, to lick the lips, express, thresh; prevarication.

অভিমান, অহঙ্কার, pride, self-esteem, individual consciousness, sullen resentment of an affront.
অভিমুখ, সম্মুখ, facing, approaching; towards.
অভিযোগ, লাগান, বিবাদ, an application of one thing to another, attack in war, sueing at law, perseverance.
অভিরত, আসক্তমনাঃ, আবিষ্ট, zealous, delighted with, devoted to.
অভিরাম, মনোহর; রম্য, beautiful, engaging, agreeable.
অভিরুচি, স্পৃহা, তুষ্টি, taste, relish, inclination, delight, attachment.
অভিলাষ, ইচ্ছা, কাম, wish, desire, lust.
অভিলেখন, লিপি করণ, to write down, to insert.
অভিশস্তি, নিন্দা, censure, blame, reproach, accusation.
অভিশাপ, অনিষ্ট প্রার্থনা, a curse, imprecation, malediction.
অভিষব, যজ্ঞের পূর্বস্নান, ablution, previous to a sacrifice, distillation.
অভিষেক, পদার্পণ, installation by anointing.
অভিষেণন, শত্রুর প্রতি প্রস্থান, a march to repel an enemy.
অভিষ্টুত, প্রশংসিত, flattered, praised, applauded.
অভিসন্ধি, গ্রন্থি, a joint, juncture.
অভিসম্পাত, অভিশাপ, curse, imprecation, war, devastation.
অভিসর, অধীন, মিত্র, a follower, attendant, companion, ally.
অভিসার, জারের গুপ্ত সঙ্গতি, *idem;* an assignation (of lovers).
অভিহিত, উক্ত, প্রকাশিত, spoken, disclosed.
অভীক, কামুক, wanton, lascivious.
অভীক্ষ্ণ পুনঃঃ, repeatedly, frequently, again and again.
অভীপ্সিত, অভীষ্ট, বাঞ্ছিত, desired, wished for, agreeable.
অভেদ, ঐক্য, similarity; similar, alike, indiscriminable.
অভ্যঙ্গ, অভ্যঞ্জন,—তৈললেপন, unction, anointing.
অভ্যধিকফল, অধিকফলযুক্ত, attended with more advantage.
অভ্যনুজ্ঞা-ন, অনুমতি, permission, consent.
অভ্যন্তর, মধ্য, inward, internal.
অভ্যবহরণ, ভক্ষণ, act of taking or eating food.
অভ্যর্ণ, নিকট, near, approached.
অভ্যর্থনা, প্রার্থনা, a petition, request, welcoming.
অভ্যাগত, অতিথি, a guest; come, approached, descended, hereditary.

অভ্যাপাৎ, আপদ, misfortune, ruin, disappointment.
অভ্যাস, আবৃত্তি, frequent repetition, study, pains, practice.
অভ্যুত্থান, সম্বর্দ্ধনা, a rising towards, rising to welcome, preparedness.
অভ্যুদয়, কল্যাণ, welfare, happiness, prosperity.
অভ্যুদাহরণ, উল্টের উদাহরণ, an exemplification by the opposite.
অভ্যুপগম, স্বীকার, consent, acquiescence, concession, admission.
অভ্যুপায়, শ্রেষ্ঠোপায়, a good expedient or method.
অভ্র, মেঘ, the sky, a cloud; talk mineral.
অভ্রিয় মেঘজাত, produced from the sky or clouds.
অমু, শীঘ্রতা, ক্রত, swiftness; quick, small.
অম, কাঁচা, অপক্ক, raw, unbaked (pottery), unripe.
অমত, অসম্মতি, disapprobation, dislike.
অমত্র, পাত্র, a vessel.
অমন্, এমন, এই প্রকার, thus, so.
অমনি, সদৃশ, বিমামূল্য, thus, so, the same, gratis, gratuitous.
অমর, নিত্য; চিরস্থায়ী, immortal, permanent; a god.
অমরাবতী, ইন্দ্রের পুরী, the residence of Indra, abounding with immortals.
অমর্ষ, অতুষ্টি, ক্রোধ, displeasure, impatience, anger.
অমর্ষণ, অতুষ্ট, ক্রোধিত, displeased, fretful, angry, impatient.
অমা, নিকট; সঙ্গে, near; with; edge of the new moon.
অমাত্য, বন্ধু, মিত্র, a friend, adviser, courtier, statesman.
অমাবস্যা, অমাবাস্যা, } প্রতিপৎ, change of the moon, day of the new moon.
অমামসী, অমামাসী, }
অমায়, বাস্তবিক, real, free from illusion or sorcery.
অমিয়া, অমৃত, nectar, water of life.
অমী, পীড়িত, অসুস্থ, sick, diseased.
অমুক, বুদ্ধিস্থিত, সম্মুখাগত, such a one, a certain person.
অমুত্র, পরলোকে, in another state or world.
অমূনি, এমনি, এই প্রকারে, thus, in the same manner, as, gratis.
অমৃত, জীবন্ত; সুধা, not dead; ambrosia, water, poison, immortality.
অমৃত্তি, পানপাত্র, an oblong drinking vessel.
অমেধ্য, অশুদ্ধ, impure, unclean, ordure, impurity.

অম্বক, চক্ষু, অক্ষি, an eye. [bergris.
অম্বর, আকাশ, মেঘ, the sky, a cloud, cotton, clothing, am-
অম্বল, অম্ল, অম্ল,—টক, acid, sour.
অম্বা, অম্বিকা, অম্বালিকা,—মাতা, a mother.
অম্বু, জল, water.
অম্বুজ, পদ্ম, চন্দ্র, the water-lily, the moon.
অম্বুদ, অম্বুবাহ,—মেঘ, a cloud.
অম্বুধি, সমুদ্র, the sea.
অম্বুভৃৎ, মেঘ, a cloud.
অম্বুর, গোবরাট, শিলা, a threshold.
অম্ভস্, জল, water.
অম্ভোজ, পদ্ম, the water-lily.
অম্ভোদ, জলদ; মেঘ, giving water; a cloud.
অম্ভোধর, অম্ভোধি,—জলধর, মেঘ, holding water; a cloud.
অম্ময়, জলবৎ, জলময়; ফেণা, aqueous, watery; froth, spume.
অম্র, আম, a mango.
অম্রত, অমৃত, ambrosia, water of life.
অম্ল, টক, acid, sour.
অম্লিকা তিন্তিড়ী, the tamarind tree.
অয়, ভাগ্য, good luck, fortunate turn. [portioned.
অযথা, অতুল্য, অনুপযুক্ত, dissimilar, inconsistent, dispro-
অয়ন, গমন, অর্দ্ধবৎসর, motion, course, a road, circuit, half
a year.
অয়মপি, অথচ, ইহাও, also, that also, even that.
অয়স, লৌহ, iron.
অয়স্কান্ত, চুম্বকপাথর, লৌহকান্ত, a sort of stone, the loadstone.
অয়োগ্র, মুষল, বাণাদি অস্ত্র, a pestle, or iron pointed weapon.
অয়োঘন, নিহানী, নিহাণী, an anvil.
অযোনি, অযোনিজ,—যোনিবিনা জাত, not born in the common
way of generation, equivocally produced.
অর, শীঘ্র, দ্রুত, quick, speedy.
অরক, জলজাত বৃক্ষ, a water plant, moss. [a well.
অরঘট্ট-ক, জলাকর্ষণ যন্ত্র, a machine for drawing water, a pit.
অরণা, মহিষ, a buffalo. [by friction.
অরণি, অগ্নি জ্বলনের কাষ্ঠ, a piece of dry wood to excite fire
অরণ্য, বন, a forest, wilderness, thicket.

অরণ্যানি, বৃহদারণ্য, নিবিড়বন, a large extensive forest.
অরত্নি, অমুষ্টহস্ত পরিমাণ, a long cubit.
অরমান, অপমান, dishonor, disappointment, distress.
অরর, অররি,—দ্বার, a door.
অরাতি, অরি,—শত্রু, an enemy.
অরাল, বক্রীকৃত, bent, crooked; rosin, pitch.
অরিত্র, হালি, কর্ণ, a rudder, helm.
অরিন্দম, জয়ী, conquering; a conqueror.
অরিমিত্র, শত্রুবন্ধু, প্রত্যন্তদেশের রাজা, an enemy's friend or ally; a sovereign whose possessions border on an enemy's territory.
অরিষ্ট, আনন্দ, সন্তোষ, আপদ, happiness, pleasure, women's apartment, misery, calamity, sign of death, a crow, liquor.
অরুংষিকা, মুখমস্তকের বিস্ফোট, eruption on the head or face.
অরুক, অরুগ,—অরোগী, বৃক্ষ, healthy, not diseased; a tree.
অরুণ, প্রত্যুষ, সূর্য্য, the dawn; the sun; purple or fawn colour.
অরুন্তুদ, অরুষ্কর,—ক্ষয়কারী, corrosive, sharp, corroding.
অরুস, ঘা, ক্ষত, a sore, wound, vital part; the sun.
অরোহী, খাটধ্বনি, descending note in music.
অর্ক, সূর্য্য, the sun, a species of plant.
অর্গল-া, খিল, a bar, bolt.
অর্ঘ, পূজা, ভজন, adoration, respect; a price.
অর্ঘ্য, উপহার, an oblation to a guest or superior.
অর্চন, পূজন, ভজন, to worship, adore, pay homage.
অর্চিস্, তেজঃ, দীপ্তি, radiance, splendor, light, flame.
অর্জ্জন, সঞ্চয়ন, to accumulate, collect, acquire.
অর্জ্জুন, শুক্লবর্ণ, white colour; white.
অর্ণব, সমুদ্র, the ocean, a sea.
অর্ণস্ জল, water.
অর্ণা, বন্যপশু, wild, untamed (of animals).
অর্ত্তন, নিন্দা, ঘৃণা, censure, reproach, hatred; abhorrence.
অর্ত্তি, দুঃখ, পীড়া, pain, the end of a bow.
অর্ত্তিক, মিষ্টান্ন, পীড়িত, cake, gingerbread; pained. [meaning.
অর্থ, অভিপ্রায়, ধন, a scope, object, motive, reason, wealth,
অর্থতঃ, অর্থাৎ, namely, viz., in fact, in fine.

অর্থনা, প্রার্থনা, petition, request, scope, desire.
অর্থবত্ত্ব, প্রয়োজনার্হতা, suitableness to a purpose.
অর্থবাদ, নিবেদন পত্র, ফলবাদ, ফলশ্রুতি, petition, plea, declaration or extolling of an object or treatise.
অর্থবান, প্রয়োজনীয়, অর্থপ্রাপক, suited, answering a purpose, relevant, apposite.
অর্থাৎ, ফলতঃ, that is to say.
অর্থান্তরে, অন্যথা, otherwise.
অর্থিত, বাঞ্ছিত, desired, requested, petitioned.
অর্থী, যাচক; বাদী, supplicating, desirous, having an object to accomplish; plaintiff, petitioner; rich.
অর্থ্য, বাঞ্ছিতব্য, to be requested, desirable; scope, end, object, desire.
অর্দনা, যাচ্ঞা, যন্ত্রণা, request, prayer, begging, suffering.
অর্দিত, যাচিত, যন্ত্রণাযুক্ত, requested, &c., tormented; convulsions.
অর্দ্ধ আধা, half, *pref.* out of tune, lispingly.
অর্দ্ধরথী, একরথারূঢ় যোদ্ধা, a warrior fighting with a single chariot.
অর্দ্ধরাত্র, মহানিশা, midnight.
অর্দ্ধশরীর, পত্নী, বনিতা, half the body, a wife.
অর্দ্ধসীরী, অর্দ্ধফলপ্রাপ্ত কৃষক, cultivating for the landowner for half the crop.
অর্দ্ধাঙ্গ, পত্নী, স্ত্রী, half the body, half one's self; a wife.
অর্দ্ধাবভেদক, শিরঃপীড়া, a voilent headache.
অর্দ্ধার্দ্ধ, আধাআধি, half and half, share and share alike.
অর্দ্ধার্দ্ধি, আধাংশী, a partner with an equal share.
অর্দ্ধেক, আধাংশ, আধা, half a thing, half.
অর্দ্ধেন্দু, অর্দ্ধচন্দ্র, a half moon, crescent.
অর্পণ, নিযুক্ত করণ, প্রদান; to appoint, employ, delegate, make an oblation, place, deposit with, commit in charge.
অর্বন, অশ্ব; নীচ, a horse; low, inferior, base.
অর্বাক, পূর্ব্ব, prior, former, antecedent; antecedently.
অর্বাচীন, বিরুদ্ধ, নূতন, অজ্ঞান, contrary, opposed to, modern, recent, unskilled, inexperienced; contrariwise.
অর্ভক ছা, ছানা, পোত, the young of an animal.
অর্য্য স্বামী, কর্ত্তা, a master, lord, owner; a Vyse.

অর্য্যমা, সূর্য্য, পূর্ব্বপুরুষ, the sun; ancestors as objects of worship.
অর্শন, অধিকার হওন, to belong to, pertain, appertain, devolve.
অর্শ, অর্শস্ —আরিশ, hemorrhoids or piles.
অর্শস, অর্শরোগযুক্ত, afflicted with the piles.
অর্শী উত্তরাধিকারী, coming into possession, succeeding to property.
অর্হ, অর্হিত,—যোগ্য, right, fit, capable, liable to, belonging to, deserving of.
অর্হণ, উপযুক্ত হওন, to be right, proper, becoming, or deserving of. [possible, probable.
অর্হণীয়, অর্হ্য,—যোগ্য, সাধ্য, capable, right, worthy, adorable
অল, পীত, হুল, yellow orpiment; sting of a bee, fang of a centipede: a tenon. [mentally.
অলং, বৃথা, uselessly, in vain; enough, sufficient; orna-
অলংক্রিয়া, ভূষণ, an ornamenting, adorning.
অলক, কেশের কোঁকড়া, চুল্‌কী, a ringlet, curl.
অলক্ত, আলতা, lac; paper impregnated with lac.
অলঙ্করণ, ভূষণ, to adorn.
অলঙ্করিষ্ণু, ভূষণাকাঙ্ক্ষী, fond of ornaments, gaudy, shewy.
অলঙ্কার, আভরণ, an ornament, ornament of speech.
অলঞ্জর, কলিঞ্জর,—ঘট, a jar, large pitcher.
অলবড্ডু, জড়, অবুদ্ধি, stupid, ignorant, awkward, clumsy.
অলবাল, বাঁধাল, a mound round the root of a tree.
অলবোলা, ধূমপান যন্ত্র, a hooka.
অলর্ক, উন্মত্ত কুকুর, a mad dog, white swallow-wort.
অলস-ক, কুণ্ঠিত, জড়, idle, slothful, indolent.
অলাত, পোড়াকাষ্ঠ, অঙ্গার, a firebrand, charcoal.
অলাবু, তুম্বী, the bottle-gourd plant and fruit.
অলি, ভ্রমর, মদ্য, a bee, scorpion, crow, cuckoo; wine.
অলিক, নিষ্ফল, কপাল, useless, in vain; the forehead.
অলিজিহ্বা, উপজিহ্বা, the root of the tongue, epiglottis.
অলিন, অলী,—বৃশ্চিক, হুলবিশিষ্ট, a centipede, scorpion, bee; stinging, having a sting.
অলিন্দ, চাতাল, a terrace.
অলীক, মিথ্যা, নিষ্ফল, false, useless, vain, trifling, not beloved.
অলীকতা, মিথ্যাকথা, falsehood, disagreeableness.

অলুহ, অলোপনীয়, not suffering elision, not omissible.
অলুক, আলুআদি, potatoe or other tuberous root.
অল্গা, এলুয়া, loose, unconnected.
অল্প, কিঞ্চিত, small, few, little; a little.
অল্পাল্প, অত্যল্প, a very few, a few.
অল্পিষ্ঠ, অল্পীয়স্,-অতিক্ষুদ্র, very small or few, minute, fewest.
অল্পীকৃত, অল্পীভুত,—ন্যূনীকৃত, হ্রস্বিত, diminished, reduced, lessened, become few.
অল্পীন, অল্পেং, ক্রমেং, by little and little, gradually.
অশন, ভোজন, to eat; a meal, boiled rice.
অশনায়া, ক্ষুধা, ভোজনেচ্ছা, hunger, appetite.
অশনি, বজ্র. বাজ, a thunderbolt.
অশাস্ত্র-ক, বেদবিরুদ্ধ, unlawful, illegal, irregular, inconsistent.
অশ্মগর্ভ, শ্যামবর্ণ মণি, an emerald.
অশ্মজ, গেরী, red chalk, red ochre.
অশ্মন্ অশ্মা,—পাষাণ, প্রস্তর, a stone.
অশ্মন্ত, চুলা, উনন, a portable hearth or fire-place.
অশ্মতাল, খলন্থষল, pestle and mortar.
অশ্মরী, পাথরী, the stone or gravel.
অশ্র, অস্র,—নেত্রাম্বু, a tear.
অশ্রি, অস্ত্রের অগ্রভাগ, ধার, কোণ, edge or point of a sword, corner, angle.
অশ্লীল, নীচ, প্রাকৃত, vulgar, low, coarse (of language).
অশ্লেষ, অসখ্য, অপ্রীতি, discord, dislike, separation, misunderstanding.
অশ্ব, ঘোটক, ঘোড়া, a horse.
অশ্বতর, খচর, a mule, a swift elephant.
অশ্বস্বন, তুরঙ্গধ্বনি, the neighing of a horse.
অশ্বীন, অশ্বের দিবসিক গতি, a day's journey for a horse; having a horse.
অষুধ, ঔষধ, medicine.
অষ্টময়সিদ্ধি, সাঙ্গতা, পরিপূর্ণতা, completeness, perfection.
অষ্টাঙ্গ, অষ্টাবয়ব, the eight members; having the eight requisites.
অষ্টাবক্র, অতিবক্র, কুরূপ, deformed, bent in eight directions.
অষ্টি, অঠী,—আঠি, the stone of a fruit.
অষ্টেপৃষ্টে, সকল দিগে, সর্বাঙ্গে, on eight sides, on every part, all over.
অষ্ঠীলিকা, অষ্ঠীলা,-কোষ্ঠবদ্ধ, costiveness, constipation.

অষ্ঠীবৎ, জানু, হাঁটু, the knee.
অসকৃত, পুনঃ২, often, repeatedly, frequently.
অসত্তামী, পাপ, অধর্ম্ম, sin, turpitude, unholiness.
অসন, ক্ষেপণ, to throw, cast.
অসি, খড়্গ, a scymetar.
অসিক্লী, অন্তঃপুরের দাসী, a female servant in the seraglio.
অসিপত্র, ইক্ষু, কোষ, sugar-cane; sword-blade, sheath.
অসু, প্রাণ, শীঘ্র. life, breath; swift.
অসুর, দৈত্য, a dæmon, evil spirit; very wicked.
অসূয়া, পরিবাদ, দ্বেষ, detraction, slander, malice.
অসূর্য্য, সূর্য্যবদৃশ্য, parhelion, destitute of the sun.
অসূর্য্যম্পশ্য, অন্তঃপুরস্থিতা স্ত্রীলোক, the women of the seraglio.
অসৃক, রক্ত, blood.
অসেচনক, মনোহর, very beautiful, heart engaging.
অস্ত, অস্তম্,—অন্তর্ধান, the setting of the heavenly bodies.
অস্তগত, অন্তর্হিত, set, gone below the horizon.
অস্তগিরি, অস্তাচল, চরম পর্বত, the western mountains.
অস্তাবলম্বন, অস্ত, the setting of a luminary.
অস্তাবলম্বী, অস্তগত, setting, set.
অস্তি, সম্প্রতি, আছে, present, now, at this time; it is.
অস্তু, হউক, be it so, let it be. [instrument.
অস্ত্র, খড়্গাদি, a missile weapon, arms, edge tool, sharp
অস্ত্রচিকিৎসা, ক্ষতাদিনাশক বিদ্যা, surgery.
অস্ত্রজ্ঞ, অস্ত্রবিৎ, skilled in arms.
অস্ত্রবৈদ্য, অস্ত্রচিকিৎসক, a surgeon.
অস্ত্রীক, স্ত্রীরহিত, unaccompanied by or without a wife.
অস্থান, স্থানরাহিত্য, want of place, wrong place; pudenda.
অস্থায়, অস্থায়ী,—অতলস্পর্শ, very deep, unfathomable.
অস্থি, হাড়, a bone. [the Ganges.
অস্থিসমর্পণ, গঙ্গাতে হাড় ত্যাগ ক-, to commit a man's bones to
অস্মদ্, আমারদের, আমাদিগকে, *in compos.* our, us.
অস্মদীয়, আমারদের, our, belonging to us.
অস্যপর, ইহার পরে, after this, hereafter.
অস্ব, অনিজ, দরিদ্র, not one's own; poor, needy.
অস্বপ্ন, দুঃস্বপ্ন, a bad or ominous dream, want of sleep.
অস্বভাব, দুঃস্বভাব, ill nature, profligate disposition.

অস্বর, কুধ্বনি, disagreeable sound.
অহং, অহম্,—আমি, I.
অহংযু, গর্ব্বী, আত্মশ্লাঘী, proud, self-important.
অহঃ, অহন,—দিবস, a day.
অহঃপতি, সূর্য্য, the sun, lord of the day.
অহঙ্কার, অভিমান, pride, self-importance, egotism, consciousness of séparate existence. [vaunting.
অহমহমিকা, আত্মশ্লাঘা, egotism, vanity, mutual or military
অহমিকা, গর্ব্ব, egotism, pride, vanity.
অহম্মতি, স্বার্থপরতা. self-love, selfishness, self-opinionatedness.
অহরহ, প্রতিদিন, daily, every day.
অহর্নিশি, দিবারাত্রি, day and night.
অহর্মণি, অহস্কর,—সূর্য্য, the sun.
অহর্ম্মুখ, প্রাতঃ, প্রত্যুষ, the dawn, morning.
অহি, সর্প, a serpent. [version.
অহিতুণ্ডিক, সাপুড়্যা. a juggler who exhibits serpents for di-
অহিনকুলতা, অহিনকুলিকা,--শত্রুতা, mortal enmity, implacableness.
অহিফেণ, সর্পফেণ, আফিম, hood of the cobra capella; a poppy, opium.
অহিভুক্, ভুজঙ্গাশন, ময়ূর, feeding on serpents; a peacock.
অহ্নায়, অবিলম্বে, instantly, soon, presently.

আ.

আইজ, অদ্য, to-day.
আইবড়, অবিবাহিত, unmarried.
আইসন, আগমন, to come, approach.
আই, . মাতামহী, a maternal grandmother.
আউখ, ইক্ষু, a sugar-cane.
আওড়ন, আওড়ান,—পড়ন, to read, repeat, recite, celebrate.
আওতা, আবৃত্ত, shady, covered close, concealed.
আগুচাও, অভ্যর্থনা, a welcome.
আংশিক, ভাগযোগ্য, entitled to a share, relating to a share.
আঁক, অঙ্ক, a mark, numeral figure, goal.
আঁখি, অক্ষি, চক্ষু, an eye.
আঁচ, শিখা, উত্তাপ, flame, heat.

আঁচমন, ভোজনোত্তর মুখক্ষালন, to wash the mouth after eating, to sip water (in worship), to guess.
আঁচল-া, বস্ত্রের শেষভাগ, border of a garment.
আঁজন, অঞ্জন, antimony, lead ore.
আঁজলা, অঞ্জলি, the palms of the hands joined so as to hold [water.
আঁটন, শক্তবন্ধন, to bind, tighten, pull tight, speak sharply.
আঁড়ি, শিশুর ক্ষীণতা, দ্বেষ, the pining or wasting of a weaned child; envy.
আঁড়িয়া, অনড্বান্, a bull; diseased from being weaned.
আঁড়েত, ক্ষীণতাগ্রস্ত, দ্বেষী, pining (as a weaned child), envious.
আঁত্, অন্ত্র, the bowels, entrails.
আঁতুড়, প্রসবগৃহ, the room of a lying-in woman.
আঁৎকান, ভয় করণ, আতঙ্ক, to fear, dread; horror.
আঁধলা, অন্ধ, blind.
আঁধার, অন্ধকার, darkness, gloom.
আঁব, আম্র, a mango.
আঁশ, তন্তু, fibres in the bark of trees, or in fruits, nap [of cloth, &c.
আঁশাল, আঁশুয়া,—আঁশবিশিষ্ট, stringy, full of fibres.
আকণ্ঠাপর্য্যন্ত, পেটুক, eating till overfilled.
আকম্র, অল্পাকাঙ্ক্ষী, asking or praying but little; indifferent.
আকর, আদি, মূল, origin, root, source, spring, mine, quarry, grit, grittiness.
আকর্ণন, শ্রবণ, to hear, listen.
আকর্ষ, আঁকড়ি, a tendril.
আকর্ষণ, টানন, গ্রহণ, to draw, attract, seize, drag, plough.
আকর্ষণী, অঙ্গগ্রহ, বিদ্যা, a spasm; science, whatever engages the mind or attracts; a tendril.
আকর্ষিণী, আকর্ষক, attractive.
আকস্মিক, হঠাৎ উপস্থিত, unexpected, coming unexpectedly.
আকা, চুলা, a hearth, furnace, kiln.
আকাঁড়া-ন, বলবান, strong, lusty, jolly, plump, imperfectly cleansed from the husk.
আকাঙ্ক্ষা, ইচ্ছা, প্রত্যাশা, desire, wish, expectation, hope.
আকাট, অনাবৃষ্টি, drought, want of rain, cessation of a shower, cessation from charity or other virtue.
আকামাহিয়া, অমুণ্ডিত, unshaven, not bereft of its fangs.

আকার, মূর্ত্তি, form, shape, figure, appearance, statue, likeness.
আকারাদি, আদ্যাকারযুক্ত, beginning with আ.
আকারান্ত, অন্ত্যাকারযুক্ত, ending with আ.
আকাল, দুর্ভিক্ষ্য, a famine.
আকালিক, অসময়. premature, unseasonable, out of season.
আকাশ, শূন্য, the sky, atmosphere, air, space.
আকাশদীপ, অন্তরীক্ষস্থদীপ, a light in the air, elevated lanthorn, a beacon.
আকাশী, আকাশস্থ, অবস্তু, airy, aërial, celestial, unsubstantial.
আকিঞ্চন, আকুঞ্চন,-চেষ্টা, প্রয়াস, endeavour, labour, exertion, contortion.
আকীর্ণ, জলপ্রোক্ষিত, sprinkled or overspread with, interspersed.
আকুণ্ঠিত, অবাক্, লজ্জিত, non-plussed, confounded, shrinking with shame.
আকুণ্ডকুণ্ড, বিবাদবর্দ্ধন, aggravation of a quarrel by interference.
আকুল, কাতর, troubled, agitated, confused, distressed.
আকৃতি, মূর্ত্তি, shape, form, likeness, image.
আকৃষ্টি, টান, মানানি, attraction, persuasion.
আক্রম, চড়াও, গ্রহণ, invasion, seizing upon, attack.
আক্রা, দুর্মূল্য, dear in price, not cheap.
আক্রান্ত, বলদ্বারাগৃহীত, invaded, seized, held, engrossed, occupied with.
আক্রামক, চড়াওকারক, invading, &c.; an invader, usurper.
আক্রোশ, কোপ, শোক, resentment, cry, lamentation, regret, reproof, imprecation, reproach, censure.
আস্কারণা, আক্রম, an aggression, attack, abuse, provocation.
আস্কুটী, নির্দয়, কাষ্ঠী, merciless, implacable, savage, barbarous; a virago, vixen.
আক্ষেপ, নিন্দা, খেদ, reproof, reproach, grief, sarcasm, irony; a comprizing.
আখড়া, গায়কসমূহ, choir of singers, company of smokers or talkers; the place where such meet.
আখণ্ড, অটুট, whole, entire, perfect, unbroken.
আখা, চুলা, a furnace, kiln.
আখু, উন্দুর, a rat, mouse.
আখুটে, অকস্মাদ্বাসনা, whim, caprice, peevishness.
আখুভুক্, উন্দুরভুক্. বিড়াল, feeding on rats; a cat.

আখেট, মৃগয়া, ভয়, the chase, hunting, pursuit, terror.
আখেটা, ভয়ানক, alarming, terrific.
আখ্যা-ন, নাম, খ্যাতি, a name, title, term, description, renown.
আখ্যায়িকা, ইতিহাস, a history, tale.
আগ্, অগ্রভাগ, first or fore part, introduction, end, point, extremity; priority, excess, odd number, the place immediately before.
আগড়া, ভুষী, ভুসী, chaff, husk.
আগড়ী, অগ্রসর, preceding, situated before; *adv.* first.
আগ্তোলন, পরফলদর্শন, to ascertain a result by a sort of lot.
আগন্তব্য, সম্ভাব্য, সাধ্য, likely to come, practicable, proveable, approachable.
আগন্তু-ক,উত্তীর্ণ, বিদেশী, arrived, come, foreign, unknown.
আগন্তুজ্বর, ব্যামোহ, affliction from calamity, witchcraft or imprecation; suffering from fever or distress.
আগ্বাড়ান, আগেবাগুন, to stretch forward, proceed, advance; ambition.
আগম, আইসন, বেদ, a coming, arrival, an inserted letter or syllable, science, the veds, legal deed or voucher, lawful mode of acquiring property.
আগমন, পৌছন, আইসন, ঘটন, arrival, coming, occurrence.
আগমনীয়, আগন্তব্য, approachable, practicable, vincible.
আগমিত, অভ্যস্ত, studied, read, acquired by study.
আগল, অগল, অক্রত, undissolved, not crumbling.
আগলন, বারণ, to restrain, prevent.
আগলি, অগ্রসর, before, preceding.
আগস্ পাপ, sin, guilt.
আগা, অগ্রভাগ, the tip, peak, point, extremity.
আগাও, আগুড়ী, anticipation of payment or revenue.
আগাম, আগোস্তরা, given in advance; pre-payment.
আগামী, অগ্রগ, *id*: preceding, coming, about to come.
আগার, গৃহ, আধার, a house, room, receptacle.
আগু অগ্রগ, পূর্ব, preceding, before, first, onward.
আগুড়ী, আগাম, advance of money, any thing prematurely done; before, preceding.
আগুন, অগ্নি, অনল, fire.

আগুনখাগি, সতী, সহগামিনী, burning with a husband.
আগুয়ান, অগ্রসর, preceding; a precursor.
আগে, পূর্ব্বে, first, before, forwards, onwards. [sitatingly.
আগেপাছে, অগ্রপশ্চাৎ, before and behind, sooner or later, he-
আগোড়, ঝাঁপ, a door of mats to a common hut.
আগ্নেয়, অগ্নিবৎ, পাচক, fiery, igneous, provocative.
আগ্র, ব্যগ্র, eager, urgent, zealous. [tenacity.
আগ্রহ, ব্যগ্রতা, eagerness, zeal, perseverance, obstinacy,
আঘাট, কুঘাট, a bad wharf.
আঘাত, তাড়ন, ক্ষতি, a blow, hurt, stroke, injury, plague.
আঘাবিঘা, বাধা. hindrance, obstrucion, opposition.
আঘার, ঘৃত, ghee; an oblation of ghee.
আঘূর্ণন, ফিরণ, a whirling round.
আঘোষণ, প্রচারণ, a proclaiming, proclamation.
আঘ্রাণ, গন্ধগ্রহণ, a scent, a smelling.
আঙ্গটী, আঙ্গুটী,—অঙ্গুরি, a toe or finger ring.
আঙ্গরা, দগ্ধকাষ্ঠ, coals, cinders. [finger.
আঙ্গলন—আন, অঙ্গুলি দ্বারা স্পর্শকরণ, to finger, stir with the
আঙ্গার—ই, দগ্ধকাষ্ঠ, a coal, charcoal, cinder.
আঙ্গিনা, উঠান, a court-yard, square court.
আঙ্গুল—ী, অঙ্গুলী, a finger, toe.
আচক্ষণ, কথন, a speaking; eloquence.
আচমন, ভোজনোত্তর মুখ ক্ষালন, to wash the mouth after eating, or as a religious rite.
আচম্বিত, হঠাৎ, suddenly, unawares.
আচরণ, ব্যবহার, চলন, custom, course of conduct, habit, usage; to act, pursue as conduct.
আচার, দাঁড়া, রীতি, conduct, practice, good conduct, the established line of conduct, usage; pickle, sauce.
আচারী, ব্যবহারী, acting, conducting. [observed.
আচার্য্য, উপদেষ্টা, a teacher, prophet; proper to be done or
আচার্য্যাণী, গুরুপত্নী, উপদেষ্ট্রী, a prophetess, preceptress, wife of a prophet.
আচালা, অচালিত, unsifted.
আচোট, আঘাত, পতিত, a blow, stroke; uncultivated, desert.
আচ্ছন্ন, ঢাকা, গুপ্ত, covered, protected, invested, affected with.

আচ্ছা, ভাল, উত্তম, good, unexceptionable; well.

আচ্ছাদক, ঢাকনা, a covering, protection, lid, case, roof.

আচ্ছাদন, আবরণ, to cover, protect; a covering, coverlid, clothes, cloth.

আচ্ছেদ, কাটন, a cutting off, amputation, confiscation.

আচ্ছোদন, মৃগয়া, game, hunting, the chase.

আছড়ন-আন, মারণ, অবক্ষেপণ, to strike, smite, dash to the ground, thresh, wash, sprinkle.

আছাড়, আঘাত, a blow, stroke, forcible dash against a thing.

আছোলা, অকাটা, অপরিষ্কৃত, unlopped, untrimmed, not stripped of its bark.

আজ, আজু,—অদ্য, to-day.

আজন্ম, জন্মাবধি, from one's birth. [a sail.

আজাড়ন, পরিষ্কারকরণ, পাল, to clear of incumbrances, cleanse;

আজান, অজ্ঞাত, unknown.

আজানু, জঙ্ঘাপর্য্যন্ত, reaching to the thigh (the hands.)

আজি, অদ্য; যুদ্ধ, to-day; war, conflict.

আজীব, বৃত্তি, উপজীবিকা, means of support, livelihood.

আজীবন্, উপজীবী, living on, supporting life by.

আজুর, আজু,-বেতনব্যতিরেকে পরিশ্রম, অবেতন, labour without pay.

আজ্ঞপিত, আজ্ঞপ্ত,—আদেশিত, ordered, commanded.

আজ্ঞা, আদেশ, order, command, decree, precept.

আজ্ঞাপন, আদেশন, to give orders, command, enjoin.

আজ্ঞাবর্ত্তী, আজ্ঞাবশ,—বশীভূত, subject to orders, obedient.

আজ্ঞাবহ, অধীন, bearing orders, obedient; obedient servant.

আজ্য, ঘৃত, clarified butter, ghee.

আঝালা, অঝাল, not hot or pungent.

আটক, ব্যাঘাত, obstacle, hindrance, prohibition, stoppage.

আটকপালিয়া, দুর্ভাগ্যযুক্ত, destined to suffering, constantly ill.

আট্‌কোল, অনুমান, a guess, feeling one's way, a doing in uncertainty.

আট্‌পটাঙ্গ, প্রাগল্ভ্য, pomp, pageantry, shew.

আট্‌পলিয়া, অষ্টকোণ, octagonal.

আট্‌পিটা, উদ্যোগী, পরিশ্রমী, active, sedulous, laborious.

আটল, দুঁড়িয়া, a bamboo fish-trap.

আটলা, বিড়া, a pad for the head of a porter.

আট্সটা, গণনা, accounts, book-keeping.
আটা, গোধূমচূর্ণ, flour, meal, bird-lime, viscid matter.
আটাপারা, নেজ্নেজিয়া, ropy, stringy.
আটাল, আঠাবৎ viscid, gluey, gummy.
আটালু, আঁটালী, a tick. [in the eighth month.
আটাসীমি, নির্বুদ্ধিতা, stupidity, folly; character of one born
আটাসীয়া, অষ্টম মাসজাত, born in the eighth month.
আটি, পুলা, a sheaf, bundle of straw, fruit-stone.
আটোপ, দর্প, pride, self-importance, assumption.
আট্কন, রুদ্ধ হওন, to be obstructed, entangled, detained.
আট্কান, প্রতিবন্ধন, to obstruct, impede, arrest, imprison, tighten, curb, withhold support.
আঠা, নির্যাস, bird-lime, gum, slime,paste, size.
আঠি, অস্থি, বীজ, a fruit-stone. [or bend, width.
আড়, টেবুচা, হেলা, aslant, leaning across, sideways; a crook
আড়কাটি, কাণ্ডারী, . a pilot; a rod.
আড়কাঠ-া, কড়িকাঠ, a cross beam in a building.
আড়গড়া, অশ্বশালা, stabling; temporary erection.
আড়ঙ্গ, গঞ্জ, a mart, manufactory, collection of idols.
আড়চা, লালসা, strong desire, covetousness, communication.
আড়ট, আড়ষ্ট, cramped, stiff, benumbed.
আড়ৎ, আড়র, the warehouse of a monopolist. [cross.
আড়ন, বেঁকন, to bend, become crooked, lie athwart, to
আড়পাপড়া, গদা, লাঠী, a cudgel, bludgeon.
আড়পার, অবচ্ছেদে, through and through, obliquely, across.
আড়বাড়, সর্বত্রে, all over, through width and heigth.
আড়ম্বর, যুদ্ধে ঢাকের শব্দ, আরম্ভ, a trumpet charge, war drum, roar of an elephant; commencement, excessive preparation, excitement, pride, anger, apology, passion, pleasure, eye-lid, friction to remove pain.
আড়র, বাণিজ্যালয়, warehouse of a forestaller or monopolist.
আড়রী, কূল, কাঁধা, brink or edge of a bank.
আড়ষ্ট, অবশ, শক্ত, cramped, stiffened, benumbed.
আড়সা, অজ্ঞানযুক্ত, neglected, unnoticed, lying as refuse.
আড়া, বক্রীভূত, bent, laid across; a fish-trap, a beam.

আড়াই, সার্দ্ধদ্বয়, two and a half.
আড়ানি, আতপত্র, a large fan or screen. [sleep.
আড়ামোড়া, গাত্রভঙ্গ, জৃম্ভা, a yawning and stretching after
আড়াল, আচ্ছাদন, a cover, screen, shelter.
আড়ি, পণ, ক্রোধ, দ্বেষ, a wager, anger, grudge, hatred, threat, promise, resolution. [secretly.
আড়িপাতন, আড়ালে থাকন, to lie in wait, lurk, peep, observe
আড়িপাতনীয়া, গুপ্তঘাতক, lurking, &c.; an assassin.
আড়ুমাড়ু, অন্ত্রপাক, পেটবেদনা, contortion of the bowels.
আড়ুরা, বিলম্বনের অপদেশ, pretext for delay, apology. [cliff.
আড়ুরি, আড়ুলি,— ভৃগু, precipice, upright sides of a river or
আড়োষ্ট, আড়ষ্ট, cramped, stiff, benumbed.
আড্ডা, উত্তরণস্থান, station, post, stage, stand, rest.
আঢ়ি, পরিমাণ বিশেষ, a measure of capacity.
আঢ্য, সম্পন্ন, ধনী, rich, opulent.
আণ্টাল, ভাঁটা, গোলা, a ball of earth or wood, bowl for play.
আণ্ডা, অণ্ড, ডিম্ব, an egg.
আণ্ডেল, ধনবান, rich, wealthy. [drum.
আতঙ্ক, আতঙ্গ,—ভয়, শঙ্কা, fear, dread, disease, sound of a
আতঞ্চন, দ্রাবক, আপদ, a menstruum, chemical test; calamity, pestilence, danger, destruction, rejection, speed, gratification. [crimes.
আততায়ী, অনিষ্ট করিতে উদ্যত, ready to perpetrate the greatest
আতপ, রৌদ্র, heat, sunhine, sun-dried (rice).
আতপত্র, ছত্র, an umbrella.
আতর, পার হইবার মূল্য, ferriage, hire of a ferry.
আতর্পণ, আদীপন, a white pigment.
আতস, অতসীনির্ম্মিত, flaxen.
আতা, আতৃপ্য, a custard apple. [pay.
আতাই, বেতন বিনা বাদ্যকর, performing (in music) without
আতান্তরে, অত্র, এইদশায়, in this, in these circumstances.
আতায়িপনা, ধূর্ত্ততা, craftiness, knavery, swindling.
আতায়ী, ধূর্ত্ত, deceitful, crafty, swindling; a kite.
আতারিকাতারি, যাতনা, groan, agony, writhing with pain.
আতালি, মাচা, a long shelf, receptacle on high. [below.
আতালিপাতালি, সর্বত্র, everywhere, high and low, above and

আতিথেয়, অতিথি সেবারত, hospitable.
আতিথ্য, অতিথ্যাদর, *id:* hospitality.
আতিদেশিক, আরোপকারী, imputing or transferring the property of one person or thing to another.
আতুর, পীড়িত, দুঃখিত, sick, afflicted, distressed.
আতৃপ্য, আতা, the custard apple.
আতেলা, তৈলরহিত, without oil, destitute of oil.
আত্ত, গৃহীত, প্রাপ্ত, accepted, received.
আত্তি, শ্রম, উদ্যোগ, labour, exertion, endeavour.
আত্ম, স্বয়ং, নিজ, self, own, private; spirit.
আত্মকলহ, নিজবিবাদ, a domestic quarrel.
আত্মগরিমা, দর্প, অহমিকা, self-conceit, a vaunt.
আত্মগ্রাহী, স্বার্থপর, আত্মাবাদী, selfish; believing in spirit.
আত্মঘাত, স্বহত্যা, suicide.
আত্মজ, পুত্র, springing from one's self; a son.
আত্মতা, তত্ত্ব; বন্ধুতা, identity, spirituality, strong friendship.
আত্মদেবতা, ইষ্টদেবতা, a guardian deity, family god.
আত্মবশ, স্বাধীন, under one's own controul, independent.
আত্মবান্ধব, পিতৃব্যাদিরপুত্রপুত্রী, a first cousin.
আত্মবিস্মৃত, ভোলা, forgetful of one's own words or actions.
আত্মম্ভরি, উদরম্ভরি selfishly voracious.
আত্মসাৎ, স্বকীয়, own, proper.
আত্মহা, স্বঘাতক, self-destroying, a suicide.
আত্মা, ব্রহ্ম, জীব, Brahma, spirit, the soul, self.
আত্মাধীন. স্বতন্ত্র, subject to one's self, independent.
আত্মাভিমত, আত্মশ্লাঘী, self-approved or applauded, self-complacent.
আত্মীয়, স্বজন, স্বকীয়, related to one's self, belonging to one's self, one's own.
আত্মীয়তা, সম্পর্ক, বন্ধুতা, relationship, friendship, intimacy.
আত্রেয়ী, রজস্বলা, ঋতুমতী, a menstruous woman.
আদ, অর্দ্ধ, অর্দ্ধেক, half.
আদকপালিয়া, শিরঃপীড়া, a violent head-ache. [depraved.
আদখেঁচড়া, অসমাপ্ত, মন্দ, half done, unfinished, bad, vile,
আদর, সম্মান, respect, veneration. honor, esteem.
আদরা, চিহ্ন, a mark, sign, land-mark.

আদর্শ, দর্পণ, নিদর্শনপত্র, a mirror, specimen, sign, original from which any thing is to be copied.
আদা, আর্দ্রক, ginger.
আদাআদি, অর্দ্ধার্দ্ধ, half and half, in half shares.
আদাড়, বাহ্যস্থান, a privy, a jakes, a place for filth.
আদান, গ্রহণ, প্রাপণ, a receiving, obtaining.
আদায়, প্রাপণ, ঋণগ্রহণ, a receiving, obtaining, borrowing.
আদি, প্রথম, initial, prior, first; et cætera.
আদিত্য, সূর্য্য, দেবতা, the sun in a particular sign, a god.
আদিত্ব, প্রাথমিকতা, প্রবৃত্তি, priority, precedence, commencement of a work.
আদিম, আদো, আদ্য,—প্রাথমিক, initial, first, prior, preceding.
আদীপন, আতর্পণ, জ্বলান, a pigment of flour or chalk; to stir up, inflame.
আদুড়, আদুল,—অনাচ্ছাদিত, uncovered, exposed, open, bare.
আদুড়ীয়, অপরিপক্ব, half-grown, immature.
আদৃত, সম্মানিত, honoured, respected, esteemed.
আদৃষ্টি, ঈক্ষণাবধি, as far as the sight reaches.
আদেশ, আজ্ঞা, অনুমতি, a command, precept, ordinance, law.
আদৌ, প্রথমে, in the first place.
আদ্দাশ, নিবেদন, অভিযোগ, a complaint, petition, law-suit.
আদ্যন্ত, আদ্যান্ত,—মূল শেষ, the beginning and the end; from beginning to end; inclusively.
আদ্যপ্রান্ত, মূলাবধি, from first to last, all along, always.
আদ্যা, দেবী কারণীভূতা, the goddesses accounted divine energies.
আদ্যূন, পেটুক, স্বার্থপর, gluttonous, luxurious, selfish.
আদ্যোপান্ত, মূলাবধি, from the first, from first to last.
আদ্রিয়মান, সম্ভ্রান্ত, obtaining or shewing respect, honoured.
আধ, আধা,—অর্দ্ধ, অর্দ্ধভাগ, half; the half, moiety.
আধমন, আধি, a pledge, pawn.
আধর্ষণ, পরিজ্ঞান, দোষণ, conviction (in law or argument).
আধলা, ইষ্টকার্দ্ধ, a half or broken piece of brick, half a pice.
আধল্লি, অর্দ্ধটাকা, half a rupee.
আধান, ধারণ, প্রাপণ, a containing, being put in possession, pregnancy, a pledge.

আধার, পাত্র, a receptacle, canal, supporter, basis, location, comprehension.
আধি, মনঃপীড়া, বন্ধক, anxiety, mental distress, expectation, calamity; a pledge, pawn, scite, a placing.
আধিক্য, আতিশয্য, abundance, overplus.
আধিদৈবিক, দেবপ্রযুক্ত, arising from or relating to the influence of a god.
আধুড়ীয়, অপরিপক্ক, immature, half-grown.
আধুনিক, ইদানীন্তন, recent, modern, novel, belonging to the present time.
আধূত, কম্পিত, shaken, agitated.
আধেক, অর্দ্ধেক, half, half a one.
আধেয়, ধারণীয়, requiring or fit to be supported or contained.
আধোবা, অধৌত, অপ্রক্ষালিত, unwashed.
আধোরণ, মাহুত, an elephant driver.
আধ্মাত, বায়ুরোগ, flatulence, a swelling and rumbling of the bowels, war, battle; sounding, sonorous, burnt.
আধ্মান, বায়ুরোগ, flatulence, distension of the abdomen from wind.
আধ্যাত্মিক, স্বাভাবিক, আন্তরিক, arising from the subject, internal.
আধ্যান, চিন্তা, thought, meditation, contemplation.
আন, আর, অন্য, other, another.
আনক, ভেরী, ঢাক, a sort of trumpet, a drum.
আনখা, অনক্ষিত, not seen before, seen for the first time.
আনদ্ধ, বদ্ধ, bound, tied, fastened, shut, imprisoned, confined; a drum.
আনন, লইয়া আইসন, মুখ, to bring; the face, mouth.
আনন্তর্য্য, পশ্চাভাব, posteriority, succession to, posterity.
আনন্দ, আনান্দ,—হর্ষ, আহ্লাদ, joy, pleasure, mirth, gladness, felicity.
আনয়ন, আনন, to bring, fetch.
আনল, অগ্নি, fire.
আনা, আনন; ষোড়শ অংশের এক, a bringing; a sixteenth part.
আনাগোনা, গমনাগমন, a coming and going, intercourse.
আনাজ, শাক, তরকারী, greens, vegetables, corn.
আনাড়, অপ্রকাশ; দুর্জ্ঞেয়, secret, not easily discovered, out of place.
আনাড়িপনা, মূর্খতা, awkwardness, clumsiness.

আনাড়ী, মূঢ়, clumsy, inexpert, ignorant, clownish.
আনামৎ, পূর্ব্বমতে, as it was.
আনায়, জাল, a fishing net.
আনায্য, দক্ষিণাগ্নি, consecrated fire placed to the south.
আনাহ, কোষ্ঠবদ্ধ, constipation, suppression of urine, the length of cloth.
আনি, আনা, the sixteenth part.
আনুকূল্য, সহায়তা, help, assistance, patronage, co-operation.
আনুপূর্ব—ী, অনুক্রম, uninterrupted succession, regularity, rank, row.
আনুপূর্ব্বক, ক্রমানুসারে, in succession or order, from the beginning.
আনুভব্য, অনুভবনীয়, cognizable by experience, specious, hypothetical.
আনুমানিক, যুক্তিসিদ্ধ, inferrible, probable; specious.
আনুরক্তি, প্রণয়, attachment, pleasure.
আনেতা, আহর্ত্তা, one who brings.
আনোখা, অনীক্ষিত, seen for the first time.
আনোট, আমোঠা,—অঙ্গুরী, a toe or finger ring.
আন্তরীণ, অন্তরিত, inward, internal, enclosed, included.
আন্ত্রিক, আন্তরিক,—অন্তরিত, inward, affecting the bowels.
আন্দোলন, দোলন, তর্ক, a swinging, oscillating, agitation, investigation.
আন্ধসিক, পাচক, a cook.
আন্বীক্ষিকী, তর্কশাস্ত্র, logic, metaphysics, investigation.
আন্যমনা, অন্যমনস্ক, otherwise-minded.
আপগা, নদী, a river.
আপণ, হাট, a market, a shop.
আপত্তি, বিপদ, বাধকতা, calamity, misfortune, adversity, danger, an objection, remonstrance, excuse.
আপদ, বিপদ, misfortune, calamity, danger, evil, accident.
আপন, নিজ, আত্মীয়, own, proper.
আপনাআপনি, আপনইচ্ছাতে, সম্বন্ধীয়, spontaneously, of one's self: a relative, friend.
আপনি, নিজে, মহাশয়, self; he or you, (respectfully.)
আপন্ন, প্রাপ্ত, গ্রস্ত, affected with, seized by, wrought upon.
আপন্নসত্ত্বা, গর্ভিণী, a pregnant woman; pregnant.

আপাক, পোয়ান, a potter's kiln.

আপাত, পড়া, উপস্থিতকাল, a falling, present time, passing instant, appointed time, opportunity.

আপাতক, এখনকার, হঠাৎ, now, off hand; sudden.

আপাততঃ, সম্প্রতি, হঠাৎ, now, instantly, immediately.

আপাদনীয়, প্রাপ্য, যোগ্য, obtainable, liable to, liable to suffer.

আপান, মদ্যপসমূহ, an assembly of drunkards, company of tipplers.

আপার, অসীম, অগণনীয়, boundless, innumerable.

আপীড়, শিরোমালা, a chaplet for the head, a diadem, &c.

আপীন, গোস্তন, an udder, large or full breast.

আপূপিক, পিষ্টকাদিকারক, a baker.

আপ্ত, হিতকারী, জ্ঞাতি, beneficent, free from error, obtained, revealed, antnentic, own; a relation.

আপ্তগ্রাহী, স্বার্থপর, selfish, greedy, avaricious.

আপ্তসার, স্বার্থপর—তা, a self-seeking; selfish, self-seeking.

আপ্যায়িত, অতিতৃপ্ত, refreshed, re-animated.

আপ্রপদীন, আপাদপতিত, reaching to the foot.

আপ্লব-ন, জলব্যাপ্তি, স্নান, an overflowing or suffusing, bathing.

আপ্লাবন, বন্যা, স্নান, an overflowing, a flood, bathing.

আফা, মৎস্যোৎপ্লবন, the leaping of fish over a weir, &c.

আফাকল, বাড়, a weir or bank for catching fish.

আফালি, মৎস্যস্পন্দন, the flouncing of fish, sudden motion, a starting, struggling.

আফিঙ্গ, আফিম,—অহিফেণ, opium.

আফিমী, আফিমভোক্তা, addicted to the use of opium. [up.

আবজন-আন, বাঁধন, to shut a door, close an opening, cover

আবটন, গলান, to smelt, temper metals, stir or move round liquids, inspissate, become thick, receive a temper, turn round, return to the same point. [read, repeat.

আবড়ন, আবর্ত্তন, ঘূরণ, to turn round as a whirlpool, to

আবডাল, ব্যবধান, a skreen; pretence.

আবদার, সোৎকণ্ঠ, ছাওলামি, a pet, sulkiness, humoursomeness, peevishness, repining.

আবদারীয়, নেকামিয়া, humoursome, cross, peevish.

আবন্ধ, বন্ধন, a binding or tying tight, a yoke, tie.
আবপন, আধার, পাত্র, a receptacle, a vessel. [credulous.
আবর, ক্ষুদ্র, a mean ignorant person, implicitly obedient,
আবরণ, আচ্ছাদন, to screen, conceal, veil, interpose, cover, guard. [as the eyes.
আবরণ, অল্পবর্ষণ, ক্ষরণ, to rain slightly, trickle, ooze, water
আবরা-ণ, সূক্ষ্মজলপাত, a slight shower, oozing or trickling of water. [rubbish.
আবর্জ্জনা, নিক্ষেপণ, জঞ্জাল, a rejection as useless, sweepings,
আবর্ত্ত-ন, ঘূরণ, a returning, turning round, circular motion, whirlpool, eddy, spiral turn of a screw or shell.
আবর্ত্তনী, মূষী, a crucible.
আবলী, শ্রেণী, a row, range, rank, succession of things.
আবশ্য, নিশ্চয়, certainly, assuredly, necessarily.
আবশ্যক, নিশ্চিত কর্ত্তব্য, প্রয়োজন, necessary, indispensable, expedient, certain; necessity, expediency.
আবহমান, স্রোত, চিরকালীন, flowing or passing on, flowing or bringing in, usual, uniform.
আবাচ্য, উপস্থ, the pudenda. [at the foot of a tree.
আবাপ, মধ্যেলেখা, আপা, an insertion, interlineation, bason
আবাপন, নাটা, বোনা, a reel or frame for winding thread; a sowing of seed.
আবাল, বালকীয়, childish, belonging to a child.
আবালবৃদ্ধ, বালবৃদ্ধসমুদায়, from the youngest to the oldest.
আবালবৃদ্ধবনিতা, সপরিবার, including children, old persons and women; wholly.
আবাল্য, বালককালাবধি, from infancy.
আবাস, বাসস্থান, dwelling-place, residence, house.
আবাহন, আহ্বান, an invitation; to bring near, approach.
আবিধ, তুরপণ, an awl, auger, drill, piercer.
আবির্ভাব, প্রকাশ, অধিষ্ঠান, an unfolding, development, inhabitation of an image.
আবিল, অপরাধী, মলযুক্ত, sinful, guilty, filthy.
আবিষ্কার, প্রকাশ, আক্ষেপণ, to bring to light, make apparent, manifest, reprove. [sessed by a dæmon.
আবিষ্ট, অভিনিযুক্ত, engaged in, engrossed, devoted to, pos-

আবিস্, ব্যক্ত, apparent; apparently, manifestly.
আবু, গরগণ্ড, a wen.
আবৃত্তি, ঘূরণ, অভ্যাস, a returning to a point, revolving, repetition, spiral turn.
আবেদন, জ্ঞাপন, an informing, representation, declaration, complaint, suit.
আবেশ, মনোযোগ, devotedness, engagedness of mind, zeal or ardour in a pursuit.
আবেশন, শিল্পাগার, workshop, manufactory, an entrance; a halo round the sun.
আবোর, মেঘ; মূর্খ, a cloud; clownish, stupid.
আভরণ, অলঙ্কার, an ornament, jewel.
আভা, দীপ্তি, splendour, brilliancy, glossiness.
আভাষ, ভূমিকা, a preface, preamble, prologue.
আভাষণ, আলাপ, সম্ভাষণ, conversation.
আভাস্, আভা, splendor, clearness, semblance, appearance.
আভিজাত্য, কুলীনতা, greatness of birth, nobility.
আভিমুখ্য, সম্মুখতা, the front of an object, a fronting position.
আভীর, গোপ, a cow-keeper, milkman.
আভ্যাসিক, শ্রুতিধর, eminent in committing to memory.
আম, রোগ, অপক্ব, a disease, crudity in the stomach, a diarrhœa; a mango; raw, unbaked.
আমন, ব্রীহি, winter rice.
আমন্ত্রণ, আহ্বান, a call, invitation.
আময়, রোগ, a disease, sickness.
আময়াবী, পীড়িত, রোগী, sick, diseased, unwell.
আমরক্ত, উদরাময়, the dysentery, bloody flux.
আমশূল, পেটশূল, the cholic.
আমা, অপক্ব ইষ্টকা, unburnt or half-burnt bricks.
আমাত্য, অমাত্য, পাত্র, a courtier, counsellor.
আমানী, কাঁজি, rice gruel, second rice-water.
আমাশয়, অতিসার, পেট, a diarrhœa; the paunch.
আমিষ, মাংসাদি, কাম, flesh, food, a bribe, pleasing object, covetousness, lust, desire.
আমীক্ষা, ছেনা, cheese, pressed curds.
আমুক্ত, পরিচ্ছন্ন, পরিহিত, clothed, accoutred.
আমূল, কারণ, মূলাবধি, a cause, origin; to the root, radically.

আমোদ, হর্ষ, গন্ধ, enjoyment, festivity, pleasure, perfume, fame, good report.

আমোদন, আহ্লাদ উৎপাদন, to give pleasure or enjoyment.

আমোদী, আহ্লাদদায়ী, gratifying, enlivening, pleasurable, sweet-scented.

আম্নায়, বেদ, the Veda, received doctrine, tradition, custom, usage, the Ágama.

আম্বল, টক, অম্ল, sour, acid.

আম্র, চ্যূত, আম্, a mango.

আম্রেড়ন, পুনরুক্তি, tautology, foolish repetition.

আম্ল, ধাত্রীবৃক্ষ, the tamarind tree; acidity.

আম্লকী, আম্লিকা, আম্লী—তেঁতুল, the tamarind fruit or tree.

আয়, অর্থাগম, income, revenue, imports.

আয়ত, দীর্ঘ, প্রস্থ, long, wide; a parallelogram.

আয়তন, পরিসর, size, length and breadth, extent; an altar, shed for sacrifices.

আয়তি, দীর্ঘতা, আগামিকাল, length, future state or time, majesty, composure, junction.

আয়ত্ত, বশীভূত, subject to, dependant.

আয়ত্তি, প্রীতি, প্রণয়, love, attachment, subjection; a limit, power, futurity, a day.

আর্য্য, পিতামহ, a paternal grandfather.

আয়াতন, আয়তন, dimensions, a ground-plot.

আয়াম, প্রসর, প্রস্থ, extent, width, length.

আয়াস, পরিশ্রম, ক্লেশ, exertion, labour, endeavour, fatigue, the hair.

আয়ু, আয়ুঃ, আয়ুস্—জীবনকাল, the period of life, age, lifetime.

আয়ুধ, যুধাস্ত্র, বাণ, armour, arms, an arrow.

আয়ুধীয়, অস্ত্রধারী, fighting with weapons.

আয়ুর্দ্দায়, জীবনকাল, allotted period of life, life time, age.

আয়ুর্ব্বেদ, চিকিৎসা, the science of medicine.

আয়ুষ্টোম, আয়ুর্ব্বৃদ্ধ্যর্থ যজ্ঞ, a sacrifice to ensure longevity.

আয়ুষ্মান, দীর্ঘজীবী, long-lived.

আয়ুষ্য, আয়ুর্বর্দ্ধক, life-preserving; aged, health.

আয়োজন, আহরণ, সঞ্চয়ন, to collect together, make provision for an undertaking.

আয়োধন, যুদ্ধ, war, battle.

আর, এবং, অন্য, and, also, furthermore; other, another.
আরক্ত, রক্ত, reddish, flesh-coloured.
আরণা, বন্য মহিষ, a wild buffalo.
আরণ্য, বন্য, wild, sylvan.
আরতি, নিবৃত্তি, দীপদর্শান, cessation; a wave-offering.
আরব্ধ, উপক্রান্ত, begun, commenced. [sentations.
আরভটী, কাপক্রীড়া, dramatic machinery, magical repre-
আরমান, অপমান, dishonor, disappointment, distress.
আরম্ভ-ণ, উপক্রম, a beginning, commencement.
আরহলা, তৈলপায়িকা, a cockroach.
আরা, ক্ষুরপণ, করাত, an auger, awl, knife, saw.
আরাকষ, করাতী, a sawyer.
আরাৎ, সমীপ, দূর, near, distant.
আরাতি, বিপক্ষ, শত্রু, an opponent, enemy, opposer.
আরাধন, ভজন, to worship, supplicate, pray.
আরাধনা, উপাসনা, worship, prayer, respect, attendance on.
আরাম, স্বাস্থ্য, উপবন, ease, health, comfort; a pleasure-garden.
আরিশ, অর্শরোগ, the piles, hemorrhoids.
আরু. শূকর, a hog, a crab, a pitcher.
আরূঢ়, আরোহিত, mounted upon.
আরোগ্য, রোগরাহিত্য, অরোগ, health; healthy.
আরোপ, মিথ্যাদেশ, গুণকল্পনা, an attributing the properties of one thing to another, a transfer, imputation, substitution, change, transformation.
আরোহ, চড়ন, a mounting upon, ascension, embarkation, climbing; length; a stair-case, ladder, vehicle.
আর্জন, প্রাপণ, সঞ্চয়ন, a procuring, accumulation, planting of trees.
আর্জব, সারল্য, straightness, rectitude, honesty, sincerity.
আর্ত্ত, খেদিত, পীড়িত, distressed, grieved, vexed, afflicted with; distress, pain. [to a season.
আর্ত্তব, পুষ্পরোগ, the menses, a flower; menstrual, relating
আর্ত্তি, পীড়া, দুঃখ, pain, distress, the end of a bow.
আর্ত্বিজ্য, পৌরোহিত্য, the office of a family priest.
আর্থিক, জ্ঞাত, নিপুণ, acquainted with, versed in, wealthy.
আর্দ্র, আর্দ্রিত,—ভিজা, wet, moist, clammy, cool.

আর্দ্রক, আদা, ginger.
আর্য্য, মান্য, গুরু, noble, venerable, respectable, excellent, apposite, proper; friend, preceptor.
আর্য্যক, পিতামহ, paternal grandfather.
আর্শি, দর্পণ, a mirror, looking-glass.
আর্ষ, আর্ষ্য,—ঋষিপ্রণীত, authorized by, of or belonging to the ancient sages.
আর্ষভ্য, উৎসর্জ্জণীয় বৃষ, a bull let loose as an offering.
আল, পীত, yellow orpiment; a sting, fang, barb, tenon; rice not boiled in its separation from the husk.
আলআলুনি, নির্লবণ, insipid, fresh; insipid food, food without salt.
আল্গা, এলুয়া, খোলা, loose, unconnected, uncovered.
আল্গামী, আল্গা—অবদ্ধতা, looseness, unconnectedness, inattention, mildness. [talking at random.
আল্গামুখ, দুর্বাক্যবাদী, foul-mouthed, obscene, scurrilous,
আল্গোচ, উদ্ধ, উত্থিত, upright, poised, raised, making efforts to rise.
আল্গোচি, উঠনি, উঠানি, the first effort of a child to rise on its feet, a lifting up a thing without touching another thing. [tiptoe.
আল্গোচে, অস্পৃষ্টে, without touching, in equipoise, on
আল্জি, আল্জিহ্বা,—উপজিহ্বা, the uvula or soft palate.
আলতা, অলক্ত, lac, leaves impregnated with lac.
আলন, পচন, to moulder or fall to decay, spoil, become tainted, rancid, be exhausted, fatigued, &c.
আলবাল, আবাপ, a mound round the root of a tree.
আলম্ব, ঠেস্, আশ্রয়, a prop, support, fulcrum, protector, object of dependance; peg, nail.
আলম্বন, আশ্রয়ণ, a depending upon, dependance, trust.
আলম্বরূঢ়, লতা, a parasitical or climbing plant, creeper.
আলয়, গৃহ, বাসস্থান, a house, habitation.
আলসিয়া, অচতুর, কুণ্ঠ, inactive, indolent, idle.
আলস্য, আলস্যামি, } জড়তা, inactivity, indolence, idleness, fatigue.
আলস্যছাড়ন, জৃম্ভা, a yawning and stretching.

আলাই, আপদ্, misfortune, calamity, affliction.

আলাৎপালাৎ, অসংলগ্নবাক্য, ভঙ্গিমা, an irrelevant reply, a turning into ridicule, ludicrous perversion of meaning.

আলান, শৃঙ্খলী, বেড়ী, a fetter, tie, rope, a tie-post. [quisition.

আলাপ, কথোপকথন, discourse, conversation, proposal, re-

আলাপিনী, বীণা বিশেষ, a lute formed of a single gourd.

আলাপী, গল্পীয়া, ভাষী, chatty, affable, conversing.

আলাবু, তুম্বী, the bottle-gourd. [fatuus.

আলায়া, পরচ্ছায়া, an apparition, will-o'-the-wisp, ignis

আলি, সেতু, শ্রেণী, সখী, a dam, dike, ridge, range, row, race, family, confidante, a tenon.

আলিঙ্গন, কোলাকোলি, an embrace, hug, clasp.

আলিঞ্জর, অলিঞ্জর, জালা, a large earthen water-jar.

আলিন্দ, বেদী, মঞ্চ, a raised terrace, a platform.

আলিপনা, আলিম্পন,—মঙ্গলাবলেপন, a white-washing or plastering on festivals.

আলীঢ়, লেহিত, lapped by the tongue.

আলু. কন্দ বিশেষ a potatoe, yam, tuberous root.

আলুণি, নির্লবণ, fresh, not salted, insipid.

আলুবা, আলে,—জীর্ণ, পচিত, mouldered, fallen to decay, dissolved, fatigued.

আলো, আলোক,—দীপ্তি, প্রকাশ, light, brightness.

আলোকন-1, দৃষ্টিপাত, দর্শন, perception, sight, vision, view, discovery. [perception.

আলোচন-1, বিবেচনা, examination, investigation, trial, view,

আলোড়ন, মন্থন, to stir up (a liquid), agitate in conversation; maceration. [desire.

আশংসা, অনুভব, সন্দেহ, supposition, doubt, uncertainty,

আশঙ্কা, ভয়, আপত্তি, awe, fear, terror, danger, peril.

আশ্পাশ্, চতুর্দিক্, on all sides, all around.

আশয়, অভিপ্রায়, an aim, scope, object, tendency, a collection, receptacle. [length, a region.

আশা, অপেক্ষা, লাভেচ্ছা, hope, expectation, trust, desire;

আশাবন্ধ, আশ্বাসজনিতবন্ধ, attachment arising from hope, an obligation; a cobweb.

আশাভঙ্গ, প্রাপ্তিভঙ্গ, disappointment.

আশিত, ভক্ষিত, তৃপ্ত, eaten, satisfied.
আশিস্, আশীঃ,—পরমমঙ্গলপ্রার্থনা, a blessing.
আশী, অহিবিষ, সর্পদন্ত, the poison or fangs of a serpent; so.
আশীবিষ, সর্প. a serpent.
আশীর্বাদ, মঙ্গলবাদ, a benediction, blessing, salutation.
আশু, শীঘ্র, soon, quickly; early (rice), easily or soon procured.
আশুগ, দ্রুতগামী, বায়ু, বাণ, fleet, swift; the wind, an arrow.
আশুভাব, শীঘ্রতা, অর্থভক্তি, swiftness, vagary, whim.
আশ্চম্বিত, হঠাৎ, suddenly, unexpectedly.
আশ্চর্য্য, অদ্ভুত, অলৌকিক, marvellous, strange, astonishing, supernatural, miraculous.
আশ্চর্য্যজ্ঞান,-বোধ, বিস্ময়জ্ঞান, wonder, surprize, astonishment.
আশ্রম, বনবাসস্থান, দশা, a hermitage, religious retreat, state or condition of life. [defence, protection.
আশ্রয়, শরণ, অবলম্বন, an asylum, refuge, recourse, shelter,
আশ্রিত, শরণাগত, অধীন, secured, placed in safety, dependant.
আশ্লেষ, আলিঙ্গনা, মিলন, an embrace, hug, union, mixture.
আশ্বসিত, আশ্বস্ত,—ভরসান্বিত, animated, encouraged, comforted. [mation.
আশ্বাস, ভরসা, প্রত্যাশা, hope, comfort, encouragement, ani-
আশ্বাসী, প্রত্যাশা, relying on, hoping.
আস্, ধনু, a bow; ah! oh!
আসক্ত, অত্যন্তরত, attached to, enamoured, devoted to.
আসক্তি, অভিনিবেশ, প্রণয়. attachment, devotion to, love.
আসঙ্গ, সংসৃষ্টি, সম্ভোগ, নিত্য, society, fellowship, copulation; incessant, constant, *adv.* —ly.
আসত্তি, আগমন, লাভ, approach, meeting, junction, close union, acquisition, gain, profit.
আসন, পীঠাদি, বসন, a seat, carpet, mat, stool, market-stall, elephant's neck; a sitting, halting of an army, sitting posture of a devotee.
আসন্দী, বেদী, a small stool or chair. [concluded.
আসন্ন, নিকটাগত, নিকটবর্ত্তী, approached, approaching, near,
আসব, মদ্য, spirits, rum.
আসাদিত, প্রাপ্ত, gained, obtained.

আসাধন, সিদ্ধি, complete accomplishment of an object.
আসাপ, কট্‌কটিয়াবেঙ্গ, a toad.
আসিদ্ধ, বন্ধিত, সাধিত, taken into custody, imprisoned, restrained, finished, accomplished.
আসুর, দৈত্য; চিকিৎসা, a dæmon, surgery, mustard; dæmoniacal, barbarous, savage. [savage.
আসুরী, আসুরিক,—দৈত্যসম্বন্ধীয়, নির্দয়, dæmoniacal, barbarous,
আসেদ্ধা, বন্ধনকারক, বন্দী প্রেরক, one who takes or gives into custody.
আসেধ, বন্ধন, কারাগার, custody, confinement, arrest, prison.
আস্কন্দিত, বল্গিত, প্লুতগতি, a gallop.
আস্ত, অখণ্ড, প্রক্ষিপ্ত, whole, unbroken, cast, thrown.
আস্তব্যস্ত, ব্যাকুল, ব্যগ্র, distracted, troubled, anxious, hurried.
আস্তর, পাতিতবস্ত্র, a covering spread out, horse-rug, mat, lining of a garment, plastering of a wall.
আস্তরণ, বিছানা, carpet, bed, bed-clothes. [trusting.
আস্তিক, ঈশ্বরবাদী, ঈশ্বরনিষ্ঠ, believing in a God, believing,
আস্তীর্ণ, আস্তৃত,—বিস্তৃত, পাতিত, spread out, extended, laid out in order.
আস্থা, বিশ্বাস, শ্রদ্ধা, যত্ন, faith, confidence, trust, dependance, respect, regard, an assembly, a prop, stay, continuance, effort. [rious, attentive, firm.
আস্থিক, বিশ্বাসাপন্ন, শ্রমী, believing, trusting, depending, labo-
আস্পদ, বিষয়, পদ, affair, business, situation, dignity, office, authority, boast. [ambition, defiance.
আস্পর্দ্ধা, আত্মশ্লাঘা, self-exaltation, boast, emulation, rivalry,
আস্ফালন, লম্ফন, স্পন্দন, দম্ভযুক্ত বাক্য, to flounce, flap, clap; a boasting, self-importance.
আস্ফোট, তাল, the slapping of one hand on the opposite arm in defiance. [pansion.
আস্ফোটন, বিকাশ, the blowing of a flower, opening, ex-
আস্ফোটনী, তুরপণ, a gimlet, auger, drill.
আস্য, মুখ, the face, visage, mouth; *in comp.* towards.
আস্বাদ, রস, রসানুভব, a savour, relish, taste.
আস্বাদু, আস্বাদী,—সুরস, delicious, well-tasted, savoury.
আহত, ঘাতিত, smitten, hurt, injured, killed, uttered falsely.

আহনন, মারন, ঘাতন, to smite, wound, kill, hammer, beat out metal.

আহব, যজ্ঞ, যুদ্ধ, a sacrifice, war, combat, attack.

আহরণ, সঞ্চয়ন, আনয়ন, to collect together, bring, remove.

আহর্ত্তা, আনেতা, ভোক্তা, one who brings, an eater.

আহার, ভোজন, food, diet, a meal, repast.

আহারক, সংগ্রাহক, collecting together, bringing.

আহারী, ভোজনকারক, feeding, feeding freely, gluttonous.

আহার্য্য, ভোজনার্হ, আনয়নীয়, fit to be eaten or brought, incidental, accessary.

আহিত, স্থাপিত, সমর্পিত, placed, deposited.

আহিতাগ্নি, সাগ্নিক, a Brahmin who preserves the consecrated fire of his family.

আহীরী, গোপাল, a cowherd.

আহুত, উৎসৃষ্ট, offered, sacrificed.

আহুতি, হোম, a burnt sacrifice.

আহূত, নিমন্ত্রিত, invited, called, summoned.

আহৃত, গৃহীত, সঞ্চিত, ভুক্ত, taken, brought, collected, eaten.

আহোপুরুষিকা, অহমিকা, self-exaltation, a vaunting of one's own valour and depreciation of another's.

আহ্নিক, দিবসিক, daily, diurnal; daily ceremonies.

আহ্লাদ, হর্ষ, joy, mirth, festivity, exultation.

আহ্লাদী, আনন্দিত, joyous, festive, mirthful, glad.

আহ্বয়, সংজ্ঞা, appellation, name, a law-suit, a sporting dispute.

আহ্বান, নিমন্ত্রণ, সম্বোধন, an invitation, call, summons.

ই.

ই, নিশ্চয়বোধক, *an emphatic affix*—even, indeed, self, very.

ইকড়, নিরাট, solid, not hollow or fistulous; a sort of reed.

ইকড়া, ইন্দুর, a bandicote rat.

ইকুণ, ডেঙ্গর, a louse.

ইক্ষু, আকু, a sugar-cane.

ইঙ্গন, সঙ্কেতন, ঠারণ, to nod, wink, express by signs or allusions.

ইঙ্গিত, সঙ্কেত, ঠার, a nod, wink, signal, sign.

ইচ্ছা, স্পৃহা, will, desire, wish, choice, inclination, bias.

ইচ্ছান্বিত, বাসনাকারী, voluntary, unconstrained, wilful.
ইচ্ছু, ইচ্ছুক,—আকাঙ্ক্ষী, desirous, willing, solicitous.
ইজ্যা, যাগ, a sacrifice, oblation, worship, reverence.
ইঞ্চাক, চিঙ্গড়িমৎস্য, a shrimp or prawn.
ইট্, ইটল, ইটাল, ইঁট,—পাটিকেল, a brick.
ইটময়, ইটীয়,—ইষ্টকনির্ম্মিত, brick, built of bricks.
ইটমন-আন, ইষ্টকক্ষেপণ, to pelt with bricks.
ইতঃ, এখানহইতে, এইহেতুক, hence, from this.
ইতর, ভিন্ন, তুচ্ছ, other, another, different, low, mean.
ইতরেদ্যুঃ, পরদিবস, on another day.
ইতস্ততঃ, এদিকওদিক, hither and thither.
ইতি, এইপর্য্যন্ত, এমন, thus far, hitherto, thus, this.
ইতিমধ্যে, ইতোমধ্যে,—এইকালে, তন্মধ্যে, during this, at this time, in the meanwhile. [advice.
ইতিহ, পুরাতনকথা, গল্প, traditional instruction, legend,
ইতিহাস, পুরাণ, পূর্ব্ববৃত্তান্ত, a history, tale, fable.
ইত্থম্ভূত, এইপ্রকার, এতাদৃশ, thus, such, like.
ইত্যবসরে, এইকালে, এইঅবকাশে, at this time or opportunity, during this.
ইদং, এই, ঐ, this, that, the same.
ইদানী, এখন, now.
ইদানীন্তন, আধুনিক, এখনকার, recent, modern, present.
ইন্দারা, কূপ, a well, large well or pit.
ইন্দু, চন্দ্র, the moon.
ইন্দুর, মূষিক, a rat, a mouse. [night, an organ of sense.
ইন্দ্র, স্বর্গাধিপতি, জীবাত্মা, the sovereign of the gods: the soul,
ইন্দ্রজাল, মায়া, ভোজবিদ্যা, legerdemain, magic, conjuring.
ইন্দ্রজালিক, মায়িক, deceptive, juggling, illusive.
ইন্দ্রলুপ্ত, টাক, morbid baldness, the falling off of the hair.
ইন্দ্রায়ুধ, রামধনুক, the rain-bow, the weapon of Indra.
ইন্দ্রাশন, গঞ্জা, an intoxicating preparation of hemp.
ইন্দ্রিয়, চক্ষুঃকর্ণাদি দশ, the senses, the organs of sensation or perception.
ইন্দ্রিয়ঘ্ন, ইন্দ্রিয়নাশক, debilitating, stupifying, enfeebling the senses. [selfdenial.
ইন্দ্রিয়দমন, কামাদি নিগ্রহ, উপাদান, suppression of sensuality,

ইন্দ্রিয়দোষ, কুবাসনা, an evil propensity, concupiscence.
ইন্দ্রিয়ার্থ, গোচর, an object of the senses.
ইন্ধন, কাষ্ঠাদি জ্বলনীয়দ্রব্য, fuel.
ইপ্সু, ঈপ্সিত,—লোভী, ইচ্ছুক, desirous, wishing for.
ইব, সাদৃশ্যবোধক, *an affix:* like, resembling, &c.
ইভ, হস্তী, an elephant.
ইমন, স্বরমিল, concord (of notes in music).
ইয়ৎ, এত, so much, thus much.
ইয়ত্তা, পরিমিতত্ব, সীমা, an assigned quantity, definiteness.
ইরম্মদ, বিদ্যুৎ, বজ্রাগ্নি, a flash of lightning, submarine fire.
ইরা, বাক্য, সরস্বতী, ভূমি, জল, language, speech, goddess of speech, the carth, water, ardent spirits.
ইলেক, রেখা, ডোরা, a line, streak, stroke, dash of the pen.
ইষু, বাণ, an arrow, a versed sine.
ইষুধি, তূণ, তূণীর, a quiver.
ইষ্ট, অভিলষিত, desired, cherished, beloved, respected, approved, sacrificed to, worshipped.
ইষ্টক-া, ইট্, a brick.
ইষ্টদেব-তা, পূজ্যদেব, the particular god worshipped by any individual.
ইষ্টি, ইচ্ছা, যাগ, গুরু, volition, will, desire; a sacrifice, oblation, spiritual guide.
ইস্তক, এঅবধি, from this place.
ইস্ত্রি, বস্ত্রঘর্ষণার্থবস্তু, a smoothing iron. [present time.
ইহকাল, ইহলোক,—মর্ত্যলোক, the present life, this world,

ঈ.

ঈক্ষণ, দর্শন, to see, view, behold.
ঈতি, অতিবৃষ্ট্যাদি ষট্, agricultural calamity, as drought, &c.
ঈদৃক, ঈদৃশ,—এইরূপ, এইপ্রকার, thus, such, resembling this.
ঈর্ষ্যা, দ্বেষ, হিংসা, envy, spite, malice.
ঈর্ষ্যী, দ্বেষী, হিংসক, spiteful, malicious, envious.
ঈশ, প্রভু, শিব, a lord, God, the Supreme, Shiva.
ঈশ, ঈশা,—লাঙ্গলদণ্ড, the beam of a plough.
ঈশান, দীপ্তি, শিব, light, splendour, Shiva; north-eastern.

ঈশ্বর, সর্ব্বস্রষ্টা, প্রভু, God, the Supreme, a lord.
ঈশ্বরনিষেধ, নাস্তিকতা, the denial of a God, atheism.
ঈশ্বরনিষ্ঠ, ঈশ্বরভক্ত, firmly relying on God, established in his service. [absorption.
ঈশ্বরসাধন, মুক্তিসাধন, a securing of the divine favour or
ঈশ্বরী, দেবী, শক্তি, a goddess, a queen.
ঈষ, ঈষা,—ইশ, the beam of a plough.
ঈষৎ, অল্প, কিঞ্চিৎ, a little, somewhat; *pref.* slight, &c.
ঈষদ্দর্শন, কটাক্ষ, অল্পদৃষ্টি, a glance, slight view.
ঈহা, চেষ্টা, ইচ্ছা, endeavour, attempt, study, wish.

উ.

উই, বল্মীক, a white ant
উঁচ, উচ্চ, high, lofty. [thatch.
উঁচন, উত্থাপন, উঠান, to stir up, lift up, loosen, strip off
উঁচনীচ, উচ্চনীচ, অসমান, rough, uneven, not level or smooth.
উঁচলন-আন, চালন, to toss corn in a sieve, to sift.
উঁছান, উঠান, অবগোরণ, to take up, lift up, unthatch, to threaten to strike.
উক, উকা,—উল্কা, খোলা, a meteor, torch, firebrand; stray, going at large, strange, unknown. [retching.
উঁকি, গুপ্তদৃষ্টি, উদ্গার, a peep, prying, attentive gaze, a
উঁকিউঠন, উদ্গারণ, to retch, to strain.
উকিমারণ, গোপনেদর্শন, to pry, watch, peep.
উকুণ কেশকীট, a louse.
উক্করী, উক্কলী,—ঢক্কাবিশেষ, a sort of drum.
উক্ত, কথিত, said, spoken, related.
উক্তি. বাক্য, কথন, speech, a word, sentence, expression.
উক্ষা, বৃষ, a bull.
উখ, উখা,—ঘর্ষণী, a rasp, file.
উখন, ঘর্ষণ, to rasp, file.
উখড়ন, কালবহন, ছুটন, to go or pass away as time, to get or break loose, to encrust with sugar.
উখড়া, মুড়কী, a preparation of parched rice and treacle.
উখড়ী, দর্ব্বী, হাতা, a ladle, a skimmer.

উখা, হাঁড়ি, a pot, saucepan.
উগরণ, বমন, to vomit, bring up the cud ; vomit.
উগ্র, ঝাল, কঠিন, ক্রোধী, hot, pungent, peevish, surly, cross, passionate.
উঘারণ, উলঙ্গকরণ, কেলান, to uncover, strip, lay bare.
উকুন, উকুণ, a louse. [course.
উঙ্কোশ, প্রসঙ্গ, introduction of a topic or subject of dis-
উচকা, উচক্কা,—অবাধ্য, headstrong, unruly, mischievous, bold, insolent.
উচলন-আন, চালন, to toss up in a sieve, to sift.
উচিত, ন্যায্য, যোগ্য, right, fit, proper, suitable, convenient.
উচোট, ঠোকর, a trip, stumble.
উচ্চ, ঊর্দ্ধ, উন্নত, high, lofty, loud.
উচ্চটা, অহংকার, ব্যবহার, pride, arrogance, a custom, usage.
উচ্চণ্ড, শীঘ্র, দ্রুত, quick, hasty, expeditious.
উচ্চমনাঃ, চিন্তান্বিত, uneasy, restless, troubled, flighty, vain.
উচ্চণ্ড, রসিক, কৌতুকী, droll, comical, jocose.
উচ্চরিত, উক্ত, কথিত, uttered, pronounced, said, spoken.
উচ্চাটন, বিষাদ, উৎপাত, sadness, gloom, sullenness, ruin, oppression ; to vex, harrass, cause to remove.
উচ্চাটী, বিষণ্ণ, উৎকণ্ঠিত, inclined to gloom or sullenness.
উচ্চাবচ, অসমান, নানাবিধ, uneven, not level, various, multiform.
উচ্চার, বিষ্ঠা, মল, excrement, filth, manure.
উচ্চার-ণ, উল্লেখ, শব্দপ্রয়োগ, utterance, pronunciation.
উচ্চৈঃ, বৃহৎ, ঊর্দ্ধ, loud; aloud, on high.
উচ্চৈশ্রবা, কালা, deaf, high-eared. [relinquished.
উচ্ছন্ন, বিনাশিত, ruined, destroyed, laid waste, stript of,
উচ্ছিন্ন, খণ্ডিত, নষ্ট, cut off, ruined. [leavings.
উচ্ছিষ্ট, অবশিষ্ট, ত্যক্ত, left, remaining, rejected after tasting;
উচ্ছিষ্টতা, অবশেষ, a remnant, orts, leavings.
উচ্ছৃঙ্খল, ক্রমরহিত, অবাধ্য, irregular, confused, self-willed, licentious, loose, unrestrained.
উচ্ছেদ, বিনাশ, ruin, destruction, devastation, excision.
উচ্ছ্রয়, উচ্ছ্রায়,—ঊর্দ্ধতা, height, elevation, a height.

উচ্ছ্রিত, উন্নত, উৎপন্ন, elevated, exalted, born, produced, grown, increased, prosperous.

উহড়ন, বমন, to vomit.

উজু, উজা,—সরল, straight, direct, sincere, honest, upright.

উপড়ন, উৎপাটন, বমন, to tear up by the roots, to vomit.

উজান, বিলোম, against the grain, in an opposite direction.

উজান, বিলোমসন্তরণ, to swim against the stream, to flood as the tide.

উজানীয়, নদ্যাদিত্যাগী, wandering (as fish from the rivers into pools).

উজল, জলের উর্দ্ধাধোগমন, উর্ম্মিমত্তা, the dashing of the waves, a tossing or agitation.

উজলন, উঠন, to rise as a wave, to be tossed, agitated.

উজলান, উৎক্ষেপণ, উচলান, to toss, agitate, sift.

উজাড়, বন, অরণ্য, a wilderness, deserted place.

উজান, ডাঙ্গা, an upper country, hill-country.

উজি, জনরব, জনশ্রুতি, a common report, rumour.

উজুবীয়া, উজানীয়, wandering (as fish in the rains).

উচ্ছট, শূন্য, উপক্রুত, waste, ruined, desolate, desert.

উজড়-ন, উৎপাটন, বিনাশ, eradication, tearing up by the roots, ruin, destruction.

উজড়ীয়, অপব্যয়ী, অপচয়ী, wasteful, lavish, expensive, ruinous.

উজ্জ্বল, দীপ্তিমান, প্রকাশ, luminous, splendid, bright; splendor, brightness, blaze.

উজ্জ্বলন, উদ্দীপন, জ্বলন, to blaze up, enkindle.

উজ্ঝিত, ত্যক্ত, left, abandoned, relinquished.

উঞ্ছ-ন, কুড়ান, a gleaning, collecting of grains.

উঞ্ছন, ধান্যশুকান, to dry rice by the fire for unhusking.

উট, উষ্ট্র, খড়াদি, a camel; dried leaves, grass, thatch.

উটকারা, বিদেশীয়, আগন্তুক, foreign, unknown, vagrant.

উটজ, পর্ণশালা, খড়াচ্ছাদিত গৃহ, a thatched house.

উটন, ধারে কেনন, to take goods on credit.

উটন, ফুলন, to heave or swell from moisture, to scale off as scurf.

উট্‌কন, অন্বেষণ, search, enquiry, a tracing out.

উট্‌কো, খোলা, straying, wandering, unknown.

উদ্দেশ, সূত্র, পন্থ, a clue, guide.

উঠ, উদ্গম, a rising up, mounting, elevation.

উঠন, গাত্তোলন, আঙ্গিনা, to rise, to mount; a court-yard.
উঠনি, উঠানি, গাত্তোলন, চড়ন, a rising up, mounting, arrival at a place. [eradicate; a court-yard.
উঠান, তোলান, to raise, exalt, elevate, remove, dismiss,
উঠানে, বাহিরে, without, out of doors.
উঠাউঠি, পুনঃ২, বার্‌বার্, repeatedly, importunately.
উঠ্‌তি, বিক্রী, সভাভঙ্গ, a vent or sale for goods, the breaking up of an assembly.
উড়কুড়, আদ্যন্ত, শেষ, the beginning and end, termination, end: from beginning to end.
উড়ঞ্চড়ীয়, অপব্যয়ী, squandering, wasting, throwing away.
উড়ন, আকাশে ভ্রমন, চড়ন, to fly, mount in the air, soar, be wasted, be scattered. [garment.
উড়নী, একপাটা, উত্তরীয়, a sheet, the Hindoo outer flowing
উড়নীয়, পলায়িত, পক্ষবান, taking flight, flying, fledged.
উড়পড়ন, উড়িয়াপড়ন, a flying up and settling or falling.
উড়া, আকাশচলন, অপব্যয়, flight, waste, the venereal.
উড়ানী, অপব্যয়, উড়নী, waste, extravagance, outer garment.
উড়ানীয়, অপব্যয়ী, wasteful, extravagant.
উড়ী, বন্যধান্য, গুঞ্জনি, wild rice; the repairing of thatch.
উডু, নক্ষত্র, any constellation in the moon's path.
উডুউডু, চিন্তান্বিত, আকুল, anxious, agitated, eager.
উডুক্কা, পক্ষবান, able to fly, fledged.
উডুপ, চন্দ্র, তরণী, ভেলা, the moon, a raft, a float.
উডুপতি, চন্দ্র, the moon. [of leprosy.
উডুম্বর, তাম্র, যজ্ঞডুম্বর, copper, a threshold, wild fig, species
উড্ডী, অস্থির, আকাশী, flighty, airy, light, vain.
উড্ডয়ন. উড়ন, flight, a soaring, rising into the air.
উড্ডীং, উল্লম্ফ, a bound or upward leap.
উড্ডীয়মান, আকাশগামী, flying.
উত, তাপ, অগ্নি, বুনান, heat, fire: sewed, woven.
উতরণ, আগমন, আইসন, পার হ-, to arrive, come to, cross over.
উতলন, উতুলন,—উত্তপন, to overflow, boil over, run over.
উতলা, উতালা,—ব্যস্ত, রাগী, distressed, agitated, touchy, passionate. [river, arrival.
উতার-1, প্রতিলিপি, পারায়ণ, a copy, duplicate; passage of a

উৎক, উদ্বিগ্ন, উৎকণ্ঠিত, anxious, regretting.

উৎকট, দুঃসহ, মত্ত, disagreeable, troublesome, bad, excessive, furious, drunk, mad.

উৎকণ্ঠা, উদ্বেগ, anxiety, regret, care, vexation, sullenness, melancholy.

উৎকর্ষ, অতিশয়, উত্তমতা, excessive; excellence, abundance, late performance.

উৎকলিকা, ভাবনা, উৎকণ্ঠা, thought, anxiety, care.

উৎকুণ, কেশরাদি, a louse.

উৎকৃষ্ট, উত্তম, excellent, good. elevated.

উৎকৃষ্টার্হ, উত্তমার্হ, capable of improvement, improvable.

উৎকোচ, ঘুষ, a bribe.

উৎক্রম, উল্লম্ফ, বিলোম, উল্লঙ্ঘ, a leap, jump, bound, departure from order, irregularity, transgression.

উৎক্রান্ত, উল্লম্ফিত, উল্লঙ্ঘিত, leaped up, transgressed.

উৎক্রোশ, ক্রোরপক্ষী, কুরর, কুরল, an eagle.

উৎক্ষেপ-ণ, ঊর্দ্ধনিক্ষেপ, a toss, a throwing up.

উৎখাত, উৎপাটন, উপদ্রব, eradication, rooting up, ruin, destruction.

উৎখাতী, নাশক, উপদ্রবী, subversive, ruinous.

উত্তম, শ্রেষ্ঠ, প্রধান, best, chief, excellent, superior, very good.

উত্তমর্ণ, ঋণদাতা, a creditor, lender.

উত্তমসাহস, পঞ্চ মহাদণ্ড, the five capital punishments.

উত্তমাঙ্গ, মস্তক, the head.

উত্তমার্হ, উৎকৃষ্টার্হ, capable of amelioration, improvable.

উত্তর, পশ্চাৎ, প্রতিবাক্য, উদক্, আগমন, subsequent, posterior, behind, last, hinder, future, northern; an answer, apology, consequence, remainder or difference, arrival, the north.

উত্তরণ, পারায়ণ, পৌঁছন, to arrive at, land, cross a river, alight.

উত্তরক্রিয়া, অন্ত্যেষ্টিক্রিয়া, funeral obsequies.

উত্তরখণ্ডন, প্রত্যুক্তি, বাক্যখণ্ডন, rejoinder, confutation.

উত্তরপক্ষ, প্রতিবাদ, a reply to an argument, refutation.

উত্তরপ্রত্যুত্তর, কথোপকথন, বিবাদ, dialogue, dispute, law-pleading.

উত্তরসংজ্ঞিত, উত্তরসাক্ষী,—শ্রুতসাক্ষী, a witness testifying from hearsay or the report of others.

উত্তরসাধক, মধ্যস্থ, সহায়, an umpire, prompter, auxiliary, director of religious ceremonies. [lers.
উত্তরস্থান, পথিকাশ্রম, an inn, place of refreshment for travel-
উত্তরাধিকার, পৈতৃকাধিকার, an inheritance, succession.
উত্তরাভাস, অপ্রকৃতোত্তর, a prevarication, deceptive reply.
উত্তরায়ণ, সূর্য্যের উত্তরগতি, the sun's path N. of the equator.
উত্তরাসঙ্গ, উড়নী, the outer Hindoo garment.
উত্তরী, উত্তরীয়,—উড়নী, পৈতা, the outer Hindoo garment, brahminical thread. [wards, subsequently.
উত্তরেণ, উদীচীন, পশ্চাৎ, northern, posterior, northerly, north-
উত্তরেদ্যুঃ, কল্য, ইহারপর, to-morrow, on a future day. [ther.
উত্তরোত্তর, অধিকাধিক, পরপর, more and more, further and fur-
উত্তর্জনা, ধম্কান, ঘেঙ্গানি, a threatening, importunity, dunning.
উত্থলন, উপচন, ছাপন, an overflowing, running or boiling over.
উত্তান, চিৎ. উন্মুখ, having the face or palm upwards, shallow.
উত্তানশয়, উন্মুখ, অবগণ্ড, lying face upwards; an infant.
উত্তাপ, উগ্রতা, তাপ, heat, ardour, zeal, distress.
উত্তাপন, তাপন, to heat, make hot. [or alight.
উত্তারণ, পার ক-, পৌঁছান, নামান, to ferry over, cause to arrive
উত্তীর্ণ, আগত, উদ্ধৃত,, পারপ্রাপ্ত, arrived, delivered, rescued, having surmounted a difficulty.
উত্তুঙ্গ, উচ্চৈঃ, high, lofty, tall.
উত্তেজনা, মার্জ্জনা, ঘর্ষা, a furbishing, polishing, dunning.
উত্তোলন, উন্নয়ন, উপচন, to raise a weight, elevate, boil over, overflow.
উত্ত্যক্ত, বর্জ্জিত, বিরক্ত, rejected, abandoned, vexed, disgusted.
উত্থন, গাত্রোত্থান, to rise, stand erect.
উত্থলন, উচ্ছলন, উপচন, to overflow, boil over.
উত্থান, উত্থাপন,—উন্নামন, to raise, elevate, excite, stir up.
উত্থিতি, উত্তোলন, গাত্রোত্থান, erection, elevation, rising up.
উৎপতন, উৎপ্লবন, চড়ন, to leap up, mount.
উৎপত্তি, জন্ম, production, a production.
উৎপন্ন, জন্মপ্রাপ্ত, produced, arisen from.
উৎপল, নালি, কুমুদ, a blue lotus, water-lily.
উৎপলিনী, কুমুদিনী, *id*: a collection of water-lilies.
উৎপাটন, উপড়ন, to root up, eradicate, eradication.

উৎপাত, উপদ্রব, ruin, destruction, calamity, outrage, violence, tumult, danger, ruin, provocation, evil omen, portent, something disagreeable.

উৎপাদন, জন্মান, to produce, create, excite, occasion.

উৎপ্রেক্ষা, সাদৃশ্য, উপমা, a resemblance, simile, metaphor, illustration, indifference, carelessness.

উৎপ্লব-ন, উৎফাল,—লম্ফ, কুঁদন, a leap, jump, bound.

উৎফুল্ল, স্ফুটিত, বিকশিত, হর্ষিত, blown, expanded, gladdened.

উৎস, নির্ঝর, a fountain, spring.

উৎসঙ্গ, ক্রোড়, অঙ্ক, the hips, the lap.

উৎসব. পরব, আনন্দ, a festival, festivity, feast.

উৎসর্গ, উৎসর্জন,—নৈবেদ্য, দান, an offering, oblation, presenting of an oblation, gift.

উৎসাহ, উদ্যম, উদ্যোগ, promptness, enterprize, zeal, energy, effort, perseverance, confidence, eagerness.

উৎসুক, উৎসাহশীল, অনুতাপী, eager, zealous for, regretting, penitent.

উৎসৃষ্ট, আহুত, ত্যক্ত, দত্ত, offered in sacrifice, given.

উৎসেচন, জলোৎক্ষেপণ, to spout or throw up water.

উদ, উদক,—জল, উদ্বিড়াল, water, an otter.

উদক্, উত্তরদিক্, the north.

উদকদান, জলদান, a bestowing of water, an offering of water to the manes of one's ancestors.

উদগ্র, উন্মুখ, উচ্চ, উন্নত, pointing upwards, high, tall, (*ironically*) a dwarf.

উদধি, উদন্বা,—সমুদ্র, সাগর, the sea, the ocean.

উদন্যা, তৃষ্ণা, পিপাসা, thirst, desire to drink.

উদপান, কূপ, a well, tank, &c.

উদম, অবশ, অবারিত, অনাবৃত, uncontrouled, unrestrained, free, open, uncovered.

উদমাদা, অবিচারক, মূঢ়, সরল, thoughtless, simple, unreflecting, sincere, unsuspecting, docile, cheerful.

উদয়, অধোহইতে প্রকাশ, a rising into view, rise of a heavenly body, coming into vogue.

উদয়গিরি, উদয়াচল,—পূর্বপর্বত, the eastern mountains.

উদয়াস্ত, দিনমান, the day, day-time.

উদর, জঠর, পেট, the abdomen or belly, paunch, womb, an enlargement of the abdomen.

উদরনাড়ী, অন্ত্র, an entrail, gut.

উদরভঙ্গ, উদরাময়,—অতিসার, a diarrhœa, dysentery.

উদরম্ভরি, আত্মম্ভরি, পেটুক, selfishly voracious, gluttonous, voluptuous.

উদররস, উদরস্থিত পাচকরস, the gastric juice.

উদরসর্ব্বস্ব, পেটসর্ব্বস্ব, পেটুক, পেটার্থী, gluttonous, voluptuous; an epicure.

উদরী, পেটাল, তুন্দিল, abdominous, corpulent, dropsical.

উদরে, অভ্যন্তরে, inwardly, internally, inclusively.

উদর্ক, পরফল, পরকাল, লাভ, remote consequence, future time, profit, advantage.

উদান, কণ্ঠস্থিত বায়ু. one of the five airs of an animal body.

উদার, অকপট, সরল, দাতা, মহৎ. candid, frank, generous, liberal, noble, grand, gentle, unperplexed.

উদারা, ঘোরতরা স্বর, the deepest notes in music.

উদারাখ্যা, উদারসংজ্ঞক,—ঘোরার্থ, অস্পষ্ট, ambiguous, of doubtful or double meaning.

উদাস, সমাধি, বৈরাগ্য, ব্যাকুলতা, religious abstraction, solitude, unconnectedness, retirement, misanthrophy, anxiety, regret.

উদাসী, বৈরাগী, নিঃসঙ্গ, ভাবিত, abstracted, lonely, retired, misanthrophic, anxious, regretting, crazy.

উদাসীন, সন্যাসী, বিদেশী, withdrawn from society, austere; a recluse, pilgrim, religious mendicant, cynic, misanthrophe, stranger, foreigner.

উদাহরণ, উদাহার,—দৃষ্টান্ত, an illustration, instance, exemplification of a rule.

উদাহৃত, উৎপ্রেক্ষিত, উক্ত, adduced in exemplification, exemplified, mentioned, spoken, famed.

উদিত, প্রকাশিত, কথিত, বদ্ধ, risen (as a heavenly body), come into notice or fashion, spoken, expressed, bound, tied.

উদীচী উত্তরদিক্, the north quarter.

উদীচীন, উত্তরেণ, northern.

উদীচ্য, উত্তরপশ্চিমদেশ, the north-west, north country.

উচ্চরিত, উচ্চারিত, spoken, uttered, said, announced.
উদূখল, মর্দ্দনপাত্র, a wooden mortar for husking rice.
উদ্গত, উদিত, বর্দ্ধিত, ascended, risen, increased, vomited.
উদ্গম, ঊর্দ্ধ্বগমন, বৃদ্ধি, জ্ঞান, ascension, rising, mounting, increase, knowledge, idea.
উদ্গাঢ়, অতিশয়, অধিক, exceeding, very, great, excessive.
উদ্গাতা, বেদগায়ক, সামগ, a chanter or reciter, particularly of the Sáma Veda.
উদ্গার-ণ, ঢেকুর, বমন, a belching, retching, vomiting.
উদ্গীথ, সামবেদাংশ, প্রণবোচ্চারণ, a portion of the Sáma Veda, the utterance of the mystic ওঁ.
উদ্গীর্ণ, বমিত, vomited, thrown up.
উদ্গূর্ণ, উদ্যত, prepared for, or engaged in action, exerted, stimulated, raised, held up.
উদ্গ্রহন, গঠন, the building up of a wall, edification.
উদ্গ্রাহ্য, সাধ্য, প্রাপ্য, an object accomplishable or attainable.
উদ্ঘন, কাষ্ঠছেদনাধার, a chopping-block, carpenter's bench.
উদ্ঘাটন, জল উত্তোলনের যন্ত্র, প্রসারণ, the rope and bucket of a well, the opening out as of a shutter.
উদ্ঘাত, আরম্ভ, অস্ত্র, commencement, a weapon, club, mallet.
উদ্দংশ, মশা, ডাঁশ, a mosquito, a gadfly, a bug.
উদ্দন্তুর, বৃহদ্দন্তী, দাঁতাল, ভয়ানক, having large teeth or tusks, formidable, tall.
উদ্দাম, অবাধিত, স্বতন্ত্র, unrestrained, unconfined, free.
উদ্দিষ্ট, অভিপ্রেত, designed, intended, regarded, done with regard to.
উদ্দীপন, জ্বলন, প্রকাশন, a blazing, glowing, shining, illumination.
উদ্দেশ, অভিপ্রায়, অন্বেষণ, কামনা, an object, view, motive, incentive, vestige, trace, search; lust, love; sake, account of; for.
উদ্দেশক, উদ্দেশকর্ত্তা,—চেষ্টাকারক, acting from a motive, or with regard to an object.
উদ্দেশ্য, প্রয়োজন, অন্বেষণীয়, an incentive; fit to be made an object of regard, deserving to be traced out.
উদ্দেষ্টা, চেষ্টাকারক, one who acts with a design or scope.
উদ্ধত, অন্যমনস্ক, দুরন্ত, মন্দাচারী, absent, ill-behaved, capricious, audacious, mischievous, self-important.

উদ্ধতামি, দুরাচরণ, নির্লজ্জতা, ill-behaviour, effrontery, audacity, mischievousness.

উদ্ধরণ, উদ্ধার,—রক্ষা, মুক্তি, ত্রাণ, deliverance, rescue, extrication, acquittal, beatitude, freedom, extract from a book, raising up from a pit.

উদ্ধুত, উদ্ধূত,—উৎক্ষিপ্ত, tossed or cast up.

উদ্বদ্ধ, টাঙ্গা, বদ্ধ, hung, tied up to a thing.

উদ্বন্ধন, ফাঁসী দেওন, to hang (a criminal.)

উদ্বমন, উদ্গারণ, to vomit, throw up, retch.

উদ্বর্ত্ত, অবশেষ, অবশিষ্ট, a remainder, overplus; remaining, left.

উদ্বর্দ্ধন, বাড়ন, অধিক-হ-, to be over, abound, be more than enough.

উদ্বাহ, বিবাহ, a marriage, wedding, nuptials.

উদ্বিগ্ন, ব্যাকুল, ভাবিত, troubled, anxious, perplexed, thoughtful, dejected.

উদ্বিড়াল, জলমার্জার, an otter.

উদ্বৃত্ত, অবশিষ্ট, অধিক, left, remaining over and above.

উদ্বেগ, ব্যাকুলতা, ভাবনা, perplexity, anxiety, hesitation, grief, care, dejection; the betelnut.

উদ্বোধ -ন, স্মরণ, জ্ঞান, remembrance, recognition, a conception of the mind, sentiment.

উদ্ভট, অলিখিত শ্লোক, সমুদ্গত, unwritten but current, well known, renowned, excellent: a tortoise, the sun.

উদ্ভব, উৎপত্তি, জন্ম, production, birth, a coming into existence.

উদ্ভাব, উষ্মা, বাষ্প, heat, steam, a thing tending upwards.

উদ্ভিজ্জ, উদ্ভিদ্,—বৃক্ষলতাদি, a tree, plant, shrub: sprouting, germinating.

উদ্ভিদ্বিদ্যা, বৃক্ষাদিবিদ্যা, botany, the science of plants.

উদ্ভিন্ন, ভেদিত, বিদ্ধ, perforated, split, opened upwards.

উদ্ভূত, উৎপন্ন, জাত, produced, arisen from, born, consequent.

উদ্যত, প্রস্তুত, প্রবৃত্ত, ready, prompt, about or prepared for an act.

উদ্যম, উদ্যোগ, exertion, readiness for action, preparedness.

উদ্যমভঙ্গ, চেষ্টাধ্বংস, নিরাশ্বাস, dissuasion, discouragement, desisting.

উদ্যমী, উদ্যোগী,—চেষ্টাবান্, active, busy, prompt, ready.

উদ্যান, উপবন, a garden, park, grove, pleasure-ground.

উদ্যাপন, ব্রতনিষ্পাদন, সম্পাদন, fulfilment of a vow, performance, accomplishment of a design.

উদ্যুক্ত, প্রস্তুত, সম্প্রবৃত্ত, ready, on the point of, engaged in.

উদ্যোগ, প্রয়াস, চেষ্টা, endeavour, exertion, enterprize, zeal, readiness, industry.

উদ্র, জলমার্জ্জার, an otter.

উদ্রেক, উন্মুখ, আরম্ভ, attempt, commencement, appearance, [perception.

উদ্রেকভঙ্গ, আশাভঙ্গ, disappointment, discouragement, dissuasion, desisting.

উদ্রেকী, উদ্যত, উদিত, about, ready, coming into view, gain- [ing ground.

উধস্, গোস্তন, the udder of a cow.

উধার, ঋণ, ধার, a loan, debt, trust, credit.

উনন, v.n. }
উনান, v.a. } গলন, গলান, চুলা, to melt, dissolve; a furnace, hearth, portable hearth.

উনুই, উৎস, নির্ঝর, a fountain, spring.

উন্দধুন্দ, গণ্ডগোল, লোকযাত্রা, a commotion, riot, tumult, confusion, anarchy, mob, multitude, procession, pomp and noise of attendants.

উন্দুর, উন্দুরু,—মূষিক, আখু, a rat, a mouse.

উন্নত, উচ্চ, সম্পন্ন, elevated, exalted, enriched, risen, ascended, increased.

উন্নতানত, উথাপড়া, risen and fallen, elevated and depressed, rising and falling.

উন্নতি, বৃদ্ধি, increase, elevation, advancement, prosperity.

উন্নয়ন, উত্তোলন, বিচার, ঊহা, to lift up, elevate; discussion, deliberation, reasoning, logic.

উন্নামন, উত্তোলন, to raise, elevate.

উন্মত্ত, উন্মদিষ্ণু, উন্মাদী,—ক্ষিপ্ত, পাগল, deranged, mad, crazy, [intoxicated.

উন্মনা, উৎকণ্ঠিত, ব্যাকুল, thoughtful, agitated, distressed, regretting.

উন্মাথ, ফাঁদ, জাল, a snare, trap, net.

উন্মাদ, বাতুলতা, বায়ুগ্রস্ত, madness, folly, extravagance; mad, [extravagant.

উন্মাদক্ষেত্র, বাতুল, a maniac, mad person.

উন্মান, উন্মিতি,—তৌলন, মাপন, a weighing, measuring; mea- [sure, value.

উন্মিষিত, প্রফুল্লিত, প্রসারিত, blown as a flower, opened as the eyes, expanded. [flower, to wink.

উন্মীলন, মুদিতের প্রকাশন, খুলন, to open as the eyes or as a

উন্মুখ, ঊর্দ্ধাস্য, উদ্যুক্ত, উদ্রেক, looking or pointing upwards, engaged in; an effort, attempt, exertion.

উন্মূলন, উৎপাটন, to root up, eradicate, abolish.

উন্মেষ, জ্ঞান, a perception, sensation, discovery.

উপকথা, ইতিহাস, a story, tale, tattle.

উপকরণ, অপ্রধানাঙ্গ, সাধন, a thing superadded, as vegetables or sauce to food ; materials, means, help, supplemental oblation. [effect, result, success.

উপকার, আনুকূল্য, assistance, help, remedy, benefit, favour,

উপকারী, অনুকূল, সহকারী, helping, assisting, benevolent, beneficial.

উপকৃতি, সাহায্য, assistance, help, advantage, benefit.

উপক্রম, আরম্ভ, উদ্যোগ, commencement, attempt, prelude.

উপগম, আগমন, প্রণয়, approach, attachment, sexual intercourse.

উপগুরু, অপ্রধান গুরু, an inferior or under spiritual teacher.

উপচন, উচ্ছলন, to run or boil over, overflow, abound.

উপচয়, প্রচুরতা, plenty, abundance.

উপচার, ব্যবহার, ব্যবসায়, practice, custom, profession, service, practice of medicine, a bribe, imputation.

উপচিত, সঞ্চিত, বর্দ্ধিত, collected, increased, improved.

উপজন, ঘটন, জন্মন, to occur, be produced, accrue, acquire ; produced, occurred, acquired, become, &c.

উপজিহ্বা, অনিজিহ্বা, the epiglottis. [port.

উপজীবিকা, জীবনোপায়, বৃত্তি, livelihood, trade, means of sup-

উপজীবী, অবলম্বী, living upon or by, dependant on.

উপজীব্য, বৃত্তিদায়ক, অবলম্বনীয়, affording a livelihood, maintaining. [idea of a thing.

উপজ্ঞা, উপদেশবিনাজ্ঞান, আদ্যজ্ঞান, intuitive knowledge, first

উপড়ন, উৎপাটন, to root up, eradicate, abolish.

উপঢৌকন, উপহার, ভেট, a present to a superior, present of ceremony.

উপতন্ত্র, সূক্ষ্মসূত্র, a small fibre or thread.

উপতাপ, খেদ, বিপদ, রোগ, distress, misfortune, pain, disease, heat, hurry.

উপতারা, তারামণ্ডল, the iris (of the eye).

উপত্যকা, পাহাড়তল, land at the foot of a hill, a valley.

উপদল, ফুলপাত্র, the calyx of a flower.

উপদেবতা, ভূত, অপচ্ছায়া, a demi-god, phantom, apparition.

উপদেশ, শিক্ষা, মন্ত্রদান, instruction, advice, doctrine.

উপদেশী, } উপদেষ্টা, } শিক্ষক, গুরু, শিক্ষাগুরু, giving instruction, instructive, edifying; a teacher, preceptor, instructor.

উপদ্রব, বিপদ, উৎপাত, calamity, ruin, injury, oppression, tyranny, ravages, a portent.

উপদ্বীপ, পুলিন, টাপু, an island.

উপধান, বালিশ, a pillow, bolster.

উপধি, ভয়, ছলনা, চক্র, fear, dread, terror, fraud, a wheel.

উপনয়ন, উপবীতধারণ সংস্কার, investiture with the brahminical thread.

উপনাম, পদবী, a sirname, nick-name.

উপনিক্ষেপ, উপনিধি,—অর্পিতধন, a deposit of valuables with another person.

উপনিষদ্, বেদের শিরোভাগ, the philosophical partof the Vedas.

উপনিহিত, নিক্ষিপ্তধন, deposited in a sealed state.

উপনীত, উপবীতী, invested with the brahminical thread.

উপন্যাস, প্রস্তাবনা, উপকথা, an exordium, prologue, tale, story.

উপপতি, জার, গুপ্তপতি, a paramour, gallant.

উপপত্তি, নির্বাহ, সংস্কার, provision, maintenance, accomplishment of an object,, production, demonstration, supply, favour, assistance.

উপপদ, পদের নিকটবর্ত্তিশব্দ, a noun in apposition or conjunction.

উপপন্ন, সাধিত, সমাপ্ত, accomplished, completed, supplied, provided for.

উপপাতক, উপপাপ,—গোবধাদি, a crime of the third degree of guilt, venial crime.

উপপাদন, সাধন, to accomplish an object, prove, establish an argument.

উপপ্লব, সূর্য্যাদিগ্রহণ, an eclipse, portent, ascending node, assault, affray.

উপপ্লুত, গ্রস্ত, উপরক্ত, eclipsed, beheld (as a portent.)

উপবন, উদ্যান, a garden, artificial wilderness.

উপবাস, অনাহার, a religious or voluntary fast.

উপবিদ্য, শিল্পকারাদি, acquainted with inferior arts.

উপবিদ্যা, অপ্রধান বিদ্যা, শিল্পবিদ্যাদি, inferior art or science, as painting, dancing, legerdemain, handicrafts, &c.

উপবিষ্ট, আসনস্থ, seated, seated near.

উপবীত, পৈতা, the sacred brahminical thread.

উপবীতী, পৈতাপ্রাপ্ত, উপনীত, wearing the brahminical thread.

উপবেশন, বসন, নিকটবসন, to sit, sit near or by.

উপভোগ, বিষয়সুখাস্বাদন, worldly or sensual enjoyment, gratification, usufruct of another's property.

উপমা, উপমান,—দৃষ্টান্ত, সাদৃশ্য, a simile, metaphor, comparison, resemblance, picture, image, likeness.

উপমাতা, ধাত্রী, উপমাকর্ত্তা, a wet-nurse, nurse; a metaphrast, comparer. [&c.

উপমিত, উপমেত,—উৎপ্রেক্ষিত. compared, illustrated by simile,

উপমিতি, উপমা, সাদৃশ্য, similitude, comparison, resemblance, metaphor, picture, image.

উপযম, বিবাহ, marriage.

উপযাচন, নিবেদন, প্রার্থনা, a request, petition, prayer.

উপযুক্ত, যোগ্য, অর্হ, সমর্থ, fit, proper, suitable, qualified.

উপযোগ, সামর্থ্য, অনুকূলতা, আহার, suitableness, adaptation, qualification, propriety, food.

উপযোগী, অনুকূল, অর্হিত, useful, fit, suitable.

উপর, ঊর্দ্ধদেশ, the top, upper part, space above, height, upon, over, concerning.

উপরক্ত, বিপন্ন, পীড়িত, গ্রস্ত, seized by calamity, afflicted, pained, eclipsed; ascending node.

উপরত, বিরত, having ceased, ceased, stopped, desisted.

উপরতি, নিবৃত্তি, মহাহ্লাদ, cessation, stop, great enjoyment, pleasure.

উপরাউপরি, অনুক্রমে, in succession, successive, one over another. [affliction.

উপরাগ, সূর্য্যাদিগ্রহণ, বিপদ, eclipse of a planet, calamity,

উপরাম, বিরতি, শেষ, cessation, stop, a breaking off, end.

উপরি, ঊর্দ্ধে, অপর, ভূত, above, aloft, over; other, another; an evil spirit, aerial spirit, a god.

উপরিদৃষ্টি, ভূতের কুদৃষ্টি, the malignant glance of an evil spirit.
উপরিষ্টাৎ, ঊর্দ্ধহইতে, from above, above, up. [cerning.
উপরে, ঊর্দ্ধে, প্রতি, বিষয়ে, up, upwards, upon, against, con-
উপরোধ, গৌরব, সহায়তা, অনুগ্রহ, dignity, protection, defence, screen, support, favor, partiality, kindness.
উপর্য্যুপরি, ঊর্দ্ধোর্দ্ধ, higher and higher, in ascending series.
উপল, পাষাণ, a stone.
উপলক্ষ-ণ, বৃত্তি, অবলম্ব, অনুমান, a livelihood, support, prop, a synecdoche of part for the whole, or a quality for the subject; inference, deduction, clue.
উপলক্ষিত, অনুমিত, inferred, deduced. [quired.
উপলব্ধ, অনুভূত, প্রাপ্ত, guessed, understood, felt, gained, ac-
উপলব্ধি, জ্ঞান, অনুভব, প্রাপ্তি, perception, guess, surmise, the understanding; gain, acquisition.
উপশম, উপশান্তি,—রোগহ্রাস,স্বাস্থ্য, alleviation, abatement of pain or distress, relief, tranquillity, being a appeased.
উপষ্টম্ভ, আরম্ভ, commencement, beginning.
উপসংব্যান, অন্তরীয়, a lower garment.
উপসংহার, নাশ, শেষ, নিষ্পত্তি, destruction, an end, completion.
উপসর্গ, উপদ্রব, উপাধি, sudden calamity, portent, symptom of a disease, inseparable preposition.
উপসর্জ্জন, অপ্রধান, অনুগত, অমুখ্য, secondary, subordinate.
উপসর্প-ণ, আগমন, অনুবৃত্তি, an approach, access, a following.
উপসর্পক, অনুবর্ত্তী, নিকটগামী, a favourite; approximating.
উপস্ত্রী, চেমনী, a concubine. [arms; near, proximate.
উপস্থ, আবাচ্য, করকণা, organs of generation, the hip, the
উপস্থনিগ্রহ, কামদমন, continence, restraint of sensual appetite.
উপস্থাপন, নিকটে রাখন, দেখান, to place near, produce.
উপস্থান, নৈকট্য, nearness, proximity.
উপস্থিত, } আগত, প্রস্তুত, arrived, present, ready, near, oc-
উপস্থায়ী, } curred. [rent.
উপস্বত্ব, আয়, লাভ, উৎপন্ন, income, profit, proceeds, produce,
উপহত, মারা, প্রহৃত, smitten, struck. [present.
উপহার, উপঢৌকন, a present to a superior, complimentary
উপহাস, হাস্য, বিদ্রূপ, a smile, jest, ridicule, mockery.
উপাখ্যান, ইতিহাস, বৃত্তান্ত, a tale, story, narration.

উপাঙ্গ, অপ্রধান ভাগ, a subdivision, subordinate part.
উপাত্ত, সম্মত, স্বীকৃত, admitted, allowed in argument, acknowledged.
উপাদান, ইন্দ্রিয়দমন, সমাধান, কারণ, restraint of the senses, abstraction from outward objects, cause, motive. [able, admissible.
উপাদেয়, উত্তম, দাতব্য, excellent, presentable, recommend-
উপাধান, উপধান, বালিশ, a cushion, pillow. [meditation.
উপাধি, পদবী, বিশেষণ, ধর্ম্মচিন্তা, a title, attribute, affix; devout
উপাধ্যায়, অধ্যাপক, পণ্ডিত, an instructor, tutor, scholar; learned.
উপানৎ, পাদু, পাদুকা, a shoe, slipper.
উপান্ত, অন্তিক, near, proximate.
উপায়, সাধন, প্রতীকার, উপকার, উপার্জ্জন, means, method, expedient, remedy, stratagem, cure, approach, acquisition of wealth. [sent.
উপায়ন, উপহার, a present to a superior, complimentary pre-
উপায়ী, উপায়কারক, using stratagems, employing means or expedients, &c.
উপার্জ্জন, ধনসঞ্চয়ন, লাভ, accumulation of property, gain, acquisition, income, earnings.
উপাস, অনাহার, উপবাস, a voluntary fast.
উপাসক, অনুবর্ত্তী, আরাধক, an obsequious attendant, sycophant, flatterer, worshipper; propitiatory.
উপাসন-া, অনুবৃত্তি, আরাধনা, service, attendance on, respect, assiduity, petition, supplication, prayer, intercession, veneration, worship. [ous service.
উপাস্য, আরাধ্য, মান্য, placable, venerable, worthy of assidu-
উপাস্থি, কোমলাস্থি, a cartilage.
উপুড়, উল্টা, পতিত, reversed, prostrate. [slightly.
উপেক্ষণ, নামানন, অনাদরণ, to neglect, disregard, notice
উপেক্ষা, অনাদর, ত্যাগ, অবজ্ঞা, neglect, disregard, contempt, supercilious disregard. [with.
উপেত, সমীপাগত, আসন্ন, approached, come near, connected
উপোষণ, উপবাস, অনাহার, a religious fast, a fast.
উবন, প্রস্থান, অন্তর্দ্ধান, departure, disappearance; to depart, vanish, evaporate, dissolve.

উবরণ, উদ্বর্ত্তন, বিস্তর, to abound, be plentiful; abundant, plentiful.

উবরা, বিস্তর, আধিক্য, abundance, plenty. [vestige.

উৎস-ন, উথলন, অনুসন্ধান, a boiling over, search, enquiry,

উবী, উবু.—খাড়া, উচ্চ, উন্নত, erect, high, exalted, elevated.

উবুড়, উল্টা, পতিত, reversed, prostrate.

উব্জু, সরল, straight, erect, upright.

উচ্চ, ঊর্দ্ধ, খাড়া, high, erect; height.

উভ, উভয়,—দুইটা, মিলিত দুই, both.

উভয়তঃ, উভয়ে,—পরস্পর, দুইদিগে, mutually, in both respects, on both accounts, on both sides.

উভয়বিদ্যা, ঐহিক পারত্রিক দুই বিদ্যা, religious science and worldly affairs.

উভরণ, বোঝাই বহিষ্করণ, to unload a vessel.

উভরায়, উচ্চৈঃশব্দে, with a loud voice, with vociferation.

উমান, মাপন, measurement, the sounding of a depth.

উরঃ, বক্ষঃস্থল, the breast, bosom.

উরগ, পন্নগ, সর্প ইত্যাদি, a serpent, snake, worm, reptile; crawling, creeping.

উরশ্ছদ, বক্ষকবচ, a breast-plate, breast-armour, coat of mail.

উরু, বড়, মহৎ, জঙ্ঘা, great, ample, much; the thigh.

উরুজ, বৈশ্য, a vyse, a man of the third class.

ঊর্ণনাভ, মাকড়সা, মর্কট, a spider.

ঊর্ণা, মেষাদির লোম, wool, fur.

উর্বরা, ফলদ, সতেজভূমি, fertile; a rich soil.

উর্বী, পৃথিবী, the earth.

উর্ষণ, ঝরণ, to admit the rain, leak, as a roof, &c.

উলঙ্গ, বিবস্ত্র, naked. [descend.

উলন, রাখন, নামন, to set down, place on the ground,

উলূক, উল্লূক,—পেচক, পেঁচা, an owl.

উল্কা, উল্মুক, ধূমকেতু, a torch, firebrand, meteor.

উল্কামুখী, খিখি, খেঁক্‌শিয়ালা, a fox. [women.

উল্কি, স্ত্রীলোকের চিহ্নরাখা বিশেষ, a tattooing practised by

উল্টন, উপুড়বা বিপরীত করণ, to reverse, turn upside down.

উল্টা, প্রতিকূল, বিপরীত, reverse, reversed, contrary, upside downward.

উল্টাপাল্টা, ফেরেফারে, গোলমালে, confusedly, upside downwards, topsy turvey.

উল্টাপাল্টামি, ফেরফার, অন্যথাকরা, inversion, confusion, perversion.

উল্টাবুঝ, ভ্রম, কুবুদ্ধি, a misconception, misconstruction, perverted mind; misconceiving, blundering.

উল্লুল, গোলমাল, confusion, hurly burly; confusedly.

উল্মুক, উল্কা, আকাশাগ্নিপাত, a torch, meteor.

উল্লঙ্ঘন, অতিক্রমণ, বিরুদ্ধাচরণ, to trangress, violate, trespass, infringe, revolt.

উল্লম্ফ, উৎপ্লব, উৎক্রম, a jump, leap, bound, skip.

উল্লাস, হর্ষ, আনন্দ, joy, exultation, rapture, mirth, vivacity.

উলূক, উল্লূক,—পেচা, an owl.

উল্লেখ-ন, প্রস্তাব, উচ্চারণ, খনন, mention, relation, annunciation, utterance, enunciation, a description; a scratching or digging the ground.

উল্বণ, স্পষ্ট, পিত্তাদির বিকার, apparent, evident, clear; excess of bile, phlegm, &c.; a symptom.

উল্লসন, উল্লসিত হওন, to be elated, full of joy, transported.

উশীর, বেণার মূল, the root of the tattie grass.

উষঃ, উষস্, উষা,—প্রত্যূষ, the dawn, the morning.

উষণ, মরিচ, pepper.

উষিপিষি, ব্যস্ততা, চঞ্চলতা, uneasiness, restlessness, fidgets.

উস্কণ, উজ্জ্বলান, to repair or stir up a fire, trim a lamp, stir up or revive an old quarrel.

উষ্ট্র উট, a camel.

উষ্ণ, তপ্ত, গ্রীষ্ম, রাগী, hot, sultry, warm, passionate.

উষ্ণা, সিদ্ধধান্য, heated, sodden, (of rice to be husked).

উষ্ণিত, কোপী, ক্রুদ্ধ, angry, passionate, enraged, provoked.

উষ্ণীষ, পাগ, পাগড়ী, শিরোবস্ত্র, a turban.

উষ্মা, তাপ, কোপ, heat, ardour, warmth, rage, anger, cholér.

উষ্মান, কোপান, to anger, enrage.

উসন, ওষাণ, to supply the hopper of a mill or mortar, &c. with grain.

উহাড়, খাপ, আচ্ছাদন, a cover, a case.

ঊ.

ঊখলি, উদূখল, a mortar for husking rice.
ঊঢ়, বিবাহিত, married.
ঊত, বুনিত, কাপড়, বস্ত্র, woven; cloth.
ঊন, কিঞ্চিৎ ন্যূন, less, *affix:* one less than.
ঊনবুকা, অসাহসী, তেজোবিনা, spiritless, destitute of energy.
ঊয়ী, বল্মীক, রুই, a white ant.
ঊরু, ঊরুঃ,—জঙ্ঘা, the thigh.
ঊরুস্তম্ভ, জঙ্ঘাকোড়া, a painful and dangerous tumor on the thigh.
ঊর্ণনাভ, মাকড়সা, a spider.
ঊর্ণা, মেষাদির লোম, wool, fur, felt.
ঊর্দ্ধ, ঊর্দ্ধ্ব,—উচ্চ, দীর্ঘ, উন্নত, high, lofty, elevated.
ঊর্দ্ধক, উত্থিত, বায়ুরোগ, ascending, rising, (spoken of flatulency occasioning pain and giddiness).
ঊর্দ্ধজানু, ঊর্দ্ধজ্ঞু,—দীর্ঘজঙ্ঘ, sitting with his knees higher than his head.
ঊর্দ্ধবাহু, উন্নতহস্ত সন্ন্যাসী, with elevated hands, (spoken of devotees).
ঊর্দ্ধরেতা, কামত্যাগী, চতুর্থাশ্রমী, a saint living in perpetual chastity.
ঊর্দ্ধশ্বাস, বায়ুরেচন, শ্বাসরোগী, expiration, emission of the breath; asthmatical.
ঊর্বস্থি, জঙ্ঘাস্থি, the thigh bone.
ঊর্মি, বীচি, a wave, surge, billow.
ঊর্মিমৎ, বীচিমৎ, wavy, undulated, convoluted.
ঊষর, লবণভূমি, saline, salt (of land); saline earth, a salt and barren soil.
ঊষা, প্রত্যূষ, প্রাতঃ, the dawn, morning twilight.
ঊহ, ঊহা,—বিতর্ক, অধ্যাহরণ, investigation, reasoning, the supplying of an ellipsis.
ঊহ্য, অধ্যাহার্য্য, elliptical, requiring to be supplied or investigated.

ঋ.

ঋক্‌, প্রথমবেদ, the first of the four Vedas.
ঋক্ষ, ঋক,—ভালুক, a bear, the constellation Ursa Minor.

K

ঋচ্, মন্ত্র, a formula of praise or incantation, hymn to a god, invocation, a sentence of the Rig Ved.
ঋজু, সরল, straight, upright, sincere, honest.
ঋণ, ধার, a loan, debt.
ঋণগ্রহণ, ধার লওন, to borrow, receive a loan.
ঋণদান, ধার দেওন, a lending, giving in loan.
ঋণদায়ক, মহাজন, সাধু, উত্তমর্ণ, a lender, creditor; lending.
ঋণবান্, ঋণী,—খাতক, ঋণগ্রাহী, a debtor; indebted.
ঋণবিশিষ্ট, ঋণগ্রস্ত, indebted, loaded with debt.
ঋণময়, ধারেকেনা, ধারেবিক্রীত, purchased or sold on credit.
ঋত, যুক্ত, গ্রস্ত, *affix:* affected with.
ঋতু, বসন্তাদিকাল, কাল, রজস্, a season, the menstrual flux.
ঋতুমতী, রজস্বলা, menstruous, (woman.)
ঋতুরাজ, বসন্তকাল, the spring.
ঋতে, ব্যতিরেকে, ভিন্নে, except, besides.
ঋত্বিক্, ঋত্বিক্,—যাজক, পুরোহিত, a sacrificial priest, a domestic priest.
ঋদ্ধি, ধন, সম্পত্তি, riches, wealth, increase, prosperity.
ঋষভ, বৃষ, উত্তম, a bull; *affix:* excellent, great.
ঋষি, মুনি, a sage, a Muni.

এ.

এ, সম্মুখস্থিত, বুদ্ধিস্থিত, ইদং, this.
এঅবধি, ইতঃপর, এখানহইতে, এখনপর্য্যন্ত, henceforth, from here, till now.
এই, অগ্রাবস্থিত, this very, even this.
এইকারণ, তজ্জন্যে, for this reason, hence, therefore, wherefore.
এক্, অদ্বিতীয়, one.
একই, অনন্য, the same, the self-same.
এক্এক্, পৃথক২, ভিন্ন২, সমস্ত, one by one, severally, each, every one.
একক্ অদ্বিতীয়, অদ্বয়, সহায়শূন্য, one, single, alone.
এক্কর্ম্মকারক, তুল্যবিষয়ী, একাভিলাষী, of the same profession, doing the same; a competitor.
এক্কালীন, সমকালজাত, সমকালীন, coeval, simultaneous, cotemporaneous.
এক্গুঁয়া, অবাধ্য, self-willed, obstinate, headstrong, perverse.
এক্ঘরিয়া, অমিলাপী, উদাসী, unsocial, recluse, secluded, singular.

এক্চালা, ঝোপড়ী, কুটীর, a shed. [attached.
এক্চিত্ত, অনন্যমনাঃ, আবিষ্ট, unanimous, attentive, sedulous,
এক্চেটিয়া, মহাজন, a monopolizer, monopolist.
এক্জামিনপ্রত, সহলগ্নক, a joint bondsman. [cessantly.
এক্ঝাই, বারম্বার, পুনঃ২, frequently, repeatedly, often, in-
এক্টা, কেবল এক, সমুদায় এক, one, an entire one.
এক্টী, একমাত্র, one, only one, merely one.
এক্টু, একটুক, একটুকি,—অল্প, কিঞ্চিৎ, small, one, a little.
এক্ঠাঁই, একত্র, together, in one body or association.
এক্তন্ত্রী, একাভিলাষী, বিপক্ষ, a rival, opponent, competitor; having the same object.
এক্তন্ত্রী, একপ্রভুক, একতন্ত্রযুক্ত, subject to one lord, having one string.
একতম, অনেকের মধ্যে এক, অন্যতম, one of many.
একতর, দুয়ের মধ্যে এক, অন্যতর, one of two, either.
একতা, একত্ব,—ঐক্য, অনন্যতা, মিলন, oneness, sameness, union, concurrence. [dance.
একতাল, সমতাল, বাদ্যযন্ত্রের মিল harmony, unison in song and
একতুম্বী, তম্বুর, বীণা, having a single gourd (as lutes, &c.)
একত্র, একস্থানে, মিলিত, in one place, collectedly, together.
একদা, এককালে, once, at once. [dency.
এক্দিক্, সমদিক্, সমসরল, having the same direction or ten-
একধা, কেবল এক, একাকী, single, simple.
এক্নামা, স্বনামক, a namesake; having the same name.
এক্পাটা, ওড়নী, the Hindoo outer garment.
এক্পাশ্, এক্পাশীয়া,—হেলা, কাইত, inclined to one side, aslant, on one side. [ception.
এক্পেট, একপরামর্শ, united in one plan of collusion or de-
এক্প্রকার, সমান, তুল্য, uniform, of the same kind.
এক্প্রভুক, এক্তন্ত্রী, এক্রাজাধীন, subject to one lord, monarchical.
এক্প্রভুত্ব, এক্রাজত্ব, একাধিপত্য, monarchy. [stinate, firm.
এক্বাগিয়া, স্বমতাবলম্বী, অবাধ্য, dogmatical, pertinacious, ob-
এক্বার, একদা, once. [ment, awhile.
এক্বিন্দু, কণা, অল্প, কিঞ্চিৎকাল, a single drop, a little, a mo-
এক্বিষয়ী, একাভিলাষী, তুল্যব্যাপারী, সহকারী, having the same object, of the same profession; a rival, coadjutor.

একভক্ত, একাহারী, eating but one meal a day.
একযোট, সঙ্গ, সমভিব্যাহার, সঞ্চয়, an association or body of persons, a collection of things.
একযোনি, সহোদর, সমানোৎপত্তিক, of the same mother, of one origin or source.
একরূপ, সদৃশ, তুল্য, সমান, similar, like, same, resembling.
একরোখা, অতিরোষী, কোপান্বিত, blindly impelled by rage, obstinate. [private.
একল, একলা,—একাকী, নিচু, বিরল, alone, single, solitary,
একলাই, উড়নী, a sheet, wrapper, outer garment.
একলাদুকলা, দুইএক, one or two together, a few.
একসঙ্গী, সংসৃষ্ট, সহবাসী, united, collected, compact, keeping in company.
একহারা, অদ্বয়, কেবল এক, single, one.
একা, একাকী,—অদ্বিতীয়, সহায়শূন্য, বিরল, alone, single, solitary.
একাগ্র, অভিনিবিষ্ট, অনন্যমনাঃ, মনোযুক্ত, devoted to one pursuit, closely attentive; a subdivided line.
একাগ্রতা, অভিনিবেশ, devotedness to or pursuit of one object, close attention.
একাতপত্র, সম্রাট, মহারাজ, widely governing, ruling the earth.
একাত্মতা, তত্ত্ব, the unity of spiritual essence, the doctrine of one universal Spirit. [regular series.
একাদিক্রম, আনুপূর্বিক, নিরন্তর, successive, uninterrupted, in
একাদোকা, দুইএক, a few, one or two, one or two together.
একাধিপতি, সম্রাট, অধিরাজ, a monarch, sovereign.
একানিয়া, একাকী, single, only.
একান্ত, অত্যন্ত, নির্জন, অবশ্য, excessive, extreme, effectual, leading to one result, private, solitary, uninhabited; certainly.
একান্তরা, এক দিন ব্যবধানে ভোজন করা, the eating of only one meal in two days, *i. e.* every other day.
একান্ন, সহভোজী, একাহারী, a messmate; living on the same food.
একাবয়ব, সমানাকৃতি, তুল্য, having the same parts, uniform, similar, alike. [neral inundation.
একার্ণব, মেলা, সমাগম, জলপ্লাবন, a promiscuous multitude, ge-
একার্থ, তুল্যার্থ, having the same meaning or intent.

একাহ, একদিন, একদিনজীবী কীট, a singlé day; ephemeral.

ঐক, একী,—তুল্য, সমান, অনন্য, alike, same, single, together.

একুড়্যা, বিরল, অমিলাপী, solitary, unsocial, odd, single.

একুন, মোট, a sum, a total, a whole.

একেএকে, ক্রমশঃ, ক্রমে২, one by one, alternately, singly.

একেলা, অদ্বয়, একাকী, alone, single, solitary, private.

একেশ্বর, সহায়শূন্য, স্বাধীন, alone, dependent on one's self alone.

একোদ্দিষ্ট, অনন্যার্থ, performed for the same person or object.

একোপম, সদৃশ, তুল্য, similar, analagous.

এক্ষণে, সম্প্রতি, অবিলম্বে, now, instantly, this instant.

এখন, এখনি,—সম্প্রতি, অধুনা, now, immediately.

এখান, এইস্থান, this place, here.

এজন্যে, এইনিমিত্ত, hence, therefore, wherefore.

এটে, কদলির মূল, the thick root of the plantain tree.

এড়, বধির, কালা, deaf.

এড়ন, জালক্ষেপণ, ছাড়ান, বাঁচন, to cast a net, loosen, liberate, release, relinquish, fly off, escape.

এড়মূক, শ্রবণবাগিন্দ্রিয়হীন, deaf and dumb. [approbation.

এড়াকাণি, অস্বীকার, a turning away the ear in refusal; dis-

এড়াটিয়া, সমল, মন্দ, অধম, filthy, loathsome, abominable, reprobate.

এণ, হরিণ, a deer.

এত, হত, এপর্য্যন্ত, so much, so long, so many, so.

এতজ্জ, এতদ্ধেতুক, এতজ্জনিত, arising from or produced by this.

এতৎ, এই, *(in composition only :)* this, of this, his.

এতৎকাল, উপস্থিতকাল, সম্প্রতি, এখন, the present time, this time, now.

এতৎকালীন, আধুনিক, এইসময়ের, belonging to this time.

এতৎক্ষণাৎ, এইঅবধি, অব্যাজে, from this instant, henceforth, immediately.

এতৎক্ষণে, এখন, সম্প্রতি, now, at this instant.

এতত্তুল্য, এইপ্রকার, সদৃশ, equal to or like this, similar.

এতৎসম, এতাদৃশ, সেইরূপ, similar to or like this.

এতদন্তর, এই ব্যতিরেকে, besides this.

এতদবধি, এপর্য্যন্ত, ইতি, so far, from or to this.

এতদা, এখন, সম্প্রতি, now, at this time.
এতদাদি, যাহার আদি এই, beginning with this.
এতদাদিতদন্ত, আদ্যন্ত সমুদায় বিবরণ, all the circumstances of any thing from beginning to end.
এতদানীং, এখন, now, at this time. [person.
এতদিতর, এতদ্ভিন্ন, অন্য, another than or different from this
এতদুত্তম, ইহাহইতে ভাল, more excellent than this.
এতদেব, এই, অনন্য, স্বরূপ, the very same, same, identical.
এতদ্গত, ইহাগত, ইহাযুক্ত, found or existing in this, attached to this.
এতদ্ধেতুক, এহেতুক, এইজন্যে, এপ্রযুক্ত, for this cause, therefore.
এতদ্বৎ, ঈদৃশ, তুল্য, like or resembling this.
এতদ্বিশিষ্ট, ইহাপ্রাপ্ত, possessed of this. [this.
এতদ্ভিন্ন, ইহাব্যতিরেক, besides this, separate or distinct from
এতন্ন, ইহা নয়, এমন নয়, not this, not so; no.
এতন্মনাঃ, এবম্প্রকারমনাঃ, thus minded, thus disposed.
এতন্মাত্র, ইহামাত্র, merely this, only this.
এতর্হি, এখন, এমন, now, at present, thus.
এতল্লোক, ইহলোক, সেই ব্যক্তি, this world, this man, this people.
এতাদৃক্, এতাদৃশ,—তুল্য, ঈদৃক্, এইপ্রকার, similar, such, like; thus.
এতাবৎ, এত, এপর্য্যন্ত, ইতি, thus much, thus far, so much, so many.
এতাবতা, এইপ্রকারে, এইহেতুক, thus, by this means, by this.
এতাবন্মাত্র, এই কেবল, simply this, merely this.
এতাবান্, এতাদৃশ, তুল্য, such, similar.
এতেক, এত, এপর্য্যন্ত, so many, so much, so long.
এথা, এখানে, এস্থানে, অত্র, here.
এনিমিত্ত, এইকারণ, for this cause, on this account, wherefore.
এপর্য্যন্ত, এইঅবধি, thus far, hitherto, till now, still, yet.
এপ্রযুক্ত, এনিমিত্ত, therefore, wherefore, hence, on this account, because.
এব, অবধার্য্য বোধক শব্দ, নিশ্চিত, (*emphatic affix:*) even, indeed.
এবং, আর, এইপ্রকার, অধিকন্তু, and, also, likewise, moreover.
এবম্প্রকার, এবম্বিধ, এবম্ভূত,—ঈদৃশ, এইপ্রকার, such, such like, of this sort.
এবার, এসময়, this time, this once.

এবে, এখন, ইদানী, now, at this time.
এমত, এমন, এমনি,—ঈদৃশ, thus, such.
এমতে, এমনে, এমনি,—এপ্রকারে, thus, so, in this manner.
এরণ্ড, ভেরেণ্ডা বৃক্ষ, the castor shrub.
এরূপ, ঈদৃশ, এমন, such, thus, so.
এলা, এলাইচ, এলাচী, the cardamum plant, cardamums.
এলুয়া, খোলা, অসংলগ্ন, আলসিয়া, loose, unconnected, random, confused, discomposed, trifling, unengaged, idle.
এলুয়ান, খোলন, to untie, loosen, disengage.
এষ, এই, this.
এহেতুক, এইজন্যে, এইকারণ, on this account, hence.

ঐ.

ঐ, অই, কিঞ্চিৎ দূরস্থিত বস্তু, that, yon, yonder.
ঐকমত্য, সম্মতি, ঐক্য, সমানতা, a confederacy, conspiracy, agreement, sameness, similarity.
ঐকাগ্র্য, স্থৈর্য্য, অভিনিবেশ, মনোযোগ, consistency, devotedness to one object.
ঐকান্তিক, নিতান্ত, অত্যন্ত, complete, entire, excessive, much, relating to one thing.
ঐকাহিক, একদিনান্তর জ্বর, tertian, (fever and ague).
ঐক্য, একতা, মিলন, বন্ধুতা, একুন, unity, oneness, amity, reconciliation, union, agreement, total, aggregate.
ঐচ্ছিক, ইচ্ছাপূর্ব্বক, voluntary, wilful.
ঐতিহ্য, ইতিহ, পারম্পর্য্যোপদেশ, traditional knowledge, tradition.
ঐন্দ্রজালিক, মায়ী, মায়াযুক্ত, magical, pertaining to legerdemain.
ঐন্দ্রিয়ক, ইন্দ্রিয়সম্বন্ধীয়, প্রত্যক্ষ, ইন্দ্রিয়গোচর, belonging to the organs of sense, evident to the senses, perceptible.
ঐমত, ঐপ্রকার, such; so, in that manner.
ঐরাবত, ইন্দ্রের হস্তী, প্রকাণ্ড, Indra's elephant; very large, monstrously large, huge.
ঐরি. শত্রু, বিপক্ষ, an enemy, opponent, adversary.
ঐশ্বর, দৈব, ঈশ্বরসম্বন্ধীয়, divine, relating to God.

ঐশ্বর্য্য, গৌরব, মহত্ত্ব, সম্পত্তি, grandeur, state, glory, pomp, majesty, greatness, wealth. [present world.
ঐহিক, ইহলোকের, ইহকালীন, pertaining to this life or the

ও.

ও, আর, অপি, এবং; উনি, and, too, also; he, that.
ওআক, ওআকবক,—দ্রোণকাক্, the night raven or common crow.
ওআড়, বালিশের উয়াড়, a pillow-case. [Trinity.
ওঁ, প্রণব, the sacred mystical expression of the Hindoo
ওঁক্, বৃষগর্জ্জনি, the grumbling or growling of a bull.
ওঁচলা, অবকর, জঞ্জাল, sweepings, leavings, dirt, refuse.
ওঁছা, উচ্ছিষ্ট, ত্যক্ত, refuse, rejected, thrown away, cast out.
ওক, ওকস্—গৃহ, আশ্রয়, a house, residence, place, asylum, haunt.
ওঘ, সমূহ, স্রোত, জলবেগ, তালবেগ, a multitude, collection, a torrent, velocity of a stream, quick time in music.
ওঙ্কার, প্রণব, the mystic letter ওঁ.
ওজস্, প্রাণ, বল, দীপ্তি, প্রকাশ, বিষম সঙ্খ্যা, life, vitality, strength, light, manifestation, odd (number), uneven, unequal.
ওঝা, অহিতুণ্ডিক, বিষবৈদ্য, a snake-catcher, a curer of the bites of snakes by charms, a charmer, exorcist.
ওঝালি, বিষবৈদ্যকর্ম্ম, the profession of a snake-catcher or charmer. [packthread, a girth.
ওটার, ভাঁড়া, পাটার, the seam of mats or sacks joined with
ওঠন, উত্থন, আরোহণ, সুস্থ হওন, to rise up, ascend, recover from sickness, come out of disgrace or distress.
ওৎ, ওতপ্রোত,—আড়াল, a screen, ambush, ambuscade.
ওতু, বিড়াল, a cat. [freaks of a cat.
ওতুপুত, উল্ট, অক্রমযুক্ত, confused, irregular, resembling the
ওতে, আড়ালে, privately, clandestincly.
ওথা, ওখানে, তত্র, there, therein, in that place.

ওদন, অন্ন, boiled rice, food.
ওদিগে, ওখানে, তথায়, thither, on that side, yonder.
ওদেষ্ট, গায়কের অশ্রাব্য স্বর. unmusical, harsh, disagreeable; (spoken of the voice.)
ওদো, আর্দ্র. ভিজা, damp, moist, wet and soft.
ওপার, নদির ওদিগ, পার, the further bank of a river, the further side of any thing; over, across.
ওম্, প্রণব, the mystic syllable ওঁ.
ওর, শেষ, সীমা, an end, boundary. [vicious.
ওরম্বা, সাহসী, দুরন্ত, dauntless, bold, daring, irresistible,
ওলন, অবরোহণ, উত্তরণ, নামন, to dismount, alight, descend from; a plumb-line.
ওলান, নামান, উত্তারণ, মলবর্জন, to cause to descend, land from a ship, launch a vessel, evacuate by stool.
ওলাউঠা, নামাউঠা, উদরভঙ্গ, double evacuation, spasmodic cholera. [combustion.
ওষ, শিশির, হিম, দাহ, frost, dew, snow, cold, a burning,
ওষধি, বর্ষজীবীবৃক্ষ, কলা ধান্যাদি, an annual or deciduous plant, herbaceous plant.
ওষধীশ, চন্দ্র, the moon.
ওহাণ, উনন, to serve a mill or mortar with grist. [lamp.
ওকাণ, উস্কন, জ্বালান, to repair a fire, raise the wick of a
ওষ্ঠ, উপরের ঠোঁট, the upper lip, a lip.
ওষ্ঠাগত, শরীরত্যাগকরণোদ্যত, (of the soul) ready to depart.
ওষ্ঠাধর, উভয় ওষ্ঠ, the lips, (upper and lower).
ওষ্ঠ্য, ওষ্ঠোচ্চারিত বর্ণ, labial, uttered from the lips.
ওসার, চৌড়া, চৌড়াই, wide; width.
ওসারত, চৌড়া, প্রশস্ত, broad, wide.
ওহা, সঞ্চয়ন, উপার্জন, a hoarding up.
ওহানে, তত্র, ওখানে, there, thither.

ঔ.

ঔচিত্য, যোগ্যতা, উপযুক্ততা, fitness, suitableness, propriety, necessity.
ঔচ্চ, উর্দ্ধতা, height, elevation.

ঔডুম্বর, তাম্রময়, যজ্ঞডুম্বরকাষ্ঠ নির্ম্মিত, made of copper, made of fig-wood; a kind of leprosy.
ঔৎকট্য, দুঃসহ্যতা, আতিশয্য, কোপ, মত্ততা, disagreeableness, troublesomeness, excessiveness, madness, fury, drunkenness.
ঔৎকর্ষ্য, শ্রেষ্ঠত্ব, excellency, perfection, pleasantness.
ঔত্বর, মোটা, স্থূল, gross.
ঔৎপাতিক, উপদ্রবান্বিত, উপদ্রবী, portentous, prodigious, astonishing, outrageous.
ঔৎসর্গিক, যাজ্ঞিক, স্বাভাবিক, pertaining to an oblation, natural.
ঔৎসুক্য, প্রার্থর্য্য, উৎসাহ, ব্যাকুলতা, zeal, zealous exertion, ardor, anxiety, perturbation, regret.
ঔদরিক, উদরম্ভরি, পেটুক, gluttonous, selfishly voracious.
ঔদশ্বিত, জলমিশ্রিত ঘোল, buttermilk and water.
ঔদার্য্য, দাতৃত্ব, গৌরব, অকাপট্য, munificence, liberality, grandeur, nobleness of mind, candour, ingenuousness.
ঔদাস্য, ঔদাসীন্য,—সংসর্গত্যাগ, বিষয়ে বিরাগ, solitude, loneliness, misanthropy, indifference.
ঔদ্ধত্য, দুরন্তা, দৌরাত্ম্য, violence, oppression, tumult.
ঔদ্বাহিক, বৈবাহিক দান, শুল্ক, a marriage gift to a woman.
ঔপনায়িক, উপনয়ন সম্বন্ধীয়, উপনয়ন যোগ্য, pertaining to or fit to be invested with the sacred thread.
ঔপনিধিক, সমর্পিত ধন বিষয়ক, pertaining to a deposit, deposited.
ঔপম্য, দৃষ্টান্ত, সাদৃশ্য, a comparison, resemblance.
ঔপাধিক, বৈশেষিক, pertaining to attributes or properties.
ঔপায়িক, ন্যায্য, উচিত, expedient, right, fit, proper.
ঔরস, ঔরস্য,—স্বদেহজাত, legitimate, lawfully begotten.
ঔর্দ্ধদেহিক, প্রেতক্রিয়া, obsequies, funeral rites, commemorative acts.
ঔর্ব, বাড়বানল, submarine fire.
ঔল্বণ্য, অতিশয়, অধিক, excessive, superabundant; superabundance, excess.
ঔষধ, অগদ, রোগনাশক দ্রব্য, a medicine, drug, remedy.
ঔষধীয়, ঔষধ বিষয়ক, medicinal, pertaining to medicine.
ঔষ্ণ্য, তাপ, ঔৎসুক্য, heat, ardour.
ঔষ্ণাস্থূক, গ্রীষ্মাগ্রীষ্ম, temperature, climate.
ঔষ্ট্রক, উষ্ট্রের সমূহ, a herd of camels.

ক.

ক, জল, মস্তক, সূর্য্য, ব্রহ্মা, water, the head, the sun, Brahmá.

কএক, কিয়ৎ, কিঞ্চিৎ, কোন, some, a few, several.

কংস, কাঁসা, মিশ্রিতধাতু বিশেষ, পানপাত্র, bell-metal, white copper, brass. a drinking vessel.

কংসবণিক, কাঁসারী, পিত্তলকার, a brazier.

কঃ, কে, কি, who? what?

কক্, ককক্,—খিল্‌খিল্, অবকূজন, a giggling, cackling noise, as in laughter or crying.

ককান, খিক্‌খিক্-ক, অবক্রন্দন, to cackle, groan, moan, cry bitterly and noisily.

ককানি, খিক্‌খিক্ করা, ফুকরণি, a cackling, sobbing, convulsed crying.

ককুৎ, গরুর ঝুঁটী, the hump of a bull or ox.

ককুদ, ছত্রাদি রাজচিহ্ন, শৃঙ্গ, *id*: an ensign of royalty, as the royal umbrella &c. the peak of a mountain.

ককুভ, দিক্, a point of the compass, quarter, space, region.

কক্ষ, বাহমূল, পার্শ্বদেশ, কচ্ছ, the arm-pit, side, flank, the end of the garment tucked in at the waist.

কক্ষা, কক্ষ্যা,—কটিবন্ধনী, রজ্জু, হস্তীবন্ধন, কুঠরী, a woman's zone or girdle, a rope, the tie of an elephant, an apartment, room, enclosure or division of a court-yard.

কখন, কোন সময়ে, when? at any time, ever, sometimes.

কখন২, কখনও,—মধ্যে২, sometimes, occasionally, now and then.

কখাদি, কখ,—বর্ণমালা, the alphabet.

কঙ্ক, বক, ক্রৌঞ্চ, a heron.

কঙ্কণ, করভূষণ, a bracelet, armlet, small bell.

কঙ্কতিকা, চিরুণী, a hair-comb.

কঙ্কর, কর্কর, কুকরই, coarse sand, gravel, grit, pebbles.

কঙ্কাল, কটিদেশ, সংঘ, the waist, the loins, a skeleton.

কঙ্গালী, দরিদ্র, নির্ধন, poor, necessitous, needy.

কঙ্গালপনা, নৈর্ধন্য, দরিদ্রতা, poverty. penury, want.

কচ, চুল, কেশ, ক্ষতচিহ্ন, the hair, hair, a cicatrice, dried sore.

কচড়া, কাছী. দড়া, রজ্জু, a cable, rope, halter, tether.
কচন, সন্ধিচ্যুত হ-, to be dislocated, slip out of place.
কচর্কচর্, পক্ষির ধ্বনি, the chirp of the mina; a supping sound in eating. [coarse powder.
কচা, সন্ধিচ্যুত, স্তম্ভ, দণ্ড, a dislocation, a stake, staff, grit,
কচান, গজান, মুঞ্জরণ, to shoot forth, to bud.
কচাল, বিবাদ, ঝকড়া. বক্বকানি, a dispute, murmuring, haggling at a bargain.
কচি, কোমল, নবীন. delicate, tender, young.
কচুরী, পিষ্টক বিশেষ. লুচি, a sort of cake. [rustling.
কচ্কচ্. বক্বকানি. a murmuring, grumbling, clipping sound,
কচ্কচিয়া. তৃণ বিশেষ, a coarse grass used in common mats.
কচ্কচী, ঝকড়া, বক্বকানি, a brawl, contention, quarrel, grumbling, murmur.
কচ্ছ, কূল, জোল, পরিহিত বস্ত্রের শেষভাগ, a shore, a marsh, the end of a garment tucked in at the waist, the Toon tree.
কচ্ছপ, কূর্ম্ম, a tortoise, a turtle.
কচ্ছূ, চুল্কানী, কণ্ডু, the itch, a scab.
কচ্টন, কচ্টান,—ছানন, to knead.
কচ্যান, মুকুলোদ্গম, মুঞ্জরণ, the budding of a tree, to bud.
কচ্লন, ধোওন, ক্ষালন, to rub clothes &c. in washing, to rinse.
কছহরী, কছারী.—ব্যবস্থান, a court of law or justice, public office. [eye-paint.
কজ্জলী, কজ্জল,— অঞ্জন, black pigment, lead ore, lamp black,
কঞ্চী, বাঁশের শাখা, ছড়ী, a twig or branch of bamboo.
কঞ্চু, সর্পের খোলস, the skin or slough of a snake.
কঞ্চুক, কবচ, অঙ্গরাখা, বস্ত্র, *id:* armour, mail, a bodice or jacket, short drawers. a garment.
কঞ্চুকাল, কালসর্প, the black cobra de capello.
কঞ্চুলিকা, কাঁচলি. অঙ্গরাখা, a woman's bodice or jacket.
কঞ্জর, ব্রহ্মা, সূর্য্য, জঠর, রজ্জু, Brahma, the sun, the belly, a rope maker.
কট্, কাঁকালি, হস্তির গণ্ড, চাঁচ, আড়াল, the hip, the loins, the temples of an elephant, a treaty, bond, fixed period, a mat, a screen.

কট, কটাৎ,—অকস্মাৎ, suddenly, unexpectedly, hastily.
কটক, চক্র, বলয়, নগর, নিতম্ব, a circle, bracelet, ring, city, metropolis, camp, brow of a hill, table land on a mountain.
কটন, কটান,—শুকন, to fade, wither, become flaccid, sallow or wan.
কটবেল, কপিত্থ, the wood-apple.
কটা, কত, কতটা, how many? how much?
কটাক্ষ, দৃষ্টিপাৎ, a glance, side glance, leer, ogling look.
কটাল, ম্লানি, ম্লান, শুষ্ক, a fading, decaying; faded, withered; the spring tides.
কটাস্, অকস্মাৎ, হঠাৎ, unexpectedly, hastily, suddenly.
কটাহ, কড়া, নরক, কূর্ম্মপৃষ্ঠ, a caldron, pan, the infernal region, a tortoise-shell, a young buffalo.
কটি, কটী, কটিতট,—কাঁকালি, the loins, hip, waist.
কটিপ্রোথ, নিতম্ব, the buttocks or posteriors.
কটিয়া, শক্ত, দুঃসহ, অনার্য্য, hard, disagreeable, inferior in quality.
কটু, তীব্র, কঠিন, দুর্গন্ধ, দুঃসহ, মৎসর, pungent, hot (in taste), fierce, severe, harsh, impetuous, fragrant, ill-scented, disagreeable, envious, abusive, scurrilous.
কটুকাটব্য, কদুক্তি, দুর্ব্বাক্য, abusive or scurrilous language.
কটুত্ব, তীক্ষ্ণতা, pungency, heat (as of pepper).
কটোরা, পানপাত্র, a cup, drinking vessel.
কট্‌কট্, কটুকটানি,—কামড়ানি, অস্বন, a throbbing pain, a clattering sound.
কট্‌কটিয়া, খড়্‌খড়ানিয়া, clattering, croaking, making a disagreeable noise.
কট্‌কিনা, কঠিনতা, difficulty, severity, roughness, harshness, an under-farming.
কট্টার, কাটার, যমধার, a dagger, poignard.
কঠিন, কঠোর,—দৃঢ়, কর্কশ, কৃপাহীন, দুর্জ্জেয়, hard, rigid, solid, harsh, severe, austere, cruel, unfeeling, difficult, abstruse.
কড়, কটক, করভূষণ, a kind of bracelet.
কড়কচ, সামুদ্রিক লবণ, a fine sea salt obtained by evaporation.
কড়কন-আন, ক্ষতমুদন বা শুকন, কচান, to heal, close or cicatrize as a wound or sore, to bud as a tree.

কড়কা, কড়ুম,—কল, অঙ্কুর, সন্তান, বীজ, a scion, sucker, stalk, descendant, heir, cause or original; a rattle.
কড়ম্ব শাকের ডাঁটা, অগ্র, the stalk of a potherb, end, point.
কড়রা, শক্ত, hard, compact as a cement, &c.
কড়া, কটক, শৃঙ্খল, হাঁড়ী, a ring, chain, link, saucepan, a straw, a corn on the foot, a cowry.
কড়াং, আয়াসে, with effort, gratingly.
কড়ামিয়া, কাঁচা গণনা, a reckoning by cowries, keeping accounts in cowries. [composition.
কড়ার, পিঙ্গলবর্ণ, গ্রন্থক, tawny, dark-coloured; cement,
কড়ি, কপর্দ্দক, কাষ্ঠ, a cowry, wood, firewood, a beam, a ring.
কড়িকান, শুকন, কড়কান, to heal, begin to heal as a sore.
কড়িকাঠ, কড়িয়া,—আড়কাঠ, আড়া, a beam in a building.
কড়িকুষ্টা, কড়িচশুালস্য,—লোভী, কৃপণ, covetous, niggardly, venal.
কড়িয়াল, ধনী, অর্থবান্, rich, wealthy.
কড়িয়ালী, বল্গা, মুখস্, the bit of a bridle. [in taste.
কড়ুবা, কটু, তিক্ত, কুরস, pungent, rancid, bitter, disagreeable
কড়্কড়্, কটুশব্দ, অবস্বন, any harsh, rattling or grating noise.
কড়্কড়ী, কোন পাত্রেতে শুষ্কান্নাদি, a grittiness or substance dried on the sides of a vessel. [bone &c.
কড়্মড়্, কঠিন দ্রব্য চর্ব্বণশব্দ, the sound of biting or gnawing a
কণ, জীরা, অণু, বীজমণি, বীণাদির স্বর, cummin seed, an atom, particle, eye of a seed, facet or spark of a gem, note of a stringed instrument. [long pepper.
কণা, অণু, বিন্দু, পিপ্পল, a particle, spark, drop, gravel, grit,
কণাদ, স্বর্ণকার, a goldsmith; a certain Muni.
কণি, নখকোণ, the corners of the nails, the growing over of the nails at the sides.
কণিকা, লেশ, বিন্দু, অণু, a particle, grain, drop, atom.
কণুই, কফোণি, বাহুর অধোগ্রন্থি, the elbow. [hollow vessel.
কণ্কণিয়া, ঠণ্ঠনিয়া, ringing, sounding as an instrument or
কণ্টক, কাঁটা, সূচ্যগ্র, লোমাঞ্চ, ক্ষুদ্রশত্রু, দুঃখজনক, a thorn, prickle, fish-bone, the point of a pin or needle, a skewer, horripilation through fear or joy, a paltry foe, any cause of pain or trouble.

কণ্টকিকীট, শুঁয়াপোকা বিশেষ, a hairy caterpillar.
কণ্টকিফল, কণ্টাফল,—কাঁঠালবৃক্ষ, the jack-fruit tree.
কণ্টকভুক্, উষ্ট্র, উট, a camel.
কণ্ঠ, গলদেশ, গলা, the throat.
কণ্ঠভূষা, কণ্ঠমালা,—হার, মালা ইত্যাদি, a necklace, collar.
কণ্ঠা, গল, মৎস্যের কাণকুয়া, the neck above the collar-bone, the gills of fish.
কণ্ঠাগত, শরীরত্যাগকরণোদ্যত, ওষ্ঠাগত, ready to depart, (spoken of the soul of one expiring).
কণ্ঠিধারী, মাল্যবান্, গল, wearing a necklace: the neck.
কণ্ঠী, কণ্ঠ্য, হার, belonging to the throat, guttural; a necklace.
কণ্ঠ্য, কণ্ঠ,—কণ্ঠহইতে উচ্চারিত বর্ণ, guttural, belonging to [the throat.
কণ্ডন, ধান্যঝাড়ন, কাঁড়ন, to cleanse rice from its husk.
কণ্ডূ, কণ্ডূয়া—কচ্ছু, চুল্‌কনা, the itch, a pimple, eruption.
কণ্ডূয়ন, চুল্‌কান, কণ্ডুর নিঘর্ষণ, an itching; to itch, to scratch.
কণ্ডূয়মান, চুল্‌কনাগ্রস্ত, চুল্‌কানিয়া, scratching, rubbing, itching.
কণ্ডূয়িত, ঘর্ষিত, scratched, rubbed.
কত, কতি,—পরিমাণ এবং সংখ্যা জিজ্ঞাসা, কিয়ৎ, how much? how [many?
কতক, কিঞ্চিৎ, কএক, কিছু, some, a few.
কতক্ষণ, কিপর্য্যন্ত, how long?
কতরণ, ভেড়ার লোম কাটন, কর্ত্তন, to shear sheep, cut, clip, trim, [dress.
কতিপয়. কতগুলি, how many?
কতেক, কএক, কিঞ্চিৎ, a few, somewhat.
কৎকৎ, অনুতাপ, মনোদুঃখ, regret, remorse, palpitation of heart, misgiving of mind.
কথং, কেন, কিপ্রকার, why? how?
কথক, বক্তা, কিঞ্চিৎ, a speaker, narrator, reciter; some, [somewhat.
কথন, বলন, বিবরণ, to speak, utter, recount, mention, say.
কথা, উক্তি, বাক্য, প্রসঙ্গ, ভাষা, a word, speech, sentence, message, passage of a book, story, language.
কথা, কথায়,—কোনস্থানে, where? in what place?
কথাবার্ত্তা, কথোপকথন, সমাচার, conversation, colloquial intercourse, news.
কথাসচিব, প্রতিবাদী, মন্ত্রণাদাতা, a pleader, barrister, solicitor, [attorney.
কথাসঞ্চার, জনশ্রুতি, জনরব, spread of a report, report, fame.

কথোপকথন, পরস্পর আলাপ, conversation, conferenee, discourse, dialogue.

কদক্ষর, নিন্দিত লিপি, a scrawl, bad writing, ill-formed letters.

কদমা, মিষ্টান্ন বিশেষ, a kind of sweetmeat.

কদম্বক, সঙ্ঘট, সমূহ, সঞ্চয়, a crowd, multitude, collection.

কদর্য্য, কৃপণ, নিন্দিত মন্দ, পাড়িত, বিষণ্ণ, penurious, base, bad, depraved, abominable. immodest, disagreeable, unpleasant, unhealthy, ill, sad.

কদলী, কলা, রম্ভাবৃক্ষ, the plantain tree.

কদা, কোন সময়ে, when? at what time?

কদাচ, কদাচিৎ, কদাচন,—কখন, seldom, rarely, scarcely ever, at any time, sometimes. [then.

কদাপি, কখনই. মধ্যে২, at some time, sometimes, now and

কদুক্তি, দুর্ব্বাক্য, abuse, reproach.

কদুষ্ণ, কদুষ্ণ,—ঈষদুষ্ণ, lukewarm, tepid.

কধী, কধূ,—কদা, যখন, কখন, when? when, at any time.

কনক, স্বর্ণ, gold, certain shrubs or trees.

কনকচূর, শীতকালীন ধান্য, কার্ত্তিকশালি, the cold-season rice.

কনাৎ, তাম্বু বিশেষ, a kind of tent, a cloth tent-fence.

কনিষ্ঠ, অনুজ, ছোটভাই, least, youngest, junior, inferior; a younger brother.

কনিষ্ঠা, ছোট আঙ্গুলী, the little finger. [swamp.

কনী, মৎস্যখাত্ পুষ্করিণী, a fishpond dug in a morass or

কনীয়ান্, অতিযুবা, অনুজ, very young, younger, junior, inferior. [well.

কন্থা, কাঁথা, কূপ, a coat of shreds worn by devotees; a

কন্থাধারক, ভিক্ষুক, সন্ন্যাসী, wearing a coat of shreds; a religious mendicant, a devotee.

কন্থান্বিত, কাঁথাপরিহিত, clothed in a coat of shreds.

কন্দ, মূল, শর্করা, মিষ্টান্ন, a bulbous root, raw or coarse sugar, a kind of sweetmeat. [chasm, cave.

কন্দর, পর্ব্বতের মধ্যস্থল, গহ্বর, a glen, defile, deep valley,

কন্দল, নিন্দা, বিবাদ, যুদ্ধ, reproach, censure, a quarrel, dispute, war.

কন্দু, লোহার কড়া, a sauce-pan, frying-pan, boiler.

কন্দুক, গেণ্ডু, গেঁড়ু, a ball for playing with.

কন্ধর, গলা, মেঘ, the neck, a cloud.

কন্যা, কুমারী, পুত্রী, a young girl, virgin, daughter, bride, the sign Virgo. [ed to the 10th year.)

কন্যাকাল, কুমারীদশা, দশমবৎসর, the period of virginity, (reckon-

কন্যাগত, কুমারীভাবযুক্ত, inherent in or pertaining to a virgin.

কন্যারাশীয়, সলজ্জ, কন্যাবৎ, modest, timid, resembling a young woman, effeminate.

কপট, ছল, চাতুরী, ছদ্ম, deceit, a trick, stratagem, fraud.

কপটবেশ, মিথ্যাবেশ, ছদ্মবেশ, অভিনয়, an assumed part or character, a play, pantomime.

কপটবেশী, ছদ্মবেশী, ছদ্মরূপী, অভিনেতা, supporting an assumed character; a player. [an actor, player.

কপটী, প্রবঞ্চক, ধূর্ত্ত, ছলী, deceitful, hypocritical, fraudulent;

কপর্দ্দ, কপর্দ্দক,—কড়ি, শিবের জটা, a cowry, the matted hair of Shiva.

কপাট, দ্বারের আবরণ, a door, a window-shutter. [luck.

কপাল, ললাট, প্রাক্তন, the forehead, destiny, fate, fortune,

কপালী, ঝনকাট, শিব, a lintel, Shiva, a certain cast.

কপালীয়, ভাগ্যবান্, fortunate; pertaining to the cast above.

কপি, বানর, কলবিশেষ, an ape or monkey; a pulley or block.

কপিল, পিঙ্গলবর্ণ, অগ্নি, tawny, monkey-brown; the god of fire.

কপিলা, গন্ধদ্রব্য, অগ্নিকোণের হস্তিনী, a sort of perfume, the Elephant of the S. E. quarter, a Puránic cow.

কপীন, কপ্নী,—কৌপীন, the strip of cloth passed between the legs. [a young Brahmin's head.

কপুচ্ছল, দক্ষিণশিখা, the lock of hair on the right side of

কপুষ্ণিক, বামশিখা, the same on the left side.

কপোত, কপোতিকা,—পারাবত, পায়রা, a pigeon, a dove.

কপোল, গণ্ডদেশ, the cheek.

কপ্তান, কপ্টান,—কর্ত্তন, to clip, trim with shears.

কফ, শ্লেষ্মা, কাস, phlegm, a cold, catarrh.

কফী, কফযুক্ত, কাসযুক্ত, ill with a cold, subject to colds.

কব, কদা, কোন সময়ে, when?

কবচ, সজ্জা, মাদুলী, defensive armour, a charm, amulet.

কবচী, সজ্জাবিশিষ্ট, armed, clothed in armour. [demon.

কবন্ধ, মস্তকহীন দেহ, a headless trunk, the belly, a certain

কবরী, কেশবেশ, অম্লতা, a braid of hair; acidity, sourness.
কবল, গ্রাস, a morsel, a mouthful, particularly that of a beast.
কবলিত, গ্রস্ত, খাদিত, ভুক্ত, swallowed, eaten.
কবা, ছল, a pretence, deception, trick.
কবাট, কপাট, a door, a shutter.
কবি, কাব্যকর্ত্তা, পণ্ডিত, a poet, a writer of taste.
কবিতা, পদ্য, ছন্দ, কাব্য, verse, poetry, a poem.
কবিরাজ, চিকিৎসক, a physician.
কবুতর, কপোত, a pigeon.
কবে, কখন, যে সময়ে, when? when.
কব্য, পিতৃশ্রাদ্ধ, পিতৃদান, an oblation to deceased ancestors.
কভী, কখী, কোনসময়ে, at any time.
কভু, কখনো, even at any time.
কমঠ, কচ্ছপ, a tortoise, a turtle.
কমণ্ডলু, যতির জলপাত্র, the water-pot of an ascetic.
কমন, কামার্থী, রম্য, lewd, libidinous, desirous, beautiful, desirable.
কমনীয়, মনোহর, রম্য, beautiful, agreeable, desirable.
কমনে, কোথায়, কচিৎ, where? whither? somewhere.
কমল, পদ্ম, জল, তাম্র, a lotus, water, copper.
কমলা, লক্ষ্মী, নাগরঙ্গী, নারাঙ্গী, Lakshmi, an orange.
কম্প, গাত্রস্পন্দন, নড়নী, আন্দোলন, a trembling, palpitation, trepidation, agitation, vibration, tremulous motion.
কম্পজ্বর, বিষমজ্বর, a fever and ague, intermittent fever.
কম্পন, স্পন্দন, থর্থরাণ, নড়ন, to tremble, quiver, shudder, palpitate, vibrate.
কম্পবায়ু, অঙ্গাবশ, পক্ষাঘাতী, paralytic, trembling from palsy.
কম্পমান, কম্পযুক্ত, আন্দোলিত, নড়ান, trembling, quaking, vibrating, palpitating, agitated.
কম্বল, লোমনির্ম্মিত গাত্রীয়বস্ত্র, a blanket, an upper cloth.
কম্বু, শঙ্খ, কঙ্কণ, গলা, a shell, conch, bracelet, ring, the neck.
কম্বুগ্রীব, কম্বুলক্ষণাক্রান্ত, having the neck marked like a shell.
কম্বুগ্রীবা, তিনরেখাযুক্ত গলা, a neck so marked, (a sign of beauty and high fortune.)

কর, হস্ত, হস্তিশুণ্ড, নখ, রশ্মি,, রাজস্ব the hand, an elephant's trunk, the claw of a beast, a ray of light, royal revenue, tax, tribute.

করই, ভাণ্ডার, গোলা, a storehouse, a granary.

করকচ, লবণ, sea salt obtained by evaporation.

করকচি, দুর্মা, কোমল, the soft unripe shell of the cocoanut; soft, eatable.

করকটিয়া, অবৃদ্ধবৃক্ষ, stunted as a plant, checked in growth.

করকনা, কটিদেশ, বংক্ষণ, the hip.

করকা, বর্ষোপল, নারিকেলমালা, কমণ্ডলু, hail, a cocoanut-vessel; an ascetic's water-pot.

করকোষ্ঠী, হস্তরেখা, the lines in the palm of the hand.

করঙ্ক, মস্তক, অস্থি, নারিকেলমালা, the head, a bone, a cocoanut-vessel.

করচা, রাজকরলিপি. রাজস্বনিয়ম, a written assessment, levy of taxes.

করণ, সাধন, নির্ম্মাণ, করা, to do, act, make; an instrument, means, action, act, operation.

করণক, পূর্ব্বক, (*in compos:*) through, by, by means of.

করণ্ড, মৌচাক, টুকরী, a honey-comb, a bee-hive, a basket.

করতল, হস্তের উপরিভাগ, অধীন, the palm of the hand, a subjection; subject, under the power of.

করতাল, মন্দিরা, a cymbal.

করতালী, হস্তদ্বারা অনঘাত করা, *id:* the beating of time by clapping the hands.

করপত্র, করাত, আরা, a saw.

করপল্লব, সঙ্কেতে কহন, ইঙ্গন, a talking by the fingers or signs.

করপাত্র. অঞ্জলি, the joined palms formed into a cup.

করপাল, করবাল,—খড়্গ, a sword, a scymetar.

করপুট, যোড়হস্তে প্রণাম করা, the joining of the palms as an act of respect and obeisance.

করভ, উটের ছানা, শিশুহস্তী. শাবক, a young elephant or camel the young of any animal, the metacarpus..

করম, ক্রিয়া, প্রাক্তনকর্ম্ম, an action, fate, the actions of a prior birth, liability to their consequences.

করমালা, জপমালা, a rosary, a bead-roll.

করশাখা, অঙ্গুলী, a finger.

করাটিয়া, করকটিয়া, অবৃদ্ধবৃক্ষ, stunted or checked in growth.

করাণ, জন্মান, চালান, to cause, impel, oblige, cause to do, &c.

করাণী, করগ্রাহক, লেখক, a collector of revenue, a clerk, writer.
করাত, করপত্র, আরা, a saw.
করাতী, আরাকষ, a sawyer.
করাল, অরাল, বড়, উচ্চ, ভয়ানক, rosin, pitch, a mixture of oil and resin: great, large, high, lofty, terrible, having projecting teeth.
করী, হস্তী, an elephant.
করীন্দ্র, প্রধান হস্তী, the leader of a herd of elephants.
করুই, ভাণ্ডার, a granary.
করুণা, দয়া, কৃপা, compassion, clemency, tenderness, mercy, pity.
করুণাকর, কৃপানিধি, দয়াময়, a mine of pity, *i. e.* full of pity, &c.
করুণানিধান, দয়াধার, কৃপান্বিত, a sea of compassion, *i. e.* very compassionate.
করুণার্দ্র, কৃপাবান্, compassionate, tender-hearted.
করুল, ক্রোরপক্ষী, the osprey or fishing eagle.
কর্কট, কাঁকড়া, রাশি বিশেষ, নাগ, a crab, the sign Cancer, a snake, a crane, a long gourd.
কর্কটী, কাঁকুড়ফল, a cucumber, a female crab.
কর্কর, কুলুই, পাষাণবৎ মৃত্তিকা, lime-stone pebbles, gravel, a splinter, a grating noise, a grating.
কর্করিয়া, কঙ্করযুক্ত, gritty, gravelly, full of nodules.
কর্কশ, কঠিন, দৃঢ়, কঠোর, কৃপাহীন, rigid, hard, rough, harsh, violent, unkind, unmerciful, miserly.
কর্ণ, শ্রবণেন্দ্রিয়, কান, হাল, the ear, a rudder, a helm.
কর্ণগোচর, শ্রবণজ্ঞান, hearing, hearing-distance.
কর্ণধার, নাবিক, a helmsman, steersman.
কর্ণপালী, কর্ণফুল,—কুণ্ডল, কর্ণভূষণ, an ear-ornament, pendent ear-jewel.
কর্ণাকর্ণি, পরস্পর ফুস্‌ফুসনি, a whispering together.
কর্ণিক, রাজের অস্ত্র, a mason's trowel.
কর্ণিকা, কুণ্ডল, বীজকোষ, মধ্যমাঙ্গুলী, an ear-ring, the seed vessel of the lotus, the middle finger.
কর্ণেজপ, ঠক, ভেদক, a tale-bearer, whisperer, informer.
কর্ত্তন, কাটন, ছাটন, to cut, trim, clip, deduct.
কর্ত্তনী, কর্ত্তরী, ছোলা, a pair of shears or scissors, parings.
কর্ত্তব্য প্রয়োজন, সাধ্য, necessary, fit, proper to be done, practicable.

কর্ত্তরিকা, কর্ত্তরী,—কর্ত্তনী, কাতারী, a pair of scissors or shears.
কর্ত্তা, কর্ত্তৃ,—প্রভু, স্বামী, অধিকারী, কারক, lord, master, governor, owner, proprietor, agent, doer.
কর্ত্তৃক, কারক, সাধক, *(in compos :)* by, *(as an agent or doer)*.
কর্ত্তৃত্ব, প্রভুত্ব, অধিকার, কারিতা, rule, government, right, sovereignty, agency, management. [agent.
কর্ত্রী, প্রধানা গৃহিণী, কারিণী, a mistress, governess, female
কর্দ্দ, কর্দ্দম,—পঙ্ক, mud, dirt, mire, clay.
কর্পট, জীর্ণবস্ত্র, old and ragged or patched garments.
কর্পাস, তুলা, কাপাস, cotton, the cotton plant or tree.
কর্পূর, গন্ধদ্রব্য বিশেষ, সিতাভ্র, camphor. [gold, water.
কর্ব্বুর, বিচিত্র, রাক্ষস, variegated, speckled; a dæmon, imp,
কর্ম্ম, ক্রিয়া, প্রয়োজন, ব্যাপার, ধর্ম্ম, action, deed, work, matter, affair, object, employment, occupation, station, duty, obligation, meritorious act, religious rites and observances.
কর্ম্মকর্ত্তা, কারক, অধ্যক্ষ, a workman, labourer, superintendant.
কর্ম্মকার, কারক, কামার, a worker, blacksmith, armourer, shoemaker, currier. [of rents, steward, factor.
কর্ম্মচারী, প্রবৃত্ত, পাটারি, employed or engaged in; a collector
কর্ম্মঠ, কর্ম্মে নিপুণ, শ্রমী, clever, diligent, laborious.
কর্ম্মণ্য, কর্ম্মযোগ্য, অনুকূল, fit for work, serviceable.
কর্ম্মফল, প্রতিফল, the consequences of human actions.
কর্ম্মভোগ, ফলভোগ, experience of the result of good or bad actions. [counsellor.
কর্ম্মসচিব, অমাত্য, রাজমন্ত্রী, an executive minister, supreme
কর্ম্মসাধন, নির্ব্বাহ, the means of accomplishing a work.
কর্ম্মাদি, কর্ম্মফল, actions &c. *i.e.* a deed and its consequences.
কর্ম্মান্ত, কর্ম্মভোগ, কর্ম্মশেষ, the end or consequence of an action or undertaking.
কর্ম্মান্বিত, শ্রমী, পারক, ধার্ম্মিক, diligent, industrious, having a stock of merit, meritorious. [fully occupied.
কর্ম্মাবৃত, পদাশ্রিত, কর্ম্মাবিষ্ট, protected by one's employ or office,
কর্ম্মার, কাংস্যকার, লোহার, a brazier, a smith.
কর্ম্মার্হ, কর্ম্মিষ্ঠ,—কর্ম্মপটু, কর্ম্মণ্য, skilful, useful, serviceable, fit for an undertaking.

কর্ম্মী, শিল্পকর, কর্ম্মরত, কর্ম্মকুশল, an artist, an advocate for religious ceremonies; ingenious, pertaining to a work.

কর্ম্মেন্দ্রিয়, বাক্,পাণি,পাদ,পায়ু,উপস্থ, the organs of bodily action.

কর্ষ, এক তোলা, চষাণি, a certain weight of gold or silver; tillage, husbandry. [a cultivator.

কর্ষক, টানক, চাষী, কৃষাণ, drawing, ploughing; a ploughman,

কর্ষণ, টানন, চষণ, to draw, drag, pull, attract, plough.

কর্ষিণী, মুখস, চাষিণী, the bit of a bridle, a female who ploughs.

কর্হি, কদা. when? at what time?

কর্হিচিৎ, কথনং, কদাপি, sometimes, occasionally.

কল, যন্ত্র, শিল্পকর্ম্ম, অঙ্কুর, রেতঃ, গ্রাস, an engine, machine, trap, spring, mechanic art, a shoot, bud, scion, semen virile, a mouthful, a chirping, buzzing.

কল্কল্, অব্যক্তশব্দ, কোলাহল, a confused noise, buz, din, hubbub.

কলঙ্ক, চিহ্ন, দোষ, কুচ্ছা, পাপ, অপবাদ, a mark, stain, spot, rust, stigma, taint, blemish, guilt, crime, abuse, defamation, ill-fame.

কলঙ্ককর, লজ্জাকর, নিন্দনীয়, অপবাদী, staining, blemishing, disgraceful, corroding, censorious; a detractor.

কলঙ্কী, কলঙ্কযুক্ত, কুৎসিত, অপবাদগ্রস্ত, stained, blemished, impure, stigmatized, &c. [weapon.

কলঞ্জ, বিষাক্তাস্ত্রাহত জন্তু, an animal stricken by a poisoned

কলত্র, ভার্য্যা, নিতম্ব, দুর্গ, a wife, the hips and loins, a fort, a royal citadel.

কলপ, লেই, paste, starch, varnish.

কলম, লেখনী, কনকচূর, a pen, a reed, a white winter-rice.

কলম্ব, বাণ, শাকেরডাঁটা, an arrow, plant-stalk, Columba root.

কলয়, কলাই,—মাষাদি, divers species of pulse or leguminous seeds.

কলরব, পায়রা, মধুরধ্বনি, কোলাহল, a dove, pigeon, cuckoo, low sound, murmur, buz, din, clatter.

কলস-শী, ঘট, ঘড়া, অলিঞ্জর, a jar, waterpot, pitcher.

কলহংস, পাতিহংস, রাজহংস, বালিহংস, a drake, gander, teal.

কলহ, বিরোধ, যুদ্ধ, গালী, a quarrel, contention, war, battle, fighting, violence, abuse.

কলহী, বিবাদী, দ্বন্দ্বী, quarrelsome, contentious.

কলা, শিল্পকর্ম্ম, ছল, অংশ, বৃদ্ধি, a mechanic art, fraud, deceit, interest of money, part, portion, digit of the moon, eight seconds of time, a plantain, the menses.

কলান, গজান, to sprout, germinate, act or work as a machine, rehearse previous to an exhibition.

কলানিধি, চন্দ্র, the moon

কলাপ, ভূষণ, ঘুঙ্গুর, ময়ূরপুচ্ছ, তূণ, সমূহ, চন্দ্র, পটু, an ornament, zone, string of bells for the waist, peacock's tail, a quiver, a multitude, assemblage, the moon, a clever and intelligent man.

কলাপী, ময়ূর, কোকিল, a peacock, the black cuckoo.

কলায়, মটর, মাষকলায়াদি, peas, pulse, vetches, &c.

কলি, চতুর্থ যুগ, the fourth or iron age.

কলি, কলিকা, কলী,—অস্ফুট পুষ্প, an unblown flower, tobacco cup, wet lime, the receptacle of a lamp.

কলিত, গণিত, জ্ঞাত, অবগত, প্রাপ্ত, ভেদিত, calculated, numbered, reckoned, known, understood, gained, acquired, separated, divided.

কলু, তৈলিক, চক্রী, an expresser of oil.

কলুষ, পাপ, অপরাধ, মল, sin, crime, guilt, defilement, filth.

কলুষী, পাপী, অপরাধী, অধম, মলযুক্ত, guilty, sinful, vile, criminal, muddy, turbid, foul, filthy.

কলেজা, কালখণ্ড, the liver.

কলেবর, দেহ, শরীর, the body.

কল্ক, কাইট, বিষ্ঠা, খলি, পাপ, refuse, filth, sediment, ordure, ear-wax, sin, fraud, guilt.

কল্কল, জলস্রোতধ্বনি, কাকা, a rippling noise, a brawling, the cawing of a crow.

কল্কলান, কাকা করণ, গালাগালি দেওন, to caw, brawl, ripple, to sound as a falling liquid.

কল্কলানী, জলস্রোতধ্বনি, তরঙ্গধ্বনি, a rippling, surf, brawling.

কল্কলায়, ঝকড়ালু, দ্বন্দ্বী, brawling, quarrelsome, contentious.

কল্‌গা, কিরীট, শিরোভূষণ, a tiara, an ornament for the head.

কল্তানি, রসানি, ক্লেদ, পুঁজ, serum, pus, thin matter.

কল্প, উপায়, ছল, ইচ্ছা, বোধ, প্রলয়, বিধি, contrivance, scheme, purpose, determination, alternative, option, opinion, report, a day and night of Brahmá, a sacred writing or precept.

কল্পতরু, সুরক্রম, দাতা, a fabled tree of Indra's paradise : a generous man.

কল্পন, রচন, নির্ম্মাণ, টানন, to contrive, devise, plan, design, construct, arrange, feign, scheme.

কল্পনা, উপায়, ছল, আরোপ, অনুকরণ, a scheme, contrivance, plan, forgery, false imputation, imitation, the trappings of an elephant &c.

কল্পান্ত, প্রলয়, the destruction of the world or end of a Calpa.

কল্পিত, মিথ্যা, গঠিত, আরোপিত, counterfeit, feigned, fictitious, forged, artificially contrived or arranged.

কল্বল-আনি, গণ্ডগোল, কলহ, a tumultuous noise, a brawl.

কল্মষ, পাপ, মল, নরক, sin, filth, one of the infernal regions.

কল্য, প্রত্যূষ. আরোগ্য, সুস্থ, বধির, the dawn, health ; recovered from sickness, deaf and dumb.

কল্য, কল্যকা.—আগামি দিবস, গতদিবস, to-morrow, yesterday.

কল্যাণ, কুশল, শুভ, welfare, prosperity, happiness, good fortune.

কল্যাণী. ভাগ্যবান্, সুখী. prosperous, fortunate, successful, [happy.

কল্যাণীয়, কুশলার্হ, deserving success, worthy of good fortune.

কল্ল, বধির, শ্রবণেন্দ্রিয়হীন, deaf.

কল্লা, কল্লী,—দুষ্ট, অধম, অবাধ্য, wicked, abominable, froward.

কল্লোল, গড়ি, কোলাহল, মুখক্ষালন, a surge, billow, roar of the sea, tumult, a gargling or washing the mouth.

কশা, কোড়া, a whip.

কশেরু, মেরুদণ্ড, পৃষ্ঠের হাড়, the back-bone, the spine, a species [of rush.

কশ্চন, কেহ, কোন লোক, some one, a certain one.

কশ্চিৎ, কেহ, যেকেহ, some one, a certain one, whosoever, any one.

কষ, কষ্টিপাথর, পরীক্ষা, a touch-stone, test, tan, the tan- [ning principle.

কষণ, পরীক্ষণ, কষলাগান, টানন, আঁটন, ঘর্ষণ, to try, examine by a touch-stone, tan, tighten, stretch, rub in the hands.

কষণী, আঁটি, কটুতা, tightness, astringency, severity, harshness.
কষা, কটুরস, an astringent or harsh taste.
কষাণি, পুঁজ, ক্লেদ, purulent matter.
কষায়, কটুরস, কাথ, কটু, কালিষ্ট, an astringent taste or juice, infusion, extract; astringent. fragrant, tawny.
কষুবা, কটু, তিক্ত rough to the taste, astringent.
কষ্ট, পীড়া, ক্লেষ, কৃচ্ছ্র, পীড়িত, নিবিড়, pain, suffering, distress, trouble; pained, suffering pain, impenetrable, impervious.
কষ্টকল্পনা, মিথ্যাপত্তি, নিরর্থক দোষ করা, a cavil.
কষ্টসাধ্য, দুঃসাধ্য, accomplishable with difficulty.
কষ্টি, পরীক্ষা, রষাণ, a test, trial, touchstone.
কস্তুরা, সশম্বুমৎস্য বিশেষ, an oyster.
কস্তুরিকা, কস্তূরী,—মৃগনাভী, মৃগমদ, musk.
কস্মিন্‌কালে, কদা, কখন, when? at what time?
কহন, কথন, উল্লেখন, জ্ঞাপন, বিবরণ, to speak, say, tell, mention, announce, rehearse. [logue, disputation.
কহাকহি, কহাবলা,—পরস্পর আলাপ, সম্ভাষণ, conversation; dia-
কহুয়া, বক্তা, বাচাল, eloquent, talkative, garrulous.
কাই, নেই, paste, starch.
কাইট্‌, খাদ, শিটা, dross, sediment, lees, refuse.
কাইত, হেলা, আড়, standing on one edge, leaning, aslant.
কাওবা, ছল, ব্যাজ, a pretence, excuse.
কাওবান, আওটন, to boil to a consistence, to thicken.
কাংস্য, কাঁসা, কংস, ঘোড়া, a mixed metal, bell-metal, white brass, a gong.
কাংস্যকার, কাংস্যবণিক,—কাঁসারি, a brazier, brass-founder.
কাঁক, কঙ্কপক্ষী, কক্ষ, a heron; the side, the flank.
কাঁকই, চিরুণী, a comb, a carding-comb.
কাঁকড়া, কর্কট, a crab.
কাঁকরা, কর্কর, কঙ্কর, pebble, gravel, grit.
কাঁকালি, কটিদেশ, কক্ষ, the loins, hip, waist, side.
কাঁকুড়, কর্কটী, সশাবিশেষ, a species of cucumber.
কাঁচলি, কঞ্চুলিকা, স্ত্রীলোকের অঙ্গরাখা, a woman's bodice or jacket.
কাঁচা, অপক্ক, মূঢ়, অজ্ঞান, unripe, raw, imperfect, ignorant, clumsy, unskilled; a novice.

কাঁচী, কর্ত্তরিকা, কাস্তিয়া, a pair of scissors or shears, a sickle; beneath the standard weight or measure.
কাঁজি, পুরাতন আমানি, মণ্ড, sour rice-water.
কাঁটা, কণ্টক, অগ্র, শত্রু, পীড়াকর, a thorn, fish-bone, point, pin, fork, enemy, cause of pain, danger.
কাঁটাকুড়, কণ্টকী বন, গহ্বর, সঙ্কট, a brake, thicket, distressed situation, difficulty.
কাঁটাল, পনস, কণ্টকময়, the jack-fruit; thorny, brambly.
কাঁটা, কদুক্তি, scurrilous and abusive language used by women.
কাঁঠী, শুকপক্ষির গলরেখা, the coloured ring on the neck of a parrot, weights for fishing-nets.
কাঁঠীচন্দনা, রেখাযুক্ত শুকপক্ষী, a parrot having such a ring.
কাঁড়ন, ভানন, স্থির করণ, to separate grain from the husk, to settle or come to an understanding with one.
কাঁড়রা, স্থূল, মোটা, thick, clumsy.
কাঁড়ি, রাশি, স্তূপ, a heap or collection, stack, pile.
কাঁত, কাঁথ,—প্রাচীর, জীর্ণ প্রাচীর, a wall, ruin, broken wall.
কাঁতড়া, কাঁথড়া,—ভাঙ্গাপ্রাচীর, a ruinous wall, ruins of a town.
কাঁথী, আড়ূরি, the high bank or shore of a river.
কাঁদন, ক্রন্দন, রোদন, বিলাপণ, to cry, weep, lament, wail, howl.
কাঁদনি, রোদন, বিলাপ, ওঝার গান, a weeping, a howling, a snake charmer's song.
কাঁদা, তীর, কূল, a shore, margin, verge.
কাঁদাড়ি, জুলী, নালী, the water-course below the eaves of a house.
কাঁদী, গুচ্ছ, স্তবক, a cluster (of fruit).
কাঁধ, স্কন্ধ, the shoulder.
কাঁধা, কাণা, তীর, কূল, a rim, edge, border, margin, bank, shore, mound.
কাঁধাড়ি, পর্ব্বতের ধার, the brow of a hill.
কাঁস্র, ঘন, ঘণ্টা, a metal sounding-plate used for a bell.
কাঁসা, কংস, white brass, bell-metal.
কাঁসারি, কাংস্যকার, কাংস্যবণিক, a brazier, copper-smith.
কাক, বায়স, a crow.
কাকচা, সর্ষপের বিচালী, the mustard plant stript of the seed.
কাকতালীয়, অকস্মাৎ কৃত, sudden, unexpected.
কাকতন্দ্রা, লঘু নিদ্রা, a light slumber easily disturbed.
কাকতুল্য, ধূর্ত্ত, crafty, crow-like.

কাকপক্ষ, মস্তকের পার্শ্বদেশস্থ চুল, side-locks of hair on children.
কাকবন্ধ্যা, একগর্ভা, *fem.* having borne but one child, only once pregnant.
কাকলাস, জেটী, সরট, কৃকলাস, a lizard. [tle noise.
কাকলী, কলরব, মধুর ধ্বনি, a hum, buz, murmur, low and gen-
কাকা, কনিষ্ঠ পিতৃব্য, খুড়া, কাকধ্বনি, a younger paternal uncle, the note of a crow.
কাকিণী, হস্তপরিমাণ, কড়ি, a cubit, a cowry, five gandas.
কাকী, খুড়ী, বায়সী, a paternal uncle's wife, a female crow.
কাকু. খেদভয়াদির বিকারজ ধ্বনি, কদলী, the faultering of the voice in grief or fear, &c. a plantain.
কাকূক্তি, কাকুতি,—ভয়াদিজনিত ধ্বনি, মিনতি, a cry of fear or distress, scream, loud complaint, supplication.
কাকোল, কালবিষ, দাঁড়কাক, a black poison, a raven.
কাকোলী, জ্বরনাশক ঔষধ, a cooling drug.
কাকোলূকিকা, কাকের এবং উলূকের পরস্পর শত্রুতা, the natural enmity between the crow and the owl, mortal enmity.
কাগ, কাক, বায়স, a crow.
কাগারি, কাকারি,—উলূক, an owl.
কাঙ্কালী, কটিদেশ, the waist, the loins.
কাঙ্গালী, ধনহীন, দরিদ্র, poor, needy, wretched.
কাঙ্গালীপনা, দরিদ্রতা, poverty, want, wretchedness.
কাঙ্গুর, গঙ্গোদক পাত্র, a vessel for carrying Ganges water.
কাচ, স্ফটিক, কাল্পনিক বেশ, ছল, chrystal, glass, a feigned cheracter, disguise, trick.
কাচতিয়া, কাচি,—কাস্তিয়া, a sickle.
কাচন, ক্ষালন, কপটবেশ ধারণ, to wash linen, to act a feigned part, to finish the forming of an idol.
কাচা, মোটা কাপড়, coarse cloth. [pantomimic.
কাচুবা, প্রতারক, কপটবেশী, a deceiver, feigned character,
কাছ, নৈকট্য, কূল, nearness to, vicinity, a coast or shore.
কাছা, কচ্ছ, পরিহিত বস্ত্রের শেষভাগ, the part of a garment passed between the legs and tucked up behind.
কাছাকাছি, নিকটানিকটি, সঙ্গে, in company, mutually near, together, nearly, at hand. [slovenly, careless.
কাছাটীলা, আলগা, কামুক, loose, lascivious, rakish, indecent.

কাছাধরা, চাটুবাদী, উপাসক, a sycophant, a satellite.
কাছান, ঘনান, দৌড়ন, নিকটাগমন, to overtake, gain upon, approach.
কাছারী, ব্যবস্থান, বিচারস্থান, a magistrate's office, court of justice.
কাছিম, কচ্ছপ, কমঠ, a tortoise, water-turtle.
কাছী, রজ্জু, কচড়া, a rope, cable, string.
কাছে, নিকটে, সমীপে, near, at, towards, in the vicinity.
কাজ, ক্রিয়া, কর্ম্ম, work, labour, duty.
কাজল, অঞ্জন, a collyrium, stibium, eye-paint.
কাজলা, শুকপক্ষী বিশেষ, কাব্‌জ্যা, a species of parrot, a wedge.
কাঞ্চন, সুবর্ণ, স্বর্ণ, gold; the mountain ebony, the thorn-apple.
কাঞ্চী, মেখলা, a woman's zone or girdle.
কাঞ্জিক, কাঞ্জী,— মণ্ড, পুরাতন আমানি, rice-gruel, sour rice-water.
কাটন, ছেদন, চিরণ, কর্ত্তন, খনন, খণ্ডন, যাপন, to cut, tear, gnaw, hew, prune, dig, deduct from wages or an account, thwart, make void, refute, erase, spend time, spin cotton-thread.
কাটনা, সূতনির্ম্মাণ, cotton-spinning.
কাটনী, সূতনির্ম্মাণ কারিণী, a female spinner, spinster; wages of a spinner.
কাটনীয়া, সূতনির্ম্মাণ কারক, ছেদক, a spinner, cutter, hewer.
কাটাই, কাটানী,—কাটনার মূল্য, wages paid for spinning.
কাটাকাটি, বধাবধি, বধিক, অপঘাতী, mutual slaughter; murderous, bloody.
কাটান, কালযাপন, আট্‌কান, নদির পথ, to pass or spend time, impede, frustrate, cause to be cut, &c. the channel of a river.
কাটার, ছোরা, যমধার, a dagger.
কাটারী, কুড়ালি, দা, দাত্র, a cleaver, a bill-hook.
কাটী, কুচি, খণ্ড, টুকরা, a chip, bit of wood, splinter.
কাঠ, কাষ্ঠ, দারু, wood, timber.
কাঠকুয়া, কেঠুয়া, সেচনী, a cow-trough, a bailing vessel.
কাঠগড়, উদূখল, a rice mortar.
কাঠগড়া, বেড়া, গরাদিয়া, *id:* an inclosure, a stockade.
কাঠছাতা, কাঠছাতিয়া,—কোঁড়ক, a mushroom, fungus.
কাঠজালী, বিট্‌লবণ, a coarse salt.
কাঠনেকার, উকি, a straining or retching ineffectually.

কাঠকম্ম, মল্লিকা, বেলফুল, the jasmine flower.

কাঠবিড়াল, বৃক্ষমার্জ্জার, a squirrel. [stakes.

কাঠরা কাষ্ঠনির্ম্মিত গৃহ, ঘেরা, a house of wood, an inclosure of

কাঠরিয়া, কাষ্ঠছেদক, বাওয়ালী, a woodman, a wood-cutter.

কাঠা, ভূমির পরিমাণ বিশেষ, রেক, কমঠ, a measure of land or capacity, a large water-turtle.

কাঠাম, নির্ম্মিতবাস্তু, framed, (as a house or image.)

কাঠাল, দৃঢ়তর, যুবন্‌, firm (as a tree,) matured, adult.

কাঠিন্য, দৃঢ়তা, নিষ্ঠুরতা, hardness, roughness, severity, unfeelingness. [reed, key, scabbard, sheath.

কাঠী, যষ্টি, বাড়ী, লেখনী, খাপ. a wand, bamboo lath, writing

কাঠুয়া, শক্ত, কাষ্ঠবৎ, hard, hardy, wooden; a wood-cutter.

কাঠুরিয়া, বাওয়ালী, কাষ্ঠছেদক, a cutter and seller of wood.

কাড়ন, তোলন, পরিষ্করণ. ছিনন, গ্রহণ, to take or lift out, clean out, snatch, seize, usurp.

কাড়া, ধরা, পরিষ্কার, ঢক্কা, a seizure, cleansing. &c. a drum.

কাড়ান, পুষ্পপাত অপেক্ষণ, to watch for the fall of a flower from the head of an idol. [eye, perforated.

কাণ, শ্রবণেন্দ্রিয়, কর্ণ, একচক্ষুহীন, বিদ্ধ, the ear; blind of one

কাণকূয়া, মৎস্যের ফুস্ফ, the gills of a fish.

কাণখড়্‌কিয়া, শ্রবণকারী, স্মরণকারী, quick of hearing, retentive.

কাণখাড়া, শ্রবণেচ্ছুক, hearing every thing, listening, attentive.

কাণখুকসী, কাণচুম্‌কনী,—কর্ণশোধনী, an ear-pick.

কাণতড়পা, কর্ণভূষণ, an ear-ornament.

কাণপাটা, কর্ণের লোলিতাংশ, the flap of the ear.

কাণপাতলা, কাণখাড়া, বাবদূক, listening, blabbing, talkative.

কাণভাঙ্গন, গোপনে অপবাদন, কর্ণেজপন, to prejudice one against a person, to warn privately against one.

কাণা, একচক্ষুয়া, বিদ্ধ, পাত্রের ধার, blind of one eye, perforated, broken; the edge of a vessel or cup.

কাণাকাণি, ফুস্ফুসনি, চুপে কহাকহি, a whispering, planning, *tête-à-tête*; ear to ear. [eaves of a house.

কাণাচি, পরছতির নীচস্থান, ছাঁচতলা, the space overhung by the

কাণাচীয়া, কাণাড়িপাতা,—কাণখাড়া, an eaves-dropper, listener.

কাণাড়ি, গাঁচা দেওয়া, a listening, eaves-dropping.

কাণাৎ, তাম্বুর পটনির্ম্মিত প্রাচীর, the curtains or walls of a tent.

কাণি, নেকড়া, a rag, small piece or remnant of cloth; a raised moulding.

কাণুটি, কর্ণমর্দন, চেতনাকরাণ, a pinching of the ear, a warning.

কাণে ২, ধারপর্য্যন্ত, up to the brim, brimful.

কাণোড়া, উপাসক, প্রভুভক্ত, obsequious, servile, obedient.

কাণ্টী, কাণ্ঠী,—দুর্ম্মুখী, বাঘিনী, কলহকারিণী, a scold, virago, vixen.

কাণ্ড, ডাঁটা, গুঁড়ি, বাণ, গুচ্ছ, প্রকরণ, a stalk, stem, trunk of a tree, an arrow, a cluster, collection, assemblage, a section, a chapter.

কাণ্ডারী, কর্ণধার, a pilot, steersman, helmsman.

কাণ্ডী, কাঁড়ী,—স্তূপ, a heap, stack, pile.

কাণ্ডীর, কাণ্ডবান্,—ধনুর্দ্ধর, শরবিশিষ্ট, an archer; armed with an arrow.

কাৎ, মূল্য, সারগুণ. worth, value, essential quality.

কাতর, ব্যাকুল, ব্যস্ত, anxious, troubled, distressed, perplexed.

কাতরাণ, কাতরাণি,—ক্লেশ, কোঁকানি, anguish, agony, complaint, moan, distress.

কাতরোক্তি, বিলাপ, lamentation, complaint.

কাতা, কাছী, a coir cable.

কাতান, কুড়ালি, দা, দাত্র, a cleaver, a bill-hook.

কাতারি, ঘট. an earthen pot or jar.

কাতারী, কাঁচী, a pair of shears.

কাতি, শঙ্খকারের করাত, a shell-cutter's saw.

কাতুর, ঘানির ভার, জাইট, the weight in an oil-press.

কাতে, সংযোগে, নিমিত্তে, in connection with, on account of; on the side of.

কাতে ২, ছলে, গোপনে, insidiously, pryingly, leaning equally both ways.

কাদড়া, পঙ্কিল, কাদাযুক্ত, soft with rain.

কাদড়াটিয়া, ঘোলা, পঙ্কযুক্ত, turbid, muddy, thick, dirty.

কাদম্বরী, মদ্য. wine, spirituous liquor.

কাদম্বিনী, মেঘ সমূহ, a range or succession of clouds.

কাদা, কর্দ্দম, পঙ্ক, mud, dirt, soft clay,

কাদাটিয়া, কাদাড়িয়া,—ঘোলা. পঙ্কময়, turbid, muddy, dirty.

কাদান, ক্ষেত্র জলমগ্ন করণ, ভূমিসেচন. to soften a field for sowing rice by flooding it.

কাদাল, ঘোলাটিয়া, কাদাময়, muddy, dirty, soft with mud.

কাদীবাদী, বিবাদী, বিরোধী, কুট্‌কুটিয়া, litigious, contentious, disputatious, querulous.

কানন, বিপিন, বন, জঙ্গল. a thicket, grove, forest, wilderness.

কানীন, অবিবাহিতা স্ত্রীজাত, born of an unmarried woman.

কান্ত, সুন্দর, প্রিয়, পতি, চন্দ্র, লৌহ, beautiful, agreeable, pleasing, dear; a husband, a gallant, the moon, iron.

কান্তলৌহ, শুদ্ধলৌহ, সার, bright iron, steel.

কান্তা, ভার্য্যা, রমণী, প্রিয়া, অঙ্গনা, a wife, a mistress, a beautiful or beloved woman.

কান্তার, কুপথ, নিবিড়বন, a bad, difficult or dangerous road, a wood, forest, red sugar-cane.

কান্তি, সৌন্দর্য্য, শোভা, অঙ্গনা, স্পৃহা, beauty, splendour, light, brilliancy, a beautiful woman, wish, desire.

কান্দন, ক্রন্দন, রোদন, to weep, cry, bewail, lament, howl.

কান্দিশীক, পলায়মান, পলায়িত, fleeing, running away, put to flight.

কান্দুয়া, রোদনকারী, অবকূজনকারী, weeping, crying, howling.

কান্দুয়াবাঘ, চিত্রব্যাঘ্র, চিতিবাঘ, the hunting-leopard.

কাপ, ছল, ছদ্মবেশ, কৌতুক, মেচ, a pretence, disguise, pantomime, shew, the nib of a pen.

কাপট্য, শঠতা, ছল, deceitfulness, craftiness, a trick. [rel.

কাপড়, বস্ত্র, বেশ, cloth, linen-cloth, a garment, dress, appa-

কাপড়্যা, বস্ত্রব্যবসায়ী, কাপড়বিক্রেতা, a linen-draper, seller of cloth.

কাপাস, তুলা, কর্পাস, cotton wool, the cotton plant.

কাপুরুষ, ভীরু, অসাহসী, নিন্দিতব্যক্তি, a coward, mean-spirited, contemptible or worthless man.

কাপ্টায়, কাপ্ট্যা,—কৃপণ, স্বার্থপর, sordid, niggardly, parsimonious, selfish.

কাপ্ট্যাপনা, কাপ্টামি,—কার্পণ্য, niggardliness, selfishness.

কাবা, ছল, ব্যাজ, কাকপক্ষী, a false pretence, a crow.

কাবান, আওটান, গাঢ় করণ, to inspissate, thicken by boiling.

কাব্য, ছন্দ, শ্লোক, পরিহাস, poetry, a poem, raillery, ridicule.

কাব্যত্ব, ছন্দতা, শ্লোকের ধর্ম্ম, poetical propriety.

কাব্র্যা, কাজলা, কীলক, a wedge.

কাম, বাসনা, রমণেচ্ছা, আশয়, মদন, বিষয়, desire, lust, wantonness, an object of desire, the god of love, affair, business.

কামগ, অবাধিত. উদম, স্বেচ্ছাচর, unrestrained, free, going where one pleases. [spontaneous.

কামজ, অভিলাষপ্রযুক্ত, স্বেচ্ছাপ্রযুক্ত, arising from desire or lust,

কামঠা, ধনুক, a bow.

কামড়ন, দংশন, to bite, snap at in order to bite. [ing pain.

কামড়ান, দংশন, পীড়ন, শূলজন্মান, *id:* to throb, to produce a grip-

কামড়ানি, শূল, পেটবেদনা, a griping pain, the cholic.

কামদ, স্বেচ্ছানুসারে দাতা, ইচ্ছানুগত, উপাসক, giving after one's own inclinations, yielding, subservient.

কামনা, বাসনা, রমণেচ্ছা, অভিরুচি, মিনতি, desire, wish, lust, appetite, inclination for, prayer, supplication.

কামরূপ-ী, বহুরূপ ধারণে সমর্থ, সুন্দর, assuming any form at pleasure pleasing, beautiful.

কামল, লম্পট, libidinous, lustful. [of bile.

কামল, নেবা, পিত্তবৃদ্ধি, the jaundice, excess or obstruction

কামাই. উপার্জ্জন, প্রাপ্তি, earnings, gains, savings. [gain.

কামান, ক্ষৌর করণ, উপার্জ্জন, প্রাপণ, to shave, to earn, acquire,

কামানী, ক্ষৌরমূল্য, a barber's fee.

কামার, লোহার, কর্ম্মকার, a blacksmith, whitesmith.

কামার্থ, কামার্থী, } লম্পট, স্ত্রীপর, রমণার্থী অভিলাষী, lascivious,
কামাল, কামী, } lewd, wanton, libidinous, amorous,
কামুক, কামাসক্ত, } lustful, desirous.

কামিনী, স্বীয়া, লম্পটী পরগাছা, an affectionate or lascivious woman, a climbing or parasitical plant.

কাম্য, অভিলষণীয়, প্রিয়, স্বেচ্ছাপূর্ব্বক, desirable, amiable, optional, voluntary, supererogatory, performed to obtain personal advantage.

কায়-া, দেহ, শরীর, the body. [ing, quarrelsome.

কায়বারী, সাহসী, দম্ভযুক্ত, কলহী, resolute, overbearing, insult-

কায়স্থ, জাতিবিশেষ, the writer cast.

কায়িক, দৈহিক, শারীরিক, bodily, corporeal.

কারক, কর্ত্তা, হেতুক, সম্পাদক, রচক, an agent, doer; doing, acting, causing, effecting, accomplishing, making.

কারণ, হেতু, প্রয়োজন, বীজ, নিমিত্তে, জন্যে, a cause, reason, motive, occasion, principle, origin; for, because, in order to, on account of.

কারণতা-ত্ব, নিমিত্তত্ব, হেতুতা, causality. [sality, creative.
কারণীভূত, মূলীভূত, সৃষ্টিকর, become a cause, possessed of cau-
কারা, কারাগার,—বন্ধনগৃহ, a prison, place of confinement.
কারি, ক্রিয়া, খাটা, উৎপন্ন, শিল্পকর, an action, act, agency, effect, artist, artificer.
কারিকা, ক্রিয়া, ব্যবসায়, নর্ত্তকী, বিবরণ, লভ্য, যাতনা, an act, agency, art, profession; an actress, dancing-woman, an explanatory sentence, interest of money, sharp pain; *fem.* acting, causing, &c.
কারিকর, শিল্পকর, a mechanic, a workman.
কারিতা-ত্ব, কর্ত্তৃত্ব, নিমিত্ততা, agency, causality.
কারী, কারক, উৎপাদক, acting, doing, causing, occasioning.
কারু, শিল্পকর, নির্ম্মায়ক, শিল্পকর্ম্ম, an artist, artificer, mechanic, agent, doer, maker, a mechanic art, a trade.
কারুজ, যন্ত্র, কল, a piece of mechanism, a manufacture.
কারুণ্য, দয়া, কৃপা, compassion, kindness, tenderness.
কারুন্দিয়া, পটু, চালাক, কর্ম্মণ্য, expert, active, diligent, useful, fit for use.
কার্কশ্য, ক্রূরতা, কৃপণতা, দুরবস্থা, cruelty, hard-heartedness, roughness, niggardliness, difficulty, want.
কার্ত্তিক, শরদের দ্বিতীয় মাস, the seventh Hindoo month.
কার্পণ্য, ব্যয়কুণ্ঠতা, parsimony, niggardliness.
কার্পাস, তুলা, কাপাস, cotton, the cotton plant.
কার্ম্মণ, মায়া, কুহক, ডাইনপনা, magic, sorcery, witchcraft.
কার্ম্মুক, ধনুক, বাঁশ, পটু, a bow, a bamboo; expert, skilful.
কার্য্য, ক্রিয়া, প্রয়োজন, কর্ত্তব্য, a work, deed, business, affair, employment, undertaking, effect, duty.
কার্ষাপণ, ষোড়শ পণ, কাহন, sixteen Pans of cowries.
কাল্, সময়, অবকাশ, মৃত্যু, যম, time, tense, season, period, opportunity, weather, death, regent of death.
কাল, কৃষ্ণবর্ণ, নীলবর্ণ, মলিন, black, dark-blue, swarthy, tarnished, dirty.
কালকিষ্ট, মলিন, filthy, squalid, dirty.
কালকূট, তীব্র বিষ, a mortal poison, a subtle venom.
কালখণ্ড, যকৃৎ, the liver. [season.
কালধর্ম্ম, মরণ, সময় ঔচিত্য, death, a suitable regard to time or

কালবেলা, অশুভকাল, certain periods in each day unpropitious for any undertaking.

কালশিরা, ঘাচিহ্ন, the livid mark from a bruise.

কালসূত্র, নরক বিশেষ, a Hindoo hell.

কালা, কৃষ্ণবর্ণ, সমল, বধির, black, swarthy, soiled, unclean, deaf.

কালাগ্নি, কালানল,—প্রলয়কালের অগ্নি, the final conflagration of the universe.

কালান্তক, যম, Yama the regent of death.

কালাশুদ্ধি, কালাশৌচ,—অশুদ্ধি সময়, any period of ceremonial impurity.

কালি, মোট, প্রসর, product or result of a sum, dimensions of a piece of land.

কালিকা, কালীদেবী, মসী, মেঘসমূহ, কল্য, the goddess *Káli*, ink, cloudiness, the morrow, an instalment of interest, the credit-price of an article.

কালিচা, কালীচা,—ঘাচিহ্ন, the livid mark of a bruise.

কালিঞ্জা, জীর্ণচাল, decayed thatch.

কালিনী, মৃত্যুকর, নাশক, deadly, ruinous, destructive.

কালিমা, কৃষ্ণতা, তমস, blackness, darkness.

কালিষ্ঠ, রৌদ্রপোড়া, পিঙ্গলবর্ণ, sun-burnt, weather-beaten, tawny.

কালী, দেবী, মসী, কলঙ্ক, the goddess, ink or blacking, a stain, stigma; black, filthy, unclean.

কালীন, সাময়িক, pertaining to time, of a particular time.

কাল্পনিক, মিথ্যা, আরোপিত, feigned, fictitious, false, forged, contrived; a hypocrite.

কাল্য, মলিন, মঙ্গলবার্ত্তা, squalid, dingy; auspicious or pleasant discourse.

কাশ, কফ, শ্লেষ্মা, তৃণ বিশেষ, a cough, cold, catarrh; a grass.

কাষ্ঠ, দারু, ইন্ধন, wood, timber, fuel.

কাষ্ঠা, দিক্, দেশ, স্থান, সীমা, প্রকর্ষ, a quarter, region of the world, space, tract, place, scite, limit, a measure of time, excellence, superiority.

কাসী, কফ, শ্লেষ্মা. a cough, cold, rheum.

কাসন, খুষণ, খুকাণ, to cough.

কাসন্দি, কফ নাশক আচার বিশেষ, a cough-mixture of tamarinds and mustard.

কাসীস, পুষ্পক, copperas or green vitriol.

কাসুয়া, কাসরোগী, কফী, afflicted with a cough.

কাস্তিয়া, দাত্র, শস্যকর্ত্তনী, a sickle.
কাহণ, কার্ষাপণ, a denomination of money.
কাহার, বেহারা, a palkee bearer. [report:
কাহিনী, ইতিহাস, বিবরণ, জনরব, a tale, story, narration, history,
কি, জিজ্ঞাসা বোধক শব্দ, *(an interrogative particle:)* what? which? (*repeated*), whether—or? either—or?
কিং, কিম,—প্রশ্নসূচক, *in compos:* what? which?
কিঙ্কর, দাস, ভৃত্য, a servant, a slave.
কিঙ্কিণী, ঘুঙ্গুর, a girdle of small bells, any tinkling ornament:
কিচড়, কিচা,—পঙ্ক, কর্দ্দম, mud, slime, dirt.
কিচির ২, কিচ্ ২, বানরধ্বনি, পক্ষীধ্বনি, the chattering of monkeys; the chirping of birds.
কিচ্মিচান, কিচ্ ২ করণ, to chatter, to chirp. [something:
কিছু, কিয়ৎ, অল্প, কিঞ্চিৎ, some, any, a little, somewhat,
কিজাত, কিপ্রকার, what sort of! (*in ridicule.*)
কিজানি, বুঝি, পাছে, perhaps, lest, for fear that, lest perchance, suppose.
কিঞ্চন, কিঞ্চিৎ,—কোন, কিছু, অল্প, some, any, a little, a few.
কিঞ্চিদপেক্ষা, শীঘ্র, অবিলম্বে, প্রায়, within a little, soon, almost.
কিঞ্চুলুক, কেঁচো, পোকা, a worm.
কিট্‌কিট্, মল, মূত্র, কফাদি, filth, dirt, any animal excretion.
কিট্‌কিটা, মলযুক্ত, মলিন, dirty, filthy, squalid. [insect.
কিণ, ক্ষতচিহ্ন, অঙ্গকড়া, তিল, a scar, wart, corn, mole; a wood-
কিণন, ক্রয়ণ, মূল্য দেওন, to purchase, to buy.
কিনা, অর্থাৎ, সন্দেহ বোধক, that is to say, videlicet, or not?
কিন্তু, পরন্তু, অথো, but, moreover, further.
কিন্নর, স্বর্গের গায়ক, celestial quiristers, demigods with the heads of horses on a human figure.
কিপর্য্যন্ত, কত দূর, কত কাল, how far? how long? till when?
কিবা, কি, কি আশ্চর্য্য, what? what! how excellent! [tion?
কিমর্থে, কেন, কিজন্যে, why? wherefore? with what inten-
কিমাকার, কিরূপ, অদ্ভুতাকৃতি, what sort of! how formed! of an unusual form.
কিম্পচান, কৃপণ, miserly, niggardly, avaricious.
কিম্পুরুষ, কিন্নর, half-human demigods, choristers of heaven.
কিম্বদন্তি, জনশ্রুতি, জনরব, a rumour, report.

কিম্বা, অথবা, or, else, otherwise.
কিম্ভূত, কি, কিপ্রকার, what? how? what kind of? [long?
কিয়ৎ, কিঞ্চিৎ, কত, some, a few, a little; how much? how
কিরণ, রশ্মি, কাটন, লোপন, a ray of light, sun or moon beam; to expunge, erase, cross out.
কিরা, দিব্য, an oath.
কিরাট, বেপারী, কৃপণ, a dealer, a miser; miserly, penurious.
কিরাত, চুয়াড়, মূল বিশেষ, a savage mountaineer; gentian-root.
কিরীচ, কত্তার, a dagger.
কিরীট, চূড়া, মুকুট, a crest, a diadem. [manner.
কিরূপ, কিপ্রকার, কেমন, of what sort or kind? how? in what
কিল, নিশ্চিত, আবশ্য, বটে, certainly, possibly, indeed, verily?
কিলাস, ছুলীরোগ, a blotch, white scab. [mal, a youth.
কিশোর, শিশু ঘোটক, শাবক, যুবন, a colt, the young of any ani-
কীকট, কৃপণ, দরিদ্র, miserly, avaricious, sordid, poor.
কীকস, অস্থি, হাড়, a bone.
কীচক, শব্দকর বাঁশ, a hollow bamboo whistling in the wind.
কীট, কীড়া,—পোকা, an insect, worm, maggot.
কীদৃক্, কীদৃশ,—কিপ্রকার, of what sort? in what manner? how?
কীর, শুকপক্ষী, কশ্মীর দেশীয় ব্যক্তি a parrot; a Cashmirian.
কীরাট, কৃপণ, লোভী, penurious, miserly, avaricious.
কীর্ত্তন, গাওন, গুণবর্ণন, to sing, celebrate, shout for joy.
কীর্ত্তি, যশঃ, সুখ্যাতি স্তুতি, fame, renown, celebration, praise.
কীল-ক, খিল, খোঁটা, মুষ্টি, মুষ্ট্যাঘাত, a pin, bolt, wedge, nail, stake, the fist, a thump, a blow.
কীলন-আন, ঘুষণ, মারণ, খিলন, বাঁধন, to strike with the fist, thump, pummel, to nail, pin, wedge up, fasten to a stake.
কীলাল, জল, সলিল, water.
কীলালধি, সাগর, সমুদ্র, the sea, the ocean. [little, &c.
কু, নিন্দিত, কুৎসিত, ঈষৎ, *a prefix:* evil, base, badly, a
কুআড়া, কুআশা,—কুজ্ঝটী, কুজ্ঝটিকা, a mist, a fog.
কুঁকড়ন, যড় বা কুঞ্চিত হওন, to contract, shrink, shrivel up.
কুক্, নাদ, ভষণ, a voice, the bark of a dog.
কুকর, নুলা, বিকৃতহস্ত, having a crooked or withered arm.
কুকর্ম্মা, কুকর্ম্মী,—দুরাচার, পাপী, wicked, vicious, profligate, sinful.

কুকাপ, ঝঞ্ঝাট, উদ্বেগ, a difficulty, perplexity, dilemma; difficult, perplexing, troublesome.

কুকিল, পিকপক্ষী, the black cuckoo.

কুকুড়া, কুক্কুট, the common fowl, a cock.

কুকুন্দর, নিতম্বগহ্বর, the cavities of the loins.

কুক্কুর, কুকুর,—কুত্তা, শ্বা, গাঁঠিয়াল, a dog, a vegetable perfume.

কুক্কুট, কুকুড়া. উল্কা, a cock, a firebrand, a lighted wisp of straw; a man of mixed cast.

কুক্কুভ, জঙ্গলী কুক্কুট, কলপ, a wild cock, varnish, glossiness.

কুক্কুরব, কুক্কুটধ্বনি, পায়রাধ্বনি, a cackling sound, a cooing.

কুক্ষি, জঠর, পেট. the belly, the abdomen.

কুজী, কুঙ্গী,—দুর্বাক্য, নিন্দা, offensive speech, scurrilous expression, abuse, reproach.

কুঙ্কুম, কেশর, saffron.

কুচ, স্তন, মাই, চেলাকাঠ, a breast, a pap, a chip of wood.

কুচকলিকা, কুচকোরক,—স্ত্রীস্তন. a woman's breast.

কুচক্র, কুমণ্ডলী. কুমন্ত্রণা, evil society, a circle of evil companions, evil advice.

কুচক্রী, কুমন্ত্রী, an evil adviser.

কুচন, চেলান, কুঁকড়ন to cut in pieces, to chip, gnaw, shrink, [contract.

কুচল, ক্ষুদ্র. অল্প, সূক্ষ্ম, small, little.

কুচা, কুচি,—চেলা, খণ্ড,টুকি, a chip, shaving, splinter, fragment, shred, piece.

কুচাগ্র, চুচুক, a nipple.

কুচ্ছন্দ, কুকাব্য, কুৎসিত শ্লোক, doggrel poetry.

কুচ্ছা. নিন্দা, অপবাদ, কলঙ্ক, calumny, slander, censure, accusation, blame, a blot, disgrace.

কুচ্ছিত, মন্দ, অধম, কুরূপ, মলিন, evil, bad, abominable, ugly, deformed, squalid.

কুছু, কিছু. কিঞ্চিৎ, অল্প, some, any, a little.

কুজ, গাড়ু, মঙ্গলগ্রহ, মঙ্গলবার, a hump or curvature of the spine, the planet Mars, Tuesday.

কুজড়-া, তুচ্ছ, অধম, মূঢ়, low, base, mean, vulgar, stupid.

কুজা, বক্র, ন্যুব্জ, জলপাত্র, deformed, crooked, hump-backed an earthen water vessel.

কুজ্ঝটিকা, কুজ্ঝটী,—কুআশা, কুহেড়ী, a mist, a fog.

কুঞ্চিত, বক্র, বাঁকা, curved, bent, crooked, tortuous, curled.
কুঞ্জ, লতাচ্ছাদিত স্থান, উদ্যান, বিষাণ, a bower, arbour, grove, an elephant's tusk, ivory.
কুঞ্জর, হস্তী, মত্ত, an elephant; *in comp*: chief, eminent.
কুট্, দংশন, ব্যথা, শূল, a sting, bite, sudden gripe or pinch.
কুট, কুটা,—চেলা, খণ্ড, a chip, bit, fragment, shred.
কুটন, চূর্ণন, গুঁড়ন, দলন, to beat or pound to powder or pulp, to tread down, to trample.
কুটনী, কুট্টনী, দূতী, a bawd, a procuress, an herb-woman.
কুটনীপনা, দূতীপনা, the profession of a procuress. [&c.
কুটান, ভূমি দলান, to cause cattle to tread down the ground,
কুটার্থ, গুপ্তছল, দ্বৈধ, a covert design, a quibble.
কুটি, গৃহ, খণ্ড, a house, a fragment, bit, chip, morsel.
কুটিল, অসরল, বক্র, ক্রূর, insincere, disingenuous, insidious, crooked, bent, severe, cruel.
কুটী, অট্টালিকা, a European's house, a palace, factory.
কুটীর, ক্ষুদ্র গৃহ, ঝুপড়ী, a small house, hut, hovel, shed.
কুটুম্ব, সম্পর্কীয়, সন্তান, পরিবার, a kinsman, relation, connexion, offspring, family.
কুটুম্বী, গৃহস্থ, সপরিজন, a householder, master of a family.
কুট্‌কট্‌, কুট্‌কুটানি,—ব্যথা, শূল, চিড়্‌চিড়্‌, a throbbing sensation, a twinge; querulousness, peevishness.
কুট্‌কুট্যা, চিড়্‌চিড়িয়া, peevish, querulous, hard to please.
কুট্টনী, কুটনী, দূতী, a bawd, a procuress.
কুট্‌মল, মুকুল, an opening flower-bud.
কুঠ, বৃক্ষ, কুষ্ঠরোগ, a tree; the leprosy.
কুঠরী, গৃহ, ঝুপড়ী, a house, an apartment, a cottage.
কুঠার, কুড়ালি, an axe, hatchet. [bank, granary.
কুঠী, অট্টালিকা, গোলা, a European's house, palace, factory,
কুঠীয়া, কুঠ্যা,—কুষ্ঠী, জড়, leprous, dull, torpid, indolent.
কুড়, কুষ্ঠরোগ, বিঘা, স্তূপ, leprosy, a bigah measure, a heap.
কুড়ন,-আন, সঞ্চয়ন, যড়ান, to collect, pick up, glean, gather into a heap. [found; a foundling.
কুড়নীয়া, কুড়ানীয়া,—সঞ্চিত, ঘড়িত, প্রাপ্ত, collected together,
কুড়া, বিঘা, a bigah of land.
কুড়ালি, কুড়ুল,—কুঠার, an axe, a hatchet.

কুড়ি, বিশ, কুষ্ঠরোগ, a score, twenty; the leprosy.
কুড়িয়া, কুড়্যা,—কুষ্ঠী, জড়, কুটীর, leprous, dull, torpid, lazy; a hut, shed, stall.
কুড্য, প্রাচীর, লেপা, a wall, the plastering of a wall.
কুড়্যামি, আলস্যামি, জড়তা, indolence, torpor, laziness, slowness.
কুণ, বীণাদির ধ্বনি, the sound or note of a stringed instrument.
কুণপ, মৃতশরীর, শব, a dead body, a corpse, a carcase.
কুণী. শুষ্কহস্ত, আঙ্গুলহাড়া, having a withered arm; a whitlow.
কুণুয়া, কুণো,—লাজুক, ত্রাসযুক্ত, কোণস্থায়ী, shy, shrinking from sight, slinking into a corner.
কুণোমি, লাজুকতা, ভয়, shyness, a shrinking from sight.
কুণ্ঠ. কুণ্ঠিত,—অলস, মূর্খ, indolent, lazy, slow, stupid, foolish.
কুণ্ড, গর্ত্ত, যজ্ঞখাত, কূপ, জারজ, a pit, sacrificial pit, bowl, bason, pool, well; the bastard of an adultress.
কুণ্ডল, কর্ণভূষণ, আঙ্গুটা, বালা ইত্যাদি, an ear-ring, ring, bracelet, collar, fetter, coil of a rope.
কুণ্ডলী, কুণ্ডলবিশিষ্ট, কুণ্ডলাকার, সর্প, wearing an ear-ring, coiling, winding; a serpent.
কুণ্ডিকা, কুণ্ডী,—পাত্র বিশেষ, a bason, hemispherical vessel.
কুতঃ, কোথাহইতে, কেমন, whence? from which? how?
কুতপ, মধ্যাহ্ন, দুপরবেলা, বড়গ্রীষ্ম, noon-tide, great or oppressive heat.
কুতুপ, কুতূ,—কুপা, চর্ম্মনির্ম্মিত তৈলপাত্র, a leathern oil-bottle.
কুতূহল, কৌতুক, উদ্যোগ, চমৎকার, বাসনা, sport, diversion, eagerness, impetuosity, wonder, surprize, inclination, desire. [brisk, pleasurable.
কুতূহলী, খেলাড়ু, ব্যগ্র, আনন্দদ, sportive, playful, impetuous,
কুত্তা, কুকুর, শ্বা, a dog.
কুত্র, কোথায়, কাহাতে, where? wherein?
কুত্রচিৎ, যে কোনস্থানে, wherever, wheresoever.
কুত্রাপি, যেখানে ২, কোনখানে, *id.* any where, some where.
কুৎসা, নিন্দা, কলঙ্ক, কুরূপতা, reproach, censure, calumny, moral blemish, deformity, ugliness.
কুৎসিত, তুচ্ছ, নিন্দিত, মন্দ, কুরূপী, low, vile, evil, bad, ugly, deformed, disgusting.

কুথলী, হস্তিঘোটকাদির সজ্জা, an elephant's housings, horse-cloth.
কুদাল, কুদালি, কুদ্দাল,—ভূমি কাটনের অস্ত্র, a hoe, spade.
কুন্তল, কেশ, চুল, যব, hair of the head, a lock of hair, barley.
কুন্থন, কোঁকান, কাতরাণ, to groan, moan, suffer pain.
কুন্দ, চম্বেলি, মল্লিকা, jasmine, frankincense, a turner's lathe.
কুন্দকর, কুঁদারু, a turner. [to turn in a lathe.
কুন্দন, উল্লম্ফন, ফাঁদন, to prance, skip, frisk, dance for joy,
কুন্দল, নীলপদ্ম, কলহ, a blue lotus, a quarrel, dispute.
কুন্দলীয়া, কলহী, দ্বন্দ্বী, quarrelsome, litigious. [kincense.
কুন্দুরু, কন্দুরুকী,—শল্লকী, শল্লকীরস, the frankincense tree, fran-
কুপ, কুপা,—কুতুপ, চর্ম্মনির্ম্মিত তৈলপাত্র, a leathern oil-bottle.
কুপিত, ক্রোধান্বিত, বিরক্ত, angry, provoked, vexed.
কুপেঁচ, কুকুঁদিত কাষ্ঠ, কুরূপী, badly turned, deformed, ugly.
কুবলয়, জলজপুষ্প, পদ্ম, a water-lily in general.
কুবিক্রম, অত্যাচার, উপদ্রব, arbitrary power, tyranny.
কুবের, ধনাধিপতি, Cuvera or the god of wealth.
কুব্জ, বক্রপৃষ্ঠ, ন্যুব্জ, বক্রীভূত, hump-backed, crooked.
কুমড়া, কুষ্মাণ্ড, a gourd, a pumpkin.
কুমার, বালক, পুত্র, রাজপুত্র, কুলাল, a boy under five years, a lad, son, prince, a potter.
কুমারিকা, কুমারী,—কন্যা, দুর্গা, পুত্রী, কীলাধার, a virgin, maiden, girl from ten to twelve years, Durgá, a daughter, the catch of a door-latch.
কুমুদ, শুক্লপদ্ম, রক্তপদ্ম the white or red lotus.
কুম্ভীর, নক্র, জলহস্তী, a crocodile.
কুম্প, বক্রহস্ত, crooked-armed.
কুম্ভ, কলসী, রাশিবিশেষ, হস্তিগণ্ড, a water-jar, the sign Aquarius, the frontal globe of an elephant.
কুম্ভক, নিশ্বাস অবরোধ, a stoppage of the mouth and nostrils to prevent breathing; (a religious ceremony.)
কুম্ভকার, কুলাল, কুমার, a potter.
কুম্ভিল, চোর, পদহারক, টিপ্পনীকার, শ্যালক, a thief, plagiarist, paraphrast, a wife's brother.
কুম্ভীপাক, নরক বিশেষ, a Hindoo hell.
কুম্ভীর, নক্র, ঘড়িয়াল, a crocodile, an alligator.
কুরঙ্গ, মৃগ, হরিণ, a deer, antelope.

কুরণ, চাঁচন, কুচান, to scrape, pare, gnaw.
কুরণ্ড, কোষবৃদ্ধি, hernia, hydrocele, &c.
কুরর, করল.—ক্রোরপক্ষী, an eagle.
কুরুচি, বিরক্তি. ঘৃণা. disgust, distaste, dislike, disrelish.
কুরুজ, রেপ, the wards of a lock.
কুরুট, ওঁচলা, অঙ্গার, sweepings, filth, rubbish.
কুর্কুর, বুক্কন, ভষণ, শ্বা, a yelping, a barking; a dog.
কুর্দন, কুন্দন, ফাঁদন, খেলন, to skip, frisk, gambol, play.
কুর্পর, জানু, কণুই, অধীন, the knee, the elbow; under controul, subject to. [a herd, flock.
কুল, বংশ, জাতি, পাল, জন্তুসমূহ, race, lineage, family, tribe,
কুলক, উত্তমবংশজ ত, well-born; the protraction of a sentence beyond a stanza, *in poetry*.
কুলকর্ম্ম, কুলধর্ম্ম,—বংশের পরম্পারা ব্যবহার, the usages or peculiar practices of a tribe, cast, or family.
কুলজ, উত্তমবংশজাত, সদ্বংশীয়, of a good family, well-born.
কুলজী, বংশাবলি, a genealogy, pedigree.
কুলটা, অসতী, বেশ্যা, an unchaste woman, courtezan, harlot.
কুলন, নির্বাহ হওন, প্রচুর, to be in sufficient quantity for, to abound; sufficient, enough.
কুলপতি, বংশপ্রধানব্যক্তি, the head or chief of a family.
কুলবতী, সদ্বংশীয়া স্ত্রী, a woman of a reputable family.
কুলবধু. কুলস্ত্রী,—সতী, অনন্যগামিনী স্ত্রী, a virtuous wife.
কুলবধুতা, সতীত্ব. পাতিব্রত্য, chastity in a wife.
কুলশীল, বংশমর্য্যাদাবর্দ্ধক আচার, conduct honorable to a family, family honor. [marriages.
কুলাচার্য্য, ঘটক, বংশগুরু, a family genealogist who contracts
কুলায়ন, পাওন, উবরণ, নির্বাহ করণ, to possess, abound in, abound, be sufficient for, to supply, furnish.
কুলানীয়, অধ্যক্ষ, superintending; a superintendant.
কুলায়, নীড়, বাসা, বসতি, a nest, a place of residence, abode.
কুলাল, কুম্ভকার, কুমার, a potter.
কুলিশ, ইন্দ্রের বজ্র, the thunderbolt of Indra.
কুলীন, উত্তমবংশজাত, nobly born, of high descent, noble.
কুলীর, কাঁকড়া, কর্কট, a crab.
কুল্য, কুলা,—সুর্প, a winnowing fan.

কুল, মাত্র, সর্ব্বতোভাবে, only, wholly.
কুলই, কঙ্কর, gravel, lime-stone pebbles.
কুশ, যজ্ঞতৃণ, a sacred or sacrificial grass.
কুশন, কাষ্ঠকাটন, চেলান, to rough-hew timber.
কুশল, কল্যাণ, শুভ, পুণ্য, সামর্থ্য, নিপুণ, সুখী, welfare, happiness, safety, virtue, virtuous act, ability, competency; expert, clever, safe, happy.
কুশলকারী, হিতকারী, beneficent, promoting the happiness of others.
কুশলী, সুখী, ভাগ্যবান্, happy, prosperous.
কুশাসন, কুশ নির্ম্মিত যে আসন, a mat of Cusha grass.
কুশী, ফাল, ধারা, ক্ষুদ্র কোষা, a ploughshare, a cotton-pod, a libation cup.
কুশীদ, কুসীদ,—বৃদ্ধিজীবিকা, ঋণদান, usury, a loan.
কুশীল, দুরাত্মা, দুষ্ট, দুষ্কর্ম্মা, inclined to evil, evil-minded, wicked.
কুশূল, গোলা, ধান্যপাত্র, a granary, barn, vessel for grain, cupboard.
কুষ্ঠ, কুড়ি, শ্বিত্র, leprosy.
কুষ্ঠী, কুষ্ঠ বিশিষ্ট, শ্বিত্রী, leprous; a leper.
কুষ্মাণ্ড, কুমড়া, a pumpkin, a gourd.
কুসুম, পুষ্প, ফল, রজস্, a flower, fruit, the menses.
কুসুম্ভ, পীতপুষ্প বিশেষ, the safflower plant.
কুহক, ভোজবিদ্যা, কার্ম্মণ, মায়া, মোহনী, sleight of hand, sorcery, delusion, deception, fascination.
কুহকী, ভেলকী, মায়াবী, প্রতারক, ছলী, a juggler, magician, sorcerer, rogue, cheat.
কুহর, গর্ত্ত, ছিদ্র, কর্ণ, a cavity, hollow, hole, rent, the ear.
কুহু, অমাবস্যা, কোকিল রব, the new moon, the cry of the cuckoo.
কুহেড়িকা, কুহেড়ী,—কুজ্ঝটী, a fog, mist, haze.
কূট, শৃঙ্গ, রাশি, কলসী, ধাতু, হাতুড়ী, ফাল, ফাঁদ, মায়া, কপট, মিথ্যা, অধম, a mountain-peak, summit, heap of grain, water-jar, elementary substance, hammer, mallet, plough-share, a snare, trap, illusion, fraud, deceit, falsehood; false, low, vile.
কূটস্থ, স্থির, অচল, অটল, fixed, uniform, unchangeable, elementary, perpetually the same, as the soul, &c.

কূটার্থ, ঘোরার্থ, কল্পিত কথা, obscurity of meaning, ambiguity, a fiction..

কূড্য, প্রাচীর, ভিত্তি, a wall.

কূতনী, কাপড় বিশেষ, a sort of cloth half-silk half-cotton.

কূথলী, থৈলী, ঝুলী, a satchel, a wallet.

কূপ, কূয়া, ইন্দারা, গর্ত্ত, a well, a pit, a hollow.

কূর্চ্চ, ভ্রূমধ্য, the upper part of the nose.

কূর্চ্চিকা, গাঢ়দুগ্ধ, thickened milk. [amusement.

কূর্দ্দন, কুন্দন, ফাঁদন, ক্রীড়া, to prance, gambol; play, sport,

কূর্ম্ম, কচ্ছপ, a tortoise, a turtle.

কূল, নদির তট, তীর, ভেড়ী, পুষ্করিণী, a river's bank, shore, edge, mound, pond, pool, the rear of an army.

কৃকলাস, টিক্‌টিকী, শরট, a lizard, a cameleon.

কৃচ্ছ্র, কষ্ট, পীড়া, তপস্যা, ব্যামোহ, পীড়িত, পীড়াকর, পাপী, bodily pain, agony, penance, distress, difficulty; suffering pain, painful, wicked, sinful.

কৃচ্ছ্রগত, যন্ত্রণাযুক্ত, ক্লিষ্ট, তপস্যাগত, suffering anguish, in pain, tormented, doing penance.

কৃৎ, কারী, কারক, *affix:* doing, performing.

কৃত, চরিত, সাধিত, সিদ্ধ. done, performed, made, effected, accomplished. [successful.

কৃতকর্ম্মা, কৃতকৃত্য,—কর্ম্মসিদ্ধ, অভীষ্টসিদ্ধ, having performed a work,

কৃতকৃতার্থ, চরিতার্থ, ভাগ্যবান্, having succeeded, successful, fortunate.

কৃতঘ্ন, অকৃতজ্ঞ, অনুপকারজ্ঞ, ungrateful, forgetful of benefits, returning evil for good. [grateful, thankful.

কৃতজ্ঞ, উপকারজ্ঞ, প্রত্যুপকারী, mindful of benefits received,

কৃতদার, ঊঢ়, বিবাহিত, married.

কৃতবিক্রয়, বিক্রীত, বেচা, disposed of, sold.

কৃতাঞ্জলি-পুট, করপুটকারী, মর্য্যাদক, বিনয়ী, holding up the hands, respectful, humble, suppliant.

কৃতান্ত, মৃত্যু, যম, সিদ্ধান্ত, death, Yama or the universal destroyer, a demonstrated conclusion, established doctrine.

কৃতাপরাধ, অপরাধী, দোষী, guilty, criminal. [object.

কৃতার্থ, কৃতকার্য্য, সিদ্ধার্থ, successful, having accomplished an

কৃতার্থী, চরিতার্থী, কৃতজ্ঞ, desirous of success, thankful.
কৃতি, ক্রিয়া, কর্ম্ম, an act, action, deed.
কৃতিতা-ত্ব, পাণ্ডিত্য, যোগ্যতা, পুণ্য, learning, acquirement, qualification, capacity, merit, virtue, piety.
কৃতী, পণ্ডিত, গুণবান্, প্রবীণ, ক্ষমতাবান্, ধার্ম্মিক, learned, accomplished, active, expert, capable, worthy, virtuous, pious.
কৃত্তি, কৃষ্ণসারাদি চর্ম্ম, an antelope's skin, an animal hide.
কৃত্য, কর্ত্তব্যকর্ম্ম, প্রয়োজন, duty, what ought to be done, a work, motive, cause.
কৃত্রিম, রচিত, কাল্পনিক, মিথ্যা, artificial, fictitious, counterfeit, forged, false.
কৃৎস্ন, সমস্ত, সমুদায়, all, whole, entire.
কৃপণ, কৃপণাশয়,—ব্যয়কুণ্ঠ, অধম, অদাতা, penurious, miserly, sordid, vile, abject; a miser.
কৃপয়া, দয়াপূর্ব্বক, দয়াকরিয়া, graciously, with compassion.
কৃপা, দয়া, করুণা, অনুগ্রহ, compassion, pity, mercy. clemency, kindness, tenderness, favour, goodness.
কৃপালু, দয়াশীল, করুণাময়, merciful. humane, compassionate, kind, tender-hearted, &c.
কৃমি, কীট, লাক্ষা, a worm, maggot, insect, lac-dye.
কৃশ, ক্ষীণ, সূক্ষ্ম, wasted, emaciated, meagre, thin, little, small.
কৃশাঙ্গী, উত্তমাঙ্গ বিশিষ্টা স্ত্রী, a woman of a slender delicate shape or figure, well-shaped, handsome.
কৃশানু, অগ্নি, অনল, fire.
কৃষক, কৃষাণ.—চাষী, লাঙ্গলা, a cultivator, peasant, farmer, husbandman.
কৃষি, কৃষাণী,—চাষকর্ম্ম, agriculture, husbandry, cultivation, ploughing, tillage.
কৃষীবল, কৃষাণ, চাষী, a husbandman, farmer, peasant.
কৃষ্ণ, কালবর্ণ, নীলবর্ণ, মরিচ, নারায়ণ, black, dark-blue; black pepper, the god Krishna.
কৃষ্ণপক্ষ, চন্দ্রের হ্রাসকাল, the fortnight of the moon's decrease.
কৃষ্ণপক্ষীয়, চন্দ্রহ্রাসকালসম্বন্ধীয়, বিজন্মা, জারজ, pertaining to the wane of the moon; bastard, illegitimate.
কৃষ্ণসার, কালমৃগ, the black antelope.
কৃষ্ণাজিন, কৃত্তি, কৃষ্ণসারের চর্ম্ম, the hide of a black antelope.

কৢপ্ত, নিয়ত, কৃত, নামধেয়, fixed, appointed, made, denominated, called.

কে, কেবা,—কোনলোক, who? what person?

কেউ, কোনলোক, কেহ, any one, some one.

কেকা, ময়ূরধ্বনি, a peacock's note.

কেচিৎ, কোনলোকেরা, (*plural*) some persons.

কেণন, ক্রয়ণ, ক্রয়করাণ, to buy, to employ another to buy.

কেতন, ধ্বজ, চিহ্ন, নিমন্ত্রণ, নিবাস, কৃত্য, a flag, banner, sign, invitation, house, abode, place, duty.

কেতু, ধ্বজ, ধূমকেতু, নবমগ্রহ, a banner, flag, comet, falling-star, descending node, the 9th planet.

কেদার, ক্ষেত্র, a field.

কেন, কি নিমিত্ত, কি কারণ, why? wherefore?

কেননা, কারণ, যেহেতু, for, because.

কেবল, মাত্র, শুদ্ধ, নিতান্ত, simple, mere, alone; only, absolutely, certainly.

কেমন, কিপ্রকার, কিরূপ, how? in what way? what sort of?

কেয়ূর, তাড়, a metal ornament for the small of the arm.

কেরবাল, বটিয়া, বৈটা, a small oar, a paddle.

কেরায়া, ভাড়া, rent, hire.

কেলান, ছালতোলন, to strip off bark, to shell, to peel fruit, to skin an animal.

কেলি, বিহার, ক্রীড়া, play, sport, diversion.

কেল্যানী, কাঞ্জী, rice-gruel, sour rice water.

কেশ, চুল, অশ্বঘাড়লোম, the hair of the head, a lock of hair, a horse's mane.

কেশব, প্রশস্তকেশযুক্ত, বিষ্ণু, hairy, shaggy; (*epithet* of Vishnu.)

কেশবেশ, চুলের সংস্কার, খোপা, a tress or fillet of hair.

কেশমার্জ্জনী, চিরুণী, a hair-comb.

কেশর, পদ্মাদির সূক্ষ্ম সূত্র, পক্ষ্ম, কুঙ্কুম, the filaments of a flower, saffron.

কেশরী, কেশযুক্ত, সিংহ, অশ্ব, having a mane; a lion, a horse; a hair.

কেশাকেশি, পরস্পরকেশগ্রহণ, a mutual pulling of the hair and fighting, a squabble, brawl.

কেশী, প্রশস্তকেশযুক্ত, hairy, shaggy.

কেহ, কেহ,—কোনলোক, some one, any one.

কৈ, কোথায়, কুত্র, where ?
কৈঙ্কর্য্য, দাস্য, অধীনতা, servitude, slavery.
কৈটভ, দৈত্য বিশেষ, a certain evil genius or demon.
কৈতব, কপট, চাতুরী, খলতা, deceit, fraud, craftiness, imposition, swindling.
কৈবর্ত্ত, ধীবর, জালিয়া, নাবিক, a fisherman, a waterman.
কৈবল্য, মুক্তি, absorption into the deity, eternal emancipation from matter.
কৈরব, পদ্ম, the lotus.
কৈলা দুগ্ধপোষ্যবৎস, a sucking calf.
কৈলাস, কুবেরের নিবাস স্থান, mount Cailása, the residence of Cuvera and favourite haunt of Vishnu.
কৈশোর, বাল্যদশা, youth, boyhood.
কো, কোআড়া,—কুজ্ঝটী, a mist, a fog.
কোঁকড়, কোঁকড়া,—চাঁচর, কুঞ্চিত, তোবড়া, শুষ্ক, curled, crumpled, rumpled, shrunk up, shrivelled.
কোঁকড়ান, ঘড়ান, তোবড়ন, তোবড়ান, শুকান, to curl, crimp, plait, crumple, furl, shrivel up, to cause to shrivel up or contract.
কোঁকান, কুন্থন, বিলাপন, to moan, groan, grunt.
কোঁচ, পোলো বিশেষ, টেঁটা a sheaf of fish-spears, a harpoon.
কোঁচড়, পরিহিত বস্ত্রের অগ্রভাগ, the lap, the end of a garment gathered into a bag.
কোঁচা, পরিহিত বস্ত্রের কুঞ্চিতভাগ, the pendent tuck of a garment.
কোক, বৃক, শরট, মণ্ডূক, চক্রবাক, খর্জ্জূর, a wolf, a lizard, cameleon, frog, the ruddy-goose, the wild date-tree.
কোকনদ, রক্তপদ্ম, the red lotus.
কোকিল, পিকপক্ষী, the black cuckoo.
কোটন,-আন, টুকিং করণ, চূর্ণন, to mince, cut up, pound, beat to powder.
কোটনা, ভেড়ুয়া, ঘনুয়া, a pander, a pimp.
কোটনাপনা, কোটনামি,—ভেড়ুয়াপনা, a pandering to another.
কোটর, বৃক্ষের ছিদ্র, a hollow in a tree, a hollow tree.
কোটাল, প্রহরী, চৌকিয়া, a watchman, constable.
কোটালী, কোটালকর্ম্ম, কোটালসমূহ, a watchman's office or duty, a city-police.

কোটি, কোটা,—এক শত লক্ষ, অস্ত্রাগ্র, প্রতিজ্ঞা, নিয়ম, পূর্ব্বপক্ষ, a crore or 10,000,000; the point of a sword, the end of a bow, a wager, promise, engagement, assertion. proposition. [ever.

কোটিকল্প, সদাসর্ব্বক্ষণে, নিত্য, to a crore of Calpas, *i. e.* for

কোট্ট, কোট,—দুর্গ, a fort, fortress, tower.

কোট্যর্দ্ধ পঞ্চাশ লক্ষ, half a crore or five millions.

কোট্যুদ্ধার, প্রতিজ্ঞাপালন, পক্ষব্যাখ্যা, সিদ্ধান্ত, the fulfilment of a promise, solution of a proposition.

কোঠ, কুষ্ঠ, ছক, leprosy, the squares on a chess-board.

কোঠরী, কুটরী, an apartment, a room.

কোঠী, কুটী, a factory, manufactory, bank, counting-house.

কোড়ন, বিন্ধন, ভেদন, খনন, to perforate, bore, dig.

কোড়া, কশা, a scourge, a whip. [elbow.

কোণ, রেখাদ্বয়ের সন্ধিস্থান, আড়, কণুই, a corner, angle, the

কোণটানা, আড়েটানা, কোণাকোণিরেখা, a diagonal line.

কোণা, কোণ, an angle, a corner. [corner.

কোণাকোণি, আড়ে ২, diagonally, transversely, from corner to

কোণী, কোণাকৃতি, কুল্প, angular, having a crooked arm.

কোথায়, কোনখানে, কুত্রাপি, where ? whither ? anywhere.

কোন, কে, কি, কেহ, কিছু, who ? which ? what ? any, some.

কোপ, ক্রোধ, রাগ, wrath, rage, fury, anger, passion.

কোপতঃ, রাগপূর্ব্বক, angrily, through passion.

কোপন, ক্রোধন, রাগন, ক্রোধান্বিত, to be angry, to rage; passionate, angry, wrathful, furious.

কোপান, ক্রোধান, রাগান, চিড়ান, to incense, irritate, provoke, anger, enrage. [lent, wrathful.

কোপশীল, কোপী,—রাগশীল, ক্রোধান্বিত, passionate, angry, viru-

কোবিদ, পণ্ডিত, wise, learned. [flexible, delicate.

কোমল. মৃদু, অকঠিন, নরম, mild, gentle, affable, tender, soft,

কোরক, কলিকা, a flower-bud. [grate.

কোরণ.-আণ, আঁচড়ান, ঘর্ষণ, চাঁচন, to scratch, rasp, scrape,

কোল, ক্রোড়, নির্ব্বাতস্থান, করতল, দিক্, ভেলক, শূকর, the bosom, an embrace, a haven, harbour, the palm of the hand, concave side of a leaf, &c. a point of the compass, a raft, a hog.

কোলক, মরিচ, long pepper.
কোলপাতী, ক্রোড়পত্র, a postcript, codicil, slip of writing.
কোলাকেলি, আলিঙ্গন, a mutual embrace.
কোয়ালি, অভ্যর্থনা,প্রত্যাশা, a welcome, encouragement, hope.
কোলাহল, গোলমাল, গণ্ডগোল, a confused or tumultuous noise, tumult, uproar.
কোষ, মুকুল, খাপ, বীজাধার, শূক, পাত্র, পাদুকা, হস্তকুণ্ড, ধনাগার, ধন, অবিধান, জরায়ু, মুষ্ক, ডিম, মণ্ডল, অষ্টি, জাতীফল, পরীক্ষা, a bud, sheath, seed-vessel, receptacle, the beard of corn, a drinking or sacrificial vessel, a shoe, sandal, the hollow palm of the hand, a treasury, treasure, a dictionary, vocabulary, the womb, scrotum, testicle, penis, an egg, a ball or globe, fruit-stone, nutmeg, cocoon, a judicial ordeal.
কোষা, ডোঙ্গা, যজ্ঞপাত্র, হস্তকুণ্ড, a canoe, sacrificial vessel, hollow palm.
কোষী, পূজাপাত্র, a sacrificial vessel.
কোষ্ঠ-1, গোলা, কুঠরী, বুক, শৌচ, বিষ্ঠা, a granary, chamber, the body of a carriage, a' drawer, the stomach, evacuation by stool, ordure.
কোষ্ঠী, জন্মপত্রিকা, প্রাক্তন, a calculated nativity, destiny.
কোহাড়া, কুজ্ঝটী, a fog, a mist.
কৌক্কুটিক, কপটী, ভণ্ডবিটল, ভণ্ডতপস্বী, a hypocrite, a description of hypocritical devotees.
কৌট-1, ডিবা, পেটী, a canister, a box.
কৌটিল্য কাপট্য, অসারল্য, খলতা, deceit, guile, insincerity, craftiness, dishonesty.
কৌড়ি, কপর্দ্দক, কড়ি, a cowry.
কৌতর, পায়রা, পারাবত, a pigeon.
কৌতুক, লীলা, রহস্য, পরব, পরিহাস, গপ্পি, diversion, sport, fun, a show, entertainment, spectacle, festival, jest, raillery, humour, wit.
কৌতুকী, রসিক, ব্যঙ্গ, jocose, funny ; a jest, a joke.
কৌতুকীয়, রসিক, উপহাসক, jocose, funny ; a wag, a showman.
কৌপীন, কড়া, কপ্নী, ক্ষুদ্র কাপড়, a small strip of cloth covering the privities.

কৌবেরী, উত্তরদিক্, the north quarter.
কৌমার, বালককাল, যৌবন, youth, childhood, boyhood.
কৌমারী, মাতৃগণের একা, স্কন্দশক্তি, one of the seven divine mothers or personified energies of the gods.
কৌমুদী চন্দ্রিকা, moonlight: *given as a title to books.* [family.
কৌল, কুলধর্ম্মাচারী, following the practice of his tribe or
কৌলটেয়, ভ্রষ্টাস্ত্রী পুত্র, জারজ, the bastard of a married woman.
কৌলিক, বংশীয়, বংশধর্ম্ম, belonging to or customary in a family.
কৌলীন্য, বংশমর্য্যাদা, nobility of birth.
কৌশল-্য, কল্যাণ, পটুতা, উপায়, ছল, welfare, happiness, eminence in art or science, policy, art, device, stratagem, contrivance.
কৌষেয়, পট্ট নির্ম্মিত বস্ত্র, silken, made of silk.
কৌস্তুভ, বিষ্ণুর ভূষণ মণি, the breast-jewel of Vishnu.
ক্রকচ, করাত, a saw.
ক্রকর, করাত, দীন, তিত্তিরপক্ষী, a saw, a poor man, a partridge.
ক্রতু, যাগ, পূজা, a sacrifice, offering, worship.
ক্রন্দন, রোদন, বিলাপন, to weep, cry, lament, wail, howl.
ক্রন্দনীয়, রোদনীয়, বিলাপনীয়, lamentable, to be wept for.
ক্রব্য, মাংস, আমিষ, পলল, meat, raw flesh.
ক্রব্যাদ, রাক্ষস, মনুষ্যভোজী, মাংসভোজী, a goblin, giant, cannibal, flesh-eater; carnivorous.
ক্রম, পাদনিক্ষেপ, গতি, আনুপূর্ব্বী, বিধি, a step, progress, order, succession, series, degree, method, precept.
ক্রমনিম্ন, ঢাল, a slope, slant, declivity.
ক্রমশঃ, পরম্পরায়, অল্পে২, in succession, successively, gradually, regularly. [terrupted.
ক্রমাগত, আনুপূর্ব্বিক, পরম্পরাগত, successive, regular, uni-
ক্রমান্বয়ী, ক্রমানুযায়ী,—আনুপূর্ব্বিক, following in the direct order of a series or of succession.
ক্রমিক, পরম্পর, আনুপূর্ব্বিক, successive, gradual.
ক্রমী, কীট, a worm. [sively, successively.
ক্রমে২, অল্পে২, পরম্পরায়, gradually, by degrees, progres-
ক্রমোৎক্রম, ক্রমরাহিত্য, চঞ্চলতা, irregularity, disorder, confusion.
ক্রয়, কেণা, কিণন, a purchase, buying.
ক্রয়ণ, কিণন, to buy, purchase.

ক্রয়বিক্রয়, বাণিজ্য, পরিবর্ত্ত, trade, commerce, traffic, barter.
ক্রয়ী, ক্রয়কারী, ক্রেতা, purchasing, dealing; a purchaser.
ক্রয্য, ক্রেতব্য, ক্রেয়, মূল্য, purchaseable, exposed for sale.
ক্রান্ত, পাদার্পিত, গত, চলিত, stepped, gone, passed over.
ক্রান্তি, আরোহ, উদ্গম, উৎকর্ষ, ascension, a surmounting, surpassing, excelling. [trader.
ক্রায়ক, ক্রয়কারী, বণিক, purchasing; a purchaser, dealer,
ক্রিমি, কীট, পোকা, an insect, worm, maggot, lac-dye.
ক্রিয়া, কর্ম্ম, যাগাদি, পূজা, শ্রাদ্ধ, ব্যাপার, an act, action, deed, work, religious acts, worship, ablutions, offerings, &c. funeral rites, affair, business.
ক্রিয়াহনন, বাধন, ফল নিবারণ, to counteract, defeat an intention, make an act ineffectual.
ক্রীড়ন, খেলন, লীলা করণ, to play, sport, toy.
ক্রীড়া, কেলি, কৌতুক, লীলা, সম্ভোগ, sport, play, amusement, pastime, a show, game, wantonness, lasciviousness, sexual enjoyment.
ক্রীত, কেনা, purchased, bought.
ক্রুদ্ধ, কোপান্বিত, রাগাল, angry, vexed, wroth, passionate.
ক্রূর, নির্দয়, কঠিন, শক্ত, ভয়ানক, উপদ্রবী, cruel, pitiless, unfeeling, harsh, severe, hard, solid, terrible, mischievous, destructive.
ক্রূরিমা, নিষ্ঠুরতা, কাঠিন্য, cruelty, unfeelingness, hardheartedness, severity, harshness.
ক্রেতব্য, ক্রেয়,—মূল্য, বিক্রয়ণীয়, purchaseable, marketable.
ক্রেতা, ক্রয়কারী, গ্রাহক, a purchaser, buyer.
ক্রোড়, কক্ষ, কটিদেশ, বক্ষস্থল, কোল, the flanks, hips, haunches, breast, chest, bosom, embrace.
ক্রোড়পত্র, কোলপাতী, a postscript, codicil, slip of writing omitted in its due place.
ক্রোধ, কোপ, রাগ, anger, wrath, rage, fury, passion.
ক্রোধী, কোপান্বিত, রাগী, angry, passionate, furious, wrathful.
ক্রোর, কোটি, এক শত লক্ষ, a crore or ten millions.
ক্রোর, ক্রোঞ্চ,—কুরলপক্ষী, the osprey or fishing-eagle.
ক্রোশ, চারি সহস্র হস্ত পরিমাণ, a distance of 400 cubits or nearly nine furlongs.

ক্লান্ত, শ্রমার্ত্ত, শ্রান্ত, fatigued, tired, wearied, languid, exhausted.

ক্লান্তি, শ্রান্তি. শ্রম, weariness, fatigue, exhaustion.

ক্লিন্ন, আর্দ্র ভিজা, পুঁজময়, wet, damp, moist, humid, corrupted.

ক্লিশিত, ক্লিষ্ট,—কাতর, দুঃখিত, শ্রান্ত, distressed, afflicted, wretched, wearied, fatigued.

ক্লিষ্টি, দুঃখ, বিপদ, শ্রান্তি, affliction, distress, calamity, weariness.

ক্লীব, নপুংসক, নির্ব্বল, অলস, জড়, শণ্ঢ, neuter, impotent, weak, idle, slothful, stupid; an eunuch, hermaphrodite.

ক্লেদ, আর্দ্রতা, পুঁজ, রসাদি, moisture, dampness, pus, ichor, clammy filth, perspiration, &c.

ক্লেশ, আপদ, খেদ, ব্যথা, চিন্তা, বিষয়কর্ম্ম, আয়াস, affliction, distress, calamity, pain, anguish, care, trouble, worldly occupation, labour, difficulty.

ক্লেশন, তাপান, পীড়ন, জ্বালান, to distress, afflict, pain, trouble, vex, harrass, &c.

ক্লোম, কোঙ্গা, পটকা, the bladder.

ক্ব, কোথায়, where? in what place or degree?

ক্বচিৎ, কোনস্থানে, somewhere.

ক্বণ, কাণ,—বীণাদির শব্দ, sound, musical sound, chink of money.

ক্বণিত, নাদিত, বাজিত, made to sound, struck as a musical string or metallic vessel.

ক্বথিত, সিদ্ধ. পক্ব, boiled, decocted, stewed, digested.

ক্বাথ, নির্য্যাস, a decoction, a solution prepared by heat.

ক্ষণ, অত্যল্পকাল, নিমিষ, অবকাশ, বিশ্রাম, পর্ব্ব, a period of four minutes, a moment, instant, leisure, opportunity, vacation from work, a centre, the time of the new or full moon, a festival.

ক্ষণদা, রাত্রি, night.

ক্ষণপ্রভা, বিদ্যুৎ, চমক, a flash of lightning, a gleam of light.

ক্ষণিক, অস্থায়ী, নাশ্য, momentary, fleeting, perishable.

ক্ষণুরা, পদরোগী, diseased with scars in the feet.

ক্ষণো, পদরোগ বিশেষ, a particular disease of the feet.

ক্ষত, ঘা, চোট, ঘায়ুক্ত, চেরা, ভাঙ্গা, a sore, wound, hurt, scar, scarred, wounded, hurt, torn, broken.

ক্ষতজ, রক্ত, পূঁজ, blood, pus, matter.

ক্ষতি, হানি, অপকার, অনিষ্ট, a hurt, loss, injury, evil, prejudice, disadvantage, damage.
ক্ষতব্রত, ব্রতভঞ্জক, a violator of a religious vow.
ক্ষতোদর, আমাশয়. রক্তাতিসার, a bloody flux.
ক্ষত্র, ক্ষত্রিয়,—দ্বিতীয় বর্ণ, a Kshatriya, one of the second or military class.
ক্ষপা, রাত্রি, রাগ, উন্মাদ, night, passion, folly. madness.
ক্ষপাকর, চন্দ্র, the moon.
ক্ষবথু, কাসরোগ, যক্ষ্মা, a cough, sneezing, sore throat, consumption.
ক্ষম, পারক, সমর্থ, সহিষ্ণু, অনুকূল, able, capable, patient, enduring, friendly.
ক্ষম, ক্ষমতা,—যোগ্যতা, সামর্থ্য, fitness, propriety, capability, capacity.
ক্ষমা, কৃপা, পাপমোচন, সহিষ্ণুতা, পৃথিবী, forbearance, pardon, long-suffering, patience, endurance, the earth, Durgá.
ক্ষমী, সহিষ্ণু, কৃপালু, নিরস্ত, patient, forbearing, gracious, forgiving.
ক্ষয়, হ্রাস, অপচয়, প্রলয়, নাশ, রোগ, প্রায়শ্চিত্ত, যক্ষ্মা, রোগনাশ, decay, waste, loss, destruction, phthisis or consumption, sickness, removal, expiation, the cure of disease,
ক্ষয়মাস, অধিমাস, মলমাস, an intercalary month.
ক্ষয়া, জীর্ণ, অপচিত, নষ্ট, decayed, going to ruin, destroyed.
ক্ষরণ, স্রবণ, চোয়ন, to leak out, ooze, trickle.
ক্ষান্ত, সহিষ্ণু, অনুগ্রাহক, বিরত, patient, enduring, forbearing, desisting from, ceasing, having desisted, &c.
ক্ষান্তি, সহিষ্ণুতা, পাপমোচন, বিরতি, patience, endurance, forbearance, forgiveness, a cessation or desisting from.
ক্ষার, তীব্ররস, বিট্‌লবণ, ভস্ম, alkali, soda or potash, salt, ashes.
ক্ষারিত, লবণাক্ত, তীব্ররসযুক্ত, distilled from saline matter, strained through alkaline ashes.
ক্ষালন, ধৌত করণ, পরিষ্করণ, to wash, rinse, clean, cleanse.
ক্ষিপ্ত, চিন্তাকুল, ব্যস্ত, ব্যগ্র, agitated, excited, moved by some strong passion.
ক্ষিতি, পৃথিবী, নিবাস, ক্ষয়, প্রলয়, the earth, a house, abode, loss, wane, destruction.
ক্ষিতিধর, পর্বত, গিরি, a mountain.

ক্ষিতিরুহ, বৃক্ষ, দ্রুম, a tree. [tracted, mad.
ক্ষিপ্ত, প্রেরিত, ফেলিত, উন্মত্ত, sent, thrown, flung, cast, dis-
ক্ষিপ্র, শীঘ্র, দ্রুত, ত্বরায়, অবিলম্বে, quick, swift, rapid; quickly, speedily, soon.
ক্ষীণ, কৃশ, পাতলা, দুর্বল, wasted, emaciated, slender, thin, feeble, decayed, exhausted.
ক্ষীর, দুগ্ধ, গাছের দুগ্ধবৎ রস, ঘনীভূতদুগ্ধ, জল, milk, the milky sap of plants, thickened milk, water.
ক্ষীরসা, পরমান্ন, পায়স, rice-milk, frumenty.
ক্ষীরা, পরমান্ন, শশা, *id.* also a cucumber.
ক্ষুণ্ণ, ক্ষুব্ধ, ক্লিষ্ট, মর্দ্দিত, চূর্ণিত, কলঙ্কী, sad, distressed, bruised, pounded, beaten to powder, marked. branded, blemished. [bruise.
ক্ষুৎ, হাঁচি, চিহ্ন, কলঙ্ক, ঘা, a sneezing; a mark, blemish,
ক্ষুতন হাঁচন, to sneeze. [corn, &c. a scrap.
ক্ষুদ, তণ্ডুলাদিকণা, টুকি, the broken fragments of pounded
ক্ষুদন, মর্দ্দন, চূর্ণন, খনন, মুদ্রাদির চিহ্নকাটন, to pound, bruise, reduce to powder, dig, carve, engrave.
ক্ষুদিয়া, সূক্ষ্ম, ছোট, minute, little, small, trifling.
ক্ষুদ্বোধ, বুভুক্ষা, hunger, sense of hunger, appetite.
ক্ষুদ্র, সূক্ষ্ম, অল্প, তুচ্ছ, কৃপণ, small, little, insignificant, mean, petty, low, vulgar, niggardly.
ক্ষুদ্রদৃষ্টি, কার্পণ্য, কৃপণ, penuriousness; penurious, miserly.
ক্ষুদ্রশ্বাস, দুঃশ্বাস, a shortness of breathing.
ক্ষুধ্, ক্ষুধা,—ভোজনেচ্ছা, বুভুক্ষা, hunger, appetite.
ক্ষুধাতুর, ক্ষুধার্ত্ত,—বুভুক্ষু, বহুক্ষুধ, hungry, famished, voracious.
ক্ষুধার্দ্দ, অবক্ষুধা, ভুকপীড়া, a painful sense of hunger.
ক্ষুধালু, ভোজনার্থী, অবক্ষুধিত, hungry, ravenous, voracious.
ক্ষুধিত, ভোজনেচ্ছুক, ক্ষুধাবিশিষ্ট, hungry. [petite.
ক্ষুন্নিবৃত্তি, ক্ষুধার নিবৃত্তি, cessation of hunger, appeasing of ap-
ক্ষুপ, ক্ষুদ্রবৃক্ষ, গুল্ম, a bush, a shrub.
ক্ষুবরী, পায়রার খোপ, ক্ষুদ্র গৃহ, a pigeon-hole, a small hut.
ক্ষুবি, বাঁশাদিঝাড়, ঝাঁদা, a clump, a tuft, a seed-plot.
ক্ষুব্ধ, ব্যস্ত, কাতর, খেদিত, agitated, disturbed, affected, distressed, excited, pained.
ক্ষুমা, মসীনা, flax, linseed.

ক্ষুর, নাপিতের অস্ত্র, অশ্বশফ, a razor, the hoof of a horse, &c.
ক্ষুরধার, ধারাল, তীক্ষ্ণধার, শানিত, sharp, razor-edged. [grass.
ক্ষুরপা, ক্ষুরপ্র,—ঘাসকাটনের অস্ত্র, an instrument for cutting
ক্ষুরী, নাপিত, মুণ্ডক, a barber.
ক্ষেত্র, ক্ষেত,—ভূমিখণ্ড, শরীর, ভার্য্যা, পুণ্যভূমি, a field, the body, a wife, a sacred spot, a place of pilgrimage.
ক্ষেত্রজ, স্বস্ত্রীতে অন্যপুরুষ জাত পুত্র, the legitimate offspring of a wife by another man.
ক্ষেত্রজ্ঞ, আত্মা, লম্পট, কৃষাণ, প্রবীণ, the soul, a libertine, a husbandman; clever, skilful.
ক্ষেপ, ফেলা, ত্যাগ, ছাড়া, বোঝাই, ভার, a throw, cast, stroke of an oar, dismissal, a boat or carriage load of goods, a burden, a pack.
ক্ষেপণ, প্রেরণ, ফেলন, ছাড়ন, যাপন, ঢালন, বহান, রাগান, উন্মাদন, to send, cast, fling, toss, throw, dismiss, spend or pass time, shed, spill, row, be angry, fall into a passion, rage, be distracted or mad.
ক্ষেপণী, অগী, দাঁড়, জাল, an oar, a net, a fishing net.
ক্ষেপলা, ক্ষেপণীয় জাল, proper to be thrown (as a net)
ক্ষেপাণ, রাগান, to provoke, incense, enrage, distract.
ক্ষেম, কুশল, মুক্তি, good fortune, welfare, happiness, absorption or final beatitude.
ক্ষেমঙ্করী, শঙ্খচিল, শুভ, the Brahmani kite; auspicious. [ket.
ক্ষেমী, কুশলী, happy, fortunate, prosperous; a trinket-bas-
ক্ষেয়ারী, দাঁড়ী, নাবিক, a rower, a waterman.
ক্ষৈণ্য, ক্ষীণতা, কৃশতা, দৌর্ব্বল্য, leanness, emaciation, feebleness.
ক্ষোণি, ক্ষোণী,—পৃথিবী, the earth.
ক্ষোভ, ব্যস্ততা, দুঃখ, শঙ্কা, প্রবৃত্তি. agitation, distress, grief, alarm, excitation, stimulation, excitement.
ক্ষোম, পট্টবস্ত্র, wove silk.
ক্ষৌণি, ক্ষৌণী,—পৃথিবী, the earth.
ক্ষৌদ্র, মধু, জল, honey, water,
ক্ষৌম, ক্ষুমা নির্ম্মিত বস্ত্র, পট্টবস্ত্র, অট্টালিকা, linen cloth, wove silk, a room on the top of a house.
ক্ষৌর, ক্ষৌরী,—ক্ষুরিকর্ম্ম, মুণ্ডন, the shaving of the head, &c.
ক্ষ্মা, পৃথিবী, the earth.

ক্ষ্বেড়, বিষ, গরল, poison, venom.
ক্ষ্বেড়ালু, গরলী, হিংসুক, poisonous, venomous, noxious.

খ.

খ, আকাশ, শূন্য, the sky, the atmosphere.
খই, খদি, খদিকা, ভাজাধান্য, parched grain.
খইম, নৌকাগম্য, গম্ভীর, navigable, deep.
খগ, পক্ষী, গ্রহ, বায়ু, বাণ, a bird, a planet, air, an arrow.
খগেন্দ্র. খগেশ, খগেশ্বর.—গরুড়, Garuṛa the king of birds.
খগোল, আকাশমণ্ডল, the planisphere or starry heavens.
খচর, আকাশগ, মেঘ, গ্রহ, পক্ষী, অশ্বতর, aerial ; a cloud, a planet, a bird, a mule.
খচিত, বেষ্টিত, set (as precious stones,) inlaid.
খচিল, গুলী, a ball, a bullet.
খজ, খজাক-া,—দর্ব্বী, a spoon, a ladle.
খঞ্জ, খোঁড়া, নেঙ্গড়া, lame, limping, crippled.
খঞ্জন, খঞ্জরীট,—পক্ষী বিশেষ, the common wag-tail.
খঞ্জনী, খঞ্জরী,—ঢক্কাবিশেষ, ডম্ফ, a tabor or small drum.
খঞ্জর, কটার, a dagger.
খট, তৃণবিশেষ, কফ, a coarse and long thatching grass, [phlegm.
খটি, স্তূপ, রাশি, সমূহ, পরামর্শ, কল্পনা, a heap, pile, quantity, multitude, consultation, advice, scheme.
খটী, খটিকা,—খড়িমাটী, খড়, chalk, a coarse grass or straw.
খট্টাশ, গন্ধমার্জার, গন্ধগোকুলা, the civet or pole-cat.
খট্বা, খাট, শয্যা, a bedstead, couch, bier, hammock.
খট্বাঙ্গ, ত্রিশূল, শিবের অস্ত্র, the weapon of Shiva.
খট্বারূঢ়, লম্পট, অধম, পাপিষ্ঠ, lecherous, abandoned, low, vile, [iniquitous.
খড়, তৃণবিশেষ, the straw of a thatching grass.
খড়কী, গুপ্তদ্বার, a private or back door.
খড়জালী, অগ্নিসিদ্ধ লবণ, a salt prepared by boiling.
খড়ম, কাষ্ঠপাদুকা, a sandal, a clog or patten.
খড়রা, অশ্বশরীর পরিষ্কারার্থ লৌহনির্ম্মিতাস্ত্র, a curry-comb.
খড়ি, খড়িকা,—শুক্ল মৃত্তিকা বিশেষ, খড়, chalk, a coarse grass.
খড়িঞ্চ, খড়িটা,—খড়মিশ্রিত লেপ, a coarse mortar for plastering cottages.

খড়িয়া, শুক্ল, পাণ্ডুর, white, chalk-coloured, pale.
খড়ুয়া, খড়নির্ম্মিত, made of straw.
খড়্গ, অসি, যজ্ঞছুরিকা, গণ্ডারশৃঙ্গ, a scimitar, sacrificial knife, the horn of a rhinoceros.
খড়্গী, গণ্ডার, খড়্গধারী, a rhinoceros; armed with a scimitar.
খণ্ড, টুকরা, বিভাগ, প্রকরণ, খাঁড়, a fragment, piece, part, section, chapter, raw sugar, a cluster of huts.
খণ্ডন, ভাঙ্গন, বিদারণ, কাটন, দোষনাশন, অন্যথাকরণ, নিবর্ত্তন, to break, tear, divide, cut, remove or expiate, avert, refute, rescind, thwart. [ture.
খণ্ডনা, আপত্তি, দোষণ, ভঙ্গ a remonstrance, refutation, frac-
খণ্ডপ্রলয়, প্রায়প্রলয়, বিবাদ, সুহৃদ্ভেদ, a partial destruction of the universe, a quarrel, dissolution of friendship.
খণ্ডাখণ্ডি, বাধাবাধি, পরস্পর বিঘ্নবিনাশ, a reciprocal thwarting, a mutual removal of difficulties.
খতান, গণন, সংখ্যান, to calculate, reckon, cast up a sum, settle an account.
খতিয়ান্, সংখ্যার্থ বহি, an account-book.
খতুয়া, ভিন্ন, জীর্ণ, পঙ্কানিয়া, torn, tattered, decayed, rotten.
খতুয়ামারণ, or ধরণ,—পচন, দরণ, to rot, moulder away, decay.
খদরণ, তাড়ান, to chase or drive away.
খদি, খদিকা,—খৈ, ভাজাধান্য, parched corn.
খদ্যোত, জোনাকিপোকা, সূর্য্য, a fire-fly, the sun. [digger.
খনক, মূষিক, সিঁধাল, সুরঙ্গকর, a rat, house-breaker, miner,
খনন, কোড়ন, গর্ত্ত করণ, সুরঙ্গ কাটন, to dig, delve, mine.
খনা, বড়শা, নাকীকথা, a hog-spear, a snuffling; nasal.
খনি, খনী,—আকর, গর্ত্ত, a mine, quarry, cave, pit, hole.
খনিত্র, খন্তা, খন্তী,—বাঁটয়া, কুদ্দাল, a paddle, spade, hoe.
খন্দ, শস্য, ফলমুখ, a harvest, a crop.
খপরা, গৃহাচ্ছাদনের খোলা, a tile.
খপরৈল, খপরাচ্ছাদিত, tiled, covered with tiles.
খপুর, গুবাকবৃক্ষ, লশুন, তৃণ বিশেষ, কলসী, the betel-tree, garlic, a fragrant grass, a water-jar.
খপুষ্প, অসম্ভব, শশবিষাণ, a flower growing in the air, *i. e.* an impossibility, absurdity, hare's horns.
খম্বা, স্তম্ভ, a post, a pillar.

খয়রা, পিঙ্গলবর্ণ, brown, light brown.

খর, গাধা, দৈত্য, কাক, বক, ক্রোরপক্ষী, উষ্মা, তীক্ষ্ণ, কটোর, an ass, a dæmon, a crow, a heron, an osprey, heat, prickly night-shade; hot, pungent, sharp, keen, rigid, harsh, cruel, brittle.

খরণস, দীর্ঘনাসিকাবিশিষ্ট, sharp-nosed.

খরপত্র, সেগুণ, রাঙ্গাতুলসী, the teak-tree, a red basil.

খরাণ, ভাজন, পোড়ান, চোঁয়াণ, to parch, burn or over-bake, calcine or burn to powder.

খর্জ্জু, চুলকনা, কচ্ছু, cutaneous eruption, itch, scab, &c.

খর্জ্জুর, খাজুর, the wild date-tree or its fruit.

খর্পর, ছত্র, খুলী, অঞ্জন, ধূর্ত্ত, চোর, a parasol, a beggar's bowl, the crown of the cranium, a sacrificial bowl, a collyrium, a rogue, a thief.

খর্ব্ব, এক শত অর্বুদ, হ্রস্বাকার, বামন, ten thousand millions; short, low; a dwarf.

খল, ধূর্ত্ত, ছলী, পরস্পরভেদকারক, উদূখল, deceitful, artful, swindling, dishonest, mischief-making; a threshing-floor, a mortar.

খলকাহিনী, ইতিহাস, গল্প, a legend, a story.

খলৎ, কপটী, চঞ্চল, পিছল, deceitful, unsteady, slippery.

খলন, পিছলন, ভুলন, চুকন, to slip, trip, blunder, err, do wrong.

খলপা, কুশূল, গোলা, an enclosure for grain, a granary.

খলমূষল, উদূখল মোনা, a mortar and pestle. [for cattle.

খলি, কল্ক, ear-wax, refuse of an oil-press, a cake thereof

খলু, নিশ্চিত, আবশ্য, না, truly, indeed, certainly, nay.

খলখল্, অস্ফুট শব্দ, a gurgling, rippling sound, or bubbling.

খল্ল, কুলী. খাড, নালা, a trench, canal, creek, deep hole.

খল্লী, গাঁটিবাত, shooting pains in the extremities.

খসণ, ঝরণ, পড়ন, to fall as leaves, fruit or a meteor, slough or fall off. [door, &c.

খসাণ, ঝরাণ, পাড়ান, খোলন, to cause to fall, loosen, open a

খস, কচ্ছু, চর্ম্মরোগযুক্ত, the itch, a scab; rough, scabby, scaly.

খসুয়া, কচ্ছুয়াবিশিষ্ট, diseased with the itch, scabby.

খসড়া, চোতা, প্রথমলিপি, a rough copy, rough draft.
খাই, খাত, গর্ত্ত, a ditch, trench, pit.
খাইদ, খাদ,— কাইট, মলা, the slag or dross of metals.
খাউকী, ছল, ধূর্ত্ততা, a pretence, imposition, deception.
খাউড়ল, খাউড়াল,—অবক্ষুধিত, পেটুক, ravenous, voracious, gluttonous.
খাওন, ভোজন, ক্ষয়করণ, পাওন, to eat, corrode, wear away, suffer or enjoy, undergo. [hospitable.
খাওনিয়া, ভোজয়িতা, আতিথেয়, feeding others, entertaining,
খাওয়ান, চরাণ, ভোজনকরাণ, to feed cattle, graze, entertain.
খাঁই, স্পৃহা, লোভ, desire, want, greediness, covetousness.
খাঁচা, পিঞ্জর, খুয়াড়, a cage, coop, pen, case, aviary.
খাঁড়, গুড়, raw sugar, molasses.
খাঁদা, খাঁদুয়া,—ক্ষুন্ননাসিকা, having lost the nose by disease, &c.
খাগী, খাকী,—ভক্ষক, নাশক, devouring, eating, consuming.
খাজা, মিষ্টান্ন বিশেষ, শক্ত, a kind of sweetmeat; firm, hard.
খাজন, লম্ব খড়্গ বিশেষ, a long-bladed scymitar.
খাজুর, খর্জুর, ছুহারা, the wild date-tree and its fruit.
খাট, বামন, ক্ষুদ্র, তুচ্ছ, খর্ব্ব, dwarf, short, low, shallow, small, mean, humble; a bed-stead, bier.
খাটদৃষ্টি, অদূরদর্শী, কৃপণ, short-sighted, penurious, niggardly.
খাটন, শ্রমকরণ, সম্পাদন, লাগন, to labour, work, toil, serve, effect, to suit, answer the end or purpose.
খাটনী, বেতন, শ্রম, a labourer's wages, task, toil.
খাট্মল, ছারপোকা, the common bug.
খাটলা, আড়াল, ব্যবধান, চালনী, a screen, a fence, a sieve.
খাটান, চালান, পরীক্ষণ, লাগান, প্রতিপন্ন, টক, to set to or superintend work, try, put to proof, apply; an effect; acid, sour.
খাটাল, অন্তর, মধ্যস্থল, an interval, space between beams, &c.
খাটী, শুদ্ধধাতু, নির্দ্দোষী, সম্মত, স্পষ্ট, refined (as metals), pure, faultless, approved, clear, plain.
খাড়ল, গ্রীষ্মকালীন ভূমিছিদ্র, fissures in the ground from heat.
খাড়া, উর্দ্ধ, ঠাড়, দাঁড়া, erect, upright, straight, steep, standing.
খাণ, খাণি,—খণ্ড, টা, a piece, an individual thing.
খাত, খাই, গর্ত্ত, পুষ্করিণী, a ditch, moat, pit, pond.

খাতক, ঋণী, ঋণগ্রাহক, a debtor, borrower.
খাতকী, টীপ, promissory (note.)
খাতা, ভূমিখণ্ড, বহি, সমূহ, সভা, a plot of ground, account-book, multitude, assembly.
খাদন, ভক্ষণ, নাশন, to eat, devour, consume, corrode.
খাদি, লাঠী, ঠেঙ্গা, a truncheon, short piece of wood.
খান, স্থান, টা, a place, situation, individual thing, piece.
খানা, গহ্বর, গর্ত্ত, আহার, a ravine, pit, pool; food, a meal.
খাপ, অসিকোষ, a sheath, scabbard.
খাপরা, খাবরা—গৃহাচ্ছাদনের ইষ্টক, ঘটাদির খণ্ড, a tile, pantile, [potsherd.
খাবল-া, মুঠা, গ্রাস, a handful, mouthful.
খাম, খাম্বা,—স্তম্ভ, খুঁটী, a pillar, a post, a stake.
খামার, শস্যমর্দ্দনস্থান, a threshing-floor.
খারা, সরল, হণ্ডীবিশেষ, কার্পাসকোষ, upright, honest, just, payable at sight; a cotton-pod.
খাল, নালা, খাড়ি, a creek, inlet, bay.
খালাড়ী, লবণ নির্ম্মাণস্থান, a place where salt is manufactured.
খাস্ত, কদর্য্য, মন্দ, নীচ, bad, evil, inferior.
খাস্তা, কদর্য্যতা, কুৎসিত কিছু, badness, the bad or inferior part of a thing.
খিখি, উল্কামুখী, খেঁকশিয়াল, a fox.
খিচন,-আন, মুখবাঁকান, ঝকড়ন, খেঁকান, to gain, mouth, make faces, dispute about trifles, to scold, to fret, to be pettish.
খিচড়, কর্দ্দম, নীচ, কটুবাক্য, dirt; vulgar, scurrilous, obscene.
খিচড়ি, মিশ্রিতান্ন বিশেষ, a mixture of rice, pulse and spices.
খিচড়ীয়া, খিচড়া,—নীচকথা, কটুবাক্য, vulgar, low, scurrilous, obscene, ungrammatical.
খিট, মর্চ্যা, কলঙ্ক, rust, scurf, scaliness.
খিটা, খিটিয়া,—মর্চ্যাধরা, rusty.
খিট্‌খিটান, খেঁকান, বড়বড়ান, to fret, complain, be querulous, [scold.
খিট্‌খিটিয়া, চিড়্‌চিড়িয়া, বক্‌বকানিয়া, fretful, peevish, querulous, murmuring, dissatisfied.
খিড়কী, ঝরকা, গুপ্তদ্বার, a window, a back or private door.
খিদ্যমান, দুঃখিত, পীড়িত, distressed, sorrowful, grieving, regretting, in pain.

খিল, পতিতভূমি, হুড়কা, গোঁজ, waste or unploughed land, a bolt, pin, peg.

খিলধরা, কুমারিকা, a staple for a bolt. [turn an arch.

খিলন-আন, খিল মারণ, গোঁজ দেওন, to pin, nail, drive a wedge,

খিলান, মাওলা, খিলিত গৃহ, an arch, dome, arched turret, vault.

খিলী, খিলিত স্থান, পর্ণাদি গুটিকা, an arch, tunnel, funnel, a paper packet of betel, &c. [thrust, push.

খুঁচন, বেধন, ফোঁড়ান, ঠেলন, to perforate, pinch, prick,

খুঁটান, তুলনাকরণ, যোড় লাগান, to compare, match. [porter.

খুঁটা, স্তম্ভ, শঙ্কু, ঠেস, a post, wooden pillar, stake, sup-

খুঁত, কলঙ্ক, কুচিহ্ন, a blemish, a bad mark.

খুকন, থুক্‌থুকান,—থুকন, থুষণ, to expectorate, to hawk, cough, wheeze.

খুকী, গর্ভ, অবগণ্ড, a fœtus, a child in arms.

খুজন, খোজন,—অন্বেষণাকরণ, to seek, search for, seek out.

খুজী, খোজা,—অনুসন্ধান, অন্বেষণ, চেষ্টা, search, enquiry.

খুজলান, চুল্কান, to itch.

খুঞ্চিয়া, ঝুড়ী, ধামা, পাত্র, a basket, a vessel.

খুড়ন, খুঁড়ন,—সঞ্চয়ন, তুলনাকরণ, খনন, to pick up, collect, glean, compare, dig, root up the earth.

খুড়া, খুড়তত, খুড়াত,—পিতার কনিষ্ঠভ্রাতা, a junior paternal uncle.

খুড়ী, কনিষ্ঠপিতৃব্যপত্নী, the wife of a junior paternal uncle.

খুদ, তণ্ডুলকণা, refuse of corn, broken grains, trash.

খুদন,-আন, খনন, কোড়ন, কূপ কাটন, to dig, cut, sink a well.

খুন্তি, বটিয়া, কুদ্দাল, a spud, paddle, spade.

খুপ্, হঠাৎ শীঘ্র, suddenly, hastily, quickly.

খুবরি, ঝুপড়ী, ক্ষুদ্রগৃহ, একচালা, a small hut, a shed.

খুর, নাপিতাস্ত্র, অশ্বাদি শফ, a razor, the hoof of an animal.

খুরশী, চৌকী, বেদী, পশু বন্ধনরজ্জু, a stool, bench, noose or tether for cattle.

খুরী, কটোরা, পানপত্র, a cup, a small basin.

খুর্পা, ঘাসকাটনের অস্ত্রবিশেষ, a spud for grubbing up grass.

খুর্মা, খাজুরফল, a date, a kind of sweet-meat.

খুলন, প্রসরণ, ঝরণ, খষণ, to open, expand, fall from, loosen.

খুলী, খর্পর, পাত্রবিশেষ, the cranium or skull, a basin.

খুল্লতাত, কনিষ্ঠপিতৃব্য, খুড়া, a father's younger brother.

খুষণ, খুষ্‌খুষণ,—কাসন, to cough, to wheeze.
খুষ্‌খুষি, খুষ্‌খুষাণি,—কাস, a cough, a fit of coughing.
খুঁকন, খুকান,—কাসন, মেলন, উত্থাপন, প্রবৃত্তিজন্মান, to cough, hawk, prompt, excite, egg on.
খুকী, কাস, প্রবর্ত্তনা, a cough, a prompting, exerting, urging.
খুসন শস্য মর্দ্দন, to thresh barley with a pedal.
খুসনি, ডাকিনী, শস্যঝাড়ানি, a witch, the threshing of barley.
খুস্‌ড়ন, জড়াইয়া রাখন, গোপনেরাখন, to wrap up, put by, conceal.
খে, খেই,—গাচা, সূত্রাগ্র, the fibres of a thread, the end of [a thread.
খেংরা, খেঙ্গরা,—ঝাড়ুন, a broom.
খেংক্, কুক্কুরাদি ধ্বনি, the yelp of a fox, dog or jackal.
খেঁকান, গর্জ্জন, তাড়ান, খিচন, to snarl, to repel crossly, drive away with threatening, to be fretful or impatient.
খেঁকী, রাগাল, খিট্‌খিটিয়া, snarling, surly, ill-natured, fret-[ful, impatient.
খেঁক্‌চান, ঘেঙ্গান, উত্তেজনা দেওন, to teaze, importune, urge peevishly.
খেঁক্‌শিয়াল, খেঁথর,—খিখি, উল্কামুখী, a fox.
খেঁচন, কর্ষণ, টানন, আঁটন, গ্রহণ, পাক দেওন, to draw, tug, pull tight, to snatch, to writhe, to contract as in spasms, &c.
খেঁচা অঙ্গগ্রহ, টান, a spasm, stitch, cramp, pull.
খেচর, আকাশগামী, aerial.
খেট-ক, গ্রাম, উপনগর, শাখানগর, নগরপ্রান্ত, গদা, a village, suburb, the club of Balaráma.
খেট্যা, গদা, লাঠী, a club, a bludgeon.
খেড়ী, বামন, ক্ষীণ, dwarf, thin, spare.
খেদ, দুঃখ, শোক, মনস্তাপ, affliction, distress, grief, sorrow, vexation, regret, repentance.
খেদড়ন-আন, তাড়ান, জাগান, to drive or turn away, to spring game, to chase.
খেদন, তাপন, পস্তান, to grieve, regret, repent, be vexed, [&c.
খেদান, তাড়ান, হাঁকন, to repulse, drive or chase away, drive cattle.

খেমী, মণিরাখিবার ডিবা, a casket, a trinket basket.
খেয়, খাত, a ditch, a moat.
খেলন, ক্রীড়ন, খেলান, to play, sport, toy, move freely.
খেলা, খেলি,—ক্রীড়া, কৌতুক, play, sport, gambol, amusement, fun.
খেলাড়ু, খেলাড়িয়া,—কুতূহলী, ক্রীড়াবান, playful, sportive, gamesome, gambolling.
খেলাড়ী, রসিকা, লীলাকারিণী, a coquette, sportive female.
খেলানী, খাটিমাদি, a toy, plaything.
খৈ, ভাজাধান্য, parched corn.
খো, খোআ,—কঙ্কর, coarse brick-dust or gravel.
খোঁড়ন, খেংচন, to be lame, to limp.
খোঁড়-া, নেঙ্গড়া, lame, limping, halt.
খোকা, অবগণ্ড, ভ্রূণ, a child in arms, an embryo.
খোজ-া, অনুসন্ধান, উদ্দেশ, search, enquiry, trace, vestige.
খোজন, অন্বেষণাকরণ, to search, to seek for what is lost.
খোদন, খনন, মুদ্রাদি কাটন, দন্তশোধন, to dig, carve, engrave, cut stone or wood, pick one's teeth.
খোদা, মুদ্রাদিতে শিরনাম, মুদ্রাদিতে যে অঙ্ক, an inscription.
খোন, বড়শা, a spear, a hog-spear.
খোপ, পায়রাগৃহ, a pigeon-box, pigeon-hole.
খোপা, বদ্ধকেশ, the bunch or tress of hair on the crown.
খোপাল, বদ্ধকেশযুক্ত, wearing the hair tied in a bunch.
খোয়ন-আন, হারন, উড়ান, to lose, dissipate, squander, lavish.
খোয়া, অপচিত, কঙ্কর, lost, gone ; broken brick. [lavish.
খোয়ানিয়া, অপব্যয়ী, উড়ানীয়া, a loser, spendthrift; wasteful,
খোয়ার, হানি, অপচয়, loss, injury. [socket, nut-shell.
খোল, খোঁপরা, খাপ, নারিকেলমালা ইত্যাদি, hollow; a sheath,
খোলন, খযাণ, প্রসারণ, ছাড়ন, ছালতোলন, উঠান, to loosen, open, untie, unyoke, strip, pull off.
খোলস, সর্পকঞ্চুক, the slough of a serpent.
খোলা, অমুদিত, অবদ্ধ, স্পষ্ট, ক্ষেত্র, খাপরা, গুবাকাদিকোষ, open, loose, free, unobstructed, clear, plain; a field, toy, tile, potsherd, the sheath of a bamboo or betel shoot.
খোলা, খোলক,—পাকস্থালী, a baking pot.
খোস, কচ্ছু, কণ্ডু, the itch, an itching eruption.

খোসন, শস্যমর্দ্দন, to unhusk, to thresh grain.
খোসা, ছিব্‌ড়া, ছাল, তুষী, a shell, pod, peel, rind, husk, chaff, bran, a ligament.
খ্যাত, নামধেয়, প্রসিদ্ধ, denominated, called, spoken of, famous, renowned, celebrated.
খ্যাতি, নাম, পদবী, যশ, a name, title, nick-name, fame, renown.

গ.

গ, চর, *an affix:* going, moving.
গইড়, তরঙ্গ, বিস্ফোট, a wave, billow, tumour, layer of thatch.
গঁগঁ, সিংহব্যাঘ্রাদি নাদ, roar of a tiger, bellow of a buffalo.
গগণ, আকাশ, অন্তরীক্ষ, the sky, the atmosphere.
গগণভেলা, হাড়গিলা, the pelican or Indian crane.
গগান, বক্‌বকান, কাতরাণ, to complain in a dissatisfied manner, to be querulous, reiterate complaints.
গঙ্গা, ভাগীরথী, the Ganges or its personification.
গঙ্গাজলী, গঙ্গাজলস্পর্শপূর্ব্বক দিব্যকরণ, a mode of swearing by the Ganges, one who so swears.
গঙ্গাধর, শিব, মহাদেব, a name of Shiva.
গঙ্গাপ্রাপ্তি, মরণ, মৃত্যুকালে গঙ্গাতীরে গমন, an arrival at the Ganges to die there, the casting of a corpse into the Ganges.
গঙ্গাযাত্রা, গঙ্গাতীরে গমনকরা, the carrying of a sick person to the Ganges, a journey to bathe in its waters.
গঙ্গাযাত্রী, গঙ্গাতীরে গমনোদ্যত, going to the Ganges for bathing, or as a sick person to die there.
গচ, মোটা কাপড়, coarse and closely woven (as cloth.)
গচ্ছ, নিক্ষেপ, বন্ধক, বৃক্ষ, a deposit, trust, pledge, a tree.
গচ্ছিত, নিক্ষিপ্ত, আধিকৃত, given in charge or trust, deposited, pledged.
গচ্ছন, নিক্ষিপ্তদ্রব্যগ্রহণ, to receive a deposit or pledge, to receive in trust.
গছান, ধনাদিনিক্ষেপণ, to give in charge or trust, deposit, pledge.
গজ, হস্তী, দুইহাতের পরিমাণ, an elephant, a yard measure, a carpenter's rule, a spit.
গজচক্ষু-য়া, টেরা, looking askance, squint-eyed.

গজদন্ত, বিষাণ, কুঞ্জ, an elephant's tusk, ivory.

গজর, বড়্‌বড়ানি, রাগপূর্ব্বক বকনি, a murmuring under provocation or disappointment. [armlet.

গজরা, করভূষণ, বাজুবন্দ, an ornament for the wrist, an

গজা, অঙ্কুর, পল্লব, মিঠাই বিশেষ, a bud, sprout, a sort of sweetmeat; pertaining to an elephant.

গজান, কলান, কচ্যান, to sprout, bud, shoot out.

গজানন, গণেশ. Ganesha, the elephant-headed deity.

গজাল, গোঁজ, কীলক, a peg to hang things on. [ment.

গজ্‌গজান, বড়্‌বড়ান, to murmur under offence or disappoint-

গঞ্জ, আকর, ধনাগার, আড়ঙ্গ, গ্রাম, অনাদর, a mine, treasury, jewel or plate room, a mart or place for merchandise, a hut, cottage, village, disrespect, contempt, a small seed.

গঞ্জ-া, মদিরাগৃহ, মাদক দ্রব্য বিশেষ, a tavern, liquor-shop, distillery, an intoxicating preparation of the tops of hemp.

গঞ্জন-আন, হেলন, তুচ্ছকরণ, to treat with disrespect or contempt, to abuse, to vilify.

গঠন, গড়ন,—নির্ম্মাণ, রচন, to make, fabricate, mould, form, construct, build, erect. [forged.

গঠিত, নির্ম্মিত, কল্পিত, formed, fabricated, &c. fictitious,

গড়, ব্যাঘাত, ব্যবধান, খাত, দুর্গ. মাঝা, প্রণাম, an impediment, obstacle, fence, skreen, breast-work, moat, ditch, fort, fortress, a medium, average, a salutation, obeisance, the hole into which a pedal falls.

গড়ন, আকৃতি, মূর্ত্তি, নির্ম্মাণ, লুঠিয়াপড়ন, make, shape, form, figure; to make, &c. to roll down.

গড়নিয়া, নির্ম্মায়ক, রচক, an artist, maker, fabricator. [ing.

গড়নী, গড়ানি,—নির্ম্মাণমূল্য, the wages for making or build-

গড়ান, নির্ম্মাণ, গলান, ঢলন, to fabricate, make, cast metals, to lie, recline, slope, run or roll down, ooze.

গড়ানিয়া, হেলা, চঞ্চল, পিছল, sloping, rolling, unsteady, slippy.

গড়ি; তরঙ্গ, ফোড়া, a billow, wave, tumor, layer of thatch.

গড়িয়া, আলসিয়া, indolent, lazy, reclining in idleness.

গড়িয়াম, কাইত, হেলা, inclined, sloping, aslant.
গড়িয়ামি, আলস্য, indolence, sloth, torpor.
গড়ু, কুজ, গড়গণ্ড, a hump on the back, a goitre or wen.
গড়ুর, কুঁজাব্যক্তি, কুব্জ, গড়গণ্ডী, hump-backed, having a goitre.
গড়ে, মাকায়, in the gross or average, on the whole. [ter.
গড়গড়ান, গর্জ্জন, গম্ভীরনাদ করণ, to thunder, rattle, rumble, clat-
গড়গড়ি, মেঘনাদ, বজ্রনিস্বন, thunder.
গড়বড়ি, গড়বিড়ি,—গোলমাল, ব্যাঘাত, confusion, tumult, a hub-bub, hindrance, impediment.
গড্ডালিকা, ক্রমভঙ্গ, ব্যাঘাত, an interruption, impediment.
গণ, জাতি, সমূহ, স্বপক্ষ, শিবের অনুচর, সংখ্যা, a kind, genus, class, tribe, multitude, flock, troop, body, faction, cabal, side or party, sect, the attendants of Shiva, an arithmetical number.
গণক, দৈবজ্ঞ, সংখ্যাবেত্তা, a calculator of nativities, astrologer, arithmetician.
গণতা, পক্ষপাত, partiality, collusion, a plot, cabal.
গণৎকার, দৈবজ্ঞ, জ্যোতির্বিদ, an astrologer, an astronomer.
গণন, খতান, সংখ্যান, জানন, to reckon, count, add up, calculate, esteem, account,
গণনা, সংখ্যা, মোট, a calculation, sum, account, enumeration, number.
গণপতি, গণাধিপ,—গণেশ, Ganesha the god of wisdom.
গণবদ্ধ, গণাক্রান্ত,—পক্ষপাতী, bound or confined to a party, partial; a partizan.
গণাগণি, পরস্পর সংখ্যাকরা, গণমেল, ভিন্নভিন্ন, a reciprocal calculation, a coalition; by or in parties.
গণাগোষ্ঠী, গোত্র, কুল, lineage, race, descent, family.
গণিকা, বেশ্যা, a harlot, prostitute, courtezan.
গণিত, জ্যোতিঃশাস্ত্র, অঙ্কবিদ্যা, a treatise on astrology, astronomy or arithmetic.
গণীভূত, স্বপক্ষ, পক্ষপাতী, one of a party, a partizan; hereditary (as a disease.)
গণেশ, গজানন, Ganesha the god of wisdom.
গণ্ডি, গণনা, সংখ্যাবিদ্যা, a calculation, enumeration, arithmetic.

গণ্ড, কপোল, হস্তিকুম্ভ, বিস্ফোট, খড়্গী, উত্তম, the cheek, side of the face, temples of an elephant, a boil, pimple, mark, spot, a Rhinoceros; *in comp.* chief, eminent, principal.

গণ্ডক, গণ্ডার, গণনাবিশেষ, ব্যাঘাত, a Rhinoceros, a reckoning by fours, an obstacle, impediment. [tiny.

গণ্ডগোল, গোলমাল, কোলাহল, an uproar, tumult, noise, mu-

গণ্ডগ্রাম, প্রধান নগর, a principal or respectable village.

গণ্ডমূর্খ, অতিমূঢ়, অজ্ঞান, pre-eminently ignorant or stupid.

গণ্ডশৈল, ভূমিকম্পাদিদ্বারা পর্ব্বতচ্যুত, the fragment of a rock thrown down by an earthquake, &c.

গণ্ডা, চারি কড়া, four cowries; four.

গণ্ডাকিয়া, গণনাবিশেষ, a reckoning by fours.

গণ্ডার, খড়্গী, a Rhinoceros. [tree.

গণ্ডি, গড়গণ্ড, গুঁড়ি, বৃক্ষপ্রকাণ্ড, a goitre, wen, the trunk of a

গণ্ডী, ধনু, ইন্দ্রায়ুধ, মণ্ডল, a bow, rainbow, halo, circle.

গণ্ডূষ, জলাঞ্জলী, মুখক্ষালন, হস্তিশুণ্ডাগ্র, a handful of water, the rinsing of the mouth, the tip of an elephant's trunk.

গত, অতীত, জ্ঞাত, হৃত, নষ্ট, হীন, gone, past, ago, understood; *in comp.* removed, destroyed, destitute of, freed from.

গতকল্য, পূর্ব্বদিবস, yesterday. [in trust.

গতন,-আন, গচ্ছান, ধনাদি স্থাপন, to deposit in charge, deliver

গতাব্দ, অব্যবহার্য্য, অচলিত, out of use or date, antedated.

গতানুগতিক, অনুকারী, ধারাবাহিক, গণাক্রান্ত, imitating others, following custom; a blind partizan.

গতানুসূচনা, কৃতভাবনা, useless after-thought.

গতায়াত, যাতায়াত, intercourse, coming and going.

গতায়ু, মরণোদ্যত, মৃতকল্প, near death, dying, expiring.

গতার্থক, কৃতসূচক, অভিপ্রায়ত্যাগী, retrospective, having relinquished a pursuit.

গতি, চলন, যাত্রা, আশ্রয়, উপায়, বোধ, প্রাপ্তি, অবস্থা, ধারা, চালি, বয়ঃক্রম, motion, progress, march, a procession, resort, refuge, expedient, means of success, knowledge, wisdom, acquisition, the course of events, fate, fortune, behaviour, conduct, gait, manner, period of life.

গতিক, অবস্থা, রীতি, ঢপ, অভিপ্রায়, উপায়, a condition of life, circumstances, conduct, position, attitude, intention, expedient.

গতিক্রিয়া, বিলম্ব, delay, procrastination, trifling.

গতিবিধি, যাতায়াত, intercourse.

গদ, ব্যাধি, বাক্য, disease, sickness, speech, a word.

গদা, গদায়ুধ,—লাঠী, a bludgeon, club, mace.

গদি, গাদিয়া,—শিতান, বালিশ, a cushion, seat, bench, a quilted cover for a palanquin.

গদিত, উক্ত, কথিত, spoken, said. [respectable.

গদিয়ান্, শিতান বিশিষ্ট, ভাগ্যবান্, having a pillow or cushion,

গদী, লাঠীধর, বিষ্ণু, bearing a mace or club; Vishnu.

গদ্গদ্, আহ্লাদে কিম্বা খেদে অব্যক্ত কথন, an inarticulate expression of joy or grief; with sighs and sobs, interrupted by sighing.

গদ্দি, পরিহাস, ব্যঙ্গ, a jest, taunt, repartee, wit.

গদ্য, ছন্দোরহিতবাক্য, পরিহাস, prose, raillery, ridicule, jest.

গন্তব্য, সুপথ, চলিতব্য, practicable as a road, fit to be gone or travelled over.

গন্তা, পথিক, গমনকারক, a traveller, one who goes or walks.

গন্ত্রী, গরুরগাড়ী, a cart or car drawn by oxen.

গন্ধ, বাস, ঘ্রাণতর্পণ, সম্পর্ক, প্রণয়, odour, scent, smell, fragrance, perfume, connexion, relationship, friendship. [wood.

গন্ধ-ক, জ্বলনীয় দ্রব্য বিশেষ, চন্দন, sulphur, sandal-wood, aloe-

গন্ধপাষাণ, গন্ধক, brimstone, sulphur.

গন্ধপ্রিয়, বাসযুক্ত, fond of scents. [drugs.

গন্ধবণিক, পসারী, চন্দনাদি বিক্রেতা, a druggist, a vender of

গন্ধসার তিক্তরসদ্রব্য বিশেষ, worm-wood.

গন্ধরস, সুগন্ধি আটাবৎ দ্রব্য, myrrh.

গন্ধর্ব্ব, স্বর্গের গায়ক, বাদক, ভূত, demigods the choristers of heaven, a singer, musician, a ghost or spirit.

গন্ধা, দুর্গন্ধ, কুবাসী, stinking, fœtid. [stink, &c.

গন্ধান, বাসদেওন, দুর্গন্ধকরণ, to emit a scent, perfume, smell,

গন্ধী, ছারপোকা, গাঁন্ধিপোকা, a bug, the green flying bug.
গপ্প, ইতিহাস, জনশ্রুতি, কথোপকথন, বক্‌বক্‌, a story, legend, report, chit-chat, tattle, talk.
গপ্পিয়া, বাচাল, বহুভাষী, বকনিয়া, talkative, garrulous, babbling, talking.
গপ্পা, বকুয়া, বকনি, a tattler; garrulous; tittle-tattle, chit-chat.
গবড়ন, পেটফেলন, পশুশুমী হওন, to cast the young, bring forth abortively, miscarry, fail in an enterprise.
গবড়ান, বিগাড়ন, নষ্টকরণ, to spoil, vitiate, do clumsily.
গবা, গরু, নির্ব্বোধ, a cow, a simpleton.
গবাক্ষ, ক্ষুদ্র ঝরকা, a small round window, an air-hole.
গবাসন, মুচী, চর্ম্মকার, a skinner, currier, tanner.
গব্র, গর্ভিণী গো, pregnant, with young (as a cow).
গব্য, গোসম্বন্ধীয়, দুগ্ধাদি পঞ্চদ্রব্য, of, belonging to, or fit for a cow, produced from a cow, (as milk, butter, cow-dung :) a herd of cows, a bow-string.
গব্যূতি, দুই ক্রোশ, a measure of two Cos.
গভস্তি, কিরণ, রশ্মি, a ray of light, a sun or moon-beam.
গভীর, গম্ভীর,—নিম্ন, অতলস্পর্শ, নিবিড়, deep, profound, grave, thick, impervious.
গম, গোধুম, wheat.
গমন, চলন, যাত্রা, সঙ্গম, motion, movement, a going, march, progress, coition.
গমনাগমন, গমাগম,—যাতায়াত, intercourse, free communication, coming and going.
গমনার্হ, চলনার্হ, চলিতব্য, accessible, passable, fit for travelling, fit for use.
গম্য, সম্ভব্য, আগমনীয়, প্রাপ্য, প্রণয়িতব্য, practicable, accessible, attainable, worthy to be visited or associated with.
গয়ার, গয়ের,—শ্লেষ্মা, থুথু, phlegm, saliva.
গয়ালী, গয়াবাসী, residing at, or a man of Gaya.
গরগণ্ড, গলদেশে মাংসবৃদ্ধি, a goitre or wen.
গরল, বিষ, ক্ষেড়, venom, poison, virus.
গরলী, বিষালু, বিষধর, venomous, poisonous.
গরাণ, গরাণিয়া,—গভীরমূলক, deep rooted, far below the surface.
গরাদিয়া, কাটগড়া, বেড়া, a pailing, rail, palisade.

গরিমা, অহঙ্কার, দম্ভ, গুরুতা, self-importance, vanity, boasting, greatness, importance.

গরিষ্ঠ, গরীয়ান্, *m.* গুরুতর, } most important, honourable, superior, gross, indigestible.
গরীয়সী, *f.* গুরুতরা }

গরু, গো, গাবী, a cow, a simpleton.

গরুড়, বিষ্ণুর বাহন পক্ষী, the bird of Vishnu, a large vulture.

গরুৎ, পাঝ্‌ঘ, পক্ষ, a wing, a feather.

গরুত্মান্, পক্ষবান্, পক্ষপতি, winged, feathered; the regent of [birds.

গরুন্যায়, মূঢ়, জড়, অপটু, stupid, silly, aukward.

গর্গর, কোপ, ক্রোধ, redness from rage or anger.

গর্গরী, ক্ষুদ্র কলসী, a gugglet, water-vessel, pitcher.

গর্গরিয়া, রাঙ্গামুখ, কোপিত, সুপক্ক, furious, red with rage or ripeness.

গর্জ্জ, নাদ, নিস্বন, a roar, growl, bellow, loud noise.

গর্জ্জন, নাদন, বুম্‌বুনান, রাগম, ভর্ৎসন, ধক্কান, কোপ, যুদ্ধ, মেঘধনি, to roar, bellow, rumble, growl, hiss, snarl, thunder, rage, scold, threaten; passion, fury, war, battle, thunder.

গর্জ্জিত, মেঘের শব্দ. the rolling of distant thunder.

গর্ত্ত, খাত, পৃথিবীর ছিদ্র, a hole, pit, ditch, cave, burrow.

গর্দ্দভ, গাধা, গন্ধ, an ass, the dung-beetle, a scent, smell.

গর্ব, অহঙ্কার, দর্প, pride, arrogance, haughtiness, scorn.

গর্বিত, দর্পী, দম্ভক, proud, haughty, vain-glorious, scornful.

গর্ভ, অন্তরাপত্য, শিশু, উদর, মধ্য, অন্তঃপুর, গঙ্গোচ্ছ্রিত স্থল, an embryo, fœtus, impregnation, a child, the womb, belly, the inside or middle of any thing, an inner apartment, the bed of the Ganges when at the fullest, the rind of the jack fruit.

গর্ভক, মস্তকের পুষ্পমালা, a chaplet of flowers for the hair.

গর্ভচ্যুত, গর্ভপতিত,—অকালজাত, অপূর্ণকালজ, abortive.

গর্ভজ গর্ভপুত্রক, ক্ষেত্রজ, arising from pregnancy, born of one's wife by another man.

গর্ভধারণ, নিষেক, conception in the womb.

গর্ভপাত, গর্ভস্রাব,—পেটখসা, পেটফেলা, an abortion, miscarriage.

গর্ভবতী, গর্ভিণী,—গুর্বিণী, সসত্ত্বা, অন্তরাপত্যা, pregnant.

গর্ভাগার, প্রসবগৃহ, a lying-in chamber, inner apartments.

গর্ভাধান, গর্ভনিমিত্ত সংস্কার, a ceremony to ensure conception.
গর্ভাষ্টম, নিষেক হইতে অষ্টম মাস, অষ্টবর্ষ, the eighth month of pregnancy ; eight years old, fit for the thread.
গর্হ-া, নিন্দা, ভর্ৎসনা, abuse, censure, blame, reproach, reviling, scurrility, disgrace. [boat.
গল, কণ্ঠ, নৌকার গলুই, the throat, neck, prow, bow of a
গলগণ্ড, গরগণ্ড, গলদেশে মাংসবৃদ্ধি, a goitre, a wen.
গলতি, দ্রবকরা, স্রবণ, ক্ষরণ, ছাড়িয়া যাওন, the smelting of metals, the melting or dissolving of sugar, &c. a leaking out, escape of an animal from confinement.
গলন, দ্রব হওন, পাকন, পচন, এড়ন, স্রবণ, ক্ষরণ, *v. n.* to melt, dissolve, suppurate, burst, wear out, escape from a cage, or prison, ooze or leak out, fall, drop (as fruit or leaves from a tree.)
গলভঙ্গ, স্বরবদ্ধ, খোনরাশি, a hoarseness.
গলহস্ত, গলগ্রহণ, a throttling, collaring, seizing by the neck.
গলা, কণ্ঠ, the neck, throat, the neck of a pitcher.
গলা-ট, গলাটিয়া,—জীর্ণ, পচা, দ্রবীভূত, স্ফুটিত, worn out, putrid, dissolved, burst.
গলানিয়া, দ্রাবক, solvent ; a dissolving substance.
গলাভাঙ্গা, স্বরবদ্ধ, খোনরা, hoarse.
গলাস-ী, গবাদি গলবদ্ধরজ্জু, the neck-rope or tie of an animal.
গলি, অল্পপরিসর পথ, a lane, alley, street, defile, the space between the fingers or toes.
গল্‌গলিয়া, বাচাল, বাবদূক, garrulous, talkative, gulping.
গল্প. ইতিহাস, কথোপকথন, গল্পজল্প, a story, chit-chat, tattle.
গল্পীয়া, বাচাল, বহুভাষী, chatty, gossiping, tattling.
গল্লা, আটি, পুলা, a sheaf, wisp, bundle of straw. [dles.
গল্লান, আটিবান্ধন, to bind sheaves, tie up grass in bun-
গস্‌গসান, উত্তপ্ত হওন, to glow, be hot with fever, boil.
গহন, নিবিড় বন, ক্লেশ, দুর্গম, a forest, wood, grove, thicket, pain, distress, trouble ; impervious.
গহনা, অলঙ্কার, আভরণ, an ornament, jewel, trinket. [place.
গহরা, গহেরা,—গম্ভীর, গর্ত্ত, দহ, deep, profound ; depth, a deep
গহরী, ব্যাজ, বিলম্ব, delay, procrastination.

গহীন, গভীর,—গম্ভীর, অতলস্পর্শ, deep, profound.

গহ্বর. গুহা, খাদা, গর্ত্ত, কুঞ্জ, বন, a ravine, defile, hole, pit, deep valley, cave, cavern, grotto, arbour, bower, thicket.

গা, শরীর, গাত্র, বাহ্যভাগ, the body, a surface.

গাইন, গায়ক, a singer, one eminent in singing.

গাই, গরু, গাবী, a cow.

গাওন গানকরণ, to sing, to calk a boat.

গাওনী, গায়কের বেতন, the wages of a singer; a calking.

গাং, গঙ্গা, নদ, the Ganges, a river in general.

গাঁ, গ্রাম, a village, a hamlet. [bale, package.

গাঁইট, গাঁইঠ, গাঁটি,—গিরা, মোট, a knot, joint, knuckle, knob,

গাঁইটকাটা, গাঁটকাটা,—কুম্ভিল, হাটচোর, a cut-purse, pick-pocket.

গাঁজন, ফেণাউঠন, to froth, to foam.

গাঁজা, গঞ্জা, ইন্দ্রাশন, the tops of hemp mixed with tobacco and used for smoking. [by.

গাঁজিয়াল, গঞ্জাধূমপায়ী, smoking hemp-tops, intoxicated there-

গাঁটা, গাঁঠা,—গুপ্তে শ্রবণ, a listening posture, a listening.

গাঁটছাড়া, বরকন্যার বস্ত্রগ্রন্থি, the ceremony of tying a bride and bridegroom together.

গাঁঠনী, মন্ত্রপূর্ব্বক বিষবন্ধন, the prevention of the spread of poison by incantations.

গাঁথন, গাঁথন, গাঁঠন,—গ্রন্থন, গিরাদেওন, গঠন, যোড়ন, to knot, knit, string beads or flowers, arrange in rows, build, sew together in plaits, unite, admit into a society.

গাঁথান, সূত্রবিদ্ধ, গ্রন্থিত, threaded, strung, knotted, regularly arranged, &c. [body.

গাকাঁটা, রোমাঞ্চ, horripilation, erection of the hair of the

গাখসা, গর্ভস্রাব, an abortion, miscarriage.

গাগরী, ক্ষুদ্র কলসী, a small water jar.

গাগী, শুক পক্ষী বিশেষ, a beautiful species of paroquet.

গাছ, গাছী, গাছা,—বৃক্ষ, চারা, a tree, plant, a single fibre, hair or rope, &c.

গাছান, গজান, চড়ন, চারাণ, to grow, sprout, spring up, climb, clamber, train or cultivate.

গাছুড়িয়া, বৃক্ষচড়নে নিপুণ, expert at climbing trees.

গাছুয়া, বৃক্ষারোহী, বৃক্ষরুহ, climbing trees, inhabiting or belonging to trees.

গাজন, শৈব সম্প্রদায়, a company of persons who swing or otherwise torture themselves in devotion to Shiva.

গাজর, শাক বিশেষ, a carrot.

গাড়, গাড়া,—আকর, গর্ত্ত, a mine, pit, hole.

গাড়ন, পোতন, to set, plant, fix in the ground, bury.

গাড়র, গাড়ল,—মেষ, a sheep, the long-legged sheep.

গাড়ী, শকট, রথ, ইত্যাদি বাহন, a cart, wheel-carriage, coach.

গাড়ীবান্, শকটাদি চালক, a coachman, driver, carter.

গাডু, কুব্জ, গলগণ্ড, ঝারী, a humped back, a wen, a sort of water-vessel having a spout.

গাঢ়, অতিশয়, দৃঢ়, শক্ত, ঘন, excessive, much, long continued, strong, close (of an embrace), deep (of sleep), thick (of liquids).

গাঢ়া, গহ্বর, নিবিড় বন, গর্ত্ত, ঘনীভূত, a cave, dark glen, ditch, abyss; thick, coarse, opaque.

গাণপত্য, গণেশ সম্বন্ধীয়, belonging or relating to Gunesha.

গাণ্ডার, গণ্ডার, খড়্গী, a Rhinoceros.

গাণ্ডিব, গণ্ডীব,—অর্জ্জুনের ধনুক, Arjŭn's bow, a bow in general.

গাতুয়া, গাতুলসিয়া,—আলসিয়া, জড়, indolent, lazy, idle.

গাতোত্থান, উঠন গাত্রোত্থান, to rise up, arise, stir, get up.

গাত্র, শরীর, বাহ্যভাগ, the body, the surface of any thing.

গাত্রপাক, শিরঃকম্প, মাথাঘোরা, a giddiness, swimming of the head, the staggers.

গাথক, গায়ক, skilful in singing; a singer, musician, chanter.

গাথা, শ্লোক, গান, ছন্দ, a verse, stanza, poem, chant, song, metre, rhyme, rustic language.

গাদ, কাইট, মলা, শিটা, lees, sediment, scum, dregs, dross, alloy, trash.

গাদন, ঠাসন, পোতন, ঠোকন, to ram or press down, charge a gun, cram, fix in the ground, tread.

গাদা, রাশি, স্তুপ, ঠাসা, a heap, rick, stack; a charge of powder, a ream of paper.

গাদি, ঢিবি, বেদী, a heap, a raised place, seat, bench, a ream of paper.

গাদীপতি, সন্যাসী সম্প্রদায়ের শ্রেষ্ঠ, the chief of a company of religious mendicants. [gent.

গাদুলস্যা, আলসিয়া, অকর্ম্মঠ, indolent, slothful, tardy, negli-

গাধা, গর্দ্দভ, মূঢ়, an ass, a fool, blockhead, dolt.

গান, গীত, রাগ, কীর্ত্তন, a song, strain, singing, music.

গাপন, অস্বীকরণ, ছিপান, to deny, conceal or withhold; denial, concealment, &c.

গাফুলান, দম্ভ করণ, অহঙ্কারে চলন, to swell with pride, be consequential, strut, stalk, swagger.

গাফুলানী, দম্ভ, self-consequence, swaggering, stateliness, pomp of demeanour.

গাবন, ঘোলন, মর্চ্যা পড়ন, to become turbid, fœtid, filthy or rusty, be injured by filth or stench.

গাবান, ঘোলান, মর্চ্যা পড়ান, গোপনীয় প্রকাশ করণ, to stir up, make turbid, foul or rusty, divulge, blab, tell tales.

গাবানিয়া, ঠক, a tale-bearer, blabber, tatler.

গাভা, গাবা,—গর্ভ, a fœtus, gravid uterus, spatha of a plant.

গাভারী, গর্ভিণী, কফী, জ্বরগ্রস্ত, big with young, advanced in pregnancy, affected with cold or fever.

গাভিণ, গাবিণ,—গর্ভিণী, গর্ভযুক্তা, pregnant, with young.

গাভী, গাবী,—গরু, a cow.

গামখুরাণ, ভোজনে পরিতোষণ, অরুচি জন্মান, to cloy, to satiate.

গামোচা, গাম্‌চা,—গাত্রমার্জ্জনী, a towel, napkin, handkerchief.

গামোড়ান, জৃম্ভা করণ, হাই ছাড়ন, to stretch, to yawn. [ness.

গাম্ভীর্য্য, গম্ভীরতা, ধীরতা, depth, profundity, gravity, serious-

গায়, বহির্দ্দিগে, উপরে, along the surface, on, over.

গায়ক, গানকর্ত্তা, a singer, chanter; singing, chanting.

গায়ত্রী, বেদমাতা, ছন্দবিশেষ, a sacred verse of the Rig Ved, a poetical measure. [hold fire.

গার্হপত্য, গার্হস্থ্য, গৃহস্থাগ্নি, householdership, the sacred house-

গার্হস্থ্য, গৃহনিবাস, গৃহস্থধর্ম্ম, residence in a house, the condition or duty of a householder; pertaining to a householder.

গাল, গণ্ডের অধোভাগ, গল্প, the cheek, a story, talk.

গালগুজব, গালাযুষা,—জনরব, গল্প, a common report, town-talk.
গালন, দ্রবীকরণ, উনন, to melt, dissolve, pour off water from rice &c.
গালা, লা, লাক্ষা, লাবাত্তী, lac, sealing wax. [rility.
গালি, গালাগালি,—অপমানবোধকবাক্য, abusive language, scur-
গালুয়া, দাম্ভিক, an exaggerater, hyperbolist, boaster. [ing
গালুনিয়া, দুর্মুখ, কুন্দলীয়া, abusive, scurrilous, scolding, brawl-
গাহক, গায়ক, গানকর্ত্তা, a singer.
গিধর, গিধী,—শৃগাল, a jackal.
গিধিনী, শকুনিপক্ষী, a species of vulture.
গিনা, মৃত্তিকা কিম্বা ধাতুময় ক্ষুদ্র পাত্র বিশেষ, a small cup of earth or metal.
গির, গীঃ,—বাণী, বাক্য, a word, a speech.
গিরা, গাঁটি, সন্ধিস্থান, a knot, joint, tie, knuckle.
গিরি, পর্ব্বত, নেংটিয়া ইন্দুর, a hill, a mountain, a mouse.
গিরীন্দ্র, গিরীশ,—হিমালয়, the Himálayan mountains.
গিলন, কবলীকরণ, লুটন, to swallow, strip, plunder, hold, contain. [chanted.
গীত, গান, কবিতা, a song, hymn, ode, verse, poem ; sung,
গীতা, ভারতীয় উপনিষৎ, a celebrated Hindu poem.
গীর্ব্বাণ, দেবতা, a deity, a god.
গু, বিষ্ঠা, মল, পিটা, fæces, ordure, excrement, dross.
গুঁড়, চূর্ণ, টুকি, চূর্ণিত any coarse powder, a crum, fragment; pulverized, crumbled, &c. [bruize.
গুঁড়ন, চূর্ণন, ছেঁচন, to pulverize, crumble, reduce to a pulp,
গুঁড়ি, আটা, চূর্ণ, থাম, কাণ্ড, flour, powder, a block, the trunk of a tree.
গুগ্গুল, গুগ্গুলু,—ধূপ বিশেষ, a gum-resin, lignum aloes.
গুচি, গুচ্ছি, গুচ্ছ,—ঝাড়, স্তবক, আটি, হার বিশেষ, a tuft, bunch, cluster, nosegay, sheaf, bundle, collection, a necklace of 32 strings.
গুচ্ছন, থোপাথোপা উৎপন্ন হওন, to grow in tufts or bunches.
গুচ্ছান, সঞ্চয়ন, থোপেথোপে রাখন, to collect, bring together, form into clusters, &c.
গুজরী, পাদালঙ্কার, an anklet of small bells.
গুজ্গুজানি, গল্প, ঠকামি, tittle tattle, gossiping, tale-bearing.

গুঞ্জা, রক্তিকা, কলরব, মদিরাগৃহ, the rati (a small seed used by jewellers as a weight), a low buzzing or humming sound, a tavern.
গুঞ্জন, গুঞ্জরণ,—কলধ্বনি করণ, ঘুণ্‌ঘুণান, to hum, buz, echo, resound, murmur.
গুটন, জড়ান, to roll or fold up, collect together.
গুটিক, সংগ্রহ, রাশি, a collection, a quantity.
গুটিকা, গুলি, বটিকা, a ball, ballot, pellet of dung, pill, &c.
গুটিপোকা, তুঁৎপোকা, a silk-worm.
গুটী, গুটি,—গুলী, বটিকা, আঁটি, a ball, ballot, pill, cocoon, fruit-stone, fruit-germ, the small pox.
গুটীপাত, গুলিবাঁট করণ, the casting of lots, a lottery.
গুড়, ইক্ষুপাক, গাড়, molasses, treacle, raw sugar.
গুড়ত্বক্‌, দারুচিনী, cinnamon or cassia.
গুড়ন, জড়ান, to roll up, furl, pack up.
গুড়মুড়া, গুল্ফের অধোভাগ, the heel.
গুঁড়, নুইয়া পড়া, a stooping posture, a crouching. [lasses.
গুড়িয়া, মোদক, ময়রা, গুড়ময়, a confectioner; made with mo-
গুড়্গুড়ী, ধূমপান যন্ত্র বিশেষ, a kind of pipe for smoking.
গুণ, বিশেষণ, ধর্ম্ম, রূপরসাদি, সত্ত্বরজস্তম, কৃতিত্ব, বিদ্যা, নিপুণতা, ফল, ইন্দ্রিয়, রজ্জু, ছিলা, তার, ত্যাগ, a quality, property, attribute, talent, faculty, virtue, excellence, merit, accomplishment, acquirement, skill, advantage, worth, an expedient, an organ of sense, a string, track-rope, bow-string, gold or silver thread, wire, sackcloth, relinquishment; *in comp* :-fold. [&c.
গুণকথন, স্তব, প্রশংসা, eulogy, panegyric, extolling of merits
গুণকার, ফলদায়ক, উপকারক, লাভজনক, উপযোগী, advantageous, salutary, improving, productive of good qualities, profitable, effectual, multiplying.
গুণজনক, গুণদ,—গুরু, শিক্ষক, a tutor, preceptor; producing virtue, &c. [effect.
গুণদর্শন, গুণদেখন,—ফলপ্রাপণ, to avail, succeed, work, take
গুণপনা, যোগ্যতা, নিপুণতা, talent, skill, ability. [ful.
গুণবাদী, স্তাবক, কৃতজ্ঞ, eulogizing, flattering, grateful, thank-

গুণবান্, নিপুণ, পটু, পণ্ডিত, ingenious, talented, learned, &c.

গুণযোগ, বিদ্যাপ্রাপ্তি, বিদ্যাভ্যাস, the possession of talent, the study of science.

গুণা, তার, wire.

গুণাগুণ, দোষাদোষ, virtues and vices, merits and defects, good and evil qualities.

গুণী, কৃতী, পণ্ডিত, নিপুণ, সাধু, শিল্পকার, accomplished, talented, learned, virtuous; an artist.

গুণ্‌গুণান, নাকী দেওন, ভণ্‌ভণান, to snuffle, hum, buz.

গুণ্ড, লোচ্চা, নির্লজ্জ, lewd, lascivious, profligate. [ness.

গুণ্ডামি, দুরাচার, লোচ্চামি, profligacy, lewdness, lascivious-

গুণ্ডিকা, ধুলি, কাষ্ঠচূর্ণ, চূর্ণ, dust, saw-dust, powder. [down.

গুতন,-আন, ঢুকান, কোঁড়ন, to thrust, knock, stab, gore, ram

গুৎস, গুচ্ছ, স্তবক, a tuft, bunch, cluster, sheaf, nosegay.

গুদ, গুহ্যদেশ, স্ত্রীচিহ্ন, the anus, pudendum muliebre.

গুদড়ী, রেজাই, কন্থা a bed-quilt, a mendicant's rug. [zine.

গুদাম, বাণিজ্যাগার, গোলা, a ware-house, store-house, maga-

গুদার, পারঘাট, a ferry, (the place).

গুদী, নৌকা নির্ম্মাণ করিবার স্থান, a small dock for boats &c.

গুন, বোরা, ছালা, a sack, bag, pack-saddle, wallet.

গুপ্ত লুকায়িত, রক্ষিত, concealed, hidden, secret, guarded, protected, preserved.

গুপ্তবেশ, ছদ্মবেশ, a disguise, dress &c. used for concealment.

গুপ্তা, গোপনে জারগামিনী, a female who conceals her amours.

গুফ, পর্ব্বতের গহ্বর, a pass, defile, ravine.

গুবাক, সুপারী, the betel nut, the betel tree.

গুমট, গ্রীষ্ম, heat of weather, sultriness.

গুমটিয়া, দূষিত, ছাতাপড়া, tainted, musty, mouldy. [tage.

গুমর, অহঙ্কার, দম্ভ, haughtiness, desire to divulge, advan-

গুমরণ, ভুণ্‌ভুণান, to buzz, whisper, rumble, re-echo.

গুমসন, ছাতাপড়ন, পচন, to moulder, spoil, grow musty, heat (as hay in the rick).

গুয়া, গুবাক, the betel nut.

গুরী, শ্বেতবর্ণ, গৌরাঙ্গ, সুরূপ, white, fair.

গুরু, ভারী, কঠিন, শক্ত, মান্য, আর্য্য, মহৎ, দীর্ঘ, উপদেশক, মাতা পিতা, heavy, difficult, firm, important, honorable, venerable, great, long or accented (vowel;) a spiritual guide, teacher, parent, elder relation, superior, &c.

গুরুপাপ, মহাপাতক, a great crime, a heinous offence.

গুর্বঙ্গনা, গুরুপত্নী, মাতা, a preceptor's wife, mother, elder female relative.

গুর্বিণী, গর্ভবতী, pregnant, with child.

গুর্বী, গুরুপত্নী, মহতী, আর্য্যা, গর্ব্বিণী, a guru's wife; great, weighty, important, heavy, pregnant.

গুল, বর্ত্তুল, অঙ্গারগুটিকা, বটিকা, সংগ্রহ, a globe, ball, fire-ball, pill, raw sugar or molasses, a collection, multitude, number.

গুলক, গুলা, গুলাক,—সংগ্রহ সমূহ, a multitude, collection, [number.

গুলন গলান, দ্রবীকরণ to dissolve in a liquid.

গুলল, গুলাল,—গুল্লাই, a bow used to shoot earthen bullets.

গুলি-ক, গুলিন,—একটা, an individual, a single one.

গুলি, গুলী,—বাঁটুল, বটিকা, a bullet, ball, cannon ball, pill.

গুলিবাঁট, গুটিকাপাৎ, a sharing by lot or dice, a lottery.

গুলিয়া, গোলাকার, globular; a species of fish.

গুল্লাই, গুল্‌তি,—গুলিক্ষেপণার্থ ধনুক, a pellet bow.

গুল্ফ, গুল.—পার্ষ্ণির উপরি গ্রন্থি, গোড়ালি, the ancle, the heel.

গুল্ম, ঝাড়, লতা, সৈন্যের দল, প্লীহা, a shrub, bush, creeping plant, division of an army, the spleen, disease of the spleen.

গুল্মী, গুল্মযুক্ত, প্লীহারোগী, দলপতি, abounding in shrubs, having the spleen, commanding a division.

গুহা, পর্ব্বতের গহ্বর, গর্ত্ত, a ravine, deep valley, cave, cavern, pit, pass, defile.

গুহ্য, গোপনীয়, নির্জ্জন, মলদ্বার, উপস্থ, concealable, requiring concealment, solitary, secret, private; the anus, the pudenda.

গূ. বিষ্ঠা, মল, মর্চ্যা, excrement, ordure, filth, rust.

গূঢ় গুপ্ত, অপ্রকাশ্য, কঠিনার্থ, concealed, hidden, secret, private, abstruse.

গূঢ়পাদ, সর্প, a serpent, a snake.

গূঢ়পুরুষ, চর, দূত, a scout, a spy.

গূঢ়জ, জারজ, গোলক, whose father is unknown, bastard.
গূঢ়াভিমানী, অব্যক্তগর্ব্বিত, অপণ্ডিত, affecting abstruseness, proud of obscurity, ignorant.
গূয়া, মললিপ্ত. মলগন্ধযুক্ত, smeared with or having the scent of excrement.
গৃধ্র, শকুনিপক্ষী, লোলুপ, a vulture; greedy.
গৃহ, বাটী, ঘর, কুঠী, a house, habitation, dwelling, abode, chamber, building.
গৃহছিদ্র আত্মবিরোধ, কুলকলঙ্ক, a family quarrel, domestic fault.
গৃহবাজ, কপোত বিশেষ, a tumbler pigeon.
গৃহভেদী, গৃহছিদ্রজনক বা সুচক, meddling with domestic affairs, inquisitive, officious, betraying family secrets.
গৃহস্থ, গৃহী, a householder; dwelling in a house.
গৃহাচ্ছাদক, গৃহছিদ্র যে গোপনে রাখে, concealing family affairs.
গৃহিণী, পত্নী, গৃহের কর্ত্রী, a wife, a house-wife.
গৃহী, গৃহাশ্রমী, সংসারী, a householder; domestic, worldly.
গৃহ্য গৃহস্থের কর্ত্তব্যকর্ম্মোপদেশক শাস্ত্র, a ritual for householders.
গৃহীত, প্রাপ্ত, লব্ধ, ধৃত, স্বীকৃত. taken, received, acquired, obtained, caught, seized, favoured, admitted.
গেঁজ্যা, থৈলী, a purse, a grass-cutter's sickle bag.
গেঁজ্যাল, গঞ্জাধূমপায়ী, addicted to intoxicating drugs; a sot.
গেঁটা, গেঁটিয়া,—গ্রন্থিময়, knotty, full of knots or protuberances.
গেণ্ডু-ক, গেঁড়ু,—বালকের লৌটি, a ball for playing with.
গেব্যা, গেবে,—সিন্দুকের কুঠরী, a drawer, till, division of a box.
গেয়, গানযোগ্য, fit to be sung or chanted.
গেরণ, পড়ন, সূর্য্যাদিগ্রহণ, to fall down; an eclipse.
গেরী, গৈরিক,—রাঙ্গামাটী, red earth, red ochre, ruddle.
গেলন, কবলীকরণ, লুটন, to swallow, strip, plunder.
গেলান, কবলীকরাণ, ওয়াণ, to make to swallow, cause to pass through an opening, &c. to feed a mill.
গেলুয়া, বাচাল, দম্ভান্বিত, talkative, boasting.
গেহ, ঘর, বাসস্থান, a house, habitation.
গৈগাঁ পল্লীগ্রাম, খেট, গ্রাম, the country, a village.
গৈরা, গহ্বরা, দহ, a deep place, an abyss.
গৈরিক, গেরী, red chalk, red orpiment.

গো, গরু, গুবাক, সম্বোধক শব্দ, a cow or bu'l, the betel nut, a vocative particle.

গোঁজ-1, কীলক, খোঁটা, স্তম্ভ, a peg, a nail, a stake.

গোঁড়, পিণ্ড, ফুলা, a lump, ba l, prominence, swelling; prominent, gibbous. [flatterer, band-leader.

গোঁড়া স্ফীতি, পিণ্ড, স্তাবক, a prominence, ball, panegyrist,

গোঁড়াম, স্তাবকতা, panegyric, bombast, gross flattery.

গোঁফ, ওষ্ঠের উপরি রক্ষিত কেশ, a mustachio, whiskers. [deer.

গোকর্ণ, বিতস্তি, সর্প, মৃগ বিশেষ, a span, a serpent, a species of

গোকল গরুকে দত্ত ঘাস, an offering of straw or grass to a cow.

গোকুল, গরুসমূহ, গোষ্ঠ, a herd of cows, a cow-pen.

গোগা, গোঙ্গা,—বোবা, dumb. [ness or nightmare.

গোঙ্গরণ,-আণ, বোবান, to utter indistinct sounds from dumb-

গোচর, ইন্দ্রিয়ার্থ, রূপরসাদি, সাক্ষাৎ, জ্ঞাতসার, an object of sense or understanding, privity, presence, hearing, &c. [handful.

গোচা, গোছা,—থোবা, আঁটি, a nosegay, bunch, small sheaf,

গোচাণ, গোছান—আঁটিবন্ধন, to collect into heaps, bunches, bundles &c.

গোচারক, গোপালক, রাখাল, a cow-herd, cow-keeper.

গোচার-ণ, গোপালন, the feeding or tending of cows, pasture.

গোচান, আঁটিবাধা, নিকশ্রাতি, পটু, tied into sheaves or bundles, tidy, orderly, clever.

গোছ, গোচ,—স্তবক, আঁটি, ধারা, গুল্ম, a bunch, nosegay, wisp, sheaf, a custom, habit, the ring of a locket &c. the ankle.

গোটন,-আন, যড়ান, to roll up, fold up, gather into heaps.

গোটা, বাদলা, জুটী, সমুদায়, একুন, গুবাক, gold or silver lace, a clew, a whole, integer, quantity, betel-nut, a kind of sauce. [vided.

গোটা-ল, সমুদায়, অখণ্ডিত, whole, unbroken, entire, undi-

গোঠ, মেষাদির পাল, সমূহ, সভা, গোষ্ঠ, a herd, drove, flock, fold, troop, multitude, company, a cow-pen.

গোড়, পাদ, তল, মূল, the foot, a pedestal, base, foundation, bottom. [origin.

গোড়া, তল, স্তম্ভ, মূল, a base, foundation, pillar, source,

গোড়ান, কাছান, নিকটাগমন, to overtake, approach, draw near.
গোড়াগোড়ি, পুনরায়, মূলাবধি, anew, from the source or foundation, wholly.
গোড়ারী, গোড়মুড়া,—পার্ষ্ণি, গুল্ফ, the heel.
গোড়িম্ব, গোড়িম্ব,—পক্ষিশাবক, unfledged, callow.
গোণী, থলিয়া, থলী, a sack.
গোত্র, কুল, আদিপুরুষ, জাতি, গোষ্ঠাদি, পর্বত, race, lineage, descent, family, clan, a species, an ancestor, a patriarch, a mountain. [relative.
গোত্রজ, জ্ঞাতি, lineally descended, of the same descent; a
গোদ, পাদস্ফীতি, elephantiasis or swelled leg.
গোদন্ত, হরিতাল, yellow orpiment, a fossil salt, a cow's tooth.
গোদা, স্ফীতপাদ, having the elephantiasis.
গোদানী, উল্কি, a tattooing of the upper part of the nose, a branding iron. [bow arm.
গোধা, ধনুরজ্জুনিবারক চর্ম্ম, an archer's leathern fence for the
গোধা, গোধিকা,—গোসাপ, the Gangetic alligator or guana.
গোধূম, গম, wheat.
গোধূলী, সূর্য্যাস্তকাল, the evening twilight.
গোনাগোষ্ঠী, পূর্বপুরুষ, a family or lineage traced backwards.
গোপ, গোয়ালা, গোপালক, a cow-keeper, dairyman, milkman, butterman.
গোপতি, ষাঁড়, a bull. [crecy, privacy, concealment.
গোপন, লুকান, ছাপান, অপ্রকাশ, to hide, conceal, guard; se-
গোপায়িত, লুক্কায়িত, রক্ষিত, concealed, hidden, guarded.
গোপাল, গোয়ালা, কৃষ্ণ, a dairyman, &c. Krishna or his image.
গোপী গোপিনী, গোপিকা,—গোপস্ত্রী, a dairy-woman, dairyman's wife.
গোপীমাটী, অঙ্গলেপনের মাটী বিশেষ, a sacred earth used for smearing the body. [household.
গোপ্পো, পরিবার সমুদায়, children and cattle, one's whole
গোপ্তা, গোপ্ত্রী,—নিহোতা, লুকানিয়া, রক্ষক, *m. f.* a concealer, one who guards.
গোন্দা, স্থূল, ভারী, thick, clumsy, unwieldy.
গোবর, গোময়,—গোবিষ্ঠা, cow-dung, manure.
গোবরাট, অম্বুর, শিলা, the threshold or sill of a door.

গোবরাণ, পাকনে বর্ণ ফিরাণ, অবলেখন, to change color as fruit in ripening, to write illegibly, to blot.
গোবাঘা, নেকড়িয়া, নেকড়্যা, বৃক, the hyæna.
গোবিন্দ, কৃষ্ণ, a name of Vishnu as Krishna.
গোময়, গোবিষ্ঠা, গোবর, cow-dung.
গোমায়ু, শৃগাল, গরুর পিত্ত, a jackal, the bile of a cow.
গোমুখ, গঙ্গার মূল নিকট তীর্থস্থান বিশেষ, জপমালার থলী, a cow's mouth, the famous Himalayan chasm through which the Ganges flows, the bag for a rosary, a sort of musical instrument.
গোমূঢ়, গাবী. অতিঅজ্ঞানী, grossly ignorant, as stupid as a [cow.
গোমেদক, পীতাশ্ম, বিষ বিশেষ, a yellow topaz, a kind of poison.
গোর-া, শুক্ল, গৌরাঙ্গ, white, fair, european.
গোরমা, গোপ্রিয় তৃণ বিশেষ, a species of grass relished by [cows.
গোরস. দুগ্ধ, দধি, ঘোলাদি, milk, whey, butter-milk, curds, &c.
গোরু, গাবী, বলদ, a cow, an ox.
গোরোচনা, তিলকাদির নিমিত্ত রঙ্গ বিশেষ, a yellow marking pigment procured from cow's urine.
গোর্দ, মস্তকের মজ্জা, শিটা, the brain, dregs, refuse..
গোল, বর্তুল, মণ্ডলাকৃতি, a globe, circle, ball ; round, globular.
গোল-ক, বিধবাতে জারজ পুত্র, গুলি, বর্তুলাকার, the bastard of a widow, a ball ; round.
গোল, গোলমাল,—উৎপাত, কোলাহল, confusion, disorder, tumult, riot.
গোলা, বাকার, শস্যের গৃহ, বৃহৎ বটিকা, a store-house, granary, barn, ball, bullet ; dissolved in liquid.
গোলা, গোলী.—বর্তুল, গুলি, a ball, a bullet.
গোলাঙ্গুল, বানর বিশেষ, a black cow-tailed monkey.
গোলান, প্রচারণ, ঘোলান, to spread a report, divulge, to dissolve into a paste.
গোলোক, কৃষ্ণের ধাম, Krishna's paradise.
গোষ্ঠ, মেষাদি পাল, বাথান, a herd, flock, drove, pen, fold, [pasture.
গোষ্ঠী, কুটুম্ব, জ্ঞাতি, পরিবার, কুল, সভা, আলাপ, kin, kindred, family connexions, dependant relatives or family, race, lineage, genealogy, an assembly, a meeting, conversation, discourse.
গোসর্গ, প্রত্যুষ. প্রাতঃ, dawn, day-break.

গোসর্প, গোসাপ,—গোধিকা, the guana.

গোস্তনী, দ্রাক্ষা, a grape.

গোহালী, গোহাইল,—গোগৃহ, a cow-house. [or its capital.

গৌড়, ভারতবর্ষের মধ্যে এক দেশ, the central part of Bengal

গৌড়ী, গুড়জাত সুরা, rum distilled from molasses.

গৌণ, অপ্রধান, অধীনতা, বিলম্ব, inferior, subordinate; inferiority, delay. [yellow, pale red.

গৌর, গৌরাঙ্গ, শুক্লবর্ণ, পীত, রক্ত, fair, white, pure, clean,

গৌরব, গুরুতা, প্রভাব, আদর, বৃদ্ধি, greatness, importance, respectability, majesty, glory, honour, grandeur, weight, reverence, respect, increase.

গৌরাঙ্গ, শ্বেত, সুন্দর, white, fair, handsome.

গৌরী, অষ্টমবর্ষীয়া কন্যা, পার্ব্বতী, a young girl, maid, virgin, Párvatí, one of the Shaktis.

গৌরীপাট, পেনেট, the lower stone or female part of the Linga.

গৌরিকা, অরজস্কা, a girl before menstruation.

গ্রন্থ, পুস্তক, a book, writing, composition, volume.

গ্রন্থক, নির্ম্মায়ক, লেখক, কড়ার, মালার সূত্র, a builder, writer, &c. cement, the thread of a necklace.

গ্রন্থন, রচন, নির্ম্মাণ, সংগ্রহণ, to string beads, arrange, place in order, build, plat, knot, work in wicker, &c. compose, write, compile, catalogue.

গ্রন্থি, সন্ধিস্থান, গিরা, a joint, knuckle, tie, knot, knob.

গ্রন্থিত, গ্রথিত,—সূত্রবিদ্ধ, রচিত, strung, arranged, composed, &c.

গ্রন্থী, নানাবিধ পুস্তকবিশিষ্ট, possessed of many books.

গ্রস্ত, কবলিত, আক্রান্ত, রাহুগ্রস্ত, swallowed, eaten, received into a hollow or socket, involved in, affected with, eclipsed.

গ্রস্তাস্ত, রাহুগ্রস্তচন্দ্রাদির অস্ত, the setting of a luminary eclipsed.

গ্রহ, আদান, ধরা, অধ্যবসায়, জ্ঞান, বোধ, সূর্য্যাদি নব, acceptance, reception, seizure, hold, tenacity, perseverance, understanding, comprehension, a planet.

গ্রহণ, হস্তে লওন, প্রাপণ, অঙ্গীকরণ, বুঝন, রাহুগ্রস্ত চন্দ্রসূর্য্য, to seize, catch, take, receive, allow, assent, hold, apprehend, comprehend, assume; an eclipse.

গ্রহণী, আমাশয়, উদরভঙ্গ, a dysentery, diarrhœa.

গ্রহপতি, সূর্য্য, the sun.

গ্রহপীড়া, গ্রহবৈগুণ্য, অশুভ, গ্রহজনিত বিপদ, the influence of an unpropitious planet, the evils thence arising.

গ্রহীতা, গ্রাহক, প্রাপক, one who takes, a receiver, &c.

গ্রাম, নগর, পল্লী, a village, a hamlet.

গ্রামণী, মণ্ডলব্যক্তি, নাপিত, প্রধান, the headman of a village, a village-barber; best, chief, excellent, eminent.

গ্রামী, গ্রামস্থ, অশিষ্ট, a villager, a rustic; pertaining to a [village.

গ্রাম্য, পোষা, গ্রামেজাত, মূঢ়, অসভ্য, tame, domestic, village, rustic, rude, unpolished.

গ্রাম্যধর্ম্ম, স্ত্রীসংসর্গ, copulation, a villager's duty.

গ্রাস, কবল, অন্নপিণ্ড, গিলনি, a mouthful, lump, bit, a swallowing.

গ্রাসাচ্ছাদন, অন্নবস্ত্র, food and raiment.

গ্রাহ, গ্রহণকরা, প্রাপ্তি, হাঙ্গর, reception, acceptance, acquisition, taking, seizure; a shark or guana.

গ্রাহক, গ্রহণকারী, ক্রেতা, গ্রহীতা, বাজপক্ষী, receiving, &c. a purchaser, receiver, &c. a hawk or falcon.

গ্রীবা, গলদেশ, ঘাড়, the neck, the nape of the neck.

গ্রীষ্ম, উত্তাপ, গুমট্কাল, উষ্ণ, heat, warmth, the hot season; hot, sultry, warm.

গ্লানি, শ্রান্তি, কাতরতা, নিন্দা, অপবাদ, languor, lassitude, fatigue, depression of mind, reproach, censure, slander.

ঘ.

ঘট, ঘড়া, কলসী, an earthen pot, jar, jug, pitcher, a water-pot.

ঘটক, যোজক, মিলনিয়া, a match-maker, one who investigates genealogies and negociates marriages.

ঘটকালি, যোজকতা, the office of a match-maker.

ঘটন, পড়ন, অর্জ্জন, পিতৃধনপ্রাপণ, মিলন, to happen, occur, belong to, inherit or succeed to, to unite.

ঘটনা, উপস্থিত যে, দৈব, যোজনা, মেল, an occurrence, event, accident, union, bringing together, mixture.

ঘটনীয়, সম্ভাব্য, যোজনীয়, যোগ্য, অর্হণীয়. liable to happen, probable, unitable, suitable, heritable.

ঘটা, জনতা, সমূহ, সভা, আড়ম্বর, a crowd, concourse, multitude, assemblage, a procession. [tilt.

ঘটাটোপ, ডোলী ইত্যাদির আচ্ছাদন, a covering for palkees &c. a

ঘটান, উৎপাদন, জন্মান, মিলান, to cause, occasion, effect, ascribe to, join, mix, unite.

ঘটিকা, দণ্ড, দণ্ডদ্বয়, গুল্ফ, a daṇḍa of 24 or muhúrta of 48 minutes, the ankle.

ঘটী, ঘড়ী, জলপাত্র a gong, watch, clock, a small jar.

ঘটীযন্ত্র, জল উত্থাপনের যন্ত্র বিশেষ, ঘড়ী, the rope and bucket of a well, a watch.

ঘট্ট, ঘাট্, a quay, wharf, landing place.

ঘট্টী, অসাধারণ কিম্বা গুপ্ত ঘাট্, a smaller or private wharf.

ঘড়া, জলপাত্র, কলসী, a water-pot, a pitcher.

ঘড়িয়াল, গোধিকা, the guana or Gangetic alligator.

ঘড়ী, দণ্ডপলাদিনির্ণয় যন্ত্র, a gong, clock, watch, hour. [purr.

ঘড়্ঘড়ান, ঘোঙ্গরাণ, to make a rattling sound in the throat, to

ঘড়্ঘড়িয়া, গোবাঘা, an hyæna; purring, rattling.

ঘড়্ঘড়ী, অন্তকালীন কণ্ঠধ্বনি, the death-rattle in the throat, a top, whirligig.

ঘণ্ট, শাকাদির মিশ্রীভাব, a sort of sauce or condiment.

ঘণ্টা, কাঁসর, ঘড়ী, a gong, a bell, a clock, an hour.

ঘণ্টী, ক্ষুদ্র ঘণ্টা, a small bell.

ঘন, কাঁসর, ঘণ্টা, কঠিনতা, সমূহ, সংখ্যা, মেঘ, গাঢ়, নিবিড়, অবিরল, মোটা, কঠিন, a gong, cymbal, bell; solidity, hardness, extension, a multitude, number, quantity, a cloud, a fragrant grass; thick, crowded, close, impervious, coarse, near, incessant, firm, hard.

ঘনঘন, অনবরতঃ, শীঘ্র, incessantly, in thick succession.

ঘনাঘন, কঠিন, শক্ত, গাঢ়, হিংস্রক, মত্তহস্তী, solid, close, thick, impervious, &c. mischievous; a vicious elephant, a rainy cloud, collision, Indra.

ঘমান, কাছান, ধরণ, to overtake, to come up with.
ঘনাবৃত, গাঢ়, আবর্ত্তিত, inspissated, thickened by boiling.
ঘনিষ্ঠ, আসন্ন, নিকটোপস্থিত, close, very near. [fish.
ঘনী, মৎস্যধরণার্থ বংশনির্ম্মিত যন্ত্র, a bamboo-cage for catching
ঘনুয়া, জার, কোটনা, a paramour, pimp, pander.
ঘবরণ, অবাক কিম্বা ব্যাকুল হওন, to be confounded, amazed, confused, disturbed or perplexed.
ঘবরাণী, উদ্বেগ, ব্যাকুলতা, বিস্ময়, perplexity, confusion, discomposure, perturbation, amazement.
ঘর, গৃহ, বসতি, বাটী, স্থান, আধার, পরিবার, a house, dwelling, home, building, groove, loop, loop-hole, place, receptacle, a family.
ঘরকন্না, গৃহকর্ম্ম, সংসার, household business.
ঘরণী, ভার্য্যা, গৃহিণী, a wife, a housewife.
ঘরসন্ধান, পরগৃহের অনুসন্ধান, a prying into family affairs, curiosity, officiousness.
ঘরা, আধার, ছিদ্র, a receptacle, drawer, hole, passage.
ঘরাঘরি, বাটী, আপনার, স্বজনের, home, one's own house; domestic, private.
ঘরামী, গৃহনির্ম্মাতা, a thatcher, a hut-builder.
ঘরুয়া, গৃহজাত, home-made, produced at home.
ঘর্ঘর-ধ্বনি, শকটাদির শব্দ, a rattling, rumbling, creaking, roar.
ঘর্ম্ম, ঘাম,— স্বেদ, রোমকূপ নিঃসৃত জল, perspiration, sweat.
ঘর্ষণ, ঘষণ,—মার্জ্জন, ভঙ্গন, to rub, wipe, clean, file, polish, varnish, grind; friction, &c.
ঘষি, শুষ্ক গোময় চূর্ণ, the powder of dried cow-dung.
ঘা, চোট, আঘাত, ক্ষত, a blow, knock, bruize, wound, ulcer, sore, cut, scar.
ঘাইট, অপরাধ, দোষ, ন্যূনতা, ন্যূন, a fault, crime, guilt, sin, defect, abatement; less, deficient.
ঘাঁটন, আবর্ত্তন, চৎকান, to stir, mix by stirring, knead.
ঘাটান, উঠান, উত্তেজনাদেওন, চেতান, to rouse up, make to rise, stimulate, stir up.
ঘাঁটি, চোরাপথ, থানা, a by-way, cross-road, ambuscade, gap in a fence, track or trace. [&c.
ঘাঁটু, চুলকনাদির কর্ত্তা, the god of cutaneous disorders, itch

ঘাঁতন, কথাদ্বারা উত্থাপন, খেদান ইত্যাদি, to affect by speaking, to make one feel. [beaten.
ঘাগী, পুনঃ২ দণ্ডিতা, *f.* hardened by beating, frequently
ঘাঘরা, ঘুঙুর, রাঙ্গতুষ, a woman's girdle of small bells, a petticoat, a furbelow; mustard-chaff.
ঘাট, নদ্যাদির অবগাহন স্থান, পর্ব্বতের গহ্বর, a wharf, landing-place, ferry, mountain-pass, defile.
ঘাটমারণ, বিনাকরে দ্রব্য চালান, to smuggle. [way.
ঘাটন, ক্ষরণ, হ্রাস হওন, ঊনন, to be deficient, fail, waste a-
ঘাটান, হ্রাস করণ, ঊনান, সুলভ করণ, to lessen, reduce, diminish, abate, cheapen.
ঘাটী, অপরাধ, পাপ, a fault, a crime.
ঘাড়, ঘাটা,—গ্রীবা, the nape of the neck.
ঘাড়নাড়ন, শিরোনমনপূর্ব্বক গাহ্যাগাহ্য প্রদর্শন, to nod assent or dissent, object, acquiesce.
ঘাড়ান, স্বীকরণ, মানন, to nod assent, acquiesce.
ঘাত, চোট, ক্ষত, a blow, a hurt. [guinary, striking.
ঘাতক, মারক, হন্তা, বধিক, a striker, murderer; seditious, san-
ঘাতন, মারণ, হনন, to smite, hurt, strike, kill.
ঘাতুক, হিংসুক, বধী, ক্রূর, destructive, mischievous, cruel, sanguinary, ferocious.
ঘানি, তৈলযন্ত্র, an oil mill.
ঘামন, স্বেদন, ঘর্ম্মাক্ত হওন, to perspire, to sweat.
ঘামাচি, ঘর্ম্মকচ্ছু, prickly heat, itching eruption. [alone.
ঘারেঘোরে, গুপ্তে, ঠারে, ইঙ্গিতে, privately, secretly, by signs
ঘালি, ক্ষত, ঘা, a wound, an ulcer.
ঘাস, গবাদির ভক্ষণ তৃণ, meadow or pasture grass.
ঘি, ঘী,—ঘৃত, হবিঃ, ghee or clarified butter.
ঘিঞ্জি, নিবিড়, ঘন, thick, crowded, impervious.
ঘিয়া, তেলা, তৈলাক্ত, oily, butyraceous, shining, polished.
ঘিরণ, বেড়ন, to surround, hedge round, fence, skreen.
ঘুঁটি, গুলী, a ball, a ballot, a lot.
ঘুঘু, পারাবত, বন্য কপোত, a dove, a turtle-dove.
ঘুঘুর-1 উচুঙ্গা, the mole-cricket, a sort of ulcer on the legs.
ঘুঙুর, কটিদেশের অলঙ্কার বিশেষ, a waist-belt of small bells.
ঘুচন, অন্তর্হিত হওন, to disappear, remove, pass away, yield.

ঘুচন,-আন, খোলন, নাশন, উল্টন, to open, loose, remove, strip, repeal, rub out, dispel.
ঘুট, গুল্ফ, the ancle, a species of jujube.
ঘুটমণ্ডল, গোলমাল, জঞ্জাল, confusion, disorder.
ঘুটী, গুল্ফ, বড়িয়া, the ancle, a chessman, &c.
ঘুড়ন, বেড়ন, পরিবেষ্টন, to surround, fence or skreen round.
ঘুড়ী, উড়ন, অশ্বী, the flight of birds, a mare.
ঘুণ, কাষ্ঠাদি জীর্ণকারিকীট বিশেষ, an insect found in timber.
ঘুণন, খুঁড়ন, to root up the ground as a swine.
ঘুণাক্ষর, ইচ্ছাবিনা উৎপন্নকার্য্য, লেশ, an undesigned and unexpected event or circumstance, the least trace or hint, a slight intimation.
ঘুণী, আটল, a bamboo-cage to catch fish.
ঘুণ্ঘুণান, ভণ্ভণান, ঘেঁকান, গর্জ্জন, to buz, hum, growl, snarl.
ঘুণ্টী, কিঙ্কিণী, ঘণ্টিকা, গুটিকা, a small bell, a button.
ঘুম-ন, নিদ্রা, শয়ন, sleep, slumber, nap, repose; to sleep, &c.
ঘুমন্ত, নিদ্রিত, তন্দ্রালু, asleep, dozing.
ঘুরণ, ঘূরণ,—বিবর্ত্তন, ফিরণ, to whirl round, roll, revolve, [turn.
ঘুলন, আবর্ত্তন, আলোড়ন, to stir liquids, agitate a fluid.
ঘুষ-া, চিঙ্গড়ি ইত্যাদি ক্ষুদ্র মৎস্য, shrimps, prawns and other small fishes.
ঘুষ, মুষ্টি, মুষ্ট্যাঘাত, উৎকোচ, the fist, a thump, a bribe.
ঘুষড়ন, গুপ্তস্থানে আশ্রয় লওন, প্রবেশন, লোপকরণ, to retreat or creep into, enter, expunge, cancel.
ঘুষণ, কীলন, জপন, প্রচারণ, উদ্ঘোষণ, প্রবেশন, to thump, strike with the fist, repeat, declare, proclaim, utter, sound, enter, run into.
ঘুষান, ঘুষড়ন, to enter, penetrate, to retreat or creep into.
ঘূরাণ, ফিরাণ, ভুলান, to make to revolve, &c. to subvert, misguide.
ঘূর্ণ, ফেরা, পাক, শিরঃকম্প, চাকভুমী, a revolution, rolling, whirl, turn, vertigo; revolving, whirling, &c.
ঘূর্ণন, মণ্ডলাকারে ভ্রমণ, to whirl, revolve, turn round.
ঘূর্ণা, শিরঃকম্প, পাকনা, a giddiness, vertigo, whirlpool, &c.
ঘূর্ণায়মান, চাকভুমী, বিবৃত্ত, turning round, revolving, whirling.
ঘূর্ণি, বিবর্ত্ত, ফেরা, a turning or whirling round, revolution.

ঘৃণা, অত্যন্ত অশ্রদ্ধা, মন্দবাস, অনিচ্ছা, অবজ্ঞা, hatred, abhorrence, dislike, disgust, nausea, shock, sneering, spurning, contempt.
ঘৃত, অগ্নিসংস্কৃত নবনীত, ঘি, clarified butter, ghee.
ঘৃষ্ট, ঘষা, মার্জ্জিত, পরিষ্কৃত, rubbed, polished, rubbed off.
ঘেঁচন,-আন, কাটান, উৎখাতন, কাটন, পাষণ, to frustrate, supplant, shuffle cards, cut, bruise or pound.
ঘেঁটন,-আন, পরদ্রব্যে হাতদেওন, মাখান, গতিবিধি করণ, to meddle with, intermeddle, have dealings with.
ঘেঁটু, ঘণ্টাকর্ণ নামক দেবতা বিশেষ, the name of a god.
ঘেঁষড়ন,-আন, হিঁছড়ন, ভূমিতে টানন, to draw, trail on the ground, drag, run as a creeper. [tune, dun.
ঘেঙ্গান, মাঙ্গন, উত্তেজন, to pray, intreat, teaze, urge, impor-
ঘেটন, ফুরণ, অনাটন, টুটন, হারণ, to fail, fall short, be insufficient, decrease, diminish, lose or be cast, to be worsted or overcome. [close, fence.
ঘেরণ বেড়ন, বেষ্টন, to surround, encompass, invest, en-
ঘেরা, মণ্ডল, আড়াল, বেড়া, a circle, fence, hedge.
ঘৈরা, গাম্ভীর্য্য, depth.
ঘোঁটন, বিচারণ, প্রস্তাবন, বিতর্কণ, মর্দ্দন, to talk over, agitate, canvass, introduce a topic, rub in a mortar, &c.
ঘোঁটনা লোড়া, শিলাপুত্র, a pestle, muller, rolling stone.
ঘোঙ-া, ঘন নামক বাদ্য যন্ত্র বিশেষ, the chinese gong.
ঘোঙ্গরা, খাটধ্বনি, কণ্ঠ্য, গলাভাঙ্গা, deep-sounded, guttural, hoarse.
ঘোটক, ঘোড়া—অশ্ব, তুরঙ্গ, a horse.
ঘোটকী, ঘোড়ী,—অশ্বী, a mare.
ঘোড়াচড়া, অশ্বারোহী, তুরঙ্গসাদী, a horseman, trooper, cavalry.
ঘোড়ারু, অশ্বারোহণশাল, বারশৃঙ্গ, fond of riding ; an elk.
ঘোণ্টা, সেয়াকোল, সুপারী বৃক্ষ, the jujube, the betel-nut tree.
ঘোপ, ঝোপ, ঝোড়, গুল্ম, a large bush.
ঘোপাল, ঝাড়ীবন গুল্মযুক্ত, abounding with bushes, bushy.
ঘোম্‌টা, অবগুণ্ঠিকা, মুখাচ্ছাদন, a veil.
ঘোর, তমস, অন্ধকার, আতঙ্ক, দীপ্তিশূন্য, ভয়ানক, darkness, gloom, horror, dread ; dark, gloomy, deep-colored, awful, dreadful.

ঘোর, ঘোরাল,—অব্যক্ত,কঠিন, অস্পষ্ট, dark, vague, obscure, abstruse, difficult, mysterious.
ঘোরা, ফেরা, ঘূর্ণি, a circuit, peregrination, revolution.
ঘোল, তক্র, আওড়, butter-milk, an eddy, a whirlpool.
ঘোলা-লী, কাদাটিয়া, অনির্ম্মল, ঘন, turbid, muddy, thick.
ঘোলান, গালন, কাদান, to dissolve in liquid, make turbid, &c.
ঘোষ, ধ্বনি, নাদ, গর্জ্জনী, কুলীন কায়স্থ, গোপ, লতা বিশেষ, a sound, cry, low thunder, distant rumbling; a class of the writer tribe, a herdsman, a sort of creeping plant.
ঘোষণা, প্রচারণা, প্রকাশ, a proclamation, publication, sermon.
ঘোষাণ, প্রচারণ, প্রকাশন, জানান, to proclaim, publish, make known, preach, inculcate.
ঘ্রাণ, বাস, গন্ধগ্রহণ, a scent, smell, the act of smelling.
ঘ্রাণেন্দ্রিয়, নাসিকা, the organ of smell, the nose.
ঘ্রাত, গৃহীতবাস, smelled to, scented.

চ.

চক, ক্রয়বিক্রয় স্থান, a regular market place, a square.
চকিত, ভয়ান্বিত, ত্রস্ত, alarmed, startled, timorous, fearful.
চকোর, পক্ষি বিশেষ, the bartavelle or red legged partridge.
চক্‌চক্‌, স্বচ্ছতা, দীপ্তি, দীপ্তিমান, clearness, transparency, brightness, glare, flash; shining, vivid, glaring.
চক্‌মকান, ঝকন, নম্পন, to flash, glare, shine, glitter, twinkle.
চক্‌মকি-য়া, দীপ্তিমান, উজ্জ্বলিত, glaring, glittering, radiant, flashing, twinkling.
চক্‌লা, প্রদেশ, অধিকার, রাষ্ট্র, a district, province, estate.
চক্র, চাকা, ঘানি, মণ্ডল, অস্ত্র বিশেষ, আবর্ত্ত, পূর্ণ সময়, ব্যূহ বিশেষ, ঘূর্ণ, ঐকমত্য, চাতুরী, সমূহ, রাশি, রাষ্ট্র, হংস বিশেষ, খিজ, শরীরের এক দেশ, a wheel, a potter's wheel, oil-mill, circle, discus, whirlpool, period of time, an army, a circular military position, a revolution, round, convolution, a combination, conspiracy, roguery; craft, deceit, a multitude, heap, a realm, region, province, the

ruddy goose, a spot of leprosy, an anatomical division of the body, astrological figure.

চক্রপাণি, নারায়ণ, বিষ্ণু, wielding the discus ; Vishnu.

চক্রবর্ত্তী, সার্বভৌম রাজা, প্রভু, প্রদেশস্থ, অধিকারস্থিত, an emperor, king, ruler, the master of an estate ; situated in a province or estate.

চক্রবাক, হংসপক্ষি বিশেষ, a species of duck.

চক্রী, বিষ্ণু, সম্রাট, অধিপতি, কুম্ভকার, কলু, কাণাড়িপাতা, সর্প, ভাঁড়, Vishnu, an emperor, the governor of a province, a potter, oilman, expresser of oil, an informer, a serpent, the ruddy goose, a tumbler or wheel-juggler.

চক্ষাচক্ষি, মুখামুখি, face to face, eye to eye.

চক্ষু, নেত্র, অক্ষি, দর্শন, the eye, vision.

চক্ষুঃশ্রবা, সর্প, a snake, (whose eyes serve for ears.)

চক্ষুর্গোচর, দর্শনীয়, প্রত্যক্ষ, an object of sight ; visible, present to the eye. [good, sound, healthy.

চঙ্গ, সুন্দর, পটু, উত্তম, অরোগী, handsome, clever, eminent,

চঙ্গাই, স্বাস্থ্য, সৌন্দর্য্য, recovery, cure, health, beauty, &c.

চঙ্গারী, ঝুড়ী বিশেষ, a wide basket. [uneasy.

চঞ্চনিয়া টনটনিয়া, চঞ্চল, shooting (as pain), shifting, fickle,

চঞ্চল, অস্থায়ী, চপল, অস্থির, দ্রুত, moving quickly, fluctuating, unsteady, changeable, fickle, capricious, volatile, inconstant, fluid.

চঞ্চু, পক্ষির ওষ্ঠ, the bill or beak of a bird. [speedily.

চট্, টাট, শুণ, মেকলী, শীঘ্র, canvass, sackcloth ; hastily,

চটন, ফাটন, টুটন, ফকন, to break, shiver, scale off, fall off in splinters, fail, be ineffectual.

চটক, চড়ই পক্ষী, কাল্পনিক চমৎকার, a sparrow, sleight of hand, a lying wonder, show, gaudiness.

চটাচটি, রেষারেষি, a mutual grudge or desire of revenge.

চটান, মাঠ, পুলিন, ফাটন, a plain, a strand ; to scale off, &c.

চটাল, প্রশস্ত, চৌড়া, broad, wide.

চটী, টাট, শুণ, মাদুরাদি, শলা, canvass, sack-cloth, a mat, a bamboo lath for wicker work.

চট্কান, ছানন, মাখন, to knead, to temper clay.

চট্কানা, থাপড়, ছানা, a slap, a cuff, kneading, &c.
চট্চটিয়া, আটাল, viscid, viscous, ropy, clammy.
চড়, চাপড়, করতল, a slap, blow, tap, the flat palm.
চড়ই, চটই,—চটক পক্ষী, a sparrow.
চড়ক, গাজনক্রিয়া, ব্যথা, the Hindoo swinging ceremony, the machine itself, pain.
চড়কন, টনটনান, জ্বলন, to throb, twinge, smart.
চড়কল, অতিশয়, অতিব্যথাকর, excessive, very painful.
চড়ন, আরোহণ, উদ্গমন, উঠন, থাবড়ান, to mount, climb, rise, ascend, scale, embark, enter a boat, to slap, to smite with the flat palm.
চড়ান, উঠাইয়া রাখন, উগান, পূরাণ, জ্যা টানন, বাড়ান, উচ্চ, উদ্ধ, বাড়া, পুলিন, to place or set upon, load, prepare, bend a bow, add, augment, slap; high, loud, steep, exalted, increased; an island, shallow, strand.
চড়াও, আক্রমণ, পড়িয়া লুটন, an attack, onset, storm, assault, invasion, inroad, aggression.
চড়াচড়ি, পরস্পর থাপড় দেওয়া, a mutual slapping, leap-frog.
চড়াশব্দ, দীর্ঘোচ্চারিত শব্দ, উচ্চৈঃস্বর, an accented or emphatic word; loud language.
চড়চড়, কাতরতা, ব্যথা, distress of mind, vexation, pain.
চড়তি, বাড়ি, বৃদ্ধি, advance of price, accumulation.
চণক, ছোলা, a sort of pea given to horses, gram.
চণ্ড, অতিশয়কোপশীল, very passionate, furious, violent.
চণ্ডাল, জাতিচ্যুত, বিটাল, an outcast, a low unprincipled fellow, a villain.
চণ্ডী, চণ্ডিকা,—দুর্গা, Durgá, i. e. the wrathful or furious.
চণ্ডু, উন্দুর, কপি, a rat, the common small monkey.
চণ্ডুল, ভরতপাকি বিশেষ, a beautiful species of lark.
চতুর, চারি, নিপুণ, প্রজ্ঞ, চালাক, four; clever, dextrous, sly, cunning, ingenious, active.
চতুরঙ্গ, চারিভাগে বিভক্ত, সাঙ্গ, quadripartite, complete.
চতুরানন, ব্রহ্মা, a name of Brahmá.
চতুর্থ, চারির পূরণ, the fourth, offered on the fourth day.
চতুর্দ্দিক, চতুর্দ্দিক্ষু,—চারিপার্শ্বে, on all sides, all round.
চতুর্দ্দোল-া, যান বিশেষ, a litter, a palquee.

চতুর্গুণা, চতুর্গুণ, four-fold.

চতুর্বর্গ বা ভদ্র,—ধর্ম্মার্থকামমোক্ষ, the four objects of human pursuit, love, riches, religion and final beatitude.

চতুর্বর্ণ, ব্রাহ্মণাদি চার, শ্বেতকৃষ্ণাদি, the four primary casts or classes of Hindoos, the four primary colours, white, black, blue and red.

চতুষ্টয়, চারি, four.

চতুষ্পাঠী, চৌবাড়ী, a college where the four Veds are taught.

চতুষ্পাদ, চৌপায়া, পশু, four-footed ; a quadruped.

চত্বর, আঙ্গিনা, যাগস্থান, a court-yard, place for sacrifice.

চনা, কলায় বিশেষ, a sort of vetch. [powder.

চন্দন, গন্ধকাষ্ঠ বিশেষ, sandal wood, sandal perfume or

চন্দনা, শুকপক্ষি বিশেষ, a species of parrot.

চন্দা, মাথট, a subscription, a collection.

চন্দ্র, চন্দ্রমা,—চাঁদ, শশধর, the moon.

চন্দ্রকান্ত, মণি বিশেষ, a fabulous gem, chrystal, stone, jasper.

চন্দ্রচূড় বা শেখর,—শিব, Shiva or the moon-crested.

চন্দ্রব্রত, রাজধর্ম্ম, রাজ্যপালনব্রত, the duty or vow of a monarch to make his subjects happy.

চন্দ্রাতপ চাঁদোয়া, an awning. [disgrace.

চন্দ্রাদিত্যকলঙ্ক, দৃঢ়কলঙ্ক, বহুকালস্থায়ী অপমান, a lasting or indelible

চন্দ্রাভাস, মিথ্যা চন্দ্র, a paraselene or false moon. [fish-

চন্দ্রিকা, জ্যোৎস্না, চন্দ্রের তেজ, moonlight, a species of small

চপট, চপড়,—থাবড়া, দায়, the flat or extended palm, risk.

চপরাস, পদাতিকের চিহ্ন, a badge, belt-plate, buckle.

চপল, কম্পমান, অস্থির, অবিবেকী, ত্রস্ত, শীঘ্র, ক্ষণিক, tremulous, shaking, wavering, unsteady, volatile, inconsiderate, rash, alarmed, swift, momentary.

চপলা, লক্ষ্মী, বিদ্যুত, চঞ্চলা, বেশ্যা, Lakshmí, fortune, lightning, an inconstant woman, a harlot.

চপেট, চপট—করতল, চড়, the flat palm, a slap.

চবিলা, রসিক, উল্লাসময়, চালাক, blithe, buxom, active. [start-

চমক ঝল্পান, জলজল, ভয়ে টলা, a flash, glare, twinkle, glance,

চমকিত, কম্পিত, ত্রস্ত, ভাজা, startled, alarmed, parched, contracted, shrunk.

চমড়া, ত্বক, ছাল, a skin, hide, leather.

চমৎকার, বিস্ময়, আশ্চর্য্যজ্ঞান, surprize, wonder, astonishment.
চমরী, গরু বিশেষ, the yak or Tartarian ox.
চমস, চম্চা, যজ্ঞীয় জলাধার বিশেষ, a spoon, sacrificial ladle.
চমূ, সৈন্য, তিন পৃতনা, an army, a squadron, a division.
চম্কন, নন্দন, কাঁপন, ভরণ, ভাজন, to flash, glittler, twinkle, shudder, start, shrug, parch.
চম্পক, পীতপুষ্পিত বৃক্ষ, a tree bearing fragrant yellow flowers.
চম্পট, লুকান, পলায়ন, a withdrawing, retiring, absconding, vanishing, flight.
চম্বেলি, বেলিপুষ্প বিশেষ, a beautiful species of jasmine.
চয়, সমূহ, সংগ্রহ, মৃত্তিকার রাশি, পগার, a multitude, assemblage, collection, heap, mound, rampart, a raised plot.
চয়ন, পুষ্পাদির আহরণ, ছাল তোলন, to collect, gather flowers &c. put together, peel, strip off, pull off.
চর, কপটবেশধারি দূত, অস্থাবর, a spy, emissary; moveable, unsteady. [a spy.
চরক, গাজনক্রিয়া, চর, the Hindoo swinging ceremony;
চরকা, সূতকাটনের যন্ত্র, আকর্ষণার্থ চাক, a spinning wheel, capstan, windlass.
চরকি, নাটাই, ক্ষুদ্র চক্র, কার্পাস ভজনের যন্ত্র, a reel, winch, crank, small wheel, the gudgeon of a wheel, a machine for cleaning cotton.
চরণ, পশু পক্ষি প্রভৃতির অহারার্থ ভ্রমণ, পাদ, শ্লোকের চতুর্থাংশ, to graze as cattle, roam for food; the foot, leg, a poetical foot, favor, protection.
চরণদাসী, ভার্য্যা, খড়ম, a wife, a sandal. [cy.
চরণসেবা, উপাসনা, শুশ্রূষা, obsequious attendance, sycophan-
চরণামৃত, চরণোদক,—গুরুপাদপ্রক্ষালিত জল, the water in which a Guru's foot has been washed.
চরণায়ুধ, কুকুড়া, a cock, *i. e.* whose foot is his weapon.
চরতা, বিছুটিবৎ ঘাস বিশেষ, a species of nettle.
চরম, অন্তিম, শেষের, পশ্চিম, অন্ত, last, final, ultimate, west, western; an end.
চরস, মাদক দ্রব্য বিশেষ, a sort of intoxicating drug.
চরসী, চরসধূমপায়ী, using intoxicating drugs; a sot.

চরাচর, স্থাবরজঙ্গম, চলাচল, the world or things moveable and immoveable.

চরাণ, গবাদি পালন, to feed or tend cattle.

চরাণী, মাঠ, a pasture, a meadow. [customary.

চরিত, চলিত, কৃত, ব্যবহৃত, moved, acted, done, instituted,

চরিত, চরিত্র,—ব্যবহার, রীতি, স্বভাব, উপাখ্যান, conduct, behabiour, observance, custom, usage, practice, disposition of mind, history. [thankful.

চরিতার্থ, কৃতকার্য্য, কৃতার্থ, attaining one's object, successful,

চরিতার্থী, কৃতার্থী, ইষ্টসিদ্ধার্থী, desirous of success.

চরিষ্ণু, চালাক, অস্থাবর, active, mobile, moveable.

চরু, যজ্ঞীয় পায়স, an oblation, chiefly of milk and butter.

চর্চ্চা, বিবেচনা, প্রস্তাব, অঙ্গলেপ, reflection, consideration, deliberation, mention, unction with fragrant ointments.

চর্ব্বণ, দন্তের দ্বারা পেষণ, to chew, to masticate.

চর্ব্বিতচর্ব্বণ, আম্রেড়ন, tautology, repetition of the same act.

চর্ভট, চর্ভটি,—আহ্লাদ, আনন্দ, আত্মশ্লাঘা, দম্ভ, festivity, noise of merriment, self-complacency, self-applause, arrogance.

চর্ম্ম, ছাল, ত্বক, ঢাল, a skin, hide, bark, leather, a shield.

চর্ম্মকার, চামার, মুচী, a tanner, currier, skinner, shoemaker.

চর্ম্মচটিকা, চাম্‌চিকা, a bat.

চর্ম্মী, ঢালী, চর্ম্মধারী, bearing a shield; a shield-bearer.

চর্য্য, ব্যবহার্য্য, আচরণীয়, practicable, customary, incumbent, proper.

চর্য্যা, ব্যবহার, আচরণ, স্বভাব, মৌনাদি ধর্ম্ম, custom, practice, habit, conduct, disposition, character, perseverance in religious austerities, regularity of religious observances.

চল, চলৎ,—গমন, আচার, ব্যাপার, motion, action, conduct.

চলন, গমন, সরণ, বহন, আচরণ, ব্যবহার, ধারা, ব্যবহার্য্য, প্রচররূপ, to move, go on, proceed, flow, sail, blow, pass, act, behave; habit, conduct, custom; customary, habitual, current.

চলনার্হ, গমনার্হ, গন্তব্য, passable, fit to be passed over.

চলাচল, চপল, অস্থির, স্থাবরজঙ্গম, tremulous, unsteady, unfixed; the world or things moveable and immoveable.
চলান, সরাণ, বহান, ঠেলন, পথ দেখান, দৌড়ান, প্রেরণ, to cause to move or act, impel, urge on, push, row, drive, dispel, conduct, guide, dispatch, shoot an arrow, &c. an invoice, a pass.
চলাবুলা, বহুশ্রম, আনাগোনা, much ado about any thing, fuss.
চলি, গতি, যাত্রা, দৌড়, a journey, a race.
চলিত, প্রেরিত, কম্পিত, গত, প্রচরদ্রূপ, sent, moved, agitated, gone, going, current, customary.
চলিষ্ণু, চলচলিয়া,—গমনশীল, অস্থাবর, দ্রুত, moveable, unsteady, [fluid.
চুলুক, গণ্ডূষ, a handful of water, a swinging, undulation.
চহ্লন, উতলন, ঝলকন, to spill, to flow or flap over.
চল্‌তি, ক্রিয়া, ব্যবহার, an action, deed, conduct, custom, [course.
চষক, পানপাত্র, a drinking vessel.
চষণ, কর্ষণ, ভূমিবিদারণ, to plough, to till.
চষাণি, কর্ষণি, কৃষিকর্ম্ম, a ploughing, wages for ploughing.
চষী, লাঙ্গলিয়া, কর্ষক, ploughing, worming in.
চহলা, কর্দ্দম, কাদা, soft mud, dirt, mire.
চা, স্পৃহা, বাঞ্ছা, ইচ্ছা, গাছ বিশেষ, wish, desire, want, demand, will, volition; tea.
চাওন, চাহন,—মাঙ্গন. বাঞ্ছন, দেখন, to ask, wish, see, look.
চাউনি, চাওয়া,—বাঞ্ছা, দৃষ্টি, আলোকনা, desire, wish, request, look, view, glance.
চাউল, পরিষ্কৃত ধান্য, তণ্ডুল, husked paddy, sifted rice.
চাঁই, লোষ্ট্র, ঢেলা, প্রধান, অধ্যক্ষ, প্রতিপালক, a turf, loose clod, a chief, leader, protector.
চাঁচ, আসন বিশেষ, a coarse mat of reeds.
চাঁচন, ছোলন, সূক্ষ্ম করণ, to scrape, pare, peel, shave, plane.
চাঁচর, কোঁকড়, চুষ্কী, curled, crimped, crisped; a curl.
চাঁচি, চাঁচনি,—কর্ত্তনী, কুচা, ছোলা, scrapings, shavings, par- [ings.
চাঁদ, চন্দ্র, নিশাকর, the moon.
চাঁদা, মাথট, a voluntary subscription, collection, extra [assessment.
চাঁদনী, চন্দ্রাতপ, বারাণ্ডা, জ্যোৎস্না, an awning, an open portico, a moonlight night.
চাঁদী, শ্বেত, স্বচ্ছ, রূপা, white, clear; silver.

চাঁপা, চম্পক বৃক্ষ, কর্ণালঙ্কার বিশেষ, the champaca tree, an ear-ornament.

চাক-১, চক্র, মণ্ডল, মৌচাক, a wheel, circle, discus, honeycomb.

চাকন, আস্বদন, আস্বাদনের পরীক্ষণ, to taste, try the taste of.

চাকভুমী, ঘূর্ণায়মান, ঘূর্ণমান, revolving, turning, going in circles.

চাকলা, প্রদেশ, অধিকার, ফলাদির খণ্ড, গোলাকৃতি, a district, province, estate; a slice of fruit, bread, &c. circular, round.

চাকশূল, ঔষধি বিশেষ, a medicinal drug. [a small spindle.

চাকী, জাঁতা, টেকুয়ার অগ্রস্থিত চাকা, a hand mill, grinding stone,

চাক্‌চক,১, দীপ্তি, স্বচ্ছভাব, brightness, lustre, splendor, brilliancy.

চাক্তী, টিক্‌লী, a wafer, lozenge, any flat round body.

চাক্ষুষ, প্রত্যক্ষ, স্পষ্ট, visible, perceptible, evident.

চাগন, চিয়ন, উঠন, জাগন, নড়ন, to come on (as a paroxysm), to rise, get up, begin to exert one's self, set about, stir.

চাগান, উঠান, জাগান, উদ্ধরণ, চিয়ান, to raise, rouse, stimulate, urge to rise, extricate, bring on (as a paroxysm.)

চাচা, চাচ্চা,—পিতৃব্য, a father's brother, paternal uncle.

চাচাত, পিতৃব্যজাত, of or derived from a paternal uncle.

চাঞ্চল্য, অস্থিরতা, দ্রুতভাব, fickleness, unsteadiness, activity, agility, fluidity.

চাটন, জিহ্বাদ্বারা রসাকর্ষণ, লেহন, to lick, to lap.

চাটি, অশ্বের পদাঘাত, লাথী, a kick backwards from an animal.

চাটিম, লেহ্য, to be licked or sucked (as certain fruits).

চাটু, মিষ্টবাক্য, স্তোত্র, grateful or pleasing words, flattery.

চাটুয়া, করতল, the palm or flat of the hand.

চাটে, সমূলে, সর্বতোভাবে, wholly, entirely.

চাড়, আবশ্যকতা, ত্বরা, necessity, hurry, a wrench, a meal.

চাড়া, উচ্চ, উচ্চৈঃস্বর, জ্যা টানন, high, steep, loud, emphatic; the fixing of a bow-string.

চাড়ী, লগী, উত্তোলন দণ্ড, a pole for impelling a boat, a lever.

চাণ, মৎস্যের জলচিহ্ন, the track of a fish in the water.

চাণ্ডাল, ব্রাহ্মণীতে শূদ্রজাত, জাতিচ্যুত, one of the lowest cast, an outcast.

চাতক, পক্ষি বিশেষ, a species of cuckoo or swallow.
চাত্র, চোর সমূহ, দুর্মতির চক্র, a band of thieves or evil-minded men, a conspiracy.
চাতাল, বেষ্টিত স্থান, ছাত, বিল, an enclosed space, a terraced roof, a sheet of water.
চাতুরী, চাতুর্য্য,—শঠতা, ছলনা, মায়া, পারকতা, ভাব, craft, cunning, deceit, roguery, cleverness, stratagem, activity, female infidelity.
চাতুর্বর্ণ্য, ব্রাহ্মণাদি সম্বন্ধীয়, of or pertaining to the four classes [of Hindoos.
চান্দনী, জ্যোৎস্না, বারাণ্ডা, চন্দ্রাতপ, moon-light, an open porch, an awning.
চান্দ্র, চন্দ্রসম্বন্ধীয়, lunar, belonging to the moon.
চান্দ্রায়ণ, ব্রত বিশেষ, a religious expiatory observance.
চাপ, মৃৎখণ্ড, বৃহৎভার, ধনুক, a turf, clod, lump, burden, block, a bow.
চাপড়, করতল, থাপড়, the flat palm, a slap, blow, pat.
চাপড়ান, থাপড়ান, to slap, to strike with the flat palm.
চাপন-আন, আঁটন, দাবন, টিপন, চিত্রাঙ্কন, থামান, ঢাকন, to press down, compress, squeeze, smother, quash, print, imprint, delay, cover, conceal.
চাপা, ঢাকনা, ছপ্পর, ভাঁত, a cover, thatch, a press, a weight.
চাপুয়া, আবর্ত্তিত, ঘন, curdled, coagulated, in clots.
চাপ্টালি, থাবড়িয়া বৈসন, a squatting posture.
চাবন, চর্ব্বণ, দন্তদ্বারা পেষণ, দর্শন, বাঞ্ছন, to chew, masticate, look, wish.
চাবনি, দৃষ্টি, ইচ্ছা, view, sight, desire, wish.
চাবান, দর্শান, লোভান, to shew, persuade, excite desire for.
চাবী তালার কাটী, a key.
চাম-ড়া, ছাল, ত্বক, a skin, hide, leather, rind.
চামচা, চমস্, থলাকা, দর্ব্বী, a spoon.
চাম্চিকা, চর্ম্মচটিকা, a species of small bat.
চামড়, আঠাল, চিটা, adhesive, sticky, sticking to.
চামড়মাংস, দৃঢ়মাংস, gristle.
চামড়ী, খুকী, শুষ্ককাষ্ঠ, scurf, dandruff, light and dry wood.
চামনী, চামনিকী,—নিকী, a nit, the egg of a louse.
চামর, চাউরী, গোপুচ্ছ বিশেষ, a choury or fly-flap, a whisk.
চামসা, শুষ্কচর্ম্মবৎ দুর্গন্ধী, stinking like a dried skin.

চামাটী, চামাতী,—ক্ষুর ঘর্ষণার্থ চর্ম্ম, চর্ম্মবন্ধনী, a razor-strap, a thong, leathern hand-cuffs.

চামার, চর্ম্মকার, মুচী, a tanner, skinner, currier, shoemaker.

চামীকর, সুবর্ণ, স্বর্ণ, gold.

চার, গূঢ়পুরুষ, টোপ, a spy, scout, bait for fish.

চার, চারি,—চতুর, চতুষ্টয়, four.

চারণ, নর্ত্তক, ভণ্ড, শাস্ত্রপাঠক, গন্ধর্ব্ব, a dancer, actor, reciter of the shasters, celestial panegyrist.

চারণ-আণ, চারাপোতন, বীচপোতন, to plant out seedlings, raise plants from seed.

চারা, পোয়া, a plant, a seedling. [chair, stool.

চারিপায়ী, চারিপাইয়া,—চৌপায়া, খাট, four-footed; a bedstead,

চারু সুন্দর, handsome, agreeable, beautiful, elegant.

চার্ব্বী, অঙ্গনা, মনোহরা, a well proportioned or beautiful woman; well-shaped, handsome.

চার্ব্বাক, নাস্তিক বিশেষ, a sophist, sceptic, materialist.

চাল, রীতি, ব্যবহার, ছপ্পর, তণ্ডুল, conduct, course, behaviour, a sloping roof, husked rice, the blue jay.

চালক, চালাক,—সতর্ক, নিপুণ, active, lively, brisk, clever.

চালকী, তণ্ডুল বিক্রেতা, a dealer in rice.

চালন, সরাণ, প্রেরণ, স্থানান্তরে নয়ন, ঝাড়ন, to cause to move, dispel, remove, dispatch, convey, carry, winnow, sift, riddle. [strainer.

চালনী, চালুনী,—সূর্প, ছাঁকনী, a winnowing fan, riddle, sieve,

চালান, চিয়ান, বহান, পাঠান, যোগান, ছোড়ান, to urge, impel, drive, dispatch, transport goods, send, superintend, manage a business, fire a gun.

চালি, রীতি, ব্যবহার, ধারা, ডৌল, দ্রুতগতি, মাচা, custom, habit, practice, method, gait, carriage, a quick motion, a hanging shelf.

চালি, চালু,—তণ্ডুল, cleansed rice.

চাষ, কৃষিকর্ম্ম, tillage, agriculture, cultivation, ploughing.

চাষণ, কর্ষণ. to plough, cultivate, till.

চাষা, চাষী,—কৃষক, কৃষাণ, a ploughman, a husbandman.

চাষা-ড়িয়া, অনাড়ী, অসভ্য, clownish, rustic, awkward, clumsy.

চাহন, বাঞ্ছন, মাগন, ভিক্ষণ, ভালবাসন, মানন, দর্শন, to wish, ask, beg, want, need, require, like, approve, choose, mind, design, intend, see, look.

চিক, বংশনির্ম্মিত আবরণ বিশেষ, a cheek or bamboo blind.

চিকণ, স্নিগ্ধ, সূক্ষ্মকাঠ, oily, unctuous, (wood) split into thin strips. [polish, split into strips.

চিকন-আন, কেশ বিন্যাসন, মার্জ্জন, to smooth or comb the hair,

চিকাশ, নিরাহ, সুপ্রকাশ, clear or fair (weather).

চিকিৎসক, বৈদ্য, a physician, doctor, surgeon. [gery.

চিকিৎসা, ব্যাধির প্রতিকার চেষ্টা, medical science, medicine, sur-

চিকিৎস্য, চিকিৎসনীয়,—প্রতিকার্য্য, curable, remediable.

চিকীর্ষা করিবার ইচ্ছা, a desire to perform a thing, a wish.

চিকীর্ষু, করণেচ্ছুক, desirous to act or do.

চিকুর, কেশ, চুল, the hair of the head.

চিকোর, পক্ষি বিশেষ, the red partridge. [glossy.

চিক্কণ স্নিগ্ধ. তৈলাক্ত, oily, greasy, slippery, sleek, smooth,

চিকা, ছুঁচা, চুচুন্দরী, the musk rat.

চিক্কুড়, বজ্র, বজ্রধ্বনি, a thunder-bolt. [prawn.

চিঙ্গড়া, চিংড়ী,—ইচ্লামৎস্য, ইঞ্চাক, জালমৎস্য, a shrimp or

চিট, মর্চ্চা, ছাতা, rust, mouldiness. [viscous, clammy.

চিটা, মর্চ্চা, ভুয়া, আঠাল, mouldiness, smut, mildew; thick,

চিটী, চিঠী,—পত্র, টীপ, a letter, note, chit, note of hand, bank note.

চিট্যা, ছাতাপড়া, আঠাল, mouldy, rusty, viscid, thick.

চিড়, কাটা, চটা, উষ্মা, রাগ, a slit, a scaling or peeling off, vexation, passion.

চিড়ন, চটন, ফাটন, খিট্ উঠন, খিট্খিটান, কোপন, to split, scale or peel off, be exasperated, fret.

চিড়া, চিপিটক, rice when wetted, parched and flattened.

চিড়িয়া, পক্ষী, a bird. [ing, the soul, heart, mind.

চিৎ, চিত্ত,—বুদ্ধি, মন, জ্ঞান, অন্তঃকরণ, intellect, understand-

চিৎ, উত্তানশয়, supine, lying face upwards.

চিতন, চিৎ হইয়া শয়ন, to recline, lie on the back. [bald.

চিতা, শবদাহনস্থান, বিচিত্র, a funeral pile; speckled, pie-

চিৎকার, চিচ্কার,—চেঁচানি, ডাকহাঁক, a scream, squall, bawl, outcry, loud cry, noise.

চিত্তবাধ, সুহৃদ্ভেদ, মনোভঙ্গ, interruption of friendship, a falling out, disagreement.

চিত্তান্তর, পরাঙ্মুখ, বিরক্ত, averse, disgusted, dissatisfied.

চিৎপাত, চিৎ হইয়া পড়ন, a falling backwards.

চিত্র, ছবি, পট, লিপি, তিলক, অদ্ভুত, বিস্ময়, নানারঙ্গী, আশ্চর্য্য, মনোহর, a picture, drawing, print, map, chintz, variegated colour, sectarial mark on the forehead, a miracle, surprize, wonder; variegated, speckled, spotted, surprizing, wonderful, captivating.

চিত্রকার, চিত্রকর,—ছবিকর. পটুয়া, a painter, chintz-printer, designer, artist.

চিত্রগুপ্ত, যম, যমের অমাত্য, Yama, the infernal registrar.

চিত্রবিচিত্র, বহুরঙ্গ, chequered, variegated, of various colours, gaudy, tawdry.

চিত্রভানু, সূর্য্য, অগ্নি, ভৈরব, the sun, fire, Bhairava, (a form of Shiva.)

চিত্রলেখা, সুখ্যাতা গ্রন্থকারিণী বিশেষ, a celebrated female writer.

চিত্রহস্ত, উত্তানহস্ত, the hand palm upwards; with upturned palm.

চিত্রা, তারা বিশেষ, a star in the Virgin's spike, a kind of cucumber.

চিত্রিণী, চমৎকারিণী, মনোহরা, surprising, ravishing, beautiful.

চিত্রিত, বিচিত্র, নানারঙ্গ, painted, variegated, chequered, spotted, speckled.

চিদাত্মা, জ্ঞানাত্মা, the intellectual soul, spirit.

চিদ্রূপ, জ্ঞানবান্, সুশীল, intelligent, wise, amiable, kind-hearted, liberal.

চিনন, জানন, স্মরণ, to know, distinguish, recognize.

চিনান, জানান, দর্শান, to show, introduce, point out, make known.

চিনাপরিচয়, আত্মীয়তা, familiar acquaintance with a person.

চিনী, শর্করা, চিনদেশীয়, sugar; Chinese.

চিন্তক, ভাবিত, ঠাহরণিয়া, thoughtful, pondering, anxious.

চিন্তন, ঠাহরণ, to think, reflect, meditate, ponder.

চিন্তা, ভাবনা, উদ্বেগ, কাতরতা, বিষাদ, ক্লেশ, ভীতি, thought, reflection, meditation, recollection, thoughtfulness, care, anxiety, dejection, grief, trouble, uneasiness, fear.

চিন্তান, চিন্তান্বিত, ভাবিত, ব্যাকুল, anxious, dejected, pensive, uneasy, careful.

চিন্তামণি, কাল্পনিক মণি বিশেষ, ব্রহ্মা, a fabulous gem procuring its possessor whatever he wished for, Brahmá.

চিপন, চিপড়ন,—নিঙ্গড়ন, নিঃসারণ, to squeeze out, express, press, wring, wring out.

চিবণ-আণ, চর্ব্বণ, to chew, to masticate.

চিপিটক, চিড়া, rice wetted, parched and flattened.

চিবুক, দাড়ি, অধরের অধোভাগ, the chin, the hollow above it.

চিম্‌টন, গ্রহণ, থাম্‌চান, to grasp, adhere, nip, pinch.

চিম্‌টা, চিম্‌টী,—মোচনা, পাকসাঁড়াশী, খেঁচা, pincers, forceps, nippers, tongs, a vice, a pinch, spasm, cramp.

চিম্‌ড়ন, সংপৃটন, কুঁকড়ন, to stick, adhere, stick close, shrivel.

চিম্‌ড়া, চিম্‌ড়ী,—খোসা, ক্ষীণ, শুষ্ক, a pod, shell, husk, skin; lean, emaciated, dried, shrivelled up.

চিম্‌ড়ান, শুকান, নিঙ্গড়ান, to cause to shrink, to wring out.

চিয়ন,-আন, জাগান, চেতান, স্পষ্টকরণ, to rouse, awaken, stir up, stimulate, make plain.

চিয়ন, চিয়স্ত,—জাগ্রৎ, চেতান, চালাক, awakened, roused, stimulated, alive, active.

চির, বহুকাল, বহুকালীন, চেরা, long, of old; old, of long standing, long, ancient; a rent or tear.

চিরকালিক, চিরকালীন,—বহুকালিক, পুরাতন, বহুদিনস্থায়ী, long-continued, inveterate, chronic, ancient, old, lasting, perennial.

চিরণ, ফাড়ন, আঁচড়ন, to tear, rend, break, lacerate, rip up.

চিরণী, চিরুণী,—কাঁকই, a comb, a carding instrument.

চিরন্থ, চিরন্তন,—বহুকালিক, পুরাতন, of long standing, old, ancient, antique.

চিল, আতায়ী পক্ষী, the Indian kite or black falcon.

চিলম, কল্কিকা, the bowl of the Hooka.

চিলমচি, ডাবর, a wash-hand basin.

চিলা, ছাতের উপরি গৃহ, the small room or turret covering the stair-case of a house.

চিল, চিলপক্ষী, চক্ষুরোগ, চক্ষুরোগযুক্ত, the kite, a sore eye; sore-eyed, blear-eyed.

চিহ্ন, পতাকা, সঙ্কেত, অঙ্ক, উদ্দেশ, ক্ষত, a signal, standard, token, sign, mark, badge, speck, spot, stain, trace, vestige, scar.

চিহ্নিত, চিহ্নযুক্ত, নির্দ্দিষ্ট, marked, appropriated, fixed, appointed.

চীন, হরিণ বিশেষ, a kind of deer, a sort of millet, China.

চীৎকার, প্রাণিকৃত উচ্চৈঃশব্দ, a scream, outcry, loud cry.

চীনী, শক্র, শর্করা, sugar.

চীর, কাপড়, বস্ত্র, নেকড়া, ত্বক, cloth, clothes, the dress of a devotee, a rag, old cloth, bark.

চীর্ণ, ফাটা, বিদীর্ণ, split, divided, rent.

চুঅন, চুওন,—করণ, নিঃসরণ, to leak, ooze, issue, flow out.

চুঁঅন, পুড়ন, দহন, to burn away, be burned or calcined.

চুক, ভ্রম, ভুল, ত্রুটি, অম্লশাক, a mistake, error, blunder, oversight, transgression; Indian sorrel.

চুঁকন, শানন, to whet, sharpen, set an edge.

চুকন, ভুলন, ত্রুটিকরণ to mistake, err, blunder, do wrong.

চুকান, নিষ্পাদন, মিটান, to decide, adjust, settle, end, conclude, terminate.

চুক্‌চুক্, চুক্‌চুকিয়া,—স্নিগ্ধ, glossy, shining with oil, &c.

চুক্তি, নিয়ম, সমাধা, a bargain, agreement. adjustment.

চুক্র, অম্লশাক, অম্লরস, Indian sorrel; sourness; acidity, acid seasoning.

চুঁচি, চঁচী,—স্তনাগ্র, চুচুক, the nipple.

চুঙ্গী, খোল, ঘরা, কলিকা, আধার, নালী a socket, mortise hole, cup, stand, a tube, pipe, water-pipe.

চুটন, মারণ, to strike, smite, hit.

চুট্‌কিয়া, ক্ষুদ্র, তুচ্ছ, little, trifling, despicable.

চুট্‌কী, স্ত্রীপাদাঙ্গুলিভূষা, উন্দুর, মুষ্টি, a ring for the toes, a mouse, a handful.

চুড়ী, বিষাণময় ভুজভূষণ, a bracelet of ivory or horn.

চুণী, সূক্ষ্ম, মণি, বিশেষ, small, diminutive; a ruby or emerald.

চুত, চুতড়,—স্ত্রীচিহ্ন, গুহ্যদেশ, the vagina, pudendum muliebre, the anus.

চুনন, বাছন, কোঁকড়ান, to chuse, pick, select, pucker.

চুপ্, নীরব, থাক্, silence; hush! be silent! peace!

চুপন, অস্ত্রে মারণ, to strike or smite with a sword, &c.

চুপড়ী, ঝুড়ী, a basket.

চুপ্‌ষণ, ভিজন, to imbibe moisture, sink (as paper).
চুবন, বুড়ান, ডুবান, to dip, plunge, immerse.
চুম্বন, চুম্বন.—চুম্বা খাওন, চুম্বা দেওন, to kiss, give a kiss.
চুমা, চুম্বা.—স্নেহপূর্বক ওষ্ঠদ্বারা ওষ্ঠাদি স্পর্শ, a kiss.
চুমুক, স্তোকেং পিবন, a sip, sipping. [nut.
চুমুরী, নারিকেলের কোষ, the spatha or sheath of the cocoa-
চুম্কুড়ী, ওষ্ঠস্বরমিশ্রিত ধ্বনি, a chirping to a bird, a coaxing.
চুম্বক. চুম্বাখাগী, লম্পট, ছলী, আকর্ষক, নির্ঘণ্ট, সংক্ষেপ, সুপণ্ডিত, সংক্ষিপ্ত, a kisser, lecher, rogue, the load-stone, an index, abstract, summary, short hand, a general scholar; laconic, drief, concise. [mountaineers.
চুয়াড়, পাহাড়ীয়া, a mountaineer, a savage, the western
চুরুট, শুষ্কতাম্রকূটনল, a cigar.
চুল, কেশ, the hair of the head, a lock of hair. [place.
চুলা, চুল্লী.—উনান, আখা, a portable hearth, furnace, fire-
চুলুক, কোষা, গণ্ডূষ, কর্দম, the hand hollowed to hold water, a handful of water, mire, mud. [lust.
চুল্কনা, চুল্কনি,—গাত্রকণ্ডূ, কামনা, an itching sensation, itch,
চুল্কান, কণ্ডূয়ন, খুজ্‌লান, to itch, to scratch.
চুল্কানী, কণ্ডূয়ন, কণ্ডূ, ফুস্কুড়ী, an itching, the itch, a pimple.
চুল্কা, কুন্তল, কোঁকড়াকেশ, a lock of hair, a curl.
চুবুলিয়া, চঞ্চল, চতুর, fickle, inconstant, thoughtlessly changing, active, sprightly.
চূচুক, চূচক,—স্তনের বোঁটা, কুচাগ্র, the nipple.
চূড়া, সংস্কারজনক প্রথম মুণ্ডন, শিখা, শৃঙ্গ, the first tonsure of a Hindoo, the lock of hair left on the crown, a peacock's crest, a plume, crest, diadem, peak, top of a mountain, summit, pinnacle, a room on the top of a house, a kind of bracelet. [termination.
চূড়ান্ত, সিদ্ধান্ত, শেষ, a conclusion, decision, issue, result,
চূড়ামণি. শিরোরত্ন, শ্রেষ্ঠ, a crest-jewel, gem in a diadem; *in comp*. eminent, chief.
চূঁড়িয়া, উড়নী, পাছুড়ী, a mantle or wrapper.
চূড়ী, কঙ্কণ, a bracelet of gold, silver or lac.

চূণ, চূণা,—ঝিনুকাদির গুঁড়া, lime, powdered lime.
চূণবালী, ভিত্তিলেপ, plaister, mortar of sand and lime.
চূণারী, চূণানির্ম্মায়ক, a lime-burner.
চূত, আম্রবৃক্ষ, আম্রফল, the mango tree or its fruit.
চূর, চূর্ণ,—গুঁড়া, খণ্ডিত, a powder, fragment, crumb ; pulverized, pounded, crumbled, broken, bruized.
চূরচূর, চূরিয়া,—পরিপূর্ণ, উপ্‌চানিয়া, মত্ত, quite full, running over, quite drunk, intoxicated.
চূর্ণক, শ্লোকের টীকা, পক্ষপ্রতিপাদন, a prose exposition of a preceding verse, the maintaining of a thesis.
চূর্ণন, গুঁড়ন, খণ্ডন, to pulverize, bruise, break, crumble, pound, pound to powder.
চূষণ, মুখদ্বারা রসাকর্ষণ, to suck, suck up.
চূষী, পলাদিময় ক্ষুদ্র লাটিম, a coral &c. for teething children.
চেঁচন-আন, চীৎকারণ, ফুকরণ, to scream, bawl, rave, vociferate, speak loud. [expanded.
চেঙ্গড়া, ছোকরা, প্রশস্ত, প্রসারিত, a lad, a boy ; wide, spread out,
চেঙ্গড়ামি, ছাওলামি, childishness, boyishness.
চেঙ্গাড়ী, চুপড়ী, a broad flat basket.
চেট-ক, ভৃত্য, দাস, a servant, a slave.
চেটা-ই, আসন বিশেষ, a mat of palm leaves.
চেটাল, ওসার, চৌড়া, broad and flat, wide, patent, (as a dish).
চেটী, চেড়ী—দাসী, a female servant, a slave girl.
চেটো, যুবা, তরুণ, করপৃষ্ঠ, করতল, young, full-grown : the palm or the back of the hand.
চেট্টা, বয়স্থা, পৌরুষ, যৌবন, manhood, adult age.
চেড়ান, ক্ষেপাণ, জ্বলান, to provoke, exasperate, fret, irritate.
চেৎ, যদি, কিজানি, পাছে, if, though, perhaps, lest.
চেতঃ, মন, বুদ্ধি, the mind, the understanding, intellect, the reasoning faculty.
চেতন, জীব, জ্ঞান, বুদ্ধি, অনুভব, বোধ, প্রাণী, the soul, understanding, intelligence, wisdom, reflexion, idea, feeling, sensation, an animal being, a sentient or rational being.
চেতন, বুঝান, জানান, to convince, cause to learn or notice, make to attend to a thing.

চেতনা, জীব, সাম, জামানি, পরামর্শ, প্রবর্ত্তনা, জ্ঞানের উদ্রেক, বুদ্ধি, life, sensation, feeling, admonition, advice, caution, warning, stimulus or excitement, reason, wisdom, intelligence.

চেতান, প্রবৃত্তিজন্মান, জাগান, বুঝান, জানান, to stimulate, excite, stir up, convince, make to feel, awaken, admonish. [scratch.

চেরণ-আণ, ফাড়ন, বিদারণ, to tear, split, cleave, break,

চেরা, ফাড়া, নেকড়া, torn, split, cleft ; a scratch, a rag.

চেল, বস্ত্র, clothes, cloth, a garment.

চেলনা, কাপড় বিশেষ, a sort of cloth.

চেলা, সন্যাসির পালক পুত্র, শিষ্য, পেট্যাল, কুচা, one adopted by a religious mendicant, a disciple, mate or assistant, a chip of wood.

চেলান, কাটন, কুচান, to hew, to chip.

চেলি, পট্টবস্ত্র বিশেষ, silken cloth. [washed.

চেলুনী, তণ্ডুলধৌতজল, the water in which rice has been

চেষ্টন, যত্নকরণ, অন্বেষণ, আরম্ভণ, প্রবর্ত্ত হওন, to endeavour, strive, take pains, labour or engage in.

চেষ্টা, যত্ন, উদ্যোগ, শ্রম, কায়িক ব্যাপার, অন্বেষণা, application, endeavour, pains, effort, labour, search, pursuit. [rious, strenuous, active, zealous.

চেষ্টান্বিত, চেষ্টাবান,—প্রবর্ত্ত, উদ্যোগী, engaged in, eager, labo-

চেষ্টিত, প্রবৃত্ত, শ্রমী, উদ্দিষ্ট, engaged in, laborious, sought, laboured after, endeavoured.

চৈ, মরিচ বিশেষ, চবিক, a species of pepper.

চৈতন্য, চেতনা, জীব, জাগনি, প্রবর্ত্তনা, উত্তেজনা, জামানি, জীবাত্মা, sensation, feeling, life, activity, knowledge, an awaking from sleep, excitement, caution, warning, stimulus, the soul, spirit, God as the essence of all sensation, &c.

চৈত্য, গ্রামের পূজ্য বৃক্ষ, the sacred tree of a village.

চৈত্র, বসন্তের প্রথম মাস, the first spring month, Cuvera's grove.

চোআলি, চুয়ালের অস্থি, the jaw-bone. [drop as fruit, &c.

চোওন, ক্ষরণ, স্রবণ, to ooze, leak out, drip, distil, fall or

চোঁআন, ভাজন, খরাণ, পোড়ান, to parch, calcine, burn to powder.

চোক-া, তীব্র, তেজাল, strong in flavour, strong as liquors.

চোক, স্পৃহা, আনন্দ, সম্মতি, desire, delight, complacence, pleasure, approbation. [edge.

চোকান, মিটান, নিষ্পাদন, শানন, to settle, adjust, whet, set an

চোঁকান, চোখান,—শানন, to set, whet, strap as a razor, &c.

চোঁকাল, চোকাল, চোখাল,—চতুর, সুধার, শানিত, keen, clever, sharp, well-set, whetted. [bark of a tree.

চোঁচ, চোচ,—ছালের অন্তরিত ভাগ, আঁশ, the fibrous or inner

চোঁচান, বীজ চয়ন, দৌড়িয়া ধাবন, to strip off seeds, to strain in running, to run hard.

চোঁচাল, আঁশাল, full of long woody fibres. [young woman.

চোঙ্গা, নল, নলী, কন্যা, a tube, spout, barrel of a gun, a

চোট, আঘাত, ঘা, ক্ষত, ঠোকর, a blow, stroke, wound, bruize, a fall, a hurt.

চোটা, কুসীদ, exorbitant interest, usury. [wound.

চোটান, ঠোকরাণ, মারণ, ঘাতন, to strike against, smite, hurt,

চোণা, গবাদির মূত্র, the urine of a beast, or *ludicrously* of a man, an ill-scented vetch.

চোণান, মূত্রনিঃসারণ, প্রস্রবণ, to pass urine, make water.

চোনন, বাছন, to select, pick, choose.

চোপ, অস্ত্রাঘাত, a blow or stroke from a weapon.

চোপান, অস্ত্রাঘাতান, to cause to strike with weapon.

চোপ্রণ-আণ, চুপ্ষণ, ভিজন, to imbibe, moisture, sink, become soft and moist.

চোবা, ছাল, the rind of fruit, peel, tegument.

চোর, পরদ্রব্যাপহারী, সিঁধাল, a thief, robber, house-breaker.

চোরছিদ্র, উকিমারণছিদ্র, ফাট্‌লা, a peep-hole.

চোরপুষ্পী, চোরকাঁটা,—ভাঁটুইঘাস, a prickly-seeded grass troublesome to pedestrians.

চোরা, অপহৃত, গুপ্ত, অপ্রকাশ, stolen, clandestine, silent, private, hidden, unperceived.

চোরাও, চোরী,—তস্করী, অপহার, theft, thievery, robbery.

চোরাগর্ত্ত, আবৃতগর্ত্ত, গুপ্তখাত, a pitfal.

চোরাঘা-ত, অচম্‌কাঘাত, গুপ্তাঘাত, a secret blow, assassination.

চোরাবালি, গুপ্তবালি দলদলীয়াস্থান, a quick-sand. [fleece, extort.
চোষণ, মুখদ্বারা রসাকর্ষণ, নিঙড়ান, to suck, imbibe, wring,
চোহাড়. পাহাড়ীয়া, a tribe of western mountaineers.
চোহালি, চুয়ালের অস্থি, the jaw-bone.
চৌ. চতুঃ, চারি, *in comp* : four.
চৌক, নেত্র, চারি পণ, the eye ; four panas.
চৌকা, চারিকোণা পাকস্থান, a square spot for cooking on.
চৌকষ, চৌকোষ,—অনিমিষ, চতুর, অনিম্নভূমি, সমান, circumspect, vigilant, watchful, cautious, attentive, clever, square, level, even, flat.
চৌকষী, চৌকষাই,—জাগ্রৎ থাকা, সাবধানতা, মনোযোগ, vigilance, caution, watchfulness, attention. [log.
চৌকাঠ, দ্বারের চারিকাঠ, শিলা, a door frame, threshold, square
চৌকালা, পোলো বিশেষ, a four-pronged harpoon.
চৌকি, কুরশী, থানা, পহরা, রক্ষা, a bench, chair, guard, watch, station ; a guarding, keeping watch.
চৌকিয়া, পহরী, রক্ষক, গণক, a watchman ; a mode of reckoning by fours or panas.
চৌঠা, চতুর্থ, চতুর্থী, fourth, the fourth.
চৌটী, চৌঠী, চৌথ,—চতুর্থাংশ, পোয়া, a fourth, a quarter.
চৌড়া, প্রশস্ত, চটাল, broad, wide.
চৌড়াই, পরিসর, ওসার, width, breadth.
চৌধুরী, জনচতুষ্টয়ের শ্রেষ্ঠ, chief of four, (a title of honour.)
চৌপল, চৌপহল,—চারিকোণা কাঁচপাত্র, square (as a bottle ;) a case bottle.
চৌপাঠী, চৌবাড়ী,—টোল, বিদ্যালয়, a school or college.
চৌপাড়. চৌপাড়ি,—পাটি, অক্ষ, দ্যূত, a die, dice.
চৌপায়া, চতুষ্পদ, পশু, a quadruped : four footed (whether thing or animal.) [litter.
চৌপালা, চতুর্দোল বিশেষ, a sort of palkee or bridegroom's
চৌপিঠা, দক্ষ, চতুর, handy, clever, active, versatile.
চৌবাচ্চা, চতুষ্কোণা খাত, কুণ্ড, জলকুণ্ড, a square pit or cistern, a vat, a well.
চৌর, চোর, সিঁধাল, a thief, robber, housebreaker.
চৌরস, সমান, সমভূমি, smooth, even, level, flat.
চৌরী, চৌর্য্য,—চুরী, অপহার, theft, robbery, burglary.

চ্যুত, পদত্যক্ত, ভ্রষ্ট, পতিত, ক্ষরিত, ছাড়া, হীন, আম্র, dismissed, fallen from, shed, dropped, oozed out, freed, void of; a mango. [release, leave.

চ্যুতি, ক্ষরণ, ছাড়ানি, বিদায়, an oozing, dropping, freedom,

ছ.

ছক, শতরঞ্চের কোষ্ঠ, the chequer of a chess-board, a square.

ছকড়া, শকট, গাড়ী, a cart, a wheel carriage.

ছগল-ক, ছাগল, অজ, a he goat.

ছটা, দীপ্তি, শোভা, সরল রেখা, সমূহ, light, lustre, splendor, radiance; a straight line, an assemblage, number, multitude.

ছটাক, সেরের ষোড়শাংশ, the sixteenth part of a seer.

ছট্‌কন, ছাড়ান, পলান, ঠিকরণ, to slip from, desert, withdraw, run away, to fall as seed from the capsule or seed-vessel.

ছট্‌কান, নিঃসারণ, ভাঁটাদি ক্ষেপণ, বহিষ্করণ, to squeeze, press or force out, shoot a marble &c, to expel, cause to withdraw, &c.

ছটফটান, ধড়্‌ফড়ান, আস্ফালন, পাড়ায় লুঠন, to struggle for liberty, flutter, toss about in pain.

ছড়, বড়্‌শা, আঁচড়, a spear, a scratch.

ছড়ন, ছাল তোলন, পড়ন, ছিটান, এলুয়ামেলুয়া আওন, to skin an animal, fall as seed, sprinkle, straggle.

ছড়ান, ছিটান, উড়ান, প্রবাপ, বপন, এড়ান, to scatter, throw about, strew, sprinkle, disperse, squander, dissipate, sow seed, loosen, free.

ছড়া, শ্লোকের টীকা, মালা, ছিটা, কলার গুচ্ছ, অপব্যয়, a prose comment, a string of beads, shot, a sprinkling, a bunch of plantains, waste.

ছড়ানিয়া, অপব্যয়ী, উড়ানিয়া, চামার, wasteful, lavish, disorderly; a skinner.

ছড়ী, অস্থূল যষ্টি, কশা, a switch, twig, cane, scourge.

ছত্র, আতপত্র, ছাতা, an umbrella, a fungus, mushroom, mould, mouldiness.

ছত্রভঙ্গ, বৈধব্য, দুর্গতি, রাজ্যভ্রংশ, অকর্তৃত্ব, widowhood, a forlorn condition, loss of empire, anarchy, independence, wilfulness.

ছত্রী, ছপ্পর, চাঁদনী, ছত্রবিশিষ্ট, a bed-tester, awning; having an umbrella. [custom.

ছদ, পাতা, পত্র, চালি, a blade of grass, a leaf, habit,

ছদি. গৃহাচ্ছাদন, the roof of a house.

ছদ্ম, ছদ্মবেশ—বেশ. ছলতা, কপট, a disguise, concealment, covering, craft, device, trick.

ছদ্মবেশী, কপটী, কপটবেশী, wearing a disguise, crafty; a pretender, hypocrite, actor, player.

ছন্দ, শ্লোক, কাব্য, বেদ, পয়ার, verse, poetry, the Vedas, a line in verse, cadence, metre.

ছন্দস্, পদ্য, বেদ, poetical metre, the Vedas and their metre.

ছন্দোগ, বেদপাঠী. a reciter of the Vedas.

ছন্ন, আচ্ছাদিত, গুপ্ত, বিরল, উন্মত্ত, covered, concealed, secret, private, solitary, mad, foolish. [tester.

ছপ্পর, চাল, আচ্ছাদন, a sloping thatch, roof, covering, bed-

ছবি, প্রতিমূর্ত্তি, চিত্র, দীপ্তি, শোভা, a portrait, picture, painting, beauty, splendour, brilliancy, light.

ছয়, ষট্, six.

ছর্দ্দি, বমি, উদ্গার, a vomiting, reaching, belching.

ছল, ছলনা,—ফাকী, কপট, চাতুরী, প্রতারণা, দোষানুসন্ধান, a stratagem, device, trick, scheme, plot, pretence, artifice, fraud, roguery, a seeking for faults.

ছলগ্রাহক. ঠক, ধূর্ত্ত, কপটী, ছলসন্দেহক, a cheat, swindler, impostor; suspicious of fraud or trick in another. [defraud, impose upon.

ছলন, প্রতারণ, ঠকান, ভুলান, to use stratagems, &c. cheat,

ছলী, প্রতারক, ঠক, কচ্ছু, deceiving, cheating; a sharper, a cheat, a blotch or scab.

ছা, শাবক, the young of an animal.

ছাই, ভস্ম, ashes.

ছাইট কোড়া, জলছিটা, a whip, the spray or beating in of rain.

ছাউনী, শিবির, সৈন্যের আবাস, চন্দ্রাতপ, a camp, encampment, barrack, an awning.

ছাওন, গৃহাচ্ছাদন, to thatch, to roof, to bottom a chair &c, with cane.

ছাওয়াল, বালক, a child, a young child. [pranks.

ছাওয়ালামি, বালকতা, খেলা, childhood, childishness, puerility,

ছাঁকন, ঝারণ, পুষ্করিণির মৎস্যসমস্তোত্তোলন, to strain, filtrate, drain a tank of its fish.

ছাঁকনি, ঝরণী, জালী, a strainer, sieve, sieve-net.

ছাঁকা, ঝরা, নির্ম্মল, অনঘ, নিষ্পাপী, strained, clear, innocent, free from crime. [ing mould.

ছাঁচ, প্রতিমূর্ত্তি, প্রতিলিপি, a likeness, image, copy, a cast-

ছাঁচি, পরছতী. the eaves of a house. [one.

ছাঁটন, কর্ত্তন, অনাদরণ, to lop off, trim, pass by or neglect

ছাঁদ, ছন্দ, সজলদুগ্ধ, poetical metre, milk and water

ছাঁদন, গরুরপাদ বান্ধন, to tie a cow's legs while milking.

ছাগ-ল, অজ, বক্রা, a goat.

ছাগলগোত্রিয়া, অগম্যাগমক, লম্পট, cohabiting promiscuously and incestuously, lecherous.

ছাট, পাতকুড়ী, পর্ণকুটি, a switch, a brush of leaves.

ছাটন, কর্ত্তন, ঝাড়ন, to clip, lop, trim, thresh.

ছাড়ন, বিবর্জন, ত্যজন, চলিয়া যাওন, খোয়ান, ক্ষমাকরণ, পলায়ন, to leave, relinquish, cast off, forsake, abandon, desert, divorce, abstain, forego, leave off, surrender, depart, abate, liberate, loose or let go, discharge, pardon, withdraw from.

ছাড়া, ব্যতিরিক্ত, ভিন্ন, বিনা, নিবর্ত্তন, ত্যাগ, except, saving, besides, without; abolition, relinquishment, &c.

ছাড়ান, উদ্ধরণ, মোচন, নিক্ষেপণ, অবসারণ, খসাণ, to set at liberty, rescue, extricate, discharge, disperse, dismiss, cashier, disband, eject, remove, detach from.

ছাত, চাতাল, the flat roof of a house, a terrace. [breast.

ছাতা আতপত্র, বক্ষঃস্থল, an umbrella, fungus, mould, the

ছাতি, ছাতী,—আতপত্র, বুক, সাহস, an umbrella, the breast, bosom, boldness, courage.

ছাতু, যবাদিচূর্ণ, barley meal, the meal of various pulse.

ছাত্র, শিষ্য, বিদ্যার্থী, a scholar, pupil, disciple, tyro. [fish.

ছানন, চটকান, মাখন, গড়ন, to knead, work, mould, drag for

ছানা, শাবক, গোজিব, আমীক্ষা, the young of animals, a young bird, curds.

ছানী, ফুলী, a film, speck or cataract on the eye.

ছান্দস, বেদের. শ্রোত, শ্রোত্রীয়, বেদাধ্যাপক, pertaining or peculiar to the Vedas, a teacher of them.

ছাপ, মুদ্রা, ছাঁচ, a stamp, die, press, block for printing cloth.

ছাপন, বস্ত্রাঙ্কন, মুদ্রাঙ্কন, লুকান, উচ্ছলন, to print, stamp, imprint, impress; to skulk, lurk, abscond, splash up, overflow.

ছাপর, ছপ্পর, ছত্রী, a thatched roof, bed-tester, &c.

ছাপান, মুদ্রাঙ্কান, দাবন, লুকান, উচ্ছলন, to publish a book, to conceal or suppress, secrete, dissemble, to overflow.

ছাপী, লুকায়িত, concealed, suppressed.

ছাবান, গৃহাচ্ছাদন করাণ, to cause or order to thatch a house or to bottom a chair.

ছাবাল, বালক, a child.

ছায়া, রৌদ্রাভাব, আশ্রয়, প্রতিবিম্ব, সূর্য্যপত্নী, a shade, shadow, covert, refuge, protection, support, a reflected image, an apparition, a petticoat, the wife of the sun.

ছায়াটিয়া. ছায়ান্বিত,—অনাতপ, shady, umbrageous.

ছায়াপাদ, ছায়ার পরিমাণদ্বারা বেলা নিরূপণ, the measurement of time by the shadow.

ছায়াবৎ, সদানুগত, কাছাধরা, attending one like a shadow, a pet animal.

ছায়ামণ্ডপ, চান্দনীযুক্তস্থান, a space with an awning for shade.

ছার, ভস্মবৎ, অধম, অপ্রিয়, অমঙ্গল, vile as ashes, abominable, hateful, unlucky.

ছারখার. ভস্মসাৎ, সর্ব্বনাশ, নষ্ট, a heap of ashes or ruins, ruin, wretchedness; ruined, wretched.

ছারপোকা, খাটমল, গন্ধী, a bug.

ছাল. ত্বক, চর্ম্ম, bark, peel, husk, skin, rind, leather.

ছালন, কাশন্দি, sauce.

ছালনা, চান্দনী, স্ত্রীপাদাভরণ বিশেষ, a marriage awning, a ring for the toe.

ছালা, গুণ, থলিয়া, ঝুলী, a sack, bag, wallet or pair of panniers, &c.

ছাবিয়া, বালক, a child.

ছি, ছিছি,—হেয়বোধক শব্দ, fie! for shame!

ছিকল, ছিকলি,—কড়া, শৃঙ্খল, a link, a chain.

ছিকলন-আন, যোড়ান, বান্ধন, টাঙ্গান, to link, tie together, suspend by a string or noose.

ছিকা, হাঁচি, a sneezing.

ছিট, চিত্রিত কাপড়, অবশিষ্ট, chintz, a balance, a remnant.

ছিটন-আন, ছড়ান, বিকীরণ, বপন, to sprinkle, scatter, sow seed, make lattice-work.

ছিটা, বিন্দু, কণা, a drop, an atom, small shot.

ছিট্‌কন-আন, প্রক্ষেপণ, ফিন্‌কি দেওন, ছড়ান, ঠিকরণ, to jerk, spout up, spatter, sprinkle, rebound, fly up.

ছিট্‌কা, শিকা, ফাঁসী, ফাঁদ, a sling, noose, slip-knot, trap.

ছিদ্র, রন্ধ্র, গর্ত্ত, দোষ, a hole, fissure, crack, rent, flaw, blemish, fault, defect, the eye of a needle, a bore, slit, incision.

ছিনন, বলে গ্রহণ, ধরণ, to seize, take by force, detain, lay hold of.

ছিনান, ঘা লাগন, ঠেকান, to strike or run against.

ছিনাল, বেশ্যা, কুলটা, a strumpet, harlot, whore.

ছিনালপনা, গণিকাকর্ম্ম, বেশ্যামি, whoredom in a woman, harlotry.

ছিনালী, লম্পটী, a whore, whorish, relating to harlotry.

ছিন্ন, খণ্ডিত, বিদীর্ণ, বিদ্ধ, cut, cut down or off, divided, split, perforated.

ছিন্নমস্তা, মস্তকহীনা স্বরক্তপাতা সক্তি, the decapitated Káli drinking her own blood.

ছিপ, বড়শির সূত্রবন্ধন কাঠ, a fishing rod.

ছিপী, গুঁজী, মুঠী, a stopple, stopper, cork.

ছিপন-আন, লুকান, দাবন, to conceal, hide, keep close, suppress.

ছিম্‌ড়া, ছিম্‌ড়ী,—শুঁটী, অনাথ, a legume, pea-pod, bean-shell, &c., an orphan.

ছিম, বর্বটী, শিম্বী, a legume, a kidney bean.

ছিলকা, বেকলা, খোসা, ছোলা, rind, peel, skin, bark, husk.

ছিলন, খোসাতোলন, to peel, skin, strip off bark or husk.

ছিলা, জ্যা, গুণ, a bow string.

ছিলম, কলিকা, the bowl of a hooka or Indian pipe.

ছুকরী, ছুঁড়ী,—কন্যা, বালিকা, a girl.

ছুঁচ, সূঁই, সূচি, সোমাজি, a needle, a thatching skewer.

ছুঁচা, ছুঁছা, ছুছুন্দরি,—চিক্কা, the musk rat.
ছুঁচাল, আগাল, pointed, sharp-pointed.
ছুঁচিপাতন, উকি মারণ, আড়িপাতন, to listen, lie on the watch.
ছুঁবন, ছুঁওন,—স্পর্শন, ঠেকন, to touch, to feel.
ছুটন, পলান, এড়িয়া যাওন, to run away, escape, to break loose, to fly as a shot from a gun &c.
ছুটান, ছাড়ান, এড়ান, to loosen, liberate, let go, dispel.
ছুটানী, মুক্তন, ছাড়ানি, liberation, exemption. [a pedlar.
ছুটাজিয়া, ক্ষুদ্র, ফড়িয়া, small, pedling, dealing in small wares;
ছুটী, ছাড়ানি, উদ্ধার, বিদায়, বিরাম, discharge, release, dismission, leave, furlough, cessation from work.
ছুড়ন, এড়ান, প্রক্ষেপণ, to liberate, throw, pelt, cast, shoot.
ছুৎ, মারী, মড়ক, contagion, infection, communication.
ছুত-া, ব্যাজ, ছল, a pretence, excuse, artifice, concealment.
ছুতর, ঠক, খল, প্রতারক, a sharper, swindler, deceiver.
ছুপন, চাপন, জয় করণ, বাড়ন, to press down, prevail over, exceed, surpass.
ছুরী, ছুরিকা,—ক্ষুদ্র কাটনের অস্ত্র, a knife, a penknife.
ছুলী, চামড়ী, মরামাস, খুকী, scurf, dry scurf, dandruff.
ছুহারা, খর্জ্জুর, the date fruit.
ছেই, ছিছি, fie! avaunt! [sation.
ছেক্, ছেকন,—অন্তর, বিরাম, an interval, intermission, cessation.
ছেদ, বিভাগ, চেরা, রন্ধ্র, অন্তর, যতি, a dividing, a cut, tear, hole, crack, the eye of a needle, an interval, a space between words, a pause.
ছেদন, কাটন, চিরণ, ফাড়ন, বেধন, বধন, to cut, tear, break, divide, slit, bore, perforate, mutilate, slay.
ছেঁদা, রন্ধ্র, বেধ, ছিদ্র, a hole, perforation, needle's eye, slit, crack, rent, tear.
ছেনা, আমীক্ষা, curds.
ছেপ, থুথু, থুক, নিষ্ঠীব, saliva, spittle. [fant, babe.
ছেলিয়া, ছেল্যা—বালক, বালিকা, অবগণ্ড, a child, boy, maid, in-
ছেলিয়ামি, ছেল্যামি,—বালকতা, চিড়্চিড়াম, childhood, infancy, childishness, pettishness.
ছেলী, অজ, মৃগের গাত্রচিহ্ন, a goat, the spots on a deer, &c.
ছেলীপড়া, চিত্রিত, বিচিত্র, speckled, spotted.

ছোঁওন, স্পর্শন, লাগন, to feel, to touch, to come in contact with, reach to. [lass.

ছোকরা, ছোকরী,—বালক, বালিকা, *m. & f.* a boy, a girl, a lad, a

ছোট, ক্ষুদ্র, তুচ্ছ, খাট, কনিষ্ঠ, small, little, trivial, petty, common, vulgar, mean, low, short, narrow, humble, younger.

ছোটন-আন, ছাড়ন, to loose, let free, emit, discharge, shoot.

ছোট মা, কণিষ্ঠামাতা, লক্ষ্মী, সম্পত্তি, the younger wife as addressed by the children of an elder; Lakshmi, riches, wealth.

ছোড়ন, বাণাদি প্রক্ষেপণ, to shoot, fire, discharge a shot.

ছোড়ান, তালার কাঠী, a key.

ছোপ, বস্ত্রাদিতে চিহ্ন, a stain, the mark of vegetable juice.

ছোপান, বস্ত্রাঙ্কন, to print calicoes, stain, mark.

ছোবড়া, নারিকেলাদির ছাল, খোল, the rind of a cocoa or betel nut, a plantain peel.

ছোরা, ছুরিকা, যমধার, a knife, stiletto.

ছোল, ত্বক, ছাল, fruit-skin, rind, peel, integument.

ছোলঙ্গ, লেবু, a citron, a lime.

ছোলন, ছাল তোলন, to peel, skin, pare, scrape.

ছোলা, চণক, gram or corn for horses.

ছ্যা, ছি ছি, fie! for shame!

জ.

জ, জাত, উৎপন্ন, *affix:* produced or descended from, born, arisen, caused.

জগৎ, ভুবন, বিশ্ব, পৃথিবী, the world, the universe, the earth or its inhabitants, mankind. [verse.

জগদাধার, বায়ু, বাতাস, the air, wind, the support of the uni-

জগন্নাথ, বিশ্বপতি, বিগ্রহ বিশেষ, Vishnu or the Lord of the world.

জগহ্, স্থান, ভূমি, a place, situation, spot.

জঘন, উরুস্থল, বংক্ষণ, কটিদেশ, the hip and loins.

জঘন্য, চরম, অধম, নীচ, last, ultimate, low, vile, base, vulgar.

জঘন্যজ, কনিষ্ঠ, শূদ্র, youngest, low-born, mean; a shúdra.

জঙ্গম, চলৎশক্তিমন্ত, locomotive, moveable, having motion, removeable.

জঙ্গল, বনজ, শূন্য, বন, অরণ্য, বনগাছ, wild, desert, waste; a desert, forest, wilderness, the weeds &c. overrunning a garden.

জঙ্গলাট, পতিত, উৎকট, desert, wild, uncultivated, waste.

জঙ্গলী, বন্য, wild, sylvan, growing wild, untamed.

জঙ্গাল, সীমা, আলি, a limit, boundary, rice-balk, ridge.

জঙ্ঘা, ঊরু, অস্থি, the thigh, the leg.

জঙ্ঘাল, শীঘ্রগামী, a quick walker; marching well.

জঙ্ঘিয়া, জানু আচ্ছাদক বস্ত্র, short drawers, breeches.

জঞ্জাল, আবর্জ্জনা, ওঁচলা, উৎপাত, rubbish, sweepings, a nuisance, disorder, confusion, misfortune.

জঞ্জালিয়া, পাকপড়া, ঝঞ্ঝাটিয়া, intricate, confused, troublesome.

জট, উদাসীনের জড়ীভূতকেশ, the long matted and tangled hair of a devotee or ascetic.

জটলা, সংঘট্ট, লোকসমূহ, a crowd, multitude of people.

জটা, জড়িতকেশ, বৃক্ষশিকড় ইত্যাদি, the matted hair of Shiva and of ascetics, a fibrous root, the long flower stalks of the palm.

জটাজূট, শিবের বিকৃতকেশ, the matted hair of Shiva, &c.

জটাধর, শিব, জটাযুক্ত, Shiva, a devotee; having matted hair.

জটিয়া, জটিল,—জটাধারী, wearing the hair matted and clotted as an ascetic.

জটুল, জড়ুল,—ডিল, চিহ্ন, a freckle, mark, spot.

জঠর, উদর, পেট, the belly, the bowels, the womb.

জড়, স্থূলবুদ্ধি, মূঢ়, চলৎশক্তিহীন, আলসিয়া, শীত, অবসন্ন, সঞ্চিত, শুষ্ক, মূল, আদি কারণ, stupid, heavy, idiotic, decrepit, inactive, motionless, sluggish, cold, frigid, chilly, benumbed, crowded, collected, heaped together, shrivelled, contracted; a root, origin, source, first cause.

জড়ান, বেষ্টন, আঁকড়ন, মোড়ান, to wrap or wind round, clasp, cling, writhe, overlay, plate metals, set jewels.

জড়াও, মোড়ান, the plating of metals, overlaying.

জড়িত, বেষ্টিত, বসান, সঙ্কুচিত, ঘন, অস্পষ্ট, set with gems, studded, crowded, contracted, frozen, uttered thick, sputtered, inarticulate.

জড়িবটী, ঔষধ, ভেষজ, medicines, drugs.

জড়িমা, মূঢ়তা, জরা, অবসন্নতা, গতিরাহিত্য, জমতাব, stupidity, idiocy, decrepitude, numbness, stiffness, congelation, a frozen state.

জড়জড়িয়া, আটাল, viscid, tenacious, sticky.

জতু, লা, লাক্ষা, lac, red animal dye.

জতুক, লা, হিং, তিল, lac dye, assafœtida, a freckle, spot.

জতুমণি, তিল, তিলক, a freckle, a mark on the skin.

জন, ব্যক্তি, লোক, a person, individual, man, mankind.

জনক, জন্মদাতা, পিতা, পূর্বপুরুষ, producing, causing, begetting; a father, ancestor.

জনতা, লোকসমূহ, সম্মর্দ, রব, প্রকাশ, a multitude, crowd, throng, mob, mankind, a rumour, talk, report, declaration, disclosure.

জনন, উৎপত্তি, বংশ, birth, production, race, lineage.

জননী, জনয়িত্রী,—মাতা, a mother.

জনপদ, দেশ, চাকলা, a country, region, province.

জনমানব, লোক, মনুষ্য গণ, people, men.

জনরব, জনশ্রুতি,—কিম্বদন্তী, গল্প, খ্যাতি, a report, rumour, fame.

জনলোক, গতধার্ম্মিকলোকের আবাস, a division of the universe; the paradise of good men. [caused.

জনিত, জাত, উৎপন্ন, প্রযুক্ত, produced, born, occasioned,

জন্তু, প্রাণী, an animal, a brute.

জন্ম, উৎপত্তি, উৎপন্ন, birth, production, result, crop.

জন্মগত, স্বাভাবিক, পৈতৃক, inherent, from the birth, hereditary.

জন্মন, জন্মপাওন, হওন, উৎপন্ন হওন, আইসন, to be born, to be produced or caused, to spring, arise, result, proceed from.

জন্মফের, মূর্ত্ত্যান্তর, জন্মান্তর, transformation, a second birth.

জন্মশোধ, জীবধর্ম্মসমাপন, মরণ, the discharge of all the duties of life, death.

জন্মান, জন্মদেওন, উৎপাদন, করাণ, সৃজন, প্রকাশন, to beget, produce, bear or bring forth, cause, create, occasion, propagate, invent.

জন্মান্ধ, জন্মাবধি দৃষ্টিহীন, born blind, blind from the birth.

জন্য, কারণ, হেতু, মূল, cause, motive, reason, occasion.

জন্যে, প্রযুক্ত, কারণ, on account of, for, because of, for the sake of, in order to.

জপ, পুনঃ২ দেবনামকরা, frequent repetition audibly or otherwise of the name of a deity.

জপন, পুনঃ২ দেবনামোচ্চারণ, to repeat the name of a deity in the use of a rosary, to mutter prayers.

জপবটী, জপমালা,—স্মারী, করমালা. a rosary or bead-roll.

জবন, ম্লেচ্ছ, মুসলমান, a foreigner, a Mussulman; Greece.

জমক. প্রাগল্ভ্য, আড়ম্বর, ঘটা, shew, pomp, parade.

জম্বাল, কর্দম, mud, clay. [small leaved basil.

জম্বীর, জম্ভীর.—লেবু, অল্পপত্রতুলসী, a lime, lemon, citron, the

জম্বু, জম্বূ,—জাম, ভারতবর্ষ, the rose apple; a division of the earth, Hindoosthan.

জম্বুক, শৃগাল, the jackal.

জম্ভন, রতিক্রিয়া, মৈথুন, copulation, sexual intercourse.

জয়, পরাভবকরা, উন্নতি; বৃদ্ধি, conquest, victory, triumph, prosperity.

জয়ত্রী, জয়িত্রী,—জাতিফলের ছাল, mace, (the spice.)

জয়ী, জেতা, জিতনিয়া, উন্নত, victorious, conquering, triumphant, prosperous. [cay.

জর, বার্দ্ধক্য, জীর্ণতা, old age, decrepitude, infirmity, de-

জরণ, বৃদ্ধ হওন, ক্ষয়ন, পচন, পাকন, to grow old, waste or wear away, decay, digest as food.

জরদ্গব, বৃদ্ধ বলীবর্দ্দ, an old ox.

জরা, শেষাবস্থা, জীর্ণতা, জীর্ণ, পচা, পক্ক, decrepitude, old age, decay; infirm, tabid, decayed, digested.

জরাণ, পাকপাওন, গলান, পচান, to digest food, to dissolve, cause to decay.

জরায়ু, পেট, গর্ভ, the womb, the uterus.

জরায়ুজ, মনুষ্যাদি, viviparous, produced from the womb.

জরু, ভার্য্যা, স্ত্রী, পত্নী. a wife. [shattered, jarring.

জর্জ্জর, জর্জ্জরিত,—বিদীর্ণ, কাটা, অতিজীর্ণ, torn, rent, cracked,

জল, সলিল, পানী, বৃষ্টি, water, liquor, rheum; rain. [wall.

জলাই, উনুই, গজাল, a fountain, spring, a pin or peg in the

জলকষ্ট, অনাবৃষ্টি, শুষ্ক, অল্পজল, drought; arid, parched, scarce of water.

জলগণ্ড, বুড়াস্থান, জোল, a swamp, a marsh.
জলচর, জলজন্তু, মৎস্যাদি, aquatic, moving or living in water.
জলছত্র, জলটঙ্গী,—পথিকজলদান গৃহ, a temporary shed for the refreshment of travellers in the hot season.
জলতরঙ্গ, বীচি, ধাতুময় বাদ্যযন্ত্র বিশেষ তাহার স্বর, a wave, the musical sound of a glass or metal vessel rubbed with the wetted fingers.
জলদ, সজল মেঘ, সলিলদ, a cloud; giving water.
জলদোষ, জলবিকারজন্য পীড়া, শ্লেষ্মাদি, a diseased state of the fluids, phlegm &c.
জলধর, মেঘ, সমুদ্র, a cloud, the ocean.
জলধি, জলনিধি,—সমুদ্র, সাগর, the sea, the ocean.
জলপথ, নৌকা দিয়া চলা, a passage by water, a water-journey.
জলপান, অন্নব্যতিরিক্ত ভোজন, a repast, refreshment, tiffin, the drinking of water.
জলপ্রায়, জলবিশিষ্ট, জলা, abounding with water, swampy, marshy.
জলবিষুব, তুলাসংক্রান্তি, the watery or autumnal equinox.
জলভরণিয়া, পানীভরা, নাবিকাদি, living or obtaining a livelihood by the water; a waterman &c.
জলমানুষ, ভূজলউভয়চারী জন্তু বিশেষ, a seal, a mermaid.
জলমার্জার, উদ্বিড়াল, an otter.
জলযোগ, অন্নভিন্ন কিঞ্চিৎ আহার, a slight repast, refreshment, tiffin.
জলশয়-ন, জলশায়ী,—বিষ্ণু, Vishnu, (as sleeping on the ocean.)
জলসত্র, পথিকজলদান গৃহ, a shed for travellers, for the advantage of shade and the refreshment of water.
জলহরী, পুষ্করিণী, a pond.
জলহস্তী, কুম্ভীর, নক্র, গোধিকা, a crocodile or alligator.
জলা, জলগণ্ড, জলপ্লাবিত, a fen, swamp, lake; fenny, wet, marshy, swampy, swamped.
জলাকর, উনুই, জলই, a spring or fountain.
জলাধার, পুষ্করিণী আদি, জলপাত্র, a receptacle for water, a pond, lake, reservoir, a water-vessel.
জলাম, গর্ভপুষ্প, জরায়ুফুল, the secundines or after-birth.
জলাশয়, পুষ্করিণী, তড়াগ, a pond, a collection of waters, reservoir, tank.
জলিকা, জলৌকা,—জোঁক, a leech.

জলীবী, মিষ্টান্ন বিশেষ, a kind of sweetmeat. [tasteless.
জলুয়া, তরল, ফিকা, নীরস, diluted, thin, watery, fluid, wet,
জলোদরী, উদররোগ, the dropsy. [gence, lustre.
জলজল্-টি, চক্চকি, উজ্জ্বল, a glare, glow, vivid light, reful-
জল্প, গল্পসল্প, ঝকড়া, chat, talk, garrulity, dissension, wrangling. [say, tell.
জল্পন, বৃথাকথন, বকন, কহন, to talk, chat, gossip, prattle,
জহ্নুতনয়া, গঙ্গা, the Ganges.
জাওর, উগরিত গোঘাস, the cud of ruminating animals.
জাঁক, জাঁকজমক,—সঙ্ঘট্ট, সমূহ, ঘটা, a crowd, multitude, an assembly of people with their beasts, carriages, music, &c. a pompous procession.
জাঁকার, কোলাহল, গণ্ডগোল, a tumultuous noise.
জাঁত, চাপা, ছাপাকল, a press, a vice.
জাঁতন, চাপান, আঁটন, to press down, press with a vice, to compress, pull tight.
জাঁতা, চাকী, ভস্ত্রা, ক্ষেত্রসেচনের যন্ত্র বিশেষ, mill-stones, a pair of bellows, a trough for watering fields. [betel-nut.
জাঁতী, গুবাক ছেদনার্থ অস্ত্র বিশেষ, an instrument for cutting
জাগন, নিদ্রোত্থান, to awake from sleep, wake, watch.
জাগনিয়া, চৌকস, পহরী, keeping awake, watchful, vigilant; a watchman. [to awake.
জাগরণ. নিদ্রাত্যাগ, চৌকশী, waking, watchfulness, vigilance;
জাগরূক, জাগরণশীল, সচেত, wakeful, watchful, vigilant.
জাগান, ঘুমভাঙ্গান, উঠান, চেতান, পাকান, to awaken, stir up, rouse, spring game, to warm unripe grain or fruit over the fire. [sprung.
জাগ্রৎ, নিদ্রোত্থিত, সচকিত, awake, rising from sleep, roused,
জাঙ্গাল, আলি, সেতু, a balk in rice fields, dyke, dam, mound.
জাঙ্ঘী, জঙ্ঘা, the leg.
জাচন, আলোচন, to inspect, survey, examine, appraise.
জাজ্বল্যমান, দেদীপ্যমান, refulgent, brilliant, resplendent, shining, conspicuous.
জাড়-1, হিম, শীতকাল, cold, frost, winter.
জাড়ি, শীতল, শীতকালীন, মিশ্রিত, cold, belonging to cold, composed of several ingredients.

জাড়িবেঙ্গ, আসাপ, ভেক, a toad, a frog.

জাড্য, জড়তা, অবসন্নতা, মূঢ়তা, অজ্ঞানতা, coldness, congelation, numbness, stiffness, apathy, stupidity, idiocy, folly.

জাত-ক, উৎপন্ন, উদ্ভূত, born, produced, begotten, arising from, natural.

জাৎ, প্রকার, বংশ, সমূহ, উৎসব, a kind, sort, class, species, breed, a multitude, troop, festival.

জাতকর্ম্ম, উৎপত্তিকালীন সংস্কার, a ceremony at the birth of a child.

জাতান্ধ, জন্মাবধি দৃষ্টিহীন, born blind.

জাতাপত্যা, প্রসূতা স্ত্রী, a mother, one who has borne children.

জাতি, প্রকার, গণ, বর্গ, গোত্র, কুল, জন্ম, উৎপত্তি, জায়ফল, বেলফুল, a kind, sort, class, species, genus, nation, family, race, tribe, birth, nativity, production, mace, nutmeg, jasmine.

জাতিখাওয়া, বলাৎকার, কন্যাভ্রষ্টাকরা, stupration, violation, rape.

জাতিমারা, জাতিনাশ করা, বলাৎকার, the causing of a person's loss of cast, rape, &c.

জাতিস্মর, পূর্বজন্মীয় স্মারক, recollecting his rank &c in a former birth.

জাতীকোষ, জাতীফল,—জায়ফল, a nutmeg.

জাতীয়, জাতিসম্বন্ধীয়, of or belonging to a kind or species.

জাতু, কখন, কদাচিত, অবজ্ঞাদিবোধক শব্দ, sometimes, occasionally: also, *interjectionally*, an expression of contempt, reproach or doubt.

জাতেষ্টি, পুত্রজন্মকালীন যাগ, a sacrifice at the birth of a child.

জান, জীব, প্রাণ, জ্ঞান, ভেল্কী, life, animality, knowledge, a wizard, an astrologer.

জানন, চিনন, পরিচয়ন, বিবেচন, বুঝন, to know, perceive, discern, discover, apprehend, esteem, consider, imagine, suppose, reckon, think.

জানবর, জন্তু, প্রাণী, an animal, a brute.

জানহিৎ, জানত,—জ্ঞাত, পরিচিত, জানিয়া, knowing, acquainted with; wilfully, designedly, knowingly.

জানান, জ্ঞাপন, প্রচারণ, বুঝান, চেতান, দর্শান, to make known, tell, declare, acquaint, inform, advertise, proclaim, warn, admonish, demonstrate, describe, show, display, persuade, suggest.

জানানি, নিশ্চয়, দৃঢ়বোধ, সমাচার, certainty, conviction, information, persuasion.

জানারি, গণকতা, কুহক, divination, sorcery.

জানু, হাঁটু, জঙ্ঘা, the knee, the thigh. [&c.

জাপ, পুনঃ২নামকরা, the repeating or muttering of prayers,

জাপটন-আন, জাঁকড়ন, আলিঙ্গন, to clasp, to embrace.

জাবনিক, বৈদেশিক, ম্লেচ্ছদেশীয়, মৌসলমানিক, pertaining or relating to foreigners, Mussulman, Grecian.

জাবান, মৎস্য ধরিয়া জলে রাখন, to preserve fish alive in a reservoir for future use.

জাবালি, সর্পাদির ছা, ধান্যের চারা, the young of serpents, scorpions and other vermin; growing rice not yet in ear. [band.)

জামাই, জামাতা,—কন্যার পতি, a son-in-law, (daughter's hus-

জাম্বির, জামীর,—লেবু, a lime or lemon. [toe.

জামড়া, ক্ষতচিহ্ন, কঠিন মাংস, কড়া, a scar, callosity, corn on the

জায়, লেখা, বিয়োগ, a list, account. estimate. [ritual.

জায়া, ভার্য্যা, পত্নী, a wife married according to a perfect

জার, উপপতি, ব্যভিচারী, a gallant, lover, paramour, adulterer.

জারণ-আন, ক্ষয় কিম্বা জীর্ণ করাণ, গলান, পাচান, to waste, cause to decay, make decrepit or infirm, dissolve, promote digestion, consume away.

জারজ, বিজন্মা, a son by a gallant; bastard, illegitimate.

জারাশঙ্কা, দুষ্টাসন্দেহ. jealousy of a wife's infidelity.

জাল, ক্ষেপণী আদি, ফাঁদ, আশাবন্ধ, গবাক্ষ, কুহক, গর্ব, অব্যক্ত কলিকা, সমূহ, অগ্নিশিখা, a net, snare, spider's web, a lattice, window, loop hole, magic, illusion, deception, pride, arrogance, an unblown flower, a multitude, assemblage, the flame of fire, a young cucumber.

জালন, জ্বালান, উদ্দীপন, to kindle a fire, light a lamp.

জালা, জলাদি রক্ষার্থ পাত্র, দাহ, কাতরতা, a jar, a burning pain, inflammation, distress, anxiety.

জালান, জ্বালান, পোড়ান, উত্তাপন, to kindle fire, burn wood &c. to heat a fluid. [juggler, vägabond.

জালিক, কৈবর্ত্ত, ব্যাধ, মাকড়, ভাঁড়, a fisherman, fowler, spider,

জালিয়া, ধীবরাদি, gaining a livelihood by nets; a fisherman, &c.

জালী, ঝালর, ঝর্ঝরী, ছানী, a fringe, net, purse, net-work, lattice, web, a film or pearl on the eye.

জালীপড়া, জালবৎ, reticulated, net-like.

জাল্‌তি, মুখাস, a muzzle for the nose of an animal.

জাহ্নবী, গঙ্গা, the Ganges personified.

জাল্ম, নীচলোক, ক্রূর, অবিবেকী, a low man, one of a low cast; cruel, harsh, severe, rash, inconsiderate.

জিওন, জীবন, জীবন্ত থাকন, to live, be or remain alive.

জিয়ান, জীবপ্রদানকরণ, প্রাণপাওয়ান, পুষ্করিণ্যাদিতে মৎস্য ধরিয়া রাখন, to animate, give life, revive, restore to life, to keep fish in a preserve. [for use.

জিউনি, মাছুয়া, a fishmonger, one who preserves fish alive

জিওল, কচ্ছপ, a tortoise.

জিগীষা, জয়েচ্ছা, emulation, wish to excel or overcome.

জিঘাংসা, হিংসেচ্ছা, দ্বেষ, a desire to injure or kill, malice, revenge. [thirsty.

জিঘাংসু, জিঘাংসক.—হিংসেচ্ছু, malicious, revengeful, blood-

জিজ্ঞাসন, প্রশ্নন, পুছন, to question, propose, enquire, ask, require. [know.

জিজ্ঞাসা, প্রশ্ন, জানিবার ইচ্ছা, an enquiry, question, desire to

জিজ্ঞাসু, প্রশ্নকারী, enquiring, inquisitive, desirous to know.

জিত, পরাজয়ী, বশীভূত, বর্ত্তমান, conquered, overcome, surpassed, won, subdued, alive, living.

জিতন, জিনন,—দমন, প্রাপণ, উৎকর্ষণ, to conquer, triumph, subdue, win, gain, excel, transcend, surpass.

জিতনিয়া, জিননিয়া—জয়ী, প্রাপী, উৎকৃষ্ট, conquering, winning, transcending, surpassing; a winner, conqueror, victor.

জিতাহার, ধ্যানজন্য আহারত্যাগ, having by abstraction surmounted the desire and necessity for food.

জিতেন্দ্রিয়, বশীকৃতেন্দ্রিয়, of subdued appetites and feelings, continent; an ascetic.

জিন, বিশ্বের অকৃত্রিমতাবাদী ঋষি, বৌদ্ধ. a Jina, a sage of the Jaina sect, a Buddhist.

জিন্দগী, জিন্দগানী,—জীবন, life.
জিব, জিভ, জিউ, জিহ্বা,—রসনা, the tongue.
জিরজ, কচ্ছপ, a turtle, a tortoise.
জিরণ, বিশ্রমণ, to rest from labour, sit still, unbend, repose.
জিল, তীক্ষ্ণ স্বর, a shrill tone, the treble string of a violin.
জীঅন, বাঁচন, to live, be alive, revive.
জীব, প্রাণ, আত্মা, প্রাণী, উপজীবিকা, বৃহস্পতি, life, existence, the sentient soul, an animal, living creature, a livelihood, occupation, Vrihaspati.
জীবৎ, জীবন্ত,—জীবনবিশিষ্ট, বর্ত্তমান, living, alive, existent.
জীবৎমান, জীবনকাল, জীবদ্দশা, life-time, the season of life.
জীবন, প্রাণ, জন্মমৃত্যুর মধ্যকাল, উপজীব্য, প্রাণী, জল, living, life, life time, a livelihood, an animal, water.
জীবন্মৃত, জীবদ্দশাতে মৃতপ্রায়, dead while living.
জীবনাবশিষ্ট, মৃতকল্প, nearly dead, having only a remaining spark of life.
জীবনোপায়, উপজীবিকা, রক্ষা, a method of subsistence, livelihood, way of escape.
জীবলোক, মনুষ্য, a man, men.
জীবাত্মা, প্রাণ, অসু, vitality, the vital principle, the soul as an emanation of deity.
জীবাধান, প্রাণরক্ষণ, the retaining or preservation of life.
জীবিকা, উপজীব্য, a livelihood, subsistence, maintenance.
জীবিকায়ী, রাজস্বদায়ী, করদ, tributary, paying tribute.
জীবিত, বর্ত্তমান, প্রাণ, alive, enlivened, revived; life.
জীয়ন্ত, বর্ত্তমান, living, alive, existent.
জীয়ান, বাঁচান, রক্ষণ, জুড়ান, মূর্চ্ছা ভঞ্জন, to protect, save, revive, bring to life, refresh, stock a pond with fish.
জীরা, ক্ষুদ্র বীজ বিশেষ, cummin seed.
জীর্ণ, বৃদ্ধ, পুরাতন, জর্জ্জরীভূত, পরিপক্ক, old, infirm, worn, worn out, decayed, inveterate, tabid, digested.
জীর্ণধরা, গবাদির প্রথম কোষ the first stomach in ruminating animals.
জীর্ণি, বার্দ্ধক্য, জরা, অন্নপাক, infirmity, old age, decay, digestion.
জুআ, পাশক্রীড়া, gaming, play at dice, &c.
জুআর, বান, শর, the flood-tide.
জুয়ারিয়া, বানানীত, বানাপ্লাবিত, brought in or overflowed by the tide.
জুয়ারী, পাশক্রীড়ক, a gambler, a player at dice, &c.

জুগুপ্সা, নিন্দা, censure, abuse, reproach, reviling.
জুল্ম, উৎকট, দুরন্ত, confident, bold, impudent, outcast.
জুজু, ভয়প্রদর্শক মূর্ত্তি, a bugbear. [after anger.
জুড়ন, স্নিগ্ধ হওন, থামন, to grow cool, be cold, become calm
জুড়ান, স্নিগ্ধ করণ, থামান, to cool, refresh, calm, quell.
জুৎ, সৌন্দর্য্য, যোগ্যতা, beauty, symmetry, elegance, fitness for a purpose.
জুতন, পাদুকা দিয়া মারণ, to beat with a slipper.
জুতল, সুন্দর, সুঠাম, সুগঠিত, beautiful, elegant, in good order, fit for its purpose.
জুতা, জুতী,—চর্ম্মপাদুকা. a shoe, a slipper.
জুকা, ভেষজ বিশেষ, a medicinal drug.
জুবড়ন, ডুবন, ভিজান, to dip cloth, to dye, to sop or dip food into sauce, &c.
জুল, উঁকি, ঈষদ্দৃষ্টি, a peep, a glance.
জুলী, খাত, নালা, প্রণালী, a trench, a watercourse. [wood.
জুহূ, যজ্ঞীয় পাত্র বিশেষ, a semicircular sacrificial vessel of
জুচ্চু, অপদেশ, ফাঁকী, a pretence, imposture, swindling.
জুষ, ঝোল, sauce, pease soup, porridge, the water of boiled pulse. [sleep.
জৃম্ভণ, হাই ছাড়ন, to yawn, gape, stretch after fatigue or
জৃম্ভা, হাই, a yawning and stretching, a gaping, &c.
জেটী, গৃহগোধিকা, the house lizard. [sumptuousness.
জেঠামি, দম্ভ, আত্মগরিমা, self-importance, assumption, pre-
জেতা, জয়ী. a conqueror, vanquisher, victor.
জেতান, জয়ী করাণ, to cause to conquer, to procure or ensure a victory. [come.
জেয়, জেতব্য,—পরাভবনীয়, conquerable, that may be over-
জৈন. জিনমতাবলম্বী, a Jaina, or follower of the Jaina sect.
জোঁক, জলৌকা, রক্তপা, a leech.
জোকন, তুলন, তৌল করণ, to weigh articles.
জোন, বেতনগ্রাহী, a labourer, one who labours for hire.
জোনাক, জ্যোতিঃযুক্ত পোকা বিশেষ, a firefly.
জোল, জলাপ্লাবিতস্থান, খানা, খাত, a fen, marsh, low ground, pool, ravine, trench. [sink.
জোলী, বিল, খানা, নালী, a crack, ravine, gutter, sewer,

জৌ, লাক্ষা, গালা, lac, gum lac or red dye.

জ্ঞাত, বুদ্ধ প্রতীত, অবগত, বিদিত, জ্ঞানত, known, perceived, understood, comprehended, privy, knowing, acquainted with.

জ্ঞাতসার, বোধগোচর, অবগত, an object of knowledge; known.

জ্ঞাতা, যে ব্যক্তি জানে, জ্ঞানপ্রাপ্ত, one who knows or is acquainted with.

জ্ঞাতি, সপিণ্ড, কুটুম্ব, a collateral relation, a kinsman.

জ্ঞাতৃতা, নৈপুণ্য, বুদ্ধি, experience, ability, genius, intelligence, knowledge.

জ্ঞান, চৈতন্য, বুদ্ধি, অনুমান, তত্ত্ববোধ, ব্রহ্মবোধ, knowledge, wisdom, talent, perception, idea, notion, opinion, persuasion, abstract knowledge of spirit.

জ্ঞানতঃ, জানিয়া, জ্ঞানপূর্ব্বক, knowingly, with knowledge.

জ্ঞানী, বুদ্ধিমান, পণ্ডিত, প্রাজ্ঞ, wise, intelligent, able, knowing, clever, shrewd.

জ্ঞানেন্দ্রিয়, বুদ্ধীন্দ্রিয়, মনোনেত্রাদি, the organs of perception or the mind, eye, ear, nose, tongue and skin.

জ্ঞাপন, জানান, প্রচারণ, বুঝান, to make known, reveal, publish, communicate, tell, announce, acquaint, inform, teach, expound.

জ্ঞেয়, বোধগম্য, জ্ঞাতসার, capable of being known, cognizable, an object of knowledge.

জ্যা, ধনুকের গুণ, a bow-string.

জ্যেষ্ঠ, অগ্রজ, শ্রেষ্ঠ, বড়, oldest, elder, first-born, best, chief, most excellent.

জ্যেষ্ঠত্ব, অগ্রজাতত্ব, শ্রেষ্ঠত্ব, primogeniture, seniority.

জ্যেষ্ঠা, অষ্টাদশ নক্ষত্র, the eighteenth lunar mansion, the middle finger, one's best beloved wife.

জ্যৈষ্ঠ, গ্রীষ্মের প্রথম মাস, a Hindoo month, the first hot month.

জ্যৈষ্ঠী, গৃহগোধিকা, জ্যৈষ্ঠমাসের পূর্ণিমা, the house lizard, the day of the full moon in Jyaishtha.

জ্যোতিঃ, তেজঃ, অগ্নি, নক্ষত্র, সূর্য্য, তারা, নেত্রমণি, light, splendour, fire, a heavenly luminary, star, the sun, the pupil of the eye.

জ্যোতিশ্চক্র, দ্বাদশ রাশিচক্র, the zodiac.

জ্যোতিষ, গ্রহাদির গতিজ্ঞাপক শাস্ত্র, astronomy, astrology, a star, luminary.

জ্যোৎস্না, চন্দ্রের রশ্মি, moon-light, a moon-light night.
জ্যৌতিষিক, দৈবজ্ঞ, জ্যোতির্ব্বেত্তা, an astrologer, an astronomer.
জ্বর, তাপ, a fever, an ague.
জ্বরী, তাপযুক্ত, পীড়িত, feverish, aguish, diseased, weak.
জ্বলন, ধক্‌ধকান, উদ্দীপন, পোড়ন, ব্যগ্র বা কাতর বা পীড্যমান হওন, to blaze, kindle up, burn, glow, to be ardent, zealous, eager, pained or distressed in mind, to smart, or be in pain.
জ্বলনী, অতিব্যথাকর, virulent. [fuel.
জ্বলনীয়, দাহ্য, পুড়িবার যোগ্য, combustible, inflammable, fit for
জ্বলন্ত, প্রজ্বলিত, ব্যগ্র, ব্যথাকর, উত্তাপিত, burning, blazing, glowing, ardent, zealous, painful, vexed.
জ্বলা, জ্বালা,—দাহ, তাপ, পীড়া, উষ্মা, ব্যগ্রতা, a burning, inflammation, virulence, smart, anguish, torment, heat of persecution, ardour, fervour.
জ্বলান, জ্বালান,—অগ্নি ফুয়ান, ধরাণ, পোড়ান, দুঃখ দেওন, পীড়ন, কোপান, to kindle, set on fire, light a candle, burn, scald, cause pain or anguish, torment, vex, harrass, importune, weary, exasperate.
জ্বালাতন, ক্লান্ত, ক্লিষ্ট, বিরক্ত, wearied, distressed, teased, vexed.
জ্বালামুখী, আগ্নের স্থান, an inflammable pit, place where subterraneous fire breaks forth, a volcano.
জ্বালিত, উত্তপ্ত, দগ্ধ, খেদিত, inflamed, burnt, vexed, grieved.

ঝ.

ঝক্, শীঘ্র, বৃথাকথা, quickly, suddenly: nonsense, rant.
ঝকড়ন, বিবাদন, to quarrel, squabble, wrangle, dispute.
ঝকড়া, কলহ, বিবাদ, যুদ্ধ, a quarrel, dispute, strife, wrangling, fight, war. [wrangling.
ঝকড়াটিয়া, ঝকড়ালু,—কুঁদলিয়া, quarrelsome, disputatious,
ঝক্‌ঝক্, চক্‌মক্, দীপ্তি, a vivid light, luminous appearance, glare, twinkling, brightness.
ঝক্‌মারী, বৃথাবাদী, অনুতাপ, কুকর্ম্ম, talking nonsense, ranting; repentance, regret, a fault, evil deed. [&c.
ঝঙ্কার, ভ্রমরাদির ভণ্‌ভণধ্বনি, গুঞ্জন, the buzzing of bees, wasps

ঝঞ্ঝন, অব্যক্তশব্দ বিশেষ, ঠঙ্ঠনানি, a jingling, rattling, jarring, clanking, clashing.

ঝঞ্ঝনা, বাজ, বজ্র, a thunderbolt, stroke of lightning.

ঝঞ্ঝা, ঝড়, a storm, squall, hurricane, a clanking, &c.

ঝঞ্ঝাট, হয়রাণী, ক্লেশ, দুঃখ, খট্খট্, perplexity, trouble, vexation, a difficulty, dilemma.

ঝটাপটি, পাছড়াপাছড়ি, a sparring, the fighting of birds.

ঝটিতি, শীঘ্র, quickly, speedily, expeditiously, apace.

ঝট্কন-আন, কাটন, শিরোচ্ছেদন, to chop or lop off, behead.

ঝট্কা, ঝড়, ঝড়ি,—প্রচণ্ড বায়ু, a hurricane, a storm, a squall, a tempest.

ঝড়কন, ভর্ৎসন, ধম্কান, to scold, chide, reprove, bluster, [domineer.

ঝড়ুয়া, বাতাসী, tempestuous, stormy, windy.

ঝণ্ডা, পতাকা, ধ্বজ, a standard, flagstaff.

ঝন্কাট, দ্বারের কপালী, a door lintel.

ঝম্প, লাফ, উৎক্রম, a jump, leap, spring, sally.

ঝর, পর্ব্বতের জলপ্রবাহ, a cascade, a waterfall.

ঝরকা, খিড়কী, a window.

ঝরণ, ক্ষরণ, গলন, স্রবণ, to drip, ooze, exude, leak, fall off [as leaves &c.

ঝরণা, চালনী, ক্ষরণি, a sieve, a dripping, pouring, falling &c.

ঝরণী, ছাকনি, রক্তক্ষরণি, a strainer, the stream of blood from a wound, &c.

ঝরাণ, চালন, ছাকন, ঝাড়ন, to pour out, strain, shake off, [dust clothes.

ঝর্ঝর, জলাদির অজস্র পতন, ভাঙ্গা, a dripping, dropping, &c; split, cracked, ragged, leaky, full of holes.

ঝর্ঝরী, জালী, ব্যবধান, মন্দিরা, a lattice, fence, cymbals.

ঝল, তরঙ্গপাত, অগ্নির তেজ, the beating of waves, a flake of [fire.

ঝল্কন, ঝলসন, গইড় পাড়ন, to flash, glare, flap as a wave.

ঝল্ঝল্, নড়ন, the flapping of a woman's breasts or an elephant's ears, &c. a dangling and flapping.

ঝল্সন-আন, ভাজন, পোড়ান, to scorch, roast, singe.

ঝষ, মৎস্য, a fish.

ঝাঁই, চেঁয়া, ধরাভাব, a calx, a calcined state.

ঝাঁক, ঝুণ্ড, সমূহ, a swarm of bees, flock of birds, herd of [cattle.

ঝাঁটন, সম্মার্জন, to sweep, cleanse with a broom.

ঝাঁটা, সম্মার্জনী, a broom.

ঝাঁপ, তৃণাদি নির্ম্মিত আবরণ, a screen or door of mats, grass &c.
ঝাঁপন, লম্ফন, আবরণ, ঢাকন, আচ্ছাদন, ব্যাপন, to jump, leap, spring, to cover a mare, to skreen with a jhámp. shut up, cover, overspread, overrun (as climbing plants do.)
ঝাঁপী, পেঁটরা, a square covered basket, a work basket.
ঝাঝুরী, ঝাঁঝরা, ঝাঁঝরী,—জলসেচনের পাত্র, বহুছিদ্রযুক্ত দুর্বী, a waterpot, cullender. strainer.
ঝাড়, গুচ্ছ, গুল্ম, বংশ, a tuft, clump, bush, shrub, branch or chandelier, a pedigree, breed, stock.
ঝাড়ন, মলন, প্রযাণ, পাছড়ন, সম্মার্জন, মন্ত্রে বিষহরণ, মানান, কোপ নিবারণ, ভার ছাড়ন, পরিষ্করণ, to thresh, shake off fruit &c. from the tree, winnow, dust clothes, sweep, expel venom by charms, advise, persuade, appease, to throw off as an animal does its load or rider, to scrape off oil &c. from the hands by rubbing them on the sides of a vessel. [&c.
ঝাড়া, গু, বিষ্ঠা, বাহ্যস্থান, পরিষ্কার, ordure, a privy, a dusting
ঝাড়াল, গুল্মযুক্ত, গুচ্ছাল, bushy, growing in tufts or clumps.
ঝাড়ী, গুল্ম, জঙ্গল, a shrub, bush, brushwood.
ঝাড়ীপথ, বনপথ, a forest road, a path among bushes.
ঝাড়ু, সম্মার্জনী, a broom.
ঝাপ্সা, ছানী, জালী, a web or film on the eye, dimness.
ঝাবা, ঝাপ্পা,—থোপ, a tassel.
ঝামা, ঝামক,—অত্যন্তদগ্ধ ইষ্টক, a burnt or vitrified brick.
ঝামর, ক্ষুদ্র শানশিল, a small whetstone for needles &c.
ঝরণ,-আণ, আওরণ, ক্ষরণ, to run as the eyes or nose, to distil, to drop from.
ঝারী, গাডু, a spouted vessel, teapot, teakettle &c.
ঝাল, তীব্র, তীক্ষ্ণ, pungent, hot to the taste. [hot.
ঝালন, ধাতুময় পাত্র সারাণ, জ্বালান, to solder, ignite, heat red
ঝালর, জালী, মশারি. fringe, net work, a musquito net.
ঝালুয়া, তীক্ষ্ণ, তীব্র, hot, pungent, high-seasoned.
ঝিনুক, শম্বুক, শুক্তি, a muscle or cockle &c. [be drowsy.
ঝিমন,-আন, নিদ্রাপড়ন, ঢুলন, to be heavy with sleep, to nod.

ঝিল, সরোবর, জলগর্ত্ত, a lake, marsh, swamp, morass.
ঝিল্লী, ঝিঁঝীপোকা, a cricket.
ঝী, ঝি,—বালিকা, কন্যা, a daughter, female child.
ঝীপুত্র, পুত্রপুত্রী, son and daughter, children. [crest.
ঝুঁটি-ী, ককুৎ, পক্ষির শিখা, a bull's hump, camel's bunch, bird's
ঝুড়ন, ঝোড়ন,—ছাটন, কর্ত্তন, to lop or trim a tree.
ঝুড়ী, চুপড়ী, a basket.
ঝুণ্ড, যুথ, সমূহ, a multitude, flock, swarm, troop.
ঝুন-া, পরিপক্ব নারিকেল, a ripe cocoanut.
ঝুপড়ী, ঝোপড়ী,—কুড়িয়া, কুঠরী, a cabin, hut, shed, cottage.
ঝুম্‌কা, ঝুম্‌কি,—কর্ণভূষা বিশেষ, an ear-ornament for women.
ঝুরী, মিষ্টান্ন বিশেষ, a sort of sweetmeat. [pended.
ঝুলন, ঝোলন,—দোলন, লট্‌কন, to swing, hang down, be sus-
ঝুলী, থলী, থৈলী, a wallet, a satchel.
ঝুঠ-া, মিথ্যা, false, feigned, counterfeit ; a liar.
ঝোড়, ঝোপ,—গুল্মীবৃক্ষ, গুল্ম, a bushy tree, a bush.
ঝোর, পর্ব্বতের জলপ্রবাহ, a cascade, a waterfall.
ঝোল, যূষ, broth, soup.
ঝোলা, ঝোলি,—দোলা, a swing, a wallet, a wrinkle.

ট.

টক, অম্ল, অম্লরস, acid, tart, sour; acidity.
টকো, টকুয়া,—অম্ল, acid, sour.
টক্কর, ঠোকর, ঠোকা, a rap, a knock.
টঙ্ক, খন্তা, ছুরী, অসি, কুঠার, খাপ, অঙ্ঘ্রি, রাগ, দর্প, a spade, hoe, hatchet, knife, sword, stone cutter's chissel, a scabbard, the leg, anger, arrogance.
টঙ্ক ন, সোহাগা, borax.
টঙ্কপতি, টঙ্কশালার অধ্যক্ষ, a mint-master.
টঙ্কশালা, মুদ্রাঙ্কনগৃহ, a mint.
টঙ্কা, টাকা, রৌপ্য মুদ্রা, a rupee, money.
টঙ্কার, জ্যাশব্দ, বিস্ময়, প্রসিদ্ধি, the twang of a bow-string, the sound of a stringed instrument, surprize, fame, notoriety.
টঙ্কারিয়া, আকর্ষণী, অঙ্গগ্রহ, a spasm, the cramp.
টঙ্কিত, আঁচা, estimated, appraised.

টণ্ডা, টণ্ডাই,—বিবাদ, a dispute, a quarrel.
টন্ক, কঠিন, শক্ত, hard, firm, solid.
টপ্পাগান, চুম্বক গান, a short solo sung in parts.
টলন, হেলন. নড়ন. হটন, to heel as a boat, stagger, totter, reel, to slip, slide, shrink from.
টহল, টল,—ভিক্ষার্থ গানপূর্বক পর্য্যটন, a begging from house to house with singing, as practised by some religious mendicants.
টহলন, গাইতে২ পর্য্যটন, বেড়ান, to go about with singing, to walk for pleasure. [rize.
টহলান, টালন, ছলপূর্বক কালক্ষেপণ, to put off, shuffle, tempo-
টাঁকন, যাচন, অগ্রসূচন, সিঁআন, to value, appraise, to foretel, to stitch, tack together, patch.
টাক, ইন্দ্রলুপ্ত, কেশধ্বংস, baldness, especially from disease.
টাক্‌পড়া, ইন্দ্রলুপ্ত, কেশহীন, bald, bald from disease.
টাকা, রৌপ্য মুদ্রা, a rupee, money.
টাকুর, নাটাই, a reel, a machine for twisting thread.
টাক্‌রা, তালু, the palate or roof of the mouth. [rax.
টাঙ্গ কুদ্দাল, চরণ, সোহাগা, a spade, hoe, axe, the leg, bo-
টাঙ্গন, ঝুলন, পর্বতীয় অশ্ব বিশেষ, to be suspended, hang, dangle; a Bootan or hill poney.
টাঙ্গী, কুঠার, পরশু, an axe, battle-axe, halbert, pole-axe.
টাট, পূজার পাত্র বিশেষ, চট, a flat sacrificial dish of copper, canvass, sail-cloth.
টাটি, ঝাঁপ, a fence or skreen of grass, &c.
টাটী, কটোরা, বাটী, a cup, a small basin.
টাটু, ক্ষুদ্রাশ্ব, a common country poney.
টান, আকর্ষণ, খেঁচা, নদির স্রোতঃ, অপ্রাপ্তি, দুর্মূল্য, কঠিন, a pull, strain, spasm, attraction, force, the strength of a stream, scarcity, demand for; dear, scarce, harsh, severe, hard.
টানন, আকর্ষণ, খেঁচন, লট্‌কান, দাঁড় মারণ, to pull, draw, drag, stretch, attract, to tow, hang up, row a boat.
টানা, খেঁচা, বস্ত্রের দীর্ঘসূত্র, বিলম্বিত, দূর, কুস্বর, a spasm, stitch, tension, pull, &c. the warp of cloth; pulled, drawn, long, far, harsh in sound, strained.

টাপু, দ্বীপ, an island. [pretext, pretence.
টাল, ছলদ্বারা কাল হরণ, ব্যাজ, procrastination, an excuse,
টালন, ছলদ্বারাকালহরণ, বিলম্বন, কালযাপন, to procrastinate, make excuses for delay, put off, spend time.
টিকন, বহন, থাকন, রহণ, বাঁচন, to wear well, stand, last, to weather a storm.
টিকা, গুল, কপালভূষা, বসন্তাবাহন, a ball for lighting the Hooka or for other uses, an ornament for the forehead, inoculation for the small pox.
টিকারা, ঝামসা, a kettle-drum.
টিকী, চূড়া, শিখা, a tuft of hair on the crown, a crest.
টিক্‌টিকী, গৃহগোধিকা, টৈক্তৃষ্টী, the house lizard.
টিক্‌লী, কাতলী, চাক্তী, a thin slice, a wafer, a lozenge.
টিটির, টিটারি, টিট্টিভ,—পক্ষি বিশেষ, তিত্তির, a lapwing or partridge.
টিট্‌কার, অবজ্ঞা, নিন্দা, contempt, reproach, reviling.
টিপন, টীপন,—থাম্‌চান, চাপন, to pinch, squeeze, press.
টিপনী, টিপ্পনী—টীকা, চাপা, সূক্ষ্মবৃষ্টিপাত, a note, remark, comment, commentary, a pressing, squeezing, pinching, the drizzling of rain. [nick.
টিপা, চাপাচিহ্ন, a mark impressed by the finger, notch,
টীকা, অর্থের বিবরণ, সঙ্কেত, a note, commentary, inuendo, a speck. [bill of exchange.
টীপ, চিটী, হুণ্ডী, a note of hand, bank-note, draft, bond,
টুক, টুকি, টুকরা,—খণ্ড, কুচি, লেশ, a bit, morsel, piece, shred, slice, small piece, a little, a scrap, fragment, portion.
টুকরী, ঝুড়ী, a basket. [failure, a falling below par.
টুট, ন্যূনতা, ত্রুটি, মূল্যহ্রাস, a deficiency, defect, loss, breach,
টুটন, ঘাটন, অল্পীভূত হওন, শ্রমছাড়ন, ভাঙ্গন, to be defective, fail, decrease, abate, to relax, grow remiss, slacken, break, burst, snap.
টুসুক, টুসা,—মড়কা, ঠুন্‌কা, brittle, fragile, weak.
টেঁটা, কাতা, a harpoon.
টেঁটারী, কাঁসারি, a brazier. [one side, slant.
টেঁড়ন, বেঁকন, আড়ন, ঢলন, to be awry or crooked, lean to

টেড়া, বেঁকা, আড়া, crooked, awry, oblique, distorted.
টেড়াদৃষ্টি, বক্রদৃষ্টি, আড়চক্ষু, squint-eyed, squinting, looking askaunt.
টেনা, টেনী,—চীরবস্ত্র, কাণিময়, ragged, tattered, full of holes.
টেপ, চাপা, দাবা. pressure, compression, a squeeze, bruise, a quashing or suppressing.
টের, প্রান্ত, ঈষৎ উপলব্ধি, প্রমাণ, বক্রতা, a border, verge, suspicion, certainty, evidence, crookedness.
টেরা, টেরচা,—বক্র, আড়, awry, crooked, distorted, across, diagonal. [ing, thwarting.
টোকক, কুচ্ছাবাদী, নিন্দক, censorious, reproving, contradict-
টোকর, ঘা, চোট, উচোট, a rap, knock, peck of a bird's bill, a trip, slip, fall, stumble.
টোকরা, টোকরী,—ঝুড়ী, চুপড়ী, a basket. [drop, dent.
টোপ, চার, শিরস্ত্র, বিন্দু, a fish bait, a cap, hat, helmet, a
টোপবৎ, বিম্বাকার, convex, raised.
টোপর, মুকুট, শিরস্ত্র, a crown, a hat. [zenge.
টোপান, ফোঁটাকে পড়ন, করণ, to drop, fall in drops, distil ; a lo-
টোপী, শিরাচ্ছাদন, ঢাকনা, a hat, cap, top, cover, lid.
টোবান, পাঠান, চালান, to send, order, set on (as a dog.)
টোল, চৌবাড়ী, ক্ষত, a college, school, hut, a bruize, dent, depression.
টোলা, টোলী,—পাড়া, a division of a town, ward, quarter.

ঠ.

ঠক, ঠগ,—কর্ণেজপ, খল, দুষ্ট, ছলী, a backbiter, talebearer, mischief-maker, sharper, extortioner, cheat.
ঠকন-আন, কাণেজপন, প্রবঞ্চন, to backbite, tell tales, swindle, cheat, outwit. [tortion, fraud.
ঠকামি, ঠগামী,—ভোগকরা, প্রতারণা, backbiting, talebearing, ex-
ঠক্ঠকী, দায়, ঝঞ্ঝাট, difficulty, jeopardy, a dilemma.
ঠট্টা, গঞ্জি, ব্যঙ্গ, অবক্ষেপ, a jibe, taunt, sarcasm, mockery.
ঠঠনন-আন, ঝন্ঝনকরণ, বাজন, to ring, jingle, sound when struck, as a piece of metal, &c.
ঠণ্ডা, শীতল, স্নিগ্ধ, cold, cooling, refreshing, comfortable.
ঠণ্ডী, স্নিগ্ধ, কফ, cold, cool ; a cold, catarrh.

ঠমক, আড়ম্বর, প্রাগল্ভ্য, shew, pomp, parade.

ঠাওরণ, ঠাহরণ-আন,—কল্পন, বিবেচনাকরণ, চিন্তন, স্থিরকরণ, চাহন, to design, plan, contrive, consider, reflect, ponder, suppose, determine, settle, intend, view,

ঠাঁই, স্থান, নিকট, সঙ্গে, পরিবর্ত্তে. a place, situation, post, station, space, spot, stead ; near, to, with, from, about, instead of.

ঠাকুর, প্রভু. দেবতা, গুরু, মান্য, মহাশয়, a lord, god, idol, father, grandfather, respectable person, sir, master.

ঠাকুরঘর, ঠাকুরবাড়ী,—দেবালয়, a temple, chapel, image-house.

ঠাকুরঝী, শ্বশুর কন্যা, গুরুর কন্যা, a sister-in-law, the daughter of one's guru.

ঠাকুরণ, ঠাকুরাণী,—দেবী, গুরুর মাতা, মান্যা স্ত্রী, a goddess, a wife's mother, a guru's mother, a respectable lady, madam. [a sketch.

ঠাট, ঘটা, ছলনা, a procession, throng, crowd, deceit,

ঠাট্টা, বিদ্রূপ, a jibe, jeer, jest, sneer, mockery, ridicule.

ঠাণ্ডা, শীতল, কুশলী, cold, cool, refreshing, agreeable, tranquil, happy. [trical.

ঠাম, চারু, সুন্দর, beautiful, elegant, well-formed, symme-

ঠার, ইঙ্গিত, সঙ্কেত, a wink, signal, hint, nod, inuendo.

ঠারণ, সঙ্কেতে জানান, ইঙ্গন, to hint, wink, nod, beckon, point at. [&c.

ঠাসন, গাদন, ছানন to ram down, load a gun, press, knead,

ঠাহর. চিন্তা, বিবেচনা, বিতর্ক, অনুমান, অনুভব, thought, reflection, investigation, consideration, resolution, idea, conception, supposition.

ঠিক, নিশ্চিত, প্রকৃত, শুদ্ধ, পুরা, যথার্থ, নিশ্চয়, exact, accurate, correct, complete, punctual, true, just, fit, proper, cast up as a sum, reckoned ; exactly.

ঠিকা, দিবসিকবেতনগ্রাহী, working for daily hire or by the job.

ঠিকানা, শিরনাম, বসতি, নিশ্চয়, the address of a letter, a station, residence, certainty.

ঠিলি, ঠিলিয়া,—কলসী, a water-pot.

ঠুকন, ঠোকন,—থাবড়ান, চড়ান, মারণ, to rap, smite, beat.

ঠেক, আটক, ব্যাঘাত, a hindrance, obstruction, difficulty.

ঠেকন-আন, লাগন, স্পর্শন, ঘা মারণ, আট্কান, দায়ে পড়ন, to concern, belong to, touch, knock, stop, obstruct, hinder, incur, implicate.

ঠেকনা, ঠেকুয়া,—ঠেস, অবলম্ব, a prop, stake, staunchion.

ঠেকার, অহঙ্কার, দর্প, pride, haughtiness, superciliousness.

ঠেকাল, ঝঞ্ঝাটিয়া, কঠিন, difficult, full of obstacles.

ঠেঙ, চরণ, অঙ্ঘ্রি, the leg.

ঠেঙ্গা, দণ্ড, লাঠী, a staff, bludgeon, stick.

ঠেঙ্গুয়া, চিঙ্গড়াদির পাদাদি, the legs of shrimps, crabs, insects, [&c.

ঠেলন, ঠেকান, চালান, খেদান, খণ্ডন, to push, thrust, shove, drive, urge, press upon, repel, refute.

ঠেস্, অবলম্ব, আশ্রয়, a prop, stake, support, refuge, dependance, reliance.

ঠেসন, ঝোঁকন, হেলন, ঠেলন, দুষ্টকে বিবর্জন, to lean against, lean, push, press, jog, to expel, to exclude from a society.

ঠেসান, অবলম্বন, ঠেকান, to prop, support, implicate.

ঠোঁট, চঞ্চু, ওষ্ঠ, মথনা, সেতু, কাঁধা, the bill or beak of a bird, the lips of a man, a spur, a ridge, verge.

ঠোকরাণ, ঠোঁটমারণ, ঠোকন, to peck as a bird, tap, rap.

ঠোসা, কোস্কা, কোটা, ঘুণ্টী, বটী, a blister, a drop of melted metal, a button, a bead.

ঠৌর, স্থৈর্য্য, নিশ্চয়, steadfastness, certainty.

ড.

ডগর, ঢক্কা বিশেষ, ডমরু, a drum.

ডগা, আগা, অগ্রভাগ, a peak, tip, nib, point, a grass-stalk.

ডগাল, আগাল, সূচ্যগ্রাকার, pointed, peaked, ending in a point.

ডঙ্কা, বৃহৎ ঢক্কা বিশেষ, a large drum.

ডমরু, ক্ষুদ্র ঢক্কা বিশেষ, a small drum shaped like an hour-[glass.

ডমরুমধ্য, দুই দ্বীপের মধ্যস্থ সুঁড়ী পথ, an isthmus or neck of land.

ডম্ফ, খঞ্জরী বিশেষ, a small hand drum or tabor.

ডর্, ভয়, ত্রাস, শঙ্কা, fear, terror, dread, alarm.

ডরণ, ভয়পাওন, to fear, be afraid or alarmed, be terrified.

ডরালু, ডরুক,—ভয়ান্বিত, ত্রস্ত, afraid, fearful, timid, timorous, cowardly.

ডলন, শানন, মর্দ্দন, to grind on a stone, rub, rub in unguents.
ডলনা, বেলুন, নোড়া, a roller of wood or stone, a muller.
ডলক, চঙ্গারী, a fruit basket or tray slung from a pole.
ডহর-1, সরোবর, বাওর, গভীর জল, a lake, deep water.
ডাইন, দক্ষিণ, right, (opposite to the left.)
ডাইন-নী, ডাকিনী, খুসনী, a witch. [spindle.
ডাঁটা, কাণ্ড, বৃন্ত, দণ্ড, a plant-stalk, stem, shaft, handle,
ডাঁটাল, বৃন্তাল, বহুনাড়িক, abounding in stalks.
ডাঁড়, বাটিয়া, দণ্ড, an oar, bird-perch, fine, forfeit.
ডাঁড়কাক, অতক্ষ্যভুক্, বায়স, the carrion crow. [still, stop.
ডাঁড়ন-আন, দণ্ডায়মান থাকন, রহন, to stand, stand erect, stand
ডাঁড়া. রীতি, চরিত্র, মেরুদণ্ড, খাড়া, custom, habit, conduct, course, manner, way, the backbone, the seam or edge of mats; erect, perpendicular.
ডাঁড়ী, বাহক, মাঝিক, a rower, waterman, a scale-beam.
ডাঁড়ুকা, বেড়ী, নিগড়, shackles, fetters, manacles, stocks.
ডাঁশ, দংশক মক্ষিকা, a gadfly.
ডাক, আহ্বান, হাঁক, চীৎকার, পত্রবাহক, a call, summons, cry, shout, a letter carrier, the post. [bellow.
ডাকন, হাঁকন, ফুকরণ, চেঁচান, to call, hail, summon, cry out,
ডাকা-ইৎ, ডাকু,—দস্যু, বাটপাড়, a robber, highwayman, marauder. [der, marauding.
ডাকাতী, ডাকাইতী,—বাটপাড়ী, দস্যুবৃত্তি, highway robbery, plun-
ডাকাবুকা, চেঁটা, নির্লজ্জ, নির্ভয়, সাহসী, bold, insolent, impudent, undaunted, daring, valiant.
ডাকিনী, খুসনী, ভূতিনী, a witch, a female imp.
ডাঙ্গা, উচ্চস্থান, নির্জলস্থান, upland, dry land.
ডাড়, দন্ত, নখ, থাবা, হুল, দাঁত, a tooth, claw, fang, serrature, the wards of a key.
ডাড়াল, করাতবৎ, করাতবদ্দন্তবিশিষ্ট, serrated, sawlike.
ডাণ্ডা, খেলারি দণ্ড, স্তম্ভ, a cricket bat, an upright post.
ডাণ্ডী খুঁটী, নৌকার পালদণ্ড, a post, a ship's yard.
ডাব, জলপূর্ণ নারিকেল, an unripe cocoanut and full of water.
ডাবর, হস্তাদি ক্ষালনপাত্র, a washing basin. [ter-pot.
ডাবু, ডাবরী—চিলমচী, ক্ষুদ্র কলসী, a basin, a small jar or wa-
ডাল, শাখা, a branch, bough of a tree.

ডালচীনী, দারুচীনী, cinnamon.

ডালন, ছাটন, কর্ত্তন, তুলিয়া ফেলন, to lop, trim, prune, fling, throw, throw down.

ডালা, চঙ্গারী, ঢাকনা, a basket, a lid, cover, top. [peas.

ডালি, ভেটী, a basket full of articles as a present, split

ডালিম, দাড়িম ফল, a pomegranate. [frisk.

ডিঙ্গন-আন, লম্ফন, কুঁদন, to leap or jump over a fence, to

ডিঙ্গর-1, প্রতারক, ছলী, তুচ্ছ, অধম, দুষ্ট, a rogue, cheat, mean person; mean, depraved.

ডিঙ্গা, নৌকা, পোত, a barge, a ship.

ডিঙ্গাচালক, মাঝিক, পোতবাহক, a mariner, a sailor.

ডিঙ্গী, ক্ষুদ্র নৌকা, দ্রোণী, a boat, skiff, wherry.

ডিণ্ডিম, মৃদঙ্গ বিশেষ. a kind of small drum or tabor.

ডিবা, কৌটা. a small round box, a canister.

ডিম, ডিম্ব, ডিম্ভ,—অণ্ড, ছা. an egg, the spawn of fishes, the young of an animal, a chrysalis.

ডিম্বজ, ডিম্ভজ,—অণ্ডজ, oviparous, produced from an egg.

ডুকরণ. হায়ছাড়ন, ক্রন্দন, ধক্‌ধকান, to sob, to weep, to throb.

ডুঙ্গী দ্রোণী, a canoe, a ferry. [ing, diving.

ডুব, অবগাহন, স্নানকরা, immersion, washing. ablution, bath-

ডুবন, ডোবন,—বুড়ন, মজ্জন, to sink, dive, plunge, to be immersed in any fluid.

ডুবরি, ডুবড়িয়া,—বুড়নিয়া, যে ডুবে, a diver. [water, &c.

ডুবান, বুড়ান, মগ্নকরণ, to sink, immerse, dip, plunge into

ডুবারা, ডুবারু, ডুবু,—পক্ষি বিশেষ, the diver bird.

ডুমুর, ডুম্বর,—উডুম্বরবৃক্ষ, উডুম্বর, a fig-tree, a fig.

ডুরী, রজ্জু, দড়ী, a line, fine rope, pack-thread.

ডুলী. শিবিকা, পাল্‌কী, a covered litter or common palkee.

ডেগ, বাটুলাই, পাকপাত্র. a caldron, a pot.

ডেঙ্গর. উকুণ, a louse.

ডেঙ্গুরা, মৃতদার, বেটুয়া, শাক বিশেষ, a widower, a sort of potherb.

ডেড়-1, সার্দ্ধ এক, one and a half.

ডেড়ী, দরিদ্রতা, অস্বাস্থ্য, want, poverty, need, sickness.

ডেনা, পক্ষ, পাখা, a wing, a pinion.

ডেলা, লোষ্ট্র, a clod, a lump of earth.

ডোঙ্গা, ডোঙ্গী,—দ্রোণী, a canoe, a skiff, a sort of basket.

ডোবা, গর্ত্ত পুষ্করিণী, জলা, a hole, pond, place overflowed.
ডোম, বেত্যাদিনির্ম্মায়ক, মুচী, a wicker or basket-maker.
ডোর-ক, দড়ী, রজ্জু, a line, string, rope, cord, fishing-line.
ডোরা, রেখা, a streak, a stripe.
ডোরী, দড়ী, রজ্জু, রসী, a rope, string, line, halter.
ডোল, ভাণ্ডার, গোলা, a storehouse, a granary, a mast.
ডোলী, শিবিকা, a litter, a palkee.
ডৌল, প্রকার, রূপ, ধারা, ঢপ, form, figure, shape, aspect. structure, fashion, kind, manner, plan, method, attitude, mien, gait.

ঢ.

ঢক, বাট্‌খারা, বস্তু, a weight, a thing.
ঢক্কা, ঢাক,—বৃহৎ ঢোল, কাড়া, a large kind of drum, a double drum.
ঢগ, খল, শঠ, প্রতারক, a deceiver, impostor, swindler.
ঢসা, ম্লান, শুষ্ক, blasted, faded, withered, dried up.
ঢপ্, মূর্ত্তি, ধারা, প্রকার, চালি, form, shape, appearance, structure, kind, manner, method, design, attitude, gait, mien.
ঢল্, ডাঙ্গাভূমি হইতে নদ্যাগত ঘোলাজল, the red or turbid waters of the up countries flowing down into the rivers of Bengal.
ঢলন, ঠেসন হেলন, গড়ান, to lean, incline, decline, slope, slant.
ঢলনাবা, পর্ব্বতীয়জলাগমন, the descent of up country waters; tinged therewith, turbid.
ঢলান, ফোচ্কামি প্রকাশন, to be lewd, to outrage decency, to proclaim one's own or another's shame or disgrace, &c.
ঢলানী, লম্পটী, কুলটা, *f.* publishing her own disgrace by her lewdness.
ঢহ, আল্‌গা, ঢিলা, ঢিলামি, loose, not pulled tight; slackness, looseness.
ঢলকন,-আন, অস্তগমন, হেলন, ঝোঁকন, ঘূরণ, গলন, নাশন, ভাঙ্গন, to decline as a luminary from the meridian, to lean to one side, to revolve, pass away, crumble, demolish, remove, level.
ঢলঢলিয়া, দীপ্যমান, দ্রুত, brilliant, sparkling, waving, fluid.

ঢসন, গলন, ভাঙ্গন, ভাঙ্গিয়া যাওন, to wear away as a bank, crumble, break off, fall in.

ঢাকন, আচ্ছাদন, ব্যাপন, আবরণ, to cover, veil, hide, conceal, overspread, overwhelm, screen, shut, seclude, smother, swarm.

ঢাকনা, ঢাকনী,—আচ্ছাদন, a cover, covering, lid, veil.

ঢাকাযোড়া, আড়াল, আবৃত, a skreen, fence, shade: fenced, &c.

ঢাকী, ঢক্কাবাজনিয়া, one who plays or beats a large drum, a drummer.

ঢাকুনী, আবরণ, আড়াল, a skreen, a fence.

ঢাণ্ডা, লোক সমূহ, a concourse of people.

ঢাল, যোদ্ধার ফলক, ছক, হেলা, গড়ান, a shield, chess-checkers, a slope, slant, obliquity; aslant, aslope, inclined, oblique. [throw or cast down.

ঢালন, ফেলিয়া দেওন, অধঃক্ষেপণ, to pour out, spill, empty,

ঢালী, চর্ম্মধারী, wearing or using a shield; a shield-bearer.

ঢিপন, কিলান, to smite with the fist, pummel, thump.

ঢিপী, ঢিবী,—রাশি, সঞ্চয়, a heap, quantity, accumulation.

ঢিল্, লোষ্ট্র, শিথিলতা, a clod, lump of earth, procrastination.

ঢিলা, ঢীলা,—শিথিল, দীর্ঘসূত্রী, আলগা, অদৃঢ়, dilatory, lazy, negligent, indolent, slow, loose, lax, slack, flaccid, relaxed.

ঢিলান, ঢিল আদি মারণ, লোষ্ট্র ক্ষেপণ, to pelt, throw clods, &c.

ঢুকন, ঘুষড়ন, প্রবেশন, পড়িয়া লুটন, to enter, pervade, rush in, make inroads into.

ঢুকান, ঘুষড়ান, গুড়ান, to thrust or force in, tuck, stab, resist.

ঢুণ্ডুভ, ঢোঁড়া সাপ, a sort of water snake.

ঢুলন, ঝিমন, to nod with sleep, be drowsy, nap.

ঢুলান, নড়ান, কম্পান, to shake, jog, agitate. [head.

ঢুষ, ছাগমেষের মস্তকাঘাত, a butt, butting, push with the

ঢুষণ, মস্তক দিয়া ঠেলন, to butt or push with the head as a ram. [but unwilling.

ঢুষণা, ঢুষণী,— আলস্য, অকর্ম্মঠ, dronish, lazy, able to work

ঢেউ, তরঙ্গ, অকস্মাদ্বাসনা, a wave, surge, billow, whim, caprice.

ঢেঁকী, তণ্ডুলাদি করণের যন্ত্র, the pedal for cleaning rice, &c.

ঢেঁটা, অশিষ্ট, দুষ্ট, অবাধ্য, অবশীভূত, insolent, saucy, impudent, stubborn.

ঢেকান ঠেসন, ঠেলন, to shove, to push.

ঢেকুর, উদ্গার, a belch, belching, a rising in the stomach.

ঢেঙ্গা, লম্ব, দীর্ঘ. tall, long.

ঢেমন, জারজ, দুষ্ট, illegitimate, bastard, depraved.

ঢেমনা, জার, উপপতি, a lover, gallant, paramour.

ঢেমনী, উপপত্নী, উপস্ত্রী, মাগ্নী, a concubine, a mistress.

ঢের. যথেষ্ট, বিস্তর, অনেক, much, many, abundant.

ঢেরা, নাটাই, সূত্র কাটনের যন্ত্র, a reel, an instrument for spinning thread, a cross mark. [quantity.

ঢেরি, ঢেরী,—রাশি, সঞ্চয়, a heap, pile, stack, collection,

ঢেঁশা, দোষসূচক দৃষ্টান্ত, an invidious, or injurious comparison, an accusation by comparison.

ঢোওন, ভার বহন, to carry a burden, to drive a carriage.

ঢোঁড়ন, অন্বেষণ, খুঁজন, to search or rummage for, seek after.

ঢোঁড়া, ঢুণ্ডুভ, জলসাপ বিশেষ, a species of water snake.

ঢোক, জলগিলন, গলাধঃকরণ, a gulp, draught of water, &c.

ঢোকন,-আন, প্রবেশন, ঢুকান, অবলম্বন, ঠেসিয়া রাখন, to enter, thrust one's self in, force or push in, to support, prop up, apply a stay. [ing, &c.

ঢোল, ঢক্কা বিশেষ, ঝিমনি, a sort of drum; a nodding, swing-

ঢোলন, ঝিমন, ঝুলন, to nod, be drowsy, swing, oscillate.

ঢোলান, ঝুলান, হেলান, to make to swing, transport or carry goods on cattle &c, to level uneven ground.

ত.

তক্, পর্য্যন্ত, অবধি, অম্ল, খাট্টা, to, unto, till, until, from; acid, sour.

তক্র, ঘোল, buttermilk with a fourth part water.

তক্ষক, সূত্রধর, প্রধান সর্প বিশেষ, a carpenter, a fabulous serpent, one of the principal Nágas of Pátála.

তক্ষণ, চাঁচা, a paring, peeling, scraping.

তখন, তখনি,—সেইক্ষণে, then, even then, at that instant.

তঙ্কা, টাকা, রূপী, ধন, a coin, a rupee, cash, treasure.

তক্কী, তত্ত্ব, অনুসন্ধান, investigation, enquiry, search.

তদুপশমকরণ, থামান, শান্তকরণ, to tranquillize, to mollify. [that.
তজ্জ, তদুদ্ভব, তাহা হইতে জাত, a rising from or produced by
তঞ্চ, গণতা, প্রবঞ্চনা, collusion, swindling, imposition.
তঞ্চক, প্রবঞ্চক, ছলনিয়া, a deceiver, swindler, imposter; deceiving, &c. [coast, strand.
তট, তড়,—কূল, নদীতীর, a shore, bank, verge, edge,
তটস্থ, তীরস্থ, অপক্ষপাতী, অগণাক্রান্ত, on the bank, ashore; impartial, indifferent to friend or foe.
তটাক, তড়াক, তড়াগ,—বৃহৎ জলাশয়, a pond or basin deep enough for the lotus to grow in.
তড়পন, আস্ফালন, উল্লম্ফন, to flounce as a fish, jump, ramp.
তড়া, তট, কূল, তীর, a shore, coast, sea-coast.
তড়িৎ, বিদ্যুৎ, lightning.
তণ্ডুল, চালু, husked rice, cleansed rice but undressed.
তৎ, তদ,—সেই, তিনি, তাহা, *in compos*: it, he, that.
তত, এতাবৎ, so much, so many. [wards, then.
ততঃ, হইতে, অনন্তর, পরে, than, from or after that, after-
ততদিন, এতাবৎ দিবস, সেইপর্য্যন্ত, so long, just so long, so many days, till then.
তৎকরণক, তাহাতে, তাহাদ্বারা, thereby, by him or her.
তৎকর্ত্তৃক, তিনিই কর্ত্তা, done by his or her agency.
তৎকালে, সেই সময়ে, then, at that time.
তৎকৃত, তাহাহইতে রচিত ইত্যাদি, done by him, her, it or that.
তৎক্ষণ, তৎক্ষণে,—তখনি, সেই কালে, then, at that instant.
তৎক্ষণাৎ, সেইঅবধি, সেইক্ষণে, অবিলম্বে, from that instant, thenceforth, forthwith, immediately.
তত্ত্ব, আদিকারণ, মূলব্যবস্থা, সূক্ষবোধ, ভাব, ধর্ম্ম, স্বরূপতা, ব্রহ্মভাব, যথার্থ, ভেদ, অনুসন্ধান, উদ্দেশ, অন্বেষণ, a first principle, axiom, accurate idea, real or essential nature, reality, identity of the soul with God, truth, mystery, search, enquiry, object of search, investigation, scrutiny.
তত্ত্বকারক, পণ্ডিত, যথার্থ বিতর্কক, a philosopher, investigator of the essential nature or truth of things.
তত্ত্বজ্ঞান, ব্রহ্মজ্ঞান, অধ্যাত্মবিদ্যা, a knowledge of divine truth or of the identity of the soul with God.

তত্ত্ববাদী, যথার্থবক্তা, speaking correctly or philosophically.
তত্ত্ববার্ত্তা, অনুসন্ধান, বিতর্ক, enquiry, search, scrutiny.
তত্ত্বাবধারণ, রক্ষণাবেক্ষণ, অধ্যক্ষতা, মনোনিবেশ, superintendance, inspection, care, attention.
তৎপর, নিপুণ, দক্ষ, প্রয়াসী, শ্রমী, আসক্ত, expert, active, clever, prompt, diligent, sedulous, devoted to.
তৎপ্রকারক, সেইপ্রকার, তদ্রূপ, of that sort or kind.
তত্র, তাহাতে, সেখানে, there, therein, in that place.
তত্রাপি, অন্যথাসূচক শব্দ, still, yet, nevertheless, notwithstanding, even there.
তথা, সেই প্রকার, thus, so, likewise, then, also, and, ditto.
তথাচ, তথাপি,—তত্রাপি, notwithstanding, nevertheless, yet, still, even.
তথায়, সেই স্থানে, সেখানে, there, in that place.
তথাস্তু, এমনি হউক, তাহা হউক, so be it, Amen.
তথ্য, নিশ্চয়, প্রকৃতত্ত্ব, সত্য, নিশ্চিত, certainty, accuracy, reality, truth; really, indeed; sure, certain.
তদনন্তর, তাহার পর, পরে, afterwards, after that, then, next.
তদন্ত, অভিপ্রায়, উদ্দেশ, বিষয়, a scope, an object.
তদন্তর, তভিন্ন, তাহা ব্যতিরেক, besides that, besides.
তদবধি, সেই অবধি, সেই পর্য্যন্ত, so far, thence, till then, from or to that.
তদবস্থ, সেইপ্রকার দশাপন্ন, thus situated, under such circumstances.
তদা, তদানী, তদানীং,—সেই কালে, then, at that time.
তদুপরি, তাহাতে, তাহার উপরে, thereupon, upon that, him or her.
তদেব, অনন্য, সেই, the very same thing, identical, the same, the self-same.
তদ্বৎ, সেইরূপ, তৎসদৃশ, like or resembling that, similar, so.
তদ্রূপ, সেইরূপ, সেইপ্রকার, of that form, such, of that kind.
তধী, সেইক্ষণে, তৎক্ষণাৎ, precisely then, at that very time.
তনয়, তনয়া,—পুত্রপুত্রী, সন্তান, *m. f.* a son or daughter, a child, offspring.
তনিষ্ঠ, ক্ষীণ, অতিসূক্ষ্ম, very thin, very small, very narrow.
তনু, তনূ,—শরীর, চর্ম্ম, অল্প, সূক্ষ্ম, সরু, ক্ষীণ, the body, the skin; small, minute, fine, delicate, slender, thin, emaciated.

তনুকূপ, লোমকূপ, the pores of the skin.
তনুজ, শরীরজাত, পুত্র, produced from the body; a son.
তনুরুহ, লোম, পালখ, the hair of the body, feathers of a bird.
তন্তু, রজ্জু, সূত্র, a thread, string, line, the threads of a warp.
তন্তুবায়, তন্ত্রবায়,—মাকড়সা, তাঁতী, a spider, a weaver. [ciated.
তন্তুসার, গুবাক, কৃশলোক, the betel tree, a person much ema-
তন্ত্র, সূত্র, রজ্জু, তাঁত, শিবোক্ত গ্রন্থ, চিকিৎসকেরদের মন্ত্র, অধীন, পরিচ্ছদাদি, a thread, string, line, thong, the threads of a warp, strings of an instrument, a weaver's loom, a class of sacred books, a class of the Vedas treating of charms, &c. a medicinal charm; dependent, subservient.
তন্ত্রতা, ছলনা, গণ্ডা, অনেক ক্রিয়ার একত্র অনুষ্ঠান, contrivance, collusion, intrigue, a commutation of many observances for one.
তন্ত্রী, বাদ্যকর, তন্ত্রশাস্ত্রবেত্তা, বীণাদি, a musician, a stringed instrument, a Tantrist or follower of the Tantras.
তন্দ্রা, তন্দ্রী,—ঈষৎ নিদ্রা, আলস্য, গ্লানি, drowsiness, sluggishness, lassitude, exhaustion, weariness. [ful.
তন্দ্রালু, ক্লান্ত, নিদ্রাতুর, আলসিয়া, weary, sleepy, drowsy, sloth-
তন্ন, তাহা নয়, not that, not so, (*expr:* denial). [nial.)
তন্নতন্ন, তাহানয় তাহানয়, not so, (a strong and repeated de-
তন্মধ্যে, ইতোমধ্যে, during that, in the mean time, therein.
তন্মাত্র, পদার্থের আদর্শ, তাহাই কেবল, the archetypes of realities; merely that, that only.
তন্বী, ক্ষীণা, সুন্দরী, a slender or delicately formed woman.
তপ, গ্রীষ্ম, গুমটকাল, heat, warmth, the hot season, summer.
তপন, সূর্য্য, গ্রীষ্ম, দাহ, নরক বিশেষ, the sun, heat, the hot season, inflammation, burning, a hindoo hell.
তপনীয়, উত্তাপনীয়, স্বর্ণ, requiring to be heated; gold.
তপস্, তপঃ,—উপবাসাদি, চান্দ্রায়ণাদি ব্রত, পুণ্য, ধর্ম্ম, গুমটকাল, শিশিরকাল, স্বর্গ বিশেষ, penance, mortification or self-denial, religious austerities, virtue, religious merit, a special observance or particular duty, the hot season, the dewy season, the heaven of devotees.

তপস্যা, পুণ্যোদ্দেশে ক্লেশজনক কর্ম্ম, ফাল্গুন মাস, devout austerity, religious penance, the month Phálguna.

তপস্যাগত, তপস্যান্বিত—কৃচ্ছ্রগত, engaged in religious austerities.

তপস্যামৎস্য, তপস্যা মাছ, the mangoe-fish.

তপস্বী, তপস্যাকর্ত্তা, উদাসীন, সন্ন্যাসী, practising austerities ; a devotee, an ascetic, a religious mendicant.

তপাস্, তল্লাস্,—অনুসন্ধান, মৃগয়া, search, research, enquiry, the chase. [burned, pained, grieved.

তপ্ত, উষ্ণ, তাপিত, খেদান্বিত, heated, hot, warm, inflamed,

তব, তোমার, thy, thine, (Sanscrit). [standing.

তবু, তবু—তবে ও, তথাপি, then, even then, yet, notwith-

তবে, সেইক্ষণে, তদা, পরে, then, at that time, next, afterwards.

তমঃ, তমস্,—অন্ধকার, মোহাদি, মায়া, অহঙ্কার, শোক, রাহু, darkness, gloom, folly, ignorance, mental blindness, worldly delusion, pride, sorrow grief, Ráhu or the ascending node.

তমস্বিনী, রাত্রি, night.

তমা, অন্ধকার, ঘোর, darkness, obscurity.

তমাক, তমাকু,—তাম্রকূট, ধূমপানযোগ্য পত্র বিশেষ, tobacco.

তমাল, তিলক, the sectarial mark on the forehead.

তমোগুণ, মোহ ক্রোধাদির কারণ গুণ, one of the three primeval qualities of matter, darkness, inertness, ignorance. delusion. &c.

তমোগুণী, অহঙ্কারান্বিত, দর্পী, proud, haughty, supercilious.

তমোপহ, অন্ধকারঘ্ন, সূর্য্যচন্দ্র, removing darkness; the sun, moon.

তমোহর, চন্দ্র, the moon.

তম্বু, বস্ত্রগৃহ, a tent. [gourd for the shell.

তম্বুর, ত্রিসূত্রযুক্ত বীণা, a lute with three strings and having a

তরঙ্গ, ঢেউ, অকস্মাদ্বাসনা, a wave, billow, whim, caprice.

তরঙ্গিণী, নদী, a river. [son of the Charak.

তরজা, চরককালীন শিবগান, responsive songs sang at the sea-

তরণ, পার হওন, ভাসন, বাঁচন, উদ্ধার পাওন, to cross a river, pass over, to float, swim. get over a difficulty, overcome. surmount.

তরণি, তরণী,—ভেলা, নৌকা, সূর্য্য, ঘৃতকুমারী বৃক্ষ, a float, raft, boat, ferry, the sun, the succotrine aloes.

তরবার, তরবারি,—অসি, খড়্গ, a sword, scymitar, hanger.

তরল, তরলিত,—কম্পমান, চঞ্চল, অগাঢ়, তরল, দীপ্র, লম্পট, trembling, tremulous, light, wavering, fickle, liquid, fluid, thin, diluted, watery, luminous, sparkling, wanton. [row.

তরশ্ব, উত্তরশ্ব, the day before yesterday, day after tomor-

তরস্, বেগ, শীঘ্রগতি, বল, speed, velocity, strength.

তরস্বী. বেগযুক্ত, বলবান, সমর্থ, সাহসী, ধাবক, বাতাস, quick, swift, strong, valiant; a courier or express, a runner, the wind.

তরাণ, উদ্ধরণ, বাঁচান, পার করণ, to save, to help over a difficulty or out of trouble, to ferry over.

তরাস, ছত্র বিশেষ, a kind of umbrella.

তরি, তরী,—নৌকা, a boat.

তরু, বৃক্ষ, a tree, a plant.

তরুণ, নবীন, নূতন, যুবা, young, juvenile, fresh, new, novel; a young man. [trine aloe.

তরুণী. যুবতী, *f.* young, &c; a young woman, the succo-

তরে, জন্যে, নিমিত্তে, for, because of, on account of.

তরকারী, ব্যঞ্জনের যোগ্য কন্দাদি দ্রব্য, garden stuff, greens, vegetables used in stews, &c.

তর্ক, বুদ্ধিদ্বারা বিবেচনা, ন্যায় শাস্ত্র, নিষ্পত্তি, reasoning, discussion, investigation, examination of an opinion, logic, decision of a question. [on.

তর্কশাস্ত্র, ন্যায়শাস্ত্র, logic, science of reasoning, a book there-

তর্কিত, বিবেচিত, আলোচিত, শঙ্কিত, investigated, examined, discussed, surveyed, in doubt, alarmed, afraid. [with logic, &c.

তর্কী, ন্যায়ক, নৈয়ায়িক, a logician, disputant; acquainted

তর্জন, তাড়ন. ঝকড়ন, গর্জ্জন, to threaten, reprimand, scold, brawl, storm. [or threat.)

তর্জ্জনী, অঙ্গুষ্ঠের সমীপাঙ্গুলি, the forefinger, (as held up in scorn

তর্তরিয়া, চঞ্চল. অস্থির, অধীর, fickle, unstable, impatient.

তর্পণ, তোষণ, জলাঞ্জলি, to please, gratify, satisfy; an offering of water to the manes of the deceased.

তর্সা, ফাক, দূরে, অন্তরে, a chasm, void space; at a distance.

তল, গাম্ভীর্য্য, নীচত্ব, গর্ত্ত, নীচা, মূল, গোড়, আধান, থাপড়া, সেই, অনন্য, depth, lowness, a pit, hole, chasm, a floor, bottom, foundation, base, stand, support, the extended palm or flat hand, *in comp.* the very, itself.

তল-৭, অধোভাগ, the bottom or underpart, the lower part.

তলবার, তলোয়ার,—খড়্গ, অসি, a sword, a scymitar.

তলাতল, নরক বিশেষ, one of the seven divisions of hell.

তলান, ডুবন, বুড়ন, to sink or dive to the bottom.

তলাব, তল.—পুষ্করিণী, সরোবর, গর্ত্ত, খাত, a pond, reservoir, large tank, a pit, a hole.

তলাবাধা, গোড়াবাঁধন, গাছের পাকামূল, the earthing up of plants or trees, a raised seat round the roots of trees, a pavement. [bottom.

তলী, অধঃস্থ, below, lying beneath, under or at the

তলুবা, বড় হাঁড়ি, a large earthen pot.

তলে, অধস্তে, নীচে, বশে, beneath, under, subject to, under the power of.

তল্প, শয্যা, উপরিগৃহ, a bed, a tower, turret or upper room.

তল্পী, মোট, গাঁঠরি, a bundle, a package.

তল্পোষ, তল্‌শুষি,—উনুই, জলাকর, a fountain, a spring.

তলস্পর্শ, আমূলাগত, অগভীর, fathomable, touching the bottom.

তসলা, হুড়কা, বহুগুণা, a bar or bolt for a door, a sort of vessel.

তষ্টি, ঢেঁটামি, কঠিনতা, obstinacy, positiveness, unyieldingness, stiffness. [ing.

তষ্টিয়া, ঢেঁটা, কঠিন, মিষ্ট, obstinate, stiff, positive, unyield-

তসিল, ঢেঁকী আদির গোঁজ, a pivot, fulcrum, horizontal bar.

তস্কর, চোর, অপহর্ত্তা, a thief, a robber.

তস্করী, চৌর্য্য, অপহার, theft, robbery. [paper.

তা, ডিম্বকইতে ছা তোলা, the hatching of eggs, a sheet of

তাই, করতালী, সেই, a clapping of hands; even that, that very. [a sheet of paper.

তাও, কোপ, কাপড়ের ভাঁজ, anger, wrath, a fold of cloth,

তাওন-য়ান, উত্তাপন, সেকন, কোপান, to heat metals, &c. to make warm, bake, provoke. [bellows.

তাওয়া, বহুগুণা, ভস্ত্রা, ঝাঁতা, a copper or brass pot, pair of

তাঁত, বস্ত্রবুননের কল, বীণাদির তন্ত্র, a weaver's loom, a musical string.

তাঁতী, তন্তুবায়, বস্ত্রবুননিয়া, a weaver.

তাঁবা, তাম্র, তাম্রবর্ণ, রক্তবর্ণ, copper; copper-coloured, red.

তাক, তাগ,—দৃষ্টিপাত, আলোকনা, সন্ধান, a look, view, survey, aim, dextrous aim.

তাকন, তাগন-আন,—আলোচন, দর্শন, সন্ধানকরণ, to look, view, behold, survey, regard, aim at. [cord.

তাগা, মাদুলী, a charm or bandage on the arm, a bit of

তাচ্ছল্য, অবজ্ঞা, অশ্রদ্ধা, disregard, contempt, neglect.

তাজগী, নবীনতা, সরস ভাব, freshness, greenness, juiciness.

তাজা, টাট্‌কা, সদ্যোজাত, রসাল, চালাক, জীবৎ, fresh, juicy, green, active, alive.

তাজী, ক্ষুদ্র অশ্ব বিশেষ, a peculiar breed of horses.

তাড়, মুঠা, আটি, হস্তালঙ্কার, মারা, a handful of grass or corn, a sheaf, an ornament for the small of the arm, a beating, striking, threatening &c.

তাড়ঙ্ক, কর্ণালঙ্কার বিশেষ, an ornament for the ear.

তাড়ন, মারণ, ধমকান, খেদান, to beat, whip, threaten, reprove, reprimand, repel, expel, drive or chase away with blows or threats. [tumour.

তাড়স, স্ফোটকের বেদনা, জ্বালা, the virulence or pain of a

তাড়স্য, জ্বলনী, পীড়াদায়ক, virulent, sore, painful. [balcony.

তাড়া, নিগ্রহ, হুড়কা, a reprimand &c. the bar of a door, a

তাড়ান, খেদান, ধমকান, চিয়ান, to drive cattle, to threaten &c, to spring game.

তাণ্ডব, নৃত্য, a dancing with violent gesticulation. [warm.

তাত, পিতা, উষ্মা, আর্য্য, উষ্ণ, a father, heat; venerable, hot,

তাতরসী, ইক্ষুরস, খর্জ্জুরাদির রস, the juice of the sugar-cane or other saccharine juice, a sort of treacle.

তাতান, উত্তাপন, to warm, heat, make hot.

তাতালিয়া, রাগাল, খিট্‌খিটিয়া, লোমশ, choleric, cross, peevish, captious, shaggy. [time.

তাৎকালিক, তাৎকালীন,—সেইকালীন, of or belonging to that

তাৎপর্য্য, অভিপ্রায়, অর্থ, a scope, object, design, intent, purpose, meaning, moral.

তাদর্থ্য, সমানাভিপ্রায়, মনোনিবেশ, identity of object, acquisition of a habit, the fixing of a thing in the mind.
তাদাত্ম্য, তৎস্বরূপতা, identity.
তাদৃক্, তাদৃশ্,—সেইপ্রকার, তদ্রূপ, such, like, similar, same.
তান, রাগ, স্বর, a tune, a key-note.
তানা, টানাসূত্র, বুনাটের তন্ত্র, the threads of the warp in cloth.
তান্ত্রিক, তন্ত্রশাস্ত্রবেত্তা, সপণ্ডিত, তন্ত্রোক্ত, a Tantrist, a scholar, or one well versed in science generally; mentioned in the Tantras.
তাপ, উষ্ণতা, জ্বালা, মনঃপীড়া, burning heat, fever, warmth, pain, smart, distress, woe, affliction, grief.
তাপন, তপ্ত হওন, তাতান, জ্বলান, শোকযুক্ত হওন, পীড়ন, ক্লেশন, সূর্য্য, to heat or be hot, to burn, scald, warm, to grieve, fret, suffer or cause pain, affliction, anguish or distress, to persecute; the sun.
তাপস, তপস্বী, যোগী, performing religious austerities; an ascetic, a devotee.
তাপান, তাবান,—জ্বলান, পীড়ন, খেদান, কোপান, to heat, inflame, scald, give pain, afflict, distress, provoke, cause to heat,.
তাবকীন, তোমার, thv, thine. [so far, so long, until, till then.
তাবৎ, সমুদায়, এইপর্য্যন্ত, সেইঅবধি, all, so much, so many.
তামলী, কড়িয়া জাতি, the cast of retail shopkeepers.
তামস, তামসিক,—তমোগুণযুক্ত, মূঢ়, জড়, দুষ্ট, affected by or pertaining to the quality of inertness, mental darkness, vice, &c.; stupid, ignorant, inert, vicious, &c.
তামসী, রাত্রি, মূঢ়তা, night, dullness, stupidity.
তামাক, তামাকু, তাম্রকূট,—ধূমপানযোগ্য গাছ বিশেষ, tobacco.
তাম্বু, বস্ত্রগৃহ, a tent.
তাম্বুল, পর্ণ, পাণ, গুবাক, the betel leaf, the areca nut.
তাম্র, তামা,—ধাতু দ্রব্য বিশেষ, copper.
তাম্রকার, কাঁসারি, কাংস্যকার, a copper-smith, a brazier.
তাম্রচূড়, কুকুড়া, a cock, *i. e.* the copper-crested.
তার, উচ্চস্বর, বীণাদির তন্ত্র, স্বর্ণের গুণা, সুরস, a high note or tone, a musical string, wire, gold thread, sa-

vour, good taste; high (as a note), good, well-flavoured.

তারক, ত্রাণকর্ত্তা, কর্ণধার, নক্ষত্র, চক্ষুর পুত্তলিকা, প্রণব, a saviour, deliverer, &c. a pilot, helmsman, a star, the pupil of the eye, the mystical Om.

তারকষ, গুণা নির্ম্মায়ক, a wire-drawer.

তারণ, পার হওন, উদ্ধরণ, ভেলা, নৌকা, to cross over a river, save, deliver, protect, preserve, get over a difficulty; a float, raft, boat.

তারতম্য, ন্যূনাধিক্য, অনুক্রম, the state or condition of more or less, greater or less degree of a thing, difference of progress, &c. proportion, an increasing series.

তারল্য, অগাঢ়তা, চাঞ্চল্য, অস্থিরতা, fluidity, unsteadiness, fickleness, tergiversation.

তারা, নক্ষত্র, নেত্রের মণি, উচ্চৈঃস্বর, দুর্গা, a star, planet, pupil (of the eye,) an octave, alto in music, Durgá.

তারাপতি, চন্দ্র, the moon as sovereign of the night.

তারামণ্ডল, নেত্রের মণি, আকাশ, নক্ষত্রের চক্র, the iris or pupil, the starry region, a stellar orb.

তারিণী, উদ্ধারকর্ত্রী, দুর্গা, a female deliverer, Durgá.

তারী, তারময়, স্বর্ণগুণাময়, made of wire, made of gold thread.

তারুণ্য, যুবত্ব, যৌবনাবস্থা, youth, youthfulness.

তার্কিক, নৈয়ায়িক, a lawyer, logician, sophist, a philosopher of the Nyáya school. [snake.

তার্ক্ষ্য, গরুড়, অরুণ, সর্প, Garura, Aruna or the dawn, a

তাল, গানের পরিমাণ, করদ্বয়ের শব্দ, গোকর্ণ, বিস্তৃতহস্ত, মন্দিরা, বিস্তার, গুটী, ঢেলা, পীত, তৃণরাজ, তাল গাছের রস, musical time or measure, the beating of time, a clapping of hands together or against the arms, a short span, the open palm, a sort of cymbal, prolixity, a ball of thread, a clue, a clod, yellow orpiment, the palmyra, toddy or palm juice. [ment.

তালক, হুড়কা, পীত, a bolt, latch, lock, lath, yellow orpi-

তালবৃন্ত, তালপত্রনির্ম্মিত ব্যজন, a fan formed of a palm leaf.

তালব্য, তালুসংযোগে উচ্চারিত, palatine, uttered from the palate.
তালা, দ্বারাদিবন্ধনকল, অট্টালিকার থাক্, মৌন, a lock, padlock, a story in a building, silence.
তালাস্ত, গানের ছেদ, a rest in music, the close of a strain.
তালী, করদ্বয়ের শব্দ করা, পরতল, পর্বতীয় তৃণরাজ, a clapping of hands, a stunning. a patch, a mending, the mountain Palm.
তালু-কা, টাকরা, the palate or roof of the mouth.
তালুয়া, করতল, পদতল, টাকরা, ব্রহ্মতালু, the palm of the hand, or sole of the foot, the roof of the mouth, the crown of the head. [card.
তাস, স্বর্ণের গুণা, খেলার্থ চিত্রিত পত্র, gold thread, a playing
তাসন, মার্জ্জন, ঝাড়ন, to brush, dust, wipe off dust.
তিউড়ী, আখা, উনান, a furnace, a small cooking place.
তিক্ত, তিত,—কটু, তীব্ররস, bitter, fragrant; bitterness, fragrance.
তিগ্ম, তিগ্ম,—উষ্ণ, কটু, সুধার, আগাল, ঝালরস, hot, pungent, acrid, sharp, keen, pointed; heat (of spices,) pungency. [provoke.
তিতন-আন, ভিজান, চিড়ান, to wet, moisten, damp, to annoy,
তিতিক্ষা, সহিষ্ণুতা, ধৈর্য্য, ক্ষমা, ক্ষান্তি, patience, resignation, patient sufferance, forbearance.
তিতিক্ষু, সহিষ্ণু, ক্ষমাশীল, patient, resigned, forbearing. [Muni.
তিত্তিরি, টিটিরপক্ষী, যজুর্বেদ; a partridge, the Yajur Veda, a
তিথি, প্রতিপৎ অমাবস্যাদি, a lunar day. [an acid seasoning.
তিন্তিড়ী, তিন্তুড়ী,—তেঁতুল, অম্লরস, the tamarind tree or it's fruit,
তিন্দু-ক, গাববৃক্ষ, a sort of ebony producing a calking resin.
তিমি, বৃহন্মৎস্য বিশেষ, a fabulous fish of enormous size.
তিমির, অন্ধকার, অন্ধতা, darkness, obscurity, blindness or gutta serena.
তিমিত, ভিজা, আর্দ্র, ক্লিন্ন, wet, moist, damp.
তিয়র, কৈবর্ত্ত, a class of Hindoos mostly fishermen.
তিরস্কার, তিরস্ক্রিয়া,—নিন্দা, অপমান, অনাদর, abuse, reproach, insult, disrespect, contempt.
তিরোহিত, লুক্কায়িত, গুপ্ত, অন্তর্হিত, আচ্ছাদিত, hidden, concealed, removed from sight, covered.

তিরোধান, গোপন, লুকান, আচ্ছাদন, ঢাকনী, ব্যবধান, খাপ, concealment, disappearance, hiding, a cover, veil, cloak, sheath. [a brute animal.

তির্য্যক, বক্রগামী, প্রাণী, পশু, moving crookedly, going awry ;

তিল, শস্য বিশেষ, আঁচিল, অত্যল্প, কণ, নিমিষ, sesamum seed and its oil, a mole or freckle, a small quantity, a moment.

তিলক, ফোটা, জড়ুল, আঁচিল, তিলেপড়া, শ্রেষ্ঠ, প্রধান, a sectarial mark, a freckle, mole, a disease of the skin; spotted, freckled, chief, pre-eminent.

তিলকাল, অত্যল্পকাল, নিমিষ, a short time, a moment.

তিলি, তৈলকর, কলু, an oilman.

তিলিয়া, তিলযুক্ত, তিলেপড়া, dotted, spotted, speckled, freckled.

তিলেতাল, চলাবুলা, বহুশ্রমে, much ado about any thing; with much fuss. [with milk.

তিলৌদন, তিলদুগ্ধযুক্তান্ন, a mixed dish of rice and sesamum

তিষ্ঠন, থাকন, রহন, টেঁকন, থামন, বাসকরণ, বসন, to stay, stop, continue, to last, endure, tarry, wait, forbear, stand, to live or dwell in a place.

তিষ্ঠা, স্থায়িত্ব, স্থিরতা, permanence, stability, &c.

তীক্ষ্ণ, উষ্ণ, উগ্র, সূক্ষ্মধার, প্রজ্ঞ, নিপুণ, ব্যগ্র, আত্মহা, যোগী, উগ্রতেজ, রাগ, ত্বরা, hot, pungent, sharp, keen-edged, intelligent, acute, active, zealous, committing suicide, self-devoted ; an ascetic, a devotee, heat, pungency &c. passion, haste, hurry.

তীক্ষ্ণকর্ম্মা, পারক, ব্যগ্রচিত্ত, active, zealous, brisk.

তীক্ষ্ণগন্ধক, শোভাঞ্জন, শজিনা, a sort of horse-radish.

তীক্ষ্ণাগ্নি, শীঘ্রপাক, quick digestion, strong digestive power.

তীবর, তীয়র,—কৈবর্ত্ত, ব্যাধ, a cast consisting chiefly of hunters and fishermen.

তীব্র, ঝাল, উগ্র, সুধার, উচ্চৈস্বর, চালাক, উত্তেজক, ব্যগ্র, অতিশয়, অত্যুগ্ররস, warm, pungent, sharp, keen. shrill, brisk, quick, urgent, energetic, much, great, excessive ; pungency, &c.

তীয়র, উচ্চৈস্বর, shrill, sharp, loud. [tin.

তীর, তট, বাণ, রাঙ্গ, a shore, bank, margin, edge, an arrow,

তীরগত, শীঘ্রগামী, তটস্থ, fleet, rapid, placed on a shore, &c.
তীরিত, সিদ্ধ, সমাপ্ত, finished, completed, ended.
তীর্থ, পুণ্যক্ষেত্র, ঘাট, a place of pilgrimage chiefly near some sacred river or spring, a landing place or ghát. [holy place.
তীর্থকারী, তীর্থগামী,—যাত্রী, পুণ্যস্থানভূমী, a pilgrim, one visiting a
তু, ভেদ অবধারন বোধক শব্দ, তুমি, but, or, and, also, moreover ; thou, (in addressing an inferior.)
তুক, পরহিংসুক মন্ত্রপাঠ. incantations to injure another.
তুখড়, তুখার,—দক্ষ, পারগ, বলবান, clever, keen, shrewd, active, brisk, strong.
তুঙ্গ, উন্নত, উচ্চ, লম্ব, প্রধান, রাগাল, তপ্ত, ঊর্দ্ধতা, অগ্র, উপরিভাগ, সূর্য্যাদির আকাশের ঊর্দ্ধস্থলপ্রাপ্তি, high, tall, lofty, chief, principal, passionate, hot ; height, a top, vertex, a planet's greatest altitude.
তুচ্ছ, নীচ, অধম, ক্ষুদ্র, অকর্ম্মণ্য, অবজ্ঞাত, হেয়, শূন্য, low, vile, vulgar, small, worthless, despised, insignificant, empty, void. [perfectly.
তুচ্ছে, অবজ্ঞাপূর্ব্বক, বিনায়াসে, contemptuously, slightly, im-
তুচ্ছজ্ঞান, তুচ্ছতাচ্ছল্য,—হেয়জ্ঞান, অবহেলা, ঠাট্টা, sense of worthlessness, &c.; contempt, derision.
তুড়কী, ঝম্প, উলম্ফ, দক্ষ, পারগ, a leap, jump, skip ; quick, clever, active.
তুড়ন, তোড়ন,—খণ্ডন, খাটন, ভর্ৎসন, দোষান, তিরস্করণ, to break, cut up, abuse, criminate, dishonor.
তুড়ী, অঙ্গুলির ধ্বনি, ঝম্প a snapping with the fingers, a leap.
তুণ্ড, মুখ, আস্য, the mouth, the face.
তুৎ, তুত,—বৃক্ষ বিশেষ, the silk mulberry shrub.
তুৎপোকা, গুটিপোকা, the silkworm. [gle.
তুতন, স্তবন, ফুস্‌লান, ভুলন, to flatter, praise, applaud, invei-
তুত্থ-ক, তুতিয়া,—বণিক দ্রব্য বিশেষ, blue vitriol.
তুন, তুন্ন,—নন্দীবৃক্ষ, a timber tree.
তুন্দ, তুন্দি,—উদর, নাভি, the belly, the navel.
তুন্দিক, তুন্দিভ, তুন্দিল,—পেটাল, স্থূলোদর, having a prominent navel, corpulent, abdominous. [up.
তুবড়ন, কোঁকড়ন, শুকন, to shrivel, contract, wrinkle, shrink

তুমুল, গোলমাল, গণ্ডগোল, অতিশয় যুদ্ধ, uproar, tumult, clangor, tumultuous combat.
তুম্বী, অলাবু, লাউ, the long or bottle gourd.
তুম্বকী, ঢক্কা বিশেষ, a species of drum.
তুরগ. তুরঙ্গ,—অশ্ব, মন, অন্তঃকরণ, a horse, the mind, the heart.
তুরঙ্গম, অশ্ব, ঘোটক, a horse. [man, cavalry.
তুরঙ্গসাদী, তুরঙ্গারূঢ়,—অশ্বারূঢ়, riding on horseback ; a horse-
তুরপণ, তুরবণ,—বুর্মা, ভ্রমরী, a drill, gimblet, awl.
তুরপণ-আণ, তুরবণ,—ছিদ্রকরণ, to bore holes with a drill, &c.
তুরী, তুলী,—বর্ত্তি, মাকু, a hair hencil, a painter's or weaver's brush, a weaver's shuttle.
তুরীয়, তুর্য্য,—চতুর্থ, fourth, the fourth.
তুল, দাঁড়ীপাল্লা, তৌলকরা, চলাবুলা, গোল, a pair of scales, a weighing, ado, noise. [manuscripts.
তুলট, তুলাট—বর্ণিত লিখনাধার, a sort of prepared paper for
তুলন, নিক্তীদিয়া মাপন, উন্নয়ন, উঠান, to weigh, raise or lift up, elevate, draw water. [larity.
তুলনা, দৃষ্টান্ত. সাদৃশ্য, a comparison, simile, equality, simi-
তুলসী, বৃক্ষ বিশেষ, the sacred basil, a species of duck.
তুলা, নিক্তী, সপ্তম রাশি, সমতা, ঐক্যতা, কার্পাস, a weighing &c. a pair of scales, the sign Libra. resemblance, similarity, equality, cotton. [synonymous.
তুল্য, সমান, সদৃশ, একার্থ, like, similar, equal, comparable,
তুল্যজ্ঞান, সমানবোধ. the esteeming of different things alike.
তুল্যতন্ত্র, ঘণ্টাবাদ্য সমাস, a set of chimes. [bling.
তুল্যানুতুল্য, সদৃশ, অনুরূপ, exceedingly like, closely resem-
তুল্যানুমান, সমানবোধ, অনুরূপজ্ঞান, a parallel case.
তুষ, ধান্যাদির ত্বক. শিটা, chaff, bran. husk, refuse, trash.
তুষণ, আমোদন, হর্ষণ, to gratify or be gratified, to please or be pleased.
তুষার, নীহার, হিম, কুজ্ঝটিকা, কুহাড়া, শীতল, frost, rime, cold, ice, snow, mist, thin rain ; cold. frigid, frosty.
তূষ্ণীক, তুষ্ণীক,—মৌনী, ধীর, silent, taciturn, grave.
তুষ্ট, আহ্লাদিত, তৃপ্ত, হর্ষযুক্ত, pleased, glad. cheerful, satisfied, gratified, happy.
তুষ্টি, আহ্লাদ, তৃপ্তি, pleasure, enjoyment, contentment.

তুষ্টিমান, হর্ষিত, pleased, gratified, contented, happy.
তুহিন, হিম, জ্যোৎস্না, frost, hoar-frost, rime, moon-light.
তূণ, তূণীর,—বাণ রাখিবার পাত্র, a quiver.
তূরী, ক্ষুদ্র ভেরী, ভোড়ঙ্গ, a trumpet. [hastily.
তূর্ণ, শীঘ্র, দ্রুত, ঝটিতি, swift, expeditious, quick; swiftly,
তূর্ণি, বেগ, ত্বরা, speed, velocity, expedition. [fourth.
তূর্য্য, ভোড়ঙ্গ, চতুর্থ, a trumpet or similar instrument; the
তূল, তুৎ, নিক্তী, the mulberry tree and fruit, a balance.
তূল-া, বীজোদ্ধৃত কার্পাস, cotton cleared of the seeds.
তূলি, তূলিকা.—চিত্রকারের বর্ত্তি, a painter's brush, a hair pencil.
তূষ্ণীং, মৌনে, silently, in silence.
তূষ্ণীংশীল, তূষ্ণীশীল,—মৌনী, ধীর, taciturn, silent, grave. [herb.
তৃণ, ঘাস, খড়, grass, straw, any gramineous plant or
তৃণগ্রাহী, বৈক্রান্তিক, amber or other electric gem. [date, &c.
তৃণদ্রুম, গুবাক নারিকেলাদি বৃক্ষ, the palm tree, palmyra, cocoa,
তৃণধান্য, উড়ীধান্য, wild rice or other grain.
তৃণরাজ, তালবৃক্ষ, the palmyra tree.
তৃতীয়, তিনের পূরণ, third, the third. [happy.
তৃপ্ত, সন্তুষ্ট, হর্ষিত, pleased, satisfied, gratified, refreshed,
তৃপ্তি, ক্ষুন্নিবৃত্তি, পরিতোষ, আহ্লাদ, a sufficiency of food. the satisfaction of appetite, pleasure, gratification, content. [sensuality.
তৃষা, তৃষ্ণা,—পিপাসা, স্পৃহা, বিষয়েচ্ছা, thirst, appetite, desire,
তৃষ্ণক, পিপাসু, ইচ্ছুক, কামুক, thirsty, desirous, eager, sensual.
তেওড়ন, বেঁকন, to be or become warped or crooked.
তেঁই, সেইনিমিত্তে, therefore, for that reason.
তেঁতুল, তেতুল,—তিন্তিড়ী, the tamarind tree or its fruit.
তেকোনা, টেঁটা, ত্রিশূল, a harpoon, trident, fishing rod.
তেজ-স্, দীপ্তি, তাপ, প্রাখর্য্য, প্রতাপ, উগ্রতা, বেগ, বল, রেত, বীর্য্য, সত্বরতা. পরাক্রম, তীব্রতা, প্রভাব, নবনীত, splendor, light, lustre, glare, vividness, heat, ardor, impatience of affronts, fierceness, bile, vigour, spirit, rapidity, luxuriance, strength, energy, semen virile, vivacity, the active principle, pungency, sharpness of metals, freshness, power, dignity, fame, fresh butter.

তেজপত্র, দারুচীনী বিশেষ, the leaf of a species of cassia.
তেজস্বী, সচেষ্ট, প্রতাপান্বিত, লঘুতার অসহিষ্ণু, দীপ্তিমন্ত, ardent, energetic, active, high-spirited, luminous, splendid, famous. [pungent.
তেজাল, সত্বর, দীপ্তিমান, তীব্র, active. energetic, bright, hot,
তেজিত, শানিত, মার্জ্জিত, whetted, sharpened, polished. burnished. [ing.
তেড়া, বক্র, টেরচা, টেরাদৃষ্টি, crooked, warped, awry, squint-
তেভান, ভিজান, to wet, moisten, make damp.
তেতালা, তিনতালায়ুক্ত গৃহ, three storied, having three stories.
তেপান্তর, প্রশস্ত মাঠ, a wide-extended plain. [manner, so.
তেমত, তেমন,—সেইপ্রকার, such, similar, like that; in that
তেমনি, নিতান্ত সেইরূপ, so, even so, in that manner; such.
তেলচাটা, তেলাপোকা—আরসুলা, a cockroach.
তেলা, চিক্কণ, স্নিগ্ধ, oily, greasy.
তেলাঙ্গা, সৈন্য, যোদ্ধা, পিপীলিকা বিশেষ, a soldier, a native of the Telinga coast, a species of red ant.
তেলাটিয়া, তৈলাক্ত, smelling of or stained with oil, oily.
তেলী, তৈলিক,—কলু, an oilman, an oil presser or seller.
তৈজস, পিত্তলাদি নির্ম্মিত দ্রব্য, ধাতুময়, metalic, made of metal.
তৈত্তিরীয়, যজুর্ব্বেদী, of or relating to the Yajŭr Veda, studying the Yajŭr Veda.
তৈত্তিরীয়ক, যজুর্ব্বেদবেত্তা, a follower of the Yajŭr Veda.
তৈল, তেল,—তিলসার, বসা, oil, fat, unctuous matter.
তৈলঙ্গ, দেশ বিশেষ, তদ্দেশীয়, সেনা, the Telinga coast, a soldier.
তৈলপা, তৈলপায়িকা,—তেলচাটা, a cockroach.
তৈলস্ফটিক, তৃণগ্রাহী, amber or some similar gem.
তৈলাকর, তিলসর্ষপাদি, seeds &c. from which oil is expressed.
তোক, সন্ততি, পুত্রপুত্রী, a child, offspring, son or daughter.
তোড়-1, অতিশয় জলবেগ, the violence of a stream.
তোড়ন-আন, খণ্ডন, ভাঙ্গন, তিরস্করণ, নিন্দন, to break, to change money for smaller coin, to dishonor, calumniate, criminate, abuse.
তোড়নী, নদীর জীর্ণ তীর, a mouldering bank or precipice.
তোড়ল, বলয়, বালা, an ornament for the wrist. [house.
তোড়া, থৈলী, পরছতী, a purse, bag of money, the eaves of a

তোড়ানি, আমানী, কাঞ্জী, টাকাভাঙ্গা, rice-gruel, rice-water, the changing of money.

তোতলা, জড়বক্তা, অস্পষ্ট কথক, a stammerer, one who stutters.

তোপড়া, পুলিন্দা, a bundle, parcel, portmanteau.

তোবড়ন, কোঁকড়ন, শুকন, to shrivel up, wrinkle, shrink up.

তোয়, জল, সলিল, বারি, water.

তোয়ধি, তোয়নিধি,—সমুদ্র, সাগর, the sea, the ocean.

তোরণ, চাঁদনী, বারাণ্ডা, a porch, arched gateway, portal, outer door, a porch near a ghát, a mound.

তোলক, তোলা,—আশী রক্তিকা পরিমাণ, a rupee's weight, (of gold or silver.)

তোলন, উত্থাপন, উত্থান, ছোলন, উৎপাতন, উদ্গারণ, to raise a weight, lift or take up, peel, strip, pull off, erase, root up, vomit. [dresses.

তোলাকাপড়, অসাধারণ দুর্মূল্য বস্ত্র, holiday clothes, high-priced

তোষ, হর্ষ, আনন্দ, pleasure, satisfaction, happiness, joy, gladness, gaiety, vivacity.

তৌল, পরিমাণ ক্রিয়া, গুরুতা, a weighing, weight.

ত্যক্ত, বিবর্জিত, ছাড়া, বিরক্ত, ক্লিষ্ট, left, resigned, relinquished, deserted, abandoned, wearied, teased, importuned. [forsake, avoid, divorce.

ত্যজন, বিবর্জন, ছাড়ন, to leave, relinquish, quit, abandon,

ত্যাগ, ছাড়া, বিবর্জনা, উৎসর্গ, relinquishment, desertion, abandonment, the presenting of an offering or oblation to the gods.

ত্যাগী, বিবর্জক, relinquishing, abandoning, &c.

ত্যাজ্য, বিবর্জনীয়, to be left. relinquished, or avoided &c.

ত্রপা, ব্রীড়া, লজ্জা, modesty, bashfulness, shame, ignominy.

ত্রপিত, ত্রপান্বিত,—লজ্জিত, লজ্জান্বিত, ashamed, bashful, modest.

ত্রয়, তিন, তিনের পূরণ, *an affix*. three, the third.

ত্রয়ী, ঋক যজুঃ সাম এই তিন বেদ, the three Vedas.

ত্রসরেণু, অণু, অতিসূক্ষ্ম বস্তু, an atom, the mote in a sunbeam.

ত্রস্ত, ত্রস্থ,—ভয়ালু, ত্বরান্বিত, alarmed, timid, fearful, fearing, afraid, impatient, hurried, in a hurry.

ত্রাণ, রক্ষা, উদ্ধার, preservation, protection, safety, salvation, deliverance, rescue.

ত্রাত, রক্ষিত, উদ্ধৃত, saved, preserved, guarded, protected, rescued, delivered.

ত্রাতা, রক্ষাকর্ত্তা, রক্ষক, a saviour, deliverer, guardian, &c.

ত্রাস, ভয়, শঙ্কা, fear, terror, dread, awe, alarm, timidity.

ত্রাসিত, ভয়ান্বিত, শঙ্কিত, terrified, affrighted, afraid, alarmed.

ত্রাসী, ত্রাসিয়া,—ভয়যুক্ত, ভীত, শঙ্কান্বিত, fearful, timid, timorous, shy, alarmed.

ত্রাহি, রক্ষা করহ. *a Sanscrit precative* : save ! deliver !

ত্রি, তিন, কিন্তু শব্দ বিশেষের সহিত প্রয়োগ হয়, three.

ত্রিকচ্ছ, পণ্ডিতের বস্ত্র ধারণ বিশেষ, tucked in three folds, (as a Pundit's garment).

ত্রিকটু, মরিচ পিপুল শুণ্ঠ মিশ্রিত ত্রয়, the three spices, or dried ginger, with long and black pepper. [future.

ত্রিকাল, ভূত বর্ত্তমান ভবিষ্যৎ, the three times, past, present and

ত্রিকুল, পিতৃমাতৃশ্বশুরকুল, the three families of one's father, mother and wife's father.

ত্রিগুণ, সত্ত্বরজঃতমঃ, তিনবার, the three principles of matter, existence, activity and inertness, the three sentient properties of goodness, passion and stupidity ; three-fold, thrice. [of matter.

ত্রিগুণাতীত, ব্রহ্ম, Brahma as independant of the properties

ত্রিজগৎ, স্বর্গমর্ত্যপাতাল, the three worlds, or heaven, earth and hell.

ত্রিতয়, তৃতীয়, তিনের পূরণ, third, the third.

ত্রিদশ, সামান্য দেবতা, a deity or god as subject to birth, being and destruction.

ত্রিদশারি, অসুর, an infernal spirit or enemy of the gods.

ত্রিদশালয়, স্বর্গ, the abode of the gods, heaven. [phere.

ত্রিদিব স্বর্গ, আকাশ, Swarga, heaven, the sky, the atmos-

ত্রিদিবেশ, সামান্য দেবতা, a god, a deity.

ত্রিদোষ, পিত্তরক্তশ্লেষ্মবিকার, a vitiated state of the three humours, bile, blood and phlegm.

ত্রিধা, তিনপ্রকার, of three sorts or kinds. [forked.

ত্রিপত্র ক, যাহার তিন পত্র হয়, three-leaved, trifoliate, three-

ত্রিপাদী, তেপায়া, অর্ঘ্য পাত্রের আধার, a tripod, a triangular stand used in religious ceremonies.

ত্রিপুণ্ড্র, তিন রেখার তিলকযুক্ত, having three curved horizontal marks on the forehead.

ত্রিফলা, আমলকী হরীতকী বয়ড়া এই তিন, the three medicinal fruits.

ত্রিবর্গ, ত্রিগণ,—ধর্ম্মার্থকাম, উৎপত্তিস্থিতিধ্বংশ, the three objects of human pursuit or love, wealth and religious merit: also other triplets.

ত্রিবিক্রম, বিষ্ণুর বামনাবতার, Vishnu as the dwarf taking the three steps over the three worlds to the discomfiture of Bali.

ত্রিভঙ্গ, কৃষ্ণের তিনবাঁকযুক্ত মূর্ত্তি বিশেষ, having three bends, (as the images of Chrishna.)

ত্রিভুবন, ত্রিলোক,—স্বর্গমর্ত্যপাতাল, the universe or three worlds.

ত্রিমূর্ত্তি, ব্রহ্মাবিষ্ণুশিব, তিনাকার, the Hindu triad, or united form of Brahmá, Vishnú, and Shiva; having three forms.

ত্রিযামা, রাত্রি, যমুনা নদী, night, the Jumna river.

ত্রিযোনি, লোভাদিজনিত বিবাদ, a lawsuit engaged in from anger, covetousness or infatuation.

ত্রিলোচন, তেচক্ষুয়া অর্থাৎ শিব, Shiva or the three-eyed.

ত্রিশূল, তেকালা, শিবের অস্ত্র, a trident, three pronged spear, Shiva's crest.

ত্রিসন্ধ্যা, পূর্ব্বাহ্ণ মধ্যাহ্ণ অপরাহ্ণ, the three periods of the day, dawn, noon and evening.

ত্রিহায়নী, তিনবৎসরের বকনা, a three year old heifer.

ত্রুটি, ক্ষতি, নাশ, অপচয়, ন্যূনতা, টুট, আজ্ঞালঙ্ঘন, প্রতিজ্ঞার অন্যথা, ভ্রম, ভুল, loss, destruction, failure, diminution, deficiency, defect, fault, crime, transgression, violation of promises and engagements, an error, mistake.

ত্রেতা, দ্বিতীয় যুগ, সংস্কৃত গার্হপত্য দক্ষিণাগ্নিত্রয়, the second Yug, the three fires, *viz*: the southern, household and sacrificial fires.

ত্রৈলোক্য, ত্রিভুবন, the three worlds, upper, middle and lower.

ত্রোটি, ঠোঁট, চঞ্চু, the bill or beak of a bird.

ত্র্যক্ষর, প্রণব, ওঁকার, তিনঅক্ষরযুক্ত, the mystic Om; triliteral.

ত্র্যান্তর, মাঠ, তেপান্তর, an extended plain.

ত্র্যম্বক, শিব, মহাদেব, Shiva.

ত্র্যহস্পর্শ, যে তিথি তিন বারে স্পর্শহয়, a solar day containing part
of three lunar days. [every third day.
ত্র্যাহিক, তেযেইয়া জ্বর, তিন দিনের পর উপস্থিত যে, tertian, occurring
ত্বক, ত্বচ্,—স্পর্শেন্দ্রিয়, চর্ম্ম, ছাল, বাকল, the skin, bark, a rind,
integument, peel, husk.
ত্বক্‌ছেদ, মেঢ়ত্বক্‌কাটন সংস্কার বিশেষ, circumcision.
ত্বগ্‌জ্ঞান, স্পর্শজ্ঞান, feeling, touch, perception by the touch.
ত্বগ্‌জ্ঞেয়, স্পর্শনীয়, স্পর্শপ্রত্যক্ষ, স্পর্শজ্ঞেয়, palpable, perceptible
to the touch, that may be felt.
ত্বঞ্চ, প্রবঞ্চনা, ছলনা, an imposition, trick, deceit.
ত্বদীয়, তোমার, thy, thine, (*Sanscrit.*) [hurry.
ত্বরা, বেগ, শীঘ্রতা, speed, expedition, haste, quickness,
ত্বরায়, ত্বরাতে,—শীঘ্র, ক্ষিপ্র, speedily, quickly, expeditious-
ly, soon, early. [swift; soon.
ত্বরিত, বেগযুক্ত, শীঘ্র, hurried, hastened, quick, expeditious,

থ.

থই, ইষ্টকগৃহাদি নির্ম্মাতা, রাজ, a mason, a bricklayer.
থইপনা, থইমি,—রাজের কর্ম্ম, masonry, the trade of a mason.
থকা, গুচ্ছ, স্তবক, a bunch of fruit or flowers.
থম্‌কান, চম্‌কন, ভয় পাওন, to be startled, to stand still from
fear or surprize.
থর, শ্রেণী, পংক্তি, a row, rank, layer. [tottering, vibrating.
থর্‌থর-াণি, অত্যন্তকম্প, নড়নী, a trembling, shaking, palpitation.
থর্‌থরাণ, কম্পন, নড়ন, to tremble, palpitate, to be agitated,
to vibrate. [a valley.
থলী, থলিয়া,—গুণ, ছালা বিশেষ, a bag, sack, a pelican's pouch,
থলুয়া, গুচ্ছ, স্তবক, a bunch, a cluster. [udder.)
থল্‌থলিয়া, ঝুল্‌ঝুলিয়া, দোলিত, swinging, dangling, (as a cow's
থাই, নদীর তলা, শ্রেণী, মাচা, মত, পক্ষ, the bottom of a
river, &c. a row, a shelf, a sect, a party.
থাক্‌, যতি, ছেদ, শ্রেণী, রহ, তিষ্ঠ, a pause, interval, stratum,
layer, a dash in writing; stop, hush, stay.
থাকন, স্থিতিকরণ, তিষ্ঠন, রহণ, টিকন, বাসকরণ, হওন, ছেকন, to stop,
cease, stay, remain, continue, subsist, last,
endure, live, dwell, exist, be, pause, desist.

থান, থান, টুটি, স্থান, a piece, bit, morsel, a place.

থানা, আড্ডা, চৌকীস্থান, দস্যুরক্ষকাদির মিলনস্থান, a military post, a police station, watch-house, place of resort for thieves, a haunt.

থাবা, করতল. নখ, চড়, পূর্ণমুষ্টি, the hand, a paw, claw, talon, fang, a slap, blow, handful.

থাম, স্তম্ভ. a pillar, post, stake, block.

থামন, জুড়ন, শান্ত হওন, মিটন, টুটন, থিতন, to become calm or tranquil, to cool, forbear, desist, abate, decline in zeal, to slacken one's pace, settle as liquids, subside.

থাল-া, ধাতুময় ভোজনপাত্র, a metal dish, a tray, a plate.

থালী, পাত্র, বাসন, a vessel, dish, pot, basin.

থাসন, ছানন, ঠাসন, গাদন, to knead, tread, press, ram, compress, load a gun.

থিতন, চঞ্চলদ্রবদ্রব্যের স্থির হওন, to settle as liquids, to subside.

থু, থুক, থুথু.—ছেপ, পিক্, নিষ্ঠীব, ঘৃণার্হ, ছিছি, spittle, saliva, any abomination; fye! for shame!

থুওন, রাখন, স্থাপন, নাম দেওন, to place, lay down, fix, appoint, give a name to, to spit, spit out.

থুকন, থুথু ফেলন, নিষ্ঠীবন, to spit, to expectorate.

থুতনী, চিবুক, ওষ্ঠের অধোভাগ, the chin.

থুবা, গুচ্ছ, ঝাবা, a tuft, cluster, bunch, tassel.

থুরণ, কুচন অর্থাৎ কুচি২ কাটন, to cut or chop to pieces, to hack, to mince.

থৈলী, বেটুয়া, বোরা, গুণ, a purse, a bag, a sack.

থোওন, রাখন, গছান, to place, put, set down, leave with.

থোক, সঞ্চয়, রাশি, পিণ্ড, একুন, a collection, heap, lump, a whole or aggregate.

থোড়, কল্পিত কদলী বৃক্ষের গর্ভ, the spatha or sheath of the plantain, the young ear of corn or grass before it shoots from the culm or stalk.

থোড়া, কিঞ্চিৎ, অল্প, few, little.

থোড়াল, মোটা অর্থাৎ বিকশনোদ্যত, plump, or swollen as grain or as the plantain when ready to shoot from the stem or culm.

থোপ-া, থোপনা, থোবা,—ঝাবা, স্তবক, a tassel, a bunch, a cluster.

থোপলা, মুখ, আনন, আস্য, the face, the mouth.

দ.

দই, দধি, curds, thickened milk. [a gadfly.

দংশ, দন্ত, হুল, সাপ, ডাঁশ, a tooth, fang, sting, bite, a snake,

দংশন, কামড়ান, দন্তাঘাত, to bite, to sting; a bite, &c.

দংষ্ট্র, দন্ত, রদন, হুল, a tooth, a fang, a sting.

দংষ্ট্রা, বিষাণ, বৃহদ্দন্ত, a tusk, fang, large tooth. [a snake.

দংষ্ট্রী, কামড়ানিয়া, হিংসুক, শূকরসর্পাদি, biting, stinging; a hog,

দক্ষ, নিপুণ, চতুর, পণ্ডিত, clever, dextrous, able, skilful, expert, acute, ingenious; a scholar, a pundit.

দক্ষিণ, উদিত সূর্য্যের বামদিক্, ডাহিণ, যমের আবাস, the south, the right side, the right hand, the abode of Yama; south, southern, right, (not left.)

দক্ষিণা, কর্ম্মের শেষাঙ্গ, গুরুর বেতন, the fee or present to a brahmin or a preceptor. [from N. to S.

দক্ষিণায়ন, শ্রাবণাদি ছয় মাস, the period of the sun's course

দগ্ধ, পোড়া, জ্বলিত, ভাজা, অগ্নিহত, burnt, scorched, singed, consumed. [afflict.

দগ্ধন, পোড়ান, খেদড়ান, to burn, scorch. calcine distress,

দগ্ধা, অমঙ্গল তিথি বিশেষ, unpropitious, (spoken of certain lunar days.)

দগ্ধিকা, ভাজা ধান্য, scorched or half burnt rice.

দড়, দঢ়,—শক্ত, কঠিন, মড়কা, firm, hard, tough, stiff, stout, stern, brittle.

দড়া, দীর্ঘ স্থূলরজ্জু, a thick cord, a rope.

দড়ী, রজ্জু, a cord, string, thin rope, line.

দণ্ড, যষ্টি, লড়ী, হাতা, প্রকাণ্ড, নিগ্রহ, শাসন, দম, যষ্টিপল পরিমিত কাল, a pilgrim's staff, a stick, handle, the trunk of a tree, a stem, oar, sceptre, a pole of four cubits, punishment, chastisement, a fine, an hour of twenty-four minutes. [tion.

দণ্ডবৎ, দণ্ডের ন্যায়, like a stick; a bow, obeisance, prostra-

দণ্ডান, তিষ্ঠন, দাঁড়ান, to stand still, stand erect.

দণ্ডায়মান, দাঁড়ান, খাড়া, standing still, erect, upright.
দণ্ডাশ্রম, বিষয়ত্যাগ, সন্ন্যাসধর্ম্ম, the condition of a pilgrim.
দণ্ডাশ্রমী, দণ্ডী,—বিষয়ত্যাগী, সন্ন্যাসী, retiring from the world, assuming the pilgrim's staff; a pilgrim, a religious mendicant.
দণ্ড্য, দণ্ডনীয়,—শাসনীয়, দাপনীয়, নিগ্রহণীয়, punishable, deserving of punishment, liable to fine.
দত্ত, যাহার দান করা গিয়াছে, পদবী বিশেষ, given, bestowed; a title given to Vaisyas and some Káyasthas.
দত্তকপুত্র, নিজপিতৃমাতৃত্যক্ত যে পোষ্য পুত্র, an adopted son (given up by his parents.)
দত্তা, বিবাহসম্বন্ধা, বাগ্দত্তা, *f*: given in marriage, betrothed.
দত্তাত্মা, স্বদত্ত পালকপুত্র, an adopted son, (self-given).
দদ্রু, কণ্ডূরোগ, দাদুরোগ, cutaneous or herpetic eruptions, ring-worm.
দধি, ঘনীভূত দুগ্ধ, ছেনা, curds, coagulated milk.
দনুজ, অসুর, দৈত্য, an Asur or demon, an infernal being.
দন্ত, দাঁত, বিষাণ, হুল, a tooth, tusk, fang.
দন্তী, হস্তী, an elephant. [gums.
দন্তমূল, শিকড়, দাঁতের গোড়া, the root or socket of a tooth, the
দন্ত্য, দন্ত সংযোগে উচ্চারিত, dental, referring or belonging to the teeth.
দন্তুর, দাঁতাল, বৃহদ্দন্তী, having large or projecting teeth.
দম্ভ, দর্প, অহংকার, নিষ্ঠুরতা, pride, arrogance, self-importance, severity.
দবন-আন, মর্দ্দন, দলন, to trample, tread under foot.
দবকন, চমকন, হটন, to start at, be startled, retreat.
দবিষ্ঠ, অতিশয় দূর, অনিকট, very distant, remote, far off.
দবীয়ান, দূরতর, কনিষ্ঠ, farther, more distant, remote, youngest.
দম, শাস্তি, অন্তরিন্দ্রিয়ের নিগ্রহ, গরিমা, গর্ব্ব, ফুসলানি, punishment, penalty, self-command, self-restraint, command of the passions, &c. a boast, ambition, wheedling, coaxing.
দমন, বশীকরণ, শাসন, আটকান, নিগ্রহণ, ধমকান, তাড়ন, to subdue, subject, reduce, tame, restrain, suppress, punish, reprimand, torment, dethrone.

দম্কল, ভারি দ্রব্য তুলনার্থ যন্ত্র বিশেষ, a screw jack, a crane.
দম্কলী, জল প্রক্ষেপণার্থ ক্ষুদ্র কল বিশেষ, a syringe, a squirt.
দম্কান, বৈসন, to sink, fall lower, sink down, settle.
দম্পতি, জায়াপতি, স্ত্রীপুরুষ, husband and wife.
দম্ভ, অহংকার, কপট, দুষ্টামি, pride, arrogance, self-importance, boasting, bullying, deceit, cheating, hypocrisy, wickedness.
দয়া, পরদুঃখ হরণের ইচ্ছা, করুণা, ক্ষমা, অনুগ্রহ, pity, compassion, sympathy, kindness, clemency, mercy, lenity, indulgence. [cious, merciful.
দয়ালু, কৃপাবন্ত, ক্ষমাশীল, compassionate, sympathizing, gra-
দয়িত, অনুগৃহীত, favoured, compassionated, accepted.
দরণ, পক্কন, পচন, বিগড়ন, to moulder away, decay, spoil.
দর্মা, ঘাস বিশেষ, তন্নির্ম্মিত আসন, a species of long grass, a mat made of it used for building huts and fences.
দরা, জীর্ণ, পচা, mouldering, putrid.
দরিদ্র, অত্যন্ত ধনহীন, দুঃখী, poor, needy, indigent, distressed, wretched.
দরী, পর্ব্বতের ছিদ্র, গহ্বর, কন্দর, সতরঞ্চী, আধুনিক, a cave, cavern, grotto, glen, valley, a carpet; modern, new.
দর্প, অহঙ্কার, আত্মশ্লাঘা, উৎসাহ, বিক্রম, প্রভা, pride, arrogance, self-importance, a boast, courage, power, energy, splendour.
দর্পণ, আর্শি, নেত্র, a mirror, looking glass, the eye.
দর্পিত, দর্পী,—দাম্ভিক, গরিমান্বিত, proud, arrogant, boasting, self-important, insulting.
দর্ব্বী, হাতা, a ladle, a spoon.
দর্ভ, কুশ ঘাস, যজ্ঞের তৃণ, the Cusha or sacrificial grass.
দর্শন, দেখন, আলোচন, ভেটন, উদিত হওন, প্রত্যক্ষ হওন, to see, view, observe, survey, visit, appear, come into view, be seen.
দর্শন, দৃষ্টি, আলোচনা, ভেটা, স্বপ্ন, চক্ষু, বেদান্তাদি ছয় শাস্ত্র, sight, view, vision, an interview, survey, prospect, scene, a visit, a dream, the eye, a philosophical school or system. [meeting.
দর্শনী, ভেট, পারিতোষিক, a sight offering, a present at

দর্শান, দেখান, প্রকাশন, to shew, exhibit, expose, display, explain.

দর্শিত, নিরীক্ষিত, উদিত, প্রকাশ, seen, shewn, exhibited, apparent, visible.

দর্শী, নিরীক্ষক, seeing, viewing, beholding, &c.

দল, কোষ, ভাগ, খণ্ড, অনেকের ঐক্য, সৈন্যসংগ্রহ, রাশি, পর্ণ, পত্র, পাল, দাম, স্থূলতা, a sheath, scabbard, a part; portion, fragment, a party, division, body of troops, a heap or quantity, a leaf, blade of grass, petal, a sail, duckweed, &c. the thickness of a board, &c.

দলক, অনবরত বৃষ্টিপাত, কাদাযুক্ত, soaking, heavy, incessant, (as rain,) thick or heavy (as a road after rain.)

দলন-আন, মর্দন, মাড়ান, ছানন, বাটন, to tread down, trample, knead, bruise, press.

দলিত, মর্দ্দিত, বিদীর্ণ, খণ্ডিত, বিকশিত, trodden, split, divided, broken, full blown, expanded.

দলুয়া, খাঁড়, অন্নপিণ্ড, ভসভসিয়া, a sort of sugar, a ball of rice; boggy, quaking.

দশ, দ্বিগুণ পঞ্চ, ten.

দশক, দশ গণ্ডা, ten gandas (in arithmetic.)

দশকিয়া, গণিত শাস্ত্র, a small treatise on numeration.

দশন, দন্ত, রদন, a tooth.

দশমূল, পাঁচন বিশেষ, a medicament prepared from ten different roots.

দশা, অবস্থা, গতি, বয়স, দীপবর্ত্তি, বস্ত্রের শেষ, a state, condition, circumstance, situation in life, period of life, the wick of a lamp, end of a garment, &c.

দশাহীন, দুর্ভাগ্য, অনাথ, unlucky, destitute, forlorn.

দস্তা, ধাতু বিশেষ, pewter, zinc, lapis calaminaris.

দস্যু, চোর, ডাকাইৎ, সিঁধাল, দৌরাত্ম্যকারী, a robber, plunderer, thief, housebreaker, an oppressor.

দহ, গহরা, আবর্ত্ত, a deep place in a river, an abyss, eddy.

দহন, জ্বলন, অগ্নি, পোড়া, to burn, be consumed; fire, a burning, combustion.

দা, কাচি, কাতান, a sickle, bill-hook, cleaver.

দাউদ, দদ্রু, a ringworm, a tetter.

দাউদিয়া, শস্যচ্ছেদক, a reaper, a corn-cutter.

দাওন, শস্যছেদন, তৃণকাটন, to reap, to mow.
দাক্ষ্য, নৈপুণ্য, skill, cleverness, capacity, address.
দাঁড়, নৌকাদণ্ড, আড়বাড়ি, নিগ্রহ, দন্ড, an oar, a perch for birds, a fine, punishment.
দাড়-1, দন্ত, রদন, নখ, হনু, চঞ্চু, চিবুক, a tooth, fang, serrature, the claw of a crab, forceps of an insect, bill of a bird, ward of a key, the chin.
দাঁড়া, রীতি, ব্যবহার, আচার, ধারা, যষ্টি, উত্তক, মেরুদণ্ড, নিগৃহীত, দাপিত, খাড়া, a custom, practice, usage, conduct, behaviour, way, method, mode, a staff, a bat, a clew, guide, the back-bone, a balk or ridge; punished, fined, standing, upright.
দাঁড়ান, দণ্ডায়মান থাকন, তিষ্টন, to stand, stand erect or still.
দাড়ি, দাঢ়ি,—ওষ্ঠের অধোভাগ, চিবুক, তৎস্থানে ধারিত কেশ অর্থাৎ শ্মশ্রু, the chin, the beard.
দাড়িম, ডালিম বৃক্ষ, the pomegranate tree or its fruit.
দাঁড়ী, নৌকাবাহক, নাবিক, আলি, তুলাদণ্ড, মূঢ়, ছেদসূচক রেখা, a rower, boatman, waterman, a balk, ridge, scale-beam, an ignorant person, the stop (।) in writing.
দাণ্ডা, গদা, লাঠী, a club, cudgel, bat, bar.
দাঁত, দন্ত, রদন, বিষাণ, a tooth, serrature, tusk.
দাঁতাল, বৃহদ্দন্তী, বনশূকর, having large teeth or tusks; a boar.
দাঁতুয়া, বৃহদ্দন্ত বিশিষ্ট, large-toothed, having projecting teeth.
দাতা, দাতৃ,—যে দান করে, দানশীল, বদান্য, a giver, donor, bestower; generous, charitable, bountiful, munificent, liberal.
দাত্র, কাচী, কাতান, a sickle, bill-hook, cleaver.
দাদা, জ্যেষ্ঠভ্রাতা, পিতামহ, an elder brother, a grandfather.
দাদু, দদ্রু, a ring-worm. [largess, alms.
দান, অর্পণ, উৎসর্গ, ত্যাগ, ভিক্ষা, a gift, donation, present,
দানপত্র, বৃত্তিদান লিপি, উত্তরাধিকার লিপি, a deed of gift, a grant, a will, a testament.
দানব, দানো,—অসুর, a demon, evil spirit, an Asur.
দানবারি, সামান্য দেবতা, a god, a deity. [bountiful.
দানশৌণ্ড, অতিশয় দাতা, বদান্য, exceedingly generous, liberal,

দানা, দৈত্য, ভূত, দেবসৈন্য, শস্যাদি, বীজ, মুক্তা, মালা বিশেষ, a demon, spectre, ghost, the troops of the gods, corn, a seed, grain of corn or sand, a pearl, a gem. a sort of neck-lace.

দানী, দানপ্রাপ্ত, দানশীল, receiving gifts or alms, liberal, bountiful.

দানুয়া, নিবেদিত, ত্যক্ত, offered, given in oblation.

দান্ত, সুশাসিত, বশীভূত, জিতেন্দ্রিয়, তপস্যার ক্লেশ সহিষ্ণু, subdued, tamed, daunted, devoted, patient under privation or penance, &c.

দান্তি, বশতা, পরাভব, ইন্দ্রিয়নিগ্রহ, subjection, submission, humiliation, self-denial, patient endurance of austerities or privations.

দাপ. দাপাড়া, প্রতাপ, দর্প, a stamping violently, potency, pride.

দাপনীয়, দাপ্য,—দণ্ডযোগ্য, punishable, fineable, amenable.

দাপন-আন, দাপাড়ণ, দাপাড়িয়া ফেলন, to stamp, shake off by stamping.

দাপিত. অপরাধিত, বিচারসিদ্ধ, condemned, fined, adjudged, awarded.

দাবন-আন, চাপন, ঠাসন, মাড়ান, ছাপন, অপহরণ, ইন্দ্রিয়দমন, to squeeze, press down or together, flatten, smoothe, stifle; quash, conceal, peculate, to subdue or govern the passions.

দাবাগ্নি. দাবানল,—বনের অগ্নিদাহ, the conflagration of a forest.

দাম, মূল্য, রজ্জু. শেয়ালা, price, cost, a rope, a girdle, &c. pond-weed.

দামড়া, বলদ, মুষ্কমুক্ত ষণ্ড, an ox, castrated bullock, gelding.

দামন্. দামনী,—রজ্জু, দড়ী, পট্টিকা, বস্ত্রের নীচভাগ, a rope, string, cord, tethering rope, girdle, ribband, the flap or skirt of a garment.

দামা, গোঁয়ার, দড়ী, a clown, a rope, a cord, a species of bird.

দামা, দামামা,—বৃহড্ঢক্কা, a species of drum.

দামাল, কচিছেল্যা, দুরন্ত শিশু, চিড়চিড়িয়া, a brat, a cross child; peevish, changeable, capricious.

দাম্ভিক, অহংকৃত, আত্মশ্লাঘী, proud, boasting, blustering, imperious, hypocritical.

দায়, দান, বৈবাহিক ধন, অধিকার, পৈতৃক ধন, বিপত্তি, ক্লেশ. ভঙ্গ, বিভাগ, অবক্ষেপ, আঘাত, স্বত্ববাদ, ঋণাদান, মূল,

দেয়, ঋণশোধপত্র, ক্ষতিধ্বংস, a gift, donation, nuptial present, portion, inheritance, heritable property, danger, difficulty, loss, destruction, trouble, a breaking, dividing, irony, a charge, allegation, law-suit, pretension, tenure, debt, responsibility, a place, a scite, reference or relation to, a quittance, discharge, indemnification. [cent; a giver, accuser.

দায়ক, যিনি দেন, দানশীল, দোষদ, giving, bountiful, munifi-

দায়াদ, পুত্র, উত্তরাধিকারী, জ্ঞাতি, স্বত্ববাদী, a son, an heir, a kinsman who may inherit, a claimant.

দায়ার্হ, বিবাদার্হ, claimable, cognizable at law.

দায়ী, দায়ক, দানশীল, ঋণগ্রস্ত, ক্লেশযুক্ত, ভারগ্রস্ত, প্রতিবাদী, giving, liberal, responsible; a debtor, one in trouble, a defendant, (in a law suit.)

দার-া, স্ত্রী, পত্নী, জায়া, a wife, a married woman.

দারকর্ম্ম, দারক্রিয়া,—বিবাহ, পাণিগ্রহ, marriage.

দারণ, ফাড়ন, ফাটন, to tear, rend, split, divide, crack.

দারদ, বিষ বিশেষ, পারা, হিঙ্গুল, সমুদ্র, a sort of poison, quicksilver, vermillion, the ocean. [ness.

দারিদ্র্য, নির্ধনতা, poverty, indigence, distress, wretched-

দারী, সপত্নীক, ব্যভিচারী, having a wife or wives, an adulterer. [wine, gunpowder.

দারু, কাষ্ঠ, মদিরা, বারুদ, wood, timber, spirituous liquors,

দারুক, পুতুলা, a doll, a puppet, Chrishna's charioteer.

দারুচিনী, দালচীনী, cinnamon. [from wood.

দারুজ, দারুময়,—কাষ্ঠনির্ম্মিত, wooden, made of or produced

দারুণ, ভয়ানক, কঠিন, অসহ্য, অকরুণ, frightful, terrific, difficult, hard, cruel, unfeeling.

দার্ঢ্য, দৃঢ়তা, কাঠিন্য, firmness, hardness, stability, strength.

দার্শনিক, দর্শনবেত্তা, acquainted with the Darshans, of enlarged views. [simile, an archetype.

দার্ষ্টান্ত, উপমিত, উপমেয়, আদর্শ, the thing elucidated by a

দাল-ী কলায় প্রভৃতি, split peas or other pulse.

দালিম, দাড়িম্ব ফল, the pomegranate. [Shúdra, fisherman.

দাস, ভৃত্য, কিঙ্কর, কৈবর্ত্ত, শূদ্র, a servant, slave, bondsman,

দাসী, স্ত্রীভৃত্য, শূদ্রী, a slave girl, maid servant, the wife of a slave or Shúdra. [servile, slavish.
দাস্য, সেবাজীবিকা, দাসবৎ, slavery, servitude, dependance;
দাহ, জ্বালা, তাপ, a burning, a conflagration, inflammation, heat.
দাহন, পোড়ান, তাপান, to burn, sear, inflame, cauterize.
দাহস্থল, শ্মশান, a place where the dead are burned.
দিক্, দিগ্,—পূর্ব্বাদি দশ, ককুভ, দেশ, পক্ষ, a point, quarter, region, side, part, party.
দিক্পতি, দিক্পাল—ককুভাধ্যক্ষ, the regent of one of the quarters of the world.
দিকে, দিগে,—কাছে, পানে, নিকটে, to, towards.
দিগম্বর, বিবস্ত্র, উলঙ্গ, বস্ত্রহীন, শিব, সন্ন্যাসী, naked, stripped, unclad; Shiva, a naked mendicant.
দিগ্দর্শন, সর্ব্বাবলোকনা, a general view, survey, look round.
দিগ্দাহ, বিশ্বের অগ্নিদাহ, a universal conflagration of the world.
দিগ্ধ, বিষার্পিত বাণ, অক্ত, a poisoned arrow; smeared, anointed, rubbed with.
দিগ্বাসাঃ, উলঙ্গ, শিব, কালীদেবী, naked; Shiva, Kálí.
দিগ্বিজয়ী, বিশ্বজিতনিয়া, conquering the universe, invincible.
দিগ্বিদিগ্, সকলদিগ, সর্ব্বত্র, every quarter, every direction, every where.
দিগ্ভ্রমণ, পর্য্যটন, a wandering about, a roving, voyaging.
দিৎসা, দানশীলতা, generosity, a wish to give.
দিৎসু, দানশীল, বদান্য, desirous to give, generous, liberal.
দিধিষূ, দোপড়া স্ত্রী, দোপড়া স্ত্রীর পতি, a virgin widow remarried, or her husband.
দিন, সূর্য্যাবচ্ছিন্ন কাল, অহোরাত্র, day time, a day, time, date.
দিনকর, দিনপতি, দিনমণি—সূর্য্য, the sun.
দিনপাত, কাল যাপন, কালবহা, উপজীবিকা, the spending, passing or lapse of time, a livelihood.
দিনমান, দিবসকাল, day, daytime.
দিনিকা, দিবসিক বেতন, a day's wages, daily hire.
দিব, দিবি,—আকাশ, অন্তরীক্ষ, the sky, the atmosphere.
দিবস, দিন, a day.
দিবসিক, আহ্নিক, প্রতিদিনের, daily, diurnal, proper for the day.

দিবসীয়, দিবসকালের, আহ্নিক, of or belonging to the day.
দিবা, দিনমান, দিবসকালে, day; by day, in the day time.
দিবাকর, সূর্য্য, the sun. [day, an owl, &c.
দিবান্ধ, যাহারা দিনে দেখিতে না পায়, পেচকাদি, unable to see by
দিব্য, ঐশ্বরী, উত্তম, সুরূপ, শপথ, divine, excellent, beautiful; an oath. [couragement.
দিব্বি, শপথ, আশ্বাস দেওয়া, an oath, an appeal to God, en-
দিশা, দিক্, ককুভ, a point of the compass, quarter, region.
দিশাহারা, পথভুলনিয়া, lost, bewildered. [fate, destiny.
দিষ্ট, বিদিত, দর্শিত, শুভাশুভ, known, shewn, pointed out;
দীক্ষক, পুরোহিত, গুরু, a priest, a spiritual guide.
দীক্ষা, ভজনা, পূজারম্ভ, মন্ত্রগ্রহণ, the performance of worship, oblation or sacrifice, the preliminary ceremonies, the receiving of instruction or the initiatory mantra or incantation.
দীক্ষিত, ভজনাপ্রবৃত্ত, উপদেশক, মন্ত্রদায়ক, engaged in worship, sacrifice or oblation, imparting instruction, giving the initiatory mantra.
দীগী, দীঘী,—দীর্ঘিকা, দীর্ঘ জলাশয়, an oblong pond.
দীন, দীনহীন,—দরিদ্র, দুঃখিত, poor, needy, distressed, miserable, wretched.
দীনার, স্বর্ণালঙ্কার, মুদ্রা, a golden ornament, a seal, a certain coin, a dinar, a certain weight of gold.
দীপ-ক, বর্ত্তি, বাতী, উল্কা, a lamp, light, candle, torch.
দীপক, প্রকাশক, জ্বালানিয়া, শোভাকর, অলঙ্কার, enlightening, illuminating, kindling, inflaming, beautifying, perspicuous; a rhetorical beauty, elegance of expression.
দীপন, শোভন, প্রজ্বলন, to shine, blaze, be luminous or light.
দীপাধার, বাতীর আধার, a lamp stand, a candlestick.
দীপান্বিত, শোভান্বিত, brilliant, luminous, clear, perspicuous.
দীপিত, দীপ্ত,—প্রজ্বলিত, প্রকাশিত, শোভান্বিত, ব্যক্তীকৃত, lighted up, blazing, made to shine, luminous, splendid, made clear, elucidated.
দীপ্তি, শোভা, প্রকাশ, সৌন্দর্য্য, light, splendour, brilliancy, effulgence, illumination, beauty.

দীপ্তিমান, দীপ্র,—প্রকাশ্যমান, উজ্জ্বলিত, শোভান্বিত, luminous, shining, bright, refulgent, illustrious.

দীপ্যমান, শোভাকর, প্রত্যক্ষ, shining, conspicuous, clear, evident.

দীয়মান, যাহা দেওয়া যাইতেছে, under bestowment, being bestowed.

দীয়া, দীপ, প্রদীপ, a light, a lamp.

দীর্ঘ, লম্ব, উত্তুঙ্গ, উচ্চ, long, tall, lofty, prolonged.

দীর্ঘকায়, ঢেঙ্গা, প্রকাণ্ড, tall, high in stature.

দীর্ঘজঙ্ঘ, লম্বজঙ্ঘাবিশিষ্ট, সারস পক্ষী, long-thighed, spindle-shanked; a crane.

দীর্ঘজীবী, বহুকালজীবী, long-lived.

দীর্ঘদর্শী, দূরদর্শী, পণ্ডিত, গৃধ্র, seeing far, foresighted, prudent, wise; a vulture.

দীর্ঘসূত্রী, শিথিল, অসত্বর, নিড়্বিড়িয়া, tedious, dilatory, slow, procrastinating.

দীর্ঘনিশ্বাস, হাই ছাড়া, a sigh, a long drawn breath.

দীর্ঘিকা, দীর্ঘ জলাশয় বিশেষ, বাপী, a large oblong pond or tank.

দীর্ঘে, লম্বালম্বে, লম্বায়, in length, lengthwise.

দু, দুই,—দ্বি, একের দ্বিগুণ, two.

দুহন, গবাদির স্তনহইতে দুগ্ধ নিঃসারণ, to milk an animal.

দুইএক, এক কিম্বা দুই, কএক, অল্প, one or two, several, a few.

দুঃখ, পীড়া, ব্যামোহ, দরিদ্রতা, শোক, ক্লেশ, যত্ন, a pain, ache, distress, poverty, affliction, grief, sorrow, vexation, misery, trouble, labour.

দুঃখী, দুঃখিত,—ক্লিষ্ট, দরিদ্র, afflicted, in pain, distressed, wretched, miserable, poor.

দুঃশীল, দুষ্টস্বভাব, দ্বেষী, inclined to evil, ill-disposed, ill-natured, vicious, malicious.

দুঃসময়, বিপৎ কাল, a time of affliction, a season of distress.

দুঃসহ-্য, কষ্টে সহ্য, অতিশয় মন্দ, hard to be borne, scarcely endurable, intolerable.

দুঃসাহস, চাপল্য, নির্ভয়তা, ঢেটামি, rashness, temerity, presumption.

দুঃস্থ, দুরবস্থ, দুর্ভাগ্যাপন্ন, নির্ধন, দুঃখী, disagreeably circumstanced, in pain or trouble, distressed, unfortunate, poor, needy.

দুঃস্বপ্ন, দোস্বান, an unpleasant dream, nightmare.

দুগড়িয়া, প্রবঞ্চক, দ্বিদলাক্রান্ত, দুদলিয়া, an impostor, a turn-coat.

দুগ্ধ, দুধ,—পয়ঃ, ক্ষীর, milk ; milked (as an animal).
দুগ্ধপোষ্য, অতিশিশু, দুধিয়া, a sucking infant or other animal.
দুটপ্পা, চুম্বক, সংক্ষেপবক্তা, laconic, brief.
দুণ-1, দুন-1,—দ্বিগুণ, two fold, twice as much.
দুতর্ক্ক, দ্ব্যর্থ, দ্বিতয়োপায়, দ্বিধা, two objects, a thing and its alternative, a dilemma.
দুদ, দুধ, দুদু,—পয়ঃ, ক্ষীর, milk.
দুদিয়া, দুধিয়া,—দুগ্ধপোষ্য, ক্ষীরদ, পয়স্বিনী, sucking, living on milk, producing milk, milky, milch.
দুনী, দ্রোণী, ডোঙ্গা. বায়ুপ্রচালিত শস্য পেষণ কল, a sort of boat or ship, a windmill.
দুঁদিয়া, দুরন্ত, দুর্দ্দান্ত, stubborn, refractory, turbulent, unruly.
দুন্দুভি, ভেরী, a sort of long trumpet, a celebrated giant.
দুমড়ন, ভাঁজন, মোড়ন, to fold, to double, to turn as the edge of a weapon, to bend.
দুরদৃষ্ট, মন্দ ভাগ্য, bad fortune, evil destiny, a hard fate.
দুরন্ত, দুষ্ট, ঢেঁটা, অবাধ্য, উপদ্রবী, wicked, vicious, unruly, impudent, severe, oppressive.
দুরবস্থা, দুর্দ্দশা, আপদ, adversity, calamity, distress.
দুরাচার, কুব্যবহারী, profligate, vicious, wicked.
দুরাত্মা, পাপী, নির্দ্দয়, ক্রূর, উপদ্রবী, profligate, wicked, unjust, severe, tyrannical, oppressive.
দুরালাপ, কটুবাক্য, scurrilous or abusive language, abuse.
দুরাশয়, দুষ্টমনাঃ, evil-minded, malicious, evil-intentioned.
দুরিত, পাপ, পাপী, পচা, নষ্ট, sin; sinful, vitiated, tainted, musty, putrid, rotten. [ved.
দুরিষ্ট, অতিমন্দ, পাপিষ্ঠ, very bad, very wicked, very depra-
দুরূহ, গূঢ়, কঠিন, কষ্টসাধ্য, abstruse, obscure, difficult, hard.
দুর্গ, কষ্টগম্য, গড়, difficult of access, a castle, fort, fortress, tower.
দুর্গত, দুঃখী, দরিদ্র, wretched, miserable, poor, needy.
দুর্গতি, ক্লেশ, দুরবস্থা, দরিদ্রতা, distress, hardship, wretchedness, misery, poverty. [ill-scented.
দুর্গন্ধ, কুবাস, কুবাসী, a stench, unpleasant scent ; fœtid,
দুর্গম, কষ্টগম্য, inaccessible, impenetrable, impassable, difficult.

দুর্গা, ভগবতী, a goddess the consort of Shiva.

দুর্ঘট, কষ্টসাধ্য, উপদ্রবী, difficult, hard to be accomplished, calamitous. [cumstance.

দুর্ঘট-ন, দুর্ভাগ্য, calamity, misfortune, a disagreeable cir-

দুর্জন, ক্রূর, দুষ্ট, খল, উপদ্রবী, পাপিষ্ঠ, ill-natured, surly, malevolent, cruel, tyrannical, unruly, wicked, mischievous. [earned victory.

দুর্জয়, কষ্টজেয়, কষ্টলব্ধ বিজয়, difficult to be subdued ; a hard

দুর্দান্ত, কষ্টদম্য, not easily subdued or suppressed.

দুর্দিন, কুসময়, মেঘাচ্ছন্ন দিন, বিপৎকাল, bad or rainy weather, a wet or cloudy day, a season of calamity.

দুর্দর্শ, অপ্রত্যক্ষ, অস্পষ্ট, scarcely visible.

দুর্দশা, বিপত্তি, অনিষ্ট. calamity, misery, adversity, danger.

দুধুরাণ, কম্পন, গুরুগুরাণ, to tremble, shake, palpitate.

দুর্ধর্ষ, নির্লজ্জ, অত্রপ, not to be abashed, confident, bold, shameless, impudent.

দুর্নাম, অখ্যাতি, কুৎসা, নিন্দা, an ill name, bad reputation or character, obloquy, slander.

দুর্নীত, কষ্টপ্রাপ্ত, obtained with difficulty. [tration.

দুর্নীতি, অন্যায়, অবিচার, injustice, impolicy, mal-adminis-

দুর্বর্ত্ম, কুপথ, কদাচার, দুষ্ট, a bad road, evil conduct ; profligate, vicious. [ated.

দুর্বল, অসমর্থ, ক্ষীণ, weak, feeble, infirm, impotent, emaci-

দুর্বিধ, মন্দপ্রকার, দুষ্ট, of a bad sort or kind, bad, wicked.

দুর্বুদ্ধি, দুর্বোধ,—মূঢ়ত্ব, অজ্ঞান, কুমতি, দুষ্ট, প্রবঞ্চক, stupidity, obstinacy in evil ; stupid, obstinate, wicked, crafty ; a cheat, a rogue.

দুর্বৃত্ত, দুরাত্মা, উপদ্রবী, অবশ, অবাধ্য, অবক্ষুধিত, ill-disposed, wicked, oppressive, unruly, unmanageable, ungovernable, ravenous.

দুর্ব্যাপার, কুআচার, ইন্দ্রিয়নিগ্রহ, evil conduct or practice, self-denial, mortification.

দুর্ভগা, অপ্রিয়ভার্য্যা, a wife hated or disliked by her husband.

দুর্ভাগ্য, দুরদৃষ্ট মন্দকপাল, a misfortune, ill luck.

দুর্ভিক্ষ, আকাল, মহার্ঘতা, a famine, dearth, scarcity.

দুর্মদ, মোহিত, মত্ত, তমোগুণযুক্ত, অহংকৃত, infatuated, blinded by pride, intoxicated with success or praise, rejoicing in evil.

[thoughtful.

দুর্ম্মনা, উদ্বিগ্নচিত্ত, বিষণ্ণ, sad, sorrowful, dejected, anxious,

দুর্ম্মা, অর্দ্ধপক্ক নারিকেল, a cocoanut when soft or half ripe.

দুর্ম্মুখ, নিষ্ঠুরভাষী, অপ্রিয়বাদী, abusive, foul-mouthed, scurrilous.

[priced.

দুর্মূল্য, আকাল, মহার্ঘ্য, a high price, dearness; dear, high-

দুর্মেধা, অজ্ঞান, নির্ব্বোধ, dull, stupid, of slender intellect.

দুর্য্যোগ, বিলগ্ন, মন্দ সময়, কুৎসিত সন্ধি, অনেক বাধকের একত্র মিলন, badly joined, cloudy, inclement; a bad joining, an evil connection, a complication of difficulties.

দুর্লক্ষণ, অশুভসূচক চিহ্ন, an evil mark, unlucky sign, ill omen.

দুর্লভ-্য, দুষ্প্রাপ্য, মহার্ঘ্য, difficult of attainment, scarce, rare.

দুর্হৃদ, দুর্মতি, বিপক্ষ, রিপু, inimical, ill-disposed; an enemy.

দুলাল, প্রেম, অনুরাগ, a dandling, a fondling, fondness.

দুলাল্য, প্রিয়, স্নিগ্ধ, স্নেহপাত্র, dear, beloved, fondled; a darling, a beloved object.

দুলিয়া, যানবাহ, কাহার, a bearer, palkee-bearer, porter.

দুশ্চরিত্র, মন্দ প্রকৃতি, বিটল, an evil disposition; ill-disposed, vicious.

[tressing, wicked.

দুষ্কর, কঠিন, ক্লেশকর, পাপাত্মা, difficult, hard, severe, dis-

দুষ্কর্ম্ম, দুষ্ক্রিয়া,—কুক্রিয়া, পাপ, ব্যভিচার, an evil act, a crime, sin, fornication.

[cious.

দুষ্কর্ম্মা, দুষ্কৃতী,—পাপী, ভ্রষ্ট, wicked, profligate, criminal, vi-

দুষ্কৃত, পাপ, কুক্রিয়া, অঘ, পাপী, sin, wickedness, crime, guilt; evil, wicked.

[distress.

দুস্থ, পীড়া, ক্লেশ, pain, suffering, vexation, affliction;

দুস্থী, দুস্থিত,—ক্লেশবিশিষ্ট, কাতর, suffering pain, poor, afflicted, vexed, &c.

দুষ্ট, ভ্রষ্ট, পাপিষ্ঠ, অজপ, বিরুদ্ধান্তঃকরণ, অশুদ্ধ, মন্দ, vile, wicked, vicious, depraved, dissolute, impure, impudent, dishonest, turbulent, wrong, evil, improper.

[lainy, turpitude.

দুষ্টামি, ভ্রষ্টাচার, লম্পটতা, wickedness, dissoluteness, vil-

দুষ্পাচ, গুরুপাক, difficult of digestion, indigestible,

দুষ্পার, দুস্তর,—অতরণার্হ, অনিবার্য্য, impassable, insurmountable, hard to be gotten over, unavoidable.

দুষ্পূর, অসন্তোষণীয়, অসম্পূর্ণ, hard to please, nice, unfilled.

দুসূতী, মোটা কাপড় বিশেষ, a coarse cloth made of double threads.

দুস্থ, দুরবস্থা, দুঃখী, দরিদ্র, disagreeably situated, afflicted, miserable, poor.

দুহাকার, উভয়ের, of both, of two persons (referred to.)

দুহাতিয়া, সব্যসাচী, দ্বিমনাঃ, দ্ব্যর্থ, দুই হস্ত দিয়া ভক্ষণাদিকর, ambidexter, double-minded, having two objects, eating or working with both hands.

দুহিতা, পুত্রী, কন্যা, a daughter.

দুহ্যমান, যাহার দোহন হইতেছে, under the operation of milking.

দূত, প্রেরিত, চর, দূত, কোটনা, a messenger, ambassador, angel, spy, a procurer, pander, pimp.

দূতী, প্রেরিতা, কুটনী, a female messenger, procuress, bawd.

দূর, অসন্নিকট, অন্তর, অসমীপে, distant, remote; distance; far, afar, away.

দূরদর্শী, দীর্ঘদর্শী, পরিণামদর্শী, বিজ্ঞ, গৃধ্র, far-seeing, provident, sagacious, wise; a vulture.

দূরাদূর, সর্ব্বত্র, অত্যন্তান্তর, far and near, every where; very far, very distant.

দূর্ব্বা, তৃণ বিশেষ, a species of excellent grass, bent grass.

দূষণ, ত্রুটি, অপরাধ, নিন্দা, দোষ প্রকাশন, খণ্ডন, ভর্ৎসন, a fault, guilt, blame, reproach; to convict, condemn, confute, point out faults, blame, reproach.

দূষণাবহ, নিন্দনীয়, occasioning guilt, reproachful.

দূষ্য, নিন্দিত, তাম্বু, condemnable, blamable, confutable; a tent.

দৃক্, চক্ষুঃ, দর্শন, দর্শী, তুল্য, an eye, sight; *in comp.* seeing, like.

দৃক্‌পাত, অবলোকন, a look, regard, survey, view.

দৃঢ়, শক্ত, কঠিন, অচল, স্থাবর, অটল, অনড়, নিষ্ঠ, স্থির, ঠিক, firm, hard, stiff, strong, tight, tough, solid, fast, stable, fixed, sure, irrevocable, inviolable, strict, resolute, accurate.

দৃঢ়বাদী, নিষ্ঠবক্তা, সত্যভাষী, affirming, asserting confidently, faithful to his word.

দৃঢ়বোধ, দৃঢ়জ্ঞান, —অনুভাব, প্রত্যয়, নির্ভর, নিশ্চয়, firm persuasion, assurance, conviction, certainty.

দৃশ্য, চক্ষুগোচর, সুন্দর, visible, perceptible, handsome.

দৃষ্ট, ঈক্ষিত, আলোকিত, প্রত্যক্ষ, seen, viewed, beheld, observed, apparent.

দৃষ্টতঃ, অনুমানে, স্পষ্টে, seemingly, ostensibly, apparently.

দৃষ্টান্ত, উদাহরণ, উপমা, an example, illustration, proof, simile, metaphor, parable.

দৃষ্টি, আলোকনা, নিরীক্ষণ, চক্ষুপাত, a view, look, glance, regard, sight, vision, a scene, a prospect.

দৃষ্টিগোচর, আলোকনীয়, সাক্ষাতে, an object of sight; within view, in sight.

দৃষ্টিধরা, তারা, নেত্রমণি, the pupil of the eye.

দৃষ্টে, অনুমানে, অপদেশে, apparently, seemingly, in pretence.

দেউড়ী, বারাণ্ডা, দ্বার, a vestibule, entrance, porch.

দেউল, দেবালয়, চড়কপূজাকর্ত্তা, a temple, one who holds or superintends the charakpújá.

দেউলী, দেউলিয়া,—হৃতসর্ব্বস্ব, a bankrupt.

দেউলী, কার্ত্তিক মাসের পর্ব্ব বিশেষ, an illumination on the new moon of the month Kártic.

দেওন, দানকরণ, অর্পণ, নিবেদন, স্বীকরণ, to give, present, grant, offer, admit, allow.

দেখন, দর্শন, অবলোকন, মানন, to see, look, view, behold, observe, spy, regard, visit. [visit.

দেখা, দৃষ্টিপাত, আলোকনা, সাক্ষাৎ, a view, sight, look, glance,

দেখাদৃষ্টে, প্রত্যক্ষতঃ, evidently, plainly, clearly. [other.

দেখাদেখি, মুখামুখি, অনুকরণ, face to face; an imitation of an-

দেখান, দর্শান, প্রকাশন, to shew, point out, manifest, display, exhibit.

দেখারু, দৃশ্য, প্রদর্শক, perceivable, &c. one who shews, &c.

দেদীপ্যমান, জাজ্বল্যমান, অতিশয় প্রকাশ্যমান, refulgent, resplendent, conspicuous. [ought to be given.

দেনা, ধার, ত্যাগ, নিবেদনীয়, a debt, gift, oblation, what

দেনুয়া, ত্যক্ত, নিবেদিত, offered as an oblation, given to Brahmins. [king, person of rank; sir.

দেব, অমর, সুর, রাজা, প্রকাশবস্ত, ঠাকুর, ভবান্, a god, dæmon,

দেবকী, কৃষ্ণের মাতা, Chrishna's mother.
দেবকুসুম, লবঙ্গ, cloves, the clove tree. [grotto.
দেবখাত-ক, অকৃত্রিম জলাশয়, a natural pond, cave, cavern,
দেবগর্জ্জন, মেঘের শব্দ, বজ্রনিস্বন, thunder, a clap of thunder.
দেবতা, সুর, ঠাকুর, আকাশ, a god, a deity, the clouds, the heavens.
দেবতালয়, দেবালয়,—ঠাকুরবাড়ী, a temple, or image-house.
দেবত্ব, দেবনিষ্ঠধর্ম্ম, অমরপদ, দেবপ্রতিষ্ঠাকরণ, deity, godhead, divinity, deification. [lands.
দেবত্র, দেবস্ব, ঠাকুরভূমি, the endowment of a temple, temple
দেবদত্ত, নিবেদিত, দৈবাধীন, অমুক, given to or by a god, some one (name unknown), something.
দেবদারু, বৃক্ষ বিশেষ, a species of pine.
দেবদূত, দেবপ্রেরিত, ভূতাদি, an angel or messenger of the gods.
দেবনিষ্ঠ, ঈশ্বরবাদী, ঈশ্বরভক্ত, firmly believing in God, pious, religious; a theist.
দেবনিষ্ঠা, ঈশ্বরশ্রদ্ধা, theism, a firm belief in God.
দেবপূজা, পুত্তলিকারাধনা, প্রতিমাপূজা, idolatry, image-worship.
দেবদাসী, বেশ্যা, a harlot, a courtezan. [ing.
দেববাণী, দেববাক্য, ঈশ্বরোক্তি, an oracle, a divine word or say-
দেবযাত্রা, পর্ব্বকালীন যাত্রা, উৎসবকালীন দেবমূর্ত্তি বহা, an idolatrous procession or carriage of sacred images.
দেবযোনি, উপদেবতা, ভূতাদি, দেবজনিত, a demigod, dæmon, super-human being; descended from a god.
দেবর, পতির কনিষ্ঠ ভ্রাতা, a husband's younger brother.
দেবর্ষি, নারদাদি ঋষি, a Rishi or celestial saint, a divine sage.
দেবল, দেবপূজাজীবী, পূজারি ব্রাহ্মণ, an attendant on an idol, a low Brahmin who lives on the offerings to an idol which he attends for hire, a certain Muni.
দেবলোক, অমর্ত্ত্যভুবন, স্বর্গ, heaven, the abode of the gods.
দেবস্থল, দেবস্থান, দেবালয়,—মন্দির, a temple, a pagoda.
দেবস্ব, দেবতার দ্রব্য, দেবপূজার্থ সংস্থাপিত ধন, a religious endowment, consecrated property, &c. [the gods.
দেবহিংসক, অসুর, সুরারি, an infernal being, one who injures
দেবী, দেবজাতীয় স্ত্রী, রাজার অভিষিক্তা স্ত্রী, প্রকাশবতী, Durgá, any goddess, a queen, a woman of rank; madam.

দেয়, দানযোগ্য, অর্প্য, পরিশোধ্য, fit to be given, that ought to be given, due, payable.

দেশ, পৃথিবীর খণ্ড, চাকলা, স্থান, স্থল, a country, region, province, tract, spot, place, side, part of the body. [where.

দেশময়, পরিপূর্ণ, ব্যাপ্ত, সর্ব্বত্র, full, abundant, pervading, every

দেশাধিপ, দেশাধিপতি,—অধিরাজ, রাজ্যাধিকারী, a sovereign, king, ruler, governor.

দেশান্ত, দেশের সীমা, the boundary of a country, a frontier.

দেশান্তর, বিদেশ, অন্য দেশ, a foreign country.

দেশী-য়, দেশজাত, দেশসম্বন্ধীয়, দেশের, natural to or produced in a country, of or belonging to a country.

দেহ, শরীর, প্রকৃতি, the body, matter, material nature, stature, constitution.

দেহপাত, মরণ, শরীরপতন, dying, death, the falling of the body.

দেহহীন, অভৌতিক, অনঙ্গ, অশারীরিক, unembodied, spiritual, immaterial, incorporeal.

দেহাত্মবাদী, আত্মানিষেধক, নাস্তিক, attributing spirituality to matter, a materialist. [the embodied soul.

দেহী, শরীরী, শরীরযুক্ত, জীব, corporeal, material, embodied;

দেহোদ্ভূত, শরীরজ, স্বাভাবিক, born in the body, inborn, natural.

দৈত্য, অসুর, an Asur, demon, titan, an evil genius.

দৈন্য, দরিদ্রতা, কৃপণতা, poverty, want, wretchedness, cringing, meanness. [mean.

দৈন্যী, দুঃখী, নিঃস্ব, কৃপণ, indigent, poor, needy, wretched,

দৈব, অদৃষ্ট, কর্ম্মভোগ, বিধাতা, ঐশ্বরিক, দেবাধীন, destiny, fate, the consequences of the actions of a former birth, providence, an incident, misfortune; divine, celestial, religious, sacred, providential.

দৈবকর্ম্ম, যজ্ঞাদি, religious acts or ceremonies, as sacrifices, &c. [teller.

দৈবজ্ঞ, গণক, an astrologer, caster of nativities, fortune-

দৈবযোগ, বিধাতৃকর্ম্ম, a divine impulse or interposition.

দৈবযোগে, দৈবাৎ,—হঠাৎ, অকস্মাৎ, providentially, by divine interposition, by chance, accidentally, unexpectedly, from above.

দৈবাধীন, দৈবায়ত্ত, হঠাৎকার, providential, casual, accidental, subject to fate, granted by providence, chance, fortuitous.

দৈবামৃত্যু, অকস্মাৎ মৃত্যু, sudden or accidental death.

দৈবী, হঠাৎ ঘটনা, আপদ, a providential occurrence, accident, disaster, mishap. [judgement.

দৈবোৎপাত, কর্ম্মবিপাক, a providential calamity, a divine

দৈর্ঘ-s, দ্রাঘিমা, লম্বাই, length.

দো, দুই, দ্বি, two. [twice.

দোকর, পুনর্কৃত, দ্বিগুণ, পুনর্ব্বার, repeated, doubled, double;

দোথা, গাঙ্গানী, the tie of a yoke, &c. [a dilemma.

দোটানা, দুদিগে মনাকর্ষ, দ্বৈধ, a pulling or soliciting two ways,

দোঠকা, শঠ, খল, a double-dealing person, a mischief-maker.

দোতত্ত্ব, উপায়ান্তর, উভয়ের মধ্যে একেতে মনোসংযোগ, an option, alternative, a choice of two.

দোতাল্লা, যাহার দুই তালা আছে, দোপেঁচা, having two stories, double-locking, (a kind of padlock.)

দোদোল্যমান, ঝুলনিয়া, ঝুলঝুলিয়া, swinging, oscillating.

দোপড়া, দ্বিরূঢ়া, *f.* a twice married woman.

দোমালা, পরিপক্ক নারিকেল, the cocoanut &c. when ripe enough to have a double shell. [fro.

দোল-না, ঝোলনা, a swinging, oscillating, rocking to and

দোলন, ঝুলন, নড়ন, হেলন, ঝোঁকন, to swing, vibrate, rock, roll, totter, wave.

দোলনী, ঝোলা, a swing.

দোলমাল, ঝোলামি, a swinging at random. [of Chrishna.

দোলযাত্রা, কল্পোৎসব, the swinging festival in commemoration

দোলা, ঝোলা, শিবিকা, a swing, litter, dooly, palkee, a jolt.

দোলান, ঝোলান, নড়ান, to swing, cause to swing, agitate, shake, move, jolt. [to and fro.

দোলায়মান, ঝুলনিয়া, নড়নিয়া, swinging, oscillating, moving

দোলিয়া, দোলাবাহক, a palkee or litter bearer.

দোষ, ত্রুটি, ছিদ্র, কলঙ্ক, ভ্রম, পাপ, অপরাধ, অপ্রামাণ্য, আপত্তি, গ্রন্থা, নিন্দা, হিংসা, অনিষ্ট, আপদ, অশুভ, a fault, defect, blemish, flaw, mistake, error, disorder, sin, offence, vice, guilt, objection, inconclusiveness, refutation, blame, accusation, defamation, calumny, disadvantage, injury, evil, unpropitiousness, unluckiness.

দোষকর, হিংসুক, অনিষ্টকর, hurtful, injurious, prejudicial.

দোষক্ষেত্র, অপরাধস্থান, অপরাধী, ব্যাধিযুক্ত শরীর, the scene of crime, a criminal, a diseased body. [abuser.

দোষগায়ক, নিন্দক, ভর্ৎসক, calumniating; a calumniator,

দোষগ্রাহক, অপবাদক, নিন্দক, charging with faults, imputing crimes, criminating, accusing.

দোষণ-আন, দোষ দেওন, অপবাদন, ভর্ৎসন, নিন্দন, খণ্ডন, to criminate, impute a crime, find fault, accuse, blame, upbraid, invalidate, weaken, confute, condemn. [guilt.

দোষনাশ, পাপমোচন, the expiation or removal of sin and

দোষস্থান, অপরাধক্ষেত্র, নিন্দাস্পদ, the scene of crime, a criminal, guilty person. [nation.

দোষাদোষি, পরস্পর অপবাদ করা, mutual accusation or recrimi-

দোষী, অপরাধী, নিন্দনীয়, অশুদ্ধ, সছিদ্র, guilty, criminal, culpable, blamable, sinful, incorrect, faulty, inaccurate, unsound.

দোসর, দ্বিতীয়, সঙ্গী, a second, a secondary.

দোসরা, দ্বিতীয়, অন্য, আরএক, second, another.

দোহন, দুগ্ধনিঃসারণ, দুয়ান, লাভভোগকরণ, নিগড়ান, to milk an animal, to cheat, cozen, draw a revenue or advantage from, oppress. [fœtus, embryo.

দোহদ, ইচ্ছা, স্পৃহা, কলঙ্ক, গর্ভ, a longing, a desire, a stain, mark,

দোহা, শ্লোক, পদ্য বিশেষ, a couplet, a sort of verse

দোহার, সহায়, উত্তরসাধক, a second, a prompter.

দোহারা, দ্বিগুণ, দ্বিতীয়, পুনর্বার, double, two-fold, second; again.

দৌড়, অতিবেগে গমনকরা, শ্রম, চেষ্টা, প্রয়োগ, a race, running, pains, endeavour, exertion. [endeavour.

দৌড়ন, ধাবন, বেগে চলন, চেষ্টাকরণ, to run, hasten, speed, escape,

দৌড়ান, বেগান, ছুটান, চালান, to make one run, hasten, accelerate, impel, drive. [a messenger.

দৌত্য, সমাচার, প্রেরিতত্ব, an embassy, message, the office of

দৌবারিক, দ্বারপালক, a porter, a door-keeper.

দৌরাত্ম্য, উৎপাত, দুষ্টামি, violence, outrage, tyranny, oppression, wickedness.

দৌর্জন্য, দুরাচার, বিটনামী, উপদ্রব, wickedness, unprincipled conduct, villainy, violence.

দৌর্বল্য, ক্ষীণতা, শ্রান্তি, weakness, feebleness, infirmity, fatigue.

দৌহিত্র, দুহিতার পুত্র, a daughter's son, a grandson.

দ্যুতি, দীপ্তি, শোভা, light, splendor, lustre, beauty.

দ্যূত, পাশি, পাশাক্রীড়া, dice, a playing at dice.

দ্যোত, দীপ্তি, রৌদ্র, light, lustre, sunshine, heat.

দ্রব, গলতি, গলাভাব, রস, দ্রুত, গলিত, তরল, fusion, a melting, liquefaction, dissolving, solution, fluid state, a fluid; liquid, melted, fluid, dissolved.

দ্রবার্হ, গলনীয়. fusible, malleable, soluble, dissolvable.

দ্রব্য, বস্তু, পদার্থ, স্বতঃস্থায়ী, সামান্য ধন, সামগ্রী, ঔষধ, a thing, substance, matter, article, household stuff, goods, baggage, materials, a drug, a medicament.

দ্রাক্ষা, গোস্তনী, মৃদ্বীকা, a grape, a raisin.

দ্রাক্ষালতা, মৃদ্বীকার গাছ, a vine.

দ্রাবক, দ্রবকারক, গলানিয়া, a solvent, a flux for metals; solvent.

দ্রাবণ, গলান, to fuse, melt, disolve, resolve.

দ্রাবী, দ্রাব্য,—গলনীয়, fusible, malleable, soluble.

দ্রু, দ্রুম,—বৃক্ষ, গাছ, a tree.

দ্রুণ, বৃশ্চিক, অলী, ভ্রমর, বিট, a scorpion, a bee, a cheat, a rogue.

দ্রুত, শীঘ্র, ত্বরান্বিত, তরল, গলিত, ঝটিতি, quick, fleet, swift, speedy, hasty, liquid, fluid, melted, fused, dissolved; swiftly, quickly,

দ্রুমাগ্র, বৃক্ষের ডাল, the branch of a tree.

দ্রোণ, অষ্ট আঢ়ক পরিমাণ, a measure of capacity.

দ্রোণকাক, দাঁড়কাক, বায়স, the raven or carrion crow.

দ্রোণী, ডোঙ্গা, a canoe, raft, any boat-shaped vessel, tub, &c.

দ্রোহ, পরমন্দচেষ্টা, অনিষ্টাচরণ, হিংসা, বধ, malice, spite, envy, injury, mischief, murder.

দ্রোহক, দ্রোহী—হিংসুক, দ্বেষী, অনিষ্টাচারী, বধিক, injurious, hurtful, spiteful, envious, malicious, sanguinary, murderous.

দ্বন্দ্ব, যুগ্ম, যোড়, মিলিত দুই, কলহ, a pair of animals, male and female, man and wife, a couple, brace, any two opposites, as good and evil; a dispute, strife, quarrel.

দ্বন্দ্বী, কলহী, বিবাদশীল, quarrelsome, disputatious, litigious.

দ্বয়, যোড়, মিলিত দুই, *affix*. a pair, brace, couple, two.

দ্বাঃস্থ, দ্বারস্থিত, দ্বারপাল, standing at the door or gate; a doorkeeper.

দ্বাপর, তৃতীয় যুগ, সন্দেহ, the third Yug, doubt, uncertainty.

দ্বার, প্রবেশের পথ, দরজা, উপায়, a door or gate-way, passage, entrance, a door, gate, window, a way, means. [count of.

দ্বারা-অ. করণক, হেতুক, by, through, by means of, on ac-

দ্বারী, দ্বারপালক, a doorkeeper, a porter, a warden.

দ্বি. দ্বির,—দুই, *in compos:* two, twice, double.

দ্বিকর, দুই হস্ত, দুইহস্তবিশিষ্ট, two hands; having two hands.

দ্বিগুণ, দোহারা, দ্বিতয়, double, two-fold.

দ্বিজ, পুনর্জাত, অণ্ডজ, পক্ষী, দন্ত, ব্রাহ্মণাদি তিন বর্ণ, twice-born, oviparous; any oviparous animal, a bird, &c. a tooth, a man of either of the three first classes.

দ্বিজাত, দ্বিজাতি,—পুনর্বার জন্মপ্রাপ্ত, ব্রাহ্মণাদি, twice born; a brahmin, kshyatriya or vais.

দ্বিজাতীয়, ব্রাহ্মণসম্বন্ধীয়, বিজাতীয়, খচ্চর, of or belonging to brahmins, &c. mongrel, of mixed breed; a mule.

দ্বিজরাজ, চন্দ্র, গরুড়, অনন্ত, the moon, the bird of Vishnu, the serpent Ananta. [twofold.

দ্বিতয়, যুগ্ম, দুই, দ্বিবিধ, দ্বিগুণ, a couple, two; of two sorts,

দ্বিতীয়, একের পর, উপসর্জ্জন, ইতর, অন্য, অপর, second, secondary, inferior, next, different, other.

দ্বিত্র্যহ, ত্র্যহ, in two or three days, two or three days ago.

দ্বিত্ব, পুনঃকরণ, reduplication, repetition. [principled.

দ্বিদলিয়া, দুই পক্ষাক্রান্ত, দুষ্ট, belonging to two parties, un-

দ্বিধা, দুই প্রকার, ঝঞ্ঝাট, সন্দেহ, ব্যর্থ, in two ways; of two kinds; a dilemma, doubt, hesitation, ambiguity. [certain.

দ্বিধাকল্প, সন্দেহ বিষয়, অনিশ্চয়, doubtful, precarious, un-

দ্বিধাকল্পন, সন্দিগ্ধ হওন, ভাবন, বিতর্কণ, to doubt, hesitate, be in suspense, to ponder.

দ্বিপ, হস্তী, an elephant.

দ্বিপদ, দ্বিপাদ,—দুইপাদবিশিষ্ট, মনুষ্য, biped, two footed ; man.

দ্বিমুখ, যাহার দুই মুখ, সাপ বিশেষ, ধূর্ত্ত, having two heads or mouths, two faced ; a serpent, amphisbæna, an artful or deceitful person.

দ্বিরদ, হস্তী, an elephant.

দ্বিরুক্তি, পুনঃকথন, tautology, repetition. [sorts, twofold.

দ্বিরূপী, দুমূর্ত্তি, দ্বিগুণাকৃতি, দ্বিপ্রকারক, having two forms, of two

দ্বিরেফ, ভ্রমর, a bee, a large black bee.

দ্বীপ, জলমধ্যবর্ত্তি বৃহৎ স্থান, চড়া, ভুবনখণ্ড, an island, any land between two waters, a continent, a division of the world.

দ্বেষ, হিংসেচ্ছা, হিংসা, malice, enmity, hatred, injuriousness.

দ্বেষণ, ঘৃণাকরণ, to hate, dislike, bear malice. [licious.

দ্বেষী, শত্রু, হিংসেচ্ছু, hating, hostile, injurious, envious, ma-

দ্বেষ্টা, দ্বেষৈষী,—শত্রু, হিংসেচ্ছু, malevolent, malignant, malicious. [a duplication, doubt.

দ্বৈত, যোট, পুনঃকরণ, সন্দেহ, a second of the same kind,

দ্বৈতজ্ঞ, দ্বৈতবাদী,—ভিন্নেশ্বরবাদী, ব্রহ্মনিন্দক, an asserter of more gods than one, a polytheist, an antipantheist or opposer of the doctrines of Brahma.

দ্বৈতজ্ঞান, দ্বৈতবাদ,—ভিন্নেশ্বরজ্ঞান, ব্রহ্মনিষেধ, a maintaining of many gods, polytheism, an assertion of the distinction of the soul from god.

দ্বৈধ, সংশয়, দ্ব্যর্থ, ব্যঙ্গোক্তি, ইতরোপায়, যুদ্ধ, দ্বিখণ্ড, বিচ্ছিন্ন, a doubt, dilemma, ambiguity, pun, double-meaning, stratagem, a double resource, a reserve of troops, a twofold form or state, a contest, a duel ; divided, split.

দ্ব্যগ্র, অগ্রদ্বয়বিশিষ্ট, বিদীর্ণ, having two points, bifid, biceps.

দ্ব্যর্থ, অর্থদ্বয়যুক্ত, দ্ব্যর্থ, ব্যঙ্গোক্তি, having two objects, ambiguous, admitting two meanings ; a quibble, a pun, a double meaning.

দ্ব্যাহিক, ইতরেদ্যুপস্থিত, পারদিবসিক, occurring every other day.

ধ.

ধড়া, জীর্ণবস্ত্র, নেকড়া, কপ্নী, an old garment, old cloth, a rag, the strip of cloth covering the privities.

ধন, অর্থ, সম্পত্তি, বিভব, wealth, riches, property, treasure, goods, property in cattle, &c.

ধনঞ্জয়, অগ্নি, অর্জ্জুন, Agni the god of fire, a name of Arjuna.

ধনপতি, ধনাধিপ-তি,—কুবের, Cuvera the god of riches.

ধনবান্, অর্থবিশিষ্ট, wealthy, opulent, rich, affluent.

ধনমদ, বিভবগর্ব, the intoxication or pride of wealth.

ধনাঢ্য, ধনবান্, অর্থী, wealthy, rich, opulent.

ধনাধার, ধনাগার,—ভাণ্ডার, a treasury, storehouse, place for treasure.

ধনাধ্যক্ষ, অর্থরক্ষক, কুবের, a treasurer, a guardian of wealth, Cuvera the god of riches.

ধনার্জ্জন, অর্থোপায়চেষ্টা, the amassing or acquiring of wealth.

ধনাশা, অর্থের ইচ্ছা, the thirst of riches, a longing hope after wealth.

ধনিচা, পাটবৎ বৃক্ষ বিশেষ, a plant whose bark is used instead of hemp.

ধনিষ্ঠা, ত্রয়োবিংশতি নক্ষত্র, the twenty third lunar mansion.

ধনী, অর্থবিশিষ্ট, কুশলী, rich, opulent, fortunate, happy.

ধনুঃ, ধনু—চাপ, নবম রাশি, কার্পাস পরিষ্করণার্থ যন্ত্র, চতুর্হস্ত পরিমাণ, a bow, arc, curve, Sagittarius, a fiddle stick, an instrument for cleaning cotton, a measure of four cubits.

ধনুক, শর নিক্ষেপ যন্ত্র, কার্ম্মুক, কার্পাস পরিষ্করণার্থ যন্ত্র, ধনুঃ রাশি, a bow, Sagittarius, a violin or cotton bow.

ধনুবৎ, ধনুরাকার,—খিলানাকৃতি, বক্রীকৃত, curved, arched, bent.

ধনুর্গুণ, জ্যা, মৌর্বী, a bow string, the chord of an arc.

ধনুর্দ্ধর, ধনুর্বিশিষ্ট, bearing a bow; an archer, bowman.

ধনুষ্টঙ্কার, জ্যাশব্দ, অঙ্গগ্রহ, the twang of a bow, severe spasmodic affection.

ধনুস্তম্ভ, অঙ্গগ্রহজনিত মাংসকাঠিন্য, rigidity from severe spasmodic affection.

ধনেশ, কুবের, Cuvera the god of wealth, a species of bird.

ধন্দ-ন্দা, অন্ধতা, ভ্রম, ছল, dimness of sight, blindness, an oversight, over-looking, sleight, stratagem.

ধন্য, ভাগ্যবান্, প্রশংসিত, প্রশংসনীয়, ভগবান্, fortunate, happy, praised, praise worthy, estimable, blessed, glorious. [thanks.

ধন্যবাদ, স্তবকরা, সঙ্কীর্ত্তন, ascription of praise, thanksgiving,

ধন্যা, ধন্যাক,—সুক্ষ্মবীজফলক বৃক্ষ বিশেষ, the coriander plant and its seed.

ধন্বী, ধনুর্বিশিষ্ট, armed with a bow; an archer, bowman.

ধব, বস্ত্র, কাপড় বিশেষ, linen, linen cloth or clothes, a species of shrub.

ধবল, শুক্ল, সুন্দর, শ্বিত্র রোগ, white, handsome, beautiful; a leprosy appearing in white blotches.

ধবলী, শ্বেত গরু, a white cow.

ধমক, ভয়প্রদর্শক বাক্য, ভর্ৎসনা, তাড়না, a threat, threatening, censure, reprimand, chiding.

ধমন, জ্বলান, প্রজ্বলন, to kindle, light up, blaze.

ধমনী, নাড়ী, শিরা, a vein, artery, nerve, any tubular vessel.

ধম্মা, ভস্ত্রা, বায়ুপ্রবাহ, ঝড়, a pair of bellows, a gust of wind.

ধম্কান, তাড়ন, ভর্ৎসন, to threaten, rate, scold, reprimand, chide, reprove.

ধম্মিল্ল, বিন্যাসিত কেশ, the hair braided and ornamented.

ধরণ, প্রাপ্ত হওন, রাখন, গ্রহণ, পাকড়ন, আকর্ষণ, অবলম্বন, জানন, কাছান, যেন্নান, মনে রাখন, লেখন, ডিষ্টন, to have, hold, contain, possess, keep, arrest, seize, catch, assume, lay hold, adhere, uphold, support, detect, overtake, press, urge, importune, notice, write down, keep in mind, retain, continue, remain. [scaffold.

ধরণা, ভষ্টি, মঞ্চ, a dunning by sitting at one's door, a

ধরনাদায়ক, উত্তেজনাকারী, dunning; a dunner, one who duns.

ধরণি, ধরণী,—পৃথিবী, the earth. [hending.

ধরণিয়া, আঁকড়ানিয়া, গ্রাহক, taking, holding, seizing, appre-

ধরণীপতি, ধরণীপাল,—ভূপতি, রাজা, lord of the earth, a king, a sovereign. [sion, retention, &c.

ধরা, পৃথিবী, আক্রমণ, রাখা, the earth, seizure, apprehen-

ধরাট, ধার, ঋণ, উদ্ধারদণ্ড, a loan, a ransom. [plaster a wall.

ধরাণ, গ্রহণ করাণ, ভিত্তিলেপন, to cause to apprehend, &c. to

ধরাধর, পর্বত, বিষ্ণু, a mountain, Vishnu.

ধরায়, আক্রমণীয়, ধর্ত্তব্য, apprehensible, seizable.

ধরিত্রী, পৃথিবী, ক্ষৌণী, the earth.

ধর্ণা, উপবেশন, a mode of dunning by sitting down at one's door with a threat of starving if not paid.

ধর্ত্তব্য গ্রাহ্য, মান্য, দোষ্য, দণ্ডনীয়, প্রমেয়, deserving acceptance, retention, notice or animadversion, appehensible, assumable.

ধর্ম্ম, পুণ্য, কর্ত্তব্যকর্ম্ম, ন্যায়, গুণ, স্বভাব, রীতি, ভাব, নিয়মিত সদনুষ্ঠান, জাতিব্যবহার, যম, religious act or merit, duty, virtue, righteousness, justice, religion, piety, the nature or property of a thing, characteristic or distinctive quality, natural state or disposition, usage, practice, fitness, propriety, proper use or application of a thing, peculiar duty of an individual, customary observances of cast, sect, &c. Yama. [meritoriously.

ধর্ম্মতঃ, যথার্থরূপে, ন্যায়তঃ, religiously, piously, justly, rightly,

ধর্ম্মতা, দেবসেবা, সৎকর্ম্ম, religion, virtue, rectitude.

ধর্ম্মপত্তন, মরিচ, black pepper. [justice, meritorious.

ধর্ম্মযুক্ত, পুণ্যযুক্ত, পুণ্যবান্, connected with religion, virtue or

ধর্ম্মশালা, দানগৃহ, অতিথিশালা, বিচারস্থান, a religious edifice, an alms-house, hospital, receptacle for strangers, &c. a court of justice.

ধর্ম্মশাস্ত্র, স্মৃতিশাস্ত্র, পুরাণ প্রভৃতি, the great body of Hindoo laws, including moral, political, &c. religious duties and jurisprudence, holy or religious writings.

ধর্ম্মশীল, পুণ্যবান্, সুশীল, possessed of religious merit, virtuous, well-disposed.

ধর্ম্মসংহিতা, স্মৃতিসংক্ষেপ, কর্ম্মকাণ্ড, a digest or code of laws, a ritual of observances, manual of duties.

ধর্ম্মাত্মা, সাধু, পুণ্যশীল, পুণ্যাত্মা, holy, pious, virtuous, religious ; a saint or holy person, a holy spirit.

ধর্ম্মাধিকরণ, ব্যবস্থান, a court of law or justice, a tribunal.

ধর্ম্মাধিকার, বিচারাধ্যক্ষতা, the right of administering justice.

ধর্ম্মাধিকারী, বিচারকর্ত্তা, ভূপাল, an administer of the laws, judge, sheriff, a sovereign.

ধর্ম্মাধ্যক্ষ, দণ্ডকর্ত্তা, বিচারকর্ত্তা, a magistrate, a judge.

ধার্ম্মিক, ধর্ম্মী—সাধু, পুণ্যশীল, যাথার্থিক, virtuous, pious, religious, just, honest, upright.

ধর্ম্ম্য, ন্যায্য, উচিত, lawful, proper, just, right, virtuous.

ধর্ষক, বিক্রমী, সাহসিক, দুরন্ত, গর্ব্বিত, daring, bold, imposing, overbearing, overawing, arrogant, proud, contumelious.

ধর্ষণ, সাহসকরণ, ধমকান, গরিমা, to dare, challenge, browbeat, overawe, be overbearing; boldness, contumely, arrogance. [ther, midwife.

ধাই, ধাত্রী,—উপমাতা, প্রসবকারিণী, a wet-nurse, foster-mo-

ধাউড়িয়া, দ্রুতগামি ভৃত্য, দৌড়ানিয়া, running, going fast; a messenger, an express.

ধাওন, দৌড়ন, অনুধাবন, to go fast, run, pursue. [fleetness.

ধাওয়া, ত্বরা দৌড়, দ্রুতগতি, expedition, speed, running,

ধাক্কা, ঠেলা, ঠেসা, a push, thrust, shove, shock.

ধাড়িয়া, জলমার্জার, an otter.

ধাড়ী, এককালীন বহুপ্রসূতা স্ত্রীজন্তু, যাহার একত্র অনেক বৎস জন্মে, *f.* strong, robust, producing many young at a time, (spoken only of the females of animals); a dam.

ধাতা, ধাতৃ,—প্রতিপালক, পিতা, ব্রহ্মা, a nourisher, regulator, father, providence, Brahmá; nourishing, possessing, &c.

ধাতু, পঞ্চভূত, তাম্র পিত্তলাদি, জ্ঞানেন্দ্রিয়, রসপ্রভৃতি সাত, শ্লেষ্মাদি, অন্নরস, শুক্র, নাড়ী, ক্রিয়াবাচক শব্দ, a primary element, a metal, ore, mineral, fossil, a property of matter, an organ of sense, constituent part of the body, bodily humour, chyle, semen virile, a gleet, the pulse, a verbal root.

ধাতুক্ষয়, তেজহ্রাস, রসবিকার, the waste or decay of the vital functions or bodily humours, a mortal disease.

ধাতুনরম, কাসরোগ, কফ, a cold, cough, catarrh.

ধাতুপ, অন্নরস, the alimentary juice or chyle.

ধাতুপুষ্টি, রসবৃদ্ধি, মাংসবৃদ্ধি nutrition, nourishment, a fattening, strengthening.

ধাতুপোষক, হৃষ্টপুষ্টিকর, পথ্য, nutritive, nutritious, nourishing, fattening, restorative.

ধাতুবাদী, ধাতুবিদ্যাবেত্তা, ধাতুদ্রব্য পরীক্ষক, a mineralogist, miner, assayer. [humours.

ধাতুভেদ, রসবিকার, a change in the habit of the body or its

ধাতুময়. তৈজস, metallic, metal, made of metal.

ধাতুমারিণী, সোহাগা, borax, (used as a flux for metals.)

ধাতুসাম্য, সুস্বাস্থ্যতা, the equilibrium of the humours, perfect health. [foster-mother.

ধাত্রী, প্রসব করায় যে স্ত্রী, উপমাতা, a midwife, wet-nurse,

ধান্নী, অপরিষ্কৃত তণ্ডুল, rice imperfectly husked or cleaned.

ধানুষ্ক-ী, ধনুর্ধারী, an archer, a bowman.

ধান্য, ধান,—তুষেতে আবৃত তণ্ডুল, paddy or unhusked rice, corn or grain in general.

ধান্যশালী, ধান্যবপনযোগ্য ভূমি, শস্যময়, a soil favourable to the growth of rice; abounding in rice or other grain.

ধান্যাদি, শস্যযবাদি, rice and other grain, grain in general.

ধাপ, সোপানের প্রত্যেক পাদনিক্ষেপের স্থান, লম্ফ, the steps of a staircase or ladder, a leap, a jump, a spring.

ধাবক, দৌড়ানিয়া, দূত. a runner, messenger, express.

ধাবড়িয়া, দ্রুতগামী, quick, swift, fleet, running quick.

ধাবন, দৌড়ন, বেগে গমন, to run, to go with speed.

ধাবমান্, দ্রুতগামী, running, moving with speed.

ধাম, শরীর, গৃহ. বসতি, স্থান, দেশ, প্রভাব, দীপ্তি, রশ্মি, the body, a house, dwelling, spot, place, country, dignity, consequence, light, a ray of light.

ধাম্সা, টিকারা, ডঙ্কা, a sort of kettle-drum.

ধামা, ধামী,—বেত্র নির্ম্মিত পাত্র বিশেষ, a water scuttle or basket of close ratan work.

ধার, ঋণ, গহরা, গাম্ভীর্য্য, হিম, ক্ষরণি, সন্ততি, ছিদ্র, ঘোটকের পদগতি, উৎকর্ষ, সমূহ, অন্ত, শেষ, বেড়া, তীর, কূল, অস্ত্রের সূক্ষ্ম ভাগ, পুরোবর্ত্তি সেনা. a debt, loan, deep place, depth, frost, slight drizzling rain, a dripping, oozing, distillation, offspring, a leak, hole or flaw in a vessel, a horse's paces, excellence, a quantity, multitude, a sort of stone, an end, limit, boundary, garden fence, wall, hedge, the edge of a weapou, brow of a hill, a margin, brink, brim, the van of an army. [umpire, debtor.

ধারক, প্রাপ্ত, বিশিষ্ট, মধ্যস্থ, ঋণী, having. holding; a holder,

ধারণ, প্রাপ্ত হওন, গ্রহণ, অবলম্বন, রাখন, পরিধানকরণ. বেশকরণ, ঋণ লওন, to have, hold, keep, maintain, bear, support, sustain, uphold, retain, assume a dress, wear, borrow.

ধারণা, অধ্যবসায়, ন্যায্যপথাবলম্বন, মনস্থিরতা, ধ্যান, মনে রাখা, মেধা, ঋণ, perseverance, continuance in right, fortitude, firmness, resolution, immovable religious abstraction, memory, retention, debt.

ধারণাবান্, অধ্যবসায়ী. ইন্দ্রিয়দমক, persevering, firm, resolute, self-restraining. [the body.

ধারণী, সরল রেখা, নাড়ী, a straight line, any tubular vessel of

ধারযুক্ত, সুশানিত, তীক্ষ্ণ, sharp, having an edge.

ধারা, রীতি, ব্যবহার, প্রবাহ, চৌল, আচরণ. প্রকার, জলাদির অধঃপতন, প্রণালী, প্রকরণ, a custom, usage, practice, habit. course, fashion, rite, ceremony, posture, carriage, gait, conduct, behaviour, method, way, plan, order, sort, kind, drops or streams of rain, a water-course, a section, chapter.

ধারাধর, মেঘ, খড়্গ, a cloud, a sword. [follow custom.

ধারাবহন, নিত্য প্রবাহের অবলম্বন, to go with the stream, to

ধারাবাহক, ধারাবাহিক, ধারাবাহী,—গতানুগতিক, following the fashion, going with the stream of custom.

ধারায়, আক্রমণীয়, গ্রহণীয়, apprehensible, liable to be seized.

ধারাল, সুশানিত, তীক্ষ্ণ, sharp, keen-edged, pointed.

ধারী. তট, প্রাপ্ত, বিশিষ্ট, an edge, a margin; having, holding.

ধারে, তড়ায়, ঋণে, on shore, on credit, on trust.

ধার্ম্মিক, পুণ্যাত্মা. religious, pious, virtuous, righteous, just.

ধার্য্য, আক্রমণীয়, নিবার্য্য, গ্রহণার্হ, স্থির, নিয়ত, apprehensible, deserving of restraint, fit to be retained or upheld &c. fixed, settled.

ধিক্, ছিছি,-fye, out upon it, for shame, O fye!

ধিক্কার, তুচ্ছীকরা, অবজ্ঞা, নিন্দা, contempt, disrespect, reproach, censure.

ধিক্কৃত, নিন্দিত, শাপগ্রস্থ, reproached, reviled, contemned, cursed, &c.

ধিমা. ধীর, সাবধান, শান্ত, slow, cautious, pacified, lulled.

ধিমায়, ধীরে, deliberately, softly, faintly.

ধী, বুদ্ধি, understanding, intellect, knowledge, idea.

ধীন্দ্রিয়, জ্ঞানেন্দ্রিয়, an organ of perception.

ধীবর, মৎস্যবৃত্তি, কৈবর্ত্ত, a fisherman.

ধীমান্, বুদ্ধিমান, বৃহস্পতি, wise, intelligent, learned, sagacious; Vrihaspati.

ধীর, পণ্ডিত, প্রাজ্ঞ, অচঞ্চল, শান্ত, মৃদু, স্থিরমনাঃ, শিষ্ট, মন্দ, অবাধ্য, বলবান, প্রতাপান্বিত, wise, sensible, learned, sedate, grave, deliberate, serious, tranquil, quiet, serene, firm, steady, consistent, determined, temperate, docile, meek, slow, lazy, dull, headstrong, selfwilled, uncontrollable, strong, powerful, jealous yet calm.

ধীরে, মনঃস্থৈর্য্য পূর্ব্বক, deliberately, coolly, slowly, sedately.

ধীসচিব, মন্ত্রী, অমাত্য, a counsellor, minister, friendly adviser.

ধুওন, বস্ত্র প্রক্ষালন, জালাদি সারণ, to wash clothes, to repair or mend nets, &c.

ধুকন, হাঁপন, to pant with running, breathe hard.

ধুত, কম্পিত, ত্যক্ত, shaken, agitated, left, relinquished.

ধুতী, পরিধেয় বস্ত্র বিশেষ, ঘুষ, the long cloth worn about the loins, a bribe.

ধুনচি, তুলাপরিষ্কারক, a cotton cleaner.

ধুনন, কার্পাসবীজোদ্ধরণ, ফোড়ন, to card or clean cotton with the bow, to shake.

ধুম, প্রাথর্য্য, শ্রম, zeal, ardor, diligence, perseverance.

ধুমী, ব্যগ্র, বহুশ্রমী, প্রকাণ্ড, ardent, persevering, huge, great, prodigious.

ধুমমারী, গণ্ডগোল, sedition, rebellion, tumult, uproar.

ধুপী, রজক, ধোবা, a washerman.

ধুম্, ব্যগ্রতা, উৎপাত, ardour, fervour, zeal, oppression.

ধুমড়ী, চেমনী, বৈষ্ণবী, লম্পটী, a concubine, a strolling woman, a female Vaishnava.

ধুমড়ীমারা, ভ্রমণী, লম্পট, vagrant, vagabond, lecherous.

ধুম্ধাম্, ধুমাধুমি,—গণ্ডগোল, উপদ্রব, a tumult, mob, hubbub, storm.

ধুধুম, মৃদঙ্গের শব্দ, the beat or call of a drum. [song.

ধুয়া, গীতের ধ্রুবপদ, the introductory stanza or chorus of a

ধুর, ভার, ঠাহরা, ভাবনা, a load, burthen, pole of a carriage, reflexion, recollection, thought.

ধুরন্ধর, ধুরীণ,—ভারবাহক, রথশকটাদি বাহক পশু, bearing a burthen; a beast of burden.

ধুরন্ধরধুরীণ, রাজা, a king, a sovereign. [ing dish.

ধূনচি, ধূনী,—ধূপদানপাত্র, অঙ্গঠী, a censer, incense pot, chaff-

ধূনক, ধূনা,—বৃক্ষনির্য্যাস, যক্ষধূপ, the resin of the *shál* tree, pitch, incense, turpentine.

ধূপ, সর্জ্জরস, গন্ধবর্ত্তিকা, রৌদ্র, খড়্গ, resin, incense, fragrant vapour, the rays or heat of the sun, strong sun-shine, a sabre.

ধূপিত, সগন্ধ, বাসিত, perfumed with incense, scented.

ধূম, ধুঁয়া,—অগ্নিহইতে নিঃসৃত পরমাণুপুঞ্জ, বাষ্প, ভাপ, smoke, steam, vapour, tobacco vapour.

ধূমকেতু, শিখাবন্ত নক্ষত্র, অবম নক্ষত্র, অগ্নি, a comet, falling meteor, the descending node, Agni, fire.

ধূমতাল, ধূমপুঞ্জ,—স্তম্ভিত ধূম, a pillar or volume of smoke. [pour.

ধূমপান, তাম্রকূট খাওন, the smoking of tobacco, inhaling of va-

ধূমযোনি, মেঘ, a cloud. [ky, purple.

ধূম্র, কৃষ্ণরক্তমিশ্রিতবর্ণ, of a smoky or purple colour, smo-

ধূর্ত্ত, শঠ, প্রতারক, রসিক, খল, পাশাক্রীড়ক, crafty, cunning, sly, knavish, mischievous, injurious, waggish; a gamester, rogue, cheat, the thorn-apple.

ধূলা, ধূলী—শুষ্ক সূক্ষ্ম মৃত্তিকা, রেণু, dust, pollen.

ধূষরিত, ম্রক্ষিত, অক্ত, anointed, smeared.

ধূসর, ঈষৎ পাণ্ডুবর্ণ, গৃধ্র, কস্তু, a grey colour, an ass, a jackal, an oilman; of a grey colour, grey.

ধুসা, লুই, flannel. [apprehended.

ধৃত, আক্রান্ত, প্রাপ্ত, গৃহীত, held, possessed, caught, seized,

ধৃতি, প্রাপ্তি, মনঃস্থৈর্য্য, সন্তোষ, যাগ, ত্যাগ, যুগ, possession, a holding, having, firmness, steadiness, constancy, restraint, pleasure, satisfaction, happiness, sacrifice, an offering, religious rite, a species of verse, an astronomical Yog.

ধৃতিমান্, স্থির, দৃঢ়মনাঃ, সন্তুষ্ট, firm, steady, constant, restrained, satisfied, happy. [bold, insulting.

ধৃষ্ট, ধৃষ্ণু,—নির্লজ্জ, প্রগল্ভ, shameless, impudent, confident,

ধেড়িয়া, জলমার্জার, an otter.

ধেনু, সবৎসা গো, a milch-cow, a cow with a calf.

ধেয়, ধার্য্য, দমনীয়, fit or proper to be held, &c.

ধেয়ান, ঠাহরণ, চিন্তন, to think upon, ponder, meditate.

ধৈর্য্য, স্থিরতা, শান্তি, বিবেচনা, ক্ষান্তি, সহিষ্ণুতা, ইন্দ্রিয়দমন, steadiness, firmness, seriousness, gravity, deliberation, coolness, patience, forbearance, endurance, abstinence, temperance.

ধৈর্য্য, স্থির, অচঞ্চল, ক্ষমাশীল, সহিষ্ণু, steady, cool, deliberate, patient, forbearing.

ধোআট, নদ্যাগত মৃত্তিকা সঞ্চয়, alluvial soil, deposit after rain.

ধোওন, প্রক্ষালন, মার্জন, to wash, clean, rinse, clarify.

ধোঁকন, হাঁপন, to pant, be out of breath.

ধোকা, ভ্রম, মায়া, শঙ্কা, সন্দেহ, illusion, deception, error, suspicion, doubt. [linen.

ধোপ, শুভ্র, বস্ত্র প্রক্ষালন, clean, washed; the washing of

ধোপা, ধোবা,—বস্ত্রক্ষালনজীবী, রজক, a washerman.

ধোপানী, ধোবানী,—রজকী, a washerwoman, washerman's wife.

ধোপাল, কাচান, ধৌত, clean, washed. [ing.

ধোয়া, পরিষ্কৃত, প্রক্ষালন, clean, washed; a cleansing, wash-

ধোয়ানি, মলা, শিটা, washings, dregs.

ধোসা, কাপড় বিশেষ, a cloth half silk, half cotton.

ধৌত, প্রক্ষালিত, পরিষ্কৃত, washed, cleaned, purified, clean.

ধ্যাত, বিবেচিত, thought or meditated upon, pondered.

ধ্যাতা, ঠাহরণিয়া, বিবেচক, বিবেকী, one who meditates or contemplates; contemplative.

ধ্যান, চিন্তা, ভাবনা, যোগ, thought, contemplation, meditation, reflection, abstracted contemplation.

ধ্যানী, চিন্তিত, যোগী, thoughtful, contemplative, abstracted; a devotee. [stract devotion.

ধ্যানযোগ, ব্রহ্মচিন্তা, ঈশ্বরনিবেশ, religious abstraction, ab-

ধ্রুব, নিশ্চিত, স্থির, স্থাবর, নিত্য, অনবরতঃ, নিশ্চয়, নির্ণয়, বিতর্ক, স্থায়িত্ব, তারা বিশেষ, certain, ascertained, fixed, firm, stable, permanent, continual, eternal; permanently, certainly; certainty, ascertainment, logic, reasoning, discussion, permanence, the polar star, one of the twenty-seven astronomical yogs, a vasu demigod.

ধ্রুব, ধ্রুবপদ,—গানের পুনঃ২ অবলম্বন পদ, ধুয়া, an introductory stanza or chorus.

ধ্রুবকা, ধুয়া, *id:* also the longitude of a star.

ধ্রুবলোক, স্বর্গপুর, heaven and its inhabitants.

ধ্বংস-ন, নাশ, হানি, মরণ, অপমান, ভ্রংশ, destruction, ruin, loss, perishing, death, degradation, a fall or departure from virtue, &c.

ধ্বংসক, ধ্বংসী,—বিনাশক, উপদ্রবী, ruinous, destructive, destroying; a destroyer.

ধ্বজ-ং, ধ্বজী,—পতাকা, নিদর্শন, চিহ্ন, অঙ্ক, যূপ, a flag, banner, signal, standard, symbol, badge, mark, funeral pillar, monument.

ধ্বজ, পুরুষচিহ্ন, তপস্বির হস্তধৃত খুলী অর্থাৎ নৃকপাল, the penis, a scull carried in penance. [land-mark.

ধ্বজিনী, সৈন্য, উন্নত চিহ্ন, বৃক্ষাদি, an army, a tree or other high

ধ্বজবান্, পতাকাধারী, an ensign or standard-bearer.

ধ্বনি, শব্দ, রব, a sound, report, noise, voice, cry.

ধ্বনিত, শব্দিত, সংক্ষেপে কথিত, sounded, high-sounding, rhetorical, poetical. [degraded.

ধ্বস্ত, অধঃপতিত, হত, নষ্ট, ভ্রষ্ট, fallen, ruined, destroyed,

ধ্বান, অব্যক্ত শব্দ, sound in general, inarticulate sound.

ধ্বান্ত, অন্ধকার, darkness.

ন.

ন, নিষেধ বোধক শব্দ, no, not, neither, *pref.* without, free from, un, less, &c. [conversation.

নকার, অস্বীকার, নাবলা, denial, neglect, begging pardon in

নকারিয়া, নাবলিয়া, omitting one thing and doing another instead, denying, &c.

নকী, পিত্তল নির্ম্মিত পাত্র, a brass pot or pan.
নকুল, বেজী, the mongoose or ichneumon.
নক্ত, রাত্রি, রাত্রিকালে, the night; by night, at night.
নক্তব্রত, দিবসে অনাহার করিয়া রাত্রিতে ভোজনব্রত, a vow to eat only at night.
নক্র, কুম্ভীর, a crocodile or alligator.
নক্ষত্র, তারা, তারাসমূহ, a star, constellation, lunar mansion.
নক্ষত্রপতি, নক্ষত্ররাজ,—চন্দ্র, the moon.
নক্ষত্রলোক, তারামণ্ডল, the starry region. [claw, talon.
নখ, নখর,—অঙ্গুলির অগ্রোপরি ভাগ, থাবা, a finger or toe nail,
নখুনা, কুক্কুটের কাঁটা, the spur of a cock. [nails.
নখরঞ্জনী, নরুন, নখছেদনাস্ত্র, a small knife for paring the
নখশূল, আঙ্গুলহাড়া, কুণী, a whitlow.
নখায়ুধ, নখবিশিষ্ট জন্তু, furnished with talons or claws.
নখী, নখবিশিষ্ট, গন্ধদ্রব্য বিশেষ, *id:* also a dried shell fish used as a drug or perfume.
নগ, বৃক্ষপর্ব্বতাদি, a tree, a mountain, a rock. [mation.
নগণ্য, তুচ্ছ, অবজ্ঞেয়, mean, base, contemptible, of no esti-
নগর-ী, গ্রামাদি. *m. & f.* a town, a city.
নগি, মূত্র, প্রস্রাব, urine. [stopping a boat.
নগী, নৌকাচালনের দণ্ড, a pole for shoving forward or
নগ্ন, বিবস্ত্র, উলঙ্গ, naked, unclothed, stripped.
নগ্নিকা, অষ্টমবর্ষীয়া কন্যা, উলঙ্গিনী, বিবস্ত্রাস্ত্রী, a girl before menstruation, a naked woman.
নচেৎ, যদি নহে, নতুবা, if not, perhaps not, else.
নঞ, না, নয়, (*a prohibitive particle* :) no, not.
নট, নর্ত্তক, দ্রবীভূত, a dancer or *nat*, a mime; curdled.
নটন, নৃত্য, নাচকরা, a dance, exhibition of dancers.
নটবর, লম্পট, লোচ্চা, কাছাটীলা, a rake, one who dresses and acts so as to please loose women; profligate.
নটিয়া, নর্ত্তক, ভণ্ড, শাক বিশেষ, a dancer, a mime, a sort of spinage.
নটী, নর্ত্তকী, বেশ্যা, a dancing girl, an actress, a strumpet, prostitute, strolling woman.
নট্যালয়, বেশ্যালয়, গণিকাগৃহ, a brothel, a house of ill-fame.
নড়, নল, a sort of reed.

নড়ন, স্থানান্তরে চলন, দোলন, কম্পন, যুদ্ধকরণ, to move, stir, dangle, shake, remove, fight.
নড়ী, যষ্টি, লাঠী, a cane, stick, staff; mace, club, pole.
নড়ুল, নড্বাল,—নলযুক্ত দেশ, reedy, abounding in reeds.
নত, বক্রীভূত, বক্র, নম্র, ভূমিষ্ঠ, নিম্ন, শয়িত, bowed, bent, crooked, prostrate, curved, humble, descended, reclined, reclining; a nose ring.
নতা, ছলনা, ব্যাজ, an excuse, pretence.
নতি, নমস্কার, প্রণাম, নম্রতা, a bow, salutation, prostration, humility.
নতু-বা, যদি নহে, otherwise, or, but.
নথ, নাসিকাভরণ বিশেষ, a ring for the nose worn by women.
নদ, স্রোতস্বান, গাং, a male river.
নদী, স্রোতস্বতী, a female river.
নন, না, নাই, নয়, no, not.
ননদ্‌ী, ননান্দিনী, ননন্দা,—পতির ভগিনী, a husband's sister.
ননী, নবনীত, মাখন, fresh butter.
ননু, অস্বীকার সম্বোধন, বিরোধোক্তি, a particle of doubt, dissent or reply.
নন্দ, হর্ষ, কুশল, বৃদ্ধি, ইন্দ্রের উপবন, joy, pleasure, happiness, festivity, increase, prosperity, one of Cuvera's nine gems, Indra's garden.
নন্দথু, হর্ষ, আহ্লাদ, happiness, felicity, pleasure, joy, festivity.
নন্দন, পুত্র, ইন্দ্রের উপবন, হর্ষজনক, a son, Indra's gardens; rejoicing, making glad.
নন্দা, বৃদ্ধি, পার্বতী, স্বামির ভগিনী, জালা, increase, prosperity, Párvatí, a husband's sister, an earthen water-jar.
নন্দি, হর্ষ, পাশক্রীড়া, joy, happiness, gambling.
নন্দিনী, পুত্রী, পতির ভগিনী, পার্বতী, a daughter, a husband's sister, the goddess Párvatí.
নন্দিক, তুনবৃক্ষ, the Toon tree.
নন্দী আহ্লাদিত, শিবের প্রধান অনুচর, প্রস্তাবনাকথক, বৃক্ষ বিশেষ, rejoicing, glad; one of Shiva's attendants, the speaker of a prologue, the pronouncer of a benediction, the Indian fig tree.
নপুংসক, ক্লীব, ছিন্নমুষ্ক, neuter; a eunuch, an hermaphrodite.
নপ্তা, নপ্তৃ,—নাতী, a grandson.
নপ্তী, নাতিনী, a grand-daughter.

নব, নূতন, আধুনিক, একোনদশ, সঙ্কীর্ত্তন, new, recent, infant; nine; praise, panegyric, celebration.
নবদ্বার, শরীর, the body. [birth.
নবনস্তা, প্রসবদিবসাবধি নবম দিবস, the ninth day after child-
নবনী, নবনীত,—মাখন, fresh butter.
নবযৌবন, অচিরপ্রাপ্তযৌবন, very young, opening into youth.
নববধু, নবোঢ়া,—অচিরবিবাহিতা, a bride, new-married woman.
নবম, নবভক্তি, the ninth. [nourable families.
নবরঙ্গকুল, প্রধান কুলজাত, noble, connected with nine ho-
নবসূতিকা, অচিরপ্রসূতা, পয়স্বিনী গো, a woman recently deliver-ed, a milch-cow. [a harvest festival.
নবান্ন, নূতন ধান্যাদি, শস্যসংগ্রহ কালের পর্ব, new rice, new corn,
নবীন, নব্য,—নূতন, আধুনিক, সদ্য, টাট্‌কা, new, novel, recent, modern, young, tender, fresh.
নভঃ, অন্তরীক্ষ, আকাশ, the atmosphere, the sky.
নমঃ, প্রণাম, দান, ত্যাগ, a bow, obeisance, salutation, bowing, bending, a gift, present, offering.
নমন, অধোগমন, ঝোঁকন, বিনয়ী হওন, to descend, stoop, bow, bend down, become humble.
নমস্কার, প্রণাম, প্রণিপাত, a bow, obeisance, reverence, salu-tation, prostration. [tation, &c.
নমস্য, সম্মানার্হ, প্রণেয়, honourable, reverend, worthy of salu-
নম্য, বক্রীকরণীয়, অবনমেয়, flexible, depressible, that may be bent down.
নম্র, অবনত, বক্রীভূত, বিনয়ী, শিষ্ট, bent down, curved, hum-ble, lowly, condescending, gentle.
নয়, নিষেধ বোধক শব্দ, নব, নীতি, no; nine; justice, right, righteousness, virtue.
নয়ন, নেত্র, চক্ষু, আনয়ন, the eye, vision; to bring, fetch.
নয়া, নূতন, আধুনিক, টাট্‌কা, new, novel, recent, fresh.
নর, মনুষ্য, পুরুষ, a man, a male, the human kind.
নরক, পাপভোগস্থান, পাপের যন্ত্রণা, hell, the infernal regi-ons, torment, misery, punishment.
নরকী, পাপী, অতিদুষ্ট, নরকযোগ্য, অতিপীড়াকর, hellish, infernal, full of torment, tormenting, deserving of hell punishment.

নরপতি, রাজা, অধ্যক্ষ, a king, sovereign, governor.

নরম, কোমল, মৃদু, শিষ্ট, soft, tender, supple, pliant, gentle, mild, humble. [moisten.

নরমাণ, কোমল করাণ, ভিজান, to soften, mollify, make tender,

নরমী, কোমলত্ব, softness, tenderness, mildness, &c.

নরলোক, পৃথিবী, the earth, the habitation of men.

নরসিংহ, বিষ্ণুর চতুর্থাবতার, প্রধান, Vishnu's fourth avatár or lion-incarnation, a chief, a man of eminence.

নরসুন্দর, নাপিত, a barber.

নরাঙ্কিত, পরসাক্ষ্যসিদ্ধ, নির্ণীত, নিশ্চিত, confirmed by the testimony of others, ascertained, corroborated, certain. [nails.

নরুণ, নখ পরিষ্কারের অস্ত্র, an instrument for paring the

নরেন্দ্র, নরেশ্বর,—বহুদেশাধিপতি, the sovereign of men, a king.

নর্ত্তক, নাটক, ভণ্ড, a dancer, dancing-boy, mime, juggler.

নর্ত্তকী, নাটকী, নাচানী, a dancing and singing girl, an actress.

নর্ত্তন, নৃত্য, অঙ্গভঙ্গি, dancing, gesticulating, acting. [nel.

নর্দ্দমা, পয়নালা, প্রণালী, a sink, drain, gutter, trench, chan-

নর্ম্ম, কৌতুক, লীলা, পরিহাস, sport, amusement, pleasure, a joke, jibe, laughter.

নর্ম্মঠ, কৌতুকরত, লম্পট, কামুক, ক্রীড়া, মৈথুন, স্তনাগ্র, devoted to pleasure, a rake, libertine, lecher; sport, amusement, sexual intercourse, the nipple.

নল, তৃণ বিশেষ, নালী, পদ্ম, a reed, pipe, tube, spout, the wind-pipe, a hooka snake, a measuring rod, a water-lily.

নলক, নাসিকাভরণের বোটী, হস্তপাদাস্থি, the drop attached to a nose-ring, a bone of the arm or leg.

নলকিনী, নলকীল,—অষ্ঠীবদস্থি, the knee-pan or cap of the knee.

নলদ, পুষ্পরস, মকরন্দ, বেণার মূল, the honey or nectar of a flower, Indian spikenard, the root of a species of grass.

নলা, বাহু, ভুজাস্থি, the arm or arm-bone.

নলিন, পদ্ম, the lotus or water-lily.

নলিনী, পদ্মিনী, পদ্মযুক্তজলাশয়, an assemblage of water-lilies, a pond abounding in lotuses.

নলিয়া, ব্যাধ, পক্ষিমারা, a fowler, hunter, bird-catcher.

নলিয়াধনু, নলযুক্ত ধনুক বিশেষ, a kind of cross bow from which the arrow is shot through a tube.

নলী, নাড়ী, চোঙ্গা, হরিতাল, a tube, the barrel of a gun, the windpipe, red arsenic. [glare.

নল্সান-আন, চমকন, উজ্জ্বলন, ঝকন, to flash, emit flashes, lighten,

নল, চারি শত হস্ত পরিমাণ, a furlong or distance of four hundred cubits. [temporary.

নশ্বর, নাশ্য, অস্থায়ী, অচির, perishable, transitory, transient,

নষ্ট, ধ্বস্ত, পলায়িত, দূরিত, মৃত, অপচিত, ভ্রষ্ট, দুষ্ট, শঠ, annihilated, destroyed, ruined, routed, removed, spoiled, tainted, lost, dead, squandered, debauched, seduced, polluted, undone, vicious, dissolute, dishonest, roguish.

নষ্টচেতাঃ, মূঢ়, অতেজ, bereft of understanding, foolish, spiritless, without energy. [man.

নষ্টা, ব্যভিচারিণী, কুলটা, a strumpet, harlot, debauched wo-

নষ্টামি, শঠতা, দুষ্টতা, ঢেঁটামি, knavery, roguishness, profligacy, debauchery, turpitude, pollution, insolence, turbulence, sedition.

নস্য, তাম্রকূটচূর্ণ, snuff, any sneezing powder.

নহি, অস্বীকরণ বোধক শব্দ, *emphatic*—no, not.

না, অভাব কিম্বা বারণ বোধক শব্দ, নৌকা, *negative or prohibitive*—no, not, nay ; a boat.

নাই, অভাব, নাস্তি, নাপিত, no, not ; a barber, the navel.

নাইয়া, রজক, নাবিক, দাঁড়ী, a waterman, a boatman.

নাওন, স্নানকরণ, অবগাহন, ঋতু, to bathe, perform ablutions, to wash ; the menses.

নাং, উপপতি, জার, a gallant, a paramour. [harlot.

নাংচুণী, নাংচোর,—লম্পটী, কুলটা, a lewd woman, strumpet,

নাংনী, জারবিশিষ্টা, having a gallant or paramour.

নাক, নাসিকা, স্বর্গ, আকাশ, the nose, heaven, the sky.

নাকড়া, নাসিকার রোগ বিশেষ, a polypus of the nose.

নাকি, সসন্দেহ জিজ্ঞাসক শব্দ, *denoting option or alternative :* or no ? or not ? or what ? [the nose.

নাকী, নাসিকার, খনা, nasal, belonging to or uttered from

নাকুয়া, উন্নতনাসিকাযুক্ত, having a fine or prominent nose.

নাক্ষত্র, নাক্ষত্রিক,—মাসিক, নক্ষত্র সম্বন্ধীয়, lunar, belonging to the lunar mansions.

নাগ, সর্প, হস্তী, a serpent, snake, cobra capella, a race of fabulous demigods, an elephant, a species of grass. [flammable gas.

নাগকূপ, আগ্নেয় স্থল, জ্বালামুখী, a volcano or opening of in-

নাগজ, সিন্দুর, হিঙ্গুল, vermilion or red lead.

নাগর, নগর সম্বন্ধীয়, নগরজাত, চতুর, বিজ্ঞ, শঠ, দুষ্ট, মন্দ, অপহ্নব, belonging to a city or town, town-born, city-bred, waggish, clever, knowing, intriguing, bad, vile, nameless; a species of grass, a denial of knowledge.

নাগরঙ্গী, নারাঙ্গী লেবু, an orange.

নাগরালি, শঠতা, পটুতা, acquaintance with the tricks of cities, sharpness, cleverness, citizenship.

নাগরী, নগরবাসী, অক্ষরভেদ, ধূর্ত্তা স্ত্রী, belonging to a city; a sort of character, *Nágri'*, a clever, intriguing woman, a species of Euphorbia. [dras.

নাগলোক, পাতাল, Pátála or the abode of serpents and hy-

নাগা, নিকটস্থ, সসজ্জ, বিবস্ত্র উদাসীন, near, armed; a naked travelling mendicant.

নাগী. নাগিনী,—সর্পিকা, a female serpent or hydra.

নাচ, নাট,—নৃত্য, অঙ্গভঙ্গি, a dance, dancing, gesticulating, jumping. [leaf.

নাচন, নর্ত্তন, কম্পন, to dance, jump, vibrate, shake as a

নাচানী, নর্ত্তকী. a *nách* or dancing girl.

নাচানীয়া, নর্ত্তক, নাট, dancing; a dancer.

নাচুয়া, নর্ত্তনিয়া, কুঁদনিয়া, dancing or frisking about, jumping.

নাছ, গুপ্তদ্বার. খিড়কী, a back or private door for females.

নাট, নৃত্য, কৌতুক, a dance, dancing, pantomime.

নাটন, নর্ত্তন, নাচ করণ, to dance, to act in pantomime.

নাটক, কৌতুক, অভিনয়, কাব্য বিশেষ, নৃত্যজীবী, ভণ্ড, a pantomime, play, drama, dramatic writing, dancing; a dancer, pantomimic actor.

নাটকী, নাচানী, নর্ত্তকী, a dancing girl, a dramatic writing.

নাটা, লতা, খর্ব, a climbing shrub; dwarf, left-handed.
নাটা-ই, সূত্রসঙ্কলনযন্ত্র, a reel for winding silk.
নাটাম, সূত্র জড়ান, to reel or wind silk or thread.
নাটিম, ঝুমঝুমী, লাটিম, a child's rattle, a top, a bauble.
নাটুয়া, নৃত্যকারী, নর্ত্তক, dancing; a dancer.
নাট্য, নৃত্য, নৃত্যবৃত্তি, a dance, act or science of dancing.
নাড়ন, স্থানান্তরে নয়ন, পলান, to move, stir, remove, retreat.
নাড়া, ছেদিত শস্যের মূল, বিচালী, stubble, straw.
নাড়ী, ডাঁটা, বৃন্ত, ধমনী, অন্ত্র, উদরস্থ শিরা, হস্তের প্রধান শিরা, দণ্ড, নল, the culm of corn or grass, a stalk, a tubular vein, intestine, gut, navel-string, the entrails, bowels, a blood-vessel, the arteries of the arm on which the pulse is felt, the pulse, pulsation, a fistulous sore, an hour of twenty-four minutes, a blow pipe, a tube.
নাড়ীটেপা, নাড়ীধরা,—বৈদ্য, a physician, one who feels the [pulse.
নাড়ীন্ধম, স্বর্ণকার, a goldsmith, one who uses the blow pipe.
নাড়ীমরা, অক্ষুধা, inappetency, loss of appetite.
নাতী, নাতিনী,—অপত্যের পুত্রপুত্রী, *m.* & *f.* grandson and grand-daughter.
নাথ, প্রভু, কর্ত্তা, প্রতিপালক, বলদের নাসিকাবিদ্ধ রজ্জু, a lord, master, governor, protector, the rope passed through the nose of a draught ox.
নাথ, নাথি,—লাথী, a kick, a kick backwards.
নাথবান্, পরাধীন, আয়ত্ত, dependant on a master or protector, subject, subservient.
নাদ, শব্দ, গর্জ্জন, ডাক, গবাদির মল, a sound, noise, roar, call, the dung of sheep, &c.
নাদন, রব করণ, বাজন, গর্জ্জন, ডাকন, মলত্যাগন, to sound, roar, thunder, call, expel dung, (as cattle.)
নাদনা, ঠাসনা, দাজা, a rammer for ramming down earth, a [jar.
নাদবিন্দু, বিন্দুযুক্ত অর্দ্ধচন্দ্র, the nasal mark ँ over a letter.
নাদা, বৃহৎ মৃত্তিকা পাত্র, a large earthen jar.
নাদিত, কণিত, ধ্বনিত, made to sound, rung.
নাদী, অশ্বাদির মল, a pellet of dung (of horses, sheep or [goats.)
নাদেয়ী, নদ্যুৎপন্ন, জলজ, ভূমিজাম, river-born, growing near

water; a sort of cane or reed, a kind of flowering shrub. [a mother's father.

নানা, অনেক, বিবিধ, মাতামহ, many, various, different, divers;

নানাত্মা, আত্মভেদ, পৃথক২ আত্মবাদ, a distinction of Spirits or the appropriation of a distinct soul to every individual person.

নানান, বিবিধ, ভিন্ন, various, divers, different.

নানার্থ, যাহার অনেক অর্থ, অস্পষ্ট, having different meanings, ambiguous, for different purposes or objects.

নানাস্থানী, পর্য্যটনিয়া, অস্থির, ভ্রমণিয়া, strolling, wandering, vagrant, roving, unsettled.

নানী, মাতামহী, a maternal grandmother.

নান্দী, প্রস্তাবনা, the eulogium, praise, or benediction of a king or deity with which a drama opens.

নান্দীমুখ, পিতৃপিতামহাদি, আভ্যুদয়িক শ্রাদ্ধ, immediate ancestors; a species of shráddha or offering to the manes of ancestors on festive occasions.

নাপিত, ক্ষৌরকর্ম্ম কর্ত্তা, a barber.

নাবন, অধোগমন, উত্তরণ, এলন, to dismount, bend down, descend, pass off by stool.

নাবান, স্নান করাণ, ডুবান, উত্তরাণ, এলান, to bathe another, to immerse, cause to dismount, unload, take down or off.

নাবাকার, নৌকাকৃতি, boat-shaped, cymbiform.

নাবাল, অধঃস্থ, তলস্থ, low, situated beneath.

নাবি, অকাল, আগুড়ী, premature, too early in the season.

নাবিক, দাঁড়ী, কর্ণধার, a waterman, boatman, pilot, helmsman, navigator.

নাবো-তে, অধতে, তলে, down, beneath, below, under.

নাব্য, নৌকাগম্য, navigable, passable in boats.

নাভি, উদরের মধ্যস্থান, চক্রমধ্য, মধ্যস্থল, the navel, the nave of a wheel, the centre of a circle.

নাম, আখ্যা, সংজ্ঞা, পাখী, কীর্ত্তি, a name, appellation, title, term, noun, reputation, fame.

নামক, অবনত, অবনায়ক, খ্যাত, bending or causing to bend downwards, depressing, named, called.

নামতা, অঙ্কপূরণ পত্র, the multiplicatión table.
নামধর, নামধারী,—আখ্যাত, named, denominated, called.
নামধেয়, আখ্যাত, সংজ্ঞা, *id*: also a name, appellation.
নামন, অধোগমন, উত্তরণ, নমুতাচরণ, ঝোঁকন, বমন, to descend, alight, light upon, condescend, bow, bend down, pass off by stool. [Indica.
নামনা, পিপ্পল বৃক্ষের জটা, the descending roots of the Ficus
নামলুক, বিখ্যাত, famous, illustrious, renowned. [launch.
নামান, উত্তারণ, ওলান, to cause to descend, lower, unload,
নামাউঠা, ওলাউঠা, a descending and ascending, purging and vomiting. [the names of the gods.
নামাবলি, দেবনামশ্রেণীবিশিষ্ট বস্ত্র, a sort of chintz printed with
নামাশ্রয়, দেবনামাবলম্বন, refuge in a particular name.
নামো, অধোভাগ, তল, দামন, the lower or under part, the bottom, the skirt.
নামো-তে, তলে, অধতে, below, beneath, under, down.
নায়, প্রদর্শন, শিক্ষা দেওয়া, a guiding, directing, guidance, teaching, instruction.
নায়ক, প্রদর্শক, অধিপ, অধ্যক্ষ, স্ত্রীপ্রেমী পুরুষ, স্বামী, অগ্রগামী, প্রধান, a guide, conductor, leader, chief, head, general, commander, constable, seizer, the central gem of a necklace, a lover or husband, (*in amatory poems*;)—leading, conducting, principal, eminent, chief. [leader, lover, &c.
নায়কীয়, নায়কসম্বন্ধীয়, of, belonging or relating to a guide,
নায়িকা, সখী, পুরুষপ্রেমীস্ত্রী, দুর্গা, a wife or mistress, (*in amatory poems* ;) Durgá.
নারক, নরকযোগ্য, নরক, infernal, impious, hellish; hell.
নারকী, অতিমন্দ, পাপিষ্ঠ, infernal, impious, wicked, depraved.
নারাঙ্গী, জম্বীর বিশেষ, an orange.
নারাচ, লৌহময় বাণ বিশেষ, an iron arrow.
নারায়ণ, বিষ্ণু, Vishnu as moving on the chaotic waters.
নারায়ণী, লক্ষ্মী, Lakshmi as the wife of Vishnu.
নারিকেল, ডাবদুর্মা নামক ফল, the cocoanut.
নারী, স্ত্রি, অবলা, woman, a female. [menstrual flux.
নারীধর্ম্ম, স্ত্রীলোকের কর্ত্তব্যকর্ম্ম, ঋতু, the duties of women, the

নাল, নলাকার কৃত্রিম বস্তু, শিরা, অশ্বের ক্ষুরবদ্ধ লৌহ, a tube, tubular stalk, culm, any tubular vessel of the body, a horse shoe. [sink, drain.

নালা, খাল, ক্ষুদ্র নদী, জলনিঃসরণ মার্গ, a rivulet, creek, outlet,

নালী, চোঙ্গা, নলবৎ ক্ষত, নর্দ্দমা, a tube, a drain, a sluice, a fistula, a running sore.

নাশ, ধ্বংশ, ক্ষতি, মরণ, হত্যা, মোচন, destruction, perdition, annihilation, ruin, loss, death, slaughter, murder, removal, expiation.

নাশন, ধ্বংশন, ভাঙ্গন, মারণ, মোচন, to destroy, ruin, demolish, slaughter, remove, expiate, avert.

নাশনীয়, নাশ্য,—ধ্বংশনীয়, অনিত্য, perishable, destructible.

নাশিত, উচ্ছন্ন, ভ্রষ্ট, নষ্ট, যাহার প্রায়শ্চিত্ত করা গিয়াছে, ruined, destroyed, spoiled, lost, removed, expiated, &c.

নাষ্টিক, অনাথ, হৃতধনাদি, bereft of an owner, forlorn, deprived of a master, property or possessions.

নাস, তামুকূটচূর্ণ, snuff.

নাসা, নাসিকা, দ্বারের উপরিকাষ্ঠ, ঝন্‌কাঠ, the nose, a tumor of the nose, the lintel of a door.

নাসিকা, ঘ্রাণেন্দ্রিয়, কপালী, the nose, a door-lintel.

নাস্তি, নহে, তন্ন, *Sanscrit* : it is not, there is not, not so.

নাস্তিক, অনীশ্বরবাদী, an atheist, infidel, sceptic. [heresy, &c.

নাস্তিক্য, ঈশ্বরনিষেধ, infidelity, atheism, rejection of the Veds,

নাহি, না, নয়, অবশ্য নয়, no, not, certainly not.

নিঙ্কন, ধৌত বস্ত্রাদিহইতে জলনিঃসরণ. লুটন, to drip as water from wet-clothes, to strip, to plunder.

নিঙ্ড়ান, রসজলাদি নিঃসারণ, অপহরণ, লুটন, to wring out, strain or squeeze out, express the juice of grapes &c. extort, plunder. [tortioner.

নিঙ্ড়ানিয়া, দৌরাত্ম্যকারী, অপহারী grinding, rapacious ; an ex-

নিঃ, নির, নিষ,—রাহিত্য বোধক শব্দ, বাহির, *prefix:* without, free from, destitute of, out, out of, forth, not.

নিঃশব্দ, মৌনী, নীরব, অবাক্, silent, noiseless, still, downcast, speechless.

নিঃশেষ, সম্পূর্ণ, সমাপ্ত, শেষরহিত, complete, entire, finished, uttermost, without remainder.

নিঃশেষিত, ক্ষুধিত, অবসন্ন, ক্ষীণ, শ্রান্ত, spent, completely famished, exhausted.

নিঃশ্রেণী, সিঁড়ী, a ladder, staircase, flight of steps.

নিঃশ্রেয়স, মুক্তি, কুশল, final emancipation, beatitude, happiness, welfare.

নিঃসঙ্গ, সঙ্গচ্যুত, বিরল, solitary, alone, private.

নিঃসন্ধি, অখণ্ড, সুরচিত, ঘন, শক্ত, whole, entire, of one piece, seamless, inseparable, close, compact, well-knit, firm.

নিঃসরণ, বহির্গমন, ক্ষরণ, ঝরণ, মরণ, to go forth or out, exude, distil, drop; an exit, death, dying.

নিঃসান, টনটনান, a tingling or throbbing.

নিঃসার, রসহীন, তেজরহিত, pithless, sapless, unsubstantial, spiritless, destitute of energy.

নিঃসারণ, বহিষ্করণ, নির্গত করণ, নিঙড়ান, to drive or cast out, expel, express the juice of fruits, &c.

নিঃসৃত, বহির্গত, ঝরিত, উৎপন্ন, বহিষ্কৃত, gone out, gone forth, proceeding from, expelled.

নিঃস্যন্দ, নির্গত, ক্ষরিত, flowing or oozing out, trickling down.

নিঃস্ব, দরিদ্র, অনাথ, poor, indigent, destitute, forlorn.

নিঃস্বত্ব, ধনরাহিত্য, অপচয়, দণ্ড, ধনাচ্ছেদ, poverty, indigence, alienation, loss, forfeit or confiscation of property.

নিঃস্বত্বক, ধনাচ্ছেদক, লুটনিয়া, confiscating, plundering, rapacious.

নিকট, সমীপ, অনন্তর, অদূরবর্ত্তী, vicinity, nearness; near, neighbouring, adjacent.

নিকটানিকটি, কাছাকাছি, প্রায়, in company, near each other, at hand, nearly.

নিকটে, কাছে, সমীপে, near, towards, at hand, in the vicinity.

নিকড়িয়া, নির্দ্ধনী, দুঃখী, penniless, poor.

নিকন-আন, গোময় দ্বারা ম্রক্ষণ, গোময়সংস্কৃত গৃহ, to smear with cow dung, to plaister; a house so plaistered.

নিকন্ধিয়া, মস্তকহীন ভূতগণ বিশেষ, a sort of fabulous malignant beings destitute of head and shoulders.

নিকর, সমূহ, অকর, খাঁটি, ঠিক, a multitude, number; free from, taxes and deductions, clear.

নিকষা, রাক্ষস গণের মাতা, নিকটবর্ত্তী, অন্তিক. the mother of imps and goblins; near, proximate.

নিকষাত্মজ, রাক্ষস, an imp, goblin. Rákshasa, young giant.

নিকায্য, গৃহ, আলয়, a house, dwelling, habitation.

নিকার, অপকার, নিষেধ, নিন্দা, হিংসা, অনাদর, an injury, offence, a hindering or obstructing, reproach, malice, wickedness, abuse, disrespect.

নিকাশ, পরিশোধ, ব্যাঘাত ঘুচান, নালা, the payment of a debt, the discharge of an obligation, the removal of a difficulty or obstruction, an issue or outlet for water.

নিকী, নিখী,—উকুণ, চামনী, a louse, a nit.

নিকুঞ্জ, কৃপণ. গুল্মযুক্ত স্থান, নিবিড় বন, লতাচ্ছাদিত স্থান, penurious, niggardly, stingy; a thicket, a place overgrown with bushes and climbing plants, a bower.

নিকৃত, খল, শঠ, ধূর্ত্ত, দুষ্ট, অধম, প্রতারিত, পদচ্যুত, dishonest, artful, insincere, wicked, perverse, low, base, vile; cheated, deceived, tricked, removed, set aside, dismissed.

নিকৃতি, খলতা, ধূর্ত্ততা, বিবর্জ্জনা, অপবাদ, নিন্দা, ধনরাহিত্য, dishonesty, insincerity, wickedness, rejection, removal, reproach, abuse, poverty.

নিকৃত্রিম, অকল্পিত প্রকৃত, অসঙ্কীর্ণ, inartificial, genuine, not counterfeit, unadulterated.

নিকৃষ্ট, বহিষ্কৃত, অবজ্ঞাত, তুচ্ছিত, অধম, মন্দ, কৃপণ, outcast, despised, low, vile, bad, niggardly, sordid.

নিকেতন, গৃহ, আলয়, a house, habitation, abode.

নিক্তী, ক্ষুদ্র পরিমাণ যন্ত্র, a pair of small scales or balance.

নিক্বণ, নিক্বাণ—বীণাদির শব্দ, a musical tone or sound, the sound of a lute, &c.

নিক্কা, চামনী. a nit.

নিক্ষিপ্ত, ফেলিত, ছড়ান, বিবর্জ্জিত, ত্যক্ত, গচ্ছিত, cast away, thrown, dispersed, rejected, given up, abandoned, deposited, pledged.

নিক্ষেপ, ফেলা, ছড়া, আদি, গচ্ছিত ধন, a throw, cast, dispersion, an injection, a deposit, a pledge.

নিক্ষেপণ, অবক্ষেপন, ক্ষেপন, ছড়ান, বুনন, to throw down, cast away, fling, scatter, disperse, sow seed.

নিখনন, শব পোতন, the burial of a corpse, interment. [on.

নিখর্ব, খাট, বাউনিয়া, short, low, dwarfish; a dwarf, a billi-

নিখট্টু, নিকর্ম্মা, আলসিয়া, without work, idle. [landmark.

নিখাত, গর্ত্ত, পরিখা, a pit or ditch, a moat designed as a

নিখাদ, হস্তির নিনাদ, the voice or roar of an elephant.

নিখিল, সমগ্র, সমুদায়, all, whole, entire, complete.

নিগড়, লৌহনির্ম্মিত পাদবন্ধন, বেড়ী, an iron foot-chain, fetter, pair of stocks. [or charms.

নিগদ, কথা, জপকরা, speech, discourse, recitation of prayer

নিগদিত, কথিত, উক্ত, উল্লিখিত, spoken, uttered, declared.

নিগম, নগর. গ্রামাদি, হাট, পথ, বাণিজ্য, নিশ্চয়, বেদ, a town, city, market, fair, high road, trade, traffic, certainty, assurance, the Veds. [gullet.

নিগরণ, ভোজন, গিলন, গলা, to eat, swallow; the throat, the

নিগাল, ঘোটকের গলা, the throat or neck of a horse.

নিগালবান্, অশ্ব, a horse; having a horse's neck.

নিগূঢ়, দুর্জ্ঞেয়, অপ্রকাশ, শক্ত, কঠিন, obscure, hidden, profound, mysterious, close, strict, fast, tight.

নিগ্রহ, প্রহার, দণ্ড, ক্লেশ দেওয়া, বন্ধকরা, ইন্দ্রিয়দমন, তাড়না, অগ্রাহ্য করা, ঘৃণা, কুব্যবহার, a smiting, punishment; ill or severe treatment, persecution, confinement, a binding, tie, mortification of the senses, &c. reproval, chiding, disfavour, discouragement, dislike, aversion, deviation from virtue, impropriety. [&c.

নিগ্রহান্বিত, ক্লেশিত, দণ্ডিত, persecuted, ill-treated, punished,

নিগ্রাহক, নিগ্রাহী,—ক্লেশদ, শাস্তিকারক, persecuting, maltreating, punishing, &c. [tents, list.

নিঘণ্টু, অভিধান, অনুক্রমণিকা, a vocabulary, table of con-

নিঘুষ্ট, ধ্বনি, রব, শব্দ, a sound, a noise. [vient.

নিঘ্ন. শিষ্ট, আয়ত্ত. docile, domestic, dependant, subser-

নিঙড়ন, ঝরণ, ক্ষরণ. নিঃসরণ, to drip as water from clothes, &c. to distil.

নিঙড়ান, রস নিঃসারণ, নিষ্পীড়ন, চোষণ, to wring clothes, wring

out, express juice from fruit, &c. to squeeze, exact, oppress, fleece. [blage.

নিচয়, সমূহ, সঞ্চয়, a multitude, collection, heap, assem-

নিছ্, নিছু,—বিরল, কেবল, alone; only. [surtout.

নিচোল, পাছুড়ী, শীতবস্ত্র, an outer garment, mantle, wrapper,

নিচোড়, কৃপণ, অধম, তুচ্ছ, niggardly, stingy, parsimonious, illiberal, mean, contemptible. [lorn.

নিছুড়িয়া, নিঃসহায়, অনাথ, friendless, destitute, orphan, for-

নিচ্ছেদ, অচ্ছেদনীয়, indivisible, reduced to its lowest terms.

নিজ, আত্ম, আত্মীয়, আপনার, own, self, proper, belonging to one's self. [self-willed, obstinate.

নিজমতাবলম্বী, আত্মমতবাদী, একগুঁয়া, self-opinionated, dogmatic,

নিজতন্ত্রী, স্বাধীন, স্বতন্ত্র, subject only to one's own will, independant. [following him on the pile.

নিজা, পতিব্রতা, সতী, *f.* devoted to her husband in life and

নিজি, নিজে,—আপনি, one's ownself, myself, &c.

নিঝুম, নিঃশব্দ, নির্বাত, still, silent, without sound, close.

নিট্, নিশ্চিত, সত্য, certain, true. [severe.

নিঠুর, ক্রূর, কঠিন, কৃপাহীন, cruel, harsh, unfeeling, strict,

নিড়ন-আন, ঘাস উপড়ান, to weed a garden or field.

নিড়ানী, কোড়, a weeding instrument.

নিডীন, ঊর্দ্ধগমন, উড়ন, a soaring, the flight of a bird.

নিতম্ব, স্ত্রীলোকের কটিপ্রোথ, পাছা, পর্বতের কুব্জীকৃত দেশ, the posteriors of a woman, the buttocks, rump of an animal, prominence of a mountain, gibbosity.

নিতরাং, নিত্য, অনবরতঃ, always, continually, eternally.

নিতল, পাতালের এক ভাগ, a division of the infernal regions.

নিতান্ত, অত্যন্ত, একান্ত, স্থির, অবশ্য, একান্তরূপে, সম্যক প্রকারে, much, excessive, sure, inviolable, complete, unreserved; surely, clearly, certainly, of necessity, excessively, very, extremely, completely, entirely, infallibly.

নিত্য, জন্মমৃত্যুরহিত, অনবরত, নির্ণীত, স্থির, প্রতিদিনের, সর্বদা, eternal, perpetual, constant, continual, incessant, permanent, fixed, invariable, regular, daily; always, eternally, continually.

নিত্যকর্ম্ম, প্রতিদিনের অবশ্য কর্ত্তব্য ক্রিয়া, the constant duties or daily services of religion. [eternally.

নিত্যশঃ, অনবরতঃ, সর্ব্বদাই, constantly, perpetually, always,

নিথর, নিঃশব্দ, স্থির, ধীর, still, quiet, free from agitation.

নিদর্শন, আদর্শ, দৃষ্টান্ত, উদাহরণ, প্রমাণ, a pattern, copy, type, simile, example, elucidation, illustration, description, proof, authority, record.

নিদর্শনী, প্রকাশক, প্রমায়ক, চিহ্ন, সন্ধান, shewing, elucidating, proving; a token, proof, mark, trace.

নিদাঘ, গ্রীষ্ম, গুমটকাল, ঘর্ম্ম, heat, warmth, the hot season, perspiration.

নিদান, মূলকারণ, আদিকারণের অন্তর্দ্ধান, রোগের মূলানুসন্ধান, বৈদ্যগ্রন্থ বিশেষ, অন্ত, নৈর্ম্মল্য, তপস্যের ফলাকাঙ্ক্ষা, a first cause, remote cause, the disappearance, cessation or removal of a first cause, the tracing or ascertaining of the causes of diseases, a certain treatise on medicine, correctness, accuracy; an end, purity, purification, a request or desire for the reward of austerities.

নিদানীভূত, আদিকারণীভূত, become a primary cause of disease, &c. [bold.

নিদারুণ, কঠিন, দুঃসহ্য, নির্ভয়, hard, difficult, severe, fearless,

নিদার্জা, চোরের মন্ত্র বিশেষ, a charm used by house-breakers.

নিদিধ্যাসন, পুনঃ২ পরমার্থ চিন্তা, deep or intense and repeated contemplation of the Deity or other object.

নিদিষ্ট, আজ্ঞাপিত, কথিত, ordered, commanded, spoken, said.

নিদেশ, আজ্ঞা, কথা, উল্লেখ, সামীপ্য, an order, command, direction, injunction, speech, speaking, utterance, relation, a word of command, vicinity, proximity, nearness.

নিদ্রা, শয়ন, আলস্য, ঘুম, sleep, sleepiness, sloth, a nap.

নিদ্রাকর্ষণ, ঝিমনি, the overpowering influence of sleep, drowsiness, heaviness. [drowsy.

নিদ্রাতিয়া, ঘুমজনক, ঘুমানিয়া, soporific, composing, narcotic,

নিদ্রাণ, নিদ্রান্বিত,—শয়িত, ঘুমযুক্ত, asleep, sleeping, drowsy.

নিদ্রাবেশ, নিদ্রার উপক্রম, a falling asleep.

নিদ্রাভঙ্গ, জাগানি, জাগনি, the interruption or breaking of sleep, an awaking from sleep. [ful.
নিদ্রালু, নিদ্রাশীল, আলসিয়া, sleepy, drowsy, lethargic, sloth-
নিদ্রিত, শয়িত, ঘুমঘুক, asleep, laid asleep, dozing.
নিধন, কুল, বংশপ্রধান, মৃত্যু, অন্তর্ধান, নাশ, a race, family, the head of a family, death, disappearance, loss, killing, destruction.
নিধান, মণ্যাদি, আধার, a gem or other treasure, a receptacle, a vessel.
নিধার, ভোতা, blunt, dull, wanting a fine edge.
নিধি, মণি, ধন, অস্বামিক ধন, ভাণ্ডার, বৃহৎ আধার, সমুদ্র, a gem, treasure, valuables, treasure found, a treasury, granary, asylum, nest, receptacle, the ocean. [ous.
নিধু, হানিকৃৎ, নাশকর, ধ্বংসক, pernicious, destructive, ruin-
নিধুতা, ধ্বংস, নাশ, উৎপাত, perdition, ruin, destruction.
নিধুবন, ক্রীড়া, হর্ষ, কম্পনা, মৈথুন, sport, play, pleasure, enjoyment, trembling, agitation, coition.
নিনাদ, রব, শব্দ, গর্জ্জনা, a sound, a noise, roar, bellow.
নিন্দক, নিন্দুক,—পরদোষদ, ভর্ৎসনাকারী, reviling, reproaching, abusing, vilifying, &c.
নিন্দন, ভর্ৎসন, তিরস্করণ, দোষ দেওন, to revile, reproach, censure, blame, accuse, calumniate, vilify, traduce, asperse.
নিন্দা, অপবাদ, তিরস্কার, অবজ্ঞা, reproach, censure, reproof, rebuke, blame, reviling, slander, calumny, abuse, contempt.
নিন্দিত, তিরস্কৃত, কুৎসিত, অধম, অনুচিত, অবিহিত, reproached, reviled, &c. evil, bad, base, low, despicable, indecent, improper, forbidden.
নিপট, নিপটে,—সম্যক প্রকারে, মাত্রে, বস্তুতঃ, completely, altogether, entirely, merely, truly, really.
নিপত, নিপাত,—মৃত্যু, নাশ, পরাজয়, হত্যা, অধঃপতন, death, destruction, ruin, overthrow, carnage, a fall, descent, an anomaly in grammar. [ruin.
নিপতন, অধঃপতন, ক্ষরণ, to fall, descend, fall down, fall to

নিপাতন, পড়ান, নামান, ধ্বংসকরণ, হনন, অধঃক্ষেপণ, ব্যাকরণব্যতিক্রম করা, to make to fall, cause to descend, precipitate, lower, throw or knock down, ruin, kill, destroy, overset, fling : an anomaly or irregularity in grammar. [killed, destroyed, &c.

নিপাতিত. অধঃক্ষিপ্ত, নষ্ট, হত, cast down, precipitated, ruined,

নিপান, গবাদির পানার্থ জলাধার, a watering trough, a milk-pail.

নিপুণ, পটু, প্রবীণ, পারগ, শ্রেষ্ঠ. clever, expert, skilful, able, active, eminent. [a close.

নিবড়ন, সমাপ্ত হওন, to be finished or accomplished, come to

নিবড়ান, সমাপন, নিষ্পাদন, to bring to a close, complete, finish.

নিবদ্ধ, রচিত, প্রস্তাবিত, আবদ্ধ, বদ্ধ, composed, treated of, discussed, confined, fastened.

নিবন, নির্বাণ হওন, অপসয়ন, কুলান, to be extinguished, expire, go out, last, suffice.

নিবন্ধ, কর্ত্তব্যকর্ম্ম, ব্রত, বাঁধা, প্রসঙ্গ, an obligation, a vow, binding, confinement, a treatise, the subject of a composition.

নিবন্ধন, বাঁধা, রচনা, কারণ, প্রয়োজন, a binding, confining, compiling from other writings, a cause, origin, motive. [lexicographer.

নিবন্ধা, রচনকর্ত্তা, সংগ্রহকারক, অভিধানরচক, an author, compiler,

নিবর্ত্ত, বিরতি, বাধা, নিষেধ, বিরত, শান্ত, ক্ষান্ত, cessation, stoppage, restraint, desisting from ; ceased, having ceased, appeased, forgiving.

নিবর্ত্তন, স্থগন, মানাকরণ, আটকান, খণ্ডন, ক্ষমাকরণ, দমন, to stop, put a stop to, cause to cease, abolish, revoke, rescind, forgive, quell.

নিবসতি, বসতি, বাসস্থান, a dwelling, abode, residence.

নিবসন, বাসকরা, a residing, dwelling or living in a place.

নিবহ, সমূহ, সঞ্চয়, a multitude, a quantity.

কিবাড়-ন, নিষ্পত্তি সমাপ্তি, completion, finishing, conclusion, accomplishment.

নিবাত, নিবাতাস,—বায়ুশূন্য স্থান, আশ্রিত, শরণাগত, আশ্রয়, sheltered, calm, close, secure, safe, as in an asylum ; a sheltered place, place of refuge.

নিবান, নির্বাণ করাণ, মিটান, কুলান, to extinguish, quench, put out, quell, to afford, supply.

নিবানিয়া, নির্বাণকারক, অপব্যয়ী, one who extinguishes; profuse, expensive, extravagant.

নিবাপ, পিণ্ড, a funeral cake or the offering of it.

নিবারণ, আট্কান, নিষেধন মানাকরণ, রোধন, to stop, prevent, hinder, oppose, resist, forbid, restrain, restrict, obstruct.

নিবারা, নিষেধ, আটক, prevention, obstruction, restraint.

নিবাস, গৃহ, বসতি স্থান, পাড়া, a house, dwelling, habitation, a lodging, quarter.

নিবাসী, অবস্থায়ী, residing, dwelling; a resident, inhabitant.

নিবিড়, ঘন, অগম্য, গুপ্ত, thick, matted, dense, shady, umbrageous, impervious, impenetrable, retired.

নিবিষ্ট, প্রবৃত্ত, উদ্যুক্ত, রত, তৎপর, engaged in, occupied with, busy, taken up with, entered into, devoted to.

নিবীত, কণ্ঠলম্বিত উপবীতাদি, the Brahminical thread, &c. as suspended from the neck.

নিবৃত, বেষ্টিত, surrounded, enclosed, encompassed.

নিবৃত্ত, বিরত, ক্ষান্ত, বাধিত, দমিত, ceased, ceasing, desisting from, appeased, stopped, hindered, prevented, made to cease, checked.

নিবৃত্তি, বিরতি, মানাকরা, cessation, a leaving off, a stoppage, abolition, suppression.

নিবেদন, যাচ্ঞা, প্রার্থনা, সম্মান পূর্বক জানানি, দান, ত্যাগ, a request, representation, address, a communication, message, complaint, petition, an offering, a present.

নিবেদিত, জ্ঞাপিত, প্রার্থিত, ত্যক্ত, mentioned, communicated, represented, made known, requested, offered, presented.

নিবেশ, প্রবেশ, মনোযোগ, ব্যগ্রতা, আবাপ, entrance, engagedness in, devotedness to, zeal, earnestness, an insertion in writing.

নিবেশন, ভিতরে গমন, লিখন, গৃহ an entering, entrance, an entry in an account or writing, a house, habitation.

নিভ, তুল্য, সদৃশ, *affix*. like, similar, resembling.

নিভৃত, গুপ্ত, বিরল, secret, private, solitary, lonely.

নিম, নিম্ব,—বৃক্ষ বিশেষ, the Nimb tree, which has a very bitter leaf.

নিমগ্ন, ডুবিত, মজ্জিত, immersed, sunk, drowned.

নিমন্ত্র, আহ্বান, ডাকা, an invitation, a call.

নিমন্ত্রণ, আহ্বান করণ, অতিথি সেবা, to call or invite to a feast, &c. : an entertainment, a feast.

নিময়, পরিবর্ত্ত, অনুক্রম, exchange, barter, a change, alteration, a succession.

নিমিত্ত, কারণ, প্রয়োজন, মূল, অভিপ্রায়, চিহ্ন, উৎপন্ন, a cause, reason, motive, origin, spring, source, view, intent, instrumental cause, a mark, sign, token, spot, trace, a consequence.

নিমিত্ত, নিমিত্তে,—জন্যে, হেতুক, যেন, for, because of, on account of, in consequence of, for the sake of, about, that, in order that.

নিমিত্তক, হেতুক, মূলক, দ্বারা, *affix*: caused by, arising from, on account of, through or by.

নিমিষ, নিমেষ,—চক্ষুর পলক, অত্যল্প ক্ষণ, the twinkling of the eye, a wink, a moment. [a winking.

নিমীলন, নেত্র মুদ্রিত করণ, the closing or shutting of the eyes,

নিমুড়িয়া, অনাথ, friendless, forlorn, orphan, destitute.

নিম্ন, গভীর, অধঃস্থ, নীচ, বিনয়ী, deep, depressed, sunk, low, humble. [ing deep; a river.

নিম্নগ, অধোগামী, গম্ভীর, নদ, descending, going down, flow-

নিম্বু, জম্বীর, নারাঙ্গী, the common lime, an orange.

নিয়ত, নির্ণীত, আদিষ্ট, স্থিরীকৃত, অদৃষ্ট, নিত্য, সর্ব্বদা, regulated, ordered, destined, fated, regular, uniform, perpetual; constantly, incessantly.

নিয়তি, আদেশ, ব্যবস্থা, নিরূপণ, কপাল, a regulation, law, appointment, destiny, fate, luck, good or ill fortune. [master, charioteer.

নিয়ন্তা, শাসনকর্ত্তা, প্রভু, সারথি, a ruler, regulator, governor,

নিয়ন্ত্রিত, অবাধিত, স্বতন্ত্র, অবাধ্য, unrestrained, unchecked, unobstructed, unprevented, free, self-willed.

নিয়ম, নিয়াম,—আদেশ, নির্ণয়, নিরূপণ, স্বীকার, কর্ত্তব্য কর্ম্ম, ব্রত, নিশ্চয়, a regulation, rule, law, engagement, agreement, contract, bargain, condition, stipulation, league, assent, promise, religious observance, vow or voluntary penance, certainty, ascertainment.

নিয়মশালী, ক্রমাগত, স্বীকারক, regular, subject to rules, stipulating, agreeing.

নিয়মান্বিত, নিয়মিত.—নির্ণীত, নির্ধারিত, স্বীকৃত, স্থিরীকৃত, স্থাপিত, regulated, regular, subject to rule, orderly, covenanted, stipulated, agreed on, appointed, fixed, settled.

নিয়ামক, নিয়মকর্ত্তা, আদেষ্টা, দাঁড়ী, সারথি, regulating, superintending, &c. a regulator, ruler, a boatman, pilot, steersman, charioteer.

নিযুক্ত, পদপ্রাপ্ত, আজ্ঞাপিত, প্রবৃত্ত, পরায়ণ, appointed to an office, constituted, commanded, engaged in, devoted or applying to.

নিযুঞ্জান, প্রেরক, appointing to office, constituting, commanding.

নিযুৎ, দশ লক্ষ, a million.

নিযুদ্ধ, লড়ালড়ি, বাহুযুদ্ধ, a close fight, wrestling, fisty cuffs, pugilism.

নিয়োক্তা, পদসংস্থাপক, ভোক্তা, কর্ত্তা, one who appoints to office, one who enjoys, a commander.

নিয়োগ, পদস্থাপন, আজ্ঞা, বিধি, মনোনিবেশ, appointment to office, an order, command, a precept, a constitution, zealous application, devotedness to an object.

নিয়োগী, প্রেরক, ordering, commanding, appointing.

নিযোজন, পদসংস্থাপন, প্রেরণ, আদেশন, to appoint to office, designate, employ, fix, destine to a profession, enjoin, command.

নিরংশী, ভাগশূন্য, অনংশী, অসঙ্গ, not sharing, not inheriting, disinherited, without a partner, single.

নিরঙ্কুশ, অবাধিত, স্বতন্ত্র, unrestrained, unchecked, free, uncontrolled, self-willed.

নিরঞ্জন, নির্ম্মল, পুণ্য, নিষ্কলঙ্ক, দেবমূর্ত্তি বিসর্জ্জন, pure, holy, free from stain; the casting of an idol into the water after its festival.

নিরত, অতিঅনুরক্ত, অনবরতঃ, excessively delighted with, very fond of; incessantly, constantly.

নিরন্তর, নিত্য, অনবরত, আসঙ্গ, অবিচ্ছেদে, সর্বদা, incessant, endless, unintermitted; constantly, incessantly.

নিরন্তর-াল, অবিচ্ছেদ, ঘন, নিবিড়, নিরেট, having no space between, close, impervious, solid.

নিরন্বয়, সন্ততিশূন্য, অপ্রামাণ্য, without posterity, not agreeing (*in grammar*), not following as a consequence (*in logic.*) [jury.

নিরপায়, রক্ষা, নির্বিঘ্নতা, security, safety, exemption from injury.

নিরপায়ী, নির্বিঘ্ন, নিত্য, secure, safe, uninjured, permanent.

নিরপেক্ষ, স্বাধীন, অনাশাপন্ন, independent, having no expectation from a given thing or object.

নিরব, নিঃশব্দ, অবাক্, silent, quiet, taciturn, speechless

নিরবগ্রহ, স্বাধীন, স্বতন্ত্র, independent, not under controul, self-willed. [or by.

নিরবচ্ছিন্ন, অবিশিষ্ট, হীন, not possessed of, not affected with or by.

নিরবদ্য, অতুচ্ছ, উত্তম, সাঙ্গ, সম্পূর্ণ, not low or mean, superior, perfect, complete, entire.

নিরয়, নরক, hell.

নিরর্থ-ক, অফলক, মিথ্যা, অনর্থ, vain, useless, fruitless, to no purpose, without an object, absurd.

নিরসন, নিরাস,—পরাজয়, থামানি, নিবৃত্তি, তাড়ন, বিবর্জন, a defeat, subjugation, a restraining, appeasing, assuaging, a cessation, desisting from, driving away, expulsion, rejection.

নিরস্ত, পরাজিত, ক্ষান্ত, নিবৃত্ত, defeated, subdued, restrained, calmed, appeased, propitiated, desisting from, ceased, made to desist, expelled. [suaging.

নিরস্তক, বিজয়ী, থামানিয়া, subduing, calming, allaying, assuaging.

নিরহ, শান্ত, অবিবাদী, quiet, peaceable, not quarrelsome.

নিরাকরণ, খেদান, বহিষ্করণ, উৎখাতন, to drive out or away, expel, exterminate, remove. [poreal.

নিরাকার, আকাররহিত, অশরীর, without form, shapeless, incor-

নিরাকৃতি, অমূর্ত্তি, বহিষ্কৃতি, উৎখাত, *id*: also expulsion, extermination. [cealed.

নিরাট, দৃঢ়, শক্ত, অচ্ছিদ্র, শুদ্ধ, solid, not hollow, close, con-

নিরাধারা, অনবরত, আসঙ্গ, incessant; incessantly.

নিরাপদে, আশ্রিত, নির্বিঘ্ন. in safety, in security. [houseless.

নিরালয়, শূন্য, বসতিহীন, desert, destitute of habitations,

নিরালা, . একাকী, বিরল, alone, private. [hand.

নিরালা-য়, বিরলে, গোপনে, privately, in secret, aside, under-

নিরাসক, খেদানিয়া. তাড়ানিয়া, repelling, driving away, repulsive.

নিরাহার, অভোজন, উপবাস, a fasting, abstinence from food.

নিরীক্ষণ, দর্শন, দেখন, অবলোকন, to look at, see, view, gaze, observe, survey.

নিরীশ্বর, ঈশ্বরনিষেধ, নাস্তিক, the non-existence or denial of a god; without God; an atheist.

নিরীহ, অচল, স্থির, নির্ম্মল, without motion or exertion, quiet, still, fine, clear. [sary.

নিরুক্ত. বেদাঙ্গ বিশেষ, one of the Vedángas, a Vedantic glos-

নিরুত্তর, প্রতিবাক্যে অসমর্থ,, অবাক্. প্রসিদ্ধ, অখণ্ড্য, without a reply, confounded, speechless, silent, clear, evident, unanswerable. [cool.

নিরুত্তাপ, তাপশূন্য, স্নিগ্ধ, free from heat, anger or jealousy,

নিরুদ্ধ, বেষ্টিত, বদ্ধ, blocked up, obstructed, hindered.

নিরুপধি, নির্ভয়, শরণাগত. আশ্রয়প্রাপ্ত, bold, fearless, safe, secure; security, boldness.

নিরুপম, অতুল, peerless, matchless, incomparable.

নিরুপেক্ষা, আদর, সম্ভ্রম, respectful attention, regard, respect.

নিরূপক, নিয়ামক, directing, regulating, &c. a director, a regulator.

নিরূপণ, নির্ণয় করণ. বিতর্কণ. সংস্থাপন, স্থিরকরণ, আজ্ঞাপন, উপক্রমন, to ascertain, investigate, determine, decide, fix, establish, assign, appoint, prescribe, regulate, try, attempt.

নিরূহ, নিশ্চয়, নির্ণয়, ন্যায়, বিতর্ক, অনধ্যাহার বাক্য, certainty, ascertainment, logic, disputation, a complete sentence or one without ellipsis.

নিরেট, ছিদ্রশূন্য, solid, not hollow, unsplit.
নিরোধ, বেষ্টনকরা, ব্যাঘাত, a blocking up, siege, obstruction, hindrance.
নির্গত, বহির্গত, উৎপন্ন, নিঃসৃত, জনিত, অতীত, gone or sent forth, produced, extracted, expelled, proceeded, issuing, arising from, past. [outlet.
নির্গম, নিঃসরণ, নালা, a going forth, departure, an issue,
নির্গমন, বহির্গমন, উৎপন্ন হওন, জন্মন; প্রস্থান করণ, to go forth, arise, issue, proceed from, depart.
নির্গলন, দ্রব হওন, গিলন, to melt, to dissolve, to gulp.
নির্গুণ, গুণাতীত, অকর্ম্মণ্য, মূর্খ, void of all properties, destitute of good qualities, worthless, useless, foolish.
নির্গূহন, মারণ, হনন, to beat, to strike, to kill.
নির্ঘণ্ট-ন, সূচীপত্র, আলোচনা, a table of contents, catalogue, an examination, survey. [severe, hard.
নির্ঘাত, বজ্রাঘাত, পীড়াজনক, a thunderstroke, a severe blow;
নির্জন, শূন্য, নিরালয়, নিভৃত, uninhabited, desert, private, retired.
নির্জনে, গোপনে, privately, aside, secretly, underhand.
নির্জয়, সর্বাজ্জয়, a complete conquest.
নির্জর, শক্ত, দৌর্বল্যহীন, অজীর্ণ, free from the infirmities of age or decrepitude. [dued.
নির্জিত, পরাস্ত, বশীভূত, conquered, overcome, entirely sub-
নির্জীব, হতপ্রাণ, দুর্বল, শ্রান্ত, lifeless, inanimate, weak, languid, exhausted.
নির্জ্য, জ্যাশূন্য ধনুঃ, unstrung, (as a bow.)
নির্ঝর, উনুই, পর্বতের ঝোরা, পর্বতীয় জলপ্রবাহ, a fountain, spring, waterfall, cascade, mountain-torrent.
নির্ঝরী, পর্বত, জলাকরযুক্ত স্থান, a mountain, a place abounding in springs, &c.
নির্ণয়, নিশ্চয়, নিষ্পত্তি, মীমাংসা, বিতর্ক, নিয়ম, স্থিরকরা, আদেশ, ব্যবস্থা, certainty, ascertainment, a decision, positive conclusion, investigation, an agreement, engagement, promise, settlement, enactment, decree.

নির্ণায়ক, নিষ্পাদক, deciding, ascertaining, leading to a conclusion, &c.

নির্ণিক্ত, পরিষ্কৃত, পবিত্র, শুদ্ধ, cleansed, purified, cleared, corrected.

নির্ণীত, স্থিরীকৃত, সম্পন্ন, স্বীকৃত, ব্যবহারিত, নিশ্চিত, settled, fixed, determined, decided, confirmed, established, usual, agreed upon, pointed out, ascertained.

নির্ণেতা, নির্ণেতৃ,—নিষ্পাদক, one who decides or ascertains, &c.

নির্দয়, নিষ্ঠুর, ক্রুর, কঠিন, hard-hearted, void of pity, merciless, unfeeling, relentless, cruel, barbarous, inhuman.

নির্দায়, মুক্ত, অনাপদ, released, free from confinement or trouble.

নির্দিষ্ট, স্থিরীকৃত, নিরূপিত, সংস্থাপিত, চিহ্নিত, fixed upon, appointed, nominated, appropriated, described, pointed out.

নির্দেশ, নিরূপণ, নিযোজন, সাক্ষ্য, আজ্ঞা, বর্ণনা, নির্ণয়, an appointment, appropriation, designation, testimony, witness, an order, mandate, a description, ascertainment.

নির্দেশন, নির্ণয়করণ, প্রমাণসাধন, নিযোজন, to ascertain, prove by testimony, establish, designate, appoint, appropriate.

নির্ধার, নিশ্চয়, শুদ্ধতা, ভোঁতা, ঋণমুক্ত, certainty, ascertainment, accuracy ; blunt, free of debt.

নির্ধারণ, নির্ণয়করণ, নিষ্পাদন, মিটান, নিয়মন, স্থির করণ, to ascertain, settle, decide, confirm, agree, covenant, bargain, give an earnest.

নির্ধূত, ঝাড়া, বহিষ্কৃত, অনাথ, ত্যক্ত, বিবর্জ্জিত, shaken out, cast out, friendless, deserted, rejected.

নির্নিশ্চ, অস্থির, অপ্রমাণ, uncertain, not established, destitute of proof or stability.

নির্বচন, কহন, বর্ণন, to speak, describe, relate, narrate.

নির্বন্ধ-ন, কৈঙ্কর্য্য, নিয়ম, আক্রম, অভিপ্রায়, অত্যন্ত চেষ্টা, slavery, bondage, an obligation, engagement, seizure, an intention, pertinacious pursuit of an object.

নির্বন্ধী, অবদ্ধ, মুক্ত, বিষয়ত্যাগী, loosed from an obligation, freed, relinquishing the world from devotion to religious abstraction, &c.

নির্ব্ব্ক, বদ্ধজল, not flowing, not passing away, stagnant.

নির্বাচন, কহান, জিজ্ঞাসন, চুনন, to cause to speak, utter, disclose or narrate, to extort from, to interrogate, chuse, select.

নির্বাণ, বুঝান, মৃত, মোক্ষপ্রাপ্ত, extinct, extinguished, gone out, departed, defunct.

নির্বাণ, বুঝানি, জুড়ানি, লয়, অন্তর্দ্ধান, অস্তগমন, প্রস্থান, নিবৃত্তি, বিশ্রাম, মোক্ষ, সংযোগ, সঙ্গম, অন্তর, বিদ্যোপদেশ, হস্তির অবগাহন, an extinguishing, putting out, quenching, quelling, extinction, disappearance, the setting of the sun, &c. a departure, refraining or desisting from, cessation, repose, final emancipation, union, association, confluence, a blending, space, a vacuum, instruction in science, the plunging or bathing of an elephant.

নির্বাত, আশ্রয়স্থান, কোণ, নিঝুম, a sheltered place, place of refuge, a calm, close weather; sheltered from the wind, secure, close, calm.

নির্বাদ, অপবাদ, নিন্দা, নিশ্চাবাদন, নিষ্পত্তি, অবিবাদ, censure, blame, reproach, a rumour, asseveration, affirmation, decision of a controversy, absence of dispute or railing. [or put out.

নির্বাপণ, প্রাণনাশকরণ, মারণ, বুঝান, to kill, cause to extinguish

নির্বার্য্য, নিঃশঙ্ক, দুর্বৃত্ত, দুঃসাহসী, acting fearlessly or without precaution, self-willed, rash. [expatriation.

নির্বাস, বহিষ্করা, দূরকরা, expulsion, ejection, banishment,

নির্বাসন, দূরকরা, অনিচ্ছ, *id:* also indifferent to, without will or inclination, dissatisfied with.

নির্বাহ, জীবিকা, কার্য্যসাধন, বাহুল্য, উপায়, সামগ্রী, সুসার, কর্ম্মসিদ্ধি, বৃত্তি, a livelihood, sufficiency, competency, abundance, a sufficient supply of means or adequate provision for the performance of any thing, means of accomplishment, expedient, materials, management, accomplishment, maintenance, support.

নির্বাহক, প্রতিপালক, কুলানিয়া, সম্পাদক, a provider, maintainer, manager, superintendant ; effecting, accomplishing, supplying, furnishing.

নির্বাহকারী, কুলানিয়া, যোগানিয়া, providing a sufficiency, supplying a demand, furnishing. [&c.

নির্বাহচলা, বৃত্তিব্যাঘাত, a difficulty in procuring a livelihood,

নির্বিন্ন, কাতর, দুঃখিত, মুগ্ধ, overcome with fear or sorrow, distressed, senseless.

নির্বিষ্ট, শ্রমোপার্জ্জিত, earned, gained as hire or wages.

নির্বৃত, শান্ত, কুশলী, easy, tranquil, in easy circumstances, prosperous, happy.

নির্বৃতি, সুখ, শান্তি, বিশ্রাম, কুশল, বিরাম, কর্ম্মসিদ্ধি, মুক্তি, মৃত্যু, ease, tranquillity, rest, repose, safety, security, easy circumstances, happiness, a cessation, desisting from, completion, accomplishment, final emancipation, death. [done.

নির্বৃত্ত, সমাপ্ত, সিদ্ধ, finished, completed, accomplished,

নির্বৃত্তি, সিদ্ধি, নিষ্পত্তি, আগমন, সন্তোষ, তৃপ্তি, মোক্ষ, an accomplishment, completion, an approach, gratification, satisfaction, final emancipation.

নির্বেশ, বেতন, উপভোগ, বিবাহ, মূর্চ্ছা, wages, hire, enjoyment, marriage, a fainting, swooning, syncope.

নির্বোধ, অজ্ঞান, মুগ্ধ, বুদ্ধিহীন, void of understanding, silly, foolish, simple, ignorant, uninformed.

নির্ব্যূঢ, বিবর্জ্জিত, ত্যক্ত, উত্তম ব্যবসা, deserted, left, abandoned ; an approved occupation.

নির্ভর্ৎসন, নিন্দা, তিরস্কার, abuse, reproach, blame.

নির্ভয়, সাহসী, নিঃশঙ্ক, নির্বিঘ্ন, bold, fearless, undaunted, familiar, not timid, secure, safe, free from danger.

নির্ভর, অত্যন্ত, অতিশয়, নিঃশঙ্ক, নিত্য, অবলম্বন, ঠেস, একান্তরূপে, much, excessive, fearless, confident, permanent ; a fulcrum, prop, dependance, point of support ; excessively.

নির্ভাজন, অধিকারচ্যুত হওন, পদচ্যুত হওন, to be bereft of an inheritance, to be discarded from office.

নির্ভ্রান্ত, ভ্রমবিহীন, free from error or mistake.

নির্মদ, মত্ততাশূন্য, sober, not intoxicated, quiet, out of rut.

নির্মম, অনিজ, কঠিন, নির্দ্দয়, কৃপাহীন, not appropriated to one's self, not considered one's own, morose, severe, savage, brutal, cruel.

নির্মমত্ব, স্নেহরাহিত্য, স্নেহরহিত, want of natural affection or attachment, harshness, severity; without natural affection.

নির্মর্য্যাদ, অনাদরদায়ী, অসীম, disrespectful, not giving honour, unlimited.

নির্মল, পবিত্র, পরিষ্কৃত, স্বচ্ছ, নিরীহ, pure, clear, clean, bright, transparent, limpid, honest, fair or clear (as the weather).

নির্মাণ, গঠন, করণ, রচন, গাঁথন, শিল্পকর্ম্ম, রচনা, to form, make, fabricate, frame, build, construct, erect, mould, dispose; a manufacture, fabrication, production, &c.

নির্মাতা, গড়নিয়া, শিল্পকারী, a maker, fabricator, builder, architect, &c.

নির্মাপণ, করাণ, গাঁথান, to cause to make, require to fabricate, &c.

নির্মায়ক, কারক, রচক, গড়নিয়া, making, fabricating, &c; a maker, &c.

নির্মাল্য, পবিত্রতা, স্বচ্ছতা, নিবেদিত পুষ্পাদি, অগাঁথা, মাল্যরহিত, purity, cleanness, clearness, &c; flowers or other offerings to a deity; loose, not strung, destitute of a necklace or garland.

নির্ম্মিত, গঠিত, রচিত, কৃত, কৃত্রিম, made, formed, framed, built, fabricated, artificial, wrought.

নির্মুক্ত, খোলা, অবদ্ধ, উদ্ধৃত, খোলসত্যক্ত সর্প, liberated, set free, released, loose, having cast the slough (as serpents, &c.)

নির্মেধ, মূঢ়, অজ্ঞান, dull, stupid, heavy, inapt.

নির্মোক, সর্পের খোলস, the slough or cast skin of serpents, &c.

নির্যাণ, বহির্গমন, প্রস্থান, মোক্ষ, হস্তির অপাঙ্গ, a going forth, departure, final emancipation, the outer corner of an elephant's eye.

নির্যাতন, প্রতিহিংসা, হত্যা, ত্যাগ, পরিদান, পরিশোধ, revenge, killing, slaughter, a gift, donation, re-delivery of a deposit. payment of a debt.

নির্যাস, ক্বাথ, সারভাগ, বৃক্ষের রস, আঠা, মীমাংসা, অকল্প, স্পষ্ট, শক্ত, a decoction, extract, infusion, pith, quintescence, gum, resin, mucus, juice, bird-lime, a decision, conclusion, logical deduction; positive, categorical, firm, tight, close. [indecent.

নির্লজ্জ, নির্লাজ,—অনপত্রপ, shameless, impudent, immodest,

নির্হার, নির্গতকরা, উৎখাতন, উৎপাটন, মলমূত্রত্যাগ, ঘর্ম্মনিঃসরণ, দাহ, an extraction or drawing out, a rooting or grubbing up, evacuation of the fœces, of urine, sweat, &c. a burning, combustion.

নির্হারী, গন্ধকারক, diffusively or widely fragrant. [sical.

নির্হেতুক, প্রয়োজনশূন্য, দাম্বাল, চঞ্চল, causeless, capricious, whim-

নির্হ্রাদ, শব্দ, রব, ধ্বনি, a sound, a noise.

নিলয়, গৃহ, বসতিস্থান, a house, habitation, abode.

নিলয়ন, ব্রহ্মপ্রাপ্তি, মোক্ষ. absorption, final beatitude.

নিলীন, বেষ্টিত, গুপ্ত, শ্লিষ্ট, মোক্ষপ্রাপ্ত, encompassed, surrounded, wrapt up, concealed, embraced, encamped, having obtained absorption, absorpt.

নিশা, রাত্রি, রজনী, night.

নিশাকর, নিশানাথ, নিশাপতি,—চন্দ্র, the moon.

নিশাচর, পেচকাদি, গৃধ্র, প্রহরী, চোর, রাক্ষস, an owl, jackal or other nocturnal bird or animal, a watchman, a night robber, a cannibal giant or goblin prowling about in the night.

নিশাচরী, রাক্ষসী, বেশ্যা, লম্পটা, a female goblin, a street walker or prostitute, a lewd strolling woman.

নিশাপাল, প্রহরী, a watchman, a night-guard.

নিশি, রাত্রি, রাত্রিতে, at night, in the night.

নিশিত, শানিত, তীক্ষ্ণীকৃত, sharpened, whetted, set.

নিশীথ, অর্দ্ধরাত্র, midnight, deep night.

নিশীথিনী, রাত্রি, রজনী, night.

নিশুতি, গভীর নিদ্রা, the fast sleep of men in the dead of night.

নিশ্চয়, নির্ণয়, স্থিরজ্ঞান, সিদ্ধান্ত, অবধারণ, বিশ্বাস, প্রতিজ্ঞা, স্পষ্ট, ঠিক,

অবশ্য, প্রত্যক্ষতঃ, certainty, ascertainment, clear knowledge, a positive conclusion, decision, determination, resolution, belief, affirmation; clear, certain, plain, positive, sure, exact; certainly, positively, confidently, resolutely, clearly, &c. [firmation.

নিশ্চয়কথা, নিষ্ঠাবাদ, স্থিরবাক্য, an asseveration, positive af-

নিশ্চয়জ্ঞান, দৃঢ় বিশ্বাস, শ্রদ্ধা. persuasion, certainty, conviction, undoubted belief.

নিশ্চয়ত্ব, সত্যতা, যাথার্থ্য, প্রকৃতত্ব, truth, accuracy, veracity, certainty, assurance.

নিশ্চল, অজড়, স্থাবর, স্থায়ী, অচঞ্চল, immoveable, still, fixed, stationary, firm, steadfast.

নিশ্চলন, লুপ্ত, অচলিত, not current, obsolete.

নিশ্চায়ক, নির্ণায়ক, নিষ্পাদক, ascertaining, deciding, &c.; one who decides, &c. [certain, sure.

নিশ্চিত, নির্ণীত, পরিজ্ঞাত, স্থির, ascertained, certainly known,

নিশ্চিতকর্ম্মা, স্থিরধী, স্থিরবিবেকী, acting decidedly, proceeding cautiously or on sure grounds.

নিশ্চিন্ত, সুস্থির, উদ্বেগশূন্য, careless, thoughtless, unconcerned, free from anxiety. [not porous.

নিশ্চিদ্র. দোষরহিত, ছিদ্রশূন্য, faultless, pure, without holes,

নিশ্চেষ্ট, আলসিয়া, নিষ্কর্ম্মী, inactive, motionless, without exertion. [piration.

নিশ্বাস, প্রাণবায়ু, প্রশ্বাস, breath, breathing, inspiration, res-

নিষঙ্গ, তূণ, a quiver. [man.

নিষঙ্গী. তূণধারী, ধন্বী, carrying a quiver; an archer, bow-

নিষণ্ণ, উদ্বিগ্ন, উৎকণ্ঠিত, sad, dejected.

নিষাদ, উৎকণ্ঠ, চণ্ডাল, dejection, sadness, a particular class of outcasts. [bidden, denied.

নিষিদ্ধ, মানা, বারিত, অস্বীকৃত, prohibited, interdicted, for-

নিষেক, গর্ভোৎপাদন, the impregnation of the uterus, injection of sperm. [a preventive.

নিষেদ্ধা, নিষেধী,—বারণকারী, one who prevents or prohibits,

নিষেধ-ম, বারণ, অপহ্নব, a prohibition, restriction, prevention, denial or negation.

নিষেবণ, সেবা, ঔষধি পানকরা, service, attendance, the taking of medicine. [gold, a neck ornament.

নিষ্ক. এক শত আট তোলা স্বর্ণ, অলঙ্কার বিশেষ, a certain weight of

নিষ্কণ্টক, কণ্টকশূন্য, দুঃখশূন্য, free from thorns, free from trouble or anxiety.

নিষ্কর, অকরদায়ী, free from tribute or taxes, untaxed.

নিষ্কর্ম্মা, নিষ্কর্ম্মান্বিত,—অব্যবসায়ী, আলসিয়া, unemployed, unoccupied with business, idle. [useless.

নিষ্কর্ম্মী, আলসিয়া, অকর্ম্মণ্য, idle, not diligent, unemployed,

নিষ্কর্ষ, নিশ্চয়, প্রমাণ, নিষ্পত্তি, নিয়োগ, বিশ্বাস, নিশ্চিত, সত্য, প্রত্যক্ষ, ঠিক, অবশ্য, certainty, evidence, proof, decision, determination, appointment to office, trust, belief; certain, plain, clear, exact, positive; positively, clearly, expressly.

নিষ্কর্ষণ. নিষ্পত্তি করণ. মিটান, প্রত্যক্ষকরণ. বিশ্বাস রাখন, নিয়োজন, to come to a point or decision, conclude, ascertain, believe, appoint, assign.

নিষ্কল, ন্যূনীকৃত, অফল, অনংশ, অনশ্বর, diminished, waned, impoten·, barren, without parts, indestructible. [menstruation.

নিষ্কলা. নিষ্কলী,—গতরজসা, অফলা, *f.* past child-bearing, past

নিষ্কাশন, বহিষ্করণ, ছাড়ান, ব্যয় করণ, বহির্গমন, গছান, নিন্দন, বিকশন, to expel, cast out, dismiss, expend, go forth, place, deposit, revile, to blow as a flower.

নিষ্কুল, বহিষ্কৃত. বিষয়ত্যাগী, expelled or voluntarily withdrawn from all family connections.

নিষ্কৃতি, উদ্ধার, রক্ষা, মুক্তি, deliverance, salvation, acquittal, clearance from a charge, &c.

নিষ্কৃত্রিম, অগঠিত, প্রকৃত, not artificial, true, genuine.

নিষ্কৃষ্ট, নিশ্চিত, স্পষ্ট, যথার্থ, ascertained, plain, clear, positive. [expulsion.

নিষ্ক্রমণ, বহির্গমন, নিঃসারণ, a going forth, bringing out, exit,

নিষ্ক্রান্ত, গত, প্রস্থিত, বহিষ্কৃত, নিঃসারিত, gone, gone forth, departed, brought out, expelled.

নিষ্ক্রামক, বহিষ্কারক, নিঃসারক, expelling, bringing forth.

নিষ্ক্রিয়া, নিরর্থক, অফল, মিথ্যা, useless, ineffectual.

নিষ্ঠ, স্থির, অনন্যচেতাঃ, তৎপর, অভিনিবিষ্ট, ধার্ম্মিক, fixed, established, occupied, engaged in, devoted to, religious, devout, virtuous.

নিষ্ঠা, দৃঢ় ভক্তি. মনোযোগ, শ্রদ্ধা, বিশ্বাস, দৃঢ়জ্ঞান, firm establishment in religion, devotion, religious austerity, belief, confidence, affiance, certainty.

নিষ্ঠীব, থুথু, শ্লেষ্মাদি ত্যাগ, spittle, saliva, a spitting.

নিষ্ঠুর, নির্দ্দয়, কঠিন, কর্কশ, cruel, unfeeling, hard-hearted, harsh, strict, severe, morose. [saliva.

নিষ্ঠেবন, থুথু ফেলন; শ্লেষ্মাদি ত্যাগন, a spitting, spitting out of

নিষ্ণাত. প্রবীণ, পণ্ডিত, skilful, clever, conversant, learned.

নিষ্পত্তি, সমাপ্তি, পূরণ, সিদ্ধি, সিদ্ধান্ত, আদেশ, a completion, termination, conclusion, finishing, fulfilment, decision, determination, award, settlement, sentence, order. [cides, &c.

নিষ্পত্তিকর, বিচারকর্ত্তা, মধ্যস্থ, a judge, umpire, one who de-

নিষ্পন্ন, সমাপ্ত, সিদ্ধ, আদিষ্ট, উৎপন্ন, done, finished, concluded, completed, decided, settled, ordered, regulated, born, produced. [dy; a fixed gaze.

নিষ্পলক, অনবরত, স্থির, incessant, without intermission, stea-

নিষ্পাদন, সমাপন, মিটান, সিদ্ধান্তকরণ, প্রতিজ্ঞা পূরণ, to accomplish, complete, conclude, finish, decide, award, regulate, fulfil a promise.

নিষ্পীড়ন, নিঙ্গড়ান, to wring, wring out, squeeze, press out.

নিষ্পেষণ, বাটন, মর্দ্দন, to rub or grind to powder, smash, tread on, trample. [dull.

নিষ্প্রভ. দীপ্তিরহিত, অস্বচ্ছ, gloomy, dark, obscure, opake,

নিষ্প্রয়োজন, নিরর্থক, অকারণ, needless, unnecessary, causeless, groundless.

নিষ্ফল, অফলক, নিরর্থক, অকর্ম্মণ্য, fruitless, ineffectual, needless. useless, unprofitable, abortive, barren.

নিসর্গ, প্রকৃতি. ভাব, স্বীয়ধর্ম্ম, ত্যাগ, nature, natural state, peculiar character or condition, rejection, abandonment.

নিস্তরণ, পার হওন, উদ্ধার পাওন, to cross or get over, find deliverance or salvation, &c.

নিস্তার, রক্ষা, উদ্ধার, ত্রাণ, মুক্তি, salvation, preservation, deliverance, rescue, acquittal, beatitude. [&c.

নিস্তারক, ত্রাণকর্ত্তা, a saviour, deliverer, preserver; saving,

নিস্তারণ, উদ্ধরণ, বাঁচান, to save, deliver, rescue, preserve, acquit. [quitted.

নিস্তীর্ণ, রক্ষিত, উদ্ধৃত, মুক্ত, saved, rescued, delivered, ac-

নিস্তুল, অসম, অসদৃশ, অনুপম, unequal, uneven, unlike, unrivalled, peerless, matchless.

নিস্তেজ, ঘোর, ভোঁতা, প্রতাপহীন, দুর্ব্বল, obscure, dull, blunt, without energy, zeal or virtue, weak, infirm, flaccid. [dent, rude.

নিস্ত্রপ, নির্লজ্জ, অশিষ্ট, shameless, immodest, bold, impu-

নিস্পন্দ, স্পন্দনরহিত, নির্জীব, মূর্চ্ছিত, motionless, still, inanimate, senseless. [bankrupt.

নিস্ব, নির্ধন, দুঃখী, দেউলিয়া, poor, indigent, destitute,

নিস্বন, শব্দ মাত্র, গর্জ্জন, a sound, loud noise, bellow.

নিহনন, মারণ, প্রাণ নাশ করণ, to smite, kill, slaughter, murder. [guinary person.

নিহন্তা, মারক, সংহারক, বধিক, a murderer, manslayer, san-

নিহানী, নিহালী,— অয়োঘন, an anvil.

নিহার, শিশির, হিম, frost, cold.

নিহারণ, ঠাহরণ, অবলোকন, to view, behold, survey.

নিহিত, স্থাপিত, গচ্ছিত, দত্ত, placed, deposited with, entrusted to, committed to one's care, given.

নিহ্নব, অপলাপ, ফাকী, অবিশ্বাস, গুপ্তকথা, concealment, denial, secrecy, dissimulation, mistrust, suspicion, a secret. [mistrusted.

নিহ্নুত, অপলাপিত, অস্বীকৃত, গুপ্ত, denied, concealed, secret,

নিহ্নুতি, অপলাপ, গূঢ়তা, অপ্রত্যয়, denial, concealment, secrecy, reserve, mistrust. [mistrusts.

নিহ্নোতা, অপলাপী, অপ্রত্যয়ী, one who denies, conceals or

নীকাশ, তুল্য, সদৃশ, *affix*: like, resembling.

নীচ, খাট, বাউনিয়া, নিম্ন, অপকৃষ্ট, অধম, সাধারণ, অধঃস্থ, অধস্তে, তলে, low, short, dwarf, deep, vile, base, mean, common, vulgar; *in comp:* down, below, under, beneath.

নীচগ, নীচগামী,—অধোগামী, নিম্ন, অধম, descending, going down, low, deep, mean. [foundation.

নীচা, তল, গোড়, the lower part, bottom, skirt, base,

নীচাশয়, ক্ষুদ্রমনাঃ, অধম, low-minded, servile, base, of mean views. [at the bottom.

নীচু, নীচে,—অধতে, তলে, below, beneath, down, under,

নীচৈঃ, ধীরে, অনুচ্চৈঃস্বরে, slowly, softly, in a low voice.

নীড়, পক্ষির বাসা, a bird's nest.

নীড়জ, পক্ষী, a bird ; produced in a bird's nest.

নীত, গৃহীত, প্রাপ্ত, লব্ধ, taken, received, obtained, gained.

নীতি, উচিত ব্যবহার, ন্যায়, প্রাপ্তি, ধারা, রীতি, virtuous conduct, morality, justice, right, ethics, moral philosophy, an acquisition, acquirement, conduct, practice.

নীতিকথা, হিতোপদেশ, a moral tale or discourse, fable, &c.

নীতিবিদ্যা, নীতিশাস্ত্র,—হিতোপদেশক শাস্ত্র, the science of morals, ethics, political science.

নীতিমান্, যথার্থ, পুণ্যবান্, just, righteous, moral, virtuous.

নীবি, স্ত্রীলোকের কটীদেশের বস্ত্রবন্ধন, মূলধন, a woman's zone, a cloth round the waist, a stock in trade, a capital, principal. [led.

নীয়মান, গ্রাহ্যমান, যাহা গ্রহণ করা যাইতেছে, being now taken or

নীয়ন্তা, গৃহীতা, ব্যাপারী, a receiver, a taker, dealer, chapman.

নীয়া, আদান, গ্রহণ, the taking of a thing, a taking up.

নীর, জল, সলিল, রস, water, juice, liquor

নীরক্ত, রক্তহীন, bloodless, destitute of blood.

নীরজাঃ, অরেণু, অরজস্বলা, রজোগুণহীন, without pollen, without menstrual evacuations, destitute of the quality of passion or activity, without fame.

নীরদ, জলদ, মেঘ, অদন্ত, giving water, toothless : a cloud.

নীরনিধি, সমুদ্র, সাগর, the sea, the ocean.

নীরব, অবাক্, নিঃশব্দ, silent, speechless, taciturn.

নীরস, রসহীন, শুষ্ক, বিস্বাদু, without juice or moisture, withered, dry, parched, sapless, tasteless, insipid.

নীরসকারক, নিঙড়ানিয়া, নিষ্পীড়ক, rapacious, impoverishing, draining, extracting juices, &c.

নীল, কৃষ্ণ বর্ণ, নীলরসযুক্ত বৃক্ষ বিশেষ, blue, dark blue; indigo, a blue sapphire. [a blue jay.
নীলকণ্ঠ, শিব, ময়ূর, Shiva or the blue-throated, a peacock,
নীললোহিত, ধূম্র, শিব, purple, mixed red and blue; Shiva.
নীলিকা, নীলী,—নীলগাছ, the indigo plant.
নীহার, শিশির, হিম, frost, hoar frost.
নুঅন, নোঅন,—হেলন, বাঁকন, নম্রতাচরণ, to incline, bend, bend down, be bent, be humble. [gether.
নুটী, আটি, পুলিন্দা, a bundle of any thing wrapped to-
নুড়, গোচা, পণ, a wisp of straw or grass, a wager
নুড়ী, ক্ষুদ্র প্রস্তর, কঙ্কর, শিলাপুত্র, পণ, a pebble, piece of brick or stone, a muller, a stake, a gage.
নুণ, লবণ, লোণ, salt. [in salt.
নুণিয়া, সলবণ, লোণা, লাবণিক, salt, saltish, selling or dealing
নুণী, নুণিয়া,—শাক বিশেষ, purslain. [entreaty.
নুতি, স্তব, কাকুতি, প্রার্থনা, praise, flattery, solicitation,
নুন্ন, প্রেরিত, আজ্ঞাপিত, আদিষ্ট, sent, ordered, dispatched, commanded.
নুন্দি, স্থূলকায়, পেটাল, corpulent, fat, abdominous.
নুমুড়ী, ঘণ্টার জিহ্বা, নলী, the tongue or clapper of a bell, the windpipe. [down, humble.
নুয়ান, নোয়ান,—বাঁকান, নামান, to bend, bend down, bring
নুলা, ক্ষুদ্রহস্তবিশিষ্ট, lame or maimed in the hand.
নূতন, নবীন, সদ্যোজাত, আধুনিক, new, novel, recent, fresh, young, upstart.
নূন, অবশ্য, হইতে পারে, certainly, assuredly, probably, perhaps; also *a particle of doubt or recollection, an expletive.* [ancles.
নূপুর, পাদ ভূষা বিশেষ, a sounding ornament or ring for the
নৃ, পুরুষ, পুং, *in compos*: a man, a male.
নৃঘ্ন, হন্তা, ঘাতক, a manslayer, a murderer.
নৃত্য, নাচ, অঙ্গভঙ্গী, a dance, a dancing with gesture, gesticulation, an acting, jumping, skipping about.
নৃপ, নৃপতি, নৃপাল,—রাজা, a king, a sovereign.
নৃপাত্মজ, রাজকুমার, a king's son, a prince.
নৃশংস, পরমদ্বেষী, ঘাতক, হিংসুক, malicious, malignant, mur-

derous. destructive, hurtful, injurious, mischievous.

নৃসিংহ, বিষ্ণুর অবতার বিশেষ, প্রধান মনুষ্য, Vishnu's fourth incarnation as a man-lion, a noble, eminent or honourable man.

নেউট, পোষা জন্তু. a tame or pet animal.

নেউটন, ফিরণ, গতায়াত করণ, to turn, turn back, return, go and come, go back and forward.

নেউট্পাড়া, যাতায়াত, intercourse, intimacy, going and coming.

নেউল, নকুল, বেজী, the ichneumon or mongoose.

নেওন, লওন, প্রাপণ, উড়ান, to take, to receive, to spend.

নেং, অঙ্ঘ্রি, the leg.

নেংচন, নেংড়ান,—খোঁড়ান, to halt, limp, be lame.

নেংট, নেংটিয়া—উলঙ্গ, বিবস্ত্র, naked, stripped, undressed.

নেংটিয়া, উন্দুর, a mouse.

নেঙ্গা, নেঙ্গা, নেটা,—বেঙ্গা, left-handed.

নেকড়া, কানি, a rag, a bit of cloth.

নেকড়িয়া, নেকড়্যা,—গোবাঘা, কেন্দুয়াবাঘ, a hyæna, a wolf.

নেকা, পাগলামিটিয়া, ভণ্ডামীকারক, acting foolishly, silly, playing the buffoon.

নেকার, উদ্গার, বমি, a nausea, a vomiting.

নেঙ্গ, ক্রম, পাদনিক্ষেপ, a step.

নেঙ্গড়া, নেংড়া,—খঞ্জ, খোঁড়া lame, limping.

নেজ, পুচ্ছ, লাঙ্গুল, an animal's tail.

নেটুয়া, নর্ত্তক, বেঙ্গা, a dancing boy ; left-handed.

নেড়া, ন্যাড়া,—স্থাণু, মুণ্ডিত, টাক্পড়া, কৌপীনধারী ভিক্ষুক, destitute of leaves or twigs, pollard, lopped, shorn, bald ; a sect of religious mendicants.

নেড়ী, গায়কী, ধুমড়ী, a female ballad singer or religious mendicant, a vagabond woman.

নেড়্যা, যবন, a contemptuous appellation for Massalmáns.

নেত, কাপড় বিশেষ, a sort of cloth.

নেতা, নেতৃ,—গৃহীতা, অগ্রগামী, স্বামী, ঠক, খাল, নদীর বেণী, one who takes, a receiver, leader, guide, master, owner, a rogue, an inlet or branch of a river.

নেতাড়ি, অর্দ্ধশ্লোক, অর্দ্ধ, a hemistich or half stanza ; half.

নেত্র, চক্ষুঃ, the eye.
নেত্রাম্বু, চক্ষুর জল, a tear, tears.
নেদিষ্ঠ, নেদিয়ান্,—অতিনিকট, very near, nearest, nearer.
নেপা, ত্বক্, চর্ম্ম, a membrane or web.
নেপাপা, লিপ্তপা, পাতাপা, web-footed.
নেবা, পাণ্ডু রোগ, the jaundice.
নেবু, জম্বীর, জামীর, নেবু, a lime or lemon. [cle.
নেমি, চক্রের অন্তভাগ, the circumference of a wheel or cir-
নেলান, চেতান, টোবান, to excite, stimulate, encourage, set on as a dog, &c. [new, young.
নৈ, মৃত্তিকাদির পিণ্ড, নবীন, a lump of earth or dough;
নৈকট্য, সামীপ্য, nearness, vicinity, proximity.
নৈগম, বণিক, উপনিষদ্, a merchant, shop-keeper, tradesman, an Upunishad. [certainty.
নৈত্য, আনন্ত্য, চিরস্থায়িত্ব, eternity, continuance, perpetuity,
নৈধামী, অনশ্বর ভূমিচিহ্ন, an imperishable landmark. [art &c.
নৈপুণ্য, দাক্ষ্য, পটুতা, cleverness, skill, ability, eminence in
নৈবেদ্য, ত্যক্তদ্রব্য, উৎসর্গ, an offering, oblation, present.
নৈমিত্তিক, নৈমিত্তক,—উৎপাদক, হেতুক, প্রযুক্ত, causal, causing, producing, procuring, having a cause, done to accomplish an object. [cian.
নৈয়ায়িক, ন্যায়শাস্ত্রবেত্তা, তার্কিক, a Nyáya philosopher, a logi-
নৈযুক্ত্য, পদনিয়োগ, appointment to office, an appointment.
নৈর্ঋত, দক্ষিণ পশ্চিম কোণের অধিপতি, the south-west quarter or its ruler, a dæmon, a fiend.
নৈর্ণয্য, নিষ্পত্তি, সত্যবাদিতা, a decision, clearness, veracity.
নৈষ্কিক, রৌপ্যবিষয়ে নিযুক্ত, the master of the mint.
নৈষ্ঠিক, গুরুগৃহস্থায়ী, ব্রহ্মচারী, a religious student constantly resident with his spiritual tutor. [belief.
নৈষ্ঠ্য, দৃঢ়বিশ্বাস করিয়া মতাবলম্বন, firm establishment in any
নৈসর্গিক, স্বাভাবিক, natural, arising from the nature of a thing.
নৈস্ত্রিংশিক, অসিবিশিষ্ট, a swordsman; armed with a sword.
নোঙ্গরা, নোঙ্গরাটিয়া,—অপবিত্র ভোজনকারী, feeding in a filthy manner, filthy, beastly.
নোড়, ভাঁজ, মরা, alloy, base mixture, base coin.
নোণা, সলবণ, saltish, brackish; salt or brackish water.

নোনা, আতাফল, a species of custard apple.
নৌ; নৌকা,—তরি, a boat, a ship, a vessel.
ন্যক্কার, বমি, ঘৃণা, অনাদর, ধিক্কার, a nausea, loathing, disgust, abhorrence, contempt, disrespect.
ন্যক্কার্য্য, ঘৃণার্হ, বমনোৎপাদক, odious, abominable, loathsome, disgustful, nauseous. [vile.
ন্যঙ, ন্যক,—খাটন্য, অধম, dwarf, short, low, base, mean,
ন্যঙচা, নেঙড়া, খোঁড়া, club-footed, lame.
ন্যস্ত, নিক্ষিপ্ত, স্থাপিত, সঞ্চিত, deposited, pledged, placed, consigned, hoarded, accumulated.
ন্যস্তক, উপার্জ্জক, সঞ্চয়কারী, boarding, saving, accumulating.
ন্যাকা, অজ্ঞান, স্থূলবুদ্ধি, ignorant, stupid, silly, uninformed, clownish, awkward.
ন্যাকার, বমি, উদ্গার, a vomiting, a throwing up.
ন্যাটা, বেঙ্গা, left-handed.
ন্যায়, নীতি, যাথার্থ্য, তর্কশাস্ত্র, বিচার, ধর্ম্ম, ঔচিত্য, বিতর্ক, বিবেচনা, দর্শন বিশেষ, সদৃশ, তুল্য, right, justice, equity, law, righteousness, propriety, fitness, truth, logic, examination, investigation, one of the six philosophical systems; like, resembling.
ন্যায়ক, বিচারকর্ত্তা, তর্কশাস্ত্রবেত্তা, a judge, logician, just reasoner.
ন্যায়তঃ, যথার্থতঃ, বিচারতঃ, according to right, agreeably to justice or equity, equitably, righteously.
ন্যায়শাস্ত্র, তর্কশাস্ত্র, writings on the Nyáya philosophy.
ন্যায়ী, বিচারসিদ্ধ, উচিত, যাথার্থিক, rational, right, proper, just, equitable, doing right.
ন্যায্য, উচিত, উপযুক্ত, বিচারণীয়, প্রাপ্যধন, অধিকার, right, proper, fit, deserved, due, litigable, recoverable at law, a right, inheritance. [sufficient.
ন্যাজ, তৃপ্ত, ধনবান্, যথেষ্ট, satisfied, wealthy, successful,
ন্যাস, নিক্ষেপ, স্থাপ্যধনাদি, নাসিকাদি গ্রহণ করিয়া জপকরা, a deposit, a pledge, a mode of prayer.
ন্যুব্জ, বক্র, কুব্জ, অধোমুখ, দর্বী, bent, crooked, curved, hump-backed, stooping, looking downwards; a ladle. [less, little, few.
ন্যূন, অপূর্ণ, অকুলন, অল্প, deficient, wanting, defective,

ন্যূনাতিরেক, ন্যূনাধিক,—অধিকাল্প, less or more.
ন্যূনাধিক্য, তারতম্য, a deficiency or excess, less or more.

প.

পংক্তি, পংক্তি,—শ্রেণী, দশাক্ষর ছন্দ, দশ, a row, range, rank, line, a stanza of four lines of ten syllables each; *in comp:* ten.
পঁহুছন, আগমন, উত্তরণ, ব্যাপন, to arrive at, come or reach to.
পক্ক, পাকা, পরিণত, সিদ্ধ, ক্লিন্ন, উত্তম, প্রজ্ঞ, নিপুণ, ripe, mature, concocted, cooked, digested, suppurated, substantial, of good materials, of mature understanding, intelligent.
পক্ষ, পালখ, স্বগণ, পার্শ্ব, সহায়, মাসের অৰ্দ্ধেক, প্রসক্ত বাক্য, মত, অনুমান, কল্প, বিতণ্ডা, প্রতিবাদ, a feather, wing, plume, a side, flank, party, partizan, friend, proxy, a flock, an army, a fortnight, a proposition or side of an argument, thesis, position, doctrine, inference, alternative, contradiction, opposition, a reply, law-plaint.
পক্ষতি, প্রতিপৎ, পালখের মূল, the first day of the wane or increase, a pinion.
পক্ষপাত, গণতা, সহকারিতা, partiality, favouritism, collusion, aid.
পক্ষপাতী, গণবদ্ধ, অনুরোধী, partial, leaning or attached to; a partizan.
পক্ষবান্, ডেনাযুক্ত, পালখাচ্ছাদিত, winged, feathered, fledged.
পক্ষব্যাপী, প্রসঙ্গের সর্বাঙ্গব্যাপী, embracing the whole of a theme or thesis.
পক্ষলক্ষণ, আদালতের বিষয় প্রমাণক চিহ্ন, the mark of a valid plaint, a true bill.
পক্ষাঘাত, অঙ্গঅবশ, অর্দ্ধাঙ্গ রোগ, palsy, paralysis, apoplexy.
পক্ষান্তরে, অন্যপক্ষে, নতুবা, on the other side, on the contrary supposition, otherwise.
পক্ষিণী, বিহঙ্গমী, দিনদ্বয়ের সহিত রাত্রি, a hen-bird, a night with the days preceding and following.
পক্ষিমারা, ব্যাধ, বেদ্যা, a bird-catcher, a fowler.
পক্ষিরাজ, গরুড়, ময়ূর, দ্রুতগামী ঘোটক, Garura king of birds, a peacock, a swift horse.

পক্ষী, বিহঙ্গম, পক্ষবিশিষ্ট, a bird, a fowl ; having wings &c.

পক্ষ্ম, চক্ষুঃপাতার লোম, কেশর, সূত্র, an eye-lash, the filament of a flower, a thread, a fibre.

পগার, সেতু, আলি, a mound, bank, a trench and mound.

পঙ্ক, কর্দ্দম, পাপ, mud, mire, dirt, soft clay, sin, guilt.

পঙ্কজ, পঙ্কেরুহ,—পদ্ম, কমল, the lotus or water-lily.

পঙ্কিল, কাদাটিয়া, কর্দ্দমযুক্ত, muddy, miry, plashy, clayey.

পঙ্গ, ফড়িঙ্গ, লোকশ্রেণী, a grasshopher, a locust, a line or circle of people seated to eat.

পঙ্গপাল, ফড়িঙ্গ সমূহ, a flight of locusts or grasshoppers.

পঙ্গু, খেঙ্গড়া, চলৎশক্তিরহিত, lame, halt, crippled, without legs, without the power of moving.

পচন, সড়ন, গলন, ক্ষরণ, দরণ, to putrify, mortify, rot, moulder, fall to decay, be musty, spoil, stink.

পচা,. দুরিত, সড়া, নষ্ট, জরা, rotten, corrupt, putrid, musty, tainted, spoiled, digested. [steep.

পচান, জারণ, সড়ান, to promote putrifaction, to macerate,

পচাকাল, কাদাযুক্ত সময়, wet sloppy weather. [stench.

পচানী, সড়াভাব, দুর্গন্ধ, putridity, putrescence, rottenness,

পচাল, অকথ্য, কটুবাক্য, obscene, scurrilous ; indecent talk, ribaldry. [lously.

পচালিয়া, আলগামুখ, কটুবাদী, talking obscenely or scurri-

পচ্য, পাকযোগ্য, digestible. [ripening.

পচ্যমান, যাহা পাক হইতেছে, under digestion, in cooking,

পঞ্চ, পাঁচ, মধ্যস্থ, five; an arbitrator, an umpire.

পঞ্চক, পাঁচসম্বন্ধীয়, পঞ্চমাংশ কর, five, relating to five, made of five, bought with five ; a tax of a fifth part.

পঞ্চকোল, মিলিত পাঁচ কালকম্, a compound of five spices.

পঞ্চগব্য, দুগ্ধ, দধি, ঘৃত, গোময়, গোমূত্র, the five productions of the cow, milk, curds, ghee, urine and dung.

পঞ্চতপাঃ, তপস্যা বিশেষ, a sitting between four fires in the burning sun as a religious mortification.

পঞ্চত্ব, পঞ্চতা,—মৃত্যু, death considered as a resolution into the five primary elements.

পঞ্চপল্লব, ঔষধি বিশেষ, a medicinal preparation from the sprouts of five different trees.

পঞ্চপ্রাণ, প্রাণাদি পাঁচ বায়ু, the five vital airs of the body.
পঞ্চভূত, পৃথিবী, জল, তেজঃ, বায়ু, আকাশ, এই পাঁচ, the five primary elements.
পঞ্চভূতাত্মা, ব্যক্তি, প্রাণী, an individual as consisting of the five elements.
পঞ্চম, পাঁচসংখ্য, পাঁচের পূরণ, fifth ; the fifth musical note.
পঞ্চরঙ্গী, বিচিত্র, বহুরঙ্গ, motley, variegated.
পঞ্চরত্ন, স্বর্ণাদি পাঁচ, the five precious things, or gold, silver, pearls, chrystal and copper.
পঞ্চশর, মদন, কন্দর্প, Káma Deva or the Indian Cupid.
পঞ্চশাখ, হস্ত, the hand ; branching out in five directions.
পঞ্চসূনা, চুল্লীপ্রভৃতি পাঁচপ্রকার প্রাণিবধস্থান, these five,—the hearth, curry-stone, broom, pestle and mortar, and the water-pot, as accidentally destructive to insects, &c. [the castor plant.
পঞ্চাঙ্গুল, হস্তবৎ, ভেরেণ্ডা বৃক্ষ, digitated, measuring five fingers;
পঞ্চাৎ, সমাজ, সভা, an assembly, a council.
পঞ্চাতী, মিলিত পাঁচ লোকের কর্ত্তব্যকর্ম্ম, a custom in which five persons unite. [sign leo.
পঞ্চানন, শিব, সিংহ, সিংহরাশি, five-faced, *i. e.* Shiva, a lion, the
পঞ্চায়িত, মধ্য, মধ্যস্থানী, the midst, mediatorship, arbitration.
পঞ্জর, পর্শুকা, খাঁচা, a rib, the side or ribs, a cage, an aviary.
পঞ্জিকা, তিথিবারাদিজ্ঞাপক পত্র বিশেষ, an almanack, a calendar.
পট, চিত্রিত বস্ত্র, চট্, চাল, চিত্র, cloth either thick, fine or coloured, canvass, the field or canvass of a picture, an outer tent-fence, a roof, thatch, a map, picture, curtain. [the bladder.
পটকা, পটাকা,—অগ্নিখেলার টোটা, ফোপ্পা, a squib, cracker,
পটকার, চিত্রকর, তন্তুবায়, a draughtsman, limner, designer, a weaver.
পটময়, কাপড়নির্ম্মিত, তাম্বু, made of cloth ; a tent, a petticoat.
পটল, গৃহের চাল, রাশি, সমূহ, চুপড়ী, ছানী, চন্দনময় তিলক, প্রকরণ, a roof or thatch, a heap, collection, multitude, train, retinue, a basket, a film on the eye. a sandal-wood mark on the forehead, a division of certain books.

পটহ, ঢক্কা, a war-drum, a kettle-drum.

পটান, অনুকূলাচরণ, কমান, to afford facilities, to forward, to make a work successful.

পটী, পট্টী,—বস্ত্রখণ্ড, বন্ধনী, ভূমিখণ্ড, পাড়া, a slip of cloth, bandage, roller, list, edge, a strip of land, a quarter in a market.

পটীর, চন্দন, ক্ষেত্র, বায়ুগুল্ম, sandal-wood, a field, a hypochondriac.

পটু, নিপুণ, চতুর, পারগ, ঠক, বকুয়া, বিকশিত, নীরোগ, ঊর্ণা কাপড়, clever, expert, skilful, diligent, active, able, smart, shrewd, crafty, fraudulent, talkative, open, blown, expanded, hale, healthy; woollen cloth.

পটুয়া, চিত্রকর, দেবমূর্ত্তিনির্ম্মায়ক, a painter, limner, an idol or image maker.

পটুকা, কটিবন্ধনী, a girdle, sash, belt.

পটোল, ফল বিশেষ, palwal or a species of cucumber.

পট্কন, হস্তযুদ্ধে পরাস্ত হওন, হারণ, to slip or fall in wrestling, to stumble, to be thrown.

পট্কান, পাছড়ান, to throw in wrestling, overcome, displace.

পট্ট, কৌষেয় বস্ত্র, বন্ধনী, wove silk, cloth, a bandage.

পট্টরাণী, পট্টমহিষী,—রাজার প্রধানা স্ত্রী, the chief or queen among a king's wives.

পাট্টশ, অস্ত্র বিশেষ, a sort of weapon, a two-edged sword.

পট্পটী, লতা বিশেষ, a sort of club rush, a pop-gun

পঠন, পড়ন,—পাঠকরণ, অধ্যয়ন, to read, peruse, recite, repeat.

পড়ন, পোরণ, ঝরণ, লুপ্ত হওন, ঘটন, আক্রমণ, শয়ন, to fall, fall down, drop, fall into disuse or decay, to invade, fall upon, occur, happen, lie, recline.

পড়সী, প্রতিবাসী, a neighbour.

পড়া, উৎকট, শূন্য, পতিত, পাঠ, অধ্যয়, ফেলা, আক্রম, waste, uncultivated, fallen; a lesson, reading, perusal, a throw at dice, an onset, attack.

পড়ান, অধ্যাপন, ফেলন, ঢালন, to teach or make to read, to throw down, spill, pour, &c.

পড়ুয়া, শিষ্য, ছাত্র, a pupil, learner, scholar, schoolboy.

পণ, কোটি, নিয়ম, প্রতিজ্ঞা, মূল্য, বেতন, অশীতি কপর্দ্দক, a wager, bet, stake, bargain, agreement, engagement, compact, stipulation, condition, price, wages, eighty cowries.

পণাপণ, অপ্রয়োগ, অপ্রয়োজনার্হ, an indifferent matter.

পণিতব্য, পণ্য,—বেচনীয়, বিক্রয়ণীয়, to be sold, vendible, saleable, marketable. [ure, miscarriage.

পণ্ড, নপুংসক, নিরর্থক শ্রম, a eunuch, a blank in a lottery, fail-

পণ্ডশ্রম, ব্যর্থায়াস, any fruitless labour, useless or unsuccessful plodding or exertion.

পণ্ডা, পাণ্ডিত্য, বুদ্ধি, learning, philosophy, science, wisdom.

পণ্ডিত, বিদ্বান্, learned, wise; a learned man, a philosopher.

পণ্য, বিক্রেয় দ্রব্য, মূল্যানুযায়ী দ্রব্য পরিমাণ, পারাণী, any merchandize, a commodity for sale, the quantity for a given price, ferriage.

পতঙ্গ, ফড়িঙ্গ, পক্ষী, a grasshopper, a locust, a bird.

পতদ্গ্রাহ, নিষ্ঠীবাধার, a spitting pot or salivary.

পতন, অবশে অধোগমন, টলন, ক্ষরণ, চ্যবন, to fall, to fall down, to slip, drop, pour, pour out.

পতয়ালু, পতনশীল, liable or having a tendency to fall.

পতর, লৌহাদির পাত, a plate of metal, an iron hoop.

পতাকা, ধ্বজা, চিহ্ন, a flag, ensign, banner, signal. [band.

পতি, প্রভু, স্বামী, a lord, master, owner, possessor, hus-

পতিত, গেরিত, উজ্ঝিত, পরাভূত, উৎপন্ন, শূন্য, উৎকট, ভ্রষ্ট, দুষ্ট, fallen, alighted, defeated, descended, born, neglected, uncultivated, fallow, laid with grass, fallen from virtue, abandoned.

পতিপ্রাণা, পতিব্রতা,—সহগামিনী, সতী, স্বীয়া, *f.* chaste, devoted to or burning with her husband, a virtuous and affectionate wife.

পতিবত্নী, সভর্তৃকা, having a husband, a married woman.

পতিম্বরা, স্বেচ্ছামতে বিবাহিতা, a bride who chooses her own husband.

পত্তন, গ্রাম, নগর, বসতি, আরম্ভ, a city, town, colony, settlement, commencement.

পত্তি, পদাতিক, সেনার দল, a foot soldier, a troop or platoon.

পত্নী, বিবাহিতা স্ত্রী, ভার্য্যা, কর্ত্রী, a wife, a mistress, a female owner or proprietor.

পত্র, দল, পাতা, পালথ, শরপুঙ্খ, লিপি, পুস্থ, অশ্বাদি বাহন, a leaf, blade of grass, the petal of a flower, leaf of a book, door or table, a sheet or plate of metal, a sword blade or sheath, the wing of a bird or insect, feather of an arrow, a letter, writing, book, lease, any vehicle, as horse, car, &c.

পত্রী, লিপি, পক্ষী, বাণ, আরোহী, a letter, a writing, a bird, an arrow, a rider.

পত্রোল্লাস, মুকুল, a bud, a flower-bud.

পথ, বর্ত্ম, মার্গ, ধারা, মত, a road, path, way, route, journey, passage, line of conduct, course, religious sect or sentiments, profession.

পথদর্শক, ডাকুয়া, বর্ত্মোপদেষ্টা, a guide, a conductor.

পথিক, পান্থ, পর্য্যটক, a traveller, wayfaring person.

পথিকাশ্রয়, পথিকাশ্রম,—উত্তরণস্থান, an inn, baiting-place, caravansera.

পথিমধ্যে, যাইতেং, on the road, by the way.

পথী, পর্য্যটক, মতাবলম্বী, travelling, journeying, following any particular sect.

পথ্য, সুভোজ্য, পানযোগ্য, রোগির বিহিত আহার, salutary, wholesome, proper as diet, regimen or medicine.

পদ, চরণ, ক্রম, চিহ্ন, স্থান, পা, শ্লোক, কার্য্যভার, মহিমা, ব্যবসায়, শব্দ, বস্তু, সংখ্যা, চতুর্থাংশ, a foot, leg, step, pace, footstep, a mark, spot, scite, place, poetical foot or line, leg or foot of a chair, &c. station, office, rank, reign, employment, situation, stage of a law-suit, a word, inflected word, connected sentiment, thing, a number in arithmetic, the fourth part.

পদগ, পদাতিক, going on foot; a foot soldier, footman.

পদচ্যুত, মহিমাভ্রষ্ট, বিদায়প্রাপ্ত, fallen from his station, discharged from office, dismissed. [path, way.

পদবী, বংশ পরম্পরাগত উপাধি, পথ, a title, surname, road, path, way.

পদব্রজে, পায়, on foot.

পদরুধী, চরণের পরিধেয় বস্ত্র, a stocking, pair of stockings.

পদস্থ, কর্ম্মনিযুক্ত, মহিমাপ্রাপ্ত, fixed in an office or station.

having or filling a situation, invested with a dignity, reigning.

পদহর, শব্দচোর, a plagiary, plagiarism.

পদাঘাত, পাদপ্রহার, a kick.

পদাঙ্ক, পাদচিহ্ন, a footstep, print of the foot.

পদাঙ্গুলি, পদাঙ্গুষ্ঠ,—পায়ে অঙ্গুলী, a toe. [foot-soldier, infantry.

পদাতি-ক, পাদগামী ভৃত্য, পদাতিসেনা, a footman, pedestrian, peon,

পদান, সংকীর্ত্তন, স্তব করণ, লিপির চিহ্ন রাখন, to praise, celebrate. applaud, to punctuate, mark writing with points or spaces, mark the cases of nouns.

পদাবলী, পদবীশ্রেণী, ছন্দ, a list of titles or offices, metre, verse, poetical arrangement.

পদার্থ, বস্তু, ইন্দ্রিয়গোচর, শব্দের প্রতিপাদ্য, ভাব, a thing, material object, the meaning of a word, a category or predicament, viz. substance, quality, action, identity, variety, relation and non-existence.

পদার্পণ, কর্ম্মে নিযোজন, a placing or putting into office, induction, instalment, inauguration.

পদাসন, পাদপীঠ, a footstool. [or ships.

পদী, নৌকার পরিমাণ, tonnage or measurement of boats

পদীম, প্রদীপ, a lamp, a light. [quainted with words.

পদুয়া, পদবিষয়ক, শব্দজ্ঞ, belonging to office, official, ac-

পদুয়াবিক্রয়, থোকে বিক্রয়, wholesale. [nually.

পদেং, ক্রমেং, অনবরতঃ, at every step, step by step, conti-

পদ্দী, পদবী,—উপাধি, নাম, a title, epithet, surname.

পদ্ধতি, পথ, শ্রেণী, কর্ম্মানুষ্ঠান বোধক গ্রন্থ, পদবী, a road, line, row, range, a ritual or manual of ceremonies, a title, a surname.

পদ্ম, কমল, ব্যূহ বিশেষ, দশ খর্ব্ব, the lotus or water-lily, a form of battle array, ten billions.

পদ্মকলিকা, অপ্রফুল্লিত কমল, an unblown water-lily.

পদ্মবন্ধু, ভ্রমর, সূর্য্য, a bee, the sun.

পদ্মরাগ, মণি বিশেষ, চুণী, a ruby. [lotuses.

পদ্মাকর, পদ্মযুক্ত জলাশয়, a deep tank, a pond abounding in

পদ্মিনী, কমলিনী, সুন্দরী স্ত্রী, an assemblage of lotuses or place abounding in them, a beautiful woman.

পদ্য, শ্লোক, ছন্দ, ব্যবহার, চলিত, metre, verse, poetry, the idiom of a language, a custom, usage, behaviour, rite, tenet; customary, habitual.

পদ্যক্রম, চলিতাচার, customary behaviour, common practice.

পদ্যপাড়ন, আচরণ, to behave, act, conduct oneself.

পদ্যহীন, অচলিত, unprecedented, novel, unusual.

পনস, কাঁটাল, the jack fruit.

পন্থা, পথ, মার্গ, a road, way, path, route, conveyance.

পন্থী, পথিক, মতাবলম্বী, travelling, journeying, following the tenets of any particular sect.

পন্নগ, সর্প, a snake, serpent, reptile.

পন্নদ্ধী, পাদুকা, পাদরথী, a shoe, a boot.

পবন, বায়ু, the wind, the air, the god of wind.

পবিত্র, শুদ্ধ, পুণ্য, নির্ম্মল, পরিষ্কৃত, pure, holy, sanctified, purified by austerities, undefiled, nice, clean.

পম, উদ্দেশক, a clue, a guide. [prosperous.

পয়ঃ, পয়স্,—দুগ্ধ, জল, বৃদ্ধি, বর্দ্ধিত, milk, water, prosperity;

পয়নালা, পয়োনালা—প্রণালী, নল, a drain, gutter, sewer, a water-course, a tube.

পয়মন্ত, ভাগ্যবন্ত, কুশলী, prosperous, happy.

পয়সা, তাম্রমুদ্রা, a pice or $\frac{1}{4}$ of an anna, money, change.

পয়স্য, দধিআদি, made from or relating to milk, as curds, cheese, or butter.

পয়স্বিনী, দুগ্ধবতী, milch, giving milk (cow or goat, &c.)

পয়ান, গতি, প্রস্থান, a going, travelling, marching, march.

পয়োধর, স্তন, মেঘ, a woman's breast, an udder, a cloud.

পয়োধি, পয়োনিধি,—সমুদ্র, the sea, the ocean.

পর, অন্য, ইতর, ভিন্ন, দূরস্থ, উত্তর, অনুগামী, অনাত্মীয়, প্রধান, শ্রেষ্ঠ, অধিক, পশ্চাৎ, শত্রু, লীন, রত, other, another, different, remote, distant, latter, least, subsequent, following, future, inimical, hostile, adverse, estranged, best, pre-eminent, exceeding, more, after; an enemy, a gnomon. *in compos*: addicted to, intent after or upon, ready.

পরকলা, স্বচ্ছ, transparent.

পরকাল, উত্তরকাল, another world, a future state.

পরকীয়, অন্যসম্বন্ধীয়, another's, belonging or relating to another.

পরকীয়া, অন্যপুরুষগামিনী স্ত্রী, the adulterous wife or the faithless mistress of another.

পরক্ষেত্র, অন্যদীয় ক্ষেত্র, another man's wife or field.

পরখ, পরখাই,—পরীক্ষা, বিবেচনা, a trial, probation, test, experiment, ordeal.

পরচুল, অন্যদীয় কেশ, false hair. [another.

পরছায়া, স্বভিন্ন ছায়া, অপদেবতা, the shadow or apparition of

পরছতী, চালের শেষ ভাগ, the eaves of a house. [subject.

পরছন্দ, পরতন্ত্র,—অন্যাধীন, dependant on another, subservient,

পরণ, বস্ত্র পরিধান করণ, to put on clothes, to dress, pull on.

পরতঃ, অন্যতঃ, by or from another.

পরতল, বস্ত্রতালী, a patch.

পরত্র, অন্যত্র, ইতরমধ্যে, শত্রুমধ্যে, পরকালের বিষয়ে, in another, among others, among enemies, about another world, in another world.

পরদার, অন্যদীয়া ভার্য্যা, ব্যভিচার, another's wife, adultery.

পরদারগমন, পরদারাভিগমন,—ব্যভিচার করা, adultery, adulterous intercourse with another's wife. [dulterer.

পরদারী, ব্যভিচারী, committing adultery, adulterous; an a-

পরদেশ, বিদেশ, প্রবাস, a foreign country; abroad.

পরন্তু, কিন্তু, but.

পরপত্রগ, সঙ্কেতবাক্যভাষী, using a catch-word.

পরপর, আর২, উত্তরোত্তর, more and more, further and further.

পরপুরপ্রবেশক, *f.* ইকা,—ভেলকী, ডাকিনী, a wizard, a witch.

পরপূর্ব্বা, অন্যপূর্ব্বা, দ্বিরূঢ়া, *f.* married before, twice married.

পরব, উৎসব, a festival, a religious feast.

পরবশ, অস্বতন্ত্র, subject to another, dependant, subservient.

পরব্রহ্ম, পরমাত্মা, Brahma or the Supreme Deity.

পরম, উৎকৃষ্ট, উত্তম, প্রধান, শ্রেষ্ঠ, best, supreme, sublime, excellent, chief, great, exquisite. *in compos*: eminently.

পরমপুরুষ, পরমাত্মা, জগতের আদি কারণ, God, the elemental generative Spirit or creative energy.

পরমলাভ, আশ্বাস, সান্ত্বনা, consolation, comfort, happiness.

পরমহংস, যোগী, an ascetic, an abstract devotee.
পরমাণু, অতিসূক্ষ্ম বস্তু, লেশ, an atom, the smallest particle of matter. [supreme Spirit, God.
পরমাত্মা, ব্রহ্ম, আদিকারণ, Brahma as soul of the universe, the
পরমান্ন, পায়স, rice boiled with milk and sugar.
পরমায়ু, জীবনকাল, the whole period of life, life-time, age, long life.
পরমার্থ, উৎকৃষ্ট বিষয়, পরমাত্মা, an excellent or sublime object, the chief good, the divine Being, Spirit.
পরমার্থতঃ, পরমার্থ বিষয়ে, with reference to the chief object, *i. e.* God, spiritually.
পরমেশ্বর, সৃষ্টিকর্ত্তা, the supreme Being, the high God, Shiva.
পরম্পর, ক্রমাগত, উত্তর২, successive, proceeding from one to another, descending from father to son, one behind another.
পরম্পরা, গোত্র, ক্রম, আনুপূর্ব্ব, lineage, regular descent, order, continuous arrangement, successive ranks, &c. [by report.
পরম্পরায়, পূর্ব্বপুরুষানুক্রমে, অন্য২ দ্বারা, প্রমুখাৎ, traditionally,
পরম্পরাগত, ইতিহাসগত, প্রাচীনোক্ত, communicated from father to son, traditional.
পরলোক, উত্তরকাল, another world, a future state, futurity.
পরশাড়া, লতা, বান্দক, a parasitical plant, a parasite.
পরশু, কুড়ালি, a battle axe, a hatchet.
পরশ্ব, পরশু,—আগামি তৃতীয় দিন, গত তৃতীয় দিন, the day after tomorrow, or day before yesterday.
পরস্পর, অন্যোন্য, উভয়তঃ, mutual, reciprocal, alternate, interchanging; mutually.
পরাক, ব্রত বিশেষ, a certain religious vow, a sacrificial sword or scymetar.
পরাক্রম, বিক্রম, বল, প্রতাপ, চড়াও, power, energy, force, strength, valour, prowess, a going out or forth, a sally. [valorous.
পরাক্রমী, বলবান্, সাহসী, powerful, strong, active, brave,
পরাক্রান্ত, শক্তিমান, মহামহিম, পক্ষপাতী, possessed of power or influence, dignified, drawn or led by another.

পরাগ, পুষ্পরেণু, ধূলি, স্নানাদিকারণ গন্ধদ্রব্যাদি চূর্ণ, সূর্য্যগ্রহ, pollen, dust, fragrant powder, an eclipse.

পরাঙ্মুখ, বিমুখ, ঘৃণাকর, having the face averted, averse, opposed to.

পরাজয়, পরাভব, হারাণি, a defeat, repulse, failure or loss of a suit at law. [dued, cast in a suit.

পরাজয়ী, পরাজিত,—পরাস্ত, হারা, defeated, conquered, sub-

পরাণ, বস্ত্রাদি পরিধান করাণ, সাজান, to dress another, clothe, trim, deck, harness, caparison. [preme.

পরাৎপর, পরমাত্মা, পরমেশ্বর, the Most High, God, the Su-

পরান্ন, পরের অন্ন ভোজন, a living at another's expence.

পরাবজ্ঞ, তুচ্ছীকৃৎ, গর্ব্বযুক্ত, contemptuous, despising others.

পরাবর্ত্তন, প্রতিগমন, পুনরাগমন, ফিরিয়া আইসন, to return, to come back, to revert to.

পরাবৃত্ত, পুনরাগত, turned back, returned, reverted to.

পরাবৃত্তি, ফিরণ, পুনরাবৃত্তি, a turning, returning, reversion.

পরাভব, পরাজয়, হারণ, উৎখাত, a defeat, overthrow, discomfiture, repulse.

পরাভূত, পরাজিত, হারা, overcome, defeated, conquered, cast.

পরামনন, অনুবোধ, অধর্ম্মত্যাগ, a change of mind, change of religious faith, conversion, repentance.

পরামর্শ, মন্ত্রণা, বিবেচনা, counsel, advice, deliberation, plan.

পরামর্শী, মন্ত্রণাদায়ী, counselling, advising. [flowered.

পরামৃষ্ট, মন্ত্রণাপ্রাপ্ত, ভ্রষ্ট, counselled, advised, defiled, de-

পরায়ণ, অনুরাগ, তৎপর, পক্ষপাতী, devotedness to; devoted to, intent upon, zealous; a follower, votary, zealot. [others.

পরাশ্রয়, পরের অবলম্বনে থাকা, a refuge in or dependance on

পরাস্ত, জিত, হারা, defeated, vanquished, overcome, subdued. [as painting, perfuming, &c.

পরিকর্ম্ম, স্নানাদি দ্বারা অঙ্গসংস্কার, decoration of the person,

পরিকল্পনা, কৌশল, উপায়, শৈলি, a contrivance, plan, invention, machination. [commendation.

পরিকীর্ত্তন, প্রস্তাব, প্রতিষ্ঠাকরা, a mentioning, commending,

পরিক্রম, বেড়ানি, বিলাস, a walking for pleasure, a walking round, dalliance, amorous play.

পরিক্ষয়, সর্ব্বনাশ, complete or entire decay.
পরিখা, খাত, খানা, গড়, a surrounding ditch or moat.
পরিগণিত, সংখ্যাত, কলিত, counted, enumerated, calculated.
পরিগত, বিদিত, জ্ঞাত, চেষ্টিত, প্রাপ্ত, বেষ্টিত, known, understood, sought, enquired after, gained, obtained, surrounded. [acknowledged.
পরিগৃহীত, প্রাপ্ত, স্বীকৃত, received, accepted, assented to,
পরিগ্রহ, আদান, স্বীকার, পত্নী, পরিবার, সৈন্যের পৃষ্ঠভাগ, মূল, আদি, মূলধন, a taking, acceptance, assent, a wife, family, servants, dependents, retinue, the reserve of an army, the sun near the moon's node, a root, origin, stock, fund.
পরিঘ, গদা, মুদ্গর, শূল, কাচপাত্র, a bludgeon, an iron or iron-bound club, a pike, a spear, a glass vessel.
পরিচয়, বন্ধুতা, আলাপ, জ্ঞাতসার, সাক্ষাৎ করাণ, জিজ্ঞাসা, acquaintance with, knowledge of, privity, introduction to, enquiry. [dependance.
পরিচর্য্যা. সেবা, উপাসনা, service, attendance upon, respect,
পরিচায়ক, সাক্ষাৎকারী, causing to know, introducing, acquainting. [tendant, follower, servant.
পরিচারক, সেবাকর, উপাসক, অনুচর, ভৃত্য, attending on ; an at-
পরিচিত, জ্ঞাত, জানিত. acquainted with, privy to, intimate.
পরিচ্ছদ, বস্ত্র, বেশ, পরিবারসমূহ, clothing, dress, a garment, a train, retinue, attendants.
পরিচ্ছন্ন, পরিহিত, বস্ত্রধারী, বেষ্টিত, সমভিব্যাহৃত, covered, clothed, involved, surrounded with, attended by.
পরিচ্ছিত্তি, ব্যবধান, সীমা, বিচ্ছেদ, নিষ্পত্তি, a partition, boundary, separation, a space, a conclusion, completion, decision.
পরিচ্ছিন্ন, সীমাযুক্ত, পরিমিত, উৎকৃষ্ট, পরিষ্কৃত, স্বচ্ছ, bounded, limited, defined, excellent, good, polished, clean, clear, pellucid.
পরিচ্ছেদ, সীমা, বিভাগ, প্রকরণ, পরিষ্কার, স্বচ্ছতা, মুক্তি, ফাক, a limit, boundary, section or division of a book, cleanness, clearness, neatness, transparency, an acquittal, a space or break in writing.

পরিজন, পোষ্যবর্গ, স্বজন, a family, household, attendants, a member of one's family, an attendant.

পরিজ্ঞান, তত্ত্ব, নিশ্চয়জ্ঞান, দোষসন্ধানকরা, a complete idea, comprehension, accurate knowledge, detection, conviction.

পরিজ্ঞাপন, বুঝান, জানান, দোষ প্রমাণ করণ, to give a complete idea of a matter, to make to comprehend, acquaint, inform, convict. [changed.

পরিণত, বক্র, পক্ক, অবস্থান্তরপ্রাপ্ত, curved, bent down, ripe,

পরিণতি, অবনতি, বিকার, a bowing down, a change, alteration, transmutation.

পরিণয়, বিবাহ, marriage. [monial.

পরিণয়ন, পাণিগ্রহণ, the performance of the marriage cere-

পরিণাম, অবস্থান্তরপ্রাপ্তি, বিকার, ভাবান্তর, a change of form, state or quality, alteration, transmutation, the result of a chemical process. [discreet.

পরিণামদর্শী, দূরদর্শী, বিজ্ঞ, provident, prudent, forecasting,

পরিণাহ, ওসার, বেড়, width, breadth, circumference.

পরিণীতা, বিবাহিতা, married.

পরিতাপ, অতিশয় উষ্মা, যাতনা, দুঃখ, ক্লেশ, ভয়, great heat, agony, pain, distress, anguish, sorrow, fear.

পরিতোষ, হর্ষ, অতিতৃপ্তি, আনন্দ, extreme delight or pleasure, gratification, satisfaction of appetite, contentment, plenty.

পরিত্যাগ, বিবর্জনা, ক্ষেপ, নিবেদন, relinquishment, abandonment, desertion, an offering. [doning.

পরিত্যাগী, বিবর্জক, ছাড়ানিয়া, relinquishing, quitting, aban-

পরিত্রাণ, রক্ষা, উদ্ধার, আত্মরক্ষা, complete deliverance, rescue, salvation, protection, self-defence.

পরিত্রাতা, রক্ষক, নিস্তারক, a saviour, deliverer, protector.

পরিত্রায়ী, নিস্তারক, রক্ষাকারী, saving, rescuing, protecting.

পরিদান, পরিবর্ত্ত, বিনিময়, ঋণশোধ, exchange, barter, the return of a loan, &c. [mentation.

পরিদেবনা, বিবেচনা. খেদ, reflection, repentance, regret, la-

পরিধান, বস্ত্রাদি ধারণ, বস্ত্রাদি, the putting on or wearing of clothes, clothes, garments, apparel.

পরিধাপন, পরাণ, বেশ করাণ, to clothe, dress, deck.

পরিধাবন, পশ্চাৎদৌড়ন, বিবেচনা, চিন্তা, a running after, pursuit, consideration, thought. reflexion.

পরিধি, বেড়, চন্দ্রসূর্য্যমণ্ডল, a circumference, periphery, the sun or moon's disk.

পরিধেয়, পরণযোগ্য, বস্ত্র, wearable; clothes, garments.

পরিপক, পরিণত, সুজীর্ণ, সমাপ্ত, পটু, quite ripe, mature, fully digested, complete, finished, clever, shrewd.

পরিপণ, মূলধন, a stock in trade, capital, principal.

পরিপন্থী, শত্রু, ডাকাইত, a foe, enemy, antagonist, a highwayman.

পরিপাক, পকত্ব, সুজীর্ণি, ripeness, maturity, digestion, maturing.

পরিপাটী, যথাক্রম, ধারা, অঙ্কবিদ্যা, ক্রমশঃ, সুন্দর, উত্তম, order, arrangement, regularity, method, arithmetic; in order, regularly; splendid, elegant, pretty, fine, neat, excellent.

পরিপালন, প্রতিজ্ঞা পূর্ণকরা, রক্ষণ, ভরণ, পোষণ, a keeping, fulfilment, observance, preservation, maintaining, nourishing.

পরিপূর্ণ, পূরিত, ভরা, প্রচুর, সম্পন্ন, filled, full, fraught, abundant, much, complete.

পরিবর্জন, ছাড়ন, ত্যজন, to relinquish, abandon, shun, avoid.

পরিবর্ত্ত, বিনিময়, প্রতিদান, প্রতিকার, ক্রমানুসার, পালা, পরস্পর কার্য্যকরা, আদানপ্রদান, প্রকরণ, exchange, barter, requital, recompence, return, change, vicissitude, permutation, succession, lieu, stead, substitution, change of topic, reciprocity, reciprocal action, interchange, a chapter, section, &c.

পরিবর্ত্তন, প্রতিদান করণ, অন্যথাকরণ, পরের স্থানে আইসন, to requite, recompense, change, alter, exchange, transpose, succeed to, supersede.

পরিবর্ত্তী, প্রতিকারক, প্রতিনিধি, requiting, changing, &c. a substitute, successor.

পরিবর্ত্তে, স্থানে, ঠাঁই, বিনিময়ে, in lieu of, instead of, in exchange for or succession to.

পরিবাদ, নিন্দা, কলঙ্ক, an accusation, charge, ill-report, slander, reproach.

পরিবাদী, দোষদ, ভর্ৎসক, accusing, slandering, reproaching.

পরিবার, স্বজন, পোষ্যবর্গ, a dependant, follower, one of a family, a household, family, train of attendants, retinue. [compassed, married.

পরিবৃত, সমভিব্যাহৃত, বিবাহিত, attended by, surrounded, en-

পরিবেদনা, বুদ্ধি, সাবধানতা, দুঃখ, শোক, wit, prudence, caution, pain, anguish.

পরিবেশ, চন্দ্রসূর্য্যের মণ্ডল, the disk of the sun or moon.

পরিবেষণ, আহারদ্রব্য বণ্টন, to serve out, distribute or help to food, carve, wait on. [fence.

পরিবেষ্টন, বেষ্টন, বেড়ন, to surround, wrap round, enclose,

পরিবেষ্টা, আহারদ্রব্য বণ্টক, one who carves food, one who helps or serves out portions at table.

পরিব্রাজক, সন্ন্যাসী, a religious mendicant, a pilgrim.

পরিভব, অনাদর, অবজ্ঞা, পরাজয়, disrespect, disregard, irreverence, contempt, a defeat.

পরিভাষা, কথোপকথন, আলাপ, বিশেষ শাস্ত্রের সঙ্কেত, নিয়ম, conversation, discourse, speech, a glossary, compilation, an appointment, engagement. [engage.

পরিভাষণ, আলাপন, অঙ্গীকরণ, to speak to, converse with, agree,

পরিভূত, তুচ্ছীকৃত, অপমানিত, হারা, জিত, disrespected, disregarded, despised, affronted, conquered, vanquished, overcome, defeated.

পরিভোগ, উপভোগ, the possession or enjoyment of property.

পরিভ্রম, পর্য্যটন, ভুল, a wandering about, an error, mistake.

পরিভ্রষ্ট, নষ্ট, ধ্বস্ত, corrupted, deflowered, degraded, fallen.

পরিভ্রামক, পর্য্যটনিয়া, ভিক্ষুক, wandering, roving about, erring: a mendicant pilgrim. [planet.

পরিমণ্ডল, চক্র, গোল, গ্রহাদির পথ, a circle, globe, the orbit of a

পরিমল, চন্দনাদি চূর্ণ, any sweet perfume, perfumed unguents.

পরিমাণ, মাপ, কম, পরিসর, measure, admeasurement, calculation, capacity, guage, weight, depth, a measure. [sures, &c.

পরিমাতা, পরিমাপক,—মাপক, তৌলনকারী, who weighs or mea-

পরিমাপন, মাপ করাণ, to cause to weigh or measure, &c.

পরিমিত, মাপিত, পরিচ্ছিন্ন, measured, defined, limited, bounded, moderate.

পরিমেয়, মাপনীয়, সসীম, গণনীয়. measurable, finite, calculable.

পরিশুদ্ধ, পরিশোধিত, —পরিষ্কৃত, শুদ্ধ, cleansed, purified, cleared off, paid.

পরিশুষ্ক, অতিশুষ্ক, well dried up, completely dry.

পরিশেষ, অন্ত, সীমা, কঙ্কণ, a complete end, end, limit, border.

পরিশোধ-ন, ঋণাপনয়ন, নিকাশ, প্রতীকার, প্রতিদান, payment, the clearing off a debt, return of an obligation, recompense, retaliation. [exertion.

পরিশ্রম, উদ্যোগ, চেষ্টা, toil, labour, fatigue, pains, endeavour,

পরিশ্রমী, উদ্যোগী, চেষ্টাবান্. taking pains, using exertion, laborious, making efforts.

পরিশ্রান্ত, ক্লান্ত, অবসন্ন, wearied, fatigued, exhausted, tired.

পরিষৎ, সভা, an assembly, meeting. audience, court.

পরিষ্কার, নৈর্ম্মল্য, স্বচ্ছতা, শুদ্ধতা, মার্জ্জনা, সংস্কার, ভূষণপরাণ, নিরপারধী জানন, সারাণি, অমলিন, নিশ্চিত, সরল, ঠিক, প্রজ্ঞ, cleanness, purity, clearness, transparency, accuracy, a cleansing, purifying, polishing, refining, ornamenting, illustrating, acquitting, repairing of buildings &c. neat, clean, pure, nice, evident, clear, upright sincere, accurate, intelligent, clever.

পরিষ্কারী, মার্জনকারী, সারাণিয়া, cleansing, purifying, acquitting, repairing, &c.

পরিষ্কৃত, নির্ম্মল, শুদ্ধ, অতিসূক্ষ্ম, স্বচ্ছ, ভূষণযুক্ত, cleansed, acquitted, &c. superfine, clear, ornamented.

পরিসর, প্রস্থ. পরিমাণ, আয়তন, width, breadth, space, room, dimension, extent. [shot, catastrophe.

পরিসীমা, অন্ত, ইয়ত্তা, শেষ, an extreme boundary, limit, up-

পরিস্পন্দন, নড়ন, অঙ্গক্ষেপ, কম্পন, a moving, flattering, vibrating, agitation. [respect.

পরিহরণ, খণ্ডন, তুচ্ছীকরণ, to confute, disprove, repel, dis-

পরিহসিত. বিদ্রূপিত, laughed at, ridiculed, mocked.

পরিসেবন, ঔষধি পানকরণ, আলিঙ্গন, মতাবলম্বন, ভূষণধারণ, to take physic, to embrace, adhere to, adopt opinions, to put on as ornaments. [ling, disrespect.

পরিহার, খণ্ডনা, দোষণা, অনাদর, a confutation, disproof, repel-

পরিহার্য্য, খণ্ডনীয়, নিন্দনীয়, তুচ্ছ, করভূষণ, confutable, refutable, despicable; a bracelet.

পরিহাস, পরীহাস,—বিদ্রূপ, কৌতুক, খেলা, ক্রীড়া, laughter, ridicule, pleasantry, raillery, jesting, mockery, mirth, sport, pastime. [&c.

পরিহাসক, কৌতুকী, ভণ্ড, a jester, buffoon, mimic; ridiculing

পরিহিত, বস্ত্রধারী, ধারিত, clothed, clad, put on as a garment.

পরীক্ষণ, বিবেচনা করণ, প্রমাণানুসন্ধান, to try, put to the proof, prove. examine, tempt.

পরীক্ষা, গুণ ও ক্রিয়ার বিবেচনা, প্রমাণ, a trial, experiment, examination, ordeal, proof, test, temptation.

পরীবার, অসিকোষ, পোষ্যবর্গ, a sword-sheath, attendants &c.

পরুষ, নিষ্ঠুর বাক্য, নির্দ্দয়, কটু, দুর্ম্মুখ, অসমান, harsh, severe, cruel, unkind, insulting, scurrilous, abusive, rough, rugged. [more.

পরে, পশ্চাতে, শেষে, আর, after, afterwards, further, further-

পরেত, মৃতব্যক্তি, ভূতাদি, dead, defunct; a ghost, spirit, goblin.

পরেদ্যুঃ, পরেদ্যবি,—আগামী দিবস, কল্য, on the morrow, next day, tomorrow. [seen, absent.

পরোক্ষ, অদৃশ্য, অগোচর, অসাক্ষাৎ, invisible, imperceptible, un-

পর্কলা, স্বচ্ছ, transparent, pellucid. [the Palásha tree.

পর্ণ, পাতা, গুবাক পত্র, পলাশবৃক্ষ, a leaf, the Pán or betel leaf,

পর্ণশালা, পর্ণকুটীর,—মুনির আশ্রম, a hermitage, an arbour, a hut constructed of leaves.

পর্ব্ব-ন্, গিরা, গ্রন্থিদ্বয়ের মধ্যস্থান, অমাবস্যা, পূর্ণিমা, অষ্টমী, চতুর্দ্দশী, সংক্রান্তি, উৎসব, প্রস্তাব, the joint of reeds, grass or corn, a joint of the body, knuckle, knot, gibbosity or elevation, a section, chapter &c. the full and change of the moon, &c. the equinox, solstice, or entrance into a sign, a festival, a holiday, an opportunity, occasion.

পর্ব্বত, শৈল, শিখরী, a mountain, a hill, a rock.

পর্ব্বতীয়, শৈলসম্বন্ধীয়, পাহাড়ীয়া, mountain, alpine, mountainous; a mountaineer. [ment of the full or change.

পর্ব্বসন্ধি, গ্রন্থি, অমাবস্যা ও পূর্ণিমা কাল, a knuckle, joint, the mo-

পর্ব্বাহ, উৎসবদিবস, the day of a festival.

পর্য্যঙ্ক, খাট, খট্টা, a bedstead, a bed.

পর্য্যটন, ভ্রমণ, বেড়ান, to go or rove about, wander, travel; a perambulation, peregrination, tour, progress.

পর্য্যন্ত, অন্ত্যসীমা, যদবধি, যাবৎ, a limit, boundary ; to, as far as, unto, until.

পর্য্যবসান, সমাপ্তি, সীমা, a finishing, conclusion, end, limit.

পর্য্যাপ্ত, প্রাপ্ত, সমাপ্ত, যথেষ্ট, ইচ্ছাবান্, obtained, gained, finished, concluded, completed, enough, sufficient, voluntary, willing.

পর্য্যাপ্তি, প্রাপ্তি, তৃপ্তি, ইচ্ছুকতা, নিবারণ, acquisition, repletion, satisfaction, willingness, readiness, the warding off of a blow, &c.

পর্য্যায়, পালা, পরিবর্ত্ত, পরম্পরা, ক্রম, একবস্তুর নামসমূহ, প্রকার, rotation, turn, succession, regular order, a string of synonyms, a manner, an occasion.

পর্য্যায়চ্যুত, পর্য্যায়ছাড়া,—কর্ম্মচ্যুত, supplanted, superseded.

পর্য্যালোচন, অবলোকন, আচন, to look attentively, gaze, survey, examine.

পর্য্যুদস্ত, নিষিদ্ধ, অনুচিত, prohibited, ceremonially forbidden, [unsuitable.

পর্য্যুষিত, পূর্ব্বদিবসীয় অন্নাদি, দূষিত, stale, not fresh, tainted, spoiled.

পর্শুকা, পাঁজরা, a rib.

পল, অত্যল্প ক্ষণ, মাংস, খড়, a minute, a certain weight, [flesh, straw, a sloping edge.

পলক, নিমেষ, the twinkling of an eye, a wink.

পলল, মাংস, flesh, meat.

পলা, প্রবাল, দর্ব্বী, coral, beads of red amber or wax, a [ladle.

পলাণ্ডু, মূল বিশেষ, an onion.

পলাতক, পলানিয়া, ভাগোড়া, a fugitive, a run away, a deserter.

পলান, পলায়ন,—ভাগকরণ, ছুট্কন, to run away, flee, escape, take to flight, desert, elope, abscond.

পলায়মান, যিনি ভাগ করিতেছেন, running away, in the act of fleeing.

পলায়িত, যিনি ভাগ করিয়াছেন, run away, absconded, fled, [eloped.

পলাল, বিচালী, খড়, straw.

পলাশ, পত্র, শ্যাম, নির্দ্দয়, a leaf; green, unfeeling, pitiless, [cruel.

পলাশী, বৃক্ষ বিশেষ, a tree bearing red blossoms, (Butea frondosa).

পলিত, পাকাচুলবিশিষ্ট, বৃদ্ধ, hoary, grey-headed, gray-haired, wrinkled, old.

পলিতা, বর্ত্তিকা, বর্ত্তি, the wick of a candle or lamp.

পলুপোকা, গুটিপোকা, a silk worm, a chrysalis.

পল্কান, ক্ষয়ন, পচন, সড়ন, to decay, to rot, to be impaired, to suffer injury.

পল্কানিয়া, জীর্ণ, ক্ষয়া, পচা, injured, decayed, impaired, rotten.

পল্টন, সৈন্যের দল, a body of troops, a regiment.

পল্লব, অঙ্কুর, পত্রযুক্ত শাখা, ডাল, a sprout, shoot, leafy twig, a branch.

পল্লবগ্রাহী, ক্ষুদ্র দোষান্বেষী, catching at straws, objecting at trifles, carping.

পল্লবিত, পল্লবযুক্ত, covered with young shoots.

পল্লি, পল্লী,—গ্রামের এক অংশ, জেটী, a district, canton, hamlet, a lizard.

পল্লীগ্রাম, নগর ভিন্ন বসতিস্থান, a village, a country village.

পল্লীগ্রামী, অশিষ্ট, গঁওয়ার, rustic; a countryman, a rustic.

পল্বল, ক্ষুদ্র সরোবর, a small artificial pond.

পশন, প্রবেশন, ঢুকন, সাগন, to enter, to fit into.

পশু, শৃঙ্গলাঙ্গুলবন্ত প্রাণী, ছাগলাদি, উপদেবতা, an animal, any livnig being, a beast, a goat, a sacrificial victiin, a subordinate deity.

পশুতা, পশুভাব, the nature or condition of a beast.

পশ্চাৎ, পশ্চাতে,—পিছে, পরে, অনন্তর, পশ্চিমে, behind, after, last, afterwards, subsequently, westward.

পশ্চাত্তাপ, কর্ম্ম করিলে পর শোক করা, after-regret, repentance, remorse.

পশ্চাদ্বর্ত্তী, অনুবর্ত্তী, অনুচর, situated or remaining behind, following; a follower.

পশ্চাদ্ভাবনা, গতানুসূচনা, চিন্তা, after-thought, reflexion.

পশ্চিম, চরম, পিছে, the west, western; after, behind.

পশ্চিমা, প্রতীচী, দাঁতকপাটী, the western quarter, tetanus or locked jaw.

পশ্চিমাস্য, প্রতীচীদিঙ্মুখ, facing or looking to the west.

পসরা, বিক্রেয় শাকাদি বোঝা, a basket of vegetables, &c. laid out for sale.

পসলা, সূক্ষ্ম বৃষ্টি, a slight shower.

পসারী, মুদী, বণিক, a grocer, druggist, petty shopkeeper.

পস্তান, অনুতাপ, অনুশোক, অনুশোচন, repentance, regret; to repent, regret.

পহিলা, প্রথম, আগে, first, the first; first, before. [step.

পা, চরণ, পদচিহ্ন, পাদনিক্ষেপ, a foot, leg, footstep, pace,

পাই, চতুর্থাংশ, a quarter, a fourth part, a *Pie*.

পাইক, পদাতিক, ধাবক, রক্ষক, a footman, a messenger, a watchman, a guard.

পাইন্, ঝাইল, solder.

পাওন প্রাপণ, উপার্জ্জন, মিলন, ভোগকরণ, উত্তরণ, to obtain, get, receive, procure, possess, acquire, find, suffer, undergo, enjoy, to reach, to arrive at.

পাওনা, প্রাপণীয়, আদেয়, due as money, to be obtained or received. [one who should receive.

পাওনিয়া, উত্তরাধিকারী, ঋণদায়ী, an heir, successor, creditor,

পাওয়ান, প্রাপ্তিকরাণ, ভোগান, জন্মান, মিলান, সাধন, লাগান, to cause to obtain, enjoy or suffer,—to procure or obtain for, conduce, induce, reduce or bring to any state, condition or place.—to bring into contact.

পাংক্তেয়, সভাতে গ্রাহ্য, admissible to the same rank in society or the same place at a public feast.

পাংশু, ধূলি, ভস্ম, শস্যক্ষেত্রার্থ সঞ্চিত গোময়, dust, ashes, manure.

পাঁচ, পঞ্চ, একাধিক চতুষ্টয়, five. [delivery.

পাঁচট, প্রসবাবধি পঞ্চম দিবস, the fifth day after a woman's

পাঁচন, জলমিলিত বিশেষে সিদ্ধৌষধি, কাথ, a medicinal preparation, an infusion, decoction.

পাঁচনী, গোতাড়ন দণ্ড, a goad, whip, cane, twig, an incision for *inoculating* a person, &c.

পাঁচালি, ছন্দ বিশেষ, কীর্ত্তন বিশেষ, a poetic metre, a mode of singing.

পাঁচিল, বেড়, a fence wall, a balustrading of brick.

পাঁজর-1, পঞ্জর, পর্শুকা, a rib, a side of the body.

পাঁজী, পঞ্জিকা, an almanack.

পাঁঠা, পাঁঠী,—ছাগল, ছাগলী, *m.* & *f.* a he or she goat.

[illegible], পাথার,—নদীর ওসার, জলপ্লাবন, the width of a river, an inundation.

পাক, রন্ধন, জীর্ণি, পরিণতি, মোড়া, পেঁচ দেওয়া, ঘুরনি, কুণ্ঠন, আবর্ত্ত, গণতা, ছল, ঝঞ্ঝাট, উৎপাত, আটক, বিস্ফোট, a cooking, digestion, ripeness, maturity, a perfecting, twist, twisting, winding, screwing, turning round, whirling, writhing, a circular motion, revolution, eddy, collusion, cheatery, a scheme, intricacy, perplexity, an entangling, obstruction, a humour or boil.

পাকখোলা, পেঁচ খুলিবার যন্ত্র, a turn-screw.

পাকচক্র, আবর্ত্ত, চক্র, গণতা, প্রবঞ্চনা, an eddy, a circular motion, a wheel, collusion, deception, cheating.

পাকড়ন-কান, ধরণ, উপায়চিন্তন, to take, to seize, to have recourse to, to make use of a thing.

পাকড়ী, পুষ্পের দল, the petals or corolla of a flower.

পাকতঃ, অনিচ্ছা পূর্ব্বক, unwillingly, reluctantly, against one's will.

পাকন, পরিপক্ক হওন, রসন, ফাঁপন, to ripen, grow ripe, suppurate, ferment.

পাকনা, আবর্ত্ত, a whirpool, an eddy.

পাকপড়া, পেঁচাল, অস্পষ্ট, intricate, perplexed, contorted, vague.

পাকপাড়া, শঠ, খল, artful, insidious, sly, designing.

পাকল, পরিণত, পক্ক, স্থির, ripe, mature, digested, concocted, fixed.

পাকলা, পাখলা,—ধৌত, প্রক্ষালিত, washed, clean, cleansed.

পাকা, পরিণত, জরা, মোড়া, বিস্ফোট, ripe, mature, digested, cooked, twisted, &c. a tumour.

পাকাচুল, পলিত কেশ, grey or hoary hair.

পাকান, রন্ধন, পরিপাক করান, পেঁচ দেওন, মোড়ান, to cook, cause to ripen, twist, screw &c.

পাকাপাকি, পরস্পর সম্মত, স্থির, স্বীকৃত, mutually agreed on, settled, admitted on all sides.

পাকে, জন্যে, নিমিত্তে, for, for the sake of, because of.

পাখ, পাখা,—পালখ, ডেনা, ব্যজন, a wing, pinion, feather, plume, the fin of a fish, a fan.

পাখলান, প্রক্ষালন, পরিষ্করণ, মার্জ্জন, to wash, rinse, clean, cleanse.

পাখী, পক্ষী, বিহঙ্গম, a bird.

পাখ্না, পক্ষ, পালখ, a feather, plume, quill.

পাগ, পাগড়ী,—উষ্ণীষ, a turband.

পাগল-া, উন্মত্ত, মূঢ়, ক্ষেপা, mad, insane, foolish; a madman, idiot, fool.

পাঙ্গন, জানন, বুঝন, to perceive, discover, form an idea.
পাঙ্গা, লবণ বিশেষ, সৈন্ধব, rock or fossil salt.
পাচক, পাকজনক, অগ্নিবৰ্দ্ধক ঔষধ, রন্ধনকর্ত্তা, concocting, promoting digestion ; a digestive, a cook.
পাচন, রন্ধন, জারণ, to cook, dress food, concoct, digest.
পাছ-া, পশ্চাদ্ভাব, পিছাড়ী, নিতম্ব, the hinder or back part, the stern, rump, posteriors.
পাছড়ন-আন, শস্য ঝাড়ন, পট্‌কান, to winnow grain, to throw [in wrestling.
পাছু, পশ্চাদ্ভাব, পশ্চাদ্দল, পিছাড়ী, the back or hinder part, the rear of an army.
পাছুড়ী, গাত্রবস্ত্র, উড়নী, a wrapper or outside garment.
পাছে, পশ্চাৎ, পরে, কি জানি, behind, after; afterwards, subsequently ; lest, for fear that.
পাজা, ভাটী, আকা, a brick kiln.
পাজী, নীচলোক, অধম, তুচ্ছ, a low fellow ; low, base, mean.
পাঞ্চজন্য, নারায়ণের শঙ্খ, Crishna's conch.
পাঞ্চভৌতিক, পঞ্চভূতনির্ম্মিত, composed of the five primary [elements.
পাট, ওসার, প্রসর, সিংহাসন, পিড়ী, বেদী, থাক, মৃত্তিকাময় কূপবেড়, কোষ, কৌষেয়বস্ত্র, কোষ্টা, ধান্যাদির বোঝা, breadth, extension, a throne, stool, board, washing-board, terrace, altar, a fold or layer of clothes, an earthen well-hoop, a cocoon, silk, a sort of hemp, a sack or load of corn.
পাটন, নগর, আড়ঙ্গ, a city, town, a mart, seaport.
পাটনী, পারাবারের মাঝিক, a ferryman.
পাটব, নৈপুণ্য, cleverness, skill, expertness, eminence in.
পাটভাঙ্গা, ছুরিকাদির উপরে ঝম্পকরা, the ceremony of falling on knives. &c. in the month Chitra.
পাটরাণী, রাজার প্রধানা স্ত্রী, the chief or crowned queen.
পাটল, আশুধান্য, বর্ণ বিশেষ, ঈষদ্রক্ত, rainy-season rice ; pale red, pink, rose colour.
পাটলী, পারুল বৃক্ষ, the trumpet flower.
পাটা, চৌড়াকাষ্ঠ, পত্র, পটুকা, a board, the boards enclosing a native manuscript, a lease of land, a belt or sash.
পাটারি, স্থানুক, গ্রামের করগ্রাহক, a manager, agent, collector [of rents &c.

পাটী, আসন বিশেষ, বাসনাদি, বাইল, বরগা, যুগ্মের এক, অঙ্কবিদ্যা, a sort of fine mat, the plant from which it is made, any thing flat (as a plate of metal), a valve, a rafter, one of a pair, arithmetic.

পাটুলি, বৃহৎ নৌকা বিশেষ, a large boat for carrying merchandise. [a rake.

পাট্টা, পত্র, মল্ল, লম্পট, a lease for land, a patent, a wrestler,

পাঠ, অধ্যয়ন, পড়া, a reading, perusal, repeating, recital, lecture, lesson, a text, a particular reading.

পাঠক, অধ্যাপক, পড়নিয়া, a lecturer, a public reader; reading, perusing, repeating. [ness of style.

পাঠক্রম, পড়নশৃঙ্খলা, the order observed in reading, correct-

পাঠগুরু, শিক্ষক, পড়ানিয়া, a reading master, teacher, schoolmaster. [tuition.

পাঠনা, অধ্যাপনা, শিক্ষা, a causing or instructing to read,

পাঠশালা, অধ্যয়নগৃহ, টোল, চৌবাড়ী, a school, college, seminary of learning.

পাঠান, প্রেরণ, চালান, to send, delegate, remit. [text.

পাঠাপাঠ, প্রকৃত অপ্রকৃত পাঠ, the right or wrong reading of a

পাঠিত, অধ্যাপিত, শিক্ষিত, caused to be read or studied.

পাঠ্য, অধ্যয়নযোগ্য, সুলেখিত, worthy of perusal, legible.

পাড়, তট, আড়া, a coast, a breast-summer.

পাড়ন-আন, অধঃপাতন, বিছান, ডিম্ব ছাড়ন, ফলাদি সঞ্চয়ন, to lay or throw down, to spread out a mat or carpet, to lay as eggs, to gather fruits or flowers.

পাড়া, পল্লী, a canton or quarter of a town.

পাড়াগাঁ, ক্ষুদ্র গ্রাম, a hamlet, a small village.

পাড়াপড়সী, এক পাড়াতে নিবাসী, a neighbour inhabiting the same quarter.

পাণ, তাম্বূল, পর্ণ, the betel leaf.

পাণি, হস্ত, the hand.

পাণিগ্রহ-ণ, পাণিপীড়ন,—বিবাহ, a taking by the hand, a form of marriage. [appointed ritual.

পাণিগৃহীতী, বিবাহিতা স্ত্রী, a bride wedded according to the

পাণিশঙ্খ, ক্ষুদ্র শঙ্খ, a small conch used in ceremonies.

পাণ্ডব, পাণ্ডুর সন্তান, the race or descendants of Pándu.

পাণ্ডর, ফিকা, পিঙ্গল, রক্ত খড়ী, কুন্দ বিশেষ, wan, pale or yellowish white : red chalk, a species of jasmine.

পাণ্ডা, পূজারী, the proprietary priest of an idol.

পাণ্ডিত্য, বিদ্যা, learning, scholarship, wisdom.

পাণ্ডু, পাণ্ডুর,—ফিকা, শুক্লবর্ণ, নেবা, বৃক্ষ বিশেষ, pale, wan, whitish; the jaundice, a certain plant.

পাণ্ডুলিপি, খস্‌ড়া, a rough sketch, a waste book.

পাণ্ডুলেখ্য, খস্‌ড়া লেখ্য, to be sketched or written in rough.

পাত, অধঃপতন, পত্র, লিপি, হুণ্ডী, সরু, a fall, a leaf, note, writing, bill, draft, a bank-note; thin.

পাতক, পাপ, অঘ, অপরাধ, sin, guilt, crime.

পাতকী, পাপী, অপরাধী, sinful, criminal, guilty.

পাতঝিয়া, তুলাদিপূর্ণ বিছানা, a palliass, a thin mattress.

পাতঞ্জল, দর্শন বিশেষ, one of the six schools of philosophy.

পাতড়া, খাদ্যদ্রব্যের বণ্ট, খস্‌ড়া, a dole, a ration of food, a waste-book.

পাতন, অধঃক্ষেপণ, বিছান, to lay or fling down, to spread as a mat.

পাতনা, আরম্ভ, ভূমিকা, কল্পনা, খস্‌ড়া, বান্‌কী, a beginning, preface, preamble, plan, design, rough sketch, muster, specimen.

পাতল-া, সূক্ষ্ম, ক্ষীণ, তরল, thin, fine, lean, slender, light, diluted.

পাতা, পত্র, দল, the leaf of a plant, blade of grass or a knife.

পাতাপা, মেপাপা, web-footed.

পাতাল, নরক বিশেষ, নাগলোক, ছিদ্র, গহ্বর, hell, the infernal regions, a hole, chasm, a calcinatory for metals.

পাতালভেদী, জলাকর, উমুই, a fountain or spring.

পাতি, ক্ষুদ্র, অত্যল্প, little, diminutive, petty.

পাতিত, বিস্তৃত, বিছান, spread out, extended as a mat, &c.

পাতিত্য, ভ্রষ্টাবস্থা, a fallen or depraved condition.

পাতিব্রত্য, সতীত্ব, কুলবধূতা, devotedness to a husband, chastity.

পাতিমৌড়, নববিবাহিতার মুকুট, a wreath or crown worn by a bride on the day of marriage.

পাতিশিয়াল, খেঁক্‌শিয়াল, খিখি, উল্কামুখী, a fox.

পাতিহাঁস, ক্ষুদ্র হংস, the common duck.

পাতী, পত্র, লিপি, লেখা, a letter, note, epistle, writing.

পাতুক, ভৃগু, ঢাল, বৃহৎ জলজন্তু বিশেষ, পতনশীল, a precipice, declivity, a large aquatic animal; disposed or tending to fall, falling frequently or habitually.

পাতকুয়া কূপ, ইন্দারা, a well, a deep well.

পাত্র, আধার, বাসনাদি, আলা, জলপ্রবাহ, রাজমন্ত্রী, কার্য্যনিযুক্ত, ব্যক্তি, লোক, শরীর, ঔচিত্য, আজ্ঞা, দল, নৃত্য বিশেষ, নববিবাহিত, বিদ্যাদি গুণসম্পন্ন, যোগ্য, a vessel, receptacle, recipient, cup, plate, dish, jar, any sacrificial vessel, the channel or course of a river, a king's minister or counsellor, any one entrusted with an office or commission, a person, the body, propriety, fitness, an order, command, a leaf, a dance performed by a man and woman, a bridegroom. *in comp*: fit, capable, adequate, worthy, deserving, an object of.

পাত্রতা, উপযুক্ততা, প্রতিপালকতা, capacity or fitness for trust or office, trustworthiness, patronage.

পাথর, প্রস্তর, পাষাণ, a stone.

পাথরী, অশ্মরী রোগ, the stone or gravel.

পাথস্, জল, সলিল, নীর, water.

পাথেয়, পথের সম্বল, provisions or expences for a journey, &c.

পাথোধি, পাথোনিধি,—সমুদ্র, সাগর, the sea, the ocean.

পাদ, চরণ, পদনিক্ষেপ, চতুর্থভাগ, বাতকর্ম্ম, a foot, poetical foot or line, a leg, pace, step, a quarter or fourth part, wind expelled backwards.

পাদগ্রাহী, চরণসেবক, প্রণত, বিনয়ী, cringing, fawning, servile, prostrate, submissive, humble.

পাদন, ফুকী ছাড়ন, to break wind backwards.

পাদপ, বৃক্ষ, a tree.

পাদপদ্ম, পদ্মসদৃশ চরণ, the lotus-foot.

পাদবিরক্ষাঃ, জুতা, পাদুকা, পয়ধ্রী, a shoe, slipper, boot, stocking.

পাদবিহরণ, চরণ নিঃক্ষেপণ, চলন, গমন, to step, walk, proceed.

পাদরথী, পয়ধ্রী, জুতা, উপানৎ, a boot, a shoe or slipper.

পাদসেবা, চরণসেবা, স্তোত্র, উপাসনা, obsequious attendance, cringing, fawning, flattery.

পাদাঙ্ক, পদচিহ্ন, উদ্দেশ, a foot-step, print of the foot, track, trace, vestige.

পাদাতিক, পাইক, পদাতি, a footman, foot-soldier, infantry.

পাদাবন, পামারণ, to stamp with the foot.
পাদুকা, পাদূ,—পাদত্রাণ, জুতা, উপানৎ, a shoe, a slipper.
পাদ্য, পাদ প্রক্ষালনার্থ জল, water for the feet offered to a guest or superior. [suck, &c.
পান, দ্রবদ্রব্যের গলাধঃকরণ, চোক, a drinking, drink, dose,
পানমত্ত, মত্ত, মদ্যপ, drunken, sottish, drinking excessively.
পানসী, আচ্ছাদনযুক্ত ক্ষুদ্র নৌকা বিশেষ, a small covered boat, a pansway.
পানা, মিষ্ট মিশ্রিত পানীয়, ভিত্তির গোড়া, জলগাছ বিশেষ, a solution, any sweet drink seasoned with fruits, &c. the foundation of a wall, a certain aquatic plant.
পানাসক্ত, মদ্যপ্রিয়, মত্ত, devoted to drinking, sottish, drunken.
পানী, জল, পানযোগ্য, দ্রবদ্রব্য, water or other liquid fit or proper for drinking.
পানীভরণ্যা, পানীভরা,—নাবিক, জলজীবী, a waterman.
পানীয়, পানযোগ্য, জল, fit for drink, potable; water. [pid.
পানীসা, পান্স্যা,—তরল, জলুয়া, diluted, watery, serous, insi-
পানে, কাছে, দিগে, to, towards, in the direction of, at.
পান্থ, পথিক, a traveller, passenger. [religious fast.
পারণা, উপবাসের পরদিনে ভোজনকরা, the first meal after a
পাপ, অধর্ম্ম, অপরাধ, অঘ, sin, wickedness, vice, crime, guilt.
পাপগ্রহ, গ্রহবৈগুণ্য, মন্দকপাল, উৎপাত, an evil planet or destiny, ill-luck, calamity. [in guilt.
পাপভাক, পাপভাগী,—অধর্ম্মাংশী, sharing in a crime; a partner
পাপরোগ, বসন্ত রোগ, the small-pox.
পাপাত্মা, অধর্ম্মশীল, দুষ্ট, sinful, wicked, profligate, depraved.
পাপিষ্ঠ, পাপী,—অধার্ম্মিক, অপরাধী, দুষ্ট, sinful, wicked, highly wicked, most wicked, criminal, guilty.
পাপীয়ান্, পাপীয়সী,—দুষ্ট, অপরাধী, *m.* & *f.* wicked, abandoned, criminal. [a knuckle.
পাব, গ্রন্থি, পর্ব্বন্, the joint or knot of a reed &c. a joint,
পাবক, পরিষ্কারক, অগ্নি, cleansing, purifying; a purifier, fire.
পাবন, শুচিকর, purifying, cleansing, purificatory.
পাম, কণ্ডুরোগ, কন্ডূ, দদ্রু, cutaneous eruption, itch, scab, ring-worm. [pid, silly.
পামর, অধম, নীচ, অজ্ঞান, base, despicable, low, vile, stu-

পায়পড়া, চরণসেবক, কাছাধরা, servile, cringing, fawning, obsequious; a sycophant.
পায়রা, কপোত, a pigeon.
পায়স, পরমান্ন, rice milk and sugar.
পায়া, পাদ, বৃন্ত, পদ, কর্ম্ম, the leg or foot of a table, &c. a stem, a stalk, a situation, rank.
পায়ু, গুহ্যেন্দ্রিয়, গুহ্যদেশ, the anus.
পার, নদীর ওদিক্, প্রান্ত, শেষ, ওদিগে, দূর, আড়পার, the farther side or opposite bank of a river, an end, limit; over, across, beyond, far, through and through.
পারক, সমর্থ, চালাক, দক্ষ, able, capable, active, expert, [clever, free.
পারগ, সমর্থ, নিপুণ, পটু, পণ্ডিত; নদীর ওপারগামী, skilful, expert, conversant, well-versed, studious, going across, crossing over.
পারণ, সমর্থ হওন, উপবাসের পরদিনে বিহিত ভোজন, to be able; the first meal after a fast.
পারতপক্ষ, কৃতিসাধ্য, সামর্থ্য, an object within one's power, [ability.
পারতঃ, যদ্যপি পারা যায়, if in one's power, even if, though able &c.
পারতন্ত্র্য, অধীনতা, বশতা, dependance, subjection, subser- [viency.
পারত্রিক, পরলোক সম্বন্ধীয়, পারলৌকিক, relating or belonging to the next world.
পারদ, পারা, তারক, উদ্ধারক, quicksilver; extricating, deli- [vering, carrying over.
পারদারিক, পরস্ত্রীরত, ব্যভিচারী, adulterous; an adulterer.
পারদার্য্য, পরস্ত্রীগমন, ব্যভিচার, adultery.
পারমার্থিক, অধ্যাত্ম, পরমাত্মসম্বন্ধীয়, মুক্তিদ, মোক্ষপ্রাপক, spiritual, relating to the sublime Spirit, excellent, leading to or procuring absorption.
পারম্পর্য্য, ঐতিহ, ইতিহ্য, পুরাতন কথা, অনুক্রম, পরম্পরাগত, tradition, traditional instruction, continuous order or succession; traditional.
পারলৌকিক, পরলোক সম্বন্ধীয়, belonging or relating to the [next world.
পারশব, শূদ্রাণীর গর্ভে ব্রাহ্মণজাত, the son of a Shúdra woman by a Brahmin, any adulterine offspring.
পারশ্বধিক, পরশুধারী, armed with a battle axe.

পারস্ত্রৈণেয়, ক্ষেত্রজ, পরস্ত্রীতে জাত সন্তান, an adulterine, a bastard son by another's wife.

পারা, রসধাতু, সামর্থ্য, quicksilver, mercury, ability, power.

পারাণী, পার হওনের নৌকা, খেয়া, a ferry-boat, ferriage.

পারাবত, পায়রা, a dove, a pigeon.

পারাবার, নদীর উভয় তট, সমুদ্র, আড়পার, the hither and further sides of a river, a river's banks, the ocean, the sea; through and through.

পারায়ণ, তরণ, অভ্যাস, সাকল্য, সাঙ্গতা, a crossing over, application, study, totality, completeness.

পারিজাত, স্বর্গীয় বৃক্ষ বিশেষ, the coral tree of Paradise.

পারিণায্য, যৌতুক দ্রব্য, the paraphernalia or property of a new-married woman, marriage gifts.

পারিতোষিক, তুষ্টিদ, প্রতিফল, ভেট, gratifying, gratificatory, satisfactory, delighting; a remuneration, a complimentary present.

পারিষদ, পার্ষদ—দৃষ্টিকর, দর্শক, সভাসদ, সভাস্থ, সহচর, সভ্য, a spectator, one of an assembly, an attendant, a servant; relating to an assembly.

পারুষ্য, তিরস্কার, নিন্দা, গালাগালি, ক্রূরতা, মারিপিট, abuse, reproach, scurrility, defamation, harshness, severity, violence, an assault, misdemeanor.

পার্থক্য, পৃথক্ হওয়া, বিভিন্নতা, প্রভেদ, separation, division, a being separate, distinctness.

পার্থিব, পৃথিবীস্থ, জগতস্থ, মৃন্ময়, মৃত্তিকানির্ম্মিত, রাজা, earthly, terrestrial, earthen, made or derived from earth; a king, a prince. [a festival day.

পার্ব্বণ, পর্ব্বকর্ত্তব্যশ্রাদ্ধ, উৎসব, relating to the lunar festivals;

পার্ব্বণী, উৎসবকালীন দক্ষিণা, given as fees at festivals.

পার্য্য, পার্য্যমান,—কৃতিসাধ্য, possible, within one's power.

পার্শ্ব, কক্ষের অধোভাগ, ধার, তীর, the side, a side, verge, margin, bank. [friend, attendant.

পার্শ্ববর্ত্তী, পার্শ্বস্থ,—সখা, মিত্র, সহচর, a companion, associate,

পার্শ্বাস্থি, পঞ্জর, a rib, a side-bone,.

পার্শ্বে ভিতে, গোপনে, aside, privately.

পার্ষ্ণি, গোড়ারি, পিঠ, পিছাড়ী, কাছী, রাগযুক্তা, the heel, the back, the rear of an army, a violent woman, (whether from rage or liquor.)

পাল, ভরণকারী, রক্ষক, গোঠ, ঝাঁক, সজাতীয় পশ্বাদি সমূহ, পট, শৃঙ্গার, a nourisher, protector, keeper, a flock, herd, drove, swarm, a sail, sail-cloth, the copulation of beasts.

পালই, ধান্যের স্তূপ, ভাণ্ডার. a corn-rick, a stack, a store-[house, magazine.

পালক, পোষ্টা, রক্ষক, a cherisher, protector, guardian, keeper, groom, cowherd; preserving, supporting, &c.

পালকপুত্র বা বেটা,—পোষ্যপুত্র, দত্তকপুত্র. an adopted son.

পালকী, শিবিকা, মহাপা, a palankeen or Indian sedan.

পালখ, পক্ষ, ডেনা, পক্ষ্ম, a plume, feather, wing, quill, the eye-lashes.

পালঙ্গ, মূল বিশেষ, খাট, beet root, a bed or bedstead.

পালন, ভরণ, পোষণ, রক্ষণ, চরাণ, পূরণ, মানন, to nourish, support, maintain, educate, bring up, cherish, protect, preserve, defend, to tend or feed cattle, to keep, fulfil, to observe, obey.

পালা, রক্ষিত, পোষা, পল্লব, নীহার, বার, পর্য্যায়, supported, &c. domestic; a twig, a sprig, a corn-rick, hoar-frost, a time, turn, rotation, spell.

পালাঙ্গা, পালঙ্গা,—প্রাচীরের আচ্ছাদন, the thatched roof or coping of a wall.

পালাতক, পলানিয়া, ভাগুড়া, fleeing, running away; a run-[away, a deserter.

পালান, ভাগ করণ, ভরণ, রক্ষণ, to flee, run away, to nourish, maintain, keep, guard, &c.

পালি, খড়্গাদির আগা কিম্বা ধার, কোণ, শ্রেণী, চিহ্ন, আলি, দাড়িযুক্তা স্ত্রী, ক্রোড়, পরিমাণ বিশেষ, the point or sharp edge of a weapon, the tip of the ear, a corner, a line, row, range, a mark, spot, stain, a causey, ridge, raised bank, a bearded woman, the hip or haunch, a measure of five seers.

পালো, ঔষধ বিশেষ, an infusion, (*in medicine.*)

পাল্টন, উল্টান, ফিরাণ, উৎখাতন, to turn up, overturn, subvert.

পাশ, রজ্জু, জাল, ফাঁদ, পার্শ্ব, তীর, a fetter, rope, tie, a net, snare, noose, toil, a side, a margin.

পাশ-ক, অক্ষ, পাষ্টি, a die or dice for playing.
পাশকথা, ইতর আলাপ, a digression, irrelevant talking.
পাশলী, পাশুলী,—পাদাঙ্গুলিভূষা, a ring for the toes. [climbing.
পাশা, অক্ষ, কর্ণভূষা, dice, an ear-ornament, a foot-rope for
পাশাপাশী, কাছাকাছি, নিকট, নৈকট্য, side by side, near; vicinity.
পাশী, বাড়, বৃক্ষাদির নির্যাস নিঃসারক, ব্যাধ, জালী, যম, a frame, one who extracts the juice of plants &c, a fowler, hunter, one armed with a net, Yama.
পাশে, কাছে, এক দিগে, গোপনে, তটে, near, towards, to one side, out of the way, aside, on shore.
পাষণ্ড, মতান্তরগ্রাহী, ভক্তিবিহীন, প্রতারক, heretical, impious, hypocritical; an imposter, &c. [weight.
পাষাণ, প্রস্তর, বাট্‌খারা, stone, a stone, a stone used as a
পাষাণী, প্রস্তর কাটনের অস্ত্র, a mason's hammer, a pick-axe, a stone-cutter's chissel.
পাষ্টি, অক্ষ, পাশ, dice for playing.
পাসরণ, বিস্মরণ, ভ্রমন, to forget, to err, to stray.
পাসরাণ, চলন, সরণ, to walk, move, go on, stir.
পাসরা, পাসোরা,—বিস্মৃতি, forgetfulness, want of recollection.
পাহাড়, পর্বত, শিলা, a mountain, a hill, a high rock.
পাহাড়ী, কাঁধাড়ি, আড়রী, the brink of a precipice.
পাহাড়ী-য়া, পর্বতীয়, চুয়াড়, mountainous, mountain, hill; a mountaineer. [tobacco.
পিওন, জল কিম্বা ধূম পানকরণ, চোষণ, to drink, suck, smoke
পিক, কোকিল, থুথু, the black cuckoo, the spittle coloured red by chewing the betel leaf.
পিঙ্গ-ল, পিঙ্গড়া,—কালিট, কপিলবর্ণ, tawny, yellowish-brown.
পিচটী, চক্ষুর মলা, the concrete rheum of the eyes.
পিচিণ্ড, উদর, the abdomen or belly. [ral, a crest.
পিচ্ছ, ময়ূরপুচ্ছ, লাঙ্গুল, চূড়া, a peacock's tail, a tail in gene-
পিচ্ছিল, কাশন্দি, মাড়যুক্ত অন্নাদি, sauce, gravy, sauce mixed with rice-gruel.
পিছন, হটন, পলান, নিবর্ত্তন, to go behind, fall back, recede, retreat, desist.
পিছল, চিক্কণ, আর্দ্রস্থান, slippery, smooth, sloppy, wet, slimy.
পিছলন, টলন, সরিয়া পড়ন, to slip, to slide.

পিছাড়ী, সৈন্যের পশ্চাদ্দল, পাছু, অশ্বের পশ্চাৎপাদবন্ধনরজ্জু, the rear of an army, a ship's stern, a horse's hinder foot-ropes.

পিছান, হটান, থামন, পাছু, to repel, to cause to go back or desist; the stern, hinder part, rear.

পিছে, পিছু, পিছা,—পশ্চাৎ, পরে, কালক্রমে, behind, backwards, after, afterwards, by and bye.

পিছাপিছি, পরস্পর, ক্রমাগত, one behind another, one following another.

পিঞ্জন, কার্পাসাদি ফোড়ন, to card cotton or wool.

পিঞ্জর, খাঁচা, বক্ষস্থল, a bird-cage, any cage, the thorax or cavity of the breast.

পিটন, মারণ, তাড়ান, to beat, strike, beat down, hammer out, punish, chase.

পিটা, পূপ, পিষ্টক বিশেষ, a sort of thin cake or bread.

পিটালী, জলযুক্ত পেষিত তণ্ডুল, a rice-gruel or ground rice mixed with water.

পিড়া, বেদী, চাতাল, a raised terrace or portico.

পিড়ী, পিঁড়ী—কাষ্ঠাসন, বেদী, a stool, an idol-pedestal, a terrace.

পিণাক, শিবের ধনুক, ত্রিশূল, Shiva's bow, a trident.

পিণ্ড, গোলবস্তু, বর্ত্তুল, টুকি, গ্রাস, শ্রাদ্ধীয় গোলাকার অন্ন, বিকৃতাবয়ব, a ball, globe, lump, mass, block, piece, quantity, mouthful, a funeral cake; deformed, distorted.

পিণ্ডদান, নিবাপ, the offering of a funeral cake to ancestors.

পিণ্ডভাক্, শ্রাদ্ধীয়ান্নভোগী, পিত্রাদি, সপিণ্ড, partaking of the funeral cake.

পিণ্ডীশূর, আলসিয়া হইয়া পরনিন্দক a lazy censorious braggart, a cotquean.

পিতা, বাপ, জনক, a father.

পিতামহ, পিতার পিতা, ব্রহ্ম, a paternal grandfather, a name of Bramha.

পিতৃ, জনক, পিতার, *in comp*: a father; a father's, paternal.

পিতৃকর্ম্ম, বা ক্রিয়া, বা কৃত্য,—শ্রাদ্ধ, funeral obsequies, offerings to ancestors.

পিতৃধন, পৈতৃকাধিকার, পুত্রাদির প্রাপ্যধন, paternal or hereditary property, patrimony.

পিতৃপক্ষ, বাপের বন্ধুগণ, জ্ঞাতি, ভাদ্র মাসের কৃষ্ণ পক্ষ, paternal relations, the moon's wane in the month Bhádra.

পিতৃপতি, যম, Yama the regent of death.

পিতৃপুরুষ, পূর্ব্বপুরুষ, পিতাপিতামহাদি, জ্ঞাতি, the line of paternal ancestors, a paternal ancestor.

পিতৃপ্রসূ, সন্ধ্যাকাল, বৈকাল, the evening twilight, evening.
পিতৃবন, শ্মশান, a cemetery, place of burning or burial.
পিতৃব্য, পিতার ভ্রাতা, a paternal uncle. [forefathers.
পিতৃলোক, পূর্ব্বপুরুষ, an ancestor, ancestors, progenitors,
পিত্ত, ধাতু. bile, bilious humour, gall.
পিত্তল, ধাতু বিশেষ, brass.
পিত্র্য, পিতৃসম্বন্ধীয়, paternal, of or relating to a father.
পিধান, আচ্ছাদন, ঢাকনা, উড়নী, পাছুড়ী, a cover, lid, top, a wrapper, covering, dress, a cloak.
পিন্ধন, পরণ, অলঙ্কারাদি ধারণ, to put on clothes, to dress.
পিপাসা, তৃষ্ণা, ইচ্ছা, thirst, drought, desire.
পিপাসী, পিপাসিত, পিপাসু,—তৃষ্ণিত, ইচ্ছুক, athirst, thirsty.
পিপীড়া, পিপীলিকা,—ক্ষুদ্র কীট বিশেষ, an ant, the small red ant.
পিপুল, পিপ্পলী,—ঔষধ বিশেষ, the long pepper.
পিপ্পল, অশ্বত্থ বৃক্ষ, the holy or sacred fig tree.
পিয়াদা, পাদিক, প্রেরিত, দুত, a footman, a messenger.
পিয়ান, পান করাণ, জল দেওন, to give or cause to drink water.
পিয়ারা, ফল বিশেষ, a guava.
পিয়ালা, পানপাত্র, a drinking glass or cup, a tea cup.
পিয়াস, তৃষ্ণা, পানেচ্ছা, thirst, desire to drink.
পিল, পীল,—গোভিম্ব, ছা, an unfledged bird, young animal.
পিলা, পিলুই,—প্লীহা, the spleen, enlargement of the spleen.
পিশাচ, প্রেত, a fiend, imp, spectre, malignant demigod.
পিশিত, পলল, মাংস, ক্রব্য, flesh, meat.
পিশু, অব্রী, a flea.
পিশুন, কুঙ্কুম, কার্পাস, কাক, চর, খল, দুষ্ট, অধম, মূঢ়, অজ্ঞান, saffron, cotton, a crow, a spy; cruel, wicked, vile, low, stupid, foolish.
পিষণ, বাটন, to grind, rub, bruise, pound. [meats.
পিষ্টক, পূপ, পিটা, রুটী, a cake of flour or meal, bread, baked
পীটন, মারণ, চাপন, to beat, strike, hammer out, beat down.
পীঠ, পৃষ্ঠ, কাষ্ঠাসন, পিঁড়ী, চাতাল, the back, a page of a book, side of a leaf, a seat, stool, chair, an idol-pedestal, a terrace.
পীঠস্থান, দুর্গা পূজার স্থান, places where Durgá is worshipped.
পীড়ন, দুঃখ দেওন, যন্ত্রণা, খেদান, নিঙ্গড়ন, to ache, smart, give

pain, to hurt, harrass, persecute, grieve, distress, torment, to bruise seeds, express oil, &c.

পীড়া, দুঃখ, ব্যথা, ক্লেশ, ব্যামোহ, খেদ, pain, smart, anguish, torture, distress, affliction.

পীড়িত, দুঃখিত, কাতর, ক্লিষ্ট, রোগান্বিত, pained, in pain, distressed, afflicted, ill, sick.

পীত, হরিদ্রাবর্ণ, পানকৃত, পীতাভ, হরিতাল, হরিদ্রা, yellow, drunk (as a liquor), quaffed : a topaz, safflower, yellow orpiment, turmeric.

পীতরস, হরিদ্রা, turmeric.

পীতলোহ, মিশ্রিত ধাতু বিশেষ, a mixed metal, yellow brass.

পীতসার, পীতবর্ণক চন্দন বিশেষ, মণি বিশেষ, a species of yellow sandal-wood, a yellow topaz.

পীতাম্বর, কৃষ্ণ, নারায়ণ, a name of Krishna.

পীন, স্থূল, মোটা, পাতুলা, স্নিগ্ধ, চিক্কণ, বর্দ্ধিত, plump, full, large, fat, fine, close, smooth, polished.

পীনস, কফ, নাসিকার রোগ বিশেষ, a cold, a cough, a disease of the nose.

পীনোধ্নী, বড়স্তনী, *f.* having a large udder, having large breasts.

পীবন্, পীবর,—স্থূল, মোটা, স্নিগ্ধ, plump, large, full, lusty, smooth.

পীযূষ, অমৃত, সুধা, সপ্তম দিবস প্রসূতা গোদুগ্ধ, nectar, ambrosia, a cow's first seven days' milk.

পীল, পক্ষি শাবক, a young bird.

পীলক, বৃহৎ পিপীলিকা বিশেষ, the large black ant.

পীলা, প্লীহা, পীত, the spleen; yellow.

পুং, পুংস্,—পুরুষ, নর, *in comp*: man, a male, masculine (*gender*)

পুংবৎ, পুরুষবৎ, manlike, manly, masculine, as or like the masculine (*in grammar*.)

পুংলিঙ্গ, পুরুষচিহ্ন, পুরুষ জাতি, the pudenda, the masculine gender (*in grammar*).

পুংশক্তি, পুরুষত্ব, মনুষ্যত্ব, তেজ, virility, manhood.

পুংশ্চলী, লম্পটী, বেশ্যা, *f.* going to men, loose, wanton; a harlot.

পুংসবন, সংস্কার বিশেষ, a ceremony on a mother's conception.

পুংস্ত্ব, পুরুষত্ব, রেতঃ, virility, manhood, semen virile.

পুঁছন, ঘর্ষণ, মার্জন, to wipe, wipe off, rub.

পুঁজ, ক্লেদ, রসানি, matter from a sore, purulent matter, pus.

পুঁজী, মূলধন, সঞ্চয়, ঐশ্বর্য্য, স্তূপ, ফলমূলাদির চতুষ্টয়, a capital or stock in trade, a hoard, heap, wealth, four of any article, as flowers, roots, &c.

পুঁটলী, থলিয়া, গাঁঠরী, a packet, a small parcel or bundle.

পুঁটো, ঘুণ্টী, অধম, ক্ষুদ্র, কনিষ্ঠ, a button; low, mean, small, little, youngest.

পুকন, কৃমিজন্মান, to breed maggots or insects (as an ulcer, &c.)

পুকুর, জলাশয়, পুষ্করিণী, a pond, a tank.

পুঙ্খ, পুচ্ছ, the feather or feathered part of an arrow.

পুঙ্খানুপুঙ্খ, ব্যগ্র, সাবধান, উদ্যত, চালাক, সূক্ষ্ম বিবেচনা, eager, ardent, attentive, ready, active; minute consideration or investigation.

পুঞ্জ, রাশি, সঞ্চয়, শ্রেণী, ঝাঁক, a heap, collection, quantity, number, a row, line, train, flock, &c.

পুঙ্গব, বৃষ, ষাঁড়, উত্তম, প্রধান, a bull, *in comp*: excellent, eminent.

পুচ্ছ, লাঙ্গুল, an animal's tail.

পুছন, জিজ্ঞাসন, to ask, enquire, interrogate, question.

পুঞ্জ, স্তূপ, রাশি, সঞ্চয়, a heap, collection, quantity.

পুঞ্জমান, স্তূপাকৃতি, বিস্তর, increasing to a heap, much, abundant.

পুড়ন, দহন, জ্বলন, to burn, scorch, burn away, be burnt.

পুণ্ডরীক, শুক্লবর্ণ পদ্ম, পূর্বপশ্চিমদিগ্‌হস্তী, the white lotus, the elephant of the S. E. quarter.

পুণ্য, ধর্ম্ম, সুকৃতি, ধার্ম্মিক, সাধু, সুন্দর, মনোজ্ঞ, moral or religious merit, virtue, purity, a good action; virtuous, meritorious, righteous, pure, holy, beautiful, pleasing.

পুণ্যবান্‌, পুণ্যবন্ত,—ধার্ম্মিক, সৎকর্ম্মান্বিত, holy, religious, virtuous, meritorious, good.

পুণ্যভূমি, তীর্থস্থান, আর্য্যাবর্ত্ত, a holy place, place of pilgrimage, the country between the Himálaya and Vindhya mountains.

পুণ্যাচারী, ধার্ম্মিক, ধর্ম্মকারী, leading a holy life, practising religious actions.

পুণ্যাত্মা, ধর্ম্মশীল, সাধু, holy, pure, religious, virtuous.

পুণ্যাহ, পুণ্যজনক দিন, বৎসরীয় করগ্রহণের প্রথম দিন, a holy day, the first day of yearly rent payments.

পুণ্যী, ধার্ম্মিক, সাধু, ধর্ম্মবান, উত্তম, holy, pure, good, virtuous, full of merit.

পুতন, রোপণ, গাড়ন, to plant a tree, bury in the ground, to fix, set up a stake, &c.

পুতনা, চমূ, সেনার দল, a division of an army, a squadron.

পুতুল, পুতুলা, পুত্তলী, পুত্তলিকা,—মৃত্তিকাদিনির্ম্মিত মূর্ত্তি, প্রতিমা, a doll, puppet, small image, idol, the image of an object on the eye.

পুত্র, তনয়, সন্তান, বেটা, a son, a boy, a male child.

পুত্রপৌত্রাদি, সন্তানসন্ততি, sons and grandsons, posterity.

পুত্রসন্তান বা সন্ততি,—ছেল্যাপিল্যা, তনয়, বেটা, male offspring or posterity, a male child, a son.

পুত্রিকা, তনয়া, দুহিতা, পুত্তলী, a daughter, a doll, a puppet.

পুত্রী, দুহিতা, কন্যা, পুত্রবান, a daughter, a girl; *m. adj.* having a son. [a son, filial.

পুত্রীয়, পুত্রসম্বন্ধীয়, পুত্রবৎ, পুত্রের, pertaining or proper to

পুত্রেষ্টি, সন্তানার্থ যাগ, a sacrifice to procure a son.

পুথী, পুস্তক, গ্রন্থ, কাণ্ড, a book, a volume.

পুদিনা, সুগন্ধ শাক বিশেষ, mint, (the plant.)

পুন, কিন্তু, পরন্তু, but.

পুনঃ, দ্বিতীয় বার, কিন্তু, দ্বি, বারবার, again, a second time, but, on the contrary; *in comp*: re, returning, again, twice, frequent, &c. [quently.

পুনঃপুনঃ, বারবার, মুহুর্মুহু, again and again, repeatedly, fre-

পুনরপি, আর, এবং, again and again, also. [recurrence.

পুনরাগমন, পরাবৃত্তি, ফেরা, a return, coming back or again,

পুনরায়, পুনর্ব্বার,—দ্বিতীয়বার, আরবার, again, a second time, over again, another time.

পুনরুক্তি, পুনঃকথন, দ্বিরুক্তি, repetition, tautology.

পুনরুত্থান, ফিরিয়া উঠন, a rising again, resurrection.

পুনর্জন্ম, জন্মান্তর, স্বাস্থ্য, রোগ নিবৃত্তি, a second birth, regeneration, recovery from dangerous sickness.

পুনর্দয়া, পুনরায় অনুগ্রহকরা, a relenting, renewal of pity, &c.

পুনর্ব্বিবাহ, পুনরায় বিবাহকরা, নবরূঢ়ার প্রথম ঋতুকালীন সংস্কার বিশেষ, a second marriage, a ceremonial on the appearance of the menses in a new married woman. [finger or toe nail.

পুনর্ভব, জন্মান্তর, কররুহ, নখ, regeneration, a second birth, a

পুনর্ভূ, পরপূর্ব্বা, দ্বির্ব্বিবাহিতা স্ত্রী, a twice-married woman, a virgin widow remarried.

পুনশ্চ, পুনরায়, আর, এতদ্ভিন্ন, again, yet again, moreover.

পুমান্. পুরুষ, নর. a man, a male.

পুর, নগর, গৃহ, বাসস্থান, a city, town, a place, house, residence, dwelling-place, habitation.

পুরঃ, পুরস্তাৎ,—সম্মুখে, অগ্রে, পূর্ব্বে, প্রাক্, প্রাগ্দিগে, in front, before, eastwards, formerly; prior, eastward.

পুরঃসর, অগ্রগামী, পূর্ব্ববর্ত্তী, অধিপ, going before, preceding, going forward ; a leader.

পুরন্দর, ইন্দ্র, Indra sovereign of the gods.

পুরন্ধ্রী, পতিপুত্রবতী, গৃহিণী, a matron, one having husband and children living, a housewife.

পুরশ্চরণ, মন্ত্রের জপ হোমাদি ক্রিয়া বিশেষ, a mode of religious service, including prayer, sacrifice &c.

পুরস্কার, প্রতিপত্তি, বৃদ্ধি, সম্ভ্রম, প্রতিফল, রাজপ্রসাদ, advancement, promotion, honor, a reward, remuneration, a donation, a royal gift.

পুরস্কার্য্য, পুরস্করণীয়,—সম্ভ্রমার্হ, আদরণীয়, proper or deserving to be honored or promoted.

পুরস্কৃত, পূজিত, প্রতিপাদিত, অগ্রস্থাপিত, honored, promoted, rewarded, &c placed in front, facing an enemy.

পুরস্কারবস্ত্র. প্রসাদ বস্ত্র, an honorary dress.

পুরস্তাৎ, অগ্রে, সম্মুখে, before, in front. [family.

পুরস্ত্রী, পুরন্ধ্রী, গৃহিণী, a matron, housewife, mistress of a

পুরস্থ, অগ্রবর্ত্তী, গৃহস্থায়ী, situated before or in front, &c. staying at home. [plete, full.

পুরা, পূর্ব্বকালে, সমাপ্ত, ভরা, before, formerly, long ago, com-

পুরাণ, বহুকালীন, বাসি, প্রাচীন ইতিহাস গ্রন্থ বিশেষ, ancient, old, stale; the Puránas or sacred Poems. [pacity.

পুরাতন, বহুকালিক, পূর্ব্বকালীন, old, ancient; a measure of ca-

পুরাবৃত্ত, পূর্ব্ববৃত্তান্ত, ইতিহাস, history, tradition, ancient story.

পুরাতনকথা, ইতিহাস, প্রাচীন গাথা, পারম্পর্য্য, an an ient story, legend, tradition.

পুরী, নগরী, বাটী, a city, palace, habitation, building.

পুরীতত্তি, নাড়ী, অন্ত্র, an entrail, a gut.

পুরীষ, বিষ্ঠা, মল, the fœces, ordure, excrement, dung.
পুরু. মোটা, স্থূল, thick, coarse.
পুরুষ, পুমান্, মানব, মনুষ্যগণ, মানুষ, ব্রহ্ম, জীবাত্মা, সাংখ্যবিৎ, a man, a male, mankind, a generation, God, the Supreme Being, spirit, the soul, life or the sentient soul, a Sáukhya philosopher.
পুরুষকার, মনুষ্যক্রিয়া, শৌর্য্য, বীর্য্য, human conduct or exertion, manliness, courage.
পুরুষক্রম, পুরুষানুক্রম,—পিত্রাদিপরম্পরা, কুলপর্য্যায়, successive generations, succession, lineage. [courage.
পুরুষত্ব, পুংস্ত্ব, সাহস, কৃতিত্ব, manhood, virility, manliness,
পুরুষাঙ্গ, শিশ্ন, the male organ of generation, the penis.
পুরুষার্থ, ধর্ম্মার্থকামমোক্ষ, মনুষ্যত্ব, সাহস, the four objects of human life, manliness, courage.
পুরুষোত্তম, প্রধান মনুষ্য, বিষ্ণু, an excellent man, Vishnu.
পুরোগ, পুরোগম,—অগ্রগামী, প্রধান, preceding, going before, chief, principal. [in ghee.
পুরোডাশ, যজ্ঞীয় পিষ্টক বিশেষ, sacrificial cakes of meal steeped
পুরোধাঃ, পুরোহিত,—যাজক, পূজারী, a family or domestic priest.
পুরোবর্ত্তী, অগ্রসর, অগ্রস্থিত, preceding, in advance, placed before or in front.
পুলক, রোমাঞ্চ, হর্ষ, কীট, কটোরা, কাঁচপাত্র, মণিরদোষ, হরিতাল, horripilation through pleasure, delight, joy, any insect infesting animals, a wine glass, goblet, a sort of stone, a flaw in a gem, yellow orpiment.
পুলকিত, হর্ষিত, অত্যাহ্লাদিত, উল্লসিত, overjoyed, delighted, excessively pleased, joyous, gay.
পুলা, আটি, গল্লা, a sheaf.
পুলাক, তোবড়া ধান্য, তোড়ানি, সংক্ষেপ, ত্বরা, shrivelled grain, rice-water, brevity, a compendium, abbreviation, despatch, celerity.
পুলি, মিষ্টান্ন বিশেষ, a sort of cake or sweetmeat.
পুলিন, চড়া, দ্বীপ, a shoal, sand-bank, strand, island.
পুলিন্দ, গাঁঠরি, মোট, a bundle, bale, package. [fatten.
পুষণ, পালন, ভরণ, হৃষ্টপুষ্ট করণ, to nourish, nurture, feed,
পুষ্কর, আকাশ, জল, পদ্ম, জলাশয়, শর, অসির দল, অসিকোষ, খাপ, হস্তির

শুণ্ডাগ্র, যুদ্ধ, মত্ততা, সংযোগ, পিঞ্জর, কোল, নৃত্য, ঔষধি বিশেষ, the sky, heaven, atmosphere, water, a lotus, a pond, a lake, an arrow, the blade or sheathe of a sword, the tip of an elephant's trunk, war, intoxication, union, a cage, a port or haven, dancing, a sort of drug.

পুষ্করিণী, জলাশয়, a pond, lake, pool, tank.

পুষ্কল, বিস্তর, উত্তম, পুঙ্খ, much, many, eminent; the feather of an arrow. [fattened, fat, plump.

পুষ্ট, প্রতিপালিত, স্থূল, nourished, cherished, fed, well-fed,

পুষ্টি, প্রতিপালন, সাহায্য, উপায়, স্থৌল্য, বৃদ্ধি, ঠেস, আশ্রয়, nourishment, support, aid, succour, relief, plumpness, good condition, increase, prosperity, thriving, a prop, shoar, bank, abutment, reliance.

পুষ্টিকর, পুষ্টিদ,—প্রতিপালক, স্থৌল্যবর্দ্ধক, cherishing, supporting, fattening, nutritious. [sion, the menses.

পুষ্প, ফুল, ছানী, ঋতু, a flower, speck on the eye, expan-

পুষ্পক, কুবেরের বিমান, ফুল, ছানী, Cuvera's chariot, a flower, a speck on the eye, a calx of brass, copperas or green vitriol. [madeva.

পুষ্পধন্বা, পুষ্পধনু,—কন্দর্প, having a bow of flowers, *i. e.* Cá-

পুষ্পাঞ্জলি, পুষ্পপূরিত করদ্বয়, a presenting of the open hands full of flowers. [author.

পুষ্পিকা, প্রকরণ, ভণিতা, a chapter or section of a book, an

পুষ্পিত, ফুলযুক্ত, আপাততঃ রমণীয়, in flower, covered with flowers, ripe for enjoyment.

পুষ্পিতা, পুষ্পবতী,—ঋতুমতি, *f.* a woman during menstruation.

পুস্তক, গ্রন্থ, হস্তলিপি, a book, a manuscript, a volume.

পুস্তা, ঠেস, অবলম্ব, ভেড়ীবন্ধী, a shoar, prop, embankment.

পূয, ক্লেদ, রসানি, পূয়শোণিত, pus, purulent matter.

পূগ, বৃন্দ, সমূহ, রাশি, গুণ, ভাব, গুবাক বৃক্ষ, কাঁটাল বৃক্ষ, a multitude, heap, number, quantity, nature, property, disposition, the betel, the jack.

পূজক, আরাধক, উপাসক, সেবক, worshipping, serving, honouring; a worshipper. [worship.

পূজন, অর্চ্চন, সেবন, to honor, respect, venerate, serve,

পূজয়িতা, উপাসক, আরাধক, a worshipper, adorer.

পূজা, অর্চনা, সেবা, সম্মান, worship, adoration, homage, respect, honor. [priest.

পূজারী, দেবলব্রাহ্মণ, a worshipper, an officiating or temple-

পূজার্হ, পূজ্য,—অর্চনীয়, আর্য্য, আদরণীয়, worthy of worship, venerable, honorable, respectable.

পূট, দ্রাবক, a menstruum or flux for metals.

পূত, পবিত্র, শুদ্ধ, পরিষ্কৃত, সরল, pure, holy, clean, cleansed, winnowed &c. honest, true, sincere.

পূতি, শুচিতা, পবিত্রতা, সারল্য, দুর্গন্ধ, পচা, সড়া, purity, sanctity, purification, truth, sincerity, putridity, stench; musty, putrid, corrupt, fœtid. [potherb.

পূতিকা. খট্টাশ, শাক বিশেষ, a civet or pole cat, a kind of

পূতিগন্ধ, কুগন্ধ, দুর্গন্ধ, a stench, putrid scent, fœtor; fœtid.

পূত্যণ্ড, কস্তুরিবিশিষ্ট হরিণ বিশেষ, গন্ধপোকা, the musk-deer, the flying or stinking bug.

পূপ, পিষ্টক, রুটী, a cake, bread.

পূয, ব্রণচ্যুত ক্লেদ, pus, matter from a sore, putridity.

পূর, পূরী.—ঘৃতভাজা পিষ্টক, a sort of cake fried in ghee.

পূর, পুষ্করিণী, ক্ষতশৌচ, পূর্ণজুয়ার, a lake, a piece of water, the cleansing or healing of sores and ulcers; high or full (as the tide.)

পূরক, নিশ্বাসাকর্ষণ, কমলালেবু, ভরণকারী, সম্পাদক, a mode of drawing in and retaining the breath as a religious act, a citron; filling, fulfilling, completing.

পূরট, মুদিত, ভরাট, বুজা, filled up, choked up.

পূরণ, ভরণ, বুজান, গাদন, অঙ্কবৃদ্ধিকরণ, সম্পাদন, বুজন, কড়কন, সমাপ্তি, নিবাড়, to fill, make up a deficiency, fill up, stuff, load, charge, to multiply (in numbers,) to recruit, complete, accomplish, finish, to become full, to heal as a sore; completion, complement.

পূরা, ভরা, সমাপ্ত, সমুদায়, সম্যক, বিস্তর. full, complete, perfect, entire, plenary, copious.

পূরাণ, বুজান, নিরাড়ন, শুধরাণ, সাম্লান, প্রতীকার করণ, ভরাণ, to stop up, fill up a cavity, to complete, to retrieve, replace, make good what is deficient.

পূর, মোটা, ভরা, thick, full. [perfect, entire.
পূর্ণ, ভরা, সম্যক, সমাপ্ত, সাঙ্গ, full, filled, all, completed,
পূর্ণপাত্র, পূর্ণচন্দ্র,—হোমের দক্ষিণা, উৎসবকালীন দত্তবস্ত্রাদি, a vessel full of rice presented to the priest at a sacrifice, one of clothes and ornaments scrambled for by the guests at a festival. [full moon.
পূর্ণিমা, পূর্ণমাসী, পূর্ণিমা,—শুক্লপক্ষের অন্তিম তিথি, the day of the
পূর্ণমাস, পূর্ণিমা তিথিতে যে যাগ, a monthly sacrifice on the day of full moon.
পূর্ত্ত, খাতাদি পুণ্যার্থ কর্ম্ম, any act of pious liberality as digging a tank, building a temple, &c.
পূর্ত্তি, ভর্ত্তী, তৃপ্তি, সমাপ্তি, fullness, repletion, completion.
পূর্ব্ব, প্রথম, প্রাক্, আদি, আদিম, আদ্য, অগ্রসর, প্রাক্কালীন, প্রাচী, অগ্রস্থিত, আগের, আগে, প্রাক্কালে, সূর্য্যোদয়ের দিক্, পিতৃলোক, first, former, prior, initial, previous, preliminary, preceding, foregoing, ancient, east, eastern, fronting; before, ago, formerly; the east, ancestors, forefathers.
পূর্ব্বক, অগ্রগামী, দ্বারা, দিয়া, করণক, preceding; by, through, with. [duced; ancestors.
পূর্ব্বজ, জ্যেষ্ঠ, অগ্রজ, পিতৃলোক, elder, previously born or pro-
পূর্ব্বদিন, গত দিবস, গত কল্য, the preceding day, yesterday.
পূর্ব্বদেশ, প্রাচী দিক্, প্রাচ্য, বঙ্গদেশ, the east, the east country.
পূর্ব্বনির্ব্বন্ধ, প্রাক্তন, আগের কট, fate, a prior obligation, a preliminary engagement.
পূর্ব্বপক্ষ, প্রস্তাব, বাক্যানুষ্ঠান, কোটি, চন্দ্রের হ্রাসকাল, a proposition, assertion, thesis, the major term in logic, the first half of a lunar month.
পূর্ব্বপুরুষ, পিতৃপিতামহাদি, forefathers, progenitors, ancestors.
পূর্ব্ববৎ, প্রাগ্বৎ, অগ্রস্থিতের ন্যায়, as before, as the preceding.
পূর্ব্ববর্ত্তী, অগ্রসর, প্রাগ্ভূত, preceding, previously, existing.
পূর্ব্ববাদ, প্রাক্ন্যায়, অগ্রোক্তি, a former plea, former assertion.
পূর্ব্ববাদী, অগ্রবক্তা, আদাণী, speaking first; a plaintiff.
পূর্ব্বরাত্র, রাত্রির প্রথম ভাগ, গতরাত্রি, the first part of the night, last night. [long time.
পূর্ব্বাপর, অগ্রপশ্চাৎ, বহুকালীন, preceding or following; of a

পূর্ব্বাবধি, চিরকালাবধি, from former times, of old, from antiquity. [the forenoon.

পূর্ব্বাহ্ণ, দিবসের আদ্যভাগ, the first or early part of the day,

পূর্ব্বা, পূর্ব্বীয়,—প্রাচী, সূর্য্যোদয়দিগস্থ, eastern, easterly, eastward, situated to the east.

পূর্ব্বে, অগ্রে, প্রাক্কালে, সম্মুখে, প্রাচীদিগে, before, in front, previously, formerly, in or to the east, eastwards.

পূর্ব্বেদ্যুঃ, পূর্ব্বদিনে, গতকল্য, on the preceding day, yesterday.

পৃক্ত, মিশ্রিত, সংলগ্ন, মৃক্ষিত, mixed, rubbed or brought in contact with, touched, smeared.

পৃচ্ছা, জিজ্ঞাসা, প্রশ্ন, a question, enquiry, interrogation.

পৃথক্, ভিন্ন, ইতর, অন্য, ভিতে, স্বতন্ত্র, separate, distinct, different; apart, aside.

পৃথক্২, ভিন্ন২, separately, severally, distinctly.

পৃথগ্বিধ, নানাপ্রকার, বিবিধ, বিশেষ, বহুরূপী, of various kinds, various, diversified, multiform.

পৃথিবী, পৃথ্বী,—মেদিনী, ভূ, মৃত্তিকা, the earth, the ground, earth.

পৃথিবীপতি পৃথ্বীপাল,—রাজা, সম্রাট, a king, a sovereign.

পৃথুক, চিপিটক, চিড়া, rice wetted, parched and flattened.

পৃষৎ, জলবিন্দু, হরিণ বিশেষ, a drop of water or other liquid, the porcine deer. [sought.

পৃষ্ট, জিজ্ঞাসিত, যাচিত, asked, interrogated, questioned,

পৃষ্ঠ, শরীরের পশ্চাৎ ভাগ, পিঠ, পাছু, বহির্দ্দিগ্, the back, a page, side, surface, the rear.

পৃষ্ঠতঃ, পশ্চাতে, পাছে, behind the back, behind, in the rear.

পৃষ্ঠমাংসাদ, ঠক, পরোক্ষাপবাদক, পরিবাদক, কুচ্ছাকারক, a backbiter, whisperer, slanderer.

পেঁচ, ছিপীতোলা কলাদি, ঘূর্ণি, পাক, ঝঞ্ঝাট, ছল, a screw, a spiral motion, a twist, intricacy, perplexity, a deep laid scheme. [perplexer; intricate.

পেঁচাও, ছলী, ঠক, পাকপাড়া, পাকপড়া, a schemer, plotter, cheat,

পেঁচান, পাক দেওন, মোড়ান, আঁটকান, শঠতাকরণ, ছলন, to screw, turn a screw, twist, to perplex, entangle, raise difficulties, cheat, plot, scheme.

পেঁচাল, পাকপড়া, ঘুরণিয়া, ধূর্ত্ত, কুটিল, perplexed, intricate, spiral, tortuous, disingenuous, artful, cheating.

পেঁজন, কার্পাসাদি কোঁড়ন, to card wool or cotton.
পেঞন, পান করণ, to drink, drink in, smoke tobacco.
পেচক, পেচা,— উলূক, an owl, a screech owl.
পেট, উদর, গর্ভ, the belly, the womb, the fœtus, pregnancy.
পেটখসা, গর্ভপাত, গর্ভস্রাব, an abortion, miscarriage. [flux.
পেটচলা বা ভাঙ্গা,—অতিসার, আমাশয়, a dysentery, diarrhœa,
পেটজ্বালা, উদরের বেদনা, কামড়ানি, a griping, griping pain.
পেটধরা, পেটবন্ধ,—অতিসারাদি নাশ, আমাশয় নিবৃত্তি, recovery or convalescence from a dysentery or flux.
পেটন, তাড়ন, মারণ, to beat, strike, hammer. [carriage.
পেটফেলন, গর্ভখসাণ, to procure an abortion, cause a mis-
পেটসর্বস্ব, পেটার্থী,—উদরম্ভরি, very gluttonous, devoted to the belly; an epicure. [pulent.
পেটাল, পেটুয়া,—তুন্দিল, ভুঁড়িয়া, large-bellied, pot-bellied, cor-
পেটারা, পেড়িয়া,—বেত্রাদিনির্ম্মিত বস্ত্রাধার বিশেষ, a sort of travelling basket or portmanteau.
পেটা, ঝাঁপী, ডালা, a wicker basket, a box, a chest.
পেটুক, পেটকা,—খাদ্য সামগ্রীতে লোলুপ, অস্মর, উদরম্ভরি, সুভোক্তা, gluttonous, gormandizing, ravenous, intemperate or nice in eating.
পেড়া, পেটারা, ঝাঁপী, কটাহ, মিষ্টান্ন বিশেষ, a basket, portmanteau, a young buffalo, a sort of sweetmeat.
পেতনা, অপরিষ্কৃত লোক, অপরিচ্ছন্ন, ভূতাদি, a sloven, a spectre.
পেতনী, পরছায়া, অপরিষ্কৃতা, *f.* an apparition, a spectre, a slut.
পেতনীব, পেতনীবৎ,—অপরিচ্ছন্না, a slut, a slattern, a flaunting and sluttish woman.
পেনেট, লিঙ্গাধার, the female pudenda in the lingam.
পেয়, পানযোগ্য, জল, দুগ্ধ, দুগ্ধপোষ্য বৎস, drinkable; drink, water, milk, a sucking calf. [beautiful.
পেশল, নিপুণ, দক্ষ, ধূর্ত্ত, সুন্দর, clever, crafty, fraudulent,
পেশী, পক্ষিডিম্ব, মুকুল, জটামাংসী, মাংসপিণ্ড, খাপ, a bird's egg, a blown bud, Indian spikenard, a lump of meat, a muscle, a sheath, a scabbard.
পেষণ, ভজন, বাটন, গুঁড়ন, চর্বণ, ভজনা, পটী, to grind corn &c. to pulverise, pound, mash, chew, masticate; a roller, a bandage.

পেষণী, জাঁতা, নোড়া, শিল, a mill-stone, a roller, a slab for grinding paints or other substances on.

পৈঠা, সোপান, শিড়ী, a staircase, flight of steps, a ladder.

পৈতা, উপবীত, the sacred thread.

পৈতৃক; পৈত্র্য,—পিত্রাদিসম্বন্ধীয়, পূর্বপুরুষীয়, পূর্বপুরুষহইতে প্রাপ্যধন, paternal, ancestral, patrimonial.

পৈত্তিক, পিত্তরোগগ্রস্থ, পিত্তবৎ, bilious, having the nature of bile.

পৈশাচ, আসুরিক, দৈত্যোপযুক্ত, demoniacal, devilish, infernal, suited to demons or goblins.

পৈশুন্য, কর্ণে জপকরা, খলতা, ঠকামি, নিন্দা, দুষ্টতা, ক্রূরতা, tale-bearing, whispering, information, defamation, backbiting, depravity, cruelty.

পো, পুত্র, ছেল্যা, a son.

পোঁচ, বালীচুণ. লেপকরা, the plaster of a wall, a coat of whitewash.

পোঁচন-আন, ঘষণ, ঝাড়ন, মুচন, to wipe, rub, dust.

পোঁচা, মণিবন্ধ, the wrist.

পোঁটা, নাড়ী, অন্ত্র, a gut, the entrails.

পোঁদ, নিতম্ব, পাছা, কর্কনা, the posteriors, the rump, the hips.

পোকা, কীট, কৃমি, an insect, a worm, vermin.

পোগণ্ড, বক্র, বিকলাঙ্গ, দশবর্ষপর্য্যন্ত বালক, নির্দাড়ি যুবা, deformed, maimed ; a beardless boy, a youth.

পোঙ্গা, গুহ্যদেশ, গুদ, the anus.

পোট, গোড়া, তলা, the foundation of a house or wall.

পোটা, দাড়িবিশিষ্টা স্ত্রী, a woman with a beard.

পোড়ন, দহন, ভর্জ্জিত হওন, জ্বলন, to burn, be burnt, parched or inflamed.

পোড়া, দগ্ধ, ভাজা, জ্বলন্ত, burnt, roasted, parched, smarting.

পোড়াকপাল্যা, কাঙ্গাল, দুর্ভাগ্যবন্ত, wretched, unfortunate, luck-less, of an evil destiny.

পোড়ান, দাহন, ঝল্সান, ভাজন, জ্বলান, অগ্নিপরীক্ষা করণ, to burn, roast, fry, to scald, to sear, to inflame, to set on fire, to try by fiery ordeal.

পোড়ানিয়া, দাহক, জ্বালানিয়া, burning &c ; an incendiary.

পোত, তরণী, নৌকা, শাবক, দাঁড়, গোড়া, কাপড়, a boat, a ship, an oar, the young of animals, cloth, the foun-dation or scite of a house.

পোতন, গাড়, to bury, plant, set, fix in the ground.

পোতবাহ, পোতবাহক,—কাণ্ডারী, মাঝিক, দাঁড়ী, নৌচালক, তিরাধিপতি, a steersman, a mariner, seaman, boatman, rower, the master of a vessel.

পোতা, মাঝিক, পূজারী, গোড়, পল্লি, a seaman, a waterman, an officiating priest, a foundation, a district, canton.

পোতাধান, মৎস্যসংঘাত, a shoal of young fish, small fry.

পোদ, তুচ্ছ জাতি বিশেষ, a low cast of Hindoos.

পোনা, মৎস্যশাবক, মৎস্যঝাঁক, the young of fish, small fry.

পোয়া, চতুর্থাংশ, চৌথ, চারা, a quarter, a fourth part, a plantlet or young plant.

পোয়ান, অগ্নি বা সূর্য্য সেবন, to warm oneself in the sun or at the fire.

পোরণ-আণ, ভরণ, to fill, to load, to freight.

পোলো, টেঁটা, তেকালা, a kind of harpoon.

পোষণ, প্রতিপালন, লালন, ভরণ, রক্ষণ, ধারণ, to feed, rear, bring up, cherish, maintain, protect, support, uphold, sustain.

পোষা, ভরণ্য, বৃত্তি, পালা, a maintenance, support; domestic, tame.

পোষাণ, ভরাণ, পূরাণ, সাম্লান, to cause to be maintained, to recompense, to retrieve a loss.

পোষ্টা, পোষ্টৃ,—প্রতিপালক, রক্ষক, a nourisher, supporter, protector, &c.

পোষ্যপুত্র, দত্তকপুত্র, পালকপুত্র, an adopted son.

পোষ্যবর্গ, পরিবার, ভৃত্যগণ, অনুচর, a household, family, retainers.

পোহান, প্রত্যুষ হওন, দর্শন, to dawn, become light, appear.

পৌগণ্ড, পাঁচ বৎসরাবধি ষোল বৎসর পর্য্যন্ত বালক, a lad from five to sixteen years, a boy.

পৌছন, উত্তরণ, লাগন, আগমন, প্রাপণ, অর্জন, to arrive at, reach, land, to inherit, succeed to, devolve upon.

পৌছান, চালান, বহান, উত্তারণ, to convey, carry to, to land.

পৌত্র, পৌত্রী,—নপ্তা, নপ্তী, নাতী, নাতিনী, *m.* & *f.* a grandson & granddaughter.

পৌত্তলিক, সাকারসেবী, প্রতিমাপূজক, an idolator, an image-worshipper.

পৌনরুক্ত, দ্বিরুক্তি, দোহারা কথা, repetition, tautology.

পৌনর্ভব, দ্বিরূঢ়ার সন্তান, the son of a twice married woman by the last husband.

পৌর, নগরসম্বন্ধীয়, নগরবাসী, শিষ্ট, ভদ্র, belonging to or living in a town, city, civil, civilized.

পৌরাণিক, পুরাণশাস্ত্রবেত্তা, পুরাণমতাবলম্বী, one well read in the Puránas, a believer in the Puránas.

পৌরুষ, মনুষ্যত্ব, পুংশক্তি, তেজ, পরাক্রম, পুরুষপরিমাণ, manhood, virility, manliness, the measure of a man.

পৌষ, নবম মাস, the month of the sun in Sagittarius.

পৌষ্টিক, ধাতুপোষক, পুষ্টিকর, nutritious, nourishing, fattening, advancing or promoting nutrition.

পৌরোহিত্য, যাজকতা, যাজকের ক্রিয়া, যাজকসম্বন্ধীয়, যাজকের, family priesthood, priestly duty; priestly, belonging to a family priest.

প্রকট, প্রকটিত,—প্রসিদ্ধ, স্পষ্ট, ব্যক্ত, প্রচারিত, প্রসারিত, বিক্ষিপ্ত, manifest, displayed, evident, apparent, notorious, laid open, spread out, unfolded, dishevelled.

প্রকরণ, প্রস্তাবনা, কাব্য কল্পনা, প্রসঙ্গ, কাণ্ড, অধ্যায়, বিষয়, বৃত্তান্ত, ঘটনা, an introduction, preface, prologue, prelude, a poetical fiction, a treatise or its subject, a section, book, chapter, an affair, circumstance, event.

প্রকর্ষ, উত্তমতা, প্রাধান্য, excellence, superiority.

প্রকর্ষিত, উত্তমীকৃত, উদ্বর্ত্তিত, স্থাপিত ধনাদির উদ্বর্ত. made to excel; the surplus produce of a pledge.

প্রকাণ্ড, উচ্চ, ঊর্দ্ধ, বলবান্, স্থূল, অতিশয় বৃহৎ, উত্তম, প্রধান, উৎকর্ষ, মহত্ত্ব, গুঁড়ী, গাছের থাড়া, tall, high, strong, robust, stout, large, stupendous, excellent, best; excellence, greatness, the trunk of a tree, the stem of a plant.

প্রকার, ডৌল, রূপ, বিধ, মত, ধারা, বিশেষ, সাদৃশ্য, a kind, sort, species, manner, method, way, a variety, a difference, a similitude.

প্রকারান্তর, অন্যবিধ, অতুল্য, অন্য, another sort, kind, way, or manner, &c; dissimilar, other.

প্রকারান্তরে, অন্যমতে, অন্যথা, সঙ্কেতে, অস্পষ্টে, in a different or other manner, otherwise, indirectly, obscurely, ambiguously. [era.

প্রকাল, বহুকাল, প্রসিদ্ধ সময়, শক, a long time, a noted time or

প্রকাশ, বিজ্ঞাপন, ঘোষণা, প্রচার, জানানি, উদয়, উজ্জ্বল, দীপ্তি, প্রভা,

প্রসার, বাক্য পরিষ্কার, স্পষ্ট, ব্যক্ত, বিকশিত, manifestation, discovery, disclosure, publication, revelation, appearance, light, lustre, illumination, expansion, opening, diffusion, perspicuity; open, manifest, expanded, blown.

প্রকাশন, উজ্জ্বলন, দর্শন, জানান, দেখান, ব্যাখ্যান, প্রচারণ, বর্ণন, কহন, to shine, appear, illuminate, manifest, display, elucidate, utter, disclose, reveal.

প্রকাশনীয়, প্রকাশ্য,—প্রচারণীয়, জ্ঞাতব্য, দৃশ্য, capable of manifestation, &c. visible. [licly.

প্রকাশরূপে, ব্যক্তরূপে, স্পষ্টে, openly, plainly, explicitly, pub-

প্রকাশিত, প্রচারিত, প্রদর্শিত, ব্যক্তীভূত, দীপ্যমান, প্রফুল্লিত, disclosed, revealed, evident, apparent, manifest, visible, conspicuous, open, blown, expanded.

প্রকাশী, উদিত, ব্যক্ত, জাজ্বল্যমান, appearing, shining, radiant.

প্রকীর্ণ, কাণ্ড, বিক্ষিপ্ত, ব্যাপ্ত, প্রচারিত, a section, chapter; scattered, interspersed, spread, published.

প্রকীর্ণক, প্রসার, আয়াম, কাণ্ড, নিষ্পত্তি, চামর, extent, length, a section, chapter, decree at law, a decision, a chowri or cow-tail whisk.

প্রকীর্ত্তন, প্রস্তাবন, বর্ণন, কথন, ঘোষণ, বুঝান, to mention, speak, say, tell, declare, explain.

প্রকৃত, যথার্থ, যোগ্য, ঠিক, সত্য, বাস্তবিক, সরল, স্বাভাবিক, শুদ্ধ, অবশ্য, নিশ্চয়, right, proper, reasonable, accurate, certain, real, true, genuine, sincere, upright, unadulterated, pure; certainly, really, accurately.

প্রকৃতার্থ, উপযুক্ত, উচিত, বাস্তবিক, ন্যায্য, সত্য আদ্দাশ, right, proper, just, pure, genuine, true; the true object of a plaint at law. [upright.

প্রকৃতার্থিক, যাথার্থিক, ধার্ম্মিক, সরল, just, righteous, honest,

প্রকৃতি, অজা, কারণীভূতা, স্বভাব, ধর্ম্ম, চরিত্র, ধাতু, অঙ্কপূরক, original matter or plastic nature, the female principle in creation, nature, disposition, temper, natural state, habitual conduct or character, a crude noun or verb, a multiplier.

প্রকৃতিসিদ্ধ, স্বভাবজাত, স্বাভাবিক, effected by nature, natural.
প্রকৃষ্ট, উত্তম, শ্রেষ্ঠ, প্রধান, excellent, eminent, superior, chief, principal. [frame.
প্রকোষ্ঠ, বাহুর অধোভাগ, কপালী, the fore-arm, part of a door
প্রক্রম, উদ্যোগ, আরম্ভ, অনুষ্ঠান, an attempt, effort, commencement, beginning.
প্রক্রান্ত, আরব্ধ, অনুষ্ঠিত, begun, commenced, attempted.
প্রক্রিয়া, দৈবীচেষ্টা, স্বস্ত্যয়ন, ঔষধসেবন, a service to obtain some divine blessing, the taking of medicine.
প্রক্ষারক, বাষ্পোদ্গতিকারক, exhalent, that which exhales.
প্রক্ষালন, ধাবন, পরিষ্করণ, মোচন, to wash, rinse, cleanse, expiate. [jected.
প্রক্ষিপ্ত, ক্ষেপিত, ছট্‌কান, ছাড়া, thrown, cast, projected, in-
প্রক্ষেপ, ক্ষেপা, ছিটা, মূলধনের অংশ, a throw, cast, throwing off, projection, propulsion, injection, the shares in a joint stock. [clever.
প্রখর, তীক্ষ্ণ, কটু, চতুর, hot, pungent, acrid, keen, sharp,
প্রখরজ্যোতি, উৎকট দীপ্তি, চকমক্, a strong light, flash, glare.
প্রখরবুদ্ধি, সূক্ষ্মমতি, penetration, acuteness.
প্রখ্যাত, প্রসিদ্ধ, যশস্বী, famous, celebrated, notorious.
প্রগণ্ড, বাহুর উপরি ভাগ, the upper arm measured from elbow to shoulder.
প্রগত, বিস্তৃত, বেড়্যাউঠা, diverging, standing out, gibbous.
প্রগতজানু-ক, বক্রপদ, bandy-legged, having the knees divergent or far apart.
প্রগল্ভ, প্রতিভান্বিত, দাম্ভিক, নির্লজ্জ, সাহসী, বলবান্, দক্ষ, bold, insolent, audacious, impudent, shameless, confident, intrepid, wilful, haughty, firm, ready, able, strong; haughtiness, boasting, pomposity. [magant.
প্রগল্ভা, লম্পটা, ব্যাপিকা, a shameless woman, wanton, ter-
প্রগাঢ়, দৃঢ়, শক্ত, কঠিন, ধীর, প্রচুর, ব্যথা, কৃচ্ছু, hard, firm, difficult, steady, serious, much, excessive, abundant; pain, privation, penance.
প্রগুণ, সরল, straight, honest, upright, sincere.
প্রগৃহ, প্রগ্রাহ,—তুলাসূত্র, বাগ, রজ্জু, বন্ধনা, বন্দী, the string sus-

pending a balance, a rein, rope, halter, confinement, captivity, a captive, prisoner, a man or beast in confinement.

প্রগ্রীব, গৃহের জাল, ঝরকা, উপবনস্থ জলটঙ্গী, গরাদিয়া, a lattice, window, balcony, a summer-house, a painted turret, a balustrade, rail, railing.

প্রচণ্ড, দাম্ভিক, কুসাহসী, ভয়ানক, রাগান্ব, দুঃসহ্য, উগ্র, তীব্র, bold, confident, presuming, headstrong, fierce, terrible, furious, violent, passionate, intolerable, insupportable, acrid, pungent, hot.

প্রচরদ্রূপ, সামান্য, সর্ব্বত্র চলিত, প্রসিদ্ধ, common, vulgar, popular, public, notorious.

প্রচলন, সচেষ্টতা, প্রসিদ্ধি, activity, alertness, currency, notoriety.

প্রচলিত, প্রসিদ্ধ, ব্যবহার্য্য, প্রবর্ত্তিত, current, notorious, common, customary, moved, stimulated.

প্রচার, প্রসিদ্ধি, প্রকাশ, ঘোষণা, গবাদি পালন, notoriety, commonness, publicity, a publication, declaration, manifestation, the grazing or tending of cattle.

প্রচুর, ভূরি, অতিশয়, যথেষ্ট, much, many, ample, abundant, sufficient.

প্রচ্ছক, প্রশ্নকর্ত্তা, জিজ্ঞাসক, one who asks or proposes a question.

প্রচ্ছন্ন, আচ্ছাদিত, গুপ্ত, covered, concealed, disguised, secret, clandestine, retired, private.

প্রচ্ছাদন, আবরণ, ঢাকন, to screen, conceal, cover, hide.

প্রজা, রাজাধিকারস্থ লোক, বশীভূত, ভাড়াটিয়া, কৃষিবল, সন্ততি, জন, ব্যক্তি, people, subjects, dependants, land tenants, peasants, off-pring, a person, individual.

প্রজাপতি, ব্রহ্মা প্রভৃতি, বিশ্বকর্ম্মা, রাজা, জামাতা, পক্ষাবতী, Brahmá, or his ten sons, Vishwa Karmá, a king, a a prince, a son-in-law, a butterfly.

প্রজ্বলন, উদ্দীপন, পুড়ন, দহন, to blaze, take fire, burn.

প্রজ্ঞ, প্রজ্ঞাবান্,—পণ্ডিত, প্রবীণ, নিপুণ, learned, intelligent, wise, sensible, clever.

প্রজ্ঞপ্ত, মিলনের স্থিরকরা, সঙ্কেত, an assignation, appointment, sign, token, hint.

প্রজ্ঞা, বুদ্ধি, সরস্বতী, intelligence, understanding, Saraswatí.

প্রণত, পাদপতিত, নম্র, নমস্কারী, prostrate, humble, bending, inclined. [tion, prostration.

প্রণতি, প্রণাম,—নমস্কার, প্রণিপাত, a bow, obeisance, saluta-

প্রণব, বেদের আদি বীজ, ওঁকার, the mystic syllable Om.

প্রণয়, প্রেম, অনুরাগ, আত্মীয়তা, পরিচয়, মেল, সন্ধি, love, affection, fondness, regard, friendship, intimacy, familiarity, acquaintance, concord, union, agreement, peace. [timate.

প্রণয়ী, অনুরাগী, আত্মীয়, affectionate, fond, friendly, in-

প্রণষ্ট, ধ্বস্ত, ruined, spoiled, lost. [pectful.

প্রণামী, নমস্কারী, মর্য্যাদক, bowing, saluting, prostrate, res-

প্রণালিকা, নাড়ী, শিরা, ধমনী, নল, নর্দমা, a tube, tubular vessel, vein, a water-pipe, a conduit.

প্রণালী, জুলী, আনুপূর্ব্বী, রীতি, ধারাগতি, a water-course, drain, issue from a pond, a continued series, a habit, custom, the course or stream of custom.

প্রণাশ, ধ্বংস, উৎখাত, ক্ষতি, destruction, perdition, ruin, loss.

প্রণিধান, মনোযোগ, অবগতি, ধ্যান, উদ্যোগ, ব্যগ্রতা, অভিলষিত, প্রবেশ, attention, fixed thought, deep meditation, effort, stress, energy, regard, an object of desire, access, entrance.

প্রণিধি, প্রার্থনা, নিয়ম, স্থান, চর, a request, solicitation, engagement, agreement, a place, situation, a spy, an emissary. [rence, prostration.

প্রণিপাত, নমস্কার, দণ্ডবৎ প্রণাম, a salutation, obeisance, reve-

প্রণিহিত, সমর্পিত, গচ্ছিত, স্থাপিত, প্রাপ্ত, স্বীকৃত, নিষ্পন্ন, delivered, consigned, entrusted, placed, fixed, deposited, obtained, received, acquired, acknowledged, decided, settled, determined.

প্রণীত, সংস্কৃতাগ্নি, পক্ক মাংসাদি, কৃত, রচিত, প্রেরিত, ক্ষিপ্ত, প্রবিষ্ট, consecrated fire, cooked, dressed, made, done, constructed, composed, sent, thrown, entered, approached. [docile, tractable.

প্রণেয়, প্রণয়পাত্র, বশতাপন্ন, amiable, agreeable, submissive,

প্রতাপ, প্রাখর্য্য, তেজ, শৌর্য্য, অভিমান, মহিমা, উষ্মা, রৌদ্র, প্রভা, ardor, zeal, courage, high spirit, jealousy of rank or power, dignity, majesty, power, heat, warmth, splendour.

প্রতারক, বঞ্চক, ধূর্ত্ত, ভুলানিয়া, খল, cajoling, insidious, perfidious; a deceiver, imposter, cheat, knave.

প্রতারণা, বঞ্চনা, ছল, deceit, imposture, fraud, imposition, trick.

[reached.

প্রতারিত, বঞ্চিত, ভুলান, deceived, cajoled, deluded, over-

প্রতি, একং, সকল, ফের, উপর ইত্যাদি, every, each; *a prefix*: back, again, to, at, towards, with, against.

প্রতিকার, হিতাহিতপরিশোধ, উৎপন্ন, উপায়, উপশম, নিবারণ, return of a kindness, retaliation, revenge, an effect, result, remedy, preventive, alleviation, resistance.

প্রতিকূল, বিমুখ, বিরুদ্ধ, প্রতিবন্ধক, বিপরীত, ব্যতিক্রান্ত, অনিষ্ট, adverse, opposed to, contrary, opposite, reverse, inverted, contrary to one's wishes.

প্রতিকৃতি, অপকার ও উপকারের পরিশোধ, নিবারণ, প্রতিমা, আভা, ছায়া, ছবি, উপাসনা, a return of kindness, &c. revenge, retaliation, resistance, an effigy, figure, image, reflected image, reflection, shadow, picture, reverence, worship.

প্রতিক্ষিপ্ত, ছাড়া, প্রেরিত, বিবর্জ্জিত, নিবারিত, নিন্দিত, dismissed, sent, despatched, rejected, repelled, opposed, resisted, calumniated.

[wards.

প্রতিগত, এদিগ্ ওদিগ্ উড্ডীয়মান, flying backwards and for-

প্রতিগমন, বা চলন,—বাহুড়ন, হটন, to return, to come or go back, to retrograde.

প্রতিগ্রহ, প্রতিগ্রাহ,—নিষ্ঠীবাধার, a spitting pot.

প্রতিগ্রহ-ণ, আদান, দানগ্রহণ, স্বীকার, সম্মতি, a receiving, acceptance, the receiving of gifts by a brahmin, the gift itself, assent, approbation, consent.

প্রতিঘাত, মারণ, হনন, নিবারণ, মারণ পরিবর্ত্তে মারণ, a smiting, killing, resistance, opposition, a back stroke, a blow given in return.

প্রতিচ্ছায়া, প্রতিবিম্ব, প্রতিমা, a reflected image, shadow, shade, image, picture; statue, impression, facsimile.

প্রতিচ্ছেদ, বৈপরীত্য, প্রতিযোগ, opposition, traversing.

প্রতিজঙ্ঘা উরুর অগ্রভাগ, the fore part of the thigh.

প্রতিজ্ঞা, নিয়ম, স্বীকার, নিশ্চয়কথা, প্রমাণ, সাক্ষ্য, পণ, a promise, engagement, assent, agreement, an admission, acknowledgement, declaration, a testimony, deposition, law-plaint, a wager, a bet.

প্রতিজ্ঞাত, নিয়ত, অঙ্গীকৃত, নিশ্চয়কথিত, promised, engaged, deposed to, affirmed, declared, &c. [missory note.

প্রতিজ্ঞাপত্র, নিয়মলিপি, টীপ, a written engagement, bond, pro-

প্রতিজ্ঞাপন, কহান, to cause or oblige to declare, promise, &c.

প্রতিতাল, কুঁজী, তালাকাঠী, a key, a picklock. [by a look.

প্রতিদর্শন, দৃষ্টিপাতের পরিবর্ত্তে দর্শন, to return a look or a word

প্রতিদান ফিরিয়া দেওয়া, দানের পরিবর্ত্তে দান, প্রতিফল, বিনিময়, a giving back, return, recompense, exchange.

প্রতিদাপন, ফিরিয়া দেওয়ান, to cause to give back or return.

প্রতিদেয়, পুনর্দাতব্য, বন্ধক, subject to be returned; a pledge, a pawn. [verberation.

প্রতিধ্বনি, প্রত্যাগত শব্দ, শব্দজনিত শব্দ, an echo, re-echoing, re-

প্রতিনপ্তা, প্রপৌত্র, a great grandson, son's grandson.

প্রতিনিধি, পরিবর্ত্তী, বিনিময়, a substitute, representative, deputy, attorney, exchange, commutation.

প্রতিন্যাস, পরস্পর আধীকরা, a mutual deposit.

প্রতিপক্ষ, শত্রু, বিপরীত, বিরুদ্ধ বাক্য, an enemy, adversary, opponent, a contrary proposition

প্রতিপৎ, প্রতিপদ,—পক্ষের আদি তিথি, the first day of the moon's increase or wane.

প্রতিপত্তি, প্রাপ্তি, লাভ, কর্ম্মসিদ্ধি, বৃদ্ধি, সম্ভ্রম, সুখ্যাতি, নিশ্চয় জ্ঞান, সম্মতি, স্বীকার, প্রবোধ, পরিচয়, acquisition, acquirement, success, accomplishment of an object, advancement, promotion, fame, reputation, knowledge, certainty, ascertainment, demonstration, assent, acknowledgement, conviction, acquaintance with.

প্রতিপন্ন, সম্পাদিত, প্রস্তুত, প্রমাণসিদ্ধ, নিশ্চিত, প্রাপ্ত, অবগত, সম্ভ্রান্ত, effected, accomplished, proved, demonstrated, obtained, known, promoted, advanced.

প্রতিপাদন, বুঝান, জানান, বিজ্ঞাপন, ফলপ্রাপণ, সাধন, to demonstrate, ascertain, cause to acknowledge, to promote, give success to, effect, accomplish.

প্রতিপাদ্য, জ্ঞাতব্য, শব্দের অর্থ, ascertainable, &c; the meaning of a word.

প্রতিপালক, রক্ষক, পোষ্টা, protecting &c; a protector, provider, [benefactor.

প্রতিপালন, পোষণ, লোকের উপকার করণ, রক্ষণ, মানন. to nourish, provide for, support, preserve, succour, protect, observe, keep, fulfil.

প্রতিপ্রসব, নিষেধ ব্যতিরিক্ত অনুমতি বাক্য, a particular exception to a general prohibition.

প্রতিফল, বেতনাদি, সমুচিত শাস্তি, পরিশোধ, a reward, remuneration, punishment, retribution, retaliation.

প্রতিবচঃ, প্রতিবচন,—উত্তর, প্রতিধ্বনি, an answer, reply, echo.

প্রতিবন্ধ, বিঘ্ন, নিষেধ, নিবারণ, an obstacle, impediment, hindrance, resistance.

প্রতিবন্ধন, বাধন, নিবারণ, আটকান, to hinder, oppose, resist. [obstruct, impede.

প্রতিবল, সমবিক্রম, সমর্থ, বলবান্, of equal might or power, able, adequate, powerful.

প্রতিবাক্য, উত্তর, an answer, a reply.

প্রতিবাদ, উত্তর, বিরোধ, আপত্তি, a reply, answer, defence in law, litigation, a remonstrance.

প্রতিবাদী, উত্তরবাদী, বিরোধী, a defendant, respondent, pleader, [litigant.

প্রতিবাধী, প্রতিবাধক,—নিবারক, বিপক্ষ, দায়ী, resisting, opposing, preventing; an opponent, a defendant.

প্রতিবাসী, নিকটবাসী, পড়সী, neighbouring; a neighbour.

প্রতিবিম্ব, প্রতিমা, আভা, ছায়া, অনুরূপ, a reflected image, reflexion, shadow, image, picture, resemblance, counterpart.

প্রতিবিম্বিত, দৃষ্টান্তীকৃত, উপমিত, খুদিত, reflected, shadowed out, [carved.

প্রতিবীক্ষণ, কথকের প্রতি আলোকন, ফিরিয়া দেখন, to look at the speaker, return a look.

প্রতিবোধ, বিরুদ্ধানুমান, অনুভব, an opposite notion, a reflected [idea.

প্রতিবোধন, অন্যথা বুঝন, অনুধাবন, to think differently, to gather ideas from reflexion.

প্রতিবোধী, প্রতিবোধক,—বিবেচক, ধ্যাতা, অনুসূচক, বিপরীত, receiving or giving ideas from reflection, opposing.

প্রতিভা, বুদ্ধি, জ্ঞান, দীপ্তি, তেজ, প্রভাব, প্রাগল্ভ্য, understanding, intellect, wit, a conception, idea, light, reflected light, splendour, dignity, audacity, boldness, confidence, impudence.

প্রতিভান্বিত, প্রজ্ঞ, বুদ্ধিমান, প্রগল্ভ, মহৎ, গৌরবযুক্ত, দর্পিত, witty, intelligent, wise, bold, confident, impudent, dignified, arrogant, proud, haughty.

প্রতিভাষ, উত্তর, প্রত্যুত্তর, an answer, reply, defence.

প্রতিভূ, লগ্নক, a surety, security, bondsman, bail.

প্রতিমা-ন, প্রতিবিম্ব, ছবি, পুত্তলী, a reflected image, an image, likeness, picture, an idol.

প্রতিমূর্ত্তি, আকার, ছবি, অনুরূপ, পুত্তলী, প্রতিনিধি, পরিবর্ত্তী, প্রতিলিপি, a likeness, resemblance, picture, image, a deputy, representative, a transcript.

প্রতিযত্ন, উদ্যোগ, চেষ্টা, বাঞ্ছা, নিবারণ, প্রতিকৃতি, বোধ, বশীকরণ, সদাচারী, চালাক, বহুশ্রমী, নিবারক, প্রতিকারক, strenuous exertion, endeavour, wish, desire, resistance, retaliation, revenge, comprehension, a taking captive; acting right, acquiring new virtues, accomplishments, &c: active, diligent, strenuous, resisting, retaliating, revenging.

প্রতিযোগ, বিপর্য্যয়, অনুরূপ, অনুকূলতা, opposition, resistance, counteraction, a counterpart, co-operation.

প্রতিযোগী, সহকারী, অনুরূপ, বিরুদ্ধ, সাথী, তুল্যশক্তিমান, এককর্ম্মাভিলাষী, co-operating, answering to, counteracting; a co-adjutor, partner, second self, competitor.

প্রতিরব, শব্দ জনিত শব্দ, উত্তর, an echo, reverberation, reply.

প্রতিরূপ, প্রতিমা, প্রতিনিধি, an image, likeness, representation, a substitute, representative.

প্রতিরূপ-ক, সদৃশ, তুল্য, পরিবর্ত্তী, প্রতিনিধি, like, resembling, substituted, representative.

প্রতিরোধ-ন, বাধা, নগরাদি বেষ্টন, নিবারণ, নিষেধ, a blocking up, obstructing, besieging, repelling, opposition, prohibition.

প্রতিলিপি, উত্তরপত্র, অনুরূপ লেখা, a written reply, a transcript, a copy, counterpart.

প্রতিলোম, ব্যতিক্রান্ত, উল্টা, বিপরীত, অধম, দুষ্ট, ব্যুৎক্রম, ব্যত্যয়, reverse, inverted, contrary to the natural course or order, against the hair or grain, low, vile, base, depraved; an inverted order, &c.

প্রতিলোমজ, উত্তমা স্ত্রীতে অধমকর্ত্তৃকজাত, born of a woman of high by a man of low cast.

প্রতিশ্যায়, কফ, শ্লেষ্ম, a catarrh, a cold.

প্রতিশ্রব, সম্মতি, প্রতিজ্ঞা, স্বীকার, an assent, engagement, promise.

প্রতিশ্রুত, স্বীকৃত, নিয়মিত, promised, assented or agreed to, accepted, engaged by promise.

প্রতিষিদ্ধ, বারিত, অস্বীকৃত, অপহ্নুত, forbidden, prohibited, denied.

প্রতিষেধ, বারণকরা, অস্বীকার, অপহ্নব, পরিত্যাগ, a prohibition, forbidding, denial, rejection.

প্রতিষ্ঠা, সুখ্যাতি, সম্মতি, প্রশংসা, গুণানুবাদ, দেবমূর্ত্ত্যাদি স্থাপনকরা, যৌতুক দানকরা, উদ্যাপন, fame, renown, celebrity, reputation, approbation, commendation, consecration of an image, endowment of a temple &c. the portioning of a daughter, completion of a vow or ceremonial, &c.

প্রতিষ্ঠিত, সুখ্যাত্যাপন্ন, সংস্থাপিত, ধনবান্, famous, renowned, celebrated, applauded, consecrated, honourable, wealthy, endowed.

প্রতিসীরা, পটনির্ম্মিত আড়াল, কাণাৎ, যবনিকা, a cloth skreen, the outer curtains of a tent.

প্রতিসূর্য্য, কৃকলাস, কাঁকলাস, a chamelion, a lizard.

প্রতিস্পান্দন, স্পান্দনোৎপাদকানুযায়ী স্পান্দন, a vibration answering to an exciting cause.

প্রতিহত, রোধিত, নিবারিত, প্রহারিত, হত, নষ্ট, মারণের পরিবর্ত্তে মারিত, opposed, resisted, struck, hurt, killed, destroyed, spoiled, reflected back, smitten in return.

প্রতিহনন, প্রহার পরিবর্ত্তে মারণ, বারণকরা, ঘাতন, to return a blow, resist, strike, kill.

প্রতিহন্তা, বিপক্ষ, বিরোদ্ধা, an opponent in conflict, a resister, obstructer, hinderer.

প্রতিহিংসা, বৈর, অন্যায়জনিত দ্বেষ, revenge taken for an injury received, retaliation.

প্রতীক, অবয়ব, অঙ্গ, a limb, a member, a part.

প্রতীকার, প্রতিফল, পরিশোধ, উপায়, উপশম, উৎপন্ন, তপস, a return, recompense, retaliation, remedy, medicine, the effect of a medicinal remedy, alleviation of disease, a result, penance.

প্রতীকার্য্য, পরিশোধনীয়, যাহার উপায় আছে, demanding revenge or retaliation, remediable, curable.

প্রতীক্ষণ, হেরণ, চাহন, অপেক্ষণ, to regard, look upon, wait for, expect.

প্রতীক্ষা, অপেক্ষা, অন্যের প্রত্যাশা, expectation, a waiting or looking for.

প্রতীচী, পশ্চিম দিক্, the west.

প্রতীত, সুখ্যাত্যাপন্ন, সম্ভ্রান্ত, অবগত, হর্ষিত, গত, famed, renowned, celebrated, venerated, known, understood, glad, delighted, gone, past.

প্রতীতি, সুখ্যাতি, প্রতায়, নিশ্চয় জ্ঞান, fame, renown, notoriety, knowledge.

প্রতীয়মান, বিশ্বাসার্থ, সম্মত, স্বীকৃত, believed, admitted, allowed.

প্রতুল, বাহুল্য, সম্পত্তি, বৃদ্ধি, abundance, wealth, prosperity.

প্রতোদ, পাঁচনীবাড়ী, তাড়ন দণ্ড, a goad, whip, switch, cane.

প্রত্ত, দত্ত, ত্যক্ত, given, presented, bestowed.

প্রত্তা, বাগ্দত্তা, বিবাহদত্তা, *f.* betrothed, given in marriage.

প্রত্যক্, পশ্চিম, পর, অনুসর, ক্রমাগত, western, subsequent, successive, following in regular order.

প্রত্যক্ষ, ইন্দ্রিয়গোচর, স্পষ্ট, ব্যক্ত, সাক্ষাৎকার, পুরস্ত, perceptible to the senses, sensible, visible, clear, plain, evident, obvious, before the eyes, present.

প্রত্যক্ষতঃ, স্পষ্টরূপে, চক্ষুগোচরে, evidently, clearly, sensibly.

প্রত্যক্ষদর্শন, সাক্ষী, an eye-witness.

প্রত্যক্ষপ্রমাণ, ইন্দ্রিয়প্রমাণ, জ্ঞানেন্দ্রিয়, the evidence of the senses, the organs of sense.

প্রত্যক্ষর, এক২ অক্ষর, প্রতিবর্ণ, ঠিক, every letter, literally.

প্রত্যক্ষসিদ্ধ, ইন্দ্রিয়প্রমাণবোধিত, proved or established by the evidence of the senses, palpable.

প্রত্যঙ্গ, জ্ঞানেন্দ্রিয়, অন্তিমাবয়ব, এক২ অঙ্গ, an organ of perception, the extremities, every part.

প্রত্যন্ত, অন্তিক, ম্লেচ্ছদেশ, contiguous, bordering; the country of Mlechchhas.

প্রত্যবস্কন্দন, বিশেষ উত্তর, আপত্তি, a special plea in law, an excuse.

প্রত্যবায়, পাপ, বিয়োগ, sin, separation.

প্রত্যভিজ্ঞা-ন, জ্ঞান, অনুবোধ, স্মরণ, অনুমান, knowledge, recollection, recognition, an idea arising from reflection.

প্রত্যভিযোগ, বিরোধবাক্যের উত্তরবাক্য, প্রত্যপবাদ, a counter-plea, counter-accusation.

প্রত্যয়, বিশ্বাস, আশা, জ্ঞান, বোধ, রীতি, ব্যবহার, সুখ্যাতি, বিভক্তি, হেতু, প্রয়োজন, belief, faith, credit, confidence, trust, knowledge, apprehension, usage, practice, fame, celebrity, the termination of a word, a cause, motive.

প্রত্যয়িত, বিশ্বসিত, বিশ্বাসপাত্র, believed, confided in, trusted.

প্রত্যয়ী, বিশ্বাসী, শ্রদ্ধাকারী, trusting, believing, trusty, faithful; a believer.

প্রত্যর্থী, প্রতিবাদী, শত্রু, a defendant *in law*, an enemy.

প্রত্যর্পণ, ফিরিয়া দেওন, to restore, return, deliver back.

প্রত্যহ, প্রতিদিন, দিনে২, daily, every day, day by day.

প্রত্যাকর্ষণ, হঠান, উল্টিয়া টানন, to draw back or pull in a contrary direction.

প্রত্যাখ্যান, বিবর্জ্জনা, অস্বীকার, ছাড়িয়া দেওয়া, খণ্ডনা, rejection, disregard, denial, refusal, disallowing, dismissal, refutation, disannulling.

প্রত্যাগমন, পুনরাগমন, বাহুড়ন, a return, turning or coming back.

প্রত্যাদান, পুনর্গ্রহণ, প্রতিফল দেওয়া, resumption, taking back, retaliation.

প্রত্যাদিষ্ট, দেবোক্ত, প্রচারিত, পরামৃষ্ট, spoken by an oracle, published, warned.

প্রত্যাদেশ, দেবতার উপদেশ, দৈববাণী, প্রকাশ, পরামর্শ, অনুমতি, চেতনা, an oracular saying, divine warning, impulse, revelation, information, warning, caution.

প্রত্যারম্ভ, পুনরোপক্রম, a recommencement.

প্রত্যাশা, ভরসা, প্রত্যয়, অপেক্ষা, hope, trust, confidence, encouragement, expectation.

প্রত্যাশী, ভরসান্বিত, অপেক্ষী, অধীন, hoping, expecting, waiting or looking for, dependant.

প্রত্যাসন্ন, নিকটবর্ত্তী, অন্তিক, near, contiguous, proximate.
প্রত্যাহার, পুনর্গ্রহ, সমাধি, যোগ বিশেষ, ইন্দ্রিয় দমন, সংক্ষেপ, উদাহরণ, resumption, collecting the thoughts, abstraction, restraint and mortification of the senses, an abridgement, compendium, paradigm.
প্রত্যুক্তি, প্রত্যুত্তর,—প্রতিবচন, a reply, rejoinder, answer, defence.
প্রত্যুত, সম্প্রতি, স্পষ্টে, সাক্ষাতে, now, now-a-days, evidently, [before the eyes.
প্রত্যুত্থান, উঠিয়া সম্মানকরা, অভ্যর্থনা, a respectful reception, a rising up to receive one.
প্রত্যুৎপন্ন, পুনর্জ্জনিত, উদ্যত, প্রস্তুত, অঙ্কপূর্ণিত, reproduced, prompt, ready ; the product in multiplication.
প্রত্যুপকার, উপকারের পরিবর্ত্তে উপকার, কৃতজ্ঞতা, a return of kindness, gratitude, grateful return.
প্রত্যুষ, অহর্মুখ, প্রাতঃকাল, the dawn, day-break, morning [twilight.
প্রত্যূহ, বিঘ্ন, আটক, an obstacle, impediment, hindrance.
প্রত্যেক, এক এক, সর্ব্ব, সমস্ত, every one, each, every.
প্রত্যেতব্য, বিশ্বসনীয়, credible, worthy of credit or belief.
প্রথম, আদি, পূর্ব্ব, প্রধান, first, prior, previous, chief, principal.
প্রথমতঃ, প্রথমে,—পূর্ব্বে, আগে, in the first place, previously.
প্রথমাবয়ব, প্রথমোৎপন্নাংশ,—গর্ভ, ভ্রূণ, an embryo, a fœtus.
প্রথা, ধারা, ব্যবহার, সুখ্যাতি, custom, usage, habit, fame, celebrity.
প্রথিত, বিখ্যাত, প্রতিষ্ঠান্বিত, famous, celebrated, illustrious, [important.
প্রদ, দাতা, দায়ক, ফলদ, *affix :* giving, bestowing, conferring, yielding.
প্রদক্ষিণ, মণ্ডলাকারে ভ্রমণকরা বিশেষ, the ceremony of walking round a person or object, keeping the right hand towards it, as a reverent salutation.
প্রদত্ত, প্রত্ত, অর্পিত, উৎসর্জ্জিত, given, conferred, bestowed.
প্রদশ্ব, স্পষ্ট, ব্যক্ত, প্রসিদ্ধ, প্রত্যক্ষ, বিখ্যাত, clear, manifest, evident, elucidated, illustrious.
প্রদর্শন, দেখন, হেরণ, দেখান, জানান, to see, view, shew, make known, declare, point out, manifest.
প্রদর্শনী, উৎসর্গ, উপঢৌকন, বৈদ্যের পারিতোষিক, an offering, ceremonial present, medical fee.

প্রদান, ত্যাগ, বিতরণ, অর্পণ, উৎসর্গ, a gift, donation, the act of giving, offering, &c.

প্রদীপ, বর্ত্তি, পদীম, a lamp, light, lantern, taper, &c.

প্রদীপন, উজ্জ্বলন, উদ্দীপন, to make to blaze, stir or light up, cause to burn brighter, make splendid, &c.

প্রদৃপ্ত, অহঙ্কৃত, গর্ব্বিত, proud, haughty, elated.

প্রদেশ, অঞ্চল, চাকলা, স্থল, অংশ, a district, country, spot, place, part.

প্রদেশিনী, তর্জ্জনী, the fore-finger. [of the night.

প্রদোষ, রজনীমুখ, সূর্য্যাস্তের পর দ্বিমুহূর্ত্ত, evening, the first part

প্রধন, যুদ্ধ, চিরণ, war, battle, a tearing, a rending.

প্রধান, শ্রেষ্ঠ, বড়, principal, pre-eminent, chief, noble.

প্রপঞ্চ, ফেরা, বৈপরীত্য, প্রকাশ, প্রসার, বিস্তার, বাহুল্য, সঞ্চয়, প্রতারণা. a reverse, inversion, opposition, extension, expansion, dilation, extent, expanse, prolixity, copiousness of style, abundance, quantity, a heap, delusion, a trick, deceit.

প্রপঞ্চিত, প্রসারিত, বিস্তারিত, expanded, dilated, prolix, treated of at length, &c.

প্রপন্ন, প্রাপ্ত, দরিদ্র, দুঃখী, obtained, poor, needy, afflicted.

প্রপা, জলছত্র, a place where water is given to travellers.

প্রপিতামহ, পিতামহের পিতা, a paternal great-grandfather.

প্রপৌত্র, পৌত্রের পুত্র, a great-grandson in the male line.

প্রফুল্ল, বিকশিত, আহ্লাদিত, আশ্বাসিত, blown, expanded, cheerful, gay, smiling, sparkling, glad, encouraged.

প্রফুল্লিত, প্রস্ফুটিত, মুকুলিত, আমোদিত, expanded, spread, open, blown, in blossom, gay, cheerful.

প্রবক্তা, কথক, বাক্‌পটু, a speaker, an eloquent man.

প্রবচন, প্রসঙ্গ, বাক্‌পটুতা, a treatise, discourse, eloquence.

প্রবঞ্চক, ভুলানিয়া, প্রতারক, ধূর্ত্ত, deceiving, insidious; a deceiver, a cheat. [imposture.

প্রবঞ্চনা, প্রতারণা, ছলনা, deceit, fraud, swindling, imposition,

প্রবন্ধ, আনুপূর্ব্বিক বাক্যরচনা, বিবরণ, a connected discourse, treatise, narrative, tale. [cent.

প্রবর, গোত্রশ্রেণীর কারণ মুনিগণ, race, family, kindred, des-

প্রবর্ত্ত, অনুষ্ঠান, চেতানি, অনুষ্ঠাপক, উদ্যত, নিযুক্ত, a commencement, undertaking, an entering upon a business, excitation; entering upon, ready, appointed to, constituted. [tor, stimulus.

প্রবর্ত্তক, প্রয়োজক, চেতনা, exciting, stimulating; an instiga-

প্রবর্ত্তন, আরম্ভণ, উপক্রমণ, কর্ম্মেতে লাগন, to begin, commence, embark in, enter upon a work or action.

প্রবর্ত্তনা, চেতানি, প্রয়োজনা, a stimulating, exciting, instigation, subornation.

প্রবর্দ্ধন, বাড়ন, to grow in size, grow fat or wealthy.

প্রবল, বলবান্, জয়ী, অখণ্ডনীয়, প্রচণ্ড, অবাধ্য, strong, powerful, superior, victorious, cogent, valid, substantial, violent, obstinate. [man.

প্রবলা, ব্যাপিকা, a termagant, violent and self-willed wo-

প্রবাচক, অর্থবোধক, পারিভাষিক, explanatory, expository, significant, technical.

প্রবাদ, জনরব, a rumour, report, insinuation, current story.

প্রবাল, পলা, অঙ্কুর, coral, a sprout, a young shoot.

প্রবাস, বিদেশবাস, অবস্থিতি, a temporary or foreign residence, lodging, sojourn. [resident.

প্রবাসী, পর্য্যটক, বিদেশবাসী, a traveller, sojourner, temporary

প্রবাহ, স্রোত, ঘটনাক্রম, ধারা, সময় বিকার, গবাদির শ্রেণী, a stream, current, flow, course, train of circumstances, traditional custom, immemorial usage, the variations of weather, a moving line of cattle &c.

প্রবাহক, চালক, চলমিয়া, দ্রুত, carrying or flowing off, flowing.

প্রবিষ্ট, উপক্রান্ত, কর্ম্মারব্ধ, অবগত, ব্যাপক, ঘুষড়া, entered into or upon, embarked or engaged in, understanding, pervading, thrust into.

প্রবীণ, নিপুণ, পটু, বিজ্ঞ, পণ্ডিত, clever, skilled, conversant, eminent, learned.

প্রবুদ্ধ, নিদ্রোত্থিত, জাগ্রৎ, চিয়ন্ত, জ্ঞাত, পরিজ্ঞাপিত, awake, wakened, vigilant, roused, stimulated, comprehending, convinced, convicted.

প্রবৃত্ত, প্রবিষ্ট, আরব্ধ, উদ্যত, having commenced or engaged in, beginning, about.

প্রবৃত্তি, উপক্রম, উদ্যোগ, ইচ্ছা, প্রয়োজনা, শীলতা, চেতনা, উত্তেজনা,

বৃত্তান্ত, সমাচার, স্রোতঃ, a commencement, entering upon, effort, inclination, tendency, predilection, excitation, excitement, stimulus, instigation, urging, intelligence, a current, course.

প্রবেশ, অন্তরে গমন, অনুষ্ঠান, প্রতিযত্ন, অধ্যবসায়, an entrance, introduction, commencement, intense application or devotion to, persevering adherence in. [a pursuit, &c.

প্রবেশন, ঢোকন, সুবড়ন, প্রবর্ত্তন, to enter, penetrate, enter into

প্রবোদ্ধা, বুঝানিয়া, চেতানিয়া, পরিজ্ঞাপক, one who convinces, awakens or excites attention.

প্রবোধ, পরিজ্ঞান, সান্ত্বনা, জ্ঞান, বুদ্ধি, জাগ্রদ্দশা, চেতনা, conviction, demonstration, a soothing, quieting, appeasing, persuasion, knowledge, understanding, intellect, wakefulness, vigilance, attention.

প্রবোধক, প্রবোধী—পরিজ্ঞাপক, চেতানিয়া, জাগানিয়া, convincing, calling forth ideas, arresting attention, awakening, exciting to vigilance. [ments.

প্রবোধন, প্রমাণ জানান, বুঝান, to convince, push with argu-

প্রব্রজিত, তীর্থগত, gone on a pilgrimage.

প্রব্রজ্যা, তীর্থবেড়ানিয়া, উদাসীন, a pilgrim, an ascetic, a travelling or mendicant devotee.

প্রভব, উৎপত্তি, জন্মভূমি, মূল, জন্মকারণ, পিত্রাদি, birth, production, a birth-place, source, the generative cause or basis of a thing, an operative cause of existence as father or mother.

প্রভা, দীপ্তি, তেজ, light, radiance, splendour, lustre, glory.

প্রভাকর, সূর্য্য, চন্দ্র, দীপ্তিমান, জাজ্বল্যমান, the sun, the moon; splendid, radiant. [dawn.

প্রভাত, প্রাতঃকাল, অরুণ, প্রত্যূষ, morning, day-break, the

প্রভাব, মাহাত্ম্য, গৌরব, পরাক্রম, প্রতাপ, majesty, dignity, greatness, power, magnanimity, high spirit, a high and jealous sense of honour.

প্রভাস, তীর্থবিশেষ, a celebrated place of pilgrimage.

প্রভিন্ন, পৃথক্, ইতর, অন্য, বিছিন্ন, খণ্ডিত, distinct, different, separated, severed, divided, broken.

প্রভু, স্বামী, অধিপতি, কর্ত্তা, রাজা, দেশাধিপ, a master, owner, lord, governor, sovereign.
প্রভুতা, প্রধানতা, রাজত্ব, আধিপত্য, কর্ত্তৃত্ব, greatness, power, supremacy, sway, government, lordship, sovereignty, dominion.
প্রভুপণা, কর্ত্তৃত্ব, স্বামিত্বপ্রকাশ, lordship &c : a playing the lord and master. [voted, obsequious.
প্রভুভক্ত, অন্নদাতার ভজিষ্ণু, অনুগত, আজ্ঞাবহ, loyal, faithful, de-
প্রভূত, বহু, ভূরি, ভারী, বড়, উচ্চ, উর্দ্ধগত, শাসিত, রাজপালিত, প্রধানীকৃত, much, many, important, great, high, lofty, gone up, ascended, governed by a sovereign, ruled, become great. [the like.
প্রভৃতি, গণবোধক, ইত্যাদি, *affix* : et cetera, and others, and
প্রভেদ, বিশেষ, বৈলক্ষণ্য, অসাম্য, বিচ্ছেদ, পার্থক্য, বিবেক, পদবী, অপনাম, a difference, distinction, disparity, inequality, separation, a severing, discriminating, a surname, a nick-name.
প্রমত্ত, উল্লসিত, মদবিহ্বল, বিভোল, অবিবেকী, elated, joyful, intoxicated, thoughtless, precipitate.
প্রমদ, হর্ষ, উল্লাস, joy, delight, pleasure, rapture.
প্রমদা, বিশেষ লক্ষণাক্রান্তা স্ত্রী a beautiful woman.
প্রমা, সুবোধ, সত্যের অনুভব, মনস্কার, ব্রহ্মজ্ঞান, true knowledge, accurate perception, consciousness, a knowledge of the soul's identity with God.
প্রমাণ, নিশ্চয়ের কারণ, সাক্ষ্য, নিদর্শন, প্রতিপত্তি, দৃষ্টান্ত, উদাহরণ, সাক্ষী, evidence, proof, testimony, attestation, demonstration, authority or warrant for an opinion, an instance, example, a witness.
প্রমাণপত্র, নিদর্শনপত্র, সুকৃতিপত্র, a voucher, an affidavit, a deposition. [proof.
প্রমাতা, প্রমাণদায়ী, সাক্ষ্যদায়ক, one who gives evidence or
প্রমাতামহ-ী, মাতামহের পিতামাতা, *m.* & *f.* a maternal great grandfather or great grandmother.
প্রমাদ, অনবধানতা, ভ্রম, চুক, উক্তুল, উপদ্রব, আপদ, inadvertence, carelessness, precipitation, error, confusion, ruin, misfortune.

প্রমাদী, অসাবধান, অবিবেকী, উন্মত্ত, উপদ্রবী careless, inattentive, inadvertent, thoughtless, mad, ruinous.
প্রমায়ক, প্রমাণদায়ী, সাক্ষী, giving proof or evidence, testifying.
প্রমিত, প্রমাণসিদ্ধ, সপ্রমাণ, proved, established, authentic.
প্রমীত, মৃত, প্রেত, dead, defunct, deceased, departed.
প্রমুখাৎ, বাক্যদ্বারা, কথায়, from the mouth of, by word of mouth, verbally ; verbal.
প্রমুদিত, হর্ষিত, আহ্লাদিত, overjoyed, elated, pleased, happy.
প্রমেয়, উপপাদ্য, প্রতিপাদনীয়, প্রমাণসাধ্য, capable of proof, probable, demonstrable.
প্রমেহ, মেহবিকার, সততঃ মূত্রস্রাবাদি, urinary affection as gonorrhœa, gleet, diabetes, &c. [from.
প্রমোচন, রক্ষণ. তারণ, উদ্ধরণ, to liberate, free, save, detach
প্রমোদ. হর্ষ. উল্লাশ, great joy, delight, pleasure, happiness.
প্রমোদী, উল্লসিত, মনোরঞ্জক, elated, glad, causing delight, delightful. [austerities, &c.
প্রযত, পূত, পবিত্র, পুণ্যবান্, holy, pious, purified by religious
প্রযত্ন, অধ্যবসায়, পরিশ্রম, অতিপ্রয়াস, বহুচেষ্টা, persevering effort, great labour, exertion, care.
প্রয়াগ, তীর্থ স্থান বিশেষ, any place of pilgrimage at the confluence of two rivers, particularly Allahabad.
প্রয়াণ, গমন, চলন. প্রস্থান, চড়াও, অভিনির্যাণ, গতি, a going, departing, a march, attack, invasion, motion.
প্রয়াত, গত, প্রস্থিত, প্রেত, gone, proceeded, departed.
প্রয়াস, চেষ্টা, ইচ্ছা, শীলতা, রুচি, অনুরাগ, বহুশ্রম, অভিনিবেশ, an endeavour or desire after, bias, passion or taste for, love, diligent exertion, ardent pursuit.
প্রয়াসী, যত্নী, শ্রমান্বিত, সচেষ্ট, ইচ্ছুক, অভিলাষী, diligent, ardent, persevering, solicitous, desirous.
প্রযুক্ত, বিশিষ্ট, প্রাপ্ত, জনিত, নিমিত্ত, জন্য, endowed with, possessed of, resulting or arising from, excited or occasioned by; from, on account of, for, because of, for the sake of. [tible, &c.
প্রযুজ্য, উত্থাপনীয়, প্রবর্ত্তনীয়, capable of excitement, susceptible, &c.
প্রযুত, দশ লক্ষ, a million. [thor, exciter.
প্রয়োক্তা, প্রবৃত্তিজনক, প্রবর্ত্তক, চালানিয়া, a mover, instigator, author, exciter.

প্রয়োগ, উদ্যম, শ্রম, অনুষ্ঠান, অভিপ্রায়, শেষ, উৎপন্ন, শব্দের ভাব, বিষয়, শাস্ত্রপ্রমাণ, উদাহরণ, মূলধন, মন্ত্রোৎপন্ন, an effort, exertion, act, action, commencement, entrance upon, main object, end, result, consequence, application or use of a word, an affair, matter, text, authority, example, illustration, principal at interest, the effect of magical rites.

প্রয়োগী, উৎপাদক, প্রবর্ত্তক, প্রতিপাদক, causing, exciting, stimulating, promoting, advancing.

প্রয়োজক, চেতানিয়া, প্রবর্ত্তক, প্রেরক, আজ্ঞাপক, *id.* a mover, instigator, moving cause; sending, ordering.

প্রয়োজন, হেতু, নিমিত্ত, উদ্দেশ, অভিপ্রায়, আবশ্যকতা, ফল, বিষয়, কর্ম্ম, a cause, occasion, origin, motive, incentive, object, necessity, use, advantage, an affair, undertaking. [occasion, proper.

প্রয়োজনীয়, আবশ্যক, উপযুক্ত, উচিত, necessary, suited to the

প্রয়োজ্য, আবশ্যক, উচিত, মূলধন, প্রেরিত, necessary, suitable, proper; a capital or principal, a messenger.

প্রলপিত, কথিত, প্রকাশিত, said, spoken, mentioned, declared.

প্রলয়, কল্পান্ত, সৃষ্টিনাশ, বিনাশ, ধ্বংশ, মূর্চ্ছা, প্রাণে মরণ, পঞ্চত্ব, প্রকাণ্ড, অতিশয়, the end of a Calpa or universal destruction of the world, destruction, annihilation, dissolution, decomposition, resolution, loss, fainting, death; vast, excessive.

প্রলাপ, কথাবার্ত্তা, অনর্থক বাক্য, অজ্ঞানাবস্থাতে কথিত বাক্য, talk, conversation, unmeaning or incoherent talking, delirious ravings, &c. [herently.

প্রলাপদর্শী, বাতুল, অসঙ্গতবাদী, delirious, raving, talking inco-

প্রলাপী, সম্ভাষী, অসঙ্গতবাদী, speaking, conversing, discoursing, talking unconnectedly or deliriously.

প্রলেপ, ক্ষতাদিতে মাখনীয় দ্রব্য, a plaster, salve, ointment.

প্রলেপন, ক্ষতাদিতে প্রলেপ লাগান, মাখান, to dress a wound, apply a plaster or salve, &c. [bait.

প্রলোভ, স্পৃহা, লালসা, ঘুষ, desire, covetousness, a bribe, a

প্রশংসন, সদ্গুণ কথন, সঙ্কীর্ত্তন, স্তবকরণ, to praise, extol, panegyrize, celebrate, applaud, flatter.

প্রশংসনীয়, প্রশংস্য,—প্রতিষ্ঠার যোগ্য, স্তবার্হ, সঙ্কীর্ত্তনীয়, praiseworthy, laudable, commendable. [flattery.

প্রশংসা, শ্লাঘা, গুণানুবাদ, স্তব, praise, commendation, applause,

প্রশংসী, গুণানুবাদী, স্তাবক, praising, celebrating, applauding.

প্রশমন, বিনাশ, রোগনাশ, পাপমোচন, প্রায়শ্চিত্ত, destruction, slaughter, removal of disease, expiation of guilt.

প্রশস্ত, স্তুত, সম্মত, উত্তম, উপযুক্ত, সুখী, চৌড়া, বিস্তৃত, অসীম, praised, applauded, approved, excellent, good, suitable, fit, happy, wide, broad, spacious, capacious, roomy, airy, vast, unconfined.

প্রশুদ্ধ, প্রত্যক্ষ, স্পষ্ট, ব্যক্ত, প্রমেয়, clear, evident, authentic.

প্রশ্ন, জিজ্ঞাসা, পূর্ব্বপক্ষ, a question, enquiry, interrogation, proposition. [breath.

প্রশ্বাস, বায়ুত্যাগ, রেচন, expiration, respiration, breathing,

প্রশ্রয়, প্রণয়, স্নেহ, লালনকরা, অদমন, কোমলতা, affection, love, regard, over-indulgence, leniency.

প্রষ্টা, জিজ্ঞাসক, one who asks or interrogates, an enquirer.

প্রষ্ঠ, প্রধান, শ্রেষ্ঠ, অগ্রগামী, অধিপ, পক্ষপাতী, chief, principal, best, preceding, going first or before; a leader, chief, conductor, partizan.

প্রষ্ঠ-ণ, পত্রের এক দিগ্, পীঠ, a page of a book.

প্রসক্ত, অনুরক্ত, পরায়ণ, মনোনিবিষ্ট, প্রস্তাবিত, লব্ধ, প্রসারিত, অনবরত, নিত্য, সততঃ, attached to, enamoured, fond of, zealous, engaged in, conversed about, treated of, obtained, gained, expanded, opened, constant, eternal, everlasting; eternally, ever.

প্রসক্তি, প্রস্তাব, বৃত্তান্ত, ক্রীড়া, বাৎসল্য, অনুরাগ, a topic, subject of conversation, dalliance, fondling, tenderness, attachment, affection.

প্রসঙ্গ, বৃত্তান্ত, প্রস্তাব, প্রবন্ধ, পদ, আবাপ, সংযোগ, সম্বন্ধ, a topic, subject, introduction, mention, a treatise, a sentiment, passage from a book, an insertion, association, connection.

প্রসঙ্গসঙ্গতি, কথাবার্ত্তা, conversation, discourse on a topic.

প্রসন্ন, প্রনুগ্রাহী, কৃপান্বিত, ক্ষমাবান্, প্রফুল্ল, নির্ম্মল, স্বচ্ছ, জোকারণ্যেতে চলিত পথ, gracious, favourable, kind, complacent, propitious, pleased, delighted, clear, clean, bright, pellucid, frequented, (*as a road.*)

প্রসব, গর্ভত্যাগ, বিয়ন, জন্ম, উৎপত্তি, সন্ততি, ফল, পুষ্প, childbirth, parturition, yeaning &c. birth, production, offspring, a fruit, a flower.

প্রসবগৃহ, প্রসূতিকার ঘর, a lying-in chamber. [calve, &c.

প্রসবন, উৎপাদন, জন্মান, বিয়ন, to produce, bring forth, yean,

প্রসর, আয়াম, ওসার, প্রশ্রয়পূর্ব্বক অন্বেষণা, ত্বরা, বেগ, dimensions, extent, width, affectionate solicitation, speed, velocity. [violently.

প্রসহ্য, হঠাৎ, বলপূর্ব্বক, suddenly, unexpectedly, forcibly,

প্রসাদ, কৃপা, দয়া, অনুগ্রহপ্রকাশ, দান, বৃত্তি, পুরস্কার, উচ্ছিষ্ট, গুরু প্রভৃতির ভুক্তশেষ, প্রাণ, সুখাবস্থা, নির্ম্মলতা, স্বচ্ছতা, grace, favour, kindness, propitiousness, a gift, present, pension, reward, leavings, remnents of an offering, life, breath, welfare, clearness, brightness, cleanness, pellucidness.

প্রসাদভোগী, বৃত্তিভোগী, পুরস্কৃত, উচ্ছিষ্টভুক্, a pensioner; enjoying favours, &c. eating the remnants of offerings, &c. feeding on another's leavings.

প্রসাদিত, অনুগৃহীত, কৃপাপাত্র, কৃপয়া দত্ত, favoured, treated graciously, graciously bestowed, &c.

প্রসাদী, অনুগ্রাহক, কৃপাবান্, shewing favour, gracious, kind.

প্রসাদীবস্ত্র, পুরস্কারবস্ত্র, an honorary dress.

প্রসাধন, বিন্যাস, বেশভূষা, decoration, embellishment, dress.

প্রসাধিত, ভূষিত, সম্পন্ন, সমাপ্ত, ornamented, decorated, embellished, accomplished, finished.

প্রসার ওসার, আয়াম, বিস্তার, ভক্ষ্যদ্রব্যাদি লুট করা, প্রচার, সুখ্যাতি, width, extent, expansion, foraging, publicity, fame. [extend, spread out.

প্রসারণ, প্রস্ফোটন, প্রকাশন, বিস্তারণ, to open, expand, unfold,

প্রসিদ্ধ, প্রত্যক্ষ, ব্যক্ত, প্রচলিত, বিদিত, বিখ্যাত, ভূষিত, clear, evident, plain, current, noted, famous, celebrated, ornamented, adorned.

প্রসিদ্ধি, বিখ্যাতি, প্রচার, fame, celebrity, notoriety.

প্রসূ, মাতা, ব্যাপিকা লতা, a mother, a spreading creeper.

প্রসূত, জাত, উৎপন্ন, born, brought forth, engendered.
প্রসূতা, প্রসূতিকা,—অচিরকাল প্রসব হইয়াছে যে স্ত্রী, জনয়িত্রী, সন্তানবতী, *f.* recently brought to bed, having had a child.
প্রসূতি, প্রসব হওয়া, বিয়নি, জন্ম, উৎপত্তি, সন্ততি, a bringing forth, yeaning, &c: birth, production, offspring.
প্রসূন, পুষ্প, মুকুল, ফল, a flower, bud, blossom, fruit.
প্রসৃতি, নিকুব্জ করতল, চারি অঙ্গুলি পরিমাণ, গণ্ডূষ, the palm of the hand hollowed, a palmful, a handful.
প্রস্তর, পাষাণ, শিলা, মণি, পুষ্পগুচ্ছ, a stone, rock, gem, jewel, a bunch of flowers, a nosegay.
প্রস্তাব, বৃত্তান্ত, কথানুষ্ঠান, প্রসঙ্গ, উপন্যাস, পর, সময়, অবসর, mention, relation, introduction, a topic, a story, a passage, an occasion, opportunity.
প্রস্তাবনা, কথানুষ্ঠান, উপন্যাস, an introduction, commencement, a prologue, prelude.
প্রস্তাবিত, কথিত, উল্লেখিত, বর্ণিত, mentioned, told, related.
প্রস্তুত, নিষ্পন্ন, উদ্যত, উপস্থিত, উক্ত, প্রকাশিত, প্রশংসিত, পুরস্কৃত, finished, completed, prepared, ready, prompt, willing, present, at hand, said, revealed, declared, praised, eulogized, advanced.
প্রস্থ, প্রস্ত,—পাত্র, বাসনাদি, যোড়া, যুগল, চৌড়া, প্রকরণ, কাণ্ড, থল, সানু অর্থাৎ পর্ব্বতীয় ভূমি, পরিমাণ বিশেষ, a set of utensils, suit of clothes, a team, width, breadth, a volume, section, mountain table-land, a measure of quantity.
প্রস্থান, অভিনির্য্যাণ, চলন, যাত্রানুষ্ঠান, the march of an assailant, a departure, setting off.
প্রস্থাপন, চলান, যাপন, প্রেরণ, to cause to depart, send, dispatch.
প্রস্থিত, যাত, চলিত, প্রয়াত, gone, departed, marched forth.
প্রস্ফুটিত, বিকশিত, প্রফুল্লিত, open, expanded, blown.
প্রস্ফোটন, সূর্প দিয়া শস্য ঝাড়ন, উচলন, বিকাশন, to winnow corn, to open or expand as a flower.
প্রস্রবণ, ক্ষরণ, ঘামন, মূতন, উনুই, জলাকর, to ooze, leak, perspire, make water; a spring, a fountain.
প্রস্রাব মূত্র, মূত্রত্যাগ, urine, the passing of urine.
প্রহনন, মারণ, ঘাতন, জয়করণ, to smite, wound, kill, defeat, repel.

প্রহর, যাম, a watch or fourth part of the day or night.
প্রহরী, কোটাল, জাগনিয়া, a watchman, sentry; keeping watch.
প্রহর্ত্তা হন্তা, ঘাতক, মারক, one who beats, a striker, smiter.
প্রহর্ষ, আহ্লাদ, উল্লাস, joy, gladness, hilarity.
প্রহার, আঘাত, হননকরা, a blow, a stroke, a smiting.
প্রহারণ, মারণ, হনন, পিটন, to beat, strike, smite, flog.
প্রহারী, মারণিয়া, তাড়ানিয়া, পিটনিয়া, ঘাতক, beating, striking, smiting, flogging, killing.
প্রহিত, নিরস্ত, ছোটান, প্রেরিত, উপযুক্ত, উপকরণ, আচার, shot as from a bow, sent, dispatched, suitable appropriate; a sauce, gravy, condiment.
প্রহৃত, হত, মারিত, ক্ষত, beaten, struck, smitten, wounded.
প্রহৃষ্ট, সন্তুষ্ট, উল্লসিত, glad, rejoiced, pleased, happy.
প্রহেলিকা, দুরূহ ব্যঙ্গার্থ প্রশ্ন, হেঁয়ালী, a riddle, an enigma, a puzzling question.
প্রাংশু, ঊর্দ্ধতা, তুঙ্গ, উচ্চ, দীর্ঘ, height; high, tall, lofty.
প্রাক্, প্রাচীন, প্রাচী, পূর্ব, former, prior, olden, east; before.
প্রাকার, ঘেরা, বেড়, চয় অর্থাৎ গড়ের বেষ্টনপ্রাচীর, a fence, inclosure, surrounding wall, a rampart or mound.
প্রাকৃত, নীচ, সংস্কৃতেতর ভাষা, common, plebeian, vulgar, low.
প্রাক্কাল, পূর্বকাল, রোগের বৃদ্ধি কিম্বা হ্রাস লগ্ন, former or olden time, the crisis of a disease.
প্রাক্তন, অদৃষ্ট, কপাল, fate, destiny, luck. [gency.
প্রাখর্য্য, ব্যগ্রতা, নৈপুণ্য, তীক্ষ্ণতা, ardor, zeal, cleverness, pun-
প্রাগভাব, উৎপত্তির পূর্ববর্ত্তি অভাব, previous non-existence..
প্রাগল্ভ্য, জমক, আড়ম্বর, চলাবুলা, দাম্ভিকতা, দর্প, টেটামি, স্পর্দ্ধা, pomp, parade, show, bustle, arrogance, confidence, effrontery, boldness, insolence.
প্রাগ্বৎ, পূর্ববৎ, যেমন আগে, as before.
প্রাগ্ভাব, পূর্বাবস্থা, a previous state, former condition.
প্রাঙ্গণ, আঙ্গিনা, a court-yard, an outer yard.
প্রাড়্ন্যায়, আদ্দাশের পূর্ববিচার, a former trial of a cause.
প্রাঙ্মুখ, পূর্বদিঙ্মুখ, পূর্বাস্য, looking eastward, having the face turned to the eastward.
প্রাচী, পূর্বদিক্, the east. [crepit.
প্রাচীন, পুরাতন, পূর্বকালীন, বৃদ্ধ, old, ancient, olden, aged, de-

প্রাচীনগাথা, ঐতিহ্য, পুরাতনকথা, tradition, ancient story.
প্রাচীনা, পূর্বকাল, বৃদ্ধাবস্থা, antiquity, old age.
প্রাচীর, বেড়, ঘেরা. a fence, wall, hedge, inclosure.
প্রাচুর্য্য বাহুল্য, নির্বাহ, plenty, sufficiency, abundance.
প্রাচ্য, শরাবতী নদীর পূর্বদক্ষিণ দেশ, the country South and East of the Sharábatí.
প্রাজাপত্য, বিবাহ সংস্কার বিশেষ, যাগ বিশেষ, ব্রত বিশেষ, a form of marriage by gift, a particular sacrifice, a peculiar penance. [clever.
প্রাজ্ঞ, পণ্ডিত, বুদ্ধিমান্, নিপুণ, learned, wise, skilful, sensible,
প্রাঞ্জল, সরল, দাতা, honest, upright, sincere, liberal.
প্রাঞ্জলি, সংযুক্ত করকোষ, the joined hands open and hollowed.
প্রাড্বিবাক, বিচারকর্ত্তা, a judge, a magistrate.
প্রাণ, নিশ্বাস, বায়ু, জীব, breath, vital air, life, the soul.
প্রাণগ্রহণ, জীবনাশকরণ, to take away an animal's life, to kill.
প্রাণঘাতক, প্রাণঘাতী,—বধী, সংহারক, জীবনাশক, murderous, deadly, fatal, mortal, destroying life.
প্রাণত্যাগ, জীবনমাশ, মরণ, the relinquishing of life, death.
প্রাণনাথ, প্রিয়তম, স্বামী, a husband, (*so addressed by his wife.*)
প্রাণপণ, জীবদায়, অত্যন্ত প্রয়াস, যুদ্ধ, the staking or hazarding of life, great exertion, strong effort, zeal.
প্রাণপ্রতিম, প্রিয়তম, জীবসদৃশ, dear as life! resembling life!
প্রাণপ্রতিষ্ঠা, দেবতার প্রতিমাতে জীবন্যাস, the consecration or inanimation of an idol.
প্রাণপ্রিয়, প্রিয়তম, ধনমণি, *voc.* beloved of my soul!
প্রাণবস্তু, সজীব বস্তু, animated matter. [like the life.
প্রাণসম, প্রাণসমান,—প্রিয়তম, জীবতুল্য, dear as life, very dear,
প্রাণহা, সংঘাতক, হন্তা, murderous, deadly, mortal; a murderer.
প্রণহিংসা, জীবনাশ, হত্যা, an injury to life, murder.
প্রাণাধার, সজীব শরীর, a living body, the vessel of the soul.
প্রাণাধিক, অতিস্নিগ্ধ, পুত্রাদি, one dearer than life, a son, &c.
প্রাণায়াম, ধ্যানসময়ে বায়ুধারণ, a mode of breathing during mental prayer. [ing, an animal.
প্রাণী, জীবন্ত, পঞ্চভূতাত্মা, জন্তু, living, vital; an animated be-
প্রাণেশ, প্রাণেশ্বর,—স্বামিসম্বোধক বাক্য, a husband, (*so addressed by his wife,*) *i. e.* lord of my life!

প্রাতঃ, অরুণোদয়, the dawn, the morning. [after sun-rise.
প্রাতঃকাল, সূর্য্যোদয় পর ছয় দণ্ড, the morning, the two hours
প্রাতিকূল্য, বৈপরীত্য, বিরুদ্ধতা, শত্রুতা, contrariety, opposition.
প্রাতিভাব্য, লগ্নকত্ব, বন্ধকতা, security, suretiship, bail.
প্রাতিলোম্য, বৈপরীত্য, ব্যতিক্রম, contrariety to nature, opposition to the grain. [confidential.
প্রাত্যয়িক, বিশ্বাসবিষয়ক, বিশ্বাস্য, pertaining to faith or trust,
প্রাথমিক, অগ্রিম, আদিম, অগ্রগণ্য, first, prior, initial, belonging to the first, having a right to priority, entitled to precedence.
প্রাদুর্ভাব, প্রকাশ, দর্শিবা, উদয়, স্বপ্রকাশ, মহিমা, a manifestation, appearing, coming to light, rising, eliciting, a vaunting, ostentation, greatness.
প্রাদুর্ভূত, প্রকাশিত, ব্যক্ত, manifest, clear, evident, elicited.
প্রাদেশ, প্রসারিতাঙ্গুষ্ঠতর্জ্জনী পরিমাণ, the span of the thumb and forefinger.
প্রাধান্য, শ্রেষ্ঠতা, প্রকর্ষ, pre-eminence, superiority.
প্রান্ত, কূল, অঞ্চল, সীমা, শেষভাগ, a margin, shore, border, end, outskirts. [road, a desert.
প্রান্তর, দূর এবং শূন্য পথ, মাঠ, a long, dreary, unsheltered
প্রাপণ, মিলন, প্রাপ্তম, উপার্জ্জন, মিলান, ঘটান, জন্মান, to obtain, find, get, inherit, acquire, cause to obtain, procure, occasion.
প্রাপ্ত, লব্ধ, উপার্জ্জিত, মিলিত, বিশিষ্ট, আগত, obtained, gained, acquired, found; *prefix*: possessing, affected with, arrived at, &c.
প্রাপ্তপঞ্চত্ব, মৃত, প্রেত, dead, deceased, defunct.
প্রাপ্তব্যবহার, দায়গ্রস্ত, কর্ম্মভারগ্রস্ত, adult, of age, arrived at the age of legal responsibility.
প্রাপ্তযৌবন, ষোড়শাধিক বৎসর বয়স্ক যুবা, arrived at puberty.
প্রাপ্তি, লাভ, উপস্বত্ব, ফল, acquisition, possession, profit, gain, benefit, advantage. [tainable.
প্রাপ্য, পৈতৃকধন, অর্জনীয়, লভ্য, heritable, patrimonial, ob-
প্রাফুল্ল্য, পুষ্পবিকাশ, হর্ষ, the expansion of a flower or of the mind, gladness. {skreen, a shed.
প্রাবরণ, উত্তরীয় বস্ত্র, আড়াল, ঝোপড়ী, an outer garment, a

প্রাবর্ত্তক, চেতানিয়া, প্রবৃত্তিজনক, exciting, stirring up, stimulating, instigating.

প্রাবল্য, সামর্থ্য, বিক্রম, strength, power.

প্রাবিড়, প্রাবীড়—অনবসর, বিশেষ বিজ্ঞাপনা, a pressure of business, [a specification.

প্রাবৃট্ পচাকাল, বর্ষাকাল, rainy, wet ; the rains.

প্রাবৃত, ঘেরিত, ঢাকিত, আচ্ছাদিত, উড়নী, fenced, skreened, covered, defended ; an outer garment.

প্রামাণিক, শাস্ত্রসিদ্ধ, প্রমাণলব্ধ, অতিমান্য, সভাতে প্রধান, গোষ্ঠীপতি, স্বমত প্রমাণকারী পণ্ডিত, well-founded, approved, founded on evidence ; a president, chairman, the head of a trade, a learned man who supports his opinions by reference to books, &c.

প্রামাণ্য, সত্যতা, গ্রাহ্যতা, সম্ভব, নিশ্চয়সিদ্ধি, authenticity, credibility, probability, practicability, evidence.

প্রায়, প্রায়ঃ,—কিঞ্চিৎ ন্যূন সমস্ত, ময়, তুল্য, দৃক্, almost, nearly ; *in compos*: abounding in, like, resembling.

প্রায়শঃ, অল্পাপেক্ষায়, অধিকাংশতঃ, বাহুল্যরূপে, পুনঃ২, প্রায়সর্ব্বদা, almost, nearly, mostly, nearly all, largely, abundantly, frequently, generally.

প্রায়শ্চিত্ত, পাপমাত্র নাশক কর্ম্ম, a penance, expiation, atonement.

প্রায়িক, কিঞ্চিৎ ন্যূন সমস্ত, nearly all, nearly, almost.

প্রারব্ধ, অনুষ্ঠিত, অদৃষ্ট, begun, fixed by fate ; destiny, fate.

প্রারম্ভ, উপক্রম, অনুষ্ঠান, a beginning, a commencement.

প্রার্থক, নিবেদনকারী, মাঙ্গনিয়া, যাচক, বাঞ্ছয়িতা, পদাভিলাষী, supplicating, supplicatory ; a wisher, requester, solicitor, suitor, candidate.

প্রার্থন, মাঙ্গন, যাচন, বাঞ্ছন, to ask, desire, supplicate, pray.

প্রার্থনা, প্রাপ্তীচ্ছা, নিবেদন, যাচ্ঞা, বাঞ্ছা, a request, prayer, petition, supplication, desire.

প্রার্থয়িতা, যাচক, মাঙ্গনিয়া, a petitioner, one who prays, &c.

প্রালব্ধ্য, প্রালব্ধ,—অদৃষ্ট, প্রাক্তন, fate, destiny, predestination.

প্রাশন, ভক্ষণ, আহার, an eating, a meal.

প্রাশস্ত্য, বৃহত্ত্ব, বিস্তর, প্রসার, উত্তমতা, উৎকর্ষ, largeness, extent, capaciousness, excellence.

প্রাশী, ভোজনকারী, ভোক্তা, eating, feeding.

প্রাসাদ, অট্টালিকা, দেবালয়, a palace, a temple.

প্রাহ্ন, দিবসের পূর্ব্বভাগ, the forenoon, the morning.
প্রিয়, স্নেহপাত্র, হিত, মনোরম, beloved, dear, amiable, agreeable, grateful, pleasant.
প্রিয়ঙ্কর, মনোহর, মনোরঞ্জক, amiable, exciting regard, pleasant.
প্রিয়ম্বদ, প্রিয়ভাষী, মিষ্টবাদী, saying agreeable things.
প্রীণন, তৃপ্তি, অরুচি, অনিচ্ছা, satisfaction. fulness, satiety.
প্রীত, স্নিগ্ধ, প্রেমপাত্র, তৃপ্ত, তুষ্ট, beloved, esteemed, satisfied, happy, pleased.
প্রীতি, প্রণয়, স্নেহ, প্রশ্রয়, তুষ্টি, সন্তোষ, রতি, তৃপ্তি, love, affection, esteem, regard, gratification, enjoyment, pleasure, satisfaction.
প্রীতিমান, স্নেহযুক্ত, প্রণয়ী, বৎসল, loving, affectionate, kind.
প্রেক. কীলক, শঙ্কু, a nail, a peg, a pin.
প্রেক্ষণ, অবলোকন, হেরণ, to view, survey, observe, behold, see, discern.
প্রেঙ্খন, ঝুলন, দোলন, নড়ন, to hang, be pendent, swing, shake.
প্রেঙ্খা, দোলা, a swing, hammock, travelling litter.
প্রেত, মৃত, পিশাচ, নরকস্থপ্রাণী, departed, deceased ; a ghost, spirit, goblin, spectre, fiend.
প্রেতকর্ম্ম, প্রেতকার্য্য,—ঔর্দ্ধদেহিকাদিক্রিয়া, অন্ত্যেষ্টিক্রিয়া, funeral ceremonies, obsequies.
প্রেতপতি, যম, Yama or the regent of death.
প্রেত্য, পরকালে, in the next world, in the world of spirits.
প্রেতনদী, বৈতরণী, the river of hell or Hindoo Styx.
প্রেম, স্নেহ, প্রণয়, বাৎসল্য, বন্ধুতা, রতি, ক্রীড়া, love, affection, attachment, tenderness, intimacy, friendship, pleasure, enjoyment, pastime, sport, fondling, caressing.
প্রেমী, স্নেহকারী, মিত্র, পরিচিত, loving, affectionate ; a friend, acquaintance.
প্রেয়ান্, প্রেয়সী,—স্নিগ্ধ, স্নেহপাত্র, *m.* & *f.* dear, best beloved.
প্রেরণ, পাঠান, আদেশন, নিযোজন, প্রবৃত্তি জন্মান, to send, despatch, give orders, command, appoint, delegate, instigate, cause.
প্রেরয়িতা, প্রেরক, আদেশক, one who sends or orders, a commander.
প্রেরিত, পাঠান, নিযোজিত, প্রয়োজ্য, সম্বাদক, দূত, sent &c; a messenger, ambassador, apostle.
প্রেষণ, পাঠান, আদেশন, to send, order, command, direct.

প্রেষ্ঠ, অত্যন্ত স্নেহপাত্র, greatly beloved, outstripped.
প্রেষ্য, দূত, ভৃত্য, দাস, a messenger, servant, slave.
প্রোক্ত, কথিত, উল্লেখিত, said, spoken, declared, uttered.
প্রোক্ষণ, শুদ্ধ্যর্থজলপ্রক্ষেপণ, শমন, বলিদান করণ, to sprinkle ceremonially, to slaughter for sacrifice, immolate.
প্রোক্ষণীয়, যজ্ঞীয়, প্রোক্ষণ দ্বারা সংস্কার্য্য, sacrificial, requiring to be ceremonially sprinkled.. [incitement.
প্রোৎসাহ, অত্যন্ত প্রয়াস, প্রবৃত্তি, effort, exertion, a stimulus,
প্রোৎসাহক, প্রবর্ত্তক, মন্ত্রণাকর্ত্তা, an instigator, stimulator, adviser.
প্রোথিত, পোতিত, গাড়া, fixed or buried in the earth.
প্রোষিত, বিদেশস্থ, প্রবাসী, দেশান্তরবাসী, abroad, absent, away from home, sojourning in a foreign country.
প্রোষিতপতিকা বা ভর্তৃকা,— বিদেশগতস্বামিনী, a woman whose husband is absent or gone a journey.
প্রৌঢ়, বয়ঃপ্রাপ্ত, বিবাহিত, বৃদ্ধ, গর্ব্বিত, ঠেঁটা, বিতর্কিত, অস্বীকৃত, adult, full grown, married, old, arrogant, confident, controverted, disputed.
প্রৌঢ়া, বিবাহিতা, ত্রিশ বৎসরাবধি পঞ্চাশ বৎসরপর্য্যন্ত বয়স্কা, কামুকী, a married woman, one from the age of 30 to 35 years, an amorous female.
প্রৌঢ়ি, উদ্যোগ, দুঃসাহস, পূর্ব্বপক্ষ, বাদানুবাদ, বিতণ্ডা, enterprize, zeal, rashness, an affirmation, a controversy, investigation. [fig tree.
প্লক্ষ, অশ্বত্থ, পাকুড়, the holy fig tree, the wave-leaved
প্লব, ঝম্প, লম্ফ, ডুব, মজ্জনা, ভাসনি, প্রেরণ, ভেলা, ডুবারু পক্ষী, মণ্ডূকবানরমেষাদি, ঢাল, গড়ান, জলাশয়, দীর্ঘ স্বর, শত্রু, নাগরমুথা ঘাস, a jump, leap, plunging, diving, floating or swimming, a sending or directing, a raft, float, the diver bird, whatever goes by leaps or jumps, as frogs, monkies, sheep, &c. a declivity or shelving ground, a piece of water, a basket for catching fish, a protracted accent, an enemy, a sort of grass.
প্লবগ, বানরভেকাদি, প্লুতগতিকর, a monkey, a frog &c. whatever moves by leaps. [plunge.
প্লবন, লম্ফন, প্লুত দিয়া গমন, ডুব দেওন, to leap, jump, gallop,

প্লাবন, বন্যা, উপচন, বিকীর্ণন, ছিটান, a deluge, flood, inundation; to overflow, inundate, suffuse, sprinkle.
প্লীহা, পিলুই, গুল্ম, রোগ বিশেষ, the spleen, a diseased enlargement of the spleen.
প্লুত, উল্লম্ফিত, জলাকীর্ণ, ব্যাপ্ত, মাখা, ঝম্প, কুর্দ্দন, দীর্ঘস্বর, jumped, overflowed, suffused, sprinkled; a gallop, leap, a skipping or capering, a grave accent.

ফ.

ফকন, হারণ, চটন, পণ্ড হওন, নাফলন, to fail, miscarry, to disappoint, to mock expectation.
ফকান, হারাণ, ভুলান, to cause to fail, disappoint, balk.
ফক্কক, ব্যর্থ, নিরর্থক, অফলক, মিথ্যা, ছলনিয়া, বঞ্চক, ধূর্ত্ত, failing, disappointing, balking, delusive, pretending, imposing ; a rogue, a cheat. [ment.
ফক্কা, পূর্বপক্ষ, বিতণ্ডা, a position or thesis, assertion, argu-
ফক্কিকা, পূর্বপক্ষ, সিদ্ধান্তাভাস, ফাকী, ছলনা, ধূর্ত্ততা, প্রবঞ্চনা, কৌশল, বিশ্বাসঘাত, পণ্ডশ্রম, আশাভঙ্গ, *id* : also—a sophism, deception, delusion, trick, fraud, illusion, stratagem, treachery, failure, disappointment.
ফক্কা, ফক্বা,—দীনহীন, নির্ধন, কঙ্গাল, penniless, poor.
ফঙ্গ, অফলক, নিরর্থক, disappointing, failing.
ফঙ্গমানী, ফঙ্গবানী,—মিথ্যা, অসার, অপ্রকৃত, অশক্ত, unsubstantial, tinsel, slight, weak. [speckled.
ফট্কা, পথছাড়িয়া, পেঁচ, চিত্রিত, a straggler, a dilemma ;
ফট্কারী, ফট্কিরী,—স্ফট, বণিক দ্রব্য বিশেষ, alum.
ফটিক, কাচ, স্ফটিক, chrystal, quartz.
ফড়, পাশক্রীড়া বিশেষ, a peculiar game at dice.
ফড়কি, পল্লব, রলা, ক্ষুদ্র শাখা, a twig, a small branch.
ফড়িঙ্গ, পতঙ্গ বিশেষ, উচুঙ্গা, পঙ্গপাল, a grasshopper, a cricket, a locust. [petty shopkeeper.
ফড়িয়া, ছুটালিয়াব্যাপারী, ক্ষুদ্র বেপারা, a pedlar, retail dealer,
ফড়্ফড়ানী, ফড়্ফড়ানিয়া,—বাবদূক, বহুবক্তা, loquacious, talkative, garrulous, voluble. [pella.
ফণা, স্ফট, সর্পের প্রসারিত মস্তক, the hood of the cobra di ca-

ফণাধর, ফণধর, ফণী,—সর্প, a snake, the hooded snake or cobra capella. [a commencement.

ফন্দী, ছল, ছুতা, পাশ, অনুষ্ঠান, a machination, artifice, snare,

ফরসা, নির্ম্মল, স্বচ্ছ, clean, clear, limpid, transparent.

ফর্ফরুণ-আণ, দম্ভ করণ, বড়াই করণ, to assume consequence, to brag, to boast, to look big.

ফল, বৃক্ষাদির শস্য, উৎপন্ন, শেষ, হিতাহিত, প্রয়োজন, উপকার, অভিপ্রায়, গুণ, লাভ, ব্যাজ, কর্ম্মভোগ, ইষ্টসিদ্ধি, ফাল, বাণাদির অগ্রস্থিত লৌহ, ছুরিকার দল, fruit, produce, result, consequence, effect, advantage or disadvantage, utility, benefit, sense, meaning, quality, property or virtue, gain, profit, interest on money &c, reward or punishment, success, a ploughshare, a spear or arrow head, the blade of a knife, the second term in proportion. [slate, a ploughshare.

ফলক, ঢাল, লিখিবার পাট, ফাল, a shield, a writing board, a

ফলকী, ঢালী, carrying a shield, armed with a shield.

ফলতঃ, বস্তুতঃ, অর্থাৎ, in reality, indeed, that is to say, in other words.

ফলদ, ফলদায়ী,—সফল, প্রয়োজক, হিতজনক, কর্ম্মভোগদাতা, fruitful, yielding fruit, advantageous, beneficial, giving the fruit or just reward of an action.

ফলন, ফল দেওন, উৎপাদন, ইষ্ট সাধন, অনুবর্ত্তন, ঘটন, to bear fruit, yield, produce, to succeed, prosper, result, ensue as a consequence.

ফলবন্ত, ফলবন্ত,—ফলযুক্ত, লাভজনক, fruitful, advantageous.

ফলমুখ, শস্য, ক্ষেত্রোৎপন্ন, a harvest, a crop.

ফলশ্রুতি, কর্ম্মের প্রবৃত্তিনিমিত্ত প্রলোভজনক বাক্য, passages of the Veds, treating of the consequences of works.

ফলা, সংযুক্তাক্ষর, বাণাদির অগ্রস্থিত লৌহ, হাতার খুরী, ফলযুক্ত, a compound letter, the head of a dart or arrow, the bowl of a spoon ; abounding in fruit.

ফলাফ, প্লুতগতি, a moving by leaps, springs or jumps.

ফলাট, শিল, গোযোনি, a stone for grinding paint on, &c: the pudendum of a cow.

ফলান, ফলোৎপাদন, লাভ জন্মান, বাটন, to bring forth fruit, make fruitful, fructify, cause advantage, to mix or grind colours &c. on a stone.

ফলাফল, লাভালাভ, হিতাহিত, success or failure, advantage or disadvantage. [a feast, a banquet.

ফলাহার, ফলার.—বৃক্ষের শস্য ভক্ষণ, ভোজ, a feeding on fruits,

ফলিত, ফলবিশিষ্ট, fruit-bearing, filled with fruit. [say.

ফলিতার্থ, নিষ্কৃষ্টার্থ, অর্থাৎ, on the whole, in fine, that is to

ফলিন্, ফলবান্, লাভজনক, fruitful, advantageous, profitable.

ফলী, ফলযুক্ত, সফল, বাণাদির অগ্রস্থিত লৌহ, ছুরিকার দল, ফাল, fruit-bearing, in fruit; a spear or arrow head, the blade of a knife, a ploughshare.

ফলোদয়, কর্ম্মবিপাক, প্রতিফল, লাভ, প্রাপ্তি, কার্য্যসিদ্ধি, the natural consequences of actions, recompense, benefit, profit, success, accomplishment of an object.

ফল্গু, ফাগু, the red powder used at the Huli festival.

ফল্গুৎসব, দোলযাত্রা, হুলি, the Huli festival. [mockery.

ফক্কি, গাদ্দি, পরিহাস, বিদ্রূপ, a jest. joke, banter, raillery,

ফক্কড়, ভণ্ড, রসিক, a jester, banterer, wag.

ফক্কা, আলগা, ঢীলা, অশক্ত, শ্লথ, ব্যর্থ, নিরর্থক, পাণ্ডুর, loose, slack, lax, flaccid, insecure, useless, ineffectual, pale as a colour.

ফাও, ব্যাজ, an overplus, make-weight, allowance.

ফাঁড়, উদর. the belly, the belly of a pitcher, &c.

ফাঁদ, কল, পাশ, জাল, a snare, trap. noose, net.

ফাঁদনী, কৌশল, উপায়, অনুষ্ঠান, a machination, device, a commencement. [commence.

ফাঁদন, ঝাঁপন, কুঁদন, আরম্ভণ, to leap, jump, prance, skip,

ফাঁপ, ফোস্কা, বুদ্বুদ, স্ফীতি, a blister, a bubble, a hollow tumour, a puffy swelling.

ফাঁপন, ফুলন, বাড়ন, পাকন, to become tumid, swell, blister, be puffed or hollow, to rise as bread, &c.

ফাঁপা, ফোস্কা, ফুলা, a blister, bump, tumour, spungy swelling.

ফাঁপান, ফুলান, বায়ুস্ফীত করণ, to puff up, inflate, distend, fill with air. [tumidity, elasticity.

ফাঁপামী, স্ফীতভাব, ফুলামী, puffiness, hollowness, spunginess.

ফাঁস-ী, ফাঁদ, পাশ, a noose, loop, slip-knot, toil, snare.

ফাক, ফাটা, ছিদ্র, বিদার, চির, তর্‌সা, অন্তর, ভঙ্গ, a chink, fissure, cleft, chasm, split, an interval, interstice, aperture, open space, vacancy, a fracture, a rupture.

ফাকড়া, প্রবঞ্চনা, ছল, ব্যাজ, an imposition, cheat, evasion, subterfuge.

ফাকা, অনাহার, চূর্ণীকৃ দ্রব্য, a fasting from want or sickness, any powdered substance.

ফাকী, প্রতারণা, ছলনা, উপায়, কৌশল, ব্যাজ, চূর্ণ, পূর্বপক্ষ, deceit, imposture, illusion, fraud, an imposition, trick, stratagem, subterfuge, any powder, an allegation, assertion, position.

ফাকুড়িয়া, ধূর্ত্ত, ছলী, a knave; knavish, roguish, perfidious.

ফাগু, ফল্গু, রক্তবর্ণ চূর্ণ বিশেষ. a red powder.

ফাটন, স্ফুটন, বিদরণ, চিরণ, ভাঙ্গন, চটন, to crack, chap, split, break, burst, break out in spots or blotches.

ফাটল-া, ছিদ্র, ফাক, রন্ধ্র. a crack, chink, peep-hole, vent.

ফাটান, ভাঙ্গান, চিরাণ, বিদারণ, to crack, split, cleave, &c.

ফাটাল, তর্‌সা, চির, ছিদ্র, a fissure, rent, crack, split.

ফাড়ন, চিরাণ, বিদারণ, খণ্ডন, to cleave, rive, tear, divide.

ফাণিত, খাঁড়, ফেণি, raw sugar, inspissated cane juice.

ফাতা, ফাতনা,—শোলা, ছিপের শর, a net-buoy, the float of a fishing line.

ফাল-া, লাঙ্গলাগ্রণাদির অগ্রস্থিত লৌহ, ছুরিকার দল, a ploughshare, arrow-head, knife-blade.

ফালপাড়ন, চষণ, ভূমি বিদারণ, to plough.

ফালপাড়ন, ঝাঁপন, কুঁদন, to leap, jump, skip, prance.

ফালা, ফালী,—কাষ্ঠাদির দীর্ঘাকার খণ্ড, কুচি, কাণি, টুকি, a small board, a chip, slip, strip, slice.

ফাল্গুণ, শিশিরকালের দ্বিতীয় মাস, the second spring month.

ফাসা, ভূমির ছিদ্র, cracks and fissures in the soft earth.

ফাসা, ছিদ্র, ফাক, a chink, a crack, an opening.

ফিক, ফিঁক,—ঠেস, ঠেকুয়া, পুস্তা, চিতার চাপিবার বাঁশ. হঠাৎ বেদনা, খোঁচা, a prop, lever, shoar, a bamboo used to prevent a woman's escape from the funeral pile, a stitch or sharp and sudden pain.

ফিকনা, ঠেস, অবলম্ব, a prop, staunchion, stay.

ফিকা, পাণ্ডুর, ম্লান, light-coloured; pale, faded.

ফিকি, স্ফুলিঙ্গ, অণু, কণা, বিন্দু, a spark, particle, atom, drop.

ফিঙ্গা, শিকা, ছিট্‌কা, পক্ষী বিশেষ, a sling, a species of bird.

ফিচাল, ধূর্ত্ত, শঠ, নিপুণ, artful, clever, ingenious.

ফির, ঘুরণি, মণ্ডল, আশাভঙ্গ, ঝঞ্ঝাট, আপদ, a revolution, a circle, a round-about way, a disappointment, any adverse circumstance.

ফিরণ, উল্টন, বিগড়ন, ঘুরণ, বাহুড়ন, পুনর্দ্দেওন, ভ্রমণ, বেড়ান, to turn, change, alter, veer, turn or move round, revolve, return, to refund, restore, to wander, rove, travel about. [dering, &c.

ফিরণিয়া, ভ্রমণিয়া, পর্য্যটক, a traveller, rover; roaming, wan-

ফিরৎ, পুনরাবৃত্ত, পুনরাগত, পুনরানীত, পুনদত্ত, returned, come, brought or given back. [article.

ফিরতী, ঘূর্ণি, প্রত্যর্পণ, a revolving, turning, the return of an

ফিরাণ, ঘুরাণ, পুনঃপ্রদান করণ, লেপন, অন্যথাকরণ, to cause to turn, circulate or revolve, to give back, refund, to plaster, to alter, change,-কহন, to prevaricate,-লওন to receive or take back, পাওন to recover, resume.

ফিরাণিয়া, লেপনিয়া, লাগানিয়া, a plasterer; plastering.

ফিরে, পুনঃ, পুনশ্চ, আরবার, পুনরায়, again.

ফিস্‌ফিসনী, সূক্ষ্মবৃষ্টিপাত, ভুড়্‌ভুড়ানী, কর্ণেজপ, a drizzling rain, a whispering, a whisperer.

ফুঁকন, ফুৎকরণ, to blow with the mouth or breath.

ফুড়ন, বিন্ধন, ভেদন, to pierce, penetrate, pierce or pass through. [*as a serpent.*

ফুঁপন, ভুকরণ, হাঁপন, শিশ্ দেওন, to sob, breathe short, hiss

ফুকর, ফুকার,—ছিদ্র, অন্তর, a crack, fissure, vent hole, space.

ফুকরণ, হাঁকন, ডাকন, to hoot, halloo, call to, bawl, shout.

ফুট, বিন্দু, দ্রাবক, ফল বিশেষ, a drop, a solvent or menstruum, a kind of melon.

ফুটন, স্ফুটন, গজন, ফুলন, বক্তন, ঝিমকী দেওন, অকস্মাৎ প্রকাশ হওন, বিন্ধন, to burst, break, burst open, expand, swell, boil or bubble up, to gush out, to emerge, break forth, to pierce, to prick.

ফুটা, বিদীর্ণ, বিকসিত. ফট্কা, split, torn, pierced, open, blown; a straggler. [cause to boil, &c.

ফুটান. বিদারণ, বিন্ধন, ওতন, বকান, to split, tear, pierce, stab,

ফুৎকার, মুখহইতে বায়ুত্যাগ, ফুঁকন, a blast of the breath, the act of blowing. [exorcise; exorcism.

ফুয়ান, ধমান, ব্যয় করণ, উড়ান, ভূত ছাড়ান, to kindle, exhaust,

ফুরণ, ব্যয় হওন, অকুলান, টুটন, নিবড়ন, ক্ষয়ণ, পড়ন, to be expended, spent, exhausted or finished, to waste, decay. [entirely.

ফুরাণ, ব্যয়করণ, উড়ান, নিবড়ান, to exhaust, spend, finish

ফুল, পুষ্প, মুকুল, রজস্. কুষ্ঠ, ছানী, a flower, mineral flowers, a bud, blossom, the menstrual flux, leprosy, a cataract or film on the eye.

ফুলখড়ী, চূর্ণ খটিকা, pure or powdered chalk.

ফুলগন্ধক, চূর্ণ গন্ধক. flowers of sulphur. brimstone.

ফুলফুলিয়া, পরিষ্কৃত, বস্ত্রবিলাসী, বাঁকড়া, neat in dress, foppish, priggish; a beau, a fop, &c.

ফুলরী, বড়া, cakes or nuts of flour fried in oil.

ফুলা, গর্ভপুষ্প. ফাঁপা. মাংসস্ফীতি, চুকনাদি, স্ফীত. ফাঁপান, the secundines or after birth, a bump, a swelling, an eruption; tumid, spongy, swollen.

ফুলন, ফাঁপন, প্রস্ফোটন, পাকন, স্বপ্রকাশ করণ, মুকুলন, to swell, become inflated or turgid, &c. to rise, ferment, to strut, look big, to blossom, blow.

ফুলান, পুষ্পোৎপাদন, মুকুলান, ফাঁপান, to blossom, bloom, cause to bloom, cause to swell, inflate.

ফুলামী, ফাঁপামী. স্ফীতভাব, গরিমা, দাম্ভিকতা, ঠেকার, expansive, elastic; elasticity; expansiveness, sponginess, tumidity, a swelling with pride, haughtiness.

ফুলী, ছানী. a film, speck or cataract on the eye.

ফুল্ক-1, মৎস্যের কাণকুয়া, স্ফুলিঙ্গ, অগ্নিকণা, the bronchiæ or gills of a fish, a spark of fire.

ফুল্ল, বিকসিত, প্রস্ফুটিত, প্রসারিত, open, blown, expanded.

ফুল্লারবিন্দ, প্রস্ফুটিত পদ্ম, বস্ত্রবিলাসী, an expanded water-lily, a fop, a beau.

ফুস্কী, মরুৎক্রিয়া, the report of wind expelled backwards.

ফুশী, নির্ধনী, কাঙ্গাল, তুচ্ছ, penniless, poor, contemptible.

ফুস্কুড়ী, অতিক্ষুদ্র ব্রণ, a pimple, carbuncle, small boil.

ফুস্ফুস্, ফোঁপ্সা, কাণে কহা, the lungs, a whisper, a whispering.

ফুস্ফুসনি, কাণে কহা, ফুড়ফুড়ি, a whispering. [flatter, seduce.

ফুস্লান, নওয়ান, ভুলান, to coax, wheedle, cajole, inveigle,

ফেঁপন, ফুলন, বাড়ন, উঠন, to swell, rise, ferment, spring up.

ফেঁপরা, ফোঁপ্সা, ফাঁপান, স্ফীত, ফুলা, অসার, the lungs ; spongy, puffy, blown, light, hollow.

ফেকুড়া, ফেকুড়ী,—রলা, পল্লব, a sprig, slip, twig, switch.

ফেটা, নুটী, a skein or reel of thread or silk.

ফেণ-া, গাঁজ, মলা, foam, froth, spume, scum.

ফেণি, গুড়, খাঁড়, মিষ্টান্ন বিশেষ, raw sugar, inspissated cane juice, a kind of sugar-plums.

ফেণিল, গাঁজলা, মলাযুক্ত, foamy, frothy, covered with scum.

ফের, পুনঃ, পুনরায়, দায়, উল্টা, আপদ, আটক, আশাভঙ্গ, ছল, পেঁচ, বেড়, again, back, back again : a peril, reverse, obstacle, disappointment, a scheme, plot, a winding, round about, compass.

ফেরৎ, প্রতিদত্ত, পুনঃপ্রাপ্ত. given back, returned in trade.

ফেরণ, ঘুরণ, আবর্ত্তন, উল্টন্, বাহুড়ন, বেড়ান, ছাপিয়া থাকন, to turn round, spin, wind, veer, return, rove, ramble, go about, take the air, to lurk, to skulk.

ফেরতা, বিগাড়, অন্যথা, পরিবর্ত্ত, তান বিশেষ, a change, alteration, a variation of notes or sounds in music.

ফের্ফার্, অন্যথাকরা, উল্টা, বৈপরীত্য, ব্যতিক্রম, আপদ, উল্টাপাল্টামি, জঞ্জাল, a variation, transposition, vicissitude, perversion, confusion, disorder.

ফেরব, ফেরু,—শৃগাল, জম্বুক, a jackal.

ফেরা, ঘূর্ণি, চক্রগমন, পর্য্যটন, বেড়ানি, পুনরাবৃত্তি, ব্যতিকর, পরিমাণ পাত্র বিশেষ, a turn, revolution, circuit, voyage, a walk, a return, a reverse, a dry measure.

ফেলন, হস্তাদি দ্বারা নিক্ষেপণ, চালন, উল্টান, সরাণ, উড়ান, বিরাম করণ, ত্যজন, ছাড়ন, to throw, cast, fling, throw down or away, to pour, spill, shed, overset, toss, displace, to squander, dissipate ; -রাখন, to put off, adjourn, to waive, give up.

ফেলা, নিক্ষিপ্ত, ছাড়া, নিক্ষেপ, উচ্ছিষ্ট, thrown or cast away ; a throw or cast, refuse, leavings.

ফোঁড়ন, ফোটন-আন,—বিন্ধন, গুতন, আঁচড়ান, সুরঙ্গ করণ, ধুনন, সাঁতলান, to pierce, stab, transfix, run through, prick, scratch, to undermine, to card cotton, to season food or sauce with spices, &c.

ফোঁপন-আন, ডুকরণ, হাঁপন, to sob, heave, breathe short.

ফোঁপরা, ফাঁপান, ফোপ্সা,. hollow, spungy, light; the lungs.

ফোটা, বিন্দু, ছিটা, তিলক, a drop, spot, stain, sectarial mark.

ফোড়, নিড়ানী, বর্ম্মা. a weeding instrument, awl, spatula.

ফোড়া. বিস্ফোট, ব্রণ, আঁচড়, a boil, tumour, scratch.

ফোপ্সা. ফেঁপরা, পটকা, ক্লোম, the lungs, the bladder. [&c.

ফোলন, বাড়ন, স্ফীত হওন, to swell, become enlarged, distended,

ফোলান, ফাঁপান, চিড়ান, কোপাণ, to cause to swell, &c. to aggravate, fret, anger, provoke. [&c.

ফোস্কা, জলপূর্ণ স্ফীতচর্ম্ম, a blister on the skin from a burn,

ফৌতিক, আগন্তুক লাভ, উপলব্ধি, perquisites of office, avails, &c.

ব

বউ, স্ত্রী, বধু, a wife, a son's wife ; used also as a vocative in addressing any respectable female.

বংক্ষণ, কুচ্কি, কটিদেশ, ক্রোড়, করকনা, the groin, the hip, the pubic and iliac regions.

বংশ, কুল, গোত্র, পিত্রাদি পরম্পরা, সন্ততি, মেরুদণ্ড, বাঁশ, বেণু, race, lineage, family, kindred, pedigree, parentage, the spine or back-bone, a bamboo, a flute, pipe, fife. [a race.

বংশকর, কুলস্থাপক, কুলরক্ষক, founding a family, continuing

বংশজ, সদ্বংশজাত, কুলজাত, born of a noble family, of such a family. [race.

বংশজনক, আদিপুরুষ, কুলজনক, a progenitor; producing a

বংশধর, কুলযুক্ত, কুলরক্ষক, having or supporting a family.

বংশলোচন, বাঁশের মধ্যে জনিত শুভ্র বস্তু, ত্বক্ক্ষীর, bamboo manna, (so called.) [nealogical table.

বংশাবলি, কুলজী, পূর্বপুরুষনামশ্রেণী, a pedigree, genealogy, ge-

বংশী, মুরলী, বেণু, a flute, fife, pipe, whistle.
বংশীধর, বেণুধারী, কৃষ্ণ, a flute player, Crishna.
বংশীয়, বংশ্য,—কুলজ, গোত্রজ, lineal, descended from, belonging to a race or family.
বক, ক্রৌঞ্চ, কঙ্ক, a crane, a heron.
বকন-আন, নিরর্থক বাক্য কহন, জল্পন, কথন, বলন, to prate, prattle, chatter, talk idly, speak.
বকনা, অপ্রসূতা স্ত্রীগো, a heifer, a young cow.
বকনি, জল্প, গল্পসল্প, বৃথাকথা, talkativeness, prating, chattering, idle talk.
বকাশপ্রত্যাশা, বৃথাশ্বাস, মিথ্যা ভরসা. vain hope, fruitless expectation.
বকুয়া, বাবদূক, গল্পিয়া. garrulous, talkative, prating, chattering.
বক্তব্য, কহিবার যোগ্য, বচনার্হ, fit to be spoken. proper to be mentioned.
বক্তা, কথক, সুকথক, বাচাল. a speaker, a fluent person, a great talker.
বক্ত্র, মুখ, আস্য, the mouth, the face.
বক্‌বকান, বহুজল্পন, বড়্‌বড়ান, to talk much, grumble, mutter. murmur.
বক্র, বাঁকা, নত, কুটিল, টেরা, পেঁচাল, প্রতিকূল, ক্রূর, ঠেঁটা, খল, crooked, curved, bent, deformed, distorted, awry, tortuous, winding, intricate, adverse, cruel, churlish, perverse, dishonest.
বক্রদৃষ্টি, গরুচকুয়া, টেরাদৃষ্টি, squint-eyed, squinting.
বক্রা, বক্রী,—ছাগলছাগলী, অজঅজা. a goat, (male & female.)
বক্রী, বেঁকা, নত, ক্রূর, প্রতিকূল, অবশেষ, crooked, bent, &c. cruel, adverse; a remainder, overplus, arrears.
বক্রোক্তি, টালমটাল, শ্লেষ, দ্ব্যর্থকথা, an evasion, equivocation, a double entendre, a pun.
বক্ষ, বক্ষস্থল,—উরঃ, বুক, ক্রোড়, the breast, chest, bosom.
বক্ষোজ, স্তন, কুচকলিকা, the female breasts or bosom.
বক্ষ্যমাণ, যাহা কহা যাইবে, কথয়িতব্য, hereafter to be mentioned or described.
বগা, ক্ষুদ্র খড়্গ, a small sword or hanger.
বঙ্ক, নদীর বাঁক, আড়, the turn or bend of a river, a reach.
বঙ্কিম, বক্র, পেঁচাল, পাকপড়া, crooked, tortuous, winding, bending.
বঙ্গ, রাঙ্গ, সীসা, কার্পাস, বাগুন, tin, calx of tin, lead, cotton, the egg plant.

বচন, কথা, বাক্য, ভাষা, সূত্র, ঋষিপ্রণীত পদ্য, a speech, sentence, word, voice, discourse, language, a rule, an aphorism.

বচনীয়, কথনীয়, নিন্দনীয়, proper to be spoken, utterable, censurable.

বচসা, বচাবচি,—বিবাদ, ঝকড়া, বিরোধ.discord, wrangling,squabbling, disputing, altercation.

বচস্কর, আজ্ঞাবহ, বশীভূত, obedient, subordinate.

বচ্ছ, বাছুর, বৎসতর, বালক, শাবক, a calf, a steer, a child, any young animal.

বজরা, আচ্ছাদনযুক্ত বৃহৎ নৌকা বিশেষ, a Budgerow or travelling boat.

বজ্র, ঝঞ্ঝনা, হীরক, কঠিন, অভেদ্য, আড়, কোণুয়া, a thunderbolt, a diamond ; hard, adamantine, impenetrable, cross, crosswise, forked.

বজ্রনিস্বন, দেবগর্জ্জন, মেঘনাদ, a clap of thunder.

বজ্রপাণি বা হস্ত,—বজ্রবিশিষ্ট অর্থাৎ ইন্দ্র, Indra, *i. e.* wielding the thunderbolt.

বজ্রবাঁটুল, ক্ষুদ্রকায় সাহসী লোক, one small in size but hardy and resolute.

বজ্রাভ, গোদন্তবৎ মণি বিশেষ, the chalcedony or opal.

বঞ্চক, প্রতারক, ধূর্ত্ত, শৃগাল, a knave, rogue, cheat, deceiver, a jackal.

বঞ্চন, ঠকান, ভুলান, to cheat, swindle, deceive; impose upon.

বঞ্চনা, প্রতারণা, ছলনা, ঠকামি, swindling, fraud, imposition, deceit, deception.

বট, ন্যগ্রোধ বৃক্ষ, এক কড়ি, the Indian fig tree, a single cowry.

বটিকা, বটা,—ঔষধের গুলী, বর্ত্তুল, a pill or bolus, a ball.

বটিয়া, কেরবাল, ক্ষুদ্র দাঁড়, a small oar or paddle.

বটী, রজ্জু, মালার দানা, জপমালা, রাজকর, a rope, a bead, a rosary, a sort of knife, an import, excise.

বটু, পরিচারক ব্রাহ্মণ, a Brahmachári after investiture.

বটে, স্বীকার বোধক শব্দ, হাঁ, অবশ্য, বস্তুতঃ, সত্য, ভাল, yes, indeed, truly, actually, verily, true, right.

বট্‌কারা, ব্যঙ্গ, বিদ্রূপ, banter, mocking, waggishness.

বট্‌কারিয়া, রসিক, কৌতুকী, a wag, banterer, mocker.

বড়, বৃহৎ, প্রশস্ত, ভারী, শ্রেষ্ঠ, ধনী, জ্যেষ্ঠ, অতিশয়, large, big, great, spacious, important, supreme, chief, noble, wealthy, elder, senior ; very, too.

বড়বা, ঘোটকী, অশ্বিনী, দাসী, a mare, the nymph Ashwiní, a female slave.

বড়বাগ্নি, বড়বানল,—জলস্থিত অগ্নি, ঔর্ব, submarine fire, a mythological being.

বড়বাভৃত, পরদাসীর জার, the gallant of another's slave-girl.

বড়মা, আপদ, বিপত্তি, misfortune, calamity personified.

বড়শা, শূল, বল্লম, টেঁটা, a spear, javelin, harpoon.

বড়শী, বড়িশ,—মৎস্য ধরণার্থ টোপাবৃত লৌহাস্ত্র, a fish-hook.

বড়া, ফুলরী, cakes of ground pulse fried in ghee.

বড়াই, মহত্ত্ব, গৌরব, অহমহমিকা, আত্মশ্লাঘা, greatness, grandeur, assumption, vaunting. vain-glory.

বড়ী, গুলী. গুটী, a ball, pill, bolus. a gingerbread-nut.

বড়ু, সেবাতী, পরিচারক ব্রাহ্মণ, a resident officiating brahmin.

বড়বড়ান, বক্‌বকান, জল্পন, to mutter, murmur, grumble, prate, chatter.

বড়, বৃহৎ, দুঃসহ্য, great, large, severe *as a wound*.

বঢ়ই, সূত্রধর, ছুতার, a carpenter.

বণিক, বাণিজ্যকারী, বেপারী, a trader, a merchant.

বণ্ট, বিভাগ, অংশ. a part, portion, share, dole.

বণ্টন, অংশন, পরিবেষণ, বিভাগ করণ, to share, dole or portion out, distribute, divide into shares.

বণ্ঠর, তালাঙ্কুর. বংশকোষ, the Tal or palm shoot, the bamboo sheath.

বণ্ড, মুক্তমুক্ত, নিষ্কল, পঙ্গু, ছিন্ন পুচ্ছ, ত্বক্‌ছিন্ন, castrated, emasculated, impotent, defective, crippled, docked, circumcised.

বৎ, ন্যায়, সদৃশ, আঠা, *affix* : as, like, similar ; a glutinous substance.

বৎস, বাছুর, যুবা বলদ, শাবক, শিশু, a calf, steer, any young animal, a child, *(a term of endearment.)*

বৎসতর, বৎসতরী,—যুবা বলদ, বকনা, *m. & f.* a steer, a heifer.

বৎসর, বর্ষ, অব্দ, দ্বাদশ মাস পরিমিত কাল, a year.

বৎসল, স্নেহকারী, অনুরাগী, fond, affectionate, kind.

বদন, মুখ, আস্য, আকার, the face, countenance, visage, form.

বদন, কহন, বলন, প্রকাশন, to speak, say, tell, declare.

বদান্য, দাতা, দানশীল, উদার, bountiful, munificent, liberal.

বদ্ধ, বন্দী, বন্ধনযুক্ত, বাঁধা, রুদ্ধ, আটকান, অস্রোত, মোদা, শক্ত, জড়, দাবিত, চাপা, নিবৃত্ত, শীলতাপ্রাপ্ত, imprisoned, bound, tied, fastened, confined, restrained, stagnant, shut, close, firm, squeezed together, staunched, stopped, confirmed in a habit or vice, &c.

বদ্ধক, রক্তপাতনিবারক, a stiptic.

বদ্ধকফ, শ্লেষ্মাতুর, afflicted with a cold or checked perspi- [ration.

বধ, হত্যা, murder, slaughter, an execution, killing.

বধন, মারণ, ঘাতন, to kill, slay, murder, smite, wound.

বধনীয়, বধ্য,—মারণার্হ, হননীয়, deserving death, worthy of death, vulnerable.

বধাবধি, মারামারি, a promiscuous or reciprocal slaughter.

বধিক, বধী,—অপঘাতী, হন্তা, murderous, sanguinary; a murderer.

বধির, শ্রবণেন্দ্রিয়হীন, কালা, deaf, hard of hearing, stunned.

বধু, বধূ,—স্ত্রী, ভার্য্যা, পুত্রের পত্নী, a woman, a wife, a son's wife.

বন, অরণ্য, কানন, বিপিন, উচ্ছন্ন স্থান, জঙ্গল, a forest, desert, wood, grove, thicket, an uncultivated place, or one full of weeds &c.

বনচর, বনচারক,—জঙ্গলী, অরণ্যবাসী, অরণ্যবেড়ানিয়া, wild, sylvan, travelling or dwelling in forests.

বনজ, জঙ্গলী, অরণ্যোৎপন্ন, wild, sylvan, produced in a forest.

বনপ্রবেশ, তপস্যারম্ভ, an entrance upon the life of an ascetic.

বনপ্রিয়, কোকিল, পিক, the Indian cuckoo.

বনবাসী, অরণ্যস্থায়ী, তপস্বী, residing in a forest: an anchorite.

বনমানুষ, চুয়াড়, বৃহৎ বানর বিশেষ, a wild man, the ouran outan.

বনমালী, কৃষ্ণ, নারায়ণ, Crishna.

বনরাজ, সিংহ, পশুপতি, the lion or king of the forest.

বনরাজী, শোভাকর বৃক্ষাদি, forest-adorning, beautiful (shrubs [&c.)

বনস্পতি, পনস ডুম্বরাদি, পুষ্প বিনা যে বৃক্ষের ফল জন্মে, trees bearing fruit without flowers.

বনস্থ, জঙ্গলী, আরণ্য, অরণ্যগামী, উদাসীন, wild, savage, forest; a hermit, an ascetic.

বনা, অন্নপাকাদি, প্রস্তুত বস্তু, a preparation (of food, &c.) [a thing prepared.

বনান, রচন, করণ, নির্ম্মাণ, গঠন, অন্নাদি রন্ধন, to make, manufacture, build, fabricate, frame, mould, to prepare or cook food, &c.

বনায়, বন্তি,—আত্মীয়তা, প্রণয়, প্রশ্রয়, intimacy, friendship, love, affection.

বনিতা, স্ত্রী, সুভগা, প্রিয়তমা a woman, a wife, a beloved wife, [a mistress.

বন্দুয়া, জঙ্গলী, বনচর, wild, sylvan, belonging to a forest.

বন্দ, বাঁধনী, গুচ্ছি. পটী, পটুকা, রজ্জু, দড়ী, কারাগার, পগার, অনুক্রম, গিরা, ভূমিখান, a fastening, knot, bandage, roller, belt, string, custody, a mound, fence, embankment, regularity, a knuckle, a parcel of ground, a piece of land. [&c.

বন্দক, পূজক, নমস্কারী, a worshipper, one who compliments,

বন্দন, প্রণাম করণ, আদরণ, নমস্কার, পূজা, to salute. to pay reverence or respect; a salutation, reverence, bow, prostration, worship.

বন্দনা, নমস্কার, প্রণাম, আরাধনা, স্তব, গানের প্রথমে মঙ্গলাচরণ, a salutation, bow, adoration, worship, praise, flattery, an introductory ascription of praise to some god at the commencement of Poems &c.

বন্দনীয়, বন্দ্য,—নমস্য, স্তবার্হ, আদরণীয়, আরাধ্য, worthy of respect or praise, venerable, adorable.

বন্দী, স্তুতিপাঠক, শত্রুগুপ্ত, কারাবদ্ধ, a parasite, flatterer, a captive, prisoner. [in confinement.

বন্দীয়ান্, বন্দুয়ান্,—কারাবদ্ধ, আট্‌কান জন্তু, a prisoner, an animal

বন্দীশালা, কারাগার, a prison, a jail.

বন্ধ, বেড়ী, সংযম, আটক, গুচ্ছি, আঁটনি, রোধ, ব্যাঘাত, বাধা, সংযোগ, শরীর, সংযত, আট্‌কান, বদ্ধ, রুদ্ধ, bonds, imprisonment, confinement, custody, a tie, fastening, hindrance, obstruction, close connection, intimate union as of body and spirit, the body; bound, confined, fastened, tied, shut.

বন্ধন, বাঁধন, গেঁঠ্যান, রোধন, আট্‌কান, ঘেরণ, বেষ্টন, কর নিরূপণ, বেড়ী, to tie, fasten, bind, hinder, obstruct, bar, close, shut, confine, imprison, enclose, gird, impose a tax; bonds, fastenings, fetters &c.

বন্ধক, আধি, গচ্ছিত ধনাদি, a pledge, pawn, mortgage.

বন্ধগত, বন্ধনগত,—বদ্ধ, আট্‌কান, গচ্ছিত, শরীরগত, bound, confined, pledged, embodied, connected with the body.

বন্ধনশালা, বন্ধনাগার,—কারাগার, a prison, a jail.

বন্ধনী, পটী, a bandage, ligament. roller, garter.

বন্ধান, বেতন, a stipend, salary, wages.

বন্দী, শত্রুগৃহীত, কারাবদ্ধ. a captive, prisoner, felon. [lation.
বন্ধু, মিত্র আত্মীয়. জ্ঞাতি. a friend. companion. kinsman, re-
বন্ধুতা, মিত্রতা, আত্মীয়তা. জ্ঞাতিত্ব, friendship, intimacy, acquaintance, relationship. [less.
বন্ধ্য, নিষ্ফল, বাঁঝা, নিঃসন্তান, unproductive, unfruitful, child-
বন্ধ্যা, অফলা, বাঁঝী, রণ্ডা, *f.* barren, sterile, unfruitful.
বন্য, আরণ্য, জঙ্গলী, বনজাত, sylvan, rural, wild, savage.
বন্যা, জলপ্লাবন, a deluge, a flood, an overflowing of water.
বপন, বীজ ক্ষেপণ, বুনন, রোপণ, to sow seed, to weave, to plant. [flesh, a sowing.
বপা, বসা, মাংসের তৈল, বীজক্ষেপ, fat, the marrow of the
বপুঃ, শরীর, দেহ, the body. [father, progenitor.
বপ্তা, বীজক্ষেপক, রোপক, জনক, বীজপুরুষ, a sower, planter,
বভ্রু, বড় বেজী, a large mongoose.
বমন, উদ্গারণ to vomit, throw off the stomach, to retch.
বমি, বমী,—বামক ঔষধি, ছর্দ্দি, an emetic, a vomiting, the substance vomited. [gushing out.
বম্‌কী, ছর্দি, বলেতে জলাদির ঊর্দ্ধনিঃসরণ, a vomiting. spouting up,
বয়ঃ, আয়ুঃ, গতপরমায়ুকাল, যৌবন, age, time of life, youth.
বয়ঃক্রম, পরমায়ু, জীবনকাল, the allotted period of life, age.
বয়দা, বিফলাণ্ড, an egg not impregnated.
বয়প্রাপ্ত, বয়স্থ,—যুবা, যৌবনবিশিষ্ট, প্রৌঢ়, সবল, young, in the prime of life, middle aged, mature.
বয়স্থা, তারুণ্য, যৌবনাবস্থা, youth, manhood, prime of life.
বয়স্ক, বয়সীয়া,—তদ্বৎসরের, বর্ষীয়, *affix* : of such an age.
বয়স্য, সমানবয়স্ক, সমকালিক, এককালীন, বন্ধু, সখা, of the same age, cotemporary ; a contemporary, companion, friend, associate, confidant.
বয়ার, মহিষ, বায়ু, পবন, a buffalo, air, the wind.
বর, প্রদান, ইষ্টদান, প্রতিজ্ঞা, প্রার্থনা, বাঞ্ছিত, পাত্র, স্বামী, শ্রেষ্ঠ, উত্তম, a boon, gift, blessing, promise, wish, desire, request, choice, a bridegroom, husband ; *in compos* : chief, excellent, best.
বরং, বরঞ্চ,—অপেক্ষাকৃত শ্রেয়, তদপেক্ষা, অথবা, rather, or rather, but rather, in preference, but, though, nay, on the contrary.

বরগা, কড়িকাঠ, আড়কাঠ, a rafter, a beam.
বরজ, পর্ণক্ষেত্র, a field or plantation of *Pán* or betel.
বরট. হংস, রাজহংস, a gander.
বরটা, বরটী,—হংসী, বোল্তা. a goose, a wasp.
বরণ, বিবাহ নিরূপণ, দানকরণ, বিতরণ, নির্ধারণ, প্রতিনিধি নিরূপণ, তিল, ব্যবধান, to betroth, to promise in marriage, to make gifts, give earnest, to appoint a representative ; a freckle, a fence, a screen.
বরণীয়, গ্রহণীয়, উপযুক্ত. বাঞ্ছনীয়, eligible, proper to be chosen.
বরদ, প্রসন্ন. অনুগ্রাহক, বাঞ্ছিতফলদাতা, উপকারক, propitious, favourable. granting a prayer; a benefactor.
বরদা, কন্যা, কুমারী, গৌরী, a girl, virgin, maid. [damsel.
বরপাত্র, নববিবাহিত. বাগ্দত্ত, a bridegroom, one betrothed to a
বরযাত্রী, বরের সহচর, an attendant on a bridegroom.
বরলা. ভেমরুল, বোল্তা, হংসী, a hornet, a wasp, a goose.
বরশা, টেঁটা, পোলো, বর্শি, a harpoon, a spear, a fish-hook.
বরা. বরাহনী,—শূকর, শূকরী, *m. & f.* a hog, boar, pig, sow.
বরাট-ক, কপর্দ্দক, কড়ি, a cowry, money.
বরিবসিত, চরণসেবিত, উপাসিত, আরাধিত, served obsequiously, waited on. honoured, adored.
বরিবস্যা, উপাসনা, চরণসেবা, respectful service, honour, obsequious attendance. [flowers, &c.
বরিষণ, বৃষ্টিপড়ন, ঝরণ, to fall or shower down as rain, dust,
বরিষা, বর্ষাকাল প্রাবৃট্কাল, the rains, the rainy season.
বরিষ্ঠ, শ্রেষ্ঠ, অত্যুত্তম. প্রিয়তম, best, most excellent, dearest, most beloved.
বরুণ, পশ্চিমদিগের অধিপতি, Varuna the god of waters.
বরেণ্য, প্রধান, উত্তম, উৎকৃষ্ট, প্রার্থনীয়, বাঞ্ছনীয়, chief, principal, pre-eminent, choice, desirable.
বর্গ, একজাতীয় সমূহ, বর্ণ, গণ, প্রকরণ, a class, tribe. number of similar things, a section, a square in numbers.
বর্গীকৃত, বর্গীভূত,—বর্ণীকৃত, জাতীভূত, classified, become a class or genus. [&c.
বর্গীয়, বর্ণক, জাতীয়, belonging to a class, tribe or genus,
বর্জ্জন, ত্যজন, ছাড়ন, নিন্দন, নিরাকরণ, to abandon, forsake, avoid, reject, relinquish, censure, except, expel.

বর্জনীয়, নিন্দনীয়, অনুচিত, দুষ্ট, censurable, exceptionable, improper, wicked. [birds, &c.

বর্জিত, পরিত্যক্ত, শিটা, বিট, rejected &c; refuse, dung of

বর্ণ, ব্রাহ্মণাদি, জাতি, স্বজাতিসমূহ, গণ, রঙ্গ, শুক্লকৃষ্ণাদি, ঘোটকাদির চিত্রকম্বল, অঙ্গরঙ্গণ, সৌন্দর্য্য, সুখ্যাতি, স্তুতি, অক্ষর, ঘড়ি, ধর্ম্ম, ভাব, গুণ, উত্তম স্বর্ণ প্রমাণ, a class, tribe, cast, order, colour, die, tint, hue, the housings of horses, &c. a staining of the body with coloured unguents, a theatrical dress, beauty, lustre, fame, celebrity, praise, a letter, syllable, property, quality, the fineness or pure colour of gold, an arithmetical quantity.

বর্ণক, অঙ্গরাগ, ভাট, গুণগাথক, সঙ্কীর্ত্তক, বর্গীয়, জাতীয়, a perfume for the body, paint, pigment, a bard, panegyrist, poetical encomiast, describer, the standard of gold; belonging to a tribe or class.

বর্ণন, সবিশেষ কহন, বিস্তারণ, শৃঙ্খলাপূর্ব্বক কথন, স্তুতিকরণ, সঙ্কীর্ত্তন, to describe, detail, delineate, narrate, relate, to praise, extol, eulogize.

বর্ণনা, বিবরণ, বৃত্তান্ত, স্তব, গুণবাদ, a description, relation, narration, praise, panegyric.

বর্ণমালা, ক্রমিক অক্ষর সমূহ, an alphabet, the series of letters.

বর্ণসঙ্কর, মিশ্রিত জাতি, বিজাতীয়, a mixed cast; mixed, mongrel.

বর্ণী, চিত্রকর, লেখক, ব্রহ্মচারী, a painter, scribe, writer, a religious student.

বর্ত্তন, হওন, জিয়ন, থাকন, অর্পন, স্থাবরধন, বৃত্তি, জীবিকা, ব্যবসায়, স্থাবর, অটল, স্থির, থাকনিয়া, স্থায়ী, to be, exist, subsist, belong to; fixed property, a maintenance, livelihood, profession; fixed, stable, stationary, abiding, staying, remaining.

বর্ত্তনীয়, বর্ত্তিতব্য,—সম্ভাব্য, ঘটনীয়, possible, probable, likely.

বর্ত্তমান, বিদ্যমান, জীবৎ, সাক্ষাৎকার, প্রস্তুত, being, existing, alive, extant, present, ready.

বর্ত্তি, বর্ত্তিকা,—বাতী, শলিতা, প্রদীপ, তুলী, রেখা, a wick, match, candle, lamp, a paint brush, a ruled line.

বর্ত্তিত, ভূত, উপজন, been, become.

বর্ত্তী, স্থ, স্থিত, স্থায়ী, *affix*: being, existing, fixed, &c.

বর্ত্তুল, মণ্ডল, গোলাকার বস্তু, গুলী, a circle, globe, ball, sphere, a marble, bullet, ball of earth, a pea. [lid.

বর্ত্ম, বর্ত্মন্,—পথ, মার্গ, চক্ষুর পাতা, a road, path, way, an eye-

বর্দ্ধক, বাড়ানিয়া, বৃদ্ধিজনক, প্রতিপাদক, বর্দ্ধনশীল, causing increase, promoting, augmenting, growing.

বর্দ্ধন, বাড়ন, বৃদ্ধি পাওন, শ্রীমন্ত হওন, to increase, grow, thrive, improve, prosper.

বর্দ্ধনীয়, বাড়নীয়, capable of increase or improvement.

বর্দ্ধমান, বর্দ্ধনশীল, পয়মন্ত, ধনীভূত, অধিকীকৃত, স্ফীতীকৃত, increasing, growing, thriving, prosperous, rich, augmented, accelerated.

বর্দ্ধিত, বাড়িত, উন্নত, কল্যাণী, বৃদ্ধিপ্রাপ্ত, বিস্তারিত, increased, thriven, prosperous, grown, expanded, extended.

বর্দ্ধিষ্ণু, বাড়নিয়া, পয়মন্ত, বর্দ্ধনশীল, ধন বাড়ানিয়া, enlarging, increasing, growing, improving, prosperous.

বর্ব্বর, চণ্ডাল, ম্লেচ্ছ, পামর, নীচ লোক, মূর্খ, অত্যন্ত নির্বুদ্ধি, an outcast, barbarian, one of a degraded tribe or occupation, a stupidly ignorant man.

বর্ম্ম, গাত্রীয় কবচ, সজ্জা, armour, a coat of mail.

বর্ম্মা, বর্ম্মী,—সজ্জাযুক্ত, কবচী, ক্ষত্রিয়, তুরপণ, mailed, accoutred; a Cshyatriya, an awl.

বর্শি, বড়িশ, পোলো, a fish-hook, harpoon, fish-spear.

বর্ষ, হায়ন, বৎসর, বৃষ্টি, ভারতাদি নব পৃথিবীখণ্ড, a year, rain, raining, a great continental division.

বর্ষজীবী, ওষধী, ফলপাকান্ত, ধান্যাদি, annual (plants, shrubs &c.)

বর্ষণ, বৃষ্টি পড়ন, to rain, fall as rain or hail, to shower.

বর্ষবৃদ্ধি, বর্ষপ্রবেশ,—জন্মদিন, সাম্বৎসরীয় পর্ব্ব, a birth day, an anniversary. [rainy season.

বর্ষা, বৃষ্টিপাত, প্রাবৃট্কাল, rain, a shower, the rains, the

বর্ষাতি, ঘোটকের বর্ষাকালীন পাদস্ফীতি, বর্ষাকালের পরিধেয় বস্ত্র, a disease in the feet of horses appearing in the rains, an outer garment for the rainy season.

বর্ষাবৎ, প্রাবৃট্, rainy, showery.

বর্ষাভূ, বর্ষাভী,—মণ্ডূক, মণ্ডূকী, *m. & f.* a frog.

বর্ষী, বর্ষীয়,—বয়স্ক, তদ্বৎসরের, of a particular age,—old.

বর্ষোপল, করকা, শিলাবৃষ্টি, শিলাপাথর, hail, a hail-stone.
বর্হ, ময়ূরের পুচ্ছ, ময়ূরের শিখা, a peacock's tail or crest.
বর্হী, ময়ূর, শিখণ্ডী, ভুজঙ্গভুক্, a peacock.
বল, পরাক্রম, সামর্থ্য, শক্তি, তেজ, বিক্রম, অত্যাচার, সৈন্য, strength, might, power, energy, vigour, force, violence, an army, forces, a chessman.
বলদ, দামড়া, ভারবাহক গরু, an ox, a bullock.
বলন, কহন, কথন, to speak, say, tell, propose.
বলবৎ, শক্তিমান, শক্ত, প্রকাণ্ড, স্থূল, সবল, দৃঢ়, অখণ্ডনীয়, প্রমাণসিদ্ধ, চলিত, প্রচণ্ড, powerful, strong, stout, lusty, solid, firm, valid, substantial, authentic, prevalent, violent. [rous, courageous, bold.
বলবান্, বলবন্ত—শক্তিমান, বিক্রমী, সাহসী, strong, powerful, vigo-
বলয়, বালা, কঙ্কণ, করভূষণ, a bracelet, an armlet.
বলয়িত, বেষ্টিত, ঘেরিত, surrounded, encircled, encompassed.
বলাকা, উড্ডীয়মান বক শ্রেণী, ক্ষুদ্র বক বিশেষ, a flight of cranes, the black crane. [dendum of the cow.
বলাট, কলাই বিশেষ, গোযোনি, a sort of split pulse, the pu-
বলাৎকার, হঠ, দৌরাত্ম্য, অত্যাচার, স্ত্রীজাতিনাশকরা, violence, force, oppression, violation, rape. [speak.
বলান, কহান, কথন শিক্ষান, to cause to speak, teach to
বলাবলি, কহাকহি, আলাপ, conversation, chat, discourse.
বলি, দেবোদ্দেশে বধ্য পশু, ইষ্টি, উৎসর্গ, উপকরণ, লোলিত চর্ম্ম, ঝোলা, a sacrifice, victim, oblation, offering, the folds of the flesh about the navel in stout persons, (especially in women,) a wrinkle.
বলিপ্রিয়, শকুনি দ্রোণকাকাদি উচ্ছিষ্টভোজি পক্ষী, predacious, delighting in sacrificial places; any bird of prey, a vulture, crow, &c. [a crow, a crane.
বলিভুক্, বলিমাংসাহারী, কাকাদি, feeding on sacrificial food;
বলিষ্ঠ, বলী, বল্য, } শক্তিমান, তেজস্বী, সাহসী, powerful, strong,
বলীয়ান্, বলীয়স্, } able, vigorous, gallant, bold.
বলীবর্দ্দ, বলীবর্দ্ধ,—বলদ, বৃষ, দামড়া, a bull, an ox, a bullock.
বল্কন, বল্গন,—ফুটন, উথলন, to boil, simmer, bubble up.
বল্কল, বৃক্ষের ছাল, ত্বক্, the bark of a tree.
বল্কান, উত্তাপন, ফুটান, to heat gently, make to boil.

বল্কা, ঈষদুষ্ণ, tepid, lukewarm, once boiled.

বল্গু, সুন্দর, মনোহর, beautiful, captivating.

বল্গা, মুখস, বাগ, the bit of a bridle, a bridle, a rein.

বল্গিত, ঘোটকের প্লুতগতি, a horse's gallop, a canter.

বল্মীক, উইপোকা, তৎ কৃত মৃত্তিকা রাশি, a white ant, a hillock of earth thrown up by ants or moles, an ant-hill.

বল্লব, গোপ, পাচক, a cowherd, herdsman, milkman, cook.

বল্লভ-া, প্রিয়-া, ইষ্ট-া, পতিপত্নী, সখাসখী, *m. & f.* dear, desired, beloved ; a lover, one beloved, a husband, wife, mistress, friend.

বল্লী, লতা, বৃক্ষাবলম্বিত তৃণ, a creeper or climbing plant.

বশ, অধীনতা, অনুনয়, দমন, অধিকার, আয়ত্ত, অধীন, দমিত, বিনয়ী, subjection, thraldom, controul, submission, authority ; captivated, enthralled, subdued, subjugated, tamed, submissive.

বশতঃ, অধীনভাবতঃ, under subjection or controul. [tion.

বশতা, অধীনতা, দমন, জয়করা, controul, subjection, subjuga-

বশতাপন্ন, আয়ত্ত, দমিত, অধীন, brought under controul, subdued, tamed, dependant.

বশীকরণ, আয়ত্তীকরণ, মোহন, মন্ত্রাদি দ্বারা দমন, to subdue, bring into subjection, to fascinate or subdue by magical charms, incantations, &c.

বশীকৃত বা ভূত,—আয়ত্তীকৃত, দমিত, মোহিত, অধীন, বিনয়ী, অনুচর, subjugated, subdued, conquered, tamed, dependant, submissive, obedient ; a retainer.

বশ্য, আয়ত্ত, আজ্ঞাবহ, বিনয়ী, দম্য, বাধ্য, অধীন, দাস, subject, obedient, docile, tame, humble. controulable, governable ; a dependant, a slave.

বসৎ, বসতি,—গৃহ, বাসস্থান, a dwelling, abode, residence.

বসদ্বাটী, বাসালয়, ঘর, গৃহ, a dwelling-house.

বসন, বাসকরণ, থাকন, উপবেশন, তলন, থিতন, ঘন হওন, বস্ত্র, to dwell, reside, sit, sit down, sink, subside, clot, coagulate ; clothing, dress, a garment.

বসনিয়া, বসিয়া,—সপরিবারে বাসকারী, নিবাসী, dwelling, residing, resident ; an inhabitant. [small-pox.

বসন্ত, পুষ্পসময়, চৈত্র বৈশাখ, রক্তবটী, the spring months, the

বসন্তী, কমলাবৎ রঙ্গ, an orange colour. [flesh, a sitting.
বসা, - বপা, মাংসতৈল, উপবেশন, fat, suet, the marrow of the
বসান, আসনস্থীকরণ, পত্তন করাণ, সংস্থাপন, রাখন, পুতন, দাবন, ঠোকন, মণিআদি জড়াম, থিতান, ঘনীকরণ, to seat, cause to sit, settle, people, establish, place, lay, fix, flatten, compress, to lodge, drive a nail, set a stone, to precipitate, make to subside or sink, to coagulate, to candy.
বসিন্দা, নিবাসী, residing, dwelling, an inhabitant.
বসু, ধ্রুবাদি অষ্ট দেবতা, যুগের বন্ধনী, রত্ন, ধন, বিত্ত, দ্রব্য, জল, a kind of demigod, the tie of a yoke, a gem, jewel, wealth, a thing, substance, matter, water.
বসুধা, বসুন্ধরা, বসুমতী,—পৃথিবী, the earth.
বসুধারা, বৈদিক কর্ম্মের পূর্বে ভিত্তির গাজে ঘৃত ঢালন, a ceremonial pouring of oil on the wall of a house.
বস্তব্য, নিবাসোপযুক্ত স্থান, habitable, inhabitable.
বস্তি, নগর, গ্রাম, বাসস্থান, জরায়ু, জঠর, a town, village, habitation, the pelvis, the womb, the abdomen.
বস্তু, পদার্থ, দ্রব্য, সামগ্রী, নির্বাহ, প্রস্থ, a thing, substance, matter, materials, ingredients, utensils, stuff, baggage. [is to say.
বস্তুতঃ, যথার্থতঃ, ফলতঃ, অর্থাৎ, in reality, in fact, viz; that
বস্তুতস্তু, যথার্থতঃ, ফলতঃ, in reality, in a word.
বস্তুতা, পদার্থতা, দেহিত্ব, প্রকৃতত্ব, সত্যতা, substantiality, materiality, reality, fact.
বস্ত্র, কাপড়, বেশ, cloth, clothing, a garment, dress, habit.
বস্ত্রগৃহ, তাম্বু, রাউটী, a tent.
বস্ত্রবিলাস, ফুলফুল্যামি, বেশধারণেতে গর্ব, foppery, dressiness, pride in dress. [warehouse.
বস্ত্রাগার, তাম্বু, কাপড় বিক্রয়শালা, a tent, a draper's or clothier's
বহন, স্থানান্তরে লওন, ভার ধারণ, সহন, যানাদি টানন, চলান, স্রোতাদির গমন, ভাসন, চলন, ক্ষরণ, ক্ষয় হওন, to carry, to bear, to draw a carriage, transport, convey, to flow, float, sail, pass by or away, (as time or a river,) to circulate as the blood, to blow as the wind, to decay, to wear away.

বহনীয়, সহনীয়, লঘুভার, দ্রুত, that may be carried &c. portable, flowing. [width of water.

বহর, ভাসমান নৌকা সমূহ, স্রোতের প্রস্থ, a fleet of boats, the

বহান, চালান, দৌড়ান, যাপন, চলান, যানাদি টানন, উড়ান, to impel, urge forward, row, steer, guide a plough, to spend time, carry or transport goods, draw a carriage &c. to waste, lavish. [vish.

বহানিয়া, চালানিয়া, ব্যয়শীল, impelling, urging forwards, la-

বহি, বহী,—খাতা, ক্ষুদ্র পুস্তক, পুথী, লিপি, an account-book, a book, tract, register, record.

বহিঃ, বহির,— বাহির, অনভ্যন্তরে, বাহ্য, গায়স্থ, *pref*: without, outside, out, out of, outwards; external.

বহিঃস্থ, বাহ্য, বাহিরের. external, outer, situated without.

বহিত্র, ভেলা, তরণি, নৌকা, a raft, a float, boat, vessel.

বহিনী, ভগিনী, স্বসা, সহোদরা, a sister.

বহিরঙ্গ, বিদেশী, শত্রু, অনাত্মীয়, কর্ম্মের সাধারণ অঙ্গ, a stranger, a foe, one not connected by consanguinity, a preliminary ceremony.

বহিরিন্দ্রিয়, কর্ম্মেন্দ্রিয়, পাণিপাদাদি, the organs of action.

বহির্দেশ, বিদেশ, বাহ্যস্থান, a foreign country, the outskirts of a town or village used as a privy.

বহির্দ্বার, গৃহের প্রবেশ পথ, a gate, an outer door, an entrance.

বহির্বাসঃ, উত্তরীয় কাপড়, উড়নী, an external covering, the outer flowing garment of the Hindoos.

বহির্ভূত, নিঃসারিত, নিরাকৃত, বাহ্য, গত, ওদিগস্থ, অপ্রয়োজনীয়, অনবধান, excluded, expelled, external, past, gone, beyond, irrelevant, careless, inattentive.

বহির্মুখ, পাষণ্ড, কটুবাদী, পরাঙ্মুখ, বিরত, বাহড়নিয়া, অপ্রসন্ন, impious, blasphemous, scurrilous, averted, ceasing, desisting from, turning back, unpropitious. [exclusion.

বহিষ্করণ, নিঃসারণ, নিরাকরণ, to expel, exclude; expulsion,

বহিস্তল, উপরিভাগ, বাহ্য, গা, the outer surface of a thing.

বহিস্ত্বক্, উত্তরীয় মাংস চর্ম্ম, উপরিস্থ বল্কল, the epidermis or skarf-skin, the outer bark or peel of plants.

বহীকার, পুস্তক বাঁধনিয়া লোক, a book-binder.

বহু, ভূরি, অধিক, অনেক, অতিশয়, *pref*: much, many, great, long, numerous; very, exceedingly.

বহুকালীন, বহুকালিক,—চিরকালিক, প্রাচীন, of long standing, chronic, ancient, old. [dant.

বহুত, ভূরি, অনেক, বিস্তর, much, many, numerous, abun-

বহুতা, বাহুল্য, অনেকত্ব, abundance, plenty, plurality, multiplicity. [servant.

বহুদর্শক, বহুদর্শী,—জ্ঞানী, প্রাজ্ঞ, wise, knowing, prudent, ob-

বহুধা, বিবিধ, অনেকধা, নানাপ্রকারে, বারম্বার, various, manifold; in many ways, often, oftentimes.

বহুপ্রজ, মানুষময়, বিস্তর সন্তানপ্রাপ্ত, populous, prolific.

বহুপ্রজা, বহুফলা,—পুনঃপুনঃ প্রসূতা, *f.* prolific, having borne many children.

বহুবর্ষক, চিরস্থায়ী, চিরকালিক, continuing many years; perennial.

বহুবিধ, নানাপ্রকার, নানামত, বিশেষ২, of many kinds or sorts, various, multiform. [attributive.

বহুব্রীহি, অন্য পদার্থের প্রধান সমাস, a compound adjective or

বহুভার্য্য, অনেক স্ত্রী বিশিষ্ট, having many wives; a polygamist.

বহুভাষী, বাচাল, গপ্পিয়া, বাবদূক, garrulous, talkative.

বহুমর্ম্মক, ঘাঁতনিয়া, মর্ম্মভেদক, নানার্থব্যাপক, affecting, touching, piercing to the quick, comprehensive.

বহুযতি, নানাবর্ণক শব্দ, polysyllabic, of many syllables.

বহুরূপ, নানাকৃতি, সরট, multiform; a camelion, a polypus.

বহুরূপী, নানাবেশধারী, নানাকার, অনেকাকৃতি, assuming many forms, many-shaped, multiform.

বহুল, অধিক, অনেক, বিস্তর, much, abundant, prolix.

বহ্নি, অগ্নি, অগ্নিকোণের অধিপতি, fire or its deity.

বহ্নিমুখ, দেবতা, দানবারি, a god, a deity.

বহ্বাশী, অতৃপ্ত, অমর, বহুভোজনাকাঙ্ক্ষী, অবক্ষুধিত, insatiable, insatiate, voracious, ravenous, greedy.

বা, বিকল্পবোধক শব্দ, or, either, perhaps.

বাই, বাতরোগ, উন্মাদ, নাটকী, rheumatism, flatulence, enthusiasm, a dancing girl. [attempt.

বাইমারা, আলস্য, অলীকক্রিয়া, পণ্ডশ্রম, idleness, levity, a vain

বাইয়া, বাতাসীয়া, অজ্ঞান, windy, flatulent, silly, idiotic.

বাইশ, পাথুরা, ২২, আশ্চর্য্য, a chisel, 22; *interject*: amazing!

বাউমিয়া, বামন, খাট, হ্রস্ব, dwarf, pigmy, short.
বাউড়া, বাউল,—ক্ষিপ্ত, পাগল, insane, mad, foolish, idiotic.
বাওড়, বাঁওড়.—বৃহৎ জলাশয়, সরোবর, a lake.
বাওড়ী, বাঁওড়ী,—ফেরা, বায়ুগুল্ফি, পৌষমাসের অন্তিম দিবস, a circuit, a whirlwind, the last day of Paus. [sieve.
বাওরন, শস্য ঝাড়ন, উচলন, পাছড়ন, to winnow, to toss in a
বাঁউ, বাহু, ব্যাম, যুগ, ধনু. a fathom, six feet.
বাঁক, ভারের দণ্ড, বক্রতা, মোড়, নদীর ফের, পাদাভরণ বিশেষ, a carrying yoke or cooly-lathe, a crook, bend, turning in a river, a ring for the legs. [foppish.
বাঁকড়া, দুরন্ত, নির্লজ্জ, ফুল্‌ফুলিয়া bold, audacious, impudent,
বাঁকন, বক্র হওন, মোড়ন, নোয়ন, ঝোঁকন, to be crooked, to bend, turn, bow, bend down.
বাঁকা, বক্র, টেরা, ঠেটা. পাকপড়া. দুঃসাহসী, দুরন্ত, bent, crooked, awry, sinuous, winding, foolhardy, obstinate.
বাঁচন, রক্ষা পাওন, পলান, থাকন, জীবন, to escape, survive, remain, continue, live. [verance.
বাঁচাও, রক্ষা, নিস্তার, escape, safety, refuge, rescue, deli-
বাঁচান, আপদোদ্ধরণ. রক্ষণ, আশ্রয় দেওন, ক্ষমা করণ, জীয়ান, to save, preserve, protect, defend, extricate, shelter, screen, uphold, spare, revive, refresh.
বাঁজা, বাঞ্জী,—বন্ধ্যা, অফলা, barren, sterile, unproductive.
বাঁট, বিভাগ, পশুস্তনাগ্র, মুঠী, a share, portion, lot, allowance, distribution, a dug, teat, the handle of a tool.
বাঁটন, বিভাগ করণ, অংশন, পরিবেশন. to share out, distribute, portion, allot, divide into shares, dispense.
বাঁটা, বিভাগ, অংশ, কলঙ্ক, a partition, allotment, portion, share, a blot, a stigma.
বাঁটিয়া, বাঁঠিয়া—খাট, বামন, low in stature, short, dwarf.
বাঁটুল, গুলী, কর্কর, মৃৎখণ্ড, a ball, shot, pill, bolus, pebble.
বাঁটখরা বা খারা,—টক, a weight of stone or other material.
বাঁটো. ব্যাজ, an allowance on money, discount.
বাঁড়িয়া,- বণ্ড, পুচ্ছহীন, bereft of the tail, tailless, docked.
বাঁধ, সেতু, রোধন, a dam, a binding, stopping, &c.
বাঁধন, আঁটন, যড়ান, গেঁঠ্যান, রোধন, আটকান, নিবারণ, ঘেরণ, মণি বসান, গড়ন, শান করণ, রচন, কলান, to bind, fasten,

tie, shut, stop, clog, obstruct, impede, confine, hinder, staunch, to gird, inclose, set a jewel, to build, pave, invent, contrive.

বাঁধা, গচ্ছিত ধনাদি, প্রতিবন্ধক, কল্পনা, আটক, a pawn. pledge, mortgage, an invention, a hindrance.

বাঁধনী, আঁটনি, রুদ্ধকরা, সিঁড়ি. শান, a fastening, shutting, stopping, &c. a knot, a pavement. [sidered.

বাঁধাল, সেতু, সুকল্পিত, a bank, a dam; judicious, well con-

বাঁশ, বংশ, বেণু, a bamboo, a piece of bamboo.

বাঁশী, বেণু, সানায়ী, মুরলী, a flute, fife, pipe, whistle.

বাক্, কথা, ভাষা, a word, speech, language, tongue.

বাকল-া, ছাল, ত্বক্, the bark of a tree, rind, integument, husk.

বাক্চাপল্য, গল্পাসল্প, gossiping, chattering, idle talk.

বাক্চাতুরী, গল্প, ব্যঙ্গ, গরিমা, wit, a joke, sprightly sally, brag.

বাক্ছল, ব্যাজ, টালমটাল, বিবাদ, ঝকড়া, a pretence, evasion, prevarication, a quarrel. altercation.

বাক্জাল, বাগ্জাল,—বাক্যস্বরূপ ফাঁদ, বাক্যের বাহুল্য, an ensnaring speech, a maze of words, a circumlocution.

বাক্পটু, সৎকথক, বাক্য ভেদে নিপুণ, eloquent, clever in speaking, skilled in words. [eloquent.

বাক্পতি, বৃহস্পতি, সদ্বক্তা, Vrihaspati, a master of language;

বাক্প্রবন্ধ, গ্রন্থরচনা, বাক্যবাহুল্য, টাল. original composition, circumlocution, prolixity. [tiveness.

বাক্ব্যয়, দ্বিরুক্তি, বাচালতা, tautology, waste of words, talka-

বাক্সিদ্ধ, যাহার কথনেতে বহুগুণ আছে, উক্তসম্পাদনক্ষম, whose word is efficacious, able to do or make good his word or pretensions. [sion, language.

বাক্য, কথা, বলা, ভাষা, a word, speech, sentence, expres-

বাক্যজ্ঞ, মনোযোগী, আজ্ঞাবহ, ভাব, বাক্যের অভিপ্রায়, attentive to what is spoken, obedient; the meaning or design of a passage. [lime.

বাখারি, কাবারী, তণ্ডচূর্ণ, a split of bamboo, a lathe, quick-

বাগীশ, কথনে নিপুণ, বৃহস্পতি, eloquent; a master of language, Vrihaspati. [quence.

বাগীশ্বরী, বাগ্দেবী,—সরস্বতী, Saraswati the goddess of elo-

বাগুনীয়া, বাগুন ফলবৎ রঙ, ধূম্র, of a purple colour, purple.

বাগুরা, মৃগ ধরিবার জাল, a net for catching deer.
বাগুরিক, মৃগজীবী, লুব্ধক, ব্যাধ, a deer-catcher, a hunter.
বাগে, দিগে, কাছে, পানে, on the side, in the direction of.
বাগে২, এদিক্‌ওদিক্‌, দিখিদিগ্‌, on this side and that, in various directions. [scruple.
বাগ্‌ড়া, ফেরফার, সন্দেহ, শঙ্কা, intricacy, perplexity, hesitation,
বাগ্দণ্ড, অনুযোগ, বাক্য তাড়না, a reproof, admonition.
বাগ্দত্ত, প্রত্ত. বিবাহে দত্ত. betrothed. promised in marriage.
বাগ্দান, কথায় বিবাহ নিশ্চয় করা, a promising in marriage, a betrothing.
বাগ্দুষ্ট, তিরস্কৃত, ভর্ৎসিত, নিন্দিত, দুর্মুখ, বিব্রুবন্‌, দুরন্বয়বাদী, defamed, abused, evil spoken of, blamed, found fault with, abusive, speaking ill or ungrammatically.
বাগ্বজ্র. অভিশাপ, an imprecation, a curse.
বাগ্বিদগ্ধা, কথনে মোহিনী, রসিকা, *f.* bland, insinuating, fascinating in speech. [cious.
বাগ্মী, বাবদূক, বাচাল, eloquent, fluent, talkative, loqua-
বাঘ, ব্যাঘ্র, শার্দুল, a tiger. [and daring woman.
বাঘিনী, ব্যাঘ্রী, কাণ্ঠী, দুঃসাহসিনী, a tigress, a virago, a bold
বাঙ্গলা, বঙ্গদেশীয়, দ্বিচালা, Bengalese; a bungalow or thatched house. [gal, Bengali.
বাঙ্গালা, বাঙ্গালী,—বঙ্গদেশীয়. Bengalese, pertaining to Ben-
বাঙ্নিষ্ঠা. বাক্যের বিশ্বস্ততা, স্থিরবাদ, নিশ্চয়কথা, punctuality, faithfulness to one's word, an affirmation, assertion.
বাঙ্নিষ্পত্তি, কথা, উচ্চারণ, উত্তর, দৃঢ়বাদিত্ব, a speech, utterance, reply, the fulfilment of one's word.
বাঙ্ময়, বহুভাষী, কথনে নিপুণ. অলঙ্কার শাস্ত্র, সদুক্তত্ব, loquacious, talkative, eloquent, rhetorical; rhetorical composition, eloquence.
বাঙ্মল, কটুবাক্য, abuse or scurrilous language. [speech.
বাঙ্মুখ, উপন্যাস, প্রস্তাবনা, an exordium, the opening of a
বাচক, কথক, সূচক, সুস্পষ্ট, পাঠক, speaking, declaring, expressing, expressive, plain; a reader, reciter.
বাচড়া, পড়াভূমি, ঘোটকের শাবক, waste or uncultivated land; a colt, a foal.
বাচনিক, শাস্ত্রসিদ্ধ, আদিষ্ট, কথিত, কথনার্হ, enjoined by the shas-

ters, directed, expressed, mentioned, worthy of being expressed.

বাচস্পতি, ভাষাবেত্তা, বৃহস্পতি, a master of language, Vrihas- [pati.

বাচাও. বুঝাই. ব্যাখ্যা, an explanation, an exposition.

বাচান, বুঝান, প্রকাশন, কহান, to explain, unfold, cause to speak.

বাচাল, বাবদূক, বহুভাষী, talkative, garrulous, chattering, [sprightly.

বাচিক, সূচক, প্রমুখাৎ, সুস্পষ্ট, শাব্দিক, expressing, expressive, verbal, vocal.

বাচিত, উক্ত, আদিষ্ট, mentioned, expressed, declared, en- [joined.

বাচ্চা, শাবক, ছা, শিশু, the young of an animal.

বাচ্য, কথনীয়, উপাধেয়, ত্রিলিঙ্গসাধ্য, তুচ্ছনীয়, কথা, বোধ, অভিপ্রায়, fit or proper to be expressed, predicable, attributable, declinable (as an adjective,) contemptible; a word, idea, meaning, predicate.

বাছন, চুনন, পৃথক্ করণ, to pick, choose, select, to sort, separate from.

বাছা, শিশু, সন্ততি, মনোনীত, a child, offspring; selected [&c.

বাছুর, গোবৎস, বৎসতর, a calf, a steer.

বাজ, ঝঞ্ঝনা, নিনাদ, ত্বরা, পাখা, ঘৃত, শ্যেনপক্ষী, a thunderbolt, sound, speed, a wing, the feather of an arrow, ghee or clarified butter, a falcon.

বাজন, ক্বণন, শব্দ দেওন, স্বনন, পীড়ন, to sound as a musical instrument, to strike as a clock or bell, to pain or suffer pain.

বাজনা, বাজা,—বাদ্য, বাদ্যযন্ত্র, music, a musical instrument.

বাজনদার, বাদ্যকর, one who plays on a musical instrument.

বাজপেয়, যজ্ঞ বিশেষ, a sacrifice in which ghee is offered.

বাজরা, চেঙ্গারী, শস্য বিশেষ, a market-basket, a species of corn.

বাজান, বাদন, ঢকাদি পিটন, ঘণ্টাদি মারণ, শঙ্খে ফুঃ দেওন, to play on an instrument, to beat a drum, to strike a bell, to sound, blow, &c.

বাজী, ঘোটক, পক্ষী, অগ্নিবাণ, পণ, a horse, a bird, a sky-rocket, squib, a wager, stake.

বাজু, বাহু, ব্যবধানভিত্তি, the arm, a partition wall, a door [pannel.

বাজু, বাজুবন্ধ,—হস্তালঙ্কার, an ornament for the arm.

বাঞ্ছন, চাহন, মাগন, to desire, wish, long for, incline to, request. [request.

বাঞ্ছা. ইচ্ছা, শীলতা. নিবেদন, a wish, desire, will, propensity,

বাট, বর্ত্ম, পথ, a road, way, passage. [grind paint, &c.

বাটন, পেষণ,ভজন. to pound, reduce to pulp, rub on a stone,

বাটনী, পেষণকারিণী. a woman who rubs things on a stone &c.

বাট্পাড়-ীয়া. ডাকাইত, চোর, a robber, thief, highwayman.

বাটা, তাম্বূলাধার. a betel-box, a species of small fish.

বাটালি, পাথুরা, বাইশ. a chissel.

বাটিয়া, দড়ী, রজ্জু, a string, twine, a sort of cord.

বাটী, গৃহ, বাসস্থান, বাড়ী, ধাতুময় পানপাত্র, উদ্যান, নাটী, a house, habitation, residence, family dwelling. home, a metal cup, a drinking vessel, a garden, a mace, a rod. [roads.

বাটুয়া, পথিক, পথগামী, ডাকাইত. travelling, infesting the

বাট্টা, তাম্বূলাধার. ব্যাজ, a betel-box, discount on notes &c.

বাড়, কাঠাম, আফা কল, তট, ধার, অঞ্চল. প্রস্থার অর্দ্ধভাগ, আম্রের আঁঠির কোষ, a frame, a fish-dam, a weir, a margin, edge, selvage, a column or half-page, the outer covering of a mango-stone.

বাড়ন. বর্দ্ধন, উবরণ, ব্যাপন, মেলন, উদ্বর্ত্তন, পরিবেষণ, to grow, thrive. increase, abound, spread, extend, jut out, become prominent, rise above, exceed, to help or carve at table. [ded, expended.

বাড়ন্ত, বৃদ্ধিপ্রাপ্ত, ব্যাপ্ত, ফুরা, prosperous, overgrown, exten-

বাড়ব, বাড়বানল. বাড়বাগ্নি,—ঔর্ব, জলস্থিত অগ্নি, submarine fire.

বাড়া. অধিক, দুর্মূল্য, ফাঁপা, বহুল, অতিরিক্ত, বৃদ্ধি, বাহুল্য, উদ্বর্ত্ত, আতিশয্য, more, increased, exorbitant, dear, turgid, prolix, redundant ; growth, enlargement, excess, abundance, overplus.

বাড়ান, বৃদ্ধিকরণ, অধিকীকরণ, মেলান, উন্নয়ন, ধনীকরণ, স্তবন, উত্থাপন, উঠিয়া ফেলন, টানন, প্রতিপাদন, to augment, enlarge, multiply, increase, to raise a price, enhance, cause to increase, extend, to exalt, magnify, enrich, flatter, to excite, to remove a carcase, throw out, to prolong, to promote.

বাড়াবাড়ি, অতিরিক্ত কথায়, বাক্যব্যয়ে, বিস্তার পূর্ব্বক, tediously, with prolixity, much at large.

বাড়ি, বিস্তর, বৃদ্ধি, উন্নতি, দুর্ম্মূল্যতা, ব্যাজ, an increase, augmentation, improvement, an advance in price, the interest of money.

বাড়ী, গৃহ, বসতিস্থান, যষ্টি, ভূমিখাতা, বৃদ্ধিনিমিত্ত ধান্যের ঋণদান, a house, a family residence, a home, a staff, stick, rod, a plot of garden ground, an advance of grain to be repaid in kind with interest.

বাড়ুন, খেংরা, ঝাঁটা, সম্মার্জ্জনী, a broom.

বাড়্তী, বৃদ্ধি, উদ্বর্ত্ত, আতিশয্য, তাল, বহুল, increase, excess, surplus, redundance, prolixity; prolix. [cess.

বাঢ়াবাঢ়ি, অতিশয়, আধিক্য. excessively, importunately; ex-

বাণ, শর, হিংসাকর দৃষ্টিপাত, পরহিংসার্থে মন্ত্রপাঠ, an arrow, dart, versed sine, the influence of an evil eye, a malignant incantation.

বাণা, শিশুর শিশ্ন, the male organ of a child.

বাণি, বুননাদি শিল্পকর্ম্মকারির বেতন, the hire or price of wearing, jewelling, &c.

বাণিজ, ব্যবসায়ী, বেপারী, a trader, trafficker, merchant.

বাণিজ্য, ব্যাপার, বিনিময়, trade, traffic, commerce, barter.

বাণিয়া, বাণ্য,—মহাজন, বণিক, a banker, merchant, trader.

বাণী, বাক্য, কথা, সরস্বতী, speech, sound, a word, language, Saraswatí or the goddess of eloquence.

বাত, বায়ু, বায়ুরোগ, মনের বিষাদ, air, wind, gout, rheumatism, flatulency, hypocondria. [with wind.

বাতকিন্, বাতকী,—বায়ুরোগগ্রস্ত, rheumatic, gouty, troubled

বাতগ্রস্ত, উন্মত্ত, বায়ুরোগবিশিষ্ট, hypocondriac, mad, flatulent.

বাতশূল, বায়ুজনিত পেটের বেদনা, the wind-colic. [spirit.

বাতাস, বায়ু, পরচ্ছায়া, ভূত, wind, air, an apparition, vision,

বাতাসা, ক্ষুদ্র ফেণি, a species of sweet meat, sugar-plums.

বাতাসী, বহুবায়ু, ঝড়ুয়া, windy, tempestuous, boisterous.

বাতাসীয়া, বায়ুময়, বায়ুযুক্ত, হালকা, চঞ্চল, তালচঞ্চুপক্ষী, airy, windy, hysterical, light; a swallow.

বাতিক, বাতুয়া,—বায়ুজনিত, বায়ুরোগযুক্ত, ঝড়ুয়া, arising from wind, flatulent, gouty, rheumatic, stormy, windy.

বাতী, বর্ত্তি, শলিতা, বাতি, গালাকাঠি, a candle, lamp, wick, a wand, rod, a stick of wax. [foolish.
বাতুল, বায়ুগ্রস্ত, উন্মত্ত, ক্ষিপ্ত, হতজ্ঞান, insane, mad, crazy,
বাত্যা, অতিশয় বায়ু, ঝড়, দাম্ভিক, মিথ্যাবাদী, a strong wind, a gale, a storm, a hurricane, a boaster, bragger, vapourer, liar. [affection.
বাৎসল্য, অত্যন্ত স্নেহ, অনুরাগ, fondness, caressing, tenderness,
বাথান, গোশালা, গোষ্ঠ, a cow-house, cow-pen, cow-pasture.
বাদ, বাক্য, বচন, বিতণ্ডা, কলহ, দ্বেষ, আক্রোশ, দুর্নাম, a word, a sentence, a contradiction, dispute, énmity, reproof, an ill name.
বাদক, কথক, বাদ্যকর, speaking; a speaker, player of music.
বাদন, বাজান, to play on an instrument, to strike as a clock.
বাদবিতণ্ডা, বিতর্ক, বাদানুবাদ, reasoning, an argument, discussion, disputation. [cloud.
বাদল, পচাকাম, কুদিন, মেঘ, wet weather, a rainy day, a
বাদলা, মেঘ, গোটা, তারাবস্ত্র, *id*: also gold or silver lace, tissue.
বাদলীয়, প্রাবৃট্, বৃষ্টিজনিত, rainy, arising from rain &c.
বাদলীয়পোকা, প্রাবৃট্কালীন কীট বিশেষ, an ephemeral insect.
বাদানুবাদ, কলহ, বিবাদ, বিতণ্ডা, কহাবলা, a dispute, quarrel, controversy, argument, disputation.
বাদাম, ফল বিশেষ, নৌকার পাল, an almond, a ship's sail.
বাদামী-য়া, অণ্ডাকৃতি, almond-shaped, oval. [sic.
বাদি, বাদী,—গানের প্রধান স্বর, the key-note in Hindoo mu-
বাদিত, অনিচ্ছা পূর্ব্বক কথিত, ধ্বনিত, কথিত, made to be uttered, extorted, sounded as a musical instrument.
বাদিয়া, সাপুড়্যা, ওঝা, a snake-catcher, snake-charmer.
বাদী, ভাষী, বাচক, বিরোধী, আজ্ঞাশী, অর্থী, অর্থজ্ঞাপক, প্রসঙ্গকারী, speaking, asserting, quarrelsome, litigious, pleading; a plaintiff, accuser, suitor, expounder, the stater of an argument or thesis.
বাদুড়, বড় চামচিকা, a large bat or vampire.
বাদ্য, বাজনা, any musical instrument, music.
বাদ্যকর, বাজন্দর, তন্ত্রী, a musician, a musical performer.
বাদ্যভাণ্ড, } নানাবিধ বাদ্যের শব্দ, a concert of instrumental mu-
বাদ্যোদ্যম, } sic, a burst of many instruments together.

বাধক, নিবারক, প্রতিবন্ধক, ঋতুশূল, hindering, obstructing, preventive; a hinderer, &c. menstrual pains.

বাধন, নিবারণ, আট্কান, ঠেকন, কাটান, খণ্ডান, to hinder, prevent, resist, oppose, obstruct, impede, clog, detain, to frustrate, to render ineffectual.

বাধ, বাধকতা,—ব্যাঘাত, নিবারণ, আটক, opposition, hindrance, obstruction, prevention, detention.

বাধা, প্রতিবন্ধ, আটক, নিষেধ, দুঃখ, ভয়, খড়ম, an impediment, prohibition, opposition, &c. pain, danger, a sandal, clog, wooden shoe. [of Crishna.

বাধাই, কৃষ্ণজন্ম সঙ্কীর্ত্তনাত্মক গান, songs celebrating the birth

বাধ্য, বিনয়ী, দমিত, বশীভূত, নিবার্য্য, submissive, subservient, tame, captive, capable of obstruction, &c. [bore.

বান, আকস্মিক জলসমূহ, a flood, a heavy sea, a high tide, the

বানপ্রস্থ-ী, বনাশ্রমী, a hermit, anchoret, brahmin devotee.

বানর, কপি, মর্কট, শাখামৃগ, an ape, a monkey, a baboon.

বানান্, স্বরব্যঞ্জনমেল, প্রমুখাৎ বর্ণযোগ, the union of vowels and consonants, spelling.

বান্তি, বমি, ছর্দ্দি, a vomiting, a throwing up from the stomach. [knot, &c.

বান্ধন, বাঁধন, আঁটন, গেঁঠ্যান, to bind, fasten, confine, tie,

বান্ধব, জ্ঞাতি, আত্মীয়, a relation, kinsman, friend. [one.

বাপ্, বাপা, বাবা,—পিতা, a father: used, in fondness, to any

বাপ্রে, বাপ্রেবাপ্, বাপু,—দুঃখাদি সম্বোধক শব্দ, oh father! father! (an expression of pain or surprize.)

বাপ্মা, পিতামাতা, পিতরৌ, father and mother, parents.

বাপক, বীজক্ষেপক, বুনানিয়া, sowing seed; a sower, seedsman.

বাপী, দীর্ঘিকা, জলাশয়, an oblong pond, a pool, a lake.

বাবদূক, বহুবক্তা, বাচাল, talkative, garrulous, loquacious.

বাবু, মর্য্যাদাসূচক সম্বোধন, ভদ্র লোক, sire, sir; a gentleman.

বাম, সব্য, বিপরীত, বিমুখ, অপ্রসন্ন, মনোরম, left (not right), contrary, opposed, reverse, inverted, unpropitious, averse from, beautiful, pleasing.

বামক, উদ্গারজনক, an emetic; causing vomiting.

বামণ, বামণী,—ব্রাহ্মণ ব্রাহ্মণী, বিপ্র বিপ্রা, *m.* & *f.* a brahmin and brahmini.

বামন, বামনীয়,—খর্ব, খাট, হ্রস্ব, a dwarf; short, pigmy, dwarfish.
বামলোচনা, সুনয়না স্ত্রী, a woman with handsome eyes.
বামা, স্ত্রীলোক, বাম হস্ত দিয়া ঢকা বাদক, a woman, a person who beats a drum with the left hand.
বামাচার, তান্ত্রিক মত, বিরুদ্ধ ধর্ম্ম, the doctrine of the Tantras, heterodoxy. [Tantras ; heterodox.
বামাচারী, তান্ত্রিক, বিরুদ্ধধর্ম্মাচারী, a Tantrist, a follower of the
বায়ুথা, উদম স্থান, নির্জ্জন স্থান, ফাক, an open airy spot, a private place, an aperture. [gaseous.
বায়বীয়, পাবনিক, বায়ুবৎ, belonging or relating to wind,
বায়ব্য, পবনসম্বন্ধীয়, মরুৎকোণ, relating to the wind, sacred to the god of wind ; the north-west.
বায়স, বায়সী,— কাক, বলিভুক্, অরিষ্ট, *m. & f.* a crow.
বায়ু, পবন, বাতাস, মরুৎ, পরচ্ছায়া, wind, air, hypocondria, the god of wind, a spirit. [the N.W.
বায়ুকোণ, মরুৎকোণ, পশ্চিম উত্তরের মধ্য, the quarter of the wind,
বায়ুগ্রন্থি, ঘূরাণিয়া বাতাস, বাওড়ী, a whirlwind. [wind, &c.
বায়ুগ্রস্ত, বিক্ষিপ্তচিত্ত, বাতিক, hypocondriac, troubled with
বায়ুব্যজন, পাখা, পাখাঢুলানি, a fan, the act of fanning.
বায়ুভক্ষক, বায়ুভুক্,—পবনাশী, সর্প, feeding on air; a serpent.
বায্য-1, বাতগ্রস্ত, পাগল, ক্ষিপ্ত, hypocondriac, insane, crazy.
বার, দিন, পালা, পরিবর্ত্ত, সময়, প্রস্তাব, সমূহ, পাল, মদ্যপাত্র, জল, শ্রেণী, অর্দ্ধপৃষ্ঠ, a day of the week, a turn, spell, rotation, exchange, vicissitude, time, an occasion, a multitude, quantity, flock, a liquor-vessel, water, a row, a tier, a column, half a page:
বারকোষ, কাষ্ঠময় গোলপাত্র বিশেষ, a tray, a large wooden dish.
বারণ, আটক করণ, নিষেধন, মানাকরণ, নামানন, আট্কান, বাধন, খণ্ডন, to hinder, prevent, prohibit, forbid, disallow, to repel, stop, check, thwart.
বারদ্বয়, দুইবার, পুনরায়, twice, again. [often, frequently.
বারবার, বারম্বার,—পুনঃ২, মুহুর্মুহু, again and again, repeatedly,
বারবেলা, প্রতিদিনের কর্ম্মাযোগ্য সময়, certain parts of each day considered unlucky and unfit for any enterprize or work. [woman.
বারস্ত্রী, বারাঙ্গনা,—বেশ্যা, a harlot, a prostitute, a common

বারাংনিধি, বারিধি—সাগর, সমুদ্র, the sea, the ocean.
বারাণ্ডা, চাঁদনী, পিড়া, a portico, a porch, a verandah.
বারান্তর, পুনরায়, ফের, again, once again, once more.
বারি, বার্,—জল, সলিল, উদক, water.
বারিকোল, বার্কোল,—কচ্ছপ, কমঠ, a tortoise.
বারিচর, জলজাত, জলচর, মৎস্য, aquatic ; a fish.
বারিজ, জলোৎপন্ন, গুগলী, শঙ্খ, শম্বুক, পদ্ম, produced in water ; a snail, a conch shell, any bivalve shell, a lotus.
বারিদ. জলদ, জলধর, মেঘ, giving water ; a cloud.
বারিভূ, জলাকর, উনুই, মণ্ডুক, a spring of water, a frog.
বারী, জলসিঞ্চনপাত্র, দুগ্ধভাণ্ড, হস্তিবন্ধনার্থ রজ্জু. পালা, a water-pot, milking-vessel, the foot rope that fastens an elephant, a spell, a turn in rotation, watch, time of duty.
বারুণী, পশ্চিমদিক্, মদিরা, বিংশতিতম নক্ষত্র, চৈত্র মাসের কৃষ্ণা ত্রয়োদশী, the west, spirituous liquor, the 20th lunar mansion, a festival on the 13th day of the wane in Chaitra. [gunpowder.
বারুদ, অগ্ন্যস্ত্রার্থে চূর্ণদ্রব্য বিশেষ, অর্থাৎ মিশ্রিত যবক্ষার গন্ধকাঙ্গার,
বারেক, একদা. একবার, once, one time. [exchange ; for.
বারে, পালায়, পর্য্যায়ক্রমে, বিনিময়ে, in turn, in rotation, in
বারে২, পরস্পরে, ক্রমে২, পুনঃ২ alternately, in rotation, often, repeatedly, again and again.
বারোদ্বারী, দ্বাদশদ্বারযুক্ত, রাজবাড়ী, অট্টালিকা, ভিক্ষুক, ভিখারী, having twelve doors, mendicant, begging from door to door ; a palace, a mendicant, a beggar.
বারোবারী, সামান্য, সাধারণ, চলিত, general, common, frequent.
বার্ত্তা, কথা, জনরব, সম্বাদ, বৃত্তান্ত, কথোপকথন, জীবিকা, ব্যবসায়, a word, report, rumour, tidings, news, message, information, relation, account, narration, warning, conversation, a livelihood, occupation. [comment.
বার্ত্তিক, প্রেরিত, সম্বাদক, টীকা, an envoy, messenger, a gloss,
বার্দ্ধক্য, বৃদ্ধাবস্থা, বুড়ামী, old age.
বার্দ্ধীন. মেষ, মুক্তমুক্ত ভেড়া, a wild sheep, a wether.
বার্দ্ধুষিক, ব্যাজখেকুয়া, ঋণদানোপজীবী, a usurer, money-lender.

বার্ষিক, প্রতিবৎসরীয়, প্রতিবৎসর অনুষ্ঠেয়, প্রতিবৎসর লভ্য বৃত্তি, yearly, annual, belonging to a year; a yearly pension, &c.

বার্হস্পত্য, নীতিশাস্ত্র, morality, ethics; derived from Vrihaspati.

বাল, অবগণ্ড, শিশু, ছেল্যা, চুল, অন্তর্লোম অশ্বাদির পুচ্ছ, মূর্খ, an infant, child, boy, lad, a colt, hair, a lock of hair, hair on the privities, a horse's tail, any tail; infantine, childish, ignorant, uninformed.

বালক, অবগণ্ড, ছেলিয়া, শিশু, মূর্খ, an infant, child, boy, lad, a fool, a blockhead.

বালকীয়, শিশুকালীন, ছেলিয়ার, childish, infantine, relating to a child.

বালসন, বালকের তাপ হওন, to be seized with fever, (spoken of an infant.)

বালসন্ধ্যাভ, বেগুনীয়ারঙ্গ, অরুণবর্ণ, purple, the colour of the twilight.

বালসা, বালকের জ্বর হওয়া, a fever, (in a child or infant.)

বালা, মেয়্যা ছেল্যা, কন্যা, স্ত্রীলোক, বলয়, a female child, girl, young woman, a female, a woman, a bracelet.

বালাই, বিপত্তি, আপদ, an ill, misfortune.

বালাধিকার, ছেল্যার বিষয়, শিশুকালোপযুক্ত, শৈশবাবস্থা, things proper for or peculiar to children, pupillage.

বালি, কদলী আদির অপ্রসারিত পত্র, দ্বারের পাতা, সিকতা, the leaf of the plantain, palm &c. in its sheathe, a single leaf of a door, sand.

বালিকা, ষোড়শ বৎসর পর্য্যন্ত বয়স্কা স্ত্রী, সিকতা, a female child, a young girl, sand.

বালিয়া, সিকতাময়, sandy, abounding in or made of sand.

বালিশ, শিতান, শিশু, মূর্খ, a pillow, bolster, cushion; young, ignorant, uninformed.

বালিহংস বা হাঁস,—বন্য পাতিহংস, a teal or wild duck.

বালী, বালুকা,—সিকতা, কঙ্কর, sand, gravel, grit.

বালীচূণ, ইষ্টকাদি গাঁথনে লেপনীয় বস্তু, sand and lime, mortar.

বালেন্দু, শুক্লপক্ষের দ্বিতীয়াদির চন্দ্র, অর্দ্ধচন্দ্র, a crescent, new moon.

বাল্তি, দুঃখী, অনাথ, কাষ্ঠময় জলপাত্র বিশেষ, poor, destitute, forlorn, bereft; a bucket.

বাল্য, শৈশবাবস্থা, ছেল্যাম, infancy, childhood, youth.

বাল্যভোগ, প্রাতঃকালীন ভোজন, breakfast, the morning meal.

বাঁশ, বংশ, বেণু, মুরলী, a bamboo, reed, flute, pipe, fife.

বাষ্প-া, বাসি, পচা, সড়া, stale, old, stinking.

বাস, গৃহ, ঘর, গন্ধ, a residence, dwelling, abode, a smell, perfume, scent.

বাস, বাসস্,—বস্ত্র, a garment, clothing, cloth, dress, apparel.

বাসক, বসনিয়া, থাকনিয়া, dwelling, residing; an inhabitant.

বাসকসজ্জা বা সজ্জিকা,—বেশভূষাযুক্তা জারাপেক্ষিণী, a woman dressed and waiting to receive her lover.

বাসতেয়, অবস্থেয়, নিবাসযোগ্য, habitable, inhabitable.

বাসন, পাত্র, আধার, বাঞ্ছন, গ্রাহ্য করণ, উত্তম করিয়া জানন, চাহন, a plate, dish, vessel, box, receptacle; to like, approve of, wish, incline to.

বাসনা, স্পৃহা, বাঞ্ছা, অভিলাষ, কামনা, অনুশীলতা, চেষ্টা, মনস্থ, a wish, desire, choice, lust, an inclination, propensity, a passion for, a design, intention.

বাসন্ত-ী, বসন্তকালীন, vernal, belonging to the spring.

বাসর, দিবস, বিবাহরাত্রীয় সহশয়ন, a day, the sleeping together of a couple the first night after marriage.

বাসা, ঠিকানা, প্রবাস, ঘর, নীড়, ছাউনী, a lodging, temporary residence, place of abode, a nest, haunt, lair, an encampment.

বাসাগার, গৃহ, থাকিবার স্থান, শয়নঘর, a man's temporary residence while away from home, a dwelling house, a sleeping room.

বাসাড়ীয়া, প্রবাসী, বিদেশী, living in lodgings, residing from home; a temporary resident, a stranger.

বাসান, সৌঁধান, গন্ধান, to perfume, scent, smell.

বাসি, পর্য্যুষিত, অটাট্কা, পরিষ্কৃত, ধৌত, ক্ষুদ্র কুঠার, stale, not fresh, old, clean-washed (clothes); a chopper, a small hatchet, an adze.

বাসিত, সুগন্ধযুক্ত, রসযুক্ত, সুস্বাদু, ভিজান, বস্ত্রপরিহিত, perfumed, scented, spiced, seasoned, steeped, infused, clothed, dressed.

বাসিন্, বাসী,—থাকনিয়া, তিষ্ঠনিয়া, dwelling, residing, inhabiting.

বাস্তব, বাস্তবিক,—যথার্থ, প্রকৃত, স্বাভাবিক, ভৌতিক, প্রমিত, সত্য, real, genuine, substantial, material, determined, substantiated, true.

বাস্তব্য, বাস্য,—নিবাসার্হ, fit for a residence, habitable.
বাস্ত, গৃহ, ভিটা, a house, dwelling, the scite of a dwelling.
বাষ্প, ভাপ, ধূম, অশ্রু, উল্লেক, উদ্দেশ, লেশ, কিছুই, vapour, steam, reek, spray, tears, rheum, mention, relation, a trace, the least trace, an atom, any thing; any, the least, the smallest.
বাষ্পধর্ম্মক, ধূমবৎ, volatile, flying off in steam.
বাহক, ভারসহ, মোটিয়া, দাঁড়ী, হস্তী ঘোটকাদি, অশ্বারূঢ়, carrying, bearing; a porter, carrier, rower, waterman, a horse or other conveyance, a horseman.
বাহড়ন, বাহুড়ন,—প্রত্যাগমন, ফিরিয়া আইসন, to turn back, to return. [other conveyance.
বাহন, যান, হস্তী ঘোটকাদি, a carriage, vehicle, a horse or
বাহন, নৌ চালান, ভার সহন, চড়ন, to row, steer, carry, bear, clamber, climb (as a plant.)
বাহবাবাহবি, ধরাধরি, হাতাহাতি, a grappling; hand to hand.
বাহিনী, সৈন্য, দল, তিনগণ সেনা, অভিমুখী, স্রোতস্বতী, an army, cohort, body of troops, battallion; *f.* facing, flowing. [outside, out of doors.
বাহির, বাহিরে,—অনভ্যন্তরে, বহির্দিগে, বাহ্যে, without, out, abroad,
বাহির্নাম, ঠিকানা, শিরনাম, the address or direction of a letter.
বাহু, বাহ,—ভুজ, ব্যাম, the arm, a fathom.
বাহুমূল, ভুজশিরঃ, কক্ষ, the shoulder-blade, the arm-pit.
বাহুযুদ্ধ, মুষ্টামুষ্টি, হাতাহাতি, কীলাকীলি, a scuffling, wrestling, hand-fight, fisticuffs; pugilism.
বাহুল্য, আতিশয্য, প্রাচুর্য্য, প্রচুর, abundance, plenty, multiplicity, enlargement, size; plentiful, many.
বাহ্য, বহনীয়, বহির্দিগের, অনভ্যন্তর, বহিঃস্থ, to be carried, &c. external, outward, superficial.
বাহ্যে, টাটি, স্পষ্টে, out (to ease nature), openly.
বাহ্যস্থান, মলমূত্রত্যাগার্থস্থান, টাটি, a privy, a place to ease nature in, the outskirts of a town, &c. so used.
বাহ্যক্রিয়া, কোষ্ঠশুদ্ধি, শৌচ, a going to stool, evacuation.
বিউনী, বেণি, জড়িত বাল, a tail of hair.
বিউলী, নিস্তুষ মুগাদি কলায়, shelled pulse. [eye of a needle.
বিঁদ, বিঁধ,—ছিদ্র, রন্ধ্র, a perforation, bore, vent, incision, the

বিঁধন, ভেদন, ফোড়ন, খুড়ন, সিঁধ কাটন, to pierce, perforate, bore, tap, stab, prick, thrust. undermine.

বিকন-আন, বেচন, বিক্রয়, to sell, to vend ; a sale.

বিকচ, প্রস্ফুটিত, প্রসারিত, টাক্‌পড়া, blown, expanded, spread, opened, open, bald.

বিকট, দায়, ভয়, ভয়ানক, বিদ্রূপ, বিকৃত, প্রকাণ্ড, অতিবড়, সুন্দর, jeopardy, danger, fear, awe ; formidable, horrible, hideous, distorted, deformed, changed in form or appearance, huge, large, beautiful.

বিকল, চিন্তান্বিত, কাতর, ভাবিত, অবাক্, নুলা, পঙ্গু, বিগড়িত, নষ্ট, জীর্ণ, শুষ্ক, হ্রাসপ্রাপ্ত, agitated, disturbed, troubled, distressed, confused, confounded, defective, imperfect, maimed, impaired, out of order, decayed, withered, waned.

বিকলাঙ্গ, নুলা, খোঁড়া, কুভোল, maimed, crippled, deformed.

বিকলেন্দ্রিয়, হতেন্দ্রিয়, অবশ হস্তপাদাদি বিশিষ্ট, having defective or impaired organs or powers.

বিকল্প, ইচ্ছাপূর্ব্বক গ্রাহ্যাগ্রাহ্য, কাম্য, দ্বিরূপ, দ্বৈধ, সন্দেহ, optional, admitting two forms (in grammar ;) an alternative, option, doubt, suspence.

বিকল্পিত, স্বেচ্ছাপূর্ব্বক গ্রহণীয়, গ্রাহ্যতর, সন্দিগ্ধ, অনিশ্চিত, admitted as optional, chosen as an alternative, in suspence, in doubt, undecided. [blown.

বিকসিত, প্রফুল্ল, প্রসারিত, opened as a flower, expanded,

বিকাও, বিক্রেতব্য, বিক্রয়ণীয, পণিতব্য, বেচিবার, saleable.

বিকার, প্রকারান্তর, স্বভাবের অন্যথা, পরিণাম, অপকৃষ্টত্ব, বিগড়, দোষ, গ্লানি, ধাতুভেদ, পিত্তাদিবৃদ্ধি, রোগ, রজোগুণপ্রাপ্তি, রাগাদি, যোগভঙ্গ, মরণকালীন রোগবৃদ্ধি, a change of form, nature or quality, alteration, transmutation, transformation, deterioration, depravation, spoiling, fading, a dangerous symptom, an accumulation of bile or other change of natural humours, disease, sickness, passion. feeling, emotion, a transition from the quiescent state of the mind, the fatal change immediately preceding death.

বিকাররাহিত্য, পরিণামশূন্যতা, রাগহীনতা, গুণসাম্য, unchangeableness, incapability of change or deterioration, immobility by passion or emotion as of the Deity. [precedes death.
বিকাররোগ, ব্যাধি, মরণকালীন পরিণাম, disease, the change which
বিকারী, পরিণামকারী, যাহার পরিণাম হইতেছে, producing or undergoing a change, &c. [deterioration, &c.
বিকার্য্য, পরিণেয়, যাহার বিকার হইতে পারে, capable of change or
বিকাল-বেলা, গোধূলী, সন্ধ্যাকাল, evening, afternoon, twilight.
বিকাশ, প্রসার, ফুলের ফুটন, expansion, the opening of a flower.
বিকী, বিক্রয়, বেচা, sale, a sale, vent. [ter.
বিকীকিনী, ক্রয়বিক্রয়, বিনিময়, buying and selling, trade, bar-
বিকির, অস্থিদগ্ধের পিণ্ড, the funeral cake offered for one destitute of surviving relatives to do it for him.
বিকীরণ, ছড়ান, নিক্ষেপণ, ছিটান, to scatter, throw about, spread, sprinkle. [sprinkled.
বিকীর্ণ, নিক্ষিপ্ত, ছিটান, scattered, spread about, dispersed,
বিকৃত, অন্যথাভূত, মতান্তর, পরিণত, বিগড়িত, নষ্ট, অপকৃষ্ট, ম্লান, রোগী, বিকলাঙ্গ, বিমুখ, বিরক্ত, changed, altered, transformed, impaired, imperfect, faded, diseased, sick, distorted, deformed, estranged, alienated, filled with aversion or disgust.
বিকৃতি, স্বভাবের অন্যথা, বিরুদ্ধাকার, ভ্রষ্টামী, দুষ্টতা, change, transformation, distortion, depravity.
বিকুর্ব্ব, নানাপ্রকার, বিবিধ, variously done, not uniform.
বিক্রম, শক্তি, বল, প্রতাপ, সাহস, power, strength, authority, energy, valour, prowess, courage, heroism.
বিক্রমী, বিক্রান্ত,—বলবান্, বীর, সাহসী, powerful, able, courageous, bold, daring, valiant, heroic.
বিক্রয়-ণ, বেচা, বিকী, a selling, sale, vent. [able, marketable.
বিক্রয়ণীয়, বিক্রেয়, —বেচিবার যোগ্য, পণিতব্য, saleable, merchant-
বিক্রয়ী, বেচনিয়া, selling, vending; a vender, seller.
বিক্রী, বিকী,—বেচা, বেচিবা, sale, a sale, vent.
বিক্রীত, বেচা, কৃতবিক্রয়, sold, disposed of by sale.
বিক্রীড়িত, কৃতক্রীড়া, বিলসিত, পরিহসিত, played, having played, danced, joked, &c.

বিক্রেতা, বিক্রয়কারী, মূল্যগ্রাহক, পণ্যজীবী, a seller, a salesman.
বিক্লব, ভয়াকুল, বিস্মিত, ক্ষুব্ধ, অবাক্, থবরাণ, overcome by fear, surprize, agitation, shame or other passion, confused, confounded, lost, bewildered.
বিক্লান্ত, শ্রান্ত, অবসন্ন. fatigued, wearied, exhausted.
বিক্লিন্ন. শুষ্ক, ম্লান, শীর্ণ, আর্দ্র, shrivelled, withered, decayed, old, wet, moist.
বিক্লেদ, আর্দ্রতা, ভিজাভাব, পুঁজ, রসানি, wetness, dampness, an oozing with matter, suppuration. [zy, silly.
বিক্ষিপ্ত, ছড়ান, নিরস্ত, পাগল, scattered, thrown, sent, &c. cra-
বিক্ষুব্ধ, কাতর. ভাবিত, agitated, disturbed, anxious.
বিক্ষেপ, ফেলা, থবরাণী, ক্ষোভ, a throwing, propelling, casting, scattering, dispersion, confusion, perplexity, distress of mind. [scatter, disperse.
বিক্ষেপণ, ফেলন, ছুটান, ছড়ান, to throw, cast, send, shoot,
বিক্ষোভ, কাতরতা, ভাবনা, agitation, distress of mind, anxiety.
বিখারা, স্বরের অমেল, অসমন্বিত স্বর, a discord, (in music.)
বিখ্যাত, প্রসিদ্ধ, বিদিত, নামধেয়, famous, renowned, praised, celebrated, spoken of, denominated.
বিখ্যাতি. প্রসিদ্ধি, যশ, fame. celebrity, notoriety, renown.
বিগড়ন, বিকার কিম্বা নাশ পাওন, মন্দ হওন, শুকন, সড়ন, পড়ন, স্বধর্ম্ম ত্যাগ করণ, to be deteriorated, to alter for the worse, to change, alter, fade, decay, apostatize.
বিগড়ান, বিগাড়ন,—নষ্ট করণ, উল্টান, ক্ষয় করণ, মন্দ করণ, জাতি মারণ, to spoil, vitiate, impair, deteriorate, deface, ruin, mar, seduce, debauch, violate.
বিগড়, বিগাড়,—বিকার, বিনাশ, স্বধর্ম্মত্যাগ, সুহৃদ্ভেদ, বিবাদ, deterioration, ruin, a change for the worse, apostacy, a rupture, quarrel. [ruining, &c.
বিগড়ানী, বিনাশক, ধ্বংশকারী, spoiling, vitiating, seducing,
বিগণ, শত্রু, রিপু, বিপক্ষ, a foe, adversary, enemy.
বিগত, প্রেত, প্রস্থিত, অন্তর্হিত, বিযুক্ত, ঘোর, দীপ্তিরহিত, বিতস্তি, departed, gone, disappeared, severed, separated, parted, dark, gloomy, obscured; a span.
বিগম, প্রস্থান, বিচ্ছেদ, অন্তর্ধান, ত্যাগ, departure, separation, disappearance, a parting, relinquishing.

বিগর্হণ, দোষ দেওন, নিন্দা করণ, গালাগালি দেওন, ঘৃণা করণ, to censure, reproach, vilify, abuse, hate, abominate.

বিগলিত, পতিত, ঝরা, অবদ্ধ, মুক্ত, দ্রুত, সড়া, fallen, dropped, oozed, removed, loose, dishevelled, melted, putrified.

বিগামী, প্রস্থানকারী, গমনোদ্যত, departing, setting off, separating.

বিগীত, তিরস্কৃত, নিন্দিত, defamed, censured, abused, reproached, vilified.

বিগুণ, অকর্ম্মণ্য, দুষ্ট, মন্দ, নষ্ট, অমঙ্গল, অপ্রসন্ন, হিংসুক, কুস্বভাব, বিকার, worthless, ill-disposed, evil, bad, spoiled, pernicious, unpropitious, injurious; an evil quality or disposition, vitiation, deterioration.

বিগোহ, মিশাল, উল্টুল, উৎপাত, প্রণয়ভঙ্গ, বিরোধ, a mixture, confusion, ruin, a rupture, quarrel.

বিগ্রহ, যুদ্ধ, পুত্তলী, প্রতিমা, আকার, রূপ, শরীর, war, battle, a combat, an image, idol, shape, form, the body.

•বিঘটন, দৈবাধীন, আপদ, an occurrence, event, misfortune.

বিঘটিত, দৈবাৎ পড়া, উপস্থিত, দুরদৃষ্টজনিত, উৎপাত, আপদ, happened, occurred, befallen as a misfortune; an accident, calamity.

বিঘত, দ্বাদশাঙ্গুলি পরিমাণ, বিতস্তি, a long span.

বিঘা, কুড়া, বিশ কাঠা ভূমি, a measure of land, twenty Cottahs or from 80 to 87 cubits square.

বিঘাত, বাধা, আটক, ক্ষতি, ধ্বংস, হত্যা, a hindrance, obstacle, injury, hurt, destruction, murder.

বিঘাতন, হিংসা করণ, মারণ, আটকান, to hurt, injure, kill, murder, impede.

বিঘাতী, হিংসাকর, মারক, বাধক, injuring, killing, destroying, opposing, &c.

বিঘূর্ণন, আবর্ত্তন, বায়ুগ্রন্থি, পাকনা, a whirling round, a whirlwind, a whirlpool.

বিঘ্ন, আঘাত, আটক, উৎপাত, আপদ, a hindrance, impediment, obstacle, obstruction, opposition, danger, calamity, misfortune.

বিঘ্নিত, বাধিত, নষ্ট, obstructed, prevented, hindered, spoiled.

বিঘ্রাণ, গন্ধ, বাস, গন্ধবোধ, a scent, smell, smelling.

বিচক্ষণ, নিপুণ, পণ্ডিত, সুচতুর, দক্ষ, eminent, superior, excellent, learned, wise, clever, able, skilful.

বিচর্চ্চিকা, কণ্ডু, কচ্ছু, দদ্রু, the itch, scab, ringworm.

বিচল, কুব্যবহার, আজ্ঞালঙ্ঘন, অন্যথাচার, ঠেটামি, চাঞ্চল্য, পাসরা, মোচড়, সন্ধিচ্যুত, irregular conduct, disobedience, perverseness, fickleness, unsteadiness, failure, a slip, dislocation, sprain, strain, wrench.

বিচলা, পিছলা, টলা, পাসরা, a slip, a false step.

বিচলিত, পিছলিত, অপগত, টের্চা, চঞ্চল, অস্থির, সন্ধিচ্যুত, বিকৃত, নষ্ট, বিরুদ্ধ, slipped, moved in a wrong direction, bent, fickle, unstable, unsteady, unfixed, dislocated, displaced, perverted, ruined, contrary.

বিচার, বিবেচনা, চর্চ্চা, বিতণ্ডা, যথার্থের নিরূপণ, অনুমান, সিদ্ধান্ত, নিষ্পত্তি, ন্যায়, investigation, examination, deliberation, consultation, discussion, disputation, reasoning, enquiry, an opinion, determination, judgment, decision, a trial at law.

বিচারক, বিচারকর্ত্তা, ন্যায়ক, বিবেকী, বুদ্ধিমান, a judge, one who investigates, &c. investigating, reflecting.

বিচারণ, যথার্থের নিরূপণ, তর্কণ, বিবেচনা করণ, নিষ্পাদন, to investigate, examine, reason, discuss, judge, decide.

বিচারসূত্র, ব্যবস্থা, তর্কবিধান, a rule for judging, a logical aphorism.

বিচারিত, বিবেচিত, তর্কিত, নির্ণীত, examined, investigated, discussed, judged, &c.

বিচারী, ন্যায়ক, তর্কক, discussing, investigating, judging.

বিচার্য্য, বিবেচনীয়, নির্ণেতব্য, deserving examination or enquiry, &c. cognizable.

বিচালিত, স্বস্থানচ্যুত, সরাণ, অসম্পূর্ণ, displaced, unfixed, removed, unfulfilled.

বিচালী, ধান্যাদির আছড়া, straw, rice or barley straw.

বিচিকিৎসা, সংশয়, সন্দেহ, ভ্রম, ভুল, বাধা, আটক, আপদ, doubt, uncertainty, an error, mistake, obstacle, interruption, any untoward circumstance.

বিচিত্র, বিস্ময়, চমৎকার নানাবর্ণ, বহুরঙ্গ, বহুবিধ, সুশোভিত, রঞ্জিত, সুন্দর, বিলক্ষণ, চমৎকারী, আশ্চর্য্য, surprize, wonder, astonishment, a variegated colour; particoloured, spotted, speckled, variegated, varied, painted, ornamented, gaudy, splendid, beautiful, beautified, elegant, handsome, surprising, wonderful, astonishing.

বিচিত্রিত, চমৎকৃত, বিস্মিত, রঞ্জিত, নানাবর্ণ, full of wonder, surprized, astonished, variegated, spotted, &c.

বিচিন্তা, ভাবনা, উদ্বেগ, অনুধাবনা, anxiety, care, careful or mature consideration, deep reflexion.

বিচিন্তিত, কাতর,ভাবিত, উদ্বিগ্ন, সুবিবেচিত, anxious, thoughtful, full of care, well considered, maturely weighed.

বিচেষ্টিত, শ্রমপূর্ব্বক অন্বেষিত, তর্কিত, নির্ণীত, আবিষ্ট, carefully sought or laboured for, closely investigated, enquired into, ascertained, deeply engaged in.

বিচ্ছিত্তি, কাটিয়া ফেলা, বিদারণ, ভঙ্গ, ভেদ, ক্ষতি, বিনাশ, অন্তর্ধান, সীমা, ছেদ. a cutting off, excision, a cutting, dividing, fracture, rupture, loss, destruction, disappearance, limit, boundary, a cæsura or pause.

বিচ্ছিন্ন, বিদীর্ণ, কাটা, ভিন্ন. ভাঙ্গা, বিভক্ত, পৃথক্কৃত, বণ্টিত, ছড়ান, parted, divided, cut, separated, interrupted, portioned, shared out, scattered.

বিচ্ছেদ, বিয়োগ, বিভাগ, পৃথককরা, ভেদকরা, বিরহ, অমিল, চিত্তমালিন্য, অপ্রীতি, যতি, অন্তরাল, প্রকরণ, a separation, division, disjunction, parting, removal, absence, disunion, variance, interruption of friendship or love, a space between words, an intermediate space, a chapter, section, division.

বিছটী, চরভা বিশেষ, a species of nettle.

বিছড়ান, ছিটান, ছানন, to scatter, strew, sprinkle, knead.

বিছা, বৃশ্চিক, a scorpion, a centipede, the sign Scorpio.

বিছান, বিস্তারণ, পাড়ন, to spread out, lay down as a mat or carpet, to strew, to lay in beds or layers.

বিছানা, শয্যা, আস্তরণ, মাদুরী ইত্যাদি, a bed, carpet, floor-mat, &c. any thing spread out to lie upon.

বিজন, বিরল, নির্জ্জন, solitary, private, lonely, uninhabited.

বিজন্মা, জারজ, কুণ্ড, a spurious birth, bastard, natural child.

বিজয়, জিতমক্রিয়া, শত্রুদমন, conquest, victory, triumph.

বিজয়া, দুর্গা, তিথি বিশেষ, Durgá, the 10th of the increase in Ashwiní. [phant: a conqueror.

বিজয়ী, জিতনিয়া, জয়প্রাপ্ত, victorious. triumphing, trium-

বিজলী, বিদ্যুৎ, তড়িৎ, lightning.

বিজাত-ক, জারজ, ঢেমন, দ্বিজাতীয়, সঙ্কর, base-born, bastard, spurious, hybrid, mongrel, of mixed breed.

বিজাতি, অন্যপ্রকার, বিশেষ, a different kind or species.

বিজাতীয়, বিশেষ, ইতর, ভিন্ন, অসামান্য, অতুল, বিলক্ষণ, বড়, অতিশয়, অদ্ভুত, বিবিধ, দ্বিজাতীয়, জারজ, অনুচিত, ঘৃণার্হ, বিপক্ষ, of a different species, dissimilar, unparalleled, excellent, great, excessive, wonderful, various, mongrel, base-born, improper, hateful, hostile.

বিজিগীষা, পরজয়েচ্ছা, a desire of conquest, emulation, rivalry.

বিজিগীষু, পরজয়েচ্ছুক, desirous of victory, emulous, invading.

বিজিত, পরাভূত, বিখ্যাত, বিদিত, subdued, overcome, conquered, famed, wafted. [open, expanded.

বিজৃম্ভিত, হাইছাড়নিয়া, প্রসারিত, yawning, stretching, spread

বিজেতা, জয়ী, জিতনিয়া, a conqueror, vanquisher, victor.

বিজ্ঞ, সবুদ্ধি, নিপুণ, wise, experienced, learned, skilful, able.

বিজ্ঞপ্তি, সম্বাদ দেওয়া, জানানি, নিবেদন, উক্তানুমান, the communication of intelligence, information, a representation, a sentiment, a declared opinion.

বিজ্ঞাত, অবগত, বুদ্ধ, বিদিত, খ্যাত্যাপন্ন, known, understood, notorious, celebrated, famous. [ness.

বিজ্ঞাতা, অবগত, জ্ঞানপ্রাপ্ত, সাক্ষী, one who knows a thing, a wit-

বিজ্ঞান, বিদ্যা, পাণ্ডিত্য, স্মৃতিশাস্ত্রবোধ, শিল্পশাস্ত্রাদিতে বুদ্ধি, অনুভব, অনুমান, বোধ, science, learning, knowledge of books, (especially of law books,) worldly knowledge as of painting &c. or of the mechanical arts, an idea, a conception of the mind.

বিজ্ঞাপন, জানান, প্রচারণ, বিবরণ, বুঝান, to make known, inform, declare, publish, describe, explain, demonstrate. [demonstration.

বিজ্ঞাপনা, প্রকাশকরা, বুঝাজি, an advertisement, information,

বিজ্ঞেয়, জ্ঞাতব্য, বোধনীয়, cognizable, comprehensible.

বিট্, বিষ্ঠা, মল, ষিড্গু, দুষ্ট, ধূর্ত, বৈশ্য, excrement, dung, a catamite, a varlet, rascal, rogue, cheat, a Vaishya.

বিটল, বিটলিয়া, বিটাল, বিটুল, বিটোল, } অধম, দুষ্ট, নোচ্চা, দুর্বৃত্ত, অসৎ, কুশীল, মন্দলোক, vile, vicious, unprincipled, seditious, unruly; a rascal, scoundrel, villain.

বিটপ, গুচ্ছ, স্তবক, পল্লব, ষিড়্গপাল, a tuft, bunch, cluster, clump, a new shoot, a keeper of pathics.

বিটপাচরণ, দুষ্টামী, ধূর্ত্তামী, rascally conduct, villainy, fraud.

বিটলবণ, কালা নুণ, black salt, (used medicinally.)

বিঠৌর, বিহ্বল, থবরাণ, হতজ্ঞান, অবাক্, মুগ্ধ, মত্ত, discomposed, confused, confounded, fascinated, intoxicated.

বিড়ম্বন, ক্লেশন, ক্ষুগান, পীড়ান, অনুকরণ, ভেজান, বেশ ধারণ, to afflict, distress, vex, tantalize, copy after, imitate, to assume a character or dress.

বিড়ম্বনা, দুঃখ, ক্লেশ, অনুকার, affliction, distress, imitation, &c.

বিড়া, আটি, আটলা, a sheaf, a porter's pad.

বিড়াল, মার্জ্জার, আখুভুক্, a cat.

বিড়্বিড়ন, কচ্‌কচি করণ, to mutter, murmur, grumble, mumble.

বিচপ, কদর্য্যাকার, বিকলাঙ্গ, কুরূপ, deformed, distorted, ugly.

বিৎ, জ্ঞ, নিপুণ, দক্ষ, *affix*: wise, knowing, clever, skilful, acquainted with, versed in.

বিত°, বিস্তার, বৃত্তান্ত, a detail, circumstantial narration.

বিতণ্ডন, বাদানুবাদ করণ, to debate, discuss, reason upon.

বিতণ্ডা, ভাষাভাষি, বাক্‌বিরোধ, বিবাদ, খণ্ডনা, a debate, argument, controversy, contention, dispute, criticism, refutation.

বিতত, টানা, বিস্তৃত, ব্যাপ্ত, stretched, extended, expanded, spread, diffused.

বিতথ, মিথ্যা, অসত্য, অযথার্থ, false, untrue.

বিতরণ, ভিক্ষাদান করণ, বণ্টন, অর্পণ, দান, ভিক্ষা, to give alms, dole out, give. bestow ; an alms, largess, donation.

বিতরণী, ভিক্ষাদায়ী, বণ্টনকারী, giving alms, bestowing, doling out.

বিতর্ক, বিবেচনা, অনুধাবন, ঠাহরা, অনুমান, সন্দেহ, investigation, discussion, reasoning, deliberation, an inference, conjecture, supposition, doubt.

বিতর্কণ, বিতণ্ডন, বাদানুবাদ করণ, ঠাহরণ, বুঝন, to reason, discuss, weigh, deliberate, think, suspect.

বিতল, নরক বিশেষ, the second of the infernal regions.

বিতস্তি, বিগত, দ্বাদশাঙ্গুলি পরিমাণ, a span, twelve fingers breadth.

বিতান, চাঁদনী, টানা, বিস্তার, an awning, canopy, the warp of cloth, an expansion, extension, spreading out.

বিতুষ, পরিষ্কৃত ধান্যাদি, cleansed from the husk or chaff.

বিতুষ্ট, বিরক্ত, অতৃপ্তমনাঃ, অসন্মত, বিমনাঃ, রুষ্ট, ক্ষুব্ধ, displeased, dissatisfied, discontented. reluctant, unwilling, angry, piqued, offended.

বিতৃষ্ণ, নিবৃত্ততৃষ্ণা, অপিপাস, ঠাণ্ডা, তৃপ্ত, অসন্তুষ্ট, বিরক্ত, having the thirst slackened, satisfied. indifferent to, dissatisfied with, disliking, disgusted. nauseating.

বিতৃষ্ণা, অশ্রদ্ধা, অনিচ্ছা, অরুচি, ঘৃণা, indifference to, dislike, distaste, satiety, disgust, antipathy.

বিত্ত, ধন, সম্পত্তি, সঞ্চিত, উপার্জ্জিত, বিচারিত, তর্কিত, বিদিত, বিখ্যাত, wealth, property, substance; gained, acquired, discussed, judged, examined, investigated, known, notorious, famous.

বিত্তা, বিত্ত.—পাণ্ডিত্য, শাস্ত্রজ্ঞান, wisdom, acquaintance with a science.

বিত্রপ, নির্লজ্জ, ঢেঁটা, impudent, shameless, bold.

বিদগ্ধ, নিপুণ, বুদ্ধিমন্ত, বিচক্ষণ, লম্পট, ভণ্ডতাকারী, পণ্ডিত, clever, sharp, shrewd, skilful, knowing, learned, witty, intriguing, amorous, lecherous, lustful; a libertine, intriguer, a scholar.

বিদগ্ধা, মোহিনী, a woman of insinuating manners and conversation.

বিদরণ, চিরণ, ফাটন, to be torn or lacerated, split, tear, crack.

বিদল, অন্যদলস্থ, বিপক্ষ, ডালা, ডালি, ছোলা, কুচা, মিঠাই, কোবিদার বৃক্ষ, of an opposite or adverse party, inimical; a sort of basket, split peas, parings, chips, cuttings, a cake, mountain ebony.

বিদা, মই, আঁচড়ী, a garden rake, a harrow.

বিদাঁড়া, বিধিবিরুদ্ধ, অনুচিত, কদাচার, অসভ্যতা, against or contrary to rule, irregular, improper, rude; rudeness, an incivility, improper conduct.

বিদায়, গমনের অনুমতি, ছুটী, permission to depart, dismissal, leave, leave of absence; retiring or departing in health and peace.

বিদায়ী, বিদায়প্রাপ্ত, পারিতোষিক, asking leave, having obtained leave; a present on departure, a gratuity.

বিদার, চেরা, ফাক, a rent, split, laceration, chink, crack.

বিদারণ, চষণ, চিরাণ, ফাড়ন, উপড়ন, to tear, lacerate, mangle, rend, split, cleave, hew, plough, root up.

বিদিক্, বিদিগ্,—দিকের মধ্যবর্ত্তি দিক্, an intermediate point of the compass. [known, declared.

বিদিত, জ্ঞাত, পরিচিত, প্রকাশিত, knowing, acquainted with,

বিদীর্ণ, চেরা, ফাড়া, torn, lacerated, scratched, rent, cleft.

বিদুর, প্রাজ্ঞ, বুদ্ধিমান, wise, clever, intelligent, learned.

বিদূষক, নিন্দক, কুৎসাবাদী, ছলগ্রাহী, রসিক, অপবাদী, ভণ্ড, blaming, finding fault, censorious, suspicious, facetious, witty; a detractor, a wag. [tance.

বিদেশ, পরদেশ, দূর দেশ, a distant or foreign country, a dis-

বিদেশী, পরদেশী, আগন্তুক, প্রবাসী, of another country, foreign, strange; a foreigner, sojourner, stranger.

বিদ্ধ, ফোঁড়া, ভেদিত, perforated, bored, pierced, penetrated.

বিদ্বত্তা, শাস্ত্রজ্ঞান. পাণ্ডিত্য, wisdom, intelligence, erudition.

বিদ্বান্, পণ্ডিত, জ্ঞানবান্, intelligent, wise, learned; a sage.

বিদ্বিষ্ট, ঘৃণিত, নিগৃহীত, ক্লিশিত, hated, persecuted, injured, maltreated, maliciously pursued.

বিদ্বেষ, বিদ্বিষ্টি,—বৈর, পরহিংসেচ্ছা, দোষকথন, নিগ্রহ, উচ্চাটন, enmity, hatred, malice, angry abuse, persecution.

বিদ্বেষী, বিদ্বেষক,—ঘৃণাযুক্ত, হিংসেচ্ছুক, ক্লেশদ, বিপথশুক, কঠিন, malicious, hating, injurious, persecuting, captious, difficult to please, dissatisfied.

বিদ্বেষ্টা, পরহিংসেচ্ছুক. ছিদ্রগ্রাহী, নিগ্রহকারী, বৈরী, a malicious or captious person, a persecutor, an enemy.

বিদ্যমান, জীবন্ত, বর্ত্তমান, সাক্ষাৎকার, প্রস্তুত, existing, existent, extant, present, ready at hand.

বিদ্যা, পাণ্ডিত্য, শাস্ত্রজ্ঞান, wisdom, learning, knowledge, science, philosophy, a magical pill or bolus.

বিদ্যাগার, বিদ্যালয়, বিদ্যাশালা,—চৌবাড়ী, চৌপ্প, a college, a school.

বিদ্যাদাতা, শিক্ষাগুরু, অধ্যাপক, a teacher, tutor, instructor.

বিদ্যাদান, শিক্ষা, উপদেশ, অধ্যাপনা, teaching, instruction, tuition, communication of knowledge.

বিদ্যাধর, দেবযোনি বিশেষ, an order of demigods.

বিদ্যাবান্, পণ্ডিত, শাস্ত্রজ্ঞ, learned, wise, literate, proficient.

বিদ্যুৎ, তড়িত, সৌদামিনী, lightning, a flash of lightning.

বিদ্যুল্লতা, মেঘজ্যোতিঃ, flashes of forked or streaked lightning.

বিদ্যোত, প্রভা, দীপ্তি, splendour, glare, light.

বিদ্রব, গলতি, চুয়ন, পলায়ন, বাঁচাও, বুদ্ধি, অপবাদ, নিন্দা, liquefaction, a flowing, oozing, melting, flight, retreat, escape, intellect, censure, reproach.

বিদ্রাবক, গলতিজনক, পরাভূত শত্রুকে দৌড়িয়া তাড়নকারী, পরিহাসক, causing to melt or run away, putting to flight, acting the mimic, jesting, jeering.

বিদ্রুত, তরল, গলিত, পলায়িত, liquid, fluid, melted, flown, fled.

বিদ্রুম, প্রবাল, coral, a young shoot, a fabulous tree.

বিদ্রূপ, ব্যঙ্গ, কৌতুক, পরিহাস, raillery, a jest, joke, jeer, jeering, mimickry, ridicule, mockery.

বিদ্রূপী, পরিহাসক, ভণ্ড, jeering &c. a jester, droll, mimic.

বিদ্রোহ, হিংসেচ্ছা, দ্বেষ, malevolence, malice, spite, persecution.

বিধ-1, প্রকার, রীতি, ব্যবস্থা, a kind, sort, manner, form, rule.

বিধবা, রণ্ডা, স্বামিহীনা, a widow; without a husband.

বিধর্ম্ম, স্বধর্ম্মত্যাগ, বিধিবিরুদ্ধ ক্রিয়া, apostacy, heterodoxy, deviation from the rules of sect or cast. [ing, &c.

বিধর্ম্মী, অন্যমতগ্রাহী, স্বধর্ম্মোল্লঙ্ঘক, apostate, heterodox, deviat-

বিধাতা, সর্ববিধায়ক ঈশ্বর, বিশ্বস্রষ্টা, ব্রহ্মা, God as universal legislator, providence, Brahmá.

বিধান, ব্যবস্থা, অনুমতি, আদেশ, আজ্ঞা, নিরূপণ, অনুষ্ঠানের উপদেশ, কর্ত্তব্য কর্ম্ম, বিধি, কল্প, রীতি, a law, rule, order, decree, statute, injunction, precept, an ordering, commanding, enjoining, settling by law, regulation, an action, ritual observance, ordinance, form, manner. [tion, injunction.

বিধানতা, স্মৃতিসাধ্যতা, কর্ত্তব্যতা, legality, lawfulness, institu-

বিধায়ক, বিধিবাক্য, সমর্পক, সংস্থাপক, স্থিতিকারক, আদেশক, an ordinance, one who consigns, delivers over, intrusts, deposits, fixes, secures or makes sure; enjoining, commanding.

বিধারা, কুরীতি, কুব্যবহার, an evil custom or habit, ill-conduct.

বিধি, কল্প, আদিষ্ট ব্যবহার, রীতি, কর্ম্মানুষ্ঠানের উপদেশ, ব্যবস্থা, আজ্ঞা, প্রমাণ সূত্র, অদৃষ্ট, ভাগ্য, ক্রিয়া, প্রকার, ধারা, ধর্ম্মশাস্ত্র, স্মৃতি, ব্রহ্মা, a sacred precept, prescribed observance, rite, rule, formula, form, statute, injunction, order, decree, command, a sacred text or citation, fate, destiny, luck, an act, action, form, manner, a sacred writing, the law, Brahmá.

বিধু, চন্দ্র, কর্পূর, the moon, camphor.

বিধুত, বিধূত,—নড়ান, কম্পমান, ত্যক্ত, agitated, shaken, shaken out, trembling, tremulous, abandoned, left, relinquished. [destitute.

বিধুর, বিহ্বল, দুঃখী, আশ্রয়হীন, agitated, distressed, afflicted,

বিধুন্তুদ, রাহুগ্রহ, Ráhu or the ascending node.

বিধূনন, বিধুতি,—কম্পন, নড়া, পরিত্যাগ, a trembling. shaking, agitation, relinquishing, abandonment, &c.

বিধৃত, স্থিরীকৃত, অবলম্বিত, আক্রান্ত, পাকড়া, আট্কান, upheld, sustained, held, seized, withheld.

বিধেয়, কর্ত্তব্য, ধার্য্য, ব্যবস্থেয়, ব্যবহার্য্য, আচরণীয়, বিহিত কর্ম্ম, to be done, upheld or prescribed, what is to be done or practised ; a prescribed observance.

বিধ্বংস. বিনাশ, দ্বেষ, ঘৃণা, অনাদর, destruction, enmity, aversion, disrespect. [hostile, averse.

বিধ্বংসী. নাশক, নশ্বর. বিমুখ, বিপক্ষ, destroying, perishing,

বিনত. অবনত, নম্র, বশীভূত, বক্র, bowed, bent, stooping, prostrate, humble, submissive, crooked, curved.

বিনতি, বিনয়,—নম্রতাচার, অনুনয়, কোমলত্ব, শিষ্টতা, সদাচার, প্রণাম, নিবেদন, কাকুতি, অধ্যেষণা, humility, modesty, submission, compliance, mildness, affability, decorum, decency, propriety of behaviour, an obeisance, reverence, apology, humiliation, entreaty, supplication, humble solicitation.

বিনম্র, বিনয়ী,—অনুনয়ী, দর্পহীন, আজ্ঞাবহ, সুশীল, বশীভূত, আলাপী, humble, modest, submissive, yielding, tractable, compliant, suppliant, affable.

বিনশ্বর, ধ্বংস্য, অনিত্য, perishable, destructible.

বিনষ্ট, ধ্বস্ত, বিকৃত, বিগড়া, ভ্রষ্ট, দুরন্ত, দুষ্ট, ধূর্ত্ত, খল, destroyed, ruined, spoiled, corrupted, perverted, fallen, perverse, vicious, artful, dishonest.

বিনা, অভাবে, ঋতে, ব্যতিরেকে, without, beside, save, except.

বিনান, কেশ পাকান, ভাঁজান, to plat, plait or dress the hair.

বিনাম, মিথ্যা নাম, a false or assumed name.
বিনামী, মিথ্যানামধারী, bearing a false or feigned name.
বিনায়ক, গণেশ, নম্র, বশীভূত, Ganesha; humble, yielding.
বিনায়াস, অনুদ্যোগ, অকষ্ট, ease, facility.
বিনাশ, সংহার, ধ্বংস, অপচয়, উৎখাত, উৎপাত, ক্ষতি, মৃত্যু, হত্যা, গানান্ত, utter destruction, annihilation, ruin, perdition, loss, death, murder, slaughter, the close of a strain, (in music.)
বিনাশন, সংহরণ, ঘাতন, বিগাড়ন, to destroy utterly, bring to ruin, annihilate, kill, murder, spoil.
বিনাশশীল, বিনাশ্য, বিনাশনীয়, বিনশ্বর, } ধ্বংস্য, নশ্বর, ক্ষয়ণীয়, অস্থায়ী, বিকার্য্য, destructible, perishable, tending to ruin, capable of being spoiled.
বিনাশী, ধ্বংস্য, ধ্বংসী, ঘাতক, destructible, &c. destructive; a destroyer. [to decay.
বিনাশোন্মুখ, ধ্বংসশীল, পচ্যমান, verging to ruin, spoiling, going
বিনাসাধে, অনিচ্ছাপূর্ব্বক, অপর্য্যাপ্তে, involuntarily.
বিনিগমক, প্রামাণিক, প্রতিপাদক, প্রবোধক, সন্দেহনিবারক, conclusive, deciding the judgment; a decisive argument.
বিনিগমনা, সিদ্ধান্ত, মীমাংসা, নিশ্চায়ক প্রমাণ, a logical conclusion, decision, decisive argument, proof.
বিনিপাত, পতন, ভ্রংশ, আপদ, পীড়া, দুর্দশা, অপমান, a fall, fall from office or dignity, fall from innocence or virtue, calamity, evil, pain, distress, disrespect.
বিনিময়, পরিদান, পরিবর্ত্ত, প্রতিফল, barter, exchange room, substitution, stead, requital, return, retaliation.
বিনিয়োগ, পদস্থাপন, কোন কর্ম্মোদ্দেশে স্থির করিয়া রাখন, প্রতিদানাপেক্ষায় দানকরা, an appointment to office, application or appropriation to a particular purpose, a giving in expectation of remuneration or return. [ing, settling.
বিনির্ণয়, নিশ্চয়, নিষ্পত্তি, certainty, assurance, an ascertain-
বিনীত, নম্র, মৃদু, অনুনয়ী, বশীভূত, আজ্ঞাবহ, ধীর, জিতেন্দ্রিয়, শিষ্ট, সুশীল, সুব্যবহার, কৃতবেশভূষণ, সুন্দর, ধৃত, ধরিয়া আনায়িত, শাসিত, দমিত, humble, modest, unassuming, placid, meek, gentle, compliant, yielding,

tractable, of subdued passions, well-behaved, decorous, decent, well-dressed, adorned, handsome, taken, led, conveyed, punished, chastized, humbled, well-trained.

বিনেতা, শাসনকর্ত্তা, রাজা, অধিপতি, শিক্ষাগুরু, পথদর্শক, a ruler, king, leader, instructor, guide.

বিনেয়, সুশাস্য, শিষ্ট, নম্র, শান্ত, উপাস্য, দম্য, governable, tractable, submissive, humble, flexible, exorable, adorable, to be humbled, &c. [mence.

বিনোদ, হর্ষ, ক্রীড়া, ব্যগ্রতা, joy, sport, play, eagerness, vehe-

বিন্দু, পৃষত, ফোটা, কণিকা, টুকি, চিহ্ন, শূন্য, ঁ কার, অনুস্বার, ভ্রূমধ্য দেশ, a drop, atom, scrap, a spot, dot, mark, point, comma, the characters ং and ঁ, the part of the forehead between the eyebrows.

বিন্ধন, ফোঁড়ন, ভেদন, কামড়ান, to pierce, perforate, bore, penetrate, to pain, gripe. [cholic.

বিন্ধনী, ভেদক, পেটশূল, perforating, &c. griping pains, the

বিন্যস্ত, ক্রমপূর্ব্বক রাখাণ, সাজান, বেশভূষিত, বসান, স্থাপিত, গচ্ছিত, arranged in order, dressed, adorned, placed, fixed, deposited, pledged, delivered.

বিন্যাস, ক্রমপূর্ব্বক স্থাপনকরা, সাজানি, বেশভূষা পিন্ধনকরা, কেশবেশ, সমাহার, আধি, স্থান, আধার, orderly or artificial arrangement, adjustment of the dress so as to adorn the person, a dressing of the hair, an assemblage, collection, deposit, pledge, a scite, place, receptacle. [oblique.

বিপক্ব, পরিণত, মোচড়ান, টেড়া, ripened, matured, twisted,

বিপক্ষ, শত্রু, বৈরী, প্রতিবাদী, বিপরীত, বিরুদ্ধ, an enemy, adversary, opponent, disputant; hostile, adverse.

বিপণ, বিক্রয়, বিক্রয়নিয়ম, a sale, a contract of sale.

বিপণি, আপণ, পণ্যবীথিকা, হাট, a shop, stall, market, fair.

বিপত্তরণ, আপদোদ্ধার, the surmounting of a difficulty, &c.

বিপত্তারী, দায়োদ্ধৃত, surmounting difficulties, escaping from calamities. [adversity.

বিপত্তি, বিপদ্.—আপদ, দুর্দশা, a misfortune, accident, calamity,

বিপথ, চোরাপথ, কুপথ, a bye-road, wrong road, evil way.

বিপথগামী, দুষ্টাচারী, going in an evil way, vicious, perverse.
বিপন্ন, দুর্ভাগ্যপ্রাপ্ত, দুর্দশাপন্ন, ক্লিষ্ট, আপদগ্রস্ত, হারাণ, নষ্ট, বিগড়া, unfortunate, distressed, afflicted, suffering adversity, lost, destroyed, spoiled.
বিপরীত, উল্টা, বিরুদ্ধ, বিপক্ষ, শত্রুতা, contrary, reverse, opposite, adverse, hostile, repugnant to; opposition, &c.
বিপরীতে, বিপক্ষে, বিরুদ্ধে, against, in opposition, contrary to.
বিপর্য্যয়, বিপর্য্যাস,—ব্যত্যয়, অন্যথা, ব্যতিক্রম, শত্রুতা, অনিচ্ছা, প্রকাণ্ড, দারুণ, contrariety, opposition, reverse, inverted order, &c. hostility, repugnance; vast, huge.
বিপর্য্যাস-ম, মিথ্যা প্রসঙ্গ, মিথ্যানুমান, ভ্রম, আরোপ, অপ্রামাণ্য বাক্য, a false assumption, as of false for true, imaginary for real, &c. a false conception, an attributing falsely, an erroneous assertion.
বিপাক, পরিণাম, দৈবাৎ ঘটনা, কর্ম্মফল, ক্লেশ, দুঃখ, আপদ, অপচয়, বিকার, অপচার, a ripening, ripeness, maturity, an unexpected result, an occurrence, the natural or moral consequences of actions, moral retribution, distress, poverty, calamity, ruin, a change of form or state, &c. indigestion.
বিপাদিকা, পাদস্ফোট, a sore, kibe or blister on the foot.
বিপিন, বন, কানন, গহন, a forest, wood, thicket.
বিপুল, প্রকাণ্ড, বড়, স্থূল, প্রচুর, অতিশয়, গভীর, huge, vast, stupendous, great, large, much, deep.
বিপ্র, ব্রাহ্মণ, দ্বিজ, a brâhman.
বিপ্রকৃতি, তিরস্কার, নিন্দা, অপমান, কুৎসা, অপবাদ, প্রত্যপবাদ, প্রতিফল, abuse, contumely, insult, reviling, reproach, censure, a retort, retaliation.
বিপ্রকৃষ্ট, বিগড়া, মন্দ, দূর, deteriorated, inferior, bad, distant.
বিপ্রগামী, বিচলিত, প্রত্যাকৃষ্ট, moving in a contrary direction.
বিপ্রতিকারী, বিরুদ্ধ, প্রতিকূল, অসাধারণ গুণযুক্ত ঔষধ, opposed to, acting against; an antagonist, a specific.
বিপ্রতিপত্তি, বিবাদ, আপত্তি, প্রাতিকূল্য, অপমান, a dispute, objection, remonstrance, obstacle, opposition of interests, disgrace, &c. [a dispute.
বিপ্রলপন, বিপ্রলাপ,—বিতণ্ডা, বিরোধ, disputation, wrangling,

বিপ্রিয়, অপ্রিয়, অপ্রীক, ঘৃণিত, পাপ, অঘ, unbeloved, disliked, disesteemed; sin, transgression, crime.

বিফল, বিফলিত,—নির্মূল, ব্যর্থ, নিরর্থক, অলীক, unproductive, fruitless, abortive, vain, useless, ineffectual, idle.

বিফলে, নিরর্থে, ineffectually, uselessly, to no purpose.

বিফুল, বিকসিত, প্রস্ফুটিত, expanded, open, blown.

বিবক্ষা, কহিবার ইচ্ছা, বাঞ্ছা, a wish to speak, a desire.

বিবক্ষিত, কথনেচ্ছার বিষয়, বাঞ্ছিত, required or wished to be spoken, wished, desired.

বিবক্ষু, কহনেচ্ছুক, desirous of speaking, wishing to say.

বিবর, বিল, গর্ত, ছিদ্র, কুহর, a burrow, hole, chasm, cave, recess.

বিবরণ, বিস্তারিয়া কহন, বৃত্তান্ত, বর্ণনা, ব্যাখ্যা, টীকা, to tell in detail, specify, narrate, describe; circumstances, particulars, a detail, description, relation, explanation, exposition, gloss, comment.

বিবর্জন, ছাড়ন, ত্যাগ করণ, ছাড়িয়া রাখন, to relinquish, leave, desert, abandon, quit, reject, except.

বিবর্ণ, বিকৃতবর্ণ, মলিন, লজ্জিত, ব্রাত্য, নীচলোক, চণ্ডাল, changed in colour, discoloured, bedaubed, reddening, blushing; one of low cast, an outcast.

বিবর্ত্ত, নৃত্য, ঘূর্ণন, ভ্রম, রাশি, সঞ্চয়, সমূহ, a dancing, a going, turning or whirling round, an error, mistake, a heap, collection, assemblage, multitude.

বিবশ, পঙ্গু, জড়, দুর্বল, অবাধ্য, crippled, incapable of exertion, weak, helpless, not under controul.

বিবসন, বিবস্ত্র,—উলঙ্গ, naked, unclothed, without clothes.

বিবসন, বিবাস,—স্বদেশ হইতে দূরকরা, ঔদাস্য, উলঙ্গ, exile, banishment, desertion; naked, unclothed.

বিবাদ, বিরোধ, কলহ, ন্যায়করা, ঝগড়া, a dispute, quarrel, broil, wrangling, a lawsuit, controversy, an objection.

বিবাদক, বিরোধক, কলহী, disputing, litigating, controverting.

বিবাদী, বিরোধী, কুন্দলীয়া, আপদাশী, বিপক্ষ, disputing, litigious, factious, quarrelsome, disputatious, controversial; a plaintiff, complainant, opponent.

বিবাদযুক্ত, বিরোধ বিষয়ক, কুন্দলিয়া, connected with or relating to disputes, &c. captious, litigious, &c.

বিবাহ, দার পরিগ্রহ, পরিণয়, marriage, a wedding, nuptials.

বিবাহিত, ঊঢ়, কৃতবিবাহ, married, wedded.

বিবাহ্য, বিবাহযোগ্য, পরিণয়ার্হ, marriageable, fit to be married.

বিবিক্ত, নির্জ্জন, উদাসী, পবিত্র, পুণ্য, পৃথক্, ভিন্ন, বিবেচিত, বিচারিত, বিবেচক, solitary, lonely, desart, deserted, pure, holy, separate, detached, distinguished, discriminated, judged, discriminating, judicious.

বিবিধ, নানাপ্রকার, বহুরূপ, various, diverse, many, multiform.

বিবুধ, দেবতা, পণ্ডিত, a god, a deity, a learned man, a philosopher.

বিবৃত, বিস্তারিত, প্রকাশিত, প্রত্যক্ষ, প্রসারিত, detailed, narrated, particularized, amplified, displayed, made manifest, evident, expanded, extended.

বিবৃতি, ব্যাখ্যা, টীকা, প্রকাশ, an explanation, gloss, exposition, manifestation, display.

বিবৃত্ত, ঘূর্ণমান, revolving, whirling, rolling, turning round.

বিবেক, বিশেষজ্ঞান, বিবেচনা, বুদ্ধি, সদসৎবিচার, সমাধি, ঔদাস্য, discrimination, judgment, the faculty of discriminating, power of discerning good from evil, conscience, abstraction from worldly affairs, religious indifference, ascetism.

বিবেকী, সূক্ষ্মবুদ্ধি, সদসৎবিচারক, বিচারকর্ত্তা, পণ্ডিত, বৈরাগী, discriminating, discriminative, judicious; a judge, a sage, an ascetic or abstract devotee.

বিবেচক, বিশেষজ্ঞ, সদসৎবিচারশীল, তর্কক, বুদ্ধিমান, শিষ্ট, তত্ত্বাবধারক, discriminating, distinguishing, judging, examining into, reasoning, reflecting, thoughtful, rational, civil, polite; a superintendant.

বিবেচন, বিতর্কণ, বিচারণ, to deliberate, reflect, design, judge, &c.

বিবেচনা, সদসৎবিচার, অনুধাবন, চর্চা, ভাবনা, তর্ক, সদসৎঅনুসন্ধান, অনুমান, স্থিরবোধ, অভিপ্রায়, তত্ত্বাবধারণ, discrimination, reflection, thought, deliberation, consideration, examination, investigation, enquiry, trial, judgement, inference, supposition, persuasion, deliberate opinion, design, purpose, a superintendance, overlooking.

বিবেচিত, তর্কিত, ভাবিত, examined. investigated, pondered, &c.
বিব্বোক, হাব, বিলাস, a female's amorous affectation of indifference to dress, &c. amorous dalliance.
বিবৃত, ক্লেশাপন্ন, কাতর, involved in calamity, distressed.
বিভক্ত, বিভিন্ন. পৃথক্কৃত, বণ্টিত, অংশিত, divided, separated, portioned, shared, parcelled out, allotted.
বিভক্তজ, বিভাগের পর জাত পুত্র, a son born after the division of his deceased father's property.
বিভক্তি, প্রত্যয়, অংশ. বণ্ট, a grammatical termination or inflexion, a division, portion. [to share out.
বিভজন, বিভাগন,—অংশন, বণ্টন, to divide into shares or lots,
বিভব, দ্রব্য, বস্তু, পদার্থ, ধন. সম্পত্তি. ঐশ্বর্য্য, প্রতাপ, পরমা শক্তি, অণিমাদি অষ্ট, মুক্তি, a thing, substance, matter, wealth, property, grandeur, loftiness of mind, magnanimity, elevation of sentiment, supreme or superhuman power, final emancipation.
বিভবনীয়, সম্পত্তি, what may be appropriated; property.
বিভবশালী, ধনবান, মহাত্মা, rich, affluent, grand, magnanimous.
বিভা, বিবাহ, দীপ্তি, সৌন্দর্য্য, light, lustre, beauty, marriage.
বিভাকর, দিবাকর. সূর্য্য, অগ্নি, the sun, fire.
বিভাগ, বণ্ট, অংশ, বিলান, ছিট, a share, portion, part, lot, a division, allowance, a fraction.
বিভাগী, বণ্টক, বিলানিয়া, অংশী, dividing, sharing out, allotting; one who receives a share, a sharer.
বিভাজক, অংশকারী, one who divides property into shares.
বিভাত, প্রাতঃকাল, বিবাহিত, dawn, day-break ; married.
বিভাবক, বিভাবী,—ধনবান, বড় লোক, rich, wealthy, powerful.
বিভাবনা, বিবেচনা, অনুভব, প্রবোধ, পরিজ্ঞান, তর্ক, বিতণ্ডা, discrimination, perception, a seeing, discovering, conviction, examination, discussion.
বিভাবনীয়, বিবেচনীয়, পরিজ্ঞেয়, discriminable, distinguishable, discoverable, liable to conviction. [bawd.
বিভাবরী, রাত্রি, হরিদ্রা, বেশ্যা, কুট্টনী, night, turmeric, a harlot.
বিভাবিত, বিবেচিত, অনুভূত, প্রমাণসিদ্ধ, পরিজ্ঞাপিত, নিষ্পন্ন, discriminated, marked, perceived, seen, discovered, proved on evidence, convicted, judged.

বিভাষা, বিকল্প, দ্বৈধবাদ, a twofold proposal, alternative, option.
বিভাষিত, বিকল্প, উক্ত, doubtful, optional, declared, spoken.
বিভিন্ন, ভেদিত, পৃথক্, অন্য, বিপরীত, মিশ্রিত, divided, separated, distinct, different, discordant, contrary, contradictory, scattered, dispersed, intermixed.
বিভীষণ, দারুণ, ভয়ানক, formidable, fearful, terrific, alarming.
বিভু, সর্ব্বব্যাপী, নিত্য, দৃঢ়, শক্ত, কর্ত্তা, ঈশ্বর, ব্রহ্মা, omnipresent, all-pervading, eternal, firm, solid, hard; a lord, sovereign, owner, master, God, Brahmá, &c.
বিভূতি, অণিমাদি, সম্পত্তি, ঐশ্বর্য্য, গোময়ভস্ম, divine or superhuman power, affluence, property, glory, grandeur, the ashes of cowdung. [pompous.
বিভূতিমান্. ঐশ্বর্য্যবন্ত, ধনবান, affluent, glorious, splendid,
বিভূষণ, অলঙ্কার. গহনা, শোভান, ornament, decoration, trinkets, jewels ; to ornament, decorate, dress, adorn.
বিভৃত, ধৃত, ধারিত, স্থিরীকৃত, অবলম্বিত, রক্ষিত, held, retained, upheld, sustained, supported, maintained.
বিভেদ, বিচ্ছেদ, পার্থক্য, বিশেষ, বৈপরীত্য, নিক্ষেপ, a separation, division, distinction, difference, contradiction, a scattering, dispersion.
বিভ্রম, ভ্রম, চুক, সন্দেহ, শঙ্কা, মনের চাঞ্চল্য, ছেনালামী. হাব, ললিত, কামাগ্নি, সৌন্দর্য্য, ঘূর্ণি. an error, mistake, a doubt, apprehension, whim, caprice, capriciousness, wantonness, female dalliance, the power of love, beauty, a whirling round.
বিভোল, হতজ্ঞান, মূর্খ, মূর্চ্ছিত, মত্ত, বিহ্বল, foolish, senseless, faint, faintish, inseusible, drunk, transported.
বিভ্রাট্, অপ্রতুল. আপদ. an emergency, misfortune, calamity.
বিভ্রান্ত, স্খলিত, ত্রস্ত, mistaken, erring, flurried, alarmed.
বিভ্রান্তি, ভুল, ঘবরাণী, error, confusion, precipitation, flurry.
বিমত, পরাঙ্মুখ, বিপরীত, অন্যধর্ম্মাক্রান্ত, অন্যমনস্ক, averse, opposed to, hostile, contrary, of a different opinion.
বিমতি, অনিচ্ছা, অরুচি, অসম্মতি, ইতরবোধ, disinclination, dislike, disapprobation, a different opinion.
বিমনস্ক, বিমনাঃ,—অমনোযোগী, অন্যমনস্ক, বিরক্ত, ঘবরাণ, চিন্তান্বিত, বিষণ্ণ, ক্ষিপ্ত, inattentive, absent in thought,

thinking of something else, otherwise-minded, averse, dissatisfied, bewildered, perplexed, sad, broken-hearted, disordered in mind.

বিমর্দ্দন, বাটন, পীষণ, চন্দনাদি ঘর্ষণ, চাপন, দলন, দমন, ঘাতন, to triturate, rub, grind, pound, compress, trample down, subdue, destroy, kill; friction &c.

বিমর্ষ, অনুতাপ, খেদ, বিতুষ্টি, বিষণ্ণ, কাতর, উদ্বিগ্ন, regret, repentance, after-sorrow, dissatisfaction, dislike, displeasure; sad, dejected, sorrowful, anxious.

বিমর্ষী, খিদ্যমান, বিরক্ত, penitent, sorry, dissatisfied, &c.

বিমল, মলশূন্য, স্বচ্ছ, শ্বেত, সুন্দর, মনোহর, clear, transparent, limpid, clean, pure, white, beautiful.

বিমা, ঝুঁকি, দায়ঠেকা, অপচয়ভাগিত্ব, insurance of ships, &c.

বিমাতা, সপত্নীমাতা, a step-mother, (the real mother being either living or dead.) [carriage.

বিমান, দেবযান, রথ, গাড়ী, the chariot of a god, a car, vehicle,

বিমার্গ, কুপথ, চোরাপথ, ভ্রষ্টাচার, ঝাড়ুন, a wrong, bad or bye-road, an evil course, a brush, a broom.

বিমুক্ত, ছাড়ান, মোক্ষপ্রাপ্ত, liberated, redeemed, pardoned, &c.

বিমুক্তি, বিমোক্ষ,—ছাড়ানি, উদ্ধার, ত্রাণ, অপবর্গ, liberation, release, liberty, redemption, final emancipation.

বিমুগ্ধ, মায়াবদ্ধ, ভুলান, জড়ীভূত, অবাক্, fascinated, bewitched, deluded, seduced, stupified, confounded.

বিমুখ, অপ্রসন্ন, প্রতিকূল, turning away from, averted, averse.

বিমোক্তা, ত্রাণকর্ত্তা, রক্ষক, a redeemer, liberator, &c.

বিমোচন, ছাড়ান, উদ্ধরণ, ক্ষমাকরণ, to release, liberate, free, redeem, disentangle, clear, disencumber, pardon.

বিমোহ, মায়া, কুহক, ভুলানি, জড়তা, fascination, a bewitching, deluding, seducing, tempting, stupefaction.

বিম্‌কী, বলেতে জলাদির ঊর্দ্ধনিঃসরণ, a spouting up, gushing out.

বিম্ব, চন্দ্র সূর্য্যের মণ্ডল, ছায়া, প্রতিমূর্ত্তি, ছবি, বুদ্বুদ, the disk of the sun or moon, a shadow, reflection, image, picture, a bubble.

বিম্ব, বিম্বিকা,—লতা বিশেষ, তেলাকুচা, a species of gourd.

বিম্বাকার, ঢোপবৎ, গোলাকৃতি, রাঙ্গা, convex, round, ruddy, red.

বিম্বিত, কৃতপ্রতিচ্ছায়া, উপমিত, reflected, shadowed out.

বিম্বোষ্ঠ, রক্তবর্ণোষ্ঠ, having red or ruddy lips, rosy-lipped.
বিয়ৎ, আকাশ, অন্তরীক্ষ, the sky, atmosphere, the heavens.
বিয়ন-আন, প্রসবন, to bring forth young, to calve, litter.
বিযুক্ত, বিচ্ছিন্ন,বিরহী, separated, disjoined, disunited, absent.
বিয়ে, বিবাহ, পরিণয়, marriage.
বিয়োগ, বিচ্ছেদ, বিরহ. নির্বাণ, আদেশলিপি, পৃথক্‌লেখা, disunion, separation, disjunction, absence (of lovers), departure, death, a label, a prescription, a separate entry or account. [(as lovers.)
বিয়োগী, বিযোগিনী,—বিরহী, বিরহিণী, *m.* & *f.* absent, separated,
বিযোড়, অযুগ্ম, অতুল্য, odd, uneven, ill-matched, unsuitable.
বিরক্ত, অতুষ্ট, ক্রুদ্ধ. ব্যস্ত, বিপক্ষ, অননুশীল, displeased, dissatisfied, disgusted, vexed, ruffled, teased, annoyed, averse, indifferent to. [disgust.
বিরক্তি, অতুষ্টি, ঘৃণা, displeasure, dissatisfaction, dislike,
বিরচন, গ্রন্থন, গড়ন, নির্ম্মাণ, to compose, write, compile, construct, build, make, fabricate, prepare.
বিরজা, নিবৃত্তরজস্কা. সন্যাসাশ্রম কালে কর্ত্তব্য হোম, তীর্থ বিশেষ, a woman who has ceased to menstruate, a sacrifice made on renouncing the world, a certain place of pilgrimage.
বিরত, নিবৃত্ত, ক্ষান্ত, ত্যাগী, ceased, relinquished, stopped, having ceased or desisted, desisting from, abandoning. [pause.
বিরতি, নিবৃত্তি, উপরাম, a cessation, desisting, stopping;
বিরল নির্জন, দূর, প্রশস্ত, অসাধারণ, কিছু কালান্তরে উপস্থিত, ঢীলা, তনু, সরু, private, retired, remote, alone, apart, wide, rare, of infrequent recurrence, occurring at distant or repeated intervals, relaxed, loose, thin, delicate, fine.
বিরলে, গোপনে,নির্জনে, secretly, underhand, privately, apart.
বিরস, পানসা, অস্বাদু, ন্যক্কার্য্য, ঘৃণার্হ, কুস্বাদু, insipid, ill-tasted, nauseous, rank; an ill taste or flavour.
বিরহ, বিচ্ছেদ, বিয়োগ, অন্তর, নিবৃত্তি, ক্ষমা, ত্যাগকরা, ঔদাস্য, প্রেমপাত্রহীনতা, অভাব, নায়কের বিলাপ, separation, parting, absence of lovers, distance, cessation,

forbearance, relinquishment, loneliness, bereavement, destitution, a lover's lament.

বিরহী, বিরহিত,— ত্যক্ত, অনাথ, উদাসী, বিয়োগী, deserted, forsaken, destitute, bereft, lonely, absent, separate, (as lovers.)

বিরহিণী, বিয়োগিনী, ত্যক্তা, a female whose lover or husband is absent; deserted, &c.

বিরাগ, বিষয়ত্যাগ, বিবেক, ইন্দ্রিয়দমন, ঔদাস্য, অরুচি, ঘৃণা, নিন্দা, কুৎসা, indifference to the world and the pleasures of sense, absence of desire or passion, disregard, dislike, disapprobation, disrelish, disgust. slander, calumny, reproach, imputation.

বিরাগী, ঘৃণাযুক্ত, বিরক্ত, কুৎসাবাদী, বিষয়ত্যাগী, জিতেন্দ্রিয়, filled with disgust, nauseating, disrelishing, calumniating, &c. dead to pleasure, &c.

বিরাজ শোভা, সৌন্দর্য্য, সুখেতে অবস্থান, আবির্ভাব, প্রকাশ, প্রজাপতি, ক্ষত্রিয়, splendour, beauty, a life of ease, dignity, &c. freedom from care, an appearing, manifestation, a shining as an object of admiration, Brahmá or his first progeny, a Cshyatriya.

বিরাজন, প্রকাশন, শোভন, সুখে থাকন, রাজ্য ভোগকরণ, to shine, be splendid, to live in ease, dignity, &c, to reign.

বিরাজিত, প্রকাশিত, আবির্ভূত, শোভান্বিত, manifested, displayed, exhibited to view, splendid.

বিরাজমান, প্রকাশমান, দীপ্তিমান, বিলক্ষণরূপবিশিষ্ট, shining, &c. exciting admiration, appearing in a beautiful form.

বিরাট, ভারতের মধ্যবর্ত্তি দেশ, রাজা, অতিবৃহৎ, প্রকাণ্ড, a part of central India, a king; huge, large.

বিরাম, নিবৃত্তি, ক্ষান্তি, বিশ্রাম, ছুটী, বিলম্ব, অবকাশ, থাক, ছেদ, a cessation, a desisting from, cessation from labour, rest, repose, a vacation, recess, adjournment, leisure, spare time, a pause, a space.

বিরিক্ত, উদ্গীর্ণ, vomited, thrown off the stomach.

বিরিঞ্চি, ব্রহ্মা, বিষ্ণু, শিব, Brahma', Vishnŭ, Shiva.

বিরুদ্ধ, বিপরীত, প্রতিকূল, উল্টা, অসঙ্গত, ছলী, কুটিল, দুষ্ট, অমঙ্গল, মন্দ, আপদ, কলহ, বিবাদ. opposed to, hostile, reverse, contrary, absurd, artful, disingenuous, insincere, evil, vile, nasty, unlucky, bad, unfortunate; a misfortune, opposition, quarrel, dispute.

বিরূপ, বক্রতা, কুডৌল, প্রাতিকূল্য, শত্রুতা, রিপু, বিপক্ষ, বিকলাঙ্গ, বিকৃত, deformity, opposition, dislike, an enemy, opponent; hostile, adverse, deformed, hideous, ill-shaped, ugly, monstrous, mis-shapen.

বিরেক, অতিসার, পেটচলা, a diarrhœa, a purging, a looseness.

বিরেচক, ভেদক ঔষধি, সারক, cathartic, purgative.

বিরেচন, মলত্যাগ করণ, উদরভেদ, to evacuate by stool; a purging.

বিরোদ্ধা, বিপক্ষ, প্রতিবন্ধক, কুন্দলীয়া, an opposer, hinderer, disputer; quarrelsome, litigious, disputatious.

বিরোধ, ঝকড়া, কলহ, বিবাদ, বৈর, শত্রুতা, পরস্পর অনৈক্য, প্রাতিকূল্য, নিষেধ, ব্যাঘাত, প্রতিবন্ধ, আটক, a quarrel, a dispute, discord, litigation, enmity, animosity, opposition, contradiction, a hindrance, obstruction, resistance, check, restraint.

বিরোধক, বিরোধী,—প্রতিবন্ধক, কুন্দলিয়া, বিপক্ষ, opposing, &c. quarrelsome, disputatious, litigious; an opponent.

বিল, গর্ত্ত, ছিদ্র, গুহা, কুহর, জলাশয়, a hole, chasm, rent, fissure, lair, cave, cavern, ravine, a valley, a lake.

বিলক্ষণ, ভিন্ন, বিশেষ, উত্তম, অনুপম, উৎকৃষ্ট, সুন্দর, কারণশূন্য স্থিতি, নিশ্চয়, differing, different, other, excellent, unequalled, marked, select, elegant, handsome; a distinction, a state or condition without an assignable cause; full well. [at shrāddas.

বিলক্ষণা, শ্রাদ্ধকালীন দেয় দ্রব্য, gifts to a Brahmin and Brahmini

বিলগ, বিলগ্ন,—অসংলগ্ন, সংযুক্ত. loose, not joined, unconnected, not made to suit or fit, joined, connected.

বিলঙ্ঘন, উৎক্রমণ, ডিঙ্গান, অন্যথাচরণ, to overstep, to transgress.

বিলজ্জ, ধৃষ্ট, অনপত্রপ, shameless, impudent, immodest.

বিলন,-আন, বণ্টন, পরিবেষণ, পৃথক২ করিয়া রাখণ, দান করণ, লুটান, to allot, deal out, to separate, arrange, dispose, to distribute, bestow, to rob, spoil.

বিলপিত, ক্রন্দিত, রুদিত, আক্রুষ্ট, lamented, bewailed, mourned.

বিলমাছ, বিলছামাছ,—উজনীয়, fish which leave the rivers after heavy rains, and are found in ponds, &c.

বিলম্ব, গৌণ, ব্যাজ, টালমটাল, delay, tardiness, loitering, procrastination, a retarding, delaying, &c.

বিলম্বন, গৌণকরণ, টালন, to dally, loiter, delay, procrastinate.

বিলম্বিত, স্থগিত, ঢীলা, মন্দ, লট্‌কা, ঝুলিয়া, delayed, slow, tardy, slow (as music,) falling or hanging down, pendant.

বিলম্বী, অসত্বর, টালনিয়া, dallying, loitering, procrastinating.

বিলয়, কল্পান্ত, বিনাশ, মোক্ষ, the dissolution of the world, destruction, final. absorption.

বিলাপ, শোকোক্তি, ক্রন্দন, ডাকরাপি, a lamentation, loud mourning, bewailing, complaint. [plain.

বিলাপন, শোক করণ, ডাকরাণ, to lament, mourn, bewail, com-

বিলাপী, ক্রন্দনকারী, শোকী, lamenting, mourning, bewailing.

বিলাস, আমোদ, আনন্দ, ক্রীড়া, কৌতুক, শারীরিক সুখানুভব, লীলা, ভাব, enjoyment, felicity, sport, play, pastime, pleasure, amorous dalliance, wantonness, a corporeal indication of amorous sentiment.

বিলাসী, কুশলী, আনন্দিত, ক্রীড়াবান, লম্পট, happy, enjoying, sporting, dallying, wanton, sensual. [rowed.

বিলিখিত, ডোরিয়া, রেখাযুক্ত, striped, marked with lines, fur-

বিলী, অংশকরা, ধার্য্যকরা, সাজানি, পৃথক্২ করা, a division, allotment of labour. &c. adjustment, regular distribution, orderly arrangement.

বিলীন, গলিত, অন্তর্হিত, dissolved, melted, disappeared, perished.

বিলুপ্ত, অচলিত, বিস্মৃত, খাটো, স্খলিত, obsolete, extinguished, forgotten, erased, wanting. [parted, dead.

বিলোক, নির্জন, নির্বাণ, মৃত, private, apart, uninhabited, de-

বিলোকন, নিরীক্ষণ, তাকন, to view steadily, look, survey, behold.

বিলোড়ন, নড়ান, ঘাঁটন, মথন, লুণ্ঠন, to agitate, stir up, churn, to roll or wallow on the ground.

বিলোম, ব্যত্যয়, ব্যতিক্রম, পানীচর্‌কী, ব্যতিক্রান্ত, বিপরীত, প্রতিকূল, উল্টা, an opposite course or order, inversion, reverse, a wheel for raising water; reverse, opposite, contrary, backward, against the grain.

বিলোমজ, উত্তমা স্ত্রীগর্ব্ভে অধমকর্ত্তৃক জাত, born of a father inferior in cast to the mother. [wave, undulate.

বিলোলন, দোলন, নড়ন, উল্লন, to swing, oscillate, wag, shake,

বিল্ব, শ্রীফল, বেল, the bel or wood apple.

বিল্‌বিল্‌, ঝুণ্ড, ঝাঁক, a swarm of ants, &c. a swarming.

বিশঙ্ক, সাহসী, নির্ভয়, নির্বিঘ্ন, fearless, bold, safe, secure.

বিশঙ্কিত, ভীত, ত্রস্ত, সন্দিগ্ধ, অবিশ্বসিত, alarmed, fearful, suspicious, suspected, mistrusted.

বিশল্য, নিষ্পীড়া, নির্বিঘ্ন, নির্গতশূল, free from pain or distress, having the dart extracted from the wound.

বিশাখা, ষোড়শ নক্ষত্র, the 16th lunar mansion.

বিশারদ, পণ্ডিত, বিখ্যাত, পটু, প্রগল্ভ, wise, learned, famous, celebrated, eminent, confident, bold, presuming.

বিশাল, মহৎ, প্রশস্ত, প্রসারিত, large, wide, enlarged, extended.

বিশিখ, অচূড়, বাণ, কাঁটা, সূচি, not crested; an arrow, pin, needle.

বিশিষ্ট, বিবিক্ত, উত্তম, উৎকৃষ্ট, প্রসিদ্ধ, শ্রেষ্ঠ, বিলক্ষণ, শিষ্ট, ভদ্র লোক, সংযুক্ত, প্রাপ্ত, distinguished, select, superior, desirable, good, excellent, eminent, noble, elegant, polite, genteel, inherent in, having, possessed of, endowed with.

বিশিষ্য, ভেদ্য, সংযুক্ত, অনন্তর্বর্ত্তী, দ্রব্যবাচক শব্দ, requiring to be discriminated, accidental, not inherent; a substantive or word discriminable by its adjective.

বিশুদ্ধ, পরিষ্কৃত, নির্ভুল, নির্ম্মল, পবিত্র, পুণ্যবান, নম্র, বশীভূত, cleansed, purified, corrected, (as a writing,) clean, pure, holy, virtuous, pious, humble, modest, compliant.

বিশুদ্ধি, শুচিতা, পরিষ্কার, purity, holiness, the correction of a writing, &c.

বিশুষ্ক, নীরস, শুকা, ম্লান, dried, dried up, withered.

বিশূচক, ভেদক ঔষধ, সারক, purgative, cathartic.

বিশৃঙ্খল, অবদ্ধ, ক্রমরহিত, উল্টাপাল্টা, ব্যাকরণবিরুদ্ধ, অনন্বিত, unrestrained, unfettered, disorderly, ungrammatical.

বিশৃঙ্খলা, অক্রম, উল্টাপাল্টামি, ধবরাণী, disorder, irregularity, confusion, perturbation, distraction.

বিশেষ, ভেদ, অসাম্য, বৈলক্ষণ্য, প্রভেদ, গুণ, প্রকার, ব্যক্তিত্ব, উপশম, বৃত্তান্ত, ইতর, ভিন্ন, অন্য, অসাধারণ, a difference, distinction, variety, dissimilarity, peculiarity, specific difference, quality, a sort, kind, manner, species, identity, amendment or alleviation of disease, particulars, circumstances, detail; other, different, distinct, particular, peculiar, special.

বিশেষক, ভেদসূচক, প্রভেদক, উপাধি, তিলক, distinguishing, specifying, particularizing, discriminative, characteristic; an attributive, a sectarial mark.

বিশেষণ, বিলক্ষণ গুণাদি, প্রভেদক লক্ষণাদি, গুণবাচক, উপাধি, a distinctive quality, predicate, characteristic mark, attribute, epithet, an adjective, an adverb or qualifying sentence.

বিশেষণীয়, প্রভেদনীয়, বিবেচনীয়, discriminable, distinguishable, to be discriminated.

বিশেষতঃ, অধিকন্তু, particularly, peculiarly, especially, chiefly.

বিশেষিত, প্রভিন্ন, বিবেচিত, distinguished, discriminated.

বিশেষ্য, বিবেচনীয়, ভেদনীয়, দ্রব্যবাচক, প্রভেদক, উপাধি, distinguishable, requiring to be particularized, &c. a substantive, a predicate, attributive.

বিশোক, খেদহীন, অসন্তাপিত, free from grief or sorrow.

বিশোচন, পরসন্তাপ নাশ করণ, দুঃখ নিবর্ত্তন, to free from grief.

বিশোধন, শুধরাণ, to purify, cleanse, correct a writing, &c.

বিশোভ, বেশভূষা পরিধান, সাজানি, an adorning, embellishing, a setting off to advantage.

বিশোষ, শুকানি, নীরসভাব, a drying, exsiccation, dryness.

বিশ্রব্ধ, বিশ্বসিত, সহিষ্ণু, ধীর, নম্রমনাঃ, বিশ্রান্ত, অতিশয়, অধিক, ভূরি, রসিক, বিজপী, trusted, confided in, patient, tranquil, firm, steady, humble; lowly-minded, rested, reposed, excessive, exceeding, much, festive, jocular, playful.

বিশ্রম্ভ, বিশ্বাস, হর্ষ, কৌতুক, প্রণয়, trust, confidence, hilarity, festivity, mirth, affection, affectionate enquiry.

বিশ্রান্ত, শ্রমবিরত, rested, reposed, refreshed after fatigue.

বিশ্রান্তি, বিশ্রাম,—বিরাম, শ্রমত্যাগ, অবকাশ, ছুটী, rest after fatigue, relaxation, repose, refreshment, leisure, a recess, vacation.

বিশ্রী, অপ্রভ, ঐশ্বর্য্যবিহীন, bereft of splendour, glory or affluence.

বিশ্রুত, খ্যাত্যাপন্ন, বিদিত, প্রতীত, renowned, famous, celebrated.

বিশ্লেষ, বিচ্ছেদ, বিরহ, বিয়োগ, separation, distance, especially of lovers or of husband and wife, disunion, disjunction. [all, universal, entire.
বিশ্ব, জগৎ, ত্রিলোক, সর্ব্ব, সমুদায়, the world, the universe;
বিশ্বকদ্রু, মৃগয়াতে কুশল কুকুর, ধ্বনি, দুষ্ট, a hound, a dog trained to the chase, sound, noise; vile, wicked.
বিশ্বকর্ম্মা, সূর্য্য, প্রাচীন শিল্পকার, the sun, the artist of the gods.
বিশ্বখণ্ডক, কঠিন, বিদ্বেষী, hard to please, dissatisfied with every thing. [universe.
বিশ্বনাথ, বিশ্বম্ভর, বিশ্বেশ্বর,—জগৎপতি, শিব, Shiva as lord of the
বিশ্বব্যাপক, সর্ব্বত্রগামী, all-pervading, filling all things. [world.
বিশ্বভণ্ড, বিশ্ববঞ্চক,—জগৎপ্রতারক, all-deceptive, deceiving the
বিশ্বম্ভরা, পৃথিবী, মহী, ক্ষিতি, the earth.
বিশ্বরূপ, সর্ব্বাকারধারী, সর্ব্বময়, সর্ব্বব্যাপী, assuming or existing in all forms, pantomorphous, universal, omnipresent. [faithful, trusty.
বিশ্বসিত, বিশ্বস্ত,—বিশ্রব্ধ, বিশ্বাসপাত্র, trusted, confided in,
বিশ্বসৃক্ বিশ্বস্রষ্টা,—জগদুৎপাদক, পরমেশ্বর, ব্রহ্মা, all-creating; God, the creator, Brahmá.
বিশ্বস্তা, বিধবা, সাধ্বী, a widow, a trusty female.
বিশ্বাস, প্রত্যয়, বিশ্রম্ভ, trust, confidence, faith, credence.
বিশ্বাসঘাত, কৃতঘ্নতা, treachery, a betraying. [tor.
বিশ্বাসঘাতক বা ঘাতী,—কৃতঘ্ন, treacherous, betraying; a trai-
বিশ্বাসন, প্রত্যয় করণ, আশ্রয় লওন, to believe, trust, confide in.
বিশ্বাসভূমি শ্রদ্ধার বিষয়, a ground of trust, matter of faith.
বিশ্বাসী, প্রত্যয়ী, সরল, সাধু, trusting, believing, trusty, faithful, honest. [trust-worthy, &c.
বিশ্বাস্য, বিশ্বসনীয়,—বিশ্বাসপাত্র, সত্যবাদী, worthy of confidence,
বিষ, গরল, জল, গন্ধরস, মৃণাল, poison, venom, water, gum, myrrh, the fibres of the lotus-stalk, a red dye.
বিষণি, গরল, কালকূট, জ্বালা, poison, venom, virus, virulence.
বিষণ্ণ, শোকযুক্ত, ভাবিত, dejected, sad, sorrowful, pensive.
বিষধর, সর্প, অহি, ভুজঙ্গ, a serpent, a poisonous snake.
বিষবৎ, বিষতুল্য,—প্রাণঘাতক, মৃত্যুজনক, অন্তক, deadly, mortal.
বিষবৈদ্য, ওঝা, সর্পকষ্টের চিকিৎসক, a serpent-charmer or professional curer of its bite, &c.

বিষম, আপদ, দায়, সন্তাপ, পীড়া, পাড়াকর, দুস্তর, সঙ্কট, মন্দ, প্রচণ্ড, উৎকট, দুরন্ত, দুর্গম, কর্কশ, দুর্যোগ, অনুপম, অসম, ঐকাহিক, অস্থির, অশুভ, অতিশয়, calamity, danger, distress, pain ; painful, difficult, hazardous, troublesome, evil, violent, unmanageable, inaccessible, rough, inclement, unparalleled, unequal, alternate, irregular, intermittent, odd, uneven ; very, excessively. [mittent.

বিষমজ্বর, প্রবল তাপ, ঐকাহিকাদি জ্বর, a violent fever, an inter-

বিষমধাতু, অস্বাস্থ্য, রোগাপন্ন, absence of health ; unhealthy.

বিষমসাহস, দুঃসাহস, ডাকাবুকামি, temerity, rashness, daring.

বিষয়, ইন্দ্রিয়গোচর, রূপরসাদি, বস্তু, অর্থ, উদ্দেশ, আশয়, বিত্ত, ব্যাপার, সাংসারিক কর্ম্ম, পদ, প্রয়োজন, ঘটনা, প্রসঙ্গ, কার্য্য, ন্যায়, আশ্রয়, দেশ, স্থান, বাসা, বাড়ী, নায়ক, পতি, an object of sense, sensible quality, as colour, form, &c. a thing, object, object of pursuit, study or desire, &c. wealth, substance, business, trade, worldly occupation, office, employment, an affair, occasion, occurrence, topic, matter, a law-suit, a refuge, asylum, a country, province, pl ice, the element in which a thing moves, a house, home, a lover, a husband.

বিষয়ক, সম্বন্ধীয়, প্রসঙ্গাধীন, relating to, about, treating of.

বিষয়কর্ম্ম, সাংসারিক কর্ম্মাদি, ব্যাপার, worldly business, attachments, &c. office, employment.

বিষয়ান্বিত, কর্ম্মনিযুক্ত, উদ্যুক্ত, আবিষ্ট, গোচরময়, in place, employed, busy, engaged in business, occupied with an affair, &c. furnishing objects to the sense or understanding.

বিষয়ী, ব্যাপারী, ব্যবসায়ী, সংসারময়, engaged in business, having worldly pursuits or engagements, &c. worldly. [cerning, about.

বিষয়ে, প্রস্তাবে, সম্বন্ধে, উপরে, in relation, in regard to, con-

বিষাক্ত, গরলযুক্ত, poisoned, mixed or smeared with poison.

বিষাণ, কুম্ভ, শৃঙ্গ, হস্তির দন্ত, ivory, the horn of an animal, the tusk of an elephant, &c. a tooth.

বিষাদ, গ্লানি, খেদ, ভাবনা, উদ্বেগ, আশাভঙ্গ, dejection, sadness, lowness of spirits, want of energy, disappointment, anxiety, regret. [virulent.

বিষাল, বিষালু, বিষী,—গরলযুক্ত, খলমী, poisonous, venomous,

বিষুব, সমরাত্রিদিবাকাল, অয়নসঞ্চার, the equinox.

বিষ্কম্ভ, প্রথমযোগ, মণ্ডলব্যাস, বিস্তার, ব্যাঘাত, the first astronomical yog, the diameter of a circle, extension, an obstacle, hindrance.

বিষ্টম্ভ, এমুক দ্রব্যের দৃঢ়ীভাব, মলমূত্ররোধ, the hardening of cement, &c. constipation, urinary obstruction.

বিষ্টর, তরু, আসন, পিঁড়ী, চৌকি, কুশমুষ্টি, কুশাসন, a tree, a seat, stool, chair, couch, a handful or a seat of Cusha grass.

বিষ্টি, আমু, compulsory or unpaid labour, an impressing.

বিষ্ঠা, মল, গূ, ordure, excrement, dung.

বিষ্ণুপদী, অয়নসঞ্চারের পর সংক্রান্তি, the sun's entrance on a new sign after the equinox.

বিসঙ্কট, আপত্তি, দায়, calamity, danger, strait, difficulty.

বিসম্বাদ, কলহ, বিরোধ, বিতণ্ডা, কচ্‌কচি, আশাভাঙ্গা, কাপট্য, ভুষানি, a dispute, quarrel, contention, contradiction, murmuring, breach of promise, disappointing, deceiving, deception. [muring, &c.

বিসম্বাদী, কুন্দলিয়া, কচ্‌কচিয়া, disputatious, contentious, mur-

বিসরণ, বিস্তরণ,—ব্যাপন, মেলন, বাড়ন, to spread, extend, expand, diffuse.

বিসর্গ, দান, ত্যাগ, ছাড়া, মলমুক্তন, দ্বিবিন্দুমাত্র বর্ণ, মোক্ষ, a gift, donation, relinquishment, abandonment, evacuation by stool, the letter ঃ, emancipation from matter. [reject.

বিসর্জ্জন, ত্যাগ করণ, বিবর্জ্জন, to make an oblation, relinquish,

বিসর্পণ, সরণ, ব্যাপন, বাড়ন, to move, extend, spread.

বিসূচিকা, রোগলক্ষণ, উপসর্গ, কোষ্ঠবদ্ধ, the symptom of a disease, costiveness.

বিসৃত, বিসৃত,—ব্যাপ্ত, প্রসারিত, diffused, extended, spread.

বিসৃষ্ট, নিবেদিত, ত্যক্ত, নিরাকৃত, offered, given, relinquished, abandoned, expelled, cast off or out.

বিস্তর, ব্যাপ্তি, প্রসার, বাড়ি, তান, বাক্যব্যয়, বাহুল্য, প্রাচুর্য্য, প্রসারিত, বহুল, প্রচুর, যথেষ্ট, অনেক, extension, expansion, enlargement, prolixity, diffuseness, amplitude, abundance, plenty, sufficiency; extended, prolix, copious, much, abundant, large. plentiful, sufficient, ample, many, numerous.

বিস্তার, ব্যাস, প্রসার, ব্যাপ্তি, বাক্যবাহুল্য, বিবরণ, বিনোদন, মণ্ডলের মধ্যরেখা, extension, spread, diffusion, amplification, prolixity, a detail, detailed narration, divergence, the diameter of a circle.

বিস্তারণ, বিবরণ, বাড়ান, বিছান, মেলান, প্রসারণ, to describe in detail, &c. to specify, enlarge, dilate, to spread out, extend, expand.

বিস্তারী, প্রসারী, spreading out, amplifying, enlarging, &c.

বিস্তীর্ণ, প্রসারিত, বিতত, মেলান, প্রশস্ত, বড়, extended, spread, spread out, expanded, enlarged, wide, ample, large.

বিস্তৃত, প্রসারিত, মণ্ডলের মধ্যরেখা, *id*: also the diameter of [a circle.

বিস্তৃতমুখ, খোলামুখ, হাই তোলক, with open mouth, gaping.

বিস্পন্দ, অঙ্গকাঁপনি, tremulous motion, (as of the limbs, &c.)

বিস্পষ্ট, সুব্যক্ত, প্রত্যক্ষ, evident, manifest, open, clear.

বিস্ফোট-ক, বিস্ফোড়া.—ব্রণ, ফুস্কুড়ী, a boil, imposthume, pustule.

বিস্ময়, আশ্চর্য্যজ্ঞান, নিরাশ্বাস, ঘবরাণী, surprize, astonishment, wonder, discouragement, confusion.

বিস্মরণ, ভুলন, পাসরণ, to forget, to lose the recollection of.

বিস্মিত, চমৎকৃত, বিহ্বল, অবাক্, surprized, astonished, confounded, disconcerted.

বিস্মৃত, অন্তর্গত, ভোলা, ভ্রমযুক্ত, forgotten, in an error, out, [mistaken.

বিস্মৃতি, ভুল, ভ্রম, চুক, লোপ, a forgetting, mistake, error, forgetfulness, oblivion.

বিস্বাদ, রসহীনতা, তার, insipidity, tastelessness, a good taste.

বিস্বাদু, অতার, নীরস, পান্সা, insipid, tasteless.

বিহগ, বিহঙ্গ-ম.—পক্ষী, মেঘ, সূর্য্যাদি, a bird, a fowl, a cloud, [the sun, &c.

বিহনন, মারণ, আট্কান, to smite, kill, hurt, impede, &c.

বিহরণ, বিহারণ,—বেড়ান, পর্য্যটন, পরিভ্রমণ, to take a walk or airing, to wander, to go about.

বিহর্ষ, আনন্দ, আহ্লাদ, gladness, joy, pleasure, delight.
বিহসন, মুচ্‌কন, পরিহাস করণ, to smile, laugh gently, laugh at.
বিহা, বিবাহ, পরিণয়, a marriage, a wedding, nuptials.
বিহস্ত, উদ্বিগ্ন, বিহ্বল, ব্যাকুল, perplexed, bewildered, confused, confounded. [torted.
বিহাপিত, দান, উৎসর্গ, দত্ত, নিঙ্গড়া, a gift, donation, given, ex-
বিহান, প্রাতঃকাল, প্রত্যুষ, ভোর, the morning, the dawu, early.
বিহায়স্, আকাশ, অন্তরীক্ষ, শূন্য, the sky, the atmosphere.
বিহার, বেড়ানি, যাত্রা, ভ্রমণ, কেলি, লীলা, a walk for pleasure or exercise, a tour, trip, ramble, a roaming, play, pastime, sport.
বিহারক, বিহারী,—বেড়ানিয়া, লীলাকারী, খেলানীয়া, taking exercise, walking or riding for pleasure, playing, sporting, moving freely. [dicule.
বিহাস, ঈষদ্ধাস্য, বিদ্রূপ, a smile, gentle laugh, laughter, ri-
বিহিত, উচিত, শাস্ত্রোক্ত, fit, proper, right, orderly, necessary.
বিহীন, রহিত, bereft, destitute or deprived of, without.
বিহ্বল, ক্ষুব্ধ, ব্যাকুল, ব্যস্ত, ভয়াপন্ন, agitated, troubled, disturbed, alarmed. [survey.
বীক্ষণ, দেখন, অবলোকন, to see, perceive, behold, view,
বীচ, আঁটি, চারা, মূলকারণ, a seed, plant, source, origin.
বীচতলা, বীচাড়, বীচাড়ি,— মাঁদাবাঁধা, a seed-plot, seed-bed.
বীচালি, পলাল, আছড়া, নাড়া, straw, stubble.
বীচি, তরঙ্গ, ঢেউ, a wave, a ripple. [cause.
বীচী, বীজ, দানা, মূল, আদিকারণ, a seed, origin, source,
বীজ, মূলকারণ, হেতু, দানা, শস্য, আঁটি, অঙ্কুর, শুক্র, অঙ্কবিদ্যা, ওঁকার, a cause, origin, spring, source, principle, seed, kernel, fruit-stone, sprout, semen, algebraic analysis, the mystical ওঁ.
বীজডাঙ্গা, বা তলা,—মাঁদাবাঁধা, a seed-plot, seed-bed.
বীজগণিত, অঙ্কবিদ্যা, arithmetic, mensuration and algebra.
বীজন, পাখা ঢুলান, বাতাস করণ, to fan, to agitate the air.
বীজপুরুষ, বীজী,—আদিপুরুষ, a progenitor, aborigines.
বীজাঙ্কুর, গেঁজ, ডেঁপ, চণকাদির দল দ্বয়, a seed-sprout, shoot, seed-lobe or cotyledon. [from a family.
বীজ্য, বীজোৎপন্ন, কুলজ, উদ্ভব, produced from seed, sprung

বীণা, তন্ত্রবাদ্য বিশেষ, the Indian lute or guitar.
বীত, গত, শান্ত, দমিত, gone, past, tranquil. quiet, tame.
বীতরাগ, রজোগুণহীন, জিতেন্দ্রিয়, free from passion, of subdued passions. [terrace, a stall, shop.
বীথি, পথ, শ্রেণী, বেদী, আপণ, a road, a row, a line, a front
বীভৎস, ঘৃণা, ঘৃণার্হ, ক্রূর, হিংসুক, disgust, abhorrence; disgusting, cruel, mischievous.
বীর, শূর, যোদ্ধা. ভণ্ড, গুণী, গুণবান্, বামাচারী, শৌর্য্য, গার্হপত্য, সাহসী, সতেজ, বলবান্, শ্রেষ্ঠ, a hero, warrior, champion, valiant man, an actor, mime, one eminent for any moral excellence, a Tantrist, heroism, (in poetry,) the sacred domestic fire of a Brahmin; bold, valiant, brave, gallant, powerful, strong, robust, eminent.
বীরত্ব. শৌর্য্য, সাহস, বিক্রম, heroism, valour, courage.
বীরপট্ট, পটুকা, পাটার, a warrior's belt or zone, a girth.
বীরবাহু, শূরের শ্রেষ্ঠ, মল্ল, chief among heroes; a wrestler.
বীরবৌলি, কর্ণভূষণ বিশেষ, কুণ্ডল, an ear-ring having a stone between two pearls.
বীরভদ্র, বিলক্ষণ যোদ্ধা, যজ্ঞীয় ঘোটক, a distinguished hero, a sacrificial horse. [terodoxy.
বীরভাব, বামাচার, বিধর্ম্ম, the observance of the Tantras, he-
বীরহা, নষ্টাগ্নি ব্রাহ্মণ, a Brahmin whose sacred fire has been extinguished through impiety or carelessness.
বীরা, গৃহিণী, পতিপুত্রবতী, a matron, a wife and mother.
বীরাসন, হাঁটু গাড়ন, to kneel; a kneeling porture.
বীর্য্য, শৌর্য্য, সাহস, বিক্রম, প্রতাপ, তেজ, বল, শুক্র, heroism, valour, bravery, courage, energy, spirit, power, might, semen virile. [robust.
বীর্য্যবান্, সাহসী, বলবান্, heroic, courageous, spirited, strong,
বুক, বুক,—বক্ষঃস্থল, উরঃ, হৃদয়, সাহস, তেজ, the breast, bosom, chest, stomach, heart, courage, spirit.
বুকড়, বুকাড়. বুকাল, বুকাইত, } সাহসী, বিক্রমী, নির্ভয়, courageous, valourous, spirited, daring, undaunted.
বুকড়া, বক্ষঃস্থল, জীর্ণধরা, the breast, the stomach, the maw.
বুকনী, চূর্ণ, চূর্ণ শর্করা, a powder, powdered sugar.

বুকফুলন-আন, বুকবাড়ান,—দৈকারিয়া চলন, to **strut, stalk, swell** with self-consequence.

বুকন, ভষণ, ভেউ২ করণ, to bark as a dog.

বুজন, মুদন, নিবন, ভরণ, to close or shut as the eyes, to go out as a lamp, to be extinguished, to be stopped or filled up with any substance.

বুজান, নিবান, ভরাট করণ, ঢাকন, মুদন, to extinguish, put out, to fill up with rubbish as a pit or well, to stop, cover over, close up, to shut the eyes.

বুজগুড়ী, বুদ্বুদ, হতবৃদ্ধি, a bubble; stunted in growth.

বুজবুজ, বুদ্বুদ, জলবিম্ব, a bubble. [derstanding, genius.

বুঝ, অনুমান, বুদ্ধি, an idea, thought, apprehension, un-

বুঝন, জ্ঞান পাওন, অনুভব করণ, জানন, মনে করণ, বিবেচিয়া কহন, টাহরণ, বিবেচনা করণ, to understand, perceive, feel a sensation, know, infer, imagine, think, suppose, suspect, design, intend, remark, note, weigh, consider, examine.

বুঝান, বিজ্ঞাপন, বিবরণ, সমঝান, প্রবোধন, শিক্ষাণ, জানান, to explain, describe, relate, demonstrate, cause to understand, convince, persuade, instruct, to import, express, mean.

বুঝাপড়া, অন্যায়গ্রস্ত লোকের উপকার করা, তত্ত্বজিজ্ঞাসা, the redressing of a grievance; an enquiry into.

বুঝায়, বুদ্ধি, জ্ঞান, the understanding, sense. [sibly.

বুঝি, মনে করি, কদাচিৎ, হইতে পারে, I think, perhaps, pos-

বুট, কলায় বিশেষ, a sort of pulse called *Gram*.

বুড়া, বৃদ্ধ, স্থূল, old, aged, great, (toe or finger.)

বুড়ন, মজ্জন, ডুবন, আপ্লাবন, to sink, plunge, dive, dip, drown, overflow. [swamp.

বুড়া, ডুব, বন্যা, জলগণ্ড, an immersion, an inundation, a

বুড়ান, ডুবান, উড়ান, to immerse, plunge, dip, squander.

বুড়াপনা, বুড়ামি,—বার্দ্ধক্য, প্রাচীনতা, old age, agedness.

বুড়ি, বন্যা, জলপ্লাব, কাকিণী, an inundation, the drowning of land, five gandas.

বুড়ী, বৃদ্ধাবস্থা, বৃদ্ধা, আপ্লাবিকা, old age, an old woman; *f.* old, aged, inundating, overflowing.

বুদ্ধ, বিদিত, অবগত, অনুভূত, গৌতম, বিষ্ণুর নবমাবতার. known, understood, perceived, felt; Buddha, the 9th incarnation of Vishnu.

বুদ্ধি, চেতন, জ্ঞান, প্রজ্ঞা, মতি, রস, উপলব্ধি, বোধ, intellect, understanding, genius, judgment, sense, sagacity, wit, perception, an idea.

বুদ্ধিমান, জ্ঞানী, পণ্ডিত, intelligent, sagacious, sage, wise.

বুদ্ধীন্দ্রিয়, জ্ঞানেন্দ্রিয়, অর্থাৎ শ্রোত্র ত্বগাদি, an organ of intellect.

বুদ্বুদ, বিম্ব, ফোস্কা, a bubble, vesicle, blister. [a sage.

বুধ, চতুর্থ গ্রহ, পণ্ডিত, the planet mercury or its regent,

বুধবার, চতুর্থ বার, Wednesday.

বুনট, বুনাট, বুনন, বুননি,—কাপড়ের ধাত, the texture of stuffs.

বুনন, বস্ত্রনির্ম্মাণ, বপন, to weave, knit, sow seed.

বুননিয়া, তন্তুবায়, তাঁতী, বপ্তা, a weaver, a seedsman, sower.

বুনাপ, বুনা কাপড়, a web, (of cloth.)

বুনা, বুনো, বুনুয়া,—জঙ্গলী, আরণ্য, wild, sylvan, rural.

বুভুক্ষা, ভোজনের ইচ্ছা, ক্ষুধা, appetite for food, hunger.

বুভুক্ষিত, বুভুক্ষু,—ক্ষুধিত, ভোজনেচ্ছুক, hungry, eager for food.

বুভুৎসা, জ্ঞানেচ্ছা, জিজ্ঞাসা, a desire to know or understand.

বুভুৎসু, জ্ঞানেচ্ছুক, জিজ্ঞাসু, desirous of knowing, &c.

বুরুস, তিন যব পরিমাণ, অঙ্গুষ্ঠপর্ব পরিমাণ, an inch.

বুর্মা, ভ্রমরী, তুরপণ, a gimlet.

বুলন, হস্ত দিয়া মর্দ্দন, ঘর্ষণ, ঘষিয়া যাওন, বেড়ান, to stroke an animal, to rub, fret, chafe, to stroll, rove, stray.

বুলী, ভাষা, বাক্য, কথা, speech, talk.

বুস, বুষ,—ধান্যাদির আগড়া, তুষ, chaff, husk, bran.

বৃংহিত, বর্দ্ধিত, উন্নত, পুষ্ট, grown, increased, nourished.

বৃক, কোক, শৃগাল, নাকেশ্বরীবাঘ, কাক, বৃক্ষনির্য্যাস বিশেষ, a wolf, jackal, hyæna, a crow, turpentine.

বৃক্ষ, দ্রুম, তরু, ঝাড়ী, গাছ, a tree, shrub, plant. [creeper.

বৃক্ষরুহ-া, লতা, পরগাছা, a parasitical or creeping plant, a

বৃজিন, কেশ, পাপ, দুষ্কর্ম্ম, অধর্ম্ম, hair, sin, vice, wickedness.

বৃত, বাঞ্ছিত, মনোনীত, নিযুক্ত, আচ্ছাদিত, রক্ষিত, বেষ্টিত, সেবিত, selected, chosen, approved, preferred, appointed, covered, screened, defended, enclosed, surrounded, served, attended.

বৃতি, বাছনী, সম্মতি, নিয়োগ, নিবেদন, যাচ্ঞা, বেড়া, ব্যবধান, বেষ্টন, a selection, choice, approbation, appointment, a request, solicitation, a hedge, fence, enclosure, a surrounding, encompassing, covering.

বৃত্ত, ভূত, মৃত, অতীত, গোল, স্বভাব, চরিত্র, ব্যবহার, রীতি, পদ্য, মণ্ডল, been, having existed, dead, deceased, past, gone, round, (in form ;) disposition, nature, practice, custom, metre, verse, a circle.

বৃত্তান্ত, বিবরণ, বিস্তারিত কথা, বার্ত্তা, জনরব, প্রস্তাব, বিষয়, ইতিহাস, প্রকার, প্রভেদ, ধর্ম্ম, ভাব, a narration, account, detail, particulars, intelligence, news, report, a topic, subject, circumstance, story, tale, a sort, kind, manner, difference, property, nature.

বৃত্তি, বার্ষিক, জীবিকা, বেতন, নির্ব্বাহ, জীবনোপায়, ব্যবসায়, ধন, সম্পত্তি, অধিকার, ভব, স্থিতি, ব্যাখ্যা, সূত্রের বিবরণ, a pension, grant, maintenance, support, stipend, a livelihood, means of subsistence, profession, wealth, property, estate, being, existence, a gloss, comment, explanation, exposition.

বৃথা, নিষ্ফলে, অনর্থক, ব্যর্থ, অলীক, মিথ্যা, পণ্ড, in vain, idly, uselessly, to no purpose ; useless, vain, absurd, idle, false, blank. [nonsense.

বৃথাকথা, অসঙ্গত বাক্য, অনর্থক কথা, an absurdity, idle talk.

বৃদ্ধ, বর্দ্ধিত, উন্নত, বাড়ন্ত, বড়, গতযৌবন, বুড়া, encreased, enlarged, large, grown, full grown, old, aged.

বৃদ্ধকাল, বুড়ামী, বার্দ্ধক্য, old age. [old age.

বৃদ্ধতা, বাড়ি, উন্নতি, বুড়ামী, increase, greatness, opulence,

বৃদ্ধা, বুড়ামী, বুড়ী, বাড়ি, an old woman, old age, increase.

বৃদ্ধাঙ্গুষ্ঠ, বৃদ্ধাঙ্গুলি,—অঙ্গুষ্ঠ, পাদাঙ্গুষ্ঠ, the thumb, the great toe.

বৃদ্ধি, বাড়ি, উন্নতি, পুরস্কার, প্রতিপত্তি, সম্ভ্রম, ধনসঞ্চয়, ব্যাজ, চড়তি, কুরণ্ডরোগ, increase, augmentation, growth, vegetation, prosperity, success, promotion, preferment, consequence, extension of power or revenue, accumulation, interest on money, advance in price, enlargement of the scrotum.

বৃদ্ধ্যাজীব-ী, ঋণদায়ক, ব্যাজখেকুয়া, a money-lender; a usurer.

বৃদ্ধ্যাকাঙ্ক্ষী, ঐশ্বর্য্যেচ্ছুক, ambitious, aspiring.

বৃন্ত, বোঁটা, ডাঁটা, কুচাগ্র, a stalk, stem, foot-stalk, a nipple.

বৃন্দ, রাশি, সমুদায়, গণ, সমূহ, সমাজ, সভা, a heap, quantity, multitude, assemblage, congregation, company.

বৃন্দা, তুলসী বৃক্ষ, the sacred Basil.

বৃন্দারক, প্রধান, অধিপতি, দেবতা, অমর, শ্রেষ্ঠ, উত্তম, আর্য্য, বিশিষ্ট, মনোজ্ঞ, a chief, head, leader, a god, an immortal; chief, excellent, eminent, best, respectable, reputable, handsome.

বৃন্দ, এক শত ক্রোর, দশ সহস্র লক্ষ, a thousand millions.

বৃশ্চিক, কৃষ্ণ কীট, বিছা, শূয়া পোকা, অষ্টম রাশি, a scorpion, centipede, the hairy caterpillar, the sign Scorpio.

বৃষ, পুরুষগো, দ্বিতীয় রাশি, বলবান্, ধর্ম্ম, শ্রেষ্ঠ, উত্তম, a bull, the sign Taurus, a strong man, virtue, moral merit; *in comp*: excellent, eminent, best.

বৃষভ, অনড্বান্, শ্রেষ্ঠ, a bull; *in comp*: preeminent, best.

বৃষল, শূদ্র, চতুর্থ বর্ণ, a Shúdra, the lowest cast.

বৃষলী, শূদ্রী, বন্ধ্যা, মৃতপ্রসূতা, রজস্বলা কুমারী, a female Shúdra, a barren woman, the mother of a still-born child, a marriageable girl.

বৃষ্টি, মেঘের জলপাত, বর্ষা, rain, a shower.

বৃহৎ, বড়, মহৎ, বিপুল, প্রকাণ্ড, অতিবাদ, চমৎকার, great, large, important, huge, stupendous, magnificent.

বৃহস্পতি, পঞ্চম গ্রহ, সুরাচার্য্য, the planet Jupiter, the preceptor of the gods.

বেওরা, বিবরণ, বৃত্তান্ত, a narration, detail, recital, report.

বেঁকন, তেওড়ন, to become awry or crooked, warp, bend.

বেঁজী, পল্লব, অঙ্কুর, ব্রণ, নকুল, a shoot, sprout, pimple, pustule, a mongoose.

বেঁটা, বেঁটে,—খর্ব্ব, হ্রস্ব, খাট, dwarf, short, low in stature.

বেঁড়া, বেঁড়ে,—পুচ্ছহীন, destitute of a tail, tailless.

বেকলা, ছোলা, ত্বক্, the rind of fruit, integument, peel, skin.

বেগ, শীঘ্রগতি, কুতূহল, ত্বরা, স্রোত, প্রবাহ, কোঁথা, swiftness, celerity, velocity, rapidity, impetuosity, speed, haste, impetus, a stream, flow, current, a straining at stool.

বেগড়া, নষ্ট, বিকৃত, দুষ্ট, spoiled, marred, faulty, vicious.
বেগবান, বেগী,—সত্বর, দ্রুতগামী, চালাক, swift, fleet, impetuous, active. [go swiftly.
বেগন, স্রবণ, বেগে বহন, দৌড়িয়া যাওন, রড়ান, to flow, hasten,
বেগরহিত, মন্দ, ঢীলা, অসত্বর, not rapid or quick, slow, dull, inactive. [pressed.
বেগার, বিনাবেতন কর্ম্মকারী, আজুকৃত, forced into service, im-
বেগারী, আজুকরা, ধরিয়া খাটান, an impressing or forcing to work, a putting to compulsory labour.
বেগুন, হিঙ্গুলী, বার্ত্তাকী, the egg plant or its fruit.
বেগুনিয়া, অরুণবর্ণ, ধূম্র, of a purple-colour, purple.
বেঙ্গ, মণ্ডুক, ভেক, a frog.
বেঙ্গা, নেটা, left-handed.
বেঙ্গাচী, বেঙ্গের ছা, a tadpole or young frog.
বেঙ্গাপিতল, মিশ্রিত ধাতু বিশেষ, কাংস্য, white-brass, bell-metal.
বেচন, বিকণ, বিক্রয় করণ, to sell, vend, dispose of.
বেচনিয়া, বিক্রয়কারী, বিক্রেতা, বেপারী, selling, vending; a seller, salesman. [assort.
বেছন, চুনন, পৃথক্ করিয়া সাজান, to pick, choose, select,
বেজী, নকুল, a mongoose, weasel, ferret.
বেটন, বেঠন,—পরিবেষ্টন কাপড়াদি, a wrapper, an outside covering of cloth or paper. [fellow.
বেটা, বেটী,—পুত্রপুত্রী, *m. & f.* a son, a daughter; *m.* a
বেটুয়া, বেড়ানিয়া, মৃতদার, থলিয়া, a vagrant, a widower, a purse.
বেট্যা, দড়ী, রজ্জু, a string, cord, rope.
বেড়, আটন, আড়াল, ঘেরা, ফেরা, বাঁক, জুয়াচুরি, a fence, hedge, party-wall, circumference, circuit, a turn, roll, winding, a scheme, collusion.
বেড়ন, ঘেরণ, পরিবেষ্টন, জড়ান, আট্কান, পুনর্ব্বিতর্ক করণ, to surround, encircle, invest, enclose, entwine, impound, imprison, re-examine, re-consider.
বেড়া, আবরণ, ঘেরা, a screen, fence, enclosure, pound.
বেড়ান, ভ্রমণ, ফেরণ, টহলন, পর্য্যটন, to traverse, ramble, walk for exercise, lounge, rove, roam, travel.
বেড়ী, পাদবন্ধন লৌহপাশ, নিগড়, বাউনী, থর, fetters, irons, a pair of tongs, the short hair on the head.

বেড়্যা, প্রগল্‌ভ. চেঁটা, ঝাঁপিয়া, বাড়ন্ত, উৎকৃষ্ট, উত্তম, presuming, forward, overbearing, jutting out, overhanging, rising above, excelling, eminent, good.

বেড্যান, পিটন, ঠেকন, to strike, beat, strike against.

বেণী, বিউনী, কবরী, বিন্যস্ত কেশ, জলপ্রবাহ, নেতা, মুহনা, a plait or braid of hair, a tail, queue, a stream, current, the branch of a river, the conflux of rivers.

বেণু, বংশী, মুরলী, বাঁশ, a pipe or flute, a bamboo. [dealer.

বেণ্যা, মহাজন, ব্যাপারী, বণিক, a banker, merchant, trader,

বেঁত, বেত্র,—নড় বিশেষ, ছড়ী, the ratan, a reed, a cane.

বেতন, ভৃতি, ভরণ্য, খাটনি, প্রতিফল, wages, hire, fare, reward, recompense, compensation.

বেতাল, ভূত, পিশাচ বিশেষ, an evil spirit, dæmon, fiend.

বেত্তা, জ্ঞাতা, নিপুণ, *in comp*: versed in, acquainted with.

বেদ, শ্রুতি, সামাদি চার শাস্ত্র, বিদ্যা, জ্ঞান, a Veda or sacred writing, philosophy, science, knowledge.

বেদনা, পীড়া, ব্যথা, যাতনা, দুঃখ, অনুভব, জ্ঞান, pain, smart, ache, agony, torment, torture, distress, perception, sensation, feeling.

বেদনীয়, জ্ঞেয়, অনুভবনীয়, বোধ্য, চেতনাবিশিষ্ট, perceptible, that may be known or felt, sensible, sensible to.

বেদাঙ্গ, ব্যাকরণাদি ছয়, the sciences appendant on the Vedas.

বেদাঙ্গী, বেদাঙ্গবেত্তা, studying or professing the Vedángas.

বেদান্ত, বেদের উত্তম কাণ্ড, the Vedánt or speculative theology.

বেদান্তী, বেদান্তমতাবলম্বী, a Vedántist or follower of the Vedánt.

বেদি, বেদী,—যাগাদি কারণ পরিষ্কৃতা ভূমি, মঞ্চ, পিড়ী, পীঠ, an altar, pillar, terrace, platform, stool, bench.

বেদী, বেত্তা, জ্ঞ, নিপুণ, *in comp*: knowing, acquainted with.

বেদিতব্য, বেদ্য,—বোধ্য, অনুভবনীয়, perceptible, that may be felt or known.

বেদ্যা, ব্যাধ, মৃগব্যজীবী, a hunter, a fowler.

বেধ, ছিদ্র, বিঁদ, সুরঙ্গ, তল, কড়া, a perforation, hole, bore, excavation, depth, the link of a chain.

বেধন, বিঁধন, কোঁড়ন, ভেদন, সিঁধ কাটন, কোড়ন, আঁচড়ান, to perforate, pierce, bore, penetrate, excavate, &c. to prick, scratch, wound.

বেধস্, বেধা,—ব্রহ্মা, বিষ্ণু, Brahmá, Vishnu. [a hurt.

বেধা, গর্ত্ত, তল, আঁচড়, ঘা, a hole, excavation, depth, a scratch,

বেপন, কম্পন, থরথরাণী, to tremble, to quake; a tremor.

বেপার, বিকীকিনী, বাণিজ্য, ব্যবসায়, কর্ম্ম, জীবনোপায়, buying and selling, traffic, commerce, a trade, calling.

বেপারী, বণিক, ব্যবসায়ী, a trader, merchant; trading, dealing.

বের্যাণ, নির্গমন, নিঃসরণ, জন্মন, উঠন, বাড়ন, বাহির হওন, ছোটান, জন্মান, ঘটনাক্রমে সিদ্ধ হওন, to go out or forth, issue, exude, arise, proceed, shoot up, stick or jut out, slip out, emit, throw, yield, be proved by the event. [in wealth.

বের্যাপড়ন, ছাড়িয়া উঠন, বাড়ন, to overhang, jut out, increase

বেল, শ্রীফল, the Bel fruit.

বেলকার, ফোড়া গালনের অস্ত্র, a lancet. [wood or stone &c.

বেলন, বেলুন,—ভসনা, a baker's or pastry-cook's roller of

বেলা, সময়, কাল, মল্লিকা, time, tide, time of day, (*an affix to words of time,*) a jasmine.

বেল্যা, সিকতাময়, মৎস্য বিশেষ, sandy; a species of fish.

বেশ, বস্ত্র, পরিচ্ছদ, ছদ্ম, শরীরের ভূষা, a dress, habit, guise, disguise, ornament. [dress.

বেশভূষা, সাজানি, অলঙ্কারাদি, embellishment, ornaments, finery,

বেশমাল্য, গর্ভক, an ornamental garland, a chaplet.

বেশর, নোলক, নাসারন্ধ্র, an ornament for the nose, a nostril.

বেশী, কৃতবেশভূষা, ছদ্মযুক্ত, dressed, ornamented, disguised.

বেশ্মন, গৃহ, বাসা, a house, a dwelling. [prostitute.

বেশ্যা, কুলটা, বারস্ত্রী, গণিকা, a courtezan, harlot, strumpet,

বেশ্যালয়, গণিকাগৃহ, a house of ill fame, a brothel. [gum.

বেষ্ট, আটা, বৃক্ষনির্যাস, birdlime, glutinous matter, size,

বেষ্টন, ঘেরণ, বেড়ন, জড়ান, বান্ধন, কটিবন্ধনী, পটুকা, to surround, encircle, enclose, invest, wind or twine round, bind; a girdle, zone, belt, &c.

বেষ্টিত, ঘেরিত, বেড়িত, জড়ান, surrounded, invested, girt, enclosed, &c. set as a jewel.

বেস্যাড়া, বাসি, সড়া, দুর্গন্ধী, stale, rancid, old, stinking.

বেহা, বিবাহ, পরিণয়, a wedding, a marriage. [father.

বেহাই, জামাতার পিতা, পুত্রবধুর পিতা, a son or daughter-in-law's

বেহারা, কাহার, a palkee bearer. [less.

বৈ, পুথী, ছাড়া, ঋতে, ভিন্ন, a book; except, besides, un-

বৈকল্পিত, বিকল্প, দ্বিধাকল্প, differently or variously applied, (in grammar,) optional.

বৈকল্য, বিস্ময়, ভাবরাণী, ঘবরাণী, বক্রতা, বিগড়, বিকৃত ভাব, অপ্রসন্নতা, amazement, agitation, confusion, discomposure, distortion, defectiveness, an impaired or withered state, unpropitiousness.

বৈকাল, সন্ধ্যাকাল, অপরাহ্ন, the evening, afternoon.

বৈকালী, সন্ধ্যাকালীন নৈবেদ্য, the evening offering.

বৈকুণ্ঠ, বিষ্ণুর ধাম, নারায়ণ, ইন্দ্র, the paradise of Vishńu, Vishnu himself, Indra.

বৈকৃত্য, পরিণাম, বিগড়, দুষ্টামি, বক্রতা, ঘৃণা, a change, transformation, depravity, deformity, aversion, disgust.

বৈগুণ্য, প্রাতিকূল্য, অপ্রসন্নতা, দুরদৃষ্ট, অপকৃষ্টতা, কদর্য্যতা, বিমুখ, বিপক্ষ, hostility, unpropitiousness, an adverse condition, perniciousness, worthlessness; unpropitious, adverse, hostile. [fear, &c.

বৈক্লব্য, ক্ষোভ, ঘবরাণী, agitation, confusion, overpowering

বৈচিত্র্য, বিচিত্রতা, শোভা, সৌন্দর্য্য, variety, variegatedness, ornament, beauty, &c. [of garland.

বৈজয়ন্তী, পতাকা, ধ্বজ, মালা বিশেষ, a flag, banner, ensign, a kind

বৈটা, বৈঠা—কেরবাল, বটিয়া, a paddle or short oar.

বৈঠক, সভা, সমাজ, সম্প্রদায়, an assembly, a sitting, a club, a company, a hooka-bottom.

বৈণবিক, বৈণুক,—বেণুবাদ্যকর, বংশীধর, a flute player.

বৈণিক, বীণাবাদ্যকর, a lute or guitar player.

বৈতথ্য, অলীকতা, অসত্যতা, falsehood, untruth.

বৈতনিক, বেতন লইয়া কর্ম্মকর্ত্তা, ভরণ্যভুক্, a hired labourer or servant, a hireling.

বৈতরণী, নরকস্থা নদী, রাক্ষসের মাতা, the river of hell or Hindoo Styx, the mother of the Rákshasas or giants.

বৈতালিক, বেতালযুক্ত, মায়াবী, বোধকর, one who serves a dæmon or familiar, a conjurer, magician, a king's bard or musician. [a dæmon.

বৈতালিকী, কুহক, বেতালের সহিত গতিবিধি, magic, intercourse with

বৈতৃষ্ণ্য, অতিশয় পিপাসা, excessive or raging thirst.
বৈদগ্ধ্য, বৈদগ্ধ্য,—চাতুর্য্য, নৈপুণ্য, cunning, craft, subtilty, sharpness, cleverness, skill. [Vedas.
বৈদিক, বেদবেত্তা, বেদবিহিত কর্ম্ম, skilful in or enjoined by the
বৈদুষ্য, পাণ্ডিত্য, বিদ্যা, জ্ঞান, learning, wisdom. [journer.
বৈদেশী, বৈদেশিক,—আগন্তুক, পরদেশীয়, foreign; a foreigner, so-
বৈদ্য-ক, চিকিৎসক, আয়ুর্ব্বেদসম্বন্ধীয়, বেদবেত্তা, a physician; medical, relating to or well read in the Vedas.
বৈদ্যকশাস্ত্র, আয়ুর্ব্বেদ, চিকিৎসা বিষয়ক গ্রন্থ, medical science, physic, a medical treatise.
বৈধ, বিহিত, যুক্তিসিদ্ধ, lawful, consistent with law, rational.
বৈধব্য, পতিহীনতা, রণ্ডাবস্থা, widowhood, state of widowhood.
বৈধর্ম্ম্য, বামাচার, নাস্তিকতা, স্বধর্ম্মত্যাগী, heterodoxy, apostacy; heretical, apostate.
বৈধেয়, মূর্খ, অজ্ঞান, পাগল, foolish, ignorant; an ideot, a fool.
বৈনাশিক, ধ্বংসক, দেহাত্মবাদী, destructive, atheistical. [reverse.
বৈপরীত্য, প্রাতিকূল্য, বিপর্য্যয়, ব্যতিক্রম, contrariety, opposition,
বৈপিত্র, ক্ষেত্রজ ভ্রাতা, a half-brother by a different father.
বৈপুল্য, আতিশয্য, গুরুতা, greatness, hugeness, importance.
বৈবর্ণ্য, বর্ণবিকার, ভ্রষ্টতা, বিগাড়, a change of colour, complexion or character, a deviation from rules of cast.
বৈবস্বত, যম, মৃত্যু, Yama the regent of death, death.
বৈবাহিক, পারিণায্য, যাহার সঙ্গে বিবাহ নিষিদ্ধ নয়, জামাতার পিতা, স্নুষার পিতা, nuptial, relating to marriage, marriageable, (as to affinity;) a son or daughter-in-law's father.
বৈভব, ঐশ্বর্য্য, মহিমা, গৌরব, wealth, grandeur.
বৈমনস্য, বিতুষ্টি, অমনোযোগ, aversion, dislike, inattention to.
বৈমাত্র, বৈমাত্রেয়,—অসহোদর ভ্রাতা, বিমাতার সন্তান, a half-brother or sister by a different mother. [tiousness.
বৈমুখ্য, ঘৃণা, বিরক্তি, অপ্রসন্নতা, aversion, dislike, unpropi-
বৈয়র্থ্য, নিরর্থকতা, inutility, uselessness, vanity, futility.
বৈয়াকরণ, ব্যাকরণবেত্তা, skilled in grammar; a grammarian.
বৈর, শত্রুতা, প্রতিযত্ন, শৌর্য্য, hostility, enmity, revenge, heroism, prowess. [pleasure.
বৈরক্ত্য, ঘৃণা, ন্যক্কার, বিতুষ্টি, disgust, nausea, dislike, dis-
বৈরঙ্গ, অসম্বন্ধীয়, অনাত্মীয়, not related, not a relative.

বৈরনির্যাতন, বৈরশুদ্ধি,—প্রতিহিংসা, অহিতকারির অপকার, revenge, retaliation, requital of injury.

বৈরস্য, কুস্বাদ, মন্দ তার, a disagreeable taste.

বৈরাগী উদাসীন, দণ্ডী, an ascetic, devotee, religious mendicant.

বৈরাগ্য, ঔদাস্য, freedom from passion or worldly attachments.

বৈরি, বৈরী,—রিপু, শত্রু, বিপক্ষ, প্রতিকূল, দ্বেষী, an enemy, foe, adversary; hostile, vindictive, revengeful, spiteful.

বৈরূপ্য, কুডৌল, বক্রতা, ugliness, deformity.

বৈলক্ষণ্য, ভাবান্তর, বিশেষ, contrariety, disparity, a difference.

বৈশন, বিন্ধন, to pierce, run through, enter, penetrate.

বৈশাখ, আদ্য মাস, the first Indian month of Aries.

বৈশিষ্ট্য, উৎকর্ষ, ভব্যতা, স্থিরতা, প্রবলতা, excellence, goodness, urbanity, gentility, peculiarity, validity.

বৈশেষিক, দর্শন বিশেষ, one of the six Darshanas or philosophical systems of the Hindoos.

বৈশ্য, তৃতীয় বর্ণ, the third or trading and agricultural cast.

বৈশ্বানর, বহ্নি, অগ্নি, fire or the god of fire.

বৈষম্য, অসাম্য, অসমভাব, আতিশয্য, দায়, উৎপাত, ঔদাস্য, inequality, unevenness, severity, rigour, difficulty, calamity, solitariness.

বৈষয়িক, সাংসারিক, of or relating to the affairs of life.

বৈষ্ণব, বিষ্ণুর উপাসক, a Vishnavite or devotee of Vishnu.

বৈসন, উপবেশন, স্থিরণ, ঘন হওন, জমন, থিতন, অবতরণ, লাগন, to sit, sit down, rest, clot, curdle, sink, settle, subside, alight, perch, to suit or fit.

বৈসর্জনিক, বিদায়ী, a parting present to a guest.

বৈস্য, বসিবার যোগ্য, fit or intended to be sat upon.

বোঁচা, বিটল, ঢেঁটা, অশিষ্ট, a callous or unprincipled person, a villain, a rascal; insolent, rude.

বোঁচামি, বিটলামি, ঢেঁটামি, rascality, villainy, rudeness.

বোঁট-১, বৃন্ত, ডাঁটা, চূচুক, a foot-stalk, a stem, a nipple.

বোকা, নির্বুদ্ধি, মূঢ়, মুখচোরা, গবা, ছাগল, stupid, simple, silly, rustic, sheepish; a blockhead, a he-goat.

বোকামি-ী, মূর্খতা, হাবামি, stupidity, rusticity, simplicity.

বোঝা, বোঝ, বোঝা,—মোট, পুলিন্দা, ভার, a burden, load, bale, pack, package, truss, a charge, a trust.

বোঝাই, ভরা, পোরা, a cargo, lading, freight, load.
বোঝারী, বোচা,—মুটিয়া, ভারবাহক, a porter, a carrier.
বোদ, নদীর স্রোতাগত কালা মৃত্তিকা, a black alluvial earth.
বোদা, বিরস, কুস্বাদু, ill-tasted, ill-flavoured. [man, bail.
বোদ্ধা, জ্ঞানী, লগ্নক, intelligent, sensible, shrewd; a bonds-
বোধ, জ্ঞান, বুদ্ধি, উপলব্ধি, অনুমান, intellect, understanding, sense, wisdom, knowledge, perception, comprehension, sensation, a notion, idea, opinion.
বোধক, জ্ঞাতা, জ্ঞাপক, সূচক, knowing, &c: signifying.
বোধন, জানন, বুঝন, অনুভূত হওন, চেতন, to know, understand, comprehend, perceive, feel a sensation; the ceremonial waking of a god. [a paradox.
বোধাতীত, অজ্ঞেয়, নিগূঢ়, অনুপলভ্য, incomprehensible, abstruse;
বোধাল, বুদ্ধিমান, দক্ষ, intelligent, wise, sensible, able.
বোধিত, জ্ঞাপিত, প্রকাশিত, made known, published, declared.
বোনন, বীজ ছড়ান, বপন, to sow seed, to weave, to knit.
বোনাল, বৃক্ষবনময়, woody, forest, abounding in woods.
বোবা, মূক, তোতলা, dumb; a stammerer, lisper.
বোবান, তোতলান, to stammer, lisp, to make a noise like a dumb man. [waist.
বোর, কাঠের গুঁড়া, কটিভূষণ, saw-dust, an ornament for the
বোরলা, বোল্তা, বোলা,—ভেমরুল, a hornet, a wasp.
বোরা, গুণ, থলিয়া, শিম্বী বিশেষ, ধান্য বিশেষ, a sack, a bag, a bean, a species of rice.
বোল বাক্য, কথা, ভাষা, ক্ষারজল, মাটী বিশেষ, a speech, saying, sentence, word, a language, a lie or liquor for dying, a glazing earth.
বোলন, কহন, to speak, say, tell, mention, observe.
বোলান, ডাকন, ডাকান, to call, call to, send for.
বোলচাল, কথাবার্ত্তা, আলাপ, discourse, conversation. [cry.
বোলী, ভাষা, বাক্য, ধ্বনি, a language, speech, phrase, note,
বৌদ্ধ, জিন, a Buddhist or follower of Buddhism.
ব্যক্ত, স্পষ্ট, প্রত্যক্ষ, ভিন্ন, পৃথক্, কথিত, প্রকাশিত, apparent, clear, manifest, evident, distinct, specific, individual, expressed, uttered, disclosed, revealed.
ব্যক্তগণিত, অঙ্কবিদ্যা, পরিপাটী, arithmetic.

ব্যক্তি, জন, এক লোক, শব্দের প্রত্যয়, an individual, a person, a man, a case or inflexion in grammar.

ব্যক্তিত্ব, পৃথক্ভাব, বিভিন্নতা, individuality, distinct existence.

ব্যগ্র, যত্নবান, সচেষ্ট, ব্যস্ত, ব্যাকুল, eager, ardent, zealous, impatient, agitated, alarmed, affrighted, perplexed, bewildered. [plexity, &c.

ব্যগ্রতা, উদ্যোগ, প্রার্থর্য্য, ধবরাণী, eagerness, ardour, zeal, per-

ব্যঙ্গ, বিদ্রূপ, গাদ্দি, পরিহাস, শ্লেষ, বক্রতা, পঙ্গু, নুলা, মণ্ডুক, তিল, অপ্রকৃত, বিকথার, অবক্ষিপ্ত, a joke, jest, sarcasm, witticism, irony, double-meaning, pun, distortion, a cripple, a frog, a spot or freckle; misplaced, distorted, sarcastic, ironical.

ব্যঙ্গযুক্ত, বিকৃত, পরিহাস্য, অবক্ষিপ্ত, distorted, garbled, ridiculous, sarcastic, &c. [words.

ব্যঙ্গোক্তি, বিদ্রূপ, শ্লেষ, a jeer, pun, joke, sarcasm, play on

ব্যঙ্গ্য, অবক্ষেপ, শ্লেষকথা, a sarcasm, irony, covert expression of contempt, &c.

ব্যজন, পাখা, a fan of *Tal* leaves or feathers.

ব্যঞ্জক, প্রকাশক, ভেদক, সূচক, বোধক, জনক, ঘাঁটক, making clear or plain, distinguishing, indicative, expressive of passion or feeing, exciting, producing effect.

ব্যঞ্জন, লক্ষণ, চিহ্ন, হলবর্ণ, অন্নের উপকরণ, দাড়ি, a mark, sign, token, spot, a consonant, (in grammar,) sauce or condiment, the beard. [figure.

ব্যঞ্জনা-বৃত্তি, অবক্ষেপ, শ্লেষ, sarcasm, irony, a rhetorical

ব্যতিকর, আপদ, বিপর্য্যয়, ব্যতীহার, a misfortune, calamity, reverse, reciprocity, reciprocal action.

ব্যতিক্রম, প্রাতিকূল্য, ব্যত্যয়, অন্যথা, উল্টা, বিকার, প্রাতিলোম্য, লঙ্ঘন, repugnance, opposition, contrariety, reverse, change, alteration, inversion, inverted or retrogade order, transgression, violation.

ব্যতিক্রমী, অন্যথাকারী, প্রতিকূল, লঙ্ঘক, reversing, inverting, opposing, transgressing

ব্যতিপ্রস্ত, ব্যতিব্যস্ত,—বিহ্বল, বিতুষ্ট, উৎকম্পিত, উৎপাতগ্রস্ত, agitated, alarmed, disgusted, annoyed, afflicted, troubled.

ব্যতিরিক্ত, ভিন্ন, excepted, withdrawn, distinct, different.

ব্যতিরেক, ছাড়া, অভাব, উল্টার প্রমাণ, ভিন্নতা, an exception, a withholding, the absence of a thing or an inference therefrom, an inverse argument, difference.

ব্যতিরেকে, ঋতে, বিনা, except, excepting, besides, without.

ব্যতিরেকী, বিভেদক, separating, distinguishing, excepting.

ব্যতিহার, ব্যতীহার,—বাণিজ্যকরা, পরিবর্ত্ত, প্রতিকার, পরস্পর ক্রিয়া করা, মারামারি ইত্যাদি. trade, barter, mutual exchange, reciprocal action, mutual abuse or blows, &c.

ব্যতীত, গত, নিষিদ্ধ, ছাড়ান, ভিন্ন. ব্যতিরিক্ত, past, gone, withdrawn, withheld, excepted.

ব্যতীতে, ঋতে, বিনা, besides, except, without.

ব্যতীপাত, উপদ্রব, উৎপাত, ধূমকেতু ভূকম্পাদি, অনাদর, সপ্তদশম যোগ, a portentous calamity, presage, portent, as comet, earthquake, &c. disrespect, contempt, the seventeenth astronomical Yog.

ব্যত্যয়, ব্যত্যাস,—অন্যথা, বিপর্য্যয়, উল্টা, ব্যতিক্রম, বিপথগমন, ভ্রষ্টাচার, contrariety, opposition, variation, reverse, inversion, inverted or retrograde order, perverseness, deviation from, violation of.

ব্যথনীয়, পীড়নীয়, sensible to or capable of pain.

ব্যথা, পীড়া, বেদনা, ব্যামোহ, ত্রাস, ভয়, pain, smart, soreness, ache, agony, torture, distress, alarm, fear.

ব্যথিত, পীড়িত, দুঃখিত, ভীত, pained, hurt, sore, distressed, &c.

ব্যপদেশ, ছল, ব্যাজ, প্রবঞ্চনা, সংজ্ঞা, a pretence, deception, craft, fraud, dishonesty, a name, appellation.

ব্যপদেষ্টা, কপটী, প্রবঞ্চক, নামদায়ক, a deceiver, impostor, a denominator, that which denominates.

ব্যপেত, বিরুদ্ধ, বিপরীত, opposed, contrary.

ব্যবকলন, অংশহীন করণ, subtraction of numbers; to subtract.

ব্যবচ্ছেদ, পৃথক্ করণ, কাটন, খণ্ড২ করণ, a dividing, division, separating, cutting in pieces, anatomizing.

ব্যবধা-ন, আড়াল, আবরণ, অন্তর, আচ্ছাদন, ঢাকা, অন্তর্ধান, a partition, screen, fence, something intervening between two objects, intervention, interposition, intermediate space, distance, covering, a covering, concealment, disappearance.

ব্যবধাতা, বিচ্ছেদক, আবরক, মধ্যবর্ত্তী, আড়াল, the person or thing which separates or intervenes, a partition, the septum of the nose.

ব্যবধায়ক, ব্যবধায়ী,—মধ্যস্থিত, আবরক, আচ্ছাদক, intervening, intermediate, screening, concealing &c.

ব্যবধেয়, মধ্যস্থেয়, suitable to intervene or lie between.

ব্যবসা, ব্যবসায়,—বৃত্তি, কর্ম্ম, ব্যাপার, বাণিজ্য, ক্রয়বিক্রয়, উদ্যোগ, পরিশ্রম, উৎসাহ, কল্পনা, কৌশল, ছল, profession, occupation, calling, trade, traffic, barter, commerce, effort, exertion, industry, perseverance, a plan, device, trick.

ব্যবসায়স্থান, বাণিজ্য কুঠী, হাট, a factory, a fair, market, &c.

ব্যবসায়ী, বণিক, বিষয়ী, ব্যাপারী, a dealer, merchant, trader; secular, following a trade, &c.

ব্যবস্থা, বিধি, আদেশ, বিধানপত্র, রীতি, ব্যবহার, মত, বিয়োগ, পৃথককরা, a law, statute, rule, written decision, prescription, established custom, tenet, a separation, a placing apart.

ব্যবস্থান, কাছারী, বিচারস্থল, a court of law, a place of judgment.

ব্যবস্থানীয়, ব্যবস্থেয়,—বিবাদ বিষয়, বিধেয়, to be decided at law, proper as an object of legislation.

ব্যবস্থাপক, বিধায়ক, বিচারকর্ত্তা, a legislator, expounder of law; legislating.

ব্যবস্থাপন, বিধান করণ, বিধান জ্ঞাপন, to legislate, to enact or interpret laws.

ব্যবস্থাপত্র, বিধানলিপি, a written opinion or legal decision.

ব্যবস্থিত, নিষ্পন্ন, আদিষ্ট, নিয়ত, স্থির, ভিন্ন, settled, decreed, enacted, arranged, invariable, separated, distinct.

ব্যবহরণীয়, ব্যবহর্ত্তব্য,—আচরণীয়, ন্যায্য, customary, agreeable to usage, litigable.

ব্যবহর্ত্তা, মধ্যস্থ, নিষ্পাদক, বিচারকর্ত্তা, আদ্দাশী, রীতিদ, an umpire, arbitrator, judge, plaintiff, the introducer of a custom.

ব্যবহার, ধারা, চালি, লৌকিক কর্ম্ম, রীতি, আচার, বিবাদ, ব্যবসায়, a custom, usage, practice, rite, ceremony, customary observances, idiom, action, conduct, behaviour, a lawsuit, profession, business.

ব্যবহারক, ব্যবহারী,—আচারী, রীতিজ্ঞ, acting customarily, in the habit of, practising, bringing into use.

ব্যবহারজ্ঞ, গতবাল্য, রীতিজ্ঞ, one past his minority and admissible to proceed at law; acquainted with usages.

ব্যবহারতঃ, ধারাক্রমে, customarily. by common usage.

ব্যবহারিক, আচরণীয়, চলিত, calculated for use, &c: customary.

ব্যবহারিত, আচরিত, চলিত, পুরাতন, established, brought into use or practice, common, current, customary, usual, old, second-hand.

ব্যবহার্য্য, লৌকিক, চলিত, আচরণীয়, ন্যায্য, চলনার্হ, পরিধেয়, বস্ত্র, customary, usual, practicable, fit for use, to be observed or practised, actionable at law, passable, (as a road,) fit for wear; a garment.

ব্যবহিত, মধ্যস্থাপিত, ব্যবধানবিশিষ্ট, আবৃত, interposed, put between, parted, separated, covered, concealed.

ব্যবহৃত, আচরিত, চলিত, done customarily, practised, used.

ব্যভিচার, অসতীত্ব, পারদার্য্য, দুষ্ক্রিয়া, বিগাড়, স্বভাবের অন্যথা, স্বামি ত্যাগকরা, ভ্রষ্টাচার, fornication, adultery, a change of state, situation, owner or master, a straying.

ব্যভিচারী, পারদারিক, লম্পট, বিপথগামী. দুষ্টাচারী, adulterous, erring, straying, following wrong courses.

ব্যভিচারিণী, পরপুরুষগামিনী, বেশ্যা, *f.* an adultress, harlot, jilt.

ব্যয়, অর্থনিক্ষেপ, ধনক্ষয়, হ্রাস, ফুরণি, a spending, expense, expenditure, diminution, consumption.

ব্যয়কাতর, ব্যয়কুণ্ঠ,—কৃপণ, penurious, miserly, stingy, sordid.

ব্যয়শীল, ব্যয়ী,—উড়ানিয়া, দানশীল, দাতা, extravagant, expensive, lavish, generous, liberal.

ব্যয়িত, ফুরা, উড়ান, expended, spent, consumed; dissipated.

ব্যয়ীকৃত, ফুরাণ, অপচয়িত, নিক্ষিপ্ত, made an article of expenditure or consumption, expended, consumed.

ব্যর্থ, নিরর্থক, useless, vain, ineffectual, unmeaning.

ব্যলীক, অনুচিত, অপ্রিয়, মন্দ, অশুভ, বিপরীত, ঠেটা, দুঁদিয়া, ক্রূর, দুষ্ট, বিটুল, পীড়া, যাতনা, improper, offensive, disagreeable, unlucky, unnatural, contumacious, seditious, mischievous, vicious, addicted to unnatural crimes; a pathic, pain, torture.

ব্যলীকতা, বিতুষ্টি, অনৌচিত্য, বিটলামী, গণ্ডগোল, displeasure, dissatisfaction, impropriety, viciousness, unnatural lust, sedition, mutiny.

ব্যসন, পাপ, দোষ, বিপদ, vice, sin, calamity, misfortune.

ব্যসনী, দুষ্ট, ভ্রষ্ট, দুঃখী, vicious, unfortunate, distressed.

ব্যস্ত, ক্ষুব্ধ, উৎকণ্ঠিত, উদ্বিগ্ন, ব্যাকুল, বিতুষ্ট, ব্যগ্র, উদ্যত, ব্যতিক্রান্ত, উল্টা, বিচ্ছিন্ন, agitated, distressed, troubled, perplexed, confused, bewildered, annoyed, ruffled, displeased, impatient, eager, busy, inverse, reversed, separated.

ব্যাকরণ, বাক্য রচনা শাস্ত্র, grammar.

ব্যাকার, ব্যাকৃতি,—পরিণাম, বক্রতা, বৈকল্য, বিরূপ, change of form, distortion, disfiguring, deformity, mimicry.

ব্যাকুল, ব্যাকুলিত,—কাতর, উৎকণ্ঠিত, অবাক্, বিক্লব, troubled, perturbed, disturbed, agitated, distracted, confounded, perplexed, bewildered.

ব্যাকৃত, বিকৃত, বিকলাঙ্গ, deformed, distorted, disfigured.

ব্যাখ্যা, ভাষ্য, টীকা, বিবরণ, প্রশংসা, গুণপ্রস্তাব, a comment, exposition, gloss, statement, representation, commendation, eulogy.

ব্যাখ্যাত, উক্ত, কথিত, বর্ণিত, প্রশংসিত, declared, stated, said, explained, expounded, commended, extolled.

ব্যাখ্যান, বুঝাই, বর্ণনা, an expounding, explaining, stating, &c.

ব্যাখ্যেয়, বর্ণনীয়, প্রশংস্য, explainable, capable of statement, commendable, worthy of eulogy.

ব্যাঘাত, প্রতিবন্ধ, আটক, বাট্পাড়ী, রোধ, দায়, আপদ, an obstacle, impediment, hindrance, a waylaying, intercepting, cutting off, danger, &c.

ব্যাঘাতী, প্রতিবন্ধক, obstructing, hindering, opposing, &c.

ব্যাঘ্র, বাঘ, শার্দ্দূল, a tiger.

ব্যাজ, ছুতা, ছল, বিলম্ব, বাট্টা, কাণ্ড, বৃদ্ধি, an excuse, veil, artifice, deceit, pretence, stay, delay, loitering, discount, deduction, a make-weight, overplus, interest of money, usury.

ব্যাজে, বিলম্বে, গৌণে, tardily, with delay.

ব্যাধ, পক্ষিমারা, মৃগব্যজীবী, জীবহিংসক, a fowler, a hunter.

ব্যাধি, রোগ, পীড়া, ব্যামোহ, disease, sickness, disorder.

ব্যাধিত, পীড়িত, রোগী, ill, sick, diseased, indisposed.

ব্যান, সমুদায় শরীর ব্যাপক বায়ু, that among the five airs which is diffused through the whole body.

ব্যাপক, মেয়ক, বাড়ন্ত, বিস্তারক, সমুদায় পক্ষ প্রস্তাবক, বিভু, সর্বগ, কর্ত্ত্বাচ্য, প্রবল, মহৎ, প্রধানীকৃত, গর্বী, প্রগল্‌ভ, বহু, অনেক, প্রতিপালক, প্রভু, কর্ত্তা, বিশেষক, spreading, extending, diffusive, comprehensive, embracing the whole of a plea or argument, all-pervading, governing, (in grammar,) followed by, powerful, prevalent, influential, having ascendance, haughty, over-bearing, forward, impudent, much, many, long; a protector, supporter, lord, master, an accident or inherent quality.

ব্যাপকতা, প্রভুত্ব, প্রাবল্য, বিস্তার, গর্ব, প্রাগল্ভ্য, ঢেঁটামী, influence, sway, prevalence, diffusion, spread, haughtiness, overbearing, forwardness, impudence.

ব্যাপন, বিস্তরণ, বিসরণ, বিসর্পণ, মেগন, ঢাকন, লাগন, ভিজন, থাকন, বেষ্টন, বিলম্বিতান, বাড়ন, শব্দসংযোগে চাহন, to be diffused, pervade, spread, overspread, extend, to occupy space or time, to reach, last, continue, to surround, to infest, swarm, abound, increase, to govern, (in grammar.)

ব্যাপাদন, হনন, দ্বেষ, হিংসেচ্ছা, to murder, kill, injure; malice, a wish to injure others.

ব্যাপার, বিষয়, কর্ম্ম, ব্যবসায়, পদ, প্রয়োজন, ক্রিয়া, পরিশ্রম, যত্ন, ব্যবহার, রীতি, বাণিজ্য, পরিবর্ত্ত, গতিবিধি, an affair, matter, business, profession, occupation, office, operation, transaction, process, undertaking, action, effort, endeavour, practice, usage, trade, barter, commerce, intercourse.

ব্যাপারী, কর্ম্মকারী, ব্যবসায়ী, নিবিষ্ট, উদ্যুক্ত, a workman, tradesman; acting, transacting, trading, busy, occupied.

ব্যাপিকা, প্রগল্‌ভা স্ত্রী, কাণ্ডী, অযাচিতকারিণী, a termagant, vixen, a forward or officious woman.

ব্যাপী, অন্তর্যামী, বিভু, all-diffusive, omnipresent, expansive.

ব্যাপ্ত, সর্ব্বময়, সর্ব্বগত, বিসৃত, আকীর্ণ, পূরিত, সম্পূর্ণ, বেষ্টিত, প্রাপ্ত, মিলিত, সংস্থাপিত, বিখ্যাতাপন্ন, pervading, diffused throughout, filling, overspread, pervaded, penetrated, filled, full, encircled, surrounded, obtained, fixed, placed, celebrated, famous.

ব্যাপ্তি, সর্ব্বত্রগতি, বিভুত্ব, পরিপূর্ণতা, স্বাভাবিক গুণ, বিস্তার, omnipresence, pervading, fulness, an inherent quality, attribute or property, diffusion, extension.

ব্যাপ্য, পার্য্য, প্রবেশ্য, সংযোগ্য, প্রভূত, অধীন, সামিল, বিশিষ্য, pervadable, permeable, penetrable, governed, (in grammar,) amenable, subject to, comprised in, dependant; the subject of an attribute.

ব্যাবর্ত্ত, বেষ্টনি, ঘেরাণি, চক্রগতি, বাছনী, নিয়োগকরা, উল্টিয়া গুড়ন, a surrounding, encompassing, screening, going round, choosing, appointing, the rolling up of a leaf, &c. backwards.

ব্যাবর্ত্তনা, নিয়োগ, বিলি, an appointing, disposal, division.

ব্যাবহারিক, লৌকিক, আচরণার্হ, calculated for common practice or use, &c. fit to be observed or practised.

ব্যাবৃত, ব্যবধানযুক্ত, ঘেরিত, অনাচ্ছাদিত, ত্যক্ত, নিরাকৃত, ব্যতিরিক্ত, well-screened or fenced, surrounded, uncovered, excluded, removed, excepted.

ব্যাবৃত্ত, মনোনীত, নিযুক্ত, বেষ্টিত, উল্টিয়া গুড়ান, প্রশংসিত, নিরাকৃত, ব্যতিরিক্ত, chosen, appointed, surrounded, rolled back, praised, hymned, removed, excepted.

ব্যাবৃত্তি, নিয়োগ, বাছনী, উদাহরণ, নিরাকৃতি, ব্যতিরেক, বেষ্টনি, স্তব, সংকীর্ত্তন বাক্য, an appointment, choice, selection, illustration, example, exclusion, rejection, exemption, surrounding, &c. praise, eulogium.

ব্যাম, বাহু পরিমাণ, ধনু, a fathom, two yards.

ব্যামুগ্ধ, দুঃখিত, পীড়িত, ক্লিষ্ট, afflicted, distressed, pained, molested.

ব্যামোহ, দুঃখ, উৎপাত, রোগ, পীড়া, ব্যাধি, উচ্চাটন, ক্লেশ, distress, trouble, vexation, affliction, suffering, pain, ache, sickness, illness, embarrassment, persecution, molestation.

ব্যামোহক, দুষ্কর, অপকারক, afflictive, distressing, &c. a nuisance.

ব্যায়াম, পরিশ্রম, উদ্যোগ, মল্লক্রীড়াদি, পৌরুষ, কর্ম্ম, ঝঞ্ঝাট, দুর্গম্য পথ, ব্যাম, fatigue, labour, exertion, athletic exercises, manhood, manliness, business, occupation, a difficulty, impassable defile, a fathom.

ব্যাল, সর্প, ব্যাঘ্র পুরাদি হিংস্রক জন্তু, উৎকট হস্তী, রাজা, ধূর্ত্ত, দুষ্ট, a snake, a beast of prey, a vicious elephant, a king, a rogue, a cheat ; wicked, bad.

ব্যালগ্রাহী, ওঝা, সাপুড়্যা, a snake-catcher.

ব্যাস, ব্যাপ্তি, বিস্তার, diffusion, spreading, extension.

ব্যাসক্ত, বিক্লব, উদ্বিগ্ন, bewildered, confused, perplexed.

ব্যাসঙ্গ, ঘবরাণী, ঔদাস্য, confusion, perplexity, loneliness, solitariness. [the Puráns.

ব্যাসপিঁড়ী, পুরাণ পাঠকের আসন, the seat of one who recites

ব্যাহত, মারা, পরাভূত, বিহ্বল, smitten, repulsed, confused, alarmed. [tion.

ব্যাহতি, পরাজয়, ব্যাঘাত, repulse, defeat, obstacle, interrup-

ব্যাহার, ব্যাহৃতি,— বাক্য, ওঁ ভুব স্বুরাদি শব্দ, voice, speech, a word, a mystical word as *om, swar, bhur, bhuvah*.

ব্যাহৃত, উক্ত, কথিত, uttered, spoken, announced.

ব্যুৎক্রম, বিপর্য্যয়, উল্টাপাল্টামি, reverse or inverted order, irregular arrangement, confusion.

ব্যুত্থান, বৈপরীত্য, আটক, নিষেধ, অস্বীকার, স্বাধীনতা, টেঁটামি, নিষিদ্ধাচরণ, opposition, resistance, obstruction, prohibition, contradiction, independance, the following of one's own inclinations, disobedience, the doing of what is prohibited.

ব্যুৎপত্তি, পাণ্ডিত্য, নৈপুণ্য, শব্দ সাধন জ্ঞান, শব্দ রচনা, অর্থ, অভিপ্রায়, জ্ঞানবৃদ্ধি, সংস্কার, science, learning, critical knowledge, the formation of words, derivation, etymology, signification, meaning, advancement in learning, improvement, proficiency.

ব্যুৎপন্ন, নিপুণ, পণ্ডিত, জনিত, জাত, versed in, proficient, learned, derived, formed as a derivative word, begotten, generated. [ing words.

ব্যুৎপাদক, পাণ্ডিত্যজনক, শব্দরচক, perfect in knowledge, form-

ব্যুৎপাদ্য, সংস্কার্য্য, রচনীয়, improvable in science, derivable.

ব্যূহ, সমূহ, সৈন্যবিন্যাস, ন্যায়শাস্ত্র, তর্ক, বিতণ্ডা, রচনা, নির্ম্মাণ, শরীর, a multitude, flock, phalanx, line, military array, logic, reasoning, investigation, manufacture, a making, the body.

ব্যোম, আকাশ, অন্তরীক্ষ, the sky, atmosphere, the heaven.

ব্রজ, বৃন্দাবন মথুরা প্রভৃতি স্থান, the district about Agra and Mathura, the scene of Chrishna's adventures.

ব্রজন, গমন, ক্রমণ, পর্য্যটন, to go, move, step, rove, travel.

ব্রণ, ক্ষুদ্র স্ফোটক, a boil, tumour, carbuncle, pimple, bubo.

ব্রত, শাস্ত্রবিহিত নিয়ম, উপবাসাদি পুণ্যকর্ম্ম, ধর্ম্মসাধন, a religious vow, a voluntary penance or other supposed meritorious act of devotion.

ব্রতী, গৃহীতব্রত, যজমান, making or performing vows, &c.

ব্রহ্ম, পরমেশ্বর, পরমাত্মা, জগতের অনাদি কারণ, বেদ, পরমার্থজ্ঞান, তপস্, বিপ্র, Brahma or the all-pervading essence, the first cause, the Veda, sacred knowledge, the practice of austerities, a Brahmin.

ব্রহ্মচর্য্য, প্রথম আশ্রম, ব্রহ্মচারির ধর্ম্ম, বৈরাগ্য, the state or condition of a religious student, devotion to a life of austerities, ascetism, abstract devotion.

ব্রহ্মচারী, বর্ণী, প্রথমাশ্রমী, তপস্বী, বেদবেত্তা, a religious student, one who continues such through life, an ascetic, a Pandit learned in the Veda.

ব্রহ্মজীবী, বৈতনিক ব্রাহ্মণ, a mercenary or hireling Brahmin.

ব্রহ্মজ্ঞান, আত্মজ্ঞান, একাত্মবোধ, the knowledge of the all-pervading Brahma, a persuasion of the identity of the soul with the creator.

ব্রহ্মজ্ঞানী, একাত্মজ্ঞ, one possessing the knowledge of the soul as one with Brahma.

ব্রহ্মণ্য, ব্রহ্মসম্বন্ধীয়, বিষ্ণু, relating to or connected with Brahma; Vishnu.

ব্রহ্মতত্ত্ব, আত্মতত্ত্ব, the true doctrine of the All-pervading.

ব্রহ্মত্ব, ব্রহ্মপদ, নির্ব্বাণ, অপবর্গ, মোক্ষ, divinity, deity, identification with Brahma, final absorption.

ব্রহ্মতালু, টাকরা, the palate or roof of the mouth.

ব্রহ্মরন্ধ্র, মস্তকের মধ্যস্থান, the crown of the head.

ব্রহ্মদৈত্য, অনূঢ় ব্রাহ্মণের ভূত, the ghost of an unmarried Brahmin.

ব্রহ্মনিরূপণ, আত্মতত্ত্ব নির্ণয়, the investigating of spirit or ascertaining of the true nature of God.

ব্রহ্মপুত্র, নদ বিশেষ, the Burampooter river.

ব্রহ্মবাদী, ব্রহ্মোপাসক, বেদান্তমতগ্রাহী, বেদান্তী, professing to pursue the knowledge of Brahma, speaking of Brahma, a follower of the Vedánt system of spiritual worship. [ing the Veds, &c.

ব্রহ্মবিন্দু, বেদপাঠে মুখনিঃসৃত শ্লেষ্মকণা, saliva sputtered in recit-

ব্রহ্মবেদ, একাত্মজ্ঞান, knowledge of Brahma, monotheism.

ব্রহ্মর্ষি, কশ্যপাদি মুনি, a sacred sage of the first order.

ব্রহ্মলোক, ব্রহ্মার স্থান, the heaven or world of Brahmá.

ব্রহ্মযজ্ঞ, বেদাধ্যাপন, the study or teaching of the Vedas.

ব্রহ্মা, বিধাতা, বিশ্বস্রষ্টা, Brahmá or the operative creator.

ব্রহ্মাণী, ব্রাহ্মী,—ব্রহ্মার শক্তি, মাতৃগণের প্রধানা, the energy or wife of Brahmá. [verse.

ব্রহ্মাণ্ড, জগৎ, বিশ্ব, the mundáne egg, the world, the uni-

ব্রহ্মাভিমান, স্বব্রহ্মতুল্যতা প্রকাশ, a vainglorious identification of one's self with Brahma.

ব্রাহ্ম, ব্রহ্মোপাসক, বিবাহসংস্কার বিশেষ, a professor of the spiritual worship of Brahma, a mode of marriage.

ব্রাহ্মণ, প্রথম বর্ণ, বিপ্র, a brahmin, one of the sacred order.

ব্রাহ্মণী, ব্রাহ্মণের স্ত্রী, a brahminness or wife of a brahmin.

ব্রাহ্মণ্য, বিপ্র জাতির ধর্ম্ম, ব্রাহ্মণের সমূহ, the condition, quality or duties of a brahmin, brahminship, brahminity, an assembly of brahmins.

ব্রাহ্মণব্রুব, বিষয়ি ব্রাহ্মণ, a brahmin engaged in secularities.

ব্রাহ্ম্যমুহূর্ত্ত, সূর্য্যোদয়ের পূর্ব্বকাল, the hour and half preceding sunrise, dawn. [the thread, &c.

ব্রাত্য, উপনয়নাদিসংস্কারহীন ব্রাহ্মণ, a brahmin uninvested with

ব্রীড়া, লজ্জা, ত্রপা, হ্রী, modesty, shame, bashfulness.

ব্রীড়িত, সলজ্জ, ত্রপান্বিত, হ্রীযুক্ত, modest, bashful, ashamed.

ব্রীহি, শরৎপক্বধান্য, আশু, rice ripening after the rains.

ব্রুবন, ব্রুবাণ,—কথক, বচনশক্তিমান, বাক্যনিষ্পাদক, speaking, able to speak, articulating.

ব্রৈহেয়, ধান্যোদ্ভবোচিত ভূমি, land fit to be sown with rice.

ভ.

ভক্ত, অনুরক্ত, সেবক, উপাসক, সেবিত, বণ্টিত, অন্ন, ভজনশীল, attached or devoted to, serving, pious, engrossed by, worshipped, served, divided, portioned out; boiled rice, food, a zealot, votary.

ভক্তদাস, অন্নদাস, ভাতুয়া, a mercenary, one who serves for his food. [crite, false worshipper.

ভক্তবিটল, কাল্পনিক ভক্ত, কপটোপাসক, hypocritical; a hypo-

ভক্তি, ভজনশীলতা, অত্যন্ত শ্রদ্ধা, সেবা, অনুরাগ, ভঙ্গ, বিভাগ, বণ্ট, devotedness to God, zeal, strong faith, divine worship, service, attendance, homage, attachment, a fracture, division, part, portion.

ভড়্যা, নট, যুবা নর্ত্তক, a dancing-boy.

ভক্ষক, খাদক, অবক্ষুধিত, অদ্মর, an eater; eating, devouring, voracious, ravenous. [tion.

ভক্ষণ, প্রাশন, ভোজন, আহার, to eat, devour; a meal, refec-

ভক্ষণীয়, ভক্ষ্য,—ভোজনীয়, অন্ন, ধান্য ঘাসাদি, খাদ্য, edible, eatable; food, corn, pasture, prey, &c.

ভগ, কীর্ত্তি, ঐশ্বর্য্যাদি গুণ, মাহাত্ম্য, শ্রী, সম্পত্তি, বীর্য্য, সর্ব্বসামর্থ্য, বিভূতি, যত্ন, সৌন্দর্য্য, শোভা, জ্ঞান, পুণ্য, ধর্ম্ম, বৈরাগ্য, শান্তি, কাম, স্পৃহা, যোনি, চন্দ্র, সূর্য্য, fame, glory, excellence, greatness, prosperity, fortune, strength, vigour, divine power, omnipotence, effort, exertion, beauty, splendour, knowledge, virtue, moral merit, absence of passion, religious tranquillity, love, desire, a wish, pudendum muliebre, the moon, the sun.

ভগন্দর, রোগ বিশেষ, a fistula in ano.

ভগবৎ, ভগবান্,—ঐশ্বর্য্যাদিগুণ বিশিষ্ট, শোভান্বিত, বলবান, সর্ব্বশক্তিমান, ঈশ্বর, illustrious, glorious, splendid, beautiful, vigorous, omnipotent, divine; God.

ভগিনী, ভগ্নী,—স্বসা, স্ত্রীলোক, a sister, a woman in general.

ভগ্ন, খণ্ডিত, ভাঙ্গা, চেরা, পরাস্ত, তুচ্ছীকৃত, দুঃখী, broken, fractured, torn, defeated, disregarded, despised, wretched, afflicted.

ভগ্নাশ, অকৃতার্থ,নির্ভরসা, disappointed, discouraged, spiritless.

ভঙ্গ, খণ্ডন, ঢেরাণী, বিল, ফাক, বিচ্ছেদ, নাশ, জয়বিপর্য্যয়, প্রবঞ্চনা, ব্যাধি, পক্ষাঘাত, a breaking, splitting, tearing, a fissure, chasm, breach, division, breaking off, disappointment, interruption, discomfiture, rout, cheating, swindling, dishonesty, fraud, disease, the palsy, hemp.

ভঙ্গন, খণ্ডন, পরাস্ত করণ. মিটান, নাশন, to break, fracture, defeat, dispel, disperse, ruin, undo.

ভঙ্গরঙ্গ, ভঙ্গিরঙ্গী,— লীলা, ভাব, অঙ্গের মনোরম বিন্যাস, dalliance, loose toying, wanton gestures.

ভঙ্গিমা, ভঙ্গী,—খণ্ডনা, বিচ্ছেদ, ছল. ছদ্ম, বক্রতা. ইঙ্গিত, রস, অবক্ষেপ, লীলা, ভাব, কুন্দনি, a fracture, breach, division, separation, deception, a trick, disguise, distortion, hint, wit, irony, repartee, dalliance, toying, gesture, attitude, capering.

ভঙ্গুর, বেঁকা, বক্র, ছলী, টেক, বিনাশোন্মুখ, নশ্বর, নদীর বেঁক, bent, crooked, distorted, fraudulent, dishonest, crafty, swindling, mouldering, dissoluble; the bend or turning of a river, a reach.

ভজন, উপাসন, সেবন, আদর করণ, to serve attentively, worship, adore, honour, pay homage, shew respect or attention. [attention, &c.

ভজনা, অর্চনা, উপাসনা, সেবা, adoration, worship, service,

ভজনীয়, আরাধনীয়, অর্চ্য, সম্ভ্রান্ত, venerable, adorable, honourable, respectable.

ভজমান, উপাস্য, ন্যায্য, যোগ্য, honourable, right, fit, proper.

ভজিষ্ণু, উপাসক, সেবক, ঈশ্বরপরায়ণ, serving, waiting on, obsequious, attentive to, devout, pious.

ভজ্যমান, পূজ্যমান, receiving worship, homage, respect. &c.

ভঞ্জন, খণ্ডন, নাশন, ঘুচান, চুকান, মিটান, মুদ্রা ভাঙ্গান, to break, fracture, demolish, destroy, dispel, allay, solve, adjust, compose a difference, change money.

ভঞ্জী, খণ্ডক, ভাঙ্গানিয়া, breaking, changing money.

ভট, যোদ্ধা, ভেঙ্গাজা, ভূত, চাণ্ডাল, a warrior, soldier, combatant, a goblin, an outcast.

ভট্ট, মীমাংসক বিশেষ, সুপণ্ডিত, শত্রু, ভাট, স্তুতিপাঠক, রাজদূত, শ্রেষ্ঠ, a philosopher, a sage, a learned man, an enemy, a panegyrist, encomiast, a king's messenger; best, excellent.

ভট্টাচার্য্য, গৌড়ীয় পণ্ডিত ব্রাহ্মণের উপাধি, জ্ঞানী, অধ্যাপক, a title given to certain Bengal pandits, a philosopher, a teacher of philosophy.

ভট্‌ভট্‌, বক্‌বক্‌, অনর্থক বাক্য, শব্দমাত্র, প্রতিধ্বনি, gabble, nonsense, an empty sound, an echo.

ভড়, বৃহৎ ভার নৌকা বিশেষ, a sort of heavy lumber-boat.

ভড়ক, ভড়ঙ্গ,—ফাকী, চাতুরী, প্রবঞ্চনা, ধূর্ত্ততা, an imposition, deception, fraud, swindling.

ভড়কন, ভয়জন্যে ত্যাগ করণ, পলান, to relinquish from fear, to flee.

ভড়কাল, স্বপ্রকাশক, প্রবঞ্চক, ostentatious, imposing, swindling.

ভড়্ভড়ান, বক্‌বকান, to gabble, babble, talk nonsense.

ভণন, কথন, গ্রন্থ রচন, to speak, utter, compose in writing.

ভণিতা, গ্রন্থকর্ত্তা, রচক, an author, a composer.

ভণ্ড, ফাকী, ছল, কৌতুকি নর্ত্তক, প্রতারক, ধূর্ত্ত, ভক্তবিটল, deceit, imposition, swindling, a wile, a jester, buffoon, mime, actor, deceiver, cheat, dissembler, hypocrite, pretender; pretended, hypocritical [upon, mimic.

ভণ্ডন, প্রতারণ, ভুলান, ভেঙ্গান, to deceive, cozen, impose

ভণ্ডামী, ফাকী, ভেঙ্গানি, imposition, a swindling, mimickry.

ভণ্ডুর, ভণ্ডুল,—প্রবঞ্চনা, ভঙ্গ, ব্যাঘাত, deceit, imposition, interruption, impediment.

ভণ্‌ভণান, ঝঙ্কার করণ, ঘুণ্‌ঘুণান, to buzz, to hum.

ভদ্র, উত্তম, বিলক্ষণ, বিশিষ্ট, শিষ্ট, মান্য, দয়াবান, মঙ্গল, শুভ, কল্যাণ, কুশল, good, excellent, virtuous, pious, pure, polished, genteel, respectable, humane, prosperous, lucky, propitious; welfare, prosperity, happiness, good fortune. [tages.

ভদ্রাভদ্র, শুভাশুভ, good and evil, advantages and disadvan-

ভদ্রাসন, রাজসিংহাসন, বসতির বাটী, ভিটা, a throne, home, dwelling-house, home-stead.

ভন্দড়, নকুল বিশেষ, a species of weasel.

ভব, বৃদ্ধি, স্থিতি, জন্ম, সংসার, মঙ্গল, সম্পত্তি, কল্যাণ, শিব, being, existence, the place, means or state of being, birth, the world, welfare, prosperity, possessions, Shiva. [nour's.

ভবদীয়, তোমার, আপনার, আপনকার, thine, yours, your ho-

ভবন, গৃহ, ভিটা, উৎপত্তি, জন্ম, স্থিতি, a house, dwelling, abode, production, birth, being. [nour.

ভবান্, আপনি, মহাশয়, thou, (*respectfully,*) Sir, your ho-

ভবানী, দুর্গা, শিবপত্নী, Párvatí or Durga in her pacific form.

ভবিতব্য, যাহা হইবে, বিধাতার নিরূপিত, উৎপত্তিশীল, যাহা হইতে পারে, that may, will or must be, to be or become, possible, probable, likely, incidental. [py.

ভবিক-1, কল্যাণ, কুশলী, welfare, prosperity ; prosperous, hap-

ভবিষ্যৎ, যাহা হইবে, আগামিকাল, about to be or happen, future ; the future, future time.

ভবিষ্যদ্বক্তা, ভাবি কথক, a prophet, predictor of future events.

ভব্য, ভাবী, সম্ভব, উচিত, সত্য, মঙ্গল, পয়োমন্ত, কুশলী, সভ্য, শিষ্ট, স্থিতি, উৎপন্ন, কল্যাণ, ভাল, that will be, likely, certain, fit, right, proper, true, auspicious, prosperous, happy, polite, well-behaved, genteel ; existence, being, result, welfare ; well.

ভব্যতা, সৌজন্য, শিষ্টতা, politeness, urbanity, condescension.

ভমরী, বুর্মা, তুরপণ, a gimlet, an awl.

ভয়, ত্রাস, শঙ্কা, আতঙ্ক, দায়, fear, fright, alarm, terror, dread, awe, peril, danger.

ভয়খেকুয়া, শঙ্কান্বিত, fearing, dreading, (from experience.)

ভয়ঙ্কর, ভয়ানক,—শঙ্কাজনক, ঘোর, দারুণ, terrific, alarming, frightful, dangerous.

ভয়শীল, ভয়ালু, অসাহসী, ভীরু, fearful, timid, cowardly.

ভর, অতিশয়, পুরা, ঢের, অধিক, চাপ, full, complete, much, excessive ; a load, weight, pressure.

ভরণ, পূর্ণীকরণ, বুজান, গাদন, পোষণ, নিষ্পাদন, পূর্ণ হওন, উপচয়, to fill, make up a deficiency, fill or stop up, charge, load, stuff, load a gun, maintain, support, nourish, terminate, be full, abound.

ভরণ, ভরণ্য,—বেতন, পণ, জীবিকা, wages, hire, maintenance.

ভরণী, দ্বিতীয় নক্ষত্র, the second lunar mansion.
ভরণ্যভুক্, বেতনগ্রাহী, living on wages; a hireling. [name.
ভরত, পক্ষি বিশেষ, তাঁতী, a skylark, a weaver, a proper
ভরদ্বাজ, পক্ষি বিশেষ, গোত্র বিশেষ, a skylark, a proper name.
ভরপুর, পরিপূর্ণ, কাঁধা পর্য্যন্ত পূরিত, ষোড়শকলাযুক্ত, full, brimful, high, (as the tide,) full, (as the moon.)
ভরসা, আশা, আশ্বাস, প্রত্যয়, বিশ্বাস, সাহস, শৌর্য্য, hope, expectation, encouragement, trust, confidence, reliance, faith, firmness, resolution, courage.
ভরসাতী, আশাপন্ন, সাহসী, full of hope, valiant, intrepid, &c.
ভরা, পরিপূর্ণ, বোঝাই, ভার, পরিপূর্ণতা, চড়তি, full, complete; a cargo, load, charge, fulness, accumulation.
ভরাট, বুজান, the stopping or filling up of holes, &c.
ভরাণি, বেতন, ভৃতি, wages, hire.
ভরাডুবী, অতিশয় ভারে নৌকার ডুবি, অত্যন্ত ক্লেশ, a sinking from overloading, accumulated misfortune.
ভর্জ্জন, ভাজন, ঝল্সান, to parch, roast, fry, bake, scorch.
ভর্জ্জনকপাল, ভাজাখোলা, a frying pan. [ported, &c.
ভর্ত্তব্য, পোষণীয়, প্রতিপাল্য, proper to be nourished, to be sup-
ভর্ত্তা, পতি, কর্ত্তা, প্রতিপালক, রক্ষক, a husband, the master of a house, a lord, supporter, nourisher, protector.
ভর্ত্তী, বোঝাই, পরিপূর্ণতা, a load, complete cargo, fulness.
ভর্ৎসন, নিন্দন, তিরস্করণ, তাড়ন, ধম্কান, to reproach, vilify, scold, abuse, reprove, threaten, menace.
ভর্ৎসনা, তিরস্কার, নিন্দা, abusive language, reproach, abuse.
ভল্ল, ভেলা, বাণ, বস্ত্রাঙ্কনার্থ ফল বিশেষ, a lance, an arrow, the marking nut.
ভল্লুক, হিংস্র জন্তু বিশেষ, ভালুক, ঋক্ষ, a bear. [rail.
ভষণ, বুকন, ঝকড়ম, গালাগালি দেওন, to bark, (as a dog.) scold,
ভস্তা-ন, অস্বাদু, পানসা, insipid, vapid, tasteless, diluted.
ভস্ত্রা, স্বর্ণকারাদির জাঁতা, a smith's bellows.
ভস্ভসিয়া, দলদলিয়া, কাদাটিয়া, boggy, soft, plashy.
ভস্ম, ছাই, পাঁশ, ashes.
ভা, দীপ্তি, প্রভা, শোভা, সূর্য্য, প্রতিবিম্ব, light, splendour, beauty, the sun, a shadow. [friend.
ভাই, ভ্রাতা, বন্ধু, আত্মীয়, a brother, kinsman, acquaintance,

ভাও, মূল্য, অর্ঘ, the price of goods, value. cost. [or plait.
ভাঁজ, মিশ্র, মলা, পাট, mixture, alloy, adulteration, a fold
ভাঁজন, দোমড়ান, পাট করণ, মিশান, ভুজন, স্বরভেদে গান করণ, to fold, (as cloth or paper,) to mix, adulterate, interpolate, &c. to vary notes in singing.
ভাঁজা, দোমড়া, পাট, a roll, fold. plait.
ভাঁজাল, মিশ্রিত, ভাঁজযুক্ত, আরোপিত, mixed, alloyed, adulterated, sophisticated, interpolated. [ebb.
ভাঁটা, লৌটি, বর্ত্তুল, আফাকল, স্রোত, a ball, marble, a weir, the
ভাঁড়, ভণ্ড, কৌতুকী, নর্ত্তক, প্রবঞ্চক, ক্ষুদ্র মৃৎপাত্র, a deceiver, impostor, juggler, buffoon, a pitcher.
ভাঁড়ান, ভুলান, ভেঙ্গান, to deceive, impose upon, mimick,&c.
ভাঁড়ামী, ভণ্ডামী, ফাকী, প্রবঞ্চনা, কৌতুক, বাজীকরা, imposition, swindling, deceitfulness, guile, mimickry, buffoonery, juggling. [sury.
ভাঁড়ার, ভাণ্ডার, গোলা. ধনাগার, a store-room, magazine, trea-
ভাঁড়ি, উহাড়, ক্ষুরকোষ, a case, a razor-case.
ভাঁতি, বিদ্রূপ. পরিহাস, derision, mockery, sport, jeering.
ভাক, অধীন, পোষ্য, কাল্পনিক, অন্নদাস, a dependant, one fed or maintained, a hypocrite; hypocritical, mercenary. [rise or after sun set.
ভাকদিন, সূর্য্যোদয়ের পূর্ব্বকাল, অস্তের পরকাল, the time before sun
ভাগ, অংশ, বণ্ট, বিক্রী, কপাল, রাশিচক্রের দ্বাদশাংশ, পলায়ন, a part, portion, share, part of a whole given as interest, partition, distribution, luck, fortune, a zodiacal degree, flight, running away,escape.
ভাগন, পলান, ভড়কন, to escape, run away, flee.
ভাগবত, বিষ্ণুপরায়ণ, পুরাণ বিশেষ, devoted to the service of Vishnu: a Vishnavite, a celebrated poem.
ভাগাড়, মৃত গো ত্যাগস্থান, a place where dead cows are cast.
ভাগাভাগি, অংশাংশি, সাজা, having equal shares; partnership.
ভাগিনী, ভাগিনেয়ী—ভগিনীর কন্যা,a sister's daughter, a niece.
ভাগিনেয়, ভাগিন্য,—ভগিনীপুত্র, a sister's son, a nephew.
ভাগী, কপালিয়া, অংশী, দায়ী, সাথী, fortunate, lucky, partaking with; a partner, sharer, shareholder, partaker in a succession, an accomplice, comrade.

ভাগীরথী, গঙ্গা নদী, the river Ganges.

ভাগোড়া, পলানিয়া, পলাতক, a fugitive, a deserter.

ভাগ্য, অদৃষ্ট, কপাল, শুভাশুভ, অংশনীয়, সবৃদ্ধি ঋণ, fate, destiny, good or ill fortune, chance, luck; to be shared or divided, &c. bearing interest.

ভাগ্যবান, ভাগ্যবন্ত.—অদৃষ্টবান, পয়োমন্ত, ধনী, ধনবান, fortunate, lucky, prosperous, wealthy.

ভাগ্যহীন বা শূন্য,—দুকপালিয়া, দুরদৃষ্টবান, নিরাশ, unfortunate, unlucky, wretched, hopeless.

ভাগ্যভাব, দৈব, কপালক্রম, দায়, the course of fortune, risk.

ভাগ্যভাবা, দায়ঠেকা, কপালঠাহরা, a risking, running a risk, venturing, trying one's fortune.

ভাগ্যভাবিয়া, দায়ে ঠেকিয়া, নির্ভর, running a risk, venturing.

ভাঙ্গ, মাদক পত্র বিশেষ, গঞ্জা, সিদ্ধি, hemp, the leaves of hemp used for smóking.

ভাঙ্গন, ফাটন, টুটন, দেউল্যা হওন, তোড়ন, খণ্ডন, নাশন, মিটান, চুকান, বিগড়ান, বিচ্ছেদ করণ, মুদ্রা ভোড়ান, বিবরিয়া লিখন, রচন, সূত কাটন, পাকান, বিনান, ঘাসাদি দলিয়া যাওন, to burst, break, crack, shiver, fail, become bankrupt, to break, demolish, destroy, dispel, interrupt, quash, put an end to, adjust, undo, deface, separate, to change money, reduce, (in arithmetic,) to compose, write a translation, compile, spin, twist, plait, to walk through long grass or mud, &c.

ভাঙ্গচি, মিত্রতা ভঙ্গ, সুহৃচ্ছেদ, চলনত্যাগ, the breaking off of friendship or of a habit.

ভাঙ্গড়, ভাঙ্গী,—গেঁজিয়াল, addicted to smoking hemp leaves; [a sot.

ভাঙ্গা, বিচ্ছেদ, খণ্ডনা, দুঃখী, খণ্ডিত, a rupture, breach, fracture; unfortunate, wretched, broken, fractured.

ভাঙ্গনি, কড়ি, কপর্দ্দক, পয়সা, change, small coin.

ভাঙ্গিখুরী, গেঁজ্যাল, stupified with hemp leaves; a sot.

ভাজক, হারক, a divisor, (in arithmetic.)

ভাজন, ভাওন, ঝলসান, পোড়ান, জ্বলান, খরাণ, অংশন, হরণ, to bake, fry, toast, parch, scorch, roast, inflame, caleine, to share, to divide, (in arithmetic.)

ভাজন্, পাত্র, বাসন, উপযুক্ত, নিপুণ, ভারযোগ্য, any vessel, cup, plate,&c. fit, trustworthy, clever, fit for office,&c.

ভাজনত্ব, ভারযোগ্যতা, fitness for office or trust.

ভাজ, জ্যেষ্ঠ ভ্রাতার স্ত্রী, an elder brother's wife.

ভাজ্য, অংশনীয়, অংশ, বণ্ট, খণ্ড, divisible, shareable; a dividend, share, portion.

ভাট, গুণগায়ক, রাজদূত, a panegyrist, a royal messenger.

ভাটা, নদ্যাদির দিবসিক জলহ্রাস, স্রোত, the ebb or reflux tide.

ভাটিয়ারা, মদ্য ভক্ষ্যদ্রব্যাদি ব্যবসায়ী, a sutler.

ভাটী, আকা, পাজা, উনন, স্রোত, a lime or brick kiln, furnace, still, the way the tide ebbs.

ভাটীবেলা, বৈকাল, the afternoon.

ভাড়া, কেরায়া, the rent of a house, the hire of a thing, a renting, hiring. [cenary.

ভাড়াটিয়া, কেরায়ী, বাসাড়িয়া, বৈতনিক, a renter, a tenant; mer-

ভাণ, কাচ, ব্যাজ, ছল, a trumped up story, a deception, imposition, pretence.

ভাণ্ড, পাত্র, বাসন, ভাঁড়, নদীর গর্ত্ত, মূলধন, বিদ্রূপ, ভাঁড়, কৌতুকী, a vessel, pitcher, pot, cup, plate, case, razor-case, the bed of a river, a capital, stock, mimickry, buffoonery, a professional jester.

ভাণ্ডার, ভাণ্ডাগার,—গোলা, দ্রব্যাগার, a store-house, magazine, store-room. [caterer, kitchen-steward.

ভাণ্ডারী, গোলার অধ্যক্ষ, ভক্ষ্যায়োজক, a store-keeper, butler,

ভাত, অন্ন, পাকা চাউল, boiled rice.

ভাতার, পতি, স্বামী, প্রতিপালক, a husband, maintainer, provider.

ভাতি, প্রভা, শোভা, brightness, splendour, resplendence.

ভাতী, অন্নসম্বন্ধীয়, অন্নের পরিবর্ত্তে প্রাপ্ত, pertaining to or exchanged for boiled rice.

ভাতুড়িয়া, ভাতুয়া,—অন্নদাস, one who serves for his food.

ভাদ্র-পদ, বর্ষার দ্বিতীয় মাস, the Indian month of the sun in Leo or the second of the rainy season.

ভাননিয়া, কুটনিয়া, one who husks rice in a mortar.

ভানন-আন, ধান কুটন, to pound or husk rice in a mortar.

ভানু, সূর্য্য, দীপ্তি, কিরণ, the Sun, light, a ray of light.

ভাপ, বাষ্প, steam, vapour, reek.

ভাপন, বাষ্পের উঠন, to reek. throw up steam, evaporate.

ভাপসাগন্ধ, হাতাপড়া, গুমসা, বাসি, mouldy, musty, fusty, stale.

ভাব হওয়া, স্থিতি, জন্ম, উৎপত্তি, জীবাত্মা, প্রাণী, বস্তু, বস্তুতা, প্রামাণ্য, সংসার, অবস্থা, দশা, স্বীয়ধর্ম্ম, স্বভাব, গুণ, চরিত্র, ব্যবহার, প্রকার, পদ, তাৎপর্য্য, ধাতুর অর্থ, অভিপ্রায়, মানস, চিত্তবিকার, কামক্রোধাদি, প্রেম, বিলাস, হাব, অসতীত্ব, চালি, গতি, ক্রিয়া, আত্মীয়তা, প্রণয়, অধ্যাপনা. বিভব, লক্ষণ, ব্যাধির বিসূচিকা, বাষ্প, existence, being, birth. production, the soul, a being, living thing, thing, substance, reality, probability, the world, a state, condition, circumstance, predicament, natural state, innate property, temperature, nature, disposition, conduct, usage, treatment, manner, station, office, meaning, the abstract idea of a word, scope, spirit, design, intention, purpose, a state or affection of the mind, emotion, passion, love, amatory sentiments or the corporeal expression of them, wanton sport, female infidelity, gesture, movement, motion, act, action, familiarity, intimacy, friendship, instruction, superhuman power, a sign, omen, symptom of disease, steam, reek.

ভাবক, বিলাস, গানে ভাবোত্থাপক, অঙ্গভঙ্গীকর, কামাদিশীল, the external expression of amorous sentiments, a singer who excites the passions, a gesticulator; susceptible, easily moved.

ভাবচোর, পদহর, a plagiary, plagiarist.

ভাবন, উদ্বিগ্ন হওন, চিন্তন, ভয় করণ, বিষাদ, ভূষণ, to be thoughtful, dejected, apprehensive or anxious, to ponder, think, meditate on, reflect, fear; dejection, anxiety, &c. adornment, decoration.

ভাবনা, উদ্বেগ, চিন্তা, সন্দেহ, ভয়, ঠাহরা, বিবেচনা, anxiety, care, disquietude, concern, apprehension, doubt, suspence, fear, cogitation, thought, contemplation.

ভাবরুণ, থরথর, to faulter through fear, to stagger, to be confused, amazed or discomposed.

ভাবরাণী, বিস্ময়, ঘবরাণী, বৈক্লব্য, amazement, confusion, discomposure, a stand, non-plus.

ভাবসাতে, স্থিরচিত্তে, অপ্রস্থানে, without confusion, readily.

ভাবান, পরিজ্ঞাপন, দোষপ্রমাণ করণ, উত্তাপন, বাষ্পোত্থাপন, to convict, to prove a charge, to hēat or steam.

ভাবার্থ, অভিপ্রায়, তাৎপর্য্য, a scope, object, purport.

ভাবিকল্প, প্রায় ভবিষ্যৎ, সম্ভব, almost or nearly future, likely.

ভাবিত, চিন্তান্বিত, উদ্বিগ্ন, বিষণ্ণ, খেদাদিযুক্ত, দোষীকৃ, সাভ্যস্থ, thoughtful, anxious, careful, solicitous, pensive, sad, affected, moved, convicted, proved.

ভাবী, যাহা হইবেক, বিধাতার নিয়ত, future, about to be, what is to be, ordained, predestinated.

ভাবুক, হওনশীল, শুভ, মঙ্গল, ভূত, উৎকর্ষ, কল্যাণ, উপকার, tending or disposed to be, happy, right; *in comp:* being, becoming what it was not before; excellence, happiness, welfare, advantage.

ভাবুকী, ভণ্ড, কৌতুকী, অঙ্গভঙ্গীকর, a comedian, actor, harlequin.

ভাবে, ন্যায়, অনুসারে, অভিপ্রায়ে, জন্যে, as, like, in the manner of, for, in the view of, to the end that.

ভাব্রী, তাড়না, ভয় দেখান, a threatening, terrifying, &c. [ing.

ভাব্য, বর্ত্তনীয়, ভবিষ্যৎ, probable, future, necessarily exist-

ভাম, ক্রোধ, ভগিনীপতি, বনবিড়াল বিশেষ, wrath, passion, anger, a sister's husband, a species of wild cat.

ভামিনী, প্রচণ্ডা, *f.* passionate, wrathful, indignant.

ভার, বহনীয় বস্তু, বোঝ, চাপ, শিকার দণ্ড, ক্ষমতার্পণ, কর্ম্ম, পদ, অনুমতি, আপদ, ঝঞ্ঝাট, কুমন্ত্র, বাণ, a load, burden, weight, a yoke or sling for carrying burthens, a charge, trust conferred, delegated power or authority, responsibility, office, station, consequence, permission, leave, trouble, difficulty, perplexity, malignant influence or incantation, an evil eye.

ভারণ, বাড়ান, গুরু হওন, চাপন, সমর্পণ, ভার দেওন, to augment, aggravate, be heavy or weighty, press heavily, to consign, commit, entrust, invest, refer, to throw responsibility or obligation on another.

ভারত, মহাকাব্য বিশেষ, ভণ্ড, the Mahábhárata, an actor, mime.

ভারতবর্ষ, জম্বুদ্বীপের খণ্ড বিশেষ, Hindustán or India proper.
ভারতী, বাণী, সরস্বতী, মনোরম্য কাব্যোল্লেখ. speech, the goddess of speech, eloquence, dramatic recitation, a quail.
ভারবাহ-ক, মুটীয়া, a bearer of burdens, a porter.
ভারা, মাচা, অন্যকে সৌঁপিয়া দেওয়া. a scaffold, scaffolding, reference, &c. [charge.
ভারাক্রান্ত, বোঝাযুক্ত. পদনিযুক্ত, loaded, entrusted with, in
ভারিক, মুটীয়া, ভারযুক্ত, a porter; bearing burthens, &c.
ভারী, দুর্বাহ্য, গুরু, স্থূল, বড়, ধীর, উদ্বিগ্ন, ভারবাহক, heavy, burdensome, weighty, lusty, big, momentous, serious, steady, sedate, sad; a porter.
ভারিবিক্রী, বহুমূল্যে বিক্রয়, পদুয়ে বিক্রয়, a selling high, wholesale.
ভারুই, পক্ষি বিশেষ, a quail. [of the Veds.
ভার্য্যা, পত্নী, জায়া, a wife espoused according to the ritual
ভাল, কপাল, কল্যাণ. উচিত, উৎকৃষ্ট, সরল, বিলক্ষণ, সুন্দর, শিষ্ট, সুসময়, শুভ, অরোগী, সুস্থ, উত্তম, স্বীকারবোধক শব্দ, হাঁ, the forehead, fortune, destiny, welfare, good; proper, right, excellent, good, honest, upright, neat, clean, handsome, elegant, pretty, genteel, gentle, fair, fine, (as weather.) convenient, favourable, pleasant, in health, well, recovered; well, well done, very well, do so, yes. [santness.
ভালই, উৎকর্ষ, সারল্য, excellence, goodness, honesty, plea-
ভালখেকুয়া, সুভোক্তা, ব্যয়শীল, luxurious, sumptuous.
ভালবাসন, উত্তম জানন, স্নেহ করণ, মনে ধরণ, to approve, like, love, accept, chuse, prefer. [goodness.
ভালাই, কল্যাণ, উপকার, উৎকর্ষ, welfare, advantage, excellence,
ভালাবুড়া, হিতাহিত. ইষ্টানিষ্ট, শুভাশুভ, good and evil.
ভালুক, ভালূক,—হিংস্র জন্তু বিশেষ, ঋক্ষ, a bear.
ভাশুর. পতির জ্যেষ্ঠ ভ্রাতা, a husband's elder brother.
ভাষণ, কথন, বলন, to speak, talk, tell, converse, utter.
ভাষা, কথা, সংস্কৃত ভিন্ন বাক্য. প্রাকৃত, a word, speech, language, vernacular dialect, current or vulgar tongue.
ভাষা-পত্র, প্রাকৃত বাক্যময় ন্যায়পত্র, a law plaint or other writing in the vulgar tongue.
ভাষাবাদ, বিতণ্ডা, বিবাদ, a dispute, suit at law, plaint, claim.

ভাষাবাদী, আজ্ঞাপী, বিবাদী, a plaintiff, a claimant.
ভাষাণ, কহিয়া পাঠান, to send to, to send a message.
ভাষী, বাদী, কথক, আলাপী, speaking, conversing.
ভাষ্য, টীকা, সুত্রের বিবরণ, a commentary, annotation, gloss.
ভাস, বাঞ্ছা, দীপ্তি, শোভা, শকুনি পক্ষী, a wish, desire, light, lustre, splendour, a vulture.
ভাসন, না বুড়িয়া জলের উপরে থাকন, সন্তরণ,উপ্চন, to float, swim, to overflow. [appearing, floating.
ভাসমান, দীপ্যমান, প্রকাশমান, জলের বহির্দিগস্থ, luminous, shining,
ভাসান, ওজান, নৌকাদিকে জলে নামান, সাঁতরাণ, বেগে বহিয়া উপড়ান, বুড়ান, to launch, set afloat, cause to float or swim, to bear down, (as a torrent,) carry away, deluge, to waste, spend lavishly.
ভাসানিয়া, বেগবান্, আপ্লাবক,উড়ানিয়া, sweeping, (as a flood or torrent,) profuse,lavish,wasteful,extravagant.
ভাস্কর, সূর্য্য, পাষাণছেদকারী, the sun, a stone-cutter, sculptor.
ভাসা, উপ্চনিয়া,কণ্ডূ আদি,বর্ষাকালে স্রোতাগত ধান্যাদিপূরিত নৌকা সমূহ, overflowing,&c. cutaneous,(eruption); vessels coming down the river, laden with corn, &c.
ভাসাকাল, বর্ষাকাল, the rains, the time when corn and other vessels arrive from the up-country.
ভাস্বর, ভাস্বান্,—দীপ্যমান, শোভান্বিত, সূর্য্য, shining, luminous, resplendent, illustrious; the sun. [mendicant.
ভিক্ষক, ভিক্ষুক,—যাচক, সন্যাসী, a beggar, petitioner, religious
ভিক্ষণ, যাচন, to beg, ask alms. [for relief.
ভিক্ষা, ভিক, যাচ্ঞা, alms, a request, a begging, a petition
ভিক্ষাচর, বা জীবী,—সন্যাসী, পরিব্রাজক, living on alms, leading a mendicant life. [city.
ভিক্ষাটন, ভিক্ষার্থে পর্য্যটন, to travel about begging; mendi-
ভিক্ষাভোক্তা বা ভোজী, যাচিতাহারী, feeding on alms.
ভিক্ষাশন, ভিক্ষাহার,—যাচকবৃত্তি, a feeding on alms, the eating of what is obtained by begging.
ভিক্ষু-ক, পরিব্রাজক, দণ্ডী, a religious mendicant.
ভিখারী, যাচক, কাঙ্গাল, a beggar, a mendicant; poor.
ভিজন, আর্দ্র হওন, চুপ্‌ষণ, to be wet, moist or soaked, to sink, (as paper.)

ভিজা, ভিগা,—আর্দ্র, সজল, wet, moist, damp, clammy, soaked.
ভিজান, ভিতান, to wet, moisten, soak, steep, slake.
ভিটা, ঘর, বাসস্থান, a house, a homestead.
ভিটামাটী, গৃহ নির্ম্মাণার্থে উচ্চীকৃত ভূমি, the raised floor of a house.
ভিড়, লোকসমূহ, ঘেরা, a crowd, mob, a fence, an enclosing.
ভিড়ন, নিকটে আইসন, মিলন, to approach, close with, visit.
ভিড়ান, লাগান, সাক্ষাৎ করাণ, মিলান, to bring a boat to shore, close with, bring near, cause to approach.
ভিত, কাঁথ, কুড়্যা, দিক্, a wall, thickness of a wall, a way, quarter, point of the compass. [interval.
ভিতর, মধ্যস্থল, অন্তর, the middle, midst, centre, inside, an
ভিতর, ভিতরে,—মধ্যে, between, within, amidst, in, into.
ভিতরী, আন্তরিক, সামিল, inner, inward, in, comprized.
ভিতে, কাছে, নিকটে, গোপনে, towards, to; aside, apart.
ভিত্তি, কুড়্যা, কাঁথ, বিচ্ছিত্তি, ছিদ্র, খণ্ড, টুকি, দোষ, ঘরের পোত, স্থান, আশ্রয়, সময়, a wall, breadth of a wall, a breaking, tearing, dividing, a rent, fissure, something broken, fragment, broken part, bit, flaw, defect, a part, place, asylum, opportunity, occasion.
ভিদন, ঢুকন, ফোড়ন, বিন্ধন, ভাঙ্গন, ছেদন, কাটন, বিদারণ, to penetrate, enter, pierce, run through, perforate, break off, separate, divide, split.
ভিন্ন, বিচ্ছিন্ন, বিদীর্ণ, চেরা, বিকসিত, পৃথক্, অন্য, অপর, ছিট, ব্যতিরেক, separated, divided, split, broken, torn, rent, open, blown, apart, asunder, parted, distinct, different, other; a fraction; else, besides, without, except. [differently, apart.
ভিন্ন২, পৃথক্২, গোপনে, distinctly, severally, separately,
ভিন্নতা, প্রভেদ, বিশেষ, a distinction, a difference.
ভিষক, চিকিৎসক, বৈদ্য, a physician, a doctor.
ভী, ভীতি,—আতঙ্ক, ত্রাস, fear, dread, terror, panic, alarm.
ভীত, ভীতু,—ভয়যুক্ত, ত্রস্ত, অসাহসী, afraid, terrified, alarmed, frightened, timid, shy, fearful, cowardly.
ভীম, ভয়ানক, দারুণ, ঘোর, ভয়, terrifying, terrific, dreadful, awful, frightful; fear, horror, terror.
ভীমরথী, অতিশয় বুড়ামী, dotage, extreme age, *i. e.* 77 years.

ভীমরুল, দংশক কীট বিশেষ, বরুলা, a hornet.

ভীরু-ক, ভীলু-ক,—ভয়শীল, অসাহসী, timid, fearful, cowardly, [pusillanimous.

ভীষণ, ভয় দেখান, ভয়ানক, to put in fear, alarm, terrify; horrible, frightful, fearful, terrific, perilous.

ভীষ্ম, শঙ্কা, ভয়ানকতা, শিব, ভূত, দারুণ, horror, terror, horribleness, the property of inspiring terror, &c. Shiva, a goblin; frightful, terrific, horrible.

ভুঁড়ি, উদর, অন্ত্র, আঁত্. the belly, the intestines

ভুঁড়িয়া, পেটাল, abdominous, pot-bellied, corpulent.

ভুক্, ভুখ্,—ক্ষুধা, আহারী, hunger; *in comp*: eating, feeding on.

ভুকা, ভুখা,—ক্ষুধিত, ক্ষধাতুর, ভোজনেচ্ছুক, hungry.

ভুক্ত, কৃতাহার, খাদিত, গিলিত, গ্রস্ত, প্রাপ্ত, অন্তর্গত, eaten, having eaten, devoured, swallowed, enjoyed, included, comprized.

ভুক্তত্যক্ত, ভুক্তাবশেষ,—উচ্ছিষ্ট, orts, leavings, remnants of a [meal.

ভুক্তন, মূলধন বাড়ান, মিশান, ভাঁজ দেওন, to add to a capital stock, or to what is paid off, to adulterate, interpolate, foist in.

ভুক্তভোগ, কর্ম্মবিপাক, কৃতভোগ, an enjoyment or suffering already experienced; having enjoyed or suffered.

ভুক্তি, আহার, উপভোগ, a meal, food, possession, occupation, usufruct.

ভুগন, ভোগ করণ, ভুলান, to suffer or enjoy, to deceive, [impose upon.

ভুগজমী, ভুলানি, ভণ্ডামী, swindling, imposition, hypocrisy.

ভুগ্ন, বিকলাঙ্গ, বক্র, অবনত, crooked, distorted, deformed, curved, bent, stooping.

ভুজ, বাহু, হস্ত, বাঁক, the arm, the hand, a bending, a [curve.

ভুজগ, ভুজঙ্গ, ভুজঙ্গম,—সর্প, a serpent, a snake.

ভুজঙ্গভোজী, ভুজগাশন, ভুজঙ্গভুক্,—ময়ূর, নকুল, গরুড়, a peacock, an ichneumon, Garura.

ভুজন, ভাঁজ দেওন, মিশান, to interpolate, foist in, adulterate.

ভুজনজাগন, শ্রবণে চমৎকৃত হওন, to be amazed as at some wonderful relation.

ভুজশিরস্, স্কন্ধ, the shoulder, the shoulder-blade.

ভুজা, ভোজ, আহার, জলপান, a meal, food, refection.

ভুঞ্জন, সুখভোগ করণ, to enjoy, to experience pleasure.

ভুঞান, নিমন্ত্রণ করণ, খাওয়ান, to treat, entertain, feast.
ভুট, উৎপাত, উপড়, বিনাশ, খণ্ডন করা, অন্যথা, উল্টাকরা, extirpation, wreck, perdition, subversion, reversion, a rescinding, inverting, upsetting.
ভুড়ভুড়, বিম্ব, ফুস্ফুসনি, a bubble, a bubbling, whispering.
ভুড়্ভুড়ান, বিম্ব উঠন, ফুস্ফুসান, to bubble up, to whisper.
ভুণন, ভাজন, ঝল্সান, সেকন, to broil, roast, bake.
ভুনি, ঠেটী, বিধবার বস্ত্র, a widow's garment.
ভুবন, জগৎ, বিশ্ব, জল, মানুষ, লোক, a world, sphere, heaven, the universe, water, mankind.
ভুবস্, অন্তরীক্ষ, আকাশ, the atmosphere, sky, æther.
ভুবর্লোক, ঋষ্যাদির স্থান, the heaven of the sages.
ভুয়া, শস্যরাহিত্য, চিটা, অসার, আন্তরিক, mildew, smut; mildewed, hollow, without substance, internal, (disease.)
ভুর-ভার, দাম্ভিকতা, গরিমা, a boast, boasting, swaggering.
ভুরভারী, দাম্ভিক, স্বপ্রকাশক, boasting, swaggering, ostentatious.
ভুরা, শর্করা বিশেষ, a sort of brown sugar.
ভুল, বিস্মৃতি, ভ্রম, চুক, মোহ, দোষ, কুহক, a forgetting, error, mistake, oversight, blunder, slip, transgression, fascination, deception.
ভুলন, চুকন, বিস্মৃত হওন, to mistake, omit, err, sin, forget.
ভুলা, চুকনিয়া, বিস্মারক, blundering, erring, forgetful.
ভুলান, ভ্রান্ত করণ, ভোগা দেওন, ফুসলান, ঠকান, to cause to err, misguide, mislead, delude, inveigle, tempt, seduce, flatter, cpax, fascinate, deceive, cheat.
ভুলানিয়া, ঠক, কুহকী, ধূর্ত্ত, a cheat, deluder, sorcerer; insidious, &c.
ভুক্কা, উমুই, মন্ত্রপাঠ, হুল, a spring of water, an incantation, [stratagem.
ভুসা, ঝুল, ধান্যাদি, soot, lamp-black, grain, corn.
ভুসী, যব গোধূমাদির ত্বক্, chaff, bran, husk; -দেওন, to interpolate; -যোগান, to bribe one to silence.
ভূ, পৃথিবী, স্থল, তলা, জন্মস্থান, বাসস্থান, তলাতল, the earth, land, ground, a place, scite, base, birth-place, residence, the lowest hell.
ভূঁই, ভূমি, ক্ষেত্র, land, ground, a field, plantation.
ভূকম্প, ভূচল,—পৃথিবীর স্পন্দন, an earthquake.

ভূগোল, মহীমণ্ডল the globe of theearth, geography.
ভূচর, স্থলচর প্রাণী, moving on land; a land animal
ভূজলচর, কচ্ছপ কুম্ভীরাদি, amphibious, living on land and water.
ভূত, যাহা হইয়াছে, অতীত, কৃত, প্রেত, পিশাচ, পরচ্ছায়া, প্রাণী, দেবাংশ, পৃথিবী আদি পাঁচ, সত্যবৃত্তান্ত, been, gone, past, become; a phantom, malignant spirit, ghost, goblin, demon, imp, apparition, vision, an existence, living creature, being, a class of demigods, the five elements, matter of fact or the real state of the case, (in law.)
ভূতকাল, অতীতকাল, the past time, (in grammar.)
ভূতগ্রস্ত, ভূতাবিষ্ট,—ভূতের বশীভূত, possessed of a demon or evil spirit. [demons.
ভূতড়িয়া, ভূতুড়িয়া,—ভূত ছাড়ানিয়া, expelling or casting out
ভূতনাথ, ভূতেশ,—অসুরপতি, শিব, Shiva as lord of the demons.
ভূতনীব, পেতনীব, অপরিচ্ছন্না, a slut, slattern; sluttish.
ভূতবৎ, প্রেতাকার, পেতনা, like an evil spirit, ugly; a sloven.
ভূতল, ভূমি, পৃথিবী, the ground, the earth.
ভূতাত্মা, জীবাত্মা, দেহ, শিব, ব্রহ্মা, the elementary or vital principle, the human body, Shiva, Brahmá.
ভূতাবেশ, ভূতের বশীভাব, possession by an evil spirit.
ভূতানুসার, ন্যায়প্রমাণ, an agreement with matter of fact.
ভূতি, সম্পত্তি, ঐশ্বর্য্য, অণিমাদি অষ্ট, জন্ম, উৎপত্তি, ভস্ম, affluence, wealth, success, grandeur, superhuman power, birth, production, ashes.
ভূতিমান্, ধনবান্, ঐশ্বর্য্যবন্ত, মহৎ, affluent, wealthy, grand.
ভূদকচর, ভূদকবাসী,—কচ্ছপ কুম্ভীরাদি, amphibious, living on land and water, as the tortoise, crocodile, &c.
ভূদেব, ব্রাহ্মণ, a brahmin, *i. e.* a terrestrial god.
ভূধর, পর্বত, গিরি, a mountain.
ভূপ, ভূপতি, ভূপালক,—পৃথিবীরক্ষক, রাজা, a king, sovereign, prince. [king, to govern.
ভূপালন, রাজত্ব করণ, দেশ শাসন, to perform the duties of a
ভূমি, পৃথিবী, মৃত্তিকা, ক্ষেত্র, স্থল, স্থান, দেশ, চাক্লা, the earth, earth, soil, land, ground, a scite, ground, base, a country, a district.

ভূমিকম্প, পৃথিবীর স্পন্দন, an earthquake. [theatrical dress.
ভূমিকা, আভাষ, ছদ্মবেশ, a preface, preamble, introduction,
ভূমিজ, পৃথিব্যোৎপন্ন, মহীরুহ, শাকাদি, মঙ্গল গ্রহ, earth-born; a vegetable, the planet Mars. [ist.
ভূমিজীবী, কৃষিলোক, প্রজা, living by the soil; an agricultural-
ভূমিপ, ভূমিপাল,—রাজা, মহীপতি, a king, sovereign, prince.
ভূমিশির, স্থল, স্থান, a spot of ground, situation, place.
ভূমিষ্ঠ, অষ্টাঙ্গ, প্রণত, জাত, prostrate, falling down to, born.
ভূমিস্পৃশ্, ভূতলস্পর্শক, মনুষ্য, বৈশ্য, কৃষক, গুপ্তচোর, অন্ধ, পঙ্গু. touching the earth; a man, mankind, a cultivator of the soil, a skulking thief, a blind man, a cripple. [peatedly.
ভূয়ঃ, বহুল, অধিক, পুনঃ২, much, many, exceedingly, re-
ভূয়োভূয়ঃ, বারম্বার, পুনঃ২, repeatedly, frequently, again & again.
ভূর-ভার, দাম্ভিকতা, গরিমা, a boast, a boasting, bragging.
ভূরি, বহু, অধিক, প্রচুর, বড়, গুরু, ভারি, much, long, many, abundant, excessive, important.
ভূর্জপত্র, বৃক্ষত্বক্ বিশেষ, the bark of a species of birch.
ভূলোক, পৃথিবী, মর্ত্ত্যলোক, the earth, the habitation of men.
ভূকা, জলাকর, মায়া, a fountain, a spring, an enchantment.
ভূষকা, ভূষণযুক্তা, অলঙ্কৃতা, *f.* wearing ornaments, &c.
ভূষণ, অলঙ্কারাদি ধরণ, বস্ত্রাদি সাজান, শোভন, to put on jewels, dress or ornaments, to decorate oneself, shine in finery, &c. [decoration.
ভূষণ, ভূষা,—অলঙ্কারাদি, a jewel, trinket, ornament, dress,
ভূষণীয়, শোভনীয়, capable of or requiring decoration, &c.
ভূষাণ, শোভান, সাজান, to adorn, deck, dress, trim, caparison. [bellished.
ভূষিত, অলঙ্কৃত, শোভিত, adorned, ornamented, decked, em-
ভূষী, তুষ, ছাল, ত্বক্, bran, chaff, a husk, integument.
ভূস্পৃঙ্মুখ, প্রণত, নম্রাস্য, prostrate, bowing down.
ভূস্পৃশ্, কৃষক, বৈশ্য, মনুষ্য, ভূতলস্পর্শক, a cultivator, man, mankind; touching the ground. [king.
ভূস্বামী, ভূমির অধিকারী, রাজা, a proprietor of land, landlord,
ভ্রূকুটি, ভ্রূভঙ্গ, a frown, contraction of the brows. [land.
ভৃগু, পর্ব্বতের ধার, পাতুক, গ্রহ, a precipice, mountain table

ভৃঙ্গ, ভ্রমর, বোল্‌তা, কলিঙ্গ পক্ষী, স্বর্ণময় পাত্র, লম্পট, the humble bee, a wasp, a sort of shrike, a golden vase, a lecher, a libertine.

ভৃঙ্গার, স্বর্ণময় ঘট, সুবর্ণ, লবঙ্গ, a golden vase, gold, cloves.

ভৃঙ্গারী, ভৃঙ্গারিকা,—ঝিঁঝিঁপোকা, ঝিল্লী, a cricket.

ভৃঙ্গী, ভ্রমরী, the female bee.

ভৃতি, জীবিকা, বেতন, মূলধন, nourishment, maintenance, wages, hire, a capital, principal sum. [vant.

ভৃতিভুক্‌, বেতনগ্রাহী, living on wages; a hireling, hired ser-

ভৃত্য, দাস, পরিচারক, পোষ্য বর্গ, a servant, slave, dependant.

ভৃত্যা, বেতন, ভরণ্য, wages, hire.

ভৃমি, বায়ুগ্রন্থি, ঝড়, পাকনা, শিরঃকম্প, a whirlwind, hurricane, eddy, whirlpool, giddiness. [ingly, &c.

ভৃশ, প্রচুর, অতিশয়, much, excessive, abundant; exceed-

ভৃষ্ট, ভাজা, ঝল্‌সান, baked, fried, parched.

ভেঁউচন, ভেংচন,—খিচন, পরিহসন, ভেঙ্গান, to make faces, mouth, grin, mock, ridicule.

ভেক, মণ্ডুক, মেঘ, ছদ্মবেশ, a frog, a cloud, a disguise, false appearance, play, pantomime, a religious habit.

ভেক্‌টী, ভেট্‌কী,—মৎস্য বিশেষ, a species of sable-fish.

ভেকী, ভণ্ড, ভাঁড়, মণ্ডূকী, a mime, actor, player, female frog.

ভেকুয়া, পশুবৎ, মূর্খ, simple, foolish; a simpleton.

ভেঙ্গ, মুখভঙ্গ, পরিহাস, ঠাট্টা, a mouthing, making faces, mocking, ridiculing, mimicry.

ভেঙ্গান, খিচন, বিদ্রূপ করণ, ঠাট্টা করণ, পরিহসন, to make faces, mouth, ridicule, mock, mimic.

ভেজন, প্রেরণ, রুদ্ধ করণ, to send, dispatch, shut, (as a door.)

ভেজান, পাঠান, রুদ্ধ করণ, পেঁচে ফেলন, ঠেকান, to send, shut, implicate in. [meeting.

ভেট, ভেটী,—উপঢৌকন, সাক্ষাৎ, a present at meeting, a

ভেটন, মিলন, সাক্ষাৎ করণ, to meet, visit, go to see.

ভেটনিয়া, মিলনিয়া, সাক্ষাৎকারী, meeting, visiting; one who meets another, a visitor.

ভেটা, সাক্ষাৎকরা, সন্দর্শন, a meeting, a visit.

ভেটিয়াল, স্রোতে বহান, going down with the tide. [ler.

ভেটীয়ারা, ভেটেরা,—ভক্ষ্যদ্রব্য মদ্যাদি বিক্রেতা, a sutler, a victual-

ভেড়ন, মিলন, নিকটে আইসন. পুনর্বিতর্কন, to meet, approach, visit, re-weigh, reconsider. [fellow.

ভেড়া, মেষ, মূর্খ, a sheep, a ram, a blockhead, a stupid

ভেড়ামী, মূর্খতা. stupidity, doltishness, sheepishness.

ভেড়ী, মেষী,জাঙ্গাল,সেতু, a ewe, a mound, dyke, embankment.

ভেড়ুয়া, কোটনা, a pander, a pimp.

ভেত্তব্য, বেধ্য, ভেদ্য, penetrable, divisible, distinguishable.

ভেত্তা, বিরোধী. বিবাদজনক. ধর্মত্যাগী, বিশ্বাসঘাতক, a factious or contentious person, a sower of dissension, a schismatic, a heretic, a traitor.

ভেদ, ছিদ্র, বেধ, পার্থক্য, বিদারণ, বিচ্ছেদ, বিবাদ, বিশেষ, প্রকার, তত্ত্ব, মর্ম. উদরভঙ্গ, গুপ্তপ্রকাশ, সন্ধান লওন, জ্ঞান, ভিন্ন, a perforation, penetration, piercing, incision, separation, dividing, rending, breaking, dispersion, disunion, disagreement, dissent, dissension, difference, dissimilarity, distinction, a kind, sort, species, a mystery, secret, a purging by stool, a divulging, reconnoitring, spying out, knowledge; else, besides.

ভেদক, ভেদজনক, বেধক, রেচক, ঠক, বিশেষণ, অপনাম, sowing dissension, &c. piercing, purgative; an incendiary, tale-bearer, an adjective, a nickname.

ভেদজ্ঞান, বিশেষবোধ, discrimination, kuowledge of differences or distinctions, &c.

ভেদজ্ঞানী, বিশেষ বোধক, discriminating, discerning individuality, viewing the gods as distinct.

ভেদন, বিন্ধন, ছেদন, ফোড়ন, খণ্ডন, চিরণ, বিদারণ, বিশেষ জানন, to pierce, bore, penetrate, transfix, break, rend, tear, divide, distinguish.

ভেদী, বেধক, বিশেষক, বিমত, চর, ঠক, খল, piercing, distinguishing, dividing, separating, dissenting; a spy, tell-tale, tale-bearer.

ভেবরণ, ভয় পাওন, থবরণ, to be alarmed or confounded.

ভেমরুল, বোল্‌তা, বরলা, a hornet.

ভেরী, লম্বা তুরী বিশেষ, a long trumpet.

ভেরেণ্ডা, ভেরাণ্ডা,—এরণ্ড বৃক্ষ, the castor shrub.

ভেলক, মাড়. মান্দাস, প্লব, a raft, a float.
ভেলা, বড়শা, শেল, প্লব, a dart, a lance, a raft, a float.
ভেল্‌কী, কুহক, মায়া, magic, sleight of hand, delusion.
ভেষজ, ভৈষজ্য,—ঔষধ, a drug, medicine, medicament.
ভৈক্ষ্য, ভিক্ষাসমূহ, a collection of alms.
ভৈরব, ভয়ানক, দারুণ, আতঙ্ক, শঙ্কা, শিবের ভয়ঙ্কর মূর্ত্তি, horrible, terrible, terrific, dangerous; horror, terror, a terrific manifestation of Shiva.
ভৈরবী, দুর্গা, স্ত্রী অবধূতা, Durgá or the terrible; a female devotee of Shiva.
ভৈরবীচক্র, স্ত্রী অবধূতার সম্প্রদায়, a society of female devotees [of Shiva.
ভোঁতা, নির্ধার, dull, (as a tool, &c.) not sharp.
ভোঁদড়, বেজী বিশেষ, a species of weasel or ichneumon.
ভোক্‌ছানি, অনাহারে ক্ষীণতা, ক্লিষ্টতা, a famished condition, inanition, extreme faintness.
ভোক্তা, খাদক, পেটুক, ফলভুক, স্বামী, an eater, glutton, one who suffers or enjoys, a husband.
ভোগ, সুখ দুঃখের অনুভব, ফলগ্রহণ, অন্ন, পক্বনৈবেদ্য, pleasure, enjoyment or suffering, possession, use, usufruct, occupancy, food, an offering of dressed food.
ভোগগৃহ, অন্তঃপুর, the haram or female apartments.
ভোগদেহ, শরীর, the body as the seat of enjoyment or suffer- [ing.
ভোগন, সুখ দুঃখানুভব করণ, মিলন, পাওন, to enjoy or suffer, undergo, to possess, obtain, get.
ভোগবৎ, সুখজনক, মনোহর, yielding enjoyment, pleasurable.
ভোগবতী, পাতালের গঙ্গা, the infernal Ganges or river of hell.
ভোগবান্, সুখদুঃখাস্বাদক, ফলভোজী, ফলভুক্, বিশিষ্ট, নর্ত্তক, গায়ক, enjoying, suffering, seized of, occupying, possessing, dancing, singing.
ভোগস্থান, শরীর, অন্তঃপুর, the body as the seat of sensual enjoyment or suffering, women's apartments.
ভোগা, ফাকী, ছল, চার, লোভ, কৌশল, a deception, imposture, cheat, snare, bait, temptation, lure, stratagem.
ভোগান, ভোগ করাণ, ভুলান, ফুসলান, to cause to enjoy or suffer, to mislead, deceive, &c.
ভোগিনী, রাজার উপপত্নী, a king's concubine.

ভোগী, সুখদুঃখানুভূত, বিষয়সুখাসক্ত, সর্প, enjoying, possessing, suffering, sensual ; a snake.

ভোগ্য, খাদ্য, সুখদুঃখের বিষয়, ফলভোগের বিষয়, eatable, to be enjoyed or suffered, pleasurable, to be followed by enjoyment or suffering.

ভোগ্যা, বেশ্যা, ঢেমনী, a harlot, a whore, a concubine. [ver.

ভোগ্যাধি, পরোপকারার্থে কৃত বন্ধক, a loan to the use of the recei-

ভোজ, আহার, ফলার, a meal, feast, banquet, treat.

ভোজন, ভক্ষণ, আহার, to eat ; act of eating, food. [food.

ভোজনীয়, ভোজ্য,—খাদ্য, ভক্ষ্য, eatable, edible, proper for

ভোজবিদ্যা, ভেল্‌কী, কুহক, legerdemain, sleight of hand, magic.

ভোজয়িতা, নিমন্ত্রণকারী, প্রতিপালক, an entertainer, host, supporter of others. [gods, provision, &c.

ভোজ্য, দেবোদ্দেশে দেয় তণ্ডুলাদি, offerings of corn, &c. to the

ভোজ্যসম্ভব, অন্নরস, খাদ্য, chyle or digested food ; eatable.

ভোজ্যান্ন, ভক্ষণীয় দ্রব্য,একান্ন, eatable; food, a table-companion.

ভোট, রাঙ্গা কম্বল বিশেষ, a sort of red blanket from Bhotan.

ভোড়ঙ্গ, তূরী, তরণী বিশেষ, a trumpet, a kind of boat.

ভোড়ঙ্গিয়া, তূরীবাদক, a trumpeter; blowing the trumpet.

ভোতা, ত্বক্, ছাল, নির্ধার, a peel, rind, tegument ; blunt, dull, obtuse. [pot.

ভোমর, মধুমক্ষিকা, ভুরপণ, a bee, an auger, drill, a watering-

ভোমা, মূর্খ, পক্ষ্ম, foolish, stupid, ignorant ; the eye-lashes.

ভোর, প্রাতঃকাল, প্রত্যূষ, the morning, the dawn ; early.

ভোলা, বিস্মারক, সন্দিগ্ধমনাঃ, forgetful, sceptical.

ভৌতিক, ভূতসম্বন্ধীয়, অলৌকিক, অদ্ভুত, পঞ্চভূতনির্ম্মিত, প্রপঞ্চ, শিব, relating to evil spirits, supernatural, demoniacal, elemental, material ; Shiva.

ভৌম, মঙ্গলগ্রহ, পার্থিব, ভূমিসম্বন্ধীয়, the planet Mars, ambergris; earthly, terrestrial, of or belonging to land.

ভৌমিক, ভূমিজ, ভূমির, ভূস্বামী, produced from the ground, belonging to land ; a landholder. [mory.

ভ্যাকান, অভ্যাস করণ, মনে রাখণ, to study, commit to me-

ভ্রংশ, অধঃপতন, দুষ্টতা, নষ্টামি, ধ্বংস, a fall, a fall from virtue, depravity, ruin, loss, destruction.

ভ্রুকুটি, ভ্রূভঙ্গী, a frown, contraction of the brows.

ভ্রম, চুক, ভুল, ঘূর্ণি, পাকনা, বায়ুগ্রন্থি, কুঁদ, চক্র, পর্য্যটন, আদর, a misconception, error, mistake, blunder, oversight, slip, forgetfulness, a whirling or going round, an eddy, whirlpool, whirlwind, a turner's lathe, a potter's wheel, a roaming, wandering, respect, credit, reputation.

ভ্রমণ, বেড়ান, ঘুরণ, চুকন, ফেরা, যাত্রা, to wander about, roam, ramble, traverse, take the air, perambulate, turn round, whirl, err, mistake; a tour, turn, circuit, ramble, voyage.

ভ্রমণী, পর্য্যটনিয়া, travelling, wandering, roaming, roving.

ভ্রমবিশিষ্ট, চুকনিয়া, mistaken, erroneous, mistaking, &c.

ভ্রমর, ভ্রমরী,—ষট্‌পদ, মধুকর, *m. & f.* the large black bee.

ভ্রমি, ঘূর্ণি, আবর্ত্ত, ঘূর্ণবায়ু, কুঁদ, চক্র, শিরঃকম্প, মূর্চ্ছা, ভুল, চুক, a whirling or going round, an eddy, whirlpool, whirlwind, a lathe, potter's wheel, vertigo, dizziness, giddiness, fainting, a swoon, stupor, forgetfulness, error, mistake.

ভ্রমী, ঘুরণিয়া, নাস্তিক, whirling, revolving, &c. a sceptic.

ভ্রষ্ট, দুষ্ট, বিগড়িত, লম্পট, মন্দ, নষ্ট, ধস্ত, পদচ্যুত, ভাজা, fallen from virtue, depraved, corrupted, dissolute, vicious, deflowered, defiled, ravished, violated, seduced, obscene, degraded, deposed, fallen from office, displaced, superseded, parched, baked, roasted, fried, toasted.

ভ্রষ্টক, বলাৎকারী, নষ্টকর, a ravisher, defiler, violator, corrupter.

ভ্রষ্টপনা, নষ্টতা, অসম্ভ্রম, depravity, a fallen state, degradation.

ভ্রষ্টা, ব্যভিচারিণী, কুলটা, an adultress, a strumpet, a violated or dissolute female.

ভ্রষ্টাচার, দুষ্টব্যবহার, বিধর্ম্ম, depraved conduct, heterodoxy in religion.

ভ্রষ্টামি, দুষ্টামি, নষ্টতা, depravity, pollution, villainy, vice.

ভ্রষ্টাশঙ্কা, জারাশঙ্কা, jealousy of a wife.

ভ্রাজক, পিত্ত, পিত্তরস, bile, the bilious humour.

ভ্রাজিষ্ণু, শোভান্বিত, বিভ্রাট্, ধৃতভূষণ, splendid, shining, gaudy, elegant in dress, &c. decorated with ornaments.

ভ্রাতা, ভ্রাতৃ—এক পিতৃজাত, a brother, friend, kin, kindred.

ভ্রাতুষ্পুত্র-ী, ভ্রাতৃপুত্র-ী, ভ্রাতার তনয়-া, *m. & f.* a brother's son and daughter. [of a brother.
ভ্রাতৃজ, ভ্রাতৃজা,—ভ্রাতার পুত্রপুত্রী, *m. & f.* the son or daughter
ভ্রাতৃব্য, ভ্রাতার তনয়, রিপু, a brother's son, an enemy.
ভ্রাত্রীয়, ভ্রাতুষ্পুত্র, ভ্রাতার উপযুক্ত, a brother's son ; a brother's, brotherly, fraternal. [roving.
ভ্রান্ত, ভ্রমযুক্ত, চুকনিয়া, পর্য্যটক, mistaken, erring, deceived,
ভ্রান্তি, ভ্রম, ভুল, মায়া, মিথ্যাদৃষ্টি, অজ্ঞানতা, পর্য্যটন, error, mistake, blunder, delusion, ignorance, a roving, roaming, wandering about, &c.
ভ্রামক, ভ্রমজনক, ছলী, শৃগাল, চুম্বকপাথর, causing error, occasioning mistake, &c. a cheat, rogue, a jackal.
ভ্রূ, নেত্রের ঊর্দ্ধলোমশ্রেণী, the eyebrows.
ভ্রূকুটি,—বিতুষ্টি বোধক দৃষ্টিপাত, a frown, look of displeasure, forbidding aspect. [wards.
ভ্রূক্ষেপ, বিকট দৃষ্টিপাত, কটাক্ষ, a frown, a glance, a look to-
ভ্রূণ, গর্ভস্থপ্রাণী, a fœtus, embryo, unborn child.
ভ্রূণঘ্ন, ভ্রূণহা,—গর্ভনাশক, পেট্খসাকারক, causing abortion, destroying the fœtus. [abortion.
ভ্রূণহত্যা, গর্ভনাশকরা, a destruction of the fœtus, procured
ভ্রূভঙ্গ-ী, বিতুষ্টি বোধক দৃষ্টিপাত, a frown, contraction of the brows.

ম.

মই, সিড়ী, বাঁশই, a ladder, a species of harrow.
মউড়, মুকুট, a marriage crown or diadem.
মওন, মন্থন, আলোড়ন, to churn, to agitate a liquid
মকর, জলজন্তু বিশেষ, দশম রাশি, কুবেরের ধন বিশেষ, ছলনা, ফাকী, an imaginary marine monster representing the sign Capricorn, one of Cuvera's treasures, deceit, deception.
মকরকেতন, মকরধ্বজ,—কন্দর্প, the Indian Cupid, whose emblem is the foregoing animal.
মকরন্দ, পুষ্পরস, মধু, ভ্রমর, কোকিল, মল্লিকা বিশেষ, মৃণাল, the nectar of a flower, a bee, the Indian cuckoo, a species of jasmine, the filaments of a lotus.

মকরালয়, সমুদ্র, সাগর, the ocean. [head-dress.
মকুট, কিরীট, চূড়া, শিরোভূষা, a crown, diadem, tiara, crest,
মকুল, প্রকাশোন্মুখ কলিকা, কুঁড়ী, an opening bud.
মক্ষিকা, মাছী, সপক্ষ কীট, a fly, any winged insect.
মখ, যজ্ঞ, যাগ, sacrifice, oblation.
মগ্ন, ডুবিত, বুড়া, sunk, immersed, plunged, dived, drowned.
মঘা. দশম নক্ষত্র, the tenth lunar mansion.
মঙ্গল, কল্যাণ, কুশল, ভাগ্য, তৃতীয় গ্রহ, সর্বার্থ রক্ষণ, শুভ, সুখদায়ক, প্রসন্ন, welfare, prosperity, happiness, good, good-fortune, a propitious act, the planet Mars, carefulness, prudence; fortunate, prosperous, lucky, happy, propitious, auspicious.
মঙ্গলকর, শুভকর, হিতকারী, doing good, beneficent, benevolent.
মঙ্গলগাওন বা বাদন,—পরকল্যাণে সুখপ্রকাশ কথন, to congratulate, to felicitate. [thanksgiving.
মঙ্গলবাদ, পরকল্যাণ প্রার্থনা, শুভবাক্য, well-wishing, felicitating,
মঙ্গলবার, তৃতীয়বার, Tuesday.
মঙ্গলাচরণ, ঘৃতধারাদি, কর্ম্মারম্ভে কর্ত্তব্য শুভজনক ক্রিয়া, শুভবাক্য, the ornamenting of a place with garlands on festive occasions, festivity, a preliminary ceremony, an invocation, religious action, congratulation, good wishes.
মঙ্গল্য, শুভকর, প্রসন্ন, সুখদায়ক, মনোহর, পুণ্য, পবিত্র, auspicious, propitious, conferring pleasure or happiness, pleasing, beautiful, agreeable, pious, pure.
মঙ্গলৈষী, হিতৈষী, পরশুভেচ্ছুক, benevolent; a well-wisher.
মচ্‌কন, বেঁউচন, মোচড়ন, চিরণ, to be wrenched, strained, sprained, bent, torn or injured by violence. [&c.
মচ্‌কান, মোচড়ান, বেঁউচান, to wrench or pull violently, strain,
মজন, মজ্জন,—অবগাহন, ডুবন, বুড়ন, দুঃখগ্রস্ত হওন, নিবিষ্ট হওন, to bathe, sink, be immersed, plunge, dip, to be drowned, be overwhelmed with trouble, &c. to be wholly taken up with.
মজান, মজ্জান,—ডুবান, বুড়ান, ভাসান, ক্লেশন, to immerse, plunge, dip, sink, drown, overwhelm with trouble, &c. afflict, distress, destroy.

মজ্জা, অস্থির মধ্যগত ধাতু, বৃক্ষের সার বা রস, marrow, pith, sap.
মজ্জাগত, আন্তরিক, মর্ম্মপীড়ক, inward, latent, affecting the marrow.
মজ্জাভেদী, মর্ম্মপীড়ক, দুঃসহ্য, touching the quick, insupportable.
মঞ্চ, মাচা, ভারা, কুঁড়িয়া, পর্য্যঙ্ক, শয্যা, খাট, a raised stage, platform, pulpit, scaffold, an elevated shed, a table, bedstead, bed.
মঞ্জন, মার্জ্জন, পুঁচন, মিসি, নেত্রমলহারক দ্রব্য, to cleanse, clean, scour; a tooth-powder, dentifrice, eye-salve.
মঞ্জরণ, মুকুলন, গজান, to bud, put forth buds or leaves.
মঞ্জরী, শিষ, পুষ্পগুচ্ছ, অঙ্কুর, মুকুল, an ear of corn, a flower-spike, flower-stalk, a shoot, sprout, a branch-bud.
মঞ্জিষ্ট, মঞ্জিষ্ঠা,—লতা বিশেষ, মণ্ডূকপর্ণী, Indian madder.
মঞ্জীর, নূপুর, a female ornament for the feet, an anklet.
মঞ্জুল, সুন্দর, মনোজ্ঞ, beautiful. agreeable, pleasing.
মটর, কলায় বিশেষ, a pea, peas. [petticoat.
মটরাসাড়ী, বিচিত্র পট্টবস্ত্র, a spotted silk garment worn as a
মটুক, কিরীট, শিরোভূষা, a crown, diadem, head-dress, &c.
মট্‌কা, তৃণগৃহের পৃষ্ঠদণ্ড, বৃহৎ মৃন্ময় জালা, the ridge of a thatched house, a large earthen jar.
মট্‌কামারণ, ছলনিদ্রা দেখান, to sham or feign sleep. [shampoo.
মট্‌কান, গ্রন্থি ভাঙ্গন, অঙ্গ টিপন, to snap or crack the joints, to
মঠ, টোল, পাঠশালা, সন্ন্যাসিরদের বাসগৃহ, মন্দির, a college, school, monastery, temple, pagoda.
মড়ক, মারী, সমুদায় দেশ ব্যাপক ঔৎপাতিক রোগ, a pestilence, mortality, epidemic disease.
মড়ল, মণ্ডল, গ্রামের প্রধান প্রজা, the head-man of a village.
মড়া, শব, মর্ত্ত্য, মৃত, a dead carcase, corpse; mortal. dead.
মড়াকামড়ি, অন্তক দংশকরা, অধ্যবসায়, অতিশয় ক্লেশ দেওয়া, উদ্বেজনা, a mortal bite, pertinacious perseverance at all hazards, a teazing, dunning. [born child.
মড়াঞ্চিয়া, অল্পদিবস প্রসব হইয়া মৃতপুত্রী, *f.* having lost her new-
মড়্‌কচা, তৃণগৃহের পৃষ্ঠদণ্ড, the ridge of a thatched house.
মড়্‌কা, মড়্‌মড়ীয়া,—ঠুন্‌কা, টুসুক, brittle, fragile, rigid.
মণি, রত্ন, মরকত প্রবালাদি বহুমূল্য প্রস্তর, মুক্তা, পোঁচা, সূচ্যগ্র, a gem, jewel, precious stone, pearl. the wrist, the clitoris, the glans penis, the point of a needle.

মণিকর্ণিকা, কাশীর অন্তর্গত কুণ্ড বিশেষ, a holy pool at Benares.
মণিকার, রত্নজীবী, রত্নপরিষ্কারক, a jeweller, gem-cutter, lapidary.
মণিপূর, নাভি, স্ত্রীলোকের রত্নযুক্ত অঙ্গরাখা বিশেষ, দেশ বিশেষ, the navel, a sort of woman's boddice studded with gems, the country of Manipoor.
মণিবন্ধ, হাতের পোঁচা, the wrist.
মণিমন্দির, বহুমূল্য প্রস্তরযুক্ত গৃহ, a temple or house of gems.
মণিহারী, রত্নজীবী, গহনাব্যবসায়ী, রত্নচোর, a jeweller, seller of toys and trinkets, a stealer of gems.
মণ্ড, মাড়, যূষ, লেই, rice-water, gruel, paste, starch.
মণ্ডন, জড়ান, মোড়ন, অলঙ্কার, গহনা, to overlay with metal, gild, plate, cover with leather or cloth: ornament, decoration, jewels, trinkets, &c.
মণ্ডপ, উৎসবকালীন অতিথিশালা, তৃণাদি নির্ম্মিত দেবগৃহ, a temporary shed at festivals, an open temple.
মণ্ডল, বর্ত্তুল, গোল, সূর্য্যচন্দ্রের বিম্ব, পরিবেশ, চক্রবাল, চক্র, বেড়, চাকলা, ব্যূহ বিশেষ, সমূহ, রাশি, চক্রাকার কুষ্ঠ, বড়ী, গ্রামের প্রধান প্রজা, a ball, globe, sphere, orb, disk, a halo, the horizon, a wheel, circle, circumference, a province, district, region, a circular form of military array, a multitude, assemblage, quantity, heap, a round spotted leprosy, a sweet-meat ball, the head-man of a village.
মণ্ডলী, সমাজ, সমূহ, an assembly, congregation, a body of people, society, gang, flock.
মণ্ডা, বড়ী, a sort of sweet-meat balls. [comfits, &c.
মণ্ডী, অতিক্ষুদ্র গোলাকার মিষ্টান্ন বিশেষ, a smaller sort of the same,
মণ্ডূক-কী, ভেক ভেকী, বর্ষাভূ, বর্ষাম্বী, *m. & f.* a frog.
মণ্ডূর, লৌহমল, খাদ, rust of iron, dross, scoriæ.
মত, ধারা, প্রকার, ধর্ম্মপথ, পক্ষ, ব্যবহার, রীতি, অভিপ্রেত, মনস্থ, ন্যায়, a way, method, mode, manner, sort, kind, set of opinions, creed, system, doctrine, sect, habit, practice, manner of thinking or acting, purpose, wish, intention; similar, like.
মতভেদ, সম্প্রদায়, অভিপ্রেতের পার্থক্য, a distinct sect, a schism.
মতমত, একমত, of one mind, of one sect.

মতান্তর, ভিন্ন রীতি, অন্যথা, অন্যপ্রকার, another sect or method, &c. alteration; altered, otherways. [tary.

মতাবলম্বী, পক্ষপাতী, ধর্ম্মাশ্রয়ী, পন্থী, a follower, partizan, sec-

মতামত, স্বীকৃতাস্বীকৃত, গ্রাহ্যাগ্রাহ্য, the sentiments received and rejected, distinct opinions; approved and disapproved, liked and disliked.

মতামতি, স্বীকার অস্বীকার, বিভিন্ন মত, মতভেদ, approbation and disapprobation, diversity of sentiments.

মতি, অনুমান, বোধ, বুদ্ধি, জ্ঞান, প্রবৃত্তি, মুক্তা, opinion, understanding, intellect, mind, conscience, intelligence, judgment, will, inclination, desire, a pearl. [brained.

মতিচ্ছিন্ন, মতিছন্ন,—হতবুদ্ধি, ক্ষিপ্ত, deranged, delirious, cracked-

মতিমান্, বুদ্ধিমান, বিবেকী, wise, reflecting, sensible, judicious.

মতী, পন্থী, সম্প্রদায়, পক্ষ, a sect, party. [formably with.

মতে, রীত্যনুসারে, ধারায়, according to, agreeably to, con-

মত্ত, মাতাল, বিভোল, হর্ষিত, ব্যগ্রমনাঃ, উৎকট, গর্ব্বযুক্ত, কামাসক্ত, বিক্ষিপ্তচিত্ত, গর্ব্বিত, মোহযুক্ত, intoxicated, drunk, overpowered with joy, delighted, enthusiastic, eager, in rut, furious, proud, lewd, &c. mad, insane, foolish, raging, infatuated.

মৎসর, পরশ্রীকাতর, কৃপণ, দ্বেষ, মশা, envious, covetous, niggardly; envy, rancour, a gnat, musquito.

মৎস্য, মাছ, মীন, a fish, an avat'ar of Vishnu.

মৎস্যণ্ডিকা, ফেণী, উথাড়, কন্দ, coarse sugar, sugar-candy.

মৎস্যরঙ্গ, মাছরাঙ্গা পক্ষী, the kingfisher.

মথন, মন্থন, আলোড়ন, to churn, agitate violently, stir up.

মথিত, আলোড়িত, নির্জ্জল ঘোল, churned, &c; butter-milk.

মদ, মদ্য,—মত্ততাজনক পেয় বস্তু, সুরা, মত্ততা, ক্ষিপ্ততা, মোহ, ব্যগ্রতা, হর্ষ, কামক্রোধাদি, দর্প, মত্ত হস্তির গণ্ডনিঃসৃত রস, wine, spirit, intoxication, drunkenness, insanity, infatuation, enthusiasm, delight, pleasure, joy, desire, passion, pride, arrogance, a liquor flowing from the temples of an elephant in rut.

মদক, নিদ্রাকর ঔষধ, ময়রা, a narcotic medicine, an opiate, a confectioner.

মদকল, মত্ততাপ্রযুক্ত অস্পষ্ট কথক, গর্জ্জিত হস্তী, speaking inarticulately through drunkenness; an elephant in rut.

মদন, কন্দর্প, ঋতু. Cámadeva the Indian Cupid, the spring.

মদনশলাকা, কামজনক ঔষধি, a provocative medicine.

মদনা, সুরা, সারী পক্ষিণী, wine, spirits, a species of parrot.

মদপাতা, মদপায়ক,— মাতাল, সুরাপানকর্ত্তা, a drinker of wine or spirits, a drunkard.

মদসার, পুনঃ২ ক্ষরিত সুরা. highly rectified spirits, alcohol.

মদিরা, মদ্য—দ্রাক্ষারস, সুরা, wine, spirituous liquors.

মদিরাগৃহ, মদ্যগৃহ,—গঞ্জা, a tavern, a spirit or dram-shop.

মদীয়. মৎসম্বন্ধীয়, আমার, নিজ, my, mine, my own.

মদোদ্ধত, মত্ত, মদপানে বিহ্বল, মাতাল, overcome by liquor, intoxicated.

মদ্যজীবী, শুণ্ডী, সুরাদি ব্যবসায়ী, a wine-seller, vintner, tavern-keeper.

মদ্যপ, সুরাপায়ী, মাতাল, a sot, tippler, toper, drunkard.

মদ্যপঙ্ক, ক্ষরয়িতব্য পিটাযুক্ত সুরা, fermented liquor ready for distillation.

মদ্যবীজ, মদ্যপাকজনক দ্রব্য বিশেষ, a drug used to assist fermentation.

মদ্যমণ্ড, সুরাভাগ, মদের ফেণ, yeast, barm, froth.

মদ্যশালা, গঞ্জা, a tavern, a dram or liquor-shop

মধু, মৌ, পুষ্পরস, সুরা বিশেষ, চৈত্র মাস, honey, the nectar of flowers, a sort of wine, the month Chaitra.

মধুকর, ভ্রমর, নায়ক, মিঠানেবু. a bee, a lover, the sweet lime.

মধুকোষ, মৌচাক, ছাগমুষ্ক, a beehive, a honeycomb, a goat's testicles.

মধুধাতু, স্বর্ণমাক্ষিক, a sort of Pyrites, honey-stone.

মধুধৃৎ, পুষ্পরসাধার, the nectary of a flower.

মধুনাপিত, মদক, ময়রা, a confectioner.

মধুপ, মধুমক্ষিকা,—ভ্রমর, মৌমাছী, a bee.

মধুপর্ক, মধুযুক্ত দধি ত্যাগ, a religious offering of curds and honey.

মধুময়, সুস্বাদু, সুরস, মিষ্ট, honeyed, mellifluous, sweet.

মধুমল্লী, বেলফুল, the double jasmine.

মধুযষ্টিকা, যষ্টিমধু, মিষ্টরসযুক্ত কাষ্ঠ বিশেষ, liquorice-stick.

মধুর, মিষ্ট, প্রিয়, আলাপী, মৃদু, সুশ্রাব্য, মিষ্টতা, গুড়, sweet, pleasing, agreeable, courteous, mellifluous, melodious; sweetness, syrup, treacle.

মধুরাণ, মিঠান, to sweeten, to make sweet.
মধুসূদন, কৃষ্ণ, Krishna as destroyer of the giant Madhu.
মধ্য, মাজ, অন্তর, ভিতর, অন্তরালস্থান, গানের ছেদ, মাঝারী তাল, কক্কাল, ঘোটকের কক্ষদেশ, দশ মহাশঙ্খ, the middle, midst, centre, inside, an interval, common time in music, a rest, a sort of metre, the waist, a horse's flank, ten thousand billions.
মধ্যনিম্ন, মাঝে চাপান গোলাকৃতি, concave, hollow in the centre.
মধ্যবর্ত্তী, মধ্যস্থ,—অন্তরস্থিত, অন্তর্গত, অভ্যন্তর, মাঝের, পঞ্চ, ব্যবহর্ত্তা situated between, within, included, inward, internal, central; a mediator, arbitrator, umpire.
মধ্যবিত্ত, উৎকৃষ্ট হইতে ন্যূন, অপকৃষ্ট হইতে উত্তম কিম্বা অধিক, মাঝারী, পরিমিত, চলিত, সাধারণ, অনাত্যন্তিক, মধ্যস্থ, middling, moderate, temperate, indifferent, ordinary, customary, not deep in colour: an umpire.
মধ্যবিধ, অনাত্যন্তিক, মাঝারী, সামান্য, অধম নয় উত্তম ও নয়, of a middling sort, common, middling.
মধ্যম, মধ্যস্থাপিত, অন্তর্গত, মাঝারী, সামান্য, middlemost, central, included, intermediate, middling, moderate, temperate, ordinary.
মধ্যমা, মধ্যা,—অনামিকা ও তর্জ্জনীর অন্তরস্থিত অঙ্গুলি, ঋতুমতী কন্যা, the middle finger, a girl arrived at puberty.
মধ্যরাত্র, অর্দ্ধনিশা, দুইপ্রহর রাত্রি, নিশীথ, midnight.
মধ্যলোক, পৃথিবী, মর্ত্ত্যলোক, the earth, the dwelling of mortals.
মধ্যস্থ, মধ্যস্থিত,—মাঝের, অভ্যন্তর, অন্তরালস্থাপিত, central, middle, inward, intervening, interposing. [terstice.
মধ্যস্থল-ী, মাঝার, অন্তর, অন্তরাল, the centre, inward part, an in-
মধ্যস্থতা, পাঞ্চাৎ, বিরোধনিষ্পত্তি, সমাধা, mediation, arbitration.
মধ্যাপসারী, মণ্ডলের মধ্যস্থানত্যাগী, চক্রের মধ্যস্থল হইতে ভ্রমণশীল, flying off from the centre, centrifugal.
মধ্যাভিসারী, মণ্ডলের মধ্যস্থানাভিমুখে আকর্ষিত, চক্রের মধ্যস্থানে পতনশীল, tending to the centre, centripetal.
মধ্যাহ্ন, দিনের দুই প্রহর বেলা, mid-day, noon; *adj:* mid-day.
মধ্যে, মাঝে, ভিতরে, অন্তরে, সাথে, in the midst, within, between, in, among.
মধ্যে২, কখন২, now and then, sometimes, occasionally.

মধ্বাসব, মধুক কল্ক নিঃসারিত সুরা, a sort of spirituous liquor.

মন, চল্লিশ সের, a weight of 40 seers.

মন, মনঃ,—চিত্ত, বুদ্ধি, মতি, স্মৃতি, অন্তঃকরণ, প্রবৃত্তি, the mind, understanding, memory, conscience, heart, inclinations. [guish.

মনঃপীড়া, ভাবনা, চিন্তা, চিত্তশূল, inquietude, pain of mind, an-

মনঃপূত, প্রশস্তচিত্ত, শুদ্ধান্তঃকরণ, প্রবৃত্ত, pure in heart, conscientious, inclined to. [comfort.

মনঃপ্রবোধ, নিশ্চয়জ্ঞান, ভরসা, conviction of mind, assurance,

মনঃশিলা, মঞ্ছাল, red arsenic.

মনন, মন দেওন, সাবধান হওন, স্বীকরণ, চিন্তন, ঠাহরণ, ভাবন, to mind, attend to, regard, admit, think of, reflect; thought, exercise of mind, reflection.

মনসা-দেবী, বিষহরী, the goddess of serpents.

মনস্কাম-না, অন্তঃকরণের প্রবৃত্তি, চিত্তবাসনা, the desire of the mind, the wish of the heart.

মনস্কার, চর্চ্চা, মনের মধ্যে সুখদুঃখ বোধ, reflection, consciousness of pleasure or pain. [sorrow, remorse.

মনস্তাপ, চিত্তপীড়া, খেদ, দুঃখ, অনুশোক, distress of mind, grief,

মনস্থ, চিত্তবর্ত্তী, চেষ্টা, অভিপ্রায়, বাঞ্ছা, situated in the mind; a thought, design, intention, wish, inclination.

মনস্বী, বুদ্ধিমান, সাবধান, শুদ্ধান্তঃকরণ, intelligent, wise, attentive, pure-minded. [slowly.

মনাক্, ঈষৎ, অল্প, সূক্ষ্ম, মন্দ, a little; minutely, tardily,

মনীষা, বুদ্ধি, পাণ্ডিত্য, the understanding, intellect, wisdom.

মনীষী, মতিমান, প্রাজ্ঞ, পণ্ডিত, wise, intelligent, learned.

মনু, স্বয়ম্ভুবাদি চতুর্দ্দশ, মন্ত্র বিশেষ, a Manu or president of the universe, the first Manu the Indian legislator, creator of the world and progenitor of mankind; a mystical verse or incantation.

মনুজ, মনুজা,—পুরুষ এবং স্ত্রী, *m. & f.* a man, a woman.

মনুষ্য, পুরুষ, ব্যক্তি, লোক, a man, person, mankind, people.

মনুষ্যত্ব, পুরুষত্ব, সৌজন্য, manhood, manliness, humanity.

মনুষ্যভক্ষক, নরমাংসাহারী, রাক্ষস, feeding on human flesh; a cannibal. [sense of honor.

মনোবাদ, বিতুষ্টি, প্রতাপ, অভিমান, dissatisfaction, jealousy, high

মনোজ্ঞ, সুন্দর, কান্ত, প্রিয়, রমণীয়, beautiful, lovely, engaging.

মনোনিবেশ, অবধান, চিত্তসংযোগ, আবেশ, অভ্যাস, ব্যগ্রচিত্ত, fixed attention, devotedness of mind, close study, a zealous entering into a scheme, &c. ardour.

মনোনীত, মনোমত,—মনের অভিলষিত, বাঞ্ছিত, বিশিষ্ট, গ্রাহ্য, approved, chosen, choice, satisfactory.

মনোব্যথা, চিত্তপীড়া, মান, প্রতাপ, pain of mind, grief, jealousy.

মনোভঙ্গ, ধ্যানভঙ্গ, পণ্ডশ্রম, মান, বিভূতি, interruption of thought, frustration of a design, a pet, anger.

মনোময়, প্রাজ্ঞ, দীর্ঘদর্শী, intelligent, prudent, wise.

মনোযুক্ত, আবিষ্ট, সাবধান, ব্যগ্রচিত্ত, engaged in, devoted to, attentive, zealous, ardent in a pursuit.

মনোযোগ, প্রণিধান, আবেশ, সাবধানতা, devotedness of mind, application, attention. [devoted to.

মনোযোগী, সাবধান, আবিষ্ট, ব্যগ্রচিত্ত, attentive, earnest, zealous,

মনোরঞ্জন, পরিতোষ প্রদান, সন্তোষ, মিষ্টান্ন, to give pleasure, to gratify; gratification, sense of pleasure, a sweetmeat.

মনোরথ, বাসনা, ইচ্ছা, স্পৃহা, a wish, desire.

মনোরম, মনোরম্য,—উৎকৃষ্ট, সুন্দর, রমণীয়, pleasant, agreeable, charming, pleasing, beautiful, lovely, inviting.

মনোহর, মনোহারী,—কান্ত, সুন্দর, চারু, রমণীয়, বিমোহন, beautiful, lovely, amiable, engaging, enticing, winning, heart-ravishing, captivating.

মন্তব্য, বিবেচিতব্য, বিচারণীয়, মান্য, জ্ঞেয়, গ্রাহ্য, to be discussed, to be reflected on, minded or regarded, cognizable, admissible. [sage.

মন্তা, মন্তৃ,—অমাত্য, পরামর্শদ, প্রাজ্ঞ, an adviser, counsellor,

মন্ত্র, দেবতার সাধন গুপ্তকথা, গুরুপ্রণীত জপোপদেশ্য বাক্য, কুহকার্থ বর্ণসমূহ, a mode of religious invocation, a form of prayer, a formula sacred to any particular deity, a text of the Veda, a mystical verse or incantation, a charm.

মন্ত্র, মন্ত্রণা,—চাতুর, ঐকমত্য, গুপ্তবাদ, পরামর্শ, যুক্তি, secret consultation, conspiracy, private advice, instigation, persuasion, counsel, advice, policy.

মন্ত্রজ্ঞ, কুহকী, অমাত্য, acquainted with charms; an adviser, &c.

মন্ত্রণীয়, যুক্তিসিদ্ধ, মন্ত্রপাঠে বশীকরণীয়, বিবেচনীয়, advisable, requiring the use of charms, &c. demanding consideration, deserving of consultation.

মন্ত্রদাতা, গুরু, a spiritual preceptor or initiator.

মন্ত্রিত, মন্ত্রপাঠে সাধিত, পরামৃষ্ট, consecrated by religious formula, advised, counselled.

মন্ত্রী, পরামর্শদাতা, রাজপাত্র, অমাত্য, ধীসচিব, a counsellor, adviser, monitor, a king's minister, statesman.

মন্থজ, নবনীত, মাখন, produced from churning; butter.

মন্থন, মওন, আলোড়ন, ঘোঁটান, to churn, agitate violently, stir up, to agitate in conversation; a churn.

মন্থর, ঢীলা, অলস, মূঢ়, স্থূল, প্রকাণ্ড, বৃহৎ, slow, tardy, lazy, dull, stupid, large, bulky.

মন্থান, মন্থনদণ্ড, ঘাগরী, a churning-stick.

মন্দ, কদর্য্য, অপকৃষ্ট, অধম, অমঙ্গল, দুর্ভাগ্য, দুষ্ট, ভ্রষ্ট, দুরন্ত, নির্লজ্জ, খল, অপরিষ্কৃত, অলস, ঢিমা, ধীর, মৃদু, অনুষ্ণ, জড়, অপটু, মূর্খ, রোগী, অল্প, অমুজ্জ্বল, ধীরে, শনৈঃ, শনি, bad, evil, vile, sad, sinister, unlucky, infamous, scandalous, vicious, wicked, immodest, shameless, mischievous, nasty, dirty, idle, lazy, tardy, dull, sluggish; slow, gentle, mild, slow as a tune, cold, phlegmatic, stupid, foolish, ill, sick, little, small, dim; gently, slowly; Saturn.

মন্দজুয়ার, মরাকটাল, the neap-tides.

মন্দটান, অল্পভাটা, মৃদু স্রোত, slack-water, a slow and gentle stream.

মন্দবাসন, ঘৃণা করণ, হেয় জানন, to dislike, disapprove, detest, hate.

মন্দবাসনা, বিতুষ্টি, ঘৃণা, হেয়জ্ঞান, dislike, disgust, disesteem, hatred.

মন্দ২, কুৎসিতরূপে, শনৈঃ২, in a bad manner, ill, slowly.

মন্দর, পর্ব্বত বিশেষ, a fabulous mountain.

মন্দর-স্থান, নাভির এবং বুকস্থলের মধ্যদেশ, the space between the breast and the navel.

মন্দা, সুমূল্য, মৃদু, অল্প, অকর্ম্মণ্য, cheap, slow, slack, little, worthless.

মন্দাকিনী, স্বর্গগঙ্গা, the celestial Ganges.

মন্দাক্ষ, হ্রী, লজ্জা, modesty, bashfulness, shame-facedness, shame.

মন্দাগ্নি, অজীর্ণ, অপাক, a slow or bad digestion, indigestion.

মন্দাদর; অনবধান, অমর্য্যাদক, negligent, inattentive, disrespectful;
মন্দার, দেবতরু, পারিজাত বৃক্ষ, one of the trees of Paradise, the coral-tree. [ham.
মন্দির, দেবালয়, মঠ, গৃহ, হর্ম্য, a temple, pagoda, house, the
মন্দিরা, বাদ্য বিশেষ, করতাল, a cymbal. [cal, tapering.
মন্দিরাকার, করতালবৎ, শুণ্ডাকৃতি, cymbal-shaped, convex, coni-
মন্দুরা, অশ্বশালা, a stable for horses.
মন্দে, ধীরে, শিথিলে, ঢীলায়, slowly, sluggishly, feebly.
মন্দোদরী, আসন বিশেষ, a species of fine mat.
মন্মথ, কন্দর্প, প্রেম, Cámadeva or the Indian Cupid, love.
মন্বন্তর, আকাল, দেব পরিমাণে একাত্তর যুগ, a famine, dearth, a period of time or the reign of a Manu.
মন্যত, সম্মত, স্বীকৃত, অনুযায়ী, agreeing, consenting to, conformable to.
মন্যমান, বিবিচ্যমান, under consideration or observation, &c.
মন্যু, শোক, বিতুষ্টি, ক্রোধ, আক্রোশ, sorrow, regret, vexation, dislike, anger, resentment, an imprecation.
মম, আমার, পরিষ্কৃত মৌচাক, my, mine; bee's wax.
মমকার, স্বীয়বোধ, স্বীয় করা, appropriation, claim.
মমতা, স্বকীয় জানা, অত্যন্ত প্রণয়, আত্মীয় গণের উপরে স্নেহ, দয়া, মায়া, অভিমান, appropriation, attachment to a thing as one's own, relative kindness or clemency, love or affection to one's own family, &c. pity, pride, arrogance. [made of.
ময়, পূর্ণ, বিশিষ্ট, আত্মক, *affix:* full, fraught, possessed or
ময়না, পক্ষি বিশেষ, the mocking-bird, the Mina.
ময়রা, মদক, মিঠাইকর, a confectioner.
ময়লা-টিয়া, সমল, অপরিষ্কৃত, foul, unclean, dirty, filthy.
ময়ান, রুটির স্ফীতিজনক রস বিশেষ, leven.
ময়ূখ, কিরণ, প্রভা, শোভা, অগ্নিশিখা, ছায়াঘড়ির কাঁটা, a ray, light, lustre, brightness, beauty, flame, a gnomon.
ময়ূরী, ভুজঙ্গভুক, বর্হিণী, *m. & f.* a peacock, peahen.
ময়ূরারি, কৃকলাস বিশেষ, a chameleon, a lizard.
মরক, মারী, বহুলোক ব্যাপিয়া প্রাণঘাতক রোগ, contagion, infectious or epidemic disease, plague, mortality.
মরকত, হরিন্মণি, an emerald or perhaps a yellow topaz.

মরণ, প্রাণবিয়োগ, পঞ্চত্বপ্রাপ্ত হওন, বাটন, শুকিয়া যাওন, ঘা মুদন, death; to die, expire, perish, fail, decrease, wither, dry up, heal or close as a wound.

মরা, মৃত, শুষ্ক, শব, তাঁবার, dead, &c. a corpse, dead carcase, base metal or coin. [of corn.

মরাই, গোলা, ধান্যাগার, a granary, storehouse, magazine

মরাটিয়া, নিস্তেজ, worn out (soil,) impoverished, poor, stunted.

মরাধার, ভোঁতা, অতীক্ষ্ণ, blunt-edged, dull, not sharp.

মরামাংস, মরামাস,—চামড়ী, scurf, scruff, dandruff.

মরাল, মৃদু, কোমল, ধূর্ত্ত, দুষ্ট, অশ্ব, মেঘ, অঞ্জন বিশেষ, soft, mild, bland; a rogue, a scoundrel, a horse, a cloud, a collyrium of lamp-black.

মরিচ, তীব্ররসযুক্ত বর্ত্তিক বীজ বিশেষ, ধর্ম্মপত্তন, black-pepper.

মরীচি, কিরণ, কৃপণ, ব্যয়কুণ্ঠ, a ray of light, a niggard, a miser.

মরীচিকা, সূর্য্যকিরণে জলভ্রম, the mirage or delusive appearance of a sheet of water in a sandy soil. [&c.

মরীচিমালা, সূর্য্যাদির কিরণমণ্ডল, a circle of rays round the sun,

মরীচিমালী, কিরণমণ্ডলী, সূর্য্যচন্দ্র, the sun or moon.

মরু, অত্যন্ত জলকষ্ট দেশ, অনুর্ব্বরা, poor (soil,) unfruitful, barren, impoverished. [wind.

মরুৎ, বায়ু, পশ্চিমোত্তর কোণের অধিপতি, wind, air, the god of

মরুৎকোণ, পশ্চিমোত্তর কোণ, the North-west quarter.

মরুৎক্রিয়া, ফুকীছাড়া, বাতকর্ম্ম, the breaking of wind backwards.

মর্কট, বানর বিশেষ, কপি, মাকড়সা, হাড়গিলা, a monkey or ape, a spider, the Indian crane.

মর্চ্যা, লৌহমল, কলঙ্ক, মলা, কিট্ট, rust. [rusty.

মর্চ্যাধরা, মর্চ্যাপড়া,—সমলা, কলঙ্কযুক্ত, কিট্টিয়া, covered with rust,

মর্ত্তব্য, নশ্বর, অনিত্য, পাঞ্চভৌতিক, mortal. [kind, the earth.

মর্ত্ত্য, পঞ্চভূতাত্মা, মনুষ্য গণ, পৃথিবী, mortal, earthly; man, man-

মর্ত্ত্যপুর, মর্ত্ত্যলোক,—পৃথিবী, নরধাম, the earth as the residence or habitation of mortals.

মর্দ্দন, ভঞ্জন, বাটন, পিষণ, মাখন, বুনন, শস্য মলন, দলন, পরাস্ত করণ, to grind on a stone; pound in a mortar, bruise, to crush, rub in an ointment, stroke with the hand, to thresh corn, to trample, tread down, to subdue an enemy.

মর্ম, অস্থি, অঙ্গযোগ, অন্তঃকরণ, সারভাগ, গুপ্তকথা, তত্ত্ব, যোগার্থ, অভিপ্রায়, প্রয়োগ, হেতু, প্রয়োজন, বিষয়, a joint, the heart, core, essence, any vital part, member or organ, a secret, secret meaning or purpose, essential doctrine, signification, application, sense, purport, scope, spring, cause, account, personal interest or concern in a thing.

মর্মজ্ঞ, সুপণ্ডিত, তত্ত্বজ্ঞ, ভেদজ্ঞ, চর, profoundly learned, versed in essential doctrines, knowing secrets ; a spy.

মর্মভেদ, মর্মাবিদ্ধ, আন্তরিক দুঃখ দেওয়া, গুপ্তজ্ঞান, সুহৃদ্ভেদ করা, আত্যন্তিক তাড়না, a penetrating or touching to the quick, a penetrating into secrets, the sowing of dissension, severe reprehension. [marble.

মর্মর, শুষ্ক পুষ্পপত্রাদির শব্দ, the rustling of dry leaves, &c.

মর্মস্থান, শরীরের মধ্যে যে স্থানের অল্প আঘাত করাতে অত্যন্ত ব্যথা অথবা মৃত্যু হয়, অঙ্গযোগস্থল, মর্ম্ম, a vital or mortal part.

মর্মস্পৃক্, মর্মাগত, অত্যন্তপীড়াদায়ক, ব্যথাজনক, অরুন্তুদ, touching the vital parts, wounding or touching to the quick, giving pain, corrosive, keen, sharp.

মর্মাধীন, সুগুপ্ত, kept inviolably secret, lodged in the breast.

মর্মান্তিক, আন্তরিক, অন্তক, মর্মাগত, mortal, deadly, wounding or affecting a vital part, stinging to the quick.

মর্য্যাদক, সম্মানপ্রদ, শিষ্ট, shewing honor or respect, civil, polite.

মর্য্যাদা, সম্মান, সম্ভ্রম, সীমা, সদাচার, ধৈর্য্য, respect, honor, esteem, reputation, rank, dignity, a boundary, limit, rectitude, propriety of conduct, steadiness.

মর্য্যাদান্বিত, সম্ভ্রান্ত, honorable, respectable, esteemed.

মর্ষ-ণ, সহিষ্ণুতা, patience, kindness, endurance, resignation.

মল, অসারভাগ, মর্চ্যা, পিটা, বিষ্ঠা, খলি, মর্কাদি, অপরিষ্কার, অশৌচ, কলঙ্ক, পাদভূষণ, filth, dirt, rust, dregs, dross, sediment, excrement, any animal secretion as earwax, sweat, rheum, &c. a soil, defilement, an ornament for the ancles.

মলকা, কুঁড়া, খাদ, the refuse of rice after sifting, dross.

মলঘ্ন, অশুচিহর, পরিষ্কারক, filth-destroying, cleansing:

মলঙ্গী, বৈতনিক লবণকর, a labourer employed in making salt.

মলজ, পূঁজ, ক্লেদ, produced from filth ; pus, matter.
মলন, ঘর্ষণ,মার্জন, মর্দ্দন, to rub, smear, to wipe, furbish, to grind, to thresh, to pull as the ear.
মলনিয়া, শস্যমর্দ্দনিয়া, a corn-thresher.
মলবদ্ধ, কোষ্ঠবদ্ধ, শৌচরোধ, বিসূচিকা, costive ; costiveness.
মলমাস, মলিম্লুচ,—অধিমাস, an intercalary month.
মলম্বা, স্বর্ণমণ্ড,সোণাজল,the gilding of a picture or of furniture.
মলয়, পর্ব্বত বিশেষ, তন্নিকটবর্ত্তি দেশ, উদ্যান, the western Gháts; Malabar, a garden, the garden of Indra.
মলয়জ, মলয় পর্ব্বতে জাত অর্থাৎ চন্দন, sandal-wood.
মলয়ানিল, মলয়পর্ব্বতাগত বায়ু, দক্ষিণ দিকের বায়ু, the south wind blowing from the Gháts in Central India.
মলা, সমল, অপরিষ্কৃত, কিট্‌কিটা, কলঙ্ক, গাদ, খাদ, মর্চ্যা, unclean, dirty, sordid, squalid; filth, sediment, dregs, scum, slag, dross, rust.
মলাছাড়ান, মলাকাটন,—শুধরাণ, to refine, clear, clarify.
মলিন, মলাযুক্ত, অশুদ্ধ, কিট্‌কিটা, মর্চ্যাধরা, শুষ্ক, বিরস, ফিকা, কালিত, ম্লান, উদ্বিগ্ন, যোলাটিয়া, পাপযুক্ত,পাপী, foul, filthy, dirty, sullied, squalid, rusty, tarnished, faded, sallow, sunburnt, sad, melancholy, sorrowful, turbid, wicked, vile, sinful.
মলিনমুখ, পাপিষ্ঠ, ক্রূর, নিষ্ঠুর, ম্লানবদন, বিরসবক্ত্র, অগ্নি, ভূত, কপি বিশেষ, vile, wicked, cruel, savage, ferocious, hard-featured, of a sad countenance, crest-fallen; Agni,a goblin,ghost, the black-faced monkey.
মলুক, ক্রিমি বিশেষ, a kind of worm.
মলূকা, খুদ, the broken remains of rice after sifting.
মল্ল, বাহুযুদ্ধে নিপুণ, a scuffler, wrestler, boxer.
মল্লযুদ্ধ, মল্লক্রীড়া,—বাহুযুদ্ধ,a scuffle, wrestle, wrestling match.
মল্লিকা, বেলফুল, the Arabian jasmine. [bag.
মশক, চর্ম্মনির্ম্মিত জলাধার, a large leathern bottle or water-
মশক, মশা,—দংশক কীট, a musquito, a gnat.
মশহরী, মশারি,—মশানিবারণার্থ বস্ত্রাবরণ, musquito-curtains.
মসী, কালী, ink for writing. [ing; a scribe, writer.
মসীজীবী, লেখক, কেরাণী, কায়স্থ, supporting himself by writ-
মসীনা, অতসী বৃণ, উমা, ক্ষুমা, linseed, flax.

মসীপ্রসূ, মস্যাধার, কালীপাত্র, লেখনী, an ink-stand, a pen.
মসূর, কলায় বিশেষ, a species of pulse or lentil.
মসূরিকা, বসন্ত রোগ, ক্ষুদ্র গদি, the small-pox, a small cushion.
মস্করা, ভণ্ড, বিদ্রূপী, a jester, buffoon, sporter with foibles.
মস্করামী, মস্করাপণা,—ভণ্ডামী, buffoonery, jesting, sporting, &c.
মস্তক, মাথা, শিরঃ, অগ্র, শৃঙ্গ, the head, top, crown, point, peak.
মস্তিষ্ক, মস্তকের মজ্জা, the brain.
মস্তু, দধির জল, whey, the watery part of curds.
মহৎ, মহা,—বৃহৎ, স্থূল, বড়, ভারী, ভগবান্, শ্রেষ্ঠ, প্রসিদ্ধ, উত্তম, অতিশয়, আত্মা, great, large, bulky, important, sublime, chief, noble, illustrious, good, excellent, opportune, much, very; the intellectual principle.
মহতী, নারদের বীণা, বেগুন, Nárada's lute, the egg-plant.
মহত্ত্ব, মহত্তত্ত্ব,—শ্রেষ্ঠতা, ভদ্রতা, greatness, perfection, urbanity, condescension.
মহত্প্রাণ, শূদ্রকে ভূমির করত্যাগ, a remission of the land tax to [Shúdras, &c.
মহন, মন্থন, আলোড়ন, to churn, to agitate violently.
মহর্লোক, পারকালিক সুখস্থান, a celestial region or paradise.
মহর্ষি, শ্রেষ্ঠ মুনি, a great sage.
মহাশল্ক, মহাশল্ক,—চিঙ্গড়ি মৎস্য, a prawn or shrimp.
মহাকায়, বৃহৎ শরীরবিশিষ্ট, প্রকাণ্ডশরীর, large-bodied, gigantic.
মহাকাল, শিবের মূর্ত্তি বিশেষ, Shiva the destroyer, eternity.
মহাঘোর, অতিশয় অন্ধকার, নরক বিশেষ, great gloom or darkness, a division of the Hindoo hell.
মহাজন, সাধু, উত্তম লোক, বেণ্যা, উত্তমর্ণ, a great or excellent man, a merchant, banker, money-lender.
মহাজনী বাণিজ্য, ঋণদানবৃত্তি, trade, commerce, money-lending.
মহাজ্ঞানী, সুপণ্ডিত, আত্মজ্ঞ, ব্রহ্মজ্ঞ, very wise, having the knowledge of spirit.
মহাতল, পঞ্চম নরক, the fifth hell in descent.
মহাত্মা, দানশীল, প্রতাপবান, মহাশয়, ভবান্, generous, noble-minded, magnanimous; Sir, your honor.
মহাদেব, মহাদেবী,—শিব এবং দুর্গা, *m.* & *f.* Shiva and Durgá.
মহাধন, বহুমূল্যের বস্ত্রাদি, সুবর্ণ, ধূপ, কৃষিকর্ম্ম, any thing costly, costly apparel, gold, incense, agriculture.
মহান্, প্রধান, বড়, প্রকাণ্ড, great, eminent, important, vast.

RRR

মহানস, পাকস্থান, a kitchen, cook-room.
মহানাদ, অতিশয় শব্দ, ঘোর মেঘের ধ্বনি, সিংহ, হস্তী, a loud sound, a large dark cloud, a lion, an elephant.
মহানিদ্রা, মৃত্যু, death, dying, decease, the last sleep.
মহানিশা, অৰ্দ্ধরাত্র, midnight, the dead of night.
মহানুভব, দানশীল, প্রতাপবিশিষ্ট, liberal, magnanimous, high-minded.
মহাপথ, রাজমার্গ, সুপথ, মৃত্যু, a high road, principal street, an excellent way, death or the way of all flesh.
মহাপথগামী, মরণোদ্যত, going the long journey, *i. e.* dying.
মহাপা, ডুলী, দোলা, a litter, a dooly or light palanquin.
মহাপাতক, মহাপাপ,—ব্রহ্মহত্যাদি পাঁচ, a great crime, heinous offence, mortal sin.
মহাপাতকী, মহাপাপী,—ব্রহ্মহত্যাদি দোষযুক্ত, guilty of a mortal sin or great crime.
মহাপুরুষ, সাধু লোক, প্রধান ব্যক্তি, a saint, a sage, a high personage, a great man, a nobleman.
মহাপ্রভু, পুণ্যাত্মা, রাজা, শিব, a saint or holy man, a king, Shiva.
মহাপ্রলয়, কল্পান্ত, বিশ্বনাশ, a periodical destruction of the world, an entire annihilation of the universe.
মহাবল, বলবান্, তেজস্বী, মল্ল, strong, powerful ; a wrestler.
মহাবাক্য, প্রণব, ওঁকার, the mystical syllable Om.
মহাবিষুব, সূর্য্যের মেষ রাশি সঞ্চার, the vernal equinox.
মহাবীর, বিলক্ষণ শূর, সিংহ, গরুড়, বিষ্ণু, a great hero, a lion, Garura, Vishnu, &c.
মহাভূত, মৃত্তিকা, বায়ু, অগ্নি, জল, আকাশ, এইপঞ্চ, the five primary elements.
মহামনস্ক, দানশীল, liberal, munificent, magnanimous.
মহামহিম, অতিশয় মহিমান্বিত:শ্রেষ্ঠ, noble, most excellent, eminent.
মহামায়া, অনাদি অবিদ্যা, অসার সংসার, দুর্গা, worldly or material illusion, Durgá.
মহামূল্য, দুর্মূল্য, মহার্ঘ, পদ্মরাগ মণি, very costly, precious; a ruby.
মহাযজ্ঞ, অধ্যাপনাদি পঞ্চ যজ্ঞ, the five essential sacrifices.
মহারথ, বাসনা, বৃহৎ যান বিশেষ, a wish, desire, a large car.
মহারাজ, প্রধান রাজা, আপনি, a great king ; Sir, your honor, your excellency, your majesty.
মহারাজাধিরাজ, সম্রাট, চক্রবর্ত্তী, a great king, a king of kings.
মহারাত্র, অর্দ্ধরাত্র, দুইপ্রহর রাত্রি, midnight, deep night.
মহারৌরব, নরক বিশেষ, one of the divisions of Hell.

মহার্ঘ-্য, দুর্মূল্য, বহুমূল্য, dear, high-priced, precious, costly.
মহালয়, পরমব্রহ্ম, আশ্রয়, তীর্থ, God as the supreme refuge, a sanctuary, asylum, a place of pilgrimage.
মহালয়া, ভাদ্রী অমাবস্যা, the day of the change in Bhádra.
মহাশঙ্খ, ললাট, মনুষ্যাস্থি, কপালাস্থি নির্ম্মিত মালা, সহস্র খর্ব, the forehead, a human bone, a necklace of the bones of the forehead, 1000 billions.
মহাশয়, গৌরবান্বিত, আপনি, a gentleman, respectable person; Sir, your honor, master. [great courage.
মহাসাহস, অত্যাচার, অসীম সাহস, a great outrage, violent assault,
মহাসাহসিক, অত্যাচারী, বিক্রমী, দৌরাত্ম্যকারক, লুটনিয়া, দস্যু, daringly outrageous, daring, violent; an assaulter, violator, plunderer, robber.
মহাসুখ, মৈথুন, copulation.
মহিমা, মহত্ত্ব, ঐশ্বর্য্য, greatness, grandeur, dignity, glory.
মহিলা, সামান্যা স্ত্রী, মায়া, a woman, a female.
মহিষ, বয়ার, a buffalo. [to a buffalo.
মহিষা, বয়ারজাত, বয়ারসম্বন্ধীয়, produced from or belonging
মহিষী, স্ত্রী মহিষ, রাজপত্নী, রাজার অভিষিক্তা স্ত্রী, a female buffalo, a crowned queen. [gle, &c.
মহী, পৃথিবী, ভূমি, the earth, the ground, base of a trian-
মহীভুজ, মহীপাল,—রাজা, নরপতি, a king, a sovereign.
মহীরুহ, বৃক্ষ, গাছ, a tree, a vegetable.
মহীলতা, কেঁচুয়া, কিঞ্চুলুক, an earthworm, a worm.
মহু, মধু, মৌ, honey. [generous, liberal.
মহেচ্ছ, মহাত্মা, প্রতাপশালী, দাতা, magnanimous, highminded,
মহেন্দ্র, স্বর্গপতি, পর্বত বিশেষ, Indra the ruler of Swarga, the Northern Gháts.
মহেশ, মহেশ্বর,—শিব, Shiva [assembly of Vishnuvites.
মহোৎসব, বৈষ্ণব সমারোহের ভোজন, a great festival, a feast at an
মহোদধি, সাগর, সমুদ্র, the great ocean. [pride.
মহোদয়, মোক্ষ, কর্ত্তা, অহঙ্কার, final emancipation, a master, lord,
মহৌষধ, শীঘ্র রোগনাশক বস্তু, রশুন, a specific, garlic.
মা, জননী, অগো, না, a mother; madam; no, not.
মাই, স্তন, বাঁট, a woman's breast, a dug, a teat.
মাইজ, বৃক্ষের সারভাগ, the pith of a plant, heart of a tree.

মাইয়া, স্ত্রীলোক, কন্যা, a woman, a girl.
মাইয়ামথ, ঘরবোলা, কুণো, মুখচোর, মূঢ়, অলস, স্ত্রৈণ, *m.* recluse, shamefaced, ignorant, inactive, effeminate.
মাংস, পলল, আমিষ, ক্রব্য. flesh, meat.
মাংসপেশী, মাংসপিণ্ড, মাংসের পৃথক্ খণ্ড, a muscle.
মাংসল, স্থূলকায়, মোটা, বলবান্. fleshy, stout, lusty, fat, corpulent, strong.
মাংসাদ, মাংসাশী,—পললখাদক, আমিষভোজী, carnivorous, feeding on flesh.
মাঁজন, মার্জ্জন, ঘর্ষণ, পুচন, to scour, rub, polish, cleanse, wipe.
মাঁদা-বাঁধা, বীজতলা, বৃক্ষমূলের আলি, আবাপ, a seed-plot, a ridge of earth round the foot of a tree to retain water.
মাকড়, মাকড়া, মাকড়সা,—ঊর্ণনাভ, তন্তুবায়, লূতা, a spider.
মাকন্দ, আম্রফল, রসাল, চুত, a mango.
মাকাটিয়া, অদাতা, কৃপণ, unkind, ungenerous, greedy, niggardly.
মাকাটী, কার্পাসের বীজ. the seeds of cotton.
মাকু, তন্তুবায়ের তুরী, বুননযন্ত্র, a weaver's shuttle.
মাকায়, সমুদায়ে, গড়ে, সাজায়, by the lump, for the whole, altogether, on the average, in partnership.
মাখন,-আন, লেপন, মর্দ্দন, ছানন, to smear, daub, plaster, spread over, to rub in, anoint, to knead.
মাখন, নবনীত, ননী, butter.
মাখনিয়া, গোপ, ননীবিকনিয়া, লেপনিয়া, a butterman, smearer, &c.
মাগী, বৃদ্ধা স্ত্রী, বুড়ী, an old woman, (in contempt.)
মাগু, স্ত্রী, পত্নী, ভার্য্যা, a wife.
মাগ্রাম, আত্মশ্লাঘা, দম্ভ, ভুরভার, self-applause, conceit, a boast, puff, boasting, puffing, vaunting.
মাগ্রামীয়া, আত্মশ্লাঘী, দাম্ভিক, conceited, vaunting, boasting, puffing.
মাঘ, শিশিরের আদ্যমাস, the first month of the dewy season.
মাঘী, মাঘ মাসের পূর্ণিমা, the full moon in Mágha.
মাঙ্গন, মাগন,—যাচন, ভিক্ষা করণ, to ask, pray, request, solicit, petition, beg.
মাঙ্গন্তা, যাচক, প্রার্থক, one who prays, begs or solicits, a solicitor, &c.
মাঙ্গন্তেড়িয়া, ভিক্ষক, যাচক, begging, requesting, asking, soliciting.
মাঙ্গলিক, শুভ, কল্যাণজনক, auspicious, propitious, lucky, fortunate.
মাঙ্গা, প্রার্থনা, নিবেদন, a request, prayer, supplication, petition.

মাগান, যাচনে পাঠান, to send or cause one to beg, solicit, &c.
মাচা-ন, মঞ্চ, ভারা, কুঁড়িয়া, a shelf, scaffold, platform, raised shed.
মাচিয়া, পিড়ী, চৌকি, a bench, stool, chair.
মাছ, মৎস্য, মীন, ঝষ, a fish.
মাছী, মক্ষিকা, সপক্ষ কীট, a fly, any winged insect.
মাছীটেপা, মাছীটিপ্যা,—ব্যয়কুণ্ঠ, কৃপণ, penurious, parsimonious, niggardly, sordid, stingy.
মাছুয়া, মৎস্যবেপারী, জেলিয়া, a fishmonger, a fisherman.
মাছুয়ানী, জেলিয়ার স্ত্রী, a fishwoman, a fisherman's wife.
মাজ, মাঝ, মাঝার,—মধ্য, অন্তর, the midst, middle, centre.
মাজন, পুচন, মার্জন, to clean, wipe, scour, scrub, polish.
মাজনা, মার্জনীয়, পরিষ্কার্য্য, something requiring to be scoured, &c.
মাজমরা, মৃতাভ্যন্তর, অন্তক, inwardly dead, internally mortal [as a disorder.
মাজা, কটিদেশ, কঙ্কাল, the loins, the waist.
মাজী, মাঝী,—কর্ণধার, নাবিক, a steersman, helmsman, boat- [man.
মাজুরী, আসন বিশেষ, a sort of fine matting, a mat.
মাঝামাঝি, পরিমিতরূপে, মধ্যস্থলে, moderately, temperately, middlingly, midway.
মাঝারী, মধ্যবিত, মধ্যবর্ত্তী, middling, moderate, temperate, [central.
মাঝে, মধ্যে, অন্তরে, in the midst, in, within, among, between.
মাট, অলস, ঢীলা, মন্দ, slow, sluggish, lazy, bad.
মাটী, মৃত্তিকা, ভূমি, earth, soil, clay, sand, &c. the ground.
মাটীকাটা, খনক, কোদালিয়া, a digger of the ground, a pioneer.
মাটীয়া, খয়রা, মৃন্ময়, পার্থিব, earth coloured, brown, earthen.
মাঠ, তেপান্তর, গো চারণের ভূমি, a plain, field, pasture, meadow.
মাঠা, ঘোল, তক্র, buttermilk, sour milk.
মাঠান, মাঠুয়া,—মাঠ সম্বন্ধীয়, মাঠস্থিত, belonging to or situated [on a plain.
মাঠে, বাহিরে, out of doors, in the open air.
মাড়, ভেলা, মণ্ড, লেই, a raft, rice-water, rice-gruel, starch, [paste.
মাড়ন, শস্য মর্দ্দন, বাটন, দলন, দাবন, to thresh, tread out corn, to bruise, rub on a stone, grind, stamp, press, trample, beat down, flatten, make smooth.
মাড়ি, মাঢ়ি,—দ্বিশল্য, চর্ব্বণদন্ত, দন্তমূল, a back or double tooth, the gums.
মাণবক, উপনয়নযোগ্য বালক, বালকবৎ মানুষ, a youth, a mani- [kin, a childish man.

মাণিক, মাণিক্য.—পদ্মরাগ, রত্ন, a ruby, a precious stone.

মাৎ, ছানার জল, অসার গুড়, whey, a thin sort of treacle, checkmate. [mountaineer.

মাতঙ্গ, হস্তী, চণ্ডাল, চুয়াড়, an elephant, an outcast, a savage

মাতঙ্গী, হস্তিনী, পার্ব্বতী, a she-elephant, the goddess Párvatí.

মাতন, মত্ত হওন, উৎকট হওন, খেপন, to be drunk or intoxicated, become furious, rage. [hat.

মাতলা, খিলান, মাতাল, an arch or its capital, a sort of wicker

মাতলামী, মত্ততা, বিহ্বলতা. drunkenness, intoxication, a reeling, staggering from drunkenness.

মাতা, মাতৃ,—জননী, দেবী, শক্তি, গরু, a mother, a goddess or personified divine energy, a cow.

মাতা, বুক্কবটী, বসন্ত রোগ, the small-pox.

মাতান, মত্ততা জন্মান, খেপান, to intoxicate, stimulate, work up to enthusiasm. [or grandmother.

মাতামহ, মাতামহী,— জননীর পিতামাতা, a maternal grandfather

মাতাল, গেঁজ্যাল, মত্ত, মদবিহ্বল, বড়, ভারী, a sot: drunk, drunken, great, important.

মাতি, পরিমাণ, তৌল, তাল বৃক্ষের অপ্রসারিত পত্র, থোড়, measure, weight, the tender leaves of the Palm.

মাতুল, মাতার ভ্রাতা, মামা, a maternal uncle. [uncle.

মাতুলী, মতুলা-নী,—মামী, মাতুলের পত্নি, the wife of a maternal

মাতৃকা, গৌরী প্রভৃতি ষোড়শ দেবী, বর্ণমালা, অগুনির্ণীত সূত্র, a class of 16 goddesses or divine energies, an alphabet, a set of preliminary rules or axioms.

মাতৃসপত্নী, বিমাতা, a stepmother.

মাতৃস্বসা, মাসী, a mother's sister, maternal aunt.

মাতৃবন্ধু, মাতৃবান্ধব,—কুটুম্ব, a maternal cognate relation.

মাত্র, অল্প, কিঞ্চিৎ, সমুদায়, নিমিষ, ক্ষণ, এক, কেবল, তৎক্ষণাৎ, a little, the whole, a moment, a unit; one, mere; only, merely, solely, precisely; at, upon.

মাত্রা, ছন্দের উচ্চারিত ধ্বনি, পরিমাণ, মোড়ক, অক্ষরের উপরিস্থিত রেখা, a short syllable, metrical quantity, measure, an instant, a dose, a quantity, the horizontal stroke of a letter. [haughtiness.

মাৎসর্য্য, পরশ্রীকাতরতা, দ্বেষ, অহঙ্কার, envy, malice, avarice, pride,

মাথট, চাঁদা, a charitable collection, subscription, extra-assessment. [peak, pinnacle.
মাথা, মস্তক, উপরিভাগ, শিরঃ, শৃঙ্গ, the head, top, upper part,
মাথাটানা, ঢেঁটা, অবাধ্য, headstrong, self-willed, rebellious.
মাথান, পরকর্ম্মেতে হাত দেওন, মধ্যে আইসন, ঢোকন, to interfere with another's concerns, to meddle.
মাথামাথি, চুষাচুষি, মাথাপর্য্যন্ত, head to head, to the very top.
মাথাল, মাথ্লা,—স্তম্ভের শিরোভাগ, তৃণ নির্ম্মিত টুপী বিশেষ, the capital of a pillar, a wicker hat. [quential.
মাথালাড়া, ঢেঁটা, প্রগল্ভ, দাম্ভিক, insolent, overbearing, conse-
মাদক, মত্ততাজনক, নিদ্রাকর, intoxicating, inebriating, narcotic.
মাদল, মৃদঙ্গ বিশেষ, a tambour, a tabor.
মাদুর, আসন বিশেষ, a sort of fine mat, a mat,
মাদুলী, কবচ, অস্ত্রাদি নিবারণার্থ পরিধেয় ভূষণ, an amulet, a charm.
মাধব, কৃষ্ণ, Crishna. [ableness, mildness, suavity.
মাধুর্য্য, মধুরতা, মিষ্টতা, কোমলত্ব, sweetness, gentleness, agree-
মাধ্যাহ্নিক, মধ্যাহ্ন কালের কর্ত্তব্য ক্রিয়া, mid-day rites; proper or belonging to mid-day.
মান, মর্য্যাদা, সম্ভ্রম, অভিমান, ঠেকার, গর্ব্ব, ক্রোধ, বিতুষ্টি, চিত্তবাধ, তৌল, মাপ, ভাও, honor, respect, rank, reputation, respectability, sullen pride, haughtiness, indignation, resentment, a pet, anger of lovers, a weighing, measuring, weight, measure, value. [responsibility.
মানত, মানসা,—ব্রত, নিয়ম, a vow, voluntary obligation or
মানন, আদর করণ, মনোযোগ করণ, পালন, প্রত্যয় করণ, সম্মত হওন, স্বীকরণ, গ্রহণ, অর্পণ, মনে করণ, বুঝন, চাহন, to esteem, regard, respect, honor, venerate, keep, observe, mind, obey, submit, believe, own, acknowledge, agree or consent to, coincide, allow, admit, offer, present, think, suppose, wish for.
মানতা, নিয়মকারী, গৃহীতব্রত, one who vows or voluntarily takes a responsibility or obligation upon himself. [gatory, binding, &c.
মাননীয়, আদরণীয়, নিয়মিত, পাল্য, estimable, honorable, obli-
মানব, মনুষ্য, মর্ত্য, a man, human creature, a multitude.

মানভাঞ্জন, অপমান করণ, to shame, disgrace, expose, dishonour. [volition, scheme.

মানস্, বোধ, বাঞ্ছা, অভিপ্রায়, a thought, idea, wish, desire,

মানস, মানসিক,—মনস্থ,আনুমানিক,অপ্রসিদ্ধ, mental, existing in the mind, ideal, imaginary. [temptible.

মানহীন, নম্রমনাঃ, দর্পশূন্য, তুচ্ছ, humble, free from pride, con-

মানহীনা, দুষ্টা স্ত্রী, বেশ্যা, a vile woman, a harlot.

মানা, আদর, মনোযোগ, স্বীকার, বারণ, নিষেধ, আটক, regard, reverence,attention,consent.acceptance,admission,&c. a prohibition, forbidding. hindrance.

মানান, সম্মত করাণ, প্রবোধন, বুঝান, প্রমাণ আমান, ঠিক লাগান, to persuade, prevail upon, convince, enforce, to make to fit, to adjust.

মানী, অহঙ্কারী, বিরুষ্ট. সম্ভ্রান্ত, মর্য্যাদক, মনোযোগী, proud, haughty, sulky, sullen, indignant, honorable, respectable, esteeming, minding, regarding.

মানুষ, নর, মর্ত্ত্য, ব্যক্তি, man,a human being,mortal, person.

মান্দ্য, মন্দতা, দুষ্টতা,অবেগতা, হ্রাস, অল্পতা, ন্যূনতা, badness, vileness, dulness, slowness, abatement, diminution, an inferior degree. [admissible.

মান্য, আদরণীয়, গ্রাহ্য, honorable, respectable, &c. credible,

মাপ, ঝোঁক, পরিমাণ, তৌল, measure, measurement, weight.

মাপন, ঝোঁকান, তৌল করণ, উমান করণ, to measure, survey, weigh, to guage, sound, fathom.

মামক, মম. আমার, my, mine. [a seal.

মামড়ী, ক্ষতচিহ্নের শুষ্কচর্ম্ম, মুদ্রা, a scab, the dry skin of a sore,

মামা, মামী,—মাতুল, মাতুলানী, a maternal uncle and his wife.

মায়া, ছল,কপট, দুষ্টামি, কুহক, মন্ত্রপাঠ, মোহ, ইন্দ্রজাল, অবিদ্যা. ব্রহ্মার শক্তি,অজ্ঞানতা, মূঢ়তা,মমতা, স্নেহ, দয়া.কৃপা, স্ত্রী লোক. a fraud, trick, deceit, deception, villainy, wickedness, magic, a magical spell, illusion, fascination, imposition on the senses, worldly illusion or unreality of matter, idealism, the personified creative energy of Brahmá, ignorance, folly, affection, tenderness, attachment, love, sensibility. feeling, sympathy, compassion, pity, a woman.

মায়াজীবী, কুহকী, মোহনকার, a juggler, conjurer, magician.
মায়ান, মায়া লাগান, ভুলান, to fascinate, delude, deceive.
মায়াবী, ঐন্দ্রজালিক, কপটী, ধূর্ত্ত, মান্ত্রিক, কুহকী, magical, illusive, fascinating, deceptive, crafty, worldly; a magician, a conjurer. [from illusion.
মায়াশূন্য, নির্দ্দয়, কঠোর, ইন্দ্রিয়সুখহীন, unkind, unfeeling, free
মায়িক, ভ্রামক, ঐন্দ্রজালিক, বঞ্চক, স্নেহযুক্ত, কৃপাবান, কুহকী, magical, illusory, illusive, deceptive, affectionate, tender, clement; a juggler, a conjurer.
মায়ী, ঐন্দ্রজালিক, বঞ্চক, কুহকী, illusive, deceptive; a deceiver, cheat, juggler.
মায়ু, পিত্ত, gall, bile, bilious humour. [&c.
মারক, মড়ক, ঘাতক, a plague, epidemic disease, a slayer,
মারকুটীয়া, কুন্দলিয়া, quarrelsome, ever ready to fight.
মারণ, প্রহারণ, পিটন, ঘাতন, নাশন, বন্দুক লাগান, ছোড়ান, লুটন, কাটন, to strike, smite, beat, knock, rap, flog, punish, kill, slay, destroy, to hit a mark, discharge, shoot, fire, to fall upon, plunder, cut off.
মারপেঁচ, ঝঞ্ঝাট, ফেরফার, ছন্দ, a difficulty, quibble, catch.
মারা, প্রহার, শাস্তি, লুট, প্রহারিত, হত, নষ্ট, a beating, &c. chastisement, capture, plunder, &c: beaten, cast away, undone. [derous.
মারাত্মক, মারন্তক,—প্রাণঘাতক, বধিক, mortal, fatal, deadly, mur-
মারামারি, বাহুযুদ্ধ, লড়ালড়ি, a scuffle, battle, close fight.
মারী, মড়ক, দেশ ব্যাপিয়া প্রাণঘাতক ব্যাধি, a pestilence, epidemic.
মারুত, বায়ু, অনিল, the wind, air, vital air. [search.
মার্গ, পথ, চেষ্টা, a road, path, way, passage, section,
মার্গণ, অন্বেষণ, যাচন, to search, seek, enquire, ask, beg.
মার্ঘ্য, মহার্ঘ্য, দুর্মূল্য, dear, high-priced.
মার্জন, পরিষ্কার করণ, অবগাহন, লেপন, পুঁছন, ঝেঁটন, ক্ষমা করণ, to scour, rub, polish, furbish, clean, cleanse, purify, bathe, anoint, varnish, wipe, sweep, clear off, forgive. [ed, &c.
মার্জনার্হ, ক্ষমাযোগ্য, পরিষ্কার্য্য, pardonable, venial, to be cleans-
মার্জনী, গামছা, কুচি, ঝেঁটা, a towel, rubber, brush, broom.
মার্জা, পরিবর্ত্ত, বিনিময়, barter, exchange, permutation.

মার্জার, বিড়াল, খট্টাশ, a cat, a polecat.
মার্ত্তণ্ড, সূর্য্য, রবি, দিনকর, the sun.
মার্দ্দব, মৃদুতা, কোমলতা, gentleness, mildness, softness.
মার্ষ্টি, অভ্যঙ্গ বিশেষ, স্নানাদি, a cleaning of the person by bathing, anointing, &c.
মাল, বীর, মল্ল, বাহুযোদ্ধা, a hero, champion, wrestler.
মালঞ্চ, পুষ্পোদ্যান, a flower-garden.
মালা, কুণ্ডলাকারে গ্রথিত পুষ্পাদি, হার, স্মারী, স্রক, গর্ভক, নারিকেলের খোল, a necklace, bead-roll, rosary, garland, wreath, chaplet, the shell of a cocoanut.
মালাকর বা কার, পুষ্পবৃত্তি জাতি, মালী, বেত, a seller of garlands, a florist, a gardener, the ratan.
মালামী, মল্লক্রীড়া, বাহুযুদ্ধ, wrestling, pugilism.
মালিক, মালী,—উদ্যানপরিচারক, পুষ্পব্যবসায়ী, a gardener, florist, a maker and seller of flowers, garlands, &c.
মালিন্য, সমলতা, কালকুষ্টতা, অপরিষ্কার, ঘোরত্ব, filthiness, dirtiness, sordidness, squalidness, tarnish, impurity, gloominess. [rosary.
মাল্য, কণ্ঠী, গ্রথিত পুষ্পাদি, স্মারী, a necklace, garland, chaplet,
মাল্যবান, হারযুক্ত, মালাবিশিষ্ট, wearing a necklace or garland.
মালসা, অঙ্গারার্থ মৃৎপাত্র, an earthen pot for embers, &c.
মালসাট, আস্পর্দ্ধা, দম্ভ, a challenging, daring, vaunting.
মাষ, কলায় বিশেষ, a sort of pulse or kidney bean.
মাষ-1, মাষক,—পঞ্চ রতি পরিমাণ, a jeweller's weight.
মাস, দুই পক্ষ, ত্রিশ দিন, সূর্য্যের এক রাশিতে অবস্থান কাল, a month (lunar or solar,) flesh.
মাসবৃদ্ধি, মলমাস, অধিমাস, an intercalary month. [sleek.
মাসাল, অধিক মাংসযুক্ত, স্থূল, চিক্কণ, fleshy, plump, lusty, fat,
মাসিক, মাসের, মাসেং বেতনপ্রাপক, প্রতিমাস প্রাপ্য বেতনাদি, প্রতিমাস কর্ত্তব্য প্রেতশ্রাদ্ধ, অন্বাহার্য্য, monthly, belonging to a month, occurring or payable monthly, lasting a month, hired for the month ; a monthly servant, monthly wages, monthly instalment, a monthly offering to ancestors.
মাসী, মাতৃভগিনী, a maternal aunt, a mother's sister.
মাসুড়া, চক্ষুর ফুলী, ছানী, a film on the eye, a cataract.

মাসোহারা, মাসিক বেতন, monthly wages or stipend.
মাহাত্ম্য, গৌরব, প্রভাব, কীর্ত্তি, greatness, glory, dignity, magnanimity, celebrity, praise.
মাহিষ, মহিষীর দুগ্ধ, তৎকৃত নবনীত, buffaloe's milk, butter, &c.
মাহত. মাহুত,—হস্তিচালক, an elephant-driver.
মাহেশ্বরী, দুর্গা, Durgá, the Shacti or personified energy of [Shiva.
মিছা, মিথ্যা, অসত্য, false, untrue; falsehood, untruth, a lie.
মিট, মোচনা, নিষ্পত্তি, absolution, expiation, conclusion.
মিটন, থামন, টুটন, ক্ষয় হওন, নিবর্ত্তন, মুক্ত হওন, to subside, fail, wear out, be extinct, be exempted.
মিটান, ঘুচান, ছাপান, দাবন, নিবান, ভঞ্জন, নিবর্ত্তন, থামান, চুকান, ছাড়ান, ক্ষয় করাণ, মোচন, to dispel, efface, erase, suppress, quash, extinguish, put an end to, terminate, calm, moderate, decide, settle, conclude, part, separate, wear out, wipe out, expiate.
মিট্‌মিটিয়া, অল্পজ্বল, নিবিয়া, গুপ্তমনস্থ, dim, expiring, concealing his purpose, secret.
মিষ্ট, মিঠ্যা,—মিষ্ট, আলাপী, মৃদু, সুসময়, sweet, sweet-spoken, gentle, opportune.
মিঠা, মিঠানি,—মাধুর্য্য, কোমলতা, sweetness, suavity, gentleness of speech.
মিঠাই, মিষ্টান্ন, লাড়ু ইত্যাদি, sweetmeats, confectionery.
মিঠান, মধুরাণ, শুভ, সুসময়, to sweeten; seasonable, opportune.
মিত, মধ্যবিত, অল্প, measured, regular, moderate, frugal.
মিতব্যয়ী, অল্পব্যয়কারী, frugal, prudent, careful.
মিতাচার, বিহিত ব্যবহার, ধৈর্য্য, regulated conduct, moderation.
মিতাশী, মিতাহারী,—অল্পভোজী, মধ্যবিত ভক্ষণকারী, eating moderately, abstemious, temperate.
মিতি, মাপ, পরিমাণ, measure, weight, measurement.
মিত্র, মিতা,—বন্ধু, সাথী, সহায়, a friend, companion, ally.
মিত্রতা, মিতালি,—বন্ধুতা, সন্ধি, friendship, intimacy, alliance.
মিত্রনাম, একনামক, স্বনাম, a name-sake.
মিত্রাক্ষর, পদ্যের প্রতিচরণের অন্তে অভিন্ন বর্ণ, a rhyme or rhyming [syllable.
মিথস্, পরস্পর, বিরলে, mutually, reciprocally, privately.
মিথুন, যমক, তৃতীয় রাশি, দ্বন্দ্ব, যোড়া, স্ত্রীপুরুষ, সংসর্গ, twins, the sign Gemini, a couple, brace, pair, male and female, man and wife, copulation, union.

মিথ্যা, বিতথ, অসত্য, কাল্পনিক, অবাস্তবিক, মায়িক, অনর্থক, নির্মূল, অকারণ, অসত্যবাদ, অপহ্নব, ব্যাজ, false, untrue, sham, counterfeit, unreal, delusory, unsubstantial, apparent, imaginary, fruitless, useless, vain, ill founded, groundless; falsehood, a lie, untruth, denial, a pretence.

মিথ্যাদৃষ্টি, অসত্যানুমান, অসত্যকে সত্যজ্ঞান করা, ইতরধর্ম্ম, নাস্তিকতা, a false view of things, heresy, atheism.

মিথ্যাশঙ্কা, অকারণ ভয়, নির্মূল সন্দেহ, groundless fear or suspicion, imaginary danger. [reply.

মিথ্যোত্তর, অস্বীকার, অসত্য প্রতিবাদ, the denial of a charge, a false

মিনতি, মিনং,—বিনতি, যাচ্ঞা, স্তবপূর্ব্বক নিবেদন, supplication, earnest entreaty, prayer, humble request.

মিল, সংযোগ, সন্ধি, সম্প্রীতি, আলাপ, সম্মতি, সমভাব, সাদৃশ্য, union, conjunction, concord, society, consent, agreement, uniformity, comparison.

মিলন, একত্র হওন, মিশন, যুটন, সন্ধি বা সালা করণ, ভেটন, স্পর্শন, লাগন, ঐক্য হওন, অন্টন, পাওন, ঘটন, কাছান, সংযোগ, সংঘটনা, মেল, সাদৃশ্য, ঔপম্য, মিত্রাক্ষর, সাক্ষাৎ, to coalesce, be mixed, unite, come together, associate, join, combine, enter into friendship, partnership or alliance, meet, visit, touch, come in contact, suit, agree, tally, accord, resemble, to cohere, cling, embrace, to find, get, obtain, fall in with, to happen, fall to, overtake, come up with; union, junction, contact, accession, agreement, resemblance, reconciliation, rhyme, a visit, a meeting. [ing, visiting, sociable.

মিলক, মিলনিয়া,—সংযোগী, সাক্ষাৎকারী, আলাপী, uniting, coalesc-

মিলান, মিশান, একত্রীকরণ, যোড়ান, লাগান, ঘটান, পাওয়ান, প্রবন্ধ জন্মান, তুলনা করণ, যুটান, ঠিক করণ, ঐক্য করণ, to mix, mingle, adulterate, compound, join, unite, graft, cement, apply, close up to bring about, procure, reconcile, mediate, compare, collate, to adjust, check an account, to fit, make to correspond or suit, &c.

মিশাল, আলাপ, প্রণয়, সম্পর্ক, social conversation, intercourse.

মিশালী, প্রণয়ী, প্রবেশক, আলাপী, social, sociable. conversable.

মিশিত, মিশ্রিত, সংযুক্ত, সম্মিষ্ট, সংশ্লিষ্ট, প্রাপ্ত, mixed, adulterated, united, combined, connected with, united together, coherent, found, obtained.

মিস্‌মিসা, রোগ বিশেষ, হাম, the measles. [ther.

মিশন, মিলন, একত্র হওন, to be mixed, mingle, unite toge-

মিশান, একত্রীকরণ, to mix, compound, jumble together.

মিশামিয়া, মিশামিশা, স্বতঃ প্রবেশক, mixing with ; an intruder.

মিশাল, একত্রীভাব, সংশ্লেষ, উল্টাপাল্টা, মিশ্রিত, a mixture, compound medicine, a jumble ; mixed, &c.

মিশ্র, সংযোগ, একত্রীকরা, উপাধি বিশেষ, mixture, incorporation, a family name. [union, mixture.

মিশ্রণ, অঙ্কসঙ্কর, সংযোগ, arithmetical addition, chemical

মিশ্রব্যবহার, মেল, প্রণয়, সাজা, মিশাল নির্ণয়, unity, concord, partnership. investigation of mixed properties, &c.

মিশ্রিত, মিশিত, সংযুক্ত, উল্টাপাল্টা, ভাজযুক্ত, mixed, compounded, jumbled together, promiscuous, adulterated.

মিশ্রিতভাষা, ভিন্ন ২ দেশীয় জড়িত বাক্য, প্রাকৃত, অশুদ্ধ কথন, a mixed language or dialect, a jargon.

মিষ্ট, মধুর, সুস্বাদু, প্রিয়, মৃদু, সময়োচিত, আর্দ্র, sweet, pleasant, kind, agreeable, nice, gentle, seasonable, opportune, sprinkled, moistened.

মিষ্টান্ন. মিঠাই, অনুকাদি, sweetmeats, sweet sauce, frumenty.

মিসি. দন্তের মঞ্জন বিশেষ, a sort of dentifrice or tooth-powder.

মীন, মৎস্য, মাছ, দ্বাদশঃ রাশি, a fish, the sign Pisces.

মীমাংসক, মীমাংসাদর্শনবেত্তা, মধ্যস্থ, বিরোধভঞ্জক, বিতর্কক, a follower of the Mímángsá philosophy, an umpire, mediator, arbitrator ; deciding a difference, investigating. [and decided.

মীমাংসনীয়, মীমাংস্য,—বিতর্কণীয়, বিবেচনীয়, to be investigated

মীমাংসা, দর্শন বিশেষ, বিতর্ক, নিষ্পত্তি, one of the six philosophical systems, logical investigation, examination, reconciliation of discordant opinions, a decision, arbitration. [tled, investigated.

মীমাংসিত, নিষ্পন্ন, বিচারিত, বিবেচিত, decided, adjudged, set-

মুকুট, কিরীট, চূড়া, শিরোভূষা, a crest, crown, diadem, tiara.
মুকুন্দ, বিষ্ণু, Vishnu or the liberator.
মুকুর, দর্পণ, আর্শি, a looking-glass, a mirror.
মুকুল, মোচ, কুঁড়ী, অবিকসিত পুষ্প, a blossom, a bud.
মুকুলিত, ঈষৎ বিকসিত কলিকাযুক্ত, budding, in blossom.
মুক্ত, ছাড়ান, রক্ষিত, উদ্ধৃত, উত্তীর্ণ, অবদ্ধ, নির্ম্মল, বিরত, released, liberated, discharged, exempted, acquitted, delivered, rescued, ransomed, emancipated, free, open, loose, dishevelled, clear (as weather,) ceased, cleared up.
মুক্তহস্ত, দানশীল, অপব্যয়ী, open-handed, liberal, generous, [prodigal
মুক্তা, মুক্তাফল,—রত্ন বিশেষ, মতি, a pearl.
মুক্তাগার, মুক্তাস্ফোট,—শুক্তি, যে শম্বুকেতে মুক্তা জন্মে, the pearl-oys-[ter.
মুক্তাদাম, মুক্তাহার, মুক্তাবলী,—মুক্তার মালা, a string of pearls.
মুক্তি, ছাড়ানি, উদ্ধার, রক্ষা, বাঁচাও, গতি, ত্রাণ, মোক্ষ, freedom, discharge, liberty, liberation, extrication, deliverance, escape, acquittal, salvation, final emancipation or absorption.
মুখ, বক্ত্র, আস্য, বদন, দ্বার, কাক, রন্ধ্র, উপক্রম, কণ, আদ্য, প্রধান, the mouth, face, countenance, front, muzzle, an entrance, aperture, opening, orifice, commencement, the first term in progression, the eye of a plant; first, chief, principal.
মুখকটু, মুখড়,—দুর্ম্মুখ, নিন্দক, scurrilous, abusive.
মুখচোরা, লজ্জাশীল, আলাপনে ভীত, bashful, shy, sheepish.
মুখচোরামী, মুখচোর,—লজ্জাশীলতা, ভয়করা, bashfulness, shyness, sheepishness, a shrinking from.
মুখদোষী, কদাকার, কদাস্য, foul-faced, ill-looking, ugly.
মুখদোষিণী, ডাকিনী, ডাইন, a hag, a witch.
মুখবন্ধ, কথনের আটককরা অর্থাৎ ধমক ঘুষাদি, a promise or threat in order to silence one, a gag, a bribe, a gift.
মুখর, কটুভাষী, নিন্দক, অপ্রিয়বাদী, শঙ্খ, কাক, scurrilous, abusive, insolent, harsh-spoken; a conch, a crow.
মুখশোষ, শোকাদি জনিত বদনের ম্লানভাব, dryness of the face through grief or disease.
মুখস, বাগ, বল্গা, কৃত্রিম মুখ, a rein, snaffle, bit, a mask.

মুখস্থ, বদনবর্ত্তী, অভ্যস্থ, মিথ্যা, কাল্পনিক, situated in the face, in the mouth, ready to be uttered, off-book, outward, pretended.

মুখান, দিগে চাহন, নিরীক্ষণ, সন্নিকট হওন, ভিড়ন, to face, look towards, be about to take place, approach.

মুখাগ্নি, আলেয়া, শবমুখে দত্তানল, সংস্কৃতাগ্নি, a fire-visaged goblin or will-of-the-wisp, fire placed in the mouth of a corpse on the pile, sacrificial fire.

মুখাপেক্ষা, অনুরোধ, পক্ষপাত, partiality, partial regard or distinction. [posite.

মুখামুখি, দেখাদেখি, সম্মুখবর্ত্তী, face to face, front to front, op-

মুখামৃত, প্রসন্নমুখে দৃষ্টিপাত, a favourable regard, propitious countenance, (*used as a term of flattery.*)

মুখাল, ছদ্মবেশির কৃত্রিম মুখ, a mask.

মুখাস, আবৃতি, কৃত্রিম মুখ, a muzzle to prevent biting, a mask.

মুখাসব, থুথু, নিষ্ঠীব, লালা, slaver, saliva, dribbling.

মুখী, প্রবাল, অঙ্কুর, a sprout, a young shoot.

মুখ্য, আদ্য, প্রধান, primary, chief, principal, pre-eminent.

মুখে, দিগে, পানে, towards, in the direction of.

মুখে২, কাণে২, up to the brim, running over, overflowing.

মুগ, মুদ্গ,—কলায় বিশেষ, a sort of kidney-bean.

মুগরাণ, মুষ্ট্যাঘাত করণ, পিটান, to thump, to beat, to pound.

মুগুর, মুদ্গর,—লৌহময় গদা, a large mallet, a hammer, club, bludgeon. mace, a dumb-bell.

মুগ্ধ, মোহিত, মায়াযুক্ত, আসক্ত, অজ্ঞান, মূর্চ্ছাপন্ন, infatuated, deluded, blindly attached to, stupid, ignorant, stupified, bereft of sensation.

মুগ্ধা, ঋতুমতী, *f.* arrived at the age of puberty.

মুচন, মুঞ্চন,—ছাড়ান, উদ্ধরণ, অবসারণ, ছুটান, ত্যাগ করণ, পুঁছন, to liberate, set free, turn loose, disband, release, emancipate, to cast, shoot, evacuate, resign, vacate, desert, forsake, divorce, to clean, wipe.

মুচী, চামার, চর্ম্মকার, ডোম, মূষী, ক্ষুদ্র নারিকেল, a currier, skinner, tanner, shoe-maker, basket-maker, a crucible, a small cocoanut. [upon.

মুচ্কন, ঈষৎহাস্য করণ, বিহসন, to smile, simper, look kindly

মুচকি, বিহাস, ঈষৎ হাস্য, a smile, simper, kind look ; smilingly.
মুচড়ন, মোচড়ন, ভাঙ্গন, to wrench, twist, dislocate, break.
মুঞ্জ, বাণ, তৃণ বিশেষ, an arrow, a species of grass.
মুঞ্জরণ, ফুলান, গজান, to flower, to shoot up into flower, to grow luxuriantly.
মুঞ্জরী, স্তবক, পুষ্পগুচ্ছ, শিষ, a flower-spike, an ear of corn.
মুটরী, ক্ষুদ্র মোট, a small bundle or load for the head.
মুটী, গুঁজী, বাঁট, মুঠ, কীল, a cork, stopple, stopper, plug, bung, a hilt, handle, plough-handle, the fist.
মুটীয়া, ভারিক, ভারবাহক, বোঝারী, a porter, carrier of burthens, a cooly. [ling.
মুটুকি, মটকানি, অঙ্গ টিপন, the cracking of the fingers by pul-
মুঠ, মুষ্টি, খড়্গাদির বাঁট, the fist, a sword-hilt, handle.
মুঠা, মুষ্টি, কুঞ্চিত হস্ত পরিমাণ, কিঞ্চিৎ, a handful.
মুঠী, মুষ্টি, কীল, গুঁজী, ঢাকনা, a handful, the clenched fist, a hilt, plug, lid, cover. [dary, border.
মুড়, নেড়া, মাথা, সীমা, lopped, pollard; the head, a boun-
মুড়কী, উখড়া, a sweetmeat of parched rice and sugar.
মুড়ন-আন, মুণ্ডন, কেশ কাটন, কামান, বৃক্ষ কাটন, মড়ান, ফিরণ, ঢেকে ঢকন, to cut the hair in disgrace, shave the head, to lop a tree of its upper branches, to overlay, cover with leather or paper, to gild, plate, overspread, wrap up, to twist, turn, tack, shut a clasp-knife, &c. [end.
মুড়া, গুঁড়িকাট, থাম, সীমা, a stump, pollard, block, log, an
মুড়ানিয়া, কামানিয়া, নাপিত, shaving, &c. a barber, hair-cutter.
মুড়ামুড়ি, আদ্যন্ত, from end to end, all over, inclusively.
মুড়ী, ভাজা তণ্ডুল, ছিন্ন মস্তক, parched rice, the severed head of an animal.
মুণ্ড, মস্তক, কপাল, নেড়া বৃক্ষ, রাহু, the head, the forehead, a lopped tree, Ráhu or the ascending node.
মুণ্ড-ক নাপিত, মুড়ানিয়া, a barber, a shaver. [pollard.
মুণ্ড, মুণ্ডিত—কেশহীন, নেড়া, shaven, shorn, bald, lopped,
মুণ্ডন, সর্বকেশ ছেদন, বৃক্ষ মুড়ন, মড়ান, to shave the head &c, to lop a tree, to cover, overlay, gild, &c.
মুণ্ডী, মিঠাই বিশেষ, নাপিত, a sweetmeat, a barber.

মুদন, সম্মীলন, বুজান, কড়কন, to shut the eyes, fill up a pit, to close as a wound, shut, move on hinges.

মুদা, গুঁজী, ঘুণ্টী, ঢাকনা, গণকের দক্ষিণা, মূত্রকৃচ্ছ্র, a plug, a cork, a button, a cover, a covering, the offering to an astrologer, the strangury.

মুদাঘরা, ঘুণ্টীঘরা, পুঁট্যাঘরা, a loop, a button-hole.

মুদিত, বুজান, হর্ষিত, shut, filled up, &c. pleased, delighted, gratified. [petty tradesman.

মুদী, নিত্যাহারযোগ্যবিক্রেতা, পসারী, a grocer, a retail-dealer,

মুদ্গ, কলয় বিশেষ, মুগ, a species of kidney-bean.

মুদ্গর, লৌহময় গদা, মুগুর, হাতড়ী, a large mallet, an iron-headed club, a hammer, a dumb-bell.

মুদ্রা, অঙ্কিত স্বর্ণরূপাদি খণ্ড, মোহর, টাকা, ছাপ, অঙ্ক, অঙ্গুলির ভঙ্গিমা বিশেষ, a coin, stamped money, a seal, signet, medal, cash, a rupee, a stamp, die, impression, print, a mode of devotional intertwining of the fingers. [er, seal-cutter.

মুদ্রাকর, মুদ্রাকার,—মোহরাদি নির্ম্মায়ক, a carver, engraver, coin-

মুদ্রাঘটিত, ধনসম্বন্ধীয়, ধনাত্মক, pecuniary, consisting of money.

মুদ্রাঙ্কিত, অঙ্কযুক্ত, ছাপা, sealed, engraved, stampt, printed.

মুদ্রান্বিত, ছাপান, অঙ্কিত, impressed, stamped, sealed.

মুদ্রাযন্ত্র, ছাপাকল, ছাপ, a printing-press, stamping machine.

মুদ্রিত, চিহ্নযুক্ত, ছাপান, অপ্রকাশিত, অবিকসিত, sealed, stampt, cut, printed, closed, unblown.

মুনি, ঋষি, তপস্বী, যতী, a holy sage, a semi-deified devotee, an inspired philosopher, lawgiver, an ascetic.

মুমুক্ষা, অপবর্গের ইচ্ছা, a desire for final emancipation.

মুমূর্ষা, মরণেচ্ছা, a desire to die, the point of death.

মুমূর্ষু, মৃতপ্রায়, মরণোদ্যত, মরণেচ্ছুক, lying at the point of death, wishing or about to die.

মুমূর্ষুদান, মৃতদত্ত, a legacy, a gift at death.

মুরলী, বংশী, বেণু, a pipe, whistle, flute.

মুরজ, মুরজ,—মৃদঙ্গ, a small drum, a tabor.

মুষল-ী, ঢেঁকী, মোনা, মুদ্গর, a pestle for cleaning rice in a mortar, a large mallet. [death.

মুষল্য, মুষল দ্বারা বধযোগ্য, deserving to be pounded to

মুষ্ক, অণ্ডকোষ, the scrotum, a testicle.

মুষ্কমুক্ত বা শূন্য, ছিন্নাণ্ডকোষ, পণ্ড, দামড়া, castrated, gelt; a eunuch, a gelding, a wether. [geld, cut

মুষ্কমোচন বা মোষণ,—অণ্ডকোষ ছেদন, পুংস্ত্ব নাশন, to castrate,

মুষ্টামুষ্টি, হাতাহাতি, বাহুযুদ্ধ, fist to fist; fisticuffs, pugilism.

মুষ্টি, কীল, মুঠা, the fist, a handful, a hilt, handle.

মুহনা, প্রবাহযোগ, বেণী, নালা, the conflux of two rivers, a junction, rivulet. [frequently.

মুহুঃ, মুহুর্মুহু,—পুনঃ২, বারম্বার, again & again, repeatedly,

মুহূর্ত্ত, দুই দণ্ড, ক্ষণিককাল, a period of 48 minutes or the 15th part of the day or night, a short time, a moment. [demon.

মূক, বোবা, মৎস্য, দীন, দানব, dumb; a fish, a pauper, a

মূঢ়, মূর্খ, অজ্ঞান, অসভ্য, নিস্তেজ, stupid, ignorant, foolish, rude, rustic, clownish, cold, phlegmatic.

মূতন, লঘী করণ, প্রস্রাব করণ, to make water, to urine.

মূত্র, মুত,—প্রস্রাব, লঘী, urine, water discharged.

মূত্রকৃচ্ছ্র, প্রস্রাবরোধ, মুদা, a suppression of urine, strangury.

মূর্খ, বিদ্যাহীন, অজ্ঞান, আনাড়ী, ignorant, illiterate, stupid, foolish, awkward.

মূর্খতা, অজ্ঞানতা, জড়তা, ignorance, stupidity, folly, idiocy.

মূর্চ্ছনা, মূঢ়তা, পক তৈলের প্রাথমিক সংস্কার, অর্দ্ধস্বর, id: *also* the first purification of oil, a tone or semitone, the 7th part of the gamut or musical scale.

মূর্চ্ছা, হঠাৎ অচৈতন্য, মোহ, a swoon, fainting fit, loss of sensation, stupor, stupefaction.

মূর্চ্ছিত, মূর্চ্ছাপন্ন, মূর্চ্ছাগত,—হঠাৎ অচৈতন্যগ্রস্ত, মোহিত, চেতনারহিত, fallen into a faint or swoon, insensible, bereft of sensation, fainted, swooned, speechless.

মূর্চ্ছাবায়ু, মৃগী রোগ, epilepsy or the falling sickness.

মূর্ত্ত, সাকার, প্রপঞ্চ, পঞ্চভূতাত্মক, having shape or figure, material, solid.

মূর্ত্তি, বস্তু, পঞ্চ ভূত, শরীর, আকার, রূপ, ছবি, প্রতিমা, substance, matter, form, shape, figure, a resemblance, likeness, image, picture, statue.

মূর্ত্তিচিত্র, ছবি, প্রতিমূর্ত্তি, a painting, picture, portrait.

মূর্ত্তিমান, মূর্ত্তিমন্ত,—শরীরী, আকারবন্ত, দক্ষ, ক্ষমতাবান, গুণী, embodied, possessed of visible form or shape, clever, skilful, accomplished.

মূর্ত্ত্যন্তর, অন্যমূর্ত্তি, আকৃতির অন্যথা, a different form, transformation.

মূর্দ্ধা, মস্তক, মাথা, মস্তকের মজ্জা, the head, the cerebellum.

মূর্দ্ধাভিষিক্ত, ক্ষত্রিয়, রাজা, ক্ষত্রিয়া স্ত্রী গর্ভে ব্রাহ্মণজাত, a chsatriya, a king, a prince, a mixed cast half bráhmin half chsatriya.

মূর্দ্ধন্য, মূর্দ্ধাসংক্রান্তোচ্চারিত বর্ণ, টবর্গাদি, lingual or cerebral (letters.)

মূল, কন্দ, কারণ, হেতু, গৃহবৃক্ষাদির গোড়া, দেশের আদি প্রজা, জাতি, আদি সূত্র, স্থাপিত ধন, পুঁজী, প্রথম, আদি, অন্তিক, a root, bulbous root, origin, source, cause, foundation, aboriginal stock, breed, the original text as distinct from a commentary, a principal at interest, capital or stock in trade, square or cube root; original, radical, near, proximate.

মূল-1, ঊনবিংশতি নক্ষত্র, the 19th lunar mansion.

মূলা, মূলক,—কন্দ বিশেষ, a radish.

মূলক, হেতুক, উদ্ভূত, শিকড়জাত, founded upon, arising from as a cause, having origin in, springing from a root.

মূলজ, স্বাভাবিক, মূলোৎপন্ন, radical, produced from the root.

মূলধন, পুঁজী, a capital, principal, stock in trade.

মূলী, মূলঘটিত, আদি, আদিকারণ, fundamental, original; a beginner, originator.

মূলীভূত, আদিকারণ, কারণীভূত, আদর্শ, become a source, cause or origin; an antitype.

মূলোৎপাত, উৎখাত, উচ্ছেদ, subversion, overthrow, total ruin.

মূল্য, দ্রব্যের পণ, অর্ঘ, ভাও, বেতন, ভাড়া, পণ্য, ক্রয়ণীয়, value, worth, price, cost, wages, hire; valuable, purchasable.

মূষা, মূষিক,—ইন্দুর, a rat, a mouse.

মূষী, মূষা,—মুচী, স্বর্ণাদি গালায় যাহাতে, a crucible.

মৃগ, হরিণ, পশু, বন্যপশু হননকরা, a deer, stag, buck, antelope, any beast, the chase.

মৃগতৃষ্ণা, সূর্য্যকিরণে জলভ্রম, the mirage or sultry vapour in sandy deserts.

মৃগধূর্ত্তক, শৃগাল, শেয়াল, a jackal.

মৃগনয়নী, মৃগলোচনী, মৃগাক্ষী, মৃগনেত্রা,— সুনয়না স্ত্রী, হরিণবৎ চক্ষু বিশিষ্টা, stag-eyed, fawn-eyed, having deer's eyes.

মৃগনাভি, মৃগমদ—কস্তূরী, the musk of a species of deer.
মৃগব্য, মৃগয়া,—বন্য পশুর বধচেষ্টা, ব্যাধবৃত্তি, deer-hunting, the chase, game, sport.
মৃগয়ু, ব্যাধ, শৃগাল, ব্রহ্মা, a hunter, a jackal, Brahmá.
মৃগরাজ, মৃগপতি, মৃগেন্দ্র,—সিংহ, the lion or king of beasts.
মৃগশাবক, হরিণের ছা, a fawn, a young deer or antelope.
মৃগশিরা, পঞ্চম নক্ষত্র, the fifth lunar mansion.
মৃগাঙ্ক, চন্দ্র, নিশাপতি, the moon.
মৃগিত, দৌড়িয়া চেষ্টিত, অন্বেষিত, hunted, chased, pursued, sought.
মৃগী, হরিণী, মূর্চ্ছাবায়ু, চিত্রিণী, a doe, the epilepsy, a description of woman in amatory works.
মৃণাল, পদ্মাদির ডাঁটা, the stalk or fibres of the lotus.
মৃণালী, পদ্ম, পদ্মিনী, a lotus, an assemblage of water-lilies.
মৃৎ, মৃত্তিকা,—মাটী, ভূমি, earth, clay, mould, soil, ground.
মৃত, পরলোকগত, মরা, নির্বাণ, dead, deceased, defunct.
মৃতকল্প, মরণোদ্যত, নির্বাণোন্মুখ, nearly dead, dying, expiring.
মৃতদত্ত, মুমূর্ষুদান, given by one deceased; a legacy.
মৃতদার, যাহার স্ত্রী মরিয়াছে, ডেজুয়া, a widower; bereft of his wife.
মৃতপুত্র, যাহার সন্তান মরিয়াছে, having lost a son, relating to a deceased son.
মৃতপ্রায়, মরণোদ্যত, মৃততুল্য, almost dead, like one dead.
মৃতাত্তর, মৃতলোকের পরিবর্তে সাক্ষ্যদায়ী, a person who gives testimony for one deceased.
মৃতি, মৃত্যু, মরণ, প্রাণবিয়োগ, death, dying, decease.
মৃত্যু, প্রাণবিয়োগ, যম, death, demise, Yama regent of death.
মৃত্যুকর, মরণকারক, অন্তক, causing death, deadly, baneful, mortal.
মৃৎস্না, উত্তমা ভূমি, a good or rich soil, fragrant earth.
মৃদঙ্গ, মুরজ, a double drum, a tabor.
মৃদু, লঘু, কোমল, কৃপাযুক্ত, সকরুণ, ক্ষমাশীল, শান্ত, ধীর, অহিংসক, অকঠিন, মন্দ, ভোতা, gentle, mild, soft, affable, kind, tender, placable, clement, peaceable, tractable, quiet, tame, supple, pliable, slow, dim, blunt.
মৃদুদ্ভব, ভূমিজ, শাক, a production of the earth, a vegetable.
মৃদুল, কোমল, জল, soft, gentle; water.
মৃদুস্রোত, নদীর মন্দটান, slack-water, a gentle stream.

মৃদ্বীকা, দ্রাক্ষা, a grape, a raisin.

মৃন্ময়, পার্থিব,মাটীয়া,earthen, earthy, made of clay or earth.

মৃষা, বৃথা, মিথ্যায়, uselessly, in vain, falsely.

মেই, খামারের মাজকাঠ, চুচুক, the center stake of a threshing floor, a nipple.

মেইয়া, স্ত্রীলোক, কন্যা, a female, a woman, a girl.

মেইয়ামী, স্ত্রীপণা, কাপুরুষত্ব, স্ত্রীবৎ ব্যবহার, womanishness, unmanliness, effeminacy, girlishness.

মেইয়ামুখ, লজ্জাশীল, মুখচোর, shame-faced, womanish, shy.

মেখলা, স্ত্রীলোকের কটিভূষা, কাঞ্চী, মুঞ্জাদি নির্ম্মিত কটিদেশার্পিত সূত্র, খড়্গবন্ধন, শরপত্রাদি নির্ম্মিত ব্রহ্মচারির উপবীত, গুণ বিশেষ, পর্বতের ধার, a woman's girdle or zone, a sword-belt, the triple cord worn round the waist by the three first classes, the sacrificial string of a brahmin made of deer skin, a fine sort of sackcloth, the edge or swell of a mountain.

মেঘ, মেঘডুম্বুর,—জলধর, ঘনাঘন, a cloud, floating vapours.

মেঘজ্যোতিঃ, মেঘদীপ,—বিদ্যুৎ, তড়িৎ, ইরম্মদ, a flash of lightning.

মেঘনাদ, মেঘনির্ঘোষ,—গর্জ্জনী, বজ্রনিস্বন, low and distant thunder, a clap of thunder. [ing of clouds.

মেঘমালা, জলধরশ্রেণী, কাদম্বিনী, a succession of clouds, gather-

মেঘলা, বাদলা সময়, দুর্দিন, cloudy, dark, lowering, overcast.

মেঘাগম, মেঘারম্ভ, মেঘোদ্রেক,—বৃষ্টির উপক্রম, কাদম্বিনী, the gathering of clouds, a lowering sky.

মেঘাচ্ছন্ন, মেঘার, covered with clouds, lowering, overcast.

মেচ্যা, চৌকি, আসন, মোড়া, a chair, a seat, a bench.

মেছুনী, জেল্যার স্ত্রী, a fishwoman, fisherman's wife.

মেছুয়া, কৈবর্ত্ত, জেল্যা, মৎস্যধর, a fisherman, fishmonger.

মেজিয়া, মেজ্যা, মেঝেম,—ঘরের মধ্যভূমি, the floor of a house.

মেঝ, মধ্যস্থল, গৃহমধ্য, the middle, the floor of a house.

মেটা, সমাধা, নিষ্পত্তি, চুকনি, a settling, adjustment, &c.

মেটান, চুকান, খণ্ডন, সন্দেহ ভঞ্জন, to settle, adjust, obviate, remove a doubt, &c. [coloured, dim.

মেটিয়া, মৃন্ময়, কাদা, মৃৎবর্ণ, অনুজ্জ্বল, clayey, earthy, earth-

মেটিয়া, মেট্যা,—গিলা, জালা, a kidney, a jar. [petroleum.

মেটিয়াতৈল, ভূমিজ তৈলবৎ জ্বলনীয় দ্রব্য বিশেষ, earth-oil, naptha,

মেড়, কাটাম, the frame-work of an image.

মেড়া, মেঢ়া,—ভেড়া, মেষ, a ram, a sheep.

মেড়ী, ভেড়ী, মেষী, a ewe, the female sheep.

মেডুয়া, ক্ষুদ্র হাতড়ী, ভোতা, মর্চ্যাপড়া, কঠিন, অধৌত কাপড়, a small hammer; blunt, dull, rusty, stiff, starched, unwashed (cloth.)

মেড্যা, মাড়ি, দন্তমূল, the gums.

মেঢ্র, লিঙ্গ, পুরুষচিহ্ন, শিশ্ন, the penis.

মেঢ্রত্বক্, পুরুষাঙ্গের অগ্রচর্ম্ম, the prepuce or foreskin.

মেদ, মজ্জা, বসা, অতিশয় মাংসবৃদ্ধি, কস্তানি, marrow, fat, morbid corpulency, serum, lymph. [pid.

মেদা, স্থূলবুদ্ধি, ঢিলা, জড়, dull, heavy, sluggish, slow, stu-

মেদিনী, পৃথিবী, মহী, বসুধা, the earth.

মেধ, যাগ, নৈবেদ্যত্যাগ, a sacrifice, offering, oblation.

মেধা, ধী, মতি, ধারণবতী বুদ্ধি, স্মারকতা, উপলব্ধি, understanding, quickness of parts, aptness, ability, retentive power, memory, apprehension, conception.

মেধাবী, মতিমান, অভ্যাস করণে নিপুণ, স্মারক, পারগ, বুদ্ধিমন্ত, of good abilities, retentive, having a good memory, apt, quick, docile, intelligent.

মেধী, মেধি,—মেইকাঠ, the central stake of a threshing floor.

মেধ্য, যজ্ঞিয়, পূত, fit for sacrifice or oblation, pure.

মেনা, স্তন, a woman's breast, the udder of a beast.

মেনী, স্ত্রীলোক, স্ত্রীপশু, a female, (woman or beast.)

মেনীমুখা, কুণুয়া, লাজুক, shunning company, retired, bashful, shame-faced. [man, daughter, girl.

মেয়্যা, মেয়ে,—স্ত্রী, স্ত্রীলোক, দুহিতা, কন্যা, female; a female, wo-

মেরু. পর্ব্বত বিশেষ, Meru a fabulous mountain, probably the high lands of Tartary, the North Pole.

মেরুগ্রন্থি, মেটিয়া, the kidneys. [a keel.

মেরুদণ্ড, পৃষ্ঠের মধ্যস্থিত অস্থি, কশেরু, ডাঁড়া, the back-bone or spine,

মেল, সমন্বয়, ঐক্য, সন্ধি, সম্প্রীতি, সম্মতি, সংযোগ, গতিবিধি, আলাপ, সাদৃশ্য, agreement, concord, reconciliation, peace, accommodation of differences, accord, consent, accession, union, conjunction, mixture, intercourse, society, comparison, similarity.

মেলক, আলাপী, ভেটনিয়া, ঐক্যকারক, যোটক, social, meeting, coming together; a reconciler, a professional contracter of marriages.

মেলন, ভেটন, একত্র হওন, মিশান, ঐক্য জন্মান, প্রসারণ, বিস্তরণ, বাড়ন, পাওয়া যাওন, to meet, come together, join, mix, reconcile, to lay open, unfold, spread out; *v.n.* to spread, extend, to be found or met with.

মেলা, হাট, সভা, সমাজ, ঘটা, লোকসমূহ, জড়িত, সংলগ্ন, যুক্ত, প্রশস্ত, উদ্দাম, a fair, an assembly, a club, a concourse, crowd, throng, mob; thronged, cowded, close, joined, united; mixed, spacious, open, roomy, free, unrestrained.

মেলান, প্রসারণ, বাড়ান, to spread out, expand, extend.

মেলানি, সভা, জনতা, সমাজ, বিদায়, an assembly, concourse, union, association, friendly dismission.

মেলাপ, ঐক্য, সন্ধি. সম্প্রীতি, an agreement, accommodation.

মেষ, ভেড়া, মেড়া, প্রথম রাশি, a ram, a sheep, the sign Aries.

মেষঘোষ, ঘটা, ভিড়ভাড়, a crowd, a hustling noise.

মেষপাল-ক, ভেড়ারক্ষক, রাখাল, গাড়রিয়া, a shepherd.

মেসুয়া, মেসো,—মাসীর পতি, a maternal aunt's husband.

মেসগড়া, ছানী, ক্ষতস্থানের নব মাংস, a film on the eye, the new flesh formed on the healing of a wound.

মেহ, শুক্রঘটিত রোগ, প্রস্রাব, ধাতুচলা, any discharge from or inflammation of the urinary passage, urine, gleet, gonorrhœa. [charge.

মেহকর, প্রস্রাবজনক, মূত্রবর্দ্ধক, diuretic, producing urinary dis-

মেহদুষ্ট, মেহবিকার,—ধাতুবিকার, morbid urinary discharge.

মৈত্র-ী, বন্ধুতা, আত্মীয়, friendship, amity; friendly, amicable.

মৈত্র, মৈত্রেয়,—বন্ধু, মিত্রসম্বন্ধীয়, a friend, companion; of or relating to a friend, friendly.

মৈথুন, মেল, সংযোগ, বিবাহ, রতিক্রিয়া, union, association, marriage, copulation, sexual intercourse.

মোক্তা, রক্ষক, ত্রাণকর্ত্তা, a deliverer, saviour, redeemer.

মোক্ষ, নির্ব্বাণ, মুক্তি, ত্রাণ, রক্ষা, final emancipation, salvation, liberation, escape. [cipation, death.

মোক্ষণ, ব্রহ্মপ্রাপ্তি, অপবর্গ, মৃত্যু, liberation from matter, eman-

মোঘ, নিরর্থক, নিষ্ফল, ভ্রমযোগ্য, ত্যক্ত, বেড়. পুষ্প বিশেষ, useless, vain, ineffectual, fallible, left, abandoned; a fence, a hedge, the trumpet-flower.

মোচ, ওষ্ঠোপরি ধারিত কেশ, মুকুল, অগ্রভাগ, mustachioes, whiskers, a blossom, a nib, a point.

মোচঙ্গ, পুষ্পরসহারি পক্ষি বিশেষ, a small bird which sucks the honey from flowers.

মোচড়-া, বেঁউচা, মচ্কা, a twist, wrench, sprain.

মোচড়ন-আন, নিঙ্গড়ন, মচ্কান, বেঁউচান, মোড়ন, to wring, twirl, twist, wrench, sprain, to splice, twist together.

মোচন, উদ্ধরণ, ছাড়ান, ক্ষমা করণ, পুচন, ঘুচান, মার্জ্জন, ভঞ্জন, ছাল তোলন, মুক্তি, to liberate, free. emancipate, release, discharge, forgive, deliver, extricate, save, to wipe, clean, obliterate, expiate, forgive, to peel, to shell; final beatitude.

মোচনা, চিম্টা, সাঁড়াশি, a pair of pincers, tongs, tweezers.

মোচরস, শিমুলের আঠা. the gum of the silk-cotton tree.

মোচা, কদলী বৃক্ষের কাঁদী, the blossoms of the plantain tree.

মোচাফল, কদলীফল, কলা, a plantain.

মোছন, পুঁচন, মার্জ্জন, মুণ্ডন, to wipe, clean, cleanse, to shave.

মোট, ভার, গাঁঠরি. একুন, গড়, পদুয়াবিক্রী, a burden, load, bundle, package, an amount, sum, total, wholesale.

মোটকী, ক্ষুদ্র মোট, লঘু ভার, a small burden, a bundle.

মোটা, স্থূল, হৃষ্টপুষ্ট, বড়, thick, coarse, dull, plump. sleek, fat, bulky, big, great, large. [cursorily.

মোটামোটি, গড়ে, অবিশেষে, in the gross, indiscriminately,

মোটিয়া, বোঝারী, ভারবাহক, a porter, carrier, bearer of burdens.

মোড়, বেঁউচা, বেঁক, পশুর স্তন, a twist, strain, bend, turning, crook, an udder. [a dose.

মোড়ক, পুঁটলী, ঔষধের মাত্রা, a small packet, a paper-parcel,

মোড়ন-আন, ফিরণ, বেঁকন, পাকান, পেঁচান, ভিড়ান, ফিরাণ, জড়ান. to turn, bend, crooken, warp, twirl, twist, screw, turn a boat to land, turn a plough, to return goods for an abatement of price or labour for an advance of pay, to wrap up in paper, put up into a parcel, to overlay, cover with leather, &c. to plate, to gild.

মোড়া, মাচিয়া, পুঁটুলি, মাত্রা, পাক, মোচড়, a stool, foot-stool, a roll or packet, a dose, a turn, twist, &c.

মোদক, মিঠাইকর, লড্ডুকা, পুষ্টিকর ঔষধ বিশেষ, হর্ষজনক, a confectioner, a sweetmeat, a species of fattening medicine; delighting, &c.

মোদন, তোষণ, হর্ষ জন্মান, রুদ্ধ করণ, বুজন, to delight, gladden, exhilirate, enliven, to shut, to close.

মোদা, রুদ্ধ, বুজা, বদ্ধকরা, shut, closed, close; a shutting.

মোদী, পসারী, a retail-shopkeeper, a grocer.

মোনা, মুষল, ঢেঁকী, the pestle of a pedal.

মোনী, বোঝাই রাখিবার জন্যে নৌকার পরিমাণ, tonnage, burthen.

মোম, পরিষ্কৃত মৌচাক, wax, bee's wax.

মোমজামা. মোমযুক্ত কাপড়, wax-cloth.

মোষক, চোর, দস্যু, প্রবঞ্চক, a robber, plunderer, free-booter, a swindler.

মোষণ, অপহরণ, চাতুরী করণ, to steal, rob, plunder, swindle.

মোহ ন, মায়া, ভেল্কী, অচৈতন্য, মূর্চ্ছা, বিহ্বলতা, বুদ্ধির ভ্রংশ, অজ্ঞানতা, সংসারজাল, fascination, infatuation, delusion, stupefaction, loss of consciousness or sensation, fainting, transport of grief, &c. folly, ignorance, worldly illusion.

মোহগত, মুগ্ধ, মায়াবদ্ধ, fascinated, stupified, under worldly delusion.

মোহজনক, ইন্দ্রিয়মুগ্ধ, কুহকী, causing stupefaction, &c. a sorcerer, magician.

মোহনী, মন্ত্রপাঠ, কুহক, মন্থন, an incantation, fascination, a churning.

মোহন্ত, সন্ন্যাসী, দণ্ডী, ভিক্ষুক, a Sannyási or religious mendicant.

মোহপ্রাপ্ত, মোহিত,—মুগ্ধ, মায়াবদ্ধ, হতজ্ঞান, fascinated, infatuated, charmed, stupified.

মোহর, সুবর্ণ, ষোড়শ টঙ্কা, মুদ্রা, a gold coin, a seal.

মোহিনী, কান্তা, মনোরমা, *f.* charming; a fascinating woman.

মোহী, মনোহর, চারু, fascinating, infatuating, charming.

মৌ. মধু, পুষ্পরস, honey, the nectar of flowers.

মৌক্তিক. রত্ন বিশেষ, মুক্তা, মতি, a pearl.

মৌখর্য্য, মুখরতা, প্রাগল্ভ্য, নিন্দা, scurrility, abusiveness, insolence, defamation.

মৌখিক, মুখসম্বন্ধীয়, মুখস্থ, কপটী, বাহ্য, কাল্পনিক, অব্যবহিত, of or belonging to the mouth or face, lip-serving, outward, pretended, immediate.

মোচাক, মধুমক্ষিকারচিত মধুস্থান, a honey-comb, a hive.
মৌন, অভাষণ,তূষ্ণীংশীলতা;বিষাদ, ঔদাস্য, silence, taciturnity, reserve, sadness, gloom, gloominess.
মৌনব্রত, নীরব থাকার নিয়ম, a vow of silence. [tacit consent.
মৌনসম্মতি, অকথনে অনুমতি, silent sufferance or acquiescence.
মৌনী, নীরব, ধীর, তূষ্ণীক, উদাসীন, silent, taciturn, grave, reserved; a hermit, ascetic.
মৌমাছী, মধুমক্ষিকা, ভ্রমর, a bee. [as a token of honor.
মৌরছোল, ময়ূরের পাখানির্মিত ব্যজন, a fan of peacock's feathers
মৌর্বী, ধনুকের ছিলা, জ্যা, a bow-string, the chord of an arc
মৌল, মূলের, মূলজ, নিঃসঙ্কর বংশজাত, radical, proceeding from a root, of pure blood, of unmixed extraction.
মৌলা, আসন বিশেষ, চাঁচ, a sort of mat. [on the crown.
মৌলি, মস্তক,কিরীট, চূড়া, the head, a diadem, the lock of hair
মৌহূর্ত্তিক, দৈবজ্ঞ, গণক, an astrologer.
ম্রক্ষণ, মাখান, লেপন, to smear, to rub, to anoint.
ম্রিয়মাণ, মরণোদ্যত,বিষণ্ণ, খেদান্বিত, dying, expiring, at the point of death, melancholy, disconsolate.
ম্লান, শুষ্ক, বিরস, বিষণ্ণ,খেদযুক্ত,অসাহস, নিরাশ, ক্লান্ত, withered, faded, decaying, sad, melancholy, dejected, grieved, discouraged, weary, languid.
ম্লানি, বিষাদ, খেদ, ক্লান্তি,শুষ্কতা, melancholy, sadness, dejection, languor, weariness, a withering, fading, flaccidness. [sad, cheerless.
ম্লানবদন বা মুখ, বিষণ্ণ, মলিনাস্য, শোকান্বিত, downcast, dejected,
ম্লেচ্ছ, বেদাচারহীন, বিদেশী, a barbarian, foreigner, one not a Hindoo.

য

যক, যক্ষ,—কুবেরের ধনরক্ষক, a class of demigods fabled to superintend the treasury and gardens of Cúvera the god of wealth. [eased liver.
যকৃৎ, কালখণ্ড, রোগবিশেষ, the liver, liver complaint or dis-
যক্ষধূপ, বৃক, সর্জ্জরস, ধূনা, resin, turpentine, incense.
যক্ষ্মা শোষরোগ, ক্ষয়কাস, pulmonary consumption.
যক্ষ্মী, ক্ষয়কাসযুক্ত, consumptive, having diseased lungs.
যখন, যে সময়ে, যৎকাল, when, whenever, as soon as.

যজন, যাগ করণ, পূজা করণ, to perform sacrifice, to worship.

যজমান, যাজ্য, যাগাদির অনুষ্ঠাপক, পূজাদির আদেষ্টা, যে ব্যক্তি দক্ষিণা দিয়া কর্ম্ম করায়, sacrificing; one for whom and at whose expence a sacrifice is offered.

যজুঃ, যজুর্ব্বেদ,—দ্বিতীয় বেদ, the second of the four Vedas.

যজুর্ব্বেদী, দ্বিতীয় বেদ সম্বন্ধীয়, pertaining to the Yajur Ved.

যজ্ঞ, যাগ, মখ, পূজা, অশ্বমেধাদি, a sacrifice, oblation, religious worship. [altar.

যজ্ঞকুণ্ড, যাগার্থ চতুষ্কোণ গর্ত্ত, a sacrificial pit serving as an

যজ্ঞবেদি, যাগার্থ উচ্চীকৃত ভূমি, an altar for sacrifice. [thread.

যজ্ঞসূত্র, যজ্ঞোপবীত,—উপনয়ন, the characteristic or sacred

যজ্ঞাঙ্গ, যজ্ঞের অনুকূল বস্তু, যাগের অংশ, any essential article of a sacrifice, any part of a sacrificial ceremony. [longing to a sacrifice.

যজ্ঞিয়, যাগাদিকর্ম্মার্হ, যজ্ঞের উপযুক্ত. sacrificial, fit for or be-

যড়, উপার্জ্জিত, সঞ্চিত, সংলগ্ন, একত্রীকৃত, অপ্রপঞ্চিত, collected, amassed, united, squeezed together, closed up.

যড়াও, মণকরা, an enamelling.

যড়ান, কুড়ান, গুটন, আঁটন, চিপড়ান, কোঁকড়ান, সঞ্চয়ন, to collect, gather together, to fold cloth or paper, to bind, squeeze together, crumple, to furl a sail, to amass, to hoard.

যৎ, যে, যাহা, which, what, that, the, as.

যত, যাবৎ, as many as, as much as, as long as.

যতঃ, যাহাতে, যেহেতুক, wherefore, hence, because, seeing, since. [while, until.

যতকাল, যতক্ষণ, যতদিন,—যেপর্য্যন্ত, যাবৎ, as long as, whilst,

যতবার, যবার, যাবৎ পর্য্যন্ত, as often as.

যতন, চেষ্টা করণ, to endeavour, strive, labour for, aim at.

যতি, যতী,—জিতেন্দ্রিয়, সন্ন্যাসী, দণ্ডী, of subdued passions, continent; an ascetic, religious mendicant.

যতি, বিরতি, থাক, আটক, দমন, ছেদ, পরিচ্ছেদ, যুক্তবর্ণ, a cessation, rest, pause, stop, check, controul, restraint, a space in writing, a syllable.

যৌতুক, বিবাহকালে পিত্রাদি দত্ত পারিতোষিক দ্রব্য, a nuptial present to a bride, marriage favours.

যতেক, যাবৎ, যতগুলি, as many as, so many.

যৎকিঞ্চিৎ, অল্প, কিছু, কেবল, a little, a few, very little; only.

যত্ন, প্রয়াস, শ্রম, চেষ্টা, উদ্যম, অধ্যবসায়, labour, toil, application, assiduity, pains, diligence, care, effort, exertion, endeavour, energy, perseverance.

যত্নপ্রাপ্ত, কামাই, উপার্জ্জিত, obtained by labour, &c; acquisitions, earnings. [tive, zealous, &c.

যত্নবান্, যত্নযুক্ত,—চেষ্টান্বিত, পরিশ্রমী, laborious, diligent, ac-

যত্র, যেখানে, যেস্থানে, where, in which, in what place.

যৎসামান্য, সাধারণ, তুচ্ছ, অধম, common, vulgar, mean, pitiful, inferior. [for instance.

যথা, যেখানে, যে প্রকার, যেমন, where, as, according to,

যথাকাম, যেমন ইচ্ছা, as you please, at will, at pleasure.

যথাকথঞ্চিৎ, যে কোন প্রকার, in any wise, in any way.

যথাকাল, দিবসের শেষভাগ, বিহিত সময়, সময়ানুসারে, the close of day, evening, due or proper time; according to the time. [sively.

যথাক্রম, আনুপূর্ব্বিক, ক্রমশঃ, in order or succession, succes-

যথাতথা, স্থূলতঃ, যেমনতেমন, সর্ব্বস্থানে, যেখানে সেখানে, indiscriminately, as much of one as the other, the same, so as, hither and thither, in all places.

যথায়, যেখানে, যে কোন স্থানে, where, in what place.

যথাযথা, সমভাবে, in equal quantities or portions.

যথারুচি, যেমন বাঞ্ছা, according to taste, as you like.

যথার্থ, সত্য, ন্যায্য, উপযুক্ত, উচিত, true, real, genuine, right, just, proper, suitable. [diture, thrift.

যথার্থব্যয়, পরিমিতব্যয়, frugality, economy, measured expen-

যথার্হ, যেমন উচিত, as is fit or proper, as is right.

যথাসাধ্য, যথাশক্তি,—সাধ্যানুসারে, as far as possible, to the utmost of one's power. [like.

যথেচ্ছ, ইচ্ছানুসারে, যেমন ইচ্ছা, as you please, just as you

যথেপ্সিত, যেমন ইচ্ছা, ইচ্ছাপূর্ব্বক, বাহুল্যে, প্রচুর, according to one's wish or pleasure, voluntarily, as one pleases, amply, abundantly; enough.

যথেষ্ট, বহুতর, অনেক, ঢের, প্রচুর, নানা, id : *also* enough, abundant, much, ample, many, sufficient, various.

যথাসম্ভব, যেমন উপযুক্ত, উপস্থিতি মত, অতিনিষ্ঠুর রূপে, as the case may be or require, according to circumstances, with the utmost rigour.

যথোচিত, যথোপযুক্ত, —যেমন ন্যায্য, কর্ম্মসঙ্গত, as far as is proper or lawful; condign. [until, while.

যদবধি, যে কালহইতে, যে কালপর্য্যন্ত, since, from the time that,

যদা, যেকালে, যখন, যেক্ষণে, when, at what time.

যদি, যদ্যপি, যদিস্যাৎ,—চেৎ, পক্ষান্তরে, যেহেতুক, if, and if, if so be, though, although, since.

যদৃচ্ছা, স্বচ্ছন্দে. স্বতন্ত্রতা, ঢেঁটামি, agreeably to one's own will or inclination; independance, wilfulness.

যন্ত্র, শিল্পকর্ম্মার্থ কল্পিত বস্তু, কল, তন্ত্র, বীণাদি. অস্ত্র, শস্ত্র, ফাঁদ, গুপ্তার্থ রেখাময় চিহ্ন, a machine, engine, implement, instrument, tool, trap, a mystical character or caballistical diagram. [guish.

যন্ত্রক, আটক, যাতনা, পীড়া, a checking, binding, pain, an-

যন্ত্রণা, দুঃখ, ক্লেশ, বেদনা, কৃচ্ছ্র, দণ্ড, পরিশ্রম, pain, anguish, agony, torment, torture, suffering, punishment, toil, hard labour.

যন্ত্রতন্ত্র, অস্ত্রশস্ত্র. কল. বীণাদি, মন্ত্রগুহ্যাদি, instruments and machines, diagrams and caballistical figures.

যন্ত্রিত, আটকান. বদ্ধ, restrained, checked, fettered, bound.

যন্ত্রী, কলবিশিষ্ট, শিল্পকার, গুণী, ধূর্ত্ত, বাদ্যকর, having a machine, &c. mechanical, projecting, ingenious, crafty, designing; a musician. [inch.

যব, শস্য বিশেষ. সিতশূক, barley, a barley-corn, half an

যবক্ষার, লবণ বিশেষ. nitre, saltpetre. [able, fixed.

যবথব, যথস্থব,—যেমন ছিল. স্থির, স্থাবর, as it was; immov-

যবন, আরবী, বিদেশী, মুসলমান, ম্লেচ্ছ, ম্লেচ্ছদেশ, an Arabian, Grecian or other foreigner, a mussulman, Arabia. &c. [curtain.

যবনিকা, তাম্বুগৃহের বেষ্টনপট, কাণাৎ, an outer tent-screen or

যবস, ঘাস, গবাদির খাদ্য তৃণ, meadow or pasture grass.

যবাকার, বাদামীরূপ, অণ্ডাকার, oval, elliptical, like a barley-corn.

যবাগূ, যাউ, মণ্ড, a sour gruel of the broken grains of rice.

যবান্ন, পক্ক যব, ছাতু, boiled barley, barley food.

যবান, যুবন, অল্পবয়স্ক, তরুণ, young. [younger brother.
যবীয়ান্, যবিষ্ঠ,—অতি ছোট, কনিষ্ঠ, very young, youngest; a
যবার, যয়বার,—যতবার, যে কোন সময়ে, as often as, whenever.
যবে, যখন, যে কালে, when, at what time, on which day.
যব্য, যব বপনের যোগ্য ভূমি, fit for or sown with barley.
যম, অন্তক, ধর্ম্মরাজ, মৃত্যু, যোড়া, যুগ্ম, Yama regent of death and judge of hell, death, a brace, a pair.
যমক, যমজ,—মিথুন, সহজাত, যোট, twins, a twin, one of a pair.
যমক, একজাতীয় শব্দের পুনঃ২ প্রয়োগ, মিত্রাক্ষর, alliteration, harmonious recurrence of sounds, rhyme.
যমকিঙ্কর, যমদূত,—যমের ভৃত্য, a messenger of Yama or death.
যমধার, ছোরা, কটার, a dagger, a stilletto.
যমপুরী, যমালয়,—নরক, the residence of Yama, hell.
যশঃ, খ্যাতি, কীর্ত্তি, স্তব, renown, fame, celebrity, reputation, panegyric, praise, eulogium.
যশস্বান্, যশস্বী,—সুখ্যাতিমন্ত, famous, renowned, illustrious.
যশোগাথক বা গায়ক,—কীর্ত্তিগায়ক, স্তাবক, কাছাধরা, a panegyrist, eulogist, flatterer, sycophant.
যষ্টা, যজমান, পূজারী, a sacrificer, worshipper, a priest.
যষ্টি, লাঠী, দণ্ড, a stick, staff, wand, mace, club.
যষ্টিমধু, মিষ্টরসযুক্ত কাষ্ঠ বিশেষ, liquorice-root.
যা, ভ্রাতৃবর্গের পরস্পর স্ত্রী, দূর হও, a husband's brother's wife; begone! avaunt!
যাউ, যবাগূ, rice-gruel made of the broken grains.
যাওন, গমন, চলন, প্রস্থান করণ, লাগন, to go, move, go by or away, depart, reach to. [course.
যাওয়াআসা, যাতায়াত, গতিবিধি, a going and coming, inter-
যাঁতা, চাকী, ভস্ত্রা, a mill-stone, a smith's bellows.
যাঁতি, সরোতী, betel-nippers, nut-crackers.
যাগ, যজ্ঞ, হোম, মখ, পূজা, অপক্ব ফল পাচক দ্রব্য, a sacrifice, oblation, offering, act of worship, lime or other substance used to ripen green-plucked fruit.
যাচক, প্রার্থক, ভিক্ষুক, a petitioner, suitor, candidate, beggar.
যাচকবৃত্তি, ভিক্ষাজীবিকা, ভিক্ষাটন, a living on alms, mendicity.
যাচন, মাঙ্গন, চাহন, প্রার্থনা করণ, to beg, pray, solicit, ask entreat, request, petition, sue for.

যাচনা, যাচ্ঞা,—প্রার্থনা, ভিক্ষা, নিবেদন, supplication, a request, suit, entreaty, &c. [for, &c.

যাচনীয়, যাচ্য,—প্রার্থনীয়, proper to be requested or prayed

যাজক, পূজারী, ঋত্বিক্, an officiating priest, a sacrificer.

যাজকতা, পৌরোহিত্য, priesthood, the priestly office.

যাজন, পূজা করণ, যাগাদি সাধন, to perform worship, conduct a sacrifice, officiate as a priest.

যাজ্য, যজমান, যজ্ঞোপার্জ্জিত, যজ্ঞিয়, যজ্ঞোপযুক্ত, one for whom a sacrifice is offered, sacrificial acts or gains; proper for sacrifice.

যাজ্ঞিক, যজ্ঞসম্বন্ধীয়; ঋত্বিক্ ব্রাহ্মণ, যজ্ঞানুষ্ঠাপক, sacrificial, of or belonging to a sacrifice; an officiating priest, a sacrificer or institutor of a sacrifice.

যাটি, যাঠী,—যষ্টি, লাঠী, a staff, stick, wand, cane.

যাত, প্রেত, গত, প্রস্থিত, gone, departed.

যাতনা, যন্ত্রণা, অতিশয় বেদনা, অত্যন্ত আয়াস, pain, agony, anguish, torment, hard or painful labour.

যাতযাম, বাসি, জীর্ণ, ম্লান, বিবর্জ্জিত, old, stale, spent, worn out, impaired, used, faded, rejected, abandoned.

যাতা, যাতৃ,—গমনকর্ত্তা, যা, one who goes, a husband's brother's wife. [ing and coming.

যতায়াত, গমনাগমন, গতিবিধি, a frequenting, intercourse, go-

যাত্রা, চলন, গমন, প্রস্থান, কালক্ষেপ, দেশভ্রমণ, পর্য্যটন, তীর্থগমন, উৎসব, সং, a going, setting off, departure, travelling, spending or passing away of time, a march, journey, pilgrimage, a holy festival or procession of idols, theatrical representation.

যাত্রিক, যাত্রোপযুক্ত, তীর্থগামী, প্রস্থানকারী, পথিক, তীর্থভ্রমণক্রম, যাত্রাকর, proper on a march, marching, journeying, going on pilgrimage, fit to set out on pilgrimage or a journey, attending in a procession.

যাত্রী, যাত্রাকারী, তীর্থপর্য্যটনী, marching, journeying, &c. a pilgrim. [ous.

যাথার্থিক, বাস্তবিক, সত্য, সাধু, true, real, genuine, just, righte-

যাথার্থ্য, স্বরূপতা, সত্যতা, তথ্য, শুদ্ধতা, reality, truth, veracity, justness, righteousness.

যাদৃক্, যাদৃশ্,—যে প্রকার, যে রূপ, as, like as, in the manner of.
যাদৃচ্ছিক, অবাধ্য, ইচ্ছাবান, স্বতন্ত্র, wilful, obstinate, independant.
যান, বাহন, অশ্ব রথাদি, a carriage, vehicle, conveyance, as palkee, horse, &c.
যানবাহ-ক, শকটাদি চালক, অশ্বাদি, বাহন, বেহারা, an animal or person drawing or carrying a vehicle, a bearer.
যানমুখ, রথাদির অগ্রাংশ. the fore part, pole or shafts of a carriage.
যাপন, চলান, ক্ষেপণ, to cause to go, &c. to spend or pass away time.
যাপ্য, গোপনীয়, গুপ্ত, requiring to be concealed, secret, dormant.
যাবক, অর্দ্ধপক্ব যব, বোরধান্য, লা, half-ripe barley, barley without the awn, forced rice, lac.
যাবজ্জীব-ন, মৃত্যুকাল পর্য্যন্ত, through life, all one's life.
যাবৎ, যত দিন, যে পর্য্যন্ত, যত, সমুদায়, whilst, during, as long as, till, until; as much as, whatever, all, the whole.
যাবতীয়, যাবদীয়,—সমগ্র, সমুদায়, all, entire, the whole.
যাবত্তাবৎ, যত তত. as much as.
যাবদ্দেশে. সর্ব্বত্র, সমুদায় দেশে, throughout, everywhere, all over the country.
যাম, প্রহর, a watch, the fourth part of a day or night.
যামঘোষ, ঘড়ী, কুক্কুট, a gong, hour-drum, clock, a cock.
যামাতা, কন্যার স্বামী, a son-in-law, (daughter's husband.)
যামিক-ভট, প্রহরী, কোটাল, a watchman, night-guard.
যামিক, প্রহর সম্বন্ধীয়, of or belonging to the watches of day or night.
যামিনী, রাত্রি, নিশাপতি, নিশীথিনী, night.
যাম্য, দক্ষিণ দিক্, the south quarter, the south.
যিনি, যে লোক, যে ব্যক্তি, who, (honorific or respectful.)
যিয়ক্ষা, যাজনের ইচ্ছা, a desire to perform sacrifice or worship.
যুক, তুলা, a pair of scales for weighing.
যুকৎ, কৌশল, চাতুর্য্য, দাঁড়া, an art, knack, habit.
যুঁকন, মাপন, তৌলন, to measure, take dimensions, weigh.
যুক্ত, মিলিত, সশ্লিষ্ট, লগ্ন, মগ্ন, বিশিষ্ট, আবিষ্ট, আসক্ত, সিদ্ধ. উচিত, ন্যায্য, joined, combined, yoked, united with, connected, possessed of, possessing, endowed or affected with, pregnant with, attached to, engaged in, intent on, occupied with, proved, concluded, proper, right, fit, reasonable.

যুক্তি, তর্ক, বিবেচনা, সিদ্ধান্ত, মন্ত্রণা, পরামর্শ, উপায়, বৃত্তান্তলিপি, ঊহা, নিগূঢ় বাক্য, সংযোগ, ন্যায্যতা, যোগ্যতা, রীতি, ব্যবহার, reasoning, argument, inference, logical conclusion, deduction, reason, counsel, advice, policy, contrivance, a specification of circumstances in written evidence, the supplying of an ellipsis, mystical expression, union, connection, propriety, fitness, usage, custom.

যুক্তিদাতা বা পাত্র,—অমাত্য, মন্ত্রী, পরামর্শদ, a senator, counsellor, adviser, monitor, one who gives advice.

যুগ, সত্য ত্রেতা দ্বাপর কলি এই চারির অন্যতম, যোয়াল, জুল, দ্বন্দ্ব, the four ages or successive periods of the world, a yoke, team, pair, couple, brace.

যুগধর্ম্ম, বিশেষ যুগের উপযুক্ত ব্যবহার, the appropriate religious duties of a particular age.

যুগপদ্, যুগপৎ,—সকৃৎ, এক কালে, একদা, at once, at one time.

যুগল, যুগ্ম, যুক্,—দুই, যোড়া, দ্বন্দ্ব, মিথুন, যোট, সাথী, সহায়, a pair, a brace, a couple, twins, a team, a yoke, a match, a mate, fellow, helper.

যুগান্ত, যুগের অবসান, কল্পান্ত, the end of an age, periodical destruction of the universe.

যুজন, যুটন,—একত্রীকরণ, মিলান, লাগন, মেলন, জুড়ান, to join, unite, yoke, cement, to commence, overspread, reach to, to be supplied or provided with, abound.

যুড়ান, থামন, শান্ত বা তুষ্ট হওন, to cool, become cool, be gratified or comforted.

যুত, যুক্ত, লগ্ন, বিশিষ্ট, connected, joined, possessed of, full of.

যুতা, চর্ম্মপাদুকা, a shoe, (of leather.)

যুথ, যূথ,—ঝুণ্ড, পাল, সমূহ, a herd, drove, flock, multitude.

যুদ্ধ, যুধ,—রণ, লড়াই, সংগ্রাম, সমর, a battle, combat, fight, contest, conflict, war.

যুদ্ধকর্ত্তা, লড়াক, a warrior, combatant, one who makes war

যুবক, যুবা, যুবন,—যৌবনান্বিত, বয়ঃক্রমপ্রাপ্ত, সতেজ, তরুণ, প্রৌঢ়, young, youthful, arrived at puberty, in the prime of life, adult; a young man, a youth.

যুবতী, যৌবনান্বিতা স্ত্রী, তরুণী, *f.* young, adult, &c. a young girl.

x x x

যুবতা, যুবত্ব,—যৌবনাবস্থা, youth, youthfulness, adult age.
যুবরাজ, রাজার প্রধান পুত্র, a prince, an heir apparent.
যুষ্মদ, তুমি, আপনি, *sing:* you, thou.
যুষ্মদীয়, তোমার, আপনার, *sing:* thy, thine, your, yours.
যূক, উকুন, ডেঙ্গর, a louse.
যূপ, পশু বন্ধনার্থ কাষ্ঠ, the stake to which a victim is bound, a funeral post.
যূষ, ঝোল, মণ্ড বিশেষ, pulse-water, soup, broth, porridge.
যে, বিশেষ্য ব্যক্তি কিম্বা বস্তু, who, which; *conj*: that.
যেঅবধি, যৎকালহইতে, from the time that, from which time.
যেকালে, যেক্ষণে,—যৎকালে, যখন, at what time, when, whenever, as soon as.
যেকিছু, যাহা, যদ্দ্রব্য, যৎকিঞ্চিৎ, whichever, whatever, the little that.
যেকেহ, যেকেউ,—যে কোন লোক, whoever, whosoever, any one.
যেকোন, যিনি, যাহা, whoever, whatever.
যেখানে, যেস্থানে,—যৎস্থলে, যত্র, যথায়, where, whither, wherever, whithersoever.
যেথা, যত্র, যৎস্থানে, যেখানে, where, whither.
যেথাসেথা, এদিগ্ ওদিগ্, যথাতথা, hither and thither, up and down.
যেন, যাহাতে, that, in order that, to the end that, whereby.
যেপর্য্যন্ত, যাবৎ, যতদূর, till, until, whilst, as long as, as far as.
যেপ্রকার, যাদৃক্, যদ্রূপ, of what sort, what kind of, as.
যেমত, যেমন,—যে প্রকার, যদ্রূপ, যাদৃক্, as, like, like as.
যেমনতেমন, মধ্যবিত, সামান্য, indifferent, passable, middling.
যেমনতেমনই, সমভাবে, বিনাভেদে, যথোপযুক্ত, just as it was, as before, the same, as is just, agreeably to desert.
যেযে, যেকেহ, যে কোন, whoever, whosoever, whichever, whatever.
যেরূপ, যৎপ্রকার, যেমন, of what form, in what manner, as, like as.
যেহেতুক, যন্নিমিত্ত, কেননা, কারণ, as, since, because, for, for as much as.
যো, পুঁজী, মূলধন, টানাকাঠ, a stock, capital, a weaver's warp-rods.
যোঁকা, মাপ, পরিমাণ, measure, dimensions, depth, guage.
যোঁকান, মাপ বা তৌল করণ, উমান করণ, to measure, take dimensions, to weigh, to sound, to guage.
যোক্তা, যোটানিয়া, যোগানিয়া, নির্ব্বাহক, ঘটক, one who joins, &c. a provider, procurer, professional match-maker.
যোক্তু, যোত, হলবন্ধন রজ্জু, the tie of a yoke.

যোগ, মিলন, একত্রীকরা, সংশ্লেষ, মিশ্র, সম্বন্ধ, মেল, শেষোৎপন্ন, উপযুক্ততা, উপায়, প্রাপ্তি, বিশেষ সময়, যুগ্মতিথি, শুভ কাল, রাশিচক্রের সপ্তবিংশতিতম ভাগ, চিত্তের একাগ্রতা, সমাধি, পাতঞ্জল দর্শন, union, junction, uniting, combination, contact, addition, mixture, connexion (as of cause and effect, subject and predicate,) result, consequence, fitness, propriety, an expedient, acquisition, a juncture, lucky conjuncture, the 27th part of a great circle, religious abstraction, intense meditation on the divinity, one of the six philosophical systems.

যোগাড়, কর্ম্ম নির্ব্বাহকরা, a supply of materials to a bricklayer or other workman.

যোগাড়িয়া, যোগাল,—খাটনিয়া, সহকারী, a bricklayer's labourer.

যোগান, নির্ব্বাহ করণ, কুলান, চালান, খাটান, to supply or provide materials, make provision for, furnish necessaries, superintend, manage, set to work, &c.

যোগানিয়া, নির্ব্বাহক, কুলানিয়া, চালানিয়া, supplying, furnishing with, &c. a superintendant, overseer.

যোগাসন, যোগ সাধনের উপকারি আসন, a religious posture favourable to devout abstraction.

যোগনিদ্রা, লঘুনিদ্রা, কাকতন্দ্রা, a light and wakeful slumber.

যোগী, বৈরাগী, দণ্ডী, ভাক্ত সন্ন্যাসী, তাঁতী, an abstract devotee, an ascetic, a pretended devotee, a weaver.

যোগে, সময়ে, দ্বারা, করণক, সঙ্গে, in, at the time of, through, by means of, together with.

যোগ্য, উপযুক্ত, নিপুণ, দক্ষ, কর্ম্মার্হ, fit, suitable, proper, sufficient, worthy, clever, able, capable, qualified.

যোগ্যতা, উপযুক্ততা, ক্ষমতা, fitness, ability, suitableness, &c.

যোঙড়া, শম্বুক, ঝিনুকাদি, a cockle-shell, oyster-shell, any bivalve shell.

যোজক, যোড়ানিয়া, ঘটক, uniting, &c. a professional match-maker.

যোজন, মিশান, যোড়ান, চারি ক্রোশ, to add, unite, cement, match; a measure of four *cos* or 8 miles.

যোজনা, সংশ্লেষ, মিশ্র, নির্ব্বাহকরা, ঘটনা, a union, addition, supply of materials, a negociating of marriages.

যোটনী, যুগল, যুগ্মের এক, সাথী, one of a pair, a match, a fellow.
যৌতক, কার্য্যকারক, দ্বারক, ঘটক, an agent, factor, manager, a negotiator of marriages.
যোটন-আন, একত্রীকরণ, মিশান, মিলান, নির্দ্ধারণ, to join, cement, mix, incorporate, to pair, yoke, bring together, to negociate, effect a bargain.
যোড়, যুগ্ম, দ্বন্দ্ব, দ্বিপদ শ্লোক, দুয়ের এক, যোট, সংশ্লেষ, সংসর্গ, a pair, couple, couplet, one of a pair, a match, union, a pairing, cohabiting, &c.
যোড়ন, মিলান, লাগান, উদ্রেক করণ, ব্যাপ্ত হওন, বাড়ন, মেলন, কুলান, জাল বিস্তারণ, সারাণ, বস্ত্রের তালী দেওন, to join, unite, cement, to commence, spread, take up room, reach, be overspread, to be supplied with, to spread a net, to mend or patch.
যোড়া, যুগ্ম, যুগল, দুই, প্রস্থ, সম্বন্ধ, মেল, পরগাছা লাগালি, পরস্পর, a pair, a couple, a match, a suit of clothes, union, connection, a grafting, patching, joining.
যোড়ান, মিলান, সংলগ্ন করণ, একত্রীকরণ, to join, unite, connect, cement, add, affix, to graft a tree, to pair, to yoke. [broidered.
যোড়িত, মিলিত, সংযুক্ত, সংলগ্ন, united, cemented, grafted, em-
যোত, হলবন্ধন রজ্জু, the tie of a yoke.
যোত-া, চাষা ভূমি, আকাকল, plowed land, a farm, a fish-weir.
যোতন, যোয়ালেতে মিলিয়া বদ্ধ করণ, to yoke or fasten together.
যোত, সম্পত্তি, আয়, নির্ব্বাহ, stock, capital, wealth, income, means, supply. [soldier.
যোদ্ধা, যোধ—সংগ্রামকর্ত্তা, লড়াক, সেনা, a warrior, combatant,
যোধ্য, যুদ্ধের বিষয়, রণযোগ্য, worthy to be fought for.
যোনি, স্ত্রীচিহ্ন, ভগ, জরায়ু, উৎপত্তি স্থান, আকর, উনুই, হেতু, আদি কারণ, pudendum muliebre, the vulva, the place of birth or production, a mine, spring, fountain, cause, origin, original.
যোনিজ, জরায়ুজ, produced from the womb, viviparous.
যোনিকীট, লম্পট, স্ত্রীপরায়ণ, a lascivious person, a lecher, profligate, debauchee. [tion.
যোনিভ্রমণ, পুনঃ২ জন্মপরিগ্রহ, reiterated births, transmigra-

যোয়াল, যোয়ালি,—যুড়িবার কাষ্ঠ, the yoke of a plough, &c.
যোষিৎ, স্ত্রী, মেয়্যা, অবলা, a woman, a female.
যৌ, যাবক, লাক্ষা, লা, lac, gum-lac.
যৌক্তিক, তার্কিক, যুক্তিসিদ্ধ, logical, founded on reasoning.
যৌগিক, ব্যুৎপন্ন, derivative, regularly formed, (in grammar.)
যৌতুক, বিবাহ আদি সময়ে লব্ধ ধন, nuptial presents to a female, a dower, marriage portion.
যৌবন, তারুণ্য, বাল্যের পরাবস্থা, youth, manhood, maturity, adult age. [adult, vigorous.
যৌবনযুক্ত, যৌবনস্থ,—তরুণ, সতেজ, প্রৌঢ়, young, youthful,
যৌবরাজ্য, যুবরাজের পদ, the office of a prince associated with his father in the government of a kingdom.

র.

রওন, রহণ, থাকন, বাস করণ, to stay, wait, stop, reside, dwell.
রং, রঙ্গ, বর্ণ, a colour, die, paint.
রক্ত, রুধির, লোহিতবর্ণ, blood; red, scarlet, tinged.
রক্তখেকুয়া, শোণিতপ, blood-thirsty, sanguinary, fond of blood.
রক্তচন্দন, রক্তবর্ণ গন্ধকাষ্ঠ বিশেষ, red sandal-wood, red sanders.
রক্তপা, জলৌকা, জোঁক, a leech, a blood-sucker.
রক্তপিত্ত, মুখাদি হইতে হঠাৎ রক্তস্রাব, spontaneous hæmorrhage, discharge of blood from the mouth, nose, &c. a reddish eruption preceding leprosy.
রক্তবটী, বসন্তরোগ, গুটী, the small-pox. [with blood.
রক্তময়, রক্তযুক্ত,—রুধিরময়, bloody, full of blood, coloured
রক্তস্রাব, হঠাৎ রক্ত নিঃসরণ, রুধির ক্ষরণ, spontaneous hæmorrhage, a discharge or flow of blood.
রক্তাক্ত, রুধিরময়, রুধিরলিপ্ত, bloody, smeared with blood.
রক্তাম্বর, রক্তবর্ণ বস্ত্রাচ্ছন্ন, clothed in red, wearing red coloured garments. [blood.
রক্তারক্তি, পরস্পর মারামারি করাতে রক্তপাত, a mutual shedding of
রক্তিমা, রক্তভাব, redness, rosiness, a red colour.
রক্তোপল, গেরী মাটী, red-ochre.
রক্ষক, পালক, ত্রাণকর্ত্তা, আশ্রয়, প্রহরী, a keeper, preserver, saviour, deliverer, defender, protector, guardian, a watchman, a guard.

রক্ষণ, পালন, উদ্ধরণ, নিবারণ, আশ্রয় দেওন, রাখন, ত্রাণ, প্রতিপালন, to preserve, protect, save, defend, ward off, shelter, shield, cherish, take care of, tend, feed, support. [nibal imp.

রক্ষস্, হিংসুক ভূতগণ, দেবাংশ, a fabulous giant, goblin, can-

রক্ষা, প্রতিপালনকরা, আশ্রয়, উদ্ধার, ত্রাণ, বাঁচাও, preservation, protection, defence, salvation, security, rescue, deliverance, escape. [protégé.

রক্ষিত, প্রতিপালিত, আশ্রিত, preserved, defended, &c. a ward,

রক্ষিতা, রক্ষাকর্ত্তা, রাখাল, প্রতিপালক, a guardian, keeper, saviour, defender, protector, &c.

রগড়, ঢকাদিতে শীঘ্র করিয়া মারা, the quick beating of a drum.

রগড়ন-আন, অঙ্গমর্দ্দন, হস্ত দিয়া শস্য মলন, পুনঃ২ সন্ধান লওন, গৌণ করণ, টালন, to rub the body, rub clothes, to rub out corn or seed with the hand, to sift a matter, to postpone, put off, delay.

রঙ্গ, রঞ্জক দ্রব্য, বর্ণ, রাং, ক্রীড়া, পরিহাস, নৃত্য, a colour, tint, dye, paint, tin, sport, mirth, merriment, acting, dancing and singing. [painter.

রঙ্গকর, রঙ্গকার,—বর্ণক, চিত্রকর, dying, colouring, &c. a dyer,

রঙ্গকারী, রঙ্গকারক,—সংকারী, কৌতুকী, রঞ্জক, making sport, &c. colouring ; a dyer. [diness.

রঙ্গচঙ্গ, চিত্রবিচিত্রভাব, চটক, a fine or glaring colour, gau-

রঙ্গচঙ্গিয়া, চিত্রবিচিত্র, ফুলফুলিয়া, gaudy, glaring, shewy, fine, dressy. [painter,

রঙ্গজীবিক, রঙ্গজীবী,—নর্ত্তক, চিত্রকর, an actor, dancer, mime, a

রঙ্গণ, রঙ্গাণ,—রঞ্জক দ্রব্য লাগান, রঙ্গ দেওন, বর্ণীকৃত করণ, to colour, tinge, dye, paint.

রঙ্গভঙ্গ, কৌতুক, বিহার, হাবভাব, কাচ, সং, merriment, fun, wanton sport or gestures, dramatic exhibition.

রঙ্গভূমি, আখড়া, যুদ্ধস্থল, a stage, theatre. a field of battle.

রঙ্গরস, ক্রীড়া, কৌতুক, ভণ্ডামী, sport, merriment, fun.

রঙ্গশালা, নাচঘর, সংআলয়, a hall for *náches*, ball-room, theatre.

রঙ্গাশিয়া, রঙ্গকর, রঞ্জক, বর্ণকারী, colouring, &c ; a dyer, colourer.

রঙ্গাবতারী, নর্ত্তক, ভণ্ড, an actor, dancer, mime, zany.

রঙ্গিল-1, চিত্রবিচিত্র, gaudy, shewy, tawdry, gay, splendid.

রঙ্গী, রঙ্গকারক, চিত্রকারী, কৌতুকী, ভাবক, colouring, dying, painting, exhibiting sports, &c. impassioned, inclined to passion.. [passion, impassioned.

রঙ্গীন, বর্ণীকৃত, বহুরঙ্গ, ভাবক, coloured, gaudy, subject to

রচন, নির্ম্মাণ করণ, গঠন, গ্রন্থ লেখন, ভণন, কল্পন, গ্রন্থন, to make, form, build, construct, fabricate, compose, invent, to arrange, string pearls, &c.

রচনা, বিন্যাস, গ্রন্থনকরা, উৎসবকালে মাল্যাদিতে সাজান, সৈন্যব্যূহ, নির্ম্মাণ, গঠন, কল্প, ভণন, orderly arrangement or disposition, decoration of the hair, the stringing of flowers,&c. making of garlands, adornment of temples with flowers, &c. at festivals, array of troops, a fabrication, making, formation, contrivance, invention, literary composition. [ser, author.

রচয়িতা, নির্ম্মায়ক, গ্রন্থক, ভণিতা, a maker, fabricator, compo-

রচিত, গঠিত, নির্ম্মিত, কল্পিত, written, composed, fabricated, made, contrived, &c. factitious.

রজঃ, ধূলি, পুষ্পরেণু. ঋতু, বিষয়াভিলাষের কারণ গুণ, dust, powder, the farina of flowers, the menses, the quality of activity or passion or the disposition to secularity. [woman.

রজক, রজকী,—ধোবা, ধোবানী, a washerman & washer-

রজত, রূপা.হার. হস্তিদন্ত,শ্বেত, silver, a necklace, ivory; white.

রজনী. রাত্রি, হরিদ্রা, night, turmeric.

রজনীকর, নিশাপতি, চন্দ্র, the moon as sovereign of the night.

রজনীগন্ধা, পুষ্প বিশেষ, the tuberose species of polyanthus.

রজনীমুখ, প্রদোষকাল, সূর্য্যাস্তের পর চারি দণ্ড, evening, night-fall.

রজস্বা, রজস্বলা,—ঋতুমতী, বিবাহযোগ্যা, *f.* menstruating, menstruous, marriageable.

রজ্জু, দড়ী. রসী, a rope, cord, line, string, tether.

রঞ্জক, তুষ্টিকর, মনোহর, কৌতুকী, চিত্রকর, রঙ্গকার, প্রবর্ত্তক, cheering, gladdening, pleasing, exciting, moving, jovial, merry, colouring, dyeing; a painter, dyer, a stimulant, provocative, excitement.

রঞ্জক-ঘরা, অগ্ন্যস্ত্রের পলিতা দিবার ছিদ্র, the touch-hole of a gun.

রঞ্জন, হর্ষজনক,ভাবোদ্দীপক,রঙ্গকরা, pleasing,charming,moving, affecting, exciting; a painting, colouring,&c.

রটন-আন, কহন, বলন, প্রকাশন, ঘোষণ, to speak, talk, utter, declare, announce, proclaim. [fame.

রটনা, কথা, জনরব, প্রচার, talk, report, rumour, publicity,

রটিত, অগ্নির ধ্বনি, কথিত, the roaring of flame; spoken, &c.

রড়ন-আন, দৌড়ন, বেগে চলন, to run, go fast, speed.

রণ, যুদ্ধ, শব্দ, a battle, fight, conflict, war, noise, sound.

রণকৃতী, রণকুশল,—সুযোদ্ধা, সংগ্রামবেত্তা, versed in war.

রণজয়ী, শত্রুপরাজয়কর,জয়প্রাপ্ত, victorious in battle, triumphant.

রণভঙ্গ, পরাভব, পরাস্ত হওয়া, a defeat, a rout, disorder.

রণভঞ্জন, পরাস্ত করণ, to defeat an enemy, put to the rout.

রণসিংহা, যুদ্ধোপযুক্ত শঙ্খ, a war-trump, war-conch.

রণ্ড, আশ্রমহীন, ধর্ম্মহীন, যিনি পুত্রহীন হইয়া মরে, অফলা বৃক্ষ, forlorn, neglecting one's religious duties; a man dying without male issue, a barren tree.

রণ্ডা, বন্ধ্যা, বিধবা, *f.* barren, sterile, childless; a widow.

রণ্ডী, স্ত্রীলোক, বিধবা, a woman, a widow.

রত, আসক্ত, পরায়ণ, আবিষ্ট, মৈথুন, delighted with, devoted or attached to, fond of, intent upon, occupied in; sexual intercourse, copulation.

রতি, স্ত্রীসংসর্গ,বিষয়সুখভোগ,প্রসক্তি,অভিলাষ, sexual intercourse, copulation, enjoyment, pleasure, desire.

রতিক্রিয়া, রতিদান,—স্ত্রীসংসর্গ, copulation, sexual intercourse.

রতিপতি, কামদেব, মদন, Cámadeva or the Indian Cupid.

রত্যাসক্ত, রত্যার্থী,—লম্পট, কামুক, বিষয়সুখাসক্ত, lascivious, lustful, libidinous, fond of pleasure.

রত্তি-কা, গুঞ্জা, a small seed used by goldsmiths as a weight, a little, a small quantity, a grain. [pearl.

রত্ন, মণি মুক্তা প্রবালাদি, a jewel, gem, precious stone, coral,

রত্নকন্দল, প্রবাল, পলা, coral.

রত্নগর্ভা, যে স্ত্রীর গর্ভে সৎপুত্র জন্মে, পৃথিবী, a mother of excellent children, the earth. [in gems.

রত্নজীবিক বা জীবী,—মণি বিক্রেতা, a jeweller, a lapidary, dealer

রত্নময়, মণিরচিত, মণিযুক্ত, made of gems, abounding in gems.

রত্নাকর, সমুদ্র, মণির উৎপত্তিস্থান, the sea, ocean, a jewel-mine.

রত্নাবলী, গ্রথিত মণি শ্রেণী, a string of jewels.
রত্নি, মুটুমহাত, a short cubit from the elbow to the insertion of the fingers.
রথ, স্যন্দন, চক্রযুক্ত যান, গাড়ী, a war-chariot, idol-car, a car, a carriage.
রথকার, যানচক্র নির্ম্মায়ক, a wheel-wright, a car-maker.
রথযাত্রা, প্রতিবৎসর পুত্তলার যান টানন, the annual procession of an idol car.
রথাঙ্গ, চক্র, রথের অবয়ব, a wheel or other part of a car.
রথী, রথারূঢ়, স্যন্দনারোহ, সারথি, রথের স্বামী, a charioteer, a car-warrior, the owner of a car.
রথ্যা, প্রশস্ত পথ, রাজপথ, a carriage road, a public street.
রদ, রদন,—দন্ত, দাঁত, বিষাণ, a tooth, a tusk.
রদী, দন্তবিশিষ্ট. বিষাণযুক্ত, হস্তী, having tusks or teeth; an elephant.
রন্ধন, অন্নাদি পাক করণ, to cook or dress food, to seeth.
রন্ধ্র, বিবর, ছিদ্র, গহ্বর, কুহর, ফাক, দোষ, a hole, incision, the eye of a needle, cavity, fissure, chasm, a rent, a fault, defect.
রব, ধ্বনি, নাদ, জনশ্রুতি, a sound, noise, cry, voice, report, rumour.
রবাহূত, শুনিয়া আগত, অনিমন্ত্রিত, called by the voice, uninvited.
রবি, সূর্য্য, দিনপতি, দিনকর, the sun.
রবিশস্য, সূর্য্য কিরণেতে পক্ক ধান্য, a harvest or crop ripened by the sun without much rain.
রবিবার, আদ্যবার, Sunday.
রম, মনোহর, প্রিয়, *affix:* charming, pleasing, delighting, ravishing.
রমণ, সুখভোগ, ক্রীড়া, লীলা, মৈথুন, নায়ক, উপপতি, পতি, কামদেব, স্মরণ, enjoyment of pleasure, sport, play, amorous dalliance, sexual intercourse, a lover, a gallant, a husband, Cupid, memory.
রমণা, রমণী,—স্ত্রী, উপপত্নী, ভার্য্যা, মনোহরী স্ত্রী, a woman, mistress, wife, an agreeable or charming woman.
রমণা, উদ্যান, উপবন, a park, pleasure grounds.
রমণীয়, রম্য,—সুন্দর, প্রিয়, মনোহর, beautiful, lovely, charming, pleasing, pleasurable, delightful.
রমণেচ্ছা, লাম্পট্য, কামশীলতা, lasciviousness, sensual desire.
রম্ভা, কদলী, স্বর্গ বেশ্যা বিশেষ, the plantain, an Apsará.
রম্বা, ফক্কী, পল্লব a small branch, a twig, rod, shoot.

রল্লক, পক্ষ্ম, কম্বল, an eye-lash, a blanket.

রশনা, সারথির হস্তস্থিত অশ্বমুখলগ্ন রজ্জু, a reign or bridle.

রশ্মি, কিরণ, অংশু, a ray of light, a sun-beam.

রষাণ, কষ্টিপাথর, a touch-stone.

রস, জলাদি দ্রবদ্রব্য, শরীরের ধাতু, সত্ত্ব, বৃক্ষনির্য্যাস, আঠা, পারা, বীর্য্য, সার, মজ্জা, পাঙ্গা, তার, স্বাদ, জিহ্বেন্দ্রিয় গোচর অর্থাৎ কটু তিক্তাদি, জিহ্বাগ্রাহ্য, শৃঙ্গারহাস্যাদি নয়, বুদ্ধি, ভাব, মনোবিকার, রমণেচ্ছা, বিষয়সুখ বোধ, a fluid, liquid, liquor, water, moisture, humour, juice, exudation, sap, gum, myrrh, quicksilver, semen virile, pith, marrow, any mineral salt, a relish, savour, flavour, zest, taste, sentiment, literary taste, wit, passion, an affection of the mind, emotion, feeling, sensuality, carnal enjoyment.

রসকর্পূর, রসকাপর,—পারা, quicksilver, a mercurial sublimate.

রসগর্ভ, হিঙ্গুল, অঞ্জন বিশেষ, vermillion, a mineral eye-paint.

রসজ, রুধির, জলজ ক্ষুদ্র কীট, blood, animalcule in liquids.

রসজ্ঞ, স্বাদভেদবেত্তা, রসিক, উত্তম কবি, অলঙ্কারাদি শাস্ত্রবেত্তা, জিহ্বা, রসায়নবেত্তা, acquainted with tastes, &c, possessed of taste; a refined or sentimental writer, an elegant poet, an alchymist, the tongue.

রসজ্ঞা, রসনা,—জিহ্বা, জিব, the tongue.

রসন, চাকন, গর্জন, আর্দ্র হওন, তার, শব্দ, to taste, to fester, grow damp; taste, sound, noise.

রসনেন্দ্রিয়, জিহ্বা, জিব, the organ of taste, the tongue.

রসপুষ্প, মিশ্রিত পারা গন্ধক লবণ এই তিন, a preparation of mercury with sulpher and salt.

রসবৎ, রসবান্,—ভাবক, চিত্তঘাতক, স্বাদুস, সত্ত্বযুক্ত, সরস, সুস্বাদু, tasteful, touching, affecting the feelings, pithy, succulent, well-flavoured, savoury, juicy.

রসবাত, গ্রন্থিস্থিত বায়ুরোগ, rheumatism in the joints.

রসরাজ, পারা, চপলা ধাতু, quicksilver, liquid mercury. [&c.

রসসিদ্ধ, রসায়নবেত্তা, an alchemist, an adept in alchemy,

রসসিদ্ধি, তাম্রাদি ধাতুভেদ করা ও দীর্ঘকাল পর্য্যন্ত রোগ এবং মৃত্যু নিবারণ করা এই উভয়ের বিদ্যা, knowledge of alchemy, the possession of the arts of transmuting metals, prolonging life, securing health, &c.

রসা, আর্দ্র, রসবৎ, পৃথিবী, রজ্জু, দড়ী, wet, juicy; the earth, a rope, a halter, a line.

রসাঞ্জন, কজ্জল বিশেষ, a collyrium or eye-paint.

রসাতল, পাতাল, Pátála or the subterraneous world, the lowest of the infernal regions.

রসাদান, শোষাণ, শুষ্ককরা, a drying up, absorption, suction.

রসান, আর্দ্র করণ, ভিজান, সাঁতসান, ফুলান, কোড়াদি পাকান, গলান, to wet, moisten, season, cause to swell or tumefy, bring on suppuration.

রসানি, ক্লেদ, পূঁজ, matter, pus, purulent matter.

রসায়ন, বিষ, মৃত্যুনিবারণার্থ বিষঘটিত ঔষধি, তদ্পানকরাণ, তদ্বিষয়ে পাণ্ডিত্য, স্বর্ণাদির উজ্জ্বল করণের প্রস্তর, poison, a poisonous medicine to preserve life, &c. elixir vitæ, the administering of such medicines, alchemy, chemistry, a stone for polishing metals.

রসাল, রসযুক্ত, সুস্বাদু, আম্র, juicy, savoury, succulent, delicious, pithy; a mango.

রসাহ্ব, সর্জ্জরস, ধূনা, বৃক, resin, turpentine.

রসিক, রসবিশিষ্ট, নাগর,ভাবক, বিদ্রূপী, কামুক, কৌতুকী, possessed of literary taste, refined, sentimental, witty, humorous, jocose, droll, funny, merry, amorous, sensual; a wag. [coquette.

রসিকা, রসবিশিষ্টা, হাবভাবযুক্তা, খেলাড়ী, *f.* witty, jocose, &c. a

রসিত, ধ্বনিত, মুণ্ডিত, sounded, rattled, gilt, gilded, plated, washed with a metal.

রসী, দড়ী, রজ্জু, a cord, line, twine, a halter, a rope.

রসুই, রন্ধন, অন্নাদি পাক, the cooking of food, cookery.

রসুন-া, কন্দ বিশেষ, অরিষ্ট, garlic, a cive, chalot

রসেন্দ্র, পারা,পরশ পাথর,স্পর্শমণি,liquid mercury, quicksilver, the philosopher's stone.

রহণ, নিবর্ত্ত হওন, তিষ্টন, থাকন, প্রবাস করণ, টেঁকন, হওন, to stop, cease, desist, forbear, stay, tarry, remain, wait, stand still, to dwell, abide, live, continue, last, endure, to be, subsist. [bitant.

রহণিয়া, থাকনিয়া, প্রবাসী, residing, continuing, &c. an inha-

রহস্, বিরলে, alone, privately, secretly, in private.

রহস্য, ঔদাস্য, পরিহাস, কৌতুক, সং, ইতিহাস, নির্জন, গুপ্ত, retirement, solitude, a joke, diversion, shew, mirth, a story, tale, proverb ; private, clandestine.

রহিত ত্যক্ত, নিবর্ত্ত, নিবারিত, বর্জ্জিত, হীন, abandoned, quitted, left, stopped, prevented; *affix :* without, void of, -less, destitute of, bereft.

রাঁড়, বিধবা, স্ত্রীলোক, a widow, a woman.

রাঁড়া-ন, অফল, নিষ্ফল, sterile, fruitless, barren. [food.

রাঁধন, রন্ধন, অন্নাদি পাক করণ, to cook, to prepare or dress

রাইল, রাশি, সঞ্চয়, স্তূপ, a quantity, pile, heap, hoard, &c.

রাই, সর্ষপ., সর্ষপ, mustard, rape-seed.

রাউটী, তাম্বু, বস্ত্রগৃহ, a tent. [dye.

রাং, রাঙ্গ,—ধাতু বিশেষ, রঙ্গ, বর্ণ, tin, paint, a colour, tint,

রাংঝালি, রাঙ্গা গালিয়া মুড়ন, the coating or tinning of vessels.

রাংতা, রাঙ্গতা,—মুড়িবার রাঙ্গা পত্র, tin-foil. leaf-tin.

রাকা, পূর্ণচন্দ্র, পূর্ণিমা, the full moon, day of the full moon.

রাক্ষস, নরাকৃতি নরখাদক প্রাণী, a fabulous monster, a giant, titan, guebre, cannibal, goblin, fiend. [go.

রাক্ষসী, রাক্ষসের স্ত্রী, বাঘিনী, a female goblin, cannibal, a vira-

রাক্ষসীবেলা, সন্ধ্যার পূর্ব তিন মুহূর্ত্ত, the close of day, dusk, evening twilight.

রাখণ, থোওন, স্থাপন, রক্ষণ, পালন, চরাণ, প্রাপ্ত হওন, আশ্রয় দেওন, ধারণ, ভরণ, ভুঞ্জান, to put, place, station, lay, lay down, keep, preserve, protect, defend, guard, tend cattle, &c. to have, hold, possess, harbour, employ, keep, retain, treat, entertain, feast.

রাখণি, গোপালাদির বেতন, hire for tending cattle, guarding, &c.

রাখলামী, রক্ষকপদ, রাখালের কর্ম্ম, guardianship, the office of a keeper, &c. [a clown.

রাখাল, রক্ষক. গোপাল, চাষা, a keeper, shepherd, cow-keeper,

রাখালি, গবাদি পালনকরা, তদ্বেতন, the tending of cattle, wages given for it.

রাগ, ক্রোধ, দ্বেষ, কাম. দুঃখ, গানের ভেদ, রঙ্গ, বর্ণ, anger, envy, passion, love, lust, distress, a tune, musical mode, a colour, tint, dye. [the passions.

রাগকর, কোপজনক, ত্রাসক, provoking, exasperating, exciting

রাগণ, খেপণ, to redden with anger, storm, rave, rage.
রাগত, রাগাল,—কোপান্বিত, ক্রোধশীল, passionate, angry, irritable, irascible. [angry.
রাগান্ধ, অতিশয় কোপযুক্ত, blinded by passion, excessively
রাগাণ, খেপাণ, to anger, provoke, irritate, incense.
রাগান্বিত, কোপিত, প্রচণ্ড, angry, enraged. irritated, furious.
রাগিণী, গানভেদ, তান, a musical mode or tune.
রাগী, রাগাল,—ক্রোধী, উগ্র, কর্কশ, passionate, irascible, irritable, touchy, warm, vehement, virulent.
রাঘব, রবাহূত, অনিমন্ত্রিত, ভাক্ত তত্ত্বজ্ঞানী, বোদালী মৎস্য, an uninvited guest, an intruder, an imposter pretending to a knowledge of the secrets of providence, a species of fish. [paint.
রাঙ্গ-১, ধাতু দ্রব্য বিশেষ, রঙ্গ, বর্ণ, tin, a tint, dye, colour, hue,
রাঙ্গতা, মুড়িবার রাঙ্গপত্র, tin-foil, leaf-tin, tin-coating.
রাঙ্গঝাল, রাঙ্গপত্র দিয়া মুড়ন, the coating or tinning of vessels.
রাঙ্গঝালনিয়া, রাঙ্গঝালকারক, a tin-coater, a tinman.
রাঙ্গভাটিয়া, ঈষদ্রক্তবর্ণ, reddish, somewhat red.
রাঙ্গা, রক্তবর্ণ, red, rosy, scarlet; tin. [raddish.
রাঙ্গামুলা, সৌন্দর্য্যযুক্ত মূর্খ, handsome but illiterate; a red
রাঙ্গামুখ, রক্তাস্য, কোপযুক্ত, red-faced, reddening with anger.
রাঙ্গাণ, রঙ্গ দেওন, বিচিত্র করণ, বর্ণী করণ. to colour, dye, tinge.
রাজ, ইষ্টক গৃহ গাঁথক, থই, রাজার সম্বন্ধীয়. a bricklayer, a mason; *in comp:* royal, a king.
রাজকন্যা বা কুমারী,—ভূপতির তনয়া, a princess, king's daughter.
রাজকর, রাজস্ব, ভূপতির ভূম্যাদিতে লভ্য পঞ্চকাদি, royal tribute, state revenue, a king's taxes.
রাজকর্ম্ম বা কার্য্য,—রাজার কৃতকর্ম্ম,রাজার আদিষ্ট কর্ম্ম,রাজার কর্ত্তব্য,রাজার নিকটে প্রাপ্তপদ, a royal work. government works, royal duty. official station or employment.
রাজকীয়, রাজসম্বন্ধীয়, royal,kingly, belonging to government.
রাজকুমার, ভূপতির সন্তান, a king's son, a prince.
রাজকুল, নৃপতির বংশ বা গোষ্ঠী, a royal family, a royal race.
রাজজ্ঞান, দেশ শাসন বিদ্যা, the science of government, civil polity, political science. [polity.
রাজজ্ঞানী, দেশশাসনেতে নিপুণ, a politician; versed in civil

রাজটীকা বা তিলক,—নৃপপদপ্রাপ্তি, তৎকালীন সংস্কার, accession to
a throne, a mode of Indian coronation.

রাজতা, রাজত্ব,রাজতী,—নৃপপদ, রাজক্রিয়া, দেশ শাসন, royalty, sovereignty, reign, government, empire, sway, rule, legislation. [payable to the king.

রাজদণ্ড, ভূপতির যষ্টি, অপরাধ জন্যে রাজার দণ্ড, a scepter, a fine

রাজদ্রোহ,ভূপতির অনিষ্টচেষ্টা, ভূপতিহত্যা, treason, regicide.

রাজদ্বার, রাজপুরীর প্রবেশ পথ, সভা, a royal gate or door, a royal levee. [king.

রাজধর্ম্ম, ভূপতির কর্ত্তব্য অথবা নীতি, the duties or virtues of a

রাজধানী, ভূপতির বাসস্থান, যে নগরে রাজকীয় কার্য্য হয়, a royal residence, palace, a capital city.

রাজনীতি, রাজার সাধু ব্যবহার, দেশশাসন বিদ্যা, the duties of kings, political science.

রাজন্য, ভূপতির বংশোদ্ভব,ক্ষত্রিয়, a royal descendant,a prince, a Chsatriya. [highway.

রাজপথ, রাজমার্গ,—সর্বলোকগমনাগমনপথ, a public road, king's

রাজপুত্র, রাজপুত,—ভূপতির তনয়, কুমার, রাজার কুলোদ্ভব, ক্ষত্রিয়, a king's son, prince, royal descendant, a kshatriya, a soldier of mixed birth. [palace.

রাজপুরী, ভূপতির বাসস্থান, প্রাসাদ, a royal city or residence, a

রাজবাড়ী, রাজবাটী,—নৃপতির বাসগৃহ,a king's residence,a palace.

রাজযক্ষ্মা, ক্ষয়কাশ, pulmonary consumption.

রাজরাণী, রাজমহিষী,— নৃপপত্নি, a queen-consort.

রাজর্ষি, উত্তম ক্ষত্রিয়, মুনি বিশেষ, a royal sage or saint.

রাজলক্ষ্মী, রাজশ্রী,—নৃপতির কপাল, the fortune or destiny of a king or the goddess thereof.

রাজস, রজোগুণাক্রান্ত হইলে যে কর্ম্ম করা যায়, proceeding from the principal of passion or secular inclination.

রাজসভা, নৃপতির সমীপে সমারোহ, a king's court, a royal assembly or council. [&c.

রাজসী, বলিদানাদিযুক্ত ভজনা, divine worship with sacrifices,

রাজসূয়, ক্ষত্রিয়ের অনুষ্ঠেয় যজ্ঞ বিশেষ, a sacrifice performed by Chsyatriyas or by a univeral monarch with his tributaries. [royal revenue.

রাজস্ব, কর,নৃপতির ভূম্যাদিতে স্বত্ব, the king's taxes or tribute,

রাজহংসী, বৃহৎ হংস বিশেষ. *m. & f.* a gander, a goose.
রাজা, নৃপতি, ভূপাল, নরাধ্যক্ষ, a king, sovereign, prince.
রাজাজ্ঞাবর্ত্তী, ভূপতির বশীভূত, loyal, obedient to the king's will.
রাজাধিরাজ, সম্রাট, a paramount sovereign, universal king.
রাজাবলি, রাজার বংশশ্রেণী, a royal genealogy, line of kings.
রাজী, শ্রেণী, আবলী, আনুপূর্ব্বী, a row, rank, continuous line.
রাজীব, পদ্ম, পঙ্কজ, a lotus or water-lily.
রাজ্ঞী, রাণী,—রাজপত্নী, a queen.
রাজ্য, নৃপতির অধিকার, শাসিত দেশ, জনপদ, সাম্রাজ্য, রাজত্ব, a kingdom, government, realm, nation, empire, a region, dominion, reign, administration.
রাজ্যনীতি, অমুক দেশের ব্যবস্থা সমূহ, the laws and constitution of a kingdom.
রাজ্যাঙ্গ, দেশশাসনেতে উপযুক্ত বস্তু, a necessary part or member of government.
রাজ্যাভিষেক, রাজপদে নিয়োগ, an anointing or installation into the government.
রাঢ়, অশিষ্ট, গঙ্গার পশ্চিম দেশ, uncivilized; the country west of the Hooghly.
রাঢ়ামী, অশিষ্টতা, চাষাড়ামী, rudeness, clownishness, unmannerliness.
রাঢ়ি, রাঢ়ীয়,—রাঢ়দেশীয়, belonging to the country west of the Hooghly.
রাণা, ঘাটের সোপান, a flight of steps at a Ghát on a river.
রাতি, রাতারাতি,—রাত্রিকালে, নিশাতে, in the night, by night.
রাতিকাণা, ঝরুসাকাণা, রাত্র্যন্ধ, purblind, blind in the night.
রাত্রি, রজনী, নিশা, night, a night; by night, at night.
রাত্রিচর, যে প্রাণী রজনীতে আহারার্থে ভ্রমণ করে, রাক্ষস, চোর, প্রহরী, prowling by night; an imp, ghost, goblin, nocturnal prowler, thief, robber, a guard.
রাত্রিযোগ, নিশাকাল, প্রদোষকাল, চোর, তস্কর, প্রহরী, the night-season, night-fall, a thief, robber, night-prowler, a watchman, guard.
রাত্রিরক্ষক, প্রহরী, কোটাল, a watchman, a night-guard.
রাত্র্যন্ধ, যে প্রাণী রাত্রিতে দেখিতে না পায়, not seeing well at night, blind at night, purblind.
রাদ্ধান্ত, কৃতপ্রমাণে সিদ্ধান্ত, a conclusion established by facts.
রান্না, অন্নাদি পাককরা, the cooking of food, cookery.
রাব, নিনাদ, শব্দ, চীৎকার, a sound, noise, shout, howl, yell.

রাম, সুখভোগ, দশরথের জ্যেষ্ঠ পুত্র, pleasure, enjoyment, the hero of the Rámáyana.

রামকুঁড়্যা, ঝুপড়ী, a hut, a cabin.

রামখড়ী, শুক্ল মৃত্তিকা বিশেষ, a species of fine chalk.

রামচাকা, লাটিম বিশেষ, a whirligig.

রামছাগল, অজ বিশেষ. the large beardless goat.

রামদূত, হনুমান্, the monkey Hanumán, the friend and messenger of Ráma.

রামধনুক, শক্রধনুঃ, গণ্ডী, the rainbow. [fair.

রামা, মনোরমা স্ত্রী, সুন্দরী, a handsome woman ; *f.* beautiful,

রামাৎ, রাম পরায়ণ, নাগা, a follower or votary of Ráma.

রামায়ণ, রামবিষয়ক মহাকাব্য বিশেষ, a celebrated epic poem of which Ráma is the hero.

রায়, উপাধি বিশেষ, রাজকুমার, a title of honour, a prince.

রায়বাঁশ, বংশযুক্ত শূল বিশেষ, a spear with a bamboo pole.

রায়বাঁশিয়া, শূলধারী, carrying a spear ; a spearman.

রায়বাঘিনী, কাণ্ডী, ব্যাপিকা, a vixen, termagant, violent woman.

রাশি, স্তূপ, পুঞ্জ, সঞ্চয়, গাদী, অঙ্কশ্রেণী, ছিট, মেষাদি দ্বাদশ, a heap, pile, stack, store, collection, mass, quantity, ream, number, a numeration scale, a term in proportion, a fraction, a zodiacal sign.

রাশিচক্র, মেষাদি দ্বাদশ গ্রহের গমনপথ, the zodiac or circle of the signs. [occasions.

রাশিনাম, কর্ম্ম সময়েতে বাচ্যনাম, a sirname used on religious

রাশিভাগ, ছিট, মেষাদির এক অংশ, the fraction of a unit, a portion of a sign.

রাশিভোগ, সূর্য্যাদির যে কোন রাশিতে অবস্থানকাল, the passage of the sun, &c, through a sign.

রাশিভোগী বা ভোক্তা,—অমুক রাশিতে অবস্থিত. passing through a sign of the zodiac. [to heaps, abundant.

রাশীভূত বা কৃত,—সঞ্চিত, স্তূপাকৃতি, বহুল. heaped up, formed in-

রাষ্ট্র, রাজ্য, দেশ, চক্র, উৎপাত, উপদ্রব, অভিব্যক্ত, বিখ্যাত, a country, province, region, kingdom, realm, the desolation of a country, &c. inundation, plague, famine, any public calamity ; manifest, notorious, current, public.

রাষ্ট্রভঙ্গ বা ভঞ্জন,—দেশের উপদ্রব, the wasting, ravaging or desolation of a country. [of Krishna.

রাস, স্ত্রী সহিত বিহার, amorous pastime, the circular dance

রাসযাত্রা, গোপী গণের সহিত কৃষ্ণের ব্যভিচার, তদ্দিবস, a religious sporting festival in commemoration of the gambols of Krishna with the milk-maids.

রাসযাত্রী, রাসযাত্রা কালীন লোকসমূহ, celebrating the foregoing festival or *rásjátrá*. [of taste.

রাসন, রসনেন্দ্রিয় সম্বন্ধীয়, belonging to the sense or organ

রাহু, নবম গ্রহ, বিধুন্তুদ, the ascending node or dragon's head.

রাহুগ্রস্ত, কথিক কাল পর্য্যন্ত অন্তর্হিত সূর্য্যচন্দ্র. eclipsed, under eclipse.

রাহুগ্রাস, সূর্য্যচন্দ্রের অন্তর্ধান, the immersion of a luminary in an eclipse. [moon.

রাহুদর্শন, রাহুপীড়া,—সূর্য্যচন্দ্র গ্রহণকাল, an eclipse of the sun or

রিক্থ, পৈতৃক ধন, সম্পত্তি, hereditary property, wealth.

রিক্থগ্রহণ বা হরণ, পিতৃধনাদি প্রাপণ, a succession to property.

রিক্থী, অর্থী, উত্তরাধিকারী, possessed of or succeeding to hereditary property; an heir.

রিক্ত, শূন্য, হীন, শুক্তোদর, শূন্যভাব, অন্তর, বন, empty, void, destitute, poor, purged by stool; vacuity, emptiness, a void, space, a forest.

রিঙ্গণ, স্খলন, পতন, ভ্রষ্ট হওন, to slip, trip, slide, tumble, creep as a child, deviate or fall from virtue.

রিজ্জন, হর্ষণ, আনন্দিত হওন, to be glad, to rejoice.

রিঠা, বস্ত্রক্ষালন যোগ্য ফল বিশেষ, the soap-berry tree.

রিপু, শত্রু, বিপক্ষ, an enemy, foe; hostile, inimical.

রিষ্ট, অশুভ, রিঠা, evil, loss, &c. the soap-berry tree.

রিষ্টি, অশুভ, ক্ষতি, অপচয়, অভাব, নাশ, পাপ, খড়্গ, misfortune, calamity, evil, loss, injury, privation, destruction, sin, a sword.

রীতি, রীত,—চালি, প্রণালী, ব্যবহার, ধারা, ধর্ম্ম, চরিত্র, স্বভাব, গুণ, মত, দৌল, গমন, a habit, custom, usage, practice, fashion, local observance, rite, ceremony, method, way, manner, peculiarity, idiom, behaviour, conduct, disposition, natural property, tenet, maxim, carriage, gait, motion, going.

রীতিজ্ঞ, ব্যবহারী, bringing in or establishing a custom.
রুই, বল্মীক, মৎস্য বিশেষ, the white ant, a species of fish.
রুক্মিণী, লক্ষ্মী, Lakshmí the goddess of fortune.
রুক্ষ-ী, উগ্র, কষায়, উগ্রকারী, কঠিন, কটু, কঠোর, কর্কশ, rough, astringent, hard, dry, harsh, unkind, morose.
রুধ, ক্ষীণ, ক্লিষ্ট, শূন্য, lean, thin, spare, empty.
রুধণ, কোপন, বিরক্ত হওন, to be angry, to be vexed with.
রুগ্ন, রোগগ্রস্ত, পীড়িত, sick, ill, indisposed, diseased, infirm.
রুচি, ক্ষুধ্, আহারে প্রবৃত্তি, স্পৃহা, বাসনা, স্বাদ, রস, অতিশয় প্রীতি, মন, তুষ্টি, আসক্তি, দীপ্তি, শোভা, প্রিয়ত্ব, hunger, appetite, wish, desire, passion, a liking, relish, savour, taste, inclination to, pleasure, satisfaction, approbation, application to, a ray of light, light, lustre, beauty, agreeableness.
রুটী, গোধূম পিষ্টক বিশেষ, bread, wheaten bread.
রুদিত, বিলপিত, আক্রুষ্ট, wept, bewailed, lamented, deplored.
রুদ্ধ, বদ্ধ, বেষ্টিত, নিষিদ্ধ, shut, closed, blocked up, besieged, surrounded, obstructed, hindered.
রুদ্র. সূর্য্য, শিব, দেবাংশ, প্রচণ্ড, the sun. Shiva, a class of demigods; wrathful, furious, vengeful.
রুদ্রাক্ষ, জপমালাযোগ্য দানা বিশেষ, a berry used for rosaries.
রুধির, রক্ত, শোণিত, লৌ, blood.
রুপণ, রুয়ণ,—রোপণ, পোতন, বপন, to plant, to sow.
রুয়া, চালের প্রস্থবংশ, ডালিম ফলের বীজ, শাঁস, লোম, ঊর্ণা, the rafters of a thatched roof, seeds of pomegranate, &c. a kernel, hair, wool. [to fret.
রুষণ, কোপন, বিতুষ্ট হওন, to be angry, vexed or displeased,
রুষ্ট, ক্রুদ্ধ, রাগান্বিত, কোপশীল, vexed, displeased, offended, enraged, angry, wrathful, passionate, severe.
রুষ্টি, উষ্মা, কোপ, ক্রোধ, anger, wrath, rage, fury.
রুষ্টিকর, কোপজনক, প্রচণ্ড, provoking, enraging, wrathful, raging.
রূঢ়, অশিষ্ট, কটু, চলিত, বিদিত, পরম্পরাগত, উৎপন্ন, গজান, প্রস্ফুটিত, নিশ্চিত, rude, uncourteous, harsh, abusive, current, notorious, traditional, of unknown or uncertain derivation, produced, sprung, born, sprouted, budded, blown, certain, ascertained.

রূঢ়বাক্য বা শব্দ, ব্যুৎপত্তিহীন বাক্য, চলিত কথা, a word used in a peculiar traditional acceptation.

রূঢ়ি, ব্যুৎপত্তিহীন সমুদায় পদের শক্তি, the customary application of a word as opposed to its etymological notion, or where the origin is unknown, as in words of foreign derivation.

রূপ, আকার, ডৌল, মূর্ত্তি, প্রতিছায়া, চক্ষুরাদি গোচর, সৌন্দর্য্য, প্রকার, ধারা, মত, জাতি, ধর্ম্ম, গুণ, স্বভাব, পদসাধন, বিভক্তি, একটা, অভিনেয় কাব্য, অভ্যাস, তুল্য. form. figure, shape, appearance, semblance, an image, figure, reflexion, object of vision, colour, beauty, a manner, mode, way, species, kind, natural property, disposition, quality, grammatical inflexion, conjugation, declension, a unit, integer, dramatic poem, play, learning by rote; *aff:* like, resembling.

রূপক, উপমাযুক্ত, দৃষ্টান্তবান্, figurative, allegorical, metaphorical.

রূপচাঁদ, কুমারবিন্দ, a fop, prig, buck, a species of fish.

রূপবান্, রূপবন্ত,—সুন্দর, চারু, আকারবিশিষ্ট, handsome, beautiful, symmetrical, elegant, having form or shape.

রূপসী, রূপবতী,—সুন্দরী, মনোহরা, *f.* handsome, beautiful, comely.

রূপা, রূপ্য,—চাঁদী, রজত ধাতু, silver, wrought silver.

রূপী, রৌপ্যমুদ্রা, তঙ্কা, টাকা, a silver coin, a rupee.

রে, তুচ্ছজ্ঞানে সম্বোধন, *voc. of contempt*, sirrah ! soho !

রেঁদা, সূত্রধরের কাষ্ঠ সমান করণার্থ অস্ত্র, a plane ;-বুলান -দেওন, or-করণ, to plane.

রেক, অতিসার, সওয়া সের, a lax, looseness, a measure of a seer and ¼.

রেখা, লম্বা চিহ্ন, লেখা, ডোরা, ছিদ্র, a stroke, line, streak, stripe, split, slit.

রেখাকার, রেখাকৃতি, রেখাপড়া, ডোরিয়া, striped, striated, streaked.

রেখাভূমি, ভূগোলের মধ্যসূত্র, the equator or equatorial line.

রেচক, ভেদক, নিশ্বাস, purgative, cathartic, aperient; a purge, cathartic, expiration of the breath.

রেচন, অতিসার, ভেদ, শ্বাসনিশ্বাস, ক্ষরণ, a lax, looseness, purging, respiration, breathing, dropping, oozing.

রেজান, তোষণ, আহ্লাদ জন্মান, to please, gratify, rejoice.
রেণু-ক, ধূলা, পরাগ, বালুকা, কণা, dust, pollen, sand, an atom.
রেত, রেতঃ, রেতস্,—বীর্য্য, শুক্র, semen virile; রেত, sand.
রেপ, কুরুন্দ, the wards of a lock.
রেফ, রকার, অর্কফলা, the letter র, or its substitute (´).
রেবতী, সপ্তবিংশতি নক্ষত্র, the last or 27th lunar mansion.
রেল-া, সমূহ, মেলা, অপর্য্যাপ্ত, a multitude, a resort, plenty.
রৈ, ধন, সম্পত্তি, ধ্বনি, পুষ্করিণীর মধ্যস্থিত কাষ্ঠ, wealth, riches, property, sound, noise, the post erected in a pond when consecrated.
রোওন, রোপণ, পোতন, বপন, to plant, to sow. [crop.)
রোআ-নি, হৈমন্তিক ধান্য, planted, (applied to the winter rice-
রোঁআ, শরীরের লোম, the hair of the body, hair of a beast.
রোক, প্রত্যক্ষ মুদ্রা, ছিদ্র, দোষ, ready-money, cash, a purchase for cash, a slit, incision, blemish, taint.
রোকড়, আয়ব্যয় লিখিবার বহী, a cash-book.
রোকড়িয়া, রোকরক্ষক, কোষাধ্যক্ষ, বণিয়া, a cash-keeper, cashier, treasurer, banker, money-changer.
রোকণ-আন, আট্কান, নিবারণ, বেধন, রঙ্গাদি লাগান, to stop, hinder, prevent, obstruct, ward off, withstand, to bore, to paint or varnish trinkets.
রোকণিয়া, গহনার রঙ্গকার, a painter or varnisher of trinkets.
রোখাণ, কোপান, to anger, provoke, irritate, incense.
রোখা-ল, প্রচণ্ড, কোপাল, উগ্র, কর্কশ, furious, passionate, touchy, morose, wayward, cross, peevish.
রোগ, পীড়া, ব্যাধি, sickness, illness, disease, distemper.
রোগকর, পীড়াজনক, অপথ্য, causing sickness, unwholesome.
রোগগ্রস্ত, রোগী,—পীড়িত, অসুস্থ, ill, diseased, unwell, sick.
রোগশালী, সতত পীড়িত, দুর্ব্বল, sickly, ailing, infirm, diseased.
রোগা, রোগাটীয়া,—ব্যাধিত, পীড়িত, ill, diseased, sick, infirm.
রোচক, আগ্নেয়, রুচিজনক, ক্ষুধাকর, সুস্বাদু, provoking appetite, stomachic, carminative, pleasant, agreeable, palatable, savoury, relishing, grateful.
রোচনা, আহারাদিতে প্রবর্ত্তনা করা, পরতুষ্টিকরা, প্রবৃত্তি জন্মান, সম্মতি, a provocation of appetite, a stimulus, a gratifying the taste of others, persuasion, approval.

রোদন, ক্রন্দন, বিলাপ করণ, to weep, cry, lament, bewail.
রোদ্ধা, প্রতিবন্ধক, নিবারক, a hinderer, obstructer, besieger, &c.
রোধ-ন, গতি বারণ, আটক, প্রতিবন্ধ, নিষেধ, hindrance, obstruction, obstacle, stoppage, blockade, seizure, embargo, prohibition. [posing, &c.
রোধক, নিষেধক, আট্‌কানিয়া, বেষ্টক, stopping, obstructing, op-
রোধন, বেষ্টন, আট্‌কান, বন্ধন, নিবারণ, ঘেরণ, নিষেধ করণ, to besiege, obstruct, hinder, oppose, impede, to shut, staunch, stop, resist, fence round, surround, interdict, lay an embargo upon.
রোপক, বপক, পোতনিয়া, planting; a planter, (of trees &c.) a seedsman. [stake, &c. graft, insert.
রোপণ, বৃক্ষাদির পোতন, যোড়ান, to plant trees, &c. fix a
রোপণিয়া, পোতনিয়া, বীজবপ্তা, a planter, sower, seedsman.
রোম, লোম, ঊর্ণা, আঁশ, hair of the body, fur, wool, nap.
রোমকূপ, লোমের মূল, the pores of the skin.
রোমাঞ্চ, রোমহর্ষ,—হর্ষাদি জনিত লোমের কণ্টকভাবে উঠন, শিহরণ, horripilation, erection of the hair of the body from delight, &c; rapture, a bristling up.
রোমাঞ্চিত, অতিশয় আহ্লাদযুক্ত, হর্ষিত, having the hair erect from sudden emotion, enraptured, delighted.
রোমাবলী, বক্ষস্থলের লোমশ্রেণী, hairiness or a line of hair.
রোয়ালী, বীজতলা, রোপিত ধান্য, a seed-plot; planted (rice.)
রোষ, ক্রোধ, কোপ, anger, wrath, passion, choler. [rave.
রোষণ, কোপন, ক্ষেপন, to be angry or enraged, to storm,
রোষাণ, কোপান, চিড়ান, to anger, provoke, exasperate.
রোষান্ব, রোষী,—ক্রোধান্বিত, রাগান্ধ, কর্কশ, angry, enraged, wrathful, cross, peevish, waspish.
রোহিণী, চতুর্থ নক্ষত্র, the fourth lunar mansion.
রোহিত, রুই মাছ, a fish much used for the table.
রৌদ্র, রৌদ,—সূর্য্যের কিরণ, উষ্মা, উগ্ররস, ভয়ানক, দারুণ, প্রচণ্ড, পীড়াকর, প্রখর, sunshine, solar heat, warmth, wrath, rage; formidable, terrible, dreadful, wrathful, violent, sharp, severe, acute.
রৌপ্য, রূপ্যময়, রজত, made of silver; silver. [hell.
রৌরব, নরক বিশেষ, a division of the Hindoo Tartarus or

ল.

লওন, গ্রহণ, ধরণ, পাওন, মিলন, বুঝন, to take, assume, to seize, receive, accept, obtain, get, acquire, know, penetrate, realize; -আইসন, আনন, to fetch, bring; -যাওন, উঠান, to take away.

লওয়ান, প্রবোধ কিম্বা প্রবৃত্তি জন্মান, মানান, ভুলান, বুঝান, to convince, persuade, draw into an opinion or measure, prevail upon, instigate, prepossess, induce, bias, wheedle, teach, explain, instruct. [ling, &c.

লওয়ানী, প্রবোধকরা, ভুলানি, persuasion, convincing, wheed-

লকলকিয়া, লগলগিয়া,—স্পন্দিত, থরথরিয়া, vibrating, darting, (as a serpent's tongue.)

লক্ষ, চিহ্ন, শর নিক্ষেপের উদ্দেশ্য, অভিপ্রায়, শত সহস্র, তুল্য, প্রতিযোগী, sign, token, a mark, butt, object, aim, a hundred thousand, an equal, a counterpart.

লক্ষণ, চিহ্ন, কলঙ্ক, অঙ্ক, বিসূচিকা, প্রমাণ, বিশেষ গুণ, ভাব, জাতি নিদর্শ, ডৌল, আকার, a sign, mark, spot, token, badge, indication, symptom, criterion, predicate, distinguishing property, omen, portent, presage, prognostic, features, physiognomy.

লক্ষণা, দৃষ্টান্ত, অধ্যাহার, উহ্যবাক্য, a metaphor, metaphorical expression, synecdoche, metonymy, an ellipsis, word understood. [sign, &c.

লক্ষণাক্রান্ত, বিশেষ চিহ্নযুক্ত, bearing a distinguishing mark or

লক্ষ্মী, কমলা, শ্রী, সম্পত্তি, বৃদ্ধি, Lacshmí the goddess of fortune, good fortune, prosperity, success.

লক্ষ্মীছাড়া, শ্রীভ্রষ্ট, দুর্ভাগ্য, abandoned by fortune, unfortunate.

লক্ষ্মীবান্, লক্ষ্মীবন্ত,—পয়োমন্ত, ধনবান্, শ্রীল, মঙ্গল, prosperous, fortunate, successful, lucky.

লক্ষ্য, শরব্য, উদ্দেশ, চিহ্ন, ছলনা, ছদ্মবেশ, শত সহস্র, দৃশ্য, অনুভব্য, a mark, butt, aim, object, sign, token, fraud, disguise, 100,000; observable, perceptible.

লগা, বৃক্ষফল প্রহারণার্থ দণ্ড, a staff for beating down fruits.

লগী, চাড়ী, ফিকনা, a pole for shoving on boats in shallow water, a boat-hook, a lever.

লগুড়, লাঠী, লৌহযুক্ত যষ্টি, a staff, stick, an iron-bound club.
লগে, ঠাঁই, স্থানে, with, about one.
লগ্ন, সংযুক্ত, একত্রিত, স্পৃষ্ট, উদ্যুক্ত, মনোযুক্ত, জনিত, উপযুক্ত, উচিত, রাশির উদয়কাল, adhering to, joined to, connected with, touching, in contact, intent upon, consequent, applicable, relevant, suitable, proper, apposite; the oblique ascension or time of a sign's rising above the horizon.
লগ্নক, প্রতিভূ, a bondsman, surety, bail.
লগ্নপত্র, বিবাহ আদি কর্ম্মোপযুক্ত কালসূচক লিপি, a written specification of a propitious time for a marriage or other religious action.
লগ্নালগ্নি, লাগালাগি, একত্র, ধরাধরি, abreast, in contact, close together.
লগ্যগুব্যবন্ধ, মলমূত্ররোধ, a stoppage of urine, constipation.
লঘিমা, লাঘব, হ্রাস, অগুরুতা, চাপল্য, smallness, diminution, levity, lightness.
লঘীয়সী, চপল, অতিশয় তুচ্ছ যে স্ত্রী, a light and contemptible woman.
লঘু, অগুরু, অভারি, অল্প, সূক্ষ্ম, অলীক, সহজ, তুচ্ছ, হ্রস্ববর্ণ, অবিবেচক, light, not heavy, little, small, minute, trifling, trivial, easy, mean, contemptible, short, (as a vowel,) imprudent.
লঘুজ্ঞান, অবজ্ঞা, অশ্রদ্ধা, তাচ্ছল্য, অনাদর, contempt, scorn, a low opinion of, disesteem, a slighting, contemning, despising.
লঘুতেজ, দুর্ব্বল, অজ্ঞান, weak, of small power, silly, imprudent.
লঘুপাক, পাকাই, সুপচ্য, light (as food,) easy of digestion.
লঘুব্যয়, পরিমিত ব্যয়, কার্পণ্য, thrift, economy, frugality.
লঘুভার, ক্ষুদ্র মোট, অগুরু, a slight burthen; light, portable.
লঘুসমর, সহজ যুদ্ধ, a skirmish, loose fight, skirmishing.
লঘ্বীক্রিয়া, প্রস্রাব, discharge of urine, act of making water.
লঙ্কা-মরিচ, গাছ মরিচ, red-pepper, chillies, capsicums.
লঙ্গ, সং,—লবঙ্গ, দেবকুসুম, a clove, the clove tree.
লঙ্ঘন, অতিক্রমণ, ডিঙ্গান, অন্যথাচরণ, উপবাস, to overstep, pass over, leap over, go beyond, exceed, to transgress, infringe, break, violate; fasting, abstinence.
লঙ্ঘালঙ্ঘি, হাতাহাতি, মারামারি, boxing, fighting, fisticuffs.

লজ্জা, ত্রপা, হ্রী, অনাদর, তিরস্কার, অপমান, shame, modesty, bashfulness, a disgrace, scandal, ignominy, affront, insult. [scandalous.

লজ্জাকর, অনুচিত, কুৎসিত, shameful, disgraceful, ignominious,

লজ্জান্বিত, লজ্জাবান্,—ত্রপাশালী, হ্রীযুক্ত, modest, bashful, abashed, ashamed. [faced, sheepish.

লজ্জালু, লজ্জুক,—ত্রপান্বিত, কুণ্ঠুয়া, modest, bashful, coy, shame-

লজ্জাশালী,, লজ্জাশীল,—অপত্রপিষ্ণু, লাজুক, modest, bashful.

লজ্জাহীন, অত্রপ, নির্লজ্জ, ধৃষ্ট, shameless, impudent, immodest, barefaced, bold. [blush.

লজ্জিত, ত্রপিত, মুখচোরা, ashamed, abashed, coy, put to the

লট্‌কন, ঝুলন, টাঙ্গন, to be suspended, hang down, swing.

লট্‌কান, ঝুলান, টাঙ্গান, to suspend, hang, hang up.

লট্‌খট্, ঝঞ্ঝাট, ক্লেশ, perplexity, intricacy, a labyrinth.

লট্‌খটী, লট্‌খটিয়া,—ঝঞ্ঝাটিয়া, ক্লেশকর, ছলী, troublesome, vexatious, intricate, perplexing, sly, artful.

লটুয়া,, লট্টা,—লম্পট, ভ্রষ্টাচারী, lewd, profligate; a libertine.

লড়ন, স্পন্দন, কম্পন, হেলন, নিবর্ত্ত হওন, যুদ্ধ করণ, to shake, move, wag, vibrate, quiver, totter, be revoked, to fight, to war. [agitation.

লড়নী, কম্প, স্পন্দ, চপলতা, a shaking, moving, vibration,

লড়াই, যুদ্ধ, রণ, গোলমাল, a battle, fight, war, riot.

লড়াক, লড়া,—যোদ্ধা, a fighter, combatant, warrior.

লড়ান, কাঁপান, দুলান, হেলান, সরাণ, নিবর্ত্তন, যুদ্ধ করণ, to shake, stir, move, jolt, remove, revoke, go to war.

লড়ালড়ি, হাতাহাতি, বাহুযুদ্ধ, fisticuffs, scuffling, a scuffle.

লড়ী, লাঠী, যষ্টি, a staff, pole, stick, wand, rod, club.

লড়্‌কান, লোভ দেখান, চার দেওন, to lay a snare, bait a hook.

লড্ডুকা, মিষ্টান্ন বিশেষ, লাড়ু, a kind of sweet-meat balls.

লণ্ড, স্পন্দ, হেলনি, a tossing about, agitation, staggering.

লড়্‌বড়ান, ঝোঁকন, হেলন, to reel, stagger, move unsteadily.

লড়্‌বড়িয়া, লড়্‌লড়িয়া,—চঞ্চল, চপল, হেলনিয়া, fickle, wavering, unsteady, reeling, staggering.

লতা, লতিকা,—বৃক্ষাশ্রিত তৃণ, চাপ্টন, ধরণ, পরাবলম্বন করণ, a vine, creeper, climbing plant; to cling to another, to effect through another.

লতান, গাছান, পরবৃক্ষারোহণ, to creep or climb as a plant.
ননী, নবনীত, মাখন, butter.
লপটন, চাপটন, জড়ন. to cling, stick, adhere to, twine about.
লপটান, চাপটান, লাগান, জড়ান, to cause to stick, to wrap or fold together, entwine.
লব, তনু. ক্ষুদ্র, সূক্ষ্ম, অল্পতা, কিঞ্চিৎ, small, little, minute ; [a little.
লবঙ্গ, দেবকুসুম, লং., cloves, the clove tree.
লবণ, নোণ, ক্ষাররস, করকচ, সৈন্ধব, sea-salt, rock or factitious salt, saltness. [brackish.
লবণাক্ত, ক্ষাররসবিশিষ্ট বস্তু, salted, rubbed with salt, saltish,
লবণাম্বু. লবণোদ,—লবণমিশ্রিত জল, তদ্বিশিষ্ট, salt water ; abounding in brackish water.
লব্ধ, উপার্জ্জিত, প্রাপ্ত, obtained, gained, acquired, received, got ; *pref*: possessed of.
লব্ধি, লাভ, হরণোৎপন্ন, acquisition, profit, gain,a quotient.
লভ্য, প্রাপ্য, প্রাপ্তি, ফলোদয়, ব্যাজ, obtainable, &c. gain, profit, advantage, produce, interest, premium, discount. [lender ; rapacious.
লভ্যভুক্, লভ্যভোক্তা,—উত্তমর্ণ, নিরখদানিয়া, a usurer, money-
লম্পট, ভ্রষ্ট, কামুক, অসৎ, স্ত্রী বিষয়ে আসক্ত, loose, libidinous, lewd, unchaste, dissolute, lascivious, amorous ; a rake, a libertine. [ism, looseness.
লম্পটতা, ভ্রষ্টতা, কামানল, lewdness; lasciviousness, libertin-
লম্ফ, উৎফাল, উৎপ্লব, a leap, jump, gambol, caper, canter.
লম্ফঝম্ফ, উৎপ্লব, কুন্দনি, a jumping about, frisking, gambols.
লম্ফন, উৎপ্লবন, কুন্দন, to jump, leap, skip, frisk, canter.
লম্ব-1, দীর্ঘ, উচ্চ, শয়িত, ঝুলনিয়া, long, tall, lying, laid along, extended in length,pendulous,hanging down.
লম্বন, চেঙ্গন, ঝুলন, to be long, hang down, dangle.
লম্বমান, টাঙ্গা, ঝুলনিয়া, দীর্ঘ, hanging, dangling, suspended, growing in length. [ness, extravagance.
লম্বাই, দ্রাঘিমা, উচ্চতা, বহুব্যয়, length, height, expensive-
লম্বাইচৌড়াই, বাক্যবাহুল্য, আত্মশ্লাঘা, tedious detail, boasting.
লম্বালম্বি. শয়িত, পতিত, at full length, laid along.
লম্বিত, ঝুলিত, দীর্ঘভাবে স্থিত, pendent, hanging down, dangling, extended in length.

লম্বে, দীর্ঘে, longwise, in length.

লম্বোদর, পেটাল, গণেশ, corpulent, pot-bellied ; Ganesha.

লয়, বিনাশ, গল্‌তি, গুপ্তভাব, অন্তর্দ্ধান, অপবর্গ, সংশ্লেষ, নৃত্য গীতাদিতে পদবিন্যাসাদির সমতা, destruction, loss, dissolution, fusion, melting, concealment, disappearance, final absorption, an embracing, adhering, clinging to, equal time in music and dancing.

লয়গত, লয়প্রাপ্ত,—গলিত, অন্তর্হিত, লুক্কায়িত, পঞ্চত্বপ্রাপ্ত, মুক্ত. dissolved, lost, concealed, dead, absorpt.

ললাট. কপাল, ভাগ্য, the forehead, fate, destiny.

ললিত, সুন্দর, মনোহর, ঈপ্সিত, লুম্বিত, কামুক, লীলা, নায়কদর্শনে অঙ্গবিন্যাস, beautiful, lovely, desired, coveted, hanging in collops from fatness, dallying, wanton ; amorous languishing or other external expression of sensual passion in a female.

লশুন, কন্দ বিশেষ, অরিষ্ট, garlic, cives.

লশুনীয়, মণি বিশেষ, a precious stone called cat's eye.

লহরী, তরঙ্গ, ঊর্ম্মি, ঢেউ, চাঞ্চল্য, অকস্মাদ্বাসনা, a wave, surge, billow, a whim, caprice, fancy.

লা, লাক্ষা,—জতু. জৌ, গালা. lac, the lac insect, sealing-wax.

লাউ, তুম্বী, a gourd, a pumpkin.

লাক, লক্ষ, শত সহস্র. a lac or 100,000.

লাগন, ঠেকন, স্পর্শন, লপ্টন, ভিড়ন, ব্যাপন, বিঁধন, বৈসন, খাটন, ফল ধরণ, পড়ন, ঘটন, ঠিক হওন. মনোনীত হওন, যোড়ন, মিলন. চাহন, উপযুক্ত হওন, প্রবর্ত্তন, কর্ম্মেতে প্রবর্ত্ত হওন, বিরোধ করণ. শত্রুতা করণ, পীড়ান, সকলঙ্ক হওন, to come in contact with, strike, knock, strike against, touch, adhere, stick, cling, to arrive at, reach, take up space, to hit a mark, to take root, settle, take effect, catch (as fire,) to happen, befal, to fit, suit, serve, do, answer, to please, meet one's views, to close, meet, apply to, to accord, agree with, to belong, relate, concern, refer to, to require, take, be necessary, to enter upon, begin, to contend with, oppose, strive to injure, to give pain, hurt, stain, blot.

লাগা, সংযোগ, লগ্ন, প্রস্তুত, contact, effect; joined, close, spread as a table, &c.

লাগান, মিলান, যুড়ন, সংযুক্ত করণ, দণ্ডাদি দেওন, লেপন, কলঙ্ক ঘটান, যোটান, ভিড়ান, ঠিক করণ, যোড়ান, স্থাপন, খাটান, আরোপ করণ, ঠেকান, to bring into contact, apply one thing to another, unite, join, add, to inflict, lay upon, to plaster, smear, stain, blot, infect, to pair, couple, moor, bring to shore, lie to, adapt, adjust, fit, suit, mix, fasten, graft, fix in a situation, to employ, set to work, to attribute, ascribe, implicate, appropriate.

লাগানিয়া, লেপনিয়া, মিলানিয়া, a plasterer; applying, bringing into contact, &c.

লাগালাগি, নিকটানিকটি, সংলগ্ন, in close or mutual contact, abreast, adjacent, contiguous.

লাগি, লাগিয়া, লাগে,—জন্যে, কারণ, নিমিত্ত, পানে, for, for the sake of, on account of, towards.

লাগি, লাগ,—সংযোগ, ধরা, junction, contact; -পাওন, -কাছান, to reach, to come up with, overtake.

লাঘব, লঘুতা, সূক্ষ্মতা, অল্পতা, তুচ্ছতা, হ্রাস, ন্যূনতা, lightness, easiness, facility, smallness, minuteness, insignificancy, alleviation, mitigation, diminution, a lowering or reduction of price.

লাঘবী, ব্যয়কুণ্ঠ, অল্পব্যয়ী, sparing, frugal, faring hard.

লাঙ্গল, হল, ফুলগাছ বিশেষ, a plough, a flowering plant.

লাঙ্গলা, চাষী, কৃষক, হলবাহক দামড়া, a cultivator, ploughman, an ox used to the plough.

লাঙ্গলিয়া. চাষী, ploughing; a ploughman, husbandman.

লাঙ্গুল, লাঙ্গূল,—পুচ্ছ, লেজ, the tail of an animal.

লাজ, লজ্জা, হ্রী, ত্রপা, shame, modesty, bashfulness.

লাজখেকুয়া, ত্রপারহিত, shameless, impudent, immodest.

লাজুক, লাজুন্যা,—লজ্জাশীল, কুণুয়া, modest, bashful, coy, sheepish.

লাজা, লাজ,—ভাজা ধান্য, খই, rice freed from the husk by frying.

লাঞ্ছন, কলঙ্ক, চিহ্ন, a spot, mark, sign.

লাঞ্ছনা, তিরস্কার, তাড়না, reproach, disgrace, abuse, reproof, reprehension.

লাঞ্ছিত, নিন্দিত, তিরস্কৃত, সকলঙ্ক, reproached, marked, notorious.

লাট, প্যাঁচ, ঝঞ্ঝাট, কোঁকড়ানি, an entanglement, intricacy, confusion, disorder, a rumple, rumpling.

লাটিম, খেলিবার বস্তু, a plaything, a toy, a top. [pole.

লাটী, লাঠী,—যষ্টি, বাড়ী, a stick, cane, staff, mace, bludgeon,

লাড়ন, দুলান, হেলান, সরাণ, to shake, agitate, move, to wave the hand, to displace, shift, remove.

লাড়া, ছেদিত শস্যের মূল, হেলান, সরাণ, stubble, a shaking, &c; shaken, displaced, &c.

লাড়ু, গোলাকার মিঠাই, a kind of sweetmeat balls, comfits.

লাৎ, লাথী,—পদাঘাত, a kick. [caper.

লাফ-১, ঝাঁপ, লম্ফ, উৎপ্লব, কুর্দনি, a jump, leap, spring, flounce,

লাফড়িয়া, দুর্দান্ত, ঢেঁটা, overleaping all bounds, insolent, bold.

লাফন, লম্ফ করণ, কুর্দন, আস্ফালন, উৎপ্লবন, to leap, jump, frisk, spring, flounce, vault, canter, gallop.

লাবণিক, লবণাক্ত, লবণসম্বন্ধীয়, লোণা, লবণবিক্রেতা, salted, dressed with salt, of or relating to salt; a vender of salt, a salt-dealer. [saltness.

লাবণ্য, সৌন্দর্য্য, লবণরস, beauty, gracefulnes, loveliness,

লাভ, উপার্জন, প্রাপ্তি, কামাই, ফল, বৃদ্ধি, ব্যাজ, gain, profit, advantage, benefit, acquisition, earnings, income, produce, interest, discount.

লাভকর, প্রাপ্তিজনক, ফলদ, gainful, profitable, advantageous.

লাভভুক্, বৃদ্ধিজীবী, উত্তমর্ণ, living on interest; a usurer, money-lender. [cess, gains.

লাভালাভ, ফলাফল, উপার্জন, profit and loss, degree of suc-

লাম্পট্য, কামুকতা, ব্যভিচার, lewdness, lasciviousness, fornication.

লাল ১, থুথু, ছেপ, নিষ্ঠীব, slaver, dribble, saliva, spittle.

লালচ, অতিশয় স্পৃহা, লালেচ্ছা, লিপ্সা, লোভ, strong desire, covetousness, avarice, a lure, inducement.

লালচিয়া, অত্যন্তলোভী, লিপ্সু, inordinately desirous, greedy, covetous, avaricious. [carefully.

লালন, বাৎসল্য করণ, স্নেহপূর্বক পালন, to caress, fondle, nourish

লালসা, অত্যন্তপ্রাপ্তীচ্ছা, লিপ্সা, লোভ, ভোগা, ardent longing, excessive desire, eagerness for, coveting, avarice, an inducement, lure, allurement, enticement.

লালস্য, লালসিক,—লিপ্সু, লোভী, covetous, greedy, very desirous.

লালাটিক, অদৃষ্টাধীন, দৈবপরায়ণ, predestined, fated, arising from fate; a predestinarian, a fatalist.

লালিত্য, কোমলতা, রম্যতা, প্রিয়ভাব, সুরস, gentleness, sweetness, loveliness, pleasure, agreeableness, pleasantness, flavour. [thin, worn.

লালুক, লালুয়া,—থুথু ফেলক, গলাটিয়া, a slabberer, sputterer;

লাস্য, লাস,—নৃত্য, হাবভাব, dancing, dalliance, wanton gesture or other indication of passion.

লাহা, লা, লাক্ষা, জতু. lac, the lac insect, sealing wax.

লিখন, রচন, লিপি কিম্বা চিত্র করণ, লেখা, লিখিত পত্র, লিখিবার পাত, to write, compose, record, draw, paint; a writing, written document, letter, record, paper.

লিঙ্গ, চিহ্ন, পুরুষাঙ্গ, পুংস্ত্ব, রূপ, প্রকৃতি, a mark, sign, token, pudendum virile, the phallus or emblem of Shiva, gender (in grammar,) nature or the active power in creation.

লিঙ্গার্চক, শিবপরায়ণ, শিবলিঙ্গপূজক, a worshipper of the phallus or emblem of Shiva.

লিপি, লেখা, লিখিতপত্র, চিত্র, ছবি, a writing, document, letter, record, handwriting, drawing, delineation.

লিপিকর, লিপিকার,—লেখক, বর্ণক, চিত্রকর, a writer, scribe, painter, delineator. [terials.

লিপিসজ্জা, লিখিবার প্রয়োজনীয় বস্তু, stationery, writing ma-

লিপ্ত, লেপিত, অক্ত, মিলিত, সংশ্লিষ্ট নিবিড়, জড়িত, সংযুক্ত, smeared, spread, covered over, tainted or infected with, closely connected or united with, thick, close, crowded, united.

লিপ্তপা, লেপাপা, পাতাপা, web-footed.

লিপ্সা, লাভেচ্ছা, অভিলাষ, প্রণয়, cupidity, desire of gain, covetousness, wish, desire, good-will.

লিপ্সিত, লাভেচ্ছু, লিপ্ত, অভিলষিত, coveted, desired, greedily sought after, united, engaged or involved in.

লিপ্সু, লোভী, লাভেচ্ছুক, coveting, covetous, desirous of gain.

লীন, দ্রবীভূত, গলিত, যুক্ত, আবিষ্ট, তন্ময়, সংশ্লিষ্ট, dissolved, melted, absorpt, absorbed in, intimately mixed or united with.

লীলা, পরিহাস, ক্রীড়া, বিহার, শৃঙ্গার, ভাব, play, sport, pastime, diversion, amorous dalliance, toying, wanton sport, lasciviousness, a female's amorous imitation of her lover's gait, &c.

লুই, লোমময় বস্ত্র বিশেষ, a sort of flannel.

লুকন, প্রচ্ছন্ন ভাবে থাকন, পলায়ন, ছাপন, to hide, lie hid or concealed, to lurk, skulk, abscond, vanish, to elude search or discovery.

লুকান, ছাপন, গুপ্ত করণ, ঢাকন, ছাপান, *id:* also to conceal, secrete, veil, suppress, dissemble.

লুকায়িত, গুপ্ত, পলায়িত, hidden, concealed, close, absconded.

লুচি, মিষ্টান্ন বিশেষ, a sort of sweetmeat. [petticoat.

লুঙ্গী, চিত্রিত স্ত্রীবস্ত্র বিশেষ, a coloured cloth worn as a

লুট-1, বলেতে গ্রহণ, অপহার, a plundering, pillaging, capture, plunder, booty, prey, spoil, peculation.

লুটন-আন, অপহরণ, উৎকট করণ, উড়ান, to plunder, pillage, rob, ravage, forage, sack, ransack, peculate, squander, waste. [derer, robber.

লুটনিয়া, অপহারক, দস্যু, plundering, pillaging, &c; a plun-

লুটানিয়া, অপহারক, নিঙ্গড়ামিয়া, উড়ামিয়া, বহুব্যয়ী, a peculator, spendthrift; plundering, &c. rapacious, lavish.

লুটিয়ারা, লুটেরা,—দস্যু, নিঙ্গড়ামিয়া, a plunderer, open robber, rapacious person, peculator. [wadding.

লুটী, ফেটী, তাল, a skein or ball of thread, a clew, a

লুঠন, লুণ্ঠন,—ভূমিতে ইতস্ততঃ পার্শ্ব পরিবর্ত্তন, বিলোড়ন, গড়াগড়ি দেওন, to roll on the ground, wallow, tumble about, writhe or toss about in pain, &c.

লুড়ী, ক্ষুদ্র প্রস্তরখণ্ড, গুলি, গুটিকা, a small piece of stone, a pebble, a ball, a lottery ticket.

লুণিয়া, লবণবিক্রেতা, a dealer in salt.

লুপ্ত, অন্তর্হিত, গুপ্ত, মিটান,, অচলিত, নির্বাণ, পতিত, disappeared, concealed, obliterated, superseded, obsolete, disused, extinct, dropped, omitted.

লুফন, উৎক্ষিপ্ত তালাদি ধরণ, to catch a ball or other thing thrown to one. [greedy.

লুব্ধ, লোভী, লিপ্সু, desirous of, covetous, avaricious,

লুব্ধক, লোলুপ, ব্যাধ, পক্ষিমারা, *id:* also a hunter, a fowler.
লুলিত, ঝুলিত, তোবড়া, hanging in collops, wrinkled. [by it.
লূতা, মাকড়সা, তজ্জনিত জ্বালা, a spider, inflammation caused
লূতাজাল বা তন্ত্র, মাকড়সার জাল, a spider's web, a cobweb.
লেই, মণ্ড, কাই, paste, starch. [clerk.
লেখক, লিপিকর, মসীজীবী, a writer, scribe, copyist, secretary,
লেখন, লিপি কিম্বা চিত্র করণ, লিপি, to write, register, draw; a writing, document, &c. [chers.
লেখনপত্তন, লিপি, পাত্তাপত্র, প্রমাণপত্র, written documents, vou-
লেখনিক, পরপরিবর্ত্তে স্বাক্ষরকারক, one who signs a writing for another. [plement.
লেখনী, লিখিবার দণ্ড, ভাস্করের অস্ত্র, a pen, style, graving im-
লেখা, লিপি, পত্র, চিহ্ন, রেখা, সংখ্যা, লিখিত, writing, a writing, handwriting, a mark, stroke, an account, calculation; written.
লেখাপড়া, পাত্তাপত্র, লিপি, পাঠশালাতে শিক্ষাকরা, records, writings, written documents, reading and writing.
লেখালেখি, পত্র চালাচালি, written correspondence.
লেখ্য, বিষয় সম্বলিত লিপি, proper to be written; a voucher.
লেজ, লাঙ্গুল, পুচ্ছ, the tail of an animal, a crupper.
লেটা, ব্যাঘাত, ঝঞ্ঝাট, a difficulty, obstacle, embarrassment.
লেপ, মাখনীয় দ্রব্য, বালীচূণ, মাখা, পোঁচ, রেজাই, a plaister, ointment, unguent, lime, mortar, a plastering, smearing, a rug or quilt. [terer, bricklayer.
লেপক, লেপনিয়া,—মাখনিয়া, লাগানিয়া, smearing, &c; a plas-
লেপন, ম্রক্ষণ, মাখন, লাগান, to smear, anoint, plaster, spread.
লেপা, ম্রক্ষিত, মধ্যস্থিত মাংসযুক্ত, smeared, plastered, &c. connected by a membrane.
লেপাপা, পাতাপা, লিপ্তপা, web-footed.
লেবু, লেবূ,—জম্বীর, নারাঙ্গী, a lime, lemon or orange.
লেম, ঐক্য, মেল, সন্ধি, agreement, unity, peace.
লেলান, কুকুরকে ডাকন, to call a dog.
লেশ, কিঞ্চিৎ, অল্প, বিন্দু, মাত্র, সংস্রব, কণা, স্ফুলিঙ্গ, a small portion, the smallest quantity, an atom, tinge, tincture, a particle, a spark.
লেহন, জিহ্বাতে গ্রহণ, চাটন, to lick, lap, taste with the tongue.

লেহাই, লেই, মণ্ড, কাই, starch, paste.
লেহ্য, লেহনযোগ্য, চাটিম, that may be licked or lapped.
লোক, জন, ব্যক্তি, জগৎ, ভুবন, a person, man, mankind, folk, people, the world, a region. [usage.
লোকতঃ, প্রচরজ্রূপে, সর্ব্বতঃ, commonly, according to common
লোকন, দর্শন, হেরণ, নিরীক্ষণ, to view, look, see, survey.
লোকপাল, রাজা, ইন্দ্রাদি দশ, a king, a sovereign, Indra, &c.
লোকবাদ, জনরব, কথা, a rumour, report, fame, talk.
লোকভয়, লোককৃতাপবাদশঙ্কা, fear of the world, dread of public opinion.
লোকযাত্রা, লৌকিক ব্যবহার, ঘটা, the business of the world, a procession, fair, market, concourse of people.
লোকান্তর, পরলোক, মরণ, another world, futurity, hereafter, death. [opprobrium.
লোকাপবাদ, লোকতঃ তিরস্কার, public disapprobation, general
লোকারণ্য, বহুলোকের সমাগম, বহুলোক, ঘটা, a concourse of people, multitude, crowd, throng, large population.
লোকালয়, মনুষ্যের বাসস্থান, নগর, গ্রাম, a habitation of men, a town, a village. [world.
লোকালোক, পৃথিবীবেষ্টিত পর্ব্বত, the supposed boundary of the
লোচন, চক্ষু, নেত্র, দর্শন, the eye, vision, act of looking, &c.
লোটন, অবলুণ্ঠন, বলেতে পরদ্রব্য গ্রহণ, কপোত বিশেষ, বদ্ধ কেশ, to roll, wallow or tumble about, to plunder; a tumbler-pigeon, a braid of hair.
লোটা, ধাতুময় জলপাত্র, ঝুলিত, a brass pitcher or water-jug; hanging, dangling, pendant.
লোটাকাণ, ঝুলিতকর্ণ, দীর্ঘকর্ণবিশিষ্ট, flap-eared.
লোটান, ফেলিয়া দেওন, বিলোড়ন, ঝুলন, অবলুণ্ঠন, to throw down or about, toss, agitate, to lie or hang loosely, dangle, toss or roll about. [roller.
লোড়া, পিষিবার প্রস্তর খণ্ড, ভরমা, a small wooden or stone
লোণ, লবণ, সৈন্ধব, করকচ, salt.
লোণা, লবণযুক্ত, ক্ষারযুক্ত ভূমি, আতাফল বিশেষ, salt, saltish, brackish, unfruitful (land;) a species of custard-apple. [share of spoil.
লোত, লুণ্ঠিত ধনাদি, স্তেয়, plunder, booty, stolen goods, a

লোপ, বিনাশ, ধ্বংস, নির্বাণ, অন্তর্ধান, অব্যবহার, মিটামি, অধ্যাহার, ব্যয়, অপচয়, অপহরণ, destruction, perdition, extinction, oblivion, disappearance, discontinuance, disuse, obsoleteness, erasure, obliteration, disannulling, the dropping or omission of a letter, &c. an ellipsis, total expenditure, loss, squandering, embezzlement.

লোপ্ত্র, চৌর্য্যধন, লুট, a stolen article, plunder, booty. [&c.

লোপ্য, নশ্বর, ধ্বংস্য, destructible, perishable, expungible,

লোফন, উৎক্ষিপ্ত ভাঁটা ধরণ, to catch a ball, &c. thrown up.

লোভ, লিপ্সা, প্রাকাঙ্ক্ষা, আহারে অতিশয় ইচ্ছা, লোগা, লালচ, inordinate desire, cupidity, covetousness, avarice, greediness, an enticement, lure, bait, inducement, temptation, an object of desire.

লোভনীয়, যাহাতে লোভ জন্মে, লালসা প্রবর্ত্তক, alluring, tempting, exciting desire or cupidity. [epicure.

লোভা-বিত, লিপ্সু, সুলোভা, covetous, avaricious, greedy; an

লোভান, লোভ দেখান, ভুলান, প্রবৃত্তি জন্মান, to entice, allure, tempt, to incite, stimulate.

লোভামি, অত্যন্ত প্রাকাঙ্ক্ষা, সুলোভতা, a grasping, greed, greediness, covetousness, epicurism.

লোভী, লুব্ধ, লিপ্সু, অগ্রহ, very desirous, greedy, covetous, eager after, voracious. [or coveted.

লোভ্য, লোভের বিষয়, অভিলষিত, desirable ; the object desired

লোম, রোম, রোঁয়া, তনূরুহ, আঁশ, the hair of the body in men or beasts, a tuft of hair, nap, wool, fur.

লোমকূপ, তনূকূপ, লোমের মূল, the pores of the skin. [lular.

লোমকূপবৎ, তনূকূপের ন্যায় ছিদ্রময়, full of pores, porous, cel-

লোমশ, সর্বাঙ্গে লোমযুক্ত, কেশর, আঁশযুক্ত, covered with hair or fur, hairy, shaggy, woolly.

লোমাঞ্চ, রোমহর্ষণ,—পুলক, শিহরণ, গাকাঁটা, erection of the hairs of the body through fear or surprize, horripilation, a bristling up.

লোমাঞ্চিত, লোমাঞ্চযুক্ত, পুলকিতশরীর, having the hair erect through violent agitation. [breast to navel.

লোমশ্রেণী, লোমাবলি,—বক্ষস্থলের লোম, the line of hair from

লোল, কম্পমান, চপল, ঢীলা, শ্লথ, কামাতুর, ইচ্ছুক, চঞ্চল, tremulous, shaking, hanging loosely, slack, flabby, lolling, desirous, concupiscent, eager, fickle.

লোলক, ঝুলিত, নাসিকাভরণ, pendant, swinging; a nose-jewel.

লোলা, অভিলাষ, লিপ্সা, লক্ষ্মী, চপলা, desire, cupidity, eagerness, Lakshmi goddess of fortune; *f.* fickle, &c.

লোলিত, ঝুলিত, শ্লথ. কম্পিত, loose, hanging in collops, flabby, slack, pendent, tremulous.

লোলুপ, অতিশয় লোভী, বৃথাকাঙ্ক্ষী, অমর, eagerly desirous, covetous, ambitious, greedy, voracious.

লোষ্ট্র, লোষ্ট,—ঢেলা, মৃৎখণ্ড, ঘাসের গুচ্ছ, a clod, lump of earth, a tuft of grass, &c.

লোহ-1, অয়স্, স্বর্ণাদি তৈজস, iron, any metal.

লোহ, লৌ,—শোণিত, রক্ত, blood.

লোহকান্ত, চুম্বক পাথর, অয়স্কান্ত, the load-stone.

লোহকার, লোহার,—কর্ম্মকার, কামার, a blacksmith, ironfounder.

লোহাঘটিত, লৌহসংযুক্ত জল, chalybeate, impregnated with iron.

লোহিত, রাঙ্গা, রক্ত, শোণিত, red, sanguine; blood.

লোহিতনয়ন, রাঙ্গাচক্ষুয়া, প্রচণ্ড, having the eyes red with rage, angry, furious, wrathful.

লোহিতমুখ, রক্তাস্য, রাঙ্গামুখ, blushing, red-faced, inflamed with anger.

লৌকিক, লোকপ্রসিদ্ধ, চলন, ব্যবহৃত, সাংসারিক, popular, vulgar, common, current, customary, human, worldly, mundane.

লৌকিকতা, বিদায়ী, ব্যবহার্য্যতা, a parting present, popularity, common usage.

লৌটি, ভাঁটা, গেঁণ্ডুক, a ball for playing with.

লৌহ, লোহা, ঔষধ বিশেষ, iron, a medicinal preparation of iron scoriæ.

শ.

শক, শাক, বৎসরের সংখ্যা বিশেষ, চিহ্ন, কীর্ত্তি, বাঞ্ছা, one who gives name to an æra, as Shálivâhana, &c. an æra, memorial, token, fame, a wish, desire.

শকট, ক্ষুদ্র রথ, গাড়ী, চতুর্থ নক্ষত্র, a carriage, cart, cart-load, the 4th lunar mansion.

শকড়া, শকট, গাড়ী, রথ, a cart, a car.

শকরকন্দ, শর্করাকন্দ, মিষ্টরসবিশিষ্ট রক্তবর্ণ আলু, the sweet-potatoe.

শকাব্দা, বৎসরের সংখ্যা বিশেষ, শাক, a particular year of any æra chiefly of that of Shálivähana.

শকুন, শকুনি, শগুন,—গৃধ্র, গিধিনী, a vulture.

শক্ত, দৃঢ়, স্তব্ধ, কঠিন, মজবুত, চিরস্থায়ী, বলবান্, সমর্থ, দক্ষ, নিপুণ, শ্রমী, প্রচণ্ড, কর্কশ, অদাতা, নির্দয়, কঠোর, দুর্জ্ঞেয়, পীড়াকর, tight, fast, firm, compact, stiff, hard, tough, rigid, inflexible, brittle, solid, durable, strong, valid, able, powerful, vigorous, capable, clever, indefatigable, diligent, violent, vehement, austere, morose, illiberal, cruel, severe, sharp, stern, arduous, difficult, abstruse, obscure, painful, poignant.

শক্তাই, বল, দৃঢ়ভাব, কাঠিন্য, strength, tightness, hardness, severity, rigour.

শক্তি, সামর্থ্য, বল, বিক্রম, বিষমতা, যোগ্যতা, কল্প, ক্ষমতা, অনুমতি, দেবী, শেল, power, ability, energy, strength, validity, force, vigour, valour, violence, severity, worthiness, liberty, option, permission, authority, warrant, a female deity, the personified energy or wife of a god, a spear.

শক্তিমান, বলবান্, ক্ষমতাপন্ন, বিক্রমী, strong, able, powerful, mighty, energetic.

শক্তু, ভুষ্ট যবাদি চূর্ণ, ছাতু, the flour of fried barley or other grain.

শক্য, যত্নদ্বারা নিষ্পাদ্য, সাধ্য, প্রতিপাদ্য, possible, practicable, effectible; the meaning of a word.

শক্রধনুঃ, ধনুরাকারে সূর্য্যের তেজ, Indra's bow, *i. e.* the rainbow.

শঙ্কনীয়, ভয়ের বিষয়, deserving to be feared, to be dreaded or suspected.

শঙ্কর, শুভ, মঙ্গল, শিব, auspicious, propitious, fortunate; Shiva.

শঙ্কা, সন্দেহ, ভয়, ত্রাস, সঙ্কট, দায়, suspicion, fear, dread, fright, alarm, terror, awe, danger, peril.

শঙ্কান্বিত, ভয়যুক্ত, সন্দিগ্ধ, ত্রস্ত, afraid, frightened, affrighted, alarmed, timid, fearful.

শঙ্কিত, ভীত, ত্রাসযুক্ত, অনিশ্চিত, *id*: also doubtful, uncertain, doubted, suspected.

শঙ্কু, শেল, গোঁজ, কীলক, কাঁটা, a javelin, spike, pole, stake, pin, gnomon.

শঙ্খ, শাঁখ, কম্বু, এক শত খর্ব, a conch used for libations, or as a blowing-horn ; 100 billions. [shell.
শঙ্খ-ক, স্ত্রীলোকের করভূষা, a bracelet made from the conch
শঙ্খকার, শাঁখারী, a shell-worker, maker of bracelets, &c.
শঙ্খিনী, বিশেষ লক্ষণাক্রান্তা স্ত্রী, ছায়া, a poetical description or class of women, an apparition, a fairy.
শজারু, শল্লকী, a porcupine.
শজিনা, শজনা, শজন্যা,—শোভাঞ্জন বৃক্ষ, the horse-radish tree.
শটিত, বাসি, ছাতাপড়া, যাতযাম, musty. stale, old.
শটী, শঠী,—বনহরিদ্রা. zedoary or mango-scented ginger.
শঠ, ধূর্ত্ত, কুটিল, ক্রূর, দুষ্ট, বিটল, deceitful, knavish, over-reaching, swindling, artful, crafty, insincere, wicked, depraved; a rogue, knave, cheat, sharper, villain. [lusion, &c.
শঠতা, ধূর্ত্ততা, ছলনা, ভণ্ডতা, knavery, craftiness, deceit, col-
শড়-া, সূক্ষ্ম, তনু, ক্ষুদ্র, সরু, ক্ষীণ, small, minute, little, in-significant, thin, slender. [spare.
শড়ঙ্গা, শড়িঙ্গ্যা,—ডিঙ্গী, দীর্ঘ, ক্ষীণ, a canoe ; long, tall, slender,
শণ, তৃণ বিশেষ, the Bengal hemp-plant, hemp.
শণসূত্র, শণনির্ম্মিত জাল, a net made of hemp.
শণ্ড, শাঁড়,—ষাঁড়, ক্লীব, পণ্ড, a bull, an ox, a natural eunuch or hermaphrodite.
শণ্ড-া, চাষা, মূর্খ, অজ্ঞান, a clown, an ignorant bumpkin.
শণ্ডতা, মুক্তমুক্তি, ক্লীবতা, বৃষের মুক্তভাব, emasculation, impotence, the state of a bull at liberty.
শত, শতক,—শও, এক সহস্রের দশম ভাগ, a hundred.
শতপথিক, বহুপথগামী, বহুমতাবলম্বী, following many ways, embracing many doctrines.
শতপদী, কর্ণজলৌকা, কেন্নো, বিছা, a centipede.
শতভিষা, চতুর্বিংশতি নক্ষত্র, the 24th lunar mansion.
শতমূলী, লতা বিশেষ, the climbing asparagus.
শতরঞ্জ, শতরিঞ্জ,—বিচিত্র সূত্রময় আসন, দরী, a floor-cloth, a carpet, chess-carpet. [per hundred, &c.
শতিক, শত সম্বন্ধীয়, শতং, relating to or denoting a hundred,
শত্রু, রিপু, বিপক্ষ, an enemy, foe, adversary, opponent.
শত্রুতা, বৈরি ভাব, বিপক্ষতা, দ্বেষ, enmity, hostility, strife.

শনি, শনৈশ্চর,—সপ্তম গ্রহ, the planet Saturn or its regent.
শনিবার, হপ্তাহের সপ্তম দিবস, saturday.
শনৈঃ, শনৈঃশনৈঃ,—মন্দে, ধীরে, ক্রমে, slowly, tardily, gently, deliberately, gradually.
শন্য, বিন্দু, বিপ্রুষ, a dot, a point, a cypher, the mark (॰).
শপথ, দিব্য, শাঁপ, মন্দবাঞ্ছা, an oath, imprecation, curse.
শপথপত্র, দিব্যপূর্ব্বক সাক্ষ্য, an affidavit or testimony on oath.
শপ্ত, শাঁপগ্রস্ত, cursed, execrated, anathematized.
শফ, খুর, বৃক্ষমূল, a hoof, a horse's hoof, the root of a tree.
শব, মৃত শরীর, মরা, a corpse, dead body, carcase.
শবদাহ, মরার পোড়ন, the burning of a corpse.
শবর, ম্লেচ্ছ, চুয়াড়, কিরাত, a barbarian, savage, mountaineer, [outcast.
শবসাধন, মরার উপরে বসিয়া জপকরা, a superstitious exercise performed while seated on a dead body.
শব্দ, ধ্বনি, স্বর, নিনাদ, রব, বাক্য, বিশেষ্য পদ, a sound, noise, roar, report, tone, voice, word, speech, a declinable word, a noun, &c.
শব্দকর, ধ্বনিকারী, ঠনঠনিয়া, স্বরবান্, sounding, making a noise, &c. sonorous.
শব্দকোষ বা সংগ্রহ,—অভিধান, a vocabulary of nouns, &c. a [dictionary.
শব্দগ্রহ, কর্ণ, বাক্যবোধ, the ear, comprehension of words, &c.
শব্দচোর, পদহর, a plagiary, plagiarist.
শব্দযোনি, শব্দাকর,—ধাতু, a dhátu or verbal root.
শব্দাতীত, বাক্যাগম্য, ব্রহ্ম, পরমেশ্বর, God *i. e.* he who is beyond the reach of sound. [sound.
শব্দার্থ, স্বরের অভিপ্রায়, the object or meaning of a word or
শম, বহিরিন্দ্রিয়নিগ্রহ, বৈরাগ্য, কামক্রোধাদি নাশ, শান্তি, সুখ, restraint of the senses, absence of passion, stoicism, ascetic indifference, devout abstraction, quietism, mental tranquillity, placidity, calmness, calm, quiet, rest.
শমতা, শান্তি, ধৈর্য্য, উপশম, tranquillity, quietude, alleviation or amendment of a disease.
শমন, মনের ধীরতা, যজ্ঞার্থ পশু হনন, যম, প্রোক্ষণ, mental tranquillity, immolation of beasts, Yama.
শমী, ছিমড়া, বৃক্ষ বিশেষ, a pod, legume, a species of Mimosa.

শমীধান্য, মুগ মাষকলায় আদি, leguminous grain, as peas, &c.
শম্বূক, শামুক, শুক্তি, শুগলী, a bivalve shell, a snail.
শয়চান, শ্যেনপক্ষী, a hawk or falcon. [repose.
শয়ন, ঘুমন, নিদ্রা যাওন, নিদ্রা, to lie down, recline; sleep.
শয়নঘর বা গৃহ,—নিদ্রাগার, ঘুমনশালা, a bedroom, bedchamber.
শয়নীয়, শয়নের যোগ্য, proper for repose, fit for lying down.
শয়িত, নিদ্রাপ্রাপ্ত, ঘুমান, lying down, asleep, reclined.
শয্যা, যাহাতে শয়ন করা যায়, বিছানা, a bed, a couch, a sopha.
শর, তীর, বাণ, নল বিশেষ, দুগ্ধের সারভাগ, an arrow, the bore or swell of the tide, a sort of grass or reed, cream, the scum of milk.
শরজাল, বিক্ষিপ্ত তীর সমূহ, a thick discharge of arrows.
শরট, কাঁকলাস, a lizard, a chamelion.
শরণ, আশ্রয়, প্রতিপালক, রক্ষাকর্ত্তা, a refuge, shelter, defence, protection, protector.
শরণাগত, শরণাপন্ন,—আশ্রিত, অবলম্বী, অবলম্বিত, বশতাপন্ন, a refugee, one who takes refuge or shelter in another, under protection of, relying on, supported by, surrendering, calling for quarter.
শরণ্য, অবলম্বনীয়, আশ্রেয়, আশ্রয়, রক্ষক, fit to be made a refuge or shelter, worthy of dependance; a refuge, defence, protection, protector.
শরৎ-কাল, আশ্বিন কার্ত্তিক, বর্ষাকালের পর দুইমাস, the autumnal or sultry season, the two months after the rains.
শরবর্ষণ, শরবৃষ্টি,—বাণজাল, a shower of arrows.
শরব্য, লক্ষ্য, a butt, a mark to shoot at.
শরা-ব, মৃৎপাত্র বিশেষ, a shallow earthen basin or pot-cover.
শরাসন, ধনুক, a bow, *q. d.* that in which an arrow is fixed.
শরীর, দেহ, প্রাণাধার, প্রপঞ্চ, the body, a material frame, matter.
শরীরগ, কীট, a reptile, a worm, *i. e.* creeping on the body.
শরীরপণ, প্রাণভয়, ইন্দ্রিয়দমন, a staking or risking of one's life, mortification or maceration of the body.
শরীরপতন বা পাত,—মরণ, দেহনাশ, death, the fall of the body.
শরীরপাক, ক্ষীণতা, কৃশভাব, ক্লিষ্টতা, a wasting of the body, emaciation, thinness, leanness.
শরীরবন্ধক, বশ্যপ্রমাণে পরহস্তগত পুত্রাদি, a hostage.

শরীরী, দেহী, প্রাপঞ্চিক, জীব, প্রাণী, corporeal, bodily, having a body, material ; an animal, sentient being.

শর্করা, চিনী. ভুরা, উখাড়, clayed or candied sugar.

শর্করোদক, চিনির পানা, লেবুরস ও শর্করাযুক্ত জল, lemonade, sherbet, a cooling beverage.

শর্বরী, রজনী, নিশা, রাত্রি, night, a night.

শলভ, পঙ্গপাল, ফড়িঙ্গ, পতঙ্গ, a grasshopper, a locust.

শলা-কা, শেল, তীর, বাণ, গোঁজ, কাঠী, রেখাটানন দণ্ড, a javelin, dart, arrow, a skewer, peg, thin bar or rod, the ribs of an umbrella, the bars of a cage, a slip of bamboo, a match, a toothpick, a probe or boujee, a ruler.

শলি, বিশ সের পরিমাণ, a dry measure of 20 seers.

শলিতা, পলিতা, বর্ত্তিকা, বাটী, the wick of a candle or lamp.

শলুফা. শাক বিশেষ, Indian fennel.

শনৈ, ক্রমে২. মন্দে২, ধীরে২, by slow degrees, slowly, softly, gently.

শল্ক, আঁইষ, ছাল, the scales of a fish, a flake, rind, bark.

শল্কময়, আঁইষযুক্ত, scaly, covered with scales, flaky.

শল্য, শেল, বাণ, শাবল, গদা, গোঁজ, কীলক, কাঠী, হাড়, শজারু, ক্লেশ, a javelin, an arrow, an iron crow or club, a peg, pin, stake, bamboo-rod, a bone, a porcupine, difficulty, embarassment.

শল্যোদ্ধার, বাস্তুভূমিহইতে মনুষ্যাদির অস্থি উত্থাপন, a clearing of bones, &c. from the site chosen for a house.

শল্লকী, শেজারু, কুন্দুরু, a porcupine, frankincense.

শশ, শশক, শশারু,—জাকাজব, a hare or rabbit.

শশধর, শশাঙ্ক, শশী,—চন্দ্র, নিশাপতি, the moon.

শশবিষাণ, অসম্ভব, hare's horns *i. e.* a natural impossibility.

শশ্বৎ, পুনঃ২, সদা, repeatedly, frequently, perpetually.

শষ্কুলি, কর্ণের কুহর, the outer ear or opening of the ear.

শস্তা, সুমূল্য, cheap, not dear, low-priced, plentiful.

শস্ত্র, খড়্গাদি, কবচ, আয়ুধ, অস্ত্র, a weapon, sword, scymetar, arms, armor, a tool, implement, instrument.

শস্ত্রকর বা কারক, অস্ত্রনির্ম্মারক, কর্ম্মকার, an instrument-maker, a cutler, an armourer.

শস্ত্রজীবী, শস্ত্রভৃৎ,—সেনা, যোদ্ধা, living by arms *i. e.* a soldier.

শস্ত্রপাণি বা হস্ত,—অস্ত্রধারী, wielding a weapon, carrying arms.

শস্ত্রাভ্যাস, অস্ত্রবিদ্যা শিক্ষা, the study of arms, military exercise.

শস্ত্রী, অস্ত্রধারী, খড়্গাদিযুক্ত. armed, accoutred, provided with arms.

শস্য, ধান্যাদি, ফল, তৃণাদির উৎপন্ন আহারোচিত দ্রব্য, শাঁস, grain, corn, a harvest, crop, fruit, the kernel, the edible substance of fruits, nuts, grain, &c.

শস্যশালী, ধান্যময়, abounding in corn, fertile in grain.

শাঁখ, শঙ্খ, কম্বু, a conch, a univalve shell.

শাঁখচিহ্নী, শাঁখিনী,—মুখদোষিণী, পেতনী, a hag, female goblin, apparition, a slut or slovenly woman.

শাঁখা, করভূষা, a shell-ornament for the wrist, a bracelet.

শাঁখারী, শঙ্খকার, a shell-cutter, a maker of bracelets, &c.

শাঁখী, শাঁখযুক্ত, শঙ্খবিশিষ্ট, testaceous, provided with a shell.

শাঁস, ধান্যাদির সারভাগ, the edible part of fruits, &c. the substance, kernel.

শাক, ভক্ষণীয় তৃণ পত্র পুষ্পাদি, দ্বীপ বিশেষ, শকাব্দা, শাক, an esculent vegetable, pot-herb, greens, any edible leaf, flower, fruit, stalk, root, &c. used as a vegetable, one of the seven Dwípas or divisions of the world, an æra, the æra of Shálivάhana.

শাক্ত, দেবীর উপাসক, a worshipper of Durgά in her various forms as the female creative principle or personified divine energy.

শাখা, বৃক্ষের ডাল, বেদের পরিচ্ছেদ বিশেষ, a branch, a bough, a branch or subdivision of the Vedas.

শাখানগর বা পুর, উপনগর, খেট, a suburb, a village.

শাখামৃগ, বানর, কপি, a monkey, an ape.

শাখী, বৃক্ষ, বেদশাখোক্ত ধর্ম্মের অনুষ্ঠাতা, a tree; an observer of any particular branch of the Veds.

শাটী, শাড়ী,—স্ত্রী লোকের পরিধেয় বস্ত্র, the dress of the Hindoo female, consisting of a piece of cloth worn as a petticoat, the end being thrown over the left shoulder.

শাঠ্য, ছল, শঠতা, ধূর্ত্তামী, a trick, deceit, collusion, craftiness, villainy.

শাব্দ, ধ্বনি, শব্দ, রব, বাক্য, sound, voice, speech.

শাণ, শান,—কষ্টিপাথর, অস্ত্রাদি তীক্ষ্ণ করণার্থ প্রস্তর, তলাবাঁধা, কাপড় বিশেষ, a whet-stone, grind-stone, a whetting or grinding, a pavement, a paved floor or terrace, a species of cloth.

শাণন, শানন,—তীক্ষ্ণীকরণ, মার্জ্জন, to whet, sharpen, grind, polish.

শাত্রব, রিপু, বৈর, দ্বেষ, প্রাতিকূল্য, an enemy, enmity, hostility, hatred, resentment, strife, opposition.

শাদা, শ্বেত, শুক্লবর্ণ, white, of a white colour.

শান, শানকী,—মুসল্মানের ভোজনপাত্র, an earthen dish or plate.

শানা, বস্ত্র বুননের কাষ্ঠ, a weaver's slay..

শান্ত, নিবৃত্ত, ক্ষমাবান্, ক্ষান্ত, থামান, ধীর, স্থির, জিতেন্দ্রিয়, allayed, appeased, pacified, soothed, calm, quiet, tranquil, peaceable, at rest; an ascetic, a stoic.

শান্তি, শম, স্থিরতা, ধৈর্য্য, কামক্রোধাদিনাশ, বৈরাগ্য, ঔদাস্য, উপশম, স্বস্ত্যয়ন, tranquillity, calmness, quietness, rest, peace, serenity, stoicism, absence of passion, indifference to external objects or impressions, quietism, cessation or alleviation of disease, a religious ceremony to avert inauspicious accidents or procure remission of disease.

শাপ, পরের অমঙ্গলবাঞ্ছা, মন্যু, a curse, an imprecation.

শাপগ্রস্ত, অভিশপ্ত, মন্যুবিশিষ্ট, cursed, lying under a curse.

শাবক, শিশু, ছা, পোত, the young of an animal, a foal, &c.

শাবল, শল্য, an iron bar or crow.

শাব্দ, বাচনিক, বাক্যসম্বন্ধীয়, ধ্বনিকারী, nominal, of or belonging to a noun or word, sounding, sonorous.

শাব্দিক, বাচনিক, স্বরসম্বন্ধীয়, অলঙ্কারাদি শাস্ত্রবেত্তা, বৈয়াকরণ, of or belonging to words or sounds, versed in the belles-lettres, conversant in grammar, &c.

শামলা, মলিন, ধূম্র, কৃষ্ণবর্ণ, dirty, dingy, dusky, dark-coloured.

শামা, ছাতা, ঘাস বিশেষ, পক্ষী বিশেষ, mould, mouldiness, a sort of grass, a species of bird.

শামুক, গুগলি, শম্বুক, শুক্তি, a snail, a bivalve shell.

শাম্য, থাম্য, ক্ষমাশীল, appeasable, assuageable, placable.

শারদীয়া, শরৎকালীন দেবীপূজা, *f.* the autumnal worship of Durgá.

শারী, ময়না পক্ষী, two varieties of the Mina bird.

শারীরিক, দৈহিক, প্রাপঞ্চিক, bodily, corporeal, corporal, material.
শার্ঙ্গ, শৃঙ্গময়, শৃঙ্গযুক্ত, made of horn, horny, corneous.
শার্দুল, ব্যাঘ্র, বাঘ, দ্বীপিন a tiger.
শাল, বৃক্ষ বিশেষ, ফাঁসী দিবার কাঠ, শূল, শিল্পাগার, a useful timber tree, a gallows, a cross or stake for impaling criminals, a work-shop.
শালা গৃহ, আগার, ঘর, a house, edifice, hall, room, place.
শালি, হৈমন্তিক ধান্য, a variety of winter-rice.
শালিক, ময়না পক্ষী, the small Bengal *Mina*.
শালী, ঘরের, গৃহসম্বন্ধীয়, বিশিষ্ট, ময়, শোভান্বিত, শীল, শীলতাযুক্ত, domestic, belonging to a house, *affix*: possessing, having, shining with, resplendent, inclined to, tending towards, having a bias to.
শালূক, পদ্ম প্রভৃতির মূল, the bulbous root of the lotus, &c.
শালতী, এক খান শালবৃক্ষ নির্ম্মিত ডিঙ্গা, a canoe formed of the trunk of a single Shál tree.
শাল্মলি, শিমুল বৃক্ষ, the silk-cotton tree.
শাশুড়ী, শ্বশ্রূ, পতির অথবা পত্নীর মাতা, a wife's or husband's mother, a mother-in-law.
শাসক, রাজত্বকারী, দেশরক্ষক, governing, ruling, &c. a governor.
শাসন, দণ্ড, বাগ্দণ্ড, তাড়ন, রাজত্ব, অধিকার, দেশ রক্ষণ, আজ্ঞা, ইন্দ্রিয় নিগ্রহ, রাজ্য পালন, বশীকরণ, দমন, discipline, correction, punishment, rebuke, reprimand, redress, reproof, government, administration, rule, dominion, controul, authority, a police, command, edict, government of the passions, &c: to rule, subdue, suppress, punish, &c.
শাসনীয়, শাস্য,—দমনীয়, নিগ্রহার্হ, তাড়নীয়, requiring controul, to be subdued, &c. punishable, censurable.
শাসানি, নিগ্রহ, তাড়না, correction, censure, a reprimand.
শাসান, ধমকান, তাড়ান, to chide, reprove, punish, correct.
শাসিত, বশীভূত, দমিত, দণ্ডিত, controlled, governed, punished, &c.
শাস্তা, নিগ্রহকারী, দেশপতি, one who disciplines, controls or punishes, a governor, ruler.
শাস্তি, নিগ্রহ, দণ্ড, প্রতিফলদান, punishment, chastisement, correction, discipline, vengeance.

শাস্ত্র, পুস্তক, গ্রন্থ, বেদ স্মৃত্যাদি, বিধান, সূত্রসমূহ, a book, treatise, literary work, sacred writing or book of authority in religion, law, art, science or letters, a law, a set of rules or maxims, science.

শাস্ত্রকর্ত্তা, ভণিতা, ধর্ম্মগ্রন্থরচক, an author, the authors of the sacred writings, &c. [science, &c.

শাস্ত্রজ্ঞ, ধর্ম্মগ্রন্থবেত্তা, acquainted with the sacred writings,

শাস্ত্রবহির্মুখ, শাস্ত্রের বিধান লঙ্ঘক, lawless, licentious, unrestrained by laws, &c.

শাস্ত্রবিৎ, শাস্ত্রবেত্তা,—পণ্ডিত, প্রবীণ, বিদ্বান্, বিদ্যাবন্ত, versed in the Shásters, skilled in theology, science or books.

শাস্ত্রমত বা সম্মত,—শাস্ত্রপ্রমাণসিদ্ধ, approved or authorized by the Shásters. [Shásters.

শাস্ত্রসিদ্ধ, সাব্যস্ত, সপ্রমাণ, proved or established by the

শাস্ত্রীয়, শাস্ত্রসম্বন্ধীয়, শাস্ত্রসিদ্ধ, of or belonging to the Shásters, scriptural, scientifical, legal, drawn from the Shásters, (as a proof, quotation, &c.)

শাস্ত্রোক্ত, শাস্ত্রবিহিত, declared or commanded in the Shásters.

শিঁথী, সীমন্তে ধারণ করে যে ভূষণ, মাল্য, মুকুট, a female ornament worn on the forehead, a wreath, a mitre.

শিকড়, বৃক্ষাদির মূল, জড়, মাড়ি, বংশের আদি পুরুষ, a fibrous root, the gums, the origin or first of a family.

শিকল, শৃঙ্খল, নিগড়, বন্ধন, a chain, fetters, bonds.

শিকা, শিক্য,—বাঁকের রজ্জু, ফিঙ্গা, ঝুলিত মাচা, the cords of a carrying-yoke, a sling or noose, a hanging shelf.

শিক্পা, ঘোটকের স্কন্দন, the rearing up of a horse.

শিক্ষক, অধ্যাপক, গুরু, শিষ্য, ছাত্র, a teacher, instructor, spiritual guide, a learner, a student.

শিক্ষণ, শিখন, শিক্ষাকরণ, অভ্যাস করণ, to learn, study, acquire knowledge, to receive instruction.

শিক্ষা, অধ্যাপনা, অভ্যাস, বেদের অঙ্গ বিশেষ, instruction, teaching, study, learning, doctrine. [tutor.

শিক্ষাকরাণ, অধ্যাপন, পড়ান, শাসন, to teach, instruct, train,

শিক্ষাকর্ত্তা, শিষ্য, ছাত্র, পড়ুয়া, a learner, scholar, student.

শিক্ষাকারক, অধ্যাপক, ছাত্র, পড়ুয়া, a teacher, instructor, tutor, master, a learner, a student.

শিক্ষাগুরু, উপদেষ্টা, অধ্যাপক, পাঠগুরু, a tutor, preceptor, instructor, teacher, school-master.

শিক্ষিত, শিক্ষাপ্রাপ্ত, অভ্যস্ত, নিপুণ, দমিত, মৃদু, taught, instructed, learned, acquired, studied, clever, skilful, trained, docile, tame.

শিখন, শিক্ষা করণ, to learn, study, acquire knowledge.

শিখর, পর্বতের শৃঙ্গ, কূট, বৃক্ষাগ্র, আগা, অগ্রভাগ, a mountain-peak, summit, the top of a tree, the point of a sword, &c. the end, the forepart.

শিখরী, পর্বত, বৃক্ষ, গাছ, a peaked mountain, a tree, a plant.

শিখা, অগ্নির অগ্রভাগ, শিষ, মস্তকের উপরিভাগে রক্ষিতকেশ, টিকী, চূড়া, মঞ্জরী, শৃঙ্গ, flame, a blaze, a tongue of fire, a crest, tuft of feathers or grass, a lock of hair left on the crown, a spike or ear of corn, a point, pinnacle, pyramid, summit, mountain-peak.

শিখান, অধ্যাপন, দমন, নিগ্রহ করণ, to teach, instruct, tutor, train, punish, break in, &c. [ment.

শিখানি, অধ্যাপনা, নিগ্রহ, শাস্তি, teaching, training, punish-

শিখাবান্, শিখী,—অগ্নি, কেতু, উজ্জ্বলিত, চূড়াবান্. Agni or fire, the personified descending node; flaming, blazing up, crested, tufted, &c.

শিখী, শিখিনী,—ময়ূর ময়ূরী, *m. & f.* a peacock, a pea-hen.

শিগ্রু, শজিনা বৃক্ষ, the horse-radish tree or its root.

শিঙ্গ, শৃঙ্গ, an animal's horn. [horn.

শিঙ্গা, শৃঙ্গ নির্ম্মিত যন্ত্র, a cupping-horn or tube, a blowing

শিঙ্গেল, শৃঙ্গবিশিষ্ট, বিষাণযুক্ত, horned, having horns.

শিঙ্ঘাণ, শিঙ্ঘনী, নাসিকার মল, the mucus of the nose, snot.

শিঞ্জন, শিঞ্জিত,—ঝঞ্জন, অলঙ্কারের ধ্বনি, to gingle, tinkle; the gingling of ornaments, &c.

শিটা, মলা, গাদ, কাইট, dregs, refuse, scum, dross.

শিড়্শিড়্, শিড়শিড়ামী,—শিহরা, রোমাঞ্চ, অতিশয় ভয়বোধ, a tingling or creeping of the flesh thro' sudden alarm, horripilation, trepidation, cold fear.

শিড়্শিড়ান, শিঃসান, শিহরণ, to tingle or creep as the flesh.

শিড়ী, শিঁড়ী,—সোপান, a ladder, stair-case, flight of steps.

শিতাণ, বালিশ, উপধান, a cushion, a pillow, a bolster.

শিথিল, ঢীলা, অদৃঢ়, ঝোলিত, অলস, অমনোযোগী, slack, loose, flaccid, flabby, lax, relaxed, slow, dilatory, inactive, inert, inattentive.

শিব, বামদেব, মাঙ্গল্য, Shiva or the destroyer, welfare, prosperity.

শিবরাত্রি, মাঘ মাসের কৃষ্ণপক্ষের চতুর্দ্দশী, the fourteenth of the wane in Mágha, as sacred to Shiva.

শিব, শিবা,—শৃগাল, জম্বুক, a jackal.

শিবা, শিবানী,—শিবপত্নী, দুর্গা, ভবানী, Durgá consort of Shiva.

শিবালয়, শিবের পূজার্থ মন্দির, শ্মশান, a temple of Shiva, a cemetery or place where bodies are burnt.

শিবিকা, গোপ্য যান, ডুলী, পাল্‌কী, a covered litter, a palkee.

শিবির, যুদ্ধোন্মুখ সেনার বাসস্থান, a camp, a barrack.

শিম, শিম্বা, শিম্বী,—ছিম্‌ড়া, কলায়াদির খোসা, a kidney-bean, legume, a pod, pea-pod, bean-shell, &c.

শিমুল, শাল্মলিবৃক্ষ, the silk-cotton tree.

শিয়াল, শৃগাল, ফেরু, a jackal or fox.

শির-া, ধমনী, সর্বাঙ্গ রক্তের গমনপথ, ধাতু, নাড়ী, a nerve, sinew, tendon, blood-vessel, vein, artery, the pulse, any tubular vessel, a gut or entrail.

শিরঃ, মস্তক, মাথা, উপরিভাগ, the head, the top or upper-part of a thing.

শিরঃকম্প-ন, মস্তকের ঘূর্ণা, গাত্রপাক, vertigo, giddiness, swimming of the head.

শিরঃপীড়া বা শূল,—মস্তকের বেদনা, a head-ache.

শিরঃনাম, শিরোনাম,—ঠিকানা, উপরিস্থিত লেখা, the address of a letter, a superscription, title, inscription.

শিরপা, ঘোটকের স্কন্দন, restiveness in a horse, rearing up.

শিরস্ত্র, টোপ, টুপী, মুকুট, a helmet, hat, cap, turban, crown.

শিরস্থ, মস্তকস্থিত, উপরিস্থিত, প্রধান, on the head or top, topmost, chief; a leader.

শিরোনমন, নমস্কার, প্রণতি, a bowing or nodding, obeisance, reverence.

শিরোধার্য্য, অবধেয়, মান্য, আর্ষ্য, to be received and attended to with respect, to be respectfully obeyed, respectable.

শিরোমণি, চূড়ামণি, মস্তকের ভূষণ, a gem worn in the crest or on the head.

শিরোলুণ্ঠন, মরণকালীন মস্তকের পতন, the hanging or drooping of the head as in one dying.

শিল-1, প্রস্তর, পাষাণ, শিলাট, বর্ষোপল, গোবরাট, মঞ্জুল, a stone, a rock, a flat stone for grinding condiments, &c. a hail-stone, the sill of a door, arsenic.
শিলাপুত্র, নোড়া, পেষণী, a muller or stone roller.
শিলাবল্কা, শিলাবাক, a species of medicinal moss or lichen.
শিলাবৃষ্টি, বর্ষোপল, a hail-stone, hail. [labour.
শিল্প-কর্ম্ম, চিত্রকর্ম্মাদি, a manual or mechanic art, handicraft
শিল্পকর বা কার, শিল্পী,—কারিকর, কারু, চিত্রকারাদি, a mechanic, handicraftsman, artizan, artificer, workman, manufacturer, artist. [mechanics.
শিল্পবিদ্যা, চিত্রাদিকর্ম্ম, the mechanic arts, handicraft trades,
শিশির, নীহার,হিম, মাঘ ফাল্গুন, dew, frost, the dewy season.
শিশু, বালক, চেঙ্গড়া, শাবক, পোত, বৎস, ছা, a child, infant, lad, boy, the young of an animal, a calf, foal, pup, &c. [fancy, pupilage.
শিশুকাল, শিশুত্ব,—বাল্য, বালককাল, childhood, boyhood, in-
শিশুক, শিশুমার,—শুশুক, উষ্কা মৎস্য, the gangetic porpoise.
শিশ্ন, মেঢ্র, the penis or male organ. [sures, sensual.
শিশ্নোদরপরায়ণ, বিষয়সুখাসক্ত, লম্পট, devoted to bodily plea-
শিখ, মঞ্জরী, অগ্নিশিখা, an ear of corn, a flower-spike, flame.
শিষ্ট, শিক্ষিত, শাসিত, ভদ্র, সভ্য, সাধুব্যবহারান্বিত, নম্র, বশীভূত, দম্য, disciplined, instructed, trained, well-bred, polite, polished, genteel, civil, gentle, tractable, docile, obedient, submissive, manageable.
শিষ্টতা, সভ্যতা, নম্রতা, politeness, urbanity, docility, &c.
শিষ্টাচার, ভদ্রতা, সভ্যতা, polite conduct or behaviour, gentility of manners. [ing.
শিষ্টাচারী, সভ্য, ভব্য, নম্র, polite, genteel, civil, condescend-
শিষ্য, ছাত্র, পড়ুয়া, a disciple, scholar, pupil.
শিহরণ, লোমহর্ষ,লোমাঞ্চ, a glow or creeping of the flesh from sudden sensation of pleasure or pain.
শীঘ্র, সত্বর, দ্রুত, বেগবান্, ত্বরিত, আশু, অবিলম্বে, তৎক্ষণাৎ, quick, speedy, rapid, swift, fleet; quickly, harshly, speedily, fast, apace, immediately, soon. [expeditious.
শীঘ্রগ, শীঘ্রগামী,—দ্রুতগামী, আশুগ, swift-going, rapid, fleet,

শীত, হিম, তুষার, স্নিগ্ধ, অলস, জড়, স্থূলবুদ্ধি, cold, coldness; cold, chilly, frigid, idle, lazy, dull, apathetic, stupid. [winter-time.

শীত-কাল, হেমন্ত, শিশির, জাড়াদিন, the cold season, the winter,

শীতড়ী. হিমকালীন গাত্রবস্ত্র, পাছুড়ী, a cold-season garment.

শীতভীত, হিমশঙ্কিত, afraid of the cold, chilly.

শীতল, হিমকর, স্নিগ্ধ, cool, refreshing, cold, chilly, frigid.

শীতল-তা, স্নিগ্ধতা, ঠাণ্ডাই, coolness, cold, frigidity, chilliness.

শীতলপাটী, হিমকর আসন বিশেষ, a cool mat used for beds, &c.

শীতলা, রক্তবটী, the small-pox or its presiding goddess.

শীতার্ত্ত. হিমকাতর, affected by the cold, cold, chilly.

শীৎকার, ভয় কিম্বা হর্ষ হেতু শরীরের হঠাৎ স্পন্দন, শিহরা, a glow of sudden pleasure, or creeping of the flesh from an unpleasant sensation. [withered.

শীর্ণ, কৃশ, ক্ষীণ, শুষ্ক, thin, slender, emaciated, lean, dry,

শীর্ষ, মস্তক, মাথা, the head.

শীল-তা, ভাব, গুণ, স্বভাব, সুস্বভাব, চরিত্র, ধারা, প্রবৃত্তি, nature, innate property, character. disposition, *especially* good conduct or disposition, temper, inclination. bias, tendency to, propensity.

শীল-ক, ভাবযুক্ত, তৎপ্রবর্ত্তমনাঃ, অনুরক্ত, বিশিষ্ট, apt, inclined to, having a bias towards, fond of, tending to, endowed with, possessed of.

শীলবান্, সুশীল, সুস্বভাববিশিষ্ট, সদ্বৃত্ত, সুব্যবহার, well-inclined, amiable, well-disposed, well-conducted.

শুঁটী, ছিমড়া, শিম্বী, a legume, a pea-pod, bean shell, &c.

শুঁঠ, শুণ্ঠী, শুষ্ক আর্দ্রক, dried ginger.

শুঁড়, শুণ্ড, হস্তির কর, an elephant's trunk or proboscis.

শুঁড়ী, মদ্যবিক্রেতা, a distiller, vintner, vender of liquors.

শুক, টিয়া পক্ষি বিশেষ, a parrot.

শুকন, শোষণ, তোবড়ন, তাপন, বিগড়ন, শুষ্ক হওন, মাটন, ক্ষীণ হওন, to dry up, shrivel, become dry, evaporate, fade, wither, heal, waste or dwindle away.

শুকনা, নীরস, ম্লান, তোবড়া, dry, sapless, withered up, shrivelled. [drought.

শুকা, শুষ্ক, ক্ষীণ, অনাবৃষ্টি, dry, dried, emaciated; dryness,

শুকান, শোষণ, ভোবড়ান, শরীর পাক পাওন, শুঁচন, নীরস হওন, ঝাটন, to dry, cause to dry up, parch or shrivel up, to pine or dwindle away, waste away, to wipe or dry up, to fade, to fall as a river.

শুকটী, শুকটা,—শুষ্ক, নীরস, ক্ষীণ, dry, lean, thin, emaciated.

শুকড়িয়া, চনামারা, withering, fading, drying away.

শুক্ত, কাঁজী, তিক্তরস ব্যঞ্জন, অম্লরস, sour-gruel, a bitter sauce or condiment, a species of vinegar or acid preparation from fruits or roots by steeping.

শুক্তি, শুষ্কতা, শোষ, শরীরপাক, মুক্তাগার, ঝিনুক, ছানী, dryness, a shrivelling up, consumption, a pearl oyster, a cockle, a muscle, spots on the eye.

শুক্তিকা, মুক্তাগার, চুকাশাক, a pearl-oyster, a kind of sorrel.

শুক্তিজ, মুক্তা, মৌক্তিক, a pearl. [its regent; white.

শুক্র, রেতঃ, ষষ্ঠ গ্রহ, শ্বেত, semen virile, the planet Venus or

শুক্রবার, হপ্তাহের ষষ্ঠ দিবস, Friday. [bright.

শুক্ল, শ্বেতবর্ণ, নির্ম্মল, সিত, white, of a white colour, pure,

শুক্লপক্ষ, চন্দ্রের বৃদ্ধিকাল, the fortnight of the moon's increase.

শুক্লিমা, শ্বেতভাব, পরিষ্কার, whiteness, brightness, purity.

শুঙ্গ-1, শূক, শূয়া, the awn of barley, &c. an insect's bristles.

শুঙ্গন, ঘ্রাণ লওন, to smell, to scent. [of errata.

শুচনা, শুদ্ধি, শুদ্ধিপত্র, the correction of a writing, a table

শুচি, শুদ্ধ, পবিত্র, পূত, নির্ম্মল, পরিষ্কার, pure, holy, purified by ablution, clean, correct. [purity.

শুচিতা, শুদ্ধতা, পবিত্রতা, purity of mind, sanctity, outward

শুণ্ঠী, শুঁঠ, শুষ্ক আর্দ্রক, dried ginger.

শুণ্ড, শুঁড়, হস্তিকর, an elephant's trunk or proboscis.

শুণ্ডিক, মদ্যবিক্রেতা, a vintner, vender of liquors, distiller.

শুদ্ধ, পবিত্র, পূত, শুচি, নির্দোষ, পরিষ্কৃত, যথার্থ, নির্ভাজ, মাত্র, কেবল. pure, purified, upright, clean, cleansed, corrected, correct, right, proper, unmixed, unadulterated, mere; alone, only.

শুদ্ধি, পবিত্রতা, শুচিতা, পূতি, প্রকৃতভাব, পরিষ্কার, যথার্থতা. purity, purification, cleanness, sanctity, rectitude. uprightness, simplicity, uuadulteratedness, correction of a writing, correctness.

শুধরণ, শুদ্ধ হওন, সারণ, to amend, grow better, improve.

শুধরাণ, শুদ্ধ করণ, পরিষ্কার করণ, সারাণ, মার্জ্জন, প্রতীকার করণ, to correct a writing, free from faults or errors, amend, reform, repair, rectify, modify, cleanse, purify, refine, expiate, forgive, remedy.

শুধু, কেবল, মাত্র, ব্যতিরিক্ত, only, merely, alone, except.

শুন, শুনী,—শ্বা, কুকুর, কুকুরী, *m. f.* a dog, a bitch.

শুনন, শ্রবণ, মানন, to hear, listen, mind, regard, attend to.

শুনান, শ্রবণ করাণ, বলন, বর্ণন, to cause to hear, &c. to tell, to relate, to repeat.

শুভ, হিত, মঙ্গল, ভদ্র, প্রিয়, উত্তম, কল্যাণ, কুশল, প্রসন্নতা, good, happy, auspicious, lucky, propitious, favourable, agreeable, pleasant, handsome; good, good fortune, welfare, auspiciousness.

শুভকর, প্রসন্ন, মঙ্গলকারী, অঙ্কবিদ্যাবেত্তা, auspicious, propitious, lucky, conferring good or welfare; an accountant, arithmetician.

শুভকর্ম্ম, মঙ্গল্যক্রিয়া, a good or auspicious act, a lucky action.

শুভক্ষণ, শুভলগ্ন,—ক্রিয়ার উপযুক্ত কাল, a lucky moment, a favourable time.

শুভগ্রহ, উত্তম কপাল, a propitious planet or favourable aspect of affairs.

শুভধ্যায়ী, শুভানুধ্যায়ী,—পরহিতৈষী, পরমঙ্গলচেষ্টক, benevolent, seeking the good of others; a well-wisher.

শুভচিন্তক, পরমঙ্গলভাবক, devising or contriving good, thinking of another's good.

শুভাদৃষ্ট, সুভাগ্য, good fortune, good luck, a lucky destiny.

শুভান্বিত, কল্যাণী, ভাগ্যবন্ত, মঙ্গল্য, কুশলসূচক, prosperous, fortunate, lucky, auspicious.

শুভিতা, সুখ, সুভাগ্য, প্রসন্নতা, সুসময়, ease in circumstances, favourableness, opportuneness, propitiousness, seasonableness, calmness or serenity of weather, &c. fine weather.

শুভ্র, শুক্ল, শ্বেত, দীপ্তিবিশিষ্ট, white, fair, bright, shining.

শুভ্রদন্তী, উত্তমদন্তবিশিষ্টা, উত্তর দক্ষিণ দিকের হস্তিনী, having white teeth; the female elephant of the N. W.

শুভ্রাংশু, চন্দ্র, নিশাপতি, the moon.

শুল্ক, মূল্য, দান, কর, ঘাটানিতে দেয়, যৌতুক, বিবাহকালে প্রাপ্য, বরং, পণ নির্দ্ধারণার্থ দেয়, price, a toll, duty, impost, inland customs, a wife's marriage present from her husband, a wife's legal perquisites arising from the profits of household labour, &c. purchase money given to a bride's parents, earnest-money given in a contract or purchase in order to bind or ratify the bargain.

শুশুক, শিশুমার, the Gangetic porpoise.

শুশ্রূষক, চরণসেবক, পরিচারক, ছাত্র, দাস, চাকানিয়া, closely or obsequiously attentive; a servant, disciple, apprentice, hireling, slave, superintendant.

শুশ্রূষা, চরণসেবা, উপাসনা, পরিচর্য্যা, শ্রবণেচ্ছা, obsequiousness, close attention, prompt service or attendance, obedience, desire to hear and obey.

শুষণা, শোষ, শুষ্কতা, a drying, drying up, exsiccation.

শুষ্ক, ম্লান, তোবড়া, পোড়া, নীরস, ক্লিষ্ট, dry, dried up, withered, shrivelled, scorched, sapless, juiceless, pale, sallow, thin.

শূক, শূঙ্গা,—শূয়া, the awn of barley, &c. an insect's bristles.

শূককীট, কণ্টকী কীট, শূয়াপোকা, বৃশ্চিক, the hairy caterpillar.

শূকধান্য, যব গমাদি, bearded grain, as barley, &c.

শূকময়, শূকী,—কণ্টকী, কণ্টকবৎ লোম বিশিষ্ট, শূয়াবিশিষ্ট, awned, bearded, bristly, setaceous.

শূকর, শূকরী,—শোয়ার, বরাহ, *m. f.* a hog, boar, sow.

শূদ্র-1, চতুর্থ বর্ণ, বৃষল, *m. f.* one of the fourth or lowest order of Hindoos, the Shúdra or serving class.

শূদ্রী, শূদ্রাণী,—শূদ্রের পত্নী, বৃষলী, the wife of a Shúdra.

শূন্য, উচ্চট, পতিত, ত্যক্ত, নির্জন, রিক্ত, আকাশ, ছিদ্র, রহিত, বিন্দু, desert, waste, uncultivated, lonely, still, empty, void, blank, vacant, hollow, unoccupied; the atmosphere, sky, heaven, a vacuum, void space, the hollow in a tree, a dot, a cypher: *affix*: destitute of, void of, without, free from.

শূন্যতা, রিক্তভাব, emptiness, vacancy, vacuity.

শূন্যদর্শন, শিরঃকম্পন, giddiness, sudden failure of sight.

শূন্যবাদী, নাস্তিক বিশেষ, দেহাত্মবাদী, an atheist who denies the reality of matter. [place.

শূন্যস্থান, রিক্তস্থল, নির্জনস্থান, an empty, desert or uninhabited

শূন্যহস্ত, রিক্তহস্ত, অদাতা, empty-handed, sparing. [of corn.

শূয়-া, শূক, শূঙ্গা, an insect's bristles, the awn or beard

শূয়াপোকা, বৃশ্চিক, কণ্টকী কীট, the hairy caterpillar.

শূয়ার, শূকর, বরাহ, a hog, a boar.

শূর, বীর, যোদ্ধা, সূর্য্য, বলবান্, সাহসী, a hero, warrior, champion, the sun; bold, brave, intrepid.

শূরতা, সাহস, বিক্রম, heroism, bravery, intrepidity, courage.

শূরণ, ওল, অর্শঘ্ন. an esculent root.

শূল, শলাকা, শেল, ভেলা, হঠাৎ বেদনা, a stake, pale, pike, spit, spear, dart, a sharp pain.

শূলব্যথা বা রোগ, পেটব্যথা, বায়ুরোগ, sharp pain, a cholic, rheumatic pains. [spearman.

শূলধারী, শেলযুক্ত, রায়বাঁশিয়া, bearing a pike or javelin; a

শূলন-আন, বিঁধন, পীড়ান, to bore, pierce, excite acute pain.

শূলকী, শেল, শলাকা, রায়বাঁশ, a javelin, spear, pike, dart.

শূলী, শূলবিশিষ্ট, পেটবেদনাযুক্ত, armed with a spear, afflicted with cholic, &c.

শৃগাল, শেয়াল, জম্বুক, ফেরু, a jackal, a fox.

শৃঙ্খল-া, শিকলী, বেড়ী, বন্ধন, a chain, a fetter, a tie.

শৃঙ্খলা, শৃঙ্খলতা,—পরিপাটী, orderly arrangement, connection, concatenation, order.

শৃঙ্খলী, হস্তিপাদ বন্ধন, a chain for the feet of an elephant.

শৃঙ্গ, শিঙ্গ, বিষাণ, পর্ব্বতাগ্র, শিখর, কূট, the horn of an animal, a mountain peak or summit.

শৃঙ্গার, আদ্যরস, ভাব, কাম, মৈথুন, amatory sentiment, passion, love, sexual intercourse, copulation, coition. [civious.

শৃঙ্গারী, ভাবশীল, কামুক, an impassioned lover; fond, las-

শৃঙ্গী, শৃঙ্গবন্ত জন্তু, শিঙ্গেল, শিখরী, horned, crested, peaked.

শেখর, শৈলশৃঙ্গ, পর্ব্বতাগ্র, কূট, a crest, summit, mountain-peak.

শেজারু, শল্লকী, a porcupine.

শেয়ান, ধূর্ত্ত, দক্ষ, crafty, cunning, subtle, artful, clever.

শেয়াল, শৃগাল, ফেরু, a jackal or fox.

শেয়ালা, শৈবাল, an aquatic plant, conferva, moss.
শেল, রায়বাঁশ, শলাকা, a pike, spear, dart, spit.
শেষ, অন্ত, সীমা, সমাপ্তি, বিরতি, বক্রী, উদ্বর্ত্ত, অবশেষ, ফল, কর্ম্মপাক, নাগেশ্বর, অন্ত্য, অবশিষ্ট, নিষ্পন্ন, ভাবী, an end, limit, termination, finish, conclusion, cessation, the latter part, rest, residue, remnant, remainder, balance, sequel, what is left, omitted or rejected, leavings, a surviver, result, consequence, doom, the king of serpents; last, latest, final, ultimate, utmost, surviving, over, done, finished, future.
শেষকাল, অন্ত্যসময়, মরণকাল, the last time, latter end, time of death.
শেষাবস্থা, শেষদশা.—বৃদ্ধকাল, old age, the last state.
শেষবেলা, বৈকাল, দিনাবসান, afternoon, close of day.
শেষভুক্ বা ভোক্তা, উচ্ছিষ্টভোজী, eating another's leavings, eating after others.
শেষমন্দ, দুর্গতি, ফল বিরুদ্ধ, a catastrophe, ill result, bad consequence.
শেষরাত্রি, রাত্রির অবসান, the close or last watch of the night.
শেষে, অন্তে, পরে, পশ্চাৎ, পরলোকে, finally, lastly, at length, at last, &c. afterwards, then, next, hereafter.
শৈত্য, শীতগুণ, হিমত্ব, coldness, chilliness, frigidity, rigour.
শৈথিল্য, ঢীলামি, শ্লথভাব, আলস্য, অনবধানতা, গৌণ, চেষ্টার ন্যূনতা, slackness, looseness, flaccidity, remissness, inattention, delav, procrastination, dilatoriness.
শৈব, শিবের উপাসক, a shivite or devotee of Shiva.
শৈবাল, শেয়ালা, an aquatic plant, conferva, moss.
শৈল, পর্ব্বত, শিল, a rock, crag, mountain.
শৈলী, কৌশল, উপায়, কল্প, a contrivance, device, stratagem, easy method, art, knack.
শৈল্য, কাঠিন্য, পাষাণত্ব, hardness, stoneness, a stony substance.
শৈশব, বাল্য, তারুণ্য, infancy, childhood, boyhood, minority.
শোওন, শয়ন, ঘুমন, to lie down, to sleep, repose, nap.
শোঁকন-ান, ঘ্রাণ লওন, to smell, to scent.
শোক, দুঃখ, খেদ, বিলাপ, অনুতাপ, grief, sorrow, lamentation, wailing, mourning, woe, regret.
শোকান্বিত, শোকী,—খেদযুক্ত, বিলাপী, sorrowful, grieving, &c.

শোকার্ত্ত, শোচক,—খেদান্বিত, দুঃখিত, অনুতপ্ত, grieved, sad, anxious, sorrowful, unhappy, sorry, repentant.

শোচনা, দুঃখ, অনুতাপ, ভাবনা, grief, sorrow, regret, repentance, anxiety.

শোণ, তৃণ বিশেষ, a shrub of whose bark a sort of cord is [made.

শোণা, শোণাপাত, শোণামুখী,—ভেদক গাছ বিশেষ, senna.

শোণিত, রক্ত, লোহু, blood.

শোথ, পাদাদির স্ফীততা, a swelling, intumescence.

শোধ, ঋণের অপনয়ন, নিকাশ, প্রতিদান, payment of a debt, paying off of arrears, retaliation of injuries.

শোধন, দায় দেওন, ঋণাপনোদন, প্রতিদান করণ, পরিষ্কার করণ, অঙ্কহ্রাস, to pay, liquidate, clear off, discharge, retaliate, correct a writing, purify, cleanse; refining of metals, arithmetical subtraction.

শোধনীয়, শোধ্য,—দেয়, দেনা, পরিষ্কার্য্য, payable, due, requiring to be cleared off, to be corrected, &c.

শোধরাণ, শুদ্ধকরণ, সুস্থ হওন, দুষ্টতা ত্যাগ করণ, to correct, rectify, amend, *v. n.* to recover, reform, improve in character and conduct.

শোভন, প্রকাশন, ভাল লাগন, সৌন্দর্য্য, মনোরম্য, সুন্দর, দীপ্ত, মঙ্গল, to shine, appear to advantage, be comely or pleasing to the sight, befit, become; beauty, elegance; beautiful, comely, handsome, splendid, shining, auspicious, propitious.

শোভনীয়, বিভূষণীয়, to be adorned or beautified, &c.

শোভা, দীপ্তি, প্রভা, কান্তি, সৌন্দর্য্য, light, lustre, brightness, radiance, splendour, glory, beauty.

শোভাকর, ভাস্বান্, দীপ্যমান, সুন্দর, shining, resplendent, comely, beautiful, ornamental.

শোভাঞ্জন, শজিনা বৃক্ষ, the Shajiná or horse-radish tree.

শোভান্বিত, দীপ্ত, যশস্বী, কান্ত, splendid, illustrious, comely, beautiful.

শোভিত, বিভূষিত, প্রভাযুক্ত, beautified, adorned, made splen- [did.

শোয়া, নিদ্রা যাওয়া, ঘুম, a reclining, reposing, sleep, repose.

শোয়ান, শয়ন করাণ, ঘুমান, to make to lie down, cause to repose, to put or lay to sleep.

শোলা, জলজ তৃণ বিশেষ, Indian cork, a spungy plant used for forming floats for fishing nets.
শোষ, শুষ্কতা, ক্ষয়, ক্ষয়রোগ, যক্ষ্মা, চোষাণি, dryness, a wasting or drying up, pulmonary consumption, exhaustion, suction. [rapacious.
শোষক, শুষ্ককর, নিঙড়ানিয়া, drying up, absorbent, avaricious,
শোষণ, শুষ্ক করণ, চোষণ, to dry up, become dry or exhausted, to imbibe, dry, suck up, exact, extort, fleece, plunder, impoverish. [exacter.
শোষণকা, অপহারক, নিঙড়ানিয়া, an extortioner, plunderer,
শোষ্টান, চোষণ, ধূমপান, নিঙড়া, a sucking up, a long draught or pull in drinking or smoking, extortion,&c.
শৌচ, পবিত্রতা জনক ক্রিয়া, স্নানাদি, ভেদ, শুদ্ধি, a purificatory rite, purification, ablution, washing, evacuation by stool, purity, cleanness. [spirits.
শৌণ্ডিক, শুঁড়ী, মদ্যজীবী, মগুহারক, a vintner, distiller, dealer in
শৌন, শৌনিক,—মাংসাদিজীবী, a butcher, poulterer, vender of flesh. [elegance, beauty, learning.
শৌভ্য, প্রিয়ত্ব, সৌন্দর্য্য, পাণ্ডিত্য, pleasantness, agreeableness,
শৌভ্যভব্য, শিষ্ট, ভদ্র, polite, well-behaved, well-bred, of polished manners. [courage.
শৌর্য্য, শূরত্ব, পরাক্রম, heroism, prowess, valour, bravery.
শ্মশান, শবদাহ স্থান, পিতৃবন, a place for burning or burying the dead, a cemetery, a sepulchre.
শ্মশ্রু, দাড়ির লোম, the beard.
শ্মশ্রুমুখী, দাড়িবিশিষ্টা স্ত্রী, a female with a beard.
শ্যাম, শ্যামল,—কৃষ্ণবর্ণ, নীলবর্ণ, হরিদ্বর্ণ, dark in colour, dark-blue, black, green.
শ্যামা-দেবী, দুর্গা, কালী, Durgá or the black goddess.
শ্যামা-ক, শ্যামক,—ঘাস বিশেষ, a species of grass or its seeds.
শ্যালা, শৈবাল, a water-plant, conferva, moss.
শ্যালাপড়া, শেয়ালাময়, শৈবালাচ্ছাদিত, overrun with moss, moss-grown, mossy. [or sister.
শ্যাল-ক, শ্যালকী,—পত্নীর ভ্রাতা ভগিনী, *m.* & *f.* a wife's brother
শ্যেন, বাজপক্ষী, the hawk or falcon. [nerating.
শ্রদ্ধাম, শ্রদ্ধাযুক্ত, আরাধক, possessed of faith, trusting, ve-

শ্রদ্ধা, দৃঢ় বিশ্বাস, প্রত্যয়, ভক্তি, সেবা, স্পৃহা, শুদ্ধি, faith, strong belief, trust, reverence, respect, a wish, desire, liking, inclination for, purity.

শ্রদ্ধান্বিত, দৃঢ় বিশ্বাস বিশিষ্ট, ভক্ত, possessed of faith, having veneration for. [liking.

শ্রদ্ধালু, বিশ্বাসকারী, ভক্ত, believing, trusting, venerating,

শ্রবণ, শুনন, শব্দের গ্রহণ, কর্ণ, to hear; hearing, attention, the ear. [serving attention.

শ্রবণীয়, শুনিবার যোগ্য, মান্য, audible, fit to be heard, de-

শ্রবণা, দ্বাবিংশতি নক্ষত্র, the twenty-second lunar mansion.

শ্রবণেন্দ্রিয়, কর্ণ, কাণ, the organ of hearing, the ear.

শ্রম, আয়াস, উদ্যম, বহুচেষ্টা, ক্লান্তি, toil, exertion, industry, diligence, application, pains, fatigue, weariness.

শ্রমান্বিত, শ্রমাসক্ত, শ্রমী,—বহুচেষ্টান্বিত, উদ্যমী, sedulous, industrious, laborious, assiduous, diligent.

শ্রাদ্ধ, পিতৃলোকের উদ্দেশে অন্নাদি দান, পিণ্ডদান, funeral obsequies or offerings to the manes of deceased ancestors. [obsequies.

শ্রাদ্ধীয়, ঔর্দ্ধদৈহিক, অন্ত্যেষ্টি সম্বন্ধীয়, of or belonging to funeral

শ্রান্ত, শ্রমকাতর, অবসন্ন, ক্লান্ত, fatigued, tired, weary, spent, jaded, languid. [relaxation, refreshment.

শ্রান্তি, অবসাদ, শ্রম, বিরাম, lassitude, weariness, fatigue,

শ্রাবণ, চতুর্থ মাস, পরগোচরে কথন, শুনান, শ্রবণপ্রাপ্ত, the first month of the rainy season, a causing to hear or speaking in another's hearing; acquired by hearing, oral.

শ্রাব্য, শ্রবণীয়, শুননের যোগ্য, শ্রবণেন্দ্রিয়গোচর, fit or proper to be heard, audible.

শ্রী, ধনাদির বৃদ্ধি, সুভাগ্য, প্রতিপত্তি, সুখ্যাতি, প্রভা, সৌন্দর্য্য, লক্ষ্মী, প্রভান্বিত, শ্রেষ্ঠ, fortune, prosperity, luck, good fortune, success, riches, elevation, consequence, fame, glory, beauty, splendour, Lakshmí the goddess of fortune; *prefix:* glorious, illustrious, excellent, eminent. [perity.

শ্রীকাতর, মৎসর, দ্বেষী, envious, vexed at another's pros-

শ্রীফল, বিল্ব, বেল, the Bel or wood-apple.

শ্রীভ্রষ্ট, দুঃখী, দুর্ভাগ্য, পতিত, পদচ্যুত, poor, unfortunate, ill-fated, luckless, fallen, degraded. [letter.

শ্রীমুখ, পত্রের চিহ্ন বিশেষ, the inscription শ্রী on the back of a

শ্রীমান, শ্রীমন্ত, শ্রীল, শ্রীযুক্ত, শ্রীযুত, শ্রীযুৎ, } প্রভান্বিত, ভাগ্যবান, সুখ্যাত, বর্দ্ধিষ্ণু, ভাগ্যবন্ত, সুন্দর, illustrious, eminent, famous, glorious, wealthy, prosperous, fortunate, beautiful.

শ্রুত, যাহা শুনা গিয়াছে, শ্রবণে অবগত, heard, reported.

শ্রুতমশ্রুত, তুচ্ছীকৃত, অনাদৃত, শুনিলে যাহা মানা যায় না, despised, disregarded, overlooked, connived at.

শ্রুতি, শ্রবণ, রব, কর্ণ, বেদ, hearing, audience, rumor, report, the ear, the Vedas. [sant sound.

শ্রুতিকটু, কুশ্রাব্য, অপ্রিয় ধ্বনি, a cacophony, harsh or unplea-

শ্রুতিপাঠ, বেদাধ্যয়ন, বেদবাক্য, the reading or study of the Vedas, the text of the Vedas.

শ্রুব, যজ্ঞের দর্বী, যাগ, a sacrificial ladle, sacrifice, oblation.

শ্রেণী, পংক্তি, আবলী, ক্রম, আনুপূর্বী, a line, row, tier, range, rank, an avenue, regular order.

শ্রেণীভূত, শ্রেণীমত,—ক্রমাগত, আনুপূর্ব্বিক, disposed in regular order, ranged in a line.

শ্রেয়ঃ, ধর্ম্ম, শ্রী, কল্যাণ, মুক্তি, ভাল, অতি উত্তম, উচিত, virtue, moral merit, good fortune, prosperity, beatitude; good, excellent, best, preferable, proper.

শ্রেষ্ঠ, প্রধান, মহৎ, অত্যুত্তম, অধিপ, best, excellent, chief, superior, great, eminent, principal, prime, select, capital, pre-eminent ; a chief.

শ্রেষ্ঠতা, প্রাধান্য, প্রভাব, উৎকর্ষ, greatness, eminence, superiority, excellence.

শ্রোণি, কটিদেশ, the hip, the loins. [to, audible.

শ্রোতব্য, শুনিবার যোগ্য, কর্ণগোচর, fit to be heard or attended

শ্রোতঃ, জল প্রবাহ, a stream, current, the flow of a river.

শ্রোতা, শ্রবণকর্ত্তা, শুননিয়া, a hearer, an auditor.

শ্রোত্র, শ্রবণেন্দ্রিয়, কর্ণ, কাণ, the ear.

শ্রোত্রিয়, সংস্কার ও বিদ্যাবিশিষ্ট ব্রাহ্মণ, ছান্দস, নম্র, শিষ্ট, ভদ্র, a Brahmin versed in the Vedas; modest, docile, well-behaved. [Vedas.

শ্রৌত, বেদসম্মত, বেদোক্ত, any observance prescribed by the

শ্লথ, কস্কা, শিথিল, অদৃঢ়, অনবধান, অলস, ঢীলামি, slack, loose, lax, soft, flaccid, flabby, relaxed, careless, indifferent, lazy; slackness, &c.

শ্লাঘা, সঙ্কীর্ত্তন, স্তুতিবাদ, praise, eulogy, applause, flattery.

শ্লাঘী, স্তুতিবাদী, সঙ্কীর্ত্তক, দাম্ভিক, praising, applauding, flattering, thankful, boasting, conceited.

শ্লাঘ্য, শ্লাঘনীয়,—প্রশংসনীয়, স্তবার্হ, আদরণীয়, praise-worthy, laudable, to be praised, respectable.

শ্লিষ্ট, সংযুক্ত, মিলিত, আলিঙ্গিত, বেষ্টিত, connected, joined, combined, embraced, surrounded.

শ্লেষ, ব্যঙ্গ, সঙ্কেতবাক্য, একবাক্যের অনেকার্থ, অবক্ষেপ, সংযোগ, সন্ধি, আলিঙ্গন, a jest, double-entendre, pun, paronomasia, irony, sarcasm, union, combination, connexion, association, contact, an embrace, embracing or clinging to.

শ্লেষকথা, দ্ব্যর্থবাক্য, ব্যঙ্গ, a word or speech bearing a double [meaning.

শ্লেষ্মজনক, কফকারক. causing or producing phlegm.

শ্লেষ্মল, কফযুক্ত, কফী, abounding with phlegm, phlegmatic.

শ্লেষ্মা, কফ, কাস, phlegm, rheum, serum, a cold.

শ্লোক, পদ্য, দোহা, কীর্ত্তি, যশঃ, a verse, couplet, stanza, fame.

শ্লোকরচক, কবি, পদ্যকর, a composer of verses, poet, versifier.

শ্বঃ, আগাম দিবস, কল্য, to-morrow.

শ্ববৃত্তি, কৈঙ্কর্য্য, দাসত্ব, সেবা, servitude, slavery, service.

শ্বশুর, পতির কিম্বা পত্নীর পিতা, a wife's or husband's father.

শ্বশ্রূ, শাশুড়ি, পতিপত্নির মাতা, a wife's or husband's mother.

শ্বসন, বায়ু, রেচন, নিঃশ্বাসপ্রশ্বাস, wind, air, breath, breathing.

শ্বা, কুকুর, কুত্তা a dog.

শ্বাস, মুখনাসিকা নির্গত বায়ু, হাইছাড়া, কাসরোগ বিশেষ, breath, respiration, breathing, sighing, a sigh, a wheezing, shortness of breath, an asthma.

শ্বাসকাস, দুঃশ্বাসযুক্ত কাসরোগ, cough attended with wheezing.

শ্বাসরোগী, দুঃশ্বাসযুক্ত, asthmatic, afflicted with asthma.

শ্বিত্র, শ্বেত কুষ্ঠ, কোঠ, the white spotted leprosy.

শ্বিত্রী, শ্বেতকুষ্ঠবস্ত, কুঠ্যা, leprous, having the spotted leprosy.

শ্বেত, শুক্ল, শুভ্র, শুক্লতা, white, fair; whiteness.

শ্বেতবর্ণ, শুক্লবর্ণ, white-coloured, white.

ষ.

ষট্, ষড়,—ছয়, six; ষড় *is used only in composition.*
ষট্, ছয়, ষট্সংখ্যা, ছয়গুণ, six, sixfold, having six.
ষট্কন, পলায়ন, to run away, flee, escape.
ষট্কর্ণ, কর্ণ বেধহীন দুই অপত্য বিদ্যমানে তৃতীয়ের সম্ভাবনা, the condition of one whose third child is about to be born, the two first not having had the ceremonial boring of the ears performed.
ষট্কর্ম্ম, যজন, যাজন, অধ্যয়ন, অধ্যাপন, দান, প্রতিগ্রহণ, মন্ত্রপাঠে সাধ্য ছয় অর্থাৎ মারণ নিরাকরণাদি the six prescribed duties, viz. adoration, sacrifice, sacred study, religious instruction, alms-giving and the receiving of lawful gifts; also the six acts performable by magical texts, viz. killing, infatuating, enthralling, expelling, exciting animosity and privation of faculties.
ষট্কর্ম্মা, ষট্কর্ম্মযুক্ত ব্রাহ্মণ, who performs the six duties or acts.
ষট্কোণা, যে বস্তুর ছয় কোণ আছে, six-cornered, hexangular.
ষট্ক্ষণ, একদণ্ড, an hour of 24 minutes or 6 *chsanas*.
ষট্পদ, ভ্রমর, অলি, a bee, the large black bee.
ষড়ঙ্গ, ব্যাকরণাদি ছয় বেদাঙ্গ, হস্তপাদাদি ছয়, আদ্য শ্রাদ্ধে প্রেতোদ্দেশে দেয় পাদুকাদি ছয় দ্রব্য, the six sciences subordinate to the Vedas, the six parts of the body, viz. hands, feet, head and waist; the six articles offered in the first Shráddha for the manes of departed relatives.
ষড়শীতি, চার কুড়ি ছয়, ছেয়াশী, মীন মিথুন কন্যা ধনুঃ এই কয় রাশির অন্যতম রাশিতে সূর্য্যের সঞ্চার, 86; the entrance of the sun into the four signs, Pisces, Gemini, Virgo and Sagittarius.
ষড়্ষড়্, পিপীলিকাদির গতিজনিত শব্দ, চুলকানি, a rustling noise, a titillation.
ষণ্ড, ষাঁড়,—ঔৎসর্গিক বৃষভ, পণ্ড, a bull at liberty, a eunuch.
ষড়্বিধ, ষট্প্রকার,—ছয় প্রকার, six-fold, of six sorts or kinds.
ষষ্ঠ, ছয়ের পূরণ, the sixth.
ষাট্পৌরুষিক, ছয় পুরুষ সম্বন্ধীয়, of or connected with six generations.
ষিড্গ, ভ্রষ্টাচারী, লম্পট, বিটুল, a libertine, lecher, catamite.

ষোড়শ, ষোল, ভূম্যাদি ষোল দেয় দ্রব্য, sixteen ; a class of sixteen articles presented to Brahmins at Shráddhas.

ষোড়শাঙ্গ, মিশ্রিত ষোল, composed of sixteen parts or ingredients.

ষোড়শী, পিণ্ডদান ক্রিয়া বিশেষ, a particular offering to ancestors.

ষোল, ষোড়শ, দ্বিগুণ অষ্ট, sixteen.

স.

স, সহিত, ময়, সমান, একের, *pref*: with, together with, having, possessing, endowed with, full of, having the quality of, of or belonging to the same.

সই, সখী, a female friend or companion.

সং, চড়কাদিকালীন কৌতুক, লোকসমাগম, বেশ ধারণ, সহিত, উত্তমরূপে, a shew, pantomime, religious spectacle as the *Charak*, the concourse of people attending it, a disguise or pantomimic character ; *pref*: with, together with, in connection with, well, perfectly, completely.

সংক্রম, রাশি সঞ্চার, দুর্গমস্থান সঞ্চার, সাঁকো, স্থানস্থানান্তরে গমন, the passage of a heavenly body from one sign to another, a difficult passage as of torrents, steep rocks, mountain passes, &c. the means of effecting it, as a bridge of ropes, &c. removal from station to station.

সংক্রান্ত, চলিত, স্থানান্তরগত, সম্পর্কান্বিত, আকর্ষিত, অনুগত, passed over, removed from one station to another, connected with, drawn towards, transferred to, attached to, pertaining to.

সংক্রান্তি, সূর্য্যের রাশ্যন্তর গমন, স্থানান্তরে গমন, the sun's entrance into a sign, a passage, passing over, removal.

সংক্ষিপ্ত, সমস্ত, অল্পেতে কথিত, অল্পবাক্য, abridged, compressed, concise, compendious, laconic, short, brief.

সংক্ষেপ, সংগ্রহ, চুম্বক, সারবাক্য, অল্পেতে কহা, বাক্যের অবিস্তার, an abridgement, compendium, concise or laconic expression, brevity, conciseness.

সংক্ষেপে, অল্পেতে, চুম্বনে, in few words, concisely, briefly.

সংখ্যক, অঙ্কক, an accountant, reckoner; *aff:* of such a number.

সংখ্যা, এককাদি, গণনা, একুন, সমস্ত, সংগ্রহ, বিশেষলিপি, a number, numeral, calculation, numeration, reckoning, account, quantity, sum total, a muster, inventory. [calculated.

সংখ্যাত, গণিত, কলিত, numbered, enumerated, reckoned,

সংখ্যাবিদ্যা. অঙ্কশাস্ত্র, গণিত, the science of numbers, arithmetic.

সংখ্যাবেত্তা, অঙ্কশাস্ত্রে নিপুণ, গণক, versed in numbers; an arithmetician, accountant. [merable.

সংখ্যেয়, গণনীয়, that may be reckoned, calculable, nu-

সংগীত, মিলিত গান ও বাদ্যের সহিত নৃত্য, গানশাস্ত্র, a public entertainment consisting of song, dancing and music, a chorus, a concert, the science of vocal music; sung in choir. [&c.

সংগুপ্ত, ছাপান, লুক্কায়িত, রক্ষিত, concealed, hidden, guarded,

সংগুপ্তি, অপ্রকাশ, রক্ষণকরা, coucealment, a guarding.

সংগৃহীত, সমুদ্ধৃত, সঞ্চিত, collected, gathered, compiled, &c.

সংগোপন, ছাপান, লুকান, রক্ষণ, অপ্রকাশ, to conceal, hide, guard, defend; concealment, &c.

সংগ্রহ, সমুদ্ধার, সংক্ষেপ, সঞ্চয়, একত্র করা, মুষ্টিবন্ধন, a selection, compilation, abridgment, collection, accumulation, a gathering together, a clenching of the fist. [pile; a catalogue.

সংগ্রহণ, সঞ্চয়ন, সমাহার করণ. to collect, bring together, com-

সংগ্রাম, যুদ্ধ, আক্রম, a battle, conflict, war, attack. [editor.

সংগ্রাহক, সঞ্চয়কর্ত্তা, সারগ্রন্থরচক, নিবন্ধা, a collector, compiler,

সংঘটন-। সঙ্গতি, পক্ষপাত, সম্মতি, মিলন, সংযোগ, মেল, যোজনা, শ্লেষ, আলিঙ্গন, উপায়, সম্ভব, accession or going over to a party, adoption of party measures, acceding to a proposal, concurrence, adherence, coherence, a meeting, occurring, encountering, union, combination of circumstances, close contact, an intertwining, embracing, a medium, means, probability.

সংঘট্ট, সংঘট,—ঘটা, বহুলোকাগম, কোটনা, a crowd, concourse, conflux of people, a pimp.

সংঘটিত, যুক্ত, মিলিত, সঙ্গত, সংশ্লিষ্ট, দ্বারা, joined, together with, met, fallen in with, occurred, concurring, acceded to, &c. through, by means of.

সংঘট্টিকা, সংঘটিকা,—কুট্টনী, a procuress, a bawd.

সংজ্ঞা, নাম, আখ্যা, বিশিষ্য, সূচনা, জ্ঞান, চেতন, a name, title, class, appellation, denomination, term, a noun, a sign, mind, intellect, sensation, thought.

সংবৎসর, দ্বাদশ মাস, হায়ন, a whole year, a twelvemonth.

সংবর্ত্ত, প্রলয়, a destruction of the universe.

সংঘ, কঙ্কাল, অস্থিমাত্র মনুষ্যাকার, a skeleton.

সংযত, বদ্ধ, আটকান, জড়ীভূত. জিতেন্দ্রিয়, বিবেকী, bound, confined, restrained, fettered, imprisoned, frozen, of restrained passions, temperate, moderate, judicious, reflecting. [erces.

সংযন্তা, নিবারক, আট্‌কাইয়া, বাধক, one who restrains or co-

সংযম, বন্ধন, আটক. ধৈর্য্য, অল্পাহার, সম্বরা, বৈধক্রিয়া পূর্ব্বদিন কর্ত্তব্য নিয়ম, জড়ীভাব, confinement, imprisonment, restraint, self-restraint, moderation, forbearance, ceremonial abstinence, concretion, coagulation.

সংযম্য, জড়ীভবনীয়, coagulable, capable of concretion, &c.

সংযুক্ত, সংলগ্ন, মিশ্রিত, বিশিষ্ট, অনুরক্ত, united, joined or connected with, conjoined, mixed or united with, endued with, possessed of, attached to.

সংযোগ, মিলন, মিশ্রণ, সঙ্গ, সংসর্গ, সংশ্লেষ, union, contact, junction, connection, admixture, association, adhesion, cohesion, coherence.

সংযোগী, মিলাইয়া, সংলগ্ন, joining, uniting, adhering, &c.

সংযোজিত, সংলগ্ন, মিলিত, connected, joined, united, attached.

সংরম্ভ, যুদ্ধ, কোপ, war, battle, wrath, rage.

সংরুদ্ধ, বদ্ধ, আট্‌কান, বাধিত, confined, shut up, hindered, prevented, obstructed.

সংলগ্ন, সংলগ্নিত,—যুক্ত, স্পৃষ্ট, সংশ্লিষ্ট, সঙ্গত, united, connected, in contact, joined, close, adhering to, attached, applicable, relevant, appropriate.

সংশয়, দ্বৈধজ্ঞান, সন্দেহ, শঙ্কা, uncertainty, doubt, incertitude, hesitation, suspicion, apprehension.

সংশয়াপন্ন, সংশয়ী,—দ্বিধাপ্রাপ্ত, শঙ্কান্বিত, সন্দিগ্ধমনাঃ, in doubt, uncertain, entertaining doubts, suspicious, hesitating, irresolute, doubtful, sceptical.

সংশ্রব, স্বীকার সম্মতি, a promise, engagement, agreement, assent. [defence, protector.

সংশ্রয়, আশ্রয়, উপায়, রক্ষক, a refuge, asylum, protection,

সংশ্রিত, শরণাপন্ন, রক্ষিত, protected, defended, sheltered, secured. [braced.

সংশ্লিষ্ট, সশ্লিষ্ট, আলিঙ্গিত, united, intimately connected, em-

সংশ্লেষ, সংযোগ, মিশ্র, সঙ্গ, আলিঙ্গন, union, connection, junction, combination, mixture, association, an embrace, embracing.

সংসক্ত, উপেত, সংলগ্ন, অব্যবহিত, বিশিষ্ট, পরিচিত, আসক্ত, বন্ধু, সঙ্গী, near, adjoining, contiguous, connected or endowed with, affected by, acquainted with, attached to, enamoured of; an intimate friend, an acquaintance.

সংসক্তি, সংযোগ, নৈকট্য, পরিচয়, বন্ধুতা, union, connexion, proximity, intercourse, acquaintance, intimacy.

সংসর্গ, শ্লেষ, সামীপ্য, সঙ্গ, সম্বন্ধ, পরিচয়, মৈথুন, union, contact, proximity, connexion, intercourse, acquaintance, association, society, intimacy, sexual intercourse.

সংসর্গী, সঙ্গী, বন্ধু, মিত্র, পরিচিত, আলাপী, a companion, intimate, acquaintance; keeping company with, familiar, friendly, social, &c.

সংসার, জগৎ, বিশ্ব, বিষয়কর্ম্ম, গার্হস্থ্য, গৃহাশ্রম, পরিবার, the world, the universe, the mundane state, a domestic life, a secular condition, worldly concerns, a family, household, household possessions.

সংসারাশ্রম, গৃহস্থাশ্রম, বিষয়ভোগ, the embracing of a secular life or profession, secularity.

সংসারাশ্রমী, বিষয়ী, গৃহস্থাশ্রমী, secular, leading a domestic life.

সংসারী, গৃহাশ্রমী, বিষয়মগ্ন, গৃহস্থ, secular, worldly, engaged in social life, occupied in temporal concerns: a householder, the master of a family.

সংসৃষ্ট, সশ্লিষ্ট, সংযুক্ত, ভাগী, সহজ, বিভাগের পর সহবাসী, connected, united, combined, engaged in partnership, connate, reunited, co-resident as relatives after partition of common property.

সংসৃষ্টি, বিভাগের পর একত্র বাসকরা, ভাগাভাগি, union, connexion, voluntary reunion of relatives after division of property, co-partnership.

সংসৃষ্টী, সমভাগী, বিভাগান্তর একত্রবাসী, a co-partner, a relative who returns to reside with his relations after a division of property.

সংস্কার, সিদ্ধি, প্রতিযত্ন, যজ্ঞোপবীত বিবাহাদি দশ, শোভা, শোধন, বিন্যাস, ভূষণ, পরিষ্কার, মার্জ্জনা, অনুভব, বোধ, স্মৃতির কারণ, বুদ্ধি, বিবেক, অন্ন কিম্বা ঔষধ প্রস্তুত করণ, completion, accomplishment, perfection, consecration, purification, a purificatory rite or sacrament or sacred ceremony of initiation, embellishment, decoration, elegance, cleaning, cleansing, a conception, idea, notion, impression, persuasion, recollection, memory, the power of habit, instinct, faculty in general, conscience, the preparation of food or medicine.

সংস্কারক, সংস্কারী,—দশ সংস্কার কর্ত্তা, পরিষ্কারক, শোধক, completing, purifying, consecrating, embellishing, &c.

সংস্কারযুক্ত, সিদ্ধ, শুদ্ধ, পরিষ্কৃত, কৃতোপবীতাদি, pure, holy, consecrated, initiated, complete, one who has gone through the ten sacraments.

সংস্কৃত, প্রাপ্তোৎকর্ষ, পরিষ্কৃত, সম্যক প্রকারে নির্ম্মিত, মার্জ্জিত, দেববাণী, perfected, accomplished, perfect, purified, exquisitely wrought, highly polished or refined; the sacred language of the Brahmins.

সংস্থ, পড়সী, নিবাসী, চর, a neighbour, an inhabitant, a spy.

সংস্থা-ন, দ্রব্য, সম্পত্তি, আয়, নির্ব্বাহ, উপায়, সঞ্চয়, রচনা, রূপ, goods, property, an income, means of living, subsistence, provision, stock, a heap, quantity, fabrication, form, figure.

সংস্থাপন, বসান, স্থিরীকরণ, রক্ষণ, to fix, place, establish, settle, defend.

সংস্থাপক, স্থিতিকর্ত্তা, পত্তনকারক, বিশেষ মত কল্পনাকারক, establishing, &c. a founder, author.

সংস্থিত, সঞ্চিত, একত্রীকৃত, collected, stored up, heaped together.

সংস্থিতি, যোত্র, কল্যাণ, বাস, থাকা, a stock of goods or money, well-being, welfare, a station, residence, abode, continuance.

সংস্পর্শ, শ্লেষ, সম্মিলন, ধরা, ছুঁয়ন, close contact, union, a grasp, touch, feel.

সংস্পৃশ্য, স্পর্শনে বোধগম্য, ছুঁয়নেয়, ধার্য্য, tangible, palpable, to be felt or grasped.

সংস্পৃষ্ট, সংলগ্ন, স্পৃষ্ট, হস্তধৃত, brought into contact, touched, grasped.

সংস্রব, মিশ্রণ, সংযোগ, mixture, union, connexion.

সংহত, প্রহারিত, ক্ষত, নষ্ট, সংলগ্ন, যুক্ত, struck, wounded, killed, destroyed, compact, close, inclined, brought together, joined.

সংহতজানুক, সংলগ্ন জানুবিশিষ্ট ব্যক্তি, knock-kneed.

সংহতি, সমূহ, রাশি, সঞ্চয়, an assemblage, heap, collection.

সংহরণ, সংহার—বিনাশ, অবঘাত, বধ, destruction, ruin, murder.

সংহর্ত্তা, বধকর্ত্তা, অপঘাতক, a destroyer, a murderer.

সংহারক, সংহারী, সংহারু,—বিনাশক, বধিক, সাংঘাতিক, *id: also* destructive, ruinous, murderous, fatal.

সংহারণ, বিনাশন, ঘাতন, to destroy, ruin, annihilate, murder.

সংহিত, সঞ্চিত, একত্রীভূত, সংযুক্ত, collected, joined, attached.

সংহিতা, শাখা, বেদের পরিচ্ছিন্ন বাক্য বিন্যাস, a peculiar arrangement of the Vedas into short divisions.

সকণ্টক, কণ্টকী, দুষ্কর, thorny, prickly, troublesome, difficult.

সকর, রাজস্বাধীন, paying revenue, chargeable with a tax.

সকরুণ, দয়াবান্, বিলাপসূচক, merciful, compassionate, plaintive.

সকর্ম্মক, ক্রিয়াসূচক ধাতু, active or transitive, (in grammar.)

সকল, সমুদায়, সমস্ত, অখিল, অখণ্ড, প্রত্যেক, all, whole, entire, with all its parts, every, each.

সকলে, একুনে, গড়ে, in amount, altogether, in the gross.

সকলঙ্ক, কলঙ্কযুক্ত, তিরস্কৃত, full of stains, defiled, disgraced, &c.

সকাম, ভাবযুক্ত, লম্পট, অভীষ্টসিদ্ধ, ফলার্থ ক্রিয়া, full of desire, sensual, amorous, possessed of the desired object, performed from the desire of future fruition or recompense.

সকারবকার, পচালবাক্য, অনর্থক বাক্য, obscene talk, nonsense.
সকাল, প্রাতঃ, ভোর, প্রত্যূষ, the morning, the early dawn.
সকালে, ভোরে, early, betimes, in the morning. [cent.
সকুল, জ্ঞাতি, a kinsman, one of the same family or des-
সকুল্য, সপ্তম পুরুষের পর দশম পুরুষ পর্য্যন্ত, a kinsman within the three degrees from the 8th to the 10th generation inclusive from a common ancestor.
সকৃৎ, একবার, বিষ্ঠা, once, at once; fæces, ordure, excrement.
সক্ষম, ক্ষমতাপন্ন, নিপুণ, উপযুক্ত, able, qualified, clever, expert, fit for, competent. [on, intimate.
সখা, সখি,—বন্ধু, পরিচয়, মিত্র, a friend, associate, compani-
সখী, সই, স্ত্রীবন্ধু বয়স্যা, মিত্রা, a female friend, a confidante.
সখ্য, সখিতা,—বন্ধুতা, মিত্রতা, close intimacy, friendship.
সগড়-ী, শকট, গাড়ী, a cart, car, waggon. [or smell.
সগন্ধ, বাসিত, বাসযুক্ত, perfumed, scented, having a scent
সগর্ভ, সহোদর ভ্রাতা, a brother of whole blood.
সগর্ভা, গর্ভিণী, সসত্ত্বা, pregnant, with child, impregnated.
সগুণ, গুণবান্, পণ্ডিত, ব্রহ্ম, খরপত্র বৃক্ষ, possessed of attributes or qualities, learned, skilful, clever, God as possessing the three properties or powers of creation, preservation and provision, Teak-wood.
সগোত্র, জ্ঞাতি, বান্ধব, গোত্র যুক্ত, one of the same family descent, a kinsman; with all one's race.
সঙ্কট, দায়, বিপদ, অগম্য, কঠিন, অপ্রশস্ত, সঙ্কীর্ণ, ঘন, a difficulty, perplexity, danger, calamity; impervious, impassable, difficult, narrow, unsafe, crowded.
সঙ্কর, উভয় বর্ণ হইতে উৎপন্ন সন্তান, চণ্ডাল, মিশ্রকর, মিশ্রিত, মিলন, দোষ, of mixed race or cast, of impure origin from intermixture of the casts, mixing, blending, mixed, compound; mixture, a blending.
সঙ্কলন, একুনকরা, সঞ্চয়ন, মিশ্রণ, একত্রীকরণ, মিলান, সংযোগ, arithmetical addition, a collecting, heaping up, intermixing, blending, intertwining, contact, junction.
সঙ্কলিত, একত্রীকৃত, মিশ্রিত, যুক্ত, যোড়ান, স্তূপীকৃত, added, blended, intermixed, joined, intertwined, collected, piled or heaped up as corn,

সঙ্কল্প, প্রবৃত্তি, মানস, কল্পনা, বৈদিক কর্ম্মের প্রতিজ্ঞা. ব্রত, intention, will, volition, thought, contrivance. a religious vow. [ed, contrived, &c.

সঙ্কল্পিত, অভিপ্রেত, নিয়মিত, কৌশলসৃষ্ট, intended, willed, vow-

সঙ্কাশ, দীপ্তি, সদৃশ, light, splendour; *affix :* like, similar.

সঙ্কীর্ণ, অপ্রশস্ত, সরু, সঙ্কট, অল্প, ব্যাপ্ত, সঞ্চিত, মিশ্রিত, সঙ্কর, অশুদ্ধ, confined, limited, close, narrow, scanty, small, crowded, spread, diffused, collected, compounded, mixed, impure.

সঙ্কীর্ত্তন, গুণকথন, স্তবন, to celebrate, praise, extol, magnify.

সঙ্কুচিত, তোবড়া, সঙ্কীর্ণ, অপ্রকাশিত, অপ্রফুল্ল, ত্রাসশীল, লাজুক, shrivelled, contracted, narrowed, closed, unblown, timid, diffident, shrinking. [crowded.

সঙ্কুল, আকুল, ব্যস্ত, সঙ্কট, agitated, perplexed, distressed,

সঙ্কেত, ঠার, শব্দের অর্থ প্রকাশক শক্তি অর্থাৎ প্রকারান্তরে কহা, ইঙ্গিত, a sign, signal, token, wink, nod, assignation, hint, inuendo, allusion, obscure intimation. indirect expression. [gestion.

সঙ্কেতবাক্য, ইঙ্গিতবাক্য, ঠারাদি, a hint, slight allusion, sug-

সঙ্কেতে, ইঙ্গিতে, প্রকারান্তরে, কৌশলে, indirectly, by signs or hints, by collusion or secret agreement.

সঙ্কোচ, তোবড়ানি, কুঁকড়ন, কুণ্ঠতা, সমাদর, a shrivelling up, contraction, withdrawing or shrinking from, backwardness, diffidence, respect.

সঙ্কোচী, কুণুয়া, কুণ্ঠিত, সম্মানকর, diffident, timid, drawing back, respectful. [junction.

সঙ্গ, সাহিত্য, মেল, সংযোগ, society, association, meeting.

সঙ্গত, যথাযোগ্য, সংলগ্ন, যথার্থ, সম্ভব, সংযুক্ত, proper, just, adequate, appropriate, relevant, apposite, applicable, coherent, consistent, probable, united, come together. [economy.

সঙ্গতব্যয়, পরিমিতব্যয়, অল্পব্যয়, prudent expenditure, thrift,

সঙ্গতি, মেল, সুযোগ, সম্ভাবনা, সময়, যোত, প্রতুল, association, meeting, accession to a party, agreement with, appropriateness, relevancy, probability, opportunity, income, means, property.

সঙ্গম, মেলন, সন্ধি, প্রণয়, সমারোহ, সংযোগ, মৈথুন, a meeting, union, association, coming together, concourse, confluence, junction, sexual intercourse.

সঙ্গী, সখা, মিত্র, অনুচর, সাথী, অনুগামী, a companion, friend, accomplice, attendant, adherent; attached to, accompanying, uniting with.

সঙ্গে, সহিত, সাথে, মধ্যে, in company or together with, with, along with, conjointly, together, among.

সঙ্গ্য, সখা, ভাগী, অনুগত, a companion, accomplice, adherent.

সঙ্ঘ, সঙ্ঘাত,—সমূহ, পাল, সঞ্চয়, রাশি, a multitude, assemblage, number, flock, herd, collection, quantity, heap. [sprung as game.

সচকিত, সভয়, তটস্থ, জাগ্রৎ, startled, awakened, vigilant,

সচরাচর, বিশ্ব, স্থাবরজঙ্গম, সাধারণ, প্রসিদ্ধ, the universe or things moveable and immoveable, or animate and inanimate, universal, immemorial, common.

সচল, চলৎশক্তিমন্ত, moving, possessed of motion.

সচিন্ত, উদ্বিগ্ন, কাতর, ভাবিত, sad, uneasy, thoughtful, anxious.

সচিব, মিত্র, সহায়, অমাত্য, মন্ত্রী, a friend, associate, companion, a minister, counsellor, adviser, monitor.

সচেত-ন, প্রাণী, জ্ঞানবিশিষ্ট, জাগ্রৎ, animate, sensitive, sensible, feeling, vigilant, wary, sprung as game.

সচেষ্ট, উদ্যুক্ত, বহুশ্রমী, উদ্দেশক, zealous, prompt, ready, strenuous, active, endeavouring after.

সচ্চিদানন্দ, পরব্রহ্ম, নিত্যজ্ঞানানন্দস্বরূপ, পরমার্থ, Brahma or the Supreme Spirit, God as the fount of being, intelligence and happiness, *q. d.* the good, the wise and the happy Being.

সচ্ছ. নির্ম্মল, শুদ্ধ, সরল, clear, transparent, pure, sincere.

সহৃদ, হিতৈষী, দাতা, benevolent, kind, generous, liberal.

সজল, জলুয়া, আর্দ্র, জলবিশিষ্ট, watery, wet, moist, having or abounding in water.

সজাগ, জাগ্রৎ, ঈষৎ নিদ্রিত, awake, vigilant, wakeful.

সজাতি, একজাতি, of the same tribe, class or kind. [lar.

সজাতীয়, একজাতীয়, তুল্য, belonging to the same species, simi-

সজীব, জীবনপ্রাপ্ত, বিদ্যমান, মূর্ত্তিমন্ত, having life, living, alive.

সজ্জ-া, বেশ, ভূষা, সাজ, কবচ, আয়োজন, dress, decoration, ornaments, furniture, equipage, trappings, harness, accoutrements, armour, apparatus, preparation. [dorned, &c.

সজ্জিত, কবচযুক্ত, কৃতবেশভূষা, armed, accoutred, dressed, a-

সঞ্চয়, সংগ্রহ, উপার্জ্জনা, a collection, accumulation, heap, hoard. [hoard.

সঞ্চয়ন, সগ্রহ করণ, উপার্জ্জন, to collect, gather together, save,

সঞ্চয়ী, সংগ্রাহক, উপার্জ্জক, collecting, accumulating, &c. thrifty; a collector, accumulator.

সঞ্চার-ণ, গতি অথবা শক্তি দান, ব্যাপার, আগম, উপস্থিতি, অনুষ্ঠান, সংক্রম, সন্ধিচ্যুত, communication of power or motion, production of things by the power of motion, an infecting by contagion, access of disease, a commencement, transition, entrance into a sign, a dislocation.

সঞ্চারী, ব্যাপক, স্পর্শে ঘটানিয়া, অনুষ্ঠাপক, acting upon, infecting, commencing. [lated, saved.

সঞ্চিত, সংগৃহীত, উপার্জ্জিত, collected, heaped up, accumu-

সটীক, টিপ্পনী যুক্ত, accompanied with a commentary.

সটকন, পলায়ন, to run away, flee, escape, slip away.

সড়ক, বর্ত্ম, সরু পথ, a way, path, road, narrow path.

সড়কা, শড়িঙ্গা, দীর্ঘাকার, লম্বা, long and narrow, tall and thin, oblong, perpendicular.

সড়কীপথ, গলী, সুড়ীপথ, a narrow lane, an alley.

সড়ঙ্গা, সড়িঙ্গা,—শড়ঙ্গা, দীর্ঘাকার তরণি, a long narrow canoe.

সড়ন, পচন, বিগড়ন, to rot, putrify, become tainted, spoil.

সড়া, পচা, বিগড়া, নষ্ট, দূষিত, rotten, spoiled, tainted, musty.

সড়গড়, অভ্যাস, সাধন, a committing to memory, practice.

সড়্সড়ান, নিঃসান. চুলকান, to tingle, to itch.

সৎ, উত্তম, শুদ্ধসত্ত্ব. পবিত্র, সাধু, সত্য, যথার্থ, বর্ত্তমান, পরমার্থ, good, excellent, pure, holy, virtuous, true, proper, right, being, existing, God or the ever-present and all-holy Being.

সতত, সর্ব্বদা, নিরন্তর, নিত্য, always, ever, continually, incessantly; eternal, incessant, continual, perpetual.

সতর্ক, চালাক, জাগ্রৎ, প্রজ্ঞ, দক্ষ, সাবধান, বিবেচক, active, alert, wary, vigilant, clever, acute, discreet, circumpect, investigating, sagacious. [tom.

সতল, সমান, চৌরস, smooth, even, square, having a bot-

সতা, সতিন,—সপত্নী. a co-wife, one of several wives.

সতী, পতিব্রতা, সাধ্বী. সহগামিনী, *f.* chaste, pure, virtuous; a woman who burns with the body of her husband. [same teacher.

সতীর্থ, এক গুরুর শিষ্য, a fellow-student or pupil of the

সতৃষ, সতৃষ্ণ,—পিপাসু, লোভী, thirsty, covetous, rapacious.

সতেজ, বলবান্, তেজস্বী, শোভান্বিত, উর্বরা, strong, vigorous, energetic, powerful, splendid, brilliant, dignified, luxuriant, rich, fertile as land.

সৎকথক, বাক্‌পটু, a good speaker; eloquent.

সৎকর্ম্ম, সৎকার, সৎক্রিয়া, সৎকৃতি, } উত্তম ক্রিয়া, দানাদি, অতিথিসেবা, সম্মান, উপাসনা, শবদাহ, শুচিজনক কর্ম্ম, a good act, acts of piety or charity, virtue, courtesy, respectful salutation, kind welcome to a guest, homage, worship, funeral obsequies, a purificatory ceremony.

সত্তম, সাধুর মধ্যে শ্রেষ্ঠ, শুদ্ধসত্ত্ব, most excellent, most pure, very holy. [lence, goodness.

সত্তা, বিদ্যমানতা, সদ্‌গুণবিশিষ্টতা, existence, being, excel-

সত্ত্ব, সত্ব,—বর্ত্তমানতা, উৎকর্ষ, সদ্ভাব, ধর্ম্ম, স্বভাব, সার, রস, প্রাণ, তেজ, ধন, অধিকার, existence, goodness, holiness, nature, disposition, essence, substance, pith, sap, life, breath, vigour, wealth, proprietary right.

সত্ত্বগুণ, সৎকর্ম্মেতে প্রবৃত্তিজনক গুণ, moral goodness, the principle or quality of truth or goodness.

সৎমা, বিমাতা, a step-mother.

সত্য, যথার্থ, নিশ্চয়, সরল, তথ্য, নির্ণয়, শপথ, অবশ্য, নিতান্ত, true, real, certain, honest, sincere; truth, certainty, an oath; yes, verily, true, indeed.

সত্যতা, যথার্থতা, নিশ্চয়, নির্ণয়, truth, certainty, fact.

সত্যপ্রতিজ্ঞা, স্থিরবাদ, তথ্যবাক্য, an asseveration, assertion of the truth of a matter. [honest.

সত্যব্রত, সরলাত্মাকরণ, অকুটিল, devoted to truth, true, sincere,

সত্যযুগ, প্রথম যুগ, the first of the four ages.
সত্যানৃত, বাণিজ্য, trade, commerce, *q. d.* truth and falsehood.
সত্বর, ত্বরান্বিত, শীঘ্র, সতর্ক, আশু, swift, quick, speedy, hasty, active, clever; quickly.
সদং, সদা,—সর্ব্বদা, নিত্য, always, ever, continually, perpetually.
সদন, সদ্মন,—গৃহ, ঘর, বাস, a house, dwelling, residence.
সদয়, কৃপান্বিত, দয়াবান, করুণাযুক্ত, উদার, দাতা, merciful, compassionate, kind, affectionate, tender, liberal.
সদর্থ, বাক্যসার, যথাযোগ্য অর্থ, অভিপ্রায়, the substance of an argument, meaning, scope, object.
সদর্প, অহঙ্কারী, দাম্ভিক, proud, haughty, arrogant.
সদসৎ, ভদ্রাভদ্র, উত্তমাধম, good and evil, right and wrong.
সদস্য, কর্ম্মানুষ্ঠানের ন্যূনাধিক বিবেচক, সদসৎ বিবেচনা কর্ত্তা, বিধিদর্শী, সাক্ষী, the inspector and director of a sacrifice, a by-stander, spectator, one present.
সদাচার, সাধুব্যবহার, virtuous conduct, correct deportment.
সদানন্দ, সর্ব্বদা হর্ষযুক্ত, always happy, ever-blest.
সদার, স্ত্রীবিশিষ্ট, স্ত্রী যুক্ত, having a wife; with a wife.
সদৃক্, সদৃশ,—তুল্য, সমান, like, alike, similar, resembling.
সদেশ, নিকট, অন্তিক, উপেত, near, nigh, proximate, adjoining.
সদেশী-য়, একদেশবাসী, পড়সী, of the same place or country; a countryman, a neighbour.
সদ্গতি, মুক্তি, স্বর্গবাস, beatitude, absorption, salvation, future bliss.
সদ্বক্তা, সুকথক, বাক্পটু, a fine speaker, an orator; eloquent.
সদ্বৃত্ত, সচ্চরিত্র, সুশীল, virtuous, well-conducted, amiable.
সদ্ভাব, বিদ্যমানতা, সত্ত্ব, দয়া, শিষ্টাচার, প্রণয়, existence, goodness, kindness, politeness, courtesy, friendship, love.
সদ্যঃ, তৎক্ষণাৎ, তদ্দিবস, immediately, instantly, forthwith, quickly.
সদ্যোজাত, তদ্দিনোৎপন্ন, নবীন, new, recent, fresh, sound.
সধবা, যে স্ত্রীর পতি জীবন্ত আছে, পতিবত্নী, a married woman whose husband is living, a wife.
সধর্ম্মী, তুল্য, সমান, সমস্বভাব, সমগুণ, তুল্যব্যবহারী, সজাতীয়, like, similar, equal, of the same nature, having the same properties, observing the same rites and duties, of the same sect or cast.

সনাতন, নিত্য, নিরন্তর, চিরস্থায়ী, eternal, perpetual, incessant, constant, fixed, permanent.

সনাম, একনাম, সমানাখ্যা, of the same name; a namesake.

সন্তত, নিত্য, বিতত, perpetual, continual, eternal, extended.

সন্ততি, সন্তান,—পুত্র কন্যা, বংশ, পুত্রাদি পরম্পরা, a child, offspring, son or daughter, posterity, progeny, descendants, lineage, race.

সন্তপ্ত, সন্তাপিত, সন্তাপী,—তাপযুক্ত, খেদান্বিত, দুঃখিত, heated, pained, grieved, distressed, afflicted.

সন্তরণ, সাঁতরণ, ভাসন, to swim, float, wade.

সন্তর্পণ, তোষণ, বহুচেষ্টা করণ, যত্ন, to satisfy, please, to take pains; care, attention.

সন্তাপ, জ্বলা, পীড়া, খেদ, দুঃখ, মনঃপীড়া, বিতুষ্টি, heat, burning pain, smart, anguish, affliction, sorrow, distress of mind, vexation, passion.

সন্তুষ্ট, হৃষ্ট, তৃপ্ত, আহ্লাদযুক্ত, উল্লসিত. pleased, gratified, satisfied, glad, happy, delighted.

সন্তুষ্টি, সন্তোষ,—হর্ষ, তৃপ্তি, আনন্দ, উল্লাস, pleasure, satisfaction, gratification, gladness, joy, delight.

সন্তোলন, ফোড়ন, সম্বরণ, to season, spice, add seasoning to food in cooking.

সন্তোষক, তুষ্টিকর, হর্ষজনক, giving pleasure, gratifying, de- [lighting, &c.

সন্তোষী, তুষ্টিকর, আনন্দিত, pleasing, &c. pleased, happy, glad.

সন্দংশ, চাঁড়ী, সাঁড়াশী, pincers, nippers, tweezers, tongs.

সন্দর্ভ, ক্রম, আনুপূর্ব, গ্রন্থন, orderly arrangement, a stringing of beads, weaving of garlands, &c. [meeting.

সন্দর্শন, নিরীক্ষণ, সাক্ষাৎকার, a looking, seeing, surveying,

সন্দিগ্ধ, অনিশ্চিত, সংশয়যুক্ত, অশ্রদ্ধ, শঙ্কান্বিত, doubted, questionable, uncertain, doubtful, in doubt, suspecting, suspicious, sceptical, afraid, diffident.

সন্দেশ, মিষ্টান্ন বিশেষ, সমাচার, a sort of sweetmeat, a message, news, report.

সন্দেহ, সংশয়, এক বস্তুতে উভয় বোধ, বিচিকিৎসা, শঙ্কা, অশ্রদ্ধা, doubt, uncertainty, scepticism, suspense, hesitation, a scruple, apprehension, fear, suspicion, mistrust.

সন্দেহী, সংশয়ী, শঙ্কালু, অপ্রত্যয়ী, in doubt, uncertain, suspicious, sceptical, jealous, mistrustful, scrupulous.

সন্দেহকল্প, অনির্ণয়, uncertainty, contingency, precariousness.

সন্ধান, অন্বেষণ, চেষ্টা, শরব্য, মর্ম্ম, অনুমান, তত্ত্ব, উদ্দেশ, সম্বাদ, ধরণ, enquiry, search, endeavour, an aim, object, a scope, butt, a secret, a guess, trace, tidings of a person or thing sought, information, discovery, recovery, capture, seizure.

সন্ধানী, উদ্দেশী, তত্ত্বকারক, অন্বেষণে পটু, অবগত, চর, aiming, guessing, searching for, expert at discovering or tracing, privy to, acquainted with, having knowledge of; a spy, a scout.

সন্ধি, উভয়ের মেলন, সংযোগ, গ্রন্থি, মেল, ঐক্য, ছিদ্র, সুরঙ্গ, যতি, junction, union, alliance, coalition, connexion, a joint, knuckle, joining, reconciliation, an agreement, treaty, peace, a hole in a wall, &c. made by house-breakers, a breach, a mine, a stop, a pause.

সন্ধিচ্যুত, গ্রন্থির যোগভেদ, বিচলিত, a dislocation; dislocated.

সন্ধ্যা, প্রত্যূষ, প্রদোষ, ত্রিকালীন উপাসনা বিশেষ, morning or evening twilight, morning, mid-day and evening devotions. [of day.

সন্ধ্যাকাল, সায়ংকাল, দিনাবসান, evening, afternoon, dusk, close

সন্নদ্ধ, উদ্যুক্ত, সাজযুক্ত, সসজ্জ, কবচাদিযুক্ত, armed, accoutred, wearing an amulet.

সন্নাহ, সজ্জা পরিধানকরা, the binding on of armour, arming.

সন্নিকট, সমীপ, অন্তিক, উপেত, near, nigh, at hand, close, proximate, adjoining, contiguous, adjacent.

সন্নিকর্ষ, নৈকট্য, সামীপ্য, আকর্ষণ, সংলাগ, nearness, vicinity, proximity, contiguity, attraction, cohesion.

সন্নিকৃষ্ট, আকর্ষিত, সংলগ্ন, নিকটস্থ, সমীপ, attracted, drawn close or together, near, adjacent, adjoining.

সন্নিধান, সন্নিধি,—নৈকট্য, nearness, proximity, vicinity.

সন্নিপাত, ত্রিদোষজন্যবিকার, a morbid state of the 3 humors.

সন্নিবিষ্ট, উদ্যুক্ত, নিকটবর্ত্তী, engaged in, intent upon, near, neighbouring, close at hand.

সন্নিবেশ, সামীপ্য, গ্রাম অথবা বাটীর নিকট গমনাদি স্থান, vicinity, neighbourhood, an open space or plain near a town or dwelling. [adjacent.

সন্নিহিত, নিকটবর্ত্তী, উপেত, near, neighbouring, close at hand,

সন্ন্যাস, চতুর্থাশ্রম, তপস্যা, ঔদাস্যভাব, ভিক্ষুকধর্ম্ম, monachism, ascetism, abandonment of the duties of active life for one of voluntary penance or mortification.

সন্ন্যাসী, চতুর্থাশ্রমী, ভিক্ষুক, দণ্ডী, one who has renounced the world for a monastic life, a religious mendicant, a monk, an ascetic. [winged.

সপক্ষ, অনুকূল, পক্ষবান, of the same side or party, partial,

সপক্ষতা, অনুকূলতা, পক্ষপাত, aid, help, assistance, partiality.

সপত্নী, পতির অন্য স্ত্রী, a co-wife, one of several wives.

সপত্নীপুত্র, পতির অন্যস্ত্রীজাত, the son of a co-wife, a half-son.

সপরিবার, সংসারযুক্ত, দারাপুত্রাদি সহিত, having a family; with all his family.

সপদি, তৎক্ষণ, আশু, instantly, in a moment, quickly.

সপিণ্ড, সপ্তম পুরুষপর্য্যন্ত জ্ঞাতি, পিণ্ডভাগী, a kinsman to the 7th generation in descent from a common ancestor, having a right to partake of the funeral cake.

সপ্ত, সপ্তম,—সাত, সাতঞি, seven, the seventh.

সপ্ততি, সত্তর সংখ্যা, seventy.

সপ্তদশ, সতের সংখ্যা, seventeen, the seventeenth. [fold.

সপ্তধা, সাত প্রকারে, সাত ভাগে, in seven ways or parts, seven-

সপ্তপদীগমন, বিবাহের শেষকর্ম্ম সাধন, a ceremony in which a bride, followed by the bridegroom, walks over seven steps marked with chalk, &c. on the floor of the husband's house. [night.

সপ্তমী, সাতঞি তিথি, the seventh day of each lunar fort-

সপ্তর্ষি, মরীচি প্রভৃতি সাত মুনি, সপ্ততারা বিশেষ, a class of seven *Rishis* or saints, forming the constellation of Ursa major or the great Bear.

সপ্তাস্র, সপ্তকোণ, সাতকোণা, a heptagon; heptagonal, seven-cornered, septangular.

সপ্তাহ, সপ্তবার—সাত দিন, a week, seven days. [athentic.

সপ্রমাণ, সাব্যস্ত, সত্য, প্রশুদ্ধ, proved, established, evident, true,

সফল, ফলবান্, লাভজনক, হিতকর, সিদ্ধার্থ, bearing fruit, productive, fruitful, effectual, advantageous, useful, profitable, successful.

সব, সবানি, সভে,—সর্ব, সকলে, প্রত্যেক, all, the whole, every, [each.

সবর্ণ, সমানবর্ণ, of the same class, tribe or colour.

সবল, বলবান্, তেজস্বী, যুবক, strong, powerful, able, hale, energetic, in full vigour, in his prime.

সব্লোট, কামুক, লম্পট, lewd, lascivious, debauched.

সবিশেষ, বিশেষযুক্ত, বিবৃত, বিস্তারিত, অসাধারণ, particular, special, circumstantial; a special object, request or circumstance.

সব্য, বাম, left, (opposed to right;) the left hand.

সব্যসাচী, দুহাতিয়া, ambidexter, using the left hand as well as the right.

সভয়, ভীরু, শঙ্কান্বিত, ভয়ঙ্কর, fearful, timid, afraid, alarmed, [dangerous, perilous.

সভর্তৃকা, সধবা, স্বামিবিশিষ্টা, *f.* having a husband.

সভা, সমাজ, রাজদ্বারে সমাগম, সমারোহ স্থান, an assembly, company, meeting, place of meeting, royal court or council, a levee, a session, the outer portion or court of an idol-temple.

সভাকার, সবাকার,—সকলকার, সকলের, তাবৎ সভাস্থদের, of or belonging to all, of or by the whole assembly.

সভাসদ্, সভাসৎ,—সভাস্থ পণ্ডিতাদি, মন্ত্রী, সামাজিক, a courtier, adviser, one of a company, a member of an assembly; having a right to a place therein.

সভাস্থ, সামাজিক, সভাতে বর্ত্তমান, having a place in an assembly, present at meeting.

সভ্য, সভারঞ্জক, সজ্জন, ভদ্র, উত্তম বংশোদ্ভব, সামাজিক, polite, polished, genteel, well-bred, courteous, fit for or admissible into society, &c.

সম, সদৃশ, তুল্য, সমান, চৌরস, like, alike, similar, same, equal, even, smooth, level.

সমক্ষ, প্রত্যক্ষ, সুব্যক্ত, নিকটবর্ত্তী, সাক্ষাৎ, visible, evident, clear, near, before, in sight, in presence of.

সমগ্র, সকল, অখণ্ড, পূর্ণ, all, whole, entire, full, complete.

সমঝন, সমজন,—বুঝন, জানন, to comprehend, perceive, know.

সমঞ্জস, উপযুক্ততা, সমন্বয়, সংলগ্নতা, তথ্য, অবিরোধ, পরিমিত ব্যয়, ন্যায়, বিচার, উপযুক্ত, ন্যায্য, fitness, propriety, agreement, consistency, accuracy, truth, reconciliation, accommodation of differences, &c. frugality, impartiality, equal justice, a trial, investigation; proper, right, condign.

সমঞ্জস্য, অল্পব্যয়ী, পরিণামদর্শী, frugal, economical, prudent.

সমতা, সমভাব,—অভিন্নাবস্থা, সাম্য, সাদৃশ্য, সম্ভব, সম্পূর্ণতা, উপশম, similarity, sameness, equality, evenness, uniformity, analogy, equilibrium, completeness, likelihood, perfection, abatement of disease.

সমধাতু, আরোগ্য, সর্বধাতুর সাম্যভাব, health, equilibrium of bodily humours, &c.

সমধিক, অতিরিক্ত, অত্যধিক, exceeding, excessive. [sic.

সমতাল, লয়, তালের সাম্য, chime, harmony, even time in mu-

সমদর্শী. তুল্যজ্ঞানী, regarding all alike, indifferent, impartial.

সমদিবারাত্রিকাল, বিষুবকাল, the time of the equinoxes.

সমন্বয়, অনেকের পরস্পর মিলন, সংলগ্নতা, সম্বন্ধ. সংযোগ, সভাতে গ্রহণকরা, agreement, concord, consistency, consequence, connection, combination, union, restoration to society or cast, &c.

সমন্বিত, পরস্পর মিলিত, তজ্জন্য সংলগ্ন, যুক্ত, বিশিষ্ট, পংক্তিগৃহীত, in concord with, following, consequent upon, consistent with, united, full of, possessing, endued with, restored to cast or society.

সমবায়, সম্বন্ধ, মেল, যোগ, সঞ্চয়, সংগ্রহ, গণ, relation or connexion, as between subject and attribute, the whole and its parts, &c. aggregation, collection, assemblage. [bled, comprized.

সমবেত, সংগৃহীত, সঞ্চিত, সামিল, aggregated, collected, assem-

সমভাবী, তদবস্থান্বিত, অটল, পরিণামশূন্য, তুল্য, সাথী, continuing the same, unmoved, uncorrupted, analogous, similar; a colleague.

সমভিব্যাহার, সমভ্যার,—সাহিত্য, সঙ্গ, মিত্রতা, পরিজন, সহচরের সমূহ, association, society, converse, intimacy, company, a retinue, train.

সমভিব্যাহারী, সমভ্যারী,—সঙ্গী, অনুচর, accompanying, &c; a comrade, attendant, retinue. [with.

সমভিব্যাহৃত, সমেত, সহিত, সঙ্গে, accompanied by, in company

সমভূমি, চৌরস স্থান, মাঠ, level ground, a plain, a flat surface.

সময়, কাল, অবকাশ, প্রতিজ্ঞা, পণ, time, season, juncture, age, period, opportunity, occasion, leisure, weather, an appointment, contract.

সময়ক্রমে বা গুণে, কিছুকালগতে, উপযুক্ত সময়ে, in course or process of time, opportunely.

সময়শিরে, উপযুক্ত সময়ে, শুভযোগে, just in time, seasonably.

সময়োচিত, কালোপযুক্ত, যথাকাল, suitable to the occasion, &c.

সমর, যুদ্ধ, রণ, বিগ্রহ, a battle, fight, conflict, war.

সমর্জু, সমসরল, parallel, (as lines.)

সমর্থ, বলবান্, ক্ষমতাপন্ন, উপযুক্ত, হিত, তুল্যার্থ, powerful, strong, able, capable, fit, proper, adequate, connected in sense or object.

সমর্পণ, সোঁপণ,—গছান, রক্ষার্থে ত্যাগ করণ, ছাড়ন, ভারণ, প্রদান করণ, দেওন, to commit, give in charge, deliver over, surrender up, to entrust, delegate, consign, to offer in sacrifice, to bestow, give.

সমল, মলিন, অপরিষ্কার, কাদাটিয়া, dirty, foul, filthy, squalid, sordid, muddy.

সমসমকাল, তৎতৎক্ষণ, প্রাক্কাল, the very time, a crisis.

সমসূত্রপাত, ঋজুসূত্র বিন্যাস, a disposing in parallel lines.

সমস্ত, সকল, সমুদায়, সংক্ষিপ্ত, মিশ্রিত, মিশ্র, একুন, all, entire, every, abridged, thrown together, compounded; an aggregate, the whole. [filled up.

সমস্যা, পদ্যের পূরণার্থ এক দেশ, part of a stanza given to be

সমা, বৎসর, সম্বৎসর, a year.

সমাগম, আগমন, উপস্থিতি, ঘটা, a coming, arrival, coming together, meeting, assembling, concourse.

সমাজ, সভা, ছাত্রাদির সমূহ, ঘটা, সম্প্রদায়, অনেক প্রামাণিক লোকের বাসস্থান, an assembly, meeting, multitude, concourse, flock, congregation, society, association, community, the district or place of abode of a respectable community.

সমাচার, সম্বাদ,রব, বিবরণ, বিজ্ঞাপন, news, tidings. intelligence, report, information, an account, notice.

সমাদর, সম্মান, মর্য্যাদা, respect, esteem, honor, reverence, veneration, reputation. [&c.

সমাদৃত, মর্য্যাদান্বিত, সম্ভ্রান্ত, respected, esteemed, reputable,

সমাধা-ন, নিষ্পত্তি, নির্ণয়, বিরোধ ভঞ্জন, মিটানি, decision of an affair, determination. award, settlement of differences,reconciliation, adjustment, completion, termination.

সমাধি. পরমেশ্বরেতে চিত্তের একাগ্রতা, ধ্যান, যোগ, *id*: *also* deep meditation on the Deity, devout abstraction, silence, burial, a grave.

সমান, তুল্য, এক, অভিন্ন, সদৃশ, সরল, শরীরস্থ বায়ু বিশেষ, equal, similar, alike, same, uniform, even, smooth, level. straight; a vital air.

সমানোদক. চতুর্দ্দশ পুরুষের পর জন্মনামস্মৃতি পর্য্যন্ত পুরুষের সন্তান, তর্পণ জলভাগী, a kinsman within 14 descents from a common ancestor, but specially the last seven, (some say the last 4,) so called from participating in the offerings of water to the manes.

সমাপন, মিটান, নিষ্পাদন, চুকান, to finish, conclude, complete, terminate, end, accomplish. [&c.

সমাপ্ত, নিষ্পন্ন, সাঙ্গ, ইতি, concluded, terminated, finished,

সমাপ্তি, শেষ, বিরোধভঞ্জন, conclusion &c. reconciliation of differences, disputes, &c.

সমাবর্ত্তন, বেদাধ্যয়নান্তের যে বৈদিক কর্ম্ম করিলে গৃহস্থ ধর্ম্মে অধিকারী হয়, a ceremony on a brahmin pupil's leaving his teacher to enter upon a life of secularity.

সমাবেদন, নিবেদন, সম্যক্ প্রকারে জানান, a respectful communication of full and explicit information. [in.

সমাবিষ্ট, একাগ্রচিত্ত, নিবিষ্টমনাঃ, engrossed by. closely engaged

সমাবেশ, স্বচ্ছন্দরূপে অবস্থান, উচিত বিভাগ, নিষ্পত্তি, প্রবেশ, একাগ্রতা, room, accommodation in a common dwelling, a just distribution, proper division, termination of differences. entrance, close or undivided attention, devotion to.

সমারোহ, বহুলোকাগম, ঘটা, লোকযাত্রা, ঠমক, a concourse, crowd; mob, multitude, procession, pomp.

সমাস, দুই তিন পদের একপদ করা, সংশ্লেষ, একুন, the composition of words, formation of compound terms, a compound word or term, aggregation.

সমাহার, সমাহৃতি,—সংগ্রহ, সংশ্লেষ, সংক্ষেপ, বর্ণবিন্যাস বিশেষ, দ্বন্দ্বসমাস বিশেষ, an aggregation, collection, assemblage, union, abridgement, an artificial arrangement of the alphabet, any two letters in which form a technical enunciation of all the intermediate ones, a string of words connected by the omission of the conjunctive particle.

সমাহিত, সাবধান, চৌকষ, ধীর, যোগাবিষ্ট, attentive, cautious, temperate, engaged in devout meditation.

সমিধ, যজ্ঞিয় কাষ্ঠ, ইন্ধন, sacrificial fuel, wood, &c. for a sacrifice. [ing even, &c.

সমীকার, তুল্যকরা, চৌরস করা, equalization, a levelling, mak-

সমীক্ষ, সাঙ্খ্য দর্শন, অবলোকন, বিতর্ক, সাক্ষাৎ, the Sánksya philosophy, a survey, investigation, presence.

সমীচীন, উত্তম, উপযুক্ত, সত্য, যথার্থ, good, right, correct, accurate, proper, fit, real, true, genuine.

সমীপ, নৈকট্য, সন্নিধান, নিকট, সন্নিকৃষ্ট, vicinity, proximity; near, adjacent, contiguous, close by.

সমীর-ণ, বায়ু, পবন, বাতাস, air, wind.

সমীহা, ব্রীড়া, বহুচেষ্টা, modesty, reserve, earnest endeavour.

সমুখ, বাক্‌পটু, মুখামুখি, প্রত্যক্ষ, eloquent, opposite, over against, facing, obvious.

সমুচিত, সমোচিত,—যথা যোগ্য, ন্যায্য, উপযুক্ত, proper, right, fit, just, deserved, suitable, condign.

সমুচ্চয়, অনেকের মিলন, সংগ্রহ, সমাহার, a collection, assemblage, union, conjunction. [total.

সমুদায়, সমুদয়,—সমস্ত, অখণ্ড, একুন, all, entire; the whole,

সমুদ্ধার, উচ্চীকরণ, উত্থাপন, উৎপাটন, দর্শান, সংগ্রহ, a raising, lifting or pulling up, a bringing to light, an extracting, a compilation.

সমুদ্র, সাগর, মুদ্রাঙ্কিত, the ocean, the sea; stamped, sealed.

সমুদ্রীয়, সাগর সম্বন্ধীয়, সামুদ্রিক, marine, ocean, of or relating to the ocean. [the roots.

সমূল, শিকড়বান্, মূলযুক্ত, মূল সুদ্ধ, having a root; by or with

সমূহ, অনেক, সংঘাত, যূথ, সঞ্চয়, স্তূপ, a multitude, number, flock, gang, cluster, heap, quantity.

সমৃদ্ধ, ধনাঢ্য, বর্দ্ধিত, prosperous, wealthy, increased.

সমৃদ্ধি, সম্পত্তি, মাহাত্ম্য, সম্ভ্রম, ঘটা, increase, prosperity, greatness, success, a crowd. [brought together.

সমেত, সঙ্গে, সহিত, সুদ্ধ, with, together with, along with,

সম্পত্তি, সম্পদ্,—বিভব, ঐশ্বর্য্য, শ্রী, বৃদ্ধি, সম্ভ্রম, wealth, affluence, prosperity, success, advancement, increase of power or fame, &c. promotion.

সম্পন্ন, প্রতুলান্বিত, শ্রীমান, পরিপূর্ণ, ভাগ্যবন্ত, সাধিত, নিষ্পন্ন, বিশিষ্ট, wealthy, prosperous, successful, advanced, promoted, enriched, happy, obtained, acquired, accomplished, effected, done, finished, completed, endowed with, possessed of.

সম্পর্ক, সম্বন্ধ, মেল, মিশ্র, অধিকার, union, connexion, contact, mixture, relationship, affinity, concern, relation, reference. claim, right to.

সম্পর্কী, সম্পর্কীয়,—সম্বন্ধীয়, কুটুম্ব, relative to, connected with, relating to; a relative. [factor, overseer.

সম্পাদক, সমাপক, কর্ম্মসাধক, স্থায়ুক, finishing, &c. a manager,

সম্পাদন, নিষ্পাদন, সমাপন, অভীষ্ট সাধান, ফলান, চালান, খাটান, to finish, complete, accomplish, to effect, to give success to, prosper, succeed, procure, to manage, conduct.

সম্পূর্ণ, পরিপূর্ণ, ভরা, ময়, অখণ্ড, সিদ্ধ, সমাপ্ত, প্রচুর, filled, full, full of, replete, perfect, plenary, complete, whole, entire, fulfilled, accomplished, finished, plenty, enough. [quickly.

সম্প্রতি. ইদানী, আশু, now, at present, in the present day,

সম্প্রদান, দান, অর্পণ, পারম্পর্য্য জ্ঞাপন, দানের পাত্র, a giving, bestowing, conferring, communicating traditionally, the dative case in grammar, the person to whom a thing is given, a grantee.

সম্প্রদা-য়, ভিন্নমত, সমাজ, গোষ্ঠ, সঙ্গ, পরম্পরায় প্রাপ্ত ধর্ম, a sect, party, company, club, association, a band of singers, &c. traditional doctrine.

সম্প্রদায়ী, পক্ষপাতী, সমাজস্থ, সধর্ম্ম, সামাজিক, পাংক্তেয়, সুব্যবহারী, a sectary, partizan, one of a band or company; admissible to a society, exemplary.

সম্বৎসর, হায়ন, a whole year, a full twelvemonth.

সম্বন্ধ, সম্পর্ক, সংলাগ, যোগ্যতা, জ্ঞাতিত্ব, যোগ, অধিকার, natural or essential connexion, as of quality and substance, &c. relation, relevancy, fitness, propriety, affinity, consanguinity, kindred, the possessive case in grammar.

সম্বন্ধী, সম্পর্কী, কুটুম্ব, শ্যালক, having relation to or connexion with; a relative, kinsman, a wife's brother.

সম্বন্ধীয়, সম্পর্কীয়, বিষয়ক, connected with, relating to, &c.

সম্বরণ, লুকান, চাপিয়া রাখন, ইন্দ্রিয়দমন, ফোড়ন, to conceal, withdraw, to govern or restrain the passions, to spice or season food. [self-controul.

সম্বরা, ফালফাস্, ধৈর্য্য, পরিমিতাচরণ, spice, seasoning of food,

সম্বর্দ্ধক, মর্য্যাদক, বাড়ানিয়া, honoring, &c. augmenting.

সম্বর্দ্ধনা, সম্ভ্রম, অভ্যর্থনা, honor, respect, respectful welcome.

সম্বল, পাথেয়, ব্যয়োচিত দ্রব্য, provision for a journey.

সম্বলিত, সমেত, মিলিত, বিষয়ক, accompanied with, containing, mixed with, connected with, relating to.

সম্বাদ, বার্ত্তা, সমাচার, কথোপকথন, a report, tidings, news, intelligence, information, conversation, converse, a dialogue.

সম্বোধন, অভিমুখীকরণ, an addressing, speaking or calling to, the vocative case, an interjection.

সম্বেগ, শীঘ্রগতি, উদ্দধুন্দ, rapidity, rapid flow, a commotion.

সম্ভব, সত্তা, জন্ম, উৎপত্তি, হেতু, কারণ, মূল, হইবার যোগ্যতা, প্রামাণ্য, হইবার যোগ্য, উপক্ত, উদ্ভব, existence, birth, production, cause, motive, origin, possibility, probability; possible, credible, likely, probable, suitable, adequate, arising from, produced from, descending from.

সম্ভবন, মিলন, লাগন, to accord, suit, do, answer, apply.

সম্ভাবনা, হইবার যোগ্যতা, প্রামাণ্য, উপযুক্ততা, ফল, ঘটনা, উপায়, যোত্র, possibility, likelihood, probability, fitness, suitableness, adequacy, result, circumstance, means, estate, stock, &c.

সম্ভাবনীয়, সম্ভাব্য,—হইবার যোগ্য, সপ্রমাণ, উপযুক্ত, possible, practicable, probable, likely, fit, suitable.

সম্ভাবিত, যোগ্য. সাধ্য, যোত্রযুক্ত, বিবেচিত, adequate, adapted to, possible, solvent, able to pay, reflected upon.

সম্ভাষণ, সম্ভাষা,—আলাপ, কথোপকথন, converse, discourse, conversation, communication. [from.

সম্ভূত, জাত, উৎপন্ন, born, arisen, sprung or produced

সম্ভূয়সমুত্থান, সাঝা, ভাগাভাগি, partnership in trade, fellowship in business, joint-commerce.

সম্ভোগ, ফলোভভোগ, বিষয়সুখগ্রহণ, মৈথুন, usufruct, enjoyment, possession, successful love, cohabitation, coition.

সম্ভোগী, ফলভুক্, কামুক, সংসর্গী, enjoying, possessing the use of, sensual, cohabiting with.

সম্ভ্রম, আদর, মর্য্যাদা, সুখ্যাতি, গুরুত্ব, মহত্ত্ব, ভয়, ত্বরাণী, ঘূর্ণি, honor, respect, reverence, esteem, reputation, note, rank, weight, consequence, dignity, hurry, confusion, flurry, a whirling round.

সম্ভ্রান্ত, সম্মানিত, সুখ্যাত্যাপন্ন, honored, respected, respectable.

সম্মত, অনুমত, প্রিয়, সঙ্গত, স্বীকৃত, approved, chosen, agreeable or conformable to, consistent with, consenting to, admitting, agreed, approving of.

সম্মতি, স্বীকার, ঐকমত্য, অনুমতি, ক্ষমতা, আজ্ঞা, বাঞ্ছা, প্রণয়, consent, approbation, acquiescence, assent, agreement in opinion or purpose, accord, leave, permission, an order, a wish, regard, affection.

সম্মান, আদর, মর্য্যাদা, সম্ভ্রম. প্রতিপত্তি, honor, respect, esteem, reverence, veneration, reputation, promotion, dignity, advancement.

সম্মার্জ্জনী, খেংরা, ঝাঁটা, a broom, a brush.

সম্মীলন, বুজন, বদ্ধ করণ, to shut, close as the eyes or a door.

সম্মুখ, অভিমুখ, সমক্ষ, সাক্ষাৎ, the front, sight, presence, face.

সম্মুখে, সমক্ষে, সাক্ষাৎ, before, in presence of, opposite, over
against. [ciliation, a meeting.
সম্মিলন, মেল, অবিরোধ, সাক্ষাৎ, union, concord, peace, recon-
সম্যক্, সমগ্র, তাবৎ, অখণ্ড, উচিত, all, whole, entire, perfect,
due, fit, proper. [rightly, properly.
সম্যক্প্রকারে, সর্ব্বতোভাবে, উত্তমরূপে, wholly, entirely, duly,
সম্শ্লিষ্ট, মিশ্রিত, সংযুক্ত, অনুগত, mixed with, adulterated, joined, attached to, connected with.
সম্রাট্, রাজাধিরাজ, a paramount sovereign, an emperor.
সযুত, বিনয়ী, বশীভূত, দমিত, খেদান্বিত, শুদ্ধ, সরলীকৃত, submissive, humble, subdued, penitent, sorry, rectified, set right, straightened.
সযোনি, জাঁতী, সখী, বয়স্যা, a pair of betel-nippers, a female confidante or intimate friend.
সর, ছানা, ঘনীভূত দুগ্ধসার, cream, curds, thick milk.
সরক, গলিপথ, গামী, a road, narrow way; going, moving, &c.
সরণ, গমন, চলন, স্খলন, টলন, ক্ষরণ, দূর হওন, ব্যবহারে পড়ন, to move, go, remove, stir, slip, trip, slide, trickle, escape, be removed, to be in use or wear.
সরজস্কা, ঋতুমতী, রজস্বলা, menstruous, in her courses.
সরতা, জাঁতী, betel-nippers, nut-crackers.
সরভাগ, পক্ক দুগ্ধসার, boiled cream, a thick custard.
সরমা, কুক্কুরী, শুনী, *f.* a bitch, *a term of reproach.*
সরল, ঋজু, ডাঁড়া, অকপট, স্থূলবুদ্ধি, অজ্ঞান, straight, perpendicular, upright, honest, sincere, frank, candid, artless, simple, foolish.
সরস্, সরসী,—তড়াগ, পুষ্করিণী, a sheet of water, a pond, a lake.
সরস, জলুয়া, রসযুক্ত, সুস্বাদু, রসিক, কোমল, জয়ী, watery, succulent, juicy, sappy, pithy, savoury, tasty, sentimental, gentle, soft, good, victorious.
সরসিজ, সরসীরুহ,—পদ্ম, a lotus or water-lily. [quence.
সরস্বতী, বাণী, বাগ্দেবী, speech, the goddess of speech and elo-
সরাগ, ক্রোধী, কোপশীল, কামনাবন্ত, ভাবযুক্ত, passionate, angry, impassioned, sentimental, under the influence of passion, desire, &c.
সরা, পরিবার বস্ত্র, জীর্ণ, in use or wear, second-hand.

সরাণ, চলান, লাড়ন, স্থানান্তরে রাখন, বৃহৎ পন্থা, রাজমার্গ, to move, cause to move, bring into use, remove, stir, displace; a high-way, high-road.

সরিৎ, নদী, স্রোতস্বতী, সূত্র, a river, stream, a thread, clue.

সরিৎপতি, সমুদ্র, সাগর, the ocean, the sea.

সরিষা, সরিষপ,—সর্ষপ, mustard-seed, the mustard plant.

সরু, তনু, ক্ষীণ, সূক্ষ্ম, সুন্দর, thin, slender, small, minute, shrill, fine, nice. [of similar form.

সরূপ, আকারবন্ত, সদৃশ, সমানাকৃতি, having form or shape, like,

সরোজ, সরোরুহ,—পদ্ম, a lotus or water-lily. [water.

সরোবর, পুষ্করিণী, জলাশয়, তড়াগ, a pond, tank, lake, sheet of

সর্গ, সৃষ্টি, স্বভাব, ধর্ম্ম, প্রকরণ, খণ্ড, creation, nature, natural property or disposition, tendency, a section, chapter, canto. [itself.

সর্জরস, ধুনা, শালবৃক্ষ, the resin of the Shál tree, the tree

সর্জ্জন, সৃষ্টি করণ, গঠন, নির্ম্মাণ, উৎপাদন, পালন, to create, make, form, produce, to rear a plant, &c.

সর্প, অহি, সাপ, a serpent, snake, a serpentine motion.

সর্পভ্রম, মিথ্যানুভব, রজ্জুকে সর্পজ্ঞান, an error in the perception of natural objects, as of a rope for a snake.

সর্পমণি, মাণিক্য, the snake-stone or carbuncle.

সর্পিস্, ঘৃত, ঘি, হবিঃ, ghee or clarified butter.

সর্ব্ব, বিশ্ব, সকল, সমস্ত, তাবৎ, অখিল, all, whole, universal, every, entire, complete. [Brahmá.

সর্ব্বকর্ত্তা, বিশ্বস্রষ্টা, ব্রহ্মা, all-creating, omnipotent, Lord of all,

সর্ব্বক্ষণ, সদা, নিরন্তর, অনবরতঃ, always, perpetually.

সর্ব্বগ, সর্ব্বত্রগামী, বিশ্বব্যাপী, আত্মা, ব্রহ্ম, শিব, going every where, all-pervading; the universal Spirit, the soul, Brahma, Shiva. [nipresent.

সর্ব্বগত, বিশ্বব্যাপ্ত, universally expanded, all-pervading, om-

সর্ব্বকাল, তাবৎ সময়, ঋতু সমস্ত, all times, all seasons.

সর্ব্বজিৎ, বিশ্বজয়ী, সকলের দমনকর্ত্তা, সকলহইতে উৎকৃষ্ট, all-conquering, all-subduing, all-surpassing.

সর্ব্বজ্ঞ, যিনি সকলি জানেন, all-wise, all-knowing, omniscient, knowing all things. [on all sides.

সর্ব্বতঃ, সমন্ততঃ, চতুর্দ্দিকে, universally, in all respects, wholly,

সর্বতোভদ্র, যন্ত্র মণ্ডল বিশেষ, দেবতার গৃহ বিশেষ, রাজসদন, a mystical square or diagram, a square temple or palace. [completely, perfectly.

সর্বতোভাবে, সম্যক্ প্রকারে, in every respect, wholly, entirely,

সর্বত্র, সকল স্থানে, every where, in all places.

সর্বত্রগ বা গামী, বিশ্বগ, অন্তর্যামী, going every where, all-pervading, omnipresent. [suredly.

সর্বথা, সকল প্রকারে, অবশ্য, in every way, by all means, as-

সর্বদর্শী, যিনি সকলি দেখেন, সর্বজ্ঞ, all-seeing, omniscient.

সর্বদা-ই, সতত, নিরন্তর, সদা, always, continually, constantly, ever, at all times, &c.

সর্বনাম, সর্ব বিশ্বাদি পঞ্চ বিংশৎ শব্দ, a pronoun or other word of universal signification, as *all, the whole, &c.*

সর্বনাশ, সমুদায়ের ধ্বংস, লোপ, উচ্ছেদ, entire or universal ruin, complete destruction, extermination, annihilation, total wreck. [&c.

সর্বনাশী, উচ্ছিন্নকারক, বিনাশক, all-destructive, exterminating,

সর্বপ্রিয়, সকলের অভীষ্ট, beloved by all, universally beloved.

সর্ববল্লভা, বেশ্যা, বারস্ত্রী, কুলটা, a common woman, a strumpet.

সর্ববিৎ, সর্বজ্ঞ, বিশ্বজ্ঞাতা, all-knowing, all-wise.

সর্ববিধ, সম্যক্ প্রকার, of every sort, of all kinds.

সর্ববেশী, ভণ্ড, ভাঁড়, সংকারী, assuming all characters; a buffoon, an actor, a zany.

সর্বব্যাপক, সর্বব্যাপী,—বিশ্বগ, অন্তর্যামী, সমুদায় পক্ষব্যাপক, all-pervading, omnipresent, embracing all the particulars of a case or subject.

সর্বময়, তাবৎস্বরূপ, বিশ্বরূপ, সকলের অন্তর্যামী, universally expanded, in every thing, abounding in every thing, general, universal. [body's mouth.

সর্বমুখী, খেংরা, চলিত, প্রচারিত, a broom, current, in every

সর্বশক্তিমান, অসীম সামর্থ্যযুক্ত, যিনি সকলি করিতে পারেন, almighty, all-powerful. [at once.

সর্বশুদ্ধ, একুনে, গড়ে, একেবারে, taken all together, inclusively,

সর্বসম্মত, সকলের স্বীকৃত, সকলের প্রিয়, universally received or approved, popular. [the sun.

সর্বসাক্ষী, সর্বজ্ঞ অর্থাৎ পরমেশ্বর, সূর্য্য, God the universal witness,

সর্বসাধারণ, যাহাতে সকলের অধিকার আছে, সামান্য, চলিত, ব্যবহৃত, common to all, general, current, staple.
সর্বসাধারণে, প্রচরদ্রূপে, in common, currently, commonly.
সর্বস্ব, সমুদায় ধন, one's whole property or entire fortune.
সর্বসিদ্ধ, প্রসিদ্ধ,বিদিত, universally known and approved, noted.
সর্বসিদ্ধি, তাবৎ প্রার্থনীয় বস্তুর প্রাপ্তি, অভীষ্টসিদ্ধি, entire success, accomplishment of all one's wishes or prayers.
সর্বাঙ্গ, সমুদায় শরীর, অবয়ব সমস্ত, বেদাঙ্গ সমুদায়, the whole body from head to foot, all the parts of a thing collectively, all the sciences appendent on the Vedas.
সর্বাঙ্গী, সমুদায় শরীর ব্যাপ্ত, diffused through the whole body.
সর্বান্তর্যামী, সর্বগ, বিশ্বময়, all-pervading, all-in-all.
সর্বীয়, সাধারণ, সকলের, তাবতীয়, relating or belonging to all, general, universal.
সর্বেন্দ্রিয়, কর্ম্মেন্দ্রিয় জ্ঞানেন্দ্রিয় যুদ্ধ অর্থাৎ হস্তপাদাদি পঞ্চ ও মনোনে ত্রাদি পঞ্চ, all the organs of perception and action.
সর্বেশ্বর, সকলের কর্তা, বিশ্বনাথ, Lord of all, God, Shiva.
সর্বোপরি, সকলহইতে উত্তম, শ্রেষ্ঠ, superior to all, above all, chief, eminent. [cinal drugs.
সর্বৌষধি, মুরা জটামাংসী প্রভৃতি দশ দ্রব্য, a class of ten medi-
সর্ষপ, সর্ষ্য,—সরিষা, mustard-seed, the mustard plant.
সলগ্ন, উপযুক্ত, সঙ্গত, apposite, suitable, pertinent, appropriate, relevant, consistent.
সলিল, জল, উদক, পানী, নীর, water. [cloud.
সলিলদ, সলিলদায়ী,—জলদায়ক, জলার্পক, মেঘ, giving water; a
সলিলধি, সমুদ্র, সাগর, অব্ধি, বারিধি, the ocean, the sea.
সবর্ণ, একজাতি, সমানবর্ণ, of the same tribe or colour; a letter of the same class.
সব্য, বাম, বামাঙ্গ, দক্ষিণদিক্‌, left; the left hand, the south.
সশা, ক্ষীরা, a cucumber.
সসজ্জ, কৃতবেশধারণ, সনদ্ধ, প্রস্তুত, dressed, harnessed, armed, accoutred, ready, willing.
সসত্ত্বা, গর্ভিণী, *f.* pregnant, quick, with child.
সস্ত্রীক, স্ত্রীবান্‌, স্ত্রীসহিত, ভার্য্যাকে সঙ্গে করিয়া, having a wife, with his wife, accompanied by his wife.

সস্য, বৃক্ষাদির ফল, শাঁস, corn, grain, fruit, the kernel, &c.
সহ, সহিত, সমভিব্যাহারে, প্রভু, ভোগী, with, together with, in company with; *affix*: enduring, suffering.
সহকার, সহকারিতা,—সাহায্য, অনুকূলতা, প্রতিপালক, aid, assistance, help, instrumentality, co-operation, patronage, a patron, helper, &c.
সহকারী, অনুকূল, সহায়, সঙ্গী, মিত্র, উপকারী, co-operating, &c; an assistant, helper, co-adjutor, ally, patron.
সহক্রীড়, বয়স্য, খেলাড়ু ভাই, a play-fellow, play-mate
সহগত্রী, সহগামিনী,—সতী, চিতারূঢ়া, চিতারোহিণী, a Satí or woman who burns on the funeral pile of her husband.
সহগমন, চিতারোহণ, concremation, or burning of a widow.
সহচর, অনুগত, সঙ্গী, সাথী, বন্ধু, an attendant, follower, associate, companion, friend.
সহচর, সহচারী,—সমভিব্যাহারী, অনুগামী, attending, accompanying, moving with. [confidante.
সহচরী, দূতী, সখী, বয়স্যা, a female attendant, companion,
সহজ, অকঠিন, লঘু, সামান্য, স্বাভাবিক, নিশ্চ, অন্তর্জাত, এককালীন জাত, সহোদর, easy, trivial, common, light, slight, trifling, ordinary, natural, inherent, innate, born with one, cognate; a full brother, a twin.
সহজে, অনায়াসে, ধীরে, সুখে, easily, without force, quietly, tranquilly, at ease.
সহধর্ম্মিণী, বেদ প্রমাণে বিবাহিতা স্ত্রী, a wife married according to the ritual of the Veds, and a sharer in her husband's merits. [tain, endure.
সহন, দুঃখভোগ করণ, ভার বহন, to bear, suffer, support, sus-
সহনশীল, সহিষ্ণু, স্থিরমনাঃ, ধীর, সহনে ক্ষম, enduring, patient of, capable of suffering, &c. [able, &c.
সহনীয়, সহ্য,—সহিবার যোগ্য, endurable, tolerable, support-
সহবর্ত্তী, সঙ্গী, অনুচর, মিত্র, সহায়, সখা, attending, present with; a follower, attendant, adherent, friend, associate, companion.
সহবাস, একত্র থাকা, সংসর্গ, সঙ্গকার, a co-residence, dwelling together, associating. [ing of a widow.
সহমরণ, প্রজ্বলিত চিতাগ্নিতে প্রবেশ, concremation or the burn-

সহমান, দুঃখবিশিষ্ট, ভারগ্রস্ত, enduring, suffering, sustaining.
সহমৃতা, যে স্ত্রী সতী হইয়াছে, a woman who, becoming a satí, has burned with her husband's body.
সহসা, আশু, হঠাৎ, অকস্মাৎ, বিনা বিবেচনাতে, প্রমাদে, hastily, unawares, suddenly, precipitately, rashly.
সহস্র, দশ শত, a thousand. [time, at once.
সহযোগে, সঙ্গে, একেবারে, together, in company, at the same
সহায়, সহকারী, অনুকূল, মিত্র, বন্ধু, অনুচর, আনুকূল্য, উপকার, a helper, assistant, co-adjutor, ally, auxiliary, patron, friend, follower, patronage, assistance, succour, help, relief, co-operation.
সহায়তা, সহকারিতা, উপকার, alliance, co-operation, help, aid.
সহায়ী, অনুকূল, উপকারক, aiding, &c. an assistant, helper, &c.
সহিত, সমভিব্যাহৃত, সহ, একসঙ্গে, সাথে, accompanied by, associated with, with, together with, in company with. [patient.
সহিষ্ণু, সহনশীল, ক্ষমাশীল, patient of, enduring, resigned,
সহিষ্ণুতা, সহনশীলতা, ধৈর্য্য, ক্ষমাশীলতা, patient endurance, resignation, constancy, patience, long-suffering.
সহোদর, একমাতৃজাত, সগর্ভ, a full-brother, one of whole blood.
সাংশয়িক, অনিশ্চিত, সন্দিগ্ধ, doubtful, doubting, suspicious.
সাংসারিক, সংসার অথবা পরিবার সম্বন্ধীয়, বিষয়ী, কামুক, mundane, earthly, worldly, secular, domestic, sensual.
সাঁকো, সংক্রম, a bridge. [sketch, a blank-book.
সাঁচ, ছাঁচ, ছাপ, ঠাট, খসড়া, a mould, form, die, print,
সাঁচা, সত্য, যথার্থ, সরল, true, genuine, honest, sincere.
সাঁচি, নবীন, টাট্কা, যথার্থ, অত্যুত্তম, new, recent, fresh, genuine, superior, excellent, best.
সাঁঝ, সাঁঝ,—সন্ধ্যাকাল, প্রদোষ, evening, close of day, dusk.
সাঁজো, সাজো,—সদ্যোজাত, নবীন, টাট্কা, new, new-made, fresh, sound, recent.
সাঁজোয়া, অস্ত্র নিবারণার্থ পরিধেয় কবচ, armour, a coat of mail.
সাঁড়াশী, সন্দংশ, a pair of tongs, pincers, tweezers, forceps.
সাঁজড়ন, সাজান, যোটান, সাজ লাগান, to yoke, to harness.
সাঁতরণ-আণ, সাঁতারণ,—সন্তরণ, ভাসন, to swim, to float.
সাঁতার, সন্তার,ভাসা, a swimming, floating, act of swimming.

সাঁটন, লুণ্ঠন, ভরণ, বৃদ্ধি পাওন, ঝাঁটন, to writhe, toss about, to be full as the stomach, to be wealthy, to threaten. [gravy or condiment.
সাঁতলান, ফোড়ন, সম্বরণ, to season, spice, add seasoning to a
সাঁধন-আন, প্রবেশ করণ, ঢুকন, ঘুষণ, to enter, go in, penetrate, creep into.
সাঁধি, সন্ধি, ফাক, ছিদ্র, a crevice, chink, hole, crack.
সাকল্য, সমুদায়, সমূহের ঐক্য, মোট, একুন, the whole, all, entire, a total, sum, amount, totality.
সাকাঙ্ক্ষ, ইচ্ছুক, অভিলাষী, willing, desirous, having desire.
সাকার, আকারবিশিষ্ট, রূপবান্, প্রপঞ্চ, দৈহিক, having shape or form, material, bodily. [idolatry.
সাকারসেবা, পুত্তলাপূজা, worship of images or material forms,
সাক্ষাৎ, গোচরে, সম্মুখে, অগোপনে, মিলন, আলাপ, পরম্পরা বিনা, প্রস্তুত, সমক্ষ, প্রত্যক্ষ, বাস্তবিক, in sight, view or presence of, before, visibly, manifestly, openly, publickly; an interview, visit, audience, meeting; immediate, present, visible, direct, before the eyes, obvious, very, real, own.
সাক্ষাৎকার, সম্মুখ, সন্দর্শন, a person's presence, interview, audience. [bearing testimony.
সাক্ষী, প্রত্যক্ষদর্শী, জ্ঞাতা, প্রমাণকারী, a witness, eye-witness;
সাক্ষাৎকারক বা কারী,— ভেটনিয়া, মিলানিয়া, a visitor; visiting, introducing, procuring an interview.
সাক্ষাৎদ্রষ্টা বা দর্শী, সাক্ষী, দৃশ্যপ্রমাণে জ্ঞাতা, an eye-witness; having ocular proof. [a deposition.
সাক্ষ্য, প্রত্যক্ষ দর্শন, প্রমাণ, eye-witness, testimony, evidence,
সাগর, সমুদ্র, সিন্ধু, অর্ণব, the ocean, the sea.
সাগ্র, অগ্রবিশিষ্ট, অগ্রের সহিত, আগাল, pointed, having a point.
সাঙ্খ্য, কপিল মুনি কল্পিত দর্শন বিশেষ, one of the six philosophical systems, an atheistical philosophy.
সাঙ্গ, অঙ্গের সহিত, সমাপ্ত, ইতি, having all its parts, perfect, complete, finished, concluded, exhausted; finis. [in all its parts, the whole.
সাঙ্গোপাঙ্গ, সম্পূর্ণ, সর্বাঙ্গ, সমুদায়, perfect, entire, complete
সাঙ্গাৎ, বন্ধু, সখা, সঙ্গী, a friend, an associate.

সাংঘাতিক, প্রাণনাশক, বধিক, deadly, fatal, murderous.
সাচিব্য, মন্ত্রিত্ব, আনুকূল্য, সুসার, আধিক্য, ministry, administration, assistance, friendship, cheapness, advantage in purchasing, &c. overplus.
সাজ, বেশ, সজ্জা, প্রয়োজনীয় দ্রব্য, অস্ত্রশস্ত্রাদি, dress, decoration, harness, accoutrements, necessaries, implements, instruments, tools.
সাজন, বেশধারণ, শোভন, to put on as a dress, to deck, adorn or accoutre oneself, to become, befit.
সাজা, দুগ্ধ ঘনীকরণার্থ অম্লীভূত দধি, sour curd, rennet, &c.
সাজান, সুবেশকরণ, পরাণ, শোভান, সাজ লাগান, প্রস্তুত করণ, ভূষাণ, কর্ত্তন, to dress, adorn, deck, caparison, harness, accoutre, prepare, lay out, spread a table, arrange, set in order, garnish, trim, adjust.
সাজা, সাঝাই,—ভাগাভাগি, partnership, coparceny.
সাজী, সাঝী,—ভাগী, অংশী, a partner, copartner.
সাজী, পুষ্পাধার, a flower-basket.
সাড়, চৈতন্য,ব্যথনীয়ত্ব, feeling, sense of feeling, sensibility [to the touch.
সাড়া, শব্দ, উত্তর, চিহ্ন, ঠার, sound, speech, voice, an answer when called, a sign, signal, nod, &c.
সাড়ে, সার্দ্ধ, and a half, (an affix to numerals.)
সাত, সপ্ত, seven.
সাতে, সাত্তি, সাথ, সাথে,—সহিত, সমভিব্যাহারে, মধ্যে, with, together with, in company with, among.
সাত্ত্বিক, সাত্বিক,—সত্ত্বগুণাবলম্বী, সুশীল, সাধু, হিতৈষী, সরল, সত্য, সত্ত্বগুণজ, virtuous, amiable, well-disposed, pious, holy, benevolent, true, sincere, authentic, relating to or proceeding from the quality of goodness or truth.
সাথী, সঙ্গী, সহায়, অনুচর, a companion, comrade, mate, associate, ally, attendant, adherent.
সাদ, সাধ,—আকাঙ্ক্ষা, প্রার্থনা, a wish, desire, prayer.
সাদী, গামী, আরোহী, *affix:* moving, going, riding upon.
সাদৃশ্য, তুল্যতা, ঐক্য, সাম্য, উপমা, দৃষ্টান্ত, উদাহরণ, likeness, similarity, similitude, resemblance, comparison, an instance, example, authority for.

সাদা, সরল, সাধু, শ্বেত, candid, sincere, frank, artless, inoffensive, honest, white, blank, plain.

সাধক, নিষ্পাদক, ভক্ত, উপাসক, effecting, &c. devout; a worshipper, a devotee.

সাধন, নিষ্পাদন, নির্বাহন, ঘটান, প্রতিপাদন, সাভ্যস্ত করণ, অভীষ্টসিদ্ধ হওন, অভ্যাস করণ, যাচন, পরমার্থের অনুষ্ঠান, প্রতিযত্ন, প্রয়াস, যদ্দ্বারা হয়, উপায়, অস্ত্রশস্ত্রাদি, হেতার, দ্রব্য, বস্তু, প্রমাণ, দণ্ড দাপন, মৃতসংস্কার, অন্ত্যেষ্টিক্রিয়া, to effect, effectuate, accomplish, procure, bring about, perform, prove, establish, prevail upon, obtain one's wishes, to exercise oneself in a thing, to solicit; exercise, especially devotional exercise, effort, labour to accomplish an object, means of doing so, an expedient, contrivance, instrument, instrumental cause, material, matter, substance, proof, authority, logical premises, enforcement of legal sentence, levying of fines, &c, funeral obsequies.

সাধনা, আরাধনা, প্রার্থনা, মানাপনয়নবাক্য, worship, adoration, prayer, humble entreaty, solicitation.

সাধনীয়, নিষ্পাদ্য, সম্ভাবনীয়, accomplishable, practicable, possible.

সাধারণ, সামান্য, তুচ্ছ, অবিভক্ত, দুর্লভ্য, common, ordinary, held in common, undivided, general, joint, scarce.

সাধারণ্য, এক বস্তুতে অনেকের অধিকার, a common right.

সাধিত, নিষ্পন্ন, সিদ্ধ, সম্মতীকৃত, অভ্যস্ত, সুশিক্ষিত, accomplished, effected, made effectual, persuaded, wrought upon, practised, well-versed.

সাধু, সদ্ব্যবহারবন্ত, সজ্জন, সরলান্তঃকরণ, মহাকুলীন, শুদ্ধ, উত্তম, উত্তমর্ণ, pious, holy, pure, righteous, good, honest, well-born, proper, correct, classical; a usurer, money-lender, creditor.

সাধ্য, যত্নদ্বারা নিষ্পাদ্য, সম্ভব, অভিপ্রেত, উপাস্য, ক্ষমতা, কল্প, practicable, possible, accomplishable; the object to be accomplished, &c. the object of worship or supplication, ability, power, option, permission, leave, liberty.

সাধুবৃত্তি, সদ্ব্যবহার, observance of prescribed ordinances, &c. correct conduct. [as far as possible.

সাধ্যক্রমে বা মতে, যথাশক্তি, to the utmost of one's ability,

সাধ্যসাধনা, মানাপনয়ন বাক্য সমূহের প্রয়োগ, নিতান্ত প্রার্থনা, earnest intreaty, urgent supplication.

সাধে২, অপ্রয়োজনে, not urgent or necessary, not pressing.

সাধ্যসিদ্ধি, অভিপ্রেত প্রাপ্তি, অভীষ্ট সাধন, বাঞ্ছিত লাভ, success in a suit, accomplishment of an object.

সাধ্বী, পতিব্রতা, সতী, সুচরিত্রা, *f.* a chaste or virtuous wife, a good or pious woman. [of feeling.

সান, সাড়, চৈতন্য, feeling, sensibility to touch, sense

সানন্দ, আহ্লাদিত, উল্লসিত, joyful, happy, festive, gay.

সানায়ী, মুরলী, বংশী, বেণু, a flute, fife, pipe, whistle.

সানু, পর্ব্বতের সমান স্থান, প্রস্থ, শৈলশৃঙ্গ, flat or table land on a mountain. [ble, favouring.

সানুকূল, প্রসন্ন, উপকারী, প্রতিযোগী, propitious, kind, favoura-

সান্নিপাতিক, সন্নিপাত সম্বন্ধীয় রোগ, consisting in or relating to morbid inflammation of the humours.

সান্ত্বন-1, আশ্বাস, প্রবোধকরা, থামানি, শান্তি, দমন, উপশম, comfort, consolation, condolence, soothing, pacification, reconciliation, quieting, quelling, abatement of disease. [orable, &c.

সান্ত্বনীয়, আশ্বসনীয়, থাম্য, to be comforted or pacified, ex-

সান্নিধ্য, নৈকট্য, সামীপ্য, nearness, vicinity, proximity.

সাপ, সর্প, ভুজঙ্গ, a serpent, a snake. [rupt.

সাপকর্ষ, মন্দ, অপকৃষ্ট, দুঃশীল, দুষ্ট, evil, bad, ill-disposed, cor-

সাপত্ন্য, সপত্নীর ভাব, পতির অন্য স্ত্রী সাহিত্য, রিপু, plurality of wives or the condition of a co-wife, an enemy.

সাপরাধ, দণ্ডযোগ্য, কৃতাপরাধ, দোষী, guilty, in fault; an offender.

সাপুড়্যা, ওঝা, a snake-charmer, snake-catcher.

সাপেক্ষ, পরাধীন, আশান্বিত, আশাসম্বলিত, dependant, expectant, attended with expectation. [tighten.

সাপ্টন, সংগ্রহ করণ, আঁটন, to gather, put together, bind,

সাপ্টা, মিশ্রিত, গড়, mixed, promiscuous; medly, bulk, gross.

সাফল্য, ফলের সাহিত্য, ফলোৎপত্তি, প্রয়োজন সিদ্ধি, অভীষ্টসিদ্ধি, fruitfulness, productiveness, efficacy, success.

সাবকাশ, নিষ্কর্ম্মা, প্রাপ্তবিশ্রাম, বিরাম কাল, idle, unoccupied, at leisure, disengaged, affording leisure; vacation, interval of occupation, spare time.

সাবধান, সমাহিতান্তঃকরণ, মনোযোগী, প্রজ্ঞ, বিবেকী, সতর্ক, attentive, studious, diligent, careful, prudent, intelligent, circumspect, discreet, cautious, wary, vigilant, reserved. [days.

সাবন, ত্রিশ দিবস পরিমাণ কাল, সৌরমাস, a month of 30 solar

সাবনদিন, সূর্য্যোদয় অবধি উদয় পর্য্যন্ত, a full solar day.

সাবিত্রী, গায়ত্রী, the Gávatrí or sacred hymn to the sun.

সাভ্যস্ত, সাব্যস্ত,—স্থিরীকৃত, প্রমাণসিদ্ধ, নির্ণীত, প্রমাণ, নিদর্শন, confirmed, established, settled, proved, evident: a warrant, proof, certain evidence.

সাম, তৃতীয় বেদ, শান্তকরা, the 3d. of the Veds, conciliation.

সামগ, সামবেদ পাঠক, a chanter or reciter of the Sáma Ved.

সামগ্রী, দ্রব্য, বস্তু, অস্ত্রপাত্রাদি, a thing, article, material, ingredient, stuff, utensil, furniture, goods.

সামঞ্জস্য, মেল, বিরোধাভাব, সমন্বয়, সাধারণ্য, অধিকারেতে সমানভাব, অল্পব্যয়ী, সাধু, reconciliation, settlement of differences, agreement, consistency, equality or community of rights; frugal, just, virtuous.

সামন্ত, সীমাস্থ, প্রতিবাসী, নিকটবর্ত্তি দেশের রাজা, প্রজা, bordering, neighbouring; a neighbouring prince, subjects.

সাময়িক, সময়োচিত, কালোপযুক্ত, ক্ষণিক, উক্তকালোপস্থিত, তৎকালীন, যথাকাল, স্বকাল ভাবিয়া, seasonable, opportune, temporary, provisional, punctual, exact to the time, adapted to the time or season, timeserving. [fitness.

সামর্থ্য, বল, ক্ষমতা, ability, power, strength, adequacy,

সামাজিক, সমাজস্থ লোক, সভাসদ্, সভ্য, সভাস্থ, পাংক্তেয়, of or belonging to a society or community, of respectable rank, admissible to society.

সামান্য, সাধারণ, প্রচলিত, উত্তম নয়, অপকৃষ্ট, তুচ্ছ, ক্ষুদ্র, জঘন্য, সামঞ্জস্য, common, held in common, general, usual, ordinary, inferior, low plebeian, trivial, insignificant, vulgar; community of rights.

সামাল, অবধান, বিলীকরা, care, caution, careful arrangement.

সামালন, সঞ্চয়ন, বিলীকরণ, স্ব২ স্থানে রাখন, মনোযোগ করণ, সুস্থ হওন, to collect together, arrange, place in order, stow carefully, attend, be careful, to amend.

সামিল, সম্বলিত, অন্তর্গত, শ্লেষ, সমুদায়, connected with, comprized in, included; a connection, a whole.

সামীপ্য, নৈকট্য, nearness, neighbourhood, contiguity.

সামুদ্র, সামুদ্রিক,—সাগরসম্বন্ধীয়, সমুদ্রোদ্ভব, marine, sea-born.

সামুদ্রক, সামুদ্রিক,—শরীরগতচিহ্নবেত্তা, তৎসম্বন্ধীয়, a chiromancer; relating to palmistry.

সাম্লন-আন, নিবারণ, প্রতীকার করণ, সহকারিতা করণ, to withstand, ward off, retrieve, defend, assist.

সাম্বৎসরিক, প্রতিবৎসর, বার্ষিক, আব্দিক, annual, yearly, relating to a year, occurring yearly.

সাম্প্রদায়িক, সামাজিক, সম্প্রদায়ের এক, সভ্য, পাংক্তেয়, পরম্পরাগত, প্রচলিত, of or belonging to a band, sect or society, reputable, respectable, in or admissible to good society, traditional, customary.

সাম্য, ঐক্য, সমভাব, সুসময়, শান্তি, স্থৈর্য্য, উপশম, হ্রাস, ন্যূনতা, equality, similarity, likeness, sameness, evenness, equilibrium, serenity, calmness, alleviation, moderation, moderating, diminution.

সাম্রাজ্য, রাজত্ব, অধিকার, প্রভুত্ব, empire, sway, rule, sovereign dominion.

[ment.

সায়, সম্মতি, স্বীকার, assent, acquiescence, acknowledge-

সায়ং, সায়ঙ্কাল, সায়াহ্ন,—সন্ধ্যাকাল, দিনাবসান, evening, eventide, close of day.

সায়ক, বাণ, তীর, a dart, an arrow.

[evening.

সায়ঙ্কালীন, সন্ধ্যাকালীন, belonging to or in the evening,

সার, স্থিরাংশ, উত্তমাংশ, শ্রেষ্ঠ ভাগ, মর্ম্ম, কাষ্ঠাদির মাঝ, মজ্জা, রস, শর, শক্তভাব, তেজ, বল, বিক্রম, অতিসার, জ্ঞাতসার, ফল, গুণ, নৈপুণ্য, essence, substance, the best, essential or vital part, heart, pith, marrow, sap, cream, curds, solidity, strength, vigour, prowess, valour, manure, a dysentery, the object of knowledge, &c. use, worth, cleverness, skill.

সারক, ভেদজনক দ্রব্য, cathartic, laxative, purgative; a purge.
সারকুড়, গোবরকুণ্ড, ওঁচলা, a heap of manure. a dung-hill.
সারথি, স্যন্দনারোহ, রথী, a car-warrior, charioteer, coachman.
সারণ, সুস্থ হওন, শুধরণ, স্থুল বা শক্ত হওন, শুধরাণ, শুদ্ধ করণ, নিষ্পাদন, দমন, পরাস্ত করণ, মারণ; নষ্ট করণ, পরিষ্কার করণ, ঝাড়ন, শাসন, দণ্ড করণ, *v. n.* to amend, get well, recover, reform, be repaired, to grow fat, acquire substance, to grow, become firm; *v. a.* to mend, repair, refit, amend, improve, correct, remedy, rectify, finish, accomplish, to humble, overthrow, defeat, despatch, kill, exterminate, to clean, winnow, reclaim, retrieve, to punish, reform.
সারমাটী, গোময়যুক্ত মৃত্তিকা, ওঁচলা, manure, a dung-hill.
সারল্য, ঋজুভাব, অবক্রতা, অন্তঃকরণের শুদ্ধতা, straightness, uprightness, honesty, integrity, sincerity.
সারসংগ্রহ, সমুদ্ধার, একত্রীকৃত উত্তমাংশ, a compilation, collection.
সারসনী, পক্ষী বিশেষ, *m. f.* the Siberian or Indian crane.
সারহীন, অসার, অশক্ত, নির্গুণ, অনর্থ, অকর্ম্ম, অকার্য্য, অলীক, unsubstantial, worthless, useless, superficial.
সারা, শুদ্ধকরা, হত্যা, সমুদায়, improvement, slaughter, &c. all, the whole, entire. [mended.
সারাণ, শুধরাণ, শুদ্ধীকৃত, to repair or cause to repair, &c.
সারাৎসার, অত্যুত্তমাংশ, শুদ্ধসার, সর্ব্বশ্রেষ্ঠ, essence, quintescence; most excellent, essential.
সারাল, সারযুক্ত, শক্ত, মজ্জাল, উর্ব্বরা, substantial, vital, solid, firm, close, pithy, vigorous, fertile.
সারার্থ, স্থিরাংশ, শক্তা, মজ্জা, বিশেষ অভিপ্রায়, substance, pith, proper meaning, chief intention.
সারি, শ্রেণী, পংক্তি, a line, row, rank, tier, range. column.
সারিন্দা, বাদ্যযন্ত্র বিশেষ, a sort of lute or guitar. [the Mina.
সারী, সারিকা,—পক্ষিণী বিশেষ, ময়না, *f.* a species of parrot,
সারূপ্য, তুল্যাকৃতি, অনন্যতা, ঐক্য, perfect resemblance, identity.
সারোদ্ধার, সংক্ষেপ গ্রন্থ, সংগ্রহ, উত্তমাংশ, মর্ম্ম, অভিপ্রায়, নিশ্চয়, স্থির, a compilation in which is compressed the substance of a work, substance, drift, whole matter; peremptory, positive.

সার্থক, অর্থযুক্ত, সপ্রয়োজন, মর্ম্মগ, সফল, হিতজনক, having a meaning, significant, to the purpose, effectual, profitable, useful. [significancy.

সার্থক্য, প্রয়োজন, সফলতা, অভিপ্রেত, usefulness, effectiveness,

সার্দ্ধ, দেড়, and a half; (an affix to numbers.)

সার্দ্র, ভিজা, তিমিত, wet, wetted, moist, damp.

সার্ব্বকালিক, সর্ব্বকালোপযুক্ত, চিরস্থায়ী, চিরকালিক, of or belonging to all times, suited to all seasons, permanent, perennial. [versal.

সার্ব্বত্রিক, সর্ব্বস্থানের, সর্ব্বময়, of or suited to every place, uni-

সার্ব্বভৌম, চক্রবর্ত্তি রাজা, সমুদায় পৃথিবী সম্বন্ধীয়, a universal monarch; of or relating to the whole earth.

সালগ্রাম, যে চক্রযুক্ত প্রস্তর বিষ্ণুর আধার বলিয়া মানে, the Sálgrám, a sacred stone worshipped as a representation of Vishnu, &c. [gods and sages.

সালোক্য, দেব ঋষ্যাদির সহবাস, a state of felicity among the

সাশ্রয়, সুমূল্যতা, বাহুল্য, cheapness, a low-price, plenty.

সাশ্রা, সুলভ, শস্তা, সুমূল্য, cheap, plentiful, low-priced.

সাস্র, সকোণ, কোণুয়া, angular, having an angle.

সাহঙ্কার, গর্ব্বান্বিত, দাম্ভিক, আত্মশ্লাঘী, proud, imperious, haughty, scornful, boasting, vain-glorious.

সাহচর্য্য, সাহিত্য, সঙ্গ, বন্ধুতা, সহকারিতা, company, society, association, fellowship, companionship, cooperation, attendance.

সাহস, বীর্য্য, বিক্রম, দুঃসাধ্য কর্ম্মে প্রবৃত্তি, দাম্ভিকতা, দৌরাত্ম্য, ক্রূরতা, বলাৎকার, courage, valour, resolution, daring, heroism, rashness, temerity, impudence, boasting, oppression, aggression, violence, rapine, cruelty, rape, ravishment. [rash.

সাহসশালী, বিক্রমী, নির্ভয়, bold, daring, courageous, valorous,

সাহসিক, সাহসী.—বিক্রমযুক্ত, তেজস্বী, নির্ভয়, দুরন্ত, প্রবল, ঢেঁটা, গরিমাযুক্ত, bold, resolute, gallant, spirited, courageous, undaunted, intrepid, rash, audacious, violent, insolent, imperious, boasting, &c.

সাহায্য, সহায়তা, সহকারিতা, সন্ধি, help, assistance, co-operation, aid, alliance, confederacy.

সাহিত্য, সঙ্গ, সংসর্গ, মেল, প্রণয়, society, companionship, association, connexion, friendship, intimacy.

সাহুকার, ধনাঢ্য, অঋণী, rich, opulent, independent, solvent.

সিউনী, সেচনী, a basket or other baling vessel.

সিংহ, মৃগেন্দ্র, পশুপতি, পঞ্চম রাশি, শ্রেষ্ঠ, a lion, the sign Leo; *in compos:* eminent, chief.

সিংহদ্বার, যে দ্বারে সিংহের আকার থাকে, a great gate, pillared entrance, portal.

সিংহনাদ, রণকালীন যোদ্ধাকৃত শব্দ, a war-shout, war-cry, vociferous onset.

সিংহাসন, সিংহাকারযুক্ত আসন বিশেষ, রাজাসন, a seat or throne supported by sculptured lions.

সিংহাসনস্থ, ভদ্রাসনস্থিত, রাজ্যাভিষিক্ত, seated on a throne, enthroned, reigning.

সিঁধ, সুরঙ্গ, a hole or breach made by house-breakers, a mine.

সিঁধকাটী, সিঁধালের সিঁধ কাটিবার অস্ত্র, a house-breaker's crow.

সিঁধাল, চোর, সুরঙ্গকারী, a house-breaker, a thief, a miner.

সিকতা, বালুকা, বালী, বালীময় ভূমি, অশ্মরী, sand, a sandy soil, the stone or gravel.

সিজন, সেকন, ভাপন, to boil, cook, to reek, smoke, steam.

সিজান, পাক করণ, ভিজান, স্বিন্ন করণ, ভাপোত্থাপন, to boil, cause to boil, seethe, steep, infuse, to warm, cause to throw up steam.

সিত, শুক্ল, শুভ্র, গৌর, white, bright, light-coloured.

সিদ্ধ, পক্ব, ক্বথিত, স্বিন্ন, প্রস্তুত, সম্পন্ন, নিষ্পন্ন, কৃতকার্য্য, সম্পূর্ণ, পূর্ণ, সাব্যস্ত, সত্য, অব্যর্থ, বিখ্যাত, দেবযোনি, cooked, boiled, sodden, infused, steeped, prepared, made ready, effected, accomplished, concluded, completed, decided, fulfilled, perfect, proved, established, real, right, infallible, celebrated, famous; a class of demigods.

সিদ্ধপুরুষ, যোগবলে অলৌকিক ক্ষমতা বিশিষ্ট, মহাপুরুষ, one who by devout abstraction and severe mortification has acquired spiritual perfection and superhuman powers, &c.

সিদ্ধসাধ্য, সিদ্ধার্থ,—অভীষ্টসিদ্ধ, কৃতার্থ, কৃতকার্য্য, having accomplished his object, successful.

সিদ্ধান্ত, রাদ্ধান্ত, বিতর্ক, নিষ্পত্তি, মীমাংসা দর্শন, a demonstration, a conclusive argument, established truth, logical induction, decision, the Mímángsá philosophy.

সিদ্ধান্তী, মীমাংসাদর্শনবেত্তা, a follower of the Mímángsá phi-[losophy.

সিদ্ধি, সম্পত্তি, ফলোদয়, বাঞ্ছিত প্রাপ্তি, নিষ্পত্তি, নির্ণয়, সিদ্ধান্ত, যোগবল, মাদক পর্ণ বিশেষ, accomplishment, completion, effect, fulfilment, success, decision, sentence, award. accuracy, logical proof, ascetic perfection, acquirement of supernatural powers, a leaf of a narcotic quality.

সিধা, ঋজু, সরল, শুদ্ধান্তঃকরণ, straight, even, upright, honest, [sincere.

সিন্দূর, রক্তবর্ণ চূর্ণ বিশেষ, নাগজ, vermillion, red-lead, minium.

সিন্ধু, সমুদ্র, নদ বিশেষ, তন্নিকট দেশ, the ocean, the river Indus, the country on its banks.

সিয়ন, সিঁয়ন, -আন,—বস্ত্রাদি সীবন, to sew, stitch, mend, vamp.

সিষাধয়িষা, সাধিবার ইচ্ছা, desire to accomplish an object.

সিসৃক্ষা, সৃজনের ইচ্ছা, a desire to create or produce.

সীয়ান, সীবন, to sew, to stitch, work as a taylor.

সীঁথি, সীমন্ত,—কেশের বিভাগকরা, হালকৃত রেখা, the parting of the hair on the forehead, a plough-furrow.

সীমন্তোন্নয়ন, গর্ভবতীর সংস্কার বিশেষ, a ceremonial parting of the hair, &c. at certain periods of pregnancy.

সীমন্তিনী, স্ত্রীলোক, a woman, *q. d.* one who parts the hair.

সীমা, সীমানা,—অন্ত, ধার, অবধি, পর্য্যন্ত, অঞ্চল, an end, margin, limit boundary, extent, landmark, barrier, confines, border, frontier.

সীবন, সূচিকর্ম্ম, sewing, taylor's work; to sew, to stitch.

সীসক, সীসা,—ধাতু বিশেষ, lead.

সু, ভাল, অনায়াস, অতিশয়, অতি, সহজ, উত্তম, সুন্দর, প্রিয়, *pref*: well, easily, exceedingly, quite, very, most; easy, good, excellent, agreeable, fine, handsome.

সুঁতি, চড় ও নদীকূল উভয়ের অন্তরগামি মন্দস্রোত, the space between a river's bank and a shoal.

সুকণ্ঠ, উত্তমস্বরবিশিষ্ট, সুগায়ক, having a sweet voice.

সুকর, অকষ্টে সাধ্য, সুসাধ্য, easy to be done, practicable.

সুকর্ম্মা, সাধু, সংব্যবহারী, নিপুণ, virtuous, good, skilful, active.
সুকাল, নিরীহ সময়, শুভিতা, fine weather, a serene atmosphere.
সুকৃত, অকষ্টে সাধ্য, সুন্দররূপে কৃত, পুণ্যবান্, ধন্য, easily done, well done, pious, fortunate.
সুকৃত, সুকৃতি,—পুণ্য, শ্রেয়ঃ, সৎকর্ম্ম, আনুকূল্য, সৌভাগ্য, virtue, goodness, moral merit, well-doing, a good deed, kindness, friendliness, kind offices, good fortune, auspiciousness.
সুকৃতিপত্র, শপথ লিপি, a written oath or affidavit to the truth of one's testimony. [fortunate.
সুকৃতী, পুণ্যবান্, কুশলী, ভাগ্যবন্ত, virtuous, good, pious, happy,
সুখ, আনন্দ, হর্ষ, নির্বিঘ্নতা, অনায়াস, pleasure, enjoyment, delight, happiness, ease, facility.
সুখড়, ধন্য, হর্ষিত, নির্বিঘ্ন, happy, delighted, pleasant, easy.
সুখদ, আমোদজনক, তৃপ্তিকর, conferring pleasure &c. pleasant, refreshing. [pleasant.
সুখশালী, আমোদযুক্ত, প্রিয়, happy, delightful, agreeable,
সুখসাগর, আনন্দার্ণব, হর্ষ, an ocean of pleasure, great delight.
সুখাত্মক, আনন্দস্বরূপ, সদানন্দ, identified with pleasure, essentially happy. [ing pleasure.
সুখাবহ, সুখের কারণ, আমোদজনক, affording enjoyment, bring-
সুখী, ধনী, কল্যাণী, কুশলী, happy, at ease, full of enjoyment.
সুখ্যাত, সুখ্যাত্যাপন্ন,—যশস্বী, প্রসিদ্ধ, in repute, celebrated, famed, well-spoken of, &c.
সুখ্যাতি, যশঃ, কীর্ত্তি, fame, celebrity, renown, reputation.
সুগঠন, সুন্দর আকৃতি, সুডৌল, সুঢপ, beauty of person or structure ; well-shaped, well-formed, &c.
সুগতিক, সুখ, উত্তম দশা, সুডৌল, a happy state or condition, having a good gait. [perfume.
সুগন্ধ, উত্তম বাস, সুরভি, a sweet scent, odour, fragrance,
সুগম, সুগম্য,—গন্তব্য, চলনার্হ, সুপথ, অকঠিন, সহজ, স্পষ্ট, accessible, passable, good as a road, practicable, easy, easy of comprehension.
সুগোচ, অনায়াসসিদ্ধি, সাঙ্গ, easy accomplishment, a finis.
সুগোচর, অতিস্পষ্ট, ব্যক্ত, প্রত্যক্ষ, বিদিত, very clear, obvious, evident, well-known.

সুগ্রীব, সুন্দর গলা বিশিষ্ট, having a fine or handsome neck.

সুঘটন, সুযোগ, সৌভাগ্য, an auspicious circumstance, good luck.

সুচির, বহুকাল, অতিশয় বিলম্ব, very long, a long while, very [late.

সুচেতাঃ, সুশীল, সুক্ষ্মবুদ্ধি, জাগ্রৎ, সচকিত, সতর্ক, well-disposed, of quick perception, vigilant, wary, cautious.

সুজন, সুশীল, হিতৈষী, শিষ্ট, ভদ্র, সৎলোক, good-natured, kind, benevolent, civil, polite, virtuous, good.

সুজন্মা, ঔরসজাত, সাধু লোক, lawfully begotten, well-born, virtuous, genteel, creditable, respectable.

সুজি, গোধূম চূর্ণ, আটা, coarse flour.

সুজীর্ণ, যাতযাম, পুরাতন, চিরন্তন, প্রাপ্তপাক, quite worn out, thread-bare, very old, well-digested.

সুড়ঙ্গ, সুরুঙ্গা, আকর, সিঁধ, a hole in the earth, a mine, breach, a hole in a wall, &c. made by house-breakers.

সুঠৌম, সুঢপ,—সুন্দরাকৃতি, সুদৃশ্য, well-shaped, well-formed, elegant, handsome.

সুড়ী, অপ্রশস্ত পথ, সরু, a narrow path; narrow, little, [shallow.

সুত, সুতা,—পুত্রপুত্রী, আত্মজ, *m. & f.* a son and daughter.

সুতরাং, অবশ্যই, প্রত্যক্ষে, নিতান্ত, অতএব, certainly, undoubtedly, surely, indeed, evidently, consequently, necessarily, of course.

সুতল, পোট, গোড়, নরক বিশেষ, a foundation, basement, base, [the 6th hell.

সুতান, সুস্বর, উত্তমগান, সুশ্রাব্য, melody, harmony; harmonious, &c.

সুতার, স্বাদুল, রসাল, মিষ্ট, well-flavoured, savoury, palatable, [nice.

সুদিন, উত্তম সময়, শুভকাল, a fine or auspicious day.

সুদূর, বহুব্যবধান দেশ, অতিদূর, remote, very distant, very far.

সুদ্ধ, সমেত, মাত্র, with, together with; only, merely.

সুধর্ম্মা, গৃহস্থধর্ম্মপালক, one who fulfils his family duties.

সুধা, অমৃত, ambrosia, nectar, water of immortality.

সুধাকর, সুধাংশু,—চন্দ্র, নিশাপতি, the moon.

সুধান, প্রশ্ন করণ, জিজ্ঞাসন, পুছন, to ask, enquire, question.

সুধী, সুধীর,—বুদ্ধিমান্, বিচক্ষণ, পণ্ডিত, highly learned, wise, clever, acute, sensible; a Pandit.

সুধু, কেবল, মাত্র, only, merely, entirely, purely.

সুনৃত, সত্য এবং প্রিয়বাক্য, an agreeable truth.

সুন্দর-রী, সুরূপ, চারু, কান্ত, শোভন, উত্তম, বিলক্ষণ, *m. f.* handsome, beautiful, fair, fine, good, excellent.

সুপথ, সুন্দর বর্ত্ম, সচ্চরিত্র, a good road, a virtuous course.

সুপথ্য, অপীড়াকর আহারাদি, wholesome, (diet or medicine.)

সুপাত্র, সৎ লোক, কর্ম্মোপযুক্ত, ক্ষমতাবান্, বিচক্ষণ, a good man, a suitable person ; duly qualified, able, clever.

সুপারী, গুবাক, the areca or betel-nut.

সুপ্ত, নিদ্রিত, ঘুমান, শয়িত, asleep, laid to sleep, sleeping.

সুপ্তি, নিদ্রা, ঘুম, নিদ্রাকর্ষণ, sleep, sleeping, drowsiness.

সুপ্রকাশ, মেঘরহিত, সুসময়, শুভিতা, clear or fair as weather; a bright day. [by women.

সুবচনী, স্ত্রীলোকের সেবিতা দেবী বিশেষ, a goddess worshipped

সুবর্ণ, উত্তম বর্ণ, স্বর্ণ, সোণা, কনক, উত্তম জাতি, স্বর্ণমুদ্রা, a fine colour, gold, a respectable class in society, a gold mohur. [fair weather.

সুবিধ, উত্তম প্রকার, সহজ, শুভিতা, of a good kind, good, easy;

সুবুদ্ধি, মতি, মতিমান্, বুদ্ধিমান্, প্রজ্ঞ, শিষ্ট, a good understanding; wise, intelligent, sensible, docile.

সুবেশ, সুরূপ, সুন্দর, সুশ্রী, handsome, elegantly dressed.

সুবোধ, নিশ্চয়জ্ঞান, বিজ্ঞতা, পণ্ডিত, জ্ঞানবান্, a correct idea, sound judgment, accurate knowledge, intelligence; sensible, intelligent, well-informed.

সুব্রত, উত্তম নিয়ম, নিয়মপালক, an excellent observance; strictly observant of vows, &c.

সুভগ, শুভ, প্রিয়, fortunate, auspicious, liked, beloved.

সুভগা, সৌভাগ্যবতী, পতির প্রেয়সী, *f.* fortunate ; a beloved or favourite wife. [posed to dearth.)

সুভিক্ষ, অনাকাল, শস্যাদির বাহুল্য, abundance, plenty, (op-

সুভোক্তা, সুভোগী,—উত্তমাহারী, উদরসর্ব্বস্ব, পেটুক, dainty or nice in eating ; an epicure.

সুমতি, সুমনাঃ,—সৎকর্ম্মেতে প্রবৃত্তি, উত্তম বুদ্ধি, সরলান্তঃকরণ, সুশীল, excellence of disposition, kindness, intelligence ; well-disposed, kind. [tleman.

সুমানুষ, সজ্জন, শিষ্ট লোক, a good or respectable man, a gen-

সুমুখ, উত্তমাস্য, সুন্দর, a fine face, good features ; handsome.

সুমেধাঃ, বুদ্ধিমন্ত, প্রাজ্ঞ, sensible, clever, of good parts or capacity. [a close fit, &c.

সুমেল, অবয়বের সমতা, সমভাব, সংলাগ, symmetry, proportion,

সুযোগ, সুঘটন, উত্তম সময়, যোত্র, নির্বাহ, a favourable opportunity, suitable time, good luck, means, supply.

সুর, দেবতা, স্বর, a god, a deity, a voice, a tune.

সুরঙ্গ, সুরঙ্গা—সিঁধ, গর্ত্ত, a hole in a wall, &c. made by housebreakers, an excavation, mine, breach.

সুরপুরী, সুরালয়,—ইন্দ্রের ধাম, স্বর্গ, সুমেরু পর্বত, the capital of Indra or heaven of the gods, mount Meru.

সুরভি, সুগন্ধ, বসন্ত, a perfume, odour, fragance, the spring.

সুরর্ষি, নারদাদি ঋষি, a divine sage as Nárada.

সুরলোক, স্বর্গ, ইন্দ্রধাম, the heaven of Indra & the immortals.

সুরা, মদ্য, অমৃত, spirituous liquor, nectar [king.

সুরাজক, উত্তম রাজার প্রভুত, well-governed, ruled by a good

সুরাপ-য়ী, মদ্যপ, মাতাল, drinking spirits, &c. a tipler, a sot.

সুরারি, অসুর, দৈত্য, an *Asur* or enemy of the gods, a Titan.

সুরূপ, উত্তমাকৃতি, সুন্দর, a fine form, beauty; handsome, beautiful, well-formed.

সুরেন্দ্র, ইন্দ্র, সুরপতি, Indra, the sovereign of the gods.

সুলভ, সুলভ্য,—সুসাধ্য, অকষ্টে প্রাপ্য, সুমূল্য, easy, feasible, easily obtainable, of easy acquisition, cheap.

সুশীল, সত্ত্বগুণ, সচ্চরিত্র, সংপ্রকৃতি, সুস্বভাব, উত্তম, good-nature, goodness or amiableness of disposition; well-disposed, amiable. [adept.

সুশৃঙ্খল, সানুক্রম, ক্রমাগত, নিপুণ, দক্ষ, orderly, regular, expert,

সুশ্রাব্য, শ্রবণে সুখজনক, কর্ণগোচর, agreeable to the ear, melodious, harmonious, sweet, audible.

সুশ্রী, সৌন্দর্য্যবন্ত, কান্ত, personable, handsome, beautiful.

সুষুপ্ত, ঘোরনিদ্রান্বিত, fast or sound asleep, in a dead sleep.

সুষুপ্তি, ঘোরনিদ্রা, a sound or deep sleep.

সুসজ্জ, উত্তম সজ্জাযুক্ত, সন্নদ্ধ, প্রস্তুত, well-armed, accoutred, caparisoned, prepared, in readiness, quite ready.

সুসময়, উত্তম ক্ষণ, উপযুক্ত কাল, উন্নতির কাল, a suitable or auspicious season, fit opportunity, prosperity, ease.

সুসহ, সুসহ্য,—লঘুভার, অকষ্টে সহনীয়, easy to be borne, tolerable.

সুসাধ্য, অকষ্টে সাধ্য, হওনযোগ্য, সম্ভব, সহজ, easily accomplished, quite practicable, quite possible, easy.

সসার, সম্পত্তি, যোজ, নির্বাহ, উপায়, প্রতুল, ঋণদান, উপকার, কর্ম্মচালা, substance, wealth, competency, ability to pay, an adequate provision for any undertaking, necessary means, supply, sufficiency, an accommodation, help, a loan, management.

সুস্থ, সুখী, নির্ব্বিঘ্ন, ধনবান্, প্রাপ্তকল্যাণ, আরোগ্য, well-circumstanced, comfortable, faring or living well, happy, at ease, healthy, well.

সুস্থির, স্থাবর, অটল, ধীর, চাঞ্চল্যরহিত, fixed, stable, firm, steady, calm, unmoved. [intelligible.

সুস্পষ্ট, অভিব্যক্ত, নিশ্চয়, সুবোধ্য, clear, very evident, distinct,

সুহৃদ্, মিত্র, বন্ধু, সখা, সহায়, a friend, associate, ally.

সুহৃদয়, শুদ্ধান্তঃকরণ, অনুকূল, উপকারক, kind-hearted, affectionate, friendly, favourable.

সুহৃদ্ভেদ, বিরোধ, অপ্রীতি, প্রীতিভঙ্গ, interruption of friendship, the sowing of dissension among friends.

সূক্ষ্ম, অল্প, তনু, সরু, অস্থূল, ক্ষীণ, পাতল, লঘু, প্রকৃত, ঠিক, প্রখর, ইন্দ্রিয়াতীত, little, small, minute, delicate, fine, thin, shrill, neat, exact, accurate, subtile, nice, precise, ingenious, imperceptible.

সূক্ষ্মদর্শী, বিশেষজ্ঞ, প্রখর, প্রাজ্ঞ, of quick perception, sharp-sighted, acute, intelligent. [witty.

সূক্ষ্মধী, প্রাজ্ঞ, বিবেকী, রসিক, shrewd, sharp, keen, ingenious,

সূক্ষ্মবোধ, প্রখরবুদ্ধি, নিশ্চয়জ্ঞান, বিবেক, বিশেষজ্ঞান, penetration, keenness of intellect, an accurate conception, perception of minute differences.

সূচ, সূচি,—সূঁই, বস্ত্রাদি সীবনের লৌহশলা, a needle.

সূচক, জ্ঞাপক, বোধক, চর, কর্ণেজপ, অনুজ্ঞাপক, indicating, pointing out, discovering, boding, portending, indicative of; an informer, a spy, a beginner.

সূচনা, ঠার, বিজ্ঞাপনা, প্রস্তাব, বৃত্তান্ত, রব, an indication, information, communication, mention, report.

সূচন-করণ, জানান, দেখান, প্রকাশন, লক্ষণ দর্শান, to point out, indicate, forebode, portend, forewarn.

সূচাল, সূচালু,—আগাল, সাগ্র, বেধক, pointed, sharp, piercing:
সূচিজীবী, সিঁয়ানিয়া, living by his needle ; a taylor.
সূচীপত্র,সূচিপত্র,—নির্ঘণ্ট,অনুক্রমণিকা,an index,table of contents.
সূত, সারথি, স্যন্দনারোহ, a charioteer.
সূত, সূতা,—সূত্র, তন্ত্র, তন্তু, দড়ী, thread, twine, yarn, a line.
সূতক, সূতকাশৌচ,—জননাশৌচ, কালাশৌচ, ceremonial impurity arising from childbirth or miscarriage.
সূতিকা, নবপ্রসূতা, যে স্ত্রীর প্রসব হইয়াছে, a lying-in woman; confined, delivered, brought to bed.
সূতলী, দড়ী, রজ্জু, শণসূত্র, packthread, twine, a string, cord.
সূত্র, তন্ত্র, তন্তু, দড়ী, পদ, টীকা, অনেকার্থ বোধক সংক্ষিপ্ত গদ্য, বিধান, লক্ষণ, ভূমিকা, অনুষ্ঠান, thread, yarn, twine, a line, a clue, a guide, a sentence, gloss, comment, precept, aphorism, axiom, rules, rudiments, a preamble, commencement. [scite, &c.
সূত্রপাত, স্থল মাপকরা, a marking out, planning, measuring a
সূত্রধর, সূতার,—বাড়ই, ছুতার, a carpenter, a joiner.
সূনু, পুত্র, তনয়, আত্মজ, a son.
সূনৃত, প্রীতিজনক সত্য বাক্য, true and agreeable discourse, an agreeable truth. [soup, broth.
সূপ, অন্নের উপকরণ, যূষ, ঝোল, a sauce, gravy, condiment,
সূপকার-ক, পাচক, রন্ধনকর্ত্তা, a cook.
সূর্প, কুলা, চালনী, a van or basket for winnowing corn.
সূর্য্য, আদিত্য, রবি, দিবাকর, the sun.
সূর্য্যকান্ত, কাচ মণি, a fabulous gem, chrystal. [the sun.
সূর্য্যগ্রহ, আদিত্য, রাহুগ্রস্ত সূর্য্যের অন্তর্ধান, the sun, an eclipse of
সূর্য্যমুখী, পুষ্প বিশেষ, the sun-flower.
সূর্য্যেন্দুসঙ্গম, অমাবস্যা, the day of the new moon. [sun-set.
সূর্য্যোদয়, সূর্য্যাস্ত,—আদিত্যের প্রকাশ এবং অন্তর্ধান, sun-rise and
সৃক, সৃক্কণী,—ওষ্ঠের প্রান্ত, the corners of the mouth.
সৃজন, রচন, জন্মান, উৎপাদন, গঠন, নির্ম্মাণ, to make, create, frame, form. [invented.
সৃষ্ট, উৎপন্ন, গঠিত, নির্ম্মিত, কল্পিত, made, created, formed,
সৃষ্টি, উৎপত্তি, উদ্ভব, গঠনা, কল্পনা, রচনা, জগৎ, সচরাচর, creation, formation, production, fabrication, invention, the world, the universe.

সে, বুদ্ধিস্থিত পদার্থ, তৎ, ঐ, তিনি, that, those, he, she, it.

সেই, অনন্য, তাহাই, that same, that very, the selfsame.

সেঁকটন-আন, ঘৃণার বোধে মুখ নাসিকার বেঁকন, to be distorted or turned up in disgust as the face or nose.

সেঁটন, লুণ্ঠন, to writhe through pain, &c. *see* সাঁটন.

সেঁউতী, সেঁওতী,—সেবতী ফুল, the white rose.

সেঁতান, সেঁতসেঁতা,—দলদলিয়া, জলময়, boggy, swampy, marshy.

সেক, ভিজানি, জলদান, জলপ্রক্ষেপ, তাতানি, a wetting, sprinkling, aspersion, pouring, watering, fomentation.

সেকন, তাতান, স্বিন্ন করণ, সিজন, to bake, apply heat, foment.

সেকরা, স্বর্ণকার, সোণার, a goldsmith, a worker in gold.

সেকপাত্র, সেচনী,—জল তুলিবার পাত্র, a bailing scoop, a vessel for watering fields from a tank.

সেক্তা, সেচনকর্ত্তা, one who foments, waters, bails out, &c.

সেচন, সেঁচন,—ভিজান, আর্দ্রীকরণ, জল তুলিয়া ফেলন, to water, wet, sprinkle, bail out water. [there-

সেখানে, সেথা,—ঐ স্থানে, তত্র, তথা, to or in that place, thither.

সেগুণ, খরপত্র, the teak-tree, teak-wood.

সেতু, আলি, জাঙ্গাল, ভেড়ী, সাঁকো, a walk, ridge, causey, mole, dam, dyke, bridge.

সেতুবন্ধ, তথা, তীর্থ বিশেষ, *id: also* Adam's bridge in Ceylon.

সেথুয়া, সহপথিক, একসঙ্গী, পথদর্শক, a fellow-traveller, a guide.

সেঁধান, সেঁধুয়ান,—প্রবিষ্ট হওন, ঢোকন, ঘুষড়ন, বৈসন, to enter, go or creep into, take root. [dier.

সেনা, অশ্ব পদাতি আদি, সৈন্য, তেলাঙ্গা, an army, troops, a sol-

সেনানী, সেনাপতি,—সৈন্যাধ্যক্ষ, a general, a commander.

সেপ্রকার, ঐরূপ, তেমন, তাদৃশ, of that kind, of that sort, such.

সেবক, উপাসক, দাস, পরিচারক, শিষ্য, serving, worshipping, &c. a servant, an attendant, a disciple.

সেবতী, সেঁউতী, the white rose.

সেবন, পরিচর্য্যা করণ, উপাসনা করণ, ঔষধ খাওন-ান, সিয়ন, to serve, attend or wait upon, worship, adore, to take or administer medicine, to sew, stitch.

সেবা, পরিচর্য্যা, স্ববৃত্তি, উপাসনা, পূজা, শুশ্রূষা, service, servitude, attendance, duty, worship, homage, reverence, respectful attention to.

সেবাতী, পূজারী, পাণ্ডা, the stipendiary priest of a temple.

সেবিত, উপাসিত, পূজিত, পিয়ান, served, attended on, worshipped, administered. [adorable.

সেব্য, সেবাপাত্র, উপাস্য, deserving worship &c, venerable,

সের, খাদ্যাদির পরিমাণ বিশেষ, a measure of weight, *a seer*.

সেরণ, সেরিয়া রাখন,—উপার্জন, সঞ্চয়ন, পুঁজী করণ, to lay or put buy, treasure up, set apart. [kind, such.

সেরূপ, সেমত,—তৎপ্রকার, তাদৃশ, এমন, of that sort, of that

সৈনিক, সেনাসম্বন্ধীয়, সেনারক্ষক, of or relating to an army; a centinel. [troops, soldiers.

সৈন্য, সেনা, বল, একত্রিত পদাতি হস্তী রথাদি, an army, forces,

সৈন্ধব, পর্বতীয় লবণ, পাঙ্গা, rock-salt, fossil-salt.

সৈরিন্ধ্রী, যে স্ত্রী পরের গৃহে স্ববশে থাকিয়া শিল্পকর্ম্ম করে, an independent female artist working in another's house.

সোঁটা, গদা, যষ্টি, a bludgeon, truncheon, mace, staff.

সোঁধান, বাসান, গন্ধান, to scent, to perfume, to smell.

সোঁপড়, সমূলে, সমান, with the roots; smooth, level.

সোঁপন, গছান, সমর্পণ, ভারণ, ছাড়ন, to deliver in charge, entrust, commit, refer to, submit, surrender.

সোজা, সরল, খাড়া, সমান, সহজ, স্পষ্ট, অবক্র, অকুটিল, straight, erect, upright, even, flat, smooth, level, plain, simple, easy, obvious, sincere, candid, inoffensive, artless. [ward,

সোজাসোজি, স্পষ্টে, নিষ্কপটে, plainly, sincerely, straight for-

সোণা, স্বর্ণ, কনক, হিরণ্য, gold. [with gold.

সোণালা, সোণালী,—মলম্বাকরা, মণ্ডনকরা, a gilding, overlaying

সোন্না, স্বর্ণকারের চিম্‌টা, a goldsmith's nippers, small tweezers.

সোতা, সোঁতা,—খাল, নালা, জলপ্রবাহ, a creek, inlet, rivulet, channel, stream, torrent.

সোদর-1, সোদর্য্য-1,—সহোদর-1, একমাতৃজাত, ভ্রাতৃভগিনী, a full brother or sister. [surname.

সোপাধি, সম্পর্ক, উপাধিযুক্ত, relationship, affinity; having a

সোপান, পইঠা, সিঁড়ী, নিঃশ্রেণি, প্রস্তাব, অনুষ্ঠান, a ladder, flight of steps, staircase, stairs, mention, introduction, commencement.

সোম, চন্দ্র, দ্বিতীয় গ্রহ, the moon; সোমবার, দ্বিতীয়বার, monday.

সোমন্ত, বলবান্, স্থূল, যুবন, young, lusty, adult; a youth, a lad.
সোমলতা, যজ্ঞিয় লতা বিশেষ, চন্দ্রবল্লরী, the moon-plant.
সোমাজি, ছুঁচ, a bamboo skewer or thatching needle.
সোসর, সোঁপড়, সমান, smooth, level, flat, even.
সোসরী, মই, বাঁশই, a sort of ladder-shaped harrow.
সোহাগ, বাৎসল্য, স্নেহপ্রকাশ, affection, fondness, caresses.
সোহাগা, স্বাগা, টঙ্ক, উপধাতু বিশেষ, borax.
সোহাগিনী, সুভগা, a beloved wife or woman. [perfume.
সৌগন্ধ্য, সুবাস, সুরভি, a sweet scent, fragrance, odour,
সৌচিক, সৌচিকী,—সূচিজীবী, *m.* a taylor, *f.* a seamstress.
সৌজন্য, সুজনতা, শিষ্টাচার, ভদ্রতা, civility, politeness, urbanity, complaisance, good-nature.
সৌদামিনী, বিদ্যুৎ, তড়িৎ, lightening. [ness.
সৌন্দর্য্য, লাবণ্য, রূপবত্তা, beauty, loveliness, elegance, neat-
সৌবর্ণ, স্বর্ণময়, হিরণ্যরচিত, golden, made of gold.
সৌবিদ, শণ্ড, ষণ্ড, অন্তঃপুররক্ষক, a eunuch, an attendant or guard on the women's apartments.
সৌভাগিনেয়, সুভগার গর্ভজাত, the son of a beloved wife.
সৌভাগ্য, শুভাদৃষ্ট, মাঙ্গল্য, good fortune, luck, auspiciousness.
সৌম্য, চান্দ্র, সুন্দর, মনোজ্ঞ, উত্তম, কোমল, ধীর, উত্তর দিক্, বুধ গ্রহ, lunar, handsome, pleasing, good, excellent, mild, gentle, placid; the north, Buddha or Mercury.
সৌর, সূর্য্যসম্বন্ধীয়, সূর্য্যের উপাসক, of or belonging to the sun, solar; a worshipper of the sun.
সৌরমাস, সূর্য্যের এক রাশিভোগকাল, a solar month.
সৌরভ্য, সুগন্ধ, সুবাস, সৌন্দর্য্য, সুখ্যাতি, fragrance, odour, perfume, an essence, beauty, fame, reputation.
সৌর্য্য, পাণ্ডিত্য, ব্যুৎপত্তি, learning, literary eminence.
সৌষ্ঠব, উৎকর্ষ, সৌন্দর্য্য, দ্রুতগতি, আতিশয্য, প্রতুল, excellence, comeliness, lightness, fleetness, excess, abundance, a competency.
সৌহার্দ্দ, প্রণয়, বন্ধুতা, friendship, amity, intimacy.
স্কন্ধ, কাঁধ, ভুজশিরঃ, প্রকাণ্ড, প্রকরণ, খণ্ড, the shoulder, the trunk of a tree, a large branch, a section, chapter. [speech.
স্খলদ্বাক্য, উচ্চারণে ত্রুটি, a mistake in pronunciation or

স্খলন, পিছলন, উচোট খাওন, পতন, ছাড়িয়া পড়ন, ভুলন, বিভ্রম, ভ্রষ্ট হওন, to slip, trip, stumble, fall, mistake, err, blunder, skip letters or words in reading or utterance, to sin or fall from virtue.

স্খলিত, বিচলিত, চ্যুত, পতিত, ভ্রমযুক্ত, slipped, stumbled, fallen, mistaken, &c.

স্তন, কুচ, মাই, বাঁট, a woman's breast, an animal's udder, dug, teat.

স্তনপান, স্তন্যপান,—দুগ্ধপানকরা, চোষণ, a sucking, suckling, being at the breast.

স্তনবৃন্ত, স্তনাগ্র,—চুচুক, কুচাগ্র, the nipple.

স্তন্য, স্তননিসৃত, দুগ্ধ, milk.

স্তন্যপায়ী, স্তন্যভুক্,—দুগ্ধপায়ী, দুগ্ধপোষ্য, sucking, at the breast; a suckling.

স্তব-পাঠ, স্তুতি, নুতি, গুণকথা, সঙ্কীর্ত্তন, সাধনা, praise, eulogy, panegyric, applause, flattery, a celebrating, hymning, solicitation.

স্তবক, ফুলের গোছা, গুচ্ছ, গুণগায়ক, a cluster of blossoms, a nosegay, bunch of flowers, a flatterer.

স্তবন, সঙ্কীর্ত্তন, গুণকথন, সাধন, to praise, hymn, extol, eulogise, flatter, entreat, solicit.

স্তব্ধ, স্তম্ভিত,—দৃঢ়ীভূত, জড়ীভূত, স্পন্দরহিত, মূর্চ্ছাপন্ন, অজ্ঞান, অবাক্, নিবৃত্ত, স্থগিত, স্থিরীকৃত, মুগ্ধ, stiff, hardened, rigid, benumbed, torpid, dull, motionless, insensible, astonished, stupid, stupified, amazed, silent, stopped, fixed, stupified by enchantment, petrified.

স্তম্ব, ধান্য তৃণাদির আটি, গোছা, থাম, গুচ্ছ, a sheaf, tuft, bunch, clump, a stake, post, pillar, a shrub.

স্তম্ভ, থাম, গৃহাদির খুঁটী, a post, pile, stake, pillar, column.

স্তম্ভ-ন, স্থাপন, স্পন্দ রহিত করণ, জড়ীভাব, অজ্ঞানতা, মোহ, to fix, set up, stupify, &c. rigidity, torpor, stupidity, insensibility or suppression of the faculties, the effect of enchantment.

স্তম্ভাকার, স্তম্ভাকৃতি,—থামবৎ, cylindrical, columnar, pillar-like.

স্তাবক, স্তুতিকারক, গুণগায়ক, কাছাধরা, চরণসেবক, praising, &c. thankful; a eulogist, panegyrist, flatterer, parasite, sycophant.

স্তিমিত, আর্দ্র, ক্লিন্ন, ভিজা, তুষ্ণীক, clammy, moist, wet, taciturn, silent.

স্তুত, প্রশংসিত, সঙ্কীর্ত্তিত, praised, eulogized, extolled, flattered, hymned.

স্তুতি, গুণপাঠ, স্তব, সঙ্কীর্ত্তন, প্রশংসা, স্তবপূর্ব্বক যাচ্ঞা, praise, eulogy, flattery, applause, solicitation.

স্তুতিপাঠক, স্তবকর্ত্তা, বন্দী, a flatterer, eulogist, panegyrist.

স্তূপ, সঞ্চয়, রাশি, সমূহ, a heap, pile, rick, mound, quantity.

স্তেন, চোর, দস্যু, তস্কর, চৌর্য্য, a thief, robber, theft.

স্তেয়, স্তৈন্য,—চৌর্য্য, অপহরণ, লুট, theft, robbery, plunder, booty.

স্তোক, অল্প, সূক্ষ্ম, বিন্দু, ব্যাজ, ছলনা, নিষেধ, small, little, a drop of water, an excuse, plea, palliation, an imposition, deception, prevention.

স্তোকে২, অল্পে২, বিন্দু২, ক্রমে২, ধীরে, মন্দে২, কদাচিৎ, by little and little, drop by drop, gradually, insensibly, slowly, gently, softly, seldom.

স্তোতা, স্তোতৃ,—স্তাবক, গুণগায়ক, a flatterer, panegyrist, eulogist.

স্তোত্র, স্তুতিকরা, স্তব, গুণগান, praise, eulogy, flattery, a hymn.

স্তোভ, মিথ্যাপ্রবোধ, কপটবাক্য, false encouragement, deceptive promises.

স্ত্রী, নারী, অবলা, বধু, মেনী, a female, a woman, a wife, a she-animal.

স্ত্রীআচার, বিবাহকালীন স্ত্রীলোকের ব্যবহার, a ludicrous practice of women before a man's marriage.

স্ত্রীগ্রহণ, বিবাহ করণ, সংসার করণ, to take a wife, to marry.

স্ত্রীচিহ্ন, স্ত্র্যংশ,—ভগ, যোনি, pudendum muliebre.

স্ত্রীজিত, স্ত্রীবশ,—ভার্য্যাধীন, পত্নীরত, ruled by a wife, uxorious.

স্ত্রীত্ব, যোষিদ্ভাব, নারীত্ব, womanhood, femality, feminality.

স্ত্রীধন, যে ধনে পতির নিরপেক্ষে স্ত্রীর অধিকার আছে, a woman's own property, trinkets, &c.

স্ত্রীধর্ম্ম, কেবল স্ত্রীর অনুষ্ঠেয় কর্ম্ম, রজঃ, manner or duty of women, menstruation.

স্ত্রীধর্ম্মিণী, স্ত্রীলোকের কর্ত্তব্যকারিণী, ঋতুমতী, রজস্বলা, *f.* observing the proper duties of her sex, menstruous.

স্ত্রীপুংধর্ম্ম, পতিপত্নীর পরস্পর কর্ত্তব্য, the reciprocal duties of husbands and wives.

স্ত্রীপর, নারীপ্রিয়, লম্পট, uxorious, devoted to women; a libertine.

স্ত্রীলিঙ্গ, যোষিৎ বাচক, নারীচিহ্ন, ভগ, the feminine gender, pudendum muliebre.

স্ত্রীসঙ্গ বা সম্ভোগ,—মৈথুন, রতিক্রিয়া, sexual intercourse, carnal commerce.

স্ত্রীসংগ্রহণ, বিবাহ, পরস্ত্রীসংসর্গকরা, marriage, seduction of a married woman. [man-
স্ত্রীহরণ, পরস্ত্রীকে বলাৎকার, rape, abduction of a married wo-
স্ত্রৈণ, স্ত্রী সম্বন্ধীয়, স্ত্রীবৎ, স্ত্রীবাধ্য, female, feminine, womanish, effeminate, under female rule, hen-pecked.
স্থ. স্থিত, বর্ত্তমান, বর্ত্তী, *affix*: being, situated, staying, &c.
স্থকিত, স্থগিত,—নিবৃত্ত, স্তব্ধ, নিবারিত, সম্প্রদায়বহিষ্কৃত, অব্যবহার্য্য, stopped, ceased, suspended, hindered, debarred, excluded from society, obsolete.
স্থণ্ডিল, চত্বর, যাগার্থ প্রস্তুত ভূমি, বালুকারচিত হোমীয় অগ্নি স্থান, a level piece of ground covered with sand, &c. prepared for a sacrifice, an altar. [ground.
স্থণ্ডিলশায়ী, চত্বরে শয়নকর্ত্তা, an ascetic sleeping on consecrated
স্থপতি, ইষ্টকাদি গৃহ নির্ম্মাণকর্ত্তা, a master-mason or carpenter. a builder, an architect. [firm.
স্থবির, বৃদ্ধ, স্থির, শক্ত, an old man; old, aged, steady, fixed,
স্থবিষ্ঠ, অতিশয় স্থূল, মাংসাল, very thick, very corpulent.
স্থল, স্থান, ঠিকানা, ভূমি, পদ, কর্ম্ম, এক দেশ, a place, spot, situation, dwelling, land, dry-land, a post, office, employment, station, a passage in a book, &c.
স্থলী. স্থান, ভূমি, প্রান্তর, a place, land; possessed of a place.
স্থলীয়, স্থানীয়, ভূমিসম্বন্ধীয়, of or belonging to a place or to dry-land. [room of.
স্থলে. স্থানে, পরিবর্ত্তে, ঠাঁই, instead of, in lieu of, in the
স্থলচর, ভূচর প্রাণী, ভূস্থ, moving on land, terrestrial.
স্থলপথে, পদব্রজে, by dry land, on foot.
স্থলভেদ, স্থানান্তর হওয়া, পদপরিবর্ত্ত, a change of situation, a vacancy, succession to a place or office.
স্থাণু, স্তম্ভ, শঙ্কু, শাখাশূন্য বৃক্ষ, বেক্তা, a stake, pin, a pollard.
স্থাতব্য, স্থাপনীয়. স্থেয়, to be placed, proper to be fixed, &c.
স্থাতা, স্থাতৃ, *f.* স্থাত্রী,—স্থায়ী, তিষ্ঠনিয়া, one who stays or abides.
স্থান, স্থল, ঠাঁই, পোত, ভূমি, পরিবর্ত্ত, ঠিকানা, বাসা, ঘর, দেশ, পদ, কর্ম্ম, অবকাশ, a place, situation, spot, scite, ground, space, stead, a home, abode, a passage in a book, a post, office, vacancy. [to be fixed.
স্থানীয়, স্থলসম্বন্ধীয়, পোতকীয়, of or belonging to a place, &c.

স্থাপন, পোতন, থুয়ন, বসান, রাখন, সমর্পণ, প্রতিষ্ঠা করণ, পত্তন করণ, স্থিতি করণ, রক্ষণ, ধারণ, to fix, set up, erect, place, put, give in charge, deposit, establish, found, keep, secure, defend, uphold.

স্থাপয়িতা, স্থাপনকর্ত্তা, স্থিতিকারক, রক্ষক, one who places, &c. a defender, upholder. [&c.

স্থাপিত, স্থিরীকৃত, প্রতিষ্ঠিত, fixed, settled, founded, established,

স্থাপ্য, স্থিতি করণীয়, পোতনীয়, গচ্ছিত ধন, to be placed, fixed, &c. given in charge ; a deposit.

স্থাবর, অচল, ধ্রুব, স্থায়ী, মণিমুক্তাদি, পরম্পরাগত ভূম্যাদি ধন, পর্ব্বতাদি, fixed, firm, immoveable, stable, stationary, unalienable, (as family jewels;) real property, (as lands, &c.) a fixture, a mountain.

স্থায়িত্ব, স্থিরভাব, চিরকালিকত্ব, অক্ষয়, lastingness, durability, steadiness, continuance, permanency, &c.

স্থায়ী, স্থিতিশীল, চিরকালিক, নিত্য, নিবাসী, *aff*: continuing, abiding, permanent, lasting, staying, inhabiting.

স্থায়ুক, প্রতিভূ, লগ্নক, গ্রামের অধ্যক্ষ, মণ্ডল, a bail, surety, overseer, bailiff, steward, the headman of a village.

স্থাল, ধাতুময় ভোজনপাত্র, a metallic dish or eating vessel.

স্থালী, হাঁড়ী, পাকপাত্র, an earthen cooking-vessel, a boiler.

স্থিত, বর্ত্তী, স্থায়ী, যে থাকে, স্থাপিত, যোজ, আয়, উৎপন্ন, being, staying, placed, fixed, situated, established, settled; stock, capital, funds, income, produce.

স্থিতি, সত্তা, বিদ্যমানত্ব, তিষ্ঠা, থাকা, দশা, অবস্থা, সংস্থান, অবলম্বন, স্থিরকরা, পত্তনকরা, বাসা, ঠিকানা, বিরাম, যতি, সীমা, being, existence, an abiding, stay, continuance, permanence, a state, condition, a settling, fixing, settlement, residence, abode, situation, place, cessation, a pause, a stop, a limit, boundary.

স্থিতিকর বা কারক, অবলম্বনকর্ত্তা, স্থাপনকারী, রক্ষক, ধারণকর্ত্তা, সংস্থাপক, upholding, supporting, sustaining, giving permanence or continuance.

স্থিতিশীল, স্থাবর, অটল, চিরস্থায়ী, permanent, abiding, durable.

স্থিতিস্থাপক, ধারণকর্ত্তা, রক্ষক, প্রকৃতিপ্রাপক, an upholder, supporter, protector, &c. elastic.

স্থির, সংস্থাপিত, শক্ত, অচল, অনড়, চিরস্থায়ী, নিত্য, নিশ্চল, নির্ব্বহ, নিরীহ, ধীর, শান্ত, নীরাগ, নির্ভয়, অচপল, অচঞ্চল, নিশ্চয়, নির্ণয়, সচ্চিদানন্দ, ঈশ্বর, fixed, firm, stable, immoveable, steadfast, permanent, durable, lasting, uniform, stationary, standing, (as water,) smooth, still, calm, serene, composed, unmoved, tranquil, passive, stoical, cool, collected, resolute, constant, faithful, certain, sure, settled, the enduring, *i. e.* God.

স্থিরচিত্ত, অচঞ্চল, নির্ভয়, ভরসান্বিত, firm, resolute, determined.

স্থিরতর, অতিস্থির, অক্ষয়, বহুকালস্থায়ী, quite firm, fixed, durable.

স্থিরধী বা বুদ্ধি, নিশ্চিন্তমনাঃ, প্রবুদ্ধ, resolved, resolute, determined, convinced. [tual.

স্থিরবাদী, দৃঢ়বাক্য, সত্যবক্তা, keeping his word, exact, punc-

স্থিরভাব, স্থায়িত্ব, স্থিতা, স্থৈর্য্য, ধৈর্য্য, permanency, durability, calmness, composure, equanimity.

স্থূল, অসূক্ষ্ম, মোটা, বৃহৎ, পীন, হৃষ্টপুষ্ট, অলস, জড়, large, bulky, thick, gross, coarse, lusty, sleek, fat, corpulent, portly, inactive, stupid, dull.

স্থূলতঃ, গড়ে, মোটামোটি, in the gross, altogether, indiscriminately. [sure.

স্থূলফল, সাকল্য, গড়, একুন, মোট, gross sum, amount or mea-

স্থূলবুদ্ধি, স্থূলধী,—জড়, অজ্ঞান, dull, stupid, heavy, ignorant.

স্থেয়, স্থাপনীয়, গাড়নীয়, to be placed or fixed, fixable.

স্থৈর্য্য, স্থিরতা, সমভাব, শমতা, ধীরতা, সাহস, নিশ্চয়, দৃঢ়বোধ, steadfastness, stability, steadiness, firmness, calmness, determination, resoluteness, certainty.

স্থৌল্য, বৃহত্ত্ব, স্থূলভাব, জড়তা, bulk, largeness, greatness, fatness, thickness, dulness. [by ablution.

স্নাত, কৃতস্নান, অবগাহনে পরিষ্কৃত, bathed, washed, purified

স্নাতক, যিনি সমাবর্ত্তন করিয়া গৃহস্থ হয়, a householder duly initiated after completing his studies.

স্নাতা, স্নায়ী,—স্নানকর্ত্তা, অবগাহনশীল, a bather, practiser of ceremonial ablutions.

স্নান, অবগাহনাদি অষ্ট প্রকার, সর্ব্বাঙ্গের জলোপক্ষেপ, a bathing, washing, ceremonial ablutions.

স্নানকুণ্ড, স্নানাগার,—অবগাহনস্থান, a bath, a bagnio.

স্নানযাত্রা, জগন্নাথের বৃহৎ মূর্ত্তিকে প্রতিবৎসর জলাভিষেক করা, the annual ablution of Jagannátha. [ablutions.

স্নানীয়, স্নানযোগ্য জল, অবগাহ্য, proper for bathing in, fit for

স্নাপিত, অবগাহিত, ডুবিত, made to bathe, bathed, immersed.

স্নায়ু, শিরা, মাংসপেশী, উপাস্থি, a tendon, muscle, cartilage.

স্নিগ্ধ, চিক্কণ, ক্লিন্ন, শীতল, প্রিয়, স্নেহপাত্র, স্নেহকারী, oily, smooth, soft, clammy, cool, refreshing, agreeable, beloved, amiable, kind, affectionate.

স্নিগ্ধমূর্ত্তি, ক্ষমাশীল, শান্ত, মৃদু, placable, clement, placid, mild.

স্নুষা, পুত্রবধূ, a daughter-in-law.

স্নেহ, প্রেম, প্রণয়, হার্দ্দ, বাৎসল্য, দয়া, কৃপা, লেপনীয় দ্রব্য, তৈলাদি, love, affection, fondness, tenderness, caressing, kindness, favour, mercy, sympathy, an unguent, oil, grease. [oily.

স্নেহী, প্রেমী, দয়াবান্, চিক্কণ, fond, affectionate, kind-hearted,

স্পন্দ-ন, নড়ন, কম্পন, বিধূনন, হস্তপাদাদি বিক্ষেপ. a moving, shaking, vibrating, fluttering, quivering, trembling, bodily motion, movement, agitation.

স্পন্দিত, কম্পিত, নড়িত, বিধূত, agitated, moved, shaken.

স্পর্দ্ধা সাহসবাদ, আস্পর্দ্ধা, ধমক, আত্মশ্লাঘা, স্বপ্রকাশ, ধৃষ্টতা, a daring, provoking, challenge, defiance, emulation, rivalry, arrogance, presumption.

স্পর্দ্ধিত, ধমকান, যুদ্ধে আহ্বানিত, dared, defied, provoked, challenged. [sation.

স্পর্শ-জ্ঞান, ত্বক্‌জ্ঞান, সান, touch, feel, contact, feeling, sen-

স্পর্শক, ছুঁয়নিয়া, সংলগ্ন, feeling, touching, coming in contact.

স্পর্শন, ছোঁয়ন, সংলগ্ন হওন, ঠেকন, হাত দেওন, to feel, touch, handle, come in contact, meddle with.

স্পর্শনীয়, স্পৃশ্য,—হস্তাদিগোচর, ত্বগিন্দ্রিয়ের বিষয়, tangible, palpable, that may be felt.

স্পর্শাতীত, সানবিহীন, কঠিন, হস্তাপ্রাপ্য, ত্বক্‌জ্ঞান বহির্ভূত, অপ্রপঞ্চ, past feeling, insensible, callous, impalpable, intangible, beyond the reach of touch, immaterial.

স্পষ্ট, সুব্যক্ত, প্রত্যক্ষ, সুবোধ্য, স্ফুট, clear, plain, obvious, evident, manifest, explicit, perspicuous, open.

স্পষ্টতঃ, স্পষ্টে,—নিতান্ত, সুব্যক্তে, প্রত্যক্ষতঃ, দৃষ্টেঃ, clearly, evidently, seemingly, ostensibly.
স্পষ্টবক্তা বা বাদী. সুব্যক্ত কথক, a clear or distinct speaker.
স্পষ্টবোধ, নিশ্চয়জ্ঞান, বিশেষানুভব, a clear motion or idea, distinct knowledge. [contact.
স্পৃষ্ট, স্পর্শিত.—ছোঁয়ান, সংলগ্ন, touched, felt, brought into
স্পৃহা, উৎকট ইচ্ছা, লিপ্সা, আশা, মনোরথ, wish, desire. inclination, longing, cupidity, hope, intention, supplication. [inclined.
স্পৃহী, লোভী, ইচ্ছুক, সাকাঙ্ক্ষ, wishful, desirous, longing,
স্ফট্, অহিফেণ, ফট্কিরি, the hood of a serpent, alum.
স্ফটিক, শুক্ল প্রস্তর বিশেষ, chrystal, quartz.
স্ফটিকারী, স্ফট্,—ফট্কিরি, alum. [horse.
স্ফন্দন, উল্লম্ফন, ফাঁদন, শিরপা করণ, to leap, prance, rear as a
স্ফিচ্, পাছা. নিতম্বের মাংসপিণ্ড, the buttocks, the hams.
স্ফীত, দোষজন্য পীন, ফুলান, ফাঁপান, স্থূলীভূত, উন্নত, বর্দ্ধিত, ফোস্কা, swollen, swelled, raised, fermented, blistered, inflated, distended, tumid, turgid, extended. enlarged, risen, grown rich or great; a bump or swelling. [prosperity, &c.
স্ফীতি, ফোস্কা, উন্নতি, বৃদ্ধি, a swelling, inflation, enlargement,
স্ফুট, স্ফুটিত,—ফুটিত, ফাটা, বিকসিত, প্রসারিত, প্রফুল্ল. স্পষ্ট, ব্যক্ত, burst, broken, rent, cracked, laid open, expanded, blown, clear, plain, manifest.
স্ফুটন, ফাটন, চিরণ, বিদরণ, প্রকাশ হওন, to burst, break, crack, rend, open, expand, emerge, appear.
স্ফুটি, ফল বিশেষ; ফাঁপা, a musk-melon, a kibe, a tumour.
স্ফুলিঙ্গ, অগ্নিকণা, ফিন্‌কি, a spark of fire, a drop of water.
স্ফুরণ, বিধূনন, কম্পন, উদয় হওন, উল্লেখ হওন, to tremble, quiver, shake, throb, to appear, become manifest, be uttered. [gladdened.
স্ফূর্ত্ত, প্রবর্ত্ত, চেতান, প্রফুল্লচিত্ত, excited, stimulated, sprightly,
স্ফূর্ত্তি, প্রবৃত্তি, চেতামি, প্রফুল্লতা, কম্প, প্রকাশ, উদয়, উল্লেখ, excitation, a stimulus, sprightliness, alacrity, tremulousness, palpitation, a throbbing, starting, expansion, eruption, manifestation, utterance.

স্ফোটক, ঝাঁপ, ফোস্কা, ব্রণ, a boil, imposthume, humour, pimple. [augur.

স্ফোটন, ফুটন, ভঙ্গ, তুরপণ, to burst, &c. a rupture, a gimlet,

স্ব, ধন, সম্পত্তি. নিজি, ব্যক্তিত্ব, আপনি, আত্মা, নিজ, আত্মীয়, wealth, property, identity, self, individuality, the soul; *pref:* own, self, one's self, one's own.

স্বক, স্বকীয়,—আত্ম, আত্মসম্পর্কীয়, নিজ, proper, peculiar, own.

স্বকার্য্য, আত্মকার্য্য, নিজ বিষয়, আত্মপর, one's own affairs, one's own peculiar duties; selfish. [dependant.

স্বগণ, আত্মপক্ষ, পক্ষপাতী, of one's own party; a partizan,

স্বগত, আত্মগত, নিজ মাত্র, গোপনে, kept or confined to one's self, exclusive, personal; apart, aside.

স্বঙ্গ, সুরূপ, সুডৌল, সুন্দর, handsome, well-formed.

স্বচ্ছ, নির্ম্মল, পরিষ্কার, শ্বেত, নিষ্কলঙ্ক, আরোগ্য, সুস্থ, clear, transparent, pellucid, white, pure, free from soil or stain, healthy, sound, convalescent.

স্বচ্ছন্দ, ইচ্ছাপূর্ব্বক, স্বাধীন, স্বতন্ত্র, প্রিয়, নিরুদ্বেগ, সুখ, spontaneous, voluntary, uncontrolled, self-willed, agreeable; abundance, ease, peace, security.

স্বচ্ছন্দে, ইচ্ছানুসারে, সহজে, at pleasure, agreeably to one's own will, freely, voluntarily, easily.

স্বচ্ছল, বিতরণশীল, দাতা, generous, liberal, munificent.

স্বজন, আত্মীয় ব্যক্তি, জ্ঞাতি, পরিবার, সগোত্র, বন্ধু, of one's own family; dependants, retainers, a distant relation, a friend. [class or nation.

স্বজাতীয়, নিজবর্ণ, নিজকুলোদ্ভব, স্বদেশীয়, of or belonging to one's

স্বজ্ঞান, আত্মবোধ, নিজবুদ্ধি, নিজকল্পনা, self-knowledge, one's own knowledge or invention.

স্বতঃ, স্বভাবতঃ, আপনাহইতে, অনাহূত, naturally, of, by or from itself, instinctively; uninvited.

স্বতন্ত্রী, স্বতন্তর,—স্বাধীন, আত্মবশ, ইচ্ছাবান্, প্রাপ্তব্যবহার, দুরন্ত, অবাধ, নিজমতাবলম্বী, independant, not subject to another's will, free, uncontrolled, adult, of full years, one's own master, arbitrary, despotic, capricious, whimsical, obstinate, headstrong.

স্বতন্ত্রতা, স্বতন্তরা,—আত্মবশতা, স্বেচ্ছাধীনতা, independance, freedom.

স্বত্ব, দান বিক্রয়াদির ক্ষমতা, স্বামিত্ব, ব্যক্তিত্ব, তত্ত্ব, স্বয়ংজীবিতা, proprietary right, owership. property in, title to, personal identity, self-existence, independant being. [holder.

স্বত্ববান্, স্বামী, অধিকারী, কর্তা, an owner, proprietor, rightful

স্বত্বাস্পদ, অধিকার বিষয়, the subject of a claim, &c. a right.

স্বদেশী, এক দেশস্থ, নিজদেশজ, a fellow-countryman, a native.

স্বধর্ম্ম, নিজকর্তব্য, স্বভাব, বিশেষ গুণ, one's own particular duties, natural or peculiar property, peculiarity. [or faith.

স্বধর্ম্মত্যাগ, জাতিভ্রংশ, বিধর্ম্ম, apostacy, abandonment of cast

স্বনাম, একনাম, আত্মনাম, a namesake, one's own name.

স্বপক্ষ, আত্মগণ, পক্ষপাতী, পক্ষতাকারী, of one's own side or party; a partizan, adherent.

স্বপ্ন, নিদ্রাকালীন অদ্ভুতানুভব, নিদ্রাবস্থা, a dream, vision, dreaming. sleep. [dreams.

স্বপ্নদর্শন, নিদ্রাবস্থায় প্রপঞ্চদৃষ্টি, the illusive scenery, &c. of

স্বপ্নবৎ, মায়িক, অবাস্তবিক, মিথ্যা, visionary, unreal, illusive.

স্বপ্রকাশ, আত্মশ্লাঘা, গরিমা, self-display, ostentation, boasting.

স্ববশ, নিজতন্ত্রী, স্বাধীন, not under controul, independant.

স্বভাব, নিসর্গ, স্বরূপ, পৃথক্ গুণ, চরিত্র, শীলতা, ধারা, ব্যবহার, nature, natural state, peculiarity, native property or quality, disposition, temper, inclination, tendency, bias, manner, way, custom.

স্বভাবতঃ, প্রকৃতিবশে, নিজে, naturally, by nature.

স্বভিন্ন, ইতর, অন্য, বিশেষ, পৃথক্, unconnected with one's self, distinct, different. [taneously.

স্বয়ং, আপনি, আপনাহইতে, *pref*: self, of one's self, spon-

স্বয়ংসিদ্ধ, আত্মগুণে খ্যাত, নিজকৃতকার্য্যেতে বিখ্যাত, famed for one's own acts or deserts. [tural, spontaneous.

স্বয়ংকৃত, আত্মকৃত, অকৃত্রিম, অযত্নভূত, self-done, self-formed, na-

স্বয়ন্দত্ত, দত্তকপুত্র, নিজার্পিত, self-given to adoptive parents.

স্বয়ম্বরা, স্বেচ্ছাপূর্ব্বক বিবাহ করে যে স্ত্রী, পতিম্বরা, a girl who chuses a husband for herself.

স্বয়ম্ভূ, যে আপনাহইতে হয়, নিজোদ্ভব, পরমেশ্বর, ব্রহ্মা, self-produced; the self-existent, God, Brahmá.

স্বর, গলার শব্দ, রব, ধ্বনি, তান, অ আ ইত্যাদি ষোড়শ বর্ণ, a voice, sound, noise, note, tone, tune, a vowel, an accent.
স্বরবান্, শব্দকারী, উচ্চৈঃধ্বনিকারক, গায়ক, সুকণ্ঠ, sounding, noisy, vocal, musical, having a fine or sweet voice.
স্বরবদ্ধ, স্বরভঙ্গ,—গলাভাঙ্গা, hoarse, deprived of his voice.
স্বরস, প্রেম, প্রণয়, হার্দ্দ, love, attachment.
স্বরিত, ধ্বনিত, উচ্চারিত, sounded, accented, articulated, pitched.
স্বরূপ, তদাত্মক, অনন্য, তুল্য, বেশধারী, নিসর্গ, স্বভাব, যাথার্থ্য, একাকৃতি, প্রতিনিধি, identified with, the same, like, similar, personating; the real nature of a thing, natural state, condition or purpose, truth, a definition, a representative, substitute, attorney.
স্বরূপতঃ, অনন্যতঃ, নিতান্ত, অর্থাৎ, ফলতঃ, identically, exactly, like, in the manner of, that is to say.
স্বরূপযোগ্য, পরিবর্ত্তনীয়, সদৃশ, ক্ষমতাবান্, proper to represent another, like, able, capable.
স্বরূপাখ্যান, যথার্থকথন, সত্যবৃত্তান্ত, তত্ত্ববাদ, a declaration of the truth or real facts of a matter.
স্বর্গ-পুর, স্বর্লোক,—ইন্দ্রধাম, দেবতার স্থান, Indra's paradise, heaven.
স্বর্গীয়, স্বর্গ্য,—স্বর্গগত, স্বর্গসম্বন্ধীয়, স্বর্গের যোগ্য, heavenly, paradisaical, celestial, righteous, deserving heaven.
স্বর্ণ, সোণা, সুবর্ণ, কনক, হেম, gold.
স্বর্ণকার, স্বর্ণকৃৎ,—সোণার, সেকরা, a goldsmith, a worker in gold.
স্বর্ণবর্ণ, হিরণ্যাকৃতি, পীত, gold-coloured, yellow.
স্বল্প, অত্যল্প, কিঞ্চিৎ, সূক্ষ্ম, তনু, very little, few, very small.
স্বল্পাহারী, অল্পাশী, পরিমিতভোজী, মিতভুক্, moderate in eating, abstinent, abstemious, temperate.
স্বসা, স্বসৃ,—ভগিনী, বহিনী, বহিন, a sister.
স্বস্তি, ভাল, জয়২, মঙ্গল, তথাস্তু, এমন হউক, excellent! well done! may good attend you! amen, so be it.
স্বস্তিক, মাঙ্গল্যদ্রব্য, শুভ বিষয়, any lucky or auspicious object.
স্বস্তিবচন, বিহিত কর্ম্মের আরম্ভে মন্ত্র বিশেষের পাঠাদি, a preliminary strewing of rice on the ground and invocation of a blessing on any succeeding ceremony.
স্বস্ত্যয়ন, প্রক্রিয়া, মঙ্গলোদ্দেশে দৈবকর্ম্মানুষ্ঠান, propitiatory rites for the averting of evil or obtaining of good.

স্বাক্ষর, স্বাকার,—স্বহস্তলিপি, one's own signature or hand-writing. [form; well-formed.

স্বাকার, স্বাকৃতি,—সুডৌল, সুন্দরাবয়ব, a fine form, one's own

স্বাগ্. সোহাগ, বাৎসল্য, affection, love, fondness, caresses.

স্বাতন্ত্র্য, আত্মবশতা, স্বমতাবলম্বিতা, independance, absence of restraint, wilfulness. [selfishness.

স্বাত্মভরণ, আত্মপোষণ, স্বার্থপরতা, a providing for one's self,

স্বাদ. রসনেন্দ্রিয়ের বিষয়, রস, চাকনি, flavour, taste, a tasting.

স্বাদিত. চাকিত, রসযুক্ত, tasted, having a flavour, seasoned.

স্বাদু-ল, সুরস, মধুর, সুতার, palatable, pleasant, savoury, nice.

স্বাধিকার, আপনার স্বত্ব, নিজ প্রভুত্ব, one's own right or title, dominion. [solute, despotic.

স্বাধীন, আত্মবশ, স্বতন্ত্র, independant, free, uncontrolled, ab-

স্বাধীনা, স্বৈরিণী, অসতী, *f.* self-willed, loose. unchaste.

স্বাধ্যায়, জপ, অভ্যাস, পুনঃ২ বেদাধ্যয়ন, inaudible reading, muttering of prayers, study of the Vedas.

স্বান্ত, মনঃ, চেতঃ, গহ্বর, the mind, the faculty of thought and feeling, a cave.

স্বাভাবিক, সহজ, প্রকৃতিসিদ্ধ, natural, innate, inherent, peculiar.

স্বামিত্ব, স্বাম্য,—প্রভুত্ব, কর্তৃত্ব, অধিকার, lordship, sovereignty, mastery, ownership, proprietary right.

স্বামী, প্রভু, কর্তা, পতি, গুরু, দেবতা, a lord, master, sovereign, owner, proprietor, husband, spiritual guide, a god.

স্বার্জিত, আত্মকৃত সঞ্চয়, নিজশ্রমোৎপন্ন, self-acquired, obtained or accumulated by one's own labour.

স্বার্থ, নিজমঙ্গলচেষ্টা, ফল, ধন, উপযুক্ত উদ্দেশে, আত্মনিমিত্ত, a regard to one's self, self-interest, personal benefit, wealth; for its proper object, for one's self.

স্বার্থী, স্বার্থপর,—কেবল আত্মকার্য্যেতে তৎপর, নিজলাভদর্শী, আত্মগ্রাহী, selfish, interested, living for one's self.

স্বাস্থ্য, উপশম, শান্তি, সুখ, তৃপ্তি, mitigation of disease, relief, recovery, ease, health, quietness, happiness.

স্বাস্থ্যজনক, সুপথ্য, হিতকারী, রোগঘ্ন, wholesome, healthy, salubrious, favourable to recovery, &c.

স্বিন্ন, অগ্নির উত্তাপে শিথিলীকৃত, সিজান, সিদ্ধ, পক্ক, swelled with heat, expanded, steeped, sodden, cooked.

স্বীকার, স্বীকরণ,—অঙ্গীকার, সম্মতি, প্রতিজ্ঞা, নিয়ম, বিনয়, an acknowledgement, assent, consent, agreeing to, acquiescence, confession, admission, agreement, promise, submission.

স্বীকারক, স্বীকারী,—অঙ্গীকারকর্ত্তা, মন্যত, সম্মত, acknowledging, consenting, confessing, &c.

স্বীকৃত, অঙ্গীকৃত, নিয়ত, প্রতিজ্ঞাত, admitted, acknowledged, confessed, promised, &c. accepted.

স্বীয়, নিজ, আত্ম, আত্মসম্বন্ধীয়, own, one's own.

স্বীয়া, পতিব্রতা, সাধ্বী, নিজা, *f.* virtuous, entirely devoted to her husband.

স্বেচ্ছা, আত্মেচ্ছা, নিজমত, স্বতন্ত্রতা, one's own will or pleasure, [self-will, free-will.

স্বেচ্ছাক্রমে বা পূর্ব্বক বা মতে,—আপনাআপনি, নিজমতবশতঃ, আপন ইচ্ছানুসারে, voluntarily, freely, willingly.

স্বেচ্ছাচর, স্বেচ্ছাধীন,—আত্মবশ, অনধীন, স্বৈর, uncontrolled, independant, following one's own inclinations.

স্বেদ, উত্তাপ, ভাপ, বাষ্প, ঘর্ম্ম, ঘাম, heat, warmth, vapour, steam, perspiration, sweat.

স্বেদজ বা জাত, কৃমি মশকাদি, musquitos, maggots, &c. supposed to be engendered from heat and moisture.

স্বেদন, ঘামন, ভাপন, to perspire, sweat, to steam, smoke.

স্বৈর-ী, স্বতন্ত্র, দুরন্ত, অবাধ্য, অসাধু, self-willed, obstinate.

স্বৈরিণী. অসাধ্বী, স্বাধীনা, *f.* unchaste, loose, wilful.

স্বোপার্জ্জিত, স্বয়ং আহৃত ধন, self-acquired or obtained.

স্মর, কন্দর্প, স্মরণকারী, Candarpa ; *aff:* remembering, &c.

স্মরণ, মনে করণ. পূর্ব্বানুভূতের জ্ঞান, উদ্বোধ, সংস্কার, to remember, recollect ; remembrance, recollection.

স্মরণী, স্মরণার্থ বস্তু, a keep-sake, token. memorial.

স্মরণীয়, স্মর্ত্তব্য, স্মার্য্য,—স্মরণযোগ্য, মনে ধার্য্য, memorable, worthy of remembrance, &c.

স্মরণে, অভ্যস্তে, মুখস্থ. by rote, by heart, from memory.

স্মারক, স্মরণকারী, মেধাবী, bringing to mind, &c. retentive.

স্মারী, জপমালা, করমালা, a rosary, a bead-roll.

স্মার্ত্ত, স্মৃতিশাস্ত্রসিদ্ধ, স্মৃতিশাস্ত্রবেত্তা, উদ্বোধগত, agreeable to the Smritis or divine code, legal, canonical, versed in the Smritis or laws, within memory.

স্মার্ত্তকাল, মনে ধরণের কাল, যে কাল পর্য্যন্ত মনে থাকে, the period to which memory extends or 100 years.
স্মিত, উপহাস, উপহসিত, a smile; smiled upon, smiling.
স্মৃত, মনে ধৃত, অভ্যস্ত, remembered, recollected.
স্মৃতি, স্মরণ, উদ্বোধ, ধর্ম্মসংহিতা, memory, recollection, remembrance, the code of Hindoo laws, jurisprudence.
স্মৃতিপত্র, স্মরণার্থ লিখিবার ক্ষুদ্র পুস্তক, a memorandum-book.
স্মের, উপহাস, ঈষৎহাস্য, a smile, a simper.
স্মেরানন, হাস্যযুক্ত বদন, শুভদৃষ্টি, প্রসন্নমুখ, a laughing or smiling countenance, a face of smiles.
স্যন্দক, স্রাবক,—মদ্যসন্ধানকর্ত্তা, শৌণ্ডিক, a distiller.
স্যন্দন, ক্ষরণ, স্রবণ, গলন, রথ, to ooze, trickle, drop, flow, distil; a war-chariot.
স্যন্দনারোহ, সারথি, রথী, a car-warrior.
স্যানা, নিপুণ, প্রাজ্ঞ, জ্ঞানবান্, clever, ingenious, skilful, wise.
স্যূতি, সূচিকর্ম্ম, সীবন, সন্ততি, গোত্র, a sewing, stitching; offspring, lineage.
স্রক, মালা, হার, a chaplet of flowers, a wreath, garland, [necklace.
স্রব, স্রাব, স্রবণ,—ক্ষরণ, গলতি, নিঃসরণ, ঘর্ম্ম, মূত্র, an oozing, trickling, dropping, distilling, flowing, leaking, exudation; perspiration, urine.
স্রষ্টা, স্রষ্টৃ,—নির্ম্মারক, সৃষ্টিকর্ত্তা, বিধাতা, রচক, a maker, creator, contriver, inventor.
স্রুক, স্রুব,—যজ্ঞপাত্র বিশেষ, হোমের দর্ব্বী, a sacrificial ladle or [spoon.
স্রুত, ক্ষরিত, গলিত, স্রোতবান্, flowed, dropped, oozed, leaked, flowing.
স্রোতঃ, জলপ্রবাহ, a stream, current, the flow or course of [water.
স্রোতবান্, বেগবান্, নদ, rapid, swift, flowing; a river.
স্রোতস্বতী, নদী, বেগবতী, তটিনী, a river, a flowing stream.

হ.

হওন, বর্ত্তন, বিদ্যমানে থাকন, জন্ম লওন, পড়ন, ঘটন, অর্শন, লাগন, to be, exist, become, come into existence, be born, arise, take place, occur, happen, to belong to, to serve, suit, answer.
হইতে, বর্ত্তিতে, থেক্যা, অপেক্ষা, to be; from, by, off, than.

হইবার, সম্ভবনীয়, বর্ত্তনীয়, practicable, possible, likely.
হউক, তথাস্তু, ভাল, so be it, amen, that's well, very well.
হওয়া, ভাব, স্থিতি. বিদ্যমানতা, সম্ভব, ঘটনা, being, existence, possibility, occurrence, &c.
হংস, হংসী,—হাঁস হাঁসী, বরুট বরুটা, চক্রবাকাদি, *m. & f.* a drake, a duck, a gander, goose, a swan.
হংসগামিনী, সুগতিকা, হংসমতচারিণী, a woman of a graceful gait.
হটুকা, হাটুড়িয়া বেড়ামিয়া, a market-man, a gadder about.
হট্ট, হাট, ক্রয়বিক্রয়ের প্রসিদ্ধ স্থান, a market, a fair.
হট্টবিলাসিনী, বেশ্যা, কুলটা, a prostitute, harlot, strumpet.
হঠ, দৌরাত্ম্য, বলাৎকার, violence, force, rapine, rape.
হঠন, হটন,—পিছন, দরকন, টলন, to move backwards, recede, back, fall back, retreat, shrink from.
হঠাৎ, অকস্মাৎ, দৈবাৎ, suddenly, unexpectedly, by chance, unawares, casually, accidentally, extempore.
হঠাৎ ইচ্ছা, হঠাদিচ্ছা,—অপ্রবৃত্তি, অকস্মাদ্বাসনা, a whim, caprice, fancy, sudden impulse.
হঠান, পিছান, টলান, to cause to recede or move backwards, &c.
হঠী, হটী,—পলাতক, ভাগোড়া, a runaway, fugitive, deserter.
হড়ুকা, ঠেলা, ধাক্কা, উচোট, a shove, push, slip.
হড়্গড়ান, টলন, সরিয়া লুঠন, to slip or roll on uneven ground.
হড্ড, অস্থি, নীচ, তুচ্ছ, অধম, a bone; low, mean, vulgar.
হড়্বড়ন, দর্কন, কম্পান, অব্যক্ত কথন, to be startled or alarmed, to be frightened, to start, to speak rapidly or inarticulately, to sputter.
হড়্বড়ান, চম্কান, কাঁপান, to hurry, flurry, startle, alarm.
হড্বড়ী, হড়্বড়ানী.—ঘবরাণী, বকুনি, গোলমাল, উদ্দধুন্দ, a flurry, alarm, stir, pother, noise, bustle, hubbub, disturbance, commotion, rebellion.
হড়্মড়িয়া, শক্ত, মড়্কা, ঠুক্কা, rustling, stiff, brittle.
হড়্হড়্, গর্জ্জনধ্বনি, গড়্গড়ি, a thundering or rumbling noise.
হড়্হড়ান, গর্জ্জন, গড়্গড়ান, to thunder, rumble, creak harshly.
হড়াগড়া, ঠেকা, ব্যাঘাত, চুক, পিছলন, a difficulty, obstacle, slip.
হড়াপোড়া, ভাজা বুট, parched pease or other pulse.
হড়ি, হাইড়, নিগড়, a pair of stocks, wooden fetters.
হণ্ডী, হণ্ডিকা,—হাঁড়ী, an earthen cooking-vessel or boiler.

হত, মারা, ক্ষত, আঘাতে মৃত, নষ্ট, বিহীন, রহিত, smitten, struck, hurt, killed, destroyed, lost, injured, *pref*: bereft or deprived of, void of. [spirit.

হতচিত্ত, নির্ভরসা, বুদ্ধিবিহীন, dispirited, bereft of sense or

হতজ্ঞান, অজ্ঞান, স্থূলবুদ্ধি, পাগল, foolish, silly, weak, idiotic.

হতপর, নষ্ট, দুষ্ট, অধার্ম্মিক, বিশ্বাসঘাতক, reprobate, profligate, abandoned, graceless, profane, perfidious, false, faithless, treacherous, traitorous.

হতপ্রায়, মৃতকল্প, মরণোদ্যত, almost dead, nearly killed.

হতভাগ্য, হতভাগা,—দুষ্কপালিয়া, দুঃখী, wretched, luckless, unfortunate, ill-fated. [impudent, bold.

হতলজ্জ, নির্লজ্জ, দুর্ম্মুখ, ধৃষ্ট, shameless, obscene, indecent,

হতাদর, অমর্য্যাদ, অবজ্ঞা, অসম্মান, bereft of character or honor; an undervaluing, inattention, disrespect to.

হতাশ-1, নির্ভরসা, hopeless, dispirited, desponding, despairing.

হতিয়ার, হস্তদোহার, অস্ত্র, a weapon, tool, implement.

হত্যা, অপঘাত, প্রাণনাশকরা, বধ, murder, killing, slaying, slaughter, carnage.

হত্যাশীল, হননশীল,—অপঘাতী, বধিক, ক্রূর, দ্বেষী, murderous, delighting in carnage, cruel, revengeful.

হনন, মারণ, ঘাতন, বধ করণ, to smite, strike, kill, slay.

হননীয়, হন্য,—বধযোগ্য, ঘাতিয়, মারণীয়, deserving death, intended for slaughter, vulnerable.

হনু, গণ্ডের অধোভাগ, the jaw, the jaw-bone.

হনুমান্, কৃষ্ণমুখ বানর, the black-faced monkey.

হন্তা, হন্তৃ,—বধকর্ত্তা, ঘাতক, নাশক, a murderer, slayer, smiter, destroyer; a specific. [ing.

হন্যমান, মার্য্যমাণ, now suffering death or enduring a beat-

হন্‌সা, কর্কশ, উগ্র, কঠোর, হিংসুক, কামড়ানিয়া, snappish, snarling, surly, mischievous, fierce.

হবন, হোম, a sacrifice, oblation, burnt-offering.

হবনীয়, হোমীয়, হোমার্থ, sacrificial, intended for sacrifice.

হবিঃ, হোমের দ্রব্য, ঘৃত, an oblation, ghee or clarified butter.

হবিষ্য, হবিষ্যান্ন,—ব্রতাদিতে বিহিত ভোজনীয় দ্রব্য, আহারকরা, pure or sacred food, the eating thereof.

হব্য, হোমীয় দ্রব্য, sacrificial, fit for sacrifice; an offering.

হম্বা, গোধ্বনি, the lowing of kine.

হয়, ঘোটক, অশ্ব, আছে, a horse ; *v.* it is, there is, yes.

হর, পরদ্রব্যগ্রাহক, নাশক, মোহক, *aff* : stealing, taking away, removing, captivating, &c.

হরণ, অজ্ঞাতে কিম্বা বলেতে পরদ্রব্য গ্রহণ, ধরণ, লুটন, যাপন, উড়ান, অঙ্কবিভাগ করণ, চৌর্য্য, বলাৎকার, to steal, rob, take by force, seize, carry off, purloin, plunder, to spend or pass time, expend, squander ; arithmetical division, stealth, theft, rape.

হরা, পরদ্রব্যগ্রহণকরা, দাবা, লুটকরা, চৌর্য্য, rapacity, peculation, plunder, robbery. [doe, roe.

হরিণ, হরিণী,—মৃগ, মৃগী, *m* & *f*. a deer, *m*. buck, stag, *f*. a

হরিণাক্ষী, হরিণনয়নী,—মৃগনয়নী, হরিণবৎ সুন্দরনেত্রবিশিষ্টা, *f*. having handsome eyes, fawn-eyed, stag-eyed.

হরিণবাটী, কারাগার, বন্দীশালা, a jail, a prison.

হরিৎ, পত্রাদির বর্ণ, পলাশ, শাক, আনাজ, তরকারী, কলাই, green, grassy, verdant ; greens, vegetables, corn, &c.

হরিৎখন্দ, আনাজভূমি, a bed of greens, crop of pulse, &c.

হরিতাল, উপধাতু বিশেষ, গোদন্ত, yellow orpiment, yellow ocre.

হরিতালিকা, ভাদ্রের শুক্লা চতুর্থী, the 4th of the increase in Bhádra.

হরিদ্রা, হলিদ্রা,—কন্দ বিশেষ, হলুদ, পীতবর্ণ, turmeric; yellow.

হরিমণি, মরকত, অশ্মগর্ভ, an emerald.

হরিবাসর, একাদশী তিথি, the eleventh day of a lunar fortnight.

হরীতকী, ফল বিশেষ, yellow myrobalan. [&c.

হর্ত্তব্য, অপহরণীয়, হরণের যোগ্য, that may be stolen or seized,

হর্ত্তা, হর্ত্তৃ,—চোর, বলাৎকারী, a thief, plunderer, ravisher, &c.

হর্ত্তাকর্ত্তা, পরাৎপর, সর্ব্বস্বামী, গৃহপতি, supreme lord, absolute master, a *title* given to the master of a family.

হর্ম্ম্য, ইষ্টকাদিরচিত গৃহ, অট্টালিকা, রাজসদন, a house of brick or stone, a mansion, a palace.

হর্ষ-কার, আহ্লাদ, আনন্দ, সুখ, কৌতুক, joy, delight, pleasure, mirth, festivity, merriment, sport.

হর্ষক, হর্ষকর,—আমোদক, তুষ্টিকর, delighting, giving pleasure.

হর্ষণ, রিঝন, উল্লসিত হওন, তোষণ, আমোদন, to rejoice, be glad or merry, to sport, to be happy, to give pleasure, delight, &c.

হর্ষমাণ, হর্ষান্বিত, হর্ষিত,—আহ্লাদিত, উল্লসিত, প্রমত্ত, delighted, glad, cheerful, happy, pleased, gay, merry, joyous.

হল, লাঙ্গল, a plough. [venom.

হলাহল, সাঙ্ঘাতিক বিষ, কালকূট, গরল, a kind of deadly poison,

হলিদ্রা, হলুদ, হলদী,—হরিদ্রা, পীতবর্ণ, turmeric; yellow.

হলী, লাঙ্গলধারী, কৃষক, holding a plough; a ploughman.

হলকা, ফাঁপা, অশক্ত, লঘু, সুলভ, অলীক, জন্তুপাল, যূথ, সমূহ, বহর, অগ্নিজ্বালা, light, soft, puffy, vain, trifling, cheap, silly, mean; a team, drove, flock, &c. a fleet of boats, rising flames.

হলহলনী, কম্প, দোলনা, সর্পগতি, a trembling, shaking, vibration, serpentine motion.

হসন, হাস্য করণ, মুচকন, laughter; to laugh, smile, simper.

হসনীয়, পরিহাস্য, হসনের বিষয়, laughable, ridiculous.

হসিত, স্মিত, প্রফুল্ল, বিকাশিত, বিকসিত, smiling, laughing, laughed at, open, blown.

হস্ত, হাত, কর, হস্তিশুণ্ড, ভুজ, প্রকোষ্ঠ, the hand, an elephant's trunk or proboscis, the arm, a cubit.

হস্তগত, হস্তস্থাপিত, গচ্ছিত, গতাম, বশীভূত, delivered into one's hand, in one's hand, captive.

হস্তাগত, মিলিত, প্রাপ্ত, come to hand, found, precured.

হস্তদোহার, সহকারী, দোহার, অস্ত্র, an assistant, co-adjutor, aid, a weapon, tool. [to another.

হস্তান্তরগত, পরগচ্ছিত, পরার্পিত, transferred or delivered over

হস্তিদন্ত, গজবিষাণ, কুম্ভ, an elephant's tooth, ivory.

হস্তিপাল, হস্তিপক,—গজরক্ষক, মাহুত, an elephant-driver.

হস্তী, হস্তিনী,—হাতী, হাতিনী, গজ, করী, *m. & f.* an elephant.

হস্তেকরণ, গ্রহণ, লওন, ধরণ, পরিণয়ন, পাণি গ্রহণ, to take, receive, accept, to receive in marriage.

হাঁ, স্বীকার বোধক শব্দ, অবশ্য, yes, well, indeed, surely.

হাঁই, হাই,—জৃম্ভা, a yawn, yawning, gaping and stretching.

হাঁক, ডাক, কুকরা, উচ্চৈঃস্বর, চীৎকার, a loud call, shout, loud cry, bawl, outcry, clamour.

হাঁকন, ডাকন, কুকরণ, চেঁচান, উচ্চৈঃস্বরে তাড়ান, to call aloud, shout, bawl, to drive or keep cattle together by shouting, &c. to frighten or drive away, &c.

হাঁকার, ডাক, চীৎকার, প্রয়াস, যত্ন, a shout, shouting out, energy, exertion of strength, &c.

হাঁকাহাঁকি, ডাকাডাকি, গোলমাল, clamour, noise, uproar, calling and bawling.

হাঁকাল, হাঁখাক্যা,—অশনে ঘুণ্ঘুণানিয়া, অজর, অবক্ষুত্র, growling over food, ravenous, gluttonous.

হাঁচন, ক্ষুৎকরণ, to sneeze.

হাঁচী, হাঁচা, হাচী,—ক্ষুৎ, ক্ষুৎকরা, a sneeze, sneezing.

হাঁটন, চলন, গমন, সরণ, to go on, move, walk, proceed.

হাঁটান, টহলান, to put off with excuses, delay from day to day. [or পাড়ন, to kneel.

হাঁটু, অষ্ঠীবৎ, জানুর গ্রন্থিস্থান, the knee, the pastern;-পাড়ন

হাঁড়ল, গহ্বর, a deep hole or cavity in a pond, &c.

হাঁড়া, বৃহৎ পাকস্থালী, a large cooking-vessel.

হাঁড়ী, ক্ষুদ্র পাকস্থালী, a smaller cooking-vessel, pot, pan.

হাঁপ, শ্রমজন্য নিশ্বাসের দ্রুতগতি, উদ্যম, শ্রম, a panting from exertion, toil, labour, great exertion.

হাঁপন-আন, ধোঁকন, কষ্টে নিশ্বাস ছাড়ন, to breathe short, puff, pant, wheeze, to be out of breath from over driving or from disease.

হাঁপানি, দুঃশ্বাস, শ্বাসকাস, a breathing short, shortness of breath, wheezing. [goose.

হাঁস-ী, হংসহংসী, বরট বরটা, *m. & f.* a duck, drake, gander,

হা, খেদ বোধক শব্দ, মুখ প্রসারণ, নাশক, ঘাতক, ah! oh! alas! ha! a gaping, an open mouth, non-plus; *aff:* destroying, removing, killing, slaying, &c.

হাঙ্গর, হিংসক জলজন্তু বিশেষ, a shark.

হাইল, হালি, নৌকার কর্ণ, a rudder, a helm, a stern-oar.

হাইর, হারি,পরাজয়, defeat, discomfiture, rout, loss at play.

হাজা, জলপ্লাব, বুড়াভাব, a swamping of lands or destruction of crops by flood or heavy rains.

হাট, হট্ট, ক্রয়বিক্রয় স্থান, ঘটা, a market, a fair, a crowd.

হাড়, ভদ্রু, অস্থি, a bone. [stocks, &c.

হাড়ি, অধম জাতি, ঝাঁটামিয়া, নিগড়, a sweeper, a scavenger,

হাড়ি-কাট, হাইক,—নিগড়, বলিমস্তকচ্ছেদমার্থ কাষ্ঠ, stocks, a block for holding the head of a sacrificial victim.

হাড়গিলা, বৃহৎ পক্ষি বিশেষ, the Adjutant bird or Indian crane.
হাত, হস্ত, পাণি, ভুজ, the hand, the arm, a cubit.
হাতকড়ি, হস্তবন্ধনী, বেড়ী, manacles, hand-cuffs, hand-fetters.
হাতচালা, মন্ত্রবলে হস্তক্ষেপ, movement of the hand by magic, &c.
হাতছানী, হস্ত নাড়নে ঠার দেওন, a beckoning with the hand.
হাতড়ন-আন, স্পর্শনে চলন, ঢুঁড়ন, অন্বেষণ, to feel one's way, to grope, to rummage, search for.
হাতড়ী, হাতুড়ী,—মুদ্গর, a hammer.
হাতযোড়া, সংযুক্ত হস্তদ্বয়, করপুট, the joining of the hands in supplication or respectful address.
হাতা, দর্বী, শলাকা, থাবা, হস্তাচ্ছাদন বস্ত্র, a ladle, spoon, shovel, a tiger's paw, a glove.
হাতাহাতি, হস্তযুদ্ধ, ধরাধরি, a scuffle, fisticuffs, grappling.
হাতী, হাতিনী,—হস্তী, হস্তিনী, *m. & f.* an elephant. [quack.
হাতুড়িয়া, কুচিকিৎসক, কাঁচা বৈদ্য, a pretender to medicine, a
হাতুয়া, বৎসবিনা হস্তেতে দোহনীয়া গো, a cow milked by the hand alone. [minent, prompt.
হাতেহাত, অবিলম্বিত, প্রস্তুত, অব্যবহিত, instant, immediate, im-
হাতিয়ার, অস্ত্রশস্ত্র, tools, implements. [slaughter.
হানন, প্রহারণ, মারণ, ঘাতন, to smite, strike, injure, kill,
হানা, বন্যা, জলগণ্ড, ক্ষতি, an inundation, swamping, injury, &c.
হানি, অপচয়, হ্রাস, ক্ষতি, অপকার, বিপদ, বধ, loss, lessening, diminution, alloy, injury, detriment, harm, mischief, disadvantage, ruin, slaughter.
হানিকর, অপকারক, অমঙ্গল, ক্ষতিকারক, দ্বেষী, doing injury, pernicious, injurious, spiteful.
হাপর, ধাতু গালনের চুলা, মূষী, a smelting furnace, a crucible.
হাব-ভাব, বিলাস, লীলা, বিভ্রম, বিব্বোক, amorous gesture in a female, wanton dalliance, blandishment, &c.
হাবজা, উচ্ছিষ্ট, ওঁচলা, leavings, refuse, trash.
হাবড়, কর্দ্দম, কাদা, পঙ্ক, mud, dirt.
হাবা, হাবী,—স্থূলবুদ্ধি, পাগল, প্রলাপী, মূক, *m. & f.* stupid, foolish, doltish, wild, incoherent, dumb.
হাবাৎ, সর্ব্বস্বান্ত, সর্ব্বক্ষতি, নিঃস্বত্ব, entire loss of property, reduced circumstances. [ness, dulness.
হাবামী, অজ্ঞানতা, পাগলামী, stupidity, foolishness, doltish-

হাব্যাস, আকাঙ্ক্ষা, প্রয়াস, সাদ, desire, inclination, a missing, wanting, longing for.

হাভাত্যা, হনবাত্তিয়া,—নিঃস্ব, দুঃখী, reduced, needy, poor.

হাম, মিলমিলা, the meazles. [as an infant.

হামা, বালকের হাঁটুকরে চলন, a creeping on hands and feet

হাম্লান, গরুর ডাকন, হম্মা করণ, to low as kine.

হায়, খেদ বোধক শব্দ, ah! alas!

হায়ন, বৎসর, অব্দ, a year, a twelvemonth.

হার, স্বর্ণাদি রচিত মালা, মুক্তাবলী, মাপমে অনুসার, a necklace, a string of pearls, a rate, common rate, proportion, an oil-measure.

হারক, হারী—হরণকর্ত্তা, নাশক, চোর, লুটনিয়া, বলাৎকারী, taking away, removing, &c. a thief, robber, plunderer, peculator, ravisher, a divisor.

হারণ, পরাভূত হওন, না পারণ, to lose at play, &c, to fail, be foiled or worsted, to be cast in a suit.

হারা-ণ, অপচিত, ভ্রান্ত, খোয়া, lost, stray, missing.

হারাণ, অপচয় করণ, না মিলন, পরাজয় করণ, জিতন, to lose, miss, vanquish, overcome, foil, defeat, cast, &c.

হারি, অপচয়, অভাব, পরাভব, loss, failure, defeat.

হারিত, খোয়াম, অপচিত, অপহৃত, লুটিত, পরাস্ত, রহিত, পক্ষি বিশেষ, lost, plundered, stolen, divided, defeated, bereft of, &c; the green wood-pigeon.

হার্দ্দ, প্রেম, স্নেহ, বাৎসল্য, হৃদয়সম্বন্ধীয়, affection, love, tenderness, kindness, friendship; of or belonging to the heart. [&c.

হার্য্য, হরণযোগ্য, proper to be taken, liable to be stolen,

হাল, লাঙ্গল, নৌকার কর্ণ, a plough, a rudder. [venom.

হালা, সুরা, মদ্য, গরল, বিষ, intoxicating liquors, poison,

হালাহল, সাঙ্ঘাতিক বিষ, a species of deadly poison.

হালি, নৌকা চালনের নিয়ামক দণ্ড, a rudder, a helm.

হালিক, হালসম্বন্ধীয়, লাঙ্গলিয়া, কৃষক, of or belonging to a plough; a ploughman. [man.

হালিয়া, হালবাহক, যুগাধীন, কর্ণধার, fit for the plough; a steers-

হাল্কা, হাল্কী,—কাঁপা, লঘু, অলীক, হেয়, তুচ্ছ, light, slight, trifling, empty, vain, despised, &c.

হাস, হাসি, হাস্য,—হর্ষবোধে মুখ প্রসার, কৌতুক, পরিহাস, laughter, laughing, merriment, sport, fun.
হাসকুড়্যা, সতত হাস্যকারী, সানন্দ, প্রফুল্লচিত্ত, always laughing. merry. gay, cheerful.
হাসন, হাস্য করণ, হর্ষণ, to laugh, to smile, to sport, be gay.
হাস্যরস, কৌতুক ব্যাপার, হর্ষবোধ, merriment, jocularity, sentiment of laughter.
হাহতোস্মি, খেদোক্তি, বিলাপ, alas! I am undone! lamentation, [sorrow.
হাহা, খেদোক্তি, হতোস্মি, alas! alas! ah me!
হাহাকার, অত্যন্ত বিষাদ, বিলাপ, খেদোক্তি, lamentation, wailing, grief, a sighing, cry of distress.
হিং, হিঙ্গু,—জতুক, বণিক দ্রব্য বিশেষ, assafœtida.
হিংসক, হিংস্রক,—অপকারক, দুষ্ট. দ্বেষী, ঈর্ষ্যান্বিত, ক্রূর, রিপু. মাংসাশী বন্য জন্তু, injurious, hurtful, noxious, mischievous, malignant, malicious, spiteful, vindictive, revengeful, rancorous, envious, fierce, savage, ferocious; an enemy, beast of prey, &c.
হিংসা, অপকার, পরানিষ্টচিন্তা, বৈর, বধ, দ্বেষ, দ্রোহ, injury, hurt, harm, mischief, killing, malice, envy, spite.
হিংসালু, হিংসাশীল,—অহিতৈষী, দ্বেষী, অপকারক, ক্রূর, disposed to injure, &c. malevolent, noxious, hurtful, mischievous, savage, fierce.
হিংসেচ্ছা, দ্বেষ, পরের অমঙ্গলচেষ্টা, desire to injure, malevolence.
হিংসন, ক্ষতি করণ, অনিষ্ট করণ, দ্বেষ করণ, to injure, hurt, do mischief, grudge, &c.
হিঁচড়ন-আন, কেশমার্জন, টানন, আকর্ষণ, to comb the hair, to pull, drag, lug.
হিঁয়াল, হিমানী, তুষার. snow, frost, hoar-frost.
হিঁয়ালি, প্রহেলিকা, an enigma, riddle, puzzle.
হিকা, হিঁচ্‌কি,—হেঁচ্‌কী, উদ্গার বিশেষ, hickup. hiccough.
হিঙ্গুল, হিঙ্গুলি,—উপধাতু বিশেষ, vermillion.
হিঙ্গুলী, বার্ত্তাকী বৃক্ষ, বেগুন, the egg-plant or its fruit.
হিক্কন, হিকা করণ বা তোলন, to hickup; a hiccough.
হিজড়া, ক্লীব, শণ্ড, an hermaphrodite, a natural eunuch.
হিত, ভাল, উত্তম, উচিত, প্রিয়, শুভ, মঙ্গল, অনুকূল, কল্যাণ, উপকার. good, proper, suitable, beneficial, friendly; welfare, benefit, advantage.

হিতবান্, শুভঙ্কর, উপকারক, profitable, serviceable, friendly.
হিতকারী, শুভকর, উপকারক, অনুকূল, সুপথ্য, doing good, beneficent, subservient, wholesome.
হিতজনক, শুভদায়ী, লাভকর, productive of good or advantage, lucrative. [is right.
হিতবাদী, সুমন্ত্রী, সুপরামর্শদ, giving good advice, advising what
হিতেচ্ছা, মঙ্গলচেষ্টা, the desire of good, benevolence, good-will.
হিতৈষী, প্রিয়েচ্ছু, পরশুভেচ্ছুক, benevolent; a well-wisher.
হিতোপদেশ, সুপরামর্শ, নীতিশাস্ত্র, দৃষ্টান্তকথা, ইতিহাস, good or friendly advice, useful instruction, an apologue, fable, moral tale. [fabulist.
হিতোপদেষ্টা, সৎপরামর্শদ, নীতিবাদী, a moral instructor, moralist,
হিন্তাল, হিঁতাল,—বৃক্ষ বিশেষ, a small palm, the marshy date.
হিন্দোল, দোলনা, ঝুলিবার শয্যা, a swing, a cradle.
হিম, শীত, শিশির, নীহার, ওষ, শীতল, স্নিগ্ধ, cold, frost, dew; cold, frosty, frigid, chilly. [moon.
হিমকর, স্নিগ্ধ, শীতল, ঠাণ্ডা, চন্দ্র cold, cooling, refreshing; the
হিমবান বা যুক্ত, শীতযুক্ত, জড়, তুষার, cold, frigid, frozen, frosty.
হিমাংশু, চন্দ্র, নিশাকর, ওষধীশ, the moon.
হিমাগম, জাড়া, শীতকাল, the cold season, winter. [cold fit.
হিমাঙ্গ, শীতবোধ, ঠাণ্ডাই, শীতলাবয়ব, a coldness, shivering,
হিমানী, হিঁয়াল, ওষ, হিমসমূহ, নীহার, snow, ice, hoar-frost.
হিমালয়, হিমাদ্রি,—পর্ব্বত বিশেষ, নগপতি, the Himalayan mountains, (the ancient Imaus.)
হিয়া, হৃদয়, অন্তঃকরণ, মন, চিত্ত, the heart.
হিরন্ময়, স্বর্ণাত্মক, স্বর্ণময়, golden, made of gold.
হিরণ্য, স্বর্ণ রূপ্যাদি, gold or other precious metal, bullion.
হিল্লোল, সমুদ্রের গর্জ্জন, ঝলৎঝলৎ, ঝল্কন, তরঙ্গ, জলসংস্পর্শি বায়ু, the roaring of the sea, the noise of agitated water, the flapping of waves, a wave, a cool breeze passing over water.
হিহি, হীহী,—হাস্যোক্তি, উঃ, he! he! heydey!-করা, খিল্‌খিলকরা, a cackling, giggling, chuckling.
হীন, তুচ্ছ, নীচ, নিন্দনীয়, বর্জ্জিত, ত্যক্ত, রহিত, bad, low, mean, vile, base, *aff:* left, abandoned, bereft of, without, destitute or deprived of, free from.

হীনজাতি, নীচলোক, চণ্ডাল, degraded, outcast, base; an outcast.
হীনবাদ, পূর্বোক্তের অন্যথা, অনির্ণয়, অসিদ্ধি, প্রমাণাভাব, prevarication, contradiction in evidence, failure in proof.
হীনাঙ্গ, অঙ্গরহিত, অপূর্ণাবয়ব, পঙ্গু, wanting a limb or part, maimed, crippled, defective.
হীর, হীরক, হীরা.—রত্ন বিশেষ, a diamond.
হীরামন, শুক পক্ষি বিশেষ, a beautiful species of parrot.
হুঁ, স্বীকার বোধক, অবশ্য, ay! indeed! truly! yes.
হুঁকশাস্ত্র, শীঘ্র, হঠাৎ, অবিলম্বে, speedily, quickly, forthwith, as if by magic.
হুঙ্কার, হুকার,—বিক্রম সূচক শব্দ, নিনাদ, গর্জন, a war-shout, shouting, a loud sound, a noise, rumbling, &c.
হুজুক, বড়াই, মিথ্যাকাহিনী, gasconading, blustering, vain talking or boasting, rodomontade.
হুড়, লোকবাহুল্য, গোলমাল, ঘটা, পণ, a crowd, mob, the noise of a crowd, a wager, a stake.
হুড়কা, অর্গল, the bolt or bar of a door.
হুড়কা, হুড়কী,—পতির সংসর্গ ত্যাগিনী, a woman who refuses to cohabit with her husband.
হুড়াহুড়ি, হুটাহুটি,—গণ্ডগোল, উদ্দখুদ্দ, a tumult, scuffle, fray, clamour, confused noise.
হুড়ান, ঠেকন, ঠেলন, পদাঘাত করণ, to knock, push, kick.
হুড়ুম, হুড়্হুড়ি,—গর্জনী, মেঘনির্ঘোষ, a loud or rumbling noise, distant thunder.
হুড়া, ঝকড়াটিয়া, ঢেঁটা, quarrelsome, perverse, pertinacious.
হুড়ামি, ঢেঁটামি, perverseness, pertinacity.
হুণ্ডী, অর্থসম্বলিত পত্র, চীপ, a bill of exchange at sight.
হুত, হোমে নিযুক্ত, যুক্তান্ন, offered with fire, burnt as an oblation; an offering of ghee, &c.
হুতাশ-ন, অগ্নি, fire or its deity.
হুতাশ, ভয়, শঙ্কা, নিরাশা, fear, dread, despair, despondence.
হুশাল, নির্ভয়, সাহসী, ভরসান্বিত, resolute, brave, bold, daring, undaunted, confident.
হুমা, বাণ, the bore on a river, a strong flood.
হুম্কা, হুম্কী,—ভয় দেখান, ধমক, a putting in fear, frightening, alarming, a threat.

হুমবাঘ, বৃহৎ ব্যাঘ্র, the royal tiger.
হুল, সূক্ষ্ম অগ্রভাগ, অলি, দংশ, a sharp point, a sting.
হুলা, পুংবিড়াল, সাগ্র, আগাল, a tom-cat; pointed, sharp.
হুলান, চোবান, খোঁচান, চেতান, to set on as a dog, to excite.
হুলাল, আগাল, অলী, সূচাল, pointed, sharp, having a point or sting; a skewer.
হুলু, হুলহুলী,—স্ত্রীলোকের হর্ষোক্তি ব্যবহার, a *ululatus* or inarticulate expression of pleasure practised by women on festive occasions, &c.
হুলস্থুল, গণ্ডগোল, a commotion, disturbance, fray, tumult.
হৃৎ, হৃদ্, হৃদয়,—অন্তঃকরণ, মন, চিত্ত, বক্ষঃস্থল, বুক, the heart, the mind, the seat of thought and affection, the bosom, the breast.
হৃত, হারিত, চোরা, রহিত, taken, taken away, stolen, bereft.
হৃদয়ঙ্গম, মনোগত, মর্ম্মগ, সঙ্গত, affecting, touching, pathetic, impressive, apposite.
হৃদয়ালু, বৎসল, প্রণয়ী, affectionate, kind-hearted, fond.
হৃদ্‌পদ্ম, হৃৎপিণ্ড,—বক্ষঃস্থ প্রাণাধার মাংসপিণ্ড, the heart *i. e.* the fleshy mass or fountain of the blood.
হৃদ্বোধ, প্রকৃতানুভব, নিশ্চয়জ্ঞান, প্রবোধ, ভরসা, an accurate conception, clear understanding, conviction, assurance, confidence.
হৃদ্য, প্রিয়, বৎসল, amiable, dear, beloved, affectionate, kind.
হৃদ্যতা, প্রিয়ত্ব, মিত্রতা, প্রণয়, amiableness, friendship, affection, kindness.
হৃদ্রোগ, হৃৎপিণ্ডব্যথা, heart-burn, any disease of the heart.
হৃষ্ট, হৃষিত,—আহ্লাদিত, প্রফুল্লচিত্ত, glad, cheerful, joyful, pleased, delighted, happy, exulting, rejoiced.
হৃষ্টচিত্ত, হৃষ্টমনাঃ, হৃষ্টান্তঃকরণ,—প্রফুল্লচিত্ত, হর্ষযুক্ত, glad-hearted, delighted, happy, jovial, merry.
হৃষ্টপুষ্ট, স্থূলকায়, মোটা, বলবান, plump, well-fed, sleek, fat, in good case, lusty, strong.
হৃষ্টি, আনন্দ, আমোদ, joy, pleasure, gladness, mirth, delight, exultation.
হে, সম্বোধন, *a vocative of calling, &c:* soho! ho! O!
হেঁচ্‌কী, হিক্কা, hiccough, hiccup.
হেচ্‌কন, টানন, আকর্ষণ, to drag, draw, pull, tug.

হেট, হেঠ,— নম্রকায়, অবনত, ঝোঁকা, নামিত, বিনয়ীভূত, উপুড় বা উল্টাকরা, bowed, stooping, bent, put or brought down, submissive; an upsetting, overturning, tilting. [prone.

হেটমুখ, নম্রাস্য, প্রণত, অধোবদন, with bent face, cast down,

হেটে, অধতে, নামোতে, down, below, downwards.

হেতু, কারণ, আদি, বীজ, মূল, প্রয়োজন, ব্যাজ, a cause, origin, source, occasion, spring, motive, reason, pretence, excuse, plea.

হেতু-ক, নিমিত্ত-ক, জন্যে, মূলক, জনিত, *aff:* because, for, on account of, for the sake of, originating in, arising from, caused by.

হেতুক, কর্ত্তা, কারক, যদ্দ্বারা হয়, করণক, an agent, active cause, instrument; causal, &c.

হেতুতা, কারণত্ব, কারিতা, প্রয়োজনত্ব, causation, causality, operation as a motive, &c. [tools.

হেত্যার, অস্ত্রশস্ত্রাদি, arms, weapons, implements, instruments,

হেথা, হেতা,—এখানে, অত্র, এথা, here, hither. [tank, &c.

হেদো, দামাচ্ছাদিত পুষ্করিণ্যাদি, overgrown with weeds as a

হেদান, চাহন, অতিশয় স্পৃহা করণ, প্রয়াস করণ, কৃশ হওন, to long for, fret after, pine, waste away.

হেন, সদৃশ, বৎ, তুল্য, so, as, like, the same.

হেম, স্বর্ণ, কনক, gold; হেমকার, স্বর্ণকার, a goldsmith.

হেমন্ত, অগ্রহায়ণপৌষ, শীতকাল, the cold season, winter.

হেয়, ত্যজনীয়, তুচ্ছ, লঘু, অধম, to be given up, untenable, indefensible, despicable, mean, base, vile.

হেয়জ্ঞান, লঘুজ্ঞান, অবজ্ঞা, অশ্রদ্ধা, তুচ্ছবোধ, a mean opinion, low idea, disregard of, disesteem, contempt.

হেরণ, দেখন, নিরীক্ষণ, অবলোকন, to look, behold, see, view, observe, regard steadfastly, gaze, stare, survey.

হেলন, না মানন, লঘু জানন, অনাদর করণ, লঙ্ঘন, টলন, ঝোঁকন, নড়ন, কম্পন, দোলন, নড়বড়ান, to neglect, disregard, despise, slight, transgress, violate, to heel, lean to one side, incline, bend, to totter, stagger, toss about, shake, vibrate, wave to and fro, reel, roll.

হেলা, ঝোঁক, দোল, লক্ষা, অবজ্ঞা, অনাদর, অনায়াস, ঢাল, হাব, অঙ্গভঙ্গি, a bending, inclination, oscillation, leaning, &c. motion, a jolt, neglect, contempt, disregard, disrespect, ease, facility, a slant, slope, wanton gesture, dalliance.

হেলান, আন্দোলন, নড়ান, বিলোলন, টলান, সরাণ, to agitate, to swing, shake, make to vibrate, to wave the hand, to wag, move, remove, &c.

হেলায়, অনায়াসে, চুম্বনে, easily, with ease, slightly.

হেষা, ঘোটকের ধ্বনি, গর্দ্দভের ধ্বনি, the neighing of a horse, the braying of an ass.

হৈম, শীতল, শীতবদ্ধ, জড়, স্বর্ণময়, cold, frigid, frozen, golden.

হৈমন্তিক, হেমন্তে উৎপন্ন, growing in the cold season, winter.

হোড়, পঙ্ক, কাদা, পণ, mud, mire, plashiness, a wager.

হোতা, হোতৃ, হোমী,—হোমকর্ত্তা, ঋগ্বেদপাঠক, a priest who offers a burnt sacrifice, a reciter of the Rigved.

হোথা, সেখানে, তত্র, তথা, there, thither, yonder, yon.

হোম, হোত্র,—বিধিপূর্ব্বক অগ্নিতে ঘৃতাদি প্রক্ষেপ, a burnt-offering, an offering by fire.

হোলা, ঢীলা, শ্লথ, বৃহৎ নৌকা, পুংবিড়াল, slack, loose; a large boat, [a he-cat.

হোল, অণ্ডকোষ, মুষ্ক, the scrotum, the testicles.

হোলী, ফল্গূৎসব, the festival of the red powder or ফল্গু.

হ্রদ, বৃহৎ অকৃত্রিম জলাশয়, অগাধজল, ডহর, a large sheet of deep water, a lake.

হ্রদিনী, নদী, স্রোতস্বতী, a river.

হ্রস্ব, খাট, বামন, খর্ব্ব, অদীর্ঘ, ছোট, লঘু, তুচ্ছ, অলীক, short, low in stature, dwarf, short as a vowel, small, less, light, unimportant, humble.

হ্রাস, ঘাটনি, ত্রুটি, অল্পতা, ক্ষয়, ন্যূনতা, আকাল, diminution, decrease, abatement, alleviation, wearing away, paucity, scarcity.

হ্রাসক, ন্যূনকারী, ঘাটানিয়া, diminishing, lessening, abating.

হ্রী, লজ্জা, ব্রীড়া, ত্রপা, shame, modesty, bashfulness.

হ্রীত; হ্রীমান,—লজ্জিত, ত্রপান্বিত, modest, bashful, ashamed.

হ্রেষা, ঘোটকের ধ্বনি, a neighing or braying.

FINIS.

ERRATA & ADDENDA.

Page.	*line.*	*after*	*insert*
4,	17,	অতি,	অতিবাদ,—
		for	*read*
6,	13,	হন,	হয়.
7,	14,	অবগত,	অবনত, নামিত
12,	22,	out-	in-
13,	2.	মনোবর্ত্তি,	মনোবর্ত্তী.
—	—	*add* 'মধ্যবর্ত্তী, internal.'	
—	9,	অন্তরভবন,	অন্তর্ভবন.
—	—	অন্তরভাব,	অন্তর্ভাব.
16,	34,	গ্রহন, করণ,	গ্রহণ. কারণ.
17;	34,	রাগভূত,	রাগীভূত.
20,.	35,	করাব,	করাণ.
21,	4,	গ্রহন,	গ্রহণ.
—	5,	কাপত্য,	কাপট্য.
—	30,	অক্রুবন-বান,	অক্রুবণ-বাণ.
24,	25,	প্রতিপৎ,	সূর্য্যেন্দুসঙ্গম.
27,	10,	*insert*	'ধনী.'
—	12,	*insert*	'উদ্দেশ্য,'
32,	9,	অনষ্ঠান,	অনষ্ঠান.
38,	36.	সবত্র,	সর্ব্বত্র.
44,	36,	*insert*	'ভূতগ্রস্ত.'
46,	24,	কেশ,	ক্লেশ.
—	25,	*dele*	'the hair.'
52,	1,	মারন,	মারণ.
54,	4,	ইচ্ছক,	ইচ্ছুক.
58,	12,	ভ্রমন,	ভ্রমণ.
69,	32.	উপস্থত,	উপস্থিত.
79,	14,	ঊক্য,	ঐক্য.
83,	24,	কথন,	কথন্.
92,	24,	কান,	কাণ.
94,	4,	প্রাণি.	পাণি.
96,	3,	Brahmá,	Brahma.
—	—	and	or.
97,	31,	কাঁকরা,	কাঁকর.
98,	20,	বিলাপণ,	বিলাপন.
100,	24,	নদির,	নদীর.
107,	11,	পক্ষীধ্বনি,	পক্ষিধ্বনি.
122,	35,	400,	4000.
126,	20,	রাগান,	রাগাণ.

Page.	*line.*	*for*	*read*
132,	31,	পত্র,	পাত্র.
134,	24,	হারন,	হারণ.
141,	15,	রাগন,	রাগণ.
151,	18,	গোচাণ,	গোচান.
157,	31,	চৎকান,	চট্কান.
159,	20,	ক্ষত্র,	ক্ষুদ্র.
163,	12,	উদ্ধ,	ঊর্দ্ধ.
165,	4,	পূতনা,	পৃতনা.
—	11,	মত্তিকার,	মৃত্তিকার.
—	24,	অহার,	আহার.
168,	31,	উদ্ধ,	ঊর্দ্ধ.
175,	11,	drief,	brief.
180,	22,	জাওন,	যাওন.
182,	5,	পুষ্করিণির,	পুষ্করিণীর.
—	20,	জাওন,	যাওন.
184,	24,	সক্তি,	শক্তি.
222,	17,	রহন,	রহণ.
231,	1,	্টি,	কুটি.
—	2,	আভা,	আত্মা.
—	28,	শঞ্চয়,	সঞ্চয়.
236,	1,	শস,	শস্য.
241,	4,	জাইতেছে,	যাইতেছে.
243,	35,	দুর্ভিক্ষ্য,	দুর্ভক্ষ্য.
253,	23.	doctrines,	doctrine.
258,	11,	তণ্ডল,	তণ্ডুল.
264,	12,	নরুন,	নরুণ.
272,	8,	-লুব্ধ,	-লব্ধ.
289,	11,	শ্রমোপর্জ্জিত,	শ্রমোপার্জ্জিত.
295,	3,	ত্রাণকর্ত্তা,	ত্রাণকর্ত্তা.
—	7,	অসদশ,	অশদৃশ.
296,	22,	গ্রাহ্যমান,	গ্রাহ্যমাণ.
—	—	জাইতেছে,	যাইতেছে.
298,	19,	ভণ্ডামী,	ভণ্ডামি.
308,	7,	পনন,	পনস.
312,	33,	মক্তি,	মুক্তি.
315,	34,	পরিমাপন,	পরিমাপণ.
318,	4,	পর্য্য,	পর্য্যন্ত.
320,	25,	*read* 'সিদ্ধৌষধ বিশেষ,'	

Page.	*line.*	*for*	*read*
323,	6,	rake,	garden-rake.
—	7,	লম্পট,	বিদা.
328,	30,	পার্য্যমান,	পার্য্যমাণ.
337,	3,	বক্ষ,	বৃক্ষ.
338,	27,	ঋতুমতি,	ঋতুমতী.
339,	10,	সরা,	সড়া.
340,	26,	হ্রাসকাল,	বৃদ্ধিকাল.
—	30,	অগস্থিরে,	অগ্রের.
342,	30,	নিপণ,	নিপুণ.
343,	7,	গ্রহ,	গ্রন্থ.
349,	30,	মংাস,	মাংস.
350,	18,	চবি,	ছবি.
355,	14,	শুখ্যাত-	সুখ্যাত-
356,	32,	পুনরোপক্রম,	পুনরুপক্রম.
362,	22,	প্রয়ান,	প্রয়াণ.
368,	29,	প্রণ,	প্রাণ.
372,	20,	35,	55.
376,	7,	-কৃ,	-কৃত.
377,	13,	পুনদত্ত,	পুনর্দত্ত.
386,	5,	˜ *dele*	বাঁঝা.
407,	13,	হস্তী,	হস্তি.
412,	1,	ঠেটামি,	ঠেঁটামি.
417,	12,	কোড়া,	ফোড়া.
424,	21,	ascetism,	asceticism
426,	21,	স্তল,	স্থূল.
431,	12,	ক্রন্দম,	ক্রন্দন.
436,	1,	উদ্বেব,	উদ্বেগ.
441,	8,	শোত্র,	শ্রোত্র.
445,	15,	চার,	চারি.
—	20,	চেনতা,	চেতনা.
459,	20,	ascetism,	asceticism
462,	21,	বরণ,	করণ.
466,	22,	সূয্যোদয়ের,	সূর্য্যোদয়ের.
470,	8,	-কৃ,	-কৃত.
475,	8,	ঠেটী,	ঠেঁটী
476,	5,	প্রথিবী,	পৃথিবী.
481,	34,	কুম্প,	কুম্স.
483,	13,	উদ্ধ,	ঊর্দ্ধ.
500,	2,	-মথ,	-মুখ.
—	24,	ভার্য্য,	ভার্য্যা.
502,	22,	পত্রি,	পত্নী.
510,	36,	কত্রিম,	কৃত্রিম.
524,	2,	*dele*	'কেবল.'
—	—	*dele*	'only.'
529,	11,	শুম,	ঘুম.
535,	1,	কোতুকী,	কৌতুকী.
538,	2,	reign,	rein.
539,	11,	তদ্,	তৎ.
545,	15,	রিকু,	রিক্ত.
553,	8,	ৈসন্ধব,	সৈন্ধব.
566,	20,	শরণ্য়,	শরণ্য.
575,	13,	or,	a.
585,	22,	আগাম,	আগামি.
601,	5,	ascetism,	asceticism
603,	14,	অত্যন্তিক,	আত্যন্তিক.
608,	32,	উপক্ত,	উপযুক্ত.
612,	12,	বিংশৎ,	ত্রিংশৎ.
613,	32,	সনদ্ধ,	সম্বদ্ধ.
622,	23,	-escence,	-essence.
633,	11,	হস্তী,	হস্তি.
634,	32,	সোহার্দ্দ,	সৌহার্দ্দ.
636,	7,	চোর্য্য,	চৌর্য্য.
—	26,	নিরুক্ষেপে,	নিরপেক্ষে.
637,	32,	পরিবত্ত,	পরিবর্ত্ত.
639,	3,	সচিদানন্দ,	সচ্চিদানন্দ.
—	31,	হয়,	হন.
640,	27,	ছুঁধনিয়া,	ছুঁয়নিয়া.
647,	11,	মধ্য,	মদ্য.